AF539339

RELIGION AND SOCIETY

RELIGION AND SOCIETY

Debiprasad Chattopadhyaya

AAKAR

Religion and Society
Debiprasad Chattopadhyaya

First Published by Ma-Le Prakashana, Bangalore, 1987
First Aakar Edition 2013
Reprinted 2020
Reprinted 2024

ISBN 978-93-5002-244-3 (Hb)

Published by
AAKAR BOOKS
28 E Pocket IV, Mayur Vihar Phase I
Delhi 110 091, India
www.aakarbooks.com

Printed at
D.K. Fine Art Press, Delhi

Aid to the Reader

Notes and References

The references in the footnotes are to the works given in the Bibliography. Where only one book by an author is included in the Bibliography only his name occurs in the footnote; where more than one work by the same author is included in the Bibliography, the name of the author is followed by the initials of the title of the work in Roman capitals. Contributions to journals and general reference works are indicated by the word 'in' preceding these.

Aakar Books is grateful to

Dr. Debiprasad Chattopadhyaya's daughters Aditi and Atashi for giving us the opportunity and privilege of publishing this book.

Calcutta University for according the necessary permission to publish the book.

Dr. G. Ramakrishna for his interest in the publication of this work.

K.K. Saxena

Contents

Introduction

The present work comprises the "Stephanos Nirmalendu Ghose Lectures for 1981" of the Calcutta University, which I had the honour to deliver at the auditorium of the National Library, Calcutta, in July 1986. I must at once thank Dr. Ashim Dasgupta, Director of the National Library, not only for providing me with all the facilities for delivering the lectures but also for taking personal interest in these to the extent of listening to me. I am also extremely grateful to Professor A.W. Mahmud for inaugurating the lectures and introducing me to the audience with kind words about me and my work, perhaps prompted more by his personal affection for me than my intrinsic worth. Dr. Santosh Kumar Mukherjee, Deputy Registrar (Estates and Trusts) of the Calcutta University spared himself of no drudgery for organising the lectures and to obtain from the University authorities the permission to get the lectures published in book-form by some publisher of my choice. I cannot really thank him enough.

*　*　*　*

The lectures as delivered are not published here in exactly the same form. Besides some alterations I eventually felt necessary in many places, the stipulated time for each lecture obliged me to shorten its length considerably. In the present book, however, I had the opportunity to use the lectures as drafted in full. This has enabled me to explain certain points more fully than I was able to do in the lectures as delivered.

In the present introduction, however, I shall try to discuss specially one point which, though related to the main theme of the lectures, could hardly be included in the lectures as planned.

* * * *

Rai Bahadur G.C. Ghosh, on whose funding the lectureship is instituted by the University, was clear and categorical about one point. He was honestly convinced that everything good and noble about man is derived from divine sources and hence embodied in religion. He therefore intended the present series of lectures to be a defence—or, perhaps more appropriately, to be a propagation of religion. I shall return to this basic question in the concluding portion of the present book, where I hope to discuss and also to review the contemporary world situation. In the Introduction, however, I shall try to emphasise another point. Rai Bahadur G.C. Ghosh was inclined also to believe that the noblest values of religion were most vividly expressed in Christianity. In short, he was also himself a devout Christian. Accordingly—besides perpetuating the memory of his son who died young and in whose name the lectureship is instituted—he was also motivated by the desire to propagate the noble values he was inclined to believe as embodied in Christianity. In the *Calendar of the University of Calcutta for 1956*, we read longish correspondences the donor had with the University authorities from August 1919 to November 1939 though, curiously enough, the first series of the lectures was already delivered in 1921 by Professor A.A. Macdonell. It is hard to guess from the *Calendar* why, even after the lectureship was already under progress, the donor wanted to be more specific about the subject-matter he desired to be highlighted. In any case, we read in the *Calendar* the following letter written by him to the University on September 24, 1924 and as modified on the suggestion of the Syndicate on November 29, 1939:

> Christ is one of the high manifestations of God. So the highest conception of God in the mind of man is Christ. So if man would lift up Christ in him, his spirit would enable him to live his life, expressed in loving service and sacrifice for fellowmen,

> his highest advancement and greatest happiness would be attained in the end.

We have added emphasis to the above, because the donor comes out here rather passionately as a devout Christian. What he says about Christ has been shared indeed by honest pious Christians for centuries. But things are somewhat different with honest historians when they look back at the historical Christ or Jesus of Nazareth and at early Christianity, i.e. as contrasted with the form it assumed from the time of Constantine, when it became a highly organised state religion. However, the point that I shall try to show here may sound strange to many. The expressions used by G.C. Ghosh—"if man would lift up Christ in him, his spirit would enable him to live his life, expressed in loving service and sacrifice," etc.—should remain acceptable to the honest historians, inclusive of the class-conscious revolutionary ones, though the sense in which Ghosh apparently wanted these to be understood is in need of very serious modification.

Thus modified, early Christianity appears to have been an organised revolutionary movement, aiming above all to emancipate the oppressed and exploited classes and its leader—the historical Christ—was tortured and killed by the ruling class because he was leading an armed uprising against the exploiting class. There is thus a good deal of real sense even for a contemporary communist to "lift up Christ in him", so that the essence of his teachings may acquire real truth instead of repeating only empty words concerning "loving service and sacrifice for fellowmen".

I shall try to show this by following mainly the writings of Frederick Engels, Archibald Robertson and Barrows Dunham. Their points, lying as these do under a huge heap of theology accumulated for centuries, would appear to many as outrageously absurd. The safer course for me would, therefore, be to allow these writers to speak for themselves.

Engels begins with what he calls "the German criticism of the Bible" specially by Bruno Bauer (1809-1882), whose scathing criticism of the Gospels and Epistles, according to

Engels, perhaps went too far, but who nevertheless did great service towards the demystification of the Bible:

> His greatest service consists not merely in having made a pitiless criticism of the Gospels and the Epistles of the apostles, but in having for the first time seriously undertaken an inquiry into not only the Jewish and Greco-Alexandrian elements but the purely Greek and Greco-Roman elements that first opened for Christianity the career of a universal religion. The legend that Christianity arose ready and complete out of Judaism and, starting from Palestine, conquered the world with its dogma already defined in the main and its morals, has been untenable since Bruno Bauer; it can continue to vegetate only in the theological faculties and with people who wish 'to keep religion alive for the people' even at the expense of science. The enormous influence which the Philonic school of Alexandria and Greco-Roman vulgar philosophy—platonic and mainly Stoic—had on Christianity, which became the state religion under Constantine, is far from having been defined in detail, but its existence has been proved and that is primarily the achievement of Bruno Bauer: he laid the foundation of the proof that Christianity was not imported from outside—from Judea—into the Romano-Greek world and imposed on it, but that, at least in its world-religion form, it is that world's own product. Bauer, of course, like all those who are fighting against deep-rooted prejudices, overreached his aim in this work. In order to define through literary sources, too, Philo's and particularly Seneca's influence on emerging Christianity and to show up the authors of the New Testament formally as downright plagiarists of those philosophers, he had to place the appearance of the new religion about half a century later, to reject the opposing accounts of Roman historians and take extensive liberties with historiography in general. According to him Christianity as such appears only under the Flavians, the literature of the New Testament only under Hadrian, Antoninus and Marcus Aurelius. As a result the New Testament accounts of Jesus and his disciples are deprived for Bauer of any historical background: they are diluted in legends in which the phases of interior development and the moral struggles of the first communities are transferred to more or

> less fictitious persons. Not Galilee and Jerusalem, but Alexandria and Rome, according to Bauer, are the birth- places of the New religion.[1]

In spite of the exaggerations of Bauer, his demystification of the Christian scripture proved for Engels the opening of new understanding of early Christianity. We shall first quote extensively from Engels and then return to further researches from the Marxist viewpoint of the subject, specially as carried forward by Archibald Robertson and Barrows Dunham. Engels observes:

"The history of early Christianity has notable points in common with the modern working-class movement. Like the latter, Christianity was originally a movement of oppressed people: it first appeared as the religion of slaves and emancipated slaves, of poor people deprived of all rights, of peoples subjugated or dispersed by Rome. Both Christianity and the workers' socialism preach forthcoming salvation from bondage and misery; Christianity places this salvation in a life beyond, after death, in heaven; socialism places it in this world, in a transformation of society. Both are persecuted and baited, their adherents are despised and made the objects of exclusive laws, the former as enemies of the human race, the latter as enemies of the state, enemies of religion, the family, and social order. And in spite of all persecution, nay, even spurred on by it, they forge victoriously, irresistibly ahead....

"The parallel between the two historical phenomena forces itself upon our attention as early as the Middle Ages in the first risings of the oppressed peasants and particularly of the town plebeians. These risings, like all mass movements of the Middle Ages, were bound to wear the mask of religion and appeared as the restoration of early Christianity from spreading degeneration; but behind the religious exaltation there were every time very tangible worldly interests. This appeared most splendidly in the organisation of the Bohemian Taborites under Jan Zizka, of glorious memory; But this trait pervades the whole of the Middle Ages till it gradually fades away after the German Peasant War to revive again with the working-men Communists after 1830. The French revolutionary Communists, as also in particular Weitling and his supporters, referred to early Christianity long before Ernest Renan's words: 'If I wanted to give you an idea of the early Christian communities I would tell you to look at a local section of the International Working Men's Association.'"[2]

Further: "We therefore see that the Christianity of that time, which was still unaware of itself, was as different as heaven from earth from the later dogmatically fixed world religion of the Council of Nicene; one cannot be recognised in the other. Here we have neither the dogma nor the morals of later Christianity but instead a feeling that one is struggling against the whole world and that the struggle will be a victorious one; an eagerness for the struggle and a certainty of victory which are totally lacking in Christians of today and which are to be found in our time only at the other pole of society, among the socialists.

"In fact, the struggle against a world that at the beginning was superior in force, and at the same time of the innovators among themselves, is common to the early Christians and the socialists. Neither of these two great movements was made by leaders or prophets—although there are prophets enough among both of them—they are mass movements."[3]

And who were the persons whom we meet in early Christianity struggling against the whole world? Here also Engels is inclined to see similarity between early Christianity and modern Communism:

"What kind of people were the first Christians recruited from? Mainly from the 'labouring and burdened', the members of the lowest strata of the people, as becomes a revolutionary element. And what did they consist of? In the towns of impoverished free men, all sorts of people, like the 'mean whites' of the southern slave states and the European beach-combers and adventurers in colonial and Chinese seaports, then of emancipated slaves and, above all, actual slaves: on the large estates in Italy, Sicily, and Africa of slaves, and in the rural districts of the provinces of small peasants who had fallen more and more into bondage through debt."[4]

It is thus that further studies in early Christianity from the Marxist point of view takes a new turn as it were. One of the most notable books embodying it is *The Origins of Christianity* by Archibald Robertson (London 1953). Reexamining a vast mass of materials which contain often very clear though sometimes comparatively subtle indications, and critically scaling off the frequent tendency of later amendments and alterations sought to be introduced into the Bible evidently intended to soften down the radical implications of early Christianity, he arrives at the view that the historical Jesus was so brutally killed because of the simple reason that he, after John the Baptist, was actively organising an armed insurrection of the oppressed people against the oppressors. The book requires to be read and perhaps also reread—by those honestly interested in knowing the historical Christ and his actual message, though unfortunately we do not have the scope here to reiterate all—or even the major—evidences on the basis of which the author convincingly substantiates his views. It is essential for our purpose at least to quote the author's own summing up of the view itself. As he puts it, "the earliest parts of the Gospels—proved to be such by internal evidence and by a comparative study of the Synoptics—point back to a revolutionary movement led first by John the Baptist and then by Jesus the Nazoraean, and aimed at the overthrow of Roman and Herodian rule in Palestine and the establishment of an earthly 'kingdom of God' in which the first would be last and the last first, the rich sent empty away and the poor filled with good things and given houses and land. The followers of John and Jesus were called Notzrim or Nazoraeans, not from the village of Nazareth, but from the Hebrew word *natzar*, "to keep"—...as keepers of secrets...

"The Nazoraeans were probably an offshoot of the Essenes. The Essenes, says Josephus, 'are despisers of riches...

Nor is there anyone to be found among them who has more than another; for it is a law among them that those who come to them must let what they have be common to the whole order... So there is, as it were, one patrimony among all the brethren'...

"The movement of John the Baptist was nipped in the bud by Antipas. A Nazoraean attempt to seize Jerusalem led to the crucifixion of Jesus by Pilate. According to the Synoptics, Jesus was believed by some to be John the Baptist risen from death, and by others to be Elijah or one of the ancient prophets. The whole history of the Messianic idea from Daniel onwards shows that it was the projection of the hopes of a revolutionary movement which had taken root among simple and ignorant people, attaching itself to leader after leader and able to survive the death of many such. We need not wonder that it survived the death of Jesus..."[5]

Fully acknowledging his basic indebtedness to Archibald Robertson's book, Barrows Dunham, in his *Heroes and Heretics* (New York, 1967) carries forward this new approach to the understanding of Christ. As he sums up his main point:

"Let me say at once, then, that I believe the historical Jesus to have been the leader of an armed movement for national liberation. The movement, betrayed on the eve of insurrection, was crushed, and the leader was executed. These events happened in perhaps, A.D. 30—at any rate, before Pontius Pilate's recall to Rome in the year 36.

"I am aware that it may seem alarming, and even horrifying, to think of Jesus as an active revolutionist. There is in the Gospels, however, some direct evidence for this view—evidence which is the stronger because it cannot be suspected of tendentiousness and may therefore be thought to record a tradition of fact. "[6]

The selected data on which the view is based requires to be understood in depth, bearing in mind that the Biblical passages quoted by him are from the translation of the *New English Bible* (Oxford and Cambridge University Presses, 1961). As Dunham says:

"Let us now examine the evidence for this view. We have said that the evangelists have left traces of original facts, rather like geological remnants which show what the ancient topography was. For example:

"'Ever since the coming of John the Baptist the kingdom of Heaven has been subjected to violence and violent men are seizing it.' Again, a parallel passage in Luke:

'Until John, it was the Law and the prophets: since then, there is the good news of the kingdom of God, and everyone forces his way in.'

"These are strange passages to find in narratives that purport to describe a man of non-revolutionary aims and other worldly intentions...

"My guess is that the passages assert a fact which a thousand years of experience had demonstrated—namely, that the liberation of the country required armed effort, and that thus only could one attain 'the kingdom of God.'

"Further, Luke's Gospel has a remarkable twenty-second chapter, in which among passages apparently put in later to validate the Eucharist, we get the picture of a band of revolutionaries, a sort of executive committee or general staff, supping together on the eve of insurrection. The leader announces, what he has surmised or been told, that one of them is a police agent.....

"Then, suddenly, the leader says,

'When I sent you out barefoot without purse or pack, were you ever short of anything?' 'No,' they answered. 'It is different now,' he said: 'whoever has a purse had better take it with him, and his pack too; and if he has no sword, let him sell his cloak to buy one. For scripture says, 'And he was counted among the outlaws, and these words, I tell you, must find fulfilment in me; indeed, all that is written of me is being fulfilled'. 'Look, Lord,' they said, 'we have two swords here.' 'Enough, enough!' he replied.

"It sounds like insurrection, does it not ? If that is what it was, then Judas's treason becomes for the first time intelligible. In the Gospels, his act of betrayal consists in identifying Jesus to the arresting officers. But neither they nor the Sanhedrin needed such help. Jesus was by that time a notable public figure, who had been greeted at the city gates by a throng shouting the insurrectionary cry *Ho-sanna!* (—'Deliver us.') But if Judas brought word that the insurrection was about to begin, that was news well worth thirty pieces of silver.

"Finally, that insurrection was the order of the day may be seen from two passages concerning Barabbas. Mark says (15:7), 'As it happened, the man known as Barabbas was then in custody with the rebels who had committed murder in the rising' (NEB). Luke says (23:19), 'This man had been put in prison for a rising that had taken place in the city, and for murder' (NEB). Those were tumultuous times, and only the rich were safely pro-Roman.

"If the historical Jesus was a social revolutionary, we can more readily appreciate the considerable body of radical doctrine which the Gospels contain. The Golden Rule suffices of itself to outlaw exploitation, but, besides this, there are many doctrines which envisage a precise reversal of the social order. The last are to be first; the lowly are to inherit the earth.

"Where the movement is concerned, there is to be no 'business as usual'—the money-changers are driven from the Temple. The upper class collaborators with Rome are 'whited sepulchres full of dead men's bones.' The legalists 'strain at (out) a gnat and swallow a camel.' On being asked a treacherous question whether the Roman tax ought to be paid, Jesus asks to see the sort of coin that usually serves for payment. One of his interlocutors produces a *denarius*, and then stands self-confuted, self- betrayed—for who would be so likely to have a *denarius* as a man in the pay of Roman officials?...

"Meanwhile the disciples, reminded of how much they have themselves given up, begin to worry about future rewards. According to Mark, the answer is: 'I tell you this: there is no one who has given up home; brothers or sisters, mother, father or children, or land, for my sake and for the

Gospel, who will not receive in this age a hundred times as much—houses, brothers and sisters, mothers and children, and land and persecutions besides; and in the age to come eternal life. But many who are first will be last and the last first.'

"In this age! The rewards, then, are not all transcendental and postponed to some other order of existence. Some of them, at least, are to be enjoyed in the same historical continuum in which they were striven for. These will consist in economic prosperity ('houses' and 'lands') and in a wider, more intimate brotherhood".....

"Lastly, there is no doubt that the movement had won the people. We have the priests' word for that: they told Pilate, 'His teaching is causing disaffection among the people all through Judaea. It started from Galilee and has spread as far as this city.' There is some reason to think, indeed, that the Romans and their collaborators struck at the last possible moment, and that further delay would have been perilous. For Jesus had understood the law of all such movements, that people must be enlightened about their true social interest and then organised to attain them: 'Ye shall know the truth, and the truth shall make you free.'"[7]

It is indeed tempting to quote more from Dunham's brilliant analysis of the evidences. Unfortunately, however, our scope is extremely limited.

But we should like to add that the message of armed uprising for the liberation of the oppressed did not end with the gruesome murder of Jesus. Here is a striking example of this. Thomas Munzer, the leader of the peasant war in Germany, while calling the princes of Saxony and the people to rise in arms against the Roman priests, gave the clarion call of an outright political agitator, using—as a pious Christian is only expected to do—the authority of Christ himself:

"Does not Christ say, 'I came not to send peace, but a sword? What must you (the princes of Saxony) do with that sword? Only one thing if you wish to be the servants of God, and that is to drive out and destroy the evil ones who stand in the way of the Gospel. Christ ordered very earnestly (Luke, 19: 27) 'bring hither mine enemies and slay them before me.' Do not give us any empty phrases that the power of God will do it without the aid of your sword, since then it would rust in its sheath.... Those who stand in the way of God's revelation must be destroyed mercilessly, as Hezekiah, Cyrus, Josiah, Daniel and Elias destroyed the priests of Baal, else the Christian Church will never come back to its source. We must uproot the weeds in God's vineyard at harvest time.... God said in the Fifth Book of Moses, [7], 'thou shalt not show mercy unto the idolators, but ye shall destroy their altars, and break down their images and burn them with fire that I shall not be wroth at you.'"[8]

* * * *

With these words about the new way of looking back at historical Jesus and the movement he led, we may return to the stipulation of the donor of the present lecturership. He observes: "If man would lift up Christ in him, his spirit would enable him to live his life expressed in loving service and sacrifice for fellowmen, his highest advancement and greatest happiness would be attained in the end." Whatever the donor might have had in his mind, we have only one point to add to this with the new understanding of the historical Christ, which is increasingly gaining grounds. From the viewpoint of the establishment all this is rather alarming to say, specially in these days of great social turmoil when, in spite of all the anxieties and grimness we are suffering from, we also hear the sound of suffering humanity knocking at the doors to be opened for global communism.

* * * *

In the lectures as delivered, however, I have not gone into the question of early Christianity. This is primarily because I felt that for the Indian audience, at any rate, the more important need is the reexamination of certain widespread notions about Indian religions in the general background of Indian history.

* * * *

It remains for me to add only one more point. The present book is not the first one I have written on Indian philosophy and religion. As a matter of fact, I have been writing on Indian philosophy and religion for the last three decades. Naturally enough, I cannot always have new things to say about the same subject. So I had often to repeat or reiterate some points discussed in my earlier works. Of these, I must specially mention the following, from which a considerable amount of material had to be taken and restated in the present book: *(1) Lokayata, (2) Indian Philosophy, (3) Indian Atheism, (4) What is Living and What is Dead in Indian Philosophy,* and *(5) Knowledge and Intervention.* However, as I do not expect any reader of my books to remember everything I have said in those books and, moreover, as what I have taken from these are placed in a new context, I do hope to have the indulgence allowed to say certain things I have said before.

REFERENCES

1. Engels in OR 321-2.
2. Ib. 313-15.
3. Ib. 326-7.
4. Ib. 330-31.
5. A. Robertson 93-96.
6. B. Dunham 51.
7. Ib. 53-7.
8. Quoted by Engels PWG 70.

1

Before Religion

I am profoundly grateful to the Vice-Chancellor of the University of Calcutta and his colleagues for giving me this opportunity—which indeed is also grand honour—of delivering the Stephanos Nirmalendu Ghose Lectures for the year 1981. At the same time it will be an obvious audacity on my part not to mention how diffident I feel to take the responsibility I am required to. I am fully aware of the fact that I had only been a somewhat timid teacher of philosophy compared to those who have delivered the same lectures before me. I find in the list of their names those of my own teachers like Nalini Kanta Brahma—to whom I literally owe my initiation in philosophy—and Surendra Nath Dasgupta and Sarvapalli Radhakrishnan, whose international reputation as historians and interpreters of Indian philosophy is hardly in need of any epithet. I also find in the list a few names of illustrious scholars and writers from abroad like those of A.A. Macdonell and Aldous Huxley, compared to whom my own stature is hardly of any significance. But I must not make my personal apologies too long, lest it be misconstrued as a reflection on the judicious selection of the Vice-Chancellor. I should rather proceed to discuss straight away what I am asked to.

1. 'Spirit of God in Man'

As is rather well-known, the subject intended to be covered by this lectureship is religion, or, as it is sometimes called, comparative religion. The letter of invitation I have received from the university mentions—evidently according to the desire of Rai Bahadur Ghosh on whose funding it is instituted—that "the lecturer will show that every religion is the product of the institution of the spirit of God within man." This, as I am inclined to understand, is true, though not the whole truth. Accordingly, I shall first try to show why this is true and then add a few words so that we may have some idea of the whole truth.

Obviously enough, belief in God—which, to put it in more theological terms, is the sense of the institution of the spirit of God within man—has been a necessary precondition for at least all the major organised religions in world history. Even Buddhism, which is sometimes mentioned as the perplexing phenomenon of "religion without God", is, in the ultimate analysis, not really an exception to this. Whatever might have been the original teachings of the Buddha—which, for all that we know, won the ears of a rather restricted band of followers and was presumably more in the nature of a socio-moral programme than religion as generally understood—had eventually to make room for a supreme God surrounded by a host of demigods, and only thus move towards being an organised religion in its full sense. The transformation had been momentous, so much so that it had to acquire a new name for itself, which was Mahāyāna. Perhaps to soothe an uneasy conscience, certain formalities of showing continuity with the alleged atheism of the Buddha could not be entirely done away with. Thus Nagarjuna—the great representative of Mahāyāna, if not its actual founder—professed to adduce certain theoretical considerations against the possible existence of God, as is suggested by the title *Iśvara-kartṛtva-nirākaraṇa-viṣṇoḥ- ekakartṛtva-nirākaraṇa*, a work attributed to him and surviving for us in the vast Tibetan collection called the Tanjur (bsTan-'gyur).[1] A critical survey of the book, however, shows that it is in fact not intended to reject the supreme God of Mahāyāna Buddhism—usually called Avalokitesvara, for whom

Nagarjuna is said to have had the most profound reverence. It is more in the nature of a philosophical refutation of the concept of causality as such and hence by implication also of the view of the world ever being created or coming into existence—a theoretical position required by the Śūnyavāda of Nagarjuna. In any case, notwithstanding such sporadic[2] philosophical formalities giving us the apparent impression that Mahayana retained the spirit of the original atheism of the Buddha, the fact remains that with the eventual development of Buddhism into the Mahayana so-called, God makes room for Himself in a big way, leaving undisturbed what is called in theological terminology "the spirit of God within man", taken of course not in the absolute ontological sense but in the more popular sense of the belief in God being an essential characteristic of all organised religions.

I have mentioned all this only to emphasise one point. The stipulation, namely that the lecturer will have to show that the institution of the spirit of God in man remains inescapably true from the historical viewpoint, despite the often-mentioned example of Buddhism having been a religion without God. In other words, there is hardly any scope to raise any doubt concerning the historical truth contained in the stipulation.

It is different, however, when it comes to the question of the whole truth. For this purpose one has to raise the further question concerning the very *making of the sense of God in man,* or, when such a sense is taken as an essential characteristic of religion, the question concerning the *making of religion itself.* This point—the addition proposed to have the whole truth—is important. First, ethnological researches correlated to archaeology want us to accept as a fact that there was a time when human beings had no notion of God and hence of the spirit thereof. Secondly, in one view at any rate—which, incidentally, in spite of provoking as much hope as hostility in the world today, is acquiring an ever-increasing importance—it is possible to foresee a future when men are going to do without any God, and hence of His spirit within.

Thus in short, in order to have the whole truth we have to reformulate the point and assert that though the institutions of the spirit of God in man had indeed been an essential feature of all organised religions, religion itself—along with all its concomitants—had a definite beginning, as definite again as it is going to have an end. The whole thing came into being, as it is going to pass away. If we ignore this we are left at best with wearisome theology, which had indeed a long innings for centuries, but not the hard core of what happened in history.

All this, I am at once anxious to add, is not intended to be a historical *evaluation* of religion. Though transitory after all, religion had an enormously complicated role in human history. Without its making, the very making of civilisation is not easily conceivable—a point which, as we shall see in the next lecture, has been brilliantly analysed by Gordon Childe. During the career of human civilisation, again, its role had often been most complex and contradictory—ranging from being an instrument for enforcing abject submission of the toiling masses to that of inspiring the revolt against tyranny and oppression, as was the case in early Christianity. In this medley of assorted functions of religion, one point is in need of special emphasis. Throughout the career of civilisations so far, it had in fact been a historical necessity. The career of the human beings began with a struggle against nature: men have progressively acquired the knowledge and capacity to control the forces of nature and extract from nature wealth for the satisfaction of human needs. This eventually led them to the threshold of civilisation, when emerged a new problem, namely the need for the regulations necessary in order to adjust the relations of men to one another and especially the distribution of the available wealth. At this stage, a section of the community itself could serve the function as custodians of the wealth in relation to another section, and when this section soon converted itself into the owners thereof, the product of the labour of others could be appropriated by it for its own satisfaction. It thus no longer remained the simple struggle of man against nature; to this was added another form of struggle, namely that of man against man. In short, human community was split into a privileged minority and an under privileged majority—the knowledge and power over nature going mainly in favour of the former. The impoverished masses—who in the earlier phase of civilisation were simply slaves and who in its advanced phase became the propertyless working class—were henceforth confronted with a dual uncertainty and a dual misery: those coming from the still uncontrolled nature and those coming from the exploitative machinery of the ruling class. Science and technology was left with the task of progressively delimiting the former, while religion to blunt the sense of the latter. From the historical point of view this was a necessity, for without the accumulation of wealth in the hands of the ruling minority, the spectacular achievements of civilisation so far could hardly be possible. At the same time, this made life for the masses too painful or too full of sufferings and uncertainties to be borne without some form of palliative remedy. This was supplied by religion—the belief in God who alone could assure justice, if not right now at least sometimes later, if not in this world at least in the after-world. This had gone on throughout the career of civilisation till recent times, when the knowledge of and power over nature have reached such magnificent dimensions that the concentration of wealth in the hands of the privileged minority, far from remaining a precondition for further human progress, has actually become a fetter for it. In short, conditions are created in the contemporary context for the basic restructuring of society, which can do away with the palliative remedy for miseries resulting from split-society—a historical necessity so far.

All this accounts for the fact that no amount of atheistic propaganda and no amount of philosophical criticisms could by themselves uproot the religious beliefs from the minds of the masses. Theology may add a certain amount of halo to religion but does not sustain it. Philosophy can expose its inner inconsistencies and lack of logic, but cannot uproot it. It draws its nourishment from some concrete material conditions, which, so long as they are allowed to persist, will have religion itself unaffected. That is why Karl Marx, when he was taking the first decisive step to Marxism, parted company with the 'Young Hegelians' who were spending all their energies in the philosophical criticism of religion. And he observed:

> *Religious* distress is at the same time the *expression* of real distress and the *protest* against real distress. Religion is the sigh of the oppressed creature, the heart of a heartless world, just as it is the spirit of a spiritless situation. It is the *opium* of the people.
>
> The abolition of religion as the *illusory* happiness of the people is required for their *real* happiness. The demand to give up the illusions about its condition is the *demand to give up a condition which needs illusions*. The criticism of religion is therefore *in embryo the criticism of the vale of woe*, the *halo* of which is religion......
>
> *The task of history*, therefore, once the *world beyond the truth* has disappeared, is to establish the *truth of this world*. The immediate *task of philosophy* which is at the service of history, once the *saintly form* of self-alienation has been unmasked, is to unmask self-alienation in its *unholy forms*. Thus the criticism of heaven turns into the criticism of the earth, the *criticism of religions* into the *criticism of right* and the *criticism of theology* into the *criticism of politics*.[3]

Such an attitude, as is rather well-known, eventually leads Marx to reformulate the basic task of philosophy in a totally different way: "The philosophers have only *interpreted* the world in various ways; the point, however, is to *change* it". Indeed, if philosophical thoughts are ultimately rooted in material conditions, how can there be a really radical change in it without changing the material conditions themselves? His view of religion is only an extension of this point to philosophical questions, as is evident from what has just been quoted.

Marx's view of religion is frequently distorted, wilfully or otherwise. Our purpose, however, is to try to review it as fully and clearly as we can. Only thus can we hope to understand why the sense of God in man had a definite beginning as it is destined also to have a definite end.

2. Three Basic Stages of Social Evolution

Since religion is inconceivable without man and man inconceivable without society, the starting point of our understanding of religion as viewed in Marxism is an idea of the evolution of society. We quote George Thomson for a brief account of it, if for no other reason than its piercing clarity combined with the most admirable absorption of the fundamentals of Marxism. Thomson observes:

> The evolution of human society has gone far enough for us to identify three main stages, corresponding to successive advances in the mode of production: pre-class society, class society, and the classless society of the future.
>
> In pre-class society, or primitive communism, the level of production was so low that the maximum effort of the whole community was absorbed in maintaining it at the minimum level of subsistence. There was no surplus. It was impossible for one man to live on the labour of another. There were no economic inequalities, and no social inequalities except the prestige earned by individual merit.
>
> When the technique of production had advanced far enough to leave a surplus over and above the immediate needs of the community, it became possible for different groups to specialise in different crafts, while the rest of the community supplied them food. Such divisions of labour, as they are called, led to further improvements in technique, till eventually there emerged a new division of labour—qualitatively new—a division between the actual producers and the organisers of production. The organisers of production were the chiefs or priests, the pioneers of such sciences as astronomy and mathematics, which were necessary for the development of agriculture. The nature of their work was such as to place them in a position of authority, and in time these custodians of the

> means of production converted themselves into owners. The community was divided into a working class and a ruling class. So we see that class society was brought into being by advances in the mode of production. The same is true of the successive phases of class society. Capitalism, in particular, has raised the productivity of labour to a level so high that the division of society into classes has now become an obstacle to the further development of the productive forces. Hence our modern paradox of poverty in the midst of plenty. In striving to maintain the rate of profit, the capitalist class, which is controlled by a few handful of big monopolists, is compelled to reduce wages, with the result that the workers, who form the overwhelming majority of the earth's inhabitants, are unable to buy the goods they produce. To this conflict there is only one solution—the socialist revolution. Having destroyed the capitalist state, the workers must create a new form of state power which will enable them to take over the means of production and thus abolish the system of private profit. When that has been done, the result is, as we know from the history of the Soviet Union, that production increases, uninterrupted by slumps, and at the same time, thanks to a fully planned economy, there is a continual rise in the people's standard of living. The conflict is resolved by abolishing the exploitation of man by man, and so the necessary conditions are created for the new communism, the classless society of the future.[4]

The account being very brief could touch some points only cryptically and hence there is a need for more elaboration. From the viewpoint of our present discussion, one of these is that of the transition from primitive pre-class society to class society, because, as we are going to see, it is directly connected with the making of religion. We shall return to the question of the making of religion in our next lecture where we shall have the advantage of being guided by one of the greatest archaeologists, V. Gordon Childe, who has shown why for the very making of human civilisation, the making of religion had been a historical necessity, whatever might have been the other consequences of it. For the present let us have a few other clarifications about the passage just quoted.

Put in the terminologies of Hegelian logic—to which Marx and Engels were profoundly indebted—the outlines of social evolution sketched above illustrate the fundamental laws of dialectics, namely "the negation of the negation". The primitive pre-class society is negated by class society, while class society in its turn is negated by the classless society of the future. Moreover, this process of the negation of the negation leads to something qualitatively new, for the classless society of the future, though in some sense is a return to some features of primitive pre-class society of the past, is a return to it in an incomparably higher level and hence to something qualitatively new. It is not a return to the conditions of the savages and early barbarians, where everybody is equal because of being equally poor, acquiring from nature with their rudimentary technology just enough to keep themselves alive or perishing when even that is not possible. On the contrary, it is moving forward to the stage in which everybody is equal because of being equally free from want and avoidable sufferings, thanks to the spectacular technological accomplishments man has in the meanwhile achieved and is progressively achieving. As the American lawyer-anthropologist L.H. Morgan, to whose researches Marx and Engels were basically indebted for the first full knowledge of the primitive pre-class society, observed: "Democracy in government, brotherhood in society, equality in rights and privileges and universal education foreshadow the next higher plane of society to which experience, intelligence and knowledge are steadily tending. *It will be a revival, in a higher form, of the liberty, equality and fraternity of the ancient gentes.*"[5]

Incidentally it may be mentioned here that Morgan, whose researches in primitive society went so much to the full formation of the dialectics of social evolution of Marx and Engels, wanted to remain true to Christian piety. He submitted the proofs of the *Ancient Society*, his *magnum opus*, to Rev. J.H. McLennan, with a request for deleting from it anything that could be viewed as incompatible with the Old

Testament, but who was foolish enough to congratulate Morgan for adducing "the strongest arguments against the Darwinians."[6] Nor had Hegel anything to do with materialism, whose dialectics went so much to the shaping of Marxism. The law of the negation of the negation was for Hegel only the mode of self-expression of God or Absolute, for whom Hegel was pleased to have various terminological alternatives—Spirit, Thought, Idea, Notion, etc. But the dialectics of social evolution in Marxism scraps all these in favour of the materialist standpoint. The real force that worked for the negation of the pre-class society by class society and which is going to work again for the negation of class society by classless society is technological development or development of the mode of production. It is this that gives the Marxist view of the dialectics of social evolution a real footing on earth or makes it an account of what really happened in history, shorn of fancy or phantasy.

What follows from all this is another proposition exceedingly important for our own discussion. It is concerning the life-span of class society in absolute time-scale.

Notwithstanding the grave anxiety we are having today—when researches in thermo-nuclear power and biology leave men with the alternatives of omnicide or welfare hitherto undreamt of—the normal expectation of human survival on the earth is for an immeasurably long period. Hence also of that of the classless society dawning before us. When we look back at the past, we have a somewhat similar impression: in absolute time-scale the total period covered by the primitive pre-class society is immeasurably longer than that of the class society. In a rough estimate, as Gordon Childe has shown, the latter "as at best one hundredth part of the time during which men have been active on our planet."[7]

Thus, compared to the primitive pre-class society behind us, and compared to the classless society the prospect for which is brightening in spite of the present gloom, the career of class society is somewhat insignificant, enormously complicated though our present problem is of moving forward to the classless society. L.H. Morgan already noted this in his own way: "The time which has passed away since civilisation began is but a fragment of the past duration of man's existence; and but a fragment of the ages yet to come. The dissolution of society bids fair to become the termination of a career of which property is the end and aim: because such a career contains the elements of self-destruction."[8]

From the point of view of what we propose to discuss, i.e. the phenomenon called religion, this transitoriness of class society is of material importance. The making of religion is a necessary concomitant to the making of the class society, just as with the withering away of class society religion also is going to wither away, perhaps slowly rather than dramatically or at one stroke. In short, the essential transitoriness of class society is also indicative of the transitoriness of religion, howsoever complex might have been the career of religion during the rather brief period of its history in absolute time-scale.

3. Before Religion

The first question that requires to be answered in this connection is that before the splitting of society into antagonistic classes, had there actually been the phenomenon called religon, the essential preconditions of which are the belief in God, prayers and sacrifices to whom is beneficial not only from the viewpoint of our own spiritual upliftment but also—at least in popular understanding—from the viewpoint of fulfilling our desires? The question is answered by anthropology, supplemented where possible by archaeology. And the answer is in the negative. The real savages still surviving in certain pockets of the world, i.e. insofar as they are not penetrated by the missionaries and merchants—and hence not contaminated by ideas and attitudes alien to what is inherent of their own—are not aware of any God and have no practice of prayers, propitiations or sacrifices. "Similarly, wherever we can penetrate the prehistory of civilised peoples, we reach a level at which again there are no gods, no prayer or sacrifice."[9]

What then do they do when confronted with a hostile nature, against which they have to struggle for their survival? Jane Harrison has answered the question:

> The savage is a man of action. Instead of asking a god to do what he wants done, he does it or tries to do it himself; instead of prayers he utters spells. In a word, he practises magic, and above all he is strenuously and frequently engaged in dancing magical dances. When a savage wants sun or wind or rain, he does not go to church and prostrate himself before a false god; he summons his tribe and dances a sun dance or a wind dance or a rain dance. When he would hunt and catch a bear, he does not pray to his god for strength to outwit and outmatch the bear, he rehearses his hunt in a bear dance.[10]

Jane Harrison has used the word "magic" as contrasted with religion, and that as the characteristic peculiarity of the theory and practice of the primitive peoples. What, then, is magic?

> Magic rests on the principle that by creating the illusion that you control reality you can actually control it. In its initial stages it is simply mimetic. You want rain, so you perform a dance in which you mimic the gathering clouds, the thunderclap, and the falling shower. You enact in fantasy the fulfilment of the desired reality. In its later stages the mimetic act may be accompanied by a command, an imperative 'Rain!' But it is a command, not a request. This principle of collective compulsion corresponds to a stage of society at which the community is still an undivided whole, supreme over each and all of its members, presenting a weak but united front against the hostile world of nature.[11]

Such a technique of confronting the hostile nature is illusory indeed. But though illusory, it is not entirely futile. In a sense, it can and does supplement the real technique. There is, in other words, a positive aspect of it, from the viewpoint of which Frazer's characterisation of it as the precursor of science seems to make sense. Here is how George Thomson gives us a picturesque description of this aspect of magic.

> The Maoris have a potato dance. The young crop is liable to be blasted by east winds, so the girls go into the fields and dance, simulating with their bodies the rush of wind and rain and the sprouting and blossoming of the crops and as they dance they sing, calling on the crop to follow their example. They enact in fantasy the fulfilment of the desired reality. That is magic, an illusory technique supplementary to the real technique. But though illusory it is not futile. The dance cannot have any direct effect on the potatoes, but it can and does have an appreciable effect on the girls themselves. Inspired by the dance in the belief that it will save the crop, they proceed to the task of tending it with greater confidence and so with greater energy than before. And so it does have an effect on the crop after all. It changes their subjective attitude to reality, and so indirectly it changes reality.[12]

The efficacy of magic is thus psychological. But it is not a matter of individual psychology. As Jane Harrison continues:

> One element in the rite we have already observed, and that is, that it be done collectively, by a number of persons feeling the same emotion.... Collectivity and emotional tension, two elements that tend to turn the simple reaction into a rite, are—specially among primitive peoples—closely associated, indeed scarcely separable. The high emotional tension is to him only caused and maintained by a thing felt socially; it is what the tribe feels that is sacred, that is matter for ritual.... Intensity, then and collectivity go together....[13]

But this primitive collectivity is undermined by the advance in productive technique: it creates surplus and hence also the possibility of a few to live on the labour of many. This, as we are going to discuss in the next lecture, constitutes the material conditions for the point of departure from magic to religion. For the present, however, we shall have a few more words on magic—the ideology characteristic of the primitive pre-class society. Notwithstanding the advance in the productive technique, the belief in the efficacy of magic does not immediately vanish. It survives in folk culture or the culture of the downtrodden people, specially among the female folk of the backward peasants.

There is nothing strange about it. Primitive practices rendered obsolete by economic progress often find sanctuary in folk culture, "which is of interest to the historian just because it is a stratified repository of discarded practices and discarded beliefs. Long after men have ceased in normal life to do as their forefathers did, they cling to the belief that their prosperity depends in some way on the good-will of their ancestors."[14]

So the pre-religious magic survives even in the otherwise religious climate. An example of this is what is called *Vrata* in Bengal.

We are indebted to Abanindranath Tagore[15] for his remarkable monograph (in Bengali) on the *Vrata*-s *of Bengal.* We shall broadly follow here his treatment of the subject, avoiding it only on points where his idealist preoccupations have obscured the subject.

The nucleus of a *Vrata,* he observes, is a desire. Clustering round it are rhyme, riddle, song, dance and even pictorial representations called the *Alpanas*. All these are meant to represent the desire as if it were already fulfilled. As Abanindranath has put it:

'A *Vrata* is just a desire. We see it represented in the pictures, listen to its echo in the songs and the rhymes, witness its reactions in the dramas and dances; in short, the *Vrata*-s are but desires as sung, the painted desires, desires as moving and living.'

All this is clearly magic. That is, it would be a mistake to call them religion. Abanindranath has repeatedly said that the *Vrata*-s are neither prayers not propitiations. The attitude underlying the performance of a *Vrata is* essentially an active one. It is not the attitude of prostrating oneself before the gods and begging some favour of them. It is rather the attitude of fulfilling the desire through certain definite action. In fact, the concept of the other world or heaven is alien to the *Vrata*-s. Of course, some of the *Vrata*-s, as we find them today, are but religious hotchpotch. But, as Abanindranath has insisted, these are either cunning devices of recent origin or just contaminations with later ideas. In any case, these are not genuine *Vrata*-s. The really genuine ones, as he poetically says, are attuned to the music of the earth.

One element of the *Vrata* is that it must be done collectively, by a number of people participating with the same desire. The desire of an individual and the actions designed to fulfil it cannot constitute a *Vrata*. It becomes a *Vrata* only when a number of persons cooperate to produce the same effect.

It may be possible for an individual to perform a dance but not a drama. Similarly, it may be possible for an individual to pray and propitiate: but not to perform a *Vrata*. Both prayer and *Vrata* are designed to fulfil the desires. However, the first is confined to the individual and it culminates in begging for the desire to be fulfilled; the latter is essentially collective and it ends in actually fulfilling the desire.

The peasants of Bengal perform the *vasudhārā vrata*. It is during the mid-summer drought, when, as the *vrata*- rhymes describe it 'the Ganga is sunken and the sky but a heap of ashes.' Naturally, the *vrata* is designed to fulfil the desire for rain, for plenty of water. The peasants sing. They sing of the shower and in the song they see the scorched earth submerged and the children swimming merrily. And they also act. They create the rain. They hang a jar on the tree, fill it with water and bore holes in it. The jar is the cloud. Water drips from it. It rains. That is how they enact, in fantasy, the fulfilment of the desired reality.

4. Magic Transplanted in Class Society

All this is picturesque indeed—the process of collective labour accompanied by some kind of primordial complex of song and dance and painting. In my next lecture I shall try to show how the requirement of human progress necessitated the negation of magic to make room for organised religion qualitatively different from magic, though without totally obliterating all hangover of magic—specially its negative aspect as having been essentially an illusion. In any case, the ideology *par excellence* of the primitive pre-class society is magic, which being unaware of goddesses and gods, prayers and propitiation, cannot but be looked back as pre-religious after all.

At the same time, specially for understanding Indian culture, we must not forget another point. Howsoever picturesque magic may appear in its original context of collective labour, there remains the possibility of its being transplanted in the later sharply class-divided society: when it is thus transplanted, it assumes the most monstrous and malignant form, serving the only purpose of ensuring financial gain for a negligible minority of a totally parasitical class. In Indian history, this actually happened in the comparatively later Vedic period—or, to be more specific, from the period of *Yajurveda*—when there developed the cult of what is called *yajña*.

There developed no doubt an extensive literature not only proclaiming which desire is sure to be fulfilled by the performance of which *yajña*, but also giving meticulous details of the way of performing each *yajña*, along with the spells appropriate for each. The literature that eventually grew about *yajña* acquired a fabulous bulk and looks most awesome. But if we raise the simple question, 'what exactly is *yajña*?', there is only one answer to it. It is in essence, nothing but primitive magic, because the main claim on which it is based is that the performance of certain acts automatically—i.e. by the intrinsic efficacy of its own—leads to the fulfilment of the results desired. There is no scope whatsoever in this entire process of the intervention of any divine agency granting the fulfilment of the desire. There is no question, in other words, of any prayer, propitiation or divine grace. As a matter of fact, the priest-class which alone is supposed to know the intricacies of performing *yajña*, eventually developed a powerful philosophical school, one of the main points of which is to deny the very existence of God and even to explain away the substantial reality of the famous Vedic deities like Indra, Varuṇa, Mitra and so on.

All this has proved somewhat puzzling to some of the modern scholars. Why should the most orthodox of all Indian thinkers—i.e. those who represent the Vedic "priests" ordinarily called—be at all so enthusiastic about total atheism? The answer seems to be that though we are accustomed to call them "priests", they are as a matter of fact not so, i.e. in so far as by "priests", we are inclined to understand those who are aware of the mode of prayer, propitiation, etc. for pleasing God or the gods and goddesses. On the contrary, what thy really are, are transplanters of primitive magic to the new socio-economic conditions, i.e. conditions of sharpy class-divided society, wanting to make their living by attracting financiers of *yajña,* i.e. ritual acts pure and simple, with the promise that nothing more than the performance of this is required for the fulfilment of all sorts of desires. To create conviction in these financiers, magical rituals had indeed to be adorned with a lot of mumbo jumbo—awesome as well as trivial. Thus we read in this ritual literature a detailed procedure of performing the *yajña,* of all sorts of implements required for their performance, etc. To these are added weary and wild speculations, absurd analogies, legends and etymologies, often also mock-disputations over useless trivialities. All this makes the discussions on the *yajña*-s the most unreadable and the most cumbrous specimens of Indian literary products. However, when all these concoctions added are sealed off, we are left with magic pure and simple. But it is not magic in its original context, namely the collective labour of the primitive people which, though illusory, somehow proves to be an aid to the actual productive technique. Magic transplanted to the sharply class-divided society becomes nothing more than mere economic drainage, financially beneficial only to a class of social parasites, professing or pretending to have the mysterious knowledge required for the performance of *yajña* and demanding of course fat fees from the financiers credulous enough to believe that the mere performance of it ensures the fulfilment of all sorts of desires.

In my subsequent lectures, I shall have the opportunity to discuss all this in more detail. For the present, it is perhaps enough to emphasise only one point. The evidence of magic shows that there was a stage of human development when there was no religion. Religion, as we shall see in the next lecture, is the characteristic product of class-society. Even when transplanted in the class-society, magic—now assuming the name of *yajña*—represents not merely a pre-religious attitude but also an attitude positively hostile to religion, inasmuch as it denies God and divine grace in every possible form.

Summing up

We have started with the proposition that every religion is the product of the institution of the spirit of God in man. We have observed that this is historically true at least as far as the major organised religions of the world are concerned. We have argued, however, that though true it is not the whole truth, for to this is to be added the further fact that religion itself—like the class society for which it is a historical necessity—is a transitory phenomenon after all, coming into being with the emergence of class society and destined to wither away with the transition to the classless society of the future. The first point required to be established for this view is that there was a time when there had been no religion and this was the period of the primitive pre-class society. We have tried to show that during this period there was "magic" instead of "religion"; the difference between the two is palpably qualitative.

In my next lecture I shall try to discuss the question of the making of religion, or more concretely that of the historical necessity of the beginnings of religion with the beginning of class society. For this purpose I shall follow mainly the researches of Gordon Childe.

REFERENCES

1. *Tanjur* mDo cxxxii.9. See Th. Stcherbatsky PS 1-16.
2. cf. *Iśvara-bhaṅga-kārikā* by *Śubhagupta. Tanjur* mDo cxii.11.
3. K. Marx CCHPR. Extract in Marx and Engels OR 42.
4. G. Thomson ER 7-8.
5. L.H. Morgan 561-62.
6. G. Thomson SAGS i.84.
7. V. Gordon Childe WHH 70.
8. L.H. Morgan 561.
9. G. Thomson ER 9.
10. J. Harrison 94.
11. G. Thomson ER 9.
12. G. Thomson SAGS i. 440.
13. J. Harrison 36-7.
14. G. Thomson SAGS i.66.
15. For summary of the book in English, See D. Chattopadhyaya L 113 ff.

2

The Making of Religion

1. Preliminary Remarks: Gordon Childe

For a descriptive account of the making of religion, we have to move about five thousand years back—sometime roughly to the third millennium B.C. when this gradually took full shape. This means that we have primarily to depend for the purpose mainly on the archaeologists, who, by examining the material remains of the extinct societies—though often correlating these also with ethnographical and ancient literary evidences where available—try to reconstruct an account of such hoary antiquity, inclusive of what Gordon Childe aptly calls "the spiritual equipment" of man. By this he means not only the ideas "translated into tools and weapons that work successfully in controlling and transforming external nature" but also "what is often termed society's ideology—its superstitions, religious beliefs, loyalties and artistic ideals."[1]

But there are archaeologists and archaeologists, with all sorts of theories and counter-theories—conjectures and counter-conjectures—which often give us the impression of a jungle as it were. Out of this jungle, however, came out a giant whose name was V. Gordon Childe. In the present lecture designed to discuss the making of religion, we propose to follow him, with full awareness of there being a host of his critics, inclusive of just mediocrity parading with nothing more than high-sounding jargons.

But let us first try to be clear about one point.

Marx died in 1883 and his lifelong collaborator Engels in

1895. Archaeology as a science was then hardly in its infancy. In spite of the decipherment of Egyptian writing by Champollion in 1822 and Schlieman's investigation of the origin of Greek civilisation at Troy and Mycenae in the 1870s, the excavations undertaken during the latter half of the nineteenth century, principally at Nineveh, Nirmud, Nippur and Lagash, are rightly described as " an undignified scramble for archaeological loot". The systematic method of excavation was really developed by Petrie, whose *Methods and Aims in Archaeology* was published in 1904, about ten years after Breasted—to whom we owe the concept of "the Fertile crescent"—began teaching Egyptology at the University of Chicago (1894), though whose first significant work *Ancient Records of Egypt* was first published in 1906. The first significant work on Sumerian excavation was that of the Royal Tombs at Ur by Leonard Wooley in 1926, while in 1924 John Marshall, depending on the work of Daya Ram Sahni at Harappa and R.D. Banerjee at Mohenjo-daro, announced the discovery of the ancient Indus Valley Civilisation.

We have mentioned some of the important landmarks in the making of modern archaeology or of archaeology as a science in its real sense—only to emphasise one point. It did not take shape during the lifetime of Marx and Engels.

It is therefore of considerable interest to note that though the makers of Marxism did not have the advantage of drawing on archaeology in formulating their view of social evolution, archaeology itself—in the works of no less a person than Gordon Childe—had to come to Marxism, so that the global survey of the earlier period of social evolution could become sufficiently meaningful.

In the book *Method and Theory of V. Gordon Childe*, Barbara McNairn has given us a brief sketch of how Gordon Childe's interest gradually shifted from the primarily philological—archaeological studies (the first edition of *The Dawn of European Civilisation*, 1925; *The Aryans*, 1926) to that of the understanding of the technique or the mode of obtaining the means of subsistence as determining the social relations as well as the ideological and other superstructural elements like science and religion. Though fascinating, we have neither the scope nor the need of reiterating the account of it here. What is of immediate relevance for our own discussion is his point of departure from his earlier interest to the basically socio-economic approach, because that gives us the first authentic account of the making of religion from the essentially archaeological viewpoint. This shift in Childe's interest took place in the mid-thirties of the last century. As Barbara McNairn rightly observes, "It was not till 1936 in *Man Makes Himself*, that Childe gave the first full account of his new economic ideas, and hence he emphasised his debt to Marxism."[2]

This book *Man Makes Himself* is a very brief one and, though stuffed throughout with cold archaeological data, was written in an amazingly simple style. Childe evidently intended it for a wide reading public. One reason for this was the scare then created by the rise of fascism, which threatened Europe with another impending "Dark Age", while Childe wanted people not to give up the hope for the future or in human progress. At the same time, Childe was too conscientious an archaeologist not to speak of progress in general terms; he substantiated it on the strength of the most relevant archaeological evidences on a global scale. The turn to Marxism, however, appears to have added a new dimension to his understanding of the very concept of progress. In other words, instead of viewing progress as a unilinear move forward of humanity, he viewed it from the dialectical standpoint, or, in Marxist terminology, progress that carried on its heels just its opposite. As we shall presently see, Childe himself used the phrase "dialectics of progress" while explaining how, for the most momentous march forward of humanity, it was also a historical necessity to create religious views and superstitions which, in their turn, had also an inhibitory effect on further progress, though as the Marxists add, despite this inhibitory influence, human progress did continue, ultimately creating material conditions that can finally overthrow the need for these. But let us not anticipate here our entire discussion but remain confined to the archaeological analysis of Gordon Childe for the making of religion as a historical necessity for the move forward to civilisation.

In the third year of the Second World War, Childe wrote another book primarily for popular consumption, or, in his own words, "designed for the bookshop public", tracing in it human progress from the hunting-gathering stage to the end of the Roman Empire. The book bears the title *What Happened in History* (1942). Though by far the most outstanding survey of global archaeology upto the time of its composition (magnificently combining in it archaeology with relevant ethnographical data), its "popular" form was motivated by the same anxiety to allay the apprehension of another Dark Age or, in other words, to protect the concept of "progress". As he himself observed, "I wrote it to convince myself that a Dark Age was not a bottomless cleft in which all traditions of culture were finally engulfed ...So I wrote it with more passion and consequently, more pretentions to literary style than in my other works."[3]

All this has to be accepted as true, specially when it is authenticated by Childe's own words. At the same time, it is difficult to imagine that an archaeologist of his stature would have turned to Marxism simply because he was scared by the rise of fascism. As we are inclined to understand, Childe accepted Marxism not merely because it helped him to retain confidence in human progress but also because he found in it the best model for synthesising the vast archaeological data in the most meaningful manner.

I have specially mentioned these two books, because these are for me the best specimens of the archaeologists' account of human progress, understood, as already said, from the Marxist viewpoint—an account in which the historical necessity of the making of religion is most lucidly explained. One of the key points for understanding this is what Childe calls "the Urban Revolution". Etymologically, *Urban* is derived from *urbs* or city and the word Revolution is modelled on what is called "the Industrial Revolution" in Europe, though ethnologically "Childe did in fact quite often associate his urban revolution with Morgan's stage 'civilisation'"[4]. Thus, in short, it means the momentous socio-economic transformation as a result of which man first moves forward from the neolithic villages to the earliest cities, which, as he showed, took place in the Old World in three primary centres—Egypt, Mesopotamia and India, the last in the Indus basin. In his view, all later forms of urbanisation are but linear descendants of these three primary centres. The point that interests us most for our present discussion, however, is that in Childe's archaeological analysis the making of religion is not only a concomitant of this profound socio-economic transformation but also an essential precondition of it. We shall try to sum up his analysis, elucidating it where necessary.

2. The Urban Revolution

In 1936, Childe formulated this concept in his *Man Makes Himself;* in 1942 he elaborated it in *What Happened in History,* and, perhaps for the purpose of giving us some idea of its crucial importance for his archaeological understanding, contributed an article exclusively on it in 1950 in the journal *Town Planning Review* with the title "The Urban Revolution". In 1958, again, in his *Retrospect* (published in the *Antiquary,* xxxii, 69-74) he returned to it in the context of explaining the need he felt for rewriting his earlier work *The Most Ancient East: The Oriental Prelude to European Prehistory* (1928) in the form of *New Light on the Most Ancient East: The Oriental Prelude to European Prehistory* (1934).

What, then, is the Urban Revolution and how is it connected with the making of religion?

In the book *What Happened in History,* Childe begins with an account of the differentiation of man from the rest of the animal kingdom with making of the tools, which, as compared to the purely physiological organs of the animals, are called "extracorporeal organs that he makes, uses, and discards at will".[5] But the earliest tools, made of a broken bough or a chipped stone, are too rudimentary or too crude to enable man to gather food from nature, which could at best be enough to maintain the human communities at the lowest level in spite of the best efforts on their part. So men, though leaving the stage of animal existence, were originally nothing more than hungry naked food-gathering savages. However, man moved forward in improving his tools, though of course slowly—almost imperceptibly slowly—for many many thousand years, till the quantitative accumulation of such protracted changes in technique led him to reach a new qualitative stage, with new tools efficient enough to *produce* food instead of just *gathering* it. This was a very significant move forward—significant enough to be called "revolutionary", inasmuch as man no longer remained a mere savage, and reached the stage of neolithic barbarism. In Childe's words: "The escape from the impasse of savagery was an economic and scientific revolution that made the participants active partners with nature instead of parasites on nature."[6] From this stage onwards, the pace of human progress gained new momentum, eventually attaining what Childe called the stage of "the Higher Barbarism of the Copper Age." As he put it: "The worst contradictions in the neolithic economy were transcended when farmers were persuaded or compelled to wring from the soil a surplus above their own domestic requirements, and when this surplus was made available to support new economic classes not directly engaged in producing their own food. The possibility of producing the requisite surplus was inherent in the very nature of the neolithic economy. Its realisation, however, required additions to the stock of applied science at the disposal of all barbarians, as well as a modification in social economic relations. The thousand years or so immediately preceding 3000 B.C. were perhaps more fertile in fruitful inventions and discoveries than any period in human history before the sixteenth century A.D. Its achievements made possible that economic reorganisation of society that I term the urban revolution."[7]

Elsewhere, Childe gives us a more detailed account of human achievements on the eve of the urban revolution: "The neolithic revolution, just described, was the climax of a long process. It has to be presented as a single event because archaeology can only recognise the result; the several steps leading up thereto are beyond the range of direct observation. A second revolution transformed some tiny villages of self-sufficing farmers into populous cities, nourished by secondary industries and foreign trade, and regularly organised as States. Some of the episodes which ushered in this transformation can be discerned, if dimly, by prehistory. The scene of the drama lies in the belt of semi-arid countries between the Nile and the Ganges. Here epoch-making inventions seem to have followed one another with breathless speed, when we recall the slow pace of progress in the millennia before the first revolution or even in the four millennia between the second and the Industrial Revolution of modern times.

"Between 6000 and 3000 B.C. man has learnt to harness the force of oxen and of winds, he invents the plough, the wheeled cart, and the sailing boat, he discovers the chemical processes involved in smelting copper ores and the physical properties of metals, and he begins to work out an accurate solar calendar. He has thereby equipped himself for urban life, and prepares the way for civilisation which shall require writing, processes of reckoning, and standards of measurement—instruments of a new way of transmitting knowledge and of exact sciences. In no period of history till the days of Galileo was progress in knowledge so rapid or far-reaching discoveries so frequent."[8]

3. Neolithic Revolution and "Surplus"

What was it in the neolithic revolution that ultimately made such spectacular achievements possible? The crucial point for understanding it is that the neolithic revolution "enabled human labour to produce more than was necessary for its maintenance", or, in short, what is called "surplus". It was this surplus that relieved some members of the community from being direct producers of their own means of subsistence, which could henceforth be met from the pool of the surplus produced by the rest of the community. Those who were thus freed from the need of directly producing their means of subsistence could become *whole-time* specialists in various capacities and contribute to the general fund of the spectacular achievements, leading man in certain centres to the threshold of the urban revolution.

For our present purpose, which is to understand the making of religion, it is not necessary to go into the details of the technological developments that led man to the eve of civilisation. However, two points are in need of special clarification. The full-time specialists had to be attracted to the incipient urban centres and had to be made permanent settlers there. For this purpose they had to be provided with some new mode of "protection" than before. Secondly, the social surplus produced in the villages had to be channelised to the incipient city centres and stored there, so that the means of subsistence for the whole-time specialists could be supplied from this accumulated surplus. The smoothest or by far the most convenient way for meeting both the purposes was to resort to some ideological device, and, under the given historical conditions, the most suitable ideological device then conceivable was a body of religious beliefs and practices. The preconditions for the making of this was at least partially already present in primitive magic, or, to be more specific, in its purely negative aspect, i.e. in so far as it was sheer illusion. In other words, primitive magic was itself infected with an inner contradiction. On the one hand, though an illusory technique it could and did serve as a supplement to real technique in the collective context. However, as rooted out of the collective context, it was shorn of its original economic function, though its essential illusoriness acquired a new socio-economic function, serving as the ideological device of providing with some new model of "protection" to the resident whole-time specialists made to settle in the incipient urban centres as well as for channelising the social surplus of the villagers to these centres for the maintenance of them as whole-time specialists. Incidentally, this new socio-economic function of religion as an outgrowth of magic is not to be misunderstood: it was a historical necessity for the urban revolution which was a tremendous progress for humanity—though progress not in a unilinear sense but in the dialectical sense of carrying on its heels marks of pronounced retardation.

Gordon Childe in his essay *The Urban Revolution* discussed at length the first of the two preconditions of this profound socio-economic transformation, namely "protection" in the new form without which the whole-time specialists could not be made to settle in the incipient urban centres. In his other books, specially in *Man Makes Himself* and *What Happened in History* he discussed the dialectics of progress as exemplified by the making of religion.

4. "Protection" for Full-Time Specialists

Let us first take up the question of the "protection" in new form of the resident whole-time specialists in the urban centre, borrowing freely for the purpose the expression used by Childe.

In any Stone Age Society, paleolithic or neolithic, "every member of the local community, not disqualified by age, must contribute actively to the communal food supply by personally collecting, hunting, fishing, gardening or herding. As long as this holds good, there can be no full-time specialists", for there is no surplus to feed them. "On the contrary, community of employment, the common absorption in obtaining food by similar devices guarantees a certain solidarity to the group. For cooperation is essential to secure food and shelter and for defence against foes, human and sub-human. This identity of economic interests and pursuits is echoed and magnified by identity of language, custom and belief; rigid conformity is enforced as effectively as industry in the common quest for food. But conformity and industrious cooperation need no State organisation to maintain them. The local group usually consists either of a single clan (persons who believe themselves descended from a common ancestor or who have earned a mystical claim to such descent by ceremonial adoption) or a group of clans related by habitual intermarriage.

"Now among some advanced barbarians (for instance, tattooers or wood carvers among the Maori) still technologically neolithic, we find expert craftsmen tending towards the status of full-time professionals, but only at the cost of breaking away from the local community. If no single village can produce a surplus large enough to feed a full-time specialist all the year round, each should produce enough to keep him a week or so. By going round from village to village an expert might thus live entirely from his craft. Such itinerants will lose their membership of the sedentary kinship group. They may in the end form an analogous organisation of their own—a craft clan, which if it remains hereditary, may become a caste, or, if it recruits its members mainly by adoption (apprenticeship throughout Antiquity and the Middle Ages was just temporary adoption), may turn into a guild. But such specialists, by emancipation from kinship ties, have also forfeited the protection of the kinship organisation which alone under barbarism, guaranteed to its members security of person and property. Society must be reorganised to accommodate and protect them."[9]

Thus the development of the city centres required that such specialists had to be rescued from nomadism with a guarantee of security in a new social organisation, because they had to break away from the old kinship bond and therefore also from the older mode of protection offered by the collective life. Security in this new form was provided by the state—a form of organisation totally unknown to humanity before the urban revolution, and, judged from the three primary centres of the earliest cities unearthed in the Old World—Egypt, Mesopotamia and Indus—the earliest states must have been theocratic, i.e. in theory controlled by some goddess or god though in practice by their earthly representatives—the priest, priestly corporations or sometimes the god-king. Thus the full-time craftsmen, uprooted from the older tribal collectives which provided them with the protection they required, came under the substitute protection of the state, which in its turn, required for its inner cohesion, a new ideological device: awe-inspiring organised religion. In the state organisation, the major share of the social surplus collected naturally went to the rulers—the priests or their corporations—while the actual workers were provided with barely nothing more than the means of subsistence, but the tension between the two was effectively submerged by the same ideological device, namely the making of religion. We quote Gordon Childe at some length:

"So in the city, specialist craftsmen were both provided with raw materials needed for the employment of their skill and also guaranteed security in a State organisation based now on residence rather than kinship. Itinerancy was no longer obligatory. The city was a community to which a craftsman could belong politically as well as economically.

"Yet in return for security they became dependent on temple or court and were relegated to the lower classes. The peasant masses gained even less material advantages; in Egypt, for instance, metal did not replace the old stone and wood tools for agricultural work. Yet, however imperfectly, even the earliest urban communities must have been held together by a sort of solidarity missing from any neolithic village. Peasants, craftsmen, priests and rulers form a community, not only by reason of identity of language and belief, but also because each performs mutually complementary functions, needed for the well-being (as redefined under civilisation) of the whole. In fact, the earliest cities illustrate a first approximation to an organic solidarity based on a functional complementarity and interdependence between all its members such as subsist between the constituent cells of an organism. Of course, this was only a very distant approximation. However necessary the concentration of the surplus really were with the existing forces of production, there seemed a glaring conflict on economic interests between the tiny ruling class, who annexed the bulk of the social surplus, and the vast majority who were left with a bare subsistence and effectively excluded from the spiritual benefits of civilisation. So solidarity had still to be maintained by the ideological devices appropriate to the mechanical solidarity of barbarism as expressed in the preeminence of the temple or the sepulchral shrine, and now supplemented by the force of the new State organisation. There could be no room for sceptics or sectaries in the oldest cities."[10]

We now pass on to the second—and perhaps more important—point necessitating the making of religion as a precondition for the urban revolution. It is concerning the channelisation of the social surplus from the rural producers to the growing cities.

5. Channelisation of the Social Surplus

There were three conceivable alternative techniques that could make this possible: 1) direct plunder, 2) purchase and 3) persuasion by ideological devices. We are going to see why the third of these presumably best suited the city governors and that moreover we have the clue in this to the making of religion.

Let us begin with the three possible alternatives for procurement.

The possibility of purchase of the surplus products of the direct producers by the city governors—the priests perhaps having merchants or traders under their control—is ruled out, because the proposition of purchase would presuppose accumulation of sufficient wealth (or in the ancient context, the accumulation of city-products with which to barter with the peasants), and this, in its turn, already employing full-time specialists by the merchants and traders to produce the typical urban products or commodities with which to buy or barter with the peasants, or, in other words, the accumulation of food stuff in the city granaries already accomplished.

We are thus left with the other two alternatives, namely plunder and persuasion.

Of these two, again, plunder is a cumbrous and complicated process: it presupposes the maintenance of a bureaucracy with at least a sizeably large armed force to coerce the peasants to part with their surplus products; for their maintenance we have to presuppose again sufficient food stuff already accumulated in the city granaries.

At any rate, compared to it, the method of persuasion is infinitely simpler and smoother. All that this method requires is the effective use of superstition. Thus, for example, once the peasants are made to believe that without offering a part of their products to the goddesses or gods—i.e. concretely to their earthly representatives, the priests or priestly corporations working for the god or god-king—they remain exposed to grave perils like droughts, plagues and disasters in many other forms, the peasants would willingly—and perhaps also eagerly—part with whatever they can afford from their own products. Besides, these priests or priestly corporations do not have to create such superstitions out of nothing: from the paleolithic age people with extremely rudimentary understanding and control of nature were trying to supplement their real technique with the illusory technique, namely magic, from the purely negative aspect of which goddesses, gods and all sorts of supernatural agencies could smoothly take shape. As George Thomson very lucidly explained: "The technique of magic is developed by the ruling class as a means of consolidating their privileges by investing them with supernatural sanctions. In this way the working class, being ignorant of the true causes of its subjection, is reconciled to its lot. This is the genesis of religion. Religion is an outgrowth of magic which emerges with the class struggle.

It is an inverted image of social reality. Just as magic expresses primitive man's weakness in the face of nature, so religion expresses civilised man's weakness in the face of society."[11] This must have made the task of the governors of the early nucleus of cities all the more easy. They had only to systematise—to add awe and wonder—to a pre-existing system of beliefs and practices, and thus make the technique of persuading the direct producers to part with their surplus products to city rulers from which to maintain the full-time specialists essential for the Urban Revolution.

I may perhaps be allowed here to mention a personal experience. While visiting the Tirupati temple a few years ago, I had the opportunity of looking at the devotees forming a queue—perhaps a mile long, if not longer—each patiently waiting for his turn to offer to the god either in cash or in kind something which in our terminology could be ultimately nothing but the surplus of their own labour. There was absolutely no question of any purchase or of barter. There was no question of using the police or any other coercive machinery enforcing them to part with their earnings—in short, there was nothing at all but their devotion to the deity that made them eager and anxious to part with their "surplus". Obedience to the god and offering to him assumed the status of a privilege. How absurdly simple the whole process was of accumulating wealth in the temple treasury, which ran to millions. While looking at the queue, I had myself the feeling that something like this—though perhaps not in the same grand scale—must have happened in front of the monumental structures unearthed by the archaeologists, which are relics of the temples of the earliest cities in Egypt, Mesopotamia and presumably also in the Indus basin. Strong religious beliefs effectively propagated among the masses must have been the easiest or the least cumbersome technique of getting the social surplus from the rural areas channelised to the growing cities.

The dramatic change in the nature of the archaeological materials testifies to the newly emerged organised religion:

"The most striking objects now unearthed are no longer the tools of agriculture and the chase and other products of domestic industry, but temple furniture, weapons, wheel-made pots, jewellery, and other manufactures turned out on a large scale by skilled artisans. As monuments we have, instead of huts and farmhouses, monumental tombs, temples, palaces, and workshops. And in them we find all manner of exotic substances, not as rarities, but regularly imported and used in everyday life. Evidently the change in the archaeologists' material reflects a transformation in the economy that produced the material."[12]

At the same time—i.e. notwithstanding the waste and inequities—it needs to be remembered that all this had been a historical necessity. Without the newly developed imposing religions the channelisation of wealth to the city centres could not be possible; without this channelisation there could be no provision for whole-time resident specialists in these centres, and without the whole-time resident specialists the foundation of civilisation could hardly be laid. Whatever, therefore, might have been the eventual role of religion, it would only be wrong sociology to overlook or ignore its original historical necessity.

7. The Dialectics of Progress

"It is important to remember", observes George Thomson, "as Gordon Childe has pointed out, that even the lowest paid slaves in Mesopotamia were better off than the free and equal members of any neolithic village. The urban revolution had brought about an absolute rise in the standard of living. On the other hand, if we take into account the enormous rise in the productivity of labour, it is clear that relatively they were worse off. The gains won from the revolution were unequally distributed. It was this factor that eventually brought the expansion of the new economy to a stop."[13]

Gordon Childe gives us an inventory of human achievements preceding and following the urban revolution. Before the urban revolution comparatively poor and illiterate communities had made an impressive series of contributions to man's progress. The two millennia immediately preceding 3000 B.C. had witnessed discoveries of far-reaching consequences," of which Childe mentions fifteen—beginning with artificial irrigation and ending with what belonged to "the earliest stages of the revolution"—a solar calendar, writing, numeral notations' and bronze.[14]

"The two thousand years after the revolution, say from 2600 to 600 B.C., produced few contributions of anything like comparable importance to human progress. Perhaps only four achievements deserve to be put in the same category as the fifteen just enumerated." These are: 'decimal notation' of Babylonia, an economical method for smelting iron on an industrial scale, a truly alphabetic script and aqueducts for supplying water to cities.[15]

Thus contrasting progress before and after the urban revolution, we have to admit that the latter "seems to mark, not the dawn of a new era of accelerated advance, but culmination and arrest of an earlier period of growth". Why, then, was this arrest? Curiously enough, one of the most important causes accounting for this is to be found in the same factor that caused the revolution.

The revolution was caused not merely by the human capacity to produce surplus but also by the channelisation of this surplus to the centres that grew into cities and the accumulation of it under the custody of the gods, i.e. their earthly representatives, the priests and the priestly corporations. But how did it happen like that and what were its consequences? This leads us to Gordon Childe's brilliant summing up of the "dialectics of progress", which we have to read and re-read for our own understanding of the subsequent course of ideological development.

"Almost from the outset of his career, it would seem, man used his distinctively human faculties not only to make substantial tools for use upon the real world, but also to imagine supernatural forces that he could employ upon it. He was, that is, simultaneously trying to understand, and so use, natural processes and peopling the real world with imaginary beings, conceived in his own image, that he hoped to coerce or cajole. He was building up science and superstition side by side.

"The superstitions man devised and the fictitious entities he imagined were presumably necessary to make him feel at home in his environment and to make life bearable. Nevertheless the pursuit of the vain hopes and illusory short-cuts suggested by magic and religion repeatedly deterred man from the harder road to the control of nature by understanding. Magic seemed easier than science, just as torture is less trouble than the collection of evidence.

"Magic and religion constituted the scaffolding needed to support the rising structure of social organisation and of science. Unhappily the scaffolding repeatedly cramped the execution of the design and impeded the progress of the permanent building. It even served to support a sham facade behind which the substantial structure was threatened with decay. The urban revolution, made possible by science, was exploited by superstition. The principal beneficiaries from the achievements of farmers and artisans were priests and kings. Magic rather than science was thereby enthroned and invested with the authority of temporal power.

"It is as futile to deplore the superstitions of the past as it is to complain of the unsightly scaffolding essential to the erection of a lovely building. It is childish to ask why man did not progress straight from the squalor of a 'pre-class' society to the glories of a classless paradise, nowhere fully realised as yet. Perhaps the conflicts and contradictions, above revealed, themselves constitute the dialectics of progress. In any case, they are facts of history. If we dislike them, that does not mean that progress is a delusion, but merely that we have understood neither the facts nor progress nor man. Man made the superstitions and the institutions of oppression as much as he made the sciences and the instruments of production. In both alike he was expressing himself, finding himself, making himself."[16]

8. The Pharaoh That Failed

We shall end the present lecture with a few words on the historical necessity of organised religion for the human move forward to civilisation. We have already quoted Childe's observation that in the earliest centres of the urban revolution there can be no room for sceptics or sectaries. The reason for this is also explained by him. The ideological cohesion essential for the urban revolution was affected by organised religion, which, if disturbed in any way cannot be tolerated. But what happens to one who chooses to disturb this universe of organised religion either by questioning it or by trying to replace it by some new cult, even though he has the profoundest political and financial power under his command? The answer is that his proposed reform was destined to fail and this for the simple reason that it was historically premature or that he was trying to go against history. In other words, material conditions were not yet created for the acceptance of such reform.

We are indebted to Barrows Dunham for a brilliant analysis of a case of this with which he opens his work *Heroes and Heretics*. It is the case of a pharaoh that failed. We shall follow Dunham and quote him freely for discussing this example, because all this has far-reaching implications for our understanding of the future of religion—a subject to which we propose to return in our last lecture.

By the rarest of chances—though for reasons we can at best speculate—an Egyptian king proposed to introduce some basic reform in the then prevailing organised religion of Egypt. When we look back at it today, his proposed reform may not appear to be so momentous after all. But it was not really a trifling one judged in its historical context.

The basic facts are as follows: "The king was Amenhotep IV, a pharaoh of the eighteenth dynasty, about 1372 to 1354 B.C. This name he changed, in celebration of his heresy, to Akhnaton. That is to say, he preferred being called 'Aten is well pleased' to being called 'Amon is satisfied'. The reason was that the pharaoh, having a taste for physical explanations, conceived the ruling god as a sun-disc rather than as a spirit of the sun."[17]

Being an all-powerful king after all, he had not much problem in introducing this reform. He had only to decree it. But its consequences were disastrous. As Dunham describes: "The main facts are reasonably clear. Akhnaton outlawed the old theology, closed down the temples of the traditional gods, abolished the priesthoods, services, and profits connected with them. He built in the plain of Amarna a new shrine and capital, Akhetaten, the City of the Horizon of the Sun. Priestly wrath and consternation can hardly have been less than they would be if some modern government were to abolish, all at once and all together, Catholicism, Protestantism, Judaism, and every other religion hitherto existing. Yet the priests, thus stricken had no alternative and no redress. The pharaoh's will was paramount."[18] Thus in short, Akhnaton's proposed reform amounted to an abrupt abolition of ancient rites and old theogonies, deprived the priests of their older functions and therefore also their financial interests inherited from their previous reigns. The ideological cohesion on which the urban revolution in Egypt was based was seriously disturbed, the old temples deserted. At the same time, the pharaoh's decree was absolute. There was no scope whatsoever to question or flout it—not at least so long as the pharaoh was there. Deprived of their inherited power and privileges, they were angry of course, but they were also obliged to keep this anger suppressed or subdued.

With the pharaoh's passing away, this anger burst forth with great vengeance. They erased Akhnaton's name from the calendar of kings, allowing it to appear—when at all—as "that criminal of Amarna". "The City of the Sun's Horizon was razed to the foundation, which still lingers at Amarna and the succeeding pharaoh, Tutankaten, changed his name to the celebrated Tutankhamon we now know. Thus the god Aten, the divine sun-disc, lost to the god Amon, the spirit of the sun."[19]

Such then is in broad outline the history of the innovation sought to be introduced into the official religion of Ancient Egypt, or to what may appear to us as some kind of a comparatively mild tilt to naturalism given to this official religion. The anger or vengeance of the priests provoked by this proposed innovation is, of course, easily understood: it was directly connected with their material interest—the income they derived from being the custodians of the traditional religion and performance of the older rites. However, the question that interests us most in this connection is the reaction of the people—of the vast masses of direct producers—whose surplus product was channelised to the temples and fattened the priests. Any relative relief from religious superstitions which kept them cowed to the priests—however feeble it may appear to us—is expected to be some relief for them after all. But it seems that historically speaking this did not happen and the pharaoh failed mainly because the people were not with him or that he could not mobilise the masses in favour of his proposed reform. At their stage of historical development they needed religion because of the material conditions in which they lived. And the religion they were accustomed to had deep roots in their consciousness, any sudden change in which was only to cause alarm in them and hence could not be acceptable. As Barrows Dunham observes:

"What were people to think and do when the gods they had worshipped, sworn by, lived by, were all at once declared nullities? One's child was perhaps ill, and one had always appealed to Amon on such occasions. One's husband had died, and it had always been necessary to settle such accounts with Osiris. But now, by decree of Akhnaton, Amon and Osiris were nowhere to be found. Their priests were scattered, their temples wasted grass. In the old days, Amon had healed and Osiris saved. Could one be sure that Aten would do these things?

"The people felt, one imagines, left naked to circumstance. A trusted guard had been removed, and the new seemed no protection because untried. Thus men kept a secret faith in the old religion and the old rites; they were on the priests', side whatever the pharaoh might decree. And in the end, when Akhnaton had died, priests and people did to his works what he had done to some of theirs."[20]

We have now a fuller idea of the failure of the pharaoh. Religion cannot be changed—far less uprooted—by sheer decree, so long as the material conditions of the society remain unaltered. That is why Marx called it the heart of a heartless world or a necessary palliative—the opium—required by the people in such a world. It can be uprooted only by changing the material conditions that require religion. Though today we may be nearing such material conditions, the ancient Egyptians were very far from it. Religion was a necessity for them, though not for us today. But more of the future of religion later.

REFERENCES

1. V. Gordon Childe WHH 15.
2. B. McNairn 29.
3. Quoted *ibid* 33.
4. *Ibid* 92.
5. V. Gordon Childe WHH 8.
6. *Ibid* 48.
7. *Ibid* 68.
8. V. Gordon Childe MMH 105.
9. V. Gordon Childe ACI 14.
10. *Ibid* 17.
11. G. Thomson ER 9.
12. V. Gordon Childe MMH 142.
13. G. Thomson SAGS i. 24.
14. V. Gordon Childe MMH 227.
15. *Ibid*.
16. *Ibid* 236-37.
17. B. Dunham 3.
18. *Ibid* 4.
19. *Ibid* 5.
20. *Ibid* 4-5.

3

Harappan Religion and the Aryan Question

1. Preliminary Remarks

The excavations and explorations by the archaeologist, both in India and Pakistan, during the decades after the first discovery of the Indus Valley Civilisation (often also called the Harappan Civilisation or Harappan Culture, taking Harappa as its type-site), have added more to our knowledge of it, than was contained in the three volumes edited by Marshall *(Mohenjodaro and the Indus Valley Civilization)*, the first full-length study of it based on the collaboration of a number of specialists like Mackay, Guha, Hempy and others. So has also grown a flourishing literature on the subject—literature sometimes based not merely on the analysis of cold archaeological data but also on presumptions and conjectures, inclusive unfortunately also of some apparently wild ones. In a recently published book called the *Ancient Cities of the Indus* edited by G.L. Possehl (1979), we have a *Bibliography* of the literature on the Indus valley civilisation, which contains 1607 entries. From this we have a rough idea of the dust cloud raised by scholars specially when it comes to such questions as the social organisation, ideology, decadence and final destruction of the civilisation as also on its language and script. In such circumstances it is only empty optimism to expect anybody to discuss the religion of the Harappan culture without being immediately challenged by a whole host of critics, however far they may be from agreeing with each other. Thus, for example, Marshall wrote a long chapter on the religion of the ancient Indus Civilisation the main thrust of which is that many prominent elements of what is known as later Hinduism—like the prominence of the Great Mother Goddess, the worship of Śiva sometimes conceived as Paśupati (the lord of animals) and sometimes as the mere phallic emblem, zoomorphism in varied forms, etc.—though forming prominent features of Hinduism are not at all traceable in the Vedic literature, conceived earlier as the main source of the Hindu religion. Only after the excavations of the Harappan sites have we been able to realise that these have real roots in the ancient Harappan Civilisation and somehow survived to form the later religious beliefs and practices of the Indians. Among the contemporary archaeologists the Allchins think that, though written decades ago, this essay of Marshall continues to be a "brilliant" one.[1] Childe himself summed up Marshall's essay with his own comments thus:

> Religion gives the most convincing illustration of the explicitly Indian character of the Indus Civilisation. Many objects from the ancient cities, otherwise unintelligible, can be satisfactorily explained by reference to the Hindu cult. The innumerable clay figurines, indeed, are not without parallels elsewhere. In India the majority represent a female personage, often richly bejewelled and sometimes pregnant or nursing an infant; some may be votive statuettes of deities, but others may represent petitioners, or even dolls. So, too, among clay models of animals the frequent Brahmani bulls may be regarded as sacred but others, such as oxen provided with a moveable head, are obviously toys like the equally common miniature carts, couches, loaves, and vases. But there are aniconic objects, notably huge stone phalli and rings, often wavy along the edge, that correspond to the *liṅgas* and *yonis* of Hindu fertility cults.
>
> The 'seals' and tablets of stamped clay, engraved copper or moulded fayence offer more conclusive evidence. A 'seal' from Mohenjo-daro depicts a horned deity with three faces sitting

cross-legged in the attitude of ritual meditation between various wild animals; he is obviously the prototype of Siva, 'three-faced', lord of beasts, 'prince of yogis', as Marshall has demonstrated in detail. Several clay tablets depict a male deity; one shows a river gushing out of a goddess's womb. In other cases tree spirits are clearly indicated. In contrast to such themes, all familiar to Hindu iconography, are isolated motives suggestive of Babylonia—an antithetic group of 'a hero tempting tigers and a half-human monster like the Sumerian Enkidu grappling with a bull or a tiger. The swastika and the cross, common on stamps and plaques, were religious or magical symbols as in Babylonia and Elam in the earliest prehistoric period, but preserve that character also in modern India as elsewhere.

The religious concepts suggested by the foregoing documents are familiar to modern and post-Vedic Hinduism. But they are conspicuously absent from the oldest of the Hindu sacred books, the *Rig-Veda*, while scenes illustrative of its hymns may be sought in vain in the Indus period. Śiva as depicted at Harappa and Mohenjo-daro is generally regarded as an 'aboriginal' deity taken over by the invading Vedic Aryans and verbally identified with the unimportant Vedic Prajāpati. Tree-spirits and female deities played a negligible role in Vedic mythology, and phallicism is unmentioned—all have been regarded by European scholars as post-Vedic accretions in Brahmanism.

Conversely, the celestial figures of the Vedic pantheon, like the thunder-wielding Indra, are not detectable in the Indus period. The horse, so prominent in Vedic imagery and a principal sacrificial animal, is never represented on the 'seals' which yet must have had a religious virtue.

For the above reasons alone the Indus Civilisation may be regarded as non-Aryan and pre-Aryan. In fact, it provides a documentary illustration of the sources, long inferred on comparative grounds, of those 'accretions' which distinguish modern Brahmanism from the religion and ritual illustrated in the Vedas.[2]

As against all this, A. Ghosh has come out rather sharply. As he says:

> It is useless to reiterate and scrutinise all that has been said to substantiate that many later-day Hindu religio-ritualistic practices and spiritual thoughts were derived from the Harappa. The worship of Śiva-paśupati, the liṅga and the mother-goddess, Upaniṣadic speculations, asceticism, Jainism, Tantrism, Sāṃkhya, Yoga—quite a motley of thoughts, beliefs and practices—all have been thought to be Harappan in origin. These theories are all fanciful and do not bear scrutiny. For example, Rudra has the appellation *Paśupati* in later Vedic literature not in the sense of lord of beasts in general but of cattle only, which is the primary sense of *paśu*, though a comprehensive meaning of birds and domestic and wild animals is not unknown. Nor has the Vedic Rudra anything to do with meditation. Thus, to see Śiva-paśupati in the well-known and much-spoken-of seal of Mohenjo-daro, which depicts wild animials, is unjustified. Similarly, Sankalia has shown that the so-called *liṅga*-s of Mohenjo-daro were found in streets and drains and were not enshrined in rooms, as one would expect sacred objects to be.[3]

2. The Harappan Civilisation

When archaeologists—inclusive of very eminent ones—argue among themselves so sharply, prudence demands that we better avoid at the present stage of our discussion the question concerning the *nature of* Harappan religion and of its possible survival in later Hinduism. What we nevertheless propose to argue first of all is that religion must have been a very potent factor in the administrative infrastructure of the Harappan Civilisation. It may be useful for this purpose to begin with a brief idea of the extent and population of this civilisation itself.

In 1883, depending mainly on published reports, the Allchins observe: "The area enclosed by line joining the outermost sites at which the material culture of this civilisation has been discovered is little less than half a million square miles, considerably larger than modern Pakistan."[4] Within this vast area of about 500,000 square miles, Pande and Ramachandran, in 1971, claimed that there were 258 sites as distinctly Harappan though, in 1979, D.K. Chakrabarti said, "While some sites..... should now be added to the list there is no assurance that all these 258 sites should strictly come under the category of the Harappan."[5] In 1992, M.R. Mughal observed: "The evidence shows that the area covered by the Indus Civilisation was larger than any of the known civilisations of the ancient world...This enormous area could not have been limited to only 144 sites (the number so far securely identified) and, indeed, claims have been made for the discovery of twenty-seven sites of Harappan affinity in east Punjab and the Doab near Saharanpur."[6]

It may be premature for us to expect a gazetteer of this vast region. But it is necessary to note a few points about the sites in it so far located.

First, D.K. Chakrabarti, depending on the published reports, has prepared a list of the major sites, i.e. those covering roughly over 1,25,000 square feet, along with the estimated population of each. The population-estimate is based on "a nineteenth century statistics for Srikapur in northwest Sind" which Lamrick thought "closely resembled Mohenjo-daro both in dimensions and layout." According to this estimate the total population of Mohenjo-daro could be 35,000 though according to Datta it could be 34,469 and according to Fairservis it was likely to have been 41,250. The total area covered by Mohenjo-daro was 850,000 square metres. Assuming Lamrick's estimate of the density of population of Harappan settlements, one is thus led to think that a site of 1,25,000 square feet was likely to have 5000 or more people in each. On the basis of this, Chakrabarti has observed, "One can possibly say with some emphasis that there were at least 15 Harappan settlements with more than 5000 people each. The number is likely to have been more when full data are available for most of the sites."[7]

Secondly, Fairservis has attempted to sketch the composition of the non-agricultural population of Mohenjo-daro. According to him this comprised of 1) Priests, 2) Scribes and Seal-cutters, 3) Musicians and dancers, 4) Engineers,

5) Potters, 6) Weavers, 7) Brick-makers, 8) Masons, 9) Carpenters, 10) Metallurgists and 11) Traders. To this needs to be added the amazing uniformity observed throughout all Harappan sites: "the apparent uniformity of weights and measures, the common script, the uniformity—almost common currency—of the seals, the evidence of extensive trade in almost every class of commodity throughout the whole Harappan culture zone, the common elements in architecture and town-planning, the common elements in art and religion."[8] It may not be wrong to expect the same uniformity in the population-composition pointed out by Fairservis about Mohenjo-daro in the other Indus cities.

Thirdly, admitting the same or at least very similar population-composition in major Harappan sites, it needs to be noted that none of the eleven major groups in the city mentioned was expected to be the direct producer of its own means of subsistence. In all presumption, therefore, they were likely to have lived on the food produced by the villagers within the general cultural zone—i.e. on the social surplus funnelled to the city centres.

This brings us back to the question we have previously discussed, namely that of the channelisation to the city-centres of the social surplus produced by the villagers. We have argued that there could be three conceivable modes for the machinery of this channelisation: purchase, plunder and persuasion—i.e. persuasion on the strength of religious beliefs. Of these three modes, as we have already argued, only the last was likely to have been the most feasible and least cumbrous one. Applying the same argument to the Harappan culture zone, we are left to presume that religion was likely to have been the most potent force in the administrative machinery of the vast "Harappan empire", whatever might have been the actual nature of this religion, i.e. whether its nature answered to Marshall's description of it or not.

3. Kosambi and Needham

Of the three primary centres of the urban revolution, there is now not much doubt that administrative machinery of at least two—namely Egypt and Mesopotamia—was largely under the grip of the priests or priestly corporation. But our present problem is concerning the third primary centre, namely the Indus Valley Civilisation.

By analogy, one is tempted to argue that since it was necessary for the other two primary centres of the Urban Revolution to use massive superstition for policing the state, the same must have been true also of the third primary centre. Besides, as we have already seen, the accumulation of the surplus products of the direct producers in the cities, seems to be best explained by the presumption of the use of superstition.

Nevertheless, the assumption of the vast Indus "Empire" being ruled by the priests or priestly corporations could not be a smooth one and there is literally a storm of controversy over the question of the actual socio-political organisation of Harappan culture. The main difficulty here, as about many other questions concerning the Harappan Culture, is the want of direct literary documents attesting to some view or the other. It is generally admitted no doubt that there must have been some strong centralised power enforcing its authority over the Harappan "empire", because, without assuming it there is hardly any explanation of the manifold uniformity observed throughout it. But we have no direct knowledge of the nature of this centralised authority.

Many relics of the Indus civilisation are generally viewed no doubt as indicative of religion and religious beliefs.

From the time of the publication of the first full report on the excavations of Harappa and Mohenjo-daro to that of the recent excavations at Kalibangan and Lothal, the archaeologists have shown how a large number of the relics of this forgotten civilisation cannot but be understood as pointers to the powerful religious beliefs prevalent in the period. We need not present here a list of such relics; readers interested in these may look up the recent book by the Allchins,[9] where all these are very ably summed up. This does not mean, of course, that we have now a coherent and comprehensive understanding of the nature of Harappan religion and it is no use speculating on when and how any full account of it would be reconstructed. Nor is the basic fact to be ignored that among the eminent archaeologists controversies are still going on about its general outlines. However, all these do not materially affect our main argument which requires only to be admitted that the Indus relics are unmistakably indicative of some presumably strong and widespread religious beliefs. If so, we have also to admit that the custodians of these were the priests or priestly corporations, and, on the analogy of ancient Egypt and Mesopotamia, we are naturally tempted to assume that these priests and priestly corporations could remain quite aloof from the actual administration of the vast Indus "empire". On the contrary it would be logical to think that, whatever might have been the actual nature of the social structure of the Indus civilisation, these priests or priestly corporations were only likely to have a large share—if not the decisive one—in the administrative machinery in the Harappan administration. From the remains of the imposing houses of the merchants in the Harappan cities, it is sometimes conjectured that these merchants could have formed the actual ruling class of the "empire". But the obvious difficulty about such a conjecture is that it can hardly explain the eventual internal decadence of the Harappan civilisation, about which the archaeologists are agreed. The merchant class—sensing as it does greater and still greater profitability —are drawn to improving and augmenting the production-process and hence the government under their rule is only expected to prosper rather than become a prey to eventual degeneration and decay. By contrast, a government under the priestly class is only likely to be under the grip of strong conservatism and hence also exposed to the possibility of creeping paralysis, because innovations in technique are generally frowned upon by the stereotyped religious beliefs.

Incidentally, D.D. Kosambi has advanced a new suggestion indicative of the effective use of religious superstition as an instrument for Harappan administration. As he observes,

> Finally, the tools of violence were curiously weak, though nothing is directly known of their social mechanism for wielding force, which we call the state. The weapons found in the Indus cities are flimsy, particularly the ribless leaf-blade copper spearheads which would have crumpled up at the first good thrust. There is nothing like a sword in the main Indus strata. Archers occur in the ideograms, arrowheads of stone and copper have been discovered. The bow would be a survival of the hunting age. Of course, iron was not known, so that a few weapons in the hands of a small minority might have sufficed; but the contrast with the excellent, sturdy though archaic, tools proves that the use of weapons was not very important. Therefore, the state mechanism, whatever it was must have had some powerful adjunct that reduced the need for violence to a minimum. The cities rested upon trade, not fighting; but if the army of police were not very strong what helped the trader maintain his unequal sharing of profit?
>
> The answer seems to lie in religion. Though there are no great statues of the gods, what has been called the 'citadel' mound undoubtedly corresponds to the temple-*zikkurat* structures in Mesopotamia... The Harappan site has been devastated by brick-robbing, while at Mohenjodaro, what must have been the ruins of a major building in the sacred enclosure are covered by a *Kuṣāna stūpa*. But the adjacent 'Great Bath' at Mohenjo-daro (filled with water drawn laboriously by hand from a special adjacent well, beautifully constructed with bitumen waterproofing between brick layers, a drain for emptying, and surrounded on three sides by cells) must have been a ritual tank, because of the beautiful and well-used bathrooms in every private house which distinguish the city from anything in the proto-history of Mesopotamia, or Egypt. Even a bather from the citadel could easily have descended the steps in the wall which led down to the river. I have explained this as the

> prototype of the sacred lotus pond *puṣkara* which survived in the later times.[10]

Thus one of the main points stressed by Kosambi in favour of his view of the comparatively greater need of religious superstitions for policing the Harappan "empire" is the flimsiness of the offensive weapons specially as contrasted with the excellent sturdy though archaic tools, which proves that the weapons usually needed to keep the people under control were not very important after all.

To this may be added another point.

The weapons unearthed at the Harappan sites are indeed flimsy, indicating the lesser use of direct violence and hence of comparatively greater use of religious superstitions. What could have perhaps made the argument stronger is another consideration.

Already in the introduction to the first full-length report on *Mohenjo-daro and the Indus Civilisation*, Marshall observes: "Their weapons of war and of the chase are the bow and arrow, spear, axe, dagger and mace. The sword they have not yet evolved; *nor is there any evidence of defensive body armours*."[11] We have added emphasis on the last point, because, thanks to Needham's brilliant analysis, this seems to have very decisive importance for the point Kosambi has argued in favour of the relatively greater use of religious superstitions for the Harappan rulers. The offensive weapons mentioned by Marshall—spear, axe, dagger and mace—are useful in hand-to-hand fights, or in cases of immediate confrontation of armed forces with the exploited peasants when necessary. Besides, these were flimsy after all. But not so are the bow and arrow, which are very effective long distance missiles. Now, as Kosambi admits, the bow and arrow being inherited from the hunting stage, there is nothing to prevent the assumption that the peasants were as much equipped with these as were the armed forces of the ruling class. And it is here the *defensive body armour* has supreme importance from the viewpoint of military technology in the distant past. So long, therefore, as the defensive body armour is not developed and used, some method other than direct violence is needed to keep the masses under control.

In the Chinese context, as Needham shows, the lack of inadequate development of defensive body armours was one main reason for the ruling ideology—viz. Confucianism—to preach to the people to remain submissive to the lords. As he observes,

"What was the situation, then in ancient China? There the crossbow—a most powerful weapon—was invented centuries before anywhere else. We know that the men of the feudal levies in ancient China (by that I mean between 800 and 300 B.C.) were armed with powerful bows. But at the same time protective armour was very little developed. The archaeologist Laufer has written a fine monograph on Chinese armour. It arises very late, and in early times you only get protective clothing made of bamboo and wood. Moreover, there are in the *Tso Chuan* countless stories of feudal lords being killed by arrow shots. *If the mass of the people as a whole were in possession of a powerful offensive weapon, and the ruling class were not in possession of a superior defensive means, one can see that the balance of power in society was different from what it was in, e.g. the time of the early Roman Empire, where the disciplined legions were rather well armoured, with bronze and iron. A slave population was possible because it was not in possession of the arms and armour of the legionaries,* nor did it have access to powerful bows. The principal Roman weapons were always the spear and the short sword. We know what troubles the slaves could give on the few occasions in which they did gain access to substantial stores of weapons, as in the revolt of Spartacus. In China, it was a different story, because from an early date the people had crossbows and the lords had poor defensive armour. If that was the case, it means that the people in China had to be persuaded, rather than cowed by force of arms, and hence the importance for the Confucians."[12] For, as Needham has already shown, "during what may be called the high feudal period in China, which runs roughly from the eighth century to the third century B.C. the feudal lords were assisted and counselled by a group of men who afterwards became the school of philosophers which we know as the Confucian School."[13] It preached to the people the virtue of remaining as pious law-abiding citizens.

With these points in mind, we may now return to the question of the Indus civilisation.

Not that we know of there having been any philosopher in the Harappan culture, not to speak of any school of philosophy even remotely resembling the Confucian one. Notwithstanding Marshall's expectation to the contrary, it can perhaps be safely asserted that there was nothing like that, or at least, even if there was any philosopher in the Harappan culture, we shall never know anything about him. What we do know, however, is that the *Harappans did not develop any defensive body armour*. Even imagining that they developed something like that made of flimsy materials, these could not be effective against the long-distance missiles—the arrows—possessed in common by the army and the masses. It follows, therefore, that for keeping the masses under control it was essential for the ruling class to have something more than their military technology. This something more had to have the efficacy of persuading the masses to remain as pious law-abiding citizens. In other words, in default of effective defensive armour they had to depend on ideological devices—or, to put it more bluntly, on religious superstitions on a really massive scale. Many stray objects found in the Harappan regions give us some glimpse of a rather imposing religion, though our archaeologists are yet to reconstruct any agreed view of this religion. But religion was there and so also there must have been its main accessory, namely, superstition.

Could it, then, be that this religious ideology was the main instrument in Harappan culture for the purpose of policing the state notwithstanding the controversies among the archaeologists and others concerning the actual *nature of* this religion ? This brings us back to Kosambi's hypothesis though from a different premise altogether. What Kosambi argued from the flimsiness of offensive weapons seems to be strengthened by the lack of defensive body armour.

4. End of Harappa and the Aryan Question

That after a glorious career of over five hundred years, the Indus civilisation came under the grip of decline and degeneration is archaeologically indisputable. Depending mainly on Mackay's work, Gordon Childe gives us some typical examples of this: "The last reconstructions of Harappan cities exhibit every sign of decadence. Old bricks were re-used for building mean houses on the sites formerly occupied by the spacious mansions of the bourgeoisie. The civic authority could no longer enforce the building regulations so strictly observed in more prosperous days so that the dwellings encroached upon the streets."[14] Discussing the fate of Mohenjo-daro city, Wheeler observes: " One thing at least is clear about the end of Mohenjo-daro: the city was already slowly dying before its ultimate end. Houses, mounting gradually upon the ruins of their predecessors or on artificial platforms in the endeavour to out-top the floods, were increasingly shoddy in construction, increasingly carved up into warrens for a swarming lower-grade population. Flimsy partitions subdivided the courtyards of houses. To a height of 30 feet or more, the tall podium of the Great Granary on the western side of the citadel was engulfed by rising structure of poorer and poorer quality. Re-used brickbats tended to replace new bricks. The city, to judge from excavated areas, was 'becoming a slum'."[15]

Why then was this decadence and degeneration after a splendid career of five hundred years or more? This is a question about which there is a good deal of controversy among the contemporary archaeologists. Perhaps it is premature at the present stage of research to expect any clear and definite answer to it. What is possible nevertheless is to mention some of the prominent views advanced with comments on their comparative plausibility.

To begin with, let us note that what was perhaps true of the Mohenjo-daro city was not likely to be true of the entire vast area covered by Harappan culture. Nevertheless, we cannot possibly ignore the fate of the Mohenjo-daro city itself. At least one of the factors that contributed to the decline of this city was repeated flooding of it which, as the Allchins observe, "has been long known and cannot be entirely discounted as a cause of local destruction."[16] It is true that the Harappans could and did rebuild or repair the city repeatedly after the devastating floods; but that must have sapped much of their energy and vitality, and hence also caused deviation from their main preoccupations. It is also tempting to conjecture that this could have further considerably weakened—or at least adversely affected—the prestige of the city rulers if they were priests, priestly corporations or priest-kings, because one source from which they were likely to create a belief in their supernormal power in the popular mind could have been their capacity for predicting the coming of the floods based on their astronomical knowledge and calendrical science. If, in spite of this, they failed to predict the coming of floods—not to mention preventing these with their allegedly supernatural power—the city dwellers were likely to have raised awkward questions about their authority.

So, the ravages caused by floods were likely to have been one of the factors that brought degeneration to the Mohenjo-daro city itself. But some of the archaeologists appear to go a step further and want to view the floods—along with other climatic and tectonic changes—as having been basically responsible for the degeneration and destruction of the Harappan culture as such. It is not necessary for our present purpose to attempt a re-examination of their view, because one of our most competent archaeologist-scientists, D.P. Agrawal,[17] has already done it.

We have in his discussion some knowledge of the changes in physical geography affecting the fate of the Indus civilisation At the same time, it needs to be noted that the decline and fall of the Indus civilisation must have been a complex phenomenon and to seek its full explanation only in any of these—or exclusively in one type of causal factors—remains exposed to the danger of over-simplification. As Agrawal himself says, "It may, however, be emphasised that not a single cause but several contributed towards the decline and disappearance of the mighty Harappan civilisation."[18] This is a point on which a significant number of serious archaeologists concur." Just as the creation and maintenance of the system was the outcome of the successful combination of several factors," observe the Allchins, "so too its breakdown could have been caused by the weakening of any one of these or the upsetting of their harmonious balance and interaction."[19] Even Wheeler—about one of whose points, as we shall presently see, there is a great deal of furore among our historians—substantially agrees with this.

> Let it be said at once that the factors instrumental in the dissolution of historic civilisations have never been of an uncomplicated kind. It can scarcely be supposed therefore that prehistoric or historic civilisations have endured simple destinies; in other words, here too no single explanation can convincingly claim total truth. Over-ambitious wars, barbarian invasions, dynastic or capitalistic intrigue, climate, the malarial mosquito have been urged severally in one context or another as the overall cause. Other theories have relied upon racial degeneration, variously defined or cautiously vague; an enlargement, perhaps, of Samuel Butler's plaint that 'life is one long process of getting tired'. Recently, deep floods derived from violent geomorphological changes have been blamed for the end of the Indus civilisation. In a particular context which has sometimes been amplified or decried without warrant, I once light-heartedly blamed Indra and his invading Aryans for a concluding share in this phenomenon. The list need not be extended. It is safe to affirm that any one of these answers to the problem is far more likely than not to be fallacious in isolation. The fall, like the rise, of a civilisation is a highly complex operation which can only be distorted and obscured by easy simplification.[20]

Interestingly enough among the causes of the decline and fall of the Indus "empire", Possehl mentions even the possibility of peasant revolt against the exploiters in the cities. As he says, "Political conflict which could destroy the people producing the food and/or the productive potential of the land on which the non-agricultural urbanites ultimately depended could be another such explanation. Might we not entertain such notions as peasant revolts against the ruling classes who may have been largely or even exclusively city based?"[21]

Such then, are some of the conjectures concerning the decline and end of the Indus civilisation, though also with the caution often expressed against putting an exclusive emphasis on any of these possible factors. The list of conjectures can indeed be enlarged, adding to such possibilities as the financial setback resulting from the loss of foreign trade from the time when the "Mesopotamians looked more towards Arabian and African markets than to Magan and Meluhha"—Meluhha probably having been "the generalised term for the Indus culture area." Another factor suggested is "the 'wearing out' of the land due to over-cultivation", though the Allchins observe that this " seems unlikely as the population pressure can never have been very great, and in late times the land retained great fertility."[22] At the same time, the Allchins comment, "Another possibility which cannot be ignored is of epidemic diseases following in the wake of floods."[23]

All these are conjectures, of course. Besides, it remains an open question whether these factors, taken severally or jointly, can explain only the internal decay of the civilisation or its final and full destruction. Gordon Childe thinks, "This imposing civilisation perished utterly as a result of internal decay accelerated by the shock of barbarian raids."[24] He mentions the following archaeological evidences for the last point:

> Then the civilisation was destroyed by barbarian invaders and the cities reoccupied by illiterate aliens. At Harappa these are

represented only by extended and flexed burials in Cemetery H and the queer painted vases that accompany them. At Chanhu-daro and Jhukar, in Sindh, a distinct barbarian culture, the Jhukar culture replaced the Harappa civilisation. Everywhere the literate tradition exemplified in the inscribed 'seal' was extinguished. But judging by the pottery from Cemetery H and Jhukar sites and by metalwork from the latter, some technical traditions were carried over. Presumably potters and smiths survived to work for new customers. Naturally, they produced quite novel objects to suit foreign tastes.

The pottery from Jhukar and Cemetery H is still wheel made, painted and fired in the old techniques, but shaped quite differently and adorned with new designs. Jhukar smiths made shaft-hole axe-heads and probably axe-adzes and pins with swollen necks. Button or bead seals of stone, fayence or pottery replaced the rectangular glazed steatite 'seal' and were engraved with geometric designs, including the filled cross, or rarely with conventional beasts, inscriptions and lifelike animals.

The button seal like the shaft-hole axe is plainly a north-western intruder in India. The closest parallels to the Jhukar seals, and an exact parallel to the axe-adze, comes from Hissar III in northern Iran. Putative intermediate links will be cited later from Makran and Baluchistan.

These agreements suggest that the barbarians who destroyed the Harappa civilisation included at least invaders from north-western Iran. Wheeler has boldly suggested their identification with the Vedic Aryans. In any case, the *ṛṣis* sang their Vedic hymns in a prehistoric night; for the invasion completely broke the literary tradition, and there is no fixed point in Indian history till the reign of Darius.[25]

5. Aryans and the End of the Indus Civilisation

The view expressed by Wheeler and tacitly endorsed by Childe, namely that the decaying or already largely decayed Indus civilisation came to its final end by the invasion of the Indo-Aryan speaking people—or more simply by the Vedic peoples—has provoked a great deal of controversy and even much indignation among a section of our scholars.

Wheeler fist expressed this view rather forcefully in 1947 in *Ancient India* No. 3 though in 1968 (reprinted in 1979), confronted with some strong criticisms and perhaps also taking note of other possible factors pointed out by other archaeologists as contributing to the final destruction of the Indus valley civilisation, he gave the impression of withdrawing or somehow modifying his original emphasis and observed that he had once blamed Indra rather rhetorically. The tone appears to be somewhat subdued and we shall try to see whether that is at all necessary. But let us begin by quoting his view as originally expressed. In 1947 he observed:

> The Aryan invasion of the Land of the Seven Rivers, the Punjab and it environs, constantly assumes the form of an onslaught upon the walled cities of the aborigines. For these cities the term used in the *Ṛgveda* is *pur,* meaning a "rampart", "fort" or "Stronghold". One is called "broad" *(pṛthvī)* and "wide" *(urvī).* Sometimes strongholds are referred to metaphorically as "of metal" *(āyasī).* Autumnal *(śāradī)* forts are also named: "this may refer to the forts in that season being occupied against Aryan attacks or against inundations caused by overflowing rivers". Forts "with a hundred walls" *(śatabhujī)* are mentioned. The citadel may be made of stone *(aśmamayī)*: alternatively, the use of mud-bricks is perhaps alluded to by the epithet *āma* ("raw", "unbaked".) Indra, the Aryan war-god to *puramdara.* "fort-destroyer". He shatters, "ninety forts" for his Aryan protege, Divodāsa. The same forts are doubtless referred to where in other hymns he demolishes variously ninety-nine and a hundred "ancient castles" of the aboriginal leader Śambara. In brief, he "rends forts as age consumes a garment."

Where are—or were—these citadels? It has in the past been supposed that they were mythical, or were "merely places or refuge against attack, ramparts of hardened earth with palisades and a ditch." The recent excavation of Harappa may be thought to have changed the picture. Here we have a highly evolved civilisation of essentially non-Aryan type, now known

> to have employed massive fortifications, and known also to have dominated the river system of north- western India at a time not distant from the likely period of the earlier Aryan invasions of that region. What destroyed this firmly-settled civilisation? Climatic, economic, political deterioration may have weakened it, but its ultimate extinction is more likely to have been completed by deliberate and large-scale destruction. It may be no more chance that at a late period of Mohenjo-daro men, women and children appear to have been massacred there (Mackay 1938: 94f., 116 ff. 172). On circumstantial evidence, Indra stands accused.[26]

The evidence cited by Mackay of men, women and children having been massacred at a later period of Mohenjo-daro is perhaps not so important for the central argument for viewing the Harappan cities finally ransacked by the invading Aryans. As P.V. Kane and others have shown, the presence of the scattered skeletons at Mohenjo-daro can be explained by other hypotheses. Nevertheless the question of the Aryan invasion remains and it is as strongly supported by some archaeologists as it is bitterly contested by some others. We shall first mention some of the latter.

In 1964, G.F. Dales wrote an article with the title "The Mythical Massacre at Mohenjo-daro."[27] Free use of innuendo and other rhetorics apart, the writer frequently refers to the authority of Marshall and Hargreaves, evidently ignoring the fact that some of their observations have become dated. However, from the archaeological viewpoint, his main—or at least one of his main—arguments is: ".... What is the material evidence to substantiate the supposed invasion and massacre? Where are the burnt fortresses, the arrowheads, weapons, pieces of armour, the smashed chariots and bodies of the invaders and defenders? Despite the extensive excavation at the largest Harappan sites there is not a single bit of evidence that can be brought forth as unconditional proof of an armed conquest and destruction on the supposed scale of the Aryan invasion." Depending mainly on his own theory of floods etc., Dales concludes: "The enemy of the

Harappans was Nature... —Indra and the barbarian hordes are exonerated."[28]

As if it were not enough to establish the innocence of Indra, K.M. Srivastava, depending mainly on the theories of natural calamities to explain the end of the Indus civilisation, proclaims: "Indra, therefore, stands completely exonerated."[29] However he wants to go a step further and seek the clue to the genesis of Wheeler's theory of the Aryan invasion. As he puts it:

> In retrospect, when we look at Wheeler's career as an archaeologist in England and India and we see him as a Brigadier in the British army during World War II, we feel he could not interpret the dubious evidence of Mohenjo-daro and Harappa in any other manner. He started his real archaeological career from Maiden Castle excavations and soon emerged as an authority of Roman archaeology. His *Rome Beyond the Imperial Frontiers* clearly shows how deeply involved he was in the Roman art and architecture, Roman concepts of town-planning—citadels, lower towns, assembly-halls, etc. Thus when he was confronted with the twin-mound towns of the Harappans and the huge fortification walls and mud-brick platforms as well as the photographs of the so-called 'massacre' at Mohenjo-daro he was at once reminded of Roman history and archaeology. Marshall's (1931) and Vats's (1940) reports on Mohenjo-daro and Harappa, respectively, as well as Piggott's *Prehistoric India* (1950: 244: 248) provided him sufficient speculations on Aryan warfare and Indra's attack on Harappan towns. The common textbooks on Indian history adorned his personal library. For the former army man and the Director General of Archaeology in India, as Wheeler was, the Aryan invasion of Indus towns (1961: 249) was as simple as the Roman invasion of Britain and Turkey.[30]

A. Brigadier in the British army almost obsessed with the Roman model is naturally not expected to know much of the Vedas. Wherefrom, then, did he get the Vedic materials to substantiate his theory of the Aryan invasion? Srivastava has a simple answer to this: "In fact it was V.S. Agarwal who provided these references to Dr. Wheeler when the latter requested Professor Agarwal, then an officer in the Archaeological Survey of India, on tour at Harappa, although Dr. Wheeler never acknowledged it in any of his writings."[31]

All this is evidently imputing a certain lack of honesty to Wheeler. Our point, however, is that if Wheeler is really to be criticised for not acknowledging the real source of his information about the Vedic materials (as he unfortunately did), we are to look elsewhere. The theory of the Aryan invasion of the Indus Valley Civilisation—and this based upon a considerable amount of Vedic data—(inclusive of those used by Wheeler)—was already advanced by R.P. Chanda in 1926 and 1929. Since these were published as *Memoirs of the Archaeological Survey of India*, Nos. 31 and 41, Wheeler's want of acquaintance with these is not easily conceivable.

The fact that within a few years of the discovery of the Indus Valley Civilisation the sound Vedic scholarship of R.P. Chanda led him to the view that the ruin of the cities was finally due to the attack of the Vedic people under the leadership of their war-god Indra, and this was, to say the least, a remarkable academic performance on his part. But most of the writers on Indian archaeology do not mention this and the hypothesis is generally associated with the names of Wheeler and Piggott, who more or less plagiarised R.P. Chanda. Therefore we propose to reproduce here the writing of R.P. Chanda at some length.

6. R.P. Chanda and the Theory of the Aryan Invasion

Here are some of the observations of R. P. Chanda published in 1926 in No. 31 of the *Memoirs of the Archaeological Survey of India* (pp. 1-5):

> The archaeological discoveries at Harappa in the Punjab and at Mohenjo-daro in Sind have pushed back the monumental history of India from the third century B.C. to at least the beginning of the third millennium B.C. by one single stroke. A series of literary monuments, the Vedic Saṃhitas, the Brāhmaṇas, and the Sutras have long been known, the youngest

in age among which is probably older than the third century B.C. But a wide divergence of opinion relating to the age of these works and particularly of the *Ṛgveda* among scholars renders their use as sources of history unsafe....

To facilitate the coordination of the data of Archaeology with literary evidence I propose to discuss in this paper some of the passages in the Vedic literature that throw light on the early history of the Indus valley....."Many of the stanzas of the *Ṛgveda* contain references to Pura and Pur both of which terms mean *nagara*, 'town', in classical Sanskrit. In one stanza (7.15.4) an extensive *(śatabhujī)* Pur made of copper or iron *(ayas)* is referred to. In another stanza (1.58.8) prayer is offered to Agni to protect the worshipper with Purs of *ayas*. In such passages *ayas* is evidently used in a metaphorical sense to denote strength. Śuṣṇa, a demon, is said to have a moveable *(cariṣṇva)* Pura (8.1.28). In the *Ṛgveda* Pura is much oftener connected with the enemies of the Aryan than with the Arya Ṛṣis and warriors. Two of the famous Ṛigvedic kings, Divodāsa, the chief of the Bharatas, and Purukutsa, the chief of the Purus, are found engaged in war with hostile owners of Puras. Divodāsa was the son of Vādhryasva and grandfather of the more famous Sudās who defeated a confederacy of ten tribes including the Yadus, Turvasas and Purus on the Western bank of the Puruṣṇi (Ravi). It is said (4.30.20) that Indra overthrew a hundred Puras made of stone *(aśmanmayī)* for his worshipper Divodāsa.

The Puras that Indra overthrew for Divodāsa evidently belonged to Śambara who is called a Dāsa (non-Arya or demon) of the mountain (6.26.5). In one stanza (9.61.2), among the enemies of Divodāsa are mentioned the Yadu (the Chief of the Yadus) and Turvasa (the chief of the Turvasas) with Śambara. The greatest feat that Indra performed on behalf of Purukutsa, the chief of the Purus, is thus described in a stanza (6.20.10): 'May we, O Indra, gain new (wealth) through your favour; the Purus worship thee with this hymn and sacrifices. You destroyed the seven autumnal (*śāradī*) Puras with thunder weapon, slew Dāsas and gave wealth to Purukutsa.' The epithet *śāradī*, usually translated as 'autumnal', is explained by Sāyaṇa in different ways. In his commentary on the above stanza he explains the term *śāradī* as 'belonging to a demon named Śarat.' But in other places (1.131. 4 etc.) he explains it as 'annual Puras

> of the enemies strengthened for a year with ramparts, ditches, etc.' The authors of the *Vedic Index* are of the opinion that *Śāradī* or autumnal Puras 'may refer to the forts in that season being occupied against Arya attacks or against inundations caused by overflowing rivers'. The same exploit performed by Indra on behalf of the chief of the Purus is also referred to in certain other stanzas...

"The terms Pur and Pura mean *nagara*, 'city', 'town', and not fort. The Sanskrit equivalent of 'fort' is *durga* which also occurs in the *Ṛgveda* (5.34.7; 7.25.2). In one stanza (1.41.3) not noticed by the authors of the *Vedic Index,* Durga and Pura occur side by side. Sāyaṇa here takes Pura as an epithet of Durga meaning 'neighbouring'. But if we can shake off our bias relating to the absence of towns in the Rigvedic period we can recognise in this stanza references to both fort and town. The recovery of the ruins of cities at Harappa and Mohenjo-daro leaves no room for doubt that the Rigvedic Aryans were familiar with towns and cities of aliens. It is futile to seek any more historical elements in the legends of Divodāsa and Purukutsa than perhaps the names of these heroes. But if we eliminate the mythical and fanciful additions there is no reason to doubt the possibility of the nucleus. There existed, and the folk memory remembered that there once existed, Arya worshippers of Indra who waged wars against civilised aboriginal neighbours living in towns and fighting from within strongholds. Who, then, were these enemies of the Aryas? Do the hymns of the *Ṛgveda* give us any more information about them?

"It appears to me that the aboriginal towns-folk with whom the Aryas came into collision in the Indus Valley are called Paṇis in hymns of all the books of the *Ṛgveda.* Yāska (*Nirukta* 6.27) in his comment on *Ṛgveda* 8.66.10 says, 'The Paṇis are merchants', and in his comment on R.V. 10. 108.1 (*Nirukta* 11.25) he calls the Paṇis demons. The distinction between the human and the superhuman Paṇi is also recognised by Sāyaṇa, the author of the commentary on the *Ṛgveda* and the context justifies the distinction. The word Paṇi is evidently derived from *Paṇa,* 'Price.' The human Paṇis of the *Ṛgveda* are wealthy merchants who do not offer sacrifices and do not give gifts to priests. In RV. 1.124.10 the poet addressing Dawn says, 'Let the Paṇis who do not perform sacrifices and do not give gifts sleep unawakened (for ever)'. Another poet sings, 'Ye mighty ones (Aśvins) what do you do there; why do you stay there among people who are held in high esteem though not offering sacrifices; ignore them, destroy the life of the Paṇis' (RV. 1.83.3). A poet prays to Indra (1.33.3), 'Do not behave like Paṇi' *(mā Paṇiḥ bhūḥ),* which according to the scholiast means, 'Do not demand the price of kine.' Another poet expecting a suitable reward for his offering of Soma drink, addresses the same deity as Paṇi (8.45.14). The Soma-drinker Indra does not like to make friends with the rich Paṇi who does not offer Soma sacrifice (4.28.7). A poet prays (3.58. 2), 'Destroy in us the mentality of the Paṇi' *(jarethām asmat vi Paṇeḥ manīṣām).* Sometimes the Ṛṣis (Poet) betray a conciliatory mood. In one hymn (6.53) the god Puṣan is repeatedly requested 'to soften the heart of the Paṇi' and make the Paṇis obedient. This hymn occurs in a book (6) of the *Ṛgveda* composed by *Ṛsis* of the family of Bharadvāja. In one hymn of this book (6.45.31-33) the poet, a Bharadvāja, praises Bṛbu, a Paṇi chief, for giving thousands of liberal gifts. Indian tradition long remembered this acceptance of gifts by Bharadvāja from the Paṇi Bṛbu as an exceptional case, an example of the special rule that a Brahmin who has fallen into distress may accept gifts from despicable men without being tainted by sin. We are told in the code of Manu (10.107), 'Bharadvāja, a performer of great austerities, accepted many cows from the carpenter Bṛbu, when he was starving together with his sons in a lonely forest.' (Bühler). Sāyaṇa in his commentary on RV. 6.45.31 describes Bṛbu as the carpenter of the Paṇis.

"It is evident from the hymns of the *Ṛgveda* that the Aryas were divided into two main classes, the priests and the warriors. Cattle breeding appears to be the main source of their livelihood, cows being the chief wealth. Agriculture was practised to a limited extent. A hymn (9.112) refers to the different professions followed and the crafts practised by the Aryas. Trade finds no place in the list. So the conclusion that the much maligned Paṇis were the representatives of an earlier commercial civilisation seems irresistible. Among the antiquities unearthed at Mohenjo-daro are coins with pictographic legends that indicate the very early development of commercial life in the Indus Valley. The Paṇis probably represented this pre-historic civilisation of the Indus Valley in its last phase when it came into contact with the invading Arya civilisation. During the second millennium B.C. there occurred in the Indus Valley events analogous to those that occurred in the Aegean world at about the same time, that is to say, successive waves of invaders of Aryan speech poured from the north-west. These invaders who in the *Ṛgveda* call themselves Arya met in the southern part of the valley a civilised people who lived in cities and castles and mainly depended on commerce for their livelihood. The Arya conquerors who were inferior in material culture either destroyed the cities or allowed them to fall into ruin. Their great god Indra is called Purohā or Purandra, 'sacker of cities'. Like the pre-historic civilisation of the Aegean, the pre-historic civilisation of the Indus Valley also failed to survive the shock of the Aryan invasion."

7. Archaeology an Aid to Vedic Studies

Let us briefly focus on the point we have been trying to argue. The discovery of the Indus Valley Civilisation, besides dramatically extending our knowledge of ancient Indian history, has also another dimension. It has become a tool for us for the interpretation of Vedic literature—specially parts of the *Ṛgveda*. The Vedic scholars may profitably turn to the archaeological findings to see if these can provide us with any clue to certain otherwise unexplained—or at best fancifully explained—passages of the *Ṛgveda*. Thus, for example, the *Ṛgveda* speaks of a considerable number of cities in the Land of the Seven Seas and of the ransacking of these by the Aryans under the leadership of the war-god Indra. The whole thing cannot be brushed aside as a mere figment of imagination of the Vedic poets for the simple reason that those who have never seen any city cannot refer to these: the Vedic peoples themselves could by no stretch of imagination be city-dwellers, it being overwhelmingly obvious from the internal evidence of the *Ṛgveda* that they were pastoral nomads after all. Therefore, before the discovery of Mohenjo-daro and Harappa—soon followed by the discovery of many other cities within the Harappan cultural zone—there could at best be some speculations about these *pura*-s or cities and of Indra's role as *purandara* or the sacker of cities in the *Ṛgveda*—speculations, some specimens of which are to be found in the *Vedic Index* by Macdonell and Keith. With the discovery of ruined cities in the Harappan cultural zone by the archaeologists the Vedic scholars are relieved of the obligation of indulging in such speculation, notwithstanding the circumstance that many questions concerning the archaeological findings still remain controversial or perhaps not yet fully explained. Thus, for example, the real story that the scattered skeletons found in Mohenjo-daro may remain a problem for the archaeologists, so also that of the corpses of the Aryan soldiers and their arms still eluding the archaeologists' spade. We may hope that more digging and better inferences of the archaeologists would solve such problems. What in the meanwhile is gained by archaeology in the matter of throwing light on the *Ṛgveda* must not be ignored, for the Ṛgvedic references to the cities and of the ransacking of these seem to have no better explanation than is provided by the material remains in the Harappan cultural zone. To correlate archaeology with literary evidences is often considered to be a tricky and delicate matter. However, the importance of archaeology as a tool for interpreting or understanding certain Vedic passages remains yet to be more adequately examined. As a tool it sometimes proves to be of surprising importance. We shall mention here another example.

8. D.D. Kosambi and the Vṛtra Myth

Let us not forget, however, that the Vedic poets were poets after all. And as poets, they belonged to the ancient world. So they are not expected to understand and objectively describe all phenomena; they record these in their own way. We are thus bequeathed by them with the tricky task of disentangling reality from myth in their poetry. We shall mention here one example of how D.D. Kosambi attempts it.

Like Purandara or "ransacker of cities", Indra is often called in the *Ṛgveda* Vṛtrahan or "slayer of Vṛtra." For the Vedic poets, this was apparently one of his great achievements. As Macdonell shows, "the chief and specific epithet of Indra is *Vṛtrahan*, 'Vṛtra-slayer'. It is applied about 70 times to him in the *Ṛgveda*."[32] Vṛtra is usually taken as the name of a dragon, destroying whom often with the aid of other gods, specially of the hoard of semi-deities called the Maruts, was considered one of his major performances. But there are certain peculiarities about this performance which cannot be easily overlooked. Vṛtra literally means the Obstructor, and is also described as *ahi*, literally 'serpent'. In other words, it is an obstructor, which also looked like a huge serpent. Many things are said by the Vedic poets about this serpent-like obstructor, among which some are extremely interesting. Vṛtra, it is said, was complacent with the idea that its real vulnerable part was known to none; however, along with the Maruts, Indra discovered its vulnerable part (iii. 32.4; v. 32.5) and thus he struck and destroyed the 'obstructor' with such fierceness as to shake the heaven and world. And what was the result? The whole area was flooded with water which was being obstructed by the serpent-looking obstructor. Here is how Macdonell gives some of the passages referring to the great exploits of Indra: "He smote Vṛtra who encompassed the waters (vi. 20.2; etc.); or the dragon that lay around *(pariśayānam)* the waters (v. 19.2); he overcame the dragon lying on the waters (v. 30.6). He slew the dragon hidden in the waters and obstructing the waters and the sky (ii.11.5), and smote Vṛtra who enclosed the waters, like a tree with the bolt (ii.14.2). Thus 'conquering the waters' (*apsujit*) is his exclusive attribute.... For many dawns and autumns Indra has let loose the streams after slaying Vṛtra (iv. 19.8).... He cleaves the mountain, making the streams flow or taking the cows (i. 57.6; x. 89.7), even with the sound of his bolt (vi.27.1). When he laid open the great mountain, he let loose the torrents and slew the Dānava, he set free the pent up springs, the udder of the mountain. (5.32.1-2). He slew the Dānava, shattered the great mountain, broke open the well, set free the pent up waters (i. 57.6; v. 33.1). He released the streams which are like imprisoned cows (i. 61.10), or which, like lowing cows, flow to the ocean (i. 32.2). He won the cows and Soma and made the seven rivers flow (i. 32.12; ii.12.12). He released the imprisoned waters (i. 57.6; i. 103.2), released the streams pent up by the dragon (ii.11.2)... let the flood of waters flow in the sea (ii. 19.3), caused the waters pent up by Vṛtra to flow (iii.26.6;iv. 17.1)."[33] And so on. The entire section of Macdonell dealing with Indra's exploit of destroying Vṛtra—snake-looking obstructor—needs to be read in full to see that according to the Vedic poet the main result of this was the release of pent-up water.

Incidentally, Macdonell points to the use in the *Ṛgveda* of the word *arṇas* or flood in this connection.

Shorn of poetic imagination and the inevitable proclivity to myth-making in ancient poetry, what does all this really mean? D.D. Kosambi answers:

"Vedic Indra is described again and again as freeing the streams. This was taken as a nature- myth in the days of Max Müller, a poetic representation of the rain-god letting pent-up waters loose from imprisoning clouds. Recorded but ignored details of the feat make such an explanation quite impossible. Indra freed the rivers from the grip of a demon Vṛtra. The word has been analysed by two most competent philologists [with full knowledge of Iranian (Aryan) as well as Sanskrit records] who did not trouble to theorise about the means of production. Their conclusion from purely philological considerations was that *vṛtra* meant 'obstacle', barrage', or 'bloquage', not a demon. The actual Ṛgvedic description independently bears this out in full. The demon lay like a dark snake across the slopes. The rivers were brought to a standstill *(tastabhānāḥ)*; when the 'demon' was struck by Indra's shattering weapon *(vajra)*, the ground buckled, the stones rolled away like chariot wheels, the pent-up waters flowed over the demon's recumbent body (cf. R.V. 4.19.4-8; 2.15.3). This is a good description of dams (not embankments as Piggott would have it) being broken up, while such prehistoric dams, now called Gebr-band, are still to be found on many water- courses in the western parts of the region under consideration. The evidence for Indra's breaking up dams is not merely rationalisation of the Vṛtra myth. RV. 2.15.8: *riṇag rodhāṃsi kṛtrimāṇi* = 'he removed artificial barriers' makes this clear; *rodhas* means 'dam' elsewhere in the ṚV, as in later Sanskrit. Indra is praised for restoring to its natural course the river Vibālī, which had flooded land along its banks. That is, the Pre-Aryan method of agriculture depended upon natural floods and flooding the lands on the banks of smaller rivers by means of seasonal (RV. 5.32.2) dams (without regular masonry), to obtain the fertilising deposit of silt to be stirred by the harrow. The Aryans shattered this dam system, thereby ruining the agriculture of the region and the possibility of continuing city life for long, or of maintaining the urban population. The fact of the ruin is undeniable: the causes have to be deduced from whatever data is available, which includes numerous heavy flood silt deposits that are visible in Mohenjo-daro excavations. The very floods which endangered city and hamlet had made possible the agriculture which supported the inhabitants."[34]

Kosambi's theory of the agricultural technique in the Harappan region depending on a toothed harrow rather than plough has to be discarded, of course, after the excavation at Kalibangan revealed an actual ploughed field. However, at least among a section of archaeologists the "flood theory" is receiving increasing importance. If there is substance in this theory, it helps us to understand the Ṛgvedic passages related to Indra's exploit against Vṛtra—the snake-like obstructor of water—much better than the earlier views wanting us to read this or that myth in these passages. Archaeology thus becomes a significant tool for the interpretation of Ṛgvedic passages which remain otherwise more or less mysterious for us.

9. Summing Up

One reason for the tenacious objection against the theory of the Aryan invasion as the final cause of the already decaying Indus civilisation resulting from the cumulative effect of various possible causes seems to be frankly chauvinistic. Later Indian mythology wants to feed us with the belief that Indra was the king of the gods after all. Imputing to him such a negative activity as the destruction of the glorious civilisation of ancient India can understandably hurt the feelings of some, rooted primarily on religious convictions. An example of this seems to be the article on "The Myth of the Aryan Invasion of Harappan Towns" by K.M. Srivastava. After attempting to refute elaborately the theory of the Aryan invasion, he apparently feels the need of coming out sharply against Wheeler's statement that 'on circumstantial evidence, Indra stands condemned'. As already noted, Srivastava passionately proclaims:

"Indra, therefore, stands completely exonerated."

As against such a passionate defence of the Vedic god, at least one point needs to be remembered. The *Ṛgveda* is a collection of songs and hymns of an ancient period after all, and hence it will be an anachronism to judge the standard of morality reflected in it by our contemporary standards. Sacking or destroying the Harappan cities may appear more or less deplorable if judged by the moral standards of our time. But it was not so to the Vedic poets, who saw in such actions the most magnificent feat of courage and strength, and therefore, which, in their standard, must have been a highly laudable performance. That is why, they sang of the glory of Indra as *purandara* or destroyer of the cities. They would not have surely done it had they been under the influence of our standard of morality.

So the rather emotional statement completely exonerating Indra makes no real sense. To the ancient poets of the *Ṛgveda*, the personal bravery and strength of Indra was higly honourable, though these were often exhibited under the influence of alcohol or the intoxicating drink they called *soma*.

The point is that the standard of morality changes, not only from age to age but mainly because of the social conditions in which it is expressed. In the society in which the Vedic poets lived, certain acts considered most despicable by our standards of morality are actually praised by the poets in ways that appear to us to be most shocking. Here is an extreme example of this. In one hymn of the *Ṛgveda*, a certain poet praises Indra by way of addressing him as follows:

> Who has made thy mother a widow? Who has sought to slay the sleeping and the waking? What deity has been more gracious than thou, since thou hast slain the father having seized him by the foot? (RV. iv. 18.12)

We have—from the standpoint of our own sense of morality —perhaps no adequate vocabulary to condemn such an act of abject patricide, particularly when it is associated with the story that Indra did it because his father had stolen some amount of the intoxicating stuff from Indra's stock (*Taittirīya Saṃhitā* vi. 1.3.6), to which Sāyaṇa refers.

Can we, with our sense of morality, exonerate Indra from such an act? We cannot. But such a question would have perhaps made no sense to the Vedic poet himself.

Wheeler's use of the words "Indra stands condemned" was perhaps intended to be rhetorical, and surely some kind of plagiarism. But Srivastava's retort that "Indra stands completely exonerated" is *just Aryan chauvinism.*

REFERENCES

1. B. & R. Allchin RCIP 213.
2. V. Gordon Childe NLMAE 184-85.
3. A. Ghosh 83-84.
4. B. & R. Allchin RCIP 167.
5. D.K. Chakrabarti in EIP 205.
6. M.R. Mughal in ACI 91.
7. D.K. Chakarabrti in EIP 207.
8. B. & R. Allchin BIC 129 n.
9. B. & R. Allchin RCIP 213 ff.
10. D.D. Kosambi 59-60.
11. J. Marshall MIC I. *Preface* iv, emphasis added.
12. J. Needham GT 168-69, emphasis added.
13. *Ibid* 155-56.
14. V. Gordon Childe NLMAE 187.
15. R.E.M. Wheeler IC 127.
16. B. & R. Allchin RCIP 224 .
17. D.P. Agrawal AI 188 ff.
18. *Ibid* 191.
19. B. & R. Allchin RCIP 191.
20. R.E.M. Wheeler IC 126.
21. G.L. Possehl ACI 288.
22. B. & R. Allchin RCIP 43.
23. *Ibid* 225.
24. V. Gordon Childe WHH 128.
25. V. Gordon Childe NLMAE 187-88.
26. M. Wheeler reprinted in ACI 291.
27. G.F. Dales reprinted in ACI 293-96.
28. G.F. Dales in ACI 296.
29. K.M. Srivastava in FIC 441.
30. *Ibid* 442.
31. *Ibid*.
32. A.A. Macdonell VM 60.
33. *Ibid* 59.
34. D.D. Kosambi 70-71.

4

Vedic Religion : Myth and Reality

1. Preliminary Remarks

In 1963, Leonard Woolley observed: "The Aryan conquerors were a simple, not to say a barbarous people, pastoral nomads for the most part, some perhaps petty farmers who had not even a word for 'brick' in their vocabulary; they could destroy, but could not rebuild."[1]

From the viewpoint of material culture, there is no ground to question this observation, excepting of course an unwarranted veneration for the Vedas and for those who composed these. Archaeologists with a sense of objective coercion on them imposed by the actual material remains unearthed wanted to look at the period of over a thousand years following the final destruction of the Harappan culture as the Dark Age or Dark Period, because nothing substantial was known about it even a few decades ago. Thanks to the brisk fieldwork of Indian archaeologists in recent years, we have now ampler information about this period than we had at the time of Indian independence.

In spite of this, however, the period continues to be "dark" after all, i.e. from the viewpoint of material culture. It was according to some, indicative of the beginning of the iron age. But R.S. Sharma, reviewing the relevant evidences, rightly observes, "till the sixth century B.C. northern India did not enter into a full-fledged iron age".[2] This means that the time-gap between the final decline of Harappan Civilisation and the beginning of the real iron age is over a thousand years, because on the basis of the radio-carbon dating of D.P. Agrawal it is difficult to doubt today that the former, i.e. the end of Harappan Civilisation, took place in about 1750 B.C. This intervening period of over a thousand years is the Dark Age of our archaeologists, because it is a period of an almost all round technological regression. Then slowly began the reintroduction of urban life, which , as compared to Harappan Culture, is often called the period of second urbanisation. As A. Ghosh puts it, "For her next cities, her 'second urbanisation', India had to wait for over a thousand years after the disappearance of the Indus cities—till the middle of the sixth century B.C. which saw simultaneously the beginnings of her historical period".[3] By this time, the invading Vedic people—who called themselves the *arya*-s or Aryans—had at least substantially lost their racial identity and got mingled with the local people, or as A. Ghosh very aptly puts it, "the early Aryan society had made room for the Indian society, in which it is difficult to isolate Aryan and non-Aryan elements."[4]

2. The Veda

There is thus an obvious truth in the observation of Leonard Woolley with which we began this lecture. What needs to be added to it, however, is that this truth is strictly confined to the viewpoint of material culture. From another viewpoint, however, the same Vedic people *created* something that continues to be a wonder of wonders. It consists of a vast store of songs and poems—often mentioned as "hymns"—over a thousand of which survive for us in the form of the vast collection called the *Ṛgveda-saṃhitā*. The codification of this took place many centuries later, for the composers of the songs were really pre-literate people. The songs or "hymns" were originally composed and were yet preserved meticulously by the most amazing form of sheer retentive memory without affecting even their original accents. This by itself indicates how much of importance was imputed to the songs by the Vedic people themselves. But Hindu orthodoxy—or at least a very dominant section thereof—usually goes to an extreme extent, when, without bothering to actually read or understand the real nature of these songs, proclaims that these are but repositories of the highest spiritual wisdom, revealed to the "poets" (*kavi*-s) or "seers" thereof. It is even proclaimed that these songs were too holy to be read—or even listened to—by the low-caste people and women, leading Marx to come out with the sarcastic remark: "the Indian Brahmin... proves the holiness of the Vedas by reserving for himself alone the right to read it."[5]

Marx was not, of course, a specialist in the Vedas, nor apparently was he aware of the fact that practically a microscopic minority of the Brahmins have actually the patience or diligence for really reading the Veda. For the vast majority of the Brahmins, who make a living of the professed spiritual wisdom of the Veda and who go to the extent of claiming that the Veda is the basic plank of Hindu religion, the word Veda is practically nothing more than sales talk or a political slogan to justify their privileges. Exsperated by all these, one of our foremost scholars, MM. H.P. Sastri, while writing an essay on the Veda, remarks that those who are Sanskritists by profession though without ever actually caring to read the Veda, may as well spare themselves the trouble to read his essay.

Since, the basic points that I want to make about the *Ṛgveda* are already made by Mahamahopadhyaya Hara Prasad Sastri and this with an authority many times more than I can possibly have, it may be wiser for me to allow him to speak on these instead of trying to speak myself. In short, I propose to quote here extensively from his exquisitely charming essay on the Veda, written originally in Bengali. I shall have to make a rough English rendering of it with full awareness, of course, that such a rendering is bound to miss much of his original sarcasm and his power of persuasion.

Before quoting him, however, I may mention one point. As most of you are aware, in 1885-87 was first published in Bengali the translation of the whole of the *Ṛgveda*: the translation appears to be as literal as it is perhaps possible and as translator, it bore the name of Ramesh Chandra Dutta. Though famous as a civilian as well as a pioneer worker on the economic history of India, Ramesh Chandra Dutta was not a Sanskritist—at least not essentially so. He could not translate the *Ṛgveda* on his own—a task that required a great deal of mastery of the Sanskrit language, specially the archaic Sanskrit in which the *Ṛgveda* was composed. It was therefore necessary for him to depend on the help of a very competent Sanskritist.

But there was then a formidable difficulty about getting one. Sanskritic studies were in those days mainly confined to the Brahmins, most of whom believed that only the Brahmins were entitled to Vedic studies. R.C. Dutta was by birth not a Brahmin and it appears that the orthodox Brahmin community then frowned upon the idea of a non-Brahmin meddling with the Vedas. What then could he do?

He appealed to Pandit Isvara Chandra Vidyasagara for help, who was already waging a veritable war against the obnoxious aspects of Brahmanical orthodoxy, though with a far greater mastery of the Sanskrit language than most of the orthodox Brahmins professed. From the preface to Dutta's translation of the *Ṛgveda* it appears that Vidyasagar readily moved forward to offer the assistance required. Apparently, Vidyasagar himself was then too busy with many things to take part in the stupendous task of helping Dutta to translate the whole of the *Ṛgveda*. Fortunately, however, among his own students there was then a young one who had already acquired a superb mastery of the Sanskrit language. He was Hara Prasad Sastri. So Vidyasagar sent H.P. Sastri to help Ramesh Chandra Dutta, and H.P. Sastri—himself fully free from the repelling aspects of the Brahmanical orthodoxy—moved forward to take up the arduous taks of explaining to Dutta the literal meaning of the entire *Ṛgveda*, freely depending, of course, on the commentary by Sāyaṇa. Thus was made possible the Bengali version of the entire *Ṛgveda* which eventually came out as having been translated by

R.C. Dutta. I have myself often wondered how much of it incorporates the work of H.P. Sastri, specially because of the exquisite charms of simple and direct prose in which the Bengali *Ṛgveda* came out—a literary style often reminding us of Hara Prasad Sastri.

I have mentioned all this specially to clarify one point. The long extract from H.P. Sastri's essay which we are going to use here may appear to be objectionable—even atrocious to many of our conservative readers. Let them not forget, however, that this essay was not written only with a smattering knowledge of the Veda. It was written instead on the basis of a detailed mastery of the whole of the *Ṛgveda*—a phenomenon which is rare and is becoming increasingly rarer these days. It is thus not easy to brush aside his observations, except of course on the strength of an ignorance about the Veda.

With this preliminary clarification, we proceed to quote H.P. Sastri who opens the essay with a biting satire on the orthodox way of looking back at the Veda. H.P. Sastri observes:

> The very name Veda evokes in every Indian an emotion of overwhelming awe: One is a rare-born who reads the Veda and one who understands it is a veritable incarnation of Śiva or Viṣṇu. Purity of body and mind is the precondition of Vedic study, which brings the power of achieving the impossible with the help of the spells. Viśwāmitra utters the spell, and lo, after a drought of twelve long years there comes rain in torrents. I utter a spell here and my enemy in Delhi is annihilated. With Vedic spells, the barren becomes mother, the sick cured, the poor prosperous and the dying man back to life. When you are in need of any proof, just claim that it is declared in the Veda and none will dare to contradict you. Such indeed are the ideas of the ignorant; the Veda is a miracle and a miracle-maker; it is inscrutable, unreadable, un-understandable, unapproachable. Without the grace of the goddess of learning and the accumulated merit of the pious acts of the previous births, none can have an access to the Veda.

But what exactly is the Veda? It is nothing but an anthology of some poems, songs, etc., composed by various gifted poets in different times, under diverse conditions and with various purposes. While trying to explain this, we hope that it would kindly be skipped ever by those that have high things to say about Sanskrit as a mere matter of profession and therefore who, without ever bothering to read the Veda, only know that it is composed by the God Brahmā. Actually speaking, this literature is somewhat like Palgrave's *Golden Treasury of Songs and Lyrics,* an anthology of songs and poems of many a gifted poet... An anthology of songs is of course merely an anthology; but how could the Veda being essentially so, acquire such a stupendous influence on religion? What explains this veneration for the Veda over hundreds of years?

The great antiquity of the Veda is about the main reason for this. Of all the books in the world, the Veda is surely the oldest. Moreover, for purposes of knowing anything about the age in which it was composed, we have only the Veda to depend upon... Let us imagine a situation in which after a lapse of about 3000 years all the books written by the Englishmen become extinct, leaving only the *Golden Treasury,* to survive. In such circumstances, the *Golden Treasury,* too, is likely to acquire a similar importance. It alone would then tell us about the thoughts, poetic capabilities and the social customs of the Englishmen.

The historian and the archaeologist will of course concentrate on the great antiquity and historical value of the Veda. From the poet's point of view, however, there is no other poetry in the world that can be easily compared to the Veda. The Veda is not an epic of the Homerian type; yet each poem *(sūkta)* of the Veda is an epic in its own way. It was then only the childhood of mankind and there could then be nothing to compare to the tremendous power man has acquired today on the external world.

In these circumstances, everything—fire, air, cloud, thunder, lightning, storm—appeared to the poets to be variable gods. It needs a great deal of development of abstract thinking to arrive at the conception of the presiding deities; men in their childhood were yet to develop it. They saw everything with the child's eyes, pictured everything with brightest hues. Their eyes were the eyes of the poets. At the same time the knowledge, the labour and the mastery over the external world which the composition of Homer's enormous poem presupposes were not possessed by them. They could just express the depths of their hearts, their awe and fear, their apprehension, hope and aspiration. And how did they express all these? There was nothing artificially clever, nothing deliberately thought out, nothing laboured about their expressions. Whenever they felt any fear or awe, it soon occupied the whole of their inner being. And they immediately expressed it in words. The words, like the feelings, were simple, clear and noble. There was no burden of the rhetoric, no anxiety to conceal anything or to discriminate between good and bad taste, no calculated contrivance for purposes of appealing to others. Their expressions had the same nobility as their feelings... Whatever they looked at appeared to them to be colossal, wonderful and a marvel. A hillock would have thrilled them a hundred times more than the great Himalayas thrill us today. Lest it upset the social norm, we refuse sometimes to express what we feel; these poets expressed the same feelings in a higly magnified yet simple language. They were poets, because they were full of that sense of wonder which is the universal characteristic of the poet's heart. Yet, compared to them, our poets today are but dry men of affairs.

Nevertheless, the Veda is regarded above all as a religious work... How was it that for thousands of years it was worshipped by millions of people? How could some poems and songs eventually acquire this scriptural status? It will be a folly to suggest that people were just fools to have imagined this. Really speaking, the process is indicative of some important psychological truth. Those who composed these songs believed that they could do it because of some kind of direct vision, which these days we call inspiration. Their fellowmen, too, believed that the composers worked under supernatural inspiration. Let us suppose that you are a poet while I am not and the two of us stay together. With your strong imagination you see everything as full of beauty; being not a poet I see the earth just as it is, the sky merely as the sky. Here lies the difference between the two of us. We know this to be a difference resulting from our different mental make-up. But people then were not aware of this. They could only note that when the poet sang he experienced a peculiar inner unrest which was not normally felt by him. How was this unrest to be accounted for? Accustomed as he was to see gods everywhere, the poet saw in this, too, the working of god. So he said, 'God has worked me up like this'. And the other wondered: Since he can do what we cannot, he must have been aided by god... In the course of time, the names of the poets who actually composed these songs were forgotten and the deities imagined to have helped the poets came to be known as the real inspirers of the Veda. This led Mādhavācārya to claim that a *ṛṣi* (Vedic poet) was one who saw the *mantra, the root ṛṣ* meaning 'to see'. It was because of this, again, that Bhavabhuti was somewhat annoyed with Kālidāsa's use of the word *mantrakṛt* ('the maker of *mantra*'); instead of *mantrakṛtām* he said, the word should rather be *mantradṛśām;* the *ṛṣis* never made the *mantras,* they merely saw them. Eventually, with the final supremacy of monotheism in the Brahmanical religion, the authorship of the Veda was attributed to the Supreme God. God being eternal, the Veda, too, was considered eternal. Being the work of God, the Veda can contain no error; it is all-truth, all-holy, all-illumination. Thus it was that a collection of simple songs acquired the scriptural status....

In the Vedic age, however, people were very simple and straightforward. It is extremely difficult for us to enter their mental world. We should be able to understand the Veda much better if we can project ourselves in imagination into the Vedic world. We should then have some real idea of the activities and the sociology of those days and should understand a lot of what the poets had to say. But it is not easy to enter that world. For this purpose, it is necessary to know a great deal about the ancient world and about the mental make-up of the ancient people. It is not enough to know only about India; it is also necessary to know the history of the ancient world wherever the Aryans appeared.[6]

All this—particularly the secular or near-secular view of the Veda as but a compilation of primitive poetry—will undoubtedly be outrageous for Indian orthodoxy, not to mention anything of some modern people organising a Vedic University somewhere in Switzerland wanting to prove that the Vedic "seers" intuitively anticipated what is latest in modern science. But there is no substance in it at all. In substantiation of H.P. Sastri's view, we shall rather quote in rough English rendering some of the actual songs or "hymns" from the *Ṛgveda* and try to show how the Vedic poets themselves were in close friendly terms with their own "deities", so that the "sense of the holy" which we are accustomed to imagine separates man from God, was practically unknown to the Vedic poets themselves. We shall next discuss the point that H.P. Sastri seems to skip over, namely the manipulation of our law makers and also of a great medieval politician that actually went to the making of the later awesome view of the Veda. Lastly, we shall try to discuss the most tricky point, namely why, in spite of the great veneration for the Veda, the Vedic gods had really no future even in the religious history of India.

Some specimens from the *Ṛgveda* first. It is really questionable how far any religious sentiment or spiritual value in our sense is at all to be found in the genuinely older portions of the *Ṛgveda*. There is no doubt that the hymns and songs are full of extravagant praise for all sorts of deities or *devas*. But they are often crassly human heroes, looting food and cattle for the tribesmen and sharing these out among themselves; sitting with them in their assemblies and addressed by them in endearing terms like 'friends' or 'the best of friends',—often simple natural phenomena and inanimate objects even like the hill (*parvata*), the herb *(oṣadhi)*, the tree *(vanaspati)*, the forests *(araṇyānī)*, the weapons *(āyudha)* like the bow and arrow. Sometimes, again, the deities are just the embodiments of fulfilment of purely this-worldly desires, like 'the protection against abortion',[7] 'the protection against consumptive diseases',[8] the protection against the nightmare'.[9] A fascinating deity of this kind is Pitu, i.e. food. The barbarian poets with their healthy appetite praised him for being savoury and delicious and because he 'makes the body fat';. In the general context of all sorts of traditional and modern claims attributing the highest spiritual wisdom to the *Ṛgveda*, this hymn to Pitu or food may be quoted here for its obvious interest.

Ṛ.V. I. 187. Deity Pitu or Food. Poet Agastya

> I glorify Food, the Great, the Upholder, the Strong, by whose invigorating power Tṛta (the famous) tortured the deformed Vṛtra. Savoury Food, honeyed Food, we welcome thee; become our protector. Come to us, beneficial Food, a source of delight, a friend well-respected, and having no envy. Your flavours, Food, are diffused through the regions, as the winds are spread through the sky. These (men), oh Food, who are your distributors, most sweet Food, they who are the eaters of our and your juices, they increase like you with elongating necks. The minds of the mighty gods are fixed, oh Food, upon you; by your active assistance (Indra) slew Ahi. Oh Food, the wealth which is associated with the mountains went to you; hear you, Oh sweet one, be accessible to our eating. And since we enjoy the abundance of the waters and the plants;—Therefore, Oh body, may thou grow fat, and since we enjoy, Soma, thy mixture with boiled milk or boiled barley;— therefore, Oh body, may thou grow fat....[10] And so on.

The refrain deserves special notice: 'Oh, body, may thou grow fat'—*vātāpe pīvaḥ it bhava.*

It is true, of course, that Pitu or food does not in any way rank among the major Vedic gods. As doubtless, again, is the fact that Indra is one. Here is a delightful drunken monologue of Indra, with the refrain that he had taken many draughts of the heady drink called Soma. As the world's earliest poem of drunkenness, it obviously has a great historical interest, though even the most extravagant theology can hardly extract any religious sentiment in our sense out of it.

Ṛgveda X. 119. Deity Indra. Poet Lava, the Son of Indra

> By temper I am one who gifts cows and horses; I have drunk Soma in many draughts. As winds shake and elongate the tree, so also Soma—having been drunk by me—shakes and

> elongates me. I have drunk Soma in many draughts. As the fast-moving horses make the chariot fast-moving so also Soma—having been taken by me—makes me move fast. I have drunk Soma in many draughts. As the cow moves towards the calf lowing, so are the hymns coming towards me. I have taken Soma in many draughts. As the carpenter constructs the upper part of the chariot, so have I mentally constructed the hymns. I have drunk Soma in many draughts. No man of the five classes *(pañcakṛṣṭi)* can elude my eyes. I have taken Soma in many draughts. Heaven and earth—the two taken together cannot equate even one side of mine. I have taken Soma in many draughts. My glory overflows heaven as well as this vast earth. I have taken Soma in many draughts. Lo, I will place this earth (where I will), either here or there. I have taken Soma in many draughts. I can burn this whole earth and I can destroy any place that you may name. I have taken Soma in many draughts. One part of mine is in heaven and another scratching the earth below. I have taken Soma in many draughts. I am greater than the great, I have risen towards the sky. I have taken Soma in many draughts. Receiving the offering I go, graced by hymns, carrying the oblation to the gods. I have taken Soma in many draughts.

The megalomania of the drunken god is, of course, easily understood. If you take so many draughts of the heady drink today, you are likely to be a megalomaniac. What is not so easily understood, however, in the standard of our moral values is the glorification of it in Vedic imagination. But that is only to be expected. The Vedic poets were not—and could not be—inhibited by our sense of morality and even of decency. They marvelled instead at the heroic performances of Indra, often under the influence of the drink. One of the poets went so far as to express the desire of Soma normally flowing to Indra—as normally indeed as the male genital moves to the hairy triangular organ of the female (RV. ix. 112.4). Would the great admirers of Vedic religion try to dig some religious sentiment in our sense in this? If so, they would also be obliged to flout what actually comes down to us as the *Ṛgveda*, i.e. at least its plain meaning.

It may not be irrelevant to quote here a comment of Winternitz which is likely to be far more helpful for our understanding of the Ṛgvedic mentality than heaps of theology sought to be dumped upon this primitive poetry. As he observes:

> However, we must not form too exalted an idea of the moral conditions in ancient India, and not picture these to ourselves in such an idyllic manner, as certainly Max Müller has at times done. We hear in the hymns of the *Rig Veda* of incest, seduction, conjugal unfaithfulness, the procuring of abortion, as also of deception, theft and robbery. All this, however, proves nothing against the antiquity of the *Rig Veda*. Modern ethnology knows nothing of the 'unspoiled children of nature' any more than it regards all primitive people as rough savages or cannibal monsters. The ethnologist knows that a step-ladder of endless gradations of the most widely differing cultural conditions leads from the primitive people to the half-civilised people, and right up to the civilised nations. We need not, therefore, imagine the people of the *Rig Veda* either as an innocent shepherd people, or as a horde of rough savages, nor, on the other hand, as a people of ultra-refined culture. The picture of culture which is unfolded in these songs, shows us the Aryan Indians as an active, joyful and war-like people, of simple, and still partly savage habits. The Vedic singers implore the gods for help against the enemy, for victory in battle, for glory and rich booty; they pray for wealth, heaps of gold and countless herds of cattle, for rain for their fields, for the blessing of children, and long life. As yet we do not find in the songs of the *Rig Veda* that effeminate, ascetic and pessimistic trait of the Indian character with which we shall meet again and again in later Indian literature.

3. Gods and Men: The Religious Sentiment

What is said above about the moral sentiments seems to be true also about the religious sentiments at least to a great extent. In spite of the *Ṛgveda* being crowded with a whole host of what are called the gods and demi-gods, it is really questionable if we are at all permitted to read in this vast literature religious sentiments in our sense. There are perhaps many ways in which this can be illustrated. We propose to choose in our next lecture one of these, namely the relation of god and man in the *Ṛgveda,* where the line of demarcation between the two often appears to be at best a thin one. I have quoted a fairly large number of examples of this in my book *Lokayata.*[10] Since, however, these are vital for the present discussion, I may as well reiterate some of these.

Indra is invoked simply as 'man': "I invoke Indra, the man (*naram*), who fulfils the desires of many from his ancient dwellings—in the same manner as my ancestors did in the past." (i.30.9). Agni is said to be *nṛvatsakhā sabhāvān*—a friend of the most human type and a member of the tribal assembly (iv. 2.5). Indra and Agni knew the ancient sages Kaṇva, Atri, Manu, 'who were skilled and who had an abode among the gods' (i. 139.9). The ancient seers sat in joyful company with the *devāḥ* and with true spells (*mantras*) generated Uṣas (vii. 76.4). Indra is praised as the chief among men (*nṛtamaḥ*) and one who shares out wealth (*vibhaktā*) along with other human beings (*nṛbhiḥ śākaiḥ*) (iv. 17.11). We shall return later to discuss the extremely interesting implication of the word *vibhaktā* or apportioner. For the present, the incomplete dehumanisation of the Vedic gods.

Agni is addressed as the chief human being among the human beings (*nṛṇāṃ nṛtamaḥ*) (i. 77.4), the chief among men (*nṛṇāṃ nṛpate*) (ii. 1.1), the best of men (*nṛtamaḥ*) (v.4.6). He is invoked to produce (*bṛhat kṛdhi*), like the human being (*nṛvat*), food in large quantity among human beings (*nṛṇāṃ*) (v. 18.5). Like the human being, says another *ṛk* addressed to him, he gives us wealth and cattle to our sons and grandsons (vi. 1.12). Mitra and Varuṇa are invoked to come and join the soma-drinking in the company of human beings (i.137.3). May Indra and Viṣṇu like human beings, give us houses (iv. 55. 4). Aśvins, along with Agastya, are said to be the foremost among the leading men (i. 180.8).

The epithet of being the chief man among men is, however, most frequently used in the case of Indra. He is the finest man among all human beings (*nṛṇāṃ nṛtamam*) (iii.51.4). Along with other humans he wins battles, and, in their company, he eats good food (i. 178.3). The Yajamānas (financiers of the ritual) are asked to offer cakes to Indra, who is immediately present and is the bravest of the human beings (*nṛṇāṃ vīratamāya*) (iii. 52.8). As foremost among men (*nṛṇāṃ nṛtama*) he cuts the enemies to pieces in battles (iv. 33.3). We shall prepare *soma* for Indra, who is.... the best man among men (*nare naryāya nṛtamāya nṛṇāṃ*) (iv. 25.4). He is the strongest leader among men (*saviṣṭhaṃ nṛṇāṃ naram*) (viii. 40. 2). In the past, he was the chief among men (*purā cit śūra nṛṇāṃ*) (viii.66.5). As the chief of men he rends asunder the clouds and causes showers (iv. 22.2). As the chief of the human beings, again, he has similar dwellings as of the other human beings (*mānuṣāṇām sam okaḥ nṛtamaḥ*) (vi. 18.7). He even speaks like human beings (*nṛvat vadan*) and 'comes to us and gives us food' (x.28.12). Like a human being he entered the army of the opponent (iii. 34.5). Shouting like a human being (*nṛvat nonuvanta*) he made the wind blow (iv. 22.4). Like a human being, again, he increased the strength (vi.19.1). Indra, who is like a human being, from thee do we—along with the leaders of men—desire wealth (vi. 19.10). In the matter of food-procuring, Indra is the chief among men: the *ṛk* in which this occurs runs as a refrain in the third book of the *Ṛgveda*, being the last *ṛk* of no less than twelve *sūktas* (30-32, 34-36, 38, 39, 43, 48-50) and it reoccurs twice in the tenth book (x. 89.18). Presumably, the Vedic poets attached great significance to this. In another *ṛk*, Indra is said to be not only the chief among the human beings, (*nṛṇāṃ nṛtamaḥ*) but also as 'common' among (equal to?) them (*naryaḥ*) (x. 29.1). With all these evidences, is it not safe to presume that Indra was originally only the culture-hero of some Vedic tribe, and the word *deva* originally meant only this? It is after all a postulate of comparative philology that words change more slowly than the meanings attached to them.

This conclusion will be strongly challenged by our orthodox scholars. But to them we may answer that we have in the writings of no less an orthodox commentator than Sāyaṇa himself, the rather startling admission that during the composition of the *Ṛgveda,* actual human beings were really being raised to the status of Vedic deities. The evidence is as follows. In one *ṛk* Indra is addressed as the killer in great battles and the increaser of human skill with the assistance of other human beings. But the context in which this occurs suggests that Indra was doing all this with the assistance rather of the Maruts. This naturally presented a problem to Sāyaṇa: How could the human beings of the *ṛk* mean the Maruts as well? And he answered, 'by the human beings are meant the men who, though originally men, later attained the status of the gods and were called the Maruts' *(nṛbhiḥ manuṣyaiḥ eva sadbhiḥ paścāt devatvam āpannaiḥ marudbhiḥ)* (Sāyaṇa on i. 129. 2).

This explanation is provocative and the temptation to digress slightly cannot be helped. If Sāyaṇa was here true to the Vedic tradition, then the attainment of godhead on the part of the Maruts may be looked upon as part of the living memory of the Ṛgvedic poets. And if this be true, it should be possible for us to infer the original human characteristics of the Maruts by examining the characteristics attributed to them in the *Ṛgveda*, though as gods. The special significance of this lies in the circumstance that of all the Vedic deities the Maruts alone retained the strongest marks of the primitive group-life. They were most frequently referred to as living in *gaṇa* or the tribal collectivity. They were all brothers among themselves and strict equality was believed to exist among them. They grew up together, were born at the same place, and had the same abode. They were strictly of one strength, one friendship and one birth. (i. 14.3; iii 35.9; etc.; i. 165.1; v.59.6; etc.; v. 56.5; v. 53.1; vii. 56.1; etc.)

Thus the Maruts had this special importance in the *Ṛgveda* that they retained the relics of not only a distinct history of human origin but also of the communistic or pre-class society to which, as human beings, they must have originally belonged.

The human origin of the Vedic deities is not confined to the case of Maruts. Sāyaṇa said that the Ṛbhus, too, originally human beings, were eventually raised to the status of gods. This genealogy of the Ṛbhus is not indeed an invention of Sāyaṇa. For in the Ṛgveda itself (i.110.4) we come across the startling declaration that the Ṛbhus, being yet mortal, attained immortality (*martāsaḥ santaḥ amṛtatvam ānaśuḥ*). Sāyaṇa said practically the same thing about the Vahnis—*pūrvam manuṣyatvena maraṇayogyāḥ api amṛtatva-lābhena prāṇān dhāritavantaḥ:* though previously, being human beings, they were mortal yet they later became immortal (on 1.20.8). Of course, as deities, they were only minor in importance. But the Aśvins were not so. And the Ṛgveda itself distinctly referred to the Aśvins being raised to the status of the gods (*devāḥ bhavathe*). (iii.54.17.)

Significantly enough, even after attaining the godhead, the Ṛbhus retained very clear relics of the collective life. As Sāyaṇa pointed out, in the Ṛgveda the Ṛbhus were addressed in the singular (*janmane*) because they formed a collective body *(saṁgha)*. And the Aśvins themselves maintained equality and a comradely relationship with the human beings:

> O Aśvins, our friendship with you comes down from our fathers; in friendship you are equal with us; know your and our grandfather to be the same;. (*yuvoḥ hi naḥ sakhyā pitryāṇi samānaḥ bandhuḥ uta tasya vittam:* the interpretation of *bandhuḥ* is after Sāyaṇa). (vii. 72.2).

What needs to be noted is that the Vedic poets felt this essentially friendly and human relationship also for their other important deities. Here are a few, though not very carefully chosen, examples:

Indra was a friend indeed! He was a friend with friends; the friend and benefactor and protector. (i.63.4) He was a friend coming from the heaven and honouring 'us' as his friends (i. 63.4); a friend accompanied by faithful friends (iii. 39.5); listening as a friend to the praises of his friends. (iii. 43.4). The friends of Indra poured out *Soma* for him (iii. 30.1).

Such examples are, however, too few to give us any real idea of how persistently Indra—described as 'the most human of the gods.... whom the seers most closely fashioned in their own likeness'—was addressed or invoked as a friend. For such references in the Ṛgveda are really numerous and it would be tedious to quote them all. Nevertheless, we may mention here one more *ṛk* because, over and above expressing the intensely friendly relation felt by the Vedic poets for Indra, it has, in distinctly referring to the past, some additional interest for us. 'O Indra, the giver of horses, cows, barley, wealth, as you were our wish-yielder in the past, so are you our friend and speak to us who are your friends'. (i.53.2)

Agni again was like a father, friendship with whom was the best of friendship (*sakhā sakhye vareṇyaḥ*) (i. 26.3), a friend of all peoples (*jāmiḥ janānām*) and the most praiseworthy friend among all friends (*sakhā sakhibhyaḥ īḍyaḥ*) (1.75.4). He was friend and minister and well disposed towards friends. The seers, desiring protection, called themselves his friends. 'Be favourably disposed, O Agni, on approaching us; the fulfiller like a friend or the parents; since men (enemies) are the grievous oppressors of men, do thou consume the foes who come against us.' And so on. (iii. 14. ; iii. 9.1; iii. 18.1) Indeed, the references to such extremely friendly relations to Agni in the Ṛgveda are no less numerous than those to Indra.

The Viśvadeva-s (all-gods) were addressed as comrades (iii. 29.4). This comradeship, coming down from the days of the fathers, was felt to be immensely old (iii. 54.9). Similar must have been the relationship felt by the Vedic poets for Aśvins: it was desired that the ancient comradeship with them be revived and the friendship be sealed with drinks, being delighted together on the basis of equality (*punaḥ purāṇam sakhyam kṛṇvānāḥ sakhyā madhvā madema saha nu samānāḥ*) (iii. 58.6). Again, Soma, Brahmaṇaspati, Savitṛ, Varuṇa, Mitra and Aryaman and others all maintained warm and comradely relations with the Vedic poets and their kinsmen. However, as comrades, Varuṇa, Mitra and Aryaman were the foremost. Macdonell observed:

> Aryaman though mentioned about a hundred times in the Ṛgveda is so destitute of individual characteristics, that in the *Naighaṇṭuka* he is passed over in the list of gods. Except in two passages, he is always mentioned with other deities, in the great majority of cases with Mitra and Varuṇa. In less than a dozen passages the word has only the appellative senses of 'comrade' and 'groomsman', which are occasionally also connected with the god. Thus Agni is once addressed with the words: 'Thou art *aryaman* when (the wooer) of maiden'. The derivative adjective *aryamya* 'relating to a comrade', once occurs as a parallel to *mitrya*, 'relating to a friend'. Thus the conception of Aryaman seems to have differed but little from that of the greater Āditya Mitra, 'the friend'. The name goes back to the Indo-Iranian period , as it occurs in the *Avesta*.[11]

Similarly, Varuṇa, observed Macdonell, was 'on a footing of friendship with his worshipper.'[12] How far the word 'worshipper' correctly describes the relation of the Vedic poets and their kinsmen to the Vedic gods needs really to be settled. For the present, however, we may examine an important indication—a clear and distinct reference to a past involved in this comradely mention of Varuṇa:

> What has become of our friendship with you, which was in the ancient days, without any spite? May we foster it and enter your thousand-door abode—you who are full of food. (vii. 88.5)

This reference to the past has some special significance with regard to the specific history of Varuṇa. It has also some general significance in the Ṛgveda, which we shall later take up.

The point is that 'some hundreds of years must have been needed for all the hymns found in the *Ṛgveda* to come into being'. There is no basis to think that during these hundreds of years the life and thought of the Vedic people remained unchanged. Therefore, it is only natural that the *Ṛgveda* should contain different strata of the thought reflecting also the fact of the Vedic people passing through different stages of social development. We have already before us theories concerning the different strata of the Ṛgveda as worked out by the foremost of the modern scholars. However, such theories, being based mostly on bare philological considerations, are liable to suffer from the limitation of a formal approach and may mislead us to expect a view of the earlier condition of the Vedic people only in the hymns actually composed earlier. On the other hand, the possibility remains that a hymn, even when considered later on linguistic grounds, may, nevertheless, by invoking the memory of the past, reveal something about the Vedic people during their comparatively early stage of social development. It is in such references to the past that we often come across the mention of the comradely relations of the Vedic poets with their gods, particularly Varuṇa. From these we may infer that the more we penetrate into the pre-history of the Vedic people, the clearer do we see their gods to be outspokenly human and maintaining a comradely relationship with the members of the tribe.

Philological considerations, too, corroborate this. Here is a *ṛk* of immense significance:

> O Agni, O Asura, this ritual (*yajña*) of ours is full of cows, of sheep (*avimāṅ*), of horses, of food, of offspring; may thou be always without anger being in our assembly (*sabhāvān*), a friend, like a human being (*nṛvat-sakhā*), possessing huge wealth and vast waters (iv.2.5).

Agni being addressed as an *asura* is indeed remarkable; Sāyaṇa found it too inconvenient to comment upon. It indicates that the *ṛk* dates back to a period when to the poets of the *Ṛgveda* the word *asura* had not fallen into disrepute. Probably, more significant than this is the use of the word *avimāṅ*, 'one full of sheep.' This is the solitary use of the word in the whole of the *Ṛgveda*, the only reference to the sheep as a form of wealth. This again indicates that the *ṛk* dates back to a period when the Vedic seers were still raising and tending the sheep, a practice they must have eventually given up. These, therefore, are evidences of the *ṛk* belonging to the most archaic stratum of the *Ṛgveda.* And it is also the *ṛk* in which the word *nṛvatsakhā,* 'friend-like-a-human being', occurs; in the comparatively earlier periods, the comradely relations felt by the Vedic poets for their gods were indeed overtly human.

Speaking of comradely relations, we are reminded here of a rather interesting evidence of Vedic literature. In the *Ṛgveda,* one of the words used for 'comrade' is *'jāmiḥ':* Agni was addressed as *janānām jāmiḥ* (i.75.4), the comrade of all men. Sāyaṇa, on the authority of the *Uṇādi Sūtra* explained the word as follows: *jama adane jamanti saha ekasmin pātre adanti iti jāmavaḥ, bandhavaḥ:* 'The root *jam* means to eat: those who eat together from the same plate are friends, *jāmayaḥ.*' One point is clear: the word for comrade (*jāmiḥ*) is derived from the circumstance of having eaten from the same plate. The association of the word comrade with communism is indeed very old.

To sum up our present point: How much of divinity or godhood in our sense is to be imputed to these Vedic gods? From the plain meaning of the Vedic verses the answer is that it cannot be much. And if that is so, religious sentiment as we understand it is hardly to be read in the *Ṛgveda.* However, there is a strong tendency among the followers of Vedic orthodoxy claiming that the Veda is too holy to be understood according to its plain meaning. We now pass on to see what fate awaited the Vedic gods as the result of the final development of this tendency.

4. Claim of Ritual Use (Viniyoga) of All Vedic Verses

The *Ṛgveda* apart, three other compilations come down to us claiming the general title *Veda.* These are *Sāmaveda, Yajurveda* and *Atharvaveda.* Of these, the last had to await long to be admitted to the status of the Veda: the word usually used as referring to the Vedas in the ancient sources is *trayi* or "the three", i.e. as excluding the *Atharvaveda.* The *Sāmaveda,* again, has hardly the status of an independent Veda, it being but an anthology of the songs of the *Ṛgveda* selected with an eye to their melody value. Among the other Vedas thus we are left only with the *Yajurveda,* which we are told, had once a rather fabulous number of different recensions though of these only a few actually survive today.

That the *Yajurveda* came into being much later than the *Ṛgveda* can hardly be doubted. Also palpable is the fact of the drastic change in its main theme: the be-all and end-all of the *Yajurveda* are the *yajña*-s which are usually translated as the Vedic "sacrifices", though these are generally nothing more than primitive magical rituals, often enlarged or magnified to make them look most awe-inspiring, so that the rich patrons financing for these (called *Yajamāna*-s) may be induced to part with substantial "fees" or *dakṣiṇā*-s to the varieties of priests looking after the execution of its various aspects—priests who had no other ostensible means of their own subsistence, and hence from the social viewpoint were no more than parasites. If the *yajña*-s are the be-all and end-all of the *Yajurveda,* the *dakṣiṇā*-s are so for the Vedic priests.

With these points in mind, we may pass on to a view, a powerful exponent of which was Sāyaṇa, whose stature as the commentator of the Veda often tends to obscure the fact of his also having been a powerful politician of the fourteenth century A.D. He was a very influential minister of the Vijayanagara Empire, though after retiring from the post he became the *mahānta* or Head Abbot of one of the monasteries founded by Śaṃkara.

In his introduction to the commentary on the *Ṛgveda* Śayaṇa came out with the categorical claim that all the verses in the *Ṛgveda* were intended to be but *mantra*-s or incantations for the *yajña*-s of the *Yajurveda* and hence the *Yajurveda* is the basic plank of the entire Vedic literature. The Ṛgvedic verses were thus nothing if not having a *viniyoga* or application in the Vedic *yajña*-s.

The claim is in fact so utterly absurd that it hardly deserves any serious discussion. Not that there is no quotation from *Ṛgveda* in the ritual discussions of the *Yajurveda.* What these actually are, however, are only certain scraps from the *Ṛgvedic* verses, torn out of their actual contexts and, as Keith has shown, not necessarily free from corruption or misreading. What is worse, there is often no rhyme or reason connecting such scraps with the theme of the ritual—or of the part thereof—the injunctions for which are given in the *Yajurveda*. In any case, nobody has been able to show that the *entire Ṛgveda* was actually intended to be employed in the Vedic sacrifices and this because of the simple reason that it is impossible to do it. In short, Sāyaṇa's claim that all the Ṛgvedic verses were but spells for Vedic *Yajña* is at best a fiction, evidently intended to inflate the veneration for the *yajña* which, from Sāyaṇa's viewpoint, might have served some political purpose.

What is much more interesting for our present discussion is the fact that God—or, for that matter, the Vedic deities—had to suffer their very being in the hands of the later Vedic priesthood, whom Sāyaṇa so much extolled and whose basic philosophical outlook took shape as the Pūrva-mīmāmsā. We shall in our next lecture discuss this philosophy. For the present we have to note another point. The fact remains that considerably later than the *Yajurveda* (and the vast literature called the *Brāhmaṇa*-s, the direct outcome of the Yajurvedic tradition) there emerged a new type of literature, called the Upaniṣads or Vedānta, which were somehow sought to be attached to the Vedic literature. In this there developed a new type of philosophy, inclusive of at least some sort of rudimentary monotheism. What nevertheless is not completely outside the scope of doubt is how far we are entitled to look back at the Upaniṣads as the products of the purely Vedic people. In all likelihood these are the products of a society in which, to repeat the expression of A. Ghose, "the early Aryan society had made room for the Indian society in which it is difficult to isolate Aryan and non-Aryan elements". Indeed, the internal evidences of the Upaniṣads lead us to doubt as to their purely Vedic or Aryan origin, for some of the prominent philosophers in this literature did not clearly have it.

Mahīdāsa Aitareya, from whom the name of the *Aitareya Upaniṣad* is derived, was, on the admission of the orthodox tradition itself, the son of a certain *itarā*, i.e. a low-caste woman according to the Vedic norm, perhaps meaning a woman belonging to the autochthons among whom the Vedic peoples moved and with whom they got intermingled. The story of Jābāla—uncertain of his actual father, his mother having "served" many men—is well-known. It is difficult to believe that Śakaṭavān Raikva—described as scratching his itches while sitting under his cart—could be a sage of pure Vedic origin, because he was a cart-driver rather than a charioteer of the Veda. If there is anything about the Jātaka story of the birth of Uddālaka Āruṇi, namely he owed his name to the Uddalāka tree under which his father united with an autochthon woman, it can hardly be indicative of his pure Vedic origin. Indeed, there are many peculiar names of Upaniṣadic philosophers the roots of which it is hard to trace in the Ṛgvedic tradition.

We have mentioned all this only to emphasise one point. Notwithstanding all that is said about the Upaniṣads as having been the ending portions of the Vedas, the society of which these were the products, like their basic intellectual climate, must have been a new one. Indeed, it was perhaps because of this that when Nārada approached Sanatkumāra with full knowledge of having studied the three Vedas among other subjects, Sanatkumāra bluntly declared that all these were but "mere names" *nāma eva*. A philosopher would have hardly said this about branches of learning *inclusive of the three Vedas* if he were in fact interested in carrying forward the strict Vedic outlook. So also when Śvetaketu returned to his father Uddālaka Āruṇi after having studied the Vedas for a full twelve years, the father, apparently without being impressed by this learning, started asking him philosophical questions unheard of in the Vedas. Incidentally, Śvetaketu—with all his knowledge of the Vedic lore—came to be remembered as the founder of the *Kāma-śāstra*, or the science of erotics rather than the Vedic outlook in any form.

So the evidence of the Upaniṣads—specially of those foreshadowing the monotheistic outlook—proves little or perhaps nothing about the eventual fate of the Vedic gods, though some of them were rather desultorily mentioned in the Upaniṣads. The real custodians of the Vedic tradition—if there were any—were the Vedic priests, whose philosophical view par excellence is to be found in the Pūrvamīmāṁsā. And this Pūrvamīmāṁsā philosophy summarily brushed off the basic concept of God, along with the whole host of the Vedic deities. Such was the eventual fate that the concept of divinity had to suffer at the hands of the most authentic representatives of the Vedic tradition itself.

All this cannot but raise a fundamental question. What exactly is meant by Vedic religion, about which there is so much talk—and so great reverence—in the country? The attempt to seek it in the Upaniṣads has its own problems, some of which we have just mentioned.

Such being the story of it in the Vedic tradition itself, are we then to look for it outside the rigid Vedic literature, i.e. in the beliefs and customs prevalent among the people?

It seems that we are obliged to do it. Here, however, from the strict Vedic viewpoint, perhaps the greatest disappointment awaits us. The great Vedic gods—Indra, Varuṇa, Mitra, Soma—have simply no place in the actual religious beliefs and practices of the vast Indian people. Indra is not totally forgotten, of course. But he is relegated by the Purāṇas to act—though nominally—as the king of gods, indulging mainly in dubious activities. It is evidently difficult—if not impossible—to construct any genuine religious sentiment out of the lusty Purāṇic stories about Indra. Varuṇa, Mitra, Soma and others perhaps suffer a worse fate: they are simply forgotten or perhaps squeezed out of the popular pantheon already overcrowded by all sorts of local deities. In this country of innumerable shrines and temples there is none for the great Vedic gods. As Louis Renou, talking of Varuṇa, observes, "today we have to look to the extreme limit of Indian expansion, the island of Bali, to find a temple dedicated to him".[13] Vedism as religion is simply extinct in India; the Vedic religion has become practically a misnomer. Apart from a few stray sentences or half sentences actually being used in some ritual—which do not really cohere with the rituals as a whole—what in fact survives today in the country is the word *Veda*, and this, specially in the legal literature called the *Dharmaśāstra*-s, mainly as a political instrument to keep the vast masses of the people as law-abiding or loyal citizens. Any law—just or unjust—is loudly proclaimed in the *Dharmaśāstra*-s, to be derived from or sanctioned by the Veda, regardless of course of the circumstance of even any remote vestige of such law actually being found in the Veda—particularly in the *Ṛgveda* which is supposed to have the highest status in the whole range of the Vedic literature. In short, the word Veda became only a political tool rather than the source of any genuine religious sentiment.

REFERENCES

1. L. Woolley in HMCSD I. ii. 458.
2. R.S. Sharma 72.
3. A. Ghosh 2.
4. *Ibid* 4.
5. K. Marx in OR 25.
6. H.P. Sastri HR (Bengali) 389-97.
7. M. Winternitz i. 109.
8. RV i. 122.9, x.85.31; etc.
9. M. Winternitz i. 109.
10. D. Chattopadhyaya L 534 ff.
11. A.A. Macdonell VM 45.
12. *Ibid* 27.
13. L. Renou 44.

5

The Vedic Gods and the Vedic Priests

In my last lecture I have tried to argue that the Vedic religion in its strict sense—i.e. the sense of being the direct outcome of the Vedic literature and as produced by the Vedic people themselves—is really a misnomer. The songs and hymns of the *Ṛgveda* produced by the pastoral nomads and expressing sentiments of the vigorous barbarians, looting food and drinking freely in the company of the deities or *deva*-s, had at best a thin coating of religious sentiment. That is why it could not take roots in the later agricultural communities foreshadowing what the archaeologists call the Second Urbanisation—the beginnings of the historical period. This explains why only from the time of the Upaniṣads—which were the products of a society in which the so-called Aryans were getting freely mixed up with the local people and were adapting their culture, both material and spiritual—things took a somewhat new turn. In the new intellectual climate room was made for the rudiments of religious sentiment in our sense. What is not easily understood, however, is the attitude of the Vedic "priests" themselves, who acquired some sort of abrupt prominence from the time of the *Yajurveda* and the *Brāhmaṇa*-s and claimed to be the exclusive custodians of the Vedic tradition in its strict sense; for the fact is that they preferred to scrap the concept of God altogether and, what appears to us all the more peculiar, proposed virtually to push out of the realm of reality the Vedic deities themselves.

This is so peculiar indeed that before passing on to see how the Vedic priests proposed to scrap the concept of God and virtually pushed out even the Vedic deities from the realm of reality, we may have some idea of the possible motivation of their stark atheism.

For the Vedic priests, the be all and end all is what is called *yajña*. It is usually translated as "sacrifice". Accepting this translation, however, it is necessary to remember that it has absolutely nothing to do with the religious sentiment—with prayer, propitiation, etc.—and hence also with God or any deity. On the contrary, the exclusive assumption on which Vedic *yajña* is based is that the performance of a certain specific act with its appropriate spell automatically—i.e. by the inherent potency of the act itself—ensures the fulfilment of the desires of the rich patrons financing for the sacrifice. In the vast priestly literature, this point is sought to be padded with all sorts of mumbo-jumbo-wild conjectures, weird analogies, absurd etymologies, concocted legends, etc. All this was evidently intended to create a good deal of awe for the *yajña*, obviously required to attract the patrons to pay for it. However, shorn of these mumbo-jumbo-jumbos what we are left with is nothing but the essence of ancient magic.

At the same time, it needs to be remembered that magic, as the characteristic ideology of the primitive pre-class society, had some function and even relevance specially in the context of the collective labour of the primitive society. By contrast, the Vedic *yajña*—though nothing but magic—is transplanted to the sharply class-divided society, which the priestly literature often bluntly eulogises. Thus transplanted, the function of magic passes into its opposite: instead of being an illusory technique supplementing the real technique, it becomes sheer economic drainage, fattening only the parasitical priest-class. Nevertheless, what survives in the Vedic *yajña* is the sense of total redundance of the assumption of God or even the reality of the Vedic deities, which now assumes the form of conscious and stark atheism.

The priestly ideology in its strict sense crystallised in the form of a philosophy which is known as the Pūrva-mīmāṃsā, often referred to simply as Mīmāṃsā. We have to go into some detail of this philosophy to see if it left any scope whatsoever for the religious sentiment.

As a philosophy, the Mīmāṃsā is inconceivable without the Vedas. It intends to thrive on the Vedas, it draws its entire intellectual nourishment from the Vedas, and, in its major part, professes to be nothing more than the right way of understanding the Veda. In fact, the Mīmāṃsā is nothing if not a rationalisation of the Veda. As a rationalisation of the Veda it acquired so much of prestige even in the ancient period that Bādarāyaṇa—the author of the source-book of Vedānta philosophy—with all his distaste for the ontology and epistemology of the Pūrva-mīmāṃsā, felt obliged to show a great deal of respect for Jaimini, who, if not the founder of the Mīmāṃsā philosophy, was at least the author of its source-book called the *Mīmāṃsā-sūtra*. Even in the eyes of its opponent, the Vedic orthodoxy of the Mīmāṃsā was absolute.

Nevertheless, the earlier generation of modern scholars felt clearly puzzled by its stark atheism. They wanted to convince themselves that there must have been something wrong somewhere about the professed atheism of the Mīmāṃsā. How could an Indian philosophical view, with an almost fanatical zeal for Vedic orthodoxy, at the same time be so aggressively atheistic?

Max Müller, for example, wonders and suspects some misunderstanding in the traditional view of the Mīmāṃsā attitude to God. Referring to "the charge of atheism that has been brought against Jaimini's Mīmāṃsā", he observes, "This sounds a very strange charge after what we have seen of the character of this philosophy, of its regard for the Veda, and the defence of its revealed character, nay, its insistence on the conscientious observance of all ceremonial injunctions. Still it has been brought both in ancient and in modern times... However, there seems to be a misunderstanding here". He proposes to clear up the misunderstanding with a bold suggestion: "Jaimini would not make the Lord responsible for the injustice that seems to prevail in the world, and hence reduced everything to cause and effect, and saw in the inequities of the world the natural result of the continued action of good or evil acts. This surely was not atheism, rather was it an attempt to clear the Lord from those charges of cruelty or undue partiality which have so often been brought against him.... It was but another attempt at justifying the wisdom of God, an ancient *Theodicee*, that whatever we may think of it, certainly did not deserve the name of atheism... If the Mīmāṃsakas were called atheists, it meant no more than that they tried to justify the ways of God in their own way."[1]

Such a statement, coming as it does from an Indologist of Max Müller's stature, is, to say the least, quite amazing. Far from proving any subtle or veiled defence of theism by Jaimini and his Mīmāṃsā, what it actually proves is that even the eminent modern interpreters of Indian philosophy, when they proceed to discuss the question of God in the Mīmāṃsā, sometimes show little or no interest in the actual Mīmāṃsā literature itself. How far this is due to some preconceived notion of the Vedic view is an interesting question. Into the details of this we cannot unfortunately digress at the moment. Nevertheless, what needs to be emphasised is that there is absolutely no way of reading any bias for theism in the Mīmāṃsā philosophy without resolutely ignoring the Mīmāṃsā literature, or, as Keith puts it rather mildly, "the atheism of the true Mīmāṃsā is regarded with such unanimity as to render it impossible to explain it away".[2]

The Mīmāṃsā literature is quite vast and in it are preserved not only the most determined declarations against the possible existence of God but also bold logical considerations in defence of this declaration. We are to review these in the present and the next lectures. As against Max Müller's statement just quoted, as we shall presently see, Kumārila, one of the greatest representatives of the Mīmāṃsā, far from having any anxiety of saving the almighty God from the charge of creating a world full of evils and inequities, simply laughed at the folly of those that could afford the extravagance to imagine that such a world, full of palpable evils and inequities, could at all be created by an all-powerful and all-merciful God. In other words, the observed evils in this world were for him decisive evidences for the non-existence of God, and, at least as Kumārila thought, no ingenuity of the theist could undermine the importance of these evidences.

But this was not the only evidence for atheism offered by Kumārila nor was Kumārila the only exponent of Mīmāṃsā atheism. All the older and authentic representatives of the Mīmāṃsā view clearly felt that it was necessary for them to deny God in order to make room for the fundamentals of their philosophy, which, in short, is the absolute autonomy of the rituals or yajña. On the other hand, as the right response to it, the authentic representatives of Indian theism felt obliged to argue against the Mīmāṃsā position.

In the *Gītā,* the Lord God himself was made to denounce this philosophy, though mentioning it by name.[3] It remains for us to see, however, that in spite of denunciations like these, the Mīmāṃsakas kept rationalising their atheism most stubbornly.

In the earliest available commentary on the *Mīmāṃsā-sūtra*, Śabara[4] asked, "Have the Vedic gods anything to do with the human lot, or, to be more specific, with ritual actions and their results?" His question was indeed more radical than this, for he wanted to settle even the ontological status of these gods. "Do the Vedic gods", he asked, "have any real or substantive existence?" For a Mīmāṃsaka these questions were of vital importance and Śabara wanted to discuss these with a great deal of earnestness. After satisfying himself that he had reviewed all the considerations on which any substantive being could be attributed to these gods, he came to the conclusion that they could have no existence in the real sense of the term. But, then the fact was that the Vedas mentioned these gods. As mentioned in the Vedas, therefore, what did these gods actually mean? Śabara answered that in the Vedas these stood for mere sounds or words, i.e. the only existence which the Vedic gods had was purely verbal. In his considered judgement, therefore, Agni, Indra, Mitra, Varuṇa, etc. were not divine beings at all. They were mere words instead. Therefore, if there were a hundred synonyms for the word *agni* or fire in the Vedas, these were for Śabara equivalent to a hundred different Vedic deities, the existence of each being constituted by the sound-value of one of the synonyms. It followed from this that, from the Mīmāṃsā point of view, there was no possibility of any interference by these Vedic gods with the human lot. They had nothing to do with the results of human actions. Hence, there was no sense in offering any sacrifice to them. Deprived as they were of any substantive existence, these gods could not accept any offering nor could they feel pleased with these. To try to invoke their grace was thus a senseless act. The rituals produced their result by the inherent potency of their own—rituals in which the names of the gods had value only as forming parts of the spells.

Such then was the mīmāṃsā attitude to God and to the Vedic deities: the former was nothing more than a mere myth and the latter nothing more than mere words. Yet there is no doubt that the Mīmāṃsakas were driven to this attitude by their utmost seriousness for the Vedas.

In other words, their rejection of both monotheism and polytheism followed from their adherence to the Vedas, or, to be more precise, from the way in which they themselves understood the Vedas.

To the average Indian today, all these may appear to be strange and even bewildering. It will, however, be hasty to think that the real reason for this is that the Mīmāṃsakas thoroughly misunderstood the Vedas. On the contrary, they themselves lived in the Vedic tradition and were too involved in it to misunderstand it. There was an almost unbroken continuity between at least one aspect of the Vedic tradition and the Mīmāṃsā philosophy, the latter being both historically and logically only a culmination of the former.

If, therefore, we fail to understand today how an almost fanatical zeal for the Vedas led the Mīmāṃsakas to accept a radical form of atheism, the real reason for this is likely to be that the enormous time-gap between the Vedas and ourselves has resulted for us in the loss of some vital aspect of the ancient Vedic tradition. This means, in short, that our view of the Vedic view is in need of serious revision.

We shall return later to discuss all this more fully. For the present, we may note that even some of the later representatives of the Mīmāṃsā system felt puzzled by the stark atheism of the philosophy they were themselves expounding. One of the best known examples of this was Khaṇḍadeva, a Mīmāṁsaka of the seventeenth century. After explaining the fundamentals of the Mīmāṁsā, he stood aghast as it were by what he had himself written. While trying to be faithful to the spirit of Jaimini, he found it impossible to allow even a scrap of theism in the philosophy he expounded. At the same time, evidently because of being personally cut off from something vital in the ancient Vedic tradition and perhaps also because of the strong authority of the Indian law-makers boosting the Vedānta philosophy in his own time—he clearly felt that the categorical stand against God inevitably embodied in his exposition of the Mīmāṃsā, must have been a sin or a sacrilege. He wanted, therefore, to atone for this sin and concluded his treatise with a strange prayer. "Thus", he said, "are explained the essence of Jaimini's views. Even by the mere utterance of these, my words have become polluted. So my only refuge consists in invoking the grace of God."[5]

This is how, under the changed atmosphere of the later days, a genuine Mīmāṃsaka looked back at the Mīmāṃsā atheism. Others, obviously with lesser scruple for the original spirit of the philosophy, wanted somehow or other to convert it into a theistic one. Understandably enough, the development of such a tendency among the Mīmāṃsakas themselves helps Radhakrishnan to feel somewhat relieved after all. Referring to the absence of God in the Mīmāṃsā philosophy, he comments, "This lacuna of the Pūrva-mīmāṃsā was so unsatisfactory that the later writers slowly *smuggled in God*".[6] He mentions in this connection the examples of Vedānta Deśika and Āpadeva. Of these two, the former produced a strange work called the *Seśvara-mīmāṃsā* or "Mīmāṃsā with God", while the latter advanced the thesis—also strange from the Mīmāṃsā point of view—that during the time of the universal dissolution (*pralaya*), the Vedas remained in the memory of God. What Radhakrishnan does not add, however, is that the mention of Vedānta Deśika in the context of the true Mīmāṃsā is irrelevant after all, it being well known that his real philosophical affiliation was to the Rāmānuja version of the Vedānta, which was most theistic of all the forms of Vedānta. In other words, he was perhaps trying to smuggle the Mīmāṃsā ideas into the framework of his own theism rather than trying to smuggle in God into the Mīmāṃsā philosophy. Besides, as it is rightly observed, the very title of his work, namely "Mīmāṃsā with God", shows how little the real Mīmāṃsā had to do with God. Similarly, Āpadeva's theory that God retained the Vedas during the time of *pralaya*, could be advanced only in complete disregard of the older and authentic standpoint of the Mīmāṃsā philosophy, according to which the very conception of *pralaya*, like that of *sṛṣṭi* or creation, was only a figment of the theist's imagination. Thus, in short, the later tendencies of reconciling the Mīmāṃsā philosophy with the view of god or the gods amounted only to the upsetting of the fundamentals of this philosophy.

With these introductory words, we may now pass on to discuss Mīmāṃsā atheism in some detail.

This is perhaps best done in two steps.

First, by reviewing the earliest Mīmāṃsā literature available for us. Secondly, by reviewing the works of the later philosophers of the Mīmāṃsā school when they were obliged to face the monotheistic arguments developed by their rivals.

We have proposed these two steps, because there is some substantial difference between the two.

The early Mīmāṃsā literature gives us the impression that it was the product of a period when monotheistic ideas were yet to take full shape. What the early Mīmāṃsakas were concerned with was mainly the question of the Vedic deities, or, more specifically, with the question of such deities having any substantive existence. In the history of Indian philosophy, however, in a much later period took shape distinctly monotheistic ideas—first among a section of the followers of the Vedānta and then among the later Nyāya-Vaiśeṣikas. The Mīmāṃsakas of later days could not ignore or bypass these ideas. They had to settle the account of the Mīmāṃsā position with later theism.

The earliest available Mīmāṃsā work is the *Mīmāṃsā-sūtra* attributed to a certain Jaimini. For understanding it, we are obliged to depend on Śabara's commentary on it.

The question that interested them vitally was: How were we to understand the exact nature of the Vedic *yajña*-s in relation to the Vedic *deva*-s, i.e. the Vedic rituals in relations to the Vedic gods? Were the gods primary and the ritual secondary, so that the rituals were nothing but acts of worshipping the gods? As a matter of fact, argued the Mīmāṃsakas, the actual relation between the two was just the reverse. The rituals were primary and the gods not even secondary but mere words useful for the rituals. The Mīmāṃsakas discussed the question threadbare and came to the conclusion that the actual status of the gods was that of mere words, i.e. in modern terminology, of mere sounds forming parts of the ritual spell.

The main discussion of the nature of the Vedic gods is to be found in the Mīmāṃsā-sūtra ix. 1.6-10 and Śabara's commentary on these. Following primarily Nilakantha Sastry's admirable translation[7] of these, let us first review the main arguments of the Mīmāṃsakas intended to prove that the rituals were primary compared to the gods and that the actual status of the Vedic gods was after all nominal. This discussion is in two parts. First, the *pūrvapakṣa* or the statement of the position of the opponent. Secondly, the *siddhānta* or the refutation of the opponent and the conclusion of the Mīmāṃsakas themselves. In my book *Indian Atheism*, I have quoted the entire discussion of all this. Nevertheless, in view of the importance of it for understanding the problem of Vedic religion being a myth or reality, I cannot help reiterating it here over again.

The View of the Opponent

The case of a theistic understanding of the Vedic gods:

The deity, it is claimed, is primary and the *yajña* is for the sake of the deity. The *yajña* is in fact a form of worshipping the deity. The deity causes the *yajña* to be performed. And the food offered in the *yajña* is for the sake of the deity, just as food offered to the guest.

It is wrong to imagine that Agni and others are not the inducing agents of the *yajña*. On the contrary, the deities are the instigators of the sacred acts. Why? Because the meal offered in the *yajña* is for the sake of the deity. What is known as the ritual is nothing but the offering of food to the deities. This is evident from the fact that edible things are offered to the deity, with the statement that the deity shall eat these.

Further, the name of the deity is mentioned in the ritual in the dative case and, compared to the accusative case, the use of the dative case is indicative of something more directly aimed at. Therefore, the deity is not secondary. On the contrary, the materials used in that ritual act itself are secondary with reference to the deity.

Thus, the ritual is only an act of worshipping the deity. Compared to the object of worship, the act of worshipping is always observed to be secondary. Just as in the case of the guest any entertainment is for the sake of pleasing him, so must be the ritual performed for the sake of pleasing the deity.

It may be objected that the acceptance of all these amounts to the admission of the deity having a human form for actually eating the offerings. To this objection it is replied that the deity does have a form and the deity does eat. But what is the proof of all these? The theist argues that all these are proved by Tradition (*smṛti*), Popular Belief (*upacāra*) and Circumstantial Evidence (*anyārthadarśana*).

Thus, according to tradition—which is a valid evidence—the deity does possess a form. And people believe the same to be true. Hence they paint Yama with a rod in his hands, Varuṇa with a noose and Indra with a thunderbolt. In this way, the popular belief strengthens the evidence of tradition. And circumstantial evidence also converges on the same point. Thus, for example, it is said in the *Ṛgveda:* "Oh, Indra, thy right arm we caught." This shows that Indra must have a human form, because the right arm and left arm are characteristic of the human form. If Indra is imagined to have no form, the statement of the *Ṛgveda* makes no sense. Similarly, in the *Ṛgveda* is said: "These two, heaven and earth, that are far apart, thou graspest, Oh Maghavan, thy fist is great." This also makes sense only if the deity is assumed to have human form. Again, the *Ṛgveda* says, "Indra, transported with juice of Soma, vast in his belly, strong in his neck and with stout arms smites Vṛtra down." This also presupposes that Indra has a belly, a neck and arms, which are indicative of human form alone. From all these it is clear that the Vedic gods possess human form.

But how is it claimed that the gods also eat? From tradition, popular belief and circumstantial evidence, again. Thus tradition or *smṛti* declares that the deity eats. People also believe that the deity eats, otherwise there can be no sense in their bringing all sorts of food for the deities and offering these to the deities. From circumstantial evidence also we have to infer that the deity eats. Thus, for example, are said in the *Ṛgveda*: "Eat Indra, and drink of that which stirs to meet thee." "All kinds of food within his maw he gathers." "(Indra) at a single draught drank the contents of thirty pails." All these make sense only on the admission that the gods actually eat.

It may be objected that if the gods actually eat, the food offered to them should diminish in quantity. But the foods offered to the gods are not observed to diminish in quantity.

To this it is replied that the deities actually eat the essence of the food offered to them, just as the bees take only the honey from the flower. In spite of the honey being taken from the flower by the bees, the flower is not observed to suffer any quantitative loss. So is the food offered to the deity. Nevertheless, just as the flower becomes honeyless, so does the food; the food becomes tasteless after it is offered to the gods. This proves that the gods eat the essence of the food offered to them.

Further, the worship of the gods in order to propitiate them becomes meaningful only if they are assumed to be the lords of the material objects which they bestow as favour on being entertained. In other words, the worship of the deity can have a meaning only if the deity is assumed to be lord of the material objects. Hence the theist proposes to prove that the deities are actual lords of the material objects. But how to prove this? The theist claims that this is proved by tradition, popular belief and circumstantial evidence. Tradition clearly declares that the deities are the masters of all the good things of life. This is corroborated by popular belief. Thus, people speak of "the deity's village," "the deity's field" and so on. Circumstantial evidence also indicates the actual lordship of the deity. Thus, for example, the *Ṛgveda* says: "Indra is sovereign lord of heaven and earth. Indra is lord of waters and of clouds. Indra is lord of prosperers and sages. Indra must be invoked in rest and efforts." Again: "Looker-on of everything, lord of this moving world, lord, Indra, of what moveth not." And so on. Evidently, these passages cannot make any sense if the deity is not considered the actual lord of the things.

Further, from tradition, popular belief and circumstantial evidences it is also clear that the deity does bestow favours. Tradition or *smṛti* declares this in so many words. Besides, there are expressions of the popular belief in the form: "Prajāpati is pleased with him; hence a son is born of him." "Vaiśravaṇa is pleased with him; hence he has obtained wealth." Circumstantial evidence concurs. Thus, for example, it is declared in the *Ṛgveda*: "It is as if one pleases the gods who are offering-eaters—by means of fire-offerings, etc. Gods in their pleasure give one food and sap of food." How can a passage like this make sense if we do not admit that the deity does bestow favours?

From all these it is only reasonable to conclude that the connection between the ritual acts and their results is effected by the gods. The deity connects the worshipper with the fruit of worship. Whoever approaches the deity with offerings, him the deity connects with the fruits of his deeds. The proofs of this, again, consist of tradition, popular belief and circumstantial evidence. Tradition declares that the deity favours him who sacrifices. This evidence of tradition is strengthened by popular belief. Thus, for example, according to the popular belief one obtains a son by worshipping Paśupati. Further, circumstantial evidence concurs. Thus, e.g., in the *Ṛgveda* is said: "He with his folk, his house, his family, his sons, gains booty for himself, and with the heroes, wealth, who, with oblation and a true believing heart serves Brahmaṇaspati, the father of the gods." Again, the *Ṛgveda* says, "Only when satisfied himself, does Indra satisfy this person with offering and cattle."

From all these it is clear that by offering food and prayers, the god is worshipped; being worshipped thus he is pleased; being pleased he offers the fruits or results of the worship. Agni, for example, is the lord of something particular; being worshipped in a particular form, he bestows the particular thing to the worshipper. Another god—Sūrya for example—cannot bestow the same thing. From the Vedas we learn which god can give what. Accordingly, something is said in the Vedas of Agni and not Sūrya, i.e. something else of Sūrya.

Answer to the Opponent

Refutation of the theistic understanding of the Vedic gods:

Verbal testimony (Veda) proves that the *yajña* should be held as primary and the mention of the deity secondary.

It is not correct to claim that the gods are inducing agents.

What is supremely important is the ritual act itself. The performance of the ritual act generates *apūrva*. [This being one of the basic ideas of the Mīmāṃsakas it may be explained here. Apūrva literally means "not existing before." Technically, however, it is taken by the Mīmāṃsakas to mean "the resultant of any action (*karma*) in an invisible stage which it is supposed to assume before producing visible results." Thus, the act is supposed to lead to some result, though the result is not observed to take place immediately after the performance of the act. Nevertheless, there is no discontinuity between the act and the result: during the interval between the act and its result, the *apūrva*, directly resulting from the act, remains operative in an invisible form and this *apūrva* ultimately leads to the final result].

As against the theistic understanding of the Yajña, therefore, the Mīmāṃsakas argue that its performance directly generates the *apūrva* and this *apūrva* ultimately leads to the result designed. But how is it proved that the performance of the ritual directly generates the *apūrva*? Śabara answers that this is proved by verbal testimony, i.e. specifically the Vedas. In fact, in these matters the only relevant proof is the evidence of verbal testimony or Vedas. "The knowledge that any thing gives fruits, i.e. any inducing agent gives a particular fruit, arises from verbal testimony and not from direct perception or any other source of knowledge." And, according to verbal testimony or the Vedas, the fruit is derived from the *yajña* itself and not from the *deva*-s. Thus, the Vedas declare: "He who desires heaven (incidentally, 'heaven' in the Mīmāṃsā philosophy means simply 'pleasure' not necessarily other-worldly) should perform the Darśa and Pūrṇamāsa rituals." "He who desires heaven (pleasure) should perform the Jyotiṣṭoma ritual." Thus, in the context of the desire for heaven or pleasure, what is mentioned is the *yajña* and not the *deva*. However, are not the ritual materials *(dravya)* and the deities *(deva)* also mentioned in connection with the *yajña*? That is true. However, the mention of the deity is secondary. The requisite materials and the gods are supposed to be already there, whereas the ritual is something yet to be performed. When something already existing is mentioned along with something that has to be brought into existence, the existent is mentioned for the sake of the non-existent. Therefore, the gods are not the inducing agents.

As against the claim of the opponent that the deity is directly aimed at by the use of the dative termination, Śabara argues that from the same source, namely the Vedas, it is clearly seen that the ritual act itself is directly connected with the designed result. The Vedas speak of the instrumentality of the *yajña* itself and not of the *deva* in producing the fruit. This fruit or result is the real *puruṣārtha* or that which is the aim of man and the endeavour for the sake of the *puruṣārtha* is ours and not that of the deity. Therefore, we do not perform any action on account of the inducement from the gods. And the mention of the deity's name with the dative ending easily agrees with the idea that the deity is the means to the performance of the fruitful *yajña*.

The opponent claims: "*Yajña* is worship of the deity and the object of worship is the primary thing in worship, as we see it in the world." To this Śabara answers that such a view of the *yajña* is untenable. That which is fruitful is the inducing agent and the inducing agent is the ritual itself.

In defence of the position of the opponent, namely that the *yajña* is nothing but an act of worship, the opponent has to admit that the deity has a form and that it actually eats, because there can be no gift or meal for a deity which is without any form and which it does not eat. In defence of his view, the opponent cites the proofs of tradition, popular belief and circumstantial evidences. Śabara, therefore, refutes, these proofs of the deity having a form and as actually eating.

Tradition or *smṛti*, argues Śabara, cannot prove that the deity has a form and that it eats. *Smṛti* is based on the *mantra*-s and *artha-vāda*-s: it is a matter of direct perception that all knowledge on which tradition rests is derived from these. And, we shall presently see (Śabara, on the *Mīmāṃsā-*

sūtra x. 4.23), that the *mantra*-s and *arthavāda*-s do not at all support such a view of the deities. It is useless, argues Śabara, to try to deny that the real basis of tradition is *mantra* and *arthavāda*. Only a superficial view of *smṛti* may lead one to imagine that it is independent of *mantra* and *arthavāda*. As for popular belief, Śabara argues that it can be valid only in so far as it is based on tradition or *smṛti* itself.

Thus, popular belief cannot prove that the gods have form and that they actually eat the offerings.

Śabara next takes up the question of the circumstantial evidence *(anyārthadarśana)* proving that the Vedic gods actually possess human form. The argument, in short, is simple. Without admitting the human form, a large number of Vedic passages make no sense at all. Thus, for example, the Ṛgveda declares, "Oh Indra thy right arm we caught." Does this not clearly imply that Indra does possess a right arm and, therefore, also the human form? If the Vedas are full of declarations like these, how can the Mīmāṃsakas profess fidelity to the Vedic authority and at the same time deny that the gods possess human forms?

Śabara answers that it is impossible to take these Vedic passages in these apparent or superficial senses. Thus, for example, the apparent meaning of the passages of the *Ṛgveda* is that we hold the right arm of Indra. However, does the *Ṛgveda* really mean this? The answer must be in the negative, for it is a matter of direct perception that we do not hold the right arm of Indra. These Vedic passages, therefore, lead us to face two clear-cut alternatives. Either, taking these in their apparent or superficial sense, we have to admit that what the *Ṛgveda* refers to is just an absurdity; or, we have to reject this apparent sense and accept the passages in some other deeper sense. The first of these alternatives is clearly untenable. If the Vedas refer to certain absurdities, what is the use of citing their authority? Since, therefore, the Vedas cannot contain absurdities, the apparent meaning of these passages which suggest these absurdities must be rejected. Thus, in short, the real meaning of the Vedic passages like these must be something else. What, then is this real meaning? The answer of Śabara is not difficult to see. The real implication of the passages like these must be mere praise—*stuti* or *arthavāda*. By this the Mīmāṃsakas mean some form of indirect glorification of certain ritual actions. Thus, for example, the real meaning of the passage of the *Ṛgveda* under consideration is the indirect glorification of the *yajña* or ritual in which something is referred to as the right arm of Indra and not that Indra really possesses a right arm.

As against this, the opponent may claim that the Vedic passage under consideration may be taken as the statement of a man who in the past held Indra's arm. That is, by direct perception the fact of somebody holding Indra's arm cannot be proved, because such an event does not take place at the present time. Nevertheless, it is quite conceivable that in the past somebody actually held Indra's arm and the Vedic passage under consideration is a mere record of this experience as stated by him.

Such a line of argument is rejected outright by Śabara, inasmuch as it goes directly against the fundamental Mīmāṃsā thesis that the Vedas are eternal and absolutely impersonal *(apauruṣeya)*. As a matter of fact, it is one of the fundamental theses of the Mīmāṃsā philosophy and the Mīmāṃsakas themselves are fully satisfied that they have proved it beyond any possible scope for doubt. Therefore, there can be no question from the Mīmāṃsā point of view of the possibility of the Vedas retaining any statement of anybody. In short, there is no other way but to accept the Vedic passage as an *arthavāda*, i.e. the glorification of a ritual action with the mention of Indra *(indrakarma)*. It remains for us to see what, from the Mīmāṃsā point of view, can be the real implication of the mention of a deity like Indra in a ritual act.

The opponent may argue that there is no sense in praising what does not exist. If Indra has no arm at all, it is meaningless even as praise to speak of Indra's arm. Śabara answers that the objection is not valid, for even if a thing is not necessarily connected with (i.e. does not possess) human attributes, it is sometimes praised as if it had human attributes. Thus, for example, a hymn of the *Ṛgveda* has for its deity "the stones" and in this the stones are praised as follows: "They speak out like a hundred, like a thousand men; they cry aloud to us with their green-tinted mouth. During the *yajña*, these pious stones taste the offered food even before Agni." Similarly, another hymn has for its deity "the rivers" and in this the river is praised as follows: "Sindhu hath yoked her car, light rolling, drawn by steed". In these passages, things having no likeness to human form at all, are praised as if these possessed the human form. Therefore, from the Vedic passages, there can be no presumption (*arthāpatti*) of the human likeness of the Vedic gods. Even if the human form of a deity is apparently mentioned, we cannot conclude that the passage cannot be understood without assuming that the deity does possess a human form.

The expression "broad-necked Indra" in the Veda does not mean that Indra possesses a neck. What can it mean then? It simply means the glorification of something which is simply referred to as the neck of Indra, though this something is not actually the neck of Indra.

In this way, after elaborately reviewing the Vedic passages alleged to refer to the Vedic gods as possessing human form, Śabara comes to the conclusion, "Therefore, there is no circumstantial evidence that indicates that the deity has human likeness."

Following Jaimini, he next proceeds to prove that the *yajña* is not a meal, the deity does not eat and, therefore, the claim that the deity is more important than the *yajña* because the meal is for the deity's sake, is absolutely untenable. The possibility of the deity actually eating the food offered to it is already disproved, of course, by the proof of the deity having no human form. Nevertheless, since Śabara offers in this connection a number of delightfully commonsense considerations against the popular belief of the theist, we may quote him at some length.

"As for the statement that from tradition, popular belief and circumstantial evidence we learn that the deity eats—this has already been refuted by proving that the deity has no human form." In other words, the possibility of eating presupposes the possession of a body and since the deity cannot have a body it is idle to imagine that it is capable of eating. "Further", adds Śabara, "the meal offered to a deity who actually eats should diminish in quantity. And there is no proof that the deities eat the essence of the food in the manner of the bee. There is direct perception in the case of the bee and it is not there in the case of the deity. Therefore, the deity does not eat. The statement that the meal offered to the deity becomes tasteless creates no difficulty. The food becomes tasteless and cold on account of the exposure to the air."

The theists claim that the *yajña* is a form of worship by which the deity is pleased and the deity eventually bestows the results. Such a claim rests on the assumption that the deity is actually the lord of the material goods: how can the deity give us the goods without himself possessing these or being the lord of these? However, argues Śabara, the assumption that the deity is the lord of the material goods is totally untenable.

"It cannot be claimed that from tradition, popular belief and circumstantial evidence we can infer the lordship of the deity." Tradition is based on the Vedic injunctions and the 'praise of the injunctions' *(arthavāda)* and there is nothing in the Vedic injunctions and their praises to indicate that the deity is actually the lord of things. Popular belief in the form "the deity's village," "the deity's field", etc. are mere beliefs without any real basis. Only that can be considered as one's property which one can dispose of at one's mere will. The deity, however, cannot at his mere will dispose of the village or the land. Therefore, the gods do not give anything. "And for the statement that circumstantial evidence shows the lordship of the deity—as in 'Indra is the lord of heaven', etc.—

knowing by direct perception that the deity has no lordship, we infer that these words are figurative."

It may be objected that from the Vedas we learn the lordship of the deity. Thus, for example, it is said in the Vedas that the gods distribute all good things and from this we infer that this is only because the gods will it, i.e. the will of the gods is the real cause of the distribution of all good things. To this Śabara replies that such an understanding of the verbal testimony of the Vedas must evidently be wrong. From direct perception we know that the real cause of obtaining all good things is the will of the performer of the act or of the *yajña*, which mentions the deity. This will of the performer of the act can never be secondary. Even those who describe the deity as omnipotent cannot overlook the part of the will of the performer of the act. Therefore, they say that the deity bestows the good things according to the act of the performer of the *yajña*. However, since the gods cannot bestow things according to their own will and have to follow instead the will of others, how can they be conceived as the real lords? Further, the alleged verbal testimony or the evidence of the Vedas is really not there. That is, the Vedas do not actually declare that the gods distribute all good things. On account of the statement quoted being opposed by direct perception, the only sense in which the statement can be taken is some praise of the *yajña* enjoined in the Vedas. When such expressions could be (easily) explained as intended for praise (of the ritual injunction itself), these cannot be taken as verbal testimony proving the lordship of the deity. And the deity can never connect the man with the fruit of his act.

Such then, was the attitude to the Vedic deities in the early Mīmāṃsā literature. In my next lecture I shall try to discuss the reaction of the later Mīmāṃsakas, to the monotheistic ideas, particularly of Kumārila, whom a scholar as eminent as Satkari Mukherjee considers to be the greatest of the traditional Indian philosophers.

REFERENCES

1. F. Max Müller CW. xix. 210.
2. A.B. Keith KM 60.
3. *Gītā* ii.42-44.
4. *Śabara* on MS i. 1.5.
5. *Khaṇḍadeva, Bhātta-dīpikā iii. 53.*
6. S. Radhakrishnan IP. ii. 427.
7. N. Sastry in. IA Vol. 50, 211 ff. & 240 ff.

6

God and the Later Mīmāṃsakas

According to the view which Kumārila[1] rejected first, God was the exclusive or sole-sufficient cause of everything or the creator of everything. As against such an absolute view of the creator, Kumārila began with a number of simple commonsense considerations.

The upholder of such a view must admit that God existed before the creation of anything whatsoever, i.e. he must admit that before the act of creation God and God alone existed. However, if nothing else existed at that time—no space, no universe, nothing—wherein could the creator himself conceivably stay and how can we at all know that he did exist at such a time? "At a time when all this did not exist, what could have been the condition of the universe? As for the creator (Prajāpati) himself, what could be his position? and what his form? And at that time (when none else existed), who would know him and explain his character to the later created persons? Without the perception (or knowledge in some form of God at a time before the creation) how can we at all assume (the fact of his existence at that time)?" In other words, the theist cannot in any way prove the existence of the creator before the act of creation, nor has he any satisfactory answer to the question concerning the position of God before the creation of the universe, because on his own admission nothing but God existed before creation.

Further, the theist will have to admit that this creator either possesses a body or that he does not. Both these alternatives, however are untenable. If God is viewed as being without a body, he cannot have any desire whatsoever—not even the desire for creation—and he cannot create without any desire to create. If, to avoid this difficulty, the theist admits that god does possess a body, he will have to face all sorts of troublesome questions to which there are no satisfactory answers. "Then, again," argued Kumārila, "in what manner do you believe the world to have had a beginning in time? (If it be held that it is brought about by a desire on the part of the creator), since the creator is without a material body, etc. how could He at all have any desire to create? And, if He has a body, assuredly this body would not have been created by Himself. Thus, then, we would have to postulate another creator (for His body; and so on *ad infinitum*). If the creator's body is held to be eternal (we ask) —so long as earth, etc. have not been produced, of what material would that body be composed?"

But the question of the body apart, the very assumption of any desire on the part of the creator to create our world is untenable, for the world is full of evils and why should God at all want to create an evil world? "Then, again, in the first place, how is it that He should have a desire to create a world which is to be fraught with all sorts of troubles to living beings? For at that time (i.e. at the beginning of creation), He has not got any guiding agencies in the shape of virtue (and sin), etc. of the living beings themselves. Nor can any creator create anything in the absence of any means and instruments." As the commentators explained, "People hold that all the troubles in this world are due to the vicious deeds of the living beings in their previous births. This may be quite true. However, at the beginning of creation, there being no previous birth of anybody, no such guiding principle would be available and the blame of creating a troublesome world would rest only on God himself."

More of this problem of evil later. For the present Kumārila argued that even granting the agency of virtue and vice, that alone could not have sufficed for the creation of the world. For producing something, it was necessary to have the required materials for production. The potter, for example, produced the jar, because he had the required materials in the form of clay, etc. But the creator, according to the theist, had no such material and hence it was not possible for him to create. In answer to such an objection, the stock example cited by the theist was that of the spider which spun the cobweb from out of itself, i.e. without the need of any external material required for production. And, if the spider could create something without being provided with any external material for production, it was useless to think that God was incapable of doing it. As against, this, Kumārila argued that the theist thoroughly misunderstood the example of the spider.

As a matter of fact, the spider did not produce anything from out of nothing or exclusively from itself. On the contrary, it produced the cobweb from some definite external material. In the words of Kumārila, "Even the production of the spider's web is not to be viewed as being without any material basis: the web is produced by the saliva which, in its turn is produced from the bodies of the insects eaten by the spider."

Kumārila next took up the question of the possible motive that could have led God to create the world. The usual answer of the theist to this question was that God was motivated to create the world by compassion or pity for the living beings. Such an answer, argued Kumārila, was useless. (If it is argued that God created the world out of compassion for the living beings, we reply:) In the absence of the objects of compassion (i.e. the living beings), no compassion could be possible for him. And, if he moved to create by pure compassion, he should have created only happy beings."

As against the second of these arguments, the typical defence of the theist is the theory of necessary evil: some amount of pain or evil was indispensable for the creation of the world, just as for making a golden ornament a certain amount of alloy is necessary to be mixed with gold. Kumārila replied that such a defence of theism was completely unsatisfactory. The theist himself claimed that God was omnipotent. Nothing, therefore, could impose a limit to his activity. Hence the view that some amount of evil was indispensable for creation could not be binding on him. Or, if it was really binding on him, the theist had no right to claim that God was actually omnipotent. "If it be argued", said Kumārila, "that without some pain neither creation nor the continuation of the world would be possible, (we reply:) When everything depends on the mere will of the creator himself, what could be impossible for him? And if he were to depend upon laws and agencies, this fact would deprive him of his (boasted) independence."

The alleged act of creation, continued Kumārila, must have been either without any definite purpose or with some definite purpose. If it was without any purpose, the act must have been utterly foolish and hence the alleged intelligence of God was only a fiction. If, on the other hand, it was with some definite purpose, this very purpose must have been indicative of some want in God, which could not be fulfilled without creation. In this alternative, therefore, the theist had to surrender his claim that God was all-perfect. "What is the end", asked Kumārila, "which he desires and which could not be gained without creating the world? Without some end in view, even a fool does not act. If he were to act so (i.e. without any end in view), what would be the good of his intelligence?"

To this the famous answer of Bādarāyaṇa, the Vedāntist was that the creation of the world by God was to be viewed as some kind of sport or play (*līlā*). The kings engage themselves in the act of hunting not because they want to satisfy thereby any specific want, but because it is a mere pastime for them. So are the children found to play for having the sheer fun of the game. Similarly, God's creation of the world is to be viewed as a sport or a pastime, rather than as an act designed to satisfy some definite want. This, argued Kumārila, led the theists to contradict themselves. "If the activity of the creator were due to a desire for mere amusement, that would go against his ever-contentedness. And (instead of affording any amusement), the great amount of work (required for creation) would be a source of infinite trouble for him. And his desire to destroy the world (at the time of *pralaya* or periodic cosmic dissolution), assumed by the theist would be hardly explicable."

A number of internal contradictions were thus involved in the position of the theist. However, these contradictions apart, the very assumption of the theist that there was a God who created the world, was, in Kumārila's view, beyond the scope of any possible evidence. He argued this in an apparently light mood and wanted to make fun of the theist's position.

"And such a creator could never be known by anybody. Even if he were known in form, the fact of his being the creator could never be known. Because, at that time (i.e. the time of creation), what could the living beings, appearing at the beginning of creation, understand? They could not understand wherefrom they have been born; nor could they know the state of the world prior to creation, nor the fact of God being the creator. Nor could the idea that they would derive from his own assertion—which is generally considered as scriptural evidence or evidence derived from direct revelation—with regard to his being the creator) be altogether trustworthy; because even though he may not have created the world, he might have spoken of having done so, in order to show off his great power."

For the theists—particularly for the followers of the Vedānta or the Upaniṣads—the main proof for the existence of God and of the creation of the world by him consisted of scriptural declarations. The plain meaning of many passages of the Vedas suggests that God is the creator of the universe. It was possible for the Buddhist or Jain philosophers to ignore the evidence of these passages altogether. But this could not be so for Kumārila. To the Mīmāṃsakas the validity of the Vedas was absolute. How, then, were they to stick to their atheism in spite of the Vedic passages declaring in favour of

God having been the creator, or, for that matter, of theism in general?

The question is interesting and it leads us to see the skill of the Mīmāṃsakas in contriving the principles of textual interpretation. They argued, in short, that the apparent meaning of these Vedic passages could not be their real meaning. The real meaning of all the Vedic passages was somehow or other connected with the injunctions concerning the Vedic rituals. Any passage which was not apparently so—and which was apparently descriptive instead of being imperative—was to be interpreted as being a round-about or indirect praise of some injunction, i.e. as having for its real theme the injunction itself. In Mīmāṃsā terminology, this was called *arthavāda*, which roughly meant the technique of interpreting those passages of the Vedas that had apparently no connection with the ritual injunctions in a way as to mean the indirect praise of ritual injunctions.

How far the Mīmāṃsākas actually succeeded in interpreting all the Vedic passages in this way is a different question altogether. For the present the point rather is that they refused to admit God even on scriptural evidences. Those passages of the Vedas that apparently mentioned God and described him as creating the world could prove the position of the theist only if grossly misunderstood. On the contrary, the actual implication of these passages was some indirect praise of the ritual injunctions and this implication became clear if the passages were understood in their proper context.

Therefore, Kumārila argued that the Vedic passages apparently referring to God and His creation were not to be taken as actual evidences for the existence of God. As he put it, "The idea common among ordinary people (that the Veda mentions creation as proceeding from Prajāpati) is a mistaken one, caused by certain eulogies *(stutivākya:* passages praising injunctions), because when a passage is not duly considered and interpreted together with the passages that precede and follow it, it is bound to give rise to a misconception."

Similar, argued Kumārila, was the real implication of certain passages of the *Mahābhārata* and the Purāṇas which, only as superficially understood or basically misunderstood, could be taken as referring to God and his creation. Incidentally, for the Vedāntic theists the strongest proofs for the existence of God were the scriptural or Vedic declarations in favour of him. Vedānta as a philosophy had little confidence in independent reasoning arriving at right conclusions concerning the ultimate reality and therefore intended only to be a systematisation of the real implication of the Vedic—particularly the Upaniṣadic—passages. Hence the claim of Kumārila that no Vedic passage actually proved the existence of God amounted to summarily ignoring the strongest proof of God which the Vedāntists were aware of. Incidentally, from the Mīmāṃsā viewpoint, the entire Upaniṣadic literature was to be considered as *arthavāda*—i.e. instead of being understood as what it plainly meant was rather to be understood as some way of glorifying the *yajña*!

Refuting thus the doctrine of God which was perhaps originally advanced by Bādarāyaṇa in his *Bhrama-sūtra*, Kumārila proceeded to the critical rejection of the view of God as advanced by the later Nyāya-Vaiśeṣikas. He began this discussion by pointing to certain internal inconsistencies of the Nyāya-Vaiśeṣika theology, that evidently developed in some later period.

Thus, for example, he argued that the Nyāya-Vaiśeṣika conception of *pralaya* or universal dissolution—like its theological counterpart namely the conception of creation—hardly made any sense. Further, though the Nyāya-Vaiśeṣika conceived God merely as the efficient cause of the world—and were thus comparatively free from the difficulties of the other theists who conceived God as creating the world without being provided with any material necessary for the purpose—yet they were by no means free from the difficulties of pointing to any possible motive that might have led God to create the world. The theological inconsistencies like these, which, according to Kumārila, were involved in the theism of the Nyāya-Vaiśeṣikas, do not appear to have major philosophical interest for us. We may, therefore, quote here only a brief summary of this aspect of Kumārila's criticism of the Nyāya-Vaiśeṣika position: "Against the Vaiśeṣika view of creation, exception is justly taken to the difficulty involved in holding that in some manner the action of the Supreme Lord brings to a stand at one time (i.e. at the time of *pralaya)* the potencies of all the souls, and then awakens them all when a new creation is imminent. Against this view it is contended that the activity of men arising from their past deeds can never cease, and it is absurd and needless to complicate matters by assuming both the force of men's deeds and the intervention of the desire of God. Moreover, it is impossible to explain why this desire should ever arise and it is unintelligible to think of any mode in which the creator can act without a body or acquire a body."

After explaining the nature of the theological inconsistencies like these, Kumārila took up for critical examination the Nyāya-Vaiśeṣika inference of God, according to which anything made of parts must presuppose an intelligent maker thereof and since everything in the world is made of parts (atoms), the totality of the things in nature must point to a supreme intelligent maker, viz. God. "As against those," said Kumārila, "who argue that the production of the body, etc. must presuppose the superintendence or control of an intelligent agent, because these are made of constituent parts, as for instance the house, etc.—our answer is as follows." And he proceeded to explain the number of fallacies involved in this inference.

First, what exactly is meant by this superintendence or control of an intelligent agent? Is it to be understood in its most general sense?

In that case, it can mean nothing more than the superintendence or control of an intelligent agent in some form or other without specifying the nature of this intelligent agent. In other words, is the Nyāya-Vaiśeṣika inference intended only to prove that the production of the bodies, etc. presupposes the action of some intelligent agent? Taken in this sense, however, the argument obviously suffers from the fallacy of redundance or *siddha-sādhana*. It means the effort to prove something which is already admitted by both the parties in a debate or, in more general terms, trying to prove something which is already well-proved even on the admission of the opponent. Hence it is useless to try to prove it over again. Thus, even a staunch atheist (like Kumārila) has nothing to object to the view that the production of the living bodies is due to the actions of the living beings who are intelligent agents. Or, as the Prābhākaras argue in so many words, the living bodies are produced by the actions of the parents, who are, of course, intelligent agents. What, then, is the use of posing an inference to prove this over again? Evidently, therefore, the Nyāya-Vaiśeṣikas cannot take the superintendence or control of the intelligent agent in this wide sense. The same charge of redundance will be advanced against the Nyāya-Vaiśeṣikas if they try to prove the superintendence of an intelligent agent in the sense of some desire being exercised by the intelligent agent. It is admitted by all that the actions of the living beings, which result in the production of the living bodies, are preceded by the desire on the part of these living beings. If, however, the Nyāya-Vaiśeṣikas want to prove that the production of bodies, etc. immediately follow the desire of an intelligent agent, their inference will be totally unacceptable, in as much as there is no instance whatsoever in which the production of anything is found to follow immediately the desire of an intelligent agent. (The jar, for example, is not produced immediately after the potter desires to produce it. This being the typical example on which the Nyāya-Vaiśeṣikas rely, they cannot argue that the bodies, etc. are produced immediately after God desires to produce these.)

To sum up: the intelligent control sought to be proved by the Nyāya-Vaiśeṣikas with the help of their inference can at best prove an intelligent control in the sense in which it is ordinarily observed in everyday life, i.e. the intelligent control by the living beings themselves. However, taken in the sense of creation immediately following the divine desire, the inference is clearly illegitimate.

Secondly, argued Kumārila, the Nyāya-Vaiśeṣikas had to conceive their intelligent agent either as possessing a body or as being without a body. Both the alternatives, were, however, logically untenable and there was no third alternative for them to suggest.

Following Kumārila, let us first take up the possibility of the intelligent agent or God possessing a body. On inferential ground, however, this body of God will have to be viewed as being produced by another intelligent agent. The inference is: God's body must be something produced by an intelligent agent, because it is a body, as for instance, our own bodies. In other words, according to the inference of the Nyāya-Vaiśeṣikas themselves, our own bodies are produced by some intelligent agent because these are made of parts. On the same ground, therefore, the alleged body of God also will have to be considered as produced by an intelligent agent, because, being a body after all, it must be composed of parts.

If the Nyāya-Vaiśeṣikas propose to deny this, their basic inference of the existence of God will become "irregular" *(anaikāntika)* inasmuch as they will have to admit something as being made of parts and yet without being produced by an intelligent agent. In the terminology of Indian logic, any case of the presence of the probans coexisting with the absence of the probandum makes an inference irregular. The denial on the part of the Nyāya-Vaiśeṣikas of God's body being produced by an intelligent cause amounts to the admission of a case of the presence of the probans, namely "made of parts", coexisting with the absence of the probandum, namely "produced by an intelligent agent."

In defence of their own position, however, the Nyāya-Vaiśeṣikas may argue that the divine body is produced by an intelligent cause no doubt, though this intelligent cause is nothing but God himself.

Such a claim obviously amounts to the assertion that God must have been without a body before producing his own body. This leads us to see the absurdity of viewing God as producing something in spite of not possessing a body. God without a body is, in the Nyāya-Vaiśeṣika view, a pure spirit and hence is similar to the liberated souls conceived by the Nyāya-Vaiśeṣikas themselves. But a liberated soul cannot produce anything in the Nyāya-Vaiśeṣika view itself. Thus, in short, God without a body cannot create or produce anything. Hence, there is no question of God creating his own body.

Such, then, was the dilemma of the Nyāya-Vaiśeṣikas: they had to conceive their God either as possessing a body or as being a purely disembodied soul. In the former alternative, there is no possible explanation of His acquiring a body while, in the latter alternative, God—like the liberated soul—cannot be conceived as an agent at all.

Kumārila next explained an incongruity—much more serious from the logical point of view—of the Nyāya-Vaiśeṣika inference of God. This incongruity was that the Nyāya-Vaiśeṣikas had to renounce the very thesis they sought to establish by their inference, if they meant to be serious about the corroborative instance on which their inference vitally depended.

What is the corroborative instance of the Nyāya-Vaiśeṣika inference of God? It is that of the cloth being produced by the weaver or that of the house being built by the mason or, as mentioned most frequently, that of the jar being produced by the potter. For our present purpose, let us keep ourselves confined mainly to the last of these. The jar is made of parts and it is observed to be produced by an intelligent agent in the form of the potter. On the evidence of this, the Nyāya-Vaiśeṣikas argue that all the composite objects of the world must be due to an intelligent cause, which, in the ultimate analysis, can be nothing but God.

But the simple question is: Is the jar really produced by the potter? Or, is the cloth really produced by the weaver and the house by the mason? The Nyāya-Vaiśeṣikas have no alternative other than to answer the question in the affirmative, otherwise they are to deprive their own inference of a corroborative instance while in the standard of Indian logic, an inference without a corroborative instance is quite useless.

However, if the jar is admitted to be something really produced by the potter, God cannot be considered as the creator thereof. Similar must be the cases of the cloth, house, etc. which, if seriously taken as being produced by the weaver, mason, etc. cannot at the same time be regarded as being produced by God. Nevertheless, the Nyāya-Vaiśeṣikas have to admit that the jar is actually produced by the potter, the cloth by the weaver, the house by the mason, and so on. To admit this, however, is absolutely fatal for the Nyāya-Vaiśeṣika inference of God, for it amounts to the surrender of the fundamental thesis of the inference (*sādhya-hīnatā*). The real thesis of the inference is that everything composite in the world is produced by God. The jar, cloth, house, etc. are composite things. If these are admitted to be produced by agents other than God, how can the Nyāya-Vaiśeṣikas at all stick to their main thesis that all the composite objects of the world are made or created by God? Thus, the corroborative instance of the inference, if not lightly taken, calls for the rejection of the very thesis of the inference.

Are, then, the Nyāya-Vaiśeṣikas to surrender the corroborative instance of their inference of God? This, again, is impossible, for the inference itself is impossible without the corroborative instance.

Thus, argued Kumārila, from the logical point of view, the position of the Nyāya-Vaiśeṣikas was not an enviable one. They could not be serious at the same time of their corroborative instance as well as their fundamental thesis. In any case, the Nyāya-Vaiśeṣikas could not agree to give up their corroborative instance, for, as Kumārila argued, this simply meant more troubles for them. As he put it, "if the corroborative instance is taken as valid, there results the pseudo-probans called the contradictory *(viruddha)*, inasmuch as it proves an agent which is not divine and which is perishable, etc." Let us see the implication of this argument.

The corroborative instance is that of the jar produced by the potter. Now, the potter is an intelligent agent no doubt, under whose guidance or superintendence the composite object called the jar is produced. However, what are the characteristic peculiarities of such an intelligent agent? First, it is something purely mundane and not divine. Secondly, it is something essentially perishable and not eternal. If, therefore, the Nyāya-Vaiśeṣikas propose to prove an intelligent cause of all the composite objects of the world on the strength of this corroborative instance, the characteristic peculiarities of the intelligent cause observed in the case of the corroborative instance must be admitted as characterising the intelligent cause inferred of the world. In other words, assuming the validity of the corroborative instance, the only intelligent cause of the world which the Nyāya-Vaiśeṣikas can infer is essentially mundane and perishable, and this flatly contradicts the fundamental thesis of the Nyāya-Vaiśeṣikas, namely a divine and eternal intelligent cause of the world.

Kumārila did not himself consider the possibility of the Nyāya-Vaiśeṣikas defending their own position with the argument that notwithstanding the specific peculiarities of the corroborative instance, what was actually proved by their inference was an intelligent cause in general or a bare intelligent cause. But it is not difficult for us to think how Kumārila could have easily answered such a defence of the inference of God. As against the claim that creation immediately followed the will of God, Kumārila simply argued that there was no instance of production of anything immediately following the desire of an intelligent agent. In the same way Kumārila could have easily dismissed the defence of the Nyāya-Vaiśeṣika position with the argument that there was no instance pointing to the production of anything by an intelligent cause without having any characteristic peculiarity. On the contrary, any corroborative instance that could be mentioned of the intelligent cause producing something was inevitably an instance of an intelligent cause with specific peculiarities like being mundane and perishable. Therefore, any intelligent cause that could be legitimately inferred had to be considered as mundane and perishable.

In view of all these difficulties, asked Kumārila, were the Nyāya-Vaiśeṣikas to surrender their corroborative instance of the potter? This, again, was evidently impossible, for that meant the surrender of their theory of creation altogether. How could the unconscious atoms themselves lead to the creation of the world? In other words, in defence of he theory of creation from unconscious atoms, the Nyāya-Vaiśeṣikas had no alternative other than that of depending on the instance of the potter—the intelligent agent that produced the jar from the intrinsically unconscious materials like clay, etc.

In my previous lecture, I have quoted extensively from Jaimini and Śabara to show how much in details they propose to reject the substantive reality of the Vedic gods and how they propose to look back at them as having no more than sheer verbal values. All this, along with the polemics against the existence of God by the late Mīmāṃsakas, gives us some idea of the religious sentiment among the Vedic priests themselves.

Concluding Remarks

With this rough idea of the priestly ideology as crystallised in the Mīmāṃsā philosophy it is not difficult to understand why it did not—and, as a matter of fact, could not—leave scope for any genuine religious sentiment. The only motivation of the Vedic priests was to attract the rich patrons financing for the sacrifices—the *Yajamāna*-s—so that the priests could get for themselves fat fees—*dakṣiṇā*-s—which was the only source of their livelihood. For this purpose, they had to allure the financiers with all sorts of absurd promises which, the priests argued, were *automatically* assured by the performance of the rituals. Such a view of the essence of the rituals was nothing more than primitive magic, though highly magnified and adorned with all sorts of trivialities to add awe and wonder to these. We have no data, of course, of how many financiers were actually attracted by such claims. From the epics, *purāṇa*-s, etc. we have the impression that there could be a sizeable number of them; even legends of the Upaniṣads—like that of King Janaka of Videha—want us to believe that there were many also in the Upaniṣadic age. However, whatever might have been the actual number of such financiers—big or small—the fact seems to have been that there was a sufficient number of them, because it is difficult to dismiss the entire discussion of the *Dharmaśāstra*-s about the priest class as but a figment of imagination nor is it possible to reject as mere wish-fulfilment the law-makers' dictation that receiving a sacrificial fee or *dakṣiṇā* was the only legitimate source of income for the priests.

In any case, what is of material interest for our present discussion is that the practising Vedic priests refused to take any chance about their own profession even by allowing God or any Vedic deity to interfere with their rituals. They were thus keen on impressing the financiers for the sacrifices that not even the will of God or of any deity could have anything to do with the results assured by the performance of the sacrifices. So God and the deities had to be eliminated in order to make room for a purely magical view of the sacrificial rituals. In doing this they were also obliged to eliminate the most essential function of religion, i.e. to provide people with a palliative remedy for their sufferings. To confront the fact of suffering, people needed a God and also a host of minor deities which they actually had, perhaps partly as inherited from the ancient Harappan Culture, though mostly as their local creations. Thus the word Veda remained as also the vast Vedic literature. But these had little or nothing to contribute to actual religion—or should we say religions—of India, beyond of course some sentences or half-sentences somehow grafted on such of the domestic rituals as *Śrāddha,* etc., which still form the main source of income of the rather impoverished priests today.

What follows from all this is only a simple point. According to the view of the Vedic priests—evidently the foremost custodians of the Vedic tradition—there was nothing that could be called religion in our sense from the Vedic viewpoint. Or, along with what we have already discussed in our lecture IV, the view of God and of gods of the Vedic priests discussed in lectures V and VI, the conclusion we are driven to is that "Vedic religion" is more a myth than reality.

REFERENCE

1. For *Kumārila's atheism Ślokavārtika, Sambandhākṣepaparihāra,* Verses 49 ff.

7

Buddhism: Revolutionary Sociology Passes into its Opposite

1. Preliminary Remarks

The Buddha died at about the age of 80, "probably a few years before or after 485 B.C." The earliest available evidences for the reintroduction of script after the Harappan period being found in the Aśokan inscriptions, it is easily understood why Buddha could not have left for us anything in writing; whatever he preached was orally preached, usually in the form of dialogues. How and when these were committed to writing is still more or less a matter of debate, though the tradition of Ceylon wants us to believe that Aśoka's son "Mahindra actually introduced Buddhism into Ceylon and brought with him the texts of the canon. These texts are said to have been first transmitted orally, until, under the Sinhalese king Vaṭṭagāmini, in the first century B.C., they were committed to writing."[1]

These are in the form of three great collections, and, since the language used in these is Pāli, are usually referred to as the *Pāli Tripiṭaka*-s. How far these actually contain the unmodified teachings of the Buddha we shall probably never know: there are controversies among the practising Buddhists and scholars only with academic interest on this point, which remain inconclusive. However, even admitting later interpolations and perhaps also omissions of the Buddha's teachings in these, it seems that we have no other alternative than to accept their substantial authenticity, for otherwise we shall be left with the only theory that original Buddhism is something unknown and unknowable.

But even admitting the authenticity of the *Pāli Tripiṭaka*-s, there is a sharp controversy among the modern scholars about the actual social affiliation of the Buddha. As Rhys Davids sums it up: "Some writers on Buddhism do not hesitate to ascribe to Gotama the role of a successful political reformer, by representing him as having fought for the poor and despised against the rich and privileged classes, and as having gone far to abolish caste. Other writers gird at the Buddha because most of the leaders of his order were drawn from the ranks of the respectable and the well-to-do, with an education in keeping with their social position: and disparage him for neglecting the humble and the wretched, for not using his influence to abolish, or to mitigate, the harshness of caste rules."[2]

We have quoted this mainly to emphasise one point. Whether original Buddhism was a form of religion in our sense and whether the Buddha had any real taste for philosophy and metaphysics may still be questions open to controversy. However, admitting substantial authenticity of the *Pāli Tripiṭaka*-s there is hardly any scope to doubt that he was about the only thinker in ancient India with an objective interest in sociology, i.e. sociology neither in the sense of the most unscrupulous defence of despotism as we read in the *Arthaśāstra* nor in the sense of fabricating some sort of theological halo for the Brāhmaṇa-Kṣatriya privileges, which we have in the *Dharmaśāstra*-s. The Buddha, for all that we know of him from the *Pāli Tripiṭaka*, was taking at least a precariously near-secular—if not fully secular—sociological interest, judged at least in the context of his time. Further, he was about the only thinker in ancient India with a conscious commitment to the dialectical outlook. Because of this, he also came rather near to the understanding of some "palliative remedy" required by the people in class-divided society. This he formulated in his own way; though, on retrospective analysis, he seems to have anticipated the essential function of religion as understood by Marx. It remains for us to see how, with the adoption of Buddhism as state religion, his original message had to pass into its opposite.

2. Suffering and the Way Out of It

The Buddhist tradition summed up Buddha's own teachings as the Four Noble Truths (*ārya-satya*), with which was linked up the doctrine of the dependent origination of things or *pratītya-samutpāda*. A theory of the chain of 12 causes to explain earthly miseries *(dvādaśā-nidāna)* along with the conception of *nirvāṇa* was, properly speaking, included in the former while from the latter followed the revolutionary views of universal impermanence (*anityatā-vāda*) and of the denial of a permanent soul–substance *(anātma-vāda)*.

The Four Noble Truths were: (1) everything was suffering, (2) suffering had a cause, (3) suffering could be extinguished, and (4) there was a path leading to this extinction. In the famous Sermon at Banaras, these were formulated thus:

> This, O monks, is the sacred truth of suffering: birth is suffering, old age is suffering, sickness is suffering, death is suffering; to be united with the unloved is suffering, to be separated from the loved is suffering; not to obtain what one desires is suffering; in short the five-fold clinging (to the earthly) is suffering.
>
> This, O monks, is the sacred truth of the origin of suffering: it is the thirst (for being), which leads from birth to birth, together with lust and desire, which finds gratification here and there : The thirst for pleasures, the thirst for being, the thirst for power.
>
> This, O monks, is the sacred truth of the extinction of suffering: the extinction of this thirst by complete annihilation of desire, letting it go, expelling it, separating oneself from it, giving it no room.
>
> This, O monks, is the sacred truth of the path which leads to the extinction of suffering. It is this sacred eight-fold path, to wit: Right Faith, Right Resolve, Right Speech, Right Action,

Right Living, Right Effort, Right Thought, Right Self-concentration. [3]

Everything about these obviously hinged on the first noble truth and the first question about it is: Why was the Buddha so obsessed with the idea that the world was but an ocean of miseries? I have elsewhere tried to answer this question in terms of the tremendous social upheavals of the age. It was the age in which North-East India was first witnessing the rise of the ruthless state-powers—specially those of Magadha and Kośala—on the ruins of the tribal societies. As was characteristic of such an age 'base greed, brutal sensuality, sordid avarice, selfish plunder of common possessions', taxation, usury, extortion and such things were creating new and unheard of miseries in the lives of the people in whose memory the liberty, equality and fraternity of the tribal life was still somewhat fresh and whose neighbours like Mallas, Vajjis and Śākyas were still in the state of tribal simplicity. The Buddha himself belonged to the Śākya tribe and never forgot his tribal pride. But the equality and freedom of the tribes were already threatened because the rising states could not tolerate the continued existence of such examples of democracy, primitive though these might have been. Besides, like deforestation, the expansion of the states required detribalisation of vast areas. Extermination and subjugation of the tribes thus formed the policy- objective of the early states. Vidudabha, the prince of Kośala, presumably during the life of the Buddha, unleashed the most brutal massacre on the Śākyas, the Buddha's own people, and even the children and women of the tribe were not spared. Ajātaśatru, the King of Magadha and one eulogised as a great philosopher in the Upaniṣads, declared, 'I will root out the Vajjians, I will destroy the Vajjians, I will bring these Vajjians to utter ruin'. He even sent his prime minister to the Buddha to seek his blessings for carrying out this determination. The Buddha, with his strong nostalgia for the tribal life, was naturally alarmed by such naked greed for riches and power. "The king", he said, "although he might have conquered the kingdoms of the earth, although he may be the ruler of all land this side of the sea, up to the ocean's shore, would, still insatiate, covet that which is beyond the sea."[5] He could also see how this greed of the kings recoiled back on themselves and made their power and riches unstable. Two of his early patrons were King Bimbisāra of Magadha and King Prasenajit of Kosala. The former was starved to death by his own son Ajātaśatru and the latter most treacherously betrayed by his son Vidudabha. "The princes who rule kingdoms", said the Buddha, "rich in treasures and wealth, turn their greed against one another, pandering insatiably to their desires. If these act thus restlessly, swimming in the stream of impermanence, carried along by greed and carnal desire, who then can walk on earth in peace?"[6] To these were also to be added the hitherto unheard of miseries created in the lives of the people by the new institutions of taxation, slavery, extortion, torture, mortgage, interest, usury: the voluminous *Jātakas* are full of these.

The Buddha himself saw all these. But what was to be done? He was too realistic to believe in any God, prayers and sacrifices to whom could not, he knew, bring any effective remedy to the miseries he saw all around. He did not ask people to pray and sacrifice. In the *Buddhacarita,* Aśvaghoṣa gave elaborate anti-theistic arguments supposed to have been expounded by the Buddha himself. Nor could the Buddha believe in the ascetic self-mortification, which he considered to be 'painful, unworthy and unprofitable.' He was, again, far too disturbed to take seriously the Upaniṣadic claim that the metaphysical wisdom could bring salvation.[7]

He asked his disciples to turn away from 'opinions concerning the beginning and hereafter of things.' For it was no use behaving like a fool who, with an arrow plunged unto his flank, wasted time speculating on the origin, maker, etc., of the arrow, instead of removing it outright. Therefore, when asked metaphysical questions that he considered to be unprofitable, he simply remained silent. In short, the problem that obsessed him most was essentially a practical one. It was the problem of the bewildering mass of sufferings he saw around. And he wanted to have an essentially practical solution for this. But how, under the conditions in which he lived, could such a solution at all be evolved?

There was no question, of course, of really removing the real miseries from this world. That meant skipping over stages of historical development and jumping, as it were, towards socialism which alone, on the basis of the stupendous development of the human productive power, could assure plenty and equality for all. Rather, the further development of the productive power which could eventually ensure such conditions presupposed, during the time of the Buddha, a further intensification of exploitation and all the miseries that it entailed. Therefore, the only alternative left for the prophet was to invent an ideal solution of the real problem and, as a precondition for this, to effect such psychological transformation of the personality in which the sense of the felt misery could be overcome. "A new doctrine", said the Buddha, "do I teach for subduing the mental intoxicants that are generated even in this present life."[8] Elsewhere he said that his purpose was to bring "a quietude of the heart."[9] And how was this to be achieved? Only by inventing the theory and practice of ideology appropriate for his age.

"I have gained coolness", declared the Buddha, "and have attained *nirvāṇa*. To found the Kingdom of Truth, I go to the city of Kasi: I will beat the drum of the immortal in the darkness of the world."[10] But where was this Kingdom of Truth to be found? Significantly, the Buddha did not look forward to what had already emerged and was emerging fuller and fuller every day—the pomp and grandeur of the rising state-powers.

Instead, he looked backward to the tribal collectives and wanted to revive what Marx called 'the imaginary substance of the tribe.' Apparently, he was pleading for a moral reform of the world. In the fourth noble truth, he spoke of right faith, right resolve, etc.,—values, as we can easily judge from the *Jātakas*, that were most ruthlessly trampled upon in the society in which he lived. The Buddha could clearly see the futility of practising all these in the society at large. So he asked the people to take the *pabbajjā* and the *upasampada* ordinations, i.e. 'to go out' of the actual society and 'to arrive at' the life of the *saṃgha*-s or the order of the monks. For within the *saṃgha*-s, things were different. Modelled consciously on the tribal collectives—without private property and with full equality and democracy among the brethren—these alone could offer the real scope to practise the 'simple moral grandeur of the ancient gentile society', for which the Buddha was really pleading. Thus the *saṃgha*-s, as classless societies within the bosom of the class society, could become the heart of a heartless world, the spirit of a spiritless situation.

3. Buddha's Sociology and Dialectics

We may now pass on to have some more idea of the sociology of the Buddha—particularly his view of private property, the social classes and the state which—it is perhaps not an accident—directly follows from his dialectical outlook.

For understanding his sociology as following from his dialectical outlook, it may be convenient to begin this discussion with an observation of Stcherbatsky, where he shows the radical implications on the question of private property as connected with the radical view of personality in early Buddhism.

> Where there is personality, there is property belonging to it. Where there is I, there is also my. And where there is personal property, there necessarily emerges a love for it in one form or other. This attachment to personal property is the root of all evil, the root of every personal action as well as of social injustice. Thus, by negating the existence of the soul, Buddhism gives us a very profound philosophical basis for the negation of the right of personal property.
>
> What personal property can be possible where even the

> personality itself is not there? Therefore, a real Buddhist is only he who has renounced personal property—and not merely property but also family, home, etc.—once for all. In the history of world religions, of Christianity and Islam, we frequently find doctrines which negate property and advise that this be renounced. But Buddhism gives the most radical treatment of this question.[11]

However, let us not see in the Buddha's condemnation of private property more significance than it has. It is nothing, for example, comparable to the demand for the abolition of the private ownership of the means of production as an essential precondition for the positive emancipation of man, which is above all an emancipation from class exploitation and therefore possible only by the overthrow of the class structure of society. Not to speak of this, Buddhism never comes anywhere near the positive conception of freedom, viz. freedom as attainable only by a greater mastery over nature based on a deeper insight into it and its laws. Such an understanding of freedom could not be developed during the Buddha's times. What was historically possible for him was to work out some palliative remedy for suffering, which he saw everywhere and in everything. All that he could suggest was to change the subjective attitude to the world—to subdue the 'mental intoxicants' and thereby to attain 'a quietude of the heart.' Private property is to be renounced because, as the Buddha feels, it creates these mental intoxicants—longing, clinging, attachment, and so on. The view of the unreality of personality, he thinks, helps one to realise the foolishness of pursuing personal property and is thus an incentive to renounce private property.

But private property, as the Buddha understands it, is to be avoided within the *saṃgha*–s or communities of the monks. These monks are supposed to renounce the world, which in fact means that they are supposed to leave the world as it is. It is beyond the power of the prophet to interfere: with the inexorable laws of history, which, during the Buddha's times, required a greater intensification of private property in the hands of the despots, monarchs and merchants. This is one example of what we call "the dialectic of progress."

The Buddha's demand for the abolition of private property is a demand for its abolition within the isolated pockets of society and it is not—what would have been historically premature—the demand for the abolition of private property from society as such. As the Buddha himself advises the brotherhood of monks:

> Live as islands unto yourselves, brethren, as refuges unto yourselves; take none other as your refuge; live with the Norm as your island, with the Norm as your refuge; take none other as your refuge.
>
> But how does a brother live in an island unto himself, as a refuge unto himself, taking none other as his refuge? How does he live with the Norm as his island, with the Norm as his refuge, taking none other as his refuge?
>
> Herein a brother, as to the body, as to feelings, as to thought, as to ideas, continues so to look upon these that he remains ardent, self-possessed and mindful, that he may overcome both the hankering and the dejection common in the world. Thus it is, brethren, that a brother lives as an island and as a refuge unto himself... with the Norm as an island and as a refuge, having no other refuge.[12]

So it will be an error to make of the Buddha a revolutionary in our sense of the term. At the same time, it will be another error not to see what is actually revolutionary about his sociology—particularly in so far as it follows from his dialectical outlook—his view of everything being involved in perpetual flux.

The passage just quoted forms the concluding sermon of a dialogue the whole of which is designed to discuss the question of wealth, and of wickedness, aggressiveness and war as following from it. A superficial reading of the dialogue as a whole may give one the impression of a fairy tale as it were—the dream of a golden age in the past and the fall of man from it with the growth of wealth and hence also of the greed for wealth. But that would be misunderstanding the dialogue, or the main point sought to be emphasised in it by the Buddha in his own way.

Equipped with no tool for socio-historical analysis in our sense—or, more strictly, possessing the only tool in the form of his intuitive vision of the dialectical outlook—the Buddha is trying nevertheless to understand and explain a momentous historical question, the question of the origin of wealth which, as he understands, creates wickedness, aggressiveness and war. And what is revolutionary about his understanding is not merely the total absence of any supernatural cant about the phenomena—and therefore that total absence of any tendency to invest them with any supernatural sanction as in the *puruṣasūkta* of the *Ṛgveda,* the *Brāhmaṇa*-s, *Upaniṣad*-s and above all in the *Dharmaśāstra*-s —but the view that like everything else in the universe, wealth and the consequent aggressiveness and war, are subject to the relentless law of *pratītya-samutapāda*: all these come into being subject to the collocation of a number of definite conditions and hence these are also destined to pass away.

From this point of view, Stcherbatsky's suggestion that the Buddha's rejection of private property is only a corollary of his rejection of soul and personal property, perhaps needs amendment. Still, in the Buddha's thoughts the rejection of the two is not unconnected. The soul is unreal, because there is nothing but perpetual flux—the coming into being and passing away. But so also is the power of wealth and private property. Like the soul and personality, private property too is subject to the relentless law of *pratītya-samutpāda,* which is the theoretical ground of the view of universal flux. It is, of course, understandable that the Buddha has to grope for expressions for the formulation of such a momentous idea. And the expressions he uses cannot but appear to us to be rather archaic. As Buddha is said to have preached:

> Thus brethren, from goods not being bestowed on the destitute, poverty grew great... stealing, violence, murder, lying, evil speaking, adultery, abusive and idle talk, covetousness and

ill–will, false opinion, incest, wanton greed and perverted lust.... Among the humans, brethren, keen mutual enmity will become the rule—keen ill-will, keen animosity, passionate thought even of killing, in a mother towards her child, in a child towards its mother, in a father towards his child and a child towards its father, in brother to brother, in brother to sister, in sister to brother. Just as a sportsman feels towards the game that he sees, so will they feel.

Among such humans, brethren there will arise a sword- period of seven days, during which they will look at each other as wild beasts; sharp swords will appear ready to their hands and they, thinking—This is a wild beast, 'This is a wild beast'—will with their swords deprive each other of life.

Then to some of those beings it will occur: Let us not slay just anyone; nor let just anyone slay us!..... Then this, brethren, will occur to those beings: Now only because we had gotten into evil ways, have we had this heavy loss of kith and kin. Let us now therefore do good. What can we do that is good? Let us now abstain from taking life. That is a good thing that we may take up and do. And they will abstain from slaughter, and will continue in this good way....

At that period, brethren, there will arise in the world an Exalted one named Metteyya (?Maitreya), an *arhat*, fully awakened, abounding in wisdom and goodness, happy, with knowledge of the worlds, unsurpassed as a guide to mortals willing to be led, a teacher for gods and men, an exalted one, a Buddha, even as I am now. He, by himself, will thoroughly know and see, as it were face to face, this universe, with its world of the spirits, its Brahmās and its Māras, and its world of recluses and Brahmins, of princes and peoples, even as I see now, by myself, thoroughly know and see them. The truth, lovely in its origin, lovely in its progress, lovely in its consummation, will he proclaim both in the spirit and in the letter, the higher life will he make known, in all its fullness and in all its purity, even as I do now.

He will be accompanied by a congregation of some thousands of brethren, even as I am now accompanied by a congregation of some hundreds of brethren.[13]

What is definite about all this is that the Buddha is not prophesying the coming of a leader to organise a revolutionary party for the final overthrow of a society every fabric of which is permeated with evil—evil that originally follows from the accumulation of wealth or private possession, or, as the Buddha puts, it, from 'goods not being bestowed on the destitute'. The Buddha never visualises a revolutionary trasformation of society. Nevertheless, the origin of social evil and its eventual passing away, as he understands the entire process, cannot be looked at as a mere phantasy or a mythological imagination of the fall of man from an original golden age awaiting some ultimate salvation by a future messiah. Not that such elements are not at all there in the Buddha's thought. Still, what is decisive about his thought is the vision of the law of universal causation—*pratītya-samutpāda*—the inescapable consequence of which is the view of universal flux. In accordance with this, the Buddha is trying to understand society, which he feels is permeated with greed, aggressiveness and evil in other forms. But he is also obliged to conceive its coming into being and its eventual destiny of passing away. What is significant about his understanding of social evil is not the way in which he conceives its origin and its passing away. It is rather his general theoretical position that, like everything else in the universe, social evil must itself be involved in the universal flux: it cannot but come into existence subject to definite conditions and it cannot but ultimately pass away.

Its coming into being, as far as he can trace it, is connected with wealth or private possession; but its passing away can be conceived by him only in terms of moral revival under the leadership of a great enlightened saint. This—particularly the second point—is of course the result of the inevitable historical limitations. But the basic theoretical position that there is nothing eternal about the social organisation—that everything in it has a definite beginning and therefore also a definite end—is a remarkable achievement of the dialectical outlook of early Buddhism.

And this cannot but be reminiscent of Morgan's verdict on society based on private property, with which Engels concludes his work on *The Origin of the Family, Private Property and the State:*

> A mere property career is not the final destiny of mankind, if progress is to be the law of the future as it has been of the past. The time which has passed away since civilisation began is but a fragment of the past duration of man's existence, and but a fragment of the ages yet to come. The dissolution of society bids fair to become the termination of a career of which property is the end and aim, because such a career contains the elements of self-destruction.[14]

It is no use speculating whether, given modern terminologies, the Buddha would have formulated his verdict on property-oriented society in the same way. The fact is that modern terminologies are not there for him. Nevertheless, what is there for him—and the importance of which can in no way be overlooked—is the dialectical view, the relentless law of *praṭītya-samutpāda.* This leads him to express, in his own way, the view that mere property career cannot be the final destiny of mankind: it comes into being subject to definite conditions and it is foredoomed to wither away.

In another dialogue forming part of the early canonical literature of the Buddhists, the implications of the dialectical outlook for the Buddha's sociology are worked out in a more remarkable manner. The main point of this dialogue—called the *Aggañña Suttanta*—is to explain not only the origin of kingship but the broader question of the origin of the main strata of traditional Indian society—the four traditional castes. As the Buddha is trying to explain, such society comes into being because of a number of specific conditions, and the inevitable consequence of this is that, because of the same relentless law of *partītya-samutpāda,* such a society is also destined to pass away. This significance of the dialogue may be entirely missed if we try to assess, in terms of contemporary sociology, the intrinsic worth of the Buddha's view of the origin of caste-oriented society. Weaker still is the Buddha's visualisation of the mode of the eventual passing away of this society: he can at best speak of his own *saṃgha*-s within which the rigidity of the castes is supposed to dissolve. However, all these are not the points by which we are to judge the basic significance of the sociology of early Buddhism. This significance is to be sought elsewhere, and that is the view that, like everything else in the universe, the caste-oriented society too comes into being only under certain specific conditions and hence it is also destined to pass away.

Before passing on to see how the Buddha expresses his own view of the caste-oriented society, it may be convenient to remember the other view then in circulation, i.e. the view sought to be negated by the Buddha. From the times of the *puruṣa-sūkta* of the *Ṛgveda*, the *Brāhmaṇa*-s and *Upaniṣad*-s, there develops the zeal to sanctify the caste-oriented society by claiming for it a divine origin. And since it is supposed to be divine creation, it is impossible—and of course impious—to try to change its basic structure. The caste-oriented society, in other words, is beyond the range of change altogether: if it has an origin in the divine will, the same will give it life eternal. It would be tedious to quote the passages from the *Brāhmaṇa*-s and *Upaniṣad*-s to show how such a view of the essential unalterableness of caste society takes shape, though finally in the *Dharmaśāstra*. But it may be sufficient for our purpose to quote a few couplets from Manu, in whose legal codes is summed up the Brahmanical view of the caste society with the divine sanction for it. As Manu puts it, "But in order to protect this universe, He, the most resplendent one, assigned separate duties and occupations to those who sprang from his mouth, arms, things and feet. To Brahmins He assigned teaching and studying (the Veda), sacrificing for their own benefit and of others, giving and accepting (of gifts). The Kṣatriya He commanded to protect the people, to bestow gifts, to offer sacrifices, to study (the Veda) and to abstain from attaching himself to sensual pleasures; the Vaiśya to tend cattle, to bestow gifts, to offer sacrifices, to study (the Veda), to trade, to lend money and to cultivate land. One occupation only the Lord prescribed to the Śūdra—to serve meekly even these three (other) castes."[15]

Such a view, though codified by Manu at a comparatively later date, comes down from distant antiquity and is fully known to the Buddha. The Brahmin Vāśettha tells him how the Brahmins themselves claim to prove their superiority: "Only the Brahmins are genuine children of Brahmā, born of his mouth, offspring of Brahmā, created by Brahmā, heirs of Brahmā." But the Buddha laughs at the *prima facie* absurdity of such a claim: "Surely, Vāśettha, the Brahmins have quite forgotten the past when they say so? On the contrary, the Brāhmaṇīs, the wives of Brahmins, are known to be fertile, are seen to be with child, bringing forth and nursing children. And yet it is these very womb-born Brahmins who say that.....Brahmins are genuine children of Brahmā, born from his mouth, his offspring, his creation and his heirs."[16]

Thus the ground on which the Brahmins want to prove their social superiority is to the Buddha a mere myth. Still the fact of the caste-divided society is there: "There are these four classes, Vāśettha, nobles, Brahmins, tradesfolk, work people."[17] And that needs an explanation. I have elsewhere quoted this dialogue extensively[18] and need not repeat it over again. But the essentially secular view taken in it is in need of reemphasis. So also the dialectical understanding underlying the whole discussion.

In this dialogue, the Buddha wants us to understand the origin of these social classes out of an originally homogeneous community of beings as a purely natural phenomenon, or, according to the Buddhist way of putting it, due to the operation of the universal law of causation, of *pratītya-samutpāda*. However, in the same Buddhist view, there is also the other side of the same law: anything that comes into being is also destined to pass away. The veil, once lifted on the past, also reveals a future. If caste-society comes into being subject to definite conditions, because of the instability of these conditions it is also destined to wither away. This is the revolutionary implication of the sociology of early Buddhism—an implication that inevitably follows from the view of universal flux—though it is also the severest historical limitation of the Buddha himself to have failed to visualise how exactly this caste-society is going to wither away. Still the implication is there and the Buddha is obliged to work it out.

The only way he finds it possible to work it out is to talk of his *saṃgha*-s—the pockets of classless society created by him within the general structure of class society of his times—within which the distinction of castes does not exist, thanks to the general technique of changing the subjective attitude to reality which, as he imagines, is conducive to freedom. This is an illusion no doubt. But it is also a historically inevitable limitation. Thus after elaborately describing how caste society comes into being, the Buddha describes as follows how it is going to pass away, though only within the brotherhood of monks:

> Again, Vāśettha, a Kṣatriya,....a Brahmin too... Vaiśya too... a Śūdra too, who is self-restrained in deed, word and thought, and has followed after the practice of the seven principles which are the 'wings of wisdom', attains to complete extinction of evil in this present life.
>
> For, Vāśettha, whosoever of these four classes becomes, as a *bhikṣu*, an *arhat*, who has destroyed the intoxicants, who has done that which is behoved him to do, who has laid down the burden, who has won his own salvation, who has wholly destroyed the fetter of rebirth, who through knowledge made perfect is free—he is declared chief among them, in virtue of a norm.[19]

Such then is the vision of the withering away of caste-society that the Buddha can have. This is the destiny of the dialectical outlook being extended to the understanding of society under conditions that are historically premature for the full working out of the dialectics of social transformation. However, as we have already said, the real significance of the Buddha's sociology is not to be sought in the way in which he visualises its withering away but in his general verdict on caste society. And this verdict is that like everything else in the universe, caste-society itself is nothing more than a passing phase. In this sense early Buddhism does mean a condemnation of the norm of caste society which, according to the spokesmen of the norm itself, is nothing if it has no eternal verity with a divine sanction.

4. Buddhism Becoming A State Religion

If the Buddha pronounced a devastating condemnation of private property and looked at it as the source of all evils and sufferings, private property took its revenge posthumously, as it were, on the Buddha and his teachings. For historically speaking, the fact is that specially from the time of Aśoka Buddhism started thriving more and more on the financial and political support of the monarchs, feudatory chiefs, wealthy merchants and other rich patrons, and the more it did so the more it was obliged to follow the obvious logic that he who pays the pipers calls for the tune. The metamorphosis in Buddhism was so great that it eventually had to assume a new name for it which was Mahāyāna, and which sought to justify its claim to be Buddhism proper by the fabrication of a whole host of new "scriptures", broadly called the *Mahāyāna-sūtra*-s with the story that Buddha himself wrote these, though considering that it would have been premature to preach these in his own times, kept these concealed among the Nagas, so that many centuries later, Nagarjuna was to discover these. Here is how Stcherbatsky describes the change:

> When we see an atheistic, soul-denying philosophic teaching of a path to personal Final Deliverance, consisting in an absolute extinction of life and a simple worship of the memory of its human founder—when we see it superseded by a magnificent High Church with a Supreme God, surrounded by a numerous pantheon and a host of saints, a religion highly devotional, highly ceremonious and clerical, with an ideal of Universal

> Salvation of all living creatures, a Salvation by the divine grace of the Buddhas and the Bodhisattvas, a Salvation not in annihilation, but in eternal life,—we are fully justified in maintaining that the history of religions has scarcely witnessed such a break between the new and the old within the pale of what nevertheless continues to claim common descent from the same religious founder.[20]

We do not obviously have the scope here to discuss the entire history of the subsequent development of Buddhism. But it is necessary for our purpose to have some idea of its salient points.

The first casualty of the new Buddhism which announces itself as the Mahāyāna is the Buddha himself, the memory of whose historicity is sought to be washed away with a flood of new mythology—the theory of the Buddhas and Bodhisattvas or future Buddhas. Its second casualty is the atheism of the Buddha, which, though not formally rejected, is in fact substituted by the creed of a supreme god placed at the top of a mixed pantheon of smaller deities and hobgoblins. Its third casualty is the Buddha's expressed distaste for metaphysics, now replaced by a spurt of metaphysical exuberance. One aspect of this is the tendency to develop into an extreme form of world-denying idealism. The other aspect of this is the growing resistance to the dialectical outlook—a resistance that reaches its philosophical climax in the Śūnya- vāda of Nāgārjuna.

But before we pass on to see the philosophical expression of this resistance, it is interesting to note how, in the scriptural work fabricated by the Mahāyānists, is codified the rejection of the dialectical outlook in its sociological aspect.

In early Buddhism, like everything else, kingship too comes into being because of some specific natural conditions. What inevitably follows from the general formula of *pratītya-samutpāda* is quite simple. Kingship, because it has a definite origin, has also a definite end.

Understandably enough, is becomes eventually impossible for Buddhism to retain such an attitude to the kings, on whose patronage that creed is increasingly dependent. The attitude to kingship has to be revised and revised in a direction that best suits the patrons of Buddhism. Accordingly, in the Mahāyāna scriptures, the king is viewed as a son of god and kingship is invested with a divine sanction. Thus, in the *Suvarṇaprabhāsottama sūtra*, the god Brahmā is brought to declare:

> How does a king, who is born of men, come to be called divine?
>
> Why is the king called the son of the gods?
>
> If a king is born in this world of mortals
>
> How can it be that a god rules over men?
>
> I will tell you of the origin of kings, who are born in the world of mortals, and for what reason kings exist, and rule over every province. By the authority of the great gods a king enters his mother's bomb. First he is ordained by gods–only then does he find an embryo, What though he is born or dies in the world of mortals—Arising from the gods he is called the son of gods. The thirty–three great gods assign the fortune of the king. The ruler of the men is created as the son of all the gods. To put a stop to unrighteousness, to prevent evil deeds, to establish all beings in well-doing, and to show them the way to heaven. Whether men, or god, or fairy, or demon, or outcaste—he is a true king who prevents evil deeds. Such a king is mother and father to those who do good. He was appointed by gods to show the results of *karma*.[21]

The Mahāyāna scripture just quoted is written—or, according to the pontifical expression permitted by Mahāyānists, 'came to the world'—several centuries after the Buddha. The divine origin of and divine sanction for kingship proclaimed in it are not just an ad hoc ideological grant to the great patrons of Buddhism. It is rather a symptom of the serious ideological retreat of later Buddhism—a retreat resulting from its ever-growing parasitism. In the context of our present discussion, we shall note only one aspect of this retreat, i.e. the retreat from the dialectical outlook of original Buddhism.

One expression of the tendency to flout the Buddha's view of universal flux is to reinstate the concept of soul in Buddhist philosophy. We are told that this is one of the issues that leads to the first split among the Buddhists. "The *Kathāvatthu* begins its exposition of divergent views by a long discussion of the question about the possible reality of the soul. The schools of *Ārya-Sammitīyas* and *Vātsiputrīyas* were inclined to interpret the doctrine of soullessness in a sense which admitted some, albeit very feeble, unity in the elements of personality."[22]

Understandably, much of this new controversy is scripture-oriented. Not only do the contending parties try to reinterpret the words of the Buddha in their own way; there is moreover the zeal to own or disown certain statements as genuine words of the Buddha. Thus the older or orthodox Buddhists, usually called the Theravādins, accuse the Vātsiputrīya of having suppressed the scriptural passages that go against their views, while the Vātsiputrīyas, in their turn, accuse the Theravādins of leaning upon passages that were not genuinely scriptural.[23] However, scriptures apart, some of the grounds mentioned by the Vātsiputrīyas in defence of their view of a somewhat shadowy but permanent soul are intended to be logical. For example, they argue that the fact of memory cannot be explained without the admission of a soul—an argument which in the comparatively later period is specially advanced by the Nyāya Vaiśeṣikas:

> Now, if there is absolutely no soul, how is it then that the detached moments of consciousness can remember or recognise things which had been experienced a long time ago? .... If there were absolutely nothing permanent, it would mean that one consciousness had perceived the object and another one remembers it. How is it possible? In this case, things experienced by Devadatta's consciousness would be remembered by the consciousness of Yajñadatta.... If there is no soul, whose is the recollection, whom does it belong to?[24]

There is moreover the evidence of the cognising agent on

which the Vātsiputrīyas are said to depend:

> A soul must exist, because wherever there is an activity it depends on an agent. Every action depends on an agent. Thus, in the example 'Devadatta walks', there is an action of walking which depends on Devadatta, the agent. To be conscious is likewise an action. Hence the agent who cognises must also exist.[25]

But the Vātsiputrīyas apparently hesitate to revive the concept of the permanent soul in the full sense of the term: "But in our opinion, the self means that the individual is neither one of the elements, nor is it something outside the elements."[26] Moreover, there is really no ground to think that such a hesitant step towards the reintroduction of the soul into Buddhist philosophy meets with any great success.

What we hear of them is from others—i.e. the rival Buddhists—who are moreover keen mainly on ridiculing the Vātsiputrīyas.

After the Vātsiputrīyas, the early Vijñāna-vādins make a comparatively bolder attempt at what Stcherbatsky has described as "a disguised return from the theory of stream of thought of the doctrine of a substantial soul."[27] This is expressed as their views of *ālaya-vijñāna* and *tathāgata-garbha,* of which the former is more philosophical, the latter frankly mythologico-metaphysical.

The concept of *ālaya-vijñāna* means something like the 'all conserving mind'—'a store-house, a real granary, where the seeds *(bīja)* or all future ideas and the traces of all past deeds are stored up'.[28] According to Vallée Poussin, "The *ālaya-vijñāna* is somewhat like a soul, and we know from the Tibetan authorities that the maintainers of the Hīnayāna strongly objected to this new vijñāna. It is a series of 'subliminal images'—a store of seeds that give birth to actual cognitions; it may be looked upon as a thinking entity which manifests itself in a succession of thoughts."[29]

The concept is specially emphasised by Aśvaghoṣa, who may be the same as the author of the famous *Buddhacarita* and who, we are further told, "was summoned to Kabul by Kātyāyanīputra, the alleged composer of the 'Abhidharma in Eight Sections', in order to help him in the compilation of the Great Commentary *(Mahāvibhāṣā)* on the text of Abhidharma," i.e. to help the grand metaphysical activity said to have taken place in the Council convened under the patronage of king Kaṇiṣka.

But the concept of *ālaya-vijñāna* has a prominent place also in Vijñānavāda as expounded by Asaṅga. In his philosophy, it means something precariously near the Upaniṣadic soul from which the entire complex of subjective and objective world is supposed to emanate, as Anesaki has shown.[30]

Much more peculiar is the concept of the *tathāgata-garbha*, under the cover of which practically the old Upaniṣadic concept of one eternal soul as embedded in all individual souls is sought to be smuggled in by Mahāyāna Buddhists. For understanding this concept, we have first to note the quaint transformation of the idea of the Tathāgata in Mahāyāna Buddhism. In early Buddhism, Tathāgata is simply an epithet of the historical Buddha and it means one who has gone beyond the sphere of worldly attachments or, more simply, one who has attained wisdom. In the mystical mythologies fabricated by the Mahāyānists, however, the concept of the Tathāgata is invested with an altogether new significance. It represents some kind of transcendental metaphysical reality from which all the Buddhas and Bodhisattvas are imagined to emanate or appear as *avatāra*-s. These Buddhas and future Buddhas have their histories; but the Tathāgata as such is supposed to be an eternal personality without any extinction. One of the *Mahāyāna* scriptures called the *Saddharma-puṇḍarīka* dilates much on the cumbrous theology of the eternal personality—of the Upaniṣadic soul—woven round the concept of the Tathāgata. But it will be tedious for the readers to go even through extracts from the text. The essential point, however, is that with a good deal of mumbo-jumbo, this Māhāyāna "scripture" wants to smuggle in into Buddhism, the essential features of the Upaniṣadic conception of a permanent soul or *ātma* which was unceremoniously discarded by early Buddhism.

Apparently all that is much too complicated to be readily understood by the common people. For the purpose of mass consumption, therefore, the need is felt for a more popular version of basically the same view. The Mahāyāna Buddhists hope to achieve this by identifying their Tathāgata with god Amitābha, the lord of Sukhāvatī, or with god Vairocana, and all this the people were asked to believe to be the same as the theory of soullessness of Buddhism. This represents the final theological version of the retreat from the dialectical outlook of original Buddhism, an outlook which is usually expressed as *anātma-vāda* or the theory of soullessness.

The theory completely passes into its opposite when it becomes the cult of a personal god. "Soullessness", Stcherbatsky observes, "was later on conceived in a pantheistic sense and personified as the primeval Buddha Vairocana. The same can be maintained with regard to its theistic conception personified as Buddha Amitābha, whose worship gave rise to the new religion."[31]

Such are some of the features of the ideological retreat of Mahāyāna Buddhism. Flouting the original view of universal flux, it pleads for divine sanction and therefore of unalterability of kingship. It wants to readapt the conception of the soul, first somewhat vaguely by the Vātsiputrīyas, then in the more well- defined form as the *ālaya-vijñāna* of the early Vijñāna-vādins, and finally in their quaint metaphysico-mythological conception of *tathāgata garbha*. At the same time it completely repudiates the atheism of the Buddha and preaches the cult of a personal god, identifying it mystically with soullessness as ultimate reality.

5. Concluding Remarks

We have now some idea of how in the Mahāyāna Buddhism the really revolutionary sting of the Buddha's original teaching—specially his sociology and dialectical outlook—

was practically removed, and rooms were made in the new cumbrous theology for the reintroduction of many a major factor of the official ideology intended to be rejected by the Buddha himself. Along with the internal ideological changes, there took place also external changes in the rituals of Buddhism, making it practically indistinguishable from official Hinduism. For having some idea of this we may turn to Tārānātha, the Tibetan historian of Indian Buddhism, on whom the modern historians specially of the Pāla period are obliged to depend.

He left for us, though in his own way, clear indications of the factors that contributed to the decline and fall of Buddhism in India. Buddhism, in its latest phase, as Tārānātha so vividly described it,[32] almost completely surrendered precisely to those beliefs and practices, as a direct rejection of which the Buddha himself had preached his original creed. For all we know, it was a creed concerned above all with the fact of suffering, and with the way out of suffering. As Stcherbatsky puts it, "It can hardly be said to represent a religion. Its more religious side, the teaching of a path is utterly human. Man reaches salvation by his own efforts through moral and intellectual perfection. Nor was there, for aught we know, very much of a worship in the Buddhism of that time. The community consisted or recluses possessing neither family nor property, assembling twice a month for open confession of their sins and engaged in the practice of austerity, meditation and philosophic discussions." The Buddha preached all these precisely because he had realised the futility of worshipping God or a host of demi-gods, offering sacrifices to them or trying to coerce them with magical rituals. For the Buddha himself these beliefs and practices were characteristics of the *tirthika*-s or outsiders. By contrast, Buddhism in its latest phase—if we are to trust Tārānātha—bowed down to all these beliefs and thus became practically indistinguishable from popular Hinduism, so-called. It assumed the form of being an elaborate worship of all sorts of gods and goddesses of the popular pantheon—often under new names, but sometimes caring not even to invent any new name for them—and of indulging in all sorts of ritual practices of which the Buddha himself had expressed his unambiguous repulsion.

Thus, e.g. the Vikramaśīla-Vihāra, the last grand centre of Buddhism established in India, had even the provision for a Bali-ācārya and a Homa-ācārya! Buddhajñāpāda, Tārānātha further tells us, persuaded King Dharmapāla to perform a *homa* of many years, during which period the king spent over nine lakh and two thousand *tolā*-s of silver—and all these were designed to make his dynasty last longer! And so on. Evidently, the memory of the human founder of the creed and even the vestige of his essentially human teachings were fully lost to the Buddhists and their patrons when Buddhism assumed such a queer form. The ideology, in short, passed into its opposite, and being left with no internal justification to survive as a distinct creed, the only thing on which it could then thrive was the fad of some big patron, the Pālas being about the last of them. With the withdrawal or collapse of this patronage, Buddhism had to go into pieces.

Sharing fully the creed in its latest phase, Tārānātha is of course not expected to have realised all these. As far as he understood, therefore, the end of the Vikramaśīla and the Odantapuri meant the end of Buddhism in India: with the fall of these two monasteries the Buddhist *ācārya*-s ran hither and thither, seeking shelter in Kashmir, Nepal and the Ko-ki countries. He does not ask himself how a creed can, so long as it possesses any inner vitality, become virtually extinct form such a vast country only with the fall of two centres situated somewhere in Bihar.

Such then is a possible account of the decline and end of Buddhism in the country of its birth. But the story of Buddhism does not end here. In some of the neighbouring countries—specially Tibet and Mongolia—the rising monarchical power found in the new Buddhism a very suitable ideology, not only providing with the most suitable palliative for suffering masses but also to keep them cowed with awe, wonder and fear. Thus the Tibetan historians of Tibet—who themselves profess to be devout Mahāyānists—tell us with tremendous enthusiasm about the zeal of the Tibetan monarchs to suppress the older religion of Tibet—called Bon (pronounced as Pan)—and establish Mahāyāna Buddhism as the state religion of the country. Though this is a different story altogether, we should like to add only one point to it. The Tibetan monarchs would not certainly have been so enthusiastic about the religious reform of Tibet if they did not sense in it a distinct political function.

This introduces us to another aspect of religion, namely its political function, which we propose to discuss more fully in the next lecture.

REFERENCES

1. M. Winternitz ii. 8.
2. T.W. Rhys Davids DB. i. 96.
3. Tr. H. Oldenberg BHLHTHO 128-29.
4. D. Chattopadhyaya L 459 ff; IP 122 ff.
5. Quoted by Oldenberg, *op. cit.* 64.
6. *Ibid.*
7. This is the usual view of early Buddhism accepted by modern scholars.
8. Quoted by Gaden in SBE xiii. 84-5.
9. *Ibid.*
10. *Ibid.* xiii. 91.
11. Th. Stcherbatsky FPS 26.
12. T.W. Rhys Davids DB iv. 74-5
13. T.W. Rhys Davids DB iv. 69-74.
14. Quoted by Engels OF 291-2.
15. Manu i. 87-91.
16. T.W. Rhys Davids DB iv. 78.
17. *ib.* iv. 79.
18. D. Chattopadhyaya WLWDIP 527 ff.
19. T.W. Rhys Davids DB iv. 93.
20. Th. Stcherbatsky CBN 33.
21. Quoted by de Bary 185-86.
22. Th. Stcherbatsky STB 5.
23. Th. Stcherbatsky CCB 4n & STB 33.

24. Th. Stcherbatsky STB 62.
25. *Ib.* 62.
26. *Ib. 34.*
27. Th. Stcherbatsky CBN 53.
28. *Ib.* 52.
29. Vallé Poussin in ERE ix. 851-2.
30. Anesaki in ERE ii. 62.
31. Th. Stcherbatsky STB 6.
32. For details given from *Tārānātha,* See summary of these in the introduction to THBI (ed. D. Chattopadhyaya).

8

Future of Religion

1. Preliminary Remarks

In this concluding lecture, I shall try to sum up the main point I have been trying to argue. The argument is that everything in the universe—both material and spiritual—is involved in the process of coming into existence and passing out of existence or the process of ceaseless flux. This is the essence of the dialectical method of Hegel which, as shorn of its mysticism and idealistic fantasy of Hegel himself, is accepted by Marxism as forming one of its most important components. Applying this method to the phenomenon called religion, the essential point resolves into the following.

Religion once came into being as necessarily as it is destined to pass away. In other words, for the convenience of discussion, the proposition can be split into two sub-propositions. First, religion has a definite beginning. Secondly, it has no future other than that of withering away. The first sub-proposition we have tried to substantiate in two steps. One of these is to show that there was a period when human beings were unaware of anything that we call religion. This was the period of the primitive pre-class society. The savages still surviving in certain pockets of the world and uncontaminated by the merchants and missionaries penetrating into them, have no religion. Instead of religion they rely on magic. Similarly, wherever we can successfully go back to the prehistory of civilised society, we come across magic instead of religion. For many thousands of years—how many we are yet to know precisely—man remained in such a stage of pre-class society, and this because of the extremely low level of the technique of production. The utmost labour of the entire community was required to maintain it at the minimum level of subsistence. There was no surplus and therefore no possibility of one section of the community living on the labour of another. At such a helpless stage of depending on the most rudimentary productive capacity, man felt the need for supplementing his actual technique by an illusory one, and that was magic.

In his struggle against nature, however, man was not destined to remain at such a helpless stage. He went on developing his tools of production, at first slowly—almost imperceptibly slowly—though after many thousand years, he took steps towards what the archaeologists call the neolithic revolution. From this stage onwards, the pace of human progress acquired spectacular momentum. Thanks to the improved technique of production, man eventually acquired the capacity of producing more than was necessary for his bare maintenance. In other words, he started producing surplus. When this took place, man reached a stage which can be described as the first foreshadowing of civilisation. But not yet civilisation proper. For the purpose of moving forward to civilisation, a further revolution was necessary, for which Gordon Childe used the descriptive epithet "the urban revolution". The most essential pre-condition for this revolution was the channelisation of the social surplus of the direct producers—mainly the farmers and peasants—to certain centres, which, when we look back at these, appear to be incipient cities. Without the accumulation of social surplus in these centres, there was no possibility of having whole-time specialists engaged in vairous arts and crafts who, as whole-timers, could no longer act also as the producers of their own means of subsistence. And without whole-time specialists there could not be the urban revolution. Some machinery was thus needed for the channelisation of the social surplus to the incipient city centres. We have argued that of all the conceivable machineries for the purpose, the one that was most feasible and least cumbrous must have been the creation of an ideological device, which we call religion. It was created not out of nothing but largely by the effective consolidation of the purely illusory aspect of primitive magic. Thus came into being a whole host of goddesses and gods, to whom the deliberate offering of the social surplus was not merely an act of piety but moreover supposed to ensure to the direct producers safety from various frightening calamities. To the direct producers themselves, such goddesses and gods were of course supposed to have substantive entities. Nevertheless, they also needed mundane or earthly representatives to act on their behalf and manage their affairs. Along with them, therefore, came into the social scene the class of priestesses and priests, who alone knew the secret of acting on their behalf. Such in brief is the account of the making of religion or its coming into being.

But it is also the account of the beginnings of class society. The social surplus accumulated in the city centres was not equally distributed among the actual workers (the farmers and full-time specialist craftsmen) and the priests and merchants etc., the latter forming the leisured class. It was not yet fully parasitical, inasmuch as its members remained as the organisers of production. But the organisers of production soon converted themselves into the owners of the means of production, and thus society was split into an owning class and a working class.

On archaeological evidence we now know that all this first took place about five thousand years ago in what Gordon Childe calls the three "primary centres" of the urban revolution, namely Egypt, Mesopotamia and the Indus Valley. Since then civilisation spread out practically all over the globe, though without disturbing the basic class structure of society, and, along with it, its ideological concomitant viz. religion, notwithstanding the circumstance of both class society and religion undergoing various changes within the general structure. Throughout this period, however, religion—though without foregoing its original function of extracting the surplus product of the direct producers—served also the purpose of offering consolation for avoidable miseries, or, as we have put it, providing with palliative remedies for these.

With these points in mind, we may now pass on to discuss the question we propose specially to discuss in the present lecture, namely the future of religion.

2. Class Society and its Future

As the making of religion is historically and necessarily connected with the making of class society, it is only logical for us to begin with some idea of the future of class society before passing on to the question of the future of religion. During the career of about five thousand years of civilisation the class structure of society underwent successive changes, until it assumed the form of modern capitalism. During these five thousand years, again, the technique of production underwent quantitative improvements, which assumed a qualitatively new form, as it were, under capitalism, so much so that it became basically incompatible with the class structure of society as such. Hence is the crisis in our times. Man is confronted with two irreconcilable alternatives. One of these is the abolition of the class structure of society. The other is to allow the productive technique to stagnate, or, if allowed to develop at all, developing mainly for destructive purpose or war—localised and even global. Imperialist countries have gone in for the second alternative. A brief but vivid idea of the real horror of this can be found in such fully documented books as *Monopoly Capital* by Baran and Sweezy.

What is greatly patronised by Imperialism as "social science" is often nothing but a screen to hide the ugliness of all this. But this is often torn to shreds by direct experience of the people. As Baran and Sweezy observe: "that idle men and idle machines coexist with deprivation at home and starvation abroad, that poverty grows in step with affluence, that enormous amounts of resources are wasted in frivolous and often harmful ways, that the United States has become the symbol and defender of reaction all over the world, that we are engaged in several wars and clearly headed towards more and bigger ones—the knowledge of all this, and much more, did not come to us from the social sciences but from the observation of unavoidable facts."[1]

The main point explained by the authors is quite simple. Monopoly capital is ultimately dominated by one motivation and that is maximum profit of the owners of the means of production and maximum profit is there in making or producing the weapons of destruction. As J.D. Bernal sums up: "It is the same demand for maximum profit that has given, in recent years, the heavy bias of technology and science towards military uses. Profits there are enormous: the public pays without asking awkward questions, and the resulting goods do not clog the market. They can be expended in wars or, if that fails, scrapped in a few years as obsolete. The demand for them is also reinforced by every means of propaganda needed to keep up war fever and justify military expenditure. One consequence of this has been the militarisation of science, with all its consequence of secrecy, screening and witch-hunting."[2]

All this gives us some idea of how the desperate attempts to preserve the class structure of society is wanting to misuse the tremendous technological developments of man: the knowledge of and power over nature acquired by man is threatening his very existence. As a result, there has grown the tendency in a certain section of thinkers to censure the technological development itself, its usual argument being that the lop-sided emphasis on material power and prosperity has undermined the spiritual upliftment of man, pushing him back to some new form of barbarism. Others with deeper insight into history and the laws of its development can see where the crisis actually belongs. It is not in the mastery over nature but in the class structure of society itself. Morgan's judgement (already quoted by us) pronounced over a hundred years back sounds prophetic today:

"A mere property career is not the final destiny of mankind, if progress is to be the law of the future as it has been of the past..... the dissolution of society bids fair to become the termination of a career of which property is the end and aim, because such a career contains the elements of self-destruction". Morgan said this depending mainly on the study of ancient society, but we have in the writings of Marx and Engels a very positive vision of human freedom resulting from the technological developments upto their times—a vision which enables us to understand the present and foresee the future. We quote Engels's lucid exposition of this from his *Socialism: Utopian and Scientific:*[3]

> Active social forces work exactly like natural forces: blindly, forcibly, destructively, so long as we do not understand and reckon with them. But when once we understand them, when once we grasp their action, their direction, their effects, it depends only upon ourselves to subject them more and more to our own will, and by means of them to reach our own ends. And this holds quite especially true of the mighty productive forces of today. As long as we obstinately refuse to understand the nature and the character of these social means of action, ...so long as these forces are at work in spite of us, in opposition to us, so long they master us....But when once their nature is understood, they can, in the hands of the producers working together, be transformed from master demons into willing servants. The difference is as that between the destructive force of electricity in the lightning of the storm, and the electricity under command in the telegraph and the voltaic arc: the difference between a conflagration, and fire working in the service of man.

How, then, are the working men and women going to use the knowledge of social forces and thereby attain mastery over these? The crucial point about it, as discovered by Marx and Engels, transformed socialism from the dream of the earlier utopians into an exact science. As Engels continued:

> With this recognition, at last, of the real nature of the productive forces of today, the social anarchy of production gives place to

> social regulation of production upon a definite plan, according to the needs of the community and of each individual. Then the capitalist mode of appropriation, in which the product enslaves first the producer and then the appropriator, is replaced by the mode of appropriation of the products that is based upon the nature of the modern means of production; upon the one hand, direct social appropriation, as means to the maintenance and extension of production—on the other, direct individual appropriation, as means of subsistence and of enjoyment. Whilst the capitalist mode of production more and more completely transforms the great majority of the population into proletarians, it creates the power which, under penalty of its own destruction, is forced to accomplish this revolution. Whilst it forces on more and more transformation of the vast means of production, already socialised, into state property, it shows itself the way to accomplishing this revolution. The proletariat seizes political power and turns the means of production into state property.

Social intervention thus based upon definite knowledge of social forces opens before man a new horizon of freedom. Here is the inspiring description of it given by Engels:

> With the seizing of the means of production by society, production of commodities is done away with, and, simultaneously, the mastery of the product over the producer. Anarchy in social production is replaced by systematic definite organisation. The struggle for individual existence disappears. Then for the first time man, in a certain sense, is finally marked off from the rest of the animal kingdom, and emerges from mere animal conditions of existence into really human ones. The whole sphere of the conditions of life which environ man, and which have hitherto ruled man, now comes under the dominion and control of man, who for the first time becomes the real conscious lord of Nature, because he has now become master of his own social organisation. The laws of his own social action hitherto standing face to face with man as laws of Nature foreign to and dominating him, will then be used with full understanding, and so mastered by him. Man's own social organisation, hitherto confronting him as a necessity imposed by Nature and history, now becomes the result of his own free

> action. The extraneous objective forces that have hitherto governed history pass under the control of man himself. Only from that time will man himself, more and more consciously make his own history—only from that time will the social causes set in movement by him have, in the main and in a constantly growing measure, the results intended by him. It is the ascent of man from the kingdom of necessity to the kingdom of freedom.

Such, then, is classless society or communism as understood in Marxism. It is only another world for conditions where men consciously make their own history. It is the human march forward from the realm of necessity to that of freedom.

3. Future of Religion

With this brief idea of the future of the class structure of society, we may now turn to our main problem, namely that of the future of religion.

Like the basic idea of communism, the condemnation of religion as a force wanting to keep the masses submissive to the privileged classes of society can be traced to a period much earlier than that of Marx and Engels. We shall begin with one example of this, specially because it expresses the ideas and attitudes not of the atheists and materialists but of very devout religious peoples. In books of European history they are mentioned as The Diggers. "In April 1649 about 20 poor men assembled at St. George's Hill, Surrey, and began to cultivate the common land. They held that the English Civil War had been fought against the King and the great landowners; now that Charles I had been executed, land should be made available for the very poor to cultivate". The number of the Diggers soon swelled up and their leader Gerrard Winstanley, himself a very pious Christian, came out with the most passionate denunciation of organised religion, when their movement was brutally suppressed and Winstanley was forced by bitter experience to recognise that 'organised' religion was in practice used "to reconcile the poor to their poverty by pretending to them that it was the will of God." As he put it,

> This Divining Doctrine, which you call spiritual and heavenly things, is the thief and robber that comes to spoil the vineyard of a man's peace, and does not enter at the door, but climbs up another way.... This divining spiritual doctrine is a cheat; for while men are gazing up to heaven, imagining after-happiness or fearing a hell after they are dead, their eyes are put out and they see not what is their birthright, and what is to be done by them here on earth while they are living. This is the filthy dreamer and the cloud without rain. And indeed the subtle clergy do know that if they can but charm the people by their divining doctrine to look after heavenly riches and glory after they are dead, then they shall easily be the inheritors of the earth and have the deceived people to be their servants.[4]

Winstanley, being himself a peasant after all, had neither the ability nor the taste for any sophisticated theoretical criticism of religion. But the view that "all religions, including Christianity too, were the work of deceivers"—a view that generally dominated the "free thinkers"—that religion "was no longer sufficient after Hegel who had set philosophy the task of showing a rational evolution in world history."[5] Hence, specially in Germany where the philosophers were greatly under the spell of Hegel, there came into being a flourishing literature produced by the angry young philosophers or radical thinkers showing the tendency to expose and criticise religion in sophisticated philosophical terms. This group of thinkers is generally referred to as the Young Hegelians who were the immediate predecessors of Marx. Marx himself, evidently because of his own radical bend of mind, was drawn into their movement and, even in his student days, became one of its most fiery leaders. But the alliance was not long to last. He started seeing the criticism of religion by the Young Hegelians—however passionate it might have been—had on the whole some kind of political romanticism and hence ineffective in the matter of uprooting religion. In fact, no amount of savage onslaught on religion could be the right way of fighting it. Already in 1842, he wrote to Ruge, about the Young Hegelians: "I asked them to criticise religion by criticising political conditions rather than the other way about, because religion, quite empty in itself, lives from earth and not from heaven and will disappear on its own once the inverted reality whose theory it represents is dissolved.[6]

This gives us some indication of the new turn Marx's thought was taking, which, as fully formed, found its first comprehensive expression in the book *German Ideology* drafted jointly by Marx and Engels. The decisive point of their departure from the Young Hegelians took place when they arrived at what is called the materialist conception of history or, more simply, Historical Materialism. Since the future of religion as visualised in Marxism—which as far as I understand, is the most scientific visualisation we have so far—follows from it, we may as well begin with a brief idea of it. Since Marxism is best understood in the words of Marx and Engels themselves, we quote here from the *German Ideology* at some length to see what they actually mean by Historical Materialism:

> The production of ideas, of conceptions, of consciousness, is at first directly interwoven with the material activity and the material intercourse of man, the language of real life. Conceiving and thinking, the mental intercourse of men, appear at this stage as the direct efflux of their material behaviour. The same applies to mental production as expressed in the language of politics, laws, morality, religion, metaphysics, etc., of a people. Men are the producers of their conceptions, ideas, etc.,—real, active men, as they are conditioned by a definite development of their productive forces and of the intercourse corresponding to these, up to its furthest forms. Consciousness can never be anything else than conscious existence, and the existence of men is their actual life-process. If in all ideology men and their circumstances appear upside-down as in a camera obscura, this phenomenon arises just as much from their historical life-process as the inversion of objects on the retina does from their physical life-process.

"In direct contrast to German philosophy which descends from heaven to earth, here we ascend from earth to heaven. That is to say, we do not set out from what men say, imagine, conceive, nor from men as narrated, thought of, imagined, conceived, in order to arrive at man in the flesh. We set out from real, active men, and on the basis of their real life-process we demonstrate the development of the ideological reflexes and echoes of their life-process. The phantoms formed in the human brain are also, necessarily, sublimates of their material life-process, which is empirically verifiable and bound to material premises. Morality, religion, metaphysics, all the rest of ideology and their corresponding forms of consciousness, thus no longer retain the semblance of independence. They have no history, no development; but men, developing their material production and their material intercourse, alter, along with this their real existence, their thinking and the products of their thinking. Life is not determined by consciousness, but consciousness by life. In the first method of approach the starting-point is consciousness taken as the living individual; in the second method, which conforms to real life, it is the real living individuals themselves, and consciousness is considered solely as their consciousness.[7]

Thus the philosophical views and in fact all ideological productions are, according to the Marxist analysis, ultimately conditioned by the material factors, namely the technique or mode of production and the relations of production resulting from it. It follows, therefore, that without a revolutionary transformation of these material conditions, there can be no revolutionary transformation in philosophical thought. Already in the *German Ideology*, Marx and Engels emphasised this. As they observe:

It [i.e. the materialistic conception of history] has not, like the idealistic view of history, in every period to look for a category, but remains constantly on the real ground of history; it does not explain practice from the idea but explains the formation of ideas form material practice; and accordingly it comes to the conclusion that all forms and products of consciousness cannot be dissolved by mental criticism.... but only by the

> practical overthrow of the actual social relations which gave rise to their idealistic humbug; that not criticism but revolution is the driving force of history, also of religion, philosophy and all other types of theory.[8]

To this is immediately to be added another point. Marx and Engels wanted repeatedly to draw our attention to the fact that there was something about the class structure of society as such which wanted to coerce the philosophers' consciousness to succumb to some basic illusion, without the philosophers themselves being aware of it. Therefore, the real emancipation of philosophy, as understood in Marxism, presupposes the revolutionary transformation of class society into classless society.

Already in the *Communist Manifesto*, they observe: "Does it require deep intuition to comprehend that man's ideas, views and conceptions, in one word, man's consciousness, changes with every change in the conditions of his material existence, in his social relations and in his social life?....

> ....The history of all past society has consisted in the development of class antagonisms that assumed different forms at different epochs.
>
> But whatever form they may have taken, one fact is common to all past ages, viz. the exploitation of one part of society by the other. No wonder, then, that the social consciousness of past ages, despite all the multiplicity and variety it displays, moves within certain common forms, or general ideas, which cannot completely vanish except with the total disappearance of class antagonisms.
>
> The communist revolution is the most radical rupture with traditional property relations; no wonder that its development involves the most radical rupture with traditional ideas.[9]

We can thus understand why in the Marxist understanding social revolution has an exceedingly important place even in the philosophical agenda. Without establishing the classless society, there is no effective emancipation of philosophy from the age-old illusions originating from the class structure of society itself. It is therefore imperative for the philosopher to change the world, and this even for the sake of philosophical emancipation. Hence is Marx's emphasis on *changing* the world, rather than remain satisfied merely with various attempts to understand it.

But all this is not to be misunderstood, and, in order not to misunderstand, the problem of relation between philosophical emancipation and social revolution is to be approached from the dialectical point of view.

From the dialectical point of view, consciousness—inclusive obviously of religious and philosophical consciousness—though ultimately rooted in material conditions, also reacts back on the material conditions. Consciousness, in other words, has also an active role. On this point, the founders of Marxism parted company with their materialist predecessors, who were on the whole taking a mechanical view of the environment conditioning our consciousness. As Marx very cryptically said in the *Third Thesis on Feuerbach:*

> The materialist doctrine that men are products of circumstances and upbringing, and that, therefore, changed men and products of other circumstances and changed upbringing, forgets that it is men that change circumstances and that the educator himself needs education....[10]

In Marxist understanding, thus, philosophers or theoreticians are not to await passively for the momentous social transformation to take place for the emancipation of their thought. For in the meanwhile there is something exceedingly important for them to do, which, though expected to be done in the special capacity of theoreticians or philosophers, is relevant for the social revolution. The most important thing is to change the world no doubt, but the point also is that there is no right way of changing the world with a wrong or inadequate understanding of it.

With these points in mind, let us turn to the question of how the essence as well as the future of religion is understood in Marxism. One of the best and most lucid expressions of this is found in the concluding chapter of Engels's *Anti-*

Dühring. We propose to wind up our lecture with an extract from it. Engels observed:

> All religion is nothing but the fantastic reflection in men's minds of those external forces which control their daily life, a reflection in which the terrestrial forces assume the form of supernatural forces. In the beginnings of history it was the forces of nature which were at first so reflected, and in the course of further evolution they underwent the most manifold and varied personifications among the various peoples..... But it is not long before, side by side with the forces of nature, social forces begin to be active; forces which present themselves to man as equally extraneous and at first equally inexplicable, dominating them with the same apparent necessity as the forces of nature themselves. The fantastic personifications, which at first only reflected the mysterious forces of nature, at this point acquire social attributes, become representatives of the forces of history. At a still further stage of evolution, all the natural and social attributes of the innumerable gods are transferred to one almighty god, who himself once more is only the reflex of the abstract man. Such was the origin of monotheism, which was historically the last product of the vulgarised philosophy of the later Greeks and found its incarnation in the exclusively national god of the Jews, Jehovah. In this convenient, handy and readily adaptable form religion can continue to exist as the immediate—that is, the sentimental—form of men's relation to the extraneous natural and social forces which dominate them, so long as men remain under the control of those forces. We have already seen, more than once, that in existing bourgeois society men are dominated by the economic conditions created by themselves, by the means of production which they themselves have produced, as if by an extraneous force. The actual basis of religious reflex action therefore continues to exist, and with it the religious reflex itself. And though bourgeois politcal economy has given a certain insight into the casual basis of this domination by extraneous forces, this makes no essential difference. Bourgeois economics can neither prevent crises in general, nor protect the individual capitalists from losses, bad debts and bankruptcy, nor secure the individual workers against unemployment and destitution.

> It is still true that man proposes and God (that is, the extraneous force of the capitalist mode of production) disposes. Mere knowledge, even if it went much further and deeper than that of bourgeois economic science, is not enough to bring social forces under the control of society. What is above all necessary for this is a social act. And when this act has been accomplished, when society, by taking possession of all means of production and using them on a planned basis, has freed itself and all its members from the bondage in which they are at present held by these means of production which they themselves have produced but which now confront them as an irresistible extraneous force; when therefore man no longer merely proposes but also disposes—only then will the last extraneous force which is still reflected in religion vanish; and with it will also vanish the religious reflection itself, for the simple reason that there will then be nothing left to reflect.[11]

To sum up: Religion was brought into being by the class structure of society; throughout the period of the class society religion drew its nourishment therefrom; with the active overthrow of the class structure of society, religion is destined to wither away. Religion, therefore, has no future—no more than the class society itself. In the absolute time-scale, however, class society is no more than a mere twinkling of the eye compared to the general history of the existence of human beings on the earth. So also is the life-span of religion.

"Ah! Faustus, now hast thou but one bare hour to live!"

REFERENCES

1. P.A. Baran & P.M. Sweezy 1-2.
2. J.D. Bernal iv. 1254.
3. K. Marx & F. Engels SW (Moscow 1975 edn.) 423-26.
4. Quoted by G. Thomson ER 20.
5. Engels in OR 193.
6. Marx to Ruge, Nov. 1842.
7. K. Marx & F. Engels GI 37-38.
8. *Ib.* 50.
9. K. Marx & F. Engels SW (Moscow 1977 ed). i. 125-26.
10. K. Marx TF *III*.
11. F. Engels AD 374-5.

Bibliography

ACI: *Ancient Cities of the Indus*, ed. Possehl G.L., New Delhi 1979
Agrawal, D.P. *Archaeology of India*, Copenhegen 1982
Allchin, B. & R. *The Birth of Indian Civilization*, Penguin 1968
Rise of Civilization in India and Pakistan, New Delhi 1983
Baran, P.A. & Sweezy, P.M. *Monopoly Capital*, New York 1966
Bernal, J.D. *Science in History*, Penguin 1969 edn.
Chattopadhyaya, D. *Lokayata*, New Delhi 1978 edn.
What is Living and What is Dead in Indian Philosophy, New Delhi 1976 edn.
Childe, V. Gordon *Man Makes Himself*, London 1951 ed.
New Light on the Most Ancient East, New York 1954 ed.
What Happened in History, 1957 ed.
The Urban Revolution (reprint in ACI)
de Bary, W.T. (ed.) *Sources of Indian Tradition*, New York 1958
Dunham, B. *Heroes and Heretics*, New York 1967
EIP: *Essays in Indian Proto-history*, ed D.K. Chakrabarti and D.P. Agrawal, New Delhi 1979
Engels, F. *Anti-Dühring*, Moscow 1947 edn.
Origin of Family, Private Property and the State, Moscow 1952 edn.
ERE: *Encyclopaedia of Religion and Ethics*
FIC: *Frontiers of the Indus Civilization*, ed. B.B. Lal and S.P. Gupta, Delhi 1984
Freud, S. *The Future of an Illusion*, Pelican Freud Library, Vol. 12
Ghosh, A. *The City in Early Historical India*, Simla 1973
Harrison, J.E. *Ancient Art and Ritual*, London 1935 ed.
IA: *Indian Antiquary*
Keith, A.B. *Karma-mīmāṃsā*, London 1921
Khaṇḍadeva, *Bhāṭṭa-dīpikā*
Kosambi, D.D. *An Introduction to the Study of Indian History*, Bombay 1956

Kumārila, *Śloka-vārtikā*
Macdonell, A.A. *Vedic Mythology*, Strassburg 1897
Marshall, J. *Mohenjodaro and the Indus Civilization*, London 1931
Marx, K. *Theses on Feuerbach*
Contribution to the Critique of Hegel's Philosophy of Right.
Marx, K. and Engels, F. *On Religion* (Selection), Moscow 1956
The German Ideology, Moscow 1964 ed.
Selected Works, Moscow 1975 ed.
Max Müller, F. *Collected Works*, Vol. XIX, London 1859
Mcrainu, B. *The Method and Theory of V. Gordon Childe*, Edinburgh 1980
Morgan, L.H. *Ancient Society*, Calcutta 1982 edn.
MS: *Mīmāṃsā-sūtra* of Jaimini
Needham, J. *The Grand Titration*, London 1979 ed.
Oldenberg, H. *Buddha: His Life, His Doctrine, His Order*, Calcutta 1927
Radhakrishnan, S. *Indian Philosophy*, Vol. I, London, 1923
Renou, L. *Religions of India*, London 1953
Rhys Davids, T.W.R. *Dialogues of the Buddha*, London Vol. I 1899, Vol. II 1910, Vol. III 1921
Ṛv: *Ṛgveda*
Sastri, H.P. *Haraprasāda Racanāvalī* (in Bengali), Calcutta, 1960
SBE: *Sacred Books of the East*
Sharma, R.S. *Material Culture and Social Formations in Ancient India*, New Delhi 1983
Stcherbatsky, Th. *Central Conception of Buddhism*, London 1923
Canception of Buddhist Nirvana, reprint Varanasi
Further Papers of Stcherbatsky, Calcutta 1971
Papers of Stcherbartsky, Calcutta 1969
Soul Theory of the Buddhists, reprint Varanasi 1970
Tanjur: *Catalogue of Indian Buddhist Texts in Tibetan Translation. Alphabetically Arranged* by A. Chattopadhyaya, Calcutta 1983
THBI: *Tārānātha's History of Buddhism in India*, Eng. Tr., Simla 1970
Thomson, G. *An Essay on Religion*, London 1950
Studies in Ancient Greek Society, London Vol. I 1949; Vol. II (*The First Philosophers*) 1955
Wheeler, R.E.M. *The Indus Civilization*, Cambridge 1979 ed.
Winternitz, M. *History of Indian Literature*, Calcutta Vol. I 1927, Vol. II 1933
Woolley, L. *History of Mankind: Culture and Scientific Development*, (Vol. I, Part 2) UNESCO 1963

Index

2024

लेखक की अन्य किताबें

द इलेक्शन दैट चेंज्ड इंडिया

हाउ मोदी वुन इंडिया

2024
डेमोक्रेसी की जीत

राजदीप सरदेसाई

अनुवाद

विजय त्रिवेदी

प्रथम प्रकाशन 2025

हार्पर हिन्दी

(हार्परकॉलिंस *पब्लिशर्स* इंडिया) द्वारा प्रकाशित

4th फ्लोर, टावर A, बिल्डिंग नं. 10, डीएलएफ साइबर सिटी,

डीएलएफ फेज II, गुरुग्राम, हरियाणा – 122002, भारत

www.harpercollins.co.in

P-ISBN: 978-93-6569-455-0

E-ISBN: 978-93-6569-142-9

टाइपसेटिंग : हार्परकॉलिंस *पब्लिशर्स* इंडिया

मुद्रक : थॉम्सन प्रेस (इंडिया) लि.

This book is produced from independently certified FSC® paper to ensure responsible forest management.

भारतीय मतदाता की बाज़ी पलट देने वाली क्षमता को समर्पित

विषय – सूची

भूमिका

2024: डेमोक्रेसी की जीत

अक्सर पूछे जाने वाला सवालः आप जैसे नामचीन और अनुभवी पत्रकार और सबकुछ जानने का दावा करने वाले पोलस्टर्स ने 2024 के चुनाव नतीजों को इतना ग़लत कैसे समझा?

वाराणसी जैसा कोई शांत शहर नहीं है। संकरी गलियों में फैला शोर और अराजकता उस शहर की आत्मा की खामोशी के साथ घुलमिल जाती है। पवित्र, शक्तिशाली और धीमी रफ़्तार से बहती नदी की मौजूदगी, इस पुरातन शहर को ऐसी ऊंचाई तक ले जाती है जो अलौकिक और लौकिक दोनों का अहसास कराती है। शायद यह बेहतर ही रहा कि 2024 के आम चुनाव के लिए देशभर में मेरा सफ़र गंगा के किनारे बसे इस पुरातन अनूठे शहर में ख़त्म हो रहा था। आखिरकार, वाराणसी अब नरेन्द्र मोदी और भारतीय जनता पार्टी की देश के राजनीतिक, सांस्कृतिक और वैचारिक, हर क्षेत्र में अपनी धमक जमाने की दीर्घकालीन योजना का हिस्सा है। यहीं, नदी के किनारे, 2014 में मोदी ने राजनीतिक शीर्ष पर पहुंचने के अपने उस अजेय अभियान की शुरुआत की थी, जहां से दस साल बाद भी उन्हें कोई हिला नहीं सका है। एक मज़बूत नेता, महान व्यक्तित्व और मीडिया के हीरो दुनिया में तेजी से बढ़ती अर्थव्यवस्था और फिर जनता के भारी उत्साह के बीच अयोध्या में भव्य राम मंदिर का पूजन। एक महान नेता—एक 'विश्व-गुरु'। मोदी के उदय की कहानियों ने ऐसा माहौल बना दिया था कि अब 2024 के चुनावों के नतीजे तो तय हो गए थे और भारतीय जनता पार्टी का 'चार सौ पार' का दावा कोई डींग मारने जैसा नहीं लगता, बल्कि ऐसा ही होगा; एक बिखरा हुआ विपक्ष, भीड़

में गुमनाम चेहरों की तरह मुकाबले में था। उनके समर्थकों के शोर में एक ही नारा थाः 'आएगा तो मोदी ही!' मानो सितारे भी सारे उनके पक्ष में थे।

कम से कम ऐसा माहौल बना हुआ था।

इस बुलबुले के फूटने के लिए कोई अप्रत्याशित आवाज़ की ज़रूरत थी। धीरे-धीरे नदी के पानी में समाते घाटों पर मैं अपने शो की रिकॉर्डिंग कर रहा था। ढलती शाम का तांबई रंग फैला हुआ था। शो के लिए मेरे मेहमान स्टैंड-अप कॉमेडियन श्याम रंगीला थे, जो देश की बड़ी राजनीतिक हस्तियों, खासतौर से प्रधानमंत्री नरेन्द्र मोदी की नकल, मिमिक्री की वजह से वायरल थे। हालांकि इन चुनावों के दौरान दुबले-पतले रंगीला हास्य कलाकार की वजह से सुर्खियों में नहीं थे, बल्कि इसकी वजह थी कि वाराणसी में मोदी के ख़िलाफ़ लड़ने के लिए उनके नामांकन पत्र को पीठासीन अधिकारी ने ख़ारिज़ कर दिया था। मैंने सवाल किया, क्या वह केवल लोगों का ध्यान आकर्षित करने के लिए चुनाव लड़ रहे थे? उन्होंने उलट कर जवाब दिया, 'क्या आप यह बता रहे हैं कि मैं मोदी के ख़िलाफ़ चुनाव नहीं लड़ सकता? क्या मैं भारत का नागरिक नहीं हूं?' मैंने कहा कि देश के नंबर वन नेता के ख़िलाफ़ इस तरह की प्रतीकात्मक लड़ाई राष्ट्रीय चुनाव की दिशा शायद ही बदलेगी। उनकी पंचलाइन थी: 'देखो सर, यह इंडिया है, यहां कुछ भी हो सकता है!'

इस पवित्र शहर की आभा चारों ओर फैली हुई महसूस हो रही थी, रंगीला की बात सीधी-सपाट थी, लेकिन बात में दम था। रंगीला के वाराणसी में चुनाव की बात भले ही प्रतीकात्मक थी, लेकिन हममें से जो लोग 2024 के चुनाव नतीजों की घोषणा प्रचार अभियान शुरू होने से पहले ही कर चुके थे, वे जिंदगी और राजनीति के उस प्रमुख सिद्धांत को भूल रहे थेः भविष्य अप्रत्याशित है, कुछ भी हो सकता है। खासतौर से एक उप-महाद्वीप जैसे 140 करोड़ की आबादी वाले देश में, जिसमें 97 करोड़ मतदाता हैं, यहां कई भाषाएं, जातियां, धार्मिक आस्थाएं और पंथ हैं। फिर कैसे मुट्ठीभर न्यूज़ एंकर और चुनावी पंडित एसी स्टूडियो में बैठकर इतने आत्मविश्वास के साथ देश की तकदीर की भविष्यवाणी कर सकते हैं?

जब चुनाव नतीजे आए, तो मुझे रंगीला के साथ अपनी बातचीत याद आ गई। ऐसा क्या खास है कि जो एक स्टेंडअप कॉमेडियन जनता की नब्ज़ को समझने की विशिष्ट क्षमता रखता है, लेकिन अनुभवी वरिष्ठ पत्रकार और अंहकारी सर्वेक्षणकर्ता, चुनावी विशेषज्ञ उसे नहीं देख सकते? 'चार सौ पार' तो भूल जाइए, मोदी के नेतृत्व वाली भाजपा 272 के बहुमत के 'जादुई आंकड़े' तक भी नहीं पहुंच पाई। बहुमत से दूर रहे प्रधानमंत्री को अब स्थिर सरकार बनाने के लिए सहयोगियों के भरोसे रहना होगा। मुझे इस बात को मानने में कोई संकोच नहीं है कि मैं भी उन लोगों में से था, जो कमोबेश आश्वस्त थे कि भाजपा को अपने दम पर बहुमत मिलेगा। हालांकि मैं कभी भी 'चार सौ पार' क्लब का हिस्सा नहीं था, फिर भी मुझे एक आसान जीत की

उम्मीद थी (भाजपा के लिए मेरा नंबर 280-प्लस था)। वास्तव में, जब मैंने 2023 की गर्मियों में इस किताब पर काम करना शुरू किया, तो मेरा शीर्षक था: 'हैट-ट्रिक', एक ऐसा शब्द जो क्रिकेट में बड़ी उपलब्धि के साथ जुड़ा हुआ है। बहुत से दूसरे लोगों की तरह, मैं भी 'मोदी की गारंटी' के शोर और बीजेपी के राजनीतिक तमाशे से प्रभावित था, मुझे लगता था कि बड़े संसाधनों वाली भाजपा मशीनरी बाकी सबको दबा देगी।

चुनावी सफ़र के दौरान, हमारे 'मूड ऑफ द नेशन' के सर्वेक्षणों से इतर आवाज़ें भी सुनाई दे रही थीं, आम आदमी और महिलाएं महंगाई, बेरोज़गारी, भर्ती परीक्षाओं में पेपर लीक, स्थानीय स्तर पर भ्रष्टाचार और अंहकारी नेताओं को लेकर शिकायत करते थे। वाराणसी में ही, जहां मोदी के समर्थक उनकी रिकॉर्ड जीत का दावा कर रहे थे, हम पीली कोठी में अद्भुत कुशल बुनकरों के पास पहुंचे, जो बेहतरीन बनारसी साड़ी की बुनाई के लिए मशहूर हैं। मुस्लिम बहुल इस इलाके में बुनकरों ने बताया कि कैसे कोविड के बाद उनकी आमदनी में तेजी से गिरावट आई और कैसा संघर्ष करना पड़ा। हताशा में, कुछ लोगों ने गुज़ारे के लिए आसपास के इलाकों में पान की दुकान खोल ली थी। जब ज़्यादातर पत्रकार वहां घाटों के सौंदर्यीकरण, काशी-विश्वनाथ कॉरिडोर बनने, पर्यटकों की तादाद बढ़ने की रिपोर्टिंग कर रहे थे, तब बहुत कम लोगों को वाराणसी में बुनकरों की बेहाली की परवाह थी। प्रधानमंत्री का रोड शो, पीली कोठी की पान की पीक से रंगी गलियों से नहीं गुज़रा था। इस शहर के बारे में एक बार एक लेखक ने कहा था, वाराणसी 'क्लियोपेट्रा' की तरह है, इसकी पहचान और सुंदरता इसकी प्राचीनता बरकरार रहने में ही है। लेकिन विरासत के इस शहर को, नगरपालिका की सस्ती नकल में बदल दिया गया है। बुनियादी ढांचे में तेज़ी से बदलाव की कोशिश में, इलाके के कई पारपंरिक व्यवसायों को बलि चढ़ा दिया गया। हां, शहर के कुछ हिस्से साफ हैं, लेकिन उनकी पहचान मिट गई है। स्थानीय लोगों का कहना है कि अब वाराणसी यहां जन्मे, चौदहवीं सदी के महान रहस्यवादी कवि कबीर का जादुई शहर नहीं रहा।

अयोध्या में हमने राम-मंदिर जाते तीर्थयात्रियों की भीड़ तो देखी, लेकिन साथ में हमने 'नेता-नौकरशाह-बिल्डर' गठजोड़ से 'रियल एस्टेट' के सौदों और सड़क चौड़ी करने के लिए पुराने घरों और प्राचीन मंदिरों को ढहाए जाने की कहानियां भी सुनीं। हमें देश के दूसरे इलाकों में भी असंतोष और गुस्से की आवाज़ें सुनाई दी थीं, खासतौर से नौजवानों और किसानों के बीच, लेकिन क्या वे व्यापक तौर पर मतदाताओं की नुमाइंदगी करते थे?

चुनावी पत्रकारिता का ख़तरा यह है कि वह आपको चिंतन और गहरे विश्लेषण का वक्त नहीं देता; आप बस कैमरा लिए एक प्रदेश से दूसरे प्रदेश तक भागते रहते हैं। शायद हमें उन लोगों की बातों को गंभीरता से सुनना चाहिए था, जिन पर अच्छी तरह से गढ़े हुए 'फील-गुड' फैक्टर का असर नहीं होता था। शायद मैं सोशल मीडिया और व्हाट्सएप 'इको चैंबर' में ज्यादा समय बिता रहा था, जहां असली ख़बर और शोर के बीच की रेखाएं गायब हो जाती हैं।

'जनता जनार्दन' हिंदी की लोकप्रिय कहावत है, जिसका मौटे तौर पर मतलब होता है, 'जनता ही भगवान' है। अगर इस चुनाव में राजनीति के कथित देवताओं को ज़मीन पर उतारा गया तो शायद इसलिए, क्योंकि उन्होंने जनता को, अपने मतदाताओं को हल्के में लिया था। अक्सर ऐसा होता है कि सत्ता के लिए दौड़ते राजनेता और सटीक आंकड़े देने वाले अचूक पोलस्टर्स, लोगों और उनकी परेशानियों से कट जाते हैं। इसी तरह सेलेब्रिटी पत्रकार अपना ज़्यादातर वक्त टीवी स्टुडियों में और प्रभावशाली राजनेताओं तक पहुंच बनाने में बिताते हैं और आम जनता से संपर्क खो देते हैं।

और इसलिए मैं यहां कहता हूं: मेरी गलती! मेरा दोष!

समय की मांग है कि हम तुरंत ड्राईंग बोर्ड पर लौटें और वक्त रहते सुधार करें। इससे जुड़े सभी लोगों से थोड़ा अंहकार कम करने की उम्मीद नई शुरुआत की ओर ले जा सकता है ताकि अगली बार 2024 की तरह हम मतदाता से इतने आश्चर्यचकित न हों।

═

अक्सर पूछे जाने वाला सवालः तो 2019 और 2024 के बीच टीम मोदी-शाह में क्या बदल गया?

आखिरकार मोदी की 'हैट-ट्रिक' हो गई, जिसकी उम्मीद लगाई जा रही थी। ठीक है, कुछ हद तक। कड़े चुनावी मुकाबले के बाद, जून 2024 में, नरेन्द्र मोदी ने लगातार तीसरी बार प्रधानमंत्री के रूप में शपथ ले ली। इससे पहले सिर्फ़ जवाहरलाल नेहरु लगातार तीन बार प्रधानमंत्री बने थे। ऐसे समय में जब दुनियाभर में कई सरकारें गिरी, निसंदेह यह बड़ी उपलब्धि है। लेकिन हमेशा की तरह मोदी की जीत पर होने वाली धूमधाम इस बार नहीं दिख रही थी। मोदी ने सरकार बनाई थी, पर विडंबना यह कि वे 'हार' भी गए थे। वे सत्ता विरोधी लहर से तो बच गए, लेकिन इसका निशाना भी बने, 2019 के मुकाबले 63 सीटें हार गए थे। विपक्ष, खासतौर से कांग्रेस पार्टी हार गई, लेकिन कहा गया कि 'जीत' भी गई, उसकी सीटों की तादाद इस बार करीब दोगुनी हो गई, उसका वोट शेयर भी बढ़ गया था। देश के तीन बड़े महत्वपूर्ण चुनावी राज्यों उत्तरप्रदेश, महाराष्ट्र और पश्चिम बंगाल में भाजपा ने अपनी ज़मीन खोई थी, लेकिन ओड़िशा और तेलंगाना जैसे राज्यों में उसने बढ़त हासिल की, यहां तक कि केरल में पहली बार एक सीट जीत ली। कांग्रेस ने उन जगहों पर बढ़त हासिल की, जहां उसके मजबूत क्षेत्रीय गठबंधन थे, साथ ही राजस्थान और हरियाणा जैसे राज्यों में भाजपा से सीधे मुकाबले में भी सेंध लगा दी। गुजरात और मध्यप्रदेश में भाजपा ने ज़बरदस्त जीत दर्ज़ की, लेकिन दक्षिणी राज्यों में पार्टी को मिला-जुला नतीजा मिला, खासतौर से तमिलनाडु में वो रास्ता नहीं बना सकी। जटील जातीय समीकरणों वाला

बड़ा राज्य उत्तरप्रदेश इस बार 'गेम-चेंजर' साबित हुआ। चुनाव बाद सीएसडीएस के सर्वे में इन बदलावों पर बारीक जानकारी मिलती है। (Appendix देखें)

इन नतीजों के मायने क्या हैं? 2024 में भारतीय मतदाता ने वही बताया जो भारत है या होना चाहिएः हर तरह की विविधता वाले इस देश में 'एक राष्ट्र, एक नेता, एक धर्म' के विचार को हमेशा चुनौती मिलने वाली थी। 2014 और 2019 के चुनावों को 'लहर का चुनाव' कहा जा सकता है, जब निर्णायक जनादेश हकीकत के साथ-साथ भावनाओं से भी तय होते हैं। 2014 में, नाराज़ मतदाता कांग्रेस नेतृत्व वाली सरकार से छुटकारा चाहता था, ऐसे में इस बदलाव की मांग को भुनाने के लिए मोदी के नेतृत्व वाली भाजपा 'सही समय' और 'सही जगह' पर थी। 2019 के चुनाव से ऐन पहले पाकिस्तान प्रायोजित आतंकवादी हमले के ख़िलाफ़ आक्रामक राष्ट्रवाद की लहर ने बाकी सब मुद्दों को बेमायने कर दिया। इसके विपरीत, 2024 में सामान्य हालात की वापसी हुई, राज्य-दर-राज्य चुनावी मुकाबलों में, स्थानीय सत्ता-विरोधी भावनाओं ने सरकारों या नतीजों को बदलने में अहम भूमिका निभाई। जैसे, उत्तर महाराष्ट्र किसानों की नाराज़गी केन्द्र सरकार के प्याज के निर्यात पर पाबंदी को लेकर थी, जबकि मराठवाड़ा में मराठा आरक्षण अहम मुद्दा था। एक तरह से स्थानीय मुद्दों ने चुनाव को एक राज्य में भी हरेक सीट की लड़ाई को मुश्किल बना दिया। भाजपा के कुल वोट में मामूली गिरावट आई, लेकिन अहम राज्यों में हवा बदल गई थी।

2024 के चुनावों की *द प्रिंट* में एक समीक्षा में राजनीतिक विश्लेषक योगेन्द्र यादव, शोधकर्ता श्रेयस सरदेसाई और राहुल शास्त्री ने फैसले के समाजशास्त्र की समीक्षा की। इसके मुताबिक भाजपा का सामाजिक गठबंधन काफी हद तक बरकरार है। संपन्न और शहरी मिडिल क्लास हिंदू, ओबीसी और अत्यंत पिछड़ी जातियां यानी (ईबीसी) और आदिवासी अब भी भाजपा की जीत में मददगार रहे। किसानों को नकद सहायता या गरीबों के लिए मुफ़्त राशन जैसे मोदी के कल्याणकारी कार्यक्रमों ने लाखों लाभार्थियों पर असर डाला और उससे भाजपा के ख़िलाफ़ सत्ता-विरोधी असर को कमज़ोर करने में मदद मिली। जबकि मुस्लिम मतदाता कांग्रेस और उसके सहयोगियों के साथ खड़े रहे। 2019 के मुकाबले सबसे बड़ा बदलाव दलित मतदाताओं में दिखा, जहां एनडीए के शेयर में पांच फ़ीसदी का नुकसान हुआ, यह वोट विपक्ष के खाते में गया। दलित-मुस्लिम गठजोड़ का, खासतौर से सबसे बड़े चुनावी मैदान उत्तरप्रदेश में चुनाव नतीजों पर बड़ा असर पड़ा। 2022 में 'बुल्डोजर' जनादेश से लेकर दो साल बाद 'मंडल' जातिगत जनादेश तक उत्तरप्रदेश 2024 के बदलाव की कहानी हैः यहां एनडीए का वोट शेयर करीब दस फ़ीसद तक कम हुआ है।

ज्यादातर लोगों का मानना है कि कांग्रेस के 'संविधान ख़तरे में है' के नारे ने लोगों के दिलों में जगह बना ली। खासतौर से दलितों और कमजोर ओबीसी जातियों को यह डर महसूस होने

लगा था कि भाजपा को फिर से बड़ा बहुमत मिला तो आरक्षण का फायदा मिला बंद हो जाएगा। लेकिन मुझे लगता है कि दलित वोटों में गिरावट की बड़ी वजह हाशिए पर पड़े लोगों के बिगड़ते आर्थिक हालात भी रहे। पिछले दस साल में, पिरामिड के निचले हिस्से के लोगों, विशेष रूप से असंगठित क्षेत्र में काम करने वाले लोगों की नौकरियां चली गईं और उनकी जिंदगी उजड़ गई। एक प्रमुख शोध एजेंसी 'इंडिया रेटिंग्स' की रिपोर्ट में बताया गया कि 2015-16 और 2022-23 के बीच असंगठित क्षेत्र के 63 लाख संस्थान उजड़ गए और 1.6 करोड़ से ज़्यादा लोगों की नौकरियां चली गईं। देश के मुसलमानों के लिए भी पिछला दशक मनोवैज्ञानिक तौर पर ज़ख्म देने वाला रहा, 'गोमांस' पर पाबंदी से लेकर 'लव जिहाद' जैसे अभियानों तक, मुसलमानों को अक्सर 'सरकारी हुक्म' का ख़ामियाज़ा उठाना पड़ता है। खूंखार पीली मशीन 'बुल्डोज़र', भाजपा शासित राज्यों में तुरंत न्याय की आड़ में असंवैधानिक तरीके से मुसलमानों के कई घरों को ध्वस्त करती रही। भाजपा में बहुत ही कम राजनीतिक नुमाइंदगी से मुसलमानों में यह भावना घर कर गई कि उन्हें निशाना बनाया जाएगा और वे 'दूसरे दर्ज़े' के नागरिक बन जाएंगे।

यही वजह है कि इस किताब में 2024 के आम चुनाव के नतीजों को उससे पहले की हर चीज़ के नज़रिए से देखने की कोशिश की गई हैः कोविड-19 महामारी, आर्थिक रूप से विनाशकारी लॉकडाउन, जम्मू कश्मीर में अनुच्छेद 370 को हटाना, नागरिकता संशोधन जैसे विवादास्पद क़ानून, हेट-स्पीच, साल भर चलने वाले किसानों के प्रदर्शन, मणिपुर में जातीय हिंसा और महाराष्ट्र, बंगाल, और उत्तरप्रदेश जैसे राज्यों में सत्ता का संघर्ष। एक दशक तक ध्रुवीकरण की कोशिश के बाद, देश को राहत और सांस लेने की ज़रूरत थी, जिसे स्तंभकार प्रताप भानू मेहता 'अधिनायकवाद की दमघोटूं छाया' और 'सांप्रदायिकता की घिनौनी हवाएं' कहते हैं।

2014 और 2019 के बीच मोदी सरकार ने केन्द्र में अपना बहुमत मज़बूत करने की कोशिश की, लेकिन इस बात का ध्यान रखा कि ना तो सहयोगियों और ना ही विरोधियों पर हावी होने की कोशिश दिखे। 2016 में नोटबंदी जैसे एकतरफा फ़ैसलों पर आम सहमति बनाने की परवाह नहीं की, लेकिन सिस्टम में फिर भी कुछ जांच और संतुलन के तरीके बने हुए थे। लेकिन 2019 में बड़े जनादेश ने एक अलग तरह के शासन मॉडल को जन्म दिया, जहां धीरे-धीरे निरंकुश होते सिस्टम ने एक ताकतवर 'सुप्रीमो पंथ' बना दिया और एक व्यक्ति के प्रभुत्व ने सत्ता को ज़्यादा क्रूर और केन्द्रित कर दिया। सत्ता का पूरा नियंत्रण सिर्फ़ एक कठोर नेता के हाथों में था, इसे आप ज़्यादा से ज़्यादा 'डेढ़ लोगों' की सत्ता कह सकते हैं, यदि इसमें अमित शाह को भी शामिल कर लिया जाए। दरअसल अमित शाह की बढ़ती ताकत नई सत्ता का एक महत्वपूर्ण पहलू है, इसलिए मैं अक्सर इस सिस्टम को 'मोदी-शाह टीम' कहता हूं। 2024 में उत्तर भारत के गली-मोहल्लों की बहस और चाय की दुकानों पर चर्चा में एक शब्द रहा है: 'तानाशाही'। इसका इस्तेमाल उस बड़ी ताकत के लिए किया जाता है, जो सभी असहमतियों और असंतोष

को कुचलने और लोकतांत्रिक मूल्यों को ख़तरे में डालने के लिए निकला था, ज़बरदस्ती का वह रूप, नई दिल्ली से निकलकर सभी तरह की व्यक्तिगत आज़ादी पर हमला कर रहा था।

यह किताब इस 'दबंग शासक' के क्रूर तरीकों के साथ भारतीय राजनीति पर असर को समझने की कोशिश करती है। इन पांच साल में देश को तानाशाही जैसी सत्ता में बदलने पर मजबूर किया गया, जिसमें मोदी-शाह की जोड़ी ने ज़िंदगी के हर क्षेत्र में अपना रास्ता बना लिया था। बेबाक हिंदुत्व से अचानक कोविड-लॉकडाउन तक, प्रवर्तन और जांच एजेंसियों के बेजा इस्तेमाल से लेकर मीडिया को दबाने तक, टीम मोदी-शाह के फ़ैसले लेने की यह कहानी बताती है कि कम समय में कितना कुछ बदल गया है। मेरा मानना है कि 2024 में भारतीय मतदाता एक सांस लेना चाहता है—चलिए इसे 'इंटरवल' कहते हैं—चोट पहुंचाने वाली, आज़ादी को कुचलने वाली एकतरफा राजनीति के दौर से। एक ताकतवर व्यक्ति को नियंत्रित करती और मजबूत विपक्ष यह बताता है बड़ी विघटनकारी राजनीति पर विराम लगा दिया गया है। 2024 के फ़ैसले ने लड़ाई के फिर से शुरू होने से पहले ज़्यादा शांति और ज़्यादा लोकतांत्रिक व्यवस्था की उम्मीदें जगा दी हैं।

═

अक्सर पूछे जाने वाला सवालः क्या 2024 के चुनाव स्वतंत्र और निष्पक्ष थे? क्या मीडिया ने निष्पक्षता से काम किया?

दोनों सवालों का जवाब मोटे तौर पर 'नहीं' होगा। देखा जाए तो, हमारे यहां चुनाव हमेशा सरकार में बैठी पार्टी के पक्ष में रहे हैं। कांग्रेस के सुनहरे दिनों के वक्त भी उसे विरोधियों के मुकाबले बढ़त रहती थी। फिर भी, 2024 के चुनाव को, देश की चुनावी राजनीति के इतिहास में सबसे अनुचित चुनाव के रूप में देखा जा सकता है। कोई 'समान अवसर' (लेवल प्लेइंग फील्ड) नहीं था। पैसा, मीडिया और केन्द्रीय एजेंसियों की ताकत ने इसे एक गैर-बराबरी का मुकाबला बना दिया, जहां सत्ता-पक्ष के पास अपने विरोधियों को ध्वस्त करने के लिए हर तरह के घातक हथियार थे। यहां तक कि 1977 में आपातकाल के बाद हुए चुनावों में प्रधानमंत्री इंदिरा गांधी ने निष्पक्ष तरीके से चुनाव कराने की कोशिश की, जबकि मोदी-शाह टीम ने पूरे चुनाव अभियान के दौरान विपक्ष को कुचलने, या ख़त्म करने की कोशिश की थी।

राजनेता और वकील डॉ. अभिषेक मनु सिंघवी की मानना है कि 'समान अवसर' संविधान की मूल संरचना का हिस्सा है। पिछले एक दशक में, कांग्रेस के पूर्व सांसद विपक्षी नेताओं के लिए 'गो टू' वकीलों में से एक थे, जो प्रवर्तन एजेंसियों की कार्रवाई से खुद को बचाने की कोशिश कर रहे थे। जैसा कि किताब में ज़िक्र किया गया है, केन्द्रीय एजेंसियों, खासतौर से

प्रवर्तन निदेशालय (ईडी) ने विपक्ष को डराने-धमकाने के लिए अपनी ताकत का इस्तेमाल किया, जिससे ये चुनाव और मुश्किल हो गए। मोदी-शाह टीम ने क़ानून और प्रवर्तन एजेंसियों का राजनीतिक प्रचारकों की तरह उपयोग किया। इन कार्रवाइयों को सत्ता के उस खेल की तरह से नहीं देखा जा सकता है जो सभी राजनीतिक दल करते है और उनका भी अपने-अपने समय में एजेंसियों के दुरुपयोग का इतिहास रहा है। मौजूदा पैटर्न या तरीका कुछ अलग है और बेशर्मी की हद तक परेशान करने वाला है। जो लोग पाला बदलकर भाजपा नेतृत्व वाले गठबंधन में शामिल हो गए, उनके ख़िलाफ़ मामले या तो बंद कर दिए गए या उनकी जांच को धीमा कर दिया गया, जबकि जिन्होंने इससे इंकार किया, उन्हें निशाना बनाया गया।

सरकार की इस तरह की कार्रवाई के लिए अब 'वॉशिंग मशीन' शब्द का इस्तेमाल किया जाने लगा। जब एक प्रमुख राजनेता के भाजपा से हाथ मिलाने के बाद उनके ख़िलाफ़ मामले को बंद कर दिया गया तो कांग्रेस प्रवक्ता पवन खेड़ा, पार्टी की प्रेस कॉन्फ्रेंस में एक 'वॉशिंग मशीन' लेकर ही आ गए। खेड़ा ने पहले एक गंदी टी-शर्ट दिखाई, जिस पर 'भ्रष्टाचार, धोखाधड़ी, घोटाला' लिखा था, उसे वॉशिंग मशीन में डाल दिया। एक बार जब इसे धोया गया तो खेड़ा ने जादुई तरीके से साफ टी-शर्ट निकाली, जिस पर 'बीजेपी मोदी-वॉश' लिखा था।

प्रतीक के तौर पर यह 'वॉशिंग मशीन' भारत की राजनीति में बदलाव को बताती है। 2014 में देश को बदलने के लिए मोदी भ्रष्टाचार के ख़िलाफ़ योद्धा थे। अब, वह उस सिस्टम का हिस्सा हैं, जो हर हाल में सत्ता बनाए रखना चाहता है। मल्टीमीडिया के इस युग में, मोबाइल फ़ोन पर वायरल होते वीडियो से वॉशिंग मशीन जैसे शब्द जल्दी ही रोज़मर्रा की बोलचाल में शामिल हो गए। मई 2023 में, एक लेक्चर के लिए जब मैं नासिक में था, तो यह देखकर हैरान रह गया कि मेरे 'वॉशिंग मशीन' की टिप्पणी पर बहुत से लोगों ने तुरंत प्रतिक्रिया दी। वहां, 'खोखे की सरकार, खोखे की सरकार' के नारे लगने लगे। महाराष्ट्र में 'खोखा' शब्द एक करोड़ रुपये के लिए कहा जाता है। श्रोता 2022 में महाराष्ट्र सरकार को गिराने के लिए हर विधायक को कथित पचास करोड़ रुपये दिए जाने की बात कर रहे थे। सौदेबाज़ी के इन रास्तों ने महाराष्ट्र को देश का सबसे अस्थिर राज्य बना दिया है।

कड़ा (पीएमएलए) क़ानून, मोदी सरकार में विपक्ष को काबू में करने के लिए मज़बूत हथियार बन गया है। लोकतंत्र में आमतौर पर ऐसा नहीं सुना जाता, लेकिन इंदिरा गांधी के 1975 के आपातकाल की यादों को ताज़ा कर दिया, जब पीएमएलए के तहत 2024 के चुनाव अभियान से पहले विपक्षी पार्टियों के दो मुख्यमंत्रियों को गिरफ़्तार किया गया। पीएमएलए के नए प्रावधानों की वजह से इसमें ज़मानत मिलना नामुमकिन सा हो गया है, इससे ईडी की ताकत और बढ़ गई है। महाराष्ट्र में उद्धव ठाकरे गुट के शिवसेना के नेताओं ने ईडी को अब (एक्सटोर्शन डिपार्टमेंट) यानी 'जबरन वसूली' विभाग कहना शुरू कर दिया है।

क्या चुनाव आयोग ने मोदी सरकार के इन चौकाने वाले कदमों को रोकने के लिए ज़रूरी कदम उठाए? जिन्हें निश्चित तौर पर सत्ता का बेज़ा इस्तेमाल कहा जा सकता है। दुख की बात है कि 'नहीं'। इससे पहले कभी भी, यहां तक कि टी.एन. शेषन के ज़माने से पहले, जब चुनाव आयोग की कोई मजबूत पहचान नहीं थी, तब भी चुनावों का यह अंपायर इतना कमज़ोर, अस्पष्ट और पक्षपाती नहीं रहा था। चुनाव आयोग की प्रतिष्ठा को उस वक्त बड़ा नुकसान पहुंचा, जब उसने प्रधानमंत्री मोदी के राजस्थान के बांसवाड़ा में सबसे सांप्रदायिक भाषण पर भी कोई 'रेड कार्ड' दिखाने की कोशिश नहीं की। चुनावों के दौरान नियमित प्रेस कॉन्फ्रेंस और जनता के साथ जानकारी साझा नहीं करने का तरीका भी उतना ही परेशान करने वाला था। वोटर-वेरिफाइड पेपर ऑडिट ट्रेल (वीवीपीएटी) की पूरी गिनती की विपक्ष की मांग को इतनी लापरवाही से क्यों लिया गया, यह भी हैरान करने वाला था। यहां तक कि चुनाव कार्यक्रम भी सत्तारूढ़ पार्टी के पक्ष में बनाया गया था: उदाहरण के लिए, महाराष्ट्र जैसे शांतिपूर्ण राज्य में पांच चरणों में चुनाव कराना समझ से परे था। प्रत्येक चरण के लिए अंतिम मतदान के आंकड़ों की घोषणा करने में ईसीआई की अत्यधिक देरी ने बेबुनियाद साजिश के सिद्धांतों को जन्म दिया, जो केवल उस संस्था के प्रति व्यापक विश्वास की कमी को उजागर करता है, जो भारत की लोकतांत्रिक व्यवस्था के केंद्र में है। एसोसिएशन ऑफ डेमोक्रेटिक रिफॉर्म्स की रिपोर्ट के अनुसार, इलेक्ट्रॉनिक वोटिंग मशीनों में आधिकारिक तौर पर डाले गए वोटों की संख्या और गिने गए वोटों की संख्या 543 निर्वाचन क्षेत्रों में से 537 में मेल नहीं खाती है। अस्सी के दशक में, पाकिस्तान की क्रिकेट टीम को उसके घरेलू मैदान पर हराना लगभग नामुमकिन था, क्योंकि माना जाता था कि पाकिस्तान के अंपायर टीम के बारहवें खिलाड़ी की तरह काम करते हैं। 2024 में भारत के चुनाव आयोग को भी विश्वसनीयता के इस संकट का सामना करना पड़ रहा है।

पैसे के असंतुलित इस्तेमाल को रोकने में चुनाव आयोग की नाकामी ने 2024 के चुनाव को और मुश्किल बना दिया। चुनावों में पैसे के इस्तेमाल का कोई हिसाब-किताब नहीं है। कोई नहीं बता सकता कि पार्टियों और उम्मीदवारों ने कितना पैसा खर्च किया, लेकिन यह तय है कि सत्ता में प्रमुख पार्टी के रूप में भाजपा को मुकाबले में इसका बड़ा फायदा था। फरवरी 2024 में, जब सुप्रीम कोर्ट ने 'इलेक्टोरल बॉन्ड' के खुलासे का आदेश दिया, तो पता चला कि भाजपा ने कुल बॉन्ड के करीब पचास फीसदी भुनाए थे, जो किसी भी दूसरी पार्टी से बहुत ज़्यादा था। देशभर में मेरे चुनावी सफ़र के दौरान पैसे की ताकत का यह फासला साफ दिख रहा था। भारतीय जनता पार्टी के पोस्टर और होर्डिंग्स, खासतौर से हिन्दीभाषी इलाकों में हर खंबे और कोने पर चमक रहे थे, जबकि विपक्ष की मौजूदगी नदारद सी थी। इस हिसाब से क्षेत्रीय दल अपने-अपने इलाकों में बेहतर दिख रहे थे, यानी कुल मिलाकर इससे भरोसा कम होता था। आयकर विभाग ने चुनावों से पहले जिस तरह से कांग्रेस पार्टी को नोटिसों की झड़ी लगा दी, वह इस बात को

समझने के लिए काफी है कि विपक्ष के खज़ाने को जकड़ में लेने के लिए सरकार की ताकत का इस्तेमाल कितना आसान है।

फिर भी, अगर मीडिया अपने कवरेज में निष्पक्ष होता तो, नकदी की कमी से जूझ रहे विपक्ष के पास 'आधा मौका' तो हो सकता था। मुख्यधारा के मीडिया में एक वरिष्ठ पत्रकार के रूप में मुझे नहीं समझ आता कि इस किताब में अपने ही समुदाय की आलोचना के लिए मुझे कहां तक जाना चाहिए। शायद कई मीडिया संस्थानों की प्रतिष्ठा में गिरावट पर एक अलग किताब की ज़रूरत है, जो सत्ता के चापलूस 'चीयरलीडर्स' बनने वालों में शामिल हो गए, जबकि उन्हें निडर होकर सत्ता के सामने सच बोलना था। यहां सबसे अहम शब्द 'डर' ही है। किताब में, मैंने नई दिल्ली टेलीविज़न (एनडीटीवी) की कहानी को याद किया है, जो देश के शुरुआती निजी समाचार नेटवर्कों में से एक है और फिर कैसे सरकार के करीबी कॉरपोरेट दिग्गज अडानी ने उसका अधिग्रहण कर लिया। इस मसले पर मीडिया में बहुत कम बहस हुई, जिससे अंदाज़ा होता है कि एक 'ताकतवर सरकार-बड़े व्यवसायी' का गठजोड़ पूरे समाचार उद्योग पर कैसा भयावह असर डाल सकता है। यहां हर कोई डरा हुआ है और हर कोई खुद पर ही सेंसरशिप लगा रहा है। मुझे इसका अहसास तब हुआ, जब एक न्यूज़ चैनल के मालिक ने मुझे लंच पर बुलाया। उन्होंने कहा कि 'मैं अपना फ़ोन कमरे में ना लाऊं। कौन जानता है कि कौन किस फ़ोन को, कब और कैसे टेप कर रहा है,' उन्होंने चेतावनी दी।

सरकार की 'लाइन लेने' के लगातार दबाव ने मीडिया के सामने विश्वसनीयता का संकट बढ़ा दिया है। मुझे याद है कि 2020-21 में किसानों के विरोध प्रदर्शन को कवर करते समय बड़ी तादाद में प्रदर्शनकारियों ने मुझे घेर लिया और वे मेरा माइक छीनने की कोशिश कर रहे थे। कोई चिल्लाया, 'आप गोदी मीडिया हैं।' मैंने उन्हें समझाने की कोशिश की कि मैं केवल उनकी कहानी रिपोर्ट करने आया हूं, लेकिन कोई फायदा नहीं हुआ। 'वॉशिंग मशीन' और 'खोखे' की तरह, 'गोदी मीडिया' भी आम इस्तेमाल में होने वाला शब्द है जिसका इशारा है कि मीडिया, सरकार का पालतू बन गया है। यह संबोधन मुझे असहज करता है, क्योंकि इसका मतलब है पूरे पेशे की निंदा करना, जो 'सब नेता चोर हैं,' से अलग नहीं है। आम लोगों के गोदी मीडिया शब्द का इस्तेमाल ज़्यादा चिंताजनक है। और इससे बड़ी चिंता यह कि लोगों का गुस्सा बेबुनियाद नहीं है। मीडिया के एक बड़े हिस्से ने मोदी सरकार की चापलूसी में अब निष्पक्षता का दिखावा भी छोड़ दिया है। मीडिया को चार्ल्स डिकेंस के उपन्यास *डेविड कॉपरफील्ड* के विनम्र, पाखंडी चरित्र 'उरिय्या हीप' में बदल दिया गया है जो हमेशा झुकी हुई रीढ़ और गिड़गिड़ाने वाला खलनायक है। सच तो यह है कि अगर उत्साही और हिम्मती यूट्यूबर्स और डिजिटल, सोशल मीडिया के क्रांतिकारियों का दमदार असर नहीं होता तो विपक्ष की कहानी कहीं दब गई होती।

इससे एक मुश्किल सवाल खड़ा होता है: क्या निष्पक्ष मीडिया होने पर विपक्ष का प्रदर्शन बेहतर होता, क्या वो चुनाव भी जीत जाता? लोकतंत्र के एक स्तम्भ के तौर पर, क्या मीडिया

को सत्ता में दस साल से ज़्यादा रहने वाली सरकार के कामकाज और चूक के लिए जवाबदेह ठहराने में विफल होने के बावजूद इतनी आसानी से छोड़ा जा सकता है? सिर्फ़ एक तथ्य के बारे में सोचें। मोदी ने 2024 के चुनाव अभियान में 80 से ज़्यादा साक्षात्कार दिए, लेकिन एक भी साक्षात्कार करने वाले ने उनसे, कोविड से मौत पर झूठे आंकड़ों, छोटे और मंझले उद्योगों की दुर्दशा, मणिपुर की तकलीफों या चीनी सीमा पर हमले के बारे में कोई सवाल नहीं किया, और न ही पत्रकार की तरह कोई पलटकर सवाल पूछा। इसके बजाय हिंदुस्तानी मीडिया लगातार विपक्ष से ही सवाल पूछना, उसका मज़ाक उड़ाना, उस पर तंज़ करने का काम करता है, मानो सरकार से सवाल पूछना अब हमारे काम का हिस्सा नहीं है।

2024 में सबके लिए 'बराबर का मैदान' (लेवल प्लेइंग फील्ड) रहा? शायद ही।

═

अक्सर पूछे जाने वाला सवाल: तो 2024 का चुनाव वास्तव में किसने जीता?

2024 के चुनाव नतीजे कई मायनों में असाधारण कहे जा सकते हैं, खासकर इसलिए कि इस चुनाव में कोई भी नहीं 'जीता'। यह चुनाव कोई नहीं जीता। मोदी के नेतृत्व वाली भाजपा 'हार' गई क्योंकि वे अपना घोषित लक्ष्य हासिल नहीं कर सके। 'चार सौ पार', एक आकर्षक हेडलाइन हो सकती है, लेकिन अपने दम पर उससे आधे के करीब सीटें जीतना, फिर गठबंधन के साथ चलने के लिए मजबूर होना, दरअसल मोदी सरकार के दस सालों पर जनमत के खारिज़ करने जैसा है। विपक्ष निश्चित तौर पर यह चुनाव नहीं 'जीत' पाया, क्योंकि वे सब मिलकर भी आधी से कम सीटें जीत पाये। विपक्ष का प्रदर्शन भले ही उम्मीद से बेहतर था, लेकिन वो सत्ता के दावेदार होने के लायक नहीं था। अगर इंडिया गठबंधन, बिहार के मुख्यमंत्री नीतीश कुमार को अपने पाले में रख पाता, तो यह 'गेम-चेंजर' साबित हो सकता था। अगर कांग्रेस शुरू से ही हारने की मानसिकता में नहीं फंसी होती, तो वह कई राज्यों में कड़ी टक्कर दे सकती थी। या अगर नवीन पटनायक ने ओडिशा में खुद की ताकत का ग़लत अंदाज़ा नहीं लगाया होता, तो भाजपा 240 से भी कम सीटों पर सिमट सकती थी।

लेकिन 'अगर ऐसा होता' के परे यहां एक पहेली है: अगर मोदी 'हार' गए और विपक्ष नहीं 'जीता', तो फिर 2024 में आखिरकार जीता कौन? इसका जवाब चुप रहने वाले, लेकिन सर्वव्यापी भारतीय मतदाता के पास है। यह भी आश्चर्यजनक है कि मतदाता मीडिया के बनाए मिथक और विनम्र दंबग नेताओं के धुंधलके के पार देख पाया और उसने लोकतंत्र को बचाया। एक ऐसे राजनीतिक माहौल में जहां सबके लिए समान खेल का मैदान नहीं था, 2024 का चुनाव जनता और नेताओं के बीच 'डेविड बनाम गोलियत' की लड़ाई बन गया और जनता ने नेताओं को सबक सिखा दिया, यह भारतीय मतदाता की असाधारण उपलब्धि है।

जातीय और धार्मिक पहचानों में बंटा भारत एक पारंपरिक समाज है, लेकिन उसकी ऊर्जा असीम आकांक्षाओं वाले अपने लोगों से हैं। पैसे की ताकत, मीडिया नियंत्रण और करिश्माई नेता चुनावों पर असर डालते हैं, लेकिन लोगों से जुड़ाव भी उतना ही महत्वपूर्ण है। अध्याय 13 में, मैंने ऐसी दस कहानियों की चर्चा की है, जो लोकतांत्रिक मूल्यों में हमारे सामूहिक भरोसे को बहाल करती हैं। ये ऐसे लोगों की प्रेरणादायक कहानियां हैं जिन्होंने अविश्वसनीय जीत हासिल करने के लिए बड़ी-बड़ी बाधाओं को पार कर लिया। भारत के अलावा कहीं और कहां, एक कम आमदनी वाले परिवार में दो बच्चों की छब्बीस साल की दलित मां, एक पूरी पार्टी मशीनरी को हरा सकती है? या एक युवा मुस्लिम महिला अपने समुदाय में वोट जीतने के लिए, सफल करियर को छोड़ देती है? या एक आदिवासी नेता 'क्रॉउड सोर्सिंग फंड' से एक युवा स्वयंसेवी सेना खड़ी कर लेता है? या फिर एक सत्तर साल के राजनेता भगवा सेना के ख़िलाफ़ राम के घर में जीत हासिल कर लेते हैं? या मणिपुर का एक शिक्षाविद् जख्मी और घायल लोगों को मरहम लगाने में जुटा रहता है? या फिर एक अनजान सा राजनीतिक कार्यकर्ता, जिसका पारिवारिक क्लर्क कहकर मज़ाक उड़ाया जाता हो, वह एक अति आत्मविश्वासी स्टार मंत्री को हरा देता है?

यही वजह है कि 2024 का चुनाव जिसने अपने सभी उतार-चढ़ावों से भारत को आश्चर्यचकित कर दिया, एक ऐसी खास कहानी है, जिसे बताया ही जाना चाहिए। चुनावों पर मेरी पिछली किताबों की तरह, मेरा मकसद किसी चीज़ पर अपना फ़ैसला बताने का नहीं है। यह एक ऐसे पत्रकार की किताब है जो आज भी भारतीय राजनीति को एक खास नज़रिए से देखने के लिए उत्सुक है। मैं एक उत्साही आशावादी व्यक्ति हूं और शायद यही वजह है कि मैं पिछले पैंतीस साल से चुनावों पर रिपोर्टिंग कर रहा हूं और हर बार वोटों की गिनती के दिन मुझमें ज्यादा उत्साह दिखाई देता है। यह दसवां आम चुनाव है, जिस पर मैंने रिपोर्टिंग की है और मुझे भरोसा है कि इस अविश्वसनीय देश में हर चुनाव दूसरे से अलग होता है।

निस्संदेह, 2024 अपने आप में अलग है, बेहतर श्रेणी में आता है। इसने एक ऐसा जनादेश दिया, जिसने भारतीय लोकतंत्र की ताकत और सीमाओं दोनों को उजागर किया। एक तरह से, यह वह साल था जब विनम्रता ने अंहकार को मात दी, जब अंहकार साहस के आगे झुक गया, जब निराशावाद, उम्मीद के सामने बेमायने हो गया और जब विविधता ने एकरूपता पर जीत हासिल की। यही वजह है कि इस चुनाव का असली विजेता वह गुमनाम भारतीय मतदाता है, जिसकी बुलंद आवाज़ की गूंज पांच साल में सिर्फ़ एक बार सुनाई देती है। लाखों अनजान मतदाता एक बेहद असमान समाज का ख़ामियाज़ा चुपचाप भुगतते हैं, लेकिन वे जानते हैं कि कैसे और कब अपने शांत और गरिमामय तरीके से जवाब देना है।

महान भारतीय मतदाता ने दिखाया है कि स्याही लगी उंगली की ताकत ख़त्म नहीं हुई है और न ही भारतीय लोकतंत्र।

1

‘अबकी बार चार सौ पार’: नाकाम देवता

मंगलवार, 4 जून 2024: सुबह 5 बजे, अलार्म घनघना रहा था। बाहर अंधेरा बना हुआ था। भोर होने में वक्त था। मेरा दिमाग तेजी से चल रहा था। आज क्या होगा? लंबे चुनाव अभियान का शोर आखिरकार ख़त्म होने वाला था और आज हम उस खामोश आवाज़ को सुन पाएंगे, जो हर भारतीय चुनाव का केन्द्र होती हैः मतदाता।

मैं *इंडिया* टुडे स्टुडियो पहुंचा, तो वहां हमेशा की तरह पहले से ही चहल-पहल थी। कैमरामैन, सहायक, ग्राफिक्स डिजाइनर, मेकअप आर्टिस्ट हर कोई भागदौड़ करता दिख रहा था। हरेक की कोशिश थी कि सबकुछ जितना मुमकिन हो, उतना बेहतर हो सके। आखिरकार, टीवी समाचार चैनलों में आम चुनावों के नतीजों से बड़ा कोई मौका नहीं होता।

सिर्फ़ 48 घंटे पहले सबका फोकस एग्ज़िट पोल करने वालों पर था। सभी सर्वेक्षणों ने नरेन्द्र मोदी और भारतीय जनता पार्टी को स्पष्ट बहुमत के साथ तीसरी बार सरकार बनाने का इशारा किया था। कुछ सर्वेक्षणों में तो सत्ताधारी गठबंधन यानी एनडीए को चार सौ से ज़्यादा सीटें मिलने की भविष्यवाणी की गई थी। इस चुनाव के दौरान प्रधानमंत्री के नेतृत्व में सिर्फ़ एक नारा गूंज रहा थाः ‘अबकी बार, चार सौ पार’। अब सर्वेक्षण करने वालों ने इस भविष्यवाणी में भी इज़ाफा करते हुए भाजपा को भारी बहुमत मिलने की बात की थी।

एग्ज़िट पोल करने वालों में जबलपुर, मध्यप्रदेश के प्रिंटिग टेक्नोलॉजी में स्नातक प्रदीप गुप्ता से बड़ा कोई सितारा नहीं है। एक दशक पहले कम लोगों ने उनका नाम सुना था, लेकिन पचपन साल के गुप्ता को चुनावों का ‘नास्त्रेदमस’ माना जाता है। उन्हें हर बार सही भविष्यवाणी के लिए जाना जाता है। गुप्ता जो कहते हैं, वह चुनावी पंडितों, पत्रकारों और राजनेताओं के लिए

मानो पत्थर की लकीर है। उनका दावा है कि वे सभी 543 निर्वाचन क्षेत्रों में से हरेक को कवर करते हैं: यह नंबर इतना बड़ा है कि इससे कम या ज़्यादा सटीक नहीं हो सकता।

गुप्ता का रिकॉर्ड दमदार है, उनका दावा है कि पिछले दस साल में उन्होंने 69 में 65 चुनाव नतीजों की सही भविष्यवाणी की थी। उनके सर्वेक्षण के तरीके हार्वर्ड ब्रिज़नेस स्कूल में केस स्टडी के तौर पर रखे गए हैं। उन्होंने दुनिया के कई संगठनों में विश्लेषण में हिस्सेदारी की है और गेट्स फाउंडेशन के लिए उपभोक्ता से जुड़ी परियोजना पर काम किया है। पहली पीढ़ी के उद्यमी गुप्ता ने 1998 में एक छोटी प्रिंटिग यूनिट के तौर पर काम शुरू किया। फिर 2005 में बाज़ार के लिए स्टडी और उपभोक्ता सर्वेक्षण पर काम किया और अब मुंबई के व्यस्त उपनगरों में से एक अंधेरी में एक आलीशान दफ्तर में सैकड़ों अनुंसधानकर्ताओं और बैकरूम कर्मचारियों की एक टीम उनकी अगुवाई में काम कर रही है। गुप्ता चुनाव सर्वेक्षणों के 'इट' मैन हैं, एग्ज़िट पोल्स के हीरो हैं, जब भी सही नतीजे आते हैं, वे डांस के लिए तैयार रहते हैं। आम चुनावों से पहले, उन्हें कई समाचार चैनलों ने अपने साथ करोड़ों के अनुबंध की पेशकश की थी, लेकिन वह अब भी *टीवी* टुडे नेटवर्क के साथ जुड़े रहे।

दिलचस्प बात यह है कि गुप्ता को टीवी पर चुनाव सर्वेक्षणों का हीरो बनाने में मेरी भी छोटी सी भूमिका रही है। साल 2015 के बिहार विधानसभा चुनावों में उनका एक प्रतिद्वन्दी न्यूज़ चैनल के साथ अनुबंध था। उन्होंने 234 सदस्यों वाली बिहार विधानसभा में नीतीश कुमार-लालू यादव-कांग्रेस महागठबंधन को 180 से ज़्यादा सीटें मिलने की संभावना जताई थी, जबकि ज़्यादातर दूसरे सर्वेक्षणों में कड़े मुकाबले या भाजपा की जीत की भविष्यवाणी की गई थी। उस चैनल के मालिक और संपादकीय टीम, प्रदीप गुप्ता की भविष्यवाणी देखकर घबरा गए और मोदी सरकार से प्रतिक्रिया के डर से सर्वेक्षण को प्रसारित नही करने का फ़ैसला किया। मैं *इंडिया* टुडे पर 'पोल ऑफ पोल्स' में उनके सर्वेक्षण के नंबर दिखाने के लिए तैयार हो गया। नतीजों में महागठबंधन ने बड़ी जीत हासिल की, गुप्ता बिल्कुल सही थे। अगले चुनाव से वे *टीवी* टुडे टीम का हिस्सा थे।

शनिवार, 1 जून को रात दस बजे, गुप्ता ने अपनी आखिरी टैली या नंबर बताएः उनका दावा था कि राष्ट्रीय जनतांत्रिक गठबंधन (एनडीए) को 361-401 और भाजपा को अपने दम पर 322-340 सीटें मिल सकती हैं। वे अपनी बात को लेकर आश्वस्त थे। जब मैंने सुझाव दिया कि उन्होंने पश्चिम बंगाल में महिलाओं के मतदान को कहीं कम तो नहीं आंका या सात चरणों के चुनाव के अंतिम दौर का जल्दबाज़ी में विश्लेषण तो नहीं किया, तो उन्होंने इसे ख़ारिज़ कर दिया। गुप्ता ने कहा, 'चिंता मत करो, हम एक बार फिर सही साबित होंगे।' वैसे भी ऐसे पोल्सटर्स से बहस करना आसान नहीं है, जिसका सैंपल साइज 543 संसदीय क्षेत्रों में पांच लाख लोगों से सीधे बातचीत का हो। हालांकि मेरे समेत कई रिपोर्टरों ने देशभर में चुनाव यात्रा करते समय

'मोदी की गारंटी' को लेकर कम उत्साह देखा था, लेकिन गुप्ता इससे बेपरवाह थे। उन्होंने ज़ोर देकर कहा, 'कुछ इलाकों में चुनावी मुकाबला है, लेकिन नतीजे साफ हैं। कोई बड़ा उलटफेर नहीं होगा।' वास्तव में, उन्होंने बाद में मुझे बताया कि उनके कच्चे डेटा में एनडीए को और ज़्यादा संख्या 420 सीटें बताई थीं, जिसे राजनीतिक आंकलन के बाद उन्होंने कम कर दिया था। इस बीच समाचार चैनलों पर 'मोदी मैजिक' का शोर फिर से सुनाई देने लगा, हर कोई आवाज़ बढ़ाने में शायद एक दूसरे से मुकाबला कर रहा था।

रविवार, 2 जून को सवेरे अख़बारों में एग्ज़िट पोल के 'बैनर हैडलाइन्स' टीवी स्टुडियो के मूड का असर दिखा रहे थे। 'पीएम मोदी सत्ता में वापसी के लिए तैयार', तो दूसरे में था '400 का आंकड़ा अब सपना नहीं रहा'। आह, 400! एक ऐसा जादुई आंकड़ा, जो इससे पहले 1984 में हासिल किया गया था, उस वक्त इंदिरा गांधी की हत्या के बाद हुए चुनाव में राजीव गांधी सत्ता में आए थे। क्या मोदी अब जीत की हैट-ट्रिक के साथ एक कदम और आगे जा सकते हैं? जहां सत्ता-विरोधी लहर जैसा शब्द बेमायने हो जाए। ज़ाहिर है एग्ज़िट पोल के आंकड़ों ने विरोधी दलों को परेशान कर दिया था। राहुल गांधी ने इन्हें 'मोदी-पोल' बताकर ख़ारिज़ कर दिया, एक अन्य विपक्षी नेता ने मुझे चेतावनी दी, 'वे झूठे आंकड़ों के लिए ऑन एयर सार्वजनिक माफ़ी की मांग करेंगे।' इस बीच मोदी सरकार पहले से ही ऐसे जश्न मना रही थी, मानो मैच ख़त्म हो गया हो। ख़बरों के हिसाब से सरकार ने पहले ही एक भव्य शपथग्रहण समारोह की योजना बना ली थी।

3 जून, नतीजों से एक दिन पहले सोमवार को शेयर बाज़ार उत्साह से खुला। मई के महीने में बाज़ार में काफी उतार-चढ़ाव रहा, जो चुनावों को लेकर अनिश्चितता और खासतौर से विदेशी संस्थागत निवेशकों की भारी मुनाफा वसूली का संकेत था। अब एग्ज़िट पोल ने नतीजों के बारे में संदेहों को मिटा दिया था। बीएसई सेंसेक्स सुबह खुलते ही 2,777 अंकों की छलांग लगाकर रिकॉर्ड ऊंचाई पर पहुंच गया था; कुछ मार्केट ऑपरेटर्स को भाजपा के कट्टर समर्थकों के तौर पर देखा जाता है। एक प्रमुख बाज़ार निवेशक ने कहा, 'एग्ज़िट पोल की भविष्यवाणी में मोदी की बड़ी जीत ने हमें उम्मीदों से भर दिया है।' इस बढ़त में सबसे आगे रहने वाले शेयरों में अडानी समूह से जुड़ी कंपनियां भी थीं, जिन्हें प्रधानमंत्री मोदी का करीबी माना जाता है।

मोदी समर्थकों के इस शोर के बीच, एक नरम आवाज़ वाले राजनीतिक कार्यकर्ता और शिक्षाविद् ने अपनी असहमति जाहिर की। योगेन्द्र यादव ने अपने करियर की शुरुआत प्रोफेसरनुमा राजनीतिक विश्लेषक के तौर पर की थी, जो अक्सर टीवी पर बहस में दिखाई देते थे। वे भारत के शुरुआती और मूल चुनाव विश्लेषकों में से एक हैं। साठ साल के यादव अब पूरी तरह से राजनेता और 'स्वराज अभियान' के संस्थापक हैं। योगेन्द्र यादव, राहुल गांधी की 'भारत जोड़ो' यात्रा के अहम हिस्सा थे, उन्होंने इससे पहले किसान आंदोलन में हिस्सा लिया

था और आमतौर पर मोदी सरकार के कटु आलोचक रहे हैं। एग्ज़िट पोल के बाद सवेरे जब मैंने उन्हें फ़ोन किया तो उन्होंने मुझसे कहा, 'मुझे सच में लगता है कि सभी पोलस्टर्स ग़लत हैं।' हफ्तों से हम अपनी यात्राओं के अनुभवों को एक-दूसरे से साझा कर रहे थे। दाढ़ी-मूंछ रखे और कुर्ता पहने, गले में गमछा लपेटे यादव हिंदीभाषी राज्यों में घूम रहे थे। उन्हें यकीन था कि ज़मीन पर लोगों का मूड भाजपा के ख़िलाफ़ हो रहा था, खासतौर से उत्तरप्रदेश में। हमने इससे पहले कई चुनाव कार्यक्रमों में साथ काम किया है और सभी पोलस्टर्स की तरह उनके कुछ पूर्वानुमान गलत भी रहे हैः उनमें 2004 के आम चुनावों के पूर्वानुमान शामिल हैं। उत्तरप्रदेश ऐसा राज्य हैं जहां यादव ने हमेशा राजनीतिक हवाओं को सही ढंग से समझा है। लेकिन अब वे विपक्षी राजनीति कर रहे थे तो क्या यह उनकी इच्छा भी हो सकती थी? उन्होंने कहा, 'मुझे पता है, मैं राजनीति का हिस्सा हूं, लेकिन मुझे लगता है कि भाजपा को बहुमत के आंकड़े से कम यानी 272 से नीचे सीटें मिलेंगी, शायद वो 240 से 260 के बीच कहीं अटक जाए।'

प्रदीप गुप्ता के 'चार सौ पार' के पूर्वानुमान बनाम योगेन्द्र यादव की 'भाजपा को 272 से कम सीटों की चेतावनी': एक ऐसा चुनाव जिसे अब ख़त्म यानी 'डन डील' माना जा रहा था, अचानक फिर से कुछ उत्साह पैदा कर रहा था। यही वजह थी कि 4 जून को देशभर की निगाहें अपने टीवी सेट और मोबाइल फ़ोन से हट नहीं रही थीं। देशभर में दस लाख से ज़्यादा मतगणना केन्द्रों पर सुबह आठ बजे इलेक्ट्रॉनिक वोटिंग मशीनें खोली गईं। मतगणना के पहले नब्बे मिनट 'नेट प्रैक्टिस' की तरह होते हैः टीवी चैनलों पर दिखाए जा रहे नंबर का वास्तविक मैच से कोई संबंध नहीं होता। ये आंकड़ें या तो मुट्ठी भर डाकपत्रों पर आधारित होते हैं या कुछ मामलों में, चैनल संपादक, टीवी स्क्रीन को गुलजार रखने के लिए दिखाते रहते हैं (यह अनैतिक है, जो दर्शकों को आसानी से गुमराह कर सकता है)। फिर भी वोटों की गिनती के पहले घंटे में हर कोई 'चार सौ पार' चला रहा था। एग्ज़िट पोल के दौरान भाजपा की जीत का ऐलान करने वाले अतिउत्साही एंकर अब जीत के पैमाने पर अटकलें लगा रहे थे।

सुबह दस बजे असली रुझान आने शुरू हुए। शुरुआती आंकड़ों से एकतरफा नतीज़े रहने की उम्मीद नहीं लगती थी। भाजपा के नेतृत्व वाला एनडीए आगे तो था, लेकिन विपक्षी इंडिया का सूपड़ा साफ नहीं हो रहा था। दरअसल, विपक्ष उत्तरप्रदेश, महाराष्ट्र और पश्चिम बंगाल जैसे बड़े प्रमुख राज्यों में आगे चल रहा था। दोपहर आते-आते एक बात साफ हो गई कि कोई एकतरफा जीत नहीं होने जा रही, बल्कि कड़े मुकाबले वाला चुनाव है। उत्साही एंकरों के 400 पार के दावे की आवाज़ थोड़ी कमज़ोर पड़ने लगी थी। 400 को तो भूल जाइए, अब 272 तक पहुंचना मुश्किल लग रहा था। देश के कई हिस्सों से अप्रत्याशित नतीजों के बीच, मैंने स्टुडियों में अपने सहयोगियों से फुसफुसाते हुए पूछाः 'गुप्ता जी कहां हैं?'

पिछले चुनावों में गुप्ता और मैंने स्टुडियों में अचानक डांस करके एग्ज़िट पोल के सही होने का जश्न मनाया था। हमारे इन शौकिया 'डांस मूव्स' की आलोचना उन लोगों ने की, जो समझते हैं कि चुनावी शो को घटिया मनोरंजन नहीं बना देना चाहिए। मेरे बच्चों और शुभचिंतकों ने मुझे चेताया भी था कि 'आज डांस न करें, इससे गलत संदेश जाएगा।' अब उन्हें चिंता करने की ज़रूरत नहीं थी। एग्ज़िट पोल के नतीजे गलत साबित होते लग रहे थे। दोपहर तीन बजे तक, जैसे-जैसे अंतिम नतीज़े आने लगे, फ़ैसला स्पष्ट और चौंकाने वाला था। एनडीए गठबंधन सरकार तो बनाएगा, लेकिन पिछले दो चुनावों से उलट भाजपा इस बार बहुमत के आंकड़े तक नहीं पहुंचेगी। 'चार सौ पार' की बात तो दूर 2019 की तरह 300 पार भी नहीं हो रहा था। जब एग्ज़िट पोल करने वाले ज़्यादातर लोग छिपने की जगह तलाश रहे थे, तब हैरान गुप्ता आखिरकार सामने आए। इस बार स्टुडियों में उनकी एंट्री 'बैंड, बाजा, बारात' संगीत के साथ नहीं हुई, जो एग्ज़िट पोल के दौरान था। इसके बजाय वे स्टुडियो में चुपचाप घुसे, यह जानते हुए कि एक बेहतरीन पोल ट्रैक रिकॉर्ड और उनकी प्रतिष्ठा को सबसे बड़ा झटका लगा था।

'तो बड़े राज्यों में आप इतना ग़लत कैसे हुए?' मेरा सीधा सवाल था। गुप्ता ने अपनी ग़लती मान ली। उन्होंने कहा, 'हम जातिगत समीकरणों में हो रहे बदलावों को पकड़ नहीं पाए, खासतौर से पूर्वी उत्तरप्रदेश में। पश्चिम बंगाल में हमें सही तरीके से जवाब नहीं मिले, जहां डर का माहौल है और महाराष्ट्र में दलितों और नए गठबंधन ने बड़ा फ़र्क कर दिया।' लेकिन पूरी तरह से हार मानने के बजाय उन्होंने कहा, 'कई राज्यों के विधानसभा चुनावों के नतीजे और सीटों की संख्या सही रही।' लेकिन जब मैंने बिना शर्त माफी मांगी तो गुप्ता अचानक रो पड़े। 2019 में जब उनका एग्ज़िट पोल एकदम सटीक निकला, तब खुशी में उनके आंसू निकल पड़े थे, लेकिन इस वक्त वे अलग तरह से भावुक थे। वे शर्मिंदगी में रोए, उनके आंसू दिखावटी नहीं थे। काफी समय से काम में व्यस्त रहने से शायद तनाव ने उन्हें जकड़ लिया था। उन्होंने बाद में कहा, 'हां, मैं सबके सामने रोया, क्योकि यह काम मेरा जुनून है। मैंने कड़ी मेहनत की थी, लेकिन गलतियां हुईं और आप सबको भी निराश किया।'

ऐसा नहीं है कि केवल न्यूज़ नेटवर्क ही निराश हुआ था। पिछले कुछ सालों में मैंने एग्ज़िट पोल के उतार-चढाव को स्वीकार करना सीख लिया था: वोट शेयर को सटीक सीटों में बदलना, 'स्वास्थ्य के लिए हानिकारक है' की वैधानिक पोत चेतावनी के साथ होना चाहिए। लेकिन जब मोटी-चमड़ी वाले न्यूज़ एंकर आगे बढ़ गए और एक और चुनाव के लिए चल दिए, तो शेयर बाज़ार में खुदरा निवेशकों के पास कोई सहारा नहीं बचा था। एग्ज़िट पोल के गलत साबित होने के बाद शेयर बाज़ार धड़ाम से गिर गया, हड़कंप मच गया था। वोटों की गिनती के दिन ही बाज़ार में 30 लाख करोड़ की गिरावट आई, यह एक दिन में अब तक की सबसे बड़ी गिरावट

थी। चौबीस घंटे पहले जिस एग्ज़िट पोल से शेयर बाज़ार में अचानक उछाल आया था, वही पोल अब भारी नुक़सान की वजह हो गए थे।

कांग्रेस नेता और पूर्व निवेश बैंकर प्रवीण चक्रवर्ती ने कहा, 'यह दुनिया का पहला शेयर बाज़ार घोटाला है।' व्हार्टन स्कूल से पढ़े चक्रवर्ती कांग्रेस के डेटा विशेषज्ञ और बाज़ार पर नज़र रखने वाले महारथी हैं। चक्रवर्ती ने शुक्रवार, 31 मई को शेयर बाज़ार में अचानक उछाल की ओर इशारा कियाः एग्ज़िट पोल से एक दिन पहले दोगुना से ज़्यादा का उछाल था। इसमें आधे से ज़्यादा करीब 58 फ़ीसद व्यापार विदेशी संस्थागत निवेशकों का था। 'इस एक दिन में उनकी इतनी ट्रेडिंग कैसे हुई? यह केवल संयोग नहीं हो सकता कि एग्ज़िट पोल में मोदी की भारी जीत के अनुमान से एक दिन पहले दोगुनी ट्रेडिंग हुई?' उन्होंने ज़ोर देकर कहा। एक पूर्व निवेश बैंकर के रूप में उनकी बात में दम लगता है। एग्ज़िट पोल के नतीज़ों से एक दिन पहले ट्रेडिंग वॉल्यूम दोगुना कैसे हो गया? बाज़ार विशेषज्ञों का मानना है कि यह एफ़आईआई नहीं है, जो जांच के दायरे में होना चाहिए, क्योंकि 31 मई को घरेलू निवेशकों ने ट्रेडिंग की, जिनके पास बहुत पैसा है। 1990 के दशक में हर्षद मेहता शेयर घोटाले को उजागर करने वाले देबाशीष बासु ने एक ऑनलाइन पत्रिका मनीलाइफ में लिखाः 'कुछ बड़े निवेशकों को इसका असली फायदा हुआ, क्योंकि वे छोटे निवेशकों के नाम पर ट्रेडिंग कर रहे थे। इनमें अप्रवासी भारतीय भी शामिल हैं और इनकी बड़ी तादाद है, और ऐसा आसानी से किया जा सकता है, लेकिन इनकी जांच करना कोई मुश्किल काम नहीं है।'

साज़िशों की चर्चाओं में प्रधानमंत्री मोदी और गृहमंत्री अमित शाह की वे दिलचस्प टिप्पणियां भी शामिल थीं, जिसमें उन्होंने चुनाव प्रचार के दौरान अपने अलग-अलग टीवी साक्षात्कारों में भरोसा जताया था कि मतगणना के दिन शेयर बाज़ार नई ऊंचाइयों पर होगा। शाह ने कहा, 'मेरा सुझाव है कि आप चार जून से पहले शेयर खरीद लें, क्योंकि बाज़ार में उछाल आएगा।' एक ज़माने में एक बिजनेस चैनल में रहीं, कांग्रेस की मुखर प्रवक्ता सुप्रिया श्रीनेत ने पूछा, 'हमारे प्रधानमंत्री और गृहमंत्री कब से शेयर बाज़ार के सलाहकार बन गए हैं?'

मकसद साफ हैः क्या शेयर बाज़ार में इतनी हलचल सिर्फ़ इसलिए हुई क्योंकि कुछ बड़े निवेशकों को एग्ज़िट पोल के नतीजों के सार्वजनिक होने से पहले ही इसकी ख़बर मिल गई थी? और क्या निवेशकों ने इस अंदरूनी (ग़लत) सूचना का फायदा उठाया? इससे ज़्यादा परेशान करने वाली बात यह है कि क्या पोलस्टर्स, शेयर बाज़ार के खिलाड़ियों और राजनेताओं के बीच कोई संबंध था, जिन्हें एग्ज़िट पोल के नतीजों के बारे में पहले से ही पता हो सकता था? ये निवेशक किसके पैसे और किसके पक्ष में निवेश कर रहे थे? जब मैंने प्रदीप गुप्ता से यह सवाल पूछा तो उन्होंने नाराज़गी के साथ जवाब दिया, 'घोटाले की बात तो छोड़िए, शेयर बाज़ार की किसी सट्टेबाज़ी से मेरा कोई लेना-देना नहीं हैं। मैंने शेयरों में कोई बड़ा कारोबार आखिरी

बार चुनावों से बहुत पहले, फरवरी 2024 में किया था। चुनावों के दौरान, मैंने सिर्फ़ 35,000 रुपये का निवेश किया था।' जब उनसे पूछा गया कि क्या उन्होंने एग्ज़िट पोल के प्रसारण से पहले किसी राजनीतिक दल या व्यक्ति से अपने पूर्वानुमानों को साझा किया था? वे भड़क गए। उन्होंने ज़ोर देकर कहा, 'मैंने स्टुडियो में लाइव शो शुरू होने तक आपके साथ भी नंबर साझा नहीं किए, तो इसे किसी और के साथ साझा करने का सवाल ही कहां से आता है। इस मामले में मेरे अपने सिद्धान्त हैं।'

लेकिन गुप्ता समेत, देश के दूसरे कई पोलस्टर्स के हितों में टकराव दिखाई देता है, जिसकी बारीकी से जांच की जानी चाहिए। गुप्ता भारतीय जनता पार्टी के लिए कई साल से जनमत सर्वेक्षण कर रहे हैं। उनकी उपभोक्ता शोध में लगी यूनिट मोदी सरकार की योजनाओं के ज़मीनी असर का सर्वेक्षण भी करती है। उनकी प्रिंटिग कंपनी ने एलपीजी गैस के बिलों की छपाई से लेकर विज्ञापन अधिकार, रेलवे आरक्षण टिकटों तक कई बड़े सरकारी ठेकों की बोली लगाई और जीती भी है। गुप्ता का कहना है कि 'ये सभी प्रिटिंग ठेके 2014 से पहले के हैं, जब डॉ. मनमोहन सिंह प्रधानमंत्री थे।' उन्होंने प्रधानमंत्री मोदी के चुनाव अभियान पर महारथ की तारीफ़ करने वाली एक किताब में भी योगदान दिया था। कहा जाता है कि वे मुंबई के भाजपा सांसद पीयूष गोयल और केन्द्रीय गृहमंत्री अमित शाह के करीबी रहे हैं। 'पीयूष और मैं 2013 में हार्वर्ड बिजनेस स्कूल में ऑनर/प्रेसीडेंट मैनेजमेंट प्रोग्राम के लिए एक ही क्लास में थे, लेकिन इसका मतलब यह नहीं कि मेरा उनसे या अमित शाह से या भाजपा से खास रिश्ता है। भारतीय जनता पार्टी ही नहीं, मैंने चुनावों के बीच कई राष्ट्रीय और क्षेत्रीय दलों के लिए सर्वेक्षण भी किया है और सलाह भी दी है, लेकिन जब एक बार चुनाव प्रक्रिया शुरू हो जाती है तो फिर मैं किसी पार्टी के साथ नहीं रहता, फिर मैं अपने दम पर काम करता हूं,' उनका दावा था। क्या भाजपा के सदस्यों ने उनकी कंपनी में कोई निवेश किया है? 'बिल्कुल नहीं, कंपनी का मालिकाना हक मेरे, मेरे परिवार और स्कूल के कुछ दोस्तों के पास है, इसमें भाजपा या किसी दूसरी पार्टी का कोई लेना-देना नहीं है। मैं किसी भी जांच के लिए तैयार हूं,' उन्होंने जवाब दिया।

हालांकि बाद में कहा गया कि भारतीय प्रतिभूति और विनिमय बोर्ड (सेबी) की जांच में बाज़ार में हेरफेर के कोई सबूत नहीं मिले, लेकिन एग्ज़िट पोल करने वालों पर संदेह के बादल पूरी तरह छंटे नहीं हैं। कम से कम गुप्ता ने तो खुले तौर पर इस बात को स्वीकार किया कि वे भाजपा के लिए सर्वेक्षण करते हैं, लेकिन टेलीविज़न पर चुनाव पूर्व जनमत सर्वेक्षण (ओपिनियन पोल्स) से दूर रहते हैं। सर्वेक्षण करने वाले उन दूसरे लोगों का क्या, जिन्होंने अपने राजनीतिक दलों के साथ रिश्तों का खुलासा नहीं किया। मेरी जांच से पता चलता है कि कई टीवी चैनल पोल करने वाले राष्ट्रीय और क्षेत्रीय राजनीतिक दलों के साथ मिलकर काम कर रहे थे। उदाहरण

के लिए, पोल करने वाले युवा प्रदीप भंडारी, जो अक्सर अपने जन की बात ब्राडिंग के तहत भाजपा के लिए सर्वेक्षण तो कर रहे थे, लेकिन टीवी कार्यक्रमों के दौरान उन्होंने इस बात का खुलासा नहीं किया। 2024 में उन्होंने एक एग्ज़िट पोल किया था जो एनडीटीवी पर प्रसारित हुआ, इसमें भाजपा नेतृत्व वाले एनडीए को 362 से 392 सीटें दिखाई गई थीं, जो नतीजों के आंकड़े से काफी दूर रहीं। भंडारी ने कहा, 'मैं जब भी भाजपा के लिए सर्वेक्षण का काम कर रहा था, मैंने अपने नंबर किसी भी रूप में टीवी पर साझा नहीं किए। 2024 में मुझे भाजपा के सर्वेक्षण का कोई काम नहीं मिला था।' लेकिन यहां सवाल यह है कि क्या कोई व्यक्ति जिसने पहले या वर्तमान में भाजपा के साथ काम किया हो, वह सही नंबर देने के लिए राजनीतिक दबाव में नहीं रहेगा? 2016 में सर्वेक्षण का काम शुरू करने वाले मुखर भंडारी ने कई चैनलों पर एंकरिंग की थी और अपने भाजपा के लिए झुकाव के बारे में बेबाकी से बताया। जुलाई 2024 में, वह औपचारिक तौर पर भाजपा के प्रवक्ता बन गए।

गुप्ता और दूसरे लोग जब एग्ज़िट पोल की तपन का सामना कर रहे थे, तब योगेन्द्र यादव सुर्खियों का मज़ा ले रहे थे। आखिरकार, वे अकेले पोलस्टर थे, जिन्होंने 'चार सौ पार' के शोर के बीच सही कहा था। वे नतीजों के दिन, रात को 9 बजे शो पर 'ऑन एयर' थे, लेकिन कोशिश कर रहे थे कि वे बहुत खुश दिखाई न दें। 'मेरे हिसाब से पोलस्टर्स सिर्फ़ पोस्टमैन की तरह हैं, उन्हें इसका पूरा केन्द्र नहीं माना जाना चाहिए। अगर वे सही हैं तो, वे सिर्फ़ अपना काम कर रहे हैं, अगर गलत हैं, तो उन्हें सुधार की कोशिश करनी चाहिए। अगर वे सही होते हैं, तो मुझे नहीं लगता कि इस पर स्टुडियो में नाचना कोई अच्छा आइडिया है और अगर वे ग़लत हैं तब भी स्टुडियो में किसी को रुलाना अच्छी बात नहीं है,' उनकी समझदारी भरी सलाह थी। यादव ने फिर अपनी नर्म आवाज़ में एक पंचलाइन दी, 'मैंने बारह साल पहले सेफोलॉजी छोड़ दी थी, मैं नहीं चाहता था, लेकिन मुझे राजनीतिक कार्यकर्ता के तौर पर इसलिए आना पड़ा क्योंकि मैंने देखा कि इन सर्वेक्षणों का दुरुपयोग देश को गुमराह करने के लिए किया जा रहा था, एक ऐसी कोशिश जिसमें आपके सहित दूसरे मीडिया चैनल भी शामिल थे।'

मैं उनकी बात सुनकर मुस्कुराया, मोटे तौर पर अपनी शर्मिंदगी छिपाने के लिए और आंशिक रूप से मीडिया कंपनियों के तौर पर हमारी सामूहिक विफलता को स्वीकार करने के लिए। अभी तीन दिन पहले ही, हम मोदी के नेतृत्व वाली भाजपा की भारी जीत की भविष्यवाणी करने वालों में शामिल थे। अब अपमान का घूंट भी पीना ही था।

इस बीच, वह व्यक्ति जिसके सितारे की चमक अचानक कम हो गई थी, अपनी घर वापसी के लिए मुंबई की उड़ान पर अकेला था। प्रदीप गुप्ता धीरे-धीरे एक बड़े रिस्क वाले चुनाव में एग्ज़िट पोल के बुरी तरह गलत होने वाले ख़तरों को समझ रहे थे। कुछ दिनों पहले ही एक समाचार एंकर ने गुप्ता को 'मतगणना का भगवान' (गॉड ऑफ पोलिंग) कहा था। अब भगवान

के पैर भी मिट्टी के होने का पता चला। एकमात्र राहत यह थी, वह अकेले नहीं थे। 2024 में दूसरे देवताओं के सिंहासन भी खिसक गए थे।

═

दस साल पहले, नरेन्द्र मोदी के राजनीति में राष्ट्रीय स्तर पर आने के साथ ही एक नया राजनीतिक शख्स सामने आयाः पेशेवर चुनाव रणनीतिकार-सलाहकार। चतुराई से बात करते, सलीके से कपड़े पहने, लैपटॉप के साथ आंकड़ों को बताने वाले ये सलाहकार जल्दी ही सुर्खियों में आ गए। पिछले दशक में हर राष्ट्रीय या क्षेत्रीय राजनीतिक दल ने, चुनावों के वक्त इन आंकड़ों के जाल बुनते, इवेंट मैनेजमेंट पेशेवरों का इस्तेमाल किया है। उन्हें इस विशेषज्ञता के लिए मोटी रकम मिल रही थी। परपंरागत रूप से भारत में, चुनाव से पहले, लो-प्रोफाइल वाले, स्थानीय कार्यकर्ता या पार्टी कार्यकर्ता घर-घर या मोहल्ले-मोहल्ले जाकर सभाएं और बैठकें और जनसंपर्क अभियान करते थे। लेकिन जबसे यह सलाहकार मैदान में उतरे, तो उन्होंने एक ऐसी दुनिया बनाई, जो अमेरिकी राष्ट्रपति शैली की राजनीतिक रणनीति से प्रभावित थी। बीस से तीस साल के इन मैनेजमेंट के शौकीनों ने अब अपने एसी वॉर रूम बना लिए थे, जहां की-बोर्ड की आवाज़, चार्ट और चित्रों पर फोकस है, निर्वाचन क्षेत्रों की बारीक जानकारियां इकट्ठा की जा रही हैं। उन्होंने राजनेताओं के लिए अभियान बनाना, ब्रांडिंग करना, राजनेताओं के सोशल मीडिया प्रोफाइल को फिर से सजाना और कभी-कभी शातिर तरीके से हेरफेर कर क्लिप और मीम्स से विरोधियों के ख़िलाफ गंदे अभियान भी शुरू कर दिए हैं। इन सलाहकारों की तादाद बढ़ने के बावजूद इनके बीच एक 'OG' (ओरिजनल गैंगस्टर) था, जो सभी राजनीतिक सलाहकारों का गुरु और पथ-प्रदर्शक थाः सैतालिस साल के प्रशांत किशोर, जिन्हें सत्ता के गलियारों में 'पीके' के रूप में जाना जाता है।

हमेशा मैचिंग पैंट-शर्ट और ट्रैंडी फुल-रिम चश्में में, मगर कैजुअल दिखते प्रशांत किशोर खुद को एक ईमानदार गांधीवादी पहचान के साथ दिखाना चाहते हैं, वह अक्सर ज़मीनी स्तर पर राजनीति के लिए अपनी बात को रखते वक्त महात्मा गांधी का सहारा लेते हैं। फिर भी किशोर की लाइफ-स्टाइल अलग है। अक्सर मर्सिडीज या बीएमडब्ल्यू में देश के महानगरों में पांच सितारा होटलों की लॉबी में नज़र आते किशोर, महात्मा से ज़्यादा रॉल्फ लॉरेन हैं। उनका बायोडॉटा शानदार है। उन्हें मोदी के 2014 के 'चाय पर चर्चा' कैंपेन और मोदी की एक 'चायवाले' की छवि बनाने में अहम भूमिका का श्रेय दिया गयाः एक ऐसा बाहरी शख्स, जो मंहगे शिक्षित और बेहतर परिवारों में जन्मे लोगों से भरी दिल्ली के अभिजात्य वर्ग को चुनौती दे रहा था। यह एक 'प्रामाणिक' व्यक्ति की बड़ी सफलता थी। मोदी को चाय की दुकान के मेहनती नायक के तौर पर पेश किया गया, जिसने हार्वर्ड से पढ़े, 'चांदी की चम्मच'

के साथ पैदा हुए लोगों से बेहतर प्रदर्शन किया। हालांकि चुनाव के बाद, बेहद महत्वाकांक्षी किशोर मोदी टीम से तेज़ी से अलग हो गए, जब बीजेपी के पुराने दिग्गजों ने उन्हें प्रधानमंत्री का 'चीफ ऑफ स्टॉफ' बनने से रोक दिया। उसके बाद उन्होंने अलग-अलग राजनीतिक दलों के साथ काम किया। वैचारिक रूप से अनैतिक होने के बावजूद, वह अपने ग्राहकों के लिए एक कोर ब्रांड तैयार करने और मल्टीमीडिया प्लेटफॉर्म पर उनकी ख़ासियतों को दमदार तरीके से रखने में माहिर हैं।

रणनीतिकार के तौर पर प्रशांत किशोर की सफलताओं की सूची में 2015 में बिहार में जनता दल (यूनाइटेड) के नेता नीतीश कुमार से हाथ मिलाना, 2017 में पंजाब में कांग्रेस के कैप्टन अमरिंदर सिंह के साथ जुड़ना, फिर 2019 में जगन मोहन रेड्डी की वापसी और 2021 में पश्चिम बंगाल में तृणमूल कांग्रेस की सुप्रीमो की जीत का सेहरा बांधना शामिल है। कुछ नाकामियां भी उनके नाम आती हैं, इनमें खासतौर से 2017 में विधानसभा चुनावों के दौरान किशोर ने राहुल गांधी और अखिलेश यादव के साथ 'यूपी के लड़के' अभियान चलाया, लेकिन वह नाकाम रहा। नतीजों से एक दिन पहले उन्होंने मुझे एक व्हाट्सएप संदेश भेजा था, जिसमें 405 सीटों वाली उत्तरप्रदेश विधानसभा में समाजवादी पार्टी-कांग्रेस गठबंधन को 200 से ज़्यादा सीटें मिलने का दावा किया गया था, वे सिर्फ़ 47 पर ही सिमट गए क्योंकि भाजपा तीन-चौथाई बहुमत से आगे निकल गई। लेकिन 2022 में गोवा में तृणमूल कांग्रेस की हार में किशोर की भूमिका के बारे में कम लोग ही जानते हैं। समुंदर के किनारे बसे डोना पाउला कस्बे के एक पांच सितारा होटल में ठहरे किशोर ने स्थानीय नेताओं को अपने पाले में लेने के लिए 'खरीदने' की कोशिश की। लेकिन उन्हें समझ आया कि गोवा की राजनीति भी समुद्र की लहरों की तरह ही खतरनाक है और चमकदार दिखते बाहरी लोगों के लिए इसमें आगे बढ़ना नामुमकिन जैसा है। किशोर और उनकी टीम गोवा में बुरी तरह विफल रही।

इस बड़ी नाकामी ने भी महत्वाकांक्षी किशोर को आगे बढ़ने से नहीं रोका। मई 2021 में, बंगाल में अपनी सफलता के बाद, उन्होंने धूमधाम से ऐलान किया कि अब वे राजनीतिक सलाहकार की भूमिका को छोड़ रहे हैं और एक नई भूमिका में दिखाई देंगे। उनका मंत्र है, 'हर दस साल में करियर में बदलाव के लिए तैयार रहना चाहिए।' एक साल बाद उन्होंने 'जन सुराज' आंदोलन शुरू किया, इसके लिए उन्होंने दावा किया कि यह उनके गृह राज्य बिहार की राजनीति को बदल देगा। लैपटॉप से राजनीति की अपनी छवि बदलने और ज़मीनी स्तर के कार्यकर्ता-नेता के तौर पर उभरने के लिए उन्होंने अक्टूबर 2022 में, राज्यव्यापी पदयात्रा शुरू की। लेकिन उन्होंने मुख्यधारा की राजनीतिक पार्टी का हिस्सा बनने की अपनी महत्वाकांक्षा का दरवाज़ा बंद नहीं किया थाः 2022 की गर्मियों में वह कांग्रेस में लगभग शामिल हो ही गए

थे, लेकिन उनकी भागीदारी पर कांग्रेस में तीखी असहमति के बाद उन्होंने बाहर रहना ही ठीक समझा। कांग्रेस का एक गुट, खासतौर से राहुल गांधी के करीबी लोगों का मानना था कि किशोर भाजपा के 'भेदिए' हो सकते थे और उन्हें घर में शामिल नहीं किया जा सकता। राहुल गांधी के एक सहयोगी ने कहा, 'समझने की ज़रूरत है कि वह नरेन्द्र मोदी के साथ कितने करीब रहे थे और फिर कितनी बार वह एक पार्टी से दूसरी पार्टी में जाते रहे, कोई इस तरह के राजनेता पर कैसे भरोसा कर सकता है?'

2024 के चुनाव जब करीब आए तो किशोर राजनीतिक सरगर्मियों के हाशिए पर थे, कांग्रेस ने दरवाज़ा बंद कर दिया था और मोदी-टीम का दरवाजा फिर से खुलने के आसार नहीं दिख रहे थे। तब किशोर ने अपने अंदाज़ में कहा कि उनका ध्यान 2025 के बिहार विधानसभा चुनावों पर है। दिलचस्प यह है कि उन्होंने अपने मित्र और उनके लिए काम कर चुके अभिषेक बनर्जी के साथ संवाद बरकरार रखा हुआ था, जो किशोर की सलाह पर अब भी ध्यान देते थे, भले ही किशोर के इंडियन पॉलिटिकल एक्शन कमेटी (I-PAC) से अलग हुई दूसरी टीम टीएमसी के साथ काम कर रही थी। 2023 के आखिर में किशोर आंध्रप्रदेश के पूर्व मुख्यमंत्री और तेलुगुदेशम पार्टी(टीडीपी) के नेता चन्द्रबाबू नायडु के बेटे नारा लोकेश के साथ विजयवाड़ा के लिए एक चार्टेड फ्लाइट पर थे। 2024 के लोकसभा चुनावों के साथ ही आंध्रप्रदेश में विधानसभा चुनाव होने वाले थे और कहा गया कि किशोर, नायडु को सलाह देने के लिए तैयार हो गए थे। नायडु को हाल ही में भ्रष्टाचार के एक पुराने मामले में ज़मानत मिली थी, यहां सीधी लड़ाई मुख्यमंत्री जगन मोहन रेड्डी के साथ थी। 'मैं चन्द्रबाबू से मिला, क्योंकि हम पुराने दोस्त रहे हैं। हमने नोट्स आदान-प्रदान किए, लेकिन मैं उनका चुनाव सलाहकार नहीं था, क्योंकि अब यह काम मैंने पूरी तरह छोड़ दिया था,' प्रशांत किशोर ने ज़ोर देकर कहा। लेकिन उनके पूर्व (I-PAC) सहयोगी अलग कहानी बताते हैं, 'उन्होंने निश्चित तौर पर हैदराबाद में रहकर चन्द्रबाबू के अभियान में सलाहकार की भूमिका निभाई। ऐसा लग रहा था कि वह अलग हो गए थे, लेकिन वह जगन मोहन रेड्डी के साथ अपना पुराना हिसाब बराबर करने की कोशिश में थे, साथ ही उन्हें उम्मीद थी कि बिहार के विधानसभा चुनावों के लिए चन्द्रबाबू मदद करेंगे,' एक पूर्व सहयोगी ने दावा किया। इस बड़े जोख़िम वाले आंध्रप्रदेश चुनाव ने ही किशोर की कंपनी, I-PAC टीम को विभाजित कर दिया था। I-PAC की एक टीम किशोर के 2019 के 'क्लाइंट' जगन मोहन रेड्डी के साथ काम कर रही थी, तो दूसरी अलग हुई टीम, जिसका नाम अब 'शोटाइम कंसल्टिंग' हो गया था, चन्द्रबाबू नायडु के अभियान के साथ जुड़ी थी। शोटाइम कंसल्टिंग के संस्थापक निदेशक रोबिन शर्मा ने कहा, 'प्रशांत हम सबके लिए एक गुरु हैं, उनके साथ ही हमने यह सफ़र शुरू किया था। मैं हमेशा उनके सुझावों को अहमियत दूंगा।'

हालांकि नायडु के अभियान में किशोर की भागीदारी बहुत साफ नहीं है, लेकिन टीवी पर अक्सर दिखाई देने का मतलब था कि वे कभी सुर्खियों से दूर नहीं रहते। एक चतुर चुनाव रणनीतिकार और बेहतर तरीके से अपनी बात को रखने वाले किशोर के पास राजनीतिक संभावनाओं की भविष्यवाणी करने और जटिल मुद्दों को छोटे और स्पष्ट तरीके से डिकोड करने की महारथ है। समाचार चैनलों और डिजिटल पोर्टलों को दिए गए उनके साक्षात्कार हमेशा वायरल होते हैं। वे ना केवल स्मार्ट दिखते हैं, स्मार्ट तरीके से बात करते हैं, जिसमें कहीं पंच होता है, तो कहीं खुलासा। 2024 के चुनावों से पहले प्रेस ट्रस्ट ऑफ इंडिया के संपादकों के साथ एक साक्षात्कार में किशोर ने भविष्यवाणी की कि भाजपा को 300 से ज़्यादा सीटें मिलेंगी और कांग्रेस 100 से भी कम सीटों पर सिमट जाएगी। वह 'चार सौ पार क्लब' के हिस्सा तो नहीं थे, लेकिन उन्होंने भाजपा की आसान जीत की भविष्यवाणी की। बंगाल में, जहां उन्होंने काफी काम किया था, टीएमसी के बजाय भाजपा की बड़ी जीत का इशारा किया।

हैरानी इस बात पर हो सकती है कि अपने 'रिटायरमेंट' के बावजूद किशोर मई महीने में कई टीवी चैनलों और वेब पोर्टल पर दिखाई दिए, जो एक सुनियोजित योजना का हिस्सा लग रहे थे। मतदान का चौथा चरण अभी ख़त्म हुआ था, किशोर ने फिर से भाजपा के तिहरे शतक लगाने और कांग्रेस के सौ के पार नहीं पहुंचने की बात की। करीब उसी वक्त योगेन्द्र यादव कह रहे थे कि भाजपा 272 से नीचे रहेगी। कांग्रेस के एक प्रवक्ता ने जोर देकर कहा, 'पीके को आम चुनावों के बीच भाजपा की बेहतर संभावनाओं की बात करने के लिए लाया गया, ताकि हमारी तरफ बढ़ती कहानी को एक मोड़ दिया जा सके।' जब आक्रामक करण थापर के साथ एक साक्षात्कार में किशोर के हिमाचल प्रदेश पर गलत चुनावी आंकलन को लेकर दोनों में तीखी बहस हुई, तब कांग्रेस सोशल मीडिया ने तेज़ी से काम करना शुरू कर दिया। मोदी और भाजपा से किशोर की दोस्ती वाले मीम्स और वीडियो सोशल मीडिया पर छा गए।

किशोर इस सबसे परेशान नहीं दिखे। 'देखिए, मुझे इससे कोई फ़र्क नहीं पड़ता कि सोशल मीडिया पर क्या ट्रोल हो रहा है। अगर आप मेरे सभी साक्षात्कार देखें, तो 2024 में ज़मीनी हालात पर मेरा आंकलन एक जैसा रहा है: "ब्रांड मोदी" कमज़ोर हो रहा है। गांवों के हालात और बेराज़गारी असली चिंताएं हैं। हां, मेरे आंकड़े गलत हो सकते हैं, लेकिन आप किसी पार्टी, खासतौर से भाजपा के इशारे पर मेरे इंटरव्यू का आरोप नहीं लगा सकते। बस उन पत्रकारों पर नज़र डालिए, जिनके लंबे समय से आग्रह पर मैंने साक्षात्कार दिए हैं, क्या उन्हें भाजपा समर्थक पत्रकार कहा जा सकता है? यह बहुत ही बचकाना तर्क है।'

कांग्रेस इस बात से सहमत नहीं थी। कांग्रेस का मानना था कि किशोर का मोदी सरकार और भाजपा के साथ गोपनीय संपर्क बना हुआ था। कांग्रेस के एक वरिष्ठ नेता ने कहा, 'सब जानते हैं कि राजनीतिक सलाह का काम पैसे से चलता है। मुझे बताइए कि किसी सरकारी

एजेंसी ने किशोर से कभी पूछताछ क्यों नहीं की और छापा नहीं मारा गया, जबकि वे देश के बड़े कामयाब सलाहकार हैं?' एक साक्षात्कार में जब मैंने किशोर से यह सवाल पूछा, तो उन्होंने उलटकर गुस्से में पूछा, 'कल को मैं पूछ सकता हूं कि आपके यहां कोई छापेमारी क्यों नहीं हुई? या जयराम रमेश और के.सी. वेणुगोपाल जैसे कांग्रेस नेताओं पर क्यों नहीं हाथ डाला गया? यह सब बकवास है। कुछ लोगों की हताशा भर है।'

फिर भी, 4 जून के नतीजों के तीन दिन बाद के उसी साक्षात्कार में, किशोर ने माना कि उन्होंने आंकड़ों पर ज़ोर देकर गलती की थी। 'मैं फिर कभी विशिष्ट नंबर को लेकर बात नहीं करूंगा, यह मेरी ग़लती थी,' उन्होंने स्वीकार किया। अगर पोलस्टर गुप्ता 'चार सौ पार' की बहती हवा में बहक गए थे, तो रणनीतिकार प्रशांत अपने आरामकुर्सी वाले राजनीतिक आंकलन में विशिष्ट नंबर की भविष्यवाणी के दोषी थे। चुनावी 'भविष्यवाणियों के भगवान' माने जाने वाले एक हाई-प्रोफाइल शख्स को नीचे देखना पड़ा था, वे शायद अपने को सर्वज्ञ समझने की वजह से बहक गए थे। उन्हें लगता था कि वे हमेशा सही थे, लेकिन मतदाताओं ने साबित कर दिया कि इस बार वे पूरी तरह ग़लत थे और जमीनी हक़ीकत से कोई वास्ता नहीं था। 2024 में किशोर की छवि को धक्का लगा था।

2024 में एक और 'भगवान' गलत साबित हुए।

दिल्ली में मार्च की एक ठंडी शाम थी। 2024 के आम चुनावों की तारीखों का ऐलान होने से देश का राजनीतिक तापमान बढ़ने लगा था। राजधानी के एक चमचमाते पांच सितारा होटल में, एक मीडिया हाउस के सालाना जलसे में देश और दुनिया के दिग्गज मौजूद थे। उसमें गृहमंत्री अमित शाह अपना भाषण ख़त्म करके, 'स्पीकर लाउंज' में एक सोफे पर आराम से बैठ गए। हाथ में चाय का कप और आसपास जमा पत्रकारों से बात करने लगे।

शाह कुछ ज़्यादा दुबले दिख रहे थे; खिचड़ी दाढ़ी से ढके उनके गाल पहले की तुलना में काफी धंसे हुए थे। कोविड के दौरान तबियत खराब रहने के बाद डाक्टरों ने उन्हें खाने-पीने पर ज्यादा ध्यान रखने को कहा था। उनका वज़न बीस किलो से ज़्यादा कम हो गया था। एक ज़माने में हट्टे-कट्टे दिखने वाले शाह अब काफी दुबले थे और उनका बेदाग़ सफेद कुर्ता पायजामा ढीला-ढाला लग रहा था। हालांकि, चश्मे के पीछे उनकी आंखें अब भी नहीं बदली थीं, वे इधर-उधर घूम रही थीं और बिना पलक झपकाए कड़ी निगाह बनी हुई थी। ज़्यादातर वक्त उनके हाव-भाव शून्य रहते हैं और किसी बात से कोई फ़र्क पड़ता नहीं दिखता। बात करते वक्त आवाज़ भले ही धीमी हो, लेकिन थोड़ी खतरनाक महसूस होती है, धाराप्रवाह हिंदी में खुरदुरापन महसूस किया जा सकता है।

राजनीतिक दिग्गज शाह, मोदी सरकार में असल नंबर-2 हैं और कमरे में हर कोई उनकी मौजूदगी से वाकिफ़ था। सभी की निगाहें उन पर टिकी थीं और उनकी हर बात पर ध्यान था और उसके मायने समझने की कोशिश हो रही थी। जैसे-जैसे वे खुलकर बात कर रहे थे। चुनावी जंग को लेकर उनकी उत्सुकता और समझ महसूस की जा सकती थी। डर पैदा करने वाले शाह के हाथ ज़रूरत से ज्यादा नाजुक दिखते हैं। दुर्भाग्य को दूर रखने के लिए उनकी उंगलियों में अंगूठियां है, वैसे भाग्य तो अभी उनके साथ है। अहमदाबाद के इस स्वघोषित 'विनम्र पार्टी कार्यकर्ता' को, बहुत से लोग निर्दयी, तो कुछ लोग बेईमान और चुनाव जीतने वाला मानते हैं। उन्हें पार्टियों को तोड़ने, दलबदल कराने, सरकारों को गिराने, अस्थिर करने और राजनीतिक विरोधियों को डराने-धमकाने के लिए सरकारी एजेसियों का इस्तेमाल करने के लिए जाना जाता था। मीडिया के कुछ लोग उन्हें आज के जमाने का 'चाणक्य' भी कहते है। तीसरी सदी के दार्शनिक चाणक्य को प्रसिद्ध सूत्र 'साम-दाम-दंड-भेद' का अनुकरण करने और एक सम्राट के सत्ता हासिल करने का खाका या योजना बनाने के लिए जाना जाता है। लेकिन शाह दार्शनिक नहीं है। इससे कहीं दूर, धमकियों, प्रलोभनों और ताकत के दम पर चुनावी राजनीति के विशेषज्ञ और बारीकी से प्रबंधन करने वाले हैं। प्रधानमंत्री के सबसे खास और भाजपा के राजनीतिक दिमाग के तौर पर शाह ही थे जिनसे उनके गुरु, और मार्गदर्शक के लिए 400 सीट के वादे को पूरा करने की उम्मीद थी।

हालांकि 'मिशन-400' के लिए भाजपा का नारा, 'अबकी बार, चार सौ पार' शाह ने नहीं गढ़ा था, हकीकत में तो वे इससे नाराज़ बताए जाते थे। एक व्यावहारिक राजनेता, नामुमकिन सी उम्मीदें बढ़ाने के पक्ष में नहीं थे। उनका मानना था कि 'चार सौ पार का कोई मतलब नहीं है, जब तक कि हम कोई ठोस वादा नहीं कर पाएं।' यह नारा जनवरी 2024 की शुरुआत में भारतीय जनता पार्टी के वरिष्ठ पदाधिकारियों और मुख्यमंत्रियों की बैठक में रखा गया था, इस बैठक में गृहमंत्री शाह मौजूद नहीं थे। चुनावी वर्ष की तैयारियों के लिए बुलाई गई बैठक की अध्यक्षता पार्टी के राष्ट्रीय अध्यक्ष जगत प्रकाश नड्डा ने की थी। मिलनसार, मध्यम श्रेणी के नेता नड्डा अब अचानक ताकतवर हो गए थे। बैठक में कई नेताओं ने 'अबकी बार, चार सौ पार' को लेकर बात की। 'यह चुनाव मोदी जी के नेतृत्व में इतिहास रचने के लिए होना चाहिए। हमने पिछली बार तिहरा शतक लगाया था, तो इस बार चार सौ का लक्ष्य रखा जाना चाहिए,' यह प्रस्ताव था। इस आइडिया को तुरंत समर्थन मिला। बैठक में मौजूद लोगों में असम के मुख्यमंत्री हिमंता बिस्वा सरमा भी थे। कांग्रेस से आए सरमा अब मोदी के सबसे उत्साही समर्थक हैं और गृहमंत्री के करीबी सहयोगी माने जाते हैं। क्या सरमा उन लोगों में से थे जिन्होंने 400 का लक्ष्य रखा था? उन्होंने नकारते हुए कहा, 'नहीं, नहीं, मैं किसी नंबर में नहीं पड़ता, मैं सिर्फ असम और पूर्वोत्तर में ज़्यादा से ज़्यादा सीटें जीतना चाहता था।'

दिलचस्प बात यह है कि आम चुनावों के नतीजों के बाद कोई भी चार सौ पार अभियान की नाकामी की ज़िम्मेदारी लेने को तैयार नहीं था। हालांकि उस समय इसे दिमाग पर छा जाने वाली लहर माना गया था। मानो इशारे पर, चापलूसी करने वाले टीवी चैनलों ने इस नारे को उठा लियाः पूरे शोर के साथ प्राइम टाइम बहस इस पर की जाने लगीं, जिनमें 400-प्लस के नारे का समर्थन किया जा रहा था।

चुनाव से पहले बढ़ते उत्साह के माहौल में, मैंने गृहमंत्री शाह से बातचीत की। मैंने पूछा, 'अमित भाई, क्या यह 400 पार का नारा कुछ हद तक "जुमला" है?' अनौपचारिक बातचीत को शुरू करने के लिए शायद यह ग़लत सवाल था, खासकर ऐसे राजनेता के लिए, जिसे 'सेक्यूलर' पत्रकार से नफरत है। 2015 में, भाजपा अध्यक्ष रहे शाह ने पहली बार एक साक्षात्कार में 'जुमला' शब्द का इस्तेमाल, मोदी सरकार की उन विफलता के बचाव के लिए किया था, जो विदेशों में जमा काले धन को देश में वापस लाने के बाद हर बैंक खाते में 15 लाख रुपये डालने का वादा किया गया था, और उसे पूरा करने में भाजपा नाकाम रही थी। शाह ने तब, उसे एक 'चुनावी जुमला' कहा था। यह शब्द सरकार को परेशान करता रहा और विपक्ष को इसका फायदा उठाने का मौका मिल गया। शाह को मेरा सवाल शायद पसंद नहीं आया था। 'आपको हमारे नारे से इतनी परेशानी क्यों हो रही है? उन्होंने कहा, 'मोदी जी के नेतृत्व में हम कहते नहीं, करते हैं।'

लेकिन ये अतिरिक्त नंबर कहां से आएगा? बेफ़िक्री से शाह ने कहा, 'हमने होमवर्क किया है। इस बार चुनावी नतीजे चौंकाने वाले होंगे। मोदी जी की लहर है। ऐसा कोई प्रदेश नहीं हैं, जहां हम अपनी सीटें नहीं बढ़ाएंगे। यहां तक कि पूरे दक्षिण में हम इस बार सीटें जीतेंगे। मणिपुर की दो सीटों को छोड़कर, जिन्हें आप मुश्किल कह सकते हैं, बाकी हर जगह हम बढ़त पर हैं।' मणिपुर की बात अहम थीः राज्य में मई 2023 से, जातीय हिंसा चल रही है, और केन्द्र सरकार पर वहां हो रहे खून-खराबे को रोक पाने की नाकामी की आरोप है।

मैंने बातचीत को उन राज्यों की तरफ ले जाने की कोशिश की, जहां भाजपा को अपने 2019 के प्रदर्शन को दोहराने में चुनौतियों का सामना करना पड़ सकता था। 'अमित भाई, महाराष्ट्र में भाजपा के ख़िलाफ़ विपक्षी गठबंधन बहुत मजबूत दिख रहा है। क्या आपको लगता है कि यहां कुछ सीटों का नुकसान हो सकता है?' मैंने पूछा। 'अरे, आप शरद पवार को बहुत अहमियत देते हो, क्या उन्होंने कभी अपने दम पर महाराष्ट्र जीता है? वे भ्रष्टाचार के "सरगना" हैं, जो सत्ता की सौदेबाजी के लिए स्थानीय क्षत्रपों से गठजोड़ करते हैं। और मैं आपको बता दूं कि उद्धव ठाकरे ने भी हमारे साथ फिर से जुड़ने के संकेत दिए हैं। हमने साफ कर दिया है कि हम उन्हें तब तक वापस नहीं लेंगे, जब तक कि वह 2019 में हमारे साथ संबंध तोड़ने के लिए माफ़ी नहीं मांगते,' शाह ने बेहद आत्मविश्वास के साथ कहा।

गृहमंत्री शाह और पवार-ठाकरे जोड़ी के बीच कभी ज़्यादा प्यार नहीं रहा। पिछले पांच साल के सत्ता के संघर्ष ने महाराष्ट्र की राजनीति को अस्त-व्यस्त कर दिया है। पवार परिवार पहले ही दो हिस्सों में बंट चुका था, चर्चा थी कि अजित पवार की पत्नी सुनेत्रा, शरद पवार की बेटी सुप्रिया सुले के ख़िलाफ़ उनके पारिवारिक गढ़ बारामती से चुनाव लड़ सकती हैं। शाह ने पुष्टि करते हुए कहा, 'हां, यह सही है। जब अजित पिछले साल हमारे साथ आए थे, तभी हमने साफ कर दिया था कि उन्हें यह वादा करना होगा कि वह अपने चाचा से सीधा मुकाबला करने के लिए तैयार रहेंगे, इस बार कोई आधा-अधूरा काम नहीं करेंगे।' इस दावे से शाह ब्रांड की राजनीति को समझा जा सकता है। गृहमंत्री ने कहा, उन्होंने ही बारामती में 'पवार बनाम पवार' चुनावी जंग को आगे बढ़ाया था।

बातचीत में अब थोड़ा जोश नज़र आ रहा था। मैंने अब दूसरे महत्वपूर्ण इलाके, उत्तरप्रदेश का रुख किया, शाह को यहीं से कुशल चुनाव रणनीतिकार की प्रतिष्ठा मिली थीः 2014 के चुनावों में जब भाजपा ने 80 में से 71 सीटें जीती थीं, तब वह उत्तरप्रदेश के प्रभारी थे। इसी से भाजपा को केन्द्र में आने में मदद मिली। शाह ने यहां 'सोशल इंजीनियरिंग' कर जातीय गठबंधन को भाजपा के साथ लाकर राजनीति ही बदल दी। हालांकि 2022 में, योगी आदित्यनाथ या अजय सिंह बिष्ट ने पार्टी को विधानसभा चुनावों में जीत दिलाई। नब्बे के दशक में राम मदिर आंदोलन में सक्रिय कार्यकर्ता के तौर पर, भगवाधारी पुजारी से मुख्यमंत्री बने योगी ने उत्तरप्रदेश में भाजपा की राजनीति को एक नई दिशा दीः हिंदुत्व बहुसंख्यकवाद और धर्म की अपील का इस्तेमाल कर बड़ी जीत हासिल की थी। शाह और योगी के बीच तनातनी की ख़बरें अक्सर आती रहती थीं। दरअसल वर्चस्व के लिए अगली पीढ़ी में लड़ाई की अटकलें चल रही थीं। गृहमंत्री पार्टी की अंदरूनी कलह पर चर्चा को लेकर नाराज़ दिखाई दिए। 'लगता है, आप गॉसिप ज़्यादा सुनते हैं। एक बात जान लीजिए, इस बार हम यूपी में अस्सी में से अस्सी सीटें जीतेंगे!' उन्होंने चुनौती के अंदाज़ में कहा।

बातचीत आगे चल सकती थी, लेकिन शाह के सहयोगियों ने इशारा किया कि उन्हें देर रात की एक और बैठक के लिए निकलना था। मैंने उनसे आखिरी बार धीमे से पूछा कि उन्हें अपने आंकड़ों पर कितना भरोसा था? उनकी निगाहें एक पल के लिए मुझ पर ठहर गईं। चेहरे से डर दिखाना शाह की रणनीति का हिस्सा है, जिसका मकसद विरोधियों को डराकर झुकाना होता है। 'अब 4 जून को बात करेंगे,' उन्होंने जाते-जाते कंधे उचकाते हुए कहा।

उसके बाद मैंने कई बार कोशिश की, लेकिन चुनाव प्रचार के दौरान फिर शाह से मुलाकात नहीं हो पाई। मुझे भाजपा के एक वरिष्ठ पदाधिकारी से उनके खेमे में बदलते मूड की जानकारी मिल रही थी, यह नेता शाह के नियमित संपर्क में थे। मई के आखिर में सातवें और अंतिम दौर के मतदान से ठीक पहले, जब मेरे सूत्र ने गृहमंत्री से मुलाक़ात की, तो शाह में एक अलग तरह

की बेचैनी दिख रही थी। आमतौर पर शाह कुछ घंटों की नींद लेते हैं, देर रात तक फ़ोन पर काम करना और फिर भोर होते ही चुनाव प्रचार के लिए निकल जाना। पदाधिकारी ने बताया, 'उस सुबह मैं जब उनसे मिला, तो लगा कि वे बिल्कुल सोए नहीं थे। आमतौर पर वह सुबह सात बजे पूरी ऊर्जा के साथ होते हैं, लेकिन तब वह थके हुए लग रहे थे और आत्मविश्वास की कमी झलक रही थी।' हर स्तर पर माहौल को समझने के लिए शाह केवल सर्वेक्षणों पर ही भरोसा नहीं करते, उनके पास पार्टी कार्यकर्ताओं से रोज़ाना ज़मीनी स्तर की ख़बर पाने का एक पूरा सिस्टम था। ख़बर उतनी अच्छी नहीं थी, जितनी वह चाहते थे। शाह ने पदाधिकारी को बताया, 'कुछ स्थानीय कारणों से कुछ जगहों पर समस्या है, उस पर नियंत्रण में लाने की कोशिश कर रहे हैं।'

फिर भी कुछ दिन पहले शाह ने इस आशंका को ख़ारिज़ कर दिया था कि भाजपा 272 का आंकड़ा भी पार नहीं कर पाएगी। जब एक साक्षात्कार करने वाले ने पूछा कि बहुमत के आंकड़े तक नहीं पहुंचने की स्थिति में क्या भाजपा के पास कोई 'प्लान-बी' था? तो उन्होंने आत्मविश्वास के साथ जवाब दिया, 'प्लान-बी तब बनाया जाता है जब प्लान-ए के सफल होने की 60 फ़ीसद से कम संभावना हो। मुझे भरोसा है कि प्रधानमंत्री मोदी भारी बहुमत के साथ सत्ता में आएंगे।' शाह के इस चेहरे ने उनकी टीम में बढ़ती बेचैनी को छिपा दिया।

मतगणना के दिन शाह अपने घर, दिल्ली में एक विशाल बगीचे से घिरे बंगले 6-ए, कृष्णा मेनन मार्ग पर नतीजे देखते रहे। 2004 में बड़ी हार के बाद से भाजपा के पहले प्रधानमंत्री अटल बिहारी वाजपेयी इस घर में रहा करते थे। शाह अपनी जीवनसाथी, पत्नी सोनल के साथ बैठे थे, जिन्होंने उनका हर अच्छे-बुरे वक्त में हमेशा साथ दिया। 2010 में जब उन्हें एक 'एक्स्ट्रा-ज्यूडिशियल किलिंग' में शामिल होने के आरोप में जेल भेज दिया गया और दो साल तक गुजरात में नहीं घुसने का आदेश मिला, तब अकेली सोनल उनके साथ मज़बूती से खड़ी थीं। 2014 से शाह के सितारे बुलंदियों पर हैं और हर चुनावी कामयाबी के साथ उनकी प्रतिष्ठा लगातार बढ़ रही है। तो क्या 4 जून को कुछ अलग हो सकता है? दोपहर होते-होते यह साफ हो गया कि स्थानीय कारण परेशान करने से ज़्यादा नुक़सान पहुंचा सकते थे, खासकर उत्तरप्रदेश में। 80 में से 80 जीतने की बात तो भूल जाइए, भाजपा प्रदेश में 'समाजवादी पार्टी-कांग्रेस' गठबंधन से गिनती में पीछे चल रही थी। महाराष्ट्र में भी 'पवार-ठाकरे-कांग्रेस' की तिकड़ी को तोड़ना मुश्किल लग रहा था, जो धीरे-धीरे भाजपा गठबंधन से आगे निकल रही थी। सोनल ने शाह का पसंदीदा दाल-कढ़ी-चावल लंच में तैयार किया था, लेकिन गृहमंत्री ने भूख नहीं होने की बात कर भोजन नहीं किया। उनकी इकलौती भविष्यवाणी सच साबित हुई कि संघर्ष में फंसे मणिपुर में भाजपा हार रही थी। चार सौ पार का नारा आखिरकार एक जुमला साबित हुआ। सपना बिखर गया था।

भाजपा के एक पूर्व रणनीतिकार का कहना था, 'मुझे लगता है कि इस बार गृहमंत्री पर काम का बोझ ज़्यादा था। हर काम वही देख रहे थे, इसमें चुनाव अभियान की रणनीति बनाने से लेकर संगठन के मुद्दों को संभालना, उम्मीदवारों का चुनाव, अंदरूनी मसलों को निपटाना और साथ में स्टार प्रचारक बनना भी शामिल था। नतीजतन उनकी नज़र अपने लक्ष्य से शायद एकबारगी हट गई।' मतदाताओं ने ताकतवर चाणक्य को निराश किया था। भाजपा के चुनावी महानायक के तौर पर शाह के कद को झटका लगा, 2024 उनकी सबसे बड़ी नाकामी साबित हुआ।

═

1989 में नरेन्द्र मोदी गुजरात में भाजपा के सचिव थे, जब पार्टी ने हिमाचल प्रदेश की कांगड़ा घाटी के एक छोटे से शहर पालमपुर में, एक पुराने ज़माने के रोटरी क्लब भवन में, अयोध्या में राम मंदिर निर्माण की मांग का प्रस्ताव पारित किया था। इसे 'पालमपुर घोषणापत्र' कहा गया, इससे भाजपा राम मंदिर आंदोलन के केन्द्र में आ गई और इसे 'भगवान राम' की राजनीतिक पार्टी के तौर पर देखा जाने लगा। सच तो यह है कि एक राजनीतिक पार्टी, प्रमुख पार्टी कांग्रेस के रहते हुए अपना वोट शेयर नहीं बढ़ा पा रही थी, उसने सत्ता तक पहुंचने के लिए एक विवादित मंदिर से जुड़े आंदोलन का फायदा उठाया। इस रास्ते पार्टी ने भारतीय राजनीति और सार्वजनिक विमर्श में हिंदू बहुसंख्यकवाद को सामने रखा। एक साल बाद, 1990 में नरेन्द्र मोदी ने भाजपा नेता और पार्टी के संरक्षक लालकृष्ण आडवाणी की सोमनाथ से अयोध्या की रथयात्रा में अहम भूमिका निभाई, यह उनका राष्ट्रीय राजनीति में पहला महत्वपूर्ण कदम था।

अब आते हैं 22 जनवरी 2024 पर, मोदी अब सिर्फ़ पर्दे के पीछे की भूमिका निभाने वाले या राष्ट्रीय स्वयंसेवक संघ के सिर्फ़ आदेश मानने वाले स्वयंसेवक नहीं रह गए थे। आज वे भारतीय जनता पार्टी के राजनीतिक इतिहास की सबसे महत्वपूर्ण घटना के मुख्य कलाकार, निर्देशक और यजमान थेः अयोध्या में बने नए राम मंदिर में रामलला की मूर्ति का प्राण प्रतिष्ठा समारोह। इस समारोह को हिंदू जागरण और पुनरुत्थान के प्रतीक के तौर पर पेश किया गया। यह बरसों से चल रहे ख़ूनी संघर्ष और हिंदू धर्म के सबसे पूजनीय भगवान में से एक के जन्मस्थान पर मंदिर बनाने के लिए चालाकी से तैयार राजनीतिक आंदोलन का क्लाईमेक्स था। यह 'धार्मिक-राजनीति' की दोपहर में भाजपा के सूर्य के चमकने का वक्त था, और कोई भी सितारा प्रधानमंत्री मोदी से ज़्यादा चमकदार नहीं था।

लेकिन मोदी यहां किस भूमिका में थे? राजनेता? पुजारी? या एक नेता जो अपने विचार या पंथ को बढ़ावा देने के लिए धर्म का इस्तेमाल कर रहा था? या फिर सबकुछ। यह पवित्र समारोह हिंदू मंदिर के उद्घाटन से पहले की एक महत्वपूर्ण रस्म था। धार्मिक प्रतीकवाद को

बड़ी कुशलता से टीवी के लिए बनाए गए तमाशे में बदल दिया गया, प्रधानमंत्री और उनकी टीम ने हर छोटी-बड़ी बारीकियों पर बखूबी से काम किया था। प्राण-प्रतिष्ठा समारोह से पहले प्रधानमंत्री ने ग्यारह दिनों का कठोर 'यम-नियम' अनुष्ठान व्रत भी रखा, जिसमें यजमान के तौर पर अपने कर्तव्यों का पालन करते हुए ज़मीन पर सोना भी शामिल था। मोदी ने अयोध्या जाने से पहले इस दौरान महाराष्ट्र, केरल, आंध्रप्रदेश और तमिलनाडु में पूजा-स्थलों का दौरा करते हुए महत्वपूर्ण मंदिरों में भी पूजा-अर्चना की। मोदी के हर एक्शन, हर कदम को कैमरे में कैद किया गया था और उन तस्वीरों और वीडियों को दूर-दूर तक शेयर किया गया, जिसका मकसद भगवान राम और प्रधानमंत्री के व्यक्तित्व के इर्द-गिर्द देशभर में धार्मिक चेतना जगाना था। भाजपा के एक वरिष्ठ नेता ने पुष्टि की, 'हम न केवल भारतीयों बल्कि दुनिया भर को हिंदू धर्म की भव्यता दिखाना चाहते थे और यह छवि अरबों लोगों तक पहुंचाई जा रही थी। ज़ाहिर है देश के नेता के रूप में प्रधानमंत्री इसके केन्द्र में होंगे।'

उस दिन, प्रधानमंत्री 'देव-राजा' की तरह वेशभूषा में थे, एक सुनहरी कुर्ते के साथ क्रीम धोती और पगड़ी पहनी हुई थी—एक विशेष पहचान वाले परिधान। कैमरे एक बार फिर उन पर टिके रहे। अयोध्या में सात हज़ार से ज्यादा विशिष्ट अतिथि और दुनिया भर में लाखों लोगों के सामने मंदिर के मुख्य पुजारियों के साथ उन्होंने अनुष्ठान किया। यह चुनिंदा लोग श्री रामजन्मभूमि तीर्थ क्षेत्र ट्रस्ट के विशेष आमंत्रित थे। ट्रस्ट का गठन सुप्रीम कोर्ट के नवम्बर 2019 के ऐतिहासिक फ़ैसले के बाद किया गया था। अदालत ने अपने आदेश में कहा कि विवादित भूमि, जिस पर बाबरी मस्जिद थी, उसे राम जन्मभूमि मंदिर के निर्माण की देखरेख का काम भारत सरकार एक ट्रस्ट बनाकर उसे सौंप दे। इस ट्रस्ट में संघ परिवार, खासतौर से विश्व हिन्दू परिषद् से जुड़े सदस्यों का वर्चस्व है। ट्रस्ट के एक अधिकारी ने कहा, 'हम यह सुनिश्चित करना चाहते थे कि मंदिर निर्माण अभियान में शामिल संत-साधु समाज ही नहीं, बल्कि देश के हर क्षेत्र के प्रतिष्ठित लोगों को इसमें शामिल किया जाए, ताकि इसकी विविधता और बढ़ सके।'

कारोबारी दिग्गज मुकेश अंबानी, फ़िल्मी सितारे अमिताभ बच्चन, क्रिकेट सुपर स्टार सचिन तेंदुलकर जैसे लोग भगवाधारी महंतों और साध्वियों के साथ कंधे से कंधा मिलाकर चल रहे थे। चुनिंदा आंवटित विशेष सीटें वीवीआईपी लोगों की मौजूदगी का अहसास कराने के लिए काफी थीं। मशहूर हस्तियों के लिए भी इस निमंत्रण को अस्वीकार करना विकल्प नहीं लग रहा था। मुंबई के एक प्रमुख कारोबारी की तब लंदन में एक ज़रूरी बोर्ड मीटिंग थी। इसके लिए जब उन्होंने कोई बहाना तलाशने की कोशिश की तो उन्हें एक शुभचिंतक का संदेश मिलाः 'यहां नहीं आना एक अच्छा आइडिया नहीं है, मेरे दोस्त। आपकी अनुपस्थिति दर्ज हो जाएगी।' स्पष्ट तौर पर कोई भी सबसे शक्तिशाली मेजबान को नाराज़ नहीं करना चाहता था। 'भय' और 'आस्था' एक ही सिक्के के दो पहलू हैं।

हालांकि, राजनीतिक विरोधियों को ऐसा कोई मलाल या शिकायत नहीं थी। ट्रस्ट ने देश के सभी मान्यता प्राप्त राजनीतिक दलों के प्रमुखों को व्यक्तिगत रूप से आमंत्रित करने का ध्यान रखा था। लेकिन किसी भी दल ने कार्यक्रम में शामिल होने का फैसला नहीं किया। प्रमुख विपक्षी दल कांग्रेस को लगता था कि प्रधानमंत्री को चुनावी फायदा पहुंचाने के लिए ही राम मंदिर कार्यक्रम को इस तरह से तय किया गया था। कांग्रेस के वरिष्ठ नेता दिग्विजय सिंह ने कहा, 'मंदिर अभी पूरी तरह बनकर तैयार नहीं हुआ है, फिर भी प्राण प्रतिष्ठा समारोह इसलिए किया जा रहा है ताकि प्रधानमंत्री मोदी को चुनावों से पहले फोटो खिंचाने का मौका मिल जाए।' मंदिर निर्माण समिति के अध्यक्ष नृपेन्द्र मिश्र ने इस आरोप को ख़ारिज़ किया। प्रधानमंत्री मोदी के प्रधान सचिव रहे मिश्रा ने ज़ोर देकर कहा कि मंदिर ट्रस्ट के सदस्य चाहते थे कि रामलला की प्रतिमा जल्द से जल्द गर्भगृह में प्रतिष्ठित की जाए। मिश्र ने कहा कि '2020 में मैंने ट्रस्ट की जिम्मेदारी संभाली है और हमारा लक्ष्य दिसम्बर 2023 तक मंदिर का उद्घाटन करना था। हमेशा से ही हमारी समय सीमा यही थी, इसका आम चुनावों से कोई लेना-देना नहीं था।' यह सच है कि मंदिर तैयार नहीं हुआ था: सिर्फ़ भूतल का काम पूरा हुआ था, पहली और दूसरी मंज़िल का काम अभी चल रहा था। मिश्र ने कहा कि प्रधानमंत्री कार्यालय (पीएमओ) ने मंदिर योजना पर कभी कोई दख़ल नहीं दिया। मिश्र ने कहा, 'हां, प्रधानमंत्री ने अगस्त 2020 में, भूमिपूजन किया था और अब वे प्राण प्रतिष्ठा समारोह में शामिल हो रहे हैं। आखिरकार वे देश के प्रधानमंत्री हैं, हैं ना?' आज तक भी राम मंदिर निर्माण का काम पूरा नहीं हुआ है और 2024 में राम को लेकर राजनीति भी इसी तरह अधूरी रह गई।

प्रधानमंत्री जब मंदिर समारोह के मुख्य यजमान बने तो 'धार्मिक और लौकिक' के बीच की रेखाएं धुंधली हो गईं, या शायद हमेशा के लिए मिट गईं। हालांकि मोदी ने अपने संबोधन में चुनावी मैदान से दूर रहने की ऐहतियात बरती, लेकिन सांस्कृतिक हिन्दू राष्ट्रवाद की जड़ों पर ज़ोर दिया। 'हमारे रामलला अब टेंट में नहीं रहेंगे, वे अब एक दिव्य मंदिर में रहेंगे। यह राष्ट्रीय चेतना का मंदिर है। राम आस्था हैं, भारत की नींव हैं, भारत का विचार हैं, भारत का क़ानून हैं, भारत की चेतना हैं, और भारत का गौरव हैं,' तालियों की गड़गड़ाहट सुनाई दे रही थी। इस वज़नदार भव्य संबोधन का मकसद मोदी की पीआर छवि को मौजूदा समय के राजनेता-राजा के रूप में प्रतिष्ठित करना था, जो चुनावी समय में राजनीति करते हैं, लेकिन इस वक्त वे हिंदू दार्शनिक हैं। मोदी के साथ मंच पर संघ प्रमुख मोहन भागवत, उत्तरप्रदेश के मुख्यमंत्री योगी आदित्यनाथ, राज्यपाल आनंदी बेन पटेल और मंदिर के पुजारी मौजूद थे, लेकिन उनकी भूमिका सिर्फ सहायक कलाकारों जैसी थी। केन्द्र के किसी भी मंत्री को आमंत्रित नहीं किया गया था; बल्कि उन्हें बाद में किसी उपयुक्त तिथि पर दर्शन के लिए कहा गया। यहां तक कि देश के सबसे अमीर और शक्तिशाली मौजूदा अतिथि भी, जो ज़्यादातर मोदी के

'चीयरलीडर्स' ही थे, समारोह को बड़ी टीवी स्क्रीन पर ही देख रहे थे। जब मोदी ने भगवान राम को दंडवत प्रणाम किया, तो भारतीय वायुसेना के विमानों ने ऊपर से पुष्प वर्षा की। कैमरे की नज़र सिर्फ़ एक व्यक्ति पर थीः यह 'एक नेता, एक राष्ट्र' जैसा क्षण था, जिसे ब्रांड मोदी को राम-राज्य के चेहरे के रूप में बढ़ावा देने के लिए तैयार किया गया था। धर्म का इस्तेमाल निरंकुश राजनीतिक पंथ के लिए किया गया।

कुछ दिनों बाद भारतीय जनता पार्टी के आंतरिक ट्रैकर पोल ने बताया कि हिंदुओं के एक बड़े हिस्से में राम मंदिर निर्माण को लेकर भावनाएं प्रबल थीं और प्रधानमंत्री की लोकप्रियता 70 फीसदी से ज़्यादा हो गई थी। सी-वोटर के *इंडिया टुडे* 'मूड ऑफ द नेशन' में कहा गया कि भाजपा अपने दम पर 304 सीटें जीत सकती थी, जो पिछले 2019 के चुनाव के आंकड़े 303 से एक ज़्यादा था। जब यह पूछा गया कि लोगों ने प्रधानमंत्री को किस चीज़ के लिए सबसे ज़्यादा याद रखा, तो 42 फ़ीसद लोगों के लिए राम मंदिर निर्माण मुद्दा था, तो 19 फ़ीसदी मानते थे कि मोदी की वजह से दुनिया में भारत का कद बढ़ा था। सी-वोटर पोलस्टर यशवंत देशमुख का कहना था, 'यह लोगों का प्रधानमंत्री पर भरोसा है, सिर्फ़ राम मंदिर ही नहीं दूसरे कई मुद्दे भी इसकी वजह हैं।'

दरअसल मंदिर समारोह के साथ नौ महीनों तक का वह व्यस्त समय पूरा हुआ, जब मोदी हर जगह मौजूद थे, यहां तक कि उनके समर्थकों की नज़र में चांद तक भी। 23 अगस्त 2023 को चंद्रयान-3 मिशन, चांद पर सफलतापूर्वक उतरा, जिससे भारत दुनिया का वह चौथा देश बन गया, जिसने इकतालीस दिनों के सफ़र के बाद चांद की सतह पर सॉफ्ट लैंडिंग की तकनीक में महारत हासिल की। उस समय प्रधानमंत्री जोहान्सबर्ग में ब्रिक्स शिखर सम्मेलन में हिस्सा ले रहे थे, लेकिन जैसे ही लैंडर उतरा, मोदी वीडियो-कॉन्फ्रेंस के जरिए तिरंगा लहराते हुए इस जश्न में शामिल हो गए। जब तक बेंगलुरु में भारतीय अंतरिक्ष अनुसंधान संगठन (इसरो) के मुख्यालय में उत्साहित वैज्ञानिकों तक कैमरा पहुंचता, इससे पहले ही प्रधानमंत्री फिर से केन्द्र में थे, 'हम नए भारत की उड़ान के गवाह हैं, नया इतिहास लिखा गया है। हालांकि इस वक्त मैं ब्रिक्स शिखर सम्मेलन के लिए दक्षिण अफ्रीका में हूं, लेकिन मेरा दिल और आत्मा भारत में थी,' मोदी ने जोश के साथ कहा। यह पूरी तरह से कोरियोग्राफ कार्यक्रम था, लाखों भारतीय लाइव टेलीकास्ट पर अपने सर्वोच्च नेता को देख रहे थे। मोदी ने घोषणा की, जिस जगह विक्रम मून लैंडर उतरा है, उसे 'शिव-शक्ति' कहा जाएगा। संदेश का मकसद पूरा हो गया था। केन्द्रीय विज्ञान और प्रौद्योगिकी मंत्री डॉ. जितेन्द्र सिंह ने इस आलोचना को ख़ारिज़ किया, मोदी ने देश के अंतरिक्ष वैज्ञानिकों के इस गौरवशाली क्षण को हाईजैक कर लिया। डॉ. सिंह ने कहा, 'देखिए यह भारत के लिए विशेष अवसर था और राष्ट्र के नेता के रूप में प्रधानमंत्री मोदी जी स्वाभाविक रूप से इस खुशी को साझा करने के लिए मौजूद रहना चाहते थे।' उन्होंने अंतरिक्ष

अनुसंधान क्षेत्र के लिए एक बेहतर माहौल बनाने का श्रेय प्रधानमंत्री को दिया, जिनके कार्यकाल में 200 से ज़्यादा स्टार्ट-अप को तेज़ी से आगे बढ़ते देखा गया है।

कुछ हफ्ते बाद, सितंबर 2023 की शुरुआत में, प्रधानमंत्री मोदी नई दिल्ली में जी-20 शिखर सम्मेलन के मेजबान के रूप में फिर से आकर्षण का केन्द्र थे। हर फोटो-ऑप को ध्यान से तैयार किया गया था, प्रसिद्ध कोणार्क मंदिर के पहिए की प्रतिकृति के आगे दुनिया के नेताओं का स्वागत करते प्रधानमंत्री से लेकर दिल्ली के प्रमुख प्रगति मैदान में हाल में ही अनावरण किए गए भारत मंडपम के भव्य मंच तक। एक और अहम कार्यक्रम दिल्ली की भीगी सुबह में हुआ, जब जी-20 के नेता प्रतिष्ठित राजघाट पर महात्मा गांधी की समाधि पर इकट्ठा हुए: तस्वीरें अंतराष्ट्रीय स्तर पर बेहतरीन मार्केटिंग का अवसर थीं। वरिष्ठ नौकरशाह और जी-20 शेरपा अमिताभ कांत ने कहा, 'मुझे लगता है कि इससे हम दुनिया में चल रहे संघर्षों के बीच शांति का एक शक्तिशाली संदेश भेजने में कामयाब हुए।'

एक और स्पष्ट संदेश था: 'ब्रांड मोदी यानी ब्रांड इंडिया'। देश भर में हजारों जी-20 बैनर और होर्डिंग्स पर केवल मोदी का मुस्कुराता हुआ चेहरा था। ऑनलाइन पोर्टल *न्यूज़लॉन्ड्री* के एक रिपोर्टर ने इंदिरागांधी अंतरराष्ट्रीय हवाई अड्डे से नई दिल्ली में आलीशान आईटीसी मौर्या और ताज पैलेस होटलों तक 12 किलोमीटर की सड़क पर कम से कम 963 जी-20 प्रचार पोस्टर या होर्डिंग्स की गिनती की थी। इन जगहों पर विदेशी मेहमानों को ठहराया गया था। सभी होर्डिंग्स पर केवल मोदी की तस्वीर थी। कोई दूसरे अंतरराष्ट्रीय राष्ट्राध्यक्ष का चेहरा नहीं दिखाई दिया। तो क्या अमेरिकी राष्ट्रपति चुनाव प्रचार की शैली में, जी-20 मूल रूप से 2024 के लिए 'मोदी अभियान' था? 'यह मत भूलिए कि पिछले नौ महीनों में देश के हर राज्य में जी-20 की कुल 200 बैठकें सफलतापूर्वक आयोजित की गईं, चाहे फिर वे भाजपा-शासित राज्य रहे हों या विपक्षी पार्टियों की सरकारों वाले प्रदेश। हमारा फोकस हर चीज़ से ऊपर भारत के नेतृत्व का था। प्रधानमंत्री के रूप में, स्वाभाविक तौर पर मोदी को एक वैश्विक नेता के रूप में पेश किया गया,' कांत का जवाब था।

मोदी को विश्व गुरु या वैश्विक नेता के रूप में स्थापित करने का यह जुनून इस स्तर पर पहुंच गया था, जहां विदेश मंत्रालय केवल मोदी की प्रचार मशीन की तरह काम कर रहा था। एक पूर्व राजनयिक ने स्वीकार किया कि 'विदेश मंत्रालय ने हमसे यह सुनिश्चित करने के लिए कहा था कि जिन देशों में हम तैनात हैं, वहां के राजनेता ट्वीट करें और यथासंभव प्रधानमंत्री की तारीफ करें। यहां तक कि ट्वीट के इस्तेमाल में आने वाले संदेश भी पहले से भेजे गए थे।' लेकिन कई बार ये पहले से तैयार अभियान योजना के मुताबिक काम नहीं करते। उदाहरण के लिए, जब 2019 का चन्द्रयान मिशन फेल हो गया, तो राजनयिक मुश्किल में पड़ गए। उन्होंने पहले से ही दुनिया भर के देशों की राजधानियों से भारत की उपलब्धियों और मोदी की प्रशंसा

के वीडियो संदेश और ट्वीट रिकॉर्ड कर लिए थे। जब सॉफ्टवेयर की गड़बड़ी के कारण लैंडर दुर्घटनाग्रस्त हो गया, तो संदेशों को अंतिम समय में जल्दबाज़ी में रोकना पड़ा। 'हम रातभर इन संदेशों को हटाने का काम करते रहे,' पूर्व राजनयिक ने हंसते हुए बताया। प्रवासी कार्यक्रमों से लेकर पुरस्कार समारोहों के आयोजनों की व्यवस्था छोड़कर, राजनयिकों को मोदी के लिए विदेश नीति पर जुटना पड़ा।

अचानक, *इंडिया टुडे* ने पत्रिका के 2023 के सालाना अंक में मोदी को अपना 'न्यूज़मेकर ऑफ द ईयर' चुना। इस चुनाव पर संपादकीय निदेशक और वरिष्ठ पत्रकार राज चेंगप्पा ने लिखा, 'हिंदू पौराणिक कथाओं के देवताओं की तरह, वह कई अवतारों में रहते हैं, जिनमें से कुछ 2023 में सामने आए और उन्हें उस वक्त का सबसे महत्वपूर्ण शख्स बनाया। वह 2023 को अपने सबसे उल्लेखनीय साल के तौर पर देख सकते हैं, भले ही दुनिया के ज़्यादा नेताओं के लिए यह भयानक साल रहा हो... 2023 में यह "मोदी का समय" है, और "मोदी है तो मुमकिन है"।'

आने वाले चुनावी तूफान की तैयारी कर ली गई थी: मोदी सिर्फ एक आम राजनेता नहीं थे। वह इन सबसे ऊपर हैं, स्वयं 'भगवान का अवतार'। 2024 की चुनावी जंग की रूपरेखा तैयार हो चुकी थी। विपक्षी दलों को दबाता एक शानदार और बेहतरीन तरीके से प्रचारित नायक खड़ा था, जो हमेशा मीडिया की नज़रों में चमकता रहता था। 2024 के लिए मोदी का 'विजय रथ' तैयार था, लेकिन 2004 के 'इंडिया शाइनिंग' के नाकाम अभियान जैसा नहीं था।

═

> 'पहले जब तक मां ज़िंदा थी, मुझे लगता था कि मुझे बॉयोलॉजिकली जन्म दिया गया है। मां के जाने के बाद, सारे अनुभवों को मैं जोड़कर देखता हूं तो मैं मान चुका हूं कि परमात्मा ने मुझे भेजा है।'
>
> —प्रधानमंत्री मोदी, *न्यूज़-18* को साक्षात्कार, 14 मई 2024

खुद को 'ईश्वर का दूत' बताने या 'नॉन-बॉयोलॉजिकल' की यह टिप्पणी प्रधानमंत्री मोदी ने उस दिन की, जब वह वाराणसी से अपना नामांकन दाखिल कर रहे थे। सात चरणों वाले आम चुनाव में वाराणसी में अंतिम चरण में मतदान हो रहा था। सेट सुंदर था: गंगा के ऐतिहासिक घाटों की पृष्ठभूमि में नाव की सवारी। ठीक दस साल पहले, मोदी ने हिंदू धर्म के सबसे पवित्र और पुरातन शहर और तीर्थस्थल वाराणसी से चुनाव लड़ने का फ़ैसला करके राष्ट्रीय राजनीति में नाटकीय एंट्री ली थी। 'मां गंगा ने बुलाया है,' मोदी के इस आकर्षक वन-लाइनर ने एक धर्मनिष्ठ हिन्दू के रूप में उनकी स्थिति को और मज़बूत किया था।

एक चापलूस प्रशंसक की तरह, साक्षात्कार करने वाली पत्रकार ने प्रधानमंत्री से उनकी असीम ऊर्जा का रहस्य बताने के लिए कहा, जो समय के साथ बढ़ रही है। जवाबः 'भगवान ने मुझे भेजा है।' यह अचानक आई, सहज टिप्पणी नहीं थी, जैसा कि बाद में पता चला। उसी दिन, एक और टीवी साक्षात्कार में प्रधानमंत्री अपने व्यक्तित्व की तुलना भगवान कृष्ण से करते-करते भावुक हो गए, लोककथा में चंचल और प्यारे बच्चे के रूप में और फिर महाभारत में अर्जुन के सलाहकार के रूप में। फिर कुछ दिनों बाद *न्यूज़-24* के साक्षात्कार में मोदी ने कहा, 'भगवान ने मुझे किसी खास काम के लिए यहां भेजा है, किसी खास उद्देश्य से। और इस उद्देश्य की प्राप्ति के लिए वह, शिक्षा, दिशा, क्षमता, ऊर्जा और प्रेरणा देता है... इसे दिव्य शक्ति कहें या ईश्वरीय शक्ति, उसके बिना यह सब संभव नहीं है।'

क्या यह एक कथित तानाशाह का दैवीय होने का पागलपन लिए भ्रम है? या फिर एक चतुर राजनेता का धार्मिक पंथ के नेता की छवि गढ़कर धर्म-परायण मतदाताओं को प्रभावित करने की कोशिश? 'दोनों ही,' आशीष नंदी ने कहा। डॉ. नंदी हमारे देश के बुद्धिमान और प्रमुख समाजशास्त्रियों में से एक हैं, जिनकी 90 के दशक में एक उभरते युवा राजनेता के रूप में मोदी से कुछ समय के लिए मुलाक़ात हुई थी। नंदी का मानना है कि मोदी का बार-बार भगवान का ज़िक्र करना एक आत्मप्रशंसा मानसिकता को बताता है। 'यह आत्मप्रशंसा सभी सत्ता में बैठे नेताओं का सामान्य गुण है, जो मानते हैं कि उन्हें दुनिया को बचाने के लिए लाया गया है, यहां तक कि वे जिस तरह लगातार अपने कपड़े बदलते हैं, नए जैकेट्स और ब्रांडेड एक्सेसरीज़ दिखाते हैं, वह सब यह दिखाने के लिए होता है कि वह एक सुप्रीम लीडर हैं। यह एक भव्य, अच्छी तरह से तैयार किया गया प्रदर्शन है, जिसका मक़सद उन्हें बाकी सबसे अलग करना है,' वह कहते हैं।

ख़ास मक़सद यह बताना है कि मोदी विश्वास, जादू और चमत्कारों से शासन करते हैं, वह सिर्फ़ एक ऐसे राजनेता भर नहीं है, जो चुनाव जीत जाते हैं। द *रिवेंज ऑफ पावर* के लेखक मोइसेस नाइम लिखते हैं कि ऐसे निरंकुश लोग इक्कीसवीं सदी के लिए राजनीति को फिर से रच रहे हैं, अपने समर्थकों के लिए। 'एक निरंकुश शासक के लिए सत्ता बनाए रखने की यह एक चाल है, अपने समर्थकों के लिए नेता से ज़्यादा वे अपने प्रशंसकों के लिए स्टार बन जाते हैं।' मोदी भी इस प्रशंसकों की राजनीति के लाभार्थी हैं, जो सर्वज्ञ और सर्वव्यापी हैं।

खास बात यह है कि उनके लिए जुनूनी हद तक खुद से ही प्रेम करना, कोई नई बात नहीं है। खुद को 'भगवान का दूत' बताना या खुद के बारे में किसी तीसरे व्यक्ति (थर्ड पर्सन) ('मोदी की गारंटी') में बात करना या फिर अंतहीन फोटों खिंचाने का सिलसिला, यह सब गुजरात के मुख्यमंत्री के दिनों से चली आ रही उनकी शख्सियत का हिस्सा है। मोदी पर विस्तार से जीवनी लिखने वाले नीलांजन मुखोपाध्याय याद करते हैं कि 2012 में उन्होंने उनसे जब पूछा था कि राज्य में बिजली सुधारों के लिए ज्योतिग्राम योजना का विचार उन्हें कहां से आया, तो मोदी ने

जवाब दिया, 'देखिए, कभी-कभी मुझे लगता है कि यह भगवान की देन है कि मैं अपने विचारों को एक्शन में बदल पाता हूं।' जब मुखोपाध्याय ने उनसे उनके किशोर अवस्था के दिनों के बारे में पूछा, जिसके बारे में कहा जाता है कि उन्होंने हिमालय में बिताया था, तो मोदी ने रहस्यपूर्ण अंदाज़ में जवाब दियाः 'कभी-कभी लगता है कि मैं इस भौतिक दुनिया में आया ही नहीं हूं।' मुखोपाध्याय कहते हैं कि 'मुझे लगता है कि मोदी ने खुद को भी यह यकीन दिला दिया है कि वे ईश्वर की दिव्य संतान हैं।' सितंबर 2023 में, संसद में जब महिला आरक्षण विधेयक पारित हुआ, तो मोदी ने बड़े गर्व से कहा, 'शायद भगवान ने मुझे महिलाओं को सशक्त बनाने के इस पवित्र कार्य के लिए चुना है।' दिव्य होने का दावा करना, रोज़ाना की जवाबदेही से बचने, क़ानून से ऊपर होने और जनता के सवालों से ऊपर होने का एक रास्ता है। यह इक्कीसवीं सदी के निरंकुश शासक की रणनीति है।

'मोदी पंथ' के अनुयायियों की अंध भक्ति से इस 'देवत्व' को बढ़ावा मिलता है। अगर इंदिरा गांधी अपने वफादारों (चमचों) से घिरी रहती थीं, तो मोदी भी अपने भक्तों या चापलूसों से घिरे हुए हैं। एक अधिकारी ने प्रधानमंत्री की अप्रवासी भारतीयों के एक समूह से मुलाकात को याद किया, इस प्रतिनिधिमंडल के प्रमुख मोदी को भगवान 'विष्णु का अवतार' बताते रहे। अधिकारी ने बताया कि 'उन्हें रोकने के बजाय, प्रधानमंत्री की मुस्कुराहट उस पर सहमति जता रही थी।' श्रीरामजन्मभूमि तीर्थ ट्रस्ट के सचिव चंपत राय की राय भी करीब-करीब यही थी। उन्होंने कहा कि 'हिंदू धर्म में देश के राजा को विष्णु का दर्जा दिया जाता है।' उन्होंने कहा, 'प्रधानमंत्री मोदी हमारे सर्वसम्मत नेता हैं, कोई आम आदमी नहीं।'

ईश्वर के चुने हुए या फिर एक कुशल राजनेता, हर वक्त अपने पर ध्यान केन्द्रित करने के लिए, अलग-अलग जगहों पर अपनी तस्वीरें खिंचाने में लगे रहते हैं। फिर चाहे चीतों को जंगल में छोड़ना हो, सरदार पटेल की विशाल प्रतिमा के सामने पोज देना हो, या ओलंपिक पदक विजेताओं के साथ खुश दिखना हो, मोदी सबसे ज़्यादा फोटो खिंचाने वाले भारतीय राजनेता होंगे। एक पूर्व सहयोगी ने टिप्पणी की, मुझे नहीं पता कि 'मोदी ने सेल्फी की खोज की या सेल्फी ने उन्हें खोजा, लेकिन उन्हें इस बात की पूरी समझ है कि कौन सा कैमरा एंगल बेहतर होगा।' यहां तक कि दुनिया के दूसरे नेता भी मोदी के इस फोटो जुनून से वाकिफ़ हैं और प्रधानमंत्री की इस आदत का फायदा उठाते हैं। महाबलीपुरम में भारत-चीन शिखर सम्मेलन में, राष्ट्रपति शी जिनपिंग ने मोदी की तस्वीर वाली एक पॉर्सिलिन प्लेट भेंट की, यह उनके लिए हर हिसाब से एक बहुमूल्य स्मृति चिन्ह था!

जनवरी 2024 में जब प्रधानमंत्री ने मुंबई के अटल सेतु ट्रांस-हार्बर ब्रिज का उद्घाटन किया, तो आधिकारिक वीडियो में पुल पर मोदी को अलग-अलग एंगल से दंबगई से चलते दिखाया गया—सिर्फ़ अकेले। दूसरे खास मेहमान उसमें नज़र नहीं आ रहे थे। महाराष्ट्र सरकार के एक

अधिकारी ने कहा, 'यह देश का सबसे लंबा समुद्री पुल है, जिसमें महाराष्ट्र सरकार के और हमारे उपमुख्यमंत्री देवेन्द्र फड़नवीस ने अहम भूमिका निभाई, लेकिन जब सबसे महत्वपूर्ण क्षण था, तो कैमरा केवल एक व्यक्ति पर फोकस था।'

लेकिन यह कोई एक मामला नहीं था। मई 2023 में, संसद के नए भवन का उद्घाटन किया गया। भवन अभी पूरी तरह तैयार नहीं था, यह किसी बेजान हवाई अड्डे के प्रस्थान लाउंज और किसी बेस्वाद पांच सितारा होटल लॉबी जैसा लग रहा था। विपक्षी राजनेताओं ने इसका मजाक उड़ाते हुए इसे 'द मोदी मैरियट' कहा। संसद की पुरानी इमारत का खुलापन, भव्यता और प्राचीनता इसमें गायब थी। विपक्षी राजनेताओं और सांसदों के मिलने-बैठने की खास जगह सेन्ट्रल हॉल जैसी कोई जगह नई इमारत में नहीं है। सेन्ट्रल हॉल में ही पहले प्रधानमंत्री जवाहरलाल नेहरु ने अपना मशहूर 'फ्रीडम एट मिडनाइट' का भाषण दिया था। शायद मोदी चाहते थे कि जल्दबाजी में तैयार इस इमारत को ऐसे ही डिज़ाइन किया जाए। एक किले जैसा भद्दा लगता स्मारक, जो सीमित जगह में बनाया गया है, उसमें लोकतंत्र की समावेशी भावना वाले मंदिर जैसा कुछ नहीं है। महत्वपूर्ण बात यह है कि राष्ट्रपति को नए भवन के उद्घाटन करने या समारोह में शामिल होने के लिए निमंत्रण नहीं भेजा गया, इस कारण से विपक्ष ने उस समारोह का बहिष्कार किया। जब विपक्ष के एक सांसद ने इस पर संसद सचिवालय के अधिकारी से स्पष्टीकरण मांगा तो बताया गया कि 'इसमें किसी नियम का उल्लंघन नहीं किया गया है, यह फ़ैसला सरकार के विवेक पर होता है।' ज़ाहिर है कि प्रधानमंत्री के नाम से निमंत्रण-पत्र पहले से तैयार किए गए थे, इसमें फिर से विचार की संभावना को ख़ारिज़ कर दिया गया।

इस समारोह की जब तस्वीर जारी की गई, तो उसमें प्रधानमंत्री के साथ फ्रेम में इकलौती कैबिनेट मंत्री निर्मला सीतारमण थीं, लेकिन वह भी हाशिए पर थीं। मंत्रिमंडल के दूसरे सहयोगियों के साथ सुर्खियों को साझा करने के बजाय मोदी भगवा पहने पुजारियों के साथ दिख रहे थे, जो संसद के अंदर समारोह के मुख्य अतिथि थेः भगवा रंग से ज़्यादा धार्मिक आयोजन ने मानो लोकतांत्रिक परपंराओं और मानदंडों का अपहरण कर लिया था। एक मंत्री ने हंसते हुए कहा, 'मैं इस ऐतिहासिक अवसर के लिए तैयार होकर आया, लेकिन कैमरे हमारी तरफ नहीं देख रहे थे।' आह, हां! मूविंग कैमरे का जादुई भ्रम, एक चुने हुए नेता की अच्छी तरह गढ़ी छवि से दूर नहीं होता। आश्चर्य नहीं होना चाहिए कि पीएमओ के पास एक इन-हाउस बड़ा टीवी प्रोडक्शन क्रू है जो हर समय अपने नेता पर नज़र रखता है। 'मोदी-कैम' 24×7 हमेशा उनके साथ है। इसकी हर वक्त मौजूदगी भक्त जनता को सम्मोहित करने के लिए डिज़ाइन की गई है।

सुर्खियां पाने के लिए मोदी का इवेंट मैनेजमेंट कौशल लंबे समय से काम कर रहा है। वरिष्ठ पत्रकार शीला भट्ट अस्सी के दशक में गुजरात के एक चुनाव अभियान को याद करती हैं, जब मोदी प्रदेश के उभरते हुए युवा नेता थे। कांग्रेस के वर्चस्व वाले इस राज्य में भाजपा

अक्सर मीडिया कवरेज नहीं होने की शिकायत करती थी। 'मुझे याद है कि कैसे मोदी ने एक बार सुझाया कि पार्टी राज्य की सभी 182 विधानसभा सीटों पर चुनाव अभियान शुरू करने के लिए अहमदाबाद के एक बड़े मैदान में रंग-बिरंगे 182 रथ इकट्ठा करें। इसके बड़े खर्च को लेकर पार्टी के दूसरे नेता इसके लिए तैयार नहीं थे, लेकिन मोदी अड़े रहे। निश्चित रूप से, अगले दिन अखबारों के फ्रंट पेज पर रथों के जमावड़े की तस्वीर थी। मोदी को लीक से हटकर और बड़ा सोचना पसंद है। उनके लिए सबकुछ एक भव्य 70-मिमी फ़िल्म की तरह होना चाहिए।'

इससे समझा जा सकता है कि मोदी क्यों 'अबकी बार चार सौ पार' के नारे के लिए तुरंत तैयार हो गए, क्योंकि यह सबकी नज़रों में आने के लिए एक अच्छी हेडलाइन या नारा था। जब जनवरी 2024 में, भाजपा की बैठक में पहली बार 400 पार का नारा सुझाया गया, तो सब लोग इसके पक्ष में नहीं थे। कुछ लोगों को संदेह था कि आत्मसंतुष्टि का यह नारा उल्टा भी पड़ सकता था। लेकिन उत्साहित मोदी ने इसे तुरंत मंज़ूरी दे दी और सभी संदेहों को दूर कर दिया। प्रधानमंत्री मोदी को लगा कि 'चार सौ पार' से एक साथ कई मकसद पूरे हो जाएंगे। यह नारा पार्टी मशीनरी को 2019 की तुलना में ज़्यादा सीटें हासिल करने के लिए उत्साहित करेगा, साथ ही कमज़ोर विपक्ष को हतोत्साहित भी करेगा। इससे इतर एक अनकही महत्वाकांक्षा भी थी ऐसा लक्ष्य हासिल करने की, जो इससे पहले केवल एक बार हुआ था: 1984 में तब अपनी मां इंदिरा गांधी की हत्या से उपजी सहानुभूति लहर पर सवार होकर राजीव गांधी ने रिकॉर्ड 414 सीटें जीती थीं। भाजपा के एक नेता ने माना, 'प्रधानमंत्री हमेशा खुद की तुलना नेहरू-गांधी परिवार से करते हैं और हर समय उनसे आगे निकलना चाहते हैं।' नेहरू-गांधी प्रेमी मोदी के लिए राजीव गांधी के रिकॉर्ड को तोड़ना एक आकर्षक संभावना थी।

भाजपा के चुनावी युद्ध का बिगुल फूंकने के लिए प्रधानमंत्री ने फरवरी के पहले सप्ताह में संसद का मंच चुना। जैसे ही उन्होंने 'अबकी बार' कहा, भाजपा सांसदों ने मेजें थपथपाते हुए ज़ोर से कहा, 'चार सौ पार'। यह एक और अच्छी तरह से कोरियोग्राफ की गई कोशिश थी, जिसका मकसद मोदी के नेतृत्व में भाजपा के अजेय होने की तस्वीर पेश करना था। प्रधानमंत्री ने इस चार सौ पार की कथा में अपना ट्विस्ट भी दिया। उन्होंने घोषणा की, 'ना केवल एनडीए को चार सौ से ज़्यादा सीटें मिलेंगी, बल्कि मुझे विश्वास है कि इस देश के लोग भाजपा को 370 से ज़्यादा सीटें देंगे।' 370 का आंकड़ा विशेष महत्व रखता है। अगस्त 2019 में जम्मू कश्मीर से अनुच्छेद 370 को रद्द करना भाजपा के लिए एक महत्वपूर्ण कामयाबी थी, यह भाजपा की विचारधारा और लंबे समय से चल रहे एजेंडा की जीत थी। मोदी ने कांग्रेस का मज़ाक उड़ाते हुए कहा कि अब तो उसके अध्यक्ष मल्लिकार्जुन खड़गे भी चार सौ पार के नारे में शामिल हो गए थे। सच तो यह है कि खड़गे ने अपने भाषण में भाजपा के इस ऊंचे लक्ष्य पर तंज के लिए यह नारा दोहराया था। लेकिन पार्टी की सक्रिय सोशल मीडिया टीम ने विपक्षी नेता की

टिप्पणियों को चालाकी से संपादित करते हुए दिखाया कि वे भी भाजपा के चार सौ पार के नारे को दोहरा रहे थे।

तो क्या भाजपा नेतृत्व ने अपने अंहकार में 'चार सौ पार' को पार्टी का 2024 का चुनावी कार्ड बना दिया था? दिलचस्प यह है कि भाजपा के एक पोल सर्वेक्षक ने बताया कि फरवरी के मध्य में उनके ट्रैकर पोल में पार्टी को 300 के आसपास दिखाया गया था, जो कहीं से 400 के करीब नहीं था। पोल सर्वेक्षक का कहना था, 'मुझे लगता है कि भाजपा नेताओं को भी पता था कि 400 सीटें हासिल नहीं की जा सकतीं, लेकिन वे इसे सार्वजनिक तौर पर स्वीकार करने को तैयार नहीं थे।' लेकिन मुख्यधारा के चापलूस मीडिया ने 'चार सौ पार' के प्रचार को पूरी तरह से अपना लिया, जबकि अंदरूनी सर्वेक्षण रिपोर्ट को इसका भरोसा नहीं था। फरवरी के आखिर में, प्रधानमंत्री ने मध्यप्रदेश में पार्टी कार्यकर्ताओं के एक कार्यक्रम में इस कहानी को एक और मोड़ दे दिया। मोदी ने दावा किया, 'अबकी बार, चार सौ पार का नारा, पार्टी ने नहीं जनता ने गढ़ा है। आज हर जगह एक ही बात सुनाई दे रही हैः अबकी बार, चार सौ पार। ऐसा पहली बार हुआ है कि जनता ने खुद अपनी पसंद की सरकार को फिर से लाने के लिए यह नारा दिया है। यह भाजपा ने नहीं दिया है,' उन्होंने घोषणा की।

टीम मोदी ने खुद को आश्वस्त कर लिया था कि 'चार सौ पार' के नारे की गूंज दूर तक सुनाई दे रही थी। कई राज्यों में मज़बूत विपक्ष की संभावना जताने वाले ज़मीनी स्तर के फीडबैक को पक्षपाती मानसिकता बताकर नज़रअंदाज़ किया गया। इस शोर के बीच स्थानीय सत्ता विरोधी आवाज़ें भी सुनी जा सकती थीं। रोज़गार और महंगाई का शोर तेज़ी से गली-मोहल्लों में सुनाई आ रहा था। इससे भी ज़्यादा चिंता की बात थी कि पहले चरण में कम मतदान होने से मतदाता की उदासीनता ने नई चिंताएं पैदा की। कल्पना और हकीकत के बीच बेमेल, शीर्ष नेतृत्व समझता, उससे पहले अभियान आगे तक पहुंच गया था। कांग्रेस ने इसके ख़िलाफ़ काम शुरू किया और 'चार सौ पार' के नारे को संविधान बदलने और आरक्षण ख़त्म करने के अभियान की तरफ मोड़ दिया। भाजपा जब तक इसका जवाब देने के लिए तैयार होती, तब तक काफी देर हो चुकी थी। कांग्रेस ने इस अभियान में बढ़त हासिल कर ली। भाजपा के एक अंदरूनी सूत्र ने कहा, 'मुझे लगता है कि प्रधानमंत्री और उनकी टीम खुद के इको-चैंबर में चल रही थी, जहां कुछ और सुनाई नहीं देता। वे खुद की अलौकिक शक्ति पर इतने आश्वस्त थे कि उन्होंने यह सोचा नहीं कि चार सौ पार का नारा उन्हें परेशान कर सकता है।'

प्रचार के आखिरी हफ्ते में आकर मोदी ने मान लिया था कि 'चार सौ पार' हासिल करना मुश्किल था। प्रधानमंत्री लगातार मीडिया से बात कर रहे थे। इस बार वे भाजपा नेतृत्व के करीबी माने जाने वाले पत्रकार-एंकर रजत शर्मा से बातचीत कर रहे थे। स्टुडियो में भाजपा-समर्थक दर्शक भरे हुए थे, जो हर बयान पर जोरदार तालियां बजा रहे थे। तालियों की गड़गड़ाहट से

भरोसा बढ़ने के बावजूद मोदी ने स्वीकार किया कि चार सौ पार का लक्ष्य केवल भाजपा का अपने पिछले आंकड़े को बेहतर करने के लिए था। उन्होंने कहा, 'अगर आपके परिवार में कोई बच्चा 90 नंबर लेकर आता है और दूसरे परिवार का बच्चा 30-40 नंबर लाता है, तो आप कभी भी अपने बच्चे को पचास नंबर पर संतुष्ट होने के लिए नहीं कहेंगे। आप तब बच्चे को 95 नंबर लाने के लिए प्रोत्साहित करते हैं। इसी तरह हमने अपने गठबंधन के लिए 400 सीटों का लक्ष्य रखा है।' उसी साक्षात्कार में मोदी ने फिर से ईश्वर के दूत की थीम पर बात बात की। 'मेरा मानना है कि ईश्वर ने मुझे 2047 तक चौबीसों घंटे काम करने का आदेश दिया है ताकि विकसित भारत का लक्ष्य हासिल किया जा सके... ईश्वर मुझे रास्ता दिखा रहे हैं... ईश्वर मुझे ऊर्जा दे रहे हैं।'

लेकिन कुछ दिनों बाद ही उस गुमनाम मतदाता ने भगवान के उस 'स्वयंभू सर्वशक्तिमान दूत' को एक संदेश दिया। भाजपा राम जन्मभूमि के शहर फैज़ाबाद-अयोध्या में 50,000 वोटों से हार गई थी। वाराणसी में, जहां मोदी के रिकॉर्ड तोड़ जीत की उम्मीद थी, मोदी की जीत के अंतर में तीन लाख वोटों की कमी आ गई; शुरुआती गिनती में तो वे पीछे भी चल रहे थे। 'चार सौ पार' को भूल जाइए, भाजपा 240 सीटों तक पहुंची थी और एनडीए भी 300 से कम पर। भाजपा मुख्यालय पर जीत की हैट-ट्रिक का जश्न तो मनाया गया, लेकिन उत्साह पहले जैसा नहीं था। जब प्रधानमंत्री मोदी अपने काफिले के साथ पार्टी कार्यालय पहुंचे तो 'मोदी, मोदी' के नारे सुनाई देने लगे, लेकिन उपलब्धियों का उत्साह नदारद था। जबरदस्ती की हंसी, अजीब सा सन्नाटा। 'मुझे लगता है कि भीड़ में महसूस हो रहा था कि हमने चुनाव जीता, लेकिन फिर भी हार गए!' भाजपा के एक पदाधिकारी ने स्वीकार किया।

भारत के लिए, यह सत्तावादी ताकतों के बादलों के छंटने जैसा था, लेकिन भाजपा के लिए भरी दोपहर में भी अंधेरा छाया था। चुनाव प्रचार के स्वयंभू देवताओं को सही मायने में ज़मीन पर उतार दिया गया। एक दशक तक तकलीफ देने वाली, ध्रुवीकरण वाली बहुसंख्यक राजनीति को एक झटका लगा था। अति-आत्मविश्वासी सर्वेक्षणकर्ता, तेज़-तर्रार रणनीतिकार, मजबूत और सख्त राजनेता, यहां तक कि हमारी पीढ़ी के सबसे करिश्माई नेता, वे सब 'असफल देवता' बन गए।

चुनाव इतना नाटकीय तरीके से कैसे बदल गया? अब फिर से उस जगह जाने का वक्त आ गया, जहां से यह सब शुरू हुआ था।

2

यह हिन्दुत्व की सरकार है: अमित शाह की अहमियत

साल 2024 की चुनावी जंग का पासा तो उसी दिन फेंक दिया गया था, जब 30 मई 2019 को मोदी सरकार ने दूसरे कार्यकाल के लिए शपथ ली थी। रायसीना हिल पर वैभवशाली राष्ट्रपति भवन के गुंबद पर तिरंगा शान से फहरा रहा था। प्रधानमंत्री नरेन्द्र मोदी ने अपने 57 मंत्रियों के साथ शपथ ली, लेकिन ज़्यादातर लोगों की निगाहें काली दाढ़ी के साथ सख्त गोल चेहरे पर टिकी थीं। जैसे ही अमित अनिल चन्द्र शाह मंच पर आए, तो लोग इस बात को लेकर अटकलें लगाने लगे कि भारतीय जनता पार्टी के अध्यक्ष को कौन सा मंत्रालय मिलेगा? शाह भले ही अब तक केन्द्र सरकार में नहीं रहे हों, लेकिन पांच साल तक भाजपा अध्यक्ष के तौर पर उन्हें संगठन में एक अनुभवी ज़मीनी राजनेता के तौर पर देखा गया। अब वे केन्द्र सरकार में एक बड़ी छलांग लगाने के लिए तैयार थे।

टीवी चैनलों पर ब्रेकिंग न्यूज़ चमकने लगी थी: शाह वित्त मंत्री होंगे! निवर्तमान वित्त मंत्री, भाजपा का सौम्य चेहरा और कानूनविद् अरुण जेटली लंबे समय से बीमार चल रहे थे। उन्होंने पहले ही स्पष्ट कर दिया था कि वे नई सरकार में मंत्री पद की जिम्मेदारी नहीं संभालेंगे। अमित शाह भाजपा के मुख्य रणनीतिकार होने के साथ शेयर बाज़ार के अनुभवी निवेशक भी थे, और उनके व्यवसायियों और वित्तीय समुदाय से जुड़े लोगों के साथ अच्छे संबंध थे। शायद यही वजह रही होगी कि टीवी पर अनुभवी पत्रकारों और विशेषज्ञों को लड़खड़ाती अर्थव्यवस्था को संभालने के लिए अमित शाह का नाम एक 'बेहतर पसंद' लग रहा हो। लेकिन साफ था

कि प्रधानमंत्री मोदी हर बार की तरह ऐसे क़यास लगाने वालों को ग़लत साबित करने वाले हैं। अगली सुबह शाह को गृहमंत्री बनाए जाने की औपचारिक घोषणा हुई यानी सरकार में सबसे अहम, दूसरी शक्तिशाली शख़्सियत।

संसद के विजय चौक चौराहे से रायसीना हिल पर चढ़ती सड़क पर दाईं ओर गहरे हिरमिची रंग की इमारत, भव्य 'नार्थ ब्लॉक' में एक-दूसरे से जुड़े और अंधेरे से गलियारों की भूलभुलैया सी है। दूसरे सरकारी दफ़्तरों के शोर-शराबे वाले माहौल से अलग यहां आला अफ़सर और उनके सहायक कर्मचारी 'टॉप सीक्रेट' लिखी फाइलों के साथ इधर से उधर जाते और फुसफुसाते देखे जा सकते हैं। इमारत में घुसने के बाद दाईं ओर मुख्य सीढ़ी पर चढ़ते वक्त आज़ाद भारत के पहले गृहमंत्री सरदार पटेल की एक बड़ी तस्वीर है। पटेल की शानदार विरासत ने ही गृह मंत्रालय को ताकत और अधिकार दिए हैं और उनका हर उत्तराधिकारी पटेल की उप्लब्धियों और छाया के आगे बौना सा महसूस होता है।

मोदी सरकार के पहले कार्यकाल में शाह से पहले गृहमंत्री रहे राजनाथ सिंह मिलनसार नेताओं में से माने जाते हैं, जो अटल बिहारी वाजपेयी की आम सहमति की राजनीति के रास्ते पर चलते हैं। भारतीय जनता पार्टी के दो बार अध्यक्ष रहे और साल 2000 में 49 साल की उम्र में उत्तरप्रदेश के मुख्यमंत्री रहे राजनाथ सिंह, को प्रधानमंत्री मोदी समेत मंत्रिमंडल के कई सहयोगियों से वरिष्ठ माना जाता है। मोदी सरकार के पहले कार्यकाल में वे प्रधानमंत्री की गैर-मौजूदगी में कैबिनेट बैठकों की अध्यक्षता करते थे, यानी उन्हें सरकार में 'नंबर दो' की हैसियत पर माना जा सकता था। लेकिन राजनाथ सिंह ने लोकप्रिय नेता के तौर पर अपनी हैसियत को समझते हुए राजनीति के समुंदर में तूफ़ान लाने की कोशिश नहीं की। अमित शाह हर तरह से अलग लगते हैं। 'हम जब कभी राजनाथ सिंह के सरकारी दफ़्तर में गए, तो कभी डर जैसा महसूस नहीं हुआ। इसमें कोई शक नहीं कि राजनाथ सिंह पार्टी के वरिष्ठ नेता हैं, लेकिन वे यह अपने हावभाव में कभी जताते नहीं हैं। दूसरी तरफ़, शाह अपनी ताकत को बताने में परहेज़ नहीं करते, और ये आपको उनसे मुलाक़ात में समझ भी आता है,' गृह मंत्रालय के रिटायर्ड अफसर याद करते हुए बताते हैं।

शाह की इस ताकत की बड़ी वजह उनका प्रधानमंत्री मोदी के करीब होना है। उनका यह रिश्ता अस्सी के दशक में शुरू हुआ, तब मोदी गुजरात भाजपा के सचिव थे और अमित शाह एक नौजवान उत्साही कार्यकर्ता। शाह मोदी के 'दायें हाथ' माने जाते हैं, 'संकटमोचक' हैं और ज़रूरत पड़ने पर वो किसी बुराई को अपने सिर पर लेने को भी तैयार रहते हैं ताकि मोदी की छवि पर असर ना पड़े, और इससे उलट व्यवहार भी कर सकते हैं। गुजरात की जोड़ी 'नंबर-1', विपरीत शख़्सियतों की जोड़ी, लेकिन एक जैसी महत्वाकांक्षाओं के साथः 'सत्ता', किसी भी कीमत पर।

फिर भी शाह, अपने नेता से ज़्यादा काम में आने वाले लोगों में से थे। इन दो घटनाओं से इस बात का अंदाज़ा हो जाता है कि लंबे वक्त से चल रही इस जोड़ी में शाह ज़्यादा आक्रामक हैं। उस वक्त अमित शाह अहमदाबाद में आरएसएस के छात्र संगठन अखिल भारतीय विद्यार्थी परिषद की राजनीति में सक्रिय और संयुक्त सचिव थे। कॉलेज छात्रसंघ के चुनावों में एबीवीपी के उम्मीदवार के तौर पर वे मैदान में थे। उनका सामना कांग्रेस के छात्र संगठन एनएसयूआई के उम्मीदवार से था। छात्रसंघ के एक प्रमुख पद पर महिला उम्मीदवार (एनएसयूआई) थी और कॉलेज में महिला वोटरों की तादाद अच्छी थी। उनके सहयोगी ने बताया, 'हमें लगता था कि ज्यादातर लड़कियां एनएसयूआई के उम्मीदवार को वोट देकर जिता देंगी, इसलिए हमें "प्लान बी" की ज़रूरत थी।' मतदान के दिन लड़कियां कम तादाद में कॉलेज पहुंचे, इसके लिए शाह ने एक योजना बनाई। उस ज़माने में मोबाइल नहीं होते थे, तो टेलीफ़ोन डायरेक्टरी से लड़कियों के घरों के नंबर लेकर उन्हें फ़ोन करना शुरू किया गया और उनके अभिभावकों को चेताया गया कि मतदान के दिन लड़कियों के लिए कॉलेज में कुछ परेशानी हो सकती है। नतीजतन बहुत सी लड़कियां उस दिन वोटिंग के लिए नहीं पहुंची। अमित शाह की चुनाव में यह पहली जीत थी। किस्सा सुनाते हुए वो सहयोगी बोले, 'यह अमित शाह का दिमाग़ ही है, जो हर बार कुछ नया सोचता है।' तेज़तर्रार और समझदार शाह ने चुनाव प्रबंधन का सबक बहुत जल्दी ही सीख लिया था।

दूसरा किस्सा खुद अमित शाह ने बताया कि उन्होंने 1998 में वाजपेयी सरकार के 'परमाणु परीक्षण' कार्यक्रम को आगे बढ़ाने पर सवाल उठाए थे। शाह उस समय 1997 में जीतकर गुजरात में पहली बार विधायक बने थे। उनकी पीएमओ तक पहुंच भले ही ना हो, लेकिन परमाणु ऊर्जा पर सरकार की आलोचना करने के लिए उन्होंने प्रधानमंत्री को चिट्ठी लिख दी। शाह के विरोध का कारण था कि 'अब पाकिस्तान भी परमाणु परीक्षण करेगा और हमारी सेना की मजबूती के बावज़ूद, हम पाक अधिकृत कश्मीर पर कब्ज़ा नहीं कर पाएंगे।' वाजपेयी इस युवा विधायक के बारे में जानने को उत्सुक थे, और उन्होंने शाह को मुलाकात का समय भी दिया। मीटिंग में, शाह ने फिर परमाणु मुद्दे को लेकर अपनी सहमति जताई। 'अमित भाई हमेशा देश और विचारधारा को सर्वोपरि रखते हैं। वे आरएसएस की अखंड भारत की अवधारणा के कट्टर समर्थक हैं, और इसकी रक्षा के लिए वो किसी परिणाम की परवाह नहीं करते,' पार्टी के एक सहयोगी ने कहा।

अखंड भारत का विचार, हिंदूत्व आंदोलन के नायक विनायक दामोदर सावरकर ने 1937 में हिन्दू महासभा के उन्नीसवें सालाना सत्र में रखा था। सावरकर का मानना था कि 'भारत कश्मीर से रामेश्वरम और सिंध से असम तक एक और अविभाज्य रहना चाहिए।' नई दिल्ली में शाह के आवास पर सावरकर की तस्वीर प्रमुखता से लगी हुई है। देश के नए गृहमंत्री, सावरकर की 'हिंदू राष्ट्र' और 'हिन्दुत्व' की विचारधारा को आगे बढ़ाने के लिए दृढ़ दिखाई देते हैं। शाह ने अपने एक सहयोगी से कहा, 'हमें इतना स्पष्ट बहुमत इसलिए नहीं मिला है कि हम कांग्रेस

के तौर-तरीकों से सरकार और देश चलाएं। यह हिन्दुत्व की सरकार है और हमें यह सुनिश्चित करना चाहिए कि हमारे वैचारिक लक्ष्य हासिल हों। इसमें समझौते का कोई सवाल ही नहीं है।'

गृह मंत्रालय के अफसरों के साथ देश के दूसरे लोगों को भी जल्दी समझ आ जाएगा कि हिंदुत्व की राजनीति पर बिना झिझक आगे बढ़ने के राजनीतिक मायने क्या हैं।

संघ परिवार का एजेंडा जम्मू कश्मीर को विशेष दर्ज़ा देने वाले अनुच्छेद 370 को हटाने का हमेशा से रहा है। भगवा परिवार हमेशा से यह मानता रहा है कि 1949 में नेहरू कैबिनेट का अनुच्छेद 370 को लागू करने का फ़ैसला, 'कश्मीर को भारत से अलग करने का प्रावधान है।' 1950 के दशक से ही राष्ट्रीय स्वयंसेवक संघ, जनसंघ और फिर भारतीय जनता पार्टी के हर प्रमुख राजनीतिक प्रस्ताव और चुनावी घोषणापत्रों में अनुच्छेद 370 के विरोध पर ज़ोर दिया गया और सत्ता में आने पर इसे हटाने का वादा भी किया गया। जनसंघ के संस्थापक अध्यक्ष डॉ. श्यामाप्रसाद मुखर्जी ने जम्मू कश्मीर को विशेष दर्जा देने के ख़िलाफ़ आंदोलन का नेतृत्व किया था। इसी आंदोलन के दौरान जब उन्हें पठानकोट में गिरफ्तार किया गया तो उसके कुछ दिनों बाद जून 1953 में श्रीनगर की जेल में उनकी रहस्यमय स्थितियों में मौत हो गई। उन्हें बिना 'परमिट' के राज्य में प्रवेश करने के मामले में गिरफ्तार किया गया था। इस आंदोलन के दौरान जनसंघ का नारा था: 'एक देश में दो विधान, दो प्रधान, दो निशान नहीं चलेगा।' यानी एक देश में दो संविधान, दो प्रधानमंत्री और दो झंडे नहीं हो सकते। उस समय तक जम्मू कश्मीर का संविधान, झंडा और प्रधानमंत्री अलग होता था। सबसे लंबे समय तक संघ के प्रमुख रहे एम.एस. गोलवलकर ने 1967 में इस बात को दोहराया, 'कश्मीर को बनाए रखने का सिर्फ़ एक ही तरीका है—भारत में उसका पूर्ण एकीकरण। अनुच्छेद 370, अलग झंडा और अलग संविधान ख़त्म होना चाहिए।'

भाजपा के सबसे वरिष्ठ नेता लालकृष्ण आडवाणी से साल 2009 में मैंने एक साक्षात्कार के दौरान पूछा था कि क्या आपको अपने इतने लंबे राजनीतिक जीवन में किसी मसले को लेकर कोई पछतावा है? आडवाणी का कहना था, 'अनुच्छेद 370 को ख़त्म नहीं कर पाना निश्चित तौर पर मेरे लिए अफसोस की बात रही है, इसे हटाना हमारे संस्थापक के लिए सच्ची श्रद्धांजलि होती।' साल 1998 से 2004 तक आडवाणी, वाजपेयी सरकार में ताकतवर गृहमंत्री रहे थे, लेकिन उन्होंने अफसोस के साथ माना कि तब भाजपा के पास अपने मूल वैचारिक एजेंडे को आगे बढ़ाने के लिए पर्याप्त बहुमत नहीं था। 'हम एक गठबंधन सरकार में न्यूनतम साझा कार्यक्रम पर काम कर रहे थे। अगर हमारे पास बहुमत होता तो हम निश्चित तौर पर कार्रवाई करते और अनुच्छेद 370 को हटा देते। अब भी अगर हमें बहुमत मिलता है तो हम ऐसा करेंगे,'

श्री आडवाणी ने कहा। लेकिन आडवाणी के नेतृत्व में बीजेपी साल 2009 के आम चुनाव हार गई। एक दशक बाद बीजेपी को ऐसा बहुमत मिला जिसकी वाजपेयी-आडवाणी युग में पार्टी ने कल्पना भी नहीं की होगी।

दिलचस्प बात यह है कि एक दशक बाद 2014 के आम चुनावों में बीजेपी को स्पष्ट बहुमत तो मिल गया, लेकिन उसने जम्मू कश्मीर से अनुच्छेद 370 को रद्द करने का फ़ैसला नहीं किया। न ही उसने इसके साथ जुड़े विवादास्पद प्रावधान 35ए को हटाने की कोशिश की, जो जम्मू कश्मीर के स्थायी निवासियों को खासतौर से शिक्षा, रोज़गार, संपत्ति और कुछ और मामलों में विशेष अधिकार देता है। इसके बजाय मार्च 2015 के चुनावों में जब नतीजों में 'त्रिशंकु विधानसभा' बनी तो भारतीय जनता पार्टी ने जम्मू कश्मीर के नेता मुफ़्ती मोहम्मद सईद की पीपुल्स डेमोक्रेटिक पार्टी के साथ गठबंधन में सरकार बना ली। प्रधानमंत्री नरेन्द्र मोदी ने तब इस बेमेल विचारधारा वाली साझेदारी को 'जम्मू कश्मीर के लोगों के सपनों को पूरा करने का ऐतिहासिक अवसर बताया था'। यह गठबंधन दिखने में अच्छा लग रहा था, जिसने हिंदू-बहुल जम्मू और मुस्लिम-बहुल कश्मीर घाटी की दूरियों को पाटने का वादा किया था। लेकिन दुखद पहलू यह है कि यह वादा हकीकत से दूर रहा। फिर जून 2018 में, भाजपा ने महबूबा मुफ़्ती के नेतृत्व वाली सरकार से समर्थन वापस ले लिया। (साल 2016 में उनके पिता मुफ्ती साहब के निधन के बाद महबूबा मुफ्ती मुख्यमंत्री बनी थीं।) इस राजनीतिक फ़ैसले ने एक अशांत इलाके को फिर से अराजकता और अस्थिरता की खाई में धकेल दिया।

भाजपा के एक वरिष्ठ नेता ने खुलासा किया कि 'मोदी सरकार ने अगले आम चुनावों से पहले साल 2019 की शुरुआत में ही अनुच्छेद 35ए को निरस्त करने का मन बना लिया था, लेकिन आम सहमति नहीं बनने पर, उसे टालना बेहतर समझा गया।' साल 1954 में राष्ट्रपति के एक आदेश से अनुच्छेद 370 के तहत, विशेष अनुच्छेद 35(ए) बनाया गया था। गृह मंत्रालय के एक सेवानिवृत वरिष्ठ अफसर ने इस बात की पुष्टि की कि अनुच्छेद 35(ए) को निरस्त करने की योजना आम चुनावों से पहले, जनवरी 2019 में ही तैयार कर ली गई थी। 'ऐसी चर्चा होने लगी थी कि आम चुनावों से पहले राजनीतिक माहौल बनाने के लिए प्रधानमंत्री कोई बड़ी घोषणा कर सकते हैं, लेकिन तभी पुलवामा हमला हो गया और कश्मीर से जुड़े सभी मसले ठंडे बस्ते में डाल दिए गए।' 14 फरवरी 2019 को कश्मीर के पुलवामा में हुए आतंकी हमले में एक विस्फोटकों से भरी गाड़ी सीआरपीएफ के जवानों के काफिले की बस से टकरा गई, जिसमें 40 जवान मारे गए। इस बड़ी आतंकवादी घटना ने चुनावी अभियान को पूरी तरह बदल दिया। देश में माहौल भी बदल गया था। अब राष्ट्रीय सुरक्षा और पाकिस्तान से चल रहा आतंकवाद एक महत्वपूर्ण मुद्दा हो गया था। पुलवामा मुद्दे के केन्द्र में आने के बाद कश्मीर के विशेष दर्ज़े को निरस्त करने के फ़ैसले को टाल दिया गया।

जून 2019 तक मोदी सरकार के सामने कोई बाधा नहीं थी। भाजपा ने यह चुनाव पिछली बार से भी ज़्यादा और बड़े बहुमत के साथ जीता था। इन चुनावों में अकेले भाजपा ने रिकॉर्ड 303 सीटें जीत ली थीं। पुलवामा हमले के जवाब में बालाकोट सर्जिकल स्ट्राइक से पाकिस्तान को कड़ा संदेश दे दिया गया था। कश्मीर घाटी में फिलहाल शांति दिख रही थी। प्रधानमंत्री मोदी ने अपने दूसरे कार्यकाल की पहली कैबिनेट बैठक में कहा, 'हमें पहले 100 दिनों में ही अगले पांच साल की दिशा तय करनी होगी।' हरेक कैबिनेट मंत्री को अपने मंत्रालयों की अगले 100 दिनों की कार्य योजना के साथ आने के लिए कहा गया था। गृहमंत्री अमित शाह, अपनी नई भूमिका के लिए तैयार दिख रहे थे।

जून की शुरुआत में, नई सरकार के शपथ लेने के कुछ दिनों बाद प्रधानमंत्री कार्यालय में एक अहम बैठक में सिर्फ़ तीन लोग मौजूद थेः प्रधानमंत्री मोदी, गृहमंत्री अमित शाह और राष्ट्रीय सुरक्षा सलाहकार अजीत डोवाल। सरकार में बैठे एक आला अफसर ने कहा कि यह सरकार में सबसे शक्तिशाली (पी-3) लोगों की तिकड़ी थी। एक प्रधानमंत्री जिनके पास पूरी कमान है, एक गृहमंत्री, जिन्हें नंबर दो की हैसियत पर अपनी मौजूदगी साबित करनी है और एक ताकतवर सुरक्षा सलाहकार, जिसके एजेंडा में दशकों से कश्मीर में आतंकवाद को ख़त्म करने का जुनून है। बैठक का अनकहा एजेंडा कश्मीर में अनुच्छेद 370 और 35(ए) को ख़त्म करने की समय सीमा या प्लान तैयार करना था। सुरक्षा सलाहकार डोवाल ने आश्वस्त किया कि फ़ैसले के किसी भी हिंसक परिणाम को सुरक्षा बल संभाल लेंगे। उन्होंने भरोसा दिलाया कि 'अगर ज़रूरत पड़ी तो हम अतिरिक्त सुरक्षा बल लगाएंगे।'

केन्द्र सरकार में पहली बार मंत्री बने शाह ने हाल ही में गृह मंत्रालय का कामकाज संभाला था, लेकिन वे संघ परिवार की लंबे समय से चली आ रही इच्छा के पूरा होने की उम्मीद से उत्साहित थे। बाद में, शाह ने संसद के अपने दफ़्तर में, पत्रकारों से कहा, 'हम जानते थे कि हम इतिहास बनाने जा रहे थे।' इससे उलट, प्रधानमंत्री मोदी इस महत्वपूर्ण (पी-3) बैठक में ज़्यादा नहीं बोले, वो सुरक्षा सलाहकार की बात को गौर से सुनते रहे। जब डोवाल की बात ख़त्म हुई तो प्रधानमंत्री ने कहा कि 'मैं चाहता हूं कि इसके लिए ज़रूरी प्रक्रिया 15 अगस्त तक पूरी हो जाए।' शाह और डोवाल ने आदेश पूरा करने के लिए सिर हिलाया। आज़ादी के बाद के सत्तर सालों में जो काम नहीं हो पाया था, उसे पूरा करने के लिए उनके पास सिर्फ़ दस सप्ताह का वक्त था: अनुच्छेद 370 और कश्मीर के विशेष प्रावधानों को निरस्त करना।

प्रधानमंत्री से योजना को हरी झंडी मिलने के बाद अमित शाह अपने अंदाज़ में पूरे जोश-खरोश के साथ काम को अंजाम देने में जुट गए। गृह सचिव राजीव गौबा के मातहत गृह मंत्रालय के कश्मीर विभाग को अनुच्छेद 370 को रद्द करने के लिए एक रोडमैप बनाने की ज़िम्मेदारी दी गई। इस टॉप सीक्रेट ऑपरेशन के बारे में किसी भी अफसर को कोई अतिरिक्त जानकारी नहीं

दी गई थी। केवल 'नीड टू नो' यानी सिर्फ़ जरूरी और जरूरत पर ही जानकारी दी जानी थी। सिक्योरिटी ग्रिड पर सुरक्षा सलाहकार के दफ़्तर और दिल्ली और श्रीनगर में सेना की कमान में साथ मिलकर काम किया गया था। शाह और डोवाल श्रीनगर में सेना कमांडर से मिलने के लिए अलग-अलग पहुंचे। इसके लिए आधिकारिक वजह स्वतंत्रता दिवस के मौके पर सुरक्षा व्यवस्था की समीक्षा करना बताई गई। मीडिया की नज़रों से बचने के लिए बैठकें सूर्योदय से पहले पांच बजे होती थीं। सुरक्षा बलों को संदेश साफ था कि 15 अगस्त से पहले ज़मीन पर अधिकतम सैनिकों की तैनाती सुनिश्चित की जाए।

अनुच्छेद 370 को निरस्त करने से जुड़े कानूनी पहलुओं को गृहमंत्री शाह के विश्वस्त और सॉलिसिटर जनरल तुषार मेहता देख रहे थे। तुषार मेहता गुजरात के जमाने से शाह के 'संकटमोचक' के तौर पर काम करते रहे। उन्होंने शाह के विवादास्पद 'फ़र्जी मुठभेड़' मामले सहित कई मामलों में शाह की पैरवी की थी। इस मामले में 2010 में शाह को जेल जाना पड़ा था। सॉलिसिटर-जनरल मेहता ने प्रत्येक क़ानूनी और संवैधानिक कदमों और उनके नतीजों पर चर्चा करने के लिए कई दौर की अहम और गोपनीय बैठकों की अध्यक्षता की। सरकार के सामने एक पेचीदा संवैधानिक सवाल यह था कि क्या राष्ट्रपति को अनुच्छेद 370 में बदलाव या निरस्त करने की घोषणा से पहले जम्मू-कश्मीर राज्य की संविधान सभा की सिफ़ारिश की आवश्यकता होगी? खासतौर से यह पेचीदगी इसलिए थी क्योंकि उस वक्त जम्मू कश्मीर में राष्ट्रपति शासन था और वहां कोई विधानसभा नहीं थी। ऐसे में क्या केन्द्र यह एकतरफा फ़ैसला कर सकता है? यह जटिल मुद्दा इसलिए भी बन सकता था क्योंकि साल 2018 में सुप्रीम कोर्ट ने राज्य में विधानसभा नहीं होने से अनुच्छेद 370 को स्थायित्व दे दिया था।

सभी अहम क़ानूनी मुद्दों की कड़ी जांच-परख के बाद तुषार मेहता ने सुझाव दिया कि किसी भी क़ानूनी चुनौती से निपटने के लिए, अनुच्छेद 370 को क़ानूनी क़िताबों में बनाए रखते हुए निष्क्रिय किया जा सकता है। एक और महत्वपूर्ण सुझाव, अनुच्छेद 370(3) के तहत राज्य की संविधान सभा को राज्य की विधानसभा के रूप में बदलने का था। सॉलिसिटर-जनरल के नज़रिए से जम्मू-कश्मीर की विधानसभा भंग होने की स्थिति में विधानमंडल की शक्तियां अनुच्छेद 356(1)(बी) के तहत संसद में निहित थीं। इसके मुताबिक राष्ट्रपति के आदेश से अनुच्छेद 370 में बदलाव के लिए एक संसदीय प्रस्ताव काफी होगा। दूसरी तरफ क़ानून के कई वरिष्ठ जानकारों ने बुनियादी संघीय सिद्धान्तों को ख़त्म करने के रूप में इस फ़ैसले की संवैधानिकता पर सवाल उठाया, लेकिन दिसम्बर,2023 में सुप्रीम कोर्ट ने अपने सर्वसम्मत फ़ैसले में अनुच्छेद 370 को निरस्त करने की राष्ट्रपति की शक्ति को बरकरार रखा। सर्वोच्च अदालत ने माना कि अनुच्छेद 370 केवल एक अस्थायी प्रावधान था और जम्मू कश्मीर का विशेष दर्जा हटाया जा सकता है।

इस मसले पर एक विरोधाभास यह माना गया कि जब दिल्ली में केन्द्र सरकार क़ानूनी बारीकियों पर काम कर रही थी, तब जम्मू कश्मीर के राज्यपाल सत्यपाल मलिक ने दावा किया कि उन्हें इस मामले में अंधेरे में रखा गया था। इसे निरस्त करने से पहले उनसे सलाह नहीं ली गई और उन्हें सरकार के निर्णय के बारे में केवल अंतिम चरण में ही बताया गया। समाजवादी सोच रखने वाले सत्यपाल मलिक उस वक्त की भाजपा की सत्ता व्यवस्था में असामान्य राजनेता माने जा सकते हैं। चौधरी चरण सिंह की अगुवाई में राजनीति शुरू करने वाले मलिक पश्चिमी उत्तरप्रदेश के एक प्रमुख जाट नेता माने जाते रहे। बाद में वे विश्वनाथ प्रताप सिंह के साथ जुड़ गए। सिंह के जनता दल के काफी समय बाद मलिक 2004 में वाजपेयी के नेतृत्व वाली भाजपा में शामिल हो गए और पार्टी के उपाध्यक्ष नियुक्त किए गए। मोदी सरकार ने 2017 में उन्हें पहले राज्यपाल बनाकर बिहार भेजा और फिर 2018 में उनका तबादला जम्मू कश्मीर कर दिया गया। कहा गया कि उस वक्त सरकार को जम्मू कश्मीर जैसे प्रमुख राज्य में एक अनुभवी राजनेता की तलाश थी। बाद में मलिक ने टिप्पणी की, 'मुझे जम्मू कश्नीर शायद इसलिए भेजा गया क्योंकि प्रधानमंत्री किसी ऐसे व्यक्ति को चाहते थे जिसकी पृष्ठभूमि आरएसएस से नहीं हो, ताकि वो वहां के लोगों के साथ एक विश्वसनीय चेहरे के तौर पर बातचीत कर सकें।' यूं तो सरकार में बैठे कई बड़े लोगों की तरह मलिक को भी पता था कि केन्द्र सरकार कश्मीर में कोई बड़े कदम की योजना बना रही है, लेकिन ऐन वक्त तक उनके साथ कोई विशेष अहम जानकारी साझा नहीं की गई। मलिक ने दावा किया, 'अचानक मुझे गृहमंत्री का फ़ोन आया और उन्होंने मुझसे अपने सलाहकारों की एक बैठक तुरंत बुलाने और अनुच्छेद 370 हटाने की सिफ़ारिश करने के लिए कहा। इस पर कोई सलाह नहीं ली गई थी, यह सिर्फ़ एक आदेश था, जिसे लागू करना था।'

तीन अगस्त तक गृहमंत्री शाह का 'मिशन कश्मीर' सुरक्षा बलों की तैनाती के साथ पूरी घाटी में उतरने के लिए तैयार था। संसद का बजट सत्र बढ़ा दिया गया, सुरक्षा का हवाला देते हुए अमरनाथ यात्रा रोक दी गई। स्कूलों और शैक्षणिक संस्थाओं को बंद करने के आदेश दे दिए गए। घाटी में इंटरनेट सेवाओं को निलंबित कर दिया गया। संसद के सेन्ट्रल हॉल में जब हममें से कुछ पत्रकारों की मुलाकात गृहमंत्री शाह से हुई, तो उनके हावभाव से कोई अंदाज़ा ही नहीं हुआ। एक वरिष्ठ पत्रकार ने पूछा, 'क्या सरकार कश्मीर में अनुच्छेद 35(ए) हटाने जा रही है?' दूसरे पत्रकार ने जम्मू कश्मीर में सुरक्षा बलों की तैनाती बढ़ाने पर सवाल किया। शाह ने कोई सीधा जवाब देने के बजाय कहा, 'भई, कुछ चीजें सरकार के लिए भी छोड़ दो, ज़्यादा अटकलें मत लगाओ, कुछ नहीं होने जा रहा।' जवाब की उम्मीद में बैठे पत्रकारों की तरफ सेन्ट्रल हॉल के स्वादिष्ट ढोकला की प्लेट बढ़ा दी गई थी। जब एक पत्रकार ने अनुच्छेद 35(ए) के सवाल पर फिर से ज़ोर दिया तो शाह ने टोकते हुए कहा, 'क्या आपको नहीं लगता

कि जम्मू-कश्मीर के लोगों के भी दूसरे भारतीयों की तरह समान अधिकार होने चाहिएं? अब, आप एक और ढोकला लीजिए।'

गृहमंत्री शाह का 3-4 अगस्त को सप्ताह के आखिरी दिन कभी संसदीय कार्यालय, तो कभी गृह मंत्रालय के अपने दफ्तर में आना-जाना लगा रहा। गृह सचिव गौबा इस दौरान श्रीनगर और एनएसए के कार्यालय के संपर्क में थे। शाह अपने ऑपरेशन को अंतिम रूप देने में व्यस्त थे। अफसरों से बातचीत के दौरान शाह ने जम्मू कश्मीर की परिवारवाद की राजनीति को लेकर कुछ अधीरता सी दिखाई। उनको लगता था कि 'पूरी राजनीति बदलनी पड़ेगी'। जब तक कि घाटी पर केन्द्र का अधिक नियंत्रण नहीं होगा, सिर्फ़ अनुच्छेद 370 को हटाने से काम नहीं चलेगा। प्रस्तावित समाधान कुछ ज़्यादा सख्त होने का संकेत दे रहा था। राज्य का आकार छोटा किया जाएगा, इसे दो केन्द्र शासित प्रदेशों जम्मू और कश्मीर और लद्दाख में विभाजित जाएगा। देश में पहली बार किसी राज्य का दर्जा घटाकर उसे केन्द्रशासित प्रदेश बना दिया गया। यह स्पष्ट नहीं हो पाया कि मूलतः यह किसका विचार था, लेकिन बाद में मीडिया के सामने गृहमंत्री शाह ने इसकी ज़िम्मेदारी खुद पर ली। शाह ने जोर देकर कहा, 'घाटी में हालात सामान्य होते ही पूर्ण राज्य का दर्ज़ा बहाल कर दिया जाएगा।' लेकिन सामान्य स्थिति के मायने साफ नहीं किए गए। ऐसा लग रहा था कि शाह कुछ लोगों के किए की सज़ा, सबको देना चाहते हों। केन्द्र के नजरिए से देखें तो कश्मीर घाटी के राजनेताओं और लोगों पर भरोसा नहीं किया जा सकता। भारत का इकलौता मुस्लिम बहुल राज्य बांट दिया गया था और उसका दर्जा कम कर दिया गया। शाह को प्रधानमंत्री का समर्थन हासिल था। और वे अपने काम की आलोचना से डरने और पीछे हटने वाले नहीं थे। जब मैंने केन्द्रशासित प्रदेश के फ़ैसले पर उनका ध्यान दिलाने की कोशिश की, तो उन्होंने कहा कि, 'आप सेक्युलर लिबरल लॉबी चिल्लाते रहिए, डिसीजन लेना हमारा काम है!'

राज्यपाल मलिक इस बात का दावा करते रहे कि जम्मू कश्मीर से राज्य का दर्जा वापस लेने के फ़ैसले पर किसी भी स्तर पर उनसे सलाह नहीं ली गई। मलिक का कहना था कि 'हालांकि मैंने अनुच्छेद 370 को हटाने के कदम का पूरा समर्थन किया था, लेकिन मैं राज्य को केन्द्र शासित प्रदेश में बदलने के फ़ैसले से सहमत नहीं था।' मलिक की राय थी कि 'इससे उन लोगों की भावनाएं आहत होंगी, जिन्हें लगता है कि उन्हें बेवजह सज़ा दी जा रही है।'

पांच अगस्त, सोमवार को संसद में जाने और घोषणा करने से पहले गृहमंत्री ने सॉलिसिटर जनरल तुषार मेहता के साथ आख़िरी बार सभी क़ानूनी पहलुओं पर गौर किया ताकि यह सुनिश्चित किया जा सके कि कुछ ज़रूरी छूट तो नहीं गया था। तय हुआ कि संसद में अनुच्छेद 370 पर बहस के दौरान मेहता, गृहमंत्री के संसद के कमरे में ही मौज़ूद रहेंगे, ताकि किसी क़ानूनी जटिलता या सवाल को समझने की ज़रूरत के वक्त उनसे विमर्श किया जा सके। गुजरात में

बीजेपी की 'हिन्दुत्व की प्रयोगशाला' से अपना राजनीतिक करियर बनाने वाले अमित शाह के लिए यह राष्ट्रीय पटल पर भगवा सूरज में चमकने का अवसर था। मानो हिन्दुत्व की जीत के इस क्षण में उनके राजनीतिक और धार्मिक पूर्वाग्रह एकजुट हो गए थे। बाद में उन्होंने अपनी आत्म-संतुष्टि के स्वर में कहा, 'मैंने उन लाखों भारतीयों के सपनों को पूरा किया है, जो इस दिन का इंतज़ार कर रहे थे'।

═

श्रीनगर में गुपकर रोड कश्मीर की सत्ता का ठिकाना माना जाता है। यहां घाटी के ताकतवर और शीर्ष नेताओं की कोठियां हैं। सबसे अच्छे वक्त में भी चिनार से ढकी इस सड़क पर घुसते ही सुरक्षा बलों की मौजूदगी दिखाई देती है। चार अगस्त की आधी रात शायद सबसे खराब वक्त रहा होगा। सड़क पर लोहे के बैरिकेड ऊपर कर दिए गए और मंद रोशनी वाली सड़क पर पुलिस बल की तादाद अचानक बढ़ा दी गई। जम्मू-कश्मीर के तीन बार मुख्यमंत्री रहे डॉ. फारुक़ अब्दुल्ला गहरी नींद सो रहे थे। वे उस रात जल्दी सो गए थे, क्योंकि सुबह उन्हें संसद की कार्यवाही में हिस्सा लेने के लिए दिल्ली रवाना होना था। पड़ोस के बंगले में उनके बेटे उमर टीवी देखने के बाद अब किताब पढ़ रहे थे। उमर अब्दुल्ला ने याद करते हुए कहा, 'रात 11 बजे के बाद मुझे मेरी पार्टी के सहयोगियों के फ़ोन आने लगे कि पुलिस लोगों को पकड़कर ले जा रही थी। करीब आधी रात को मोबाइल फोन बंद हो गए, तब मुझे लगा कि मामला कुछ गड़बड़ था।'

अगली सुबह तो लैंडलाइन फ़ोन भी काम नहीं कर रहे थे। जब उमर अब्दुल्ला ने अपने घर से बाहर निकलने की कोशिश की, तो पता चला कि गेट पर बाहर से ताला लगा हुआ था। 'तभी मुझे अहसास हुआ कि मेरे गार्ड अब मेरे जेलर थे। कोई आधिकारिक आदेश नहीं था, कोई सरकारी कागज़ नहीं थे और ना ही किसी ने इस बारे में कोई सूचना दी थी। उस सुबह जब संसद में गृहमंत्री ने भाषण दिया, तब हमें पता चला कि क्या हुआ था,' नाराज़गी के स्वर में उमर ने कहा। घंटों बाद, दोपहर के भोजन के वक्त अपने पिता से एक छोटी मुलाकात के बाद, उमर को कश्मीर में खूबसूरत डल झील की ओर झांकते विशाल हरि निवास में ले जाया गया, जिसे अब सरकारी गेस्ट हाउस बना दिया गया है। उनके लिए एक साथी वहां पहले से मौजूद थी, राज्य की पूर्व मुख्यमंत्री महबूबा मुफ्ती को भी वहां हिरासत में रखा गया था। 'मजिस्ट्रेट ने मेरे लिए शर्त रखी थी कि मैं महबूबा मुफ्ती से नहीं मिल सकता। हम यूं तो अच्छे दोस्त नहीं हैं, लेकिन मैंने उन्हें संदेश भेजा कि जब वे बगीचे में टहलने जा रही हो तो वो वक्त बता दें ताकि रास्ते में आमना-सामना ना हो,' उमर ने तंज के साथ हंसी में कहा।

कुछ दिनों बाद महबूबा मुफ्ती को राज्य सरकार के पर्यटन विभाग के दूसरे गेस्ट हाउस में ले जाया गया, लेकिन उमर अब्दुल्ला को अगले आठ महीने हरि निवास में एकांतवास में बिताने

पड़े। पहले पांच हफ्ते तो किसी भी अखबार या टेलीविजन चैनल को देखने की इजाज़त नहीं दी गई। उमर ने तब अपना ज़्यादातर वक्त पढ़ने, टहलने या फिर अपनी पंसदीदा 'जिग्सॉ पज़ल्स' को सुलझाने में बिताया। 'मुझे लगता है कि मेरी बोर्डिगं स्कूल में पढ़ाई मेरे काम आई। मैं खुद के साथ रहने में भी सहज रहता हूं,' उमर ने कहा। उमर को मार्च के आखिरी सप्ताह में रिहा कर दिया गया, जिसके तुरंत बाद सुप्रीम कोर्ट ने उनकी बंदी प्रत्यक्षीकरण याचिका पर नोटिस जारी किया। 'जिस दिन मुझे रिहा किया गया, उसी दिन प्रधानमंत्री ने कोविड लॉकडाउन की घोषणा की थी। मुझे लगता है कि मैं एक नज़रबंदी से दूसरी नज़रबंदी में चला गया!'

अब्दुल्ला परिवार को इतने नाटकीय घटनाक्रमों से राजनीतिक विश्वासघात की बू आ रही थी। 'कई सप्ताह से ये अफवाहें चल रही थीं कि केन्द्र सरकार कुछ योजना बना रही थी, लेकिन हममें से किसी को इस बात का अंदाज़ा नहीं था कि क्या होने जा रहा था। मेरी पार्टी के एक नेता ने जोर देकर कहा कि केन्द्र कश्मीर के विशेष दर्जा को ख़त्म करने जा रहा था और हो सकता है कि राज्य का विभाजन भी किया जाए, लेकिन हमने उनकी बात पर भरोसा नहीं किया, हमने उनकी बात को मज़ाक समझा। मेरे हिसाब से उसे वो जानकारी थी, जो मुझे पता नहीं थी,' उमर ने याद करते हुए कहा। तीन दिन पहले ही उमर और उनके पिता फ़ारूक़ अब्दुल्ला ने प्रधानमंत्री से संसद के दफ़्तर में मुलाक़ात की थी। केन्द्र सरकार के अर्ध सैनिक बलों की सौ अतिरिक्त कंपनियां भेजने और अमरनाथ यात्रा को रद्द करने के फ़ैसले ने घाटी में कुछ बड़ा होने की अटकलों को जन्म दिया था। 'हमें हर जगह कुछ मिले-जुले से संकेत मिल रहे थे। कुछ दिन पहले जब हम राज्यपाल से मिले तो उन्होंने भरोसा दिलाया कि चिंता की कोई बात नहीं थी, लेकिन ज़मीनी हक़ीकत कुछ और थी। प्रधानमंत्री से मुलाक़ात में हमने अपनी चिंता ज़ाहिर की और आश्वासन मांगा कि कश्मीर में ऐसा कुछ नहीं होगा, जिससे घाटी में कोई परेशानी बढ़ जाए,' उमर ने कहा। उमर की बात मानें तो प्रधानमंत्री ने उन्हें भरोसा दिलाया कि परेशान होने की कोई बात नहीं थी। 'हमारा ऐसा कोई इरादा नहीं है,' प्रधानमंत्री ने अपनी बातचीत में आश्वस्त किया। बैठक में ऐसा कुछ नहीं कहा गया जिससे लगे कि अब्दुल्ला परिवार की दुनिया में कोई तूफान आने वाला था। प्रधानमंत्री ने तो इस मुलाकात की तस्वीर के साथ बाद में एक ट्वीट भी किया। 'साफ है कि मिस्टर मोदी ना केवल झूठे इंसान हैं, बल्कि बहुत सफाई से झूठ बोलते हैं,' डॉ. अब्दुल्ला की आवाज़ में नाराज़गी झलक रही थी।

जम्मू कश्मीर के मुख्यमंत्री रहते हुए डॉ. फ़ारुक़ अब्दुल्ला और उमर अब्दुल्ला की नरेन्द्र मोदी से कई बार अंतर राज्यीय परिषद् की बैठकों में बातचीत होती थी। उनके बीच कोई विशेष रिश्ता या लगाव नहीं था, लेकिन डॉ. अब्दुल्ला और प्रधानमंत्री मोदी के बीच कोई दुश्मनी भी नहीं रही। डॉ. अब्दुल्ला याद करते हुए कहते हैं, 'वे हमेशा नरम लहजे और विनम्रता से बात करते हैं, और मुझे हमेशा फ़ारुक़ साहब बुलाते रहे। अगस्त में उस दिन भी कुछ अलग नहीं था। जब हमने उनसे पूछा कि ये अफवाहें तेज़ है कि केन्द्र घाटी में कुछ बड़ा बदलाव करने जा रहा

था, तो उन्होंने मुस्कुराते हुए ऐसे देखा, जिसका मतलब था कि मुझे अफ़वाह फैलाने वालों के बजाय, उन पर भरोसा करना चाहिए।'

मोदी की मीठी, लेकिन छल भरी आवाज़ को याद करते हुए डॉ. अब्दुल्ला की नाराज़गी तब और बढ़ गई, जब पता चला कि बिना किसी औपचारिक आदेश के उन्हें भी हिरासत में लिया जा रहा था। और जब अगले दिन संसद में सरकार ने कहा कि डॉ. अब्दुल्ला को नज़रबंद नहीं किया गया था, तो उनका गुस्सा और बढ़ गया। गुपकर रोड पर उनके घर के बाहर टीवी चैनलों के कैमरे लगे हुए थे। डॉ. अब्दुल्ला अपने घर की बालकनी में आकर चिल्लाए: 'गृहमंत्री संसद में झूठ बोल रहे हैं। क्या आपको लगता है कि जब मेरे प्रदेश में आग लगाई जा रही हो, तो मैं संसद जाने के बजाय अपनी इच्छा से अपने घर में रहूंगा?'

अब्दुल्ला परिवार अकेला नहीं था। अनुच्छेद 370 को निरस्त करने की घोषणा के बाद एक महीने में पांच हज़ार से ज़्यादा लोगों को ऐहतियातन गिरफ़्तार किया गया था। इनमें से ज़्यादातर गिरफ़्तारियां जम्मू कश्मीर सार्वजनिक सुरक्षा अधिनियम में की गईं, जिसके तहत किसी को भी बिना किसी वारंट, मुकदमे या अदालती सुनवाई के नज़रबंद या गिरफ्तार कर दो साल तक जेल में रखा जा सकता है। जहां प्रधानमंत्री से आश्वासन के बावजूद अब्दुल्ला परिवार के सदस्यों को गिरफ्तार किया गया था, वहीं महबूबा मुफ्ती के साथ तो और भी अपमानजनक व्यवहार करने के आरोप लगे। केन्द्र सरकार से उतार-चढ़ाव वाले रिश्तों के बावजूद साल 2018 तक महबूबा मुफ्ती बीजेपी के साथ राज्य में गठबंधन सरकार चला रही थीं। बीजेपी के साथ उनकी नाराजगी उस वक्त बढ़ गई, जब महबूबा ने पत्थरबाज़ी करने के आरोपी गुमराह कश्मीरी नौजवानों के लिए 'माफ़ी योजना' शुरू की। शाह को लगता था कि महबूबा स्थानीय उग्रवादियों का पक्ष लेती थीं और उन पर भरोसा नहीं किया जा सकता। अपने पिता मुफ्ती साहब से विरासत में मिली मुख्यमंत्री की कुर्सी पर बैठने वाली महबूबा की नाराज़गी अमित शाह को लेकर साफ दिख रही थी। महबूबा बोलीं, 'मैं उनसे एक बार दिल्ली में मिली थीं और उन्होंने मुझसे आंख भी नहीं मिलाई।' अब्दुल्ला की तरह महबूबा भी अपनी गिरफ़्तारी को लेकर खासा गुस्से में थी, 'उन्होंने मुझे अपने बैग पैक करने का वक्त भी नहीं दिया, वे मेरी अलमारियाँ तलाश रहे थे। मानो मैं पूर्व मुख्यमंत्री नहीं, कोई आतंकवादी हूं।'

राज्यपाल मलिक घाटी में राजनेताओं की गिरफ़्तारी का बचाव कर रहे थे। उन्होंने कहा, 'आप ऐसे नेताओं को सड़क पर घूमने और चिल्लाने की इजाज़त नहीं दे सकते जो उकसा रहे हों कि अगर अनुच्छेद 370 को हटाया गया तो घाटी में खून की नदियां बह जाएंगी। कोई और परेशानी बढ़ने से रोकने के लिए उन्हें गिरफ़्तार करना ही होगा।' मलिक का दावा था कि स्थानीय नेता लगातार आम आदमी से कट रहे थे और अब जनता का विश्वास उन पर से उठ गया था। 'मुझे याद है कि अनुच्छेद 370 की घोषणा से एक रात पहले महबूबा मुफ़्ती मुझसे मिलने आई थीं। उन्होंने चेतावनी दी कि यदि केन्द्र सरकार ने अनुच्छेद 370 के साथ कोई छेडछाड़ की तो

घाटी में विस्फोट हो जाएगा। अगले दिन कुछ नहीं हुआ, सड़क पर कोई नहीं निकला। हमें एक भी गोली नहीं चलानी पड़ी,' मलिक ने सफाई दी कि 'नेता भले ही हिंसा चाहते हों, लेकिन लोग अब उग्रवाद से थक चुके थे।'

कम से कम अब्दुल्ला और मुफ़्ती परिवार के लोगों को तो अच्छी जगहों पर रखा गया था। जबकि हिरासत में लिए गए कई दूसरे लोगों को एक जेल से दूसरी जेल में भेजा जाता रहा। सुरक्षा कारणों से कुछ को दिल्ली की तिहाड़ जेल में, तो कुछ को बरेली और आगरा की सेन्ट्रल जेल में रखा गया। आगरा जेल में बंद जम्मू कश्मीर के कुछ कैदियों के परिवार वालों और पत्रकारों ने जब 'सूचना के अधिकार क़ानून' के तहत उनके बारे में जानकारी मांगी तो 'गोपनीयता और सुरक्षा कारणों' का हवाला देते हुए उन्हें सूचना देने से इंकार कर दिया गया।

मई, 2022 में एक न्यूज़ वेबसाइट 'आर्टिकल 14' ने एक ख़बर छापी जिसमें आसिफ सुल्तान के मामले का ज़िक्र था, जिसे गिरफ़्तारी के 20 महीने बाद एक विशेष अदालत ने ज़मानत दे दी, लेकिन कश्मीर की काउंटर इंटेलिजेंस इकाई ने फिर से गिरफ़्तार कर लिया। कई वकीलों ने इस गिरफ़्तारी को 'रिवोलविंग डोर डिंटेशन' बताया। सरकार में अफसर रहे आसिफ के पिता सुल्तान सईद बेहद परेशान हो गए थे। उनकी तकलीफ महसूस की जा सकती थी, 'मैं अपने बेटे को गले लगाना चाहता था, लेकिन मेरी सुनने वाला कोई नहीं था'।

संसद में गृहमंत्री शाह और प्रधानमंत्री मोदी, किसी भावुकता या असहमति के लिए लिए तैयार नहीं थे। जैसे ही गृहमंत्री शाह ने सदन में अनुच्छेद 370 को रद्द करने और राज्य को विभाजित करने का प्रस्ताव पेश किया, विपक्षी सदस्य विरोध करने लगे। पीडीपी के दो सदस्यों ने तो संविधान की प्रति को फाड़ दिया। गृहमंत्री बेअसर दिख रहे थे। उन्होंने उसी जोश के साथ इसे एक महत्वपूर्ण मोड़ बताया। शाह जानते थे कि ना केवल सदन में बहुमत उनके पक्ष में था बल्कि उन्हें प्रधानमंत्री का साथ और समर्थन भी हासिल था। उसी शाम, एक ट्वीट में शाह ने प्रधानमंत्री की तारीफ करते हुए कहा, 'आज मोदी सरकार ने लंबे समय से चली आ रही एक ऐतिहासिक गलती को सुधार दिया है। मैं देश की एकता और संप्रभुता के प्रति उनकी अटूट प्रतिबद्धता के लिए प्रधानमंत्री नरेन्द्र मोदी जी को बधाई देता हूं। यह ऐतिहासिक फ़ैसला जम्मू कश्मीर और लद्दाख में शांति और विकास की एक नई सुबह लेकर आएगा।' प्रधानमंत्री मोदी ने भी प्रतिक्रिया देने में देर नहीं लगाई। प्रधानमंत्री ने लिखाः 'हमारे गृहमंत्री अमित शाह जी जम्मू कश्मीर और लद्दाख के लोगों की बेहतरी के लिए अथक कोशिश कर रहे हैं। उनकी मेहनत और प्रतिबद्धता इन बिलों में दिखाई देती है। इसके लिए मैं अमित भाई को विशेष रूप से बधाई देना चाहता हूं।' गुजरात की जोडी नंबर 1 ने आपस में एक दूसरे की तारीफ करते हुए ज़ाहिर कर दिया कि इस ऐतिहासिक फैसले के पीछे कौन था। यह महत्वपूर्ण निर्णय उनकी सरकार के दूसरे कार्यकाल की विरासत बनेगा।

संसद में शाह के अपनी छाप छोड़ने के दो दिन बाद, अब केन्द्र में आने की बारी प्रधानमंत्री मोदी की थी। राष्ट्र के नाम संबोधन में प्रधानमंत्री मोदी ने इसे जम्मू कश्मीर और लद्दाख के लिए नए युग की शुरुआत बताया। अनुच्छेद 370 को हटाने की ज़रूरत पर प्रधानमंत्री ने कहा, 'हमने एक राष्ट्र के रूप में, परिवार के रूप में ऐतिहासिक निर्णय किया है। जिस व्यवस्था की वजह से जम्मू, कश्मीर और लद्दाख में हमारे भाई-बहन बहुत से अधिकारों से वंचित थे और जो उनके विकास के लिए बड़ी बाधा थी, वो अब ख़त्म हो गया है।' प्रधानमंत्री ने सुशासन की आवश्यकता पर ज़ोर देते हुए कहा कि वो वक्त भी लौटेगा जब हिंदी सिनेमा में कश्मीर की वादियों का ज़िक्र होता था। प्रधानमंत्री ने 'नया भारत, नया जम्मू कश्मीर और नया लद्दाख' का नारा देते हुए दावा किया कि 'अनुच्छेद 370 और 35(ए) ने अलगाववाद, भ्रष्टाचार, आतंकवाद और परिवारराज के अलावा कुछ नहीं दिया।' जम्मू कश्मीर के लोगों को राज्य के दर्जे की बहाली कब होगी, पर कोई ठोस आश्वासन के बिना प्रधानमंत्री ने कहा कि धीरे-धीरे स्थिति सामान्य हो जाएगी। संदेश साफ था कि विवादास्पद अनुच्छेद 370 की वापसी के फ़ैसले से पीछे नहीं हटा जाएगा।

मोदी सरकार 2.0 ने मानो 'रेत पर रेखा' खींचकर सीमाएं तय कर दी थी। दूसरी बार शपथ लेने के करीब दो महीने बाद ही सरकार ने एक ऐसा ऐतिहासिक फ़ैसला किया, जिसने बरसों बरस से अशांत कश्मीर की 'यथास्थिति' को ख़त्म कर दिया था। इससे पहले मोदी सरकार ने पहली बार सत्ता में आने के दो साल बाद 8 नवम्बर 2016 की रात नोटबंदी का ऐलान कर 500 और 1000 के नोटों को चलन से बाहर कर दिया था। उस वक्त सरकार में बैठे और सरकार के बाहर के लोग इस फ़ैसले से चौंक गए थे। लेकिन अनुच्छेद 370 को रद्द करने का निर्णय अप्रत्याशित नहीं था। इसकी शुरुआत तो साल 2019 के चुनाव प्रचार अभियान के दौरान ही हो गई थी। वैसे भी यह मुद्दा भाजपा के एजेंडे में शुरुआत से रहा था। सरकार के एक वरिष्ठ मंत्री ने बताया कि जब नोटबंदी के निर्णय के बारे में जानकारी दी गई तो कैबिनेट बैठक में मानो सन्नाटा पसर गया और मंत्री एक-दूसरे की तरफ देखने लगे। 'मगर जब 5 अगस्त 2019 की सुबह अनुच्छेद 370 को हटाने के बारे में बताया गया तो माहौल कुछ अलग था।' वरिष्ठ मंत्री ने दावा किया कि 'कुछ मंत्रियों ने उत्साह में मेजें थपथपाकर इस फ़ैसले का स्वागत किया और प्रधानमंत्री और गृहमंत्री को बधाई दी। मोदी सरकार ने सही समय पर फ़ैसला किया था।'

लोकसभा चुनावों में एक और बड़ी जीत की चमक अभी बरकरार थी। इस जीत से प्रधानमंत्री मोदी के नेता नंबर 1 की साख पर फिर से मुहर लगी थी। इसके मुकाबले विपक्ष, खासतौर से कांग्रेस अब भी उधेड़बुन या असमंजस में थी और क़रारी चुनावी हार से निकलने की कोशिश कर रही थी। सरकार के पास एक साहसिक कदम उठाने के लिए सदन में पर्याप्त ताकत थी, चाहे

फिलहाल उसके नतीजे अराजक माने जाएं। मोदी 1.0 से उलट, मोदी 2.0 को अपने वैचारिक लक्ष्यों को आगे बढ़ाने के लिए सहयोगियों की तरफ से चिंता या दबाव महसूस नहीं हो रहा था। सरकार के भीतर या बाहर अभी किसी के असहमति जताने की स्थिति नहीं थी। फरवरी 2019 में पुलवामा में हुए आतंकी हमले के बाद से साफ था कि जनता फिलहाल पाकिस्तान के साथ रिश्तों को सुधारने या फिर कश्मीर में राजनेताओं या अलगाववादियों से बातचीत करने के ख़िलाफ़ थी। देश में अभी सिर्फ़ 'राष्ट्र प्रथम' के उत्साहित माहौल का इस्तेमाल किया जा सकता था। उत्साहित गृहमंत्री ने संसद के अपने दफ़्तर में कहा, 'मोदी सरकार ने वो फ़ैसला किया है, जिसका देश इंतज़ार कर रहा था।'

भारतीय जनता पार्टी के लिए 'इन हाउस ट्रैकर' सर्वेक्षण बता रहा था कि अनुच्छेद 370 के फ़ैसले को जनता का भारी समर्थन मिला था और 80 फ़ीसदी लोगों ने इस पर अपनी मुहर लगाई थी। इसके बाद जनवरी 2020 में हुए *इंडिया टुडे* सर्वेक्षण में 58 फ़ीसदी लोगों ने माना कि अनुच्छेद 370 को रद्द करने से कश्मीर समस्या के स्थायी समाधान की ओर बढ़ा जा सकता है। ज़्यादातर लोगों ने इसे सरकार की बड़ी उपलब्धि माना, लेकिन प्रदेश को दो हिस्सों में बांटने और उसे राज्य के दर्जे से घटाकर केन्द्र शासित प्रदेश बनाने के फ़ैसले पर लोग उस तरह सरकार के साथ दिखाई नहीं दिए। सर्वेक्षण में पचास फ़ीसदी लोगों का मानना था कि यह फ़ैसला, देश के संघीय ढांचे के ख़िलाफ था।

बीजेपी के लिए यह मसला केवल वोटों की ताकत को लेकर नही था। भाजपा के एक नेता ने मुझसे कहा कि 'इससे एक ऐसा "माहौल" बनेगा, जिससे मोदी-शाह की अगुवाई वाली बीजेपी और सरकार को अलग नज़रिए से देखा जाएगा।' यही माहौल गृहमंत्री शाह के उस जवाब में दिख रहा था, जब एक पत्रकार ने उनसे पूछा कि क्या इतने महत्वपूर्ण फ़ैसले से पहले सरकार को इससे जुडे लोगों से सलाह-मशविरा नहीं करना चाहिए था? गृहमंत्री का जवाब स्पष्ट था, 'सत्तर सालों से हम सिर्फ़ सलाह मशविरा ही तो कर रहे हैं, इसलिए कोई ठोस फ़ैसला नहीं किया गया। अब सलाह नहीं, एक्शन दिखेगा।'

देश के इकलौते मुस्लिम-बहुल राज्य को केन्द्र शासित प्रदेश में बदल दिया गया। साफ था कि यह मुस्लिम बहुल इलाके को अपने अधीन करने की छिपी हुई हिंदू भावनाओं का मसला है और इसे हिंदुत्व की ताकत बताना भी माना जा सकता है। नई सरकार के पहले 100 दिनों में कड़े राजनीतिक फ़ैसले लेने का खाका तैयार था। अपने मूल एजेंडे पर आगे बढ़ने में सरकार को कोई परेशानी नहीं थी। कश्मीर पर फ़ैसला तो पहला कदम था। देश में हिन्दुत्व की राजनीति को आगे बढ़ाने के लिए अभी बहुत कुछ पिटारे में था।

अक्टूबर 2019, दिवाली से ठीक पहले गृहमंत्री के पास एक खास मेहमान, आरएसएस के वरिष्ठ नेता चाय पर मुलाकात के लिए पहुंचे। उन्होंने अनुच्छेद 370 को निरस्त करने के सरकार के प्रभावी तरीके से फ़ैसला लेने पर बधाई दी। बात को आगे बढ़ाते हुए आरएसएस नेता ने कहा कि पाकिस्तान से आए कई हिंदू परिवार दिल्ली और उसके आसपास के इलाके में बरसों से रह रहे हैं, लेकिन उनको नागरिकता देने के मामले सरकारी फ़ाइलों में अटके हुए हैं, क्या आप उनके लिए कुछ कर सकते हैं? बिना देर लगाए शाह ने आश्वस्त किया, 'चिंता मत कीजिए, हम जल्दी ही इसको ठीक करने जा रहे हैं।'

अनुच्छेद 370 को निरस्त करना तो भाजपा के मूल एजेंडे में शामिल था, साथ ही नागरिकता क़ानून में बदलाव भी उनकी प्राथमिकताओं में था। इस बदलाव से दक्षिण एशिया में धार्मिक तौर पर उत्पीड़ित हिंदुओं को नागरिकता मिल सकती थी। 2014 के चुनावों से पहले बीजेपी ने अपने चुनावी घोषणापत्र में इस बात पर ज़ोर दिया था कि वो सरकार बनने पर पड़ोसी देशों में प्रताड़ित हिंदुओं को बसाने पर काम करेगी। सरकार ने जुलाई 2016 में नागरिकता संशोधन विधेयक को लोकसभा में पेश किया और इसे संसद की स्थायी समिति के पास विस्तार से चर्चा के लिए भेज दिया गया। फिर जनवरी 2019 में इसे लोकसभा से पास भी कर दिया गया, लेकिन राज्यसभा में पास होने से पहले ही लोकसभा का कार्यकाल ख़त्म हो जाने से वह बिल 'लैप्स' हो गया। उस वक्त राज्यसभा में पूर्वोत्तर में कई सहयोगी दल बड़ी तादाद में बांग्लादेशी शरणार्थियों को नागरिकता दिए जाने के डर से इस बिल का विरोध कर रहे थे और बीजेपी चुनावों से पहले कोई जोख़िम उठाने को तैयार नहीं थी।

वैसे शाह इसको लेकर परेशान नहीं दिख रहे थे। अप्रैल 2019 में एक प्रेस ब्रीफिंग में शाह ने स्पष्ट किया: 'पहले नागरिकता संशोधन बिल आएगा, सभी शरणार्थियों को नागरिकता मिलेगी और फिर राष्ट्रीय नागरिक रजिस्टर (एनआरसी) आएगा। इसलिए शरणार्थियों को नहीं, घुसपैठियों को चिंता करनी चाहिए। क्रोनोलोजी तो समझिए।' बातचीत में चुनाव अभियान के दौरान ही बीजेपी अध्यक्ष ने अपना इरादा जता दिया था। मई 2019 में चुनाव प्रचार के दौरान पश्चिम बंगाल में बोनगांव में एक चुनावी सभा में अमित शाह ने ज़ोर देकर कहा, 'पहले हम नागरिकता संशोधन बिल पास करेंगे और यह सुनिश्चित करेंगे कि पड़ोसी देशों के शरणार्थियों को भारतीय नागरिकता मिले। इसके बाद राष्ट्रीय नागरिकता रजिस्टर बनाया जाएगा और पहचान करके हर घुसपैठिये को बाहर कर देंगे। हम पूरे देश में एनआरसी लागू करेंगे। हम बौद्ध, सिख और हिंदुओं को छोड़कर हर घुसपैठिए को बाहर कर देंगे।' सभा में मौजूद लोग तालियां बजाकर समर्थन जता रहे थे, इनमें से ज़्यादातर आबादी बांग्लादेश से आए 'मतुआ' समाज के हिंदुओं की थी।

इससे पहले तक शाह मुस्लिम प्रवासियों का नाम साफतौर पर लेने से बचते रहे थे और अक्सर वे उनके लिए 'घुसपैठिए' शब्द का इस्तेमाल करते थे। लेकिन अब मुस्लिम बांग्लादेशियों की तरफ साफ इशारा था। शाह ने एक चुनावी रैली में चुनौती दी, 'घुसपैठिए बंगाल की ज़मीन पर दीमक की तरह हैं और बीजेपी सरकार एक-एक घुसपैठिए को उठाकर बंगाल की खाड़ी में फेंक देगी'। यह पहली बार था जब नागरिकता क़ानून को, धार्मिक रंग देने की साफ कोशिश की गई। शाह की इस टिप्पणी को बीजेपी के आधिकारिक ट्विटर हैंडल पर पोस्ट किया गया, मगर बाद में उसे हटा दिया गया। शाह के इस बयान को कई आलोचकों ने मुस्लिम विरोधी मानसिकता बताया, जिसे बाद में नागरिकता संशोधन कानून का आधार बनाया गया।

2019 के चुनावों की शानदार जीत ने शाह का भरोसा बढ़ा दिया था कि वो सही रास्ते पर थे। भाजपा अध्यक्ष के तौर पर हिन्दू शरणार्थियों के लिए नागरिकता क़ानून में जिस बदलाव की बात उन्होंने की थी, अब वे गृहमंत्री के तौर पर उसे हक़ीकत में बदल सकते थे। उन्होंने अपने एक सहयोगी को कहा भी कि 'जब जनता ने बहुमत दिया है तो फिर दबाव की राजनीति नहीं हो सकती।' वैसे शाह को भी ज़मीनी हक़ीकत पता थी कि यह बारुदी सुरंग में घुसने जैसा मसला था। अगस्त, 2019 में सुप्रीम कोर्ट की निगरानी में बीजेपी शासित असम में बनाई गई 'एनआरसी की लिस्ट' में 19 लाख से ज़्यादा आवेदकों को बाहर कर दिया गया था, इनमें हिंदुओं की तादाद भी काफी थी, जो फिर से बेघर होने की हालत में आ गए थे। अब शाह पर अपनी ही पार्टी की तरफ से इसका रास्ता निकालने का दबाव बनने लगा था। उन्हें हिंदू हितों की रक्षा करते हुए मुस्लिम घुसपैठियों को बाहर करने के लिए क़ानूनी रास्ता ढूंढना था। देश भर में 'एनआरसी' को लागू करना तो टेढ़ा काम था, लेकिन हिन्दू शरणार्थियों को नागरिकता का मसला क़ानूनी तौर पर मुमकिन था।

आर्टिकल 370 को ध्यान में रखते हुए, शाह के कानूनी सलाहकार, सॉलिसिटर जनरल तुषार मेहता को क़ानूनी मसलों पर ध्यान देने का जिम्मा दिया गया। मेहता जोश खरोश से काम को निपटाने में जुट गए। मेहता की राय स्पष्ट थीः नागरिकता देना किसी भी देश की संप्रभुता से जुड़ा मसला है। उनका मानना था कि 'यदि इसमें वर्गीकरण या भेद करने को लेकर कोई मनमानी नहीं है, तब तक इसमें कोई क़ानूनी रुकावट नहीं आएगी।' इसमें साल 2014 से पहले भारत में आने वाले चुनिंदा देशों के 'धार्मिक तौर पर प्रताड़ित' अल्पसंख्यकों को नागरिकता का मसला था, जो उनके नजरिए से कोई क़ानूनी दिक्कत नहीं थी। लेकिन कई संविधान विशेषज्ञों की राय अलग थी। क़ानून विशेषज्ञ गौतम भाटिया का मानना था कि 'प्रवासियों को मुस्लिमों और गैर-मुस्लिमों में बांटने का मतलब क़ानूनी तौर पर धार्मिक भेदभाव करना है, जो हमारे धर्मनिरपेक्ष संवैधानिक व्यवहार से मेल नहीं खाता'।

एक बार फिर ऐसा लगा कि फ़ैसला लेते वक्त बहुत कम सलाह-मशविरा किया गया था। सरकार के सबसे बड़े क़ानूनी सलाहकार यानी अटॉर्नी जनरल के.के. वेणुगोपाल को शुरुआती मसौदा तैयार करने में शामिल नहीं किया गया था। गृह मंत्रालय ने इस मसले पर पहल की थी और क़ानून मंत्रालय को सरकार की मंशा बता दी गई थी। बाद में क़ानून मंत्री रविशंकर ने दावा किया कि 'किसी तरह का कोई मतभेद नहीं है और हम सब एकमत हैं।' प्रस्तावित क़ानून की संवैधानिकता या फिर किसी राजनीतिक विरोध की चिंता को दरकिनार कर दिया गया। बताया जाता है कि गृहमंत्री शाह ने आला अफसरों के साथ एक बैठक में चिढ़ते हुए सवाल किया, 'कांग्रेस जैसी पार्टियां इस बिल पर कैसे आपत्ति जताएंगे? क्या आपको पता है कि साल 2003 में राज्यसभा में विपक्ष के नेता के तौर पर डॉ. मनमोहन सिंह ने तब की वाजपेयी सरकार से यह सुनिश्चित करने का आग्रह किया था कि बांग्लादेश से आए अल्पसंख्यकों को नागरिकता आसानी से दी जाए। अब किस मुंह से वे विरोध करेंगे?' वैसे यह बिल उससे अलग था। इसमें मुस्लिम शरणार्थियों को अपने आप नगारिकता मिलने के दायरे से बाहर कर दिया गया था। शाह ने उस चिंता को भी खारिज़ कर दिया कि उनके सहयोगी जनता दल (यूनाइटेड) इस बिल पर सरकार का साथ नहीं देंगे। शाह ने अपने अंदाज़ में कहा, 'यह बीजेपी की सरकार है, हमारे पास 303 सांसद हैं, उनके पास कितने हैं?' जनता दल (यूनाइटेड) के सोलह सांसद थे।

शाह जानते थे कि उनके पास उस व्यक्ति का समर्थन था, सिर्फ़ जिसका होना ही सरकार में मायने रखता हैः प्रधानमंत्री मोदी। वैसे नागरिकता संशोधन कानून मोदी के 2019 के चुनावी एजेंडा में शामिल नहीं था, लेकिन शाह ने प्रधानमंत्री को आश्वस्त किया कि बिल पास कराने में कोई परेशानी नहीं होगी। कश्मीर पर ऐतिहासिक फ़ैसले के बाद इसे भी सरकार के उस बड़े कदम की तरह देखा गया जो उसके हिंदुत्व और राष्ट्रवादी एजेंडा को मजबूती देगा और हताश विपक्ष को इसका विरोध करने में मुश्किल होगी। मोदी 1.0 में जहां सरकार सर्वसम्मति के रास्ते से चलती दिख रही थी वहीं मोदी 2.0 में पहले काम, फिर चर्चा के मोड में आ गई। शाह इस बदलाव को साफतौर पर जता रहे थे। अनुच्छेद 370 को रद्द करते वक्त जहां प्रधानमंत्री कार्यालय हर कदम पर बारीक नज़र रखता था, अब गृहमंत्री को संसद के शीतकालीन सत्र में इस बिल को पारित कराना था।

शाह आश्वस्त तो थे, लेकिन कोई जोखिम उठाना नहीं चाहते थे। उन्होंने अपनी 'कोर टीम'—पीयूष गोयल, धर्मेन्द्र प्रधान और भूपेन्द्र यादव को सरकार में प्रमुख सहयोगियों और विपक्षी दलों के नेताओं से बात करने की जिम्मेदारी सौंपी। लोकसभा में तो बीजेपी की ताकत मज़बूत थी, लेकिन राज्यसभा में पर्याप्त बहुमत नहीं था। ओड़िशा के बीजू जनता दल और आंध्रप्रदेश की वाईएसआर कांग्रेस ने शाह की टीम को आश्वस्त किया कि वे राज्यों में भले ही बीजेपी के विरोधी दल की भूमिका में हों, लेकिन केन्द्र में 'दोस्त' हैं और संसद में बिल

का समर्थन करेंगे। बिहार मे जनता दल यूनाइटेड के नेता और मुख्यमंत्री नीतीश कुमार से खुद अमित शाह ने बात की। नीतीश कुमार इस बिल से अपना मुस्लिम वोट खिसकने की आशंका से परेशान थे। नीतीश ने शुरू में एक बैठक में बिल पर विरोध जताया था, लेकिन गृहमंत्री के फ़ोन पर बात करने से मामला सुलझ गया। जनता दल यूनाइटेड के एक वरिष्ठ नेता कहा, 'मुझे लगता है कि नीतीश बाबू को पता था कि बिहार में विधानसभा चुनावों में एक साल का वक्त भी नहीं बचा था और वे उस वक्त भाजपा से मुकाबला करने की स्थिति में नहीं थे।'

9 दिसम्बर 2019, गृहमंत्री शाह ने बिल पेश किया, इस बिल में 31 दिसम्बर 2014 से पहले पाकिस्तान, अफ़गानिस्तान और बांग्लादेश से भारत आने वाले गैर मुस्लिमों (हिंदू, ईसाई, पारसी, जैन, सिख और बौद्ध) को अपने आप नागरिकता देने की बात की गई है। एक दिन बाद ही बिल लोकसभा में पास हो गया, उसके पक्ष में 311 वोट मिले थे, जबकि केवल 80 वोट इसके विरोध में पड़े। फिर 11 दिसम्बर को यह बिल राज्यसभा में भी पारित हो गया, हालांकि यहां 110 ख़िलाफ़ वोटों के पक्ष में 125 वोट ही मिले थे। इस क़ानून को 'धर्म निरपेक्ष' रखने की विपक्षी कोशिश नाकाम हो गई थी। दोनों सदनों में सबकी नज़र नारंगी रंग की जैकेट पहने गृहमंत्री शाह पर ही थी। गृहमंत्री ने ज़ोर देते हुए कहा, 'यह बिल मुसलमानों के ख़िलाफ़ 0.001 प्रतिशत भी नहीं है, यह घुसपैठियों के ख़िलाफ़ है।' लेकिन इसके बाद गृहमंत्री पड़ोसी इस्लामिक देशों में गैर-मुस्लिमों के साथ उत्पीड़न, हत्या, बलात्कार, जबरन धर्म परिवर्तन और पूजा स्थलों को तोड़ने की घटनाओं का ज़िक्र कर रहे थे। जब कांग्रेस सांसद शशि थरूर ने कहा कि 'जिन्होंने धर्म को राष्ट्रीयता का आधार माना, उन्होंने ही पाकिस्तान बनाया ...और यही पाकिस्तान का विचार था।' गृहमंत्री ने जवाब दिया, 'अगर कांग्रेस, धर्म के आधार पर देश को बांटने के लिए तैयार नहीं होती तो आज सीएए की ज़रूरत ही नही पड़ती। यह कांग्रेस ही थी, जिसने देश का बंटवारा किया... हमने नहीं किया।'

यह आख़िरी जवाब बिल्कुल शाह के अंदाज़ में था, जो धार्मिक राष्ट्रवाद को लेकर किसी भी हद तक हमले के लिए तैयार दिखते हैं। कट्टर हिन्दूत्व की सोच उनके दिल के करीब तो हमेशा रही, लेकिन पहली बार देशभर के लोग उनकी इस भावना को 'लाइव' देख रहे थे। एक जोशीले दक्षिणपंथी नेता के तौर पर शाह हमेशा आम सहमति के नाम पर धर्म निरपेक्षता को खारिज करते हैं और धर्मनिरपेक्ष और उदारवादी कहलाने वाले लोगों को निशाना बनाने में गर्व महसूस करते हैं। गुजरात के साम्प्रदायिक माहौल के बीच आगे बढ़ने और राजनीति में मजबूत होने के साथ हिन्दू-मुस्लिम राजनीति को उनकी दूसरी पसंद मानना चाहिए। नागरिकता क़ानून पर बहस हिन्दूत्व को अंतरराष्ट्रीय नजरिए तक पहुंचाने का एक महत्वपूर्ण कदम था, जहां मुसलमानों को दुश्मन नहीं तो कम से कम संदेह की नज़र से देखा जाएगा। बिल पारित होने के बाद जब हम उनके कक्ष में मिले, तो वे उत्साहित नज़र आ रहे थे, लेकिन अपने आक्रामक

अंदाज़ में शाह ने कहा, 'यदि आप लोगों को लगता है कि यह अल्पसंख्यक विरोधी कानून है तो आप धर्मनिरपेक्षता और तुष्टिकरण का अपना चश्मा बदलिए। यह समाज में असली एकता बनाने का क़ानून है।'

मैं चुपचाप सुनता रहा, साफगोई के साथ कड़वी बात करने वाले मंत्री के साथ बहस करने का मन फिलहाल नहीं था। पहले अनुच्छेद 370 और अब सीएए, यानी नागरिकता संशोधन क़ानून। क़ानूनों के लिए नये तरीके से रास्ता बनाती सरकार तेज़ी से आगे बढ़ रही थी। भाजपा ने संसद में तो संख्या बल के आधार पर विपक्ष की आवाज़ बंद कर दी थी, लेकिन इन संसदीय गलियारों के बाहर, देश की सड़कों और गलियों में बढ़ती नाराज़गी महसूस की जा सकती थी।

═

दक्षिणी दिल्ली में पसरा जामिया मिलिया इस्लामिया परिसर दिल्ली के शोर-शराबे के बीच शांति का नख़लिस्तान महसूस होता है। हरे-भरे और घने पेड़ों की कतारें विश्वविद्यालय को चारों ओर बसे भीड़भाड़ वाले इलाके से अलग करती हैं। नवाब पटौदी खेल परिसर और यहां का सुंदर क्रिकेट मैदान खेल गतिविधियों से चहकता रहता है। पुस्तकालय के ठीक सामने बनी मस्जिद, प्रार्थना और चिंतन के लिए बेहतर जगह है। आम्तौर पर रविवार को यहां सन्नाटा रहता है। छात्र अपने डिपार्टमेंट के पास टहलते दिखाई देते हैं या फिर पुस्तकालय में पढ़ रहे होते हैं। लेकिन 15 दिसम्बर 2019 का दिन शायद अलग होने वाला था। यहां तक कि सर्दी की बढ़ी हुई ठंडक भी राजनीतिक गर्मी को कम नही कर पाएगी।

जामिया के छात्र कई दिनों से नागरिकता संशोधन क नून के असर पर गर्मागर्म बहस कर रहे थे। जबकि जामिया में और डिपार्टमेंट्स में सब तरह के लोग थे। सुपर स्टार शाहरुख खान और क्रिकेटर वीरेन्द्र सहवाग यहां के नामी छात्रों में से रहे हैं, विश्वविद्यालय के अल्पसंख्यक चरित्र पर कोई बहस नहीं है। देशभर में कई युवा भारतीय मुसलमानों के लिए जामिया में दाखिला बेहतर शिक्षा का पासपोर्ट माना जाता है। सीएए को लेकर जैसे-जैसे राजनीतिक बहस ध्रुवीकृत होने लगी, जामिया में इसकी गर्मी का एहसास होने लगा था। उत्तेजित छात्रों को लगता था कि यह क़ानून पहली नज़र में मुसलमानों के ख़िलाफ़ भेदभाव वाला है और उन्हें अपनी आवाज़ को बुलंद करनी पडेगी। 15 दिसम्बर को रविवार के दिन विश्वविद्यालय परिसर के बाहर छात्रों ने एक विरोध मार्च निकाला। आयोजकों में से एक छात्र असगर अहमद (बदला हुआ नाम) ने कहा, 'हमारा विरोध प्रतीकात्मक और शांतिपूर्ण था। हम केवल यह बताना चाहते थे कि जिस तरह से मोदी सरकार ने एक असंवैधानिक क़ानून आगे बढ़ाया है, इससे छात्र नाराज़ हैं।'

दोपहर 2 बजते-बजते प्रदर्शन ने रफ्तार पकड़ ली थी। पड़ोसी इलाके जामिया नगर में दुकानें बंद होने लगीं। ओखला से आम आदमी पार्टी के विधायक अमानतुल्ला खान की नुमाइंदगी

में इलाके में एक 'शांतिपूर्ण' रैली निकाली गई। जैसे-जैसे लोगों की तादाद बढ़ने लगी तो तय किया गया कि प्रदर्शनकारी रिंग रोड से होते हुए इंडिया गेट की तरफ मार्च करेंगे। पुलिस ने सुरक्षा के नज़रिए से बैरिकेड्स लगाने शुरू कर दिए। तब तक भीड़ बेचैन होने लगी थी और कुछ प्रदर्शनकारियों ने बैरिकेड्स पर चढ़ने की कोशिश भी की। शाम को करीब 4 बजे कुछ अज्ञात लोगों ने डीटीसी की दो बसों और एक मोटर साइकिल में आग लगा दी। कुछ इलाकों में पथराव होने की ख़बरें आने लगी। पुलिस ने अब प्रदर्शनकारियों पर आंसूगैस के गोले छोड़े और लाठियां बरसाईं। शाम 6 बजे तक आगजनी की कई और घटनाएं हो गईं। अब साफ हो गया कि यह केवल छात्रों का शांतिपूर्ण प्रदर्शन नहीं था, स्थिति हिंसक और काबू से बाहर होने लगी थी। अहमद ने जोर देकर कहा, 'मेरी बात पर भरोसा कीजिए, इस हिंसा के पीछे छात्र नहीं, बल्कि बाहरी लोग थे, जिससे परेशानी हुई'।

प्रशासन और पुलिस के लिए छात्रों और बाहरी लोगों में कोई फ़र्क नहीं था। कुछ ही देर में पुलिस प्रदर्शनकारियों की तलाश में जामिया परिसर में घुस गई। आंसू गैस के गोले छोड़े गए। दरवाज़ों को जबरन तोड़ने की कोशिश हुई। मुख्य पुस्तकालय में भी तोड़-फोड़ की गई। एक छात्र ने कहा, 'इससे पहले कि हम कुछ समझ पाते, पुलिस, जो सामने आया उसे डंडों से पीट रही थी। कई लोगों के सिर में चोटें आईं, कुछ के ख़ून बहने लगा था।' अगले दिन जब पत्रकारों ने स्थानीय पुलिस से कॉलेज पुस्तकालय में घुसने पर सवाल किए, तो पुलिस का कहना था, 'जब आप बसें जलाते हैं, पुलिस पर हमला करते हैं तो फिर आप छात्र नहीं, दंगाई होते हैं।'

उस रविवार को जो कुछ हुआ, उस पर भले ही परस्पर विरोधी बातें सामने आ रही हों, लेकिन एक बात साफ थी कि सीएए ने समाज में मोदी सरकार के विरोधी, खासतौर से मुस्लिम समाज में गुस्सा भर दिया था। अब न केवल छात्रों के लिए बल्कि जामिया और उसके आसपास के इलाकों में रहने वाले लोगों के लिए सीएए वो राजनीतिक आदेश था, जिसकी कोशिश मुसलमानों को 'दूसरे दर्जे' का नागरिक बनाने की थी। जम्मू कश्मीर के राज्य का दर्जा खोने के बाद इस नागरिकता संशोधन क़ानून को, देश को 'हिंदू बहुसंख्यक' राज्य बनाने के कदम की तरह देखा जाने लगा। स्थानीय लोगों की नज़र में, मोदी-शाह की जोड़ी अब भी साल 2002 के गुजरात दंगों से पहचानी जाती थी। अब अतीत के भूत, नई पीढ़ी को परेशान करने के लिए लौट आए थे। सीएए के बचाव में गृहमंत्री ने जो कुछ कहा, उससे भी नाराज़गी और अविश्वास कम नहीं होने वाला था। इलाके के एक दुकानदार ने टिप्पणी की, 'खाकी वर्दी वालों के लिए जामिया में रहने और दाढ़ी रखने वाला हर आदमी दंगाई है। उनकी कार्रवाई क़ानून व्यवस्था बनाए रखने के लिए नहीं, बल्कि हमें सबक सिखाने के लिए होती हैं।'

सोमवार सुबह जामिया इलाके में पसरी शांति परेशान करने वाली थी। जली हुई बस, पुस्तकालय की टूटी हुई खिड़कियां और फर्श पर पड़े ख़ून के धब्बे पिछले दिन जो कुछ हुआ,

उसकी याद दिला रहे थे। स्थानीय लोगों का गुस्सा अभी कम नहीं हो रहा था। जामिया से कुछ दूर ही शाहीन बाग कॉलोनी में, बुजुर्ग महिलाओं का एक ग्रुप शांतिपूर्ण प्रदर्शन के लिए इकट्ठा हुआ। उनके हाथों में जामिया में हिंसा और सीएए के ख़िलाफ़ तख्तियां थीं, उनकी तादाद बहुत ज्यादा नहीं थी। एक पुलिस अफसर ने माना कि 'शुरू में हमें लगा कि कुछ छात्रों के अभिभावक सांकेतिक प्रदर्शन के लिए इकट्ठा हुए हैं, हमें इस बात की आशंका नहीं हुई कि यह इतना बड़ा मुद्दा बन जाएगा।'

जामिया नगर से सटा शाहीन बाग, कामकाजी लोगों का इलाका माना जाता है। अस्सी के दशक तक इस इलाके में हिन्दू गुर्जर समाज के लोग सब्जियां उगाते थे और उनके खेत थे। लेकिन जैसे ही उन लोगों ने यहां से ज़मीनें बेचकर जाना शुरू किया, घनी बस्ती वाले जामिया से आकर लोग यहां बसने लगे। फिर 1992 में बाबरी मस्जिद टूटने के बाद यहां आबादी का स्वरूप तेज़ी से बदलने लगा। मुसलमान (और हिंदू) अपने-अपने समुदायों के इलाकों में सुरक्षा तलाश रहे थे।

मिली-जुली आबादी वाला शाहीन बाग धीरे-धीरे एक भीड़भाड़ वाली मुस्लिम बस्ती में तब्दील हो गया, जिसमें कोई सहूलियतें नहीं थीं। गंदी सड़कें, खुले सीवर और अनियमित बिजली आपूर्ति के साथ शाहीन बाग एक ऐसी बीमार और खराब होती बस्ती लगती थी, जिससे सरकार ने मानो मुंह मोड़ लिया हो। लगता था कि सरकार ने शाहीन बाग को अपने हाल पर छोड़ दिया है। एक स्थानीय निवासी ने बताया कि 'शाहीन बाग में हमारे पास रोज़ाना सैकड़ों शिकायतें आती हैं जिन पर कोई ध्यान देने वाला नहीं। अब हमारे पास शिकायत की एक और वजह थी, इस बार हम सिर्फ़ नागरिक के तौर पर नहीं बल्कि एक गौरव के साथ भारतीय मुसलमान नागरिक होने की वजह से अपने अधिकारों के लिए एकजुट थे।'

कुछ ही दिनों बाद, सटे हुए नोएडा की तरफ जाने वाली मुख्य सड़क को बंद कर दिया गया, यहां बैठी महिलाओं के छोटे विरोध पर अब लोगों का ध्यान जाने लगा और कुछ ही दिनों में यहां रफ्तार और तादाद बढ़ने लगी थी। हर शाम कुछ युवा और बुज़ुर्ग महिलाएं भी प्रदर्शन कर अपनी बात पहुंचाने की कोशिश कर रही थीं। पुरुष प्रधान समाज में मुस्लिम महिलाओं की नुमाइंदगी में आपसी भागीदारी से चल रहा यह आंदोलन जम्हूरियत के लिए एक अनोखी मिसाल जैसा था। अस्सी की उम्र में, हिजाब या बुर्का पहनने से लेकर साड़ी पहनने वाली, दिहाड़ी मज़दूरों से लेकर सलवार-कमीज पहनकर जाने वाली लड़कियां, शाहीन बाग का यह प्रदर्शन विविधता की दुर्लभ नुमाइंदगी कर रहा था। अपने बच्चों को गोद में उठाए, लेकिन एक मजबूत संकल्प के साथ महिलाओं की नुमाइंदगी वाले इस धरने ने देशभर नें सीएए के ख़िलाफ़ हो रहे प्रदर्शनों से एक अलग पहचान बनाई थी।

यह अपने आपमें एक खास तरह का धरना स्थल था, जहां दिल्ली की सर्दी में टेंट के नीचे गद्दों और कंबलों में एक साथ लिपटे हुए अपने छोटे बच्चों के साथ, कहीं खाना बनाते, खिलाते,

हंसते और बातें करते हुए मुस्लिम महिलाएं प्रदर्शन कर रही थीं। यहां नाटक और नुक्कड़ नाटक भी हो रहे थे। सीएए और मोदी सरकार के ख़िलाफ़ नारों के साथ बैनर बनाए जा रहे थे। दीवारों पर भी प्रदर्शन का रंग नज़र आने लगा। एकजुटता दिखाने के लिए कुछ विपक्षी नेता भी कभी-कभी यहां आ जाते थे, लेकिन इस प्रदर्शन की असली स्टार महिलाएं ही थीं।

इस इलाके में रिपोर्टिंग करते वक्त मुझे यहां महिलाओं की हिस्सेदारी और उनके डटे रहने के संकल्प ने प्रभावित किया। यह उपद्रवियों का जमावड़ा नहीं, बल्कि संवैधानिक और व्यक्तिगत आज़ादी की भावना का जश्न मनाने वाली अनुशासित मंडली थी। यह उनकी हिम्मत ही थी कि वे ऐसे वक्त में एकसाथ थीं जब असहमति को अपराध सा माना जाने लगा था। मुझे याद आता है कि मैंने एक महिला से पूछा कि क्या आपके पास गृहमंत्री के लिए कोई संदेश है? महिला ने जोर देकर जवाब दिया, 'अगर अमित शाह कहते हैं कि वे सीएए पर एक इंच पीछे नहीं हटेंगे तो आप उनसे जाकर कह दीजिए कि हम इस ज़मीन से एक इंच भी पीछे नहीं हटेंगे। यह ज़मीन और देश जितना उनका है, उतना ही हमारा भी है।'

गृहमंत्री सुनने या पीछे हटने के मूड में नही दिख रहे थे। 'यह सब प्रायोजित है; इसके पीछे विपक्ष और राष्ट्रविरोधी लोगों का हाथ है,' संसद में पत्रकारों के सवालों को खारिज़ करते हुए उन्होंने कहा। शाह को लगता था कि सीएए क़ानूनों पर दबाव बनाने के लिए यह राजनीतिक 'साज़िश' थी, लेकिन पीछे हटने का सवाल ही नहीं था। इसके साथ एक और मसला था, फरवरी 2020 में दिल्ली में होने वाले विधानसभा चुनाव। पांच साल पहले आम आदमी पार्टी ने सरकार बनाई थी, उन चुनावों में बीजेपी को बड़ी हार का सामना करना पड़ा था। शाह उस बड़ी हार का बदला लेना चाहते थे। अगर कोई एक राजनेता जिसे वे सख्त नापसंद करते थे तो वह है, दिल्ली के मुख्यमंत्री अरविन्द केजरीवाल। केजरीवाल के सवाल पर शाह का सपाट जवाब था: 'वह झूठा आदमी है'।

शाह ने दिल्ली के विधानसभा चुनावों की लड़ाई आक्रामक तरीके से शुरू की। वे चुनावी रणनीति पर खुद नज़र रखे हुए थे। शाहीन बाग में सीएए का प्रदर्शन इस चुनाव अभियान के लिए बड़ा मुद्दा बन गया था। भाजपा ने कांग्रेस और आप पर 'अल्पसंख्यक तुष्टिकरण' का आरोप लगाया। शाहीन बाग का आंदोलन शांतिपूर्ण तरीके से चल रहा था, लेकिन कुछ लोगों ने कई बार उसे उकसाने की कोशिश ज़रूर की। स्थानीय भाजपा नेता शाहीन बाग के प्रदर्शनकारियों को अक्सर 'टुकड़े-टुकड़े गैंग' कहकर बुलाते थे। बीजेपी और कई 'दक्षिणपंथी' टीवी एंकर भी मोदी विरोधी लोगों के लिए इसी नारे का इस्तेमाल करते थे। सबसे पहले साल 2016 में जेएनयू कैंपस में हुए छात्रों के प्रदर्शन के वक्त इस 'टुकड़े-टुकड़े गैंग' का मुहावरे के तौर पर इस्तेमाल हुआ, फिर तो सीएए विरोधी लोगों के लिए यही नारा काम में लिया जाने लगा।

साल 2020 के गणतंत्र दिवस पर एक चुनावी रैली में शाह ने भाजपा की शाहीन बाग विरोधी भावना को स्वर दिया। उन्होंने रैली में मौजूद लोगों से आह्वान किया, 'इस बार बटन इतनी ताकत

से दबाओ के करंट शाहीन बाग में लगे और विरोध ख़त्म हो जाए। आपका वोट दिल्ली और देश को सुरक्षित बनाएगा और शाहीन बाग जैसी दूसरी घटनाओं को रोकेगा।' सरकार में सबसे दूसरे ताकतवर शख्स और गृहमंत्री अपने समर्थकों से खुलेआम वोट का इस्तेमाल शाहीन बाग आंदोलन को ख़त्म करने के लिए कह रहे थे। क्या यह 'मुस्लिम विरोध' के ख़िलाफ़ हिंदू वोट बैंक के गुस्से को भड़काने की कोशिश थी? या हिंदू वोटों को एकजुटता के लिए साम्प्रदायिक पिच का खुलेआम इस्तेमाल था?

दिल्ली से भाजपा के सांसद परवेश वर्मा ने चेतावनी दी: 'लाखों लोग वहां (शाहीन बाग) इकट्ठा होते हैं। दिल्ली की जनता को तय करना होगा, वे आपके घरों में घुसेंगे, आपकी बहन, बेटियों के साथ बलात्कार करेंगे, उन्हें मारेंगे... आज वक्त है, कल मोदी और अमित शाह आपको बचाने नहीं आएंगे।' चुनाव आयोग ने औपचारिक कार्रवाई करते हुए परवेश वर्मा का नाम बीजेपी के स्टार प्रचारकों की सूची में से हटा दिया। ऐसी गैर कानूनी ज़ुबान के लिए यह छोटा कदम था। परवेश वर्मा को कोई पछतावा नहीं था। अपनी भड़काऊ टिपण्णियों पर परवेश वर्मा का बचाव था, 'मैंने शाहीन बाग में प्रदर्शनकारियों को कहते हुए सुना कि "हम जिहाद चाहते हैं"। हम जानते हैं कि जिहाद क्या है... जो कश्मीर में हुआ, वह दिल्ली में भी हो सकता है।'

वर्मा अकेले नेता नहीं थे। गृहमंत्री के भाषण के एक दिन बाद केन्द्रीय वित्त राज्य मंत्री अनुराग ठाकुर ने इस मुद्दे को और हवा दी। एक चुनावी रैली में ठाकुर नारा लगवा रहे थे... 'देश के गद्दारों को...' भीड़ ने पूरी गर्मी के साथ जवाब दिया.. 'गोली मारो सालों को'। यह उपद्रव भड़काने, घृणा और गुस्सा बढ़ाने वाला भाषण था जो किसी बेकाबू भीड़ को हथियार उठाने के लिए भी उकसा सकता था। यह साफतौर पर चुनाव में लगी आदर्श आचार संहिता का उल्लंघन तो था ही, एक आपराधिक कृत्य था, लेकिन दिल्ली पुलिस, जिसने कुछ समय पहले ही जामिया मिलिया परिसर में घुसकर सरकार विरोधी नारे लगाने वालों की जमकर पिटाई थी, वो बेअसर और चुप थी। चुनाव आयोग ने थोड़ी हिम्मत दिखाते हुए ठाकुर का नाम भी स्टार प्रचारक की सूची से हटा दिया।

उनचास साल के स्मार्ट दिखने वाले ठाकुर को मैं उन दिनों से जानता हूं, जब वो क्रिकेट प्रशासन देख रहे थे। एक बार मैंने हिमाचल प्रदेश के धर्मशाला में उनके साथ भारत-ऑस्ट्रेलिया टैस्ट मैच भी देखा था। बर्फ से ढकी खूबसूरत वादियों की गोद में यह स्टेडियम ठाकुर ने तैयार करवाया था। भारतीय क्रिकेट कंट्रोल बोर्ड के अध्यक्ष के तौर पर उनका क्रिकेट प्रशासक का कार्यकाल विवादास्पद वजहों के साथ खत्म हुआ, जब सुप्रीम कोर्ट ने उन्हें इसलिए बर्खास्त कर दिया क्योंकि वे सुप्रीम अदालत की कमेटी के सुधारों को लागू करने में नाकाम रहे थे। इससे पहले भी विवाद तब हुआ जब हिमाचल प्रदेश क्रिकेट एसोसिएशन के मुखिया होते हुए, उन्होंने रणजी ट्रॉफी के मैच में खुद को ही प्रदेश की टीम का कप्तान बना लिया। अपने इस इकलौते

प्रथम श्रेणी मैच में वे शून्य पर आउट हो गए थे। वो क्रिकेट प्रेमी तो लगते थे, लेकिन खेलों में शामिल दूसरे कई राजनेताओं की तरह, खेल प्रशासन को अपनी 'जागीर' की तरह चलाना चाहते थे। हिमाचल प्रदेश के मुख्यमंत्री रहे प्रेम कुमार धूमल के बेटे, अनुराग ठाकुर भारतीय जनता युवा मोर्चा के अध्यक्ष भी रह चुके हैं। मोदी के पहले कार्यकाल में उन्हें कोई मौका नहीं मिला, लेकिन दूसरी बार की सरकार में 2019 में उन्हें केन्द्रीय राज्य मंत्री बनाया गया। युवा और महत्वाकांक्षी ठाकुर, लगता था कि अपने खोए हुए समय की भरपाई करना चाहते थे। मैंने उनसे उनके भड़काऊ भाषण पर सवाल किया, शुरुआत में तो उन्होंने इस भाषण के लिए इंकार कर दिया, लेकिन जब उसका वीडियो दिखाया गया, तो वे आक्रामक दिखाई दिए। 'आप इसे ज़रूरत से ज़्यादा तूल दे रहे हैं, वो एक चुनावी रैली थी, जहां बातें होती ही हैं। मैंने गोली मारो नहीं कहा, यह भीड़ का जवाब था!' ठाकुर के बचाव में दम नहीं था।

यह सच है कि मंत्री ने खुद 'गोली मारो' नहीं कहा था, लेकिन उन्होंने भीड़ को भड़काऊ नारा लगाने से रोका भी नहीं। एक अनुभवी राजनेता का भीड़ को हिंसा के लिए उकसाने का बचाव नहीं किया जा सकता। युवा मंत्री की चालाकी समझ आ रही थी। कुछ हफ्ते पहले दिल्ली के ही एक और भड़काऊ और नफरती भाषण देने वाले भाजपा नेता कपिल मिश्रा ने सीएए समर्थक रैली में शाहीन बाग के प्रदर्शनकारियों को लेकर गोली मारो कहा था। आम आदमी पार्टी के नेता रहे, कपिल मिश्रा पर पुलिस कोई कार्रवाई करने के मूड में नहीं दिखी, जबकि अब यह भाजपा नेता आए दिन मुस्लिम विरोधी नारे लगाते देखा जा सकता था। ठाकुर ने सवाल किया, 'आप मुझे किसी और के बयान से क्यों जोड़ रहे हैं?' क्योंकि साफ था कि केन्द्रीय मंत्री केवल चुनावी प्रचार की बात कर रहे थे। अल्पसंख्यकों के ख़िलाफ़ हिंसक भाषा की रणनीति का इस्तेमाल भाजपा शायद चुनाव जीतने के लिए करना चाहती थी।

ठाकुर के 'गोली मारो' के उकसावे के कुछ दिनों बाद ही शाहीन बाग विरोध प्रदर्शन के पास ही गोलियों की आवाज़ सुनी गई। गाज़ियाबाद में रहने वाले एक नौजवान कपिल गुर्जर ने इलाके में दहशत फैलाने के मकसद से हवा में तीन गोलियां चलाईं, हालांकि इस वारदात में कोई घायल नहीं हुआ। पुलिस ने गुर्जर को काबू में लेकर गिरफ़्तार कर लिया। संदेश साफ था, 'गोली मारो' के बयान को नज़रअंदाज़ नहीं किया जा सकता।

विपक्षी नेताओं को इस बात की आशंका थी कि शाहीन बाग विरोध प्रदर्शन से हिन्दू-मुस्लिम विभाजन बढ़ सकता है और भाजपा इसका चुनावी फायदा उठा सकती थी। दिल्ली के मुख्यमंत्री अरविन्द केजरीवाल भी इससे अनजान नहीं थे। केजरीवाल के लिए यह पतली रस्सी पर चलने जैसा था। इस नाज़ुक राजनीतिक परिस्थिति में उन्होंने बीच का रास्ता निकाला। वे अपने समर्थकों के दबाव के बावजूद शाहीन बाग में प्रदर्शनकारियों के सामने भाषण देने नहीं गए। आम आदमी पार्टी के लिए मुस्लिम वोटर बड़े समर्थक के तौर पर देखे जा रहे थे, लेकिन केजरीवाल शहरी

हिन्दू वोटर को अनदेखा नहीं कर सकते थे। चुनाव अभियान के दौरान जब मैंने केजरीवाल का साक्षात्कार किया तो उससे पहले उनके सहयोगी ने एक अनुरोध कियाः 'आप अरविंद जी से कोई भी सवाल कर सकते हैं, लेकिन कोशिश करें कि सिर्फ शाहीन बाग पर फोकस ना हो, यह एक संवेदनशील मसला है'। राजनीति के जानकार मानते हैं कि केजरीवाल को यकीन था कि शाहीन बाग दरअसल चुनावी माहौल को बदलने के लिए भाजपा का ही जाल था। केजरीवाल ने पलटकर पूछा, 'आपको क्या लगता है कि केन्द्र सरकार शहर के बीचों-बीच इस तरह के विरोध प्रदर्शन को जारी रखने की इजाज़त क्यों दे रही है। बीजेपी चाहती है कि शाहीन बाग आंदोलन लोगों को बांटने का काम करता रहे।'

दिल्ली में चुनाव नतीजों से एक रात पहले गृहमंत्री शाह इंडिया इंटरनेशनल सेन्टर में एक वरिष्ठ पत्रकार की बेटी की शादी के समारोह में शामिल होने पहुंचे थे। जब उनसे नतीजों की भविष्यवाणी के बारे में पूछा गया तो उन्होंने भाजपा की जीत का भरोसा जताया। अपने अंदाज़ में हंसते हुए शाह बोले, 'मैं जानता हूं आप केजरीवाल की जीत चाहते हैं, पर वो होगा नहीं'। मगर अगले दिन गृहमंत्री की भविष्यवाणी पूरी तरह गलत साबित हुई। एक बार फिर दिल्ली में आम आदमी पार्टी जीत का परचम फहरा रही थी। आम आदमी पार्टी ने दिल्ली विधानसभा की कुल 70 सीटों में से 62 सीटों पर कब्ज़ा कर लिया था। भाजपा को सिर्फ़ आठ सीटें मिली। कुछ महीनों पहले हुए लोकसभा चुनावों के नतीजों से उलट यह हैरान करने वाला था, तब भाजपा ने दिल्ली की सभी सातों संसदीय सीटें बड़े अंतर से जीती थीं। लेकिन यह पहली बार नहीं था कि मतदाताओं ने लोकसभा और विधानसभा चुनावों में अलग-अलग पंसद पर मुहर लगाई।

शाहीन बाग ने भले ही दिल्ली के चुनावी नतीजों पर कोई असर नहीं डाला हो, लेकिन यह साफ था कि दिल्ली 'ख़तरे के ढेर' पर बैठी थी। एक तरफ मुस्लिम इलाकों में बढ़ती सीएए विरोधी भावना और दूसरी तरफ राजनेताओं की हिन्दू भावनाओं को भड़काने की कोशिश, कुछ ना कुछ होने की आशंका जता रहा था। हिन्दू उग्रवाद को बनाए रखने के लिए खासतौर से ऐसे मुसलमानों की ज़रूरत होती है जो प्रतिक्रिया के नाम पर आग को भड़काते रहें। सांप्रदायिक हिंसा का यह जहरीला नाग दिल्ली में फन फैला रहा था।

═

फरवरी 2020 में जब दिल्ली में सीएए का मुद्दा गरमा रहा था, उस वक्त प्रधानमंत्री एक बड़े विदेशी मेहमान के स्वागत की तैयारी में व्यस्त थे। अमेरिकी राष्ट्रपति का भारत दौरा प्रधानमंत्री के लिए राजनीति की सड़क पर एक बड़ा मील का पत्थर था। बराक ओबामा से अलग डोनाल्ड ट्रम्प के साथ प्रधानमंत्री ने एक 'केमेस्ट्री' बनाई थी। इससे पहले सितम्बर 2019 में अपने अमेरिकी दौरे में ह्यूस्टन में 'हाउडी मोदी' कार्यक्रम में प्रधानमंत्री मोदी ने 'अबकी बार ट्रम्प

सरकार' का नारा लगाकर खुलेआम समर्थन किया था। भारत-अमेरिका बातचीत में शामिल रहे एक वरिष्ठ राजनयिक का मानना था कि ट्रंप पर प्रधानमंत्री मोदी का आकर्षण छाया हुआ था। बताया गया कि अमेरिकी राष्ट्रपति ने अपने एक सहयोगी से कहा कि 'वो बिल्कुल मेरे जैसे हैं, बातों को इधर-उधर नहीं घुमाते।' ट्रम्प और मोदी दोनों को अति राष्ट्रवादी, कट्टरपंथी और राजनीति को हकीकत में टीवी पर इस्तेमाल करने वाले अनुभवी राजनेता के तौर पर देखा जाता था, जिन्हें मीडिया में सुर्खियां बटोरने में मज़ा आता था। वहां अमेरिकी मेजबान ने मोदी का ह्यूस्टन में ज़बरदस्त स्वागत किया था, तो अब प्रधानमंत्री मोदी अपने गढ़ अहमदाबाद में अमेरिकी राष्ट्रपति और उनके परिवार के शानदार स्वागत के लिए तैयार थे।

अमेरिकी राष्ट्रपति के स्वागत के लिए अहमदाबाद को चुनना कोई अचरज वाली बात नहीं थी। 2014 में प्रधानमंत्री बनने के बाद से ही मोदी खास विदेशी मेहमानों को अहमदाबाद ले जाते रहे हैं। मोदी ने अपनी राजनीति इसी शहर से शुरू की थी। उनके अतीत से जुड़े, गुजरात से प्रधानमंत्री भावनात्मक जुड़ाव महसूस करते हैं। मोदी यहां के अनकहे नायक हैं, सम्राट जैसे हैं, सरकार उनके आदेश पर चलती है और समर्थक जनता उनके इशारे पर आने पर गौरव सा महसूस करती है। अमेरिका के 'हाउडी मोदी' कार्यक्रम के जवाब में, अहमदाबाद के बाहरी इलाके में बने विशाल मोटेरा क्रिकेट स्टेडियम में इस मेगा इवेंट 'नमस्ते ट्रम्प' का आयोजन किया गया था। दोनों ही कार्यक्रमों का आयोजन मोदी के गुजराती समर्थकों ने किया था। करीब एक लाख बीस हज़ार लोगों को बिठाने के लिए मोटेरा स्टेडियम में कई बदलाव किए गए, जिससे यह दुनिया का सबसे बड़ा क्रिकेट स्टेडियम बन गया। यह दुनिया में खेलों के नक्शे पर गुजरात को असरदार तरीके से रखने की कोशिश थी। गृहमंत्री शाह के बेटे जय शाह, अब गुजरात क्रिकेट एसोसिएशन के अध्यक्ष थे, इससे पहले मोदी और शाह भी यह जिम्मेदारी संभाल चुके थे। मोटेरा देश के मौजूदा नेतृत्व के लिए अपना इलाका था। (मोदी ब्रांड को अमर करने के लिए साल 2021 में मोटेरा स्टेडियम का नाम बदलकर नरेन्द्र मोदी स्टेडियम कर दिया गया)।

राष्ट्रपति के दौरे के लिए अहमदाबाद को नए तरीके सजाया-संवारा जा रहा था। दुनिया की बड़ी हस्तियों के रास्ते में आने वाली झुग्गी-झोपड़ियों को नज़रों से दूर रखने की कोशिश की गई। दिल्ली में भी हाई अलर्ट था। अहमदाबाद में एक दिन बिताने के बाद राष्ट्रपति आधिकारिक कार्यक्रमों के लिए दिल्ली पहुंचने वाले थे। लेकिन शांतिपूर्ण अहमदाबाद से अलग दिल्ली में कुछ हिस्सों में सीएए के विरोध प्रदर्शन हो रहे थे। रविवार 23 फरवरी, अहमदाबाद अगले दिन ट्रम्प के स्वागत के लिए तैयार था, तब दिल्ली में शाहीन बाग के समर्थन में एकजुटता दिखाने के लिए सीएए विरोधी कुछ प्रदर्शनकारियों ने उत्तर-पूर्वी दिल्ली के ज़ाफ़राबाद मेट्रो स्टेशन के पास प्रदर्शन करते हुए स्टेशन को रोकने का फ़ैसला किया। यह प्रदर्शन ऐसी चिंगारी साबित हुई,

जिससे अगले 72 घंटों तक दिल्ली में खून-खराबा होता रहा। जब अमेरिकी राष्ट्रपति भारत में उतरे, तब तक राष्ट्रीय राजधानी में कुछ हिस्से दंगे की आग में जल रहे थे।

ज़ाफ़राबाद में धरने के कुछ ही घंटों में भाजपा नेता कपिल मिश्रा अपने साथियों के साथ वहां पहुंच गए और प्रदर्शनकारियों को सड़क खाली करने की चेतावनी देते हुए भड़काऊ भाषण दिए। उनकी राजनीतिक ताकत का अंदाज़ा इस बात से लगाया जा सकता है कि मिश्रा के भाषण के वक्त उत्तर-पूर्वी दिल्ली के पुलिस उपायुक्त उनके पास ही खड़े थे। भाषण के बाद मिश्रा ने ट्वीट किया, 'दिल्ली पुलिस को तीन दिन का अल्टीमेटम दे रहा हूं। ज़ाफ़राबाद और चांद बाग में प्रदर्शनकारियों से सड़कें खाली कराएं, उसके बाद हम कोई बात नहीं सुनेंगे।' अपने ट्वीट में एक वीडियो लगाते हुए मिश्रा ने लिखाः 'जब तक डोनाल्ड ट्रम्प भारत में हैं, हम शांति बनाए रखेंगे। उसके बाद भी सड़कें खाली नहीं की गई तो हम पुलिस की बात भी नहीं सुनेंगे... हम सड़कों पर उतरने के लिए मजबूर होंगे'। सीएए विरोधी प्रदर्शनकारियों के लिए यह स्पष्ट चेतावनी थी, ख़ून खराबे के ख़तरे की चेतावनी। पुलिस की स्पेशल ब्रांच और इंटेलीजेंस विंग ने उत्तर-पूर्वी दिल्ली को कई अलर्ट और संदेश भेजे, लेकिन पुलिस ने फिलहाल कोई कार्रवाई नहीं करने का मन बना लिया था। 23 फरवरी को एक ही दिन में घबराए हुए लोगों ने 700 से ज़्यादा कॉल किए, लेकिन पुलिस ने कोई बड़ा कदम नहीं उठाया। उस शाम, सीएए समर्थक और विरोधियों के बीच पथराव और झड़पों की पहली रिपोर्ट उत्तर-पूर्वी दिल्ली के मौजपुर इलाके से आई, अगले दिन सुबह होने तक हिंसा आसपास के इलाकों में फैल गई थी। दोपहर होते-होते दिल्ली के कई इलाकों से दंगों की खबरें आने लगी, कई जगहों पर हिन्दू-मुस्लिम गुटों ने एक-दूसरे को निशाना बनाया था। पुलिस ने आंसू गैस के गोले छोड़े, लाठीचार्ज किया। इसी दौरान गोकुलपुर इलाके में एक कांस्टेबल रतन लाल की गोली लगने से मौत हो गई। इंटेलीजेंस ब्यूरो के एक कर्मचारी अंकित शर्मा का शव, उनके लापता होने के एक दिन बाद 26 फरवरी को चांदबाग के पास एक नाले में मिला। पुलिस को लगता था कि सीएए विरोधी प्रदर्शनकारियों ने पुलिस और हिंदुओं को निशाना बनाकर हमले किए। इलाके से आम आदमी पार्टी के पार्षद ताहिर हुसैन को गिरफ़्तार किया गया और शर्मा की हत्या के माम्ले में मुख्य आरोपी बनाया गया। पुलिस ने हुसैन के परिसर से भारी मात्रा में हथियार और गोला-बारूद पकड़ा था। मैं हुसैन से फोन पर बात करने में कामयाब हो गया, उस समय वह कहीं छिपा हुआ था। हुसैन ने आरोप लगाया कि उसे फंसाया जा रहा है लेकिन हुसैन के ख़िलाफ़ मजबूत सबूत थे। 'ताहिर और उसके गिरोह के लोग पहले से ही हथियारों के साथ थे। यह दंगा नहीं बल्कि हिंसा भड़काने के लिए एक पूर्व नियोजित साज़िश थी,' दिल्ली पुलिस के एक आला अफसर ने कहा।

लेकिन हिंसा एकतरफा नहीं थी। इससे अलग, एक वायरल वीडियो में दिल्ली पुलिस को कुछ नौजवान मुसलमानों को पीटते हुए और उन्हें राष्ट्रगान गाने और 'वंदे मातरम' बोलने के

लिए मजबूर करते देखा जा सकता था। उनमें से एक तेइस साल के फ़ैजान की मौत चौटों के कारण हो गई। मैं उसकी मां किस्मतुन से मिला, जो अपने बेटे की मौत की तेज़ी से और उचित जांच के लिए लड़ रही थी। उसने रोते हुए कहा, 'हमारी कोई सुनवाई नहीं है।' पुलिस ने ताहिर हुसैन को तो तुरंत गिरफ़्तार कर लिया था लेकिन फैजान की पिटाई करने और उसका वीडियो बनाने वालों की पहचान पुलिस लंबे समय तक नहीं कर पाई। दंगों के चार साल बाद जुलाई 2024 में दिल्ली उच्च न्यायालय ने फैजान की मौत की जांच सीबीआई से कराने के आदेश दिए। हिंदू बहुल इलाकों में लाठियों और तलवारों से लैस उन्मादी भीड़ भगवा झंडा फहराते और भड़काऊ नारे लगाते हुए मुस्लिम घरों और दुकानों को निशाना बना रही थी। शुरुआत मुसलमानों और पुलिस के बीच झड़पों से हुई थी, लेकिन 25 फरवरी तक हिंसा का जवाबी हमला शुरू हो गया, जिसके निशाने पर मुसलमानों की संपत्ति और उनके धार्मिक स्थल थे।

दोनों समुदायों की तरफ से एक जैसी हिंसा कैसे हो रही थी, इसको समझने के लिए शिव विहार इलाके के वो दो स्कूल काफी हैं, जिनमें एक का मालिकाना हक हिन्दू के पास था तो दूसरे के मालिक मुसलमान थे। डीआरपी कॉन्वेंट और राजधानी पब्लिक स्कूल, दोनों की दीवारें भी साझा थीं। आरोप है कि एक दूसरे समुदायों ने दोनों स्कूलों को निशाना बनाया। पुलिस दोनों जगह सबकुछ खत्म हो जाने के बाद पहुंची। स्कूल के एक अधिकारी ने आरोप लगाया, 'हम पुलिस को बार-बार फ़ोन करते रहे, लेकिन कोई नहीं पहुंचा।'

इन दंगों में 53 लोग मारे गए, पुलिस के अंतिम आंकड़े के मुताबिक मरने वालों में 38 मुस्लिम और 15 हिन्दू थे। इस हिंसा ने दोनों समुदायों के बीच गहरी दरार बना दी, लेकिन इस सवाल का जवाब मिलना बाकी था कि दिल्ली पुलिस और गृह मंत्रालय को इसके बारे में पहले जानकारी क्यों नहीं मिल पाई। ये वो सरकार थी, जिसे अपनी सख्त क़ानून व्यवस्था पर बहुत भरोसा था। लेकिन सवालों पर प्रशासन के पास कुछ साफ जवाब नहीं था। गृह मंत्रालय जब स्थिति पर काबू करने में खुद को नाकाम पा रहा था, तब राष्ट्रीय सुरक्षा सलाहकार अजीत डोवाल को 'दंगा विरोधी ऑपरेशन्स' पर निगरानी के लिए बुलाया गया। उस वक्त बहुत से आला अफसर ट्रम्प के दौरे की सुरक्षा व्यवस्था के काम में लगे थे, तब इस बढ़ती हिंसा ने कम पुलिस बल को मुश्किल और हैरानी में डाल दिया था।

सरकारी सूत्र इस बात पर ज़ोर दे रहे थे कि यह हिंसा 'पॉपुलर फ्रंट ऑफ इंडिया' जैसे, कई इस्लामिक संगठनों ने फ़ैलाई। इन राष्ट्र विरोधी ताकतों का मकसद एक बड़े विदेशी मेहमान के भारत दौरे के वक्त मोदी सरकार को बदनाम करना था। गृह मंत्रालय के एक अफसर का कहना था कि 'सीएए विरोधी प्रदर्शनकारी अपने मुद्दे पर दुनिया भर के मीडिया का ध्यान खींचना चाहते थे। ट्रंप यात्रा के दौरान हिंसा की साज़िश कर उन्होंने अपना पक्ष रखने की कोशिश की।' दिल्ली पुलिस ने अपने आरोप-पत्र में दावा किया कि इन सीएए विरोधी ताकतों जिनमें जेएनयू के छात्र

रहे उमर खालिद और शरजील इमाम का नाम शामिल है, को कड़े आतंकवाद विरोधी क़ानून (यूएपीए) के तहत गिरफ़्तार किया गया। यह क़ानून साम्प्रदायिक मंशा से लोगों की जान लेने और हिंसा से आतंकवाद पर लगाम लगाने के मकसद से बनाया गया था। पुलिस के आरोप पत्र में खालिद के उग्र स्वभाव का ज़िक्र किया गया है और कहा गया कि उसने फरवरी के महीने में महाराष्ट्र के अमरावती में एक भाषण में राष्ट्रपति ट्रम्प की यात्रा के दौरान लोगों को सड़क पर उतरने के लिए उकसाया था। खालिद के वकीलों का कहना था कि पुलिस ने असहमति की एक लोकप्रिय आवाज़ को बंद करने के मकसद से भाषण को तोड़-मरोड़कर पेश किया था। 'उस दिन का भाषण गांधी जी की एकता रखने की शिक्षा पर था, लेकिन उसे आतंक करार दिया गया।' उन्होंने दावा किया कि 'इस संपादित वीडियो को दिखाने वाले न्यूज़ चैनलों ने जांच एजेंसियों को बताया था कि इसका स्रोत भाजपा के एक नेता का ट्वीट था।'

मैं देश की राजधानी में आयोजित कुछ सेमिनारों और टीवी स्टूडियो में उमर खालिद से दो-एक बार मिला हूँ। मुझे वह दुबला-पतला चश्मा लगाए, पढ़ा-लिखा विचारशील नौजवान लगा, जो मोदी सरकार की नीतियों का मुखर आलोचक है। उसने सीएए विरोधी प्रदर्शनों के लिए समर्थन जुटाने की बात तो की, लेकिन कहा कि वो हिंसा के ख़िलाफ़ है। 'ये आप टीवी वाले लोग ही हैं, जिन्होंने मुझे "अर्बन नक्सल" करार दिया है। मैं गरीबों और वंचितों के मानवाधिकारों के लिए बोलता हूं, तो इससे मैं राष्ट्रविरोधी कैसे हो जाता हूं?' उन्होंने पूछा। खालिद को लगता है कि ऐसे ध्रुवीकृत राजनीतिक माहौल में उसके पीछे पड़े मीडिया ने उसे 'टुकड़े-टुकड़े गिरोह' के हिस्से के तौर पर पेश किया, जिसे सलाखों के पीछे होना चाहिए। खालिद के ख़िलाफ़ पुलिस का मामला कमज़ोर दिखाई देता थाः जो सिर्फ़ व्हाट्सअप संदेशों और अपराधिक बताए जाने वाले राजनीतिक भाषण पर आधारित था। मगर उसे कड़े आतंकवादी विरोधी कानून यूएपीए के तहत पकड़ने का मतलब था कि उसे ज़मानत नहीं मिल सकती थी। साल 2024 तक खालिद को जेल में रहते हुए चार साल से ज़्यादा हो गए हैं।

खालिद क़ानूनी गिरफ़्त में आने वाला इकलौता सीएए विरोधी प्रदर्शनकारी नहीं था। दिल्ली में हिंसा भड़काने के आरोप में दो युवा मुखर महिला कार्यकर्ताओं देवांगना कलिता और नताशा नरवाल को भी यूएपीए के तहत गिरफ़्तार किया गया था। दोनों ने प्रदर्शनों में हिस्सा लेने की बात तो मानी थी, लेकिन हिंसा भड़काने या उसमें शामिल होने से इंकार किया था। उन्हें एक साल जेल में रहने के बाद जमानत मिल पाई। जिस दिन वो रिहा हुई, मैंने उनका साक्षात्कार किया था। बेपरवाह सी दिखती नरवाल ने कहा कि 'सरकार हमें जेल में डालकर डरा नहीं सकती, हमनें कोई गलत काम नहीं किया है।'

इनके ख़िलाफ़ दंगों की 'साज़िश' में शामिल होने के सबूत बहुत साफ नहीं हैं लेकिन ट्रम्प की भारत यात्रा और दिल्ली दंगों के बीच तार तो जोड़े जा सकते हैं, भले ही वो कमज़ोर दिखते

हों। इतना तो साफ है कि सीएए विरोधी प्रदर्शनकारियों ने अमेरिकी राष्ट्रपति ट्रम्प की यात्रा से पहले अचानक सड़क जाम करने का आह्वान किया, जिसे ऐसे खास मौके पर विरोध प्रदर्शन तेज़ करने की रणनीति के तौर पर देखा जा सकता है। अहमदाबाद में उतरे ट्रम्प का जब भव्य स्वागत हो रहा था, तब शायद टीवी चैनलों के लिए यह तय करना मुश्किल हो रहा था कि वे किस बात पर फोकस करें: अमेरिकी राष्ट्रपति ट्रम्प और प्रधानमंत्री मोदी के बीच दोस्ताना मुलाकात पर या फिर दिल्ली में बढ़ती हिंसा पर। टीवी स्क्रीन्स पर अहमदाबाद में 'नमस्ते ट्रम्प' की रैली की शानदार तस्वीरें और दिल्ली में जलती कारों और टूटी दुकानों की तस्वीरें गड्डमड्ड हो रही थीं। जैसे ही हमने विचलित करने वाली हिंसा की तस्वीरें दिखाना शुरू किया कि सूचना प्रसारण मंत्रालय से एक 'सलाह' मिली कि ऐसी तस्वीरों से बचा जाए, जिनसे परेशानी बढ़ सकती हो। स्पष्ट है कि मोदी सरकार नहीं चाहती थी कि दिल्ली की ज़मीनी हकीकत अहमदाबाद की पार्टी को खराब करे। लेकिन यदि लोगों, खासतौर से मुस्लिम संप्रदाय के बीच सीएए को लेकर गुस्से को ज़ाहिर करने के लिए सड़क पर प्रदर्शन करना मंशा थी, तो मिशन पूरा हो गया था। दिल्ली की सड़कों पर बहे ख़ून की ज़िम्मेदारी अभी तय होनी थी।

दिल्ली में हुई हिंसा को सिर्फ़ फरवरी 2020 की घटनाओं से जोड़कर नहीं देखा जा सकता। हकीकत यह है कि मई 2019 में मोदी सरकार के दोबारा आने के बाद से उग्र हिंदुत्व की राजनीति में कोई कमी नहीं आई थी, और ना ही लोगों के बीच सौहार्द बनाए रखने की कोई परवाह की गई। राजनीतिक और धार्मिक ध्रुवीकरण के बीज तो शायद उस दिन ही बो दिए गए थे, जब देश के इकलौते मुस्लिम बहुल राज्य जम्मू-कश्मीर से अनुच्छेद 370 को निरस्त किया गया और उसे राज्य से घटाकर केन्द्र शासित प्रदेश बना दिया गया। इसके साथ ही नागरिकता संशोधन क़ानून को मुस्लिम आबादी को असुरक्षित महसूस कराने और सत्ता के दुरुपयोग की आशंका के तौर पर देखा गया। सरकार के इस दावे से कि इसका असर भारतीयों पर नहीं पड़ेगा, चिंताए कम होने वाली नहीं थीं। अगर माहौल में तनाव हो, तो लोग कई बार बेवजह की आशंका से घिरे रहते हैं। एक आक्रामक हिन्दुत्व वाली सरकार और गुस्से में भरे बैठे लोगों, खासतौर से मुसलमानों के बीच बढ़ता अविश्वास किसी अनहोनी की आशंका जता रहा था। संसद में बहुमत को धार्मिक बहुसंख्यवाद समझने की भूल सरकार को नहीं करनी चाहिए। साल 2019 में मिले प्रचंड बहुमत को मोदी-शाह टीम ने शायद हिन्दू राष्ट्र के एजेंडा को बढ़ाने और बांटने वाले कार्यक्रम के रास्ते पर चलने का जनादेश मान लिया था। सरकार का एजेंडा इससे साफ हो जाता है कि जहां एक तरफ सीएए विरोधी प्रदर्शनकारियों को गिरफ़्तार कर लिया गया, वहीं 'गोली मारो' जैसी भड़काऊ बयानबाजी करने वाले सीएए समर्थकों के ख़िलाफ़ कोई ठोस कार्रवाई नहीं की गई। जब भड़काऊ भाषणों को सामान्य मान लिया जाए और मॉब लिंचिग समेत मुसलमानों के ख़िलाफ़ दूसरी घटनाओं को तर्कसंगत

बनाने की कोशिश हो, तो ऐसी सरकार पर सबके साथ समान व्यवहार की बात पर भरोसा करना मुश्किल होता है।

दिल्ली में हिंसा के कुछ दिनों बात संसद के सेन्ट्रल हॉल में गृहमंत्री से हुई मुलाकात मुझे याद है। गृहमंत्री की आवाज़ में नाराज़गी झलक रही थी. 'इसके लिए आप सभी कथित सेक्युलर लोग ज़िम्मेदार हैं। आपने लोगों को यह भरोसा दिलाया है कि यह सरकार मुस्लिम विरोधी है।' मैंने गृहमंत्री को यह याद दिलाने की कोशिश कि अनुच्छेद **370** को हटाने और सीएए का फ़ैसला किसी सेकुलर बुद्धिजीवी वर्ग ने नहीं बल्कि उनके गृह मंत्रालय ने किया था और हिंसा से भी वो अनजान नहीं थे। शाह ने अति विश्वास के साथ जवाब दिया, 'आपको यह समझ आना चाहिए कि ज़्यादातर मतदाता इन मुद्दों पर हमारे साथ हैं।'

मोदी 2.0 के पहले नौ महीनों में बेलगाम होती अधिनायकवादी और हिन्दुत्व की टकराव वाली राजनीति की ताकत और सीमाएं नज़र आने लगी थीं। पिछली सरकारों ने शांति बनाए रखने की कोशिश के नाम पर जिन मुद्दों को टालने का काम किया था, टीम मोदी-शाह ने उन कथित विवादास्पद मुद्दों पर कड़े फ़ैसले किए थे। पिछली सरकारों के वक्त की आम सहमति की राजनीति की जगह अब टकराव की राजनीति ले रही थी। एक के बाद एक लगातार मिलती चुनावी जीत से पैदा अंहकार ने अजेय होने का भाव पैदा कर दिया था। अंहकार और धार्मिक घृणा की राजनीति से माहौल में गर्मी पैदा हो रही थी। हवा में नफ़रत फैल रही थी और लगता था कि साम्प्रदायिक ताकतों को खुला छोड़ दिया गया था। साल 2014 का 'सबका साथ, सबका विकास' का नारा मोदी 2.0 के पहले साल में ही दफ़न हो गया था। सरकार भले ही इस बात पर जोर देती रही कि उसकी कल्याणकारी योजनाएं सिर्फ़ हिन्दुओं के लिए नहीं, सभी भारतीयों के लिए थीं, लेकिन ज़मीन पर वो मुसलमानों का विश्वास खो रही थी। हिन्दू मुसलमानों के बीच की दरार साफ थी, और एक बड़ा वर्ग अपने वोट के जरिए जवाब देने के लिए 2024 का इंतज़ार करने लगा। गृहमंत्री शाह की विरोध की राजनीति ने हिंदुत्व के नाम पर एक बेशर्म चेहरे को उजागर किया था। पिछले गृहमंत्री राजनाथ सिंह के ज़माने की जिम्मेदार राजनीति का मुखौटा उतर गया था। संघ परिवार में शाह की इस कट्टर विचारधारा पर मौटे तौर पर सहमति थी, लेकिन वो जनता में लोकप्रिय राजनेता के बजाय भयभीत ज़्यादा महसूस हो रहे थे। इस बीच एक सवाल घूम रहा था कि एक आहत और आपसी संघर्ष से जूझते राष्ट्र को एकजुट करने के लिए क्या करना होगा। जिंदगी में एक बार आने वाली महामारी शायद वो हासिल करने वाली थी, जो हमारा राजनीतिक नेतृत्व नहीं कर सका। धर्म ने जिसे विभाजित किया था, एक वायरस उन सबको एकजुट करने में लग गया।

3

'ताली बजाओ, थाली बजाओ': कोविड चुनौती

मार्च का महीना दिल्ली में शादियों का सीजन होता है। गर्मियों के आने से पहले बसंत की महक के जाने का वक्त शादी-ब्याह के समारोहों के लिए बेहतर समय रहता है। मार्च 2020 में लुटिंयस दिल्ली में भारतीय जनता पार्टी के राष्ट्रीय अध्यक्ष जगत प्रकाश नड्डा के बेटे की शादी का 'रिसेप्शन' समारोह था। मोतीलाल मार्ग पर उनके आवास के बाहर कारों का काफ़िला, विशेष राजनीतिक मेहमानों में प्रधानमंत्री मोदी 'स्टार' अतिथि थे। सजे हुए लॉन में जब कैमरे चमक रहे थे, उस वक्त एक 'वीवीआईपी' कमरे में विशेष आमंत्रित मेहमानों की असली महफिल थी। गृहमंत्री अमित शाह के दरबार में पार्टी के वरिष्ठ नेता टेबल को घेरे हुए थे। उसी में शामिल थे मध्यप्रदेश के पूर्व मुख्यमंत्री शिवराज सिंह चौहान। 'अमित भाई, सिंधिया जी का क्या करना है? आप जो कहेंगे, वो होगा,' पार्टी के शोर के बीच चौहान के इस सधे हुए सवाल के जवाब में अमित शाह मुस्कुरा भर दिए। और इसके साथ ही मध्यप्रदेश में सरकार गिराने का 'ऑपरेशन लोटस' शुरू हो गया था।

एक हफ्ते बाद जब देशभर में होली का जश्न चल रहा था, तब कांग्रेस नेता ज्योतिरादित्य सिंधिया ने गृहमंत्री शाह की मौजूदगी में प्रधानमंत्री से उनके आवास पर मुलाकात की। इस मुलाक़ात से करीब चौबीस घंटे पहले 10 मार्च को अपने दिवंगत पिता माधव राव सिंधिया की 75वीं जयंती पर मध्यप्रदेश में 22 विधायकों के साथ उन्होंने कांग्रेस के दो दशकों के अपने रिश्तों को ख़त्म कर दिया था। कांग्रेस की अंतरिम अध्यक्ष सोनिया गांधी को लिखी चिट्ठी में

उन्होंने इस्तीफ़ा देते हुए कहाः 'हालांकि मेरा लक्ष्य और मकसद वही है जो हमेशा से रहा है, अपने प्रदेश और देश के लोगों की सेवा करना, लेकिन अब मैं पार्टी में रहकर ऐसा करने में खुद को असमर्थ पा रहा हूं।' ग्वालियर राजघराने के वंशज सिंधिया और उनके समर्थक विधायकों के इस्तीफ़े से पन्द्रह महीने पुरानी कांग्रेस की कमलनाथ सरकार ख़तरे में आ गई थी। राजनीतिक होली के रंग बदलने लगे थे।

सिंधिया के पार्टी बदलने की ख़बर इतनी अचरज भरी भी नहीं थी। दिसम्बर 2018 में हुए चुनावों में मध्यप्रदेश के फ़ैसले के बाद से ही वे नाराज़ चल रहे थे, जब कांग्रेस ने भाजपा को कड़ी टक्कर देकर एक नई राजनीतिक इबारत लिखी थी। यूं तो उन्होंने अनचाहे मन से कमलनाथ को मुख्यमंत्री के तौर पर स्वीकार कर लिया था, लेकिन इसके बाद वे प्रदेश कांग्रेस के संगठन में अपनी भूमिका पर आलाकमान की मुहर चाहते थे। स्टार प्रचारक और पार्टी में राहुल गांधी की युवा ब्रिगेड के अहम नेता सिंधिया को भोपाल में नई सरकार में महत्वपूर्ण भूमिका का भरोसा दिलाया गया था। 'किसी पद की बात तो छोड़िए, मैं सिर्फ़ इतना चाहता था कि संगठन में मुझे और मेरे समर्थकों को सम्मान तो मिले। वादे किए गए, लेकिन कभी पूरे नहीं हुए,' सिंधिया ने बाद में दावा किया। फिर 2019 के लोकसभा चुनावों में चौंकाने वाली खबर तब आई जब वे अपनी पारिवारिक सीट गुना से लोकसभा का चुनाव हार गए, इसके बाद उन्हें तेजी से किनारे लगा दिया गया और प्रदेश कांग्रेस के अध्यक्ष भी नहीं रह गए। यहां तक कि भोपाल में सरकारी घर देने का जो वादा किया गया था, वो भी पूरा नहीं हुआ। एक प्रमुख मीडिया दिग्गज की तब के मुख्यमंत्री कमलनाथ, पूर्व मुख्यमंत्री दिग्विजय सिंह और सिंधिया के बीच झगड़ा खत्म कराने की कोशिश रंग नहीं लाई। लगता था कि दोनों दिग्गज कांग्रेसी नेताओं ने अपने 'जूनियर' को 'हैसियत' दिखाने का मन बना लिया था। फिर राज्यसभा उम्मीदवारों की सूची में जब उनका नाम शामिल नहीं था, तो लगा कि अब पार्टी में उनका वक्त पूरा हो गया था। सिंधिया ने आरोप लगाया, 'मैंने गांधी परिवार के सामने अपनी चिंताएं रखने की कोशिश की, यहां तक कि सोनिया जी और राहुल जी से मिलने के प्रयास भी किए, लेकिन कोई मेरी बात सुनने को तैयार नहीं था।' हाशिए पर आने के बाद सिंधिया ने भाजपा में बातचीत के लिए दरवाज़ा खोला।

भारतीय जनता पार्टी के सिंधिया परिवार से रिश्तों में उतार-चढ़ाव आते रहे हैं। ज्योतिरादित्य की दादी राजमाता विजयाराजे सिंधिया जनसंघ के मज़बूत सदस्यों में से रहीं, उनकी एक बुआ वसुंधरा राजे राजस्थान में भाजपा की मुख्यमंत्री थीं, और दूसरी बुआ यशोधरा राजे पिछली मध्यप्रदेश सरकार में कैबिनेट मंत्री थीं। फिर भी, ज्योतिरादित्य के पिता माधवराव सिंधिया ने 1980 में परिवार के बाकी सदस्यों से अलग, कांग्रेस से हाथ मिला लिया और बेटा भी उसी रास्ते पर चलने लगा। उस वक्त वे 'हिन्दुत्व' की विचारधारा और भाजपा की कड़ी आलोचना करते थे। साल 2018 के चुनावों के दौरान भाजपा ने ज्योतिरादित्य के 'शाही' होने को बहुत

मुद्दा बनाया और उनकी तुलना अपने आम आदमी शिवराज सिंह चौहान से की थी। चौहान तब प्रचार के दौरान उन्हें खारिज़ करते हुए कहते कि 'महलों में रहने वाले लोग ज़मीनी हक़ीकत को नहीं समझते हैं'।

लेकिन, फिर एक नाटकीय मोड़ में, चौहान, सिंधिया की 'बगावत' के सहारे, कमलनाथ सरकार को गिराकर, एक बार फिर से मध्यप्रदेश के मुख्यमंत्री बने। भाजपा नेता और प्रवक्ता ज़फ़र इस्लाम ने ज्योतिरादित्य को भाजपा में शामिल कराने में अहम भूमिका निभाई। सिंधिया की तरह जफ़र इस्लाम भी 'इन्वेस्टमेंट बैंकर' से राजनीति में आए थे। भाजपा में कुछ खास मुस्लिम चेहरों में से एक जफ़र अपनी छाप और जगह बनाने की कोशिश कर रहे थे और टीवी चैनलों की बहस में मोदी सरकार का ज़ोरदार बचाव करते दिखते थे। सिंधिया की बगावत को अंजाम तक पहुंचाने का काम जफ़र इस्लाम को सौंपा गया। उन्होंने कांग्रेस के इस युवा नेता के साथ दूसरे बाग़ी विधायकों से मुलाकात की और उन्हें मनाने के लिए मंत्री पद और दूसरे फायदों के बारे में आश्वस्त किया। पहले अहम कदम के तौर पर सत्रह विधायकों को सुरक्षित रखने के लिए बेंगलुरु के एक रिसॉर्ट में ले जाया गया। उस वक्त कर्नाटक में भाजपा की सरकार थी, यानी सरकारी मशीनरी काबू में थी। बाद में इस्लाम ने खुलासा किया, 'पहले हम कुछ विधायकों को दिल्ली के पास गुरुग्राम लेकर गए, लेकिन वहां कांग्रेस नेतृत्व उनसे संपर्क करने और वापस अपने खेमे में लाने में कामयाब रहा। इस बार हमने सुनिश्चित किया कि ऑपरेशन पूरी तरह गोपनीय रहे और कोई भी बेंगलुरु में विधायकों तक नहीं पहुंच सके।' 'पार्टी विद ए डिफरेंस' यानी एक अलग तरह की पार्टी का नारा देने वाली भाजपा अब विधायकों को लुभाने और विरोधी पार्टियों की सरकारों को गिराने में माहिर हो गई थी। यह टीम मोदी-शाह की अगुवाई वाली नई भारतीय जनता पार्टी का एक और संकेत हैं।

विधानसभा में संख्याबल तो कांग्रेस के ख़िलाफ़ था, लेकिन राजनीतिक लड़ाइयों के लंबे अनुभव वाले चतुर कमलनाथ ने बाज़ी पलटने की एक और कोशिश की। अंतरराष्ट्रीय समाचार एजेंसियों की रिपोर्ट्स में दुनिया में तेज़ी से फैल रहे एक नए वायरस के बारे में चेतावनी थी, जिस पर तुरंत विशेष ध्यान देने की ज़रूरत थी। विश्व स्वास्थ्य संगठन ने फरवरी 2020 में इस बीमारी को कोविड-19 का नाम दिया था। यह बीमारी नए वायरस **SARS-CoV2** से फ़ैल रही थी और पहली बार 2019 के आखिर में चीन के वुआन प्रांत में इसके बारे में जानकारी मिली थी। मार्च के मध्य तक सरकारी सलाह पर बहुत से दफ्तरों, कॉलेजों और स्कूलों ने वायरस से बचाने के लिए ऐहतियात के तौर पर मास्क पहनना और सामाजिक दूरी बनाना शुरू कर दिया था। उस समय भाजपा अविश्वास प्रस्ताव रखने पर ज़ोर दे रही थी, तब मुख्यमंत्री कमलनाथ ने सुझाव दिया कि ऐहतियात के तौर पर सदन को स्थगित कर दिया जाए। कांग्रेस के नेता और मध्यप्रदेश विधानसभा के अध्यक्ष एन.पी. प्रजापति ने कोरोना वायरस की आशंका के कारण

सदन को 16 मार्च को दस दिनों के लिए स्थगित कर दिया। कमलनाथ को उम्मीद रही होगी कि इन दस दिनों से उन्हें बाग़ी विधायकों को वापस लाने के लिए कुछ और वक्त मिल जाएगा।

इस बीच, दिल्ली में संसद को भी कोरोना की वजह से सदन स्थगित करने का दबाव बन रहा था, लेकिन दोनों पीठासीन अधिकारी नरमी बरतने को तैयार नहीं थे। 18 मार्च को जब तृणमूल कांग्रेस के चार सांसद काले मास्क पहनकर राज्यसभा में पहुंचे, तो राज्यसभा के सभापति वेंकैया नायडू ने उन्हें मास्क हटाने के निर्देश देते हुए कहा कि यह संसद के नियमों के ख़िलाफ़ था। जब कई सांसदों ने सदन की अवधि कम करने की मांग की तो अल्पसंख्यक मामलों के मंत्री मुख्तार अब्बास नक़वी ने आपत्ति ज़ाहिर करते हुए कहा कि किसी तरह की घबराहट दिखाना देश के हित में नहीं होगा। विरोधाभास यह था कि एक तरफ मोदी सरकार लोगों को मास्क लगाने और बड़ी सभाओं को सीमित करने की सलाह दे रही थी, दूसरी तरफ जो सांसद सलाह पर अमल करने की बात कर रहे थे, उन पर बेवजह 'घबराहट' का आरोप लग रहा था। कांग्रेस के सांसद राजीव गौड़ा ने तंज में टिप्पणी की, 'कोरोना वायरस नहीं जानता कि हम सांसद हैं!'

कमलनाथ को लग रहा था कि संसद को जल्दी स्थगित नहीं करने का फ़ैसला प्रधानमंत्री और गृहमंत्री कार्यालय के दबाव में किया गया था। उन्होंने जोर देते हुए कहा कि 'कोरोना वायरस के मामले बढ़ने के बावजूद सरकार संसद की बैठक स्थगित नहीं कर रही, क्योंकि उसकी नज़र पहले मध्य प्रदेश सरकार को गिराने पर है। अगर संसद नहीं चल रही होती, तो मध्य प्रदेश विधानसभा भी स्थगित हो जाती और फिर भाजपा के प्लान पर पानी फिर जाता।' मोदी के नेतृत्व वाली भाजपा के सत्ता चाहने के रास्ते में महामारी को भी नहीं आने दिया जाएगा।

भाजपा नेतृत्व को जल्दी कोई कदम उठाने की ज़रूरत का अहसास हो गया था। शिवराज सिंह चौहान ने अब सुप्रीम कोर्ट का रुख किया। अदालत ने 20 मार्च को वीडियो रिकॉर्डिंग के साथ सदन में बहुमत साबित करने का आदेश दिया। कमलनाथ को जब यह लगा कि अब उनका खेल ख़त्म हो गया था तो उन्होंने बहुमत परीक्षण से कुछ घंटों पहले ही इस्तीफ़ा दे दिया। 23 मार्च को भोपाल के राजभवन में बंद कमरे में आयोजित समारोह में चौहान ने चौथी बार मध्यप्रदेश के मुख्यमंत्री पद की शपथ ली। समारोह के लिए पार्टी के किसी भी नेता और मीडिया को बुलावा नहीं भेजा गया, भोपाल में कोविड की वजह से लॉकडाउन हो गया था। अगली सुबह यानी 24 मार्च को हुए विश्वास मत का कांग्रेस ने बहिष्कार किया और शिवराज सिंह चौहान ने विधानसभा में अपना बहुमत साबित कर दिया। उसी रात आठ बजे, चार घंटे का नोटिस देते हुए प्रधानमंत्री मोदी ने देशभर में आधी रात से अगले 21 दिनों के लिए लॉकडाउन का ऐलान कर दिया। एक अरब से ज़्यादा लोगों के लिए लॉकडाउन की घोषणा। कांग्रेस सरकार गिराने और उसकी जगह भाजपा सरकार बनाने के बाद, मोदी सरकार अब सदी में एक बार आने वाली महामारी की चुनौती से लड़ने के लिए तैयार थी।

मैंने केन्द्रीय स्वास्थ्य मंत्री डॉ. हर्षवर्धन से पूछा था कि क्या मोदी सरकार ने भोपाल में ऑपरेशन लोट्स को कामयाब बनाने के लिए लॉकडाउन के ऐलान में देरी की? वाजपेयी-आडवाणी युग के भाजपा नेता मृदुभाषी, मिलनसार और ईएनटी सर्जन डॉ. हर्षवर्धन ने सवाल को टाल दिया। उन्होंने कहा, 'मेरा फोकस तब कोविड के इंतज़ामों पर था। मध्य प्रदेश में क्या हो रहा था, यह मेरा विषय नहीं था। इस राजनीतिक मसले को पार्टी और प्रधानमंत्री देख रहे थे।' मार्च 2020 में क्या विरोधी पार्टी की सरकार गिराने के लिए लॉकडाउन में देरी की गई? कोविड प्रबंधन के दौरान यह उन अहम सवालों में से एक था, जिनका जवाब नहीं मिल पाया था। इस घटनाक्रम ने मोदी की राजनीति पर 'मैकिवेलियन' राजनीति की स्याह छाप जैसे सवाल ज़रूर खड़े किए थे।

═

प्रधानमंत्री मोदी का राष्ट्र के नाम संबोधन, अब देश की अहम और बहु प्रतीक्षित 'घटनाओं' में शुमार हो गया था। इससे पहले उन्होंने नवम्बर 2016 में जिस नाटकीय तरीके से एक झटके में 500 और 1000 रुपये के नोटों को बंद करने की घोषणा की थी, उसने देश को झकझोर दिया था। उसके बाद जब भी मोदी के राष्ट्र के नाम संबोधन की चर्चा होती, तो लोगों के मन में डर के साथ उत्सुकता होती थी। हालांकि उस रात 24 मार्च का संबोधन कुछ अलग था। प्रधानमंत्री का ट्वीट ही रहस्य से भरा था: 'कोविड-19 के ख़तरे से जुड़े अहम पहलुओं पर आज रात 8 बजे राष्ट्र को संबोधित करूंगा।' न्यूज़ रूम ने राहत की सांस ली। एक बार फिर से कोई लास्ट-मिनट सरप्राइज नहीं होगा: यह कोई राजनीतिक या नाटकीय आर्थिक फ़ैसला नहीं, बल्कि वायरस पर संबोधन होना था। उस समय तक, अधिकारिक तौर पर देशभर में कोविड के 515 मामले सामने आए थे और अब तक 10 मौतें हुई थीं।

मोदी ने कोविड से निपटने के लिए सरकारी कोशिशों को लेकर 19 मार्च को राष्ट्र को संबोधित किया था। उस दिन प्रधानमंत्री ने 24 घंटे के लिए जनता कर्फ़्यू का आह्वान किया था, यानी इस दौरान कोई भी अपने घर से बाहर नहीं निकलेगा। उन्होंने स्थिति को गंभीर और किसी विश्व युद्ध से भी बदतर बताते हुए घबराहट में बेवजह की खरीदारी से बचने पर ज़ोर दिया। मोदी ने लोगों को भरोसा दिलाया कि सरकार आवश्यक वस्तुओं की आपूर्ति के लिए सभी ज़रूरी कदम उठा रही थी। प्रधानमंत्री ने लोगों को आखिरी सलाह दी: 'डॉक्टरों से लेकर नर्सों तक, अस्पताल, सफाई, एयरलाइंस, सरकारी कर्मचारियों, पुलिसकर्मियों, मीडिया, ट्रेन, बस और ऑटो रिक्शा सेवाओं से जुड़े लोग और होम डिलीवरी करने वाले, सभी अपनी परवाह किए बिना, निस्वार्थ भाव से दूसरों की सेवा कर रहे हैं। राष्ट्र उन सभी का आभारी है और नागरिकों को इनके प्रति रविवार को आभार व्यक्त करना चाहिए।' हाई अलर्ट पर घबराए हुए से देश के लिए प्रधानमंत्री

का संदेश था कि 22 मार्च की शाम पांच बजे, पांच मिनट के लिए जब प्रशासन की तरफ से साइरन बजे, तो सभी लोग अपने घरों और दफ्तरों से बाहर निकलकर, अपनी बालकनी, छतों, और दरवाजों पर खड़े होकर ताली बजाएं, घंटी बजाएं और थाली बजाएं। 'ताली बजाओ, थाली बजाओ,' महामारी के बीच एक विचित्र सा संदेश, शायद वायरस को डराने या काम में लगे लोगों को आभार के नाम पर करोड़ों भारतीयों से शोर मचाने के लिए कहा जा रहा था। जानकारों का मानना है कि मोदी अंक 8 को लेकर जुनूनी हैं, उनके कथित अंधविश्वास और कथित जादुई सोच (साल 2014 में मोदी ने दो हज़ार साल पहले की प्राचीन प्लास्टिक सर्जरी का ज़िक्र किया था, जिसमें भगवान गणेश के हाथी के सिर को लेकर चर्चा की थी) का खेल एक महामारी के वैज्ञानिक इलाज के तौर पर माना जा रहा था, या फिर इस कथित पागलपन के पीछे कोई तर्क था?

कुछ महीनों बाद एक आला सरकारी अफसर ने मुझे बताया कि 'ताली-थाली और फिर दीया जलाओ' अभियान, पूरी तरह से प्रधानमंत्री का आइडिया था। आला अफसर का तर्क था, 'मोदी ने एक कठिन दौर में इसे मनोबल बढ़ाने वाला और एकता और साझेदारी की भावना पैदा करने वाला अनूठा तरीका माना था।' जब मैंने कहा कि 'ताली-थाली' का आइडिया (ऑल इज वैल) यानी 'सब ठीक है' की कल्पना, विज्ञान विरोधी और भ्रम फैलाने वाला था, खासतौर से इतनी बड़ी बीमारी के संकट को देखते हुए, यह गलत समय पर भी था। तो जवाब में अफसर की टिप्पणी तल्ख थी, 'क्या लाखों लोग प्रधानमंत्री की सलाह पर बाहर नहीं आए और उनकी सलाह को नहीं माना? आप जैसे लिबरल एलीट लोग प्रधानमंत्री की इस सम्मोहन शक्ति को कभी नहीं सराहेंगे।' प्रधानमंत्री के इस 'आकर्षण' ने ज़्यादातर लोगों को एक तर्कहीन सलाह की तरफ धकेल दिया था। किसी भी तार्किक व्यक्ति से 'ताली-थाली' संदेश को मानने की उम्मीद नहीं की जा सकती, लेकिन देश की एक बड़ी आबादी अपने नेता के रास्ते पर चलने को लेकर खुश थी। प्रधानमंत्री मोदी सिर्फ़ एक राजनेता नहीं, बल्कि 'फील गुड गुरु', एक 'सौभाग्य' बढ़ाने वाले, ताबीज बांटने वाले ओझा या मनोवैज्ञानिक जादूगर या फिर अपने समर्थकों के लिए एक 'पंथ' के रूप में थे, जो अपने कम्युनिकेशन के ताकतवर हथियारों से देश को एक अलग तरह की 'जंग' के लिए तैयार कर रहे थे।

24 मार्च को सरकार ने औपचारिक तौर पर वायरस के ख़िलाफ़ जंग का ऐलान कर दिया। अपने गंभीर दिखते चेहरे के साथ प्रधानमंत्री ने आधी रात से अगले इक्कीस दिनों के लिए लॉकडाउन की घोषणा कर दी। 'आज आधी रात से, पूरे देश में पूर्ण लॉकडाउन हो जाएगा। देश और हर नागरिक की सुरक्षा के लिए लोगों को अपने घरों से बाहर निकलने पर पूरी तरह पाबंदी रहेगी। आपके दरवाज़े पर एक "लक्ष्मण रेखा" है। आपका घर के बाहर रखा एक कदम कोरोना वायरस को आपके घर के अंदर ले आएगा।' प्रधानमंत्री ने चेतावनी के स्वर में कहा कि 'यदि हालात इक्कीस दिन में काबू में नहीं किए गए तो भारत इक्कीस साल पीछे जा सकता है।'

'फील गुड गुरु' से निराशा और कयामत तक की भविष्यवाणी करते मोदी में यह बदलाव अचानक और नाटकीय था। सिर्फ़ दो दिन पहले देश से ताली और थाली बजाने की सलाह दी जा रही थी और अगले ही पल जश्न से बलिदान तक मोदी ने देश को 'भावनात्मक रोलर कोस्टर' पर चढ़ा दिया था। टेलीविजन चैनलों की रेटिंग्स बताती है कि मोदी का लॉकडाउन पर राष्ट्र को संबोधन देश के इतिहास में सबसे ज़्यादा देखा जाने वाला टीवी प्रसारण था, जिसे 201 चैनलों पर करीब बीस करोड़ (19.7 करोड़) लोगों ने लाइव देखा। इसे टेलीविजन की आपदा का चरम मान सकते हैं।

इस प्रसारण की ताकत को समझने में थोड़ी देर लगी। मेरे दिमाग में सबसे पहले आया कि क्या मुझे अगली सुबह के लिए तय डेंटिस्ट से मुलाकात को रद्द कर देना चाहिए? ज़ाहिर है लाखों भारतीयों की चिंताएं मुझसे ज़्यादा गहरी और गंभीर रही होंगी। रोजमर्रा के किराना सामान के मिलने में मुश्किलें, परिवहन सेवाएं ठप, स्कूल-दफ्तर बंद हो गए थे। क्या झुग्गियों, चॉल और एक कमरे में एक साथ छह से आठ रहने वाले लाखों लोग वाइरस फैलने से रोकने के लिए सामाजिक दूरी बनाने जैसी बातों को पूरा कर सकते थे? मध्यम वर्ग के लोगों के लिए यह एक लग्जरी जैसा था लेकिन झुग्गियों और छोटे-छोटे कमरों में रहने वालों के लिए नामुमकिन था। क्या ये गुमनाम से लोग 21 दिनों का लॉकडाउन झेल पाएंगे? गंभीर सवाल यह था कि दिहाड़ी मजदूर, गरीब लोग रातों-रात घर पर रहने के फरमान को लागू करने का खामियाज़ा कैसे भुगत पाएंगे? कैसे जी पाएंगे?

ज़्यादातर भारतीयों को जरूरी चीजों के बारें में सोचने के लिए वक्त नहीं दिया गया। आधी रात से लॉकडाउन का ऐलान प्रधानमंत्री के रात आठ बजे शुरू हुए राष्ट्र के नाम संबोधन में किया गया, जो करीब नौ बजे ख़त्म हुआ, यानी देश को अपनी ज़िंदगी संभालने के लिए सिर्फ़ चार घंटे मिले थे। डॉ. हर्षवर्धन ने सफाई दी, 'हमारे पास कोई और विकल्प नहीं था, यदि लॉकडाउन में देर की जाती तो अराजकता हो जाती।' स्वास्थ्य मंत्री के तौर पर उन पर ही कोविड-19 पर निगरानी की ज़िम्मेदारी थी। मगर उन लोगों के लिए आवश्यक सेवाओं, बसों और ठहरने की जगह जैसे ज़रूरी इंतज़ाम किए जा सकते थे, जो लोग अपने घरों से दूर थे और फंस गए थे। स्वास्थ्य मंत्री ने स्वीकार करते हुए कहा, 'ये सभी बड़े फ़ैसले प्रधानमंत्री कार्यालय और गृह मंत्रालय में किए गए, हम सिर्फ़ उनके निर्देशों पर काम कर रहे थे।'

मृदुभाषी डॉ. हर्षवर्धन ने लोगों के जहन में उठते संदेह की ही पुष्टि की। लॉकडाउन से संबंधित सारे निर्देश प्रधानमंत्री कार्यालय और गृहमंत्री के कार्यालय से ही आ रहे थे। दूसरे मंत्रालयों और राज्य सरकारों को भी गाइडलाइन के हिसाब से काम करना था। मार्च 2021 में बीबीसी की एक आरटीआई पर आई रिपोर्ट से पता चलता है कि केन्द्र और राज्य दोनों में ज़्यादातर सरकारी विभागों से लॉकडाउन लागू करने से पहले कोई सलाह-मशविरा नहीं किया

गया था। लेकिन गृह मंत्रालय के एक अधिकारी का दावा था, 'वो ऐसा कैसे कह सकते हैं, ज़्यादातर राज्य सरकारों से हम संपर्क में थे और उन्होंने पहले ही स्थानीय स्तर पर लॉकडाउन शुरू कर दिए थे।'

सचाई तो यह है कि सबकुछ केन्द्र के हाथ में ही था। 11 मार्च 2020 को गृह मंत्रालय ने आपदा प्रबंधन अधिनियम 2005, को लागू करते हुए आदेश जारी किया, जिसमें आपदा प्रबंधन के लिए कोई भी ज़रूरी कदम उठाने की ताकत गृह मंत्रालय को मिल गई थी। उसी दिन केन्द्र सरकार ने राज्यों को उसके निर्देश मानने के लिए महामारी रोग अधिनियम, 1897 का हवाला दिया। उन्नीसवीं सदी में बम्बई में हुए प्लेग के वक्त हज़ारों लोग मारे गए थे, तब बने इस क़ानून का इस्तेमाल सरकार इक्कीसवीं सदी में वायरस से निपटने के लिए कर रही थी। मौटे तौर पर लोगों की आज़ादी पर काबू के लिए सरकारों ने असीमित अधिकार अपने पास ले लिए थे। गृह मंत्रालय के एक आला अधिकारी का दावा था, 'उपायों को लागू करते वक्त केन्द्र और राज्य सरकारों के बीच बेहतर समन्वय था, चाहे वो क्वारन्टीन हो, ज़रूरी स्क्रीनिंग हो, सीमाओं को सील करने से लॉकडाउन नियंत्रण तक, हर मसले पर हम लगातार एक-दूसरे से बात कर रहे थे।'

बात में भले ही कितनी सचाई हो, लेकिन जल्दी ही यह साफ हो गया कि मोदी सरकार की वायरस के ख़िलाफ़ छेड़ी गई 'जंग' गरीबों के लिए विनाशकारी साबित हुई, बहुतों को नौकरी गंवानी पड़ी तो कई लोगों की अपनी जान भी खोनी पड़ी। इक्कीस दिनों का यह बलिदान कहीं ज़्यादा तकलीफ देने वाला और लंबा था। कोई 'ताली या थाली' का शोर उस वायरस को फैलने से नहीं रोक सकता था।

> 'शहरी भारत ने अब तक प्रवासी मज़दूरों की परवाह नहीं की। महामारी ने अब तक गुमनाम रहे उन लोगों को एक चेहरा दिया, और अब उनकी परवाह इसलिए की जा रही थी क्योंकि बड़े और मध्यम वर्ग के लोगों को उनके बिना मुश्किलें पैदा हो रही थी।'
>
> — पुरस्कृत पत्रकार पी. साईनाथ, 10 अप्रैल 2020 को *इंडिया* टुडे को दिए साक्षात्कार में

28 मार्च 2020 को प्रधानमंत्री के नेशनल लॉकडाउन की घोषणा के चार दिनों बाद बड़े पैमाने पर पलायन शुरू हो गया। यह 2020 का सबसे बड़ा प्रवासी पलायन था—इसे ऐतिहासिक कहा जा सकता है। देशभर में शहरों से घबराए हुए हताश-निराश लोग अपने छोटे-छोटे बच्चों और बुज़ुर्गों को साथ लेकर अपने गांवों के लिए निकल पड़े, चाहे वो पैदल हो, साइकिल या फिर गाड़ी—जो साधन मिला, बस वो निकल गए थे। नई दिल्ली से पूर्वी उत्तरप्रदेश तक, मुंबई

से असम तक, हैदराबाद से छत्तीसगढ़ तक, लोग पैदल जाने के लिए मजबूर थे, क्योंकि सरकार के आदेश से ज़्यादातर रेलगाड़ियां और बसें अब नहीं चल रही थीं।

लॉकडाउन शुरू होते ही लोग अपने घरों तक पहुंचने का रास्ता ढूंढने लगे। टीवी चैनलों पर एकाध तस्वीरें दिखने लगीं, जिसमें प्रवासी परिवार अपने ज़रूरी सामान के साथ राजमार्गों पर पैदल या साइकिल पर जा रहे थे। जैसे ही प्रवासियों को ले जाने के लिए बसों के इंतज़ाम की अफवाह फैली, लोग बस अड्डों तक पहुंचने लगे। दिल्ली की सीमा से सटे नोएडा में ज्यादातर राष्ट्रीय बड़े चैनलों के दफ्तर हैं तो प्रवासियों के पलायन का संकट टीवी चैनलों पर 'ब्रेकिंग न्यूज़' के तौर पर चमकने लगा।

उस शाम मैंने हालात देखने के लिए दफ्तर से आनंद विहार तक का एक चक्कर लगाया। ज़मीन पर हालात परेशान करने वाले थे। बिहार के सीवान ज़िले के एक नौजवान ने रुंआसी आवाज़ में बताया, 'मकान मालिक हमसे एडवांस किराया मांग रहा था, नहीं देने पर उसने कमरे से बाहर निकाल दिया। जब हमारे पास काम नहीं है तो पैसा कहां से दें?' दिहाड़ी मज़दूरों की ऐसी बहुत सी आवाज़ों में निराशा दिख रही थी, इनमें से ज़्यादातर लोग शहरों में मकान बनाने का काम करते थे। एक तरफ शहर में राशन ख़त्म हो रहा था, साथ ही वे अपने गांव को लेकर भी परेशान थे। दिल्ली में सरकार के अफसरों को भीड़ को संभालने के लिए जूझना पड़ रहा था, वे प्रवासियों से अपने गांव लौटने के लिए कह रहे थे। चार दिन पहले ही प्रधानमंत्री ने एक साथ भीड़ जुटाने के ख़िलाफ़ चेतावनी दी थी। एक सौ तीस करोड़ की आबादी वाले देश में यह हुजुम इस बात का सबूत था कि लॉकडाउन से निबटना आसान नहीं होगा। निराश लोगों की तकलीफों को आसानी से नहीं भुलाया जा सकता। बेहाल आनंद विहार आने वाले दिनों की परेशानी को समझाने के लिए काफी था।

मोदी सरकार शुरुआत में तो प्रवासी मज़दूरों के अपने घरों को लौटने की खबर को मानने को तैयार नहीं थी। जिस दिन पहली बार आनंद विहार पर मौजूद हुजूम की ख़बर आई, उस दिन एक आला अफसर ने न्यूज़ चैनलों के दफ्तरों में फ़ोन करके हिदायत दी, 'वे घबराहट फैलाने का काम नहीं करें।' शिकायती लहज़े में उन्होंने कहा, 'आप तो ऐसे दिखा रहे हैं मानो पूरा देश सड़क पर है।' राज्य सरकारें भी हालात को गंभीरता से लेने को तैयार नहीं थीं। परेशानी का इलाज ढूंढने के बजाय केन्द्र और राज्य सरकारें एक-दूसरे पर ज़िम्मेदारी डाल रही थीं और दोनों मिलकर काम करती नहीं दिखीं। दिल्ली सरकार के एक अधिकारी ने कहा, 'हम तो लोगों को उनके घर भेजने को तैयार हैं लेकिन उनके लिए बसों या दूसरे इंतज़ाम तो यूपी और बिहार सरकारों को करना होगा।'

इसे भी त्रासदी कहना चाहिए कि आमतौर पर 'सिस्टम' को हरकत में लाने के लिए किसी बड़ी दुर्घटना की ज़रूरत होती है। 9 मई, को महाराष्ट्र के औरंगाबाद के पास 16 लोग मालगाड़ी

की चपेट में आ गए, वे लंबे समय से चलते-चलते थककर पटरियों के पास ही सो गए थे। जालना कस्बे में ये लोग एक स्टील फैक्ट्री में काम करते थे, जहां मालिक ने उन्हें मजदूरी देने से मना कर दिया। बिना पैसे और भोजन के परेशान होते ये दिहाड़ी मज़दूर किसी भी तरह मध्यप्रदेश में अपने गांव लौटना चाहते थे। उनके क्षत-विक्षत शव और ख़ून पटरी पर फैला हुआ था। पीड़ित रिश्तेदारों की तकलीफ समझी जा सकती थी। एक ने कहा, 'इस देश में गरीबों की कोई सुनवाई नहीं है।' यह बातचीत सोशल मीडिया पर वायरल हो गई।

आमतौर पर मोदी सरकार मे बैठे लोग 'मीडिया नैरेटिव' को 'मैनेज' करने में ना केवल कामयाब रहते हैं बल्कि वे इस बात का खासतौर से ध्यान रखते हैं कि मुख्यधारा का मीडिया कोई परेशानी पैदा करने वाले सवाल ना उठाए और सोशल मीडिया पर उनकी विचारधारा वालों का असर ना हो। लेकिन इतने बड़े संकट को 'मीडिया मैनेजर' नहीं संभाल सकते थे। सरकार के पास अब गरीब, भूखे और बेसहारा लोगों की कुछ मदद करने के अलावा कोई रास्ता नहीं था। शुरुआत में जहां केन्द्र सरकार जनता की इस तकलीफ को मानने से बच रही थी, अब उसे उनके लिए परिवहन का इंतज़ाम बढ़ाने के लिए मजबूर होना पड़ा। यहां भी शुरू में बड़ी अराजकता सी थी, क्योंकि सरकार ने 'श्रमिक स्पेशल ट्रेन' चलाई थीं। जब हमने बताया कि मुंबई से जाने वाले प्रवासियों को किराया देने के लिए मजबूर किया जा रहा था, तो खबर को झूठी बताते हुए रेल मंत्री पीयूष गोयल नाराज़ हो गए। भारतीय जनता पार्टी के प्रवक्ता ने आरोप लगाया कि 'केवल विरोधी दलों वाली राज्य सरकारें ही प्रवासियों से रेलगाड़ी में चढ़ने का किराया वसूल रही हैं।' एक दिन बाद हमने एक और ख़बर दिखाई, जिसमें बताया कि कैसे बीजेपी शासित गुजरात से उत्तरप्रदेश जाने वाली गाड़ी में चढ़ने के लिए 600 रुपये मांगे जा रहे थे। सरकार का झूठ कैमरे पर साफ दिख रहा था।

हकीकत ये थी कि बिना कोई स्पष्ट योजना के बसें और ट्रेन शुरू करने से अराजकता और परेशानी बढ़ गई थी। रेलवे के एक आदेश में कहा गया कि 'राज्य सरकारें यात्रियों से टिकट किराया वसूलेंगी और पैसा रेलवे को सौंपेंगी।' कांग्रेस ने आरोप लगाया कि सरकार परेशान मज़दूरों से पैसे वसूल कर उनका शोषण कर रही थी जबकि भाजपा ने दावा किया कि रेलवे पहले ही 85 फ़ीसदी खर्चा उठा रही थी और बाकी 15 फ़ीसदी वो राज्य सरकारों से ले रही थी। इस राजनीतिक खींचतान का हर्जाना सैकड़ों गरीब हिन्दुस्तानी भुगत रहे थे। ज़िम्मेदारी से बचने के लिए सरकार '3-डी' फॉर्मूला (**Denial. Deflection. Distraction.**) इस्तेमाल कर रही थी—इंकार, मुंह फेरना और फिर ध्यान भटकाना। जब जान-माल का नुकसान रुक नहीं रहा था, उस वक्त मोदी सरकार राजनीतिक फायदे का हिसाब-किताब देख रही थी।

इस खींचतान का इससे बेहतर उदाहरण क्या हो सकता है जब शिवसेना नेता और महाराष्ट्र के तब के मुख्यमंत्री उद्धव ठाकरे और रेल मंत्री पीयूष गोयल के बीच सोशल मीडिया प्लेटफॉर्म,

फेसबुक और ट्विटर पर जुबानी जंग चल रही थी। मुख्यमंत्री ठाकरे ने लिखा, राज्य में केवल पैंतीस-चालीस ट्रेन ही मुहैया कराई गई थीं जबकि राज्य में अस्सी ट्रेन की ज़रूरत बताई थी। मुंबई में सबसे ज़्यादा छात्र और प्रवासी मज़दूर फंसे हुए थे। इसके जवाब में रेल मंत्री गोयल ने रात दो बजे तक एक के बाद एक 12 ट्वीट किए, जिसमें महाराष्ट्र सरकार से अलग-अलग राज्यों में जाने वाले यात्रियों की सूची देने के लिए कहा गया था। देर रात के आखिरी ट्वीट में सवाल था, 'महाराष्ट्र से 125 ट्रेनों की सूची कहां हैं? रात दो बजे तक केवल 46 ट्रेन की लिस्ट मिली है।' इस आपात स्थिति में देश को सोशल मीडिया पर इस 'जंग' की ज़रूरत तो कतई नहीं थी। हमारे रिपोर्टर ने रेल मंत्री गोयल, जो खुद मुंबईकर हैं, से पूछा कि क्या आप सीधे फ़ोन पर बात कर इस मसले को नहीं सुलझा सकते थे? 'माफ़ कीजिए, मगर मुख्यमंत्री इस मसले पर सार्वजनिक तौर पर झूठ बोल रहे थे और उन्हें इसका जवाब देना ज़रूरी था।' साल 2019 में हुए राजनीतिक झगड़े से पहले तक शिवसेना और बीजेपी महाराष्ट्र में साथ-साथ थे। ऐसा लग रहा था कि वो घाव अब भी हरे थे। ऐसे मुश्किल वक्त में जब लोगों को राहत की फौरी ज़रूरत थी, उस समय राजनीतिक पेंतरेबाज़ी ना केवल तकलीफ़ देने वाली थी, बल्कि इसे क्रूर कहना ज़्यादा ठीक होगा।

प्रधानमंत्री, राज्यों के मुख्यमंत्रियों और सरकारी अधिकारियों के साथ नियमित बैठक कर रहे थे, तो क्या वे इसमें निर्देश देकर प्रवासियों के आने-जाने का इंतज़ाम ठीक नहीं कर सकते थे? रेलवे के एक आला अफ़सर का तर्क था कि 'भारत जैसे बड़े देश में एक ही दिन में सबकुछ ठीक हो जाने की उम्मीद करना उचित नहीं है।' क्या बेहतर सहयोग नहीं हो सकता? मेरा सवाल था। 'यह अचानक आया संकट था, जिसके बारे में किसी ने सोचा भी नहीं था। देश भर में लॉकडाउन, कोविड-19 के डर के बावजूद हमारे अफसर लोगों की मदद के लिए दिन-रात लगे हुए थे। आप पत्रकारों को सिर्फ़ गलती दिखाई देती है, आप कभी इस बात की तारीफ़ नहीं करेंगे कि रेलवे ने इतने सारे लोगों को उनके घरों तक सुरक्षित पहुंचाने का पहाड़ जैसा काम किया,' वरिष्ठ अधिकारी का तर्क था।

रेलवे ने मई से जून के बीच 3740 'श्रमिक स्पेशल ट्रेन' चलाकर 60 लाख से ज़्यादा लोगों को उनके गृह राज्यों में अपने घर तक सुरक्षित पहुंचाया। रेल मंत्री इस बात को मानने को तैयार नहीं थे कि ट्रेनों की आवाजाही पहले शुरू की जा सकती थी। 'जब हमने देखा कि प्रवासी मजदूर बनाए गए शिविरों में रुकने को तैयार नहीं थे, तो फिर हमने ट्रेन शुरू की।' गोयल का तर्क था कि 'लॉकडाउन का सीधा मतलब है कि आप जहां हैं, वहीं रहें।' गोयल ने देरी के लिए राज्य सरकारों को ज़िम्मेदार ठहराया। उनका आरोप था कि 'प्रवासी स्टेशनों पर मौजूद थे, लेकिन उन्हें नहीं ले जाया जा सकता था क्योंकि कई कारणों से बहुत से राज्य इसके लिए तैयार ही नहीं थे।'

सच तो यह है कि अचानक लॉकडाउन ने ना केवल रेलवे बल्कि पूरी सरकार को हिला दिया था। इसकी बड़ी वजह किसी स्पष्ट योजना का अभाव तो था ही, साथ ही हर दिन नए 'फरमानों' के जारी होने से भ्रम बढ़ रहा था। इसमें एक उदाहरण प्रवासी यात्रियों से टिकट किराया वसूली का मामला भी था। मोदी सरकार यह दावा तो कर सकती है उसने अपनी तरफ से हरसंभव कोशिश की, यहां तक कि कई बार उसने आपदा को अवसर में बदलने का काम भी किया। मास्क, पीपीई और सैनिटाइज़र को बड़े पैमाने पर बनाकर नए अवसर भी पैदा किए, जिसे मोदी सरकार 'मिशन मोड' 'आत्मनिर्भर भारत' होने की बात कहती है। स्वास्थ्य मंत्रालय के एक अधिकारी का कहना था कि 'जब महामारी आई, तब हम पीपीई किट बनाने के लिए तैयार नहीं थे और दूसरे ज़रूरी उपकरणों के लिए भी हम आयात पर निर्भर थे। जबकि एक साल बाद हम रोज़ाना दो लाख किट और दो लाख एन-95 मास्क बना रहे थे। क्या ये बड़ी उपलब्धि नहीं है?' लेकिन रोजाना बढ़ती मौतों की तादाद के आगे यह आत्म-प्रशंसा बेमायने थी।

इक्कीस दिन के लॉकडाउन के करीब दो महीने बाद मई 2020 में सरकार धीरे-धीरे हालात पर काबू पाते दिखने लगी। सरकारी आंकड़ों के मुताबिक तब तक देश में कोविड-19 के ढाई लाख से अधिक मामले और 7200 मौतें हुई थीं। 30 जून, 2020 को कोविड महामारी आने के बाद, छठी बार प्रधानमंत्री राष्ट्र को संबोधित कर रहे थे। इस बार लॉकडाउन को अनलॉक 2.0 की घोषणा के साथ बड़ा फोकस 80 करोड़ लोगों तक मुफ्त भोजन योजना का विस्तार करना था। 'प्रधानमंत्री गरीब अन्न कल्याण योजना' पर 90 हज़ार करोड़ का खर्च आना था। प्रधानमंत्री का फोकस गरीब किसान थे और उनके सामने वे अन्नदाता बनना चाहते थे। प्रधानमंत्री कार्यालय के एक अधिकारी का कहना था कि 'हो सकता है हमने सबकुछ ठीक नहीं किया हो, लेकिन प्रधानमंत्री जी की चिंता गरीबों की तकलीफ़ कम करने की रही। इसलिए लोग उन पर भरोसा करते हैं और वोट देते हैं।' सरकार को उम्मीद थी कि 80 करोड़ लोगों को मुफ़्त अनाज योजना से लोगों का गुस्सा कम होगा।

अहम सवाल था कि क्या लॉकडाउन में रियायत से लाखों गरीब लोगों की तकलीफ़ कम हो सकती थी? ज़्यादातर चिकित्सा विशेषज्ञों की राय थी कि लॉकडाउन को बढ़ाया जाना चाहिए, इससे वायरस के संक्रमण की श्रृंखला को तोड़ने में मदद मिलती और सरकार को महामारी से निपटने के लिए ज़्यादा समय मिल जाता। केन्द्र की 'कोविड टॉस्क फोर्स' के सदस्य और अखिल भारतीय आयुर्विज्ञान संस्थान के निदेशक रहे डॉ. रणदीप गुलेरिया का मानना था कि 'यह सही काम था। लॉकडाउन के बिना तेज़ी से फैलती महामारी को संभालना भी अस्पतालों के लिए मुश्किल हो जाता।'

दूसरी तरफ ऐसे लोग थे जिनके मुताबिक बेहतर योजना और काम में रफ्तार से ऐसा करना मुमकिन था। लॉकडाउन को बढ़ाने के ख़िलाफ़ नाराज़गी ज़ाहिर करने वालों में सबसे बड़ा नाम

बजाज ऑटो के प्रबंध निदेशक राजीव बजाज का था। बजाज लॉकडाउन को 'मनमाना' और 'बेवजह की कार्रवाई' मानते थे। जून 2020 में कांग्रेस नेता राहुल गांधी के साथ एक बातचीत में राजीव बजाज ने कहा कि 'आपने गलत चीज़ों की रफ्तार को रोक दिया। इससे महामारी की रफ़्तार नहीं रुकी बल्कि इसका सीधा नुकसान सकल घरेलू उत्पाद (जीडीपी) को उठाना पड़ा है। इससे दोनों तरफ खामियाज़ा उठाना पड़ा।' उनकी बात में दम था। सरकारी आंकड़ों के मुताबिक साल 2020-21 में पहली तिमाही अप्रैल-जून में जीडीपी 23 फ़ीसदी से ज़्यादा गिर गई थी। यह दुनिया की दूसरी अर्थव्यवस्थाओं के मुकाबले सबसे खराब था। सरकार की बात मानें तो साल 2020 से 2023 के बीच 25 हज़ार से ज़्यादा छोटे उद्योग बंद हो गए, इससे खासतौर से असंगठित क्षेत्र में लाखों लोगों को अपनी नौकरी गंवानी पड़ी।

भाजपा इस बात से नाराज़ थी कि उद्योगपति, विपक्ष के नेता के साथ बातचीत में सरकार पर हमला कर रहे थे। पार्टी ने इसके ख़िलाफ़ तुरंत मोर्चा खोल दिया, बीजेपी के प्रवक्ता सैयद ज़फ़र इस्लाम ने एक टीवी बहस के दौरान मुझसे कहा, 'हर किसी को अपनी राय रखने का अधिकार है, लेकिन यह भी समझना चाहिए कि राजीव बजाज कोविड-19 और इससे निपटने के तरीकों के विशेषज्ञ नहीं हैं।' महामारी प्रबंधन पर अपनी आलोचना को बर्दाश्त नहीं करने वाली मोदी सरकार का यही तरीका था: दमदार तरीके से आलोचकों पर हमला बोलना, इसके लिए पार्टी प्रवक्ता टीवी कार्यक्रमों पर किसी भी हद तक जा सकते थे। किसी भी बड़े संकट पर सवाल के जवाब में सरकार अक्सर उसे खारिज़ कर देती थी। उदाहरण के तौर पर, सितम्बर 2020 में संसद में एक लिखित जवाब में गृह राज्य मंत्री नित्यानंद राय का दावा था कि 'बड़े पैमाने पर मजदूरों के पलायन की चर्चा, फ़र्ज़ी ख़बरें फैलने से आई है।' राय का दावा था कि 'बड़ी संख्या में मजदूरों ने पलायन इसलिए किया क्योंकि फर्जी खबरों की वजह से उन्हें यह घबराहट हो गई कि अब भोजन, पानी और रोजमर्रा की ज़रूरी चीजों के लिए परेशानी उठानी पड़ेगी।'

कई हफ्तों तक चले इस मानवीय संकट से निपटने में हुई प्रशानिक चूक का जिम्मा 'फ़र्ज़ी खबरों' पर डालना साफतौर पर अपनी जवाबदेही से पल्ला झाड़ना था। ऐसा लगता था कि मोदी सरकार उस संदेशवाहक को गोली मारने के लिए आमादा थी, जो लॉकडाउन की वजह से आर्थिक परेशानियां झेल रहे लोगों को सच सामने रख रहा था।

सरकार के श्रम और रोज़गार मंत्री संतोष गंगवार ने संसद में बताया कि 2020 के लॉकडाउन के दौरान करीब एक करोड़ चालीस लाख मजदूर अपने गृह राज्यों में लौट आए, लेकिन उन्होंने कहा कि सरकार के पास कोविड के दौरान नौकरी और जान गंवाने वाले मजदूरों का कोई आंकड़ा नहीं था। उस शाम मैंने अपने प्राइम टाइम शो पर सीधे सवाल के साथ बहस की: 'मोदी सरकार इंकार की मुद्रा में, क्या लॉकडाउन में किसी मजदूर की नौकरी और जान नहीं गई?' अगले दिन दिल्ली के इंडिया इटरनेशनल सेंटर में मेरी मुलाकात अचानक भाजपा के

एक नेता से हो गई, मिज़ाज में गर्मी के साथ उन्होंने पूछा, 'ये नकारात्मकता फैलाना आप कब बंद करेंगे? सरकार इस संकट में इतने लोगों को राहत पहुंचा रही है, वो आपको दिखाई नहीं देता?' मैं उनके इस लहज़े से हैरान तो था, लेकिन संभलते हुए कहा, संकट के वक्त लोगों की मदद करना सरकार की ज़िम्मेदारी होती है। मैंने कहा, 'हकीकत तो यह है कि लोगों को बहुत तकलीफ़ों का सामना करना पड़ा है, बहुत से लोगों की मौत हो गई, उनमें वो भी शामिल हैं जो नींद में ही पटरियों पर ट्रेन की चपेट में आ गए।' उन्होंने पलटकर जवाब दिया, 'तो अब आप हमें उन मजदूरों की मौत के लिए भी ज़िम्मेदार ठहराएंगे? क्या लोगों को पटरी पर सोने के लिए हमने कहा था?' मैं वहां से निकल तो गया, लेकिन हैरान था कि सरकारों में इतनी सहानुभूति क्यों नहीं होती, लोगों की परेशानी उन्हें क्यों तकलीफ नहीं देती। यह सच है कि लॉकडाउन का प्रबंधन कोई आसान काम नहीं था, और सरकारी संसाधनों की भी अपनी सीमा होती है, लेकिन सच से मुंह मोड़ना भी तो ठीक नहीं कहा जा सकता। इस सबके बीच में सहानुभूति गायब थी। कामकाज की आलोचना सरकार को शायद स्वीकार नहीं थी और इसका असर कामकाज पर दिख रहा था।

27 मार्च 2020 को लॉकडाउन के कुछ दिनों बाद कोविड-19 से निपटने के लिए प्रधानमंत्री ने 'पीएम केयर्स फंड' का गठन किया। प्रधानमंत्री मोदी ने लोगों से फंड में उदारता से दान देने की अपील की, इसके पैसे का इस्तेमाल कोविड के लिए राहत कार्यों में किया जाना था। हालांकि बाढ़ और भूकंप जैसी प्राकृतिक आपदाओं के मौके पर सार्वजनिक चंदा जुटाने के लिए 1984 में बना 'प्रधानमंत्री राष्ट्रीय राहत कोष' पहले से ही था। एक सरकारी अधिकारी का कहना था, 'हम एक ऐसा फंड चाहते थे जो सामान्य आपदाओं के बजाय खासतौर से कोविड की समस्याओं के निपटने के लिए इस्तेमाल किया जा सके।'

इस फंड की योजना पर मुंबई के एक वकील मनोज हरित ने पूरा ब्यौरा दिया है। हरित के मुताबिक फंड की घोषणा का पहला ट्वीट 28 मार्च की शाम 4 बजकर 51 मिनट पर आया। थोड़ी देर बाद शाम 5 बजकर 9 मिनट पर भारतीय प्रशानिक सेवा संघ ने 21 लाख रुपये फंड में देने का वादा किया। उसके दस मिनट से भी कम समय में 5 बजकर 18 मिनट पर प्रधानमंत्री के 'हार्डकोर फैन' रहे अभिनेता अक्षय कुमार ने 25 करोड़ रुपये देने का ऐलान किया और शाम 5 बजकर 34 मिनट पर 'फोनपे' ने एक लिंक साझा किया, जिससे लोग पीएम केयर्स फंड में अपना हिस्सा दे सकते थे। स्पष्ट है कि प्रधानमंत्री की घोषणा से पहले ही उसे सफल दिखाने की योजना बना ली गई थी। हरित का मानना था कि 'सरकार के मीडिया प्रबंधन को ध्यान में रखते हुए योजना के रोलआउट होने के साथ ही लोगों की यह रफ़्तार महज एक संयोग नहीं हो सकती।'

एक पत्रकार साथी ने आरटीआई के माध्यम से कई बार पीएम केयर्स फंड और इसके दानदाताओं के बारे में जानकारी मांगी, लेकिन कभी कोई जवाब नहीं मिला। जनवरी 2023

में दिल्ली हाईकोर्ट में एक हलफ़नामे में प्रधानमंत्री कार्यालय ने स्पष्ट किया, पीएम केयर्स फंड एक सार्वजनिक धर्मार्थ फंड है, जिसे केन्द्र सरकार या कोई दूसरा सरकारी संगठन नियंत्रित नहीं करता, इसलिए वो किसी तीसरे पक्ष की जानकारी देने को बाध्य नहीं है।

वैसे यह सफाई बेमायना थी। इस फंड की वेबसाइट पर जानकारी दी गई है कि भारत के प्रधानमंत्री इसके पदेन अध्यक्ष हैं। रक्षा मंत्री, गृहमंत्री और वित्त मंत्री इसके पदेन ट्रस्टी होंगे। इस फंड को पीएमओ में अतिरिक्त सचिव या संयुक्त सचिव मानद तौर पर देखेंगे। फंड में दान को विदेशी अंशदान (विनियमन) संशोधन अधिनियम (एफसीआरए) के तहत छूट दी गई थी। केन्द्र सरकार ने कॉर्पोरेट्स और सरकारी कंपनियों को भी फंड में योगदान के लिए कहा था। वेबसाइट के मुताबिक साल 2020 में कुल 3,076.62 करोड़ रुपये इकट्ठा हुए थे। फंड से हज़ारों करोड़ रुपये सरकारी मशीनरी और संसाधनों का इस्तेमाल कर वेंटिलेटर, ऑक्सीजन सिलेंडर और वैक्सीन आदि खरीदने पर खर्च किए गए।

फंड की पारदर्शिता और सरकार के दोहरे रवैये को लेकर एक और आरटीआई कार्यकर्ता, कमोडोर लोकेश बत्रा (सेवानिवृत) ने जानकारी मांगी। पीएम केयर्स फंड में सभी योगदान को सौ फीसदी आयकर से मुक्त किया गया था, तो आरटीआई में इस छूट को जानने को आधार बनाया गया। जवाब में आयकर आयुक्त (छूट) के कार्यालय ने बताया, 'पीएम केयर्स फंड को पंजीकरण अधिनियम, 1908 के तहत पंजीकृत किया गया है और यह भारत सरकार के स्वामित्व, नियंत्रण वाली संस्था है।' लेकिन यह आरटीआई अधिनियम के तहत 'सार्वजनिक संस्थान' की श्रेणी में नहीं आता। दिसम्बर 2020 में जारी फंड की ट्रस्ट डीड में कहा गया हैः 'ट्रस्ट के कामकाज में केन्द्र या किसी भी राज्य सरकार का प्रत्यक्ष या अप्रत्यक्ष तौर पर कोई नियंत्रण नहीं है।' इस मसले पर कमोडोर लोकेश बत्रा का कहना था, 'अगर इस पर कोई सरकारी निंयत्रण नहीं है, तो फिर पूरा फंड सरकारी अफसरों की देखरेख में कैसे चल रहा है? और फंड से चलने वाली कोविड से जुड़ी हर चीज़, चाहे वो वेंटिलेटर हो या वैक्सीन, उन पर प्रधानमंत्री मोदी की फोटो क्यों लगाई जा रही है?' हक़ीकत यह है कि मोदी सरकार ने अपनी छवि के लिए पीएम केयर्स फंड की मदद और उसके काम का इस्तेमाल किया। इससे कोविड से लड़ने में सरकार को मजबूती मिली, प्रधानमंत्री की छवि भी सुधरी, लेकिन उस पर सवाल नहीं किए जा सके।

सामाजिक सेवा में जुड़े लोगों के मुश्किल सवालों पर सरकार अक्सर चुप्पी साध जाती है। लेकिन कोविड के वक्त इन मुश्किल सवालों को नज़रअंदाज़ करने से संकट और बढ़ गया। मोदी सरकार की चुप्पी तब और हैरान करने वाली थी, जब कोविड फैलाने के नाम पर मुसलमानों को निशाना बनाने की कोशिश की गई। मार्च 2020 में लॉकडाउन की घोषणा के कुछ दिनों बाद दक्षिणी दिल्ली के निज़ामुद्दीन इलाके में मुस्लिम मिशनरी 'तबलीगी जमात' के एक आयोजन पर सवाल खड़ा करते हुए, इसे पूरे देश में कोविड फैलाने के लिए ज़िम्मेदार ठहराया गया। दिल्ली

नगर निगम की मंज़ूरी के बाद हुए उस सम्मेलन में कई विदेशियों समेत हज़ारों लोगों ने हिस्सा लिया था। सम्मेलन में शामिल हुए कई लोग जाने-अनजाने में कोविड का शिकार हो गए और वे इसे अपने शहरों और गांवों तक ले गए।

इस पर भाजपा के आईटी सेल के कुछ लोगों ने इसे हैशटैग #कोरोनाजिहाद नाम से बढ़ाकर, भारतीयों को निशाना बनाने की 'इस्लामिक साज़िश' कहा दिल्ली में भाजपा के नेता कपिल मिश्रा, भड़काऊ ट्वीट करने वालों में सबसे आगे थे: 'तबलीगी जमात के लोगों ने डॉक्टरों और स्वास्थ्य कर्मचारियों पर थूकना शुरू कर दिया है। ज़ाहिर है कि उनका मकसद ज़्यादा से ज़्यादा लोगों में कोरोना फैलाना और उन्हें मारना है।' हैरत की बात यह है कि राष्ट्रीय या दिल्ली के किसी भाजपा नेता ने इस तरह के भड़काऊ और साम्प्रदायिक बयान का खंडन नहीं किया। इसके साथ ही तबलीगी जमात के सदस्यों के 'क्वारंटीन' में जाने से मना करने, स्वास्थ्य कर्मचारियों पर हमला करने और हिंदुओं पर पेशाब की बोतलें फेंकने जैसी अफवाहें फैलने लगीं। तबलीगी जमात को #कोरोनाआतंकवादी बताने वाले हैशटेग चलाए जाने लगा। न्यूज़ चैनल भी पीछे नहीं थे, उन पर तबलीगी जमात को कोरोना वायरस फैलाने का दोषी बताया जा रहा था।

अफवाहों पर रोक की कोशिश के बजाय भाजपा शासित राज्यों में पुलिस ने तबलीगी जमात के सदस्यों को पकड़ना शुरू किया और उन्हें और उनके संपर्क में आए लोगों को क्वारंटीन करने लगी। उत्तरप्रदेश पुलिस तो थोड़ा और आगे बढ़ गई, उसने तबलीगी जमात के कार्यक्रम में शामिल होने वाले किसी शख्स की जानकारी देने वाले को दस हज़ार रुपये देने का ऐलान भी कर दिया। यह सच है कि तबलीगी जमात के कई लोग कोरोना पॉजिटिव मिले, लेकिन उन पर कोरोना फैलाने के लिए पूरी तरह जिम्मेदारी डालना एक विभाजनकारी राजनीतिक एजेंडे के सिवाय कुछ नहीं कहा जा सकता। प्रवासी मज़दूरों पर लॉकडाउन के असर को शुरुआत में ख़ारिज़ करने के बाद, सरकारी मशीनरी अब किसी एक समुदाय को शैतान बताने का काम कर रही थी: दाढ़ी रखने वाले मुसलमानों को अचानक कोरोना फैलाने वालों के तौर पर निशाना बनाया गया और उनका सामाजिक बहिष्कार किया जाने लगा। कर्नाटक में भाजपा के पूर्व सांसद अनंतकुमार हेगड़े ने तो तबलीगी जमात को आतंकवादी करार दे दिया। सोशल मीडिया पर एक वीडियो साझा किया गया, जिसमें फल और सब्जी बेचने वाले मुसलमानों को अपने इलाके में नहीं आने देने की बात की गई थी। आरोप लगाया गया कि वे अपने सामान से कोरोना फैलाने का काम कर रहे थे। कर्नाटक के मैंगलोर और यूपी के मेरठ जैसे शहरों में तो पोस्टर लग गए, जिनमें चेतावनी थी कि मुसलमानों को अब उस इलाके में आने की इज़ाजत नहीं थी। मजहब के आधार पर लोगों को बांटना और इतने बड़े संकट के बीच नफरत और कट्टरता फैलाना उस वायरस से कम ख़तरनाक नहीं था।

हकीक़त यह भी है कि केन्द्र और कई राज्य सरकारों ने भी ऐसे आरोपों को रोकने या नफ़रत फैलाने वालों के ख़िलाफ़ कोई कार्रवाई नहीं की। यह केवल संवैधानिक ज़िम्मेदारी से बचना भर नहीं था, बल्कि यह एक जानबूझकर किया गया आपराधिक काम था, इसे लापरवाही कहकर नहीं बचा जा सकता। इससे लगा कि कोविड की लड़ाई में हमारी नैतिकता भी कहीं गुम हो गई थी। अप्रैल 2020 के शुरू में एक मामला महबूब अली का सामने आया, जिसमें वो भोपाल में तबलीगी जमात के सम्मेलन में हिस्सा लेने के बाद उत्तर-पश्चिम दिल्ली के बवाना में अपने गांव लौटा था। पड़ोसियों ने उस पर 'कोरोना आंतकवादी' होने का आरोप ही नहीं लगाया, उसे खेत में घसीटकर लाठी-डंडों और पत्थरों से इतना पीटा कि उसकी नाक और कान से ख़ून बहने लगा। उसकी जान बड़ी मुश्किल से बची। यह कोई इकलौता मामला नहीं था। देशभर में खासतौर पर मुस्लिम सब्जी विक्रेताओं पर हमलों की ख़बरें आने लगी थीं। कोविड आपातकाल से कुछ समय पहले ही उत्तर पूर्वी दिल्ली में सांप्रदायिक दंगे हुए थे। हिंसा भले ही रुक गई हो, लेकिन घृणा की आंधी चल रही थी। यह पहला मौका नहीं था, जब मजहब के नाम पर निर्दोष लोगों को निशाना बनाया गया। परेशानी का सबब यह था कि कोविड का ख़तरा तो कुछ दिनों में टल जाएगा, लेकिन 'सांप्रदायिक वायरस' का नासूर बना रहेगा।

═

साल 2021 में एक तकलीफ़ भरे भयावह साल के बाद, नए साल की शुरुआत हो रही थी। मोदी सरकार एक नई शुरुआत के जश्न की तैयारी में थी। वायरस का असर कम होने लगा था। हालांकि सार्वजनिक स्थानों पर मास्क अब भी ज़रूरी थे, लेकिन देश के अधिकांश हिस्सों में लॉकडाउन में ढील दे दी गई थी। अस्थायी कोविड केन्द्र बंद किए जा रहे थे। दुकानें, ऑफिस और रेस्टोरेन्ट खुलने लगे थे। बाज़ारों में भीड़ बढ़ने लगी थी। एयरलाइन्स ने उड़ानें बढ़ाना शुरू कर दिया था और अब बोर्ड के इम्तिहानों के बारे में भी फ़ैसले होने लगे थे। रिज़र्व बैंक ने 'कोविड संक्रमण के कम' होने का इशारा करते हुए कहा कि 'देश की अर्थव्यवस्था अब कुहासे से निकलकर उजाले की तरफ बढ़ रही' थी। अमेरिका समेत दुनिया के ज़्यादातर हिस्से अब भी कोविड की एक और मार का सामना कर रहे थे, लेकिन भारत को कोविड की लड़ाई में एक विजेता की तरह पेश किया जा रहा था।

जनवरी 2021 में वर्ल्ड इकोनोमिक फोरम को वीडियो कॉन्फ्रेंस के माध्यम से संबोधित करते हुए प्रधानमंत्री मोदी ने दावा किया कि भारत ने कोविड से सबकुछ ख़त्म हो जाने की आशंकाओं को गलत साबित कर दिया था। प्रधानमंत्री ने कहा, 'आशंका जताई जा रही थी कि भारत पर कोरोना का असर सबसे ज़्यादा पड़ेगा। यहां तक कहा गया कि भारत में तो कोरोना की सुनामी आ जाएगी... लेकिन देश में कोरोना मरीज़ों की तादाद तेज़ी से घट रही है।' अब

बारी भारतीय जनता पार्टी की थी। 21 फरवरी को पार्टी के वरिष्ठ नेताओं और सभी प्रदेश प्रमुखों ने महामारी को हराकर देश को फिर से विकास के रास्ते पर लाने के लिए प्रधानमंत्री के दूरदर्शी नेतृत्व के प्रति एक प्रस्ताव पारित कर आभार प्रकट किया। मार्च के पहले हफ्ते में दिल्ली मेडिकल एसोसिएशन की एक बैठक में तब के स्वास्थ्य मंत्री डॉ. हर्षवर्धन तो एक कदम और आगे बढ़ गए। उन्होंने देश में कोविड-19 के अंतिम चरण में होने का ऐलान कर दिया। मंत्री जी, दुनिया भर में छाए इस संकट के वक्त प्रधानमंत्री की भूमिका की प्रशंसा करना नहीं भूले। डॉ. हर्षवर्धन ने दावा किया कि 'अंतरराष्ट्रीय सहयोग में भारत एक उदाहरण बन गया है।' विजय की घोषणा स्वरूप डिटेल साझा की गई कि 62 देशों को साढ़े पांच करोड से ज़्यादा वैक्सीन भेजकर भारत ने 'फार्मेसी की दुनिया' में महत्वपूर्ण भूमिका निभाई थी। चाटुकारिता और चापलूसी की संस्कृति में दौड़ लगाने वालों ने प्रधानमंत्री मोदी को 'वैक्सीन गुरु' और भारत को 'विश्व गुरु' घोषित कर दिया था।

सरकार का यह आत्मविश्वास कोरोना मरीज़ों की तादाद में तेजी से आई कमी की वजह से था। सितम्बर 2020 में जहां हर दिन करीब 90 हज़ार मामले सामने आ रहे थे, वो फरवरी आते-आते घटकर 11 हज़ार प्रतिदिन हो गए थे। कोविड से हर सप्ताह मरने वालों की संख्या सौ से नीचे आ गई थी। केन्द्रीय स्वास्थ्य मंत्रालय की रोज़ाना की ब्रीफिंग बंद हो गई थी। कोविड टॉस्क फोर्स की बैठकें छोटी और कम हो गई थीं। सरकार से रिटायर हुए एक अधिकारी ने बताया कि, 'सरकार में बैठे लोगों को लगने लगा था कि कोविड का बुरा दौर अब गुज़र चुका था। कुछ दिनों की बात है, बस नज़र रखने की ज़रूरत थी।'

फरवरी के आखिरी हफ्ते में चुनाव आयोग ने पांच राज्यों में विधानसभा चुनावों का ऐलान भी कर दिया। इसमें 824 विधानसभा सीटों के लिए 18 करोड़ 60 लाख लोगों को वोट डालना था। पश्चिम बंगाल में लंबी और तीखी राजनीतिक लड़ाई आठ चरणों में पूरी होनी थी। चुनाव के बाद अब क्रिकेट भी होना था। भारतीय क्रिकेट बोर्ड ने अहमदाबाद के नरेन्द्र मोदी स्टेडियम में भारत और इंग्लैंड के बीच अंतरराष्ट्रीय मैच तय कर दिए। करीब 1 लाख तीस हज़ार क्रिकेट प्रेमी मैच का आनंद ले रहे थे, इनमें ज़्यादातर 'बिना मास्क' थे। चुनावी बिगुल और क्रिकेट मैच से साफ था कि भारत के लिए ज़िंदगी कोविड के पार भी थी।

और जब देश के दो बड़े जुनून क्रिकेट और चुनाव शानदार तरीके से हो सकते थे, तो फिर धार्मिक आयोजनों को कैसे रोका जा सकता था। भले ही अब कोविड के मामले फिर से बढ़ने लगे थे, लेकिन केन्द्र की मंजूरी के साथ मार्च में उत्तराखंड सरकार ने हरिद्वार में गंगा तट पर 'कुंभ मेले' के आयोजन की घोषणा कर दी। मेले में लाखों तीर्थयात्री सामूहिक स्नान के लिए पहुंचते हैं और इसे 2020 में महामारी की शुरुआत के बाद से देश में पहले बड़े सार्वजनिक उत्सव के रूप में पेश किया गया। केन्द्र सरकार की 'कोविड टॉस्क फोर्स' में शामिल एक स्वास्थ्य

विशेषज्ञ ने खुलासा किया कि उन्होंने दिल्ली में टॉस्क फोर्स की बैठक में चिंता जताई थी कि कुंभ से कोविड़ तेजी से फैल सकता था। 'बैठक में ज़्यादातर अफसरों की राय थी कि कुंभ को या तो टाल दिया जाए या महीने भर चलने वाले इस उत्सव को छोटा कर दिया जाए। लेकिन अगले दिन अख़बारों में प्रधानमंत्री की फोटो वाले पूरे पेज के विज्ञापन को देखकर मैं चोंक गया। विज्ञापन में श्रद्धालुओं को आमंत्रित करते हुए आश्वस्त किया गया था कि यह पवित्र स्नान सभी के लिए "स्वच्छ" और "सुरक्षित" था।'

सवाल है कि इतनी चेतावनी के बावज़ूद केन्द्र सरकार ने उत्तराखंड सरकार को कुंभ मेले इज़ाजत क्यों दी? इस मसले पर भी हमेशा की तरह केन्द्र और राज्य एक-दूसरे पर ज़िम्मेदारी टालते दिखे। केन्द्रीय स्वास्थ्य मंत्रालय के एक पूर्व अधिकारी ने दावा किया, 'हमने उत्तराखंड सरकार को अधूरी तैयारियों को लेकर कई बार चेताया था, लेकिन वे भरोसा दिलाते रहे कि हालात काबू में थे।' साफ है कि केन्द्र अपनी ज़िम्मेदारी से हाथ धोने की कमज़ोर कोशिश कर रहा था। केन्द्र सरकार और खासतौर से गृह मंत्रालय के पास आपदा प्रबंधन क़ानून के तहत बहुत ताकत थी और वो राज्य सरकार की निगरानी और नियंत्रण कर सकता था। यूं भी उत्तराखंड में भाजपा की सरकार थी यानी केन्द्र के आदेश को टालने की आशंका कम थी।

हरिद्वार में कुंभ मेले के आयोजन को हरी झंडी देना एक बड़ी गलती थी। लेकिन यह मोदी सरकार का अति-आत्मविश्वास था, जिसे लग रहा था कि उसने कोविड पर काबू पा लिया था। शायद भाजपा-संघ परिवार का देश को यह बताने का तरीका भी था कि देश को अब कोविड से डरने की ज़रूरत नहीं थी। जब एक न्यूज़ शो पर मैंने भाजपा के प्रवक्ता से कुंभ मेले को स्थगित करने की ज़रूरत पर सवाल किया, तो मुझ पर ज़मीनी हकीकत से अनजान 'हिंदुओं से डरने वाला' कथित उदारवादी होने का आरोप लगाया गया। स्थानीय राजनीति की तरह यहां भी धर्म ने तर्क पर कब्ज़ा कर लिया था। उत्तराखंड में विधानसभा चुनाव एक साल दूर थे और भाजपा इसकी तैयारी में जुटी थी। मार्च की शुरुआत में भाजपा ने देहरादून में नेतृत्व में बदलाव का फ़ैसला किया और मुख्यमंत्री त्रिवेन्द्र सिंह की जगह आरएसएस से आशीर्वाद प्राप्त कमज़ोर राजनेता तीरथ सिंह रावत को बिठा दिया गया। त्रिवेन्द्र सिंह रावत ने कुंभ आयोजन में सख़्त कोविड प्रोटोकॉल पर जोर दिया था, लेकिन नए मुख्यमंत्री प्रोटोकॉल का विरोध करने वाले पुजारियों और स्थानीय व्यापारियों को खुश करने में जुट गए। ये लोग कोविड की पहचान के लिए 'आरटी-पीसीआर' टैस्ट को ज़रूरी करने का विरोध कर रहे थे। उनका मानना था कि इससे लोग कुंभ में आने से बचेंगे।

12 अप्रैल को देश में कोविड के एक लाख 69 हज़ार नए मामले दर्ज किए गए, ब्राजील को पीछे छोड़ता हुआ वो कोविड से प्रभावित दूसरा देश बन गया था, तब 30 लाख लोग हरिद्वार में पवित्र स्नान के लिए गंगा तट पर इकट्ठा थे। आस्था के बहाव में कोविड प्रोटोकॉल गंगा में बह

गया था। सामाजिक दूरी अब चिंता का विषय नहीं था, लाखों लोग एकसाथ डुबकी लगा रहे थे। इस समारोह में खुद मुख्यमंत्री तीरथ सिंह रावत भी शामिल थे, जिन्होंने सार्वजनिक रूप से यह भरोसा जताया था कि 'ईश्वर में विश्वास वायरस के डर को दूर कर देगा'। उन्होंने भी मास्क नहीं पहना था। उत्तराखंड के एक पुलिस अधिकारी ने दावा किया कि 'जब मुख्यमंत्री प्रोटोकॉल नहीं मान रहे थे तो दूसरों पर यह लागू कराना मुमकिन नहीं था, दरअसल यह बस पागलपन था।' हरिद्वार में कुंभ मेले को मोदी राज में धार्मिक उन्माद के उफान के तौर पर देखा जा सकता है।

15 अप्रैल तक दो हज़ार से ज्यादा श्रद्धालुओं में कोविड के लक्षण मिले थे। इसके दो दिन बाद मोदी सरकार पीछे हटी, और कुंभ मेले को अब 'प्रतीकात्मक' तौर पर मनाने की बात कही गई, लेकिन तब तक गंगा में बहुत पानी बह चुका था। 28 अप्रैल को जब कुंभ का समापन हुआ, तब तक 90 लाख से ज्यादा लोग पवित्र स्नान कर चुके थे। उनमें से हज़ारों लोग बिना किसी जांच या क्वारंटीन के अपने घरों तक पहुंच चुके थे। उनके वायरस को साथ ले जाने की आशंका से इंकार नहीं किया जा सकता। हालांकि कुंभ में आने वाले कितने श्रद्धालु कोरोना पॉजिटिव पाए गए, इसके आंकड़े नहीं हैं, लेकिन इस आयोजन से कोविड फैलने की आशंका से नहीं बचा जा सकता। कुंभ मेले के दौरान उत्तराखंड में कोविड के मामलों में 1800 फ़ीसदी की बढ़ोतरी हुई। लेकिन 2020 में जिन लोगों ने तबलीगी जमात के आयोजनों की कड़ी आलोचना की थी, कुंभ के दौरान प्रोटोकॉल की परवाह नहीं करने पर उसकी निंदा या आलोचना करने की हिम्मत किसी ने नहीं दिखाई। चार महीने कुर्सी पर रहे मुख्यमंत्री तीरथ सिंह ने 2 जुलाई को इस्तीफ़ा दे दिया। वजह थी कि मुख्यमंत्री बनते वक्त वे विधायक नहीं थे और उन्हें छह महीने के भीतर चुनाव लड़कर विधानसभा पहुंचना ज़रूरी था, लेकिन उस वक्त उप-चुनाव को लेकर अनिश्चितता की वजह से उन्हें कुर्सी छोड़नी पड़ी। वैसे माना जा रहा था कि कुंभ में कोविड को लेकर अव्यवस्था की जिम्मेदारी तय करने के लिए केन्द्र कोई बलि का बकरा ढूंढ रहा था।

लेकिन केन्द्र सरकार पर कोई सवाल नहीं उठा रहा था, जिसने कुंभ, क्रिकेट मैच और चुनावों की इजाज़त दी थी। फिर से तेज़ी से बढ़ते कोविड मामलों के लिए कौन जवाबदेह होगा? फरवरी में प्रधानमंत्री मोदी को उनके सहयोगियों और समर्थकों ने कोविड जंग का विजेता घोषित किया था, जिसने भारत को 'विश्व गुरु' के तौर पर उभरने में मदद की। लेकिन अब साठ दिन बाद मोदी सरकार, उस अंधेरी गुफा से गुजरने वाली थी, जिस संकट को खुद को उसने पैदा किया था। कोविड की दूसरी लहर के लिए मोदी सरकार तैयार नहीं थी।

═

मोदी चुनावों को जंग की तरह लड़ते हैं। मार्च से अप्रैल 2021 की शुरुआत तक प्रधानमंत्री चुनावी जंग के मैदान में थे। उनकी नज़र खासतौर से पश्चिम बंगाल के चुनावों पर थी, जहां इस

बार भाजपा को तृणमूल कांग्रेस की ममता बनर्जी सरकार गिराने की उम्मीद लग रही थी। इससे पहले 2019 के लोकसभा चुनावों में भाजपा ने यहां पहली बार दहाई का आंकड़ा पार किया। पार्टी ने प्रदेश की 42 लोकसभा सीटों में से 18 जीत ली थीं। खासतौर से गृहमंत्री अमित शाह को बंगाल में ममता के किले को ढहाने का भरोसा था। कोलकता में पत्रकारों से बातचीत में शाह ने कहा, अब ममता का समय ख़त्म हो गया था। शाह का आत्मविश्वास झलक रहा था, 'आप बस इंतज़ार कीजिए, देखिए, हम बंगाल में इतिहास रच देंगे।'

शाह को 'मोदी फैक्टर' पर यकीन था। मोदी भाजपा के 'शुभंकर' हैं, प्रमुख चेहरा हैं। बंगाल में अप्रैल के पहले हफ्ते तक मोदी ने नौ रैलियां पूरी कर ली थीं। आठ चरणों के इस चुनाव में वे बीस रैलियां करने वाले थे। प्रधानमंत्री समेत बीजेपी के हर वरिष्ठ नेता और केन्द्रीय मंत्री को बंगाल में एक जिले की ज़िम्मेदारी सौंपी गई थीं। अप्रैल के दूसरे पखवाड़े तक, 'कार्पेट बाम्बिंग' स्टाइल में भाजपा का हर मजबूत योद्धा बंगाल में तैनात था। पार्टी के पश्चिम बंगाल प्रभारी कैलाश विजयवर्गीय के मुताबिक, 'प्रदेश की सभी 294 सीटों को कवर करने की योजना बना ली गई थी।' उन्होंने ज़ोर देकर कहा, यह 'कमल का तूफ़ान' है।

17 अप्रैल को प्रधानमंत्री ने बंगाल के आसनसोल में रैली की। चुनाव अभियान में उनके निशाने पर मुख्यमंत्री ममता बनर्जी होती थीं, जिन्हें वे आम सभाओं में तंज के साथ 'दीदी, ओ दीदी' कहकर चिढ़ाते थे। राजनीतिक विरोधी इसे करारे हमले के तौर पर देखते थे। बंगाली राष्ट्रीय प्रतीक गुरुदेव रबीन्द्र नाथ टैगोर की तरह दिखने के लिए लंबी सफेद दाढ़ी रखे, भगवा कुर्ता पहने मोदी ने सभा में मौजूद लोगों को बड़ी तादाद में पहुंचने के लिए धन्यवाद दियाः 'जहां भी मैं देखता हूं, मुझे केवल लोग ही लोग दिखाई देते हैं। आप लोगों ने तो आज कमाल ही कर दिया।' प्रधानमंत्री ने भाषण में कोविड प्रोटोकॉल को ध्यान में रखने जैसी किसी बात का ज़िक्र नहीं किया।

जब प्रधानमंत्री आसनसोल में रैली कर रहे थे, तब लगातार दूसरे दिन देश में कोविड के दो लाख से ज़्यादा मामले दर्ज किए गए थे। पिछले चौबीस घंटों में कोविड से एक हज़ार से ज़्यादा मौतें हुई थीं, लेकिन प्रधानमंत्री नारे लगाती भीड़ को और बड़ी तादाद में आने के लिए आमंत्रण दे रहे थे। कोविड के ख़िलाफ़ लड़ाई में इससे खराब क्या हो सकता था, जब देश का शीर्ष नेतृत्व ही सुरक्षा की ज़रूरतों से बेपरवाह दिख रहा था। 'आप सिर्फ प्रधानमंत्री को ही दोष क्यों दे रहे हैं? क्या ममता बनर्जी ने अपनी रैलियां बंद कर दी हैं?' कोविड के बढ़ते मामलों के बावजूद प्रधानमंत्री की रैलियों पर सवाल के जवाब में कैलाश विजयवर्गीय ने उलटकर सवाल पूछा। विजयवर्गीय के पास भले ही अपने तर्क हों, लेकिन देश के सर्वोच्च नेता के तौर पर प्रधानमंत्री से तो लोगों के सामने मिसाल के तौर पर पेश आने की उम्मीद की जा सकती है? क्या चुनाव प्रचार अभियान ने सबकुछ बेमायना कर दिया था?

सिर्फ़ पांच दिन बाद ही सच सामने था, देश कोविड की दूसरी लहर के भंवर में पूरी तरह फंस चुका था। 22 अप्रैल को तीन लाख से ज़्यादा मामले दर्ज किए गए, जो दुनियाभर में एक दिन में दर्ज अब तक का सबसे बड़ा आंकड़ा था। राजनीतिक सभाओं में बढ़ती जनता की नाराज़गी को देखते हुए प्रधानमंत्री को अपनी कुछ रैलियों को रद्द करना पड़ा। प्रधानमंत्री कार्यालय ने इसकी वजह कोविड के इंतज़ामों पर बैठकों के लिए प्रधानमंत्री की दिल्ली में रहने की ज़रूरत बताई, इसमें मुख्यमंत्रियों के साथ होने वाली वीडियो कान्फ्रेंसिग भी शामिल थी। गृहमंत्री शाह पर अपनी रैलियों को कम करने का दबाव था। कलकत्ता हाईकोर्ट ने दख़ल देते हुए चुनाव आयोग पर टिप्पणी की और उसे 'कोविड प्रोटोकॉल' के लिए पर्याप्त कदम नहीं उठाने के लिए दोषी माना। मद्रास हाईकोर्ट की टिप्पणी तो एक कदम आगे थी, अदालत ने कहा आयोग पर 'हत्या' का आरोप लगाया जाना चाहिए, क्योंकि 'आज हम जिस स्थिति में है, उसके लिए अकेले आयोग ज़िम्मेदार है।' लेकिन तीखी टिप्पणियों के बावजूद ज़मीनी हकीकत गंभीर थी। चुनाव आयोग ही नहीं, लगता था कि पूरा सिस्टम अपनी ज़िम्मेदारी निभाने में नाकाम रहा था।

आमतौर पर अपनी छवि और संदेश देने को लेकर सचेत रहने वाले प्रधानमंत्री 2021 की गर्मियों में इतनी बुरी तरह कैसे ग़लत साबित हुए, इस सवाल का जवाब देते हुए एक आला अधिकारी ने बताया कि प्रधानमंत्री पर पार्टी की तरफ से 'आक्रामक' चुनाव अभियान के लिए बहुत दबाव था। उन्होंने समझाने की कोशिश की, देखिए, 'चुनाव के वक्त प्रधानमंत्री सबसे पहले पार्टी के कार्यकर्ता होते हैं। पार्टी चुनाव अभियान बनाती है और उम्मीद करती है कि इस समय प्रधानमंत्री, पार्टी को प्राथमिकता दें।' लेकिन इतनी बड़ी महामारी के समय देश नेतृत्व से ज्यादा जिम्मेदार, भरोसेमंद और सामाजिक तौर पर जागरुक होने की उम्मीद कर रहा था, जो दूसरों को वायरस से लड़ने के लिए ज्यादा सचेत रहने की बात कर रहा हो। अधिकारी ने माना, 'हां, हम चीज़ों को ठीक तरह से नहीं समझे।' लेकिन कहा, 'प्रधानमंत्री को दोष देना तो आसान है, बताइए किस राज्य सरकार ने कमाल का काम किया?' हमेशा की तरह, नाकामी की जवाबदेही नहीं मानने के लिए सरकार के पास जिम्मेदारी को टालना ही आखिरी तरीका होता है। इसका खामियाज़ा देश को कोरोना की दूसरी लहर से हुए भारी नुक़सान से उठाना पड़ा।

अप्रैल से जून 2021 के दस हफ्तों में सरकार बेबस दिख रही थी। कोविड 2.0 'डेल्टा स्ट्रेन', पहले से तेज़ी से फैलने वाला और ज़्यादा ख़तरनाक वायरस था, जिसने देश को हिलाकर रख दिया। देश का मेडिकल सिस्टम हांफ रहा था और ढहने की कगार पर था। तस्वीरें डराने वाली थीं। ऑक्सीजन की आपूर्ति में कमी ने कोविड की रोगियों की सांसें मुश्किल कर दी थीं। परेशान रिश्तेदार आईसीयू बैड या गैस सिलेंडर की तलाश में मारे-मारे फिर रहे थे। श्मशान घाटों में जगह कम पड़ गई थी। अस्थायी चिताओं पर होते अंतिम संस्कारों की बदबू हवा में फैल रही थी, और दिल दहलाने वाली तस्वीरें थी प्रधानमंत्री मोदी के संसदीय क्षेत्र वाराणसी सहित कई जगहों

पर गंगा में तैरती लाशें। कई गांवों में नदियों में फेकें जा रहे, फूल गए शवों की तस्वीरें, यह सच बयां कर रही थीं कि कोविड ने सिर्फ़ शहरों को ही नहीं, देश के हर इलाके को जकड़ लिया था।

कोविड 2.0 के इस भयावह संकट पर एक बार फिर सरकार सच से रूबरू होने को तैयार नहीं थी। जब वाराणसी के घाटों पर जलती लाशों की तस्वीरें पहली बार टीवी पर दिखाई गईं, तो आला अधिकारी ने शिकायती लहज़े में फ़ोन किया। उन्होंने सवाल करते हुए दावा किया, 'ये तस्वीरों आपको कहां से मिल रही हैं? इनमें से कई तस्वीरें तो पुरानी हैं, हालात उतने खराब नहीं हैं, जितने आप बता रहे हैं।' नदी किनारे रेत में दबी लाशों की तस्वीरों के बाद उत्तरप्रदेश सरकार के सूचना विभाग के अधिकारी का फ़ोन था, 'ये कोई नई बात नहीं हैं, लोग बरसों से यहां अंतिम संस्कार के लिए आते हैं और उनमें से कई समुदायों और जातियों में शव को रेत में दफ़नाने की परंपरा है। शवों को गंगा में फेंकना भी कोई नई बात नहीं है, और ना ही इसका कोविड से कोई लेना-देना है।' जब मैंने उनसे बड़ी तादाद में रेत में दफ़न शवों की संख्या के बारे में सवाल किया तो अधिकारी का जवाब नाराज़गी भरा था, 'आपको सिर्फ़ कोविड के बारे नेगेटिव ख़बरें दिखानी हैं; कुछ पॉजिटिव खबरें क्यों नहीं दिखा सकते?'

आंखों के सामने के सच को स्वीकार नहीं करने और असली आंकड़ें नहीं बताने से समझ आता है कि सरकार कोविड की दूसरी लहर का मुकाबला कितनी शिद्दत से कर रही थी। फरवरी 2022 में, तत्कालीन जल शक्ति राज्य मंत्री बिश्वेश्वर टुडू ने राज्यसभा में एक सवाल के जवाब में स्पष्ट किया, 'गंगा नदी में फेंके गए कोविड-19 से जुडे शवों की तादाद की जानकारी सरकार के पास नहीं है।'

आलोचकों ने अब एनडीए सरकार का नाम बदलकर 'नो डेटा अवेलबिल' (कोई डेटा उपलब्ध नहीं) कर दिया। उस वक्त खासतौर से कोविड से मौतों की कम गिनती को लेकर सरकार निशाने पर थी। मई 2022 में विश्व स्वास्थ्य संगठन (**WHO**) की एक रिपोर्ट में चौंकाने वाला दावा किया गया कि भारत में 2020-21 में कोविड की पहली दो लहरों में 47 लाख से ज़्यादा लोग मारे गए, जो सरकार के 4 लाख 81 हज़ार के आंकड़े से तकरीबन दस गुना ज़्यादा है। सर्वेक्षण के तरीके और सैंपल साइज में ख़ामियां बताते हुए सरकार ने रिपोर्ट को ख़ारिज़ करने में देर नहीं लगाई। लेकिन कोविड के दौरान हुई मौतों की संख्या, सरकार के आंकड़े से कहीं ज़्यादा थी। इस हक़ीकत को प्रधानमंत्री के गृह राज्य गुजरात समेत देशभर में कोशिश करके भी नहीं छिपाया जा सकता। जब अप्रैल-मई 2021 में कोविड उफान पर था, तब अहमदाबाद में तुलनात्मक तौर पर सरकारी आंकड़ों से तीन गुना ज़्यादा मौतें हुई थीं, पिछले वर्षों में औसतन 8,337 की तुलना में 30,247 मौतें। यह आंकड़ा स्थानीय प्रशासन ने दिया था। जबकि गुजरात सरकार के स्वास्थ्य विभाग के आंकड़ों के हिसाब से अप्रैल-मई 2021 में एक हज़ार से कम मौतें हुई थीं। जुलाई 2024 में, ऑक्सफोर्ड विश्वविद्यालय समेत कई विश्वविद्यालय के शोधकर्ताओं ने

राष्ट्रीय परिवार स्वास्थ्य सर्वेक्षण (एनएचएफएस) 2019-21 के मृत्यु दर के आंकड़ों के हिसाब से अनुमान लगाया कि केवल 2020 में करीब 12 लाख ज़्यादा मौतें हुईं, जो उस साल देश में कोविड-19 से होने वाली मौतों की सरकारी संख्या से आठ गुना ज़्यादा थीं।

सवाल था कि क्या मोदी सरकार ने अपनी छवि बचाने के लिए कोविड मौतों की संख्या को लेकर देश से झूठ बोला? विश्व स्वास्थ्य संगठन के आंकड़ों पर कांग्रेस के नेता राहुल गांधी ने एक ट्वीट किया, 'देश में कोविड से 47 लाख लोग मारे गए। सरकारी दावे के मुताबिक 4.8 लाख नहीं। मोदी झूठ बोलते हैं, विज्ञान नहीं।' भाजपा ने तुरंत इसका पलटवार किया, पार्टी के प्रवक्ता संबित पात्रा ने राहुल गांधी और कांग्रेस पर प्रधानमंत्री को 'बदनाम' करने और 'देश की छवि को खराब' करने का आरोप लगाया। क्या अपने ही लोगों की मौतों की संख्या ग़लत बताने से देश की छवि सुधरती है? लेकिन अब सच से इतर की राजनीति के ज़माने में 'तथ्य' और 'सत्य' कोई मायने नहीं रखते। लगता है देश झूठे गणराज्य में तब्दील हो जाता है, जहां सरकारें उनसे असहमति जताने वालों को चीखकर, उदासीन होकर या फिर धमकियां देकर जांच से बचती है। जम्हूरियत में राजनीतिक नेतृत्व लोगों के प्रति जवाबदेह होता है। सामान्य समय में सरकार भले ही झूठ बोलकर बच सकती हो, लेकिन कोविड जैसी महामारी के समय गुंज़ाइश नहीं थी। मोदी सरकार उस वक्त भी इसलिए बच निकली, क्योंकि मीडिया में ज़्यादातर लोग सीधे और सख्त सवाल पूछने वाले नहीं थे।

मोदी सरकार का कोविड पर जवाबदेही से बचने का एक और तरीका था, राज्य सरकारों को घेरना और जिम्मेदार ठहराना। कोविड मामलों में इतने बड़े उछाल पर केन्द्र ही नहीं राज्य सरकारें भी जवाब देने की हालत में नहीं थीं। दिल्ली शहर में ऑक्सीजन का संकट गहरा था, केन्द्र ने दिल्ली की केजरीवाल सरकार को निशाने पर लिया। मोदी सरकार ने दावा किया कि चार अस्पतालों में 'ऑक्सीजन प्लांट' इसलिए वक्त पर नहीं लग पाए क्योंकि दिल्ली सरकार ने 'साइट रेडिनेस सर्टिफिकेट' जमा नहीं किए थे। मैंने यह सवाल जब दिल्ली के मुख्यमंत्री अरविंद केजरीवाल से पूछा, तो उन्होंने चिढ़कर जवाब दिया, 'दिल्ली में पैसे का नियंत्रण और इंतज़ाम केन्द्र सरकार के पास है। वे ऑक्सीजन प्लांट लगाने में अपनी नाकामी को छिपाने की कोशिश कर रहे हैं।' महामारी की आपात स्थिति में एक-दूसरे पर हमला करने का यह तरीका जिम्मेदार लोगों के बीच आपसी विश्वास के संकट को बताता है।

एक दूसरे के विरोधी दावों के बीच, यह साफ था कि केन्द्र और राज्य सरकारें कोविड से निपटने के लिए बेहतर तैयारी कर सकती थीं। उदाहरण के लिए एक न्यूज़ वेबसाइट 'स्क्रॉल' के मुताबिक मार्च 2020 में महामारी आने के बाद केन्द्र सरकार को नए ऑक्सीजन प्लांट लगाने की निविदा आमंत्रित करने में ही आठ महीने लग गए। अक्टूबर 2020 में, केन्द्रीय स्वास्थ्य मंत्रालय की स्वायत संस्था, सेन्ट्रल मेडिकल सर्विसेज ने देशभर में डेढ़ सौ ज़िलों में 'प्रेशर

स्विंग एडसोर्प्शन' ऑक्सीजन प्लांट लगाने के लिए ऑनलाइन निविदा जारी की। इन 162 प्लांट (कथित तौर पर इनमें 12 को बाद में जोड़ा गया) के लिए पीएम केयर्स फंड से 201.58 करोड़ रुपये आवंटित किए गए। लेकिन अप्रैल 2021 में जब कोविड की दूसरी लहर भयावह तबाही मचा रही थी, तब स्वास्थ्य मंत्रालय ने एक ट्वीट में बताया कि केवल तैंतीस प्लांट ही लग पाए थे।

कोविड के उफान के वक्त मई 2021 में प्रसिद्ध कार्डियक सर्जन डॉ. देवी शेट्टी ने एक साक्षात्कार में मुझसे कहा, 'कोविड की दूसरी लहर की भयावहता और तीव्रता का कोई भी अंदाज़ा नहीं लगा सकता था। सरकार की आलोचना करना तो आसान है, लेकिन किसी भी देश का मेडिकल सिस्टम भारत जैसे देश को नहीं संभाल सकता। यह सच है कि सरकार ने अस्पतालों में ऑक्सीजन पहुंचाने के लिए पूरी ताकत लगा दी, वे और क्या कर सकते हैं?'

भारत जैसी बड़ी आबादी वाले देश में यह आसान काम नहीं था। लेकिन सवाल हैः क्या सरकार इस संकट का अंदाज़ा नहीं लगा सकती थी? और इसके असर को कम करने के लिए ज़्यादा तैयारी कर सकती थी? जैसे सबसे प्रमुख 'वेरिएंट' का पता लगाने के लिए 'जीनोम सीक्वेंसिग' को प्राथमिकता नहीं दी गई और ना ही उसे जल्दी ट्रैक करने के लिए राष्ट्रीय स्तर पर कोई संयुक्त प्रयास किया गया। महामारी शुरू होने के कई महीनों बाद कोविड वेरिएंट को ट्रैक करने के खास मकसद के साथ भारतीय SARS-COV-2 'जीनोमिक्स कंसोर्टियम' (INSACOG) की स्थापना दिसम्बर 2020 में की गई। मई 2021 में *इंडिया टुडे* में छपी एक रिपोर्ट के मुताबिक कंसोर्टियम को शुरुआत से मुश्किलों का सामना करना पड़ा। शुरुआती छह महीनों के लिए इसे जैव प्रोद्योगिकी विभाग के फंड से 115 करोड़ रुपये आवंटित किए गए थे, लेकिन इसमें से भी सिर्फ़ 80 करोड़ रुपये मार्च के आखिर में मिल पाए। संस्थान को कई प्रदेशों से जांच के लिए सैंपल भी नहीं मिले, क्योंकि उनके पास सैंपल रखने, प्रयोगशालाओं और कोल्ड स्टोरेज प्लांट तक उन्हें पहुंचाने के लिए नोडल अधिकारी भी नहीं थे जहां उन्हें संरक्षित रखा जा सकता हो। नतीजा रहा कि कंसोर्टियम फरवरी 2021 तक 80,000 सैंपल की 'सीक्वेंसिग' के अपने लक्ष्य से बहुत पीछे रह गया। उसने केवल साढ़े तीन हज़ार सैंपल पर काम किया। मार्च 2021 में कंसोर्टियम ने बताया कि दूसरी लहर का प्रमुख कारण, घातक बी.1.617 वेरिएंट था। ये महाराष्ट्र के बीस फ़ीसदी सैंपल में पाया गया, जो किसी भी दूसरे राज्य से कहीं ज़्यादा था।

हैदराबाद के सेंटर फॉर सेल्युलर एंड मॉलिक्यूलर बायोलोजी (सीसीएमबी) के पूर्व निदेशक डॉ राकेश ने *इंडिया टुडे* को अपने एक साक्षात्कार में बताया, 'इस तेज़ी से फैल रहे खतरनाक वेरिएंट को लेकर जब तक खतरे से आगाह किया गया, तब तक बहुत देर हो चुकी थी। इसके साथ ही मेडिकल संस्थानों के बीच अधिकारों और नियंत्रण की लड़ाई से हालात बदतर हो गए।' उदाहरण के तौर पर, बिना कोई डोमेन विशेषज्ञता के, अखिल भारतीय अनुसंधान परिषद्

महामारी का प्रबंधन देख रही थी। मई 2021 में जीनोक्स कंसोर्टिम के वैज्ञानिक सलाहकार बोर्ड से इस्तीफ़ा देने वाले वायरोलोजिस्ट डॉ. शाहिद जमील ने बताया, 'परिषद् देशभर की प्रयोगशालाओं से कोविड के सैम्पल तो इकट्ठे कर रहा था, लेकिन बिना किसी ठोस वजह के वह उसके नतीजे दूसरों के साथ साझा नहीं कर रहा था।'

इससे राष्ट्रीय टॉस्क फोर्स के कामकाज पर भी सवाल उठते हैं। इस टॉस्क फोर्स का गठन प्रधानमंत्री ने कोविड के मामले संभालने के लिए किया था। डॉ. वी.के. पॉल की अध्यक्षता में बने इस टॉस्क फोर्स में आईसीएमआर के महानिदेशक बलराम भार्गव, एम्स के निदेशक डॉ. रणदीप गुलेरिया और राष्ट्रीय रोग नियंत्रण केन्द्र के निदेशक जीत कुमार सिंह शामिल थे। एक स्वास्थ्य विशेषज्ञ ने बताया, 'हालांकि टॉस्क फोर्स के सभी सदस्य अपने अपने क्षेत्र में विशेषज्ञ थे, लेकिन उनके पास सरकार को यह बताने का अधिकार या ताकत शायद नहीं थी कि वे बता सकें कि चीज़ें कहां गलत हो रही थीं।'

दरअसल ऐसे संकट के वक्त में राजनीतिक नेतृत्व नदारद सा था। मई 2021 में *बिज़नेस स्टेंडर्ड* की रिपोर्ट में कोविड के दौरान प्रधानमंत्री के सार्वजनिक कार्यक्रमों का विश्लेषण किया गया था। रिपोर्ट के मुताबिक प्रधानमंत्री मोदी ने मार्च से सितम्बर 2020 तक सात महीनों में 80 से ज़्यादा कार्यक्रमों में हिस्सा लिया। इसके बाद अगले चार महीनों में वे 111 कार्यक्रमों में शामिल हुए। फरवरी से 25 अप्रैल 2021 तक, चुनावी रैलियों समेत 92 सार्वजनिक कार्यक्रमों में मौजूद रहे। इसके बाद करीब बीस दिनों तक वे किसी सार्वजनिक कार्यक्रम में नहीं दिखाई दिए, जो कोविड-19 शुरू होने के बाद से सबसे लंबा समय कहा जा सकता है। यानी कोविड के सबसे बड़े संकट के वक्त प्रधानमंत्री नज़र नहीं आए। कोविड की पहली लहर के वक्त लॉकडाउन के दौरान प्रधानमंत्री मोदी लगातार जनता से संवाद कर रहे थे, लेकिन दूसरे चरण में देश के 'सुप्रीम लीडर' गायब रहे, शायद भयावहता की बुरी ख़बर को सुनने से बच रहे थे। एक सरकारी अधिकारी ने बचाव करते हुए बताया कि 'इस दौरान प्रधानमंत्री हालात की निगरानी कर रहे थे और रोज़ाना ब्रीफिंग ले रहे थे। जब प्रधानमंत्री टीवी पर होते हैं तो आप उन्हें "प्राइम-टाइम प्रधानमंत्री" कहते हैं, और जब टीवी पर नज़र नहीं आते तो आपको लगता है कि वे काम नहीं कर रहे हैं। आखिर आप उनसे क्या उम्मीद करते हैं?' सरकारी अधिकारी की निगाहें सवाल पूछ रही थीं।

मई 2021 में *आउटलुक* पत्रिका के कवर पेज को खाली छोड़ा गया था, सफेद खाली पन्ने पर मोटे अक्षरों में लिखा था – 'लापता'। नीचे लिखा था, 'भारत सरकार, उम्र: 7 साल'। कहा गया कि भयावह दूसरी कोविड लहर के दौरान सरकार लापता हो गई थी, यदि मिल जाती है तो देश के नागरिकों सूचित किया जाए। उसी महीने *इंडिया टुडे* का कवर पेज भी सरकार की गंभीर आलोचना के लिए काफी था। 'द फेल्ड स्टेट' के शीर्षक वाले इस कवर पेज पर अंतिम संस्कार के इंतज़ार में सड़क पर कतार में रखे शवों की विचलित करने वाली तस्वीर थी। सत्ता

में सात साल बाद मोदी सरकार मीडिया के सवालों के घेरे में थी। सरकार की विश्वसनीयता पर सवाल उठने लगे थे। अगस्त 2021 में *इंडिया* टुडे के साल में दो बार किए जाने वाले 'मूड ऑफ द नेशन सर्वे' में देश का बदलता मूड दिख रहा था। देश के अगले प्रधानमंत्री के तौर पर मोदी को सबसे पसंदीदा मानने वाले लोग अब सिर्फ़ 24 फ़ीसदी रह गए थे, जो छह महीने पहले जनवरी 2021 के सर्वे में 38 प्रतिशत थे। पिछले सात साल में प्रधानमंत्री मोदी की लोकप्रियता की सबसे कम रेटिंग थी। कोविड की दूसरी लहर की भयावहता का असर प्रधानमंत्री की छवि पर भी पड़ता दिख रहा था। 'विश्व गुरु' की ब्रांडिग अब डरावने सपने जैसी लग रही थी। मोदी को राजनीति में नए चेहरे की सख्त ज़रूरत महसूस हो रही थी। जनता का भरोसा बहाल करने के लिए अब सिर्फ़ अच्छे भाषण काफी नहीं थे। अब उन्हें अपनी बात को ज़मीनी हकीक़त पर उतारने की ज़रूरत थी।

═

राष्ट्रीय स्वयंसेवक संघ की शाखा में जाने की आदत से डॉ. हर्षवर्धन सवेरे जल्दी उठ जाते हैं। सात जुलाई 2021 को, भोर से पहले की सैर ख़त्म करने के बाद स्वास्थ्य मंत्री दफ्तर में एक और लंबे दिन की तैयारी कर रहे थे। मिलनसार डॉक्टर-राजनेता डॉ. हर्षवर्धन को कोविड संकट ने स्वास्थ्य मंत्री के तौर पर बड़ी मुश्किल में डाल दिया था। दिल्ली में तीन दशकों से लंबे वक्त तक राजनीति करने, लोकसभा और विधानसभा के कई चुनाव जीतने, साल 2013 में मुख्ययमंत्री बनते-बनते रह गए डॉ. हर्षवर्धन को कभी ऐसी महामारी के संकट से नहीं जूझना पड़ा था। डॉ. हर्षवर्धन कोविड-19 से निपटने के लिए बनी मंत्रियों की कमेटी के अध्यक्ष थे। जिनके पास संकट से निपटने की प्रमुख जिम्मेदारी थी। उस वक्त को याद करते हुए डॉ. हर्षवर्धन कहते हैं, 'मुझे लगता है कि 2020 और 2021 में करीब 18 महीनों में मैं आधी रात के बाद ही घर पहुंचता था और कुछ घंटों की ही नींद हो पाती थी। मैं चौबीसों घंटे ड्यूटी पर रहने वाले डॉक्टर की तरह था।'

उस दौरान उन्होंने कभी कोई फ़ोन कॉल मिस नहीं किया। कोविड की दूसरी लहर के वक्त तो हर समय फोन बजता रहता था, क्योंकि कोई भी निराश, हताश परिचित, दोस्त उनसे आईसीयू बैड या ऑक्सीजन सिलेंडर की उम्मीद कर रहे थे। जुलाई की शुरुआत में ऐसा लगा कि कम से कम दिल्ली में तो कोविड का बुरा दौर ख़त्म हो गया था। फ़ोन आना अब कम हो गया था। फिर भी, उस सुबह जब घंटी बजी तो उन्होंने तुरंत फोन उठाया। फ़ोन पर कोई मरीज नहीं, बल्कि भारतीय जनता पार्टी के राष्ट्रीय अध्यक्ष जगत प्रकाश नड्डा थे। 'हर्षवर्धन जी, मुझे आपको मंत्री पद से इस्तीफ़ा देने की सूचना देने के लिए कहा गया है। क्या आप राष्ट्रपति भवन को इसकी सूचना दे देंगे? प्रधानमंत्री आपसे बाद में बात करेंगे।' बस, छोटा सा संदेश था।

राजनीति से जितना सम्मान मिलता है, उतनी ही वो निर्दयी भी होती है। महीनों से डॉ. हर्षवर्धन कोविड संकट से निपटने के लिए मोदी सरकार के सबसे प्रमुख लोगों में से थे। और अब भाजपा अध्यक्ष के एक फ़ोन ने सबकुछ एक झटके में बदल दिया, कैबिनेट में बदलाव के लिए उन्हें इस्तीफ़ा देना था। राजधानी के सत्ता के गलियारों में इस बात की चर्चा पहले से चल रही थी कि प्रधानमंत्री, डॉ. हर्षवर्धन के कामकाज से 'खुश नहीं' थे। खासतौर से दूसरी लहर के दौरान जब सरकारी मशीनरी के 'गायब' होने के आरोप लगने लगे। ऑक्सीजन संकट से जूझ रही दिल्ली में कोविड इंतज़ामों को देखने के लिए तब गृहमंत्री अमित शाह आगे आए, जबकि टॉस्क फोर्स के प्रमुख डॉ. वी.के. पॉल को मीडिया संभालने के लिए कहा गया। स्वास्थ्य मंत्री अब हाशिए पर चले गए थे। 'आप मेरे मंत्रालय के किसी भी अधिकारी से पूछिए कि कोविड संकट से निपटने के लिए मैंने कैसे दिलोजान से कोशिश की। सिर्फ़ इसलिए कि मैं हर वक्त आपके टीवी कैमरों के सामने नहीं था, तो इसका मतलब क्या यह होता है कि मैं ग़ायब था।' स्वास्थ्य मंत्री के जवाब में तकलीफ़ झलक रही थी। आमतौर पर टीवी से दूर रहने वाले स्वास्थ्य मंत्री को जब मैंने दूसरी बार साक्षात्कार के लिए आग्रह किया, तो मुश्किल से तैयार हुए थे। मैंने उन्हें पहले सवालों की सूची भेज दी। उन्होंने तब कहा था, 'मैं लाइव आने के बजाय रिकॉर्डेड इंटरव्यू दूंगा।' मीडिया की तपन उन्हें महसूस हो रही थी। सरकार पर राजनीतिक दबाव का असर उन्हें झेलना पड़ा था।

अप्रैल 2021 में डॉ. हर्षवर्धन शायद पूर्व प्रधानमंत्री डॉ. मनमोहन सिंह के सवालों के भंवर में फंस गए थे। कोविड के मामलों में तेजी से बढ़ोतरी के बाद डॉ. सिंह ने प्रधानमंत्री मोदी को एक चिट्ठी लिखकर महामारी से लड़ने के तरीके तो सुझाए ही थे, साथ ही उन्होंने केन्द्र की वैक्सीन नीति को लेकर संदेह ज़ाहिर किया था। डॉ. सिंह ने सरकार को पांच सूत्री फॉर्मूला भेजते हुए कहा कि 'कोविड के ख़िलाफ़ मजबूती से लड़ाई के लिए टीकाकरण की रफ्तार को तेज़ करने की ज़रूरत है।' हालांकि डॉ. सिंह ने यह चिट्ठी प्रधानमंत्री मोदी को लिखी थी, लेकिन उन्होंने इसका कोई जवाब नहीं दिया, मगर एक दिन बाद डॉ. हर्षवर्धन इस विवाद में कूद पड़े। अच्छे स्वभाव वाले स्वास्थ्य मंत्री यूं सार्वजनिक रूप से चिड़चिड़ापन नहीं दिखाते थे, लेकिन डॉ. सिंह को लिखे एक बयान में उन्होंने आरोप लगाया कि कांग्रेस पार्टी इस संकट के समय 'नकारात्मकता फैलाने' की कोशिश कर रही थी। डॉ. हर्षवर्धन ने लिखा, 'ऐसा लगता है कि जिन लोगों ने आपको सलाह दी या आपका पत्र लिखा, उन्होंने पहले से ही उपलब्ध सार्वजनिक जानकारी के बारे में आपको गुमराह करके आपकी प्रतिष्ठा को धक्का पहुंचाया है।' राजनीतिक गलियारों में चर्चा यह थी कि यह मसौदा तो पीएमओ में तैयार हुआ था, स्वास्थ्य मंत्री तो बस संदेशवाहक थे। डॉ. हर्षवर्धन ने बाद में मुझे बातचीत में बताया कि 'इससे फ़र्क नहीं पड़ता कि मसौदा कौन तैयार करता है। कैबिनेट की सामूहिक

ज़िम्मेदारी के तौर पर मुझे यह ज़रूरी लगा कि पूर्व प्रधानमंत्री को पत्र लिखकर स्थिति को स्पष्ट किया जाना चाहिए।'

कुल मिलाकर बात यह थी कि कोविड के बड़े संकट से निपटने की नाकामी और सिस्टम फेल होने के लिए डॉ. हर्षवर्धन दोषी ठहराए गए। नाकामियों की आलोचना को झेलती मोदी सरकार को किसी को तो जवाबदेह ठहराना ही था। मोदी सरकार में अपेक्षाकृत 'लो-प्रोफाइल' वाले डॉ. हर्षवर्धन को 'बलि का बकरा' बनाने में कोई दिक्कत नहीं हुई। कहा जाता है कि हटाए जाने से कुछ दिन पहले प्रधानमंत्री ने कैबिनेट बैठक में भी स्वास्थ्य मंत्री के ख़िलाफ़ नाराज़गी ज़ाहिर की थी। बताया गया कि प्रधानमंत्री ने बैठक में कहा, 'मैं देख रहा हूं कि आपमें से कुछ लोग कोविड के ख़िलाफ़ सरकार की कोशिशों को बताने के बजाय सोशल मीडिया पर केवल जन्मदिन की शुभकामनाएं भेजते हैं।'

दरअसल डॉ. हर्षवर्धन पुराने ज़माने के तौर तरीकों वाले राजनेता थे, और 'सोशल मीडिया आउटरीच' में उनकी कोई खास दिलचस्पी और पकड़ नहीं थी, जो मोदी सरकार की रणनीति का एक अहम हिस्सा है। 'सरकार ने टॉस्क फोर्स के उन लोगों के ख़िलाफ़ कोई कार्रवाई क्यों नहीं की, जो पीएमओ से नियुक्त किए गए थे और सारे बड़े फ़ैसले लेने में शामिल थे। हर्षवर्धन जी एक ईमानदार मिलनसार नेता हैं, जिनके लिए आज की गलाकाट राजनीति में जगह बनाना मुश्किल है,' पूर्व स्वास्थ्य मंत्री के एक सहायक कुछ और भी इशारा कर रहे थे।

दिल्ली के लिए अनजान सा चेहरा रहे गुजरात से राज्यसभा सांसद मनसुख मंडाविया को डॉ. हर्षवर्धन की जगह स्वास्थ्य मंत्री की जिम्मेदारी मिली। साल 2002 में विधानसभा चुनाव जीतने के बाद प्रधानमंत्री ने खुद उन्हें गुजरात भाजपा की अगली पीढ़ी के राजनेताओं के तौर पर चुना था। 2015 में राज्यसभा में आने के बाद भी उनका कोई बड़ा प्रभाव नही था लेकिन वे गुजरात भाजपा में सबसे कम उम्र के महासचिव बने। फिर उनचास साल की उम्र में उन्हें एक महत्वपूर्ण विभाग सौंपा गया। गुजरात भाजपा के एक सदस्य की मानें तो, 'मनसुख भाई चुपचाप काम करते हैं, लेकिन पूरी तरह से मोदी की हां में हां मिलाने वाले हैं, जो मोदी के ख़िलाफ़ कभी नहीं जाते। प्रधानमंत्री उन्हें अपनी कोर टीम में चाहते हैं।'

देश को भले ही एक नया स्वास्थ्य मंत्री मिल गया हो, लेकिन पीएमओ का दख़ल अब बढ़ गया था। मोदी सरकार ने राजनीतिक तौर पर भले ही मनमोहन सिंह पर निशाना साधा हो, लेकिन वो उनके सुझावों पर काम करने में जुट गई थी। कोविड पर काबू के लिए टीकाकरण मे तेज़ी लाने की ज़रूरत थी। यह एक ऐसा जादुई हथियार था, जिससे देश को महामारी की तबाही से बचाया जा सकता था।

═

'भारत में एक नहीं, दो नहीं, बल्कि तीन कोरोना वायरस वैक्सीन का परीक्षण किया जा रहा है... बड़े पैमाने पर इनके उत्पादन के साथ-साथ हर भारतीय को कम से कम समय में वैक्सीन देने की योजना बन गई है। जैसे ही वैज्ञानिक इसके लिए हरी झंडी देंगे। देश उन वैक्सीन का बड़े पैमाने पर उत्पादन शुरू कर देगा।'

—15अगस्त 2020 को लालकिले से स्वतंत्रता दिवस के मौके पर भाषण के दौरान प्रधानमंत्री नरेन्द्र मोदी

'दुनिया के सबसे बड़े वैक्सीन उत्पादक देश के रूप में, मैं आज दुनिया को एक और भरोसा दिलाना चाहता हूं... भारत की वैक्सीन उत्पादन और वितरण क्षमता का इस्तेमाल इस संकट से लड़ने में पूरी मानवता के लिए किया जाएगा।'

—सितम्बर, 2020 में संयुक्त राष्ट्र में पूर्व-रिकॉर्डेड भाषण के दौरान प्रधानमंत्री मोदी

मोदी सरकार की वैक्सीन बनाने की महत्वाकांक्षी योजना के बावजूद, अप्रैल-मई 2021 में जब कोविड की दूसरी लहर ने तबाही मचाई, तब भारत वैक्सीन के लिए परेशान था। केन्द्र का दावा था कि 16 जनवरी 2021 को अभियान शुरू होने के बाद से 14 करोड़ 30 लाख लोगों को टीका लगाया गया है, यानी सिर्फ़ 7.9 फ़ीसदी आबादी को वैक्सीन की पहली खुराक मिल पाई थी। तब तक अमेरिका में 57 फ़ीसदी और इंग्लैंड में 60 फ़ीसदी आबादी को टीका लग चुका था। महाराष्ट्र समेत कई राज्यों ने वैक्सीन की कमी की शिकायत की, तो केन्द्र सरकार ने उनकी ख़राब योजना और वितरण को दोषी करार दिया। उस वक्त, अचानक वैक्सीन के उत्पादन को 30-40 लाख रोज़ाना से बढ़ कर कम से कम 80-90 लाख रोज़ाना करने की ज़रूरत पड़ गई।

विडंबना यह है कि कोरोना की दूसरी लहर के पहले 'वैक्सीन मैत्री मिशन' के तहत भारत ने दुनिया भर को करीब साढ़े छह करोड़ वैक्सीन मुफ़्त भेजी थी। दुनिया भर में भारतीय दूतावासों से इस बात के लिए जोर दिया जा रहा था कि वे मोदी सरकार की वैक्सीन कूटनीति को 'सॉफ्ट पावर' और वैक्सीन चुनौती के लिए प्रतिबद्धता के तौर पर पेश करें। उस ज़माने के एक पूर्व राजनयिक ने कहा, 'हमें प्रधानमंत्री की प्रमुखता वाली तस्वीरों के साथ वैक्सीन निर्यात की भूमिका पर ज़ोर देने के लिए कहा गया। इसे एक बड़े कदम के तौर पर देखा जा रहा था।' जनवरी में जब ब्राज़ील को 20 लाख वैक्सीन पहुंचें, तो तत्कालीन राष्ट्रपति जेयर बोल्सानारो ने अपने ट्वीट पर भगवान हनुमान की छवि के साथ प्रधानमंत्री का शुक्रिया अदा करते हुए लिखाः 'धन्यवाद भारत'। प्रधानमंत्री ने तुरंत जवाब दियाः 'यह सम्मान हमारा है।'

देश में वैक्सीन की कमी के बावजूद प्रधानमंत्री मोदी की अंतरराष्ट्रीय छवि को चमकदार रखने की कोशिश हो रही थी।

अप्रैल 2021 तक, 'वैक्सीन मैत्री' का शोर मंद हो गया, क्योंकि निर्यात नीति को उलटने की ज़रूरत आ गई। कोविड से मरने वालों की तादाद तेज़ी से बढ़ने पर शिष्टाचार, अराजकता में बदलने लगा था। वैक्सीन अभियान शुरू करते वक्त जनवरी में सरकार ने करीब एक करोड़ सत्तर लाख वैक्सीन का ऑर्डर किया। कोविड संकट बढ़ने पर मार्च में फिर 11 करोड़ वैक्सीन का ऑर्डर किया गया, लेकिन 140 करोड़ की आबादी वाले देश में यह बहुत कम संख्या थी। प्रधानमंत्री कोविड टॉस्क फोर्स के एक सदस्य ने स्वीकार किया, 'किसी पर उंगली उठाने का कोई मायने नहीं हैं। सच तो यह है कि कोविड की दूसरी भयावह लहर से हम सब हैरान थे। हमने पहले कदम के तौर पर खासतौर से फ्रंटलाइन वर्कर्स और 65 साल से ऊपर के लोगों के लिए वैक्सीन देने की योजना बनाई थी, लेकिन दूसरी लहर ने तो शायद किसी को नहीं छोड़ा और हमें टीकाकरण अभियान को नए तरीके से शुरू करने की मशक्कत करनी पड़ी।'

इस अभियान में केवल यही इकलौती गड़बड़ नहीं थी।

1 मई 2021 को जब दूसरी लहर तबाही मचा रही थी, तब राज्य सरकारों के दबाव में केन्द्र सरकार ने उदार मूल्य नीति और वैक्सीन नीति में तेजी लाने का फ़ैसला किया। इसके तहत घरेलू वैक्सीन निर्माता अपना 50 प्रतिशत उत्पादन राज्य सरकारों और निजी अस्पतालों या संस्थानों को सीधा बेच सकते थे। बाकी आधा हिस्सा केन्द्र सरकार को मिलना था, जिससे सरकार पैंतालिस साल से ऊपर के लोगों को मुफ़्त टीका लगाने वाली थी। यानी अब राज्य सरकारें घरेलू और दूसरे देशों से भी वैक्सीन सीधे खरीद सकती थीं। लेकिन अभी महीना भर भी नहीं बीता था कि जून में प्रधानमंत्री ने ऐलान किया कि देश भर में अब केन्द्र ही वैक्सीन खरीदेगा और पैंतालिस साल से ज़्यादा की उम्र की सीमा के बजाय सभी वयस्कों को टीका मुफ़्त लगाया जाएगा। दरअसल यह घोषणा सुप्रीम कोर्ट के सरकार से वैक्सीन नीति पर हलफ़नामा मांगे जाने के एक हफ्ते के भीतर हुई। अदालत ने सरकार से पूछा था कि टीकों के लिए केन्द्र के बजट में रखी गई 35,000 करोड़ की रकम अब तक कैसे खर्च की गई? वैक्सीन की कीमतें अलग-अलग क्यों रखी गईं और सभी को टीके मुफ्त क्यों नहीं दिए गए?

वैक्सीन संकट और उसकी कीमतों में लूट को लेकर हो रही तीखी आलोचना के बीच, प्रधानमंत्री ने नीति में भ्रम को लेकर एक बार फिर राज्य सरकारों और मीडिया पर दोष मढ़ने की कोशिश की। प्रधानमंत्री ने जून में अपने संबोधन में कहा, 'कुछ लोगों ने राज्यों के लिए विकल्प की कमी होने पर सवाल उठाया और पूछा था कि केन्द्र सरकार ही यह सब क्यों तय कर रही थी? हरेक के लिए एक ही तरह के उपाय नहीं चल सकते और लॉकडाउन में ढील को

लेकर भी तर्क दिए गए। कई तरीके के दबाव डाले गए और कुछ मीडिया संस्थानों ने इस तरह का अभियान भी चलाया।'

प्रधानमंत्री के भाषण पर तेलंगाना के मुख्यमंत्री के. चन्द्रशेखर राव की नाराज़गी दिख रही थी। इससे पहले प्रधानमंत्री की मुख्यमंत्रियों के साथ हुई एक वर्चुअल बैठक में, राव ने शिकायत की थी कि केन्द्र उनके विचारों की अनदेखी कर रहा था। 'मुझे समझ नहीं आता, जब केन्द्र सरकार घरेलू उत्पादन बढ़ाने के बजाय वैक्सीन का निर्यात कर रही थी, तब तो प्रधानमंत्री इसका श्रेय खुद ले रहे थे। और जब कोविड की दूसरी लहर से हालात खराब हो गए हैं, तो टीकों की कमी के लिए हमें जिम्मेदार ठहरा रहे हैं। ऐसा नहीं होना चाहिए,' राव ने शिकायत दर्ज कराई थी। राव ने इस मसले पर गैर-एनडीए मुख्यमंत्रियों से समर्थन मांगा और एक गठबंधन बनाने की भी कोशिश की। केरल के मुख्यमंत्री पिनाराई विजयन ने इससे पहले ही गैर-एनडीए मुख्यमंत्रियों को केन्द्र सरकार से मुफ्त टीकों की मांग में एकजुट होने के लिए लिखा था। जब हर तरफ आलोचना हो रही थी, तो प्रधानमंत्री कार्यालय ने 'मेड इन इंडिया' वैक्सीन कार्यक्रम की प्रमुख दो कंपनियों: पुणे की सीरम इंस्टीट्यूट ऑफ इंडिया और हैदराबाद की भारत बायोटेक का रुख किया।

दोनों कंपनियां एक-दूसरे से बिल्कुल अलग हैं। एक ज़माने में घोड़ों का फार्म चलाने वाले डॉ. साइरस एस.पूनावाला की 1966 में एक पशु चिकित्सक से अचानक मुलाकात हो गई। उन्होंने डॉ. पूनावाला को वैक्सीन व्यवसाय में निवेश करने और इसे बढ़ाने की प्रेरणा दी थी। उनके बेटे और कंपनी के सीईओ अदार पूनावाला ने इसे और आगे बढ़ाया। अप्रैल 2020 में जब दुनिया कोविड के लॉकडाउन से जूझ रही थी, तब ब्रिटेन में पढ़े चालीस साल के अदार पूनावाला ने ऑक्सफोर्ड विश्वविद्यालय के प्रसिद्ध जेनर इंस्टीट्यूट के साथ वैक्सीन का इंसानों पर परीक्षण शुरू करने के लिए एक साझेदारी की घोषणा की। वैक्सीन की तुरंत और बढ़ती ज़रूरत को ध्यान में रखते हुए पूनावाला ने वित्तीय जोखिम उठाने का फ़ैसला किया और मंज़ूरी से पहले ही ऑक्सफोर्ड वैक्सीन की लाखों ख़ुराक बनाने की घोषणा की। 'यह एक जोखिम तो था, लेकिन सोच-समझकर लिया गया,' पूनावाला ने मुझे बाद में बताया। इसके साथ ही कोविशील्ड वैक्सीन परियोजना की शुरुआत हुई।

अगर अदार पूनावाला शानदार सूट पहने दूसरी पीढ़ी के बिज़नेस लीडर हैं, जो कई बार बॉलीवुड के बड़े सितारों के साथ भी देखे जाते हैं तो भारत बायोटेक के संस्थापक चेयरमैन और प्रबंध निदेशक डॉ. कृष्णा एला, इससे बिल्कुल उलट हैं। आणविक जीवविज्ञानी डॉ. एला पहली पीढ़ी के व्यवसायी हैं जो छात्रवृति पर आगे पढ़ाई करने के लिए अमेरिका गए और अपनी पत्नी सुचित्रा एला के साथ मिलकर वैक्सीन व्यवयास शुरू किया। कोविड-19 वैक्सीन में निवेश के फ़ैसले ने इस अनजान से जोड़े को अचानक सुर्ख़ियों में ला दिया। एक तरफ पूनावाला एक बहुराष्ट्रीय फार्मा कंपनी एज़ट्राजेनेका के साथ अंतरराष्ट्रीय संघ का हिस्सा थे तो दूसरी ओर

एला ने भारत की आईसीएमआर के साथ आगे बढ़ने का फ़ैसला किया। 'कोवैक्सीन' वैक्सीन परियोजना भारत सरकार के 'मेड इन इंडिया' की पहल थी, जिससे कंपनी और मोदी सरकार के रिश्तों को लेकर अटकलें लगाई जाने लगीं। क्या भारत बायोटेक ने इस मदद के बदले भाजपा को चंदा दिया था? हमने एक कार्यक्रम में कृष्णा एला से सवाल किया। उन्होंने नाराज़गी भरी आवाज़ में जवाब दिया, 'मुझे गेट्स फाउंडेशन से कोई पैसा नहीं मिला है, ना मुझे भारत सरकार से कोई पैसा मिला है। हमने अपने खर्च पर क्लिनिकल टैस्ट किए और खुद के जोखिम पर दो करोड़ वैक्सीन खुराक बनाई। मैंने कभी नहीं कहा कि केवल सरकार ही हमारी वैक्सीन खरीदे। मैंने यह वैक्सीन कारोबार के नजरिये से नहीं बनाई, बल्कि एक वैज्ञानिक के तौर पर देश के प्रति अपनी ज़िम्मेदारी पूरा करने के लिए बनाई है।'

कोविड संकट के दौरान यह एक नैतिक ज़िम्मेदारी थी या कारोबार का बेहतरीन मौका, मोदी सरकार ने वैक्सीन की कमी से निपटने के दौरान पूनावाला और एला की तरफ रुख किया। साल 2020 में फंड के मामले में कंजूसी करने वाली सरकार ने मई 2021 में थोड़ी ज़्यादा मदद 4,500 करोड़ रुपये मंज़ूर किए। इससे यह उम्मीद बन गई कि सीरम इंस्टीट्यूट जुलाई तक कोविशील्ड की ख़ुराक का उत्पादन तीन करोड़ से बढ़ाकर दस करोड़ कर देगा और भारत बायोटेक कोवैक्सीन की ख़ुराक का उत्पादन तीन करोड़ से बढ़ाकर पांच करोड़ अस्सी लाख तक कर देगा। जनवरी 2021 में अदार पूनावाला के इस बयान से बड़ा विवाद हो गया कि केवल तीन टीके ही वैज्ञानिक कसौटी पर खरे उतरे हैं, इनमें: फाइज़र-बायोएनटेक, मॉडर्ना और ऑक्सफोर्ड-एस्ट्रोजेनेका हैं। बाकी सभी 'पानी की तरह सुरक्षित' थे और वो कितना असरकारी थे, इसका परीक्षण नहीं किया गया है। नाराज़ डॉ. एला ने पलटकर जवाब देने में देर नहीं लगाई, 'हम 200 फ़ीसदी ईमानदारी से क्लिनिकल ट्रायल करते हैं और फिर भी हमें आलोचना झेलनी पड़ती है। पानी की तरह कहकर कुछ कंपनियों ने मुझे गलत तरीके से ब्रांड करने की कोशिश की है।'

विवाद के सार्वजनिक होने पर मामले को शांत करने के लिए पीएमओ को बीच-बचाव करना पड़ा। प्रधानमंत्री मोदी ने दोनों पक्षों से बात कर, साथ देने का भरोसा दिलाया। नए स्वास्थ्य मंत्री सीधे पीएमओ को रिपोर्ट करते थे और टीकाकरण के लक्ष्य पर रोजाना की प्रगति बताने के लिए एक डैशबोर्ड बनाया गया, जिसकी निगरानी सीधे साउथ ब्लॉक यानी पीएमओ से हो रही थी। अगस्त 2021 में, कोविड की दूसरी लहर का बुरा दौर ख़त्म हो चुका था। उस समय एक महीने में 15 करोड़ से ज़्यादा वैक्सीन खुराक मिल रही थी। जब अक्टूबर 2021 में भारत ने सौ करोड़ वैक्सीन खुराक का बहुत बड़ा 'मील के पत्थर' जैसा लक्ष्य हासिल किया, तो प्रधानमंत्री ने खुद पूनावाला और डॉ. एला को 'हाई-टी' पर आमंत्रित कर उनकी काफी प्रशंसा की। दोनों वैक्सीन निर्माताओं ने भी प्रधानमंत्री की बहुत तारीफ

की। अदार पूनावाला ने तारीफ करते हुए कहा, 'प्रधानमंत्री मोदी की दूरदर्शी सोच के बिना यह मुमकिन नहीं था।'

भारतीय जनता पार्टी तो एक कदम और आगे बढ़ गई। पार्टी ने देशभर में "धन्यवाद मोदी जी" अभियान शुरू कर दिया। भाजपा शासित राज्य सरकारों से कहा गया कि वे अख़बारों में विज्ञापन दें और पार्टी की स्थानीय इकाईयों ने बैनर और पोस्टर लगाए, जिनमें प्रधानमंत्री की तस्वीर के साथ भारत में एक अरब वैक्सीन की उपलब्धि की प्रशंसा की गई थी। भाजपा की सोशल मीडिया टीम ने डिजिटल प्लेटफॉर्म पर अभियान चलाया। इससे पहले विश्वविद्यालय अनुदान आयोग ने केन्द्रीय विश्वविद्यालयों से कहा कि वे अपने परिसरों में मुफ्त टीकाकरण अभियान के लिए प्रधानमंत्री का आभार ज़ाहिर करने वाले पोस्टर लगाएं। केन्द्रीय विद्यालयों के छात्रों से दूसरी लहर के दौरान फाइनल परीक्षा रद्द करने के लिए प्रधानमंत्री का शुक्रिया अदा करने वाले वीडियो बनाने के लिए कहा गया। ये स्क्रिप्टेड वीडियो **#ThankYouModiji** हैशटेग के साथ सोशल मीडिया अकाउंट पर पोस्ट किए गए। मोदी की शानदार पीआर टीम ने कुछ ही समय में माहौल बदल दिया, महामारी अब आयोजन हो गई थी और इसे प्रधानमंत्री को 'सुप्रीम लीडर' की ब्रांडिग के साथ जोड़ दिया गया। 'क्या इंदिरा गांधी ने अपनी छवि को बीस सूत्री कार्यक्रम से नहीं जोड़ा था? फिर मोदी जी की पहचान वैक्सीन की पहल से है, तो किसी को क्यों शिकायत होनी चाहिए?' एक भाजपा नेता ने पूछा।

मोदी शैली का यह इंवेट मैनेजमेंट एक बार फिर 17 सितम्बर को दिखाई दिया, जब सरकारी दावों के मुताबिक एक ही दिन में वैक्सीन की ढाई करोड़ खुराक दी गई। टीकाकरण अभियान के शुरू होने के बाद प्रधानमंत्री के जन्मदिन यानी 17 सितम्बर को सबसे ज़्यादा आंकड़ें तक पहुंचा था। इसमें से ज़्यादातर वैक्सीन ख़ुराक गुजरात में बीस लाख के आंकड़े सहित भाजपा शासित राज्यों कर्नाटक, बिहार, उत्तरप्रदेश और मध्यप्रदेश में दी गई थीं। इस पर प्रधानमंत्री ने चिकित्सा अधिकारियों, कर्मचारियों और लाभार्थियों को धन्यवाद देने में मीडिया के इस्तेमाल में देर नहीं लगाई। ट्वीटर से लेकर फेसबुक तक सभी सोशल मीडिया प्लेटफॉर्म पर हर जगह प्रधानमंत्री थे। प्रधानमंत्री ने गोवा में स्वास्थ्य कर्मियों को एक वीडियो संबोधन में कहा, 'कल मेरे लिए बहुत भावुक दिन था। आप सभी की कोशिशों से यह मेरे लिए बहुत खास दिन बन गया।' स्वास्थ्य मंत्री मंडाविया ने इस रिकॉर्ड को प्रधानमंत्री के लिए भारत का उपहार बताया, यानी 'बर्थडे गिफ्ट'। महामारी के वक्त भी 'राजनीतिक चापलूसी' का कोई मौका नहीं छूटने की कोशिशें जारी थीं।

एक और तस्वीर भी थी, उदाहरण के लिए, मध्यप्रदेश में कई जगहों पर उन लोगों को भी वैक्सीन प्रमाणपत्र जारी कर दिए गए, जिन्होंने वैक्सीन खुराक ली ही नहीं थी। एक मामले में तो एक ऐसे शख्स के नाम भी सर्टिफिकेट जारी किया गया, जो कई महीने पहले कोविड की वजह

से दुनिया से विदा हो गया था। सरकार के अपने **CoWin** पोर्टल से तस्वीर और साफ होती है कि प्रधानमंत्री के जन्मदिन के मौके पर वैक्सीन खुराकों का यह उछाल सामान्य नहीं था। जन्मदिन से पहले और बाद में वैक्सीन लेने के मामलों में बड़ी गिरावट दिख रही थी। स्वास्थ्य मंत्रालय के पूर्व अधिकारी ने माना कि 'सारी कोशिशें प्रधानमंत्री के जन्मदिन को बड़ा मौका बनाने के लिए की गई थीं, इसलिए वैक्सीन आपूर्ति को स्टॉक किया गया, ताकि 17 सितम्बर को रिकॉर्ड तोड़ने वाला दिन बनाया जा सके।'

दरअसल 2021 का 'बर्थडे वैक्सीन बैश' तो भाजपा के उस अभियान की शुरुआत करने के लिए था, जो प्रधानमंत्री के सार्वजनिक जीवन में बीस साल पूरा होने के मौके पर आयोजित किया जाना था। मोदी पहली बार 7 अक्टूबर 2001 को गुजरात के मुख्यमंत्री बने थे। इस दौरान बीस दिनों तक 'सेवा और समर्पण' अभियान चलाया जाना था। इस लंबे चलने वाले जन्मदिन समारोह में भाजपा नेताओं ने पांच करोड़ लोगों से प्रधानमंत्री को सार्वजनिक सेवा में उनके प्रयासों के लिए 'शुक्रिया अदा' करने वाले पोस्टकार्ड भेजने का इंतज़ाम भी किया था। सरकार ने पांच किलो मुफ़्त राशन योजना में 14 करोड़ लोगों को राशन दिया। इन राशन बैग पर प्रधानमंत्री की तस्वीर के साथ संदेश था: 'धन्यवाद मोदी जी'।

मानो सरकार लोगों से कोविड में हुई मौतों और उस भयावह दौर को भूलने की बात कर रही हो, इसके लिए मीडिया की मदद से एक 'फील गुड फैक्टर' का माहौल बनाया जा रहा था, जिसमें प्रधानमंत्री सुपरमैन थे। कुछ महीनों पहले ही देश ने कोविड की दूसरी लहर की भयावहता झेली थी, जिसमें सरकारी आंकड़ों के मुताबिक भी चार लाख से ज़्यादा लोगों ने जान गवांई थी। गैर-सरकारी अनुमानों में तो यह संख्या कई गुना थी। 10 जून 2021 को तो, सिर्फ़ एक दिन में कोविड से 6,148 मौतें हुई, जो दुनियाभर में एक दिन में होने वाली सबसे ज़्यादा मौतें थीं। फिर भी देश, कम से कम मोदी सरकार तो जानमाल के भारी नुकसान पर शोक जाहिर करने के बजाए जश्न के मूड में थी। ख़ैर, सबसे बुरा दौर बीत चुका था। अब प्रचार को रफ्तार देने का मौसम आ गया था।

मई 2021 में, सूचना प्रसारण मंत्री प्रकाश जावड़ेकर ने कहा, देश की वयस्क आबादी को टीका लगाने का काम दिसम्बर 2021 तक पूरा हो जाएगा। साल के आखिर तक, देश की करीब 94 करोड़ वयस्क आबादी में से 64 फ़ीसदी को पूरी तरह से टीका लगा दिया गया था और करीब 90 फ़ीसदी को पहली ख़ुराक दे दी गई थी। 2021 की गर्मियों में कोविड से आई तबाही के बाद यह एक शानदार उपलब्धि थी। हर वैक्सीन सर्टिफिकेट पर प्रधानमंत्री मोदी की तस्वीर थी, जो यह भरोसा दिलाने के लिए काफी थी कि महामारी के संकट के वक्त प्रधानमंत्री उनकी चिंता कर रहे थे। यही तस्वीर विरोधी राजनेताओं को भड़काने के लिए भी काफी थी। पश्चिम बंगाल की मुख्यमंत्री ममता बनर्जी ने अपनी नाराज़गी ज़ाहिर कर दी। उन्होंने कोविड

मसले पर प्रधानमंत्री की ओर से बुलाई गई किसी भी बैठक से दूर रहने की धमकी दी। बनर्जी ने भड़कते हुए कहा, 'जब कोविड के ख़िलाफ़ लडाई एक सामूहिक प्रयास है तो आप केवल एक व्यक्ति की तस्वीर कैसे इस्तेमाल कर सकते हैं? क्या आप कल मृत्यु प्रमाण पत्र पर भी प्रधानमंत्री की फोटो लगाएंगे?'

भारतीय जनता पार्टी के अध्यक्ष और (मोदी सरकार 1.0 और मोदी 3.0 में) स्वास्थ्य मंत्री जे.पी. नड्डा तो और आगे तक चले गए। हिमाचल प्रदेश में एक चुनावी रैली में नड्डा ने मतदाताओं से कहा, 'प्रधानमंत्री मोदी ने वैक्सीन बनाकर आपकी रक्षा की, अब भाजपा की रक्षा करने की बारी आपकी है।'

'ताली-थाली' के सुपर स्टार से लेकर 'विश्व गुरु' और अब 'वैक्सीन निर्माता-रक्षक' की छवि से मोदी राजनीतिक नुकसान से तो बच ही गए, साथ ही और मज़बूत होकर निकले। मोदी की जगह कोई और नेता होता तो आर्थिक हालात को कमज़ोर करते लॉकडाउन और दूसरी लहर से निपटने में हुई गड़बड़ियों की आलोचना से बच पाना उसके लिए मुश्किल होता, लेकिन मोदी के 'चीयरलीडर्स' ने इसे मोदी सरकार की बड़ी उपलब्धि के तौर पर पेश किया। जनवरी 2022 में हुए *इंडिया टुडे* के 'मूड ऑफ द नेशन' सर्वेक्षण में कहा गया कि जवाब देने वालों में से 82 फ़ीसदी लोगों ने माना कि केन्द्र सरकार ने टीकाकरण अभियान में ठीक काम किया था। सवाल है कि क्या जनता की याददाश्त वाकई कमज़ोर होती है? क्या सरकार के आपदा को अवसर में बदलने की नीति का असर हो गया? या विपक्ष अपनी आवाज़ ठीक तरह से उठाने में नाकाम रहा? क्या मीडिया सरकार को जवाबदेह ठहराना भूल गया? या प्रधानमंत्री मोदी 'टेफ्लॉन' जैसी शख्सियत थे, जिन पर किसी तूफान का असर नहीं हुआ और वे ज्यादातर देशवासियों का विश्वास हासिल करने में कामयाब रहे?

विपक्ष के एक नेता ने बाद में मुझसे कहा, 'अगर कोई नेता महामारी के ऐसे हालात में भी राजनीतिक मुनाफा कमा सकता है तो फिर कहने के लिए क्या बचता है।'

भारत को छोड़कर, दुनिया में हर कोई चुनौती का सामना कर रहा था। लेकिन इस बार मोदी सरकार के लिए चुनौती कोई अनजान वायरस नहीं, सामूहिक विरोध होगा।

4

'जय जवान, जय किसान': किसान आंदोलन

प्रधानमंत्री नरेन्द्र मोदी की कैबिनेट बैठकें अक्सर चौंकाती हैं। 'मोदी जी क्या सोचते हैं, यह सोचना मुश्किल है। हमारी बात तो छोड़िए, उनकी छाया को भी शायद इस बात का अहसास नहीं होता कि उनके दिमाग़ में क्या चल रहा है,' मोदी सरकार के एक कैबिनेट मंत्री ने हंसते हुए मुझे बताया। 5 जून 2020 को साउथ ब्लॉक में कैबिनेट बैठक में मंत्रियों में भविष्य को लेकर चिंता थी। देश के बहुत से हिस्सों में अब भी लॉकडाउन चल रहा था, वे प्रवासी मजदूरों और कोविड से उपजे आर्थिक संकट को लेकर अपनी बात रखना चाहते थे। लेकिन कैबिनेट बैठक का एजेंडा कोविड संकट नही, बल्कि कृषि यानी किसानी था। बैठक में प्रधानमंत्री ने घोषणा की, 'हम लंबे समय से पड़े तीन कृषि सुधारों को अध्यादेश के रूप में ला रहे हैं, उससे खेती की तस्वीर बदलेगी और किसानों की आमदनी भी बढ़ेगी।' तत्कालीन कृषि मंत्री नरेन्द्र सिंह तोमर को अब इस ख़बर से हैरान-परेशान दिख रहे कैबिनेट मंत्रियों को पूरी जानकारी देनी थी। एक बड़े संकट से जूझ रहे देश में किसानों की आमदनी पर मार करने वाले इन क़ानूनों को पारित कराने की कोशिश को तानाशाही या गलत प्राथमिकता के सिवाय क्या कहा जा सकता है। उस वक़्त जब किसान को सहारे की ज़रूरत थी, तब मोदी सरकार ने एक झटका दिया।

तीन अध्यादेश (जो अब क़ानून बन गए) किसान उपज व्यापार और वाणिज्य (संवर्धन और सुविधा) अध्यादेश, 2020; किसान (सशक्तिकरण और संरक्षण) समझौते पर मूल्य आश्वासन और कृषि सेवा अध्यादेश, 2020; और आवश्यक वस्तु (संशोधन) अधिनियम 2020 लाए गए

थे। प्रधानमंत्री ने कहा कि हमारा इरादा है कि किसानों को उपज का सरकारी मंडियों के बाहर भी बेहतर दाम मिल सके और बाज़ार के रास्ते खुल जाएं। प्रधानमंत्री मोदी ने कहा, 'हमने व्यापार और उद्योगों के लिए तो उदारीकरण कर दिया है लेकिन कृषि पर अब भी सरकारी नियंत्रण है।' मोदी ने आगे बढ़ते हुए ज़ोर देकर कहा कि 'यह सही सनय है जब किसानों को उपज का बेहतर दाम मिल सके, इसके लिए खेती को बाज़ार में ज़्यादा अवसर मिलने चाहिएं।'

प्रधानमंत्री की इस योजना से केन्द्रीय खाद्य प्रसंस्करण मंत्री और शिरोमणि अकाली दल से तीन बार सांसद रहीं हरसिमरत कौर की चिंताएं शायद बढ़ गई थीं। उनके पति सुखबीर बादल भी सांसद थे। हरसिमरत कौर साफगोई से अपने मन की बात रखती हैं। मोदी सरकार की कैबिनेट बैठकों में आमतौर पर मंत्री असहमति ज़ाहिर नहीं करते, लेकिन हरसिमरत कौर ने अपनी नाखुशी जाहिर कर दी। उन्होंने स्पष्ट किया, 'मैं इन अध्यादेशों को इस तरह से पारित नहीं करने की बात करती रही हूं, इससे परेशानी बढ़ेगी।' कौर ने कहा, 'मैं इस मसले पर पीछे इसलिए हटी, क्योंकि मुझे प्रधानमंत्री जी ने यह भरोसा दिलाया था कि किसानों से जुड़े लोगों से सलाह-मशविरा के बिना कोई बिल पास नहीं कराया जाएगा।' तब प्रधानमंत्री ने कृषि मंत्री तोमर और गृहमंत्री अमित शाह से हरसिमरत से बात कर इस मुद्दे को सुलझाने के निर्देश दिए।

अकाली दल के नेता अगले तीन महीनों तक तोमर और शाह से किसान संगठनों के साथ बैठक के लिए दबाव डालते रहे। बताया गया कि तोमर को मध्यप्रदेश में विधानसभा उप-चुनावों की वजह से वक्त नहीं मिल पा रहा और शाह कोविड की वजह से अस्पताल में भर्ती थे। हरसिमरत ने दावा किया, 'मैंने हर दरवाज़े को खटखटाया, लेकिन कोई सुनने वाला नहीं था।' वैसे मोदी सरकार में यह कोई नई बात नहीं थी। शायद इसीलिए कोई भी मंत्री, प्रधानमंत्री की मंज़ूरी के बिना किसी विवादास्पद मुद्दे पर आगे नहीं बढ़ना चाहता था। कृषि मंत्री को भी शायद कोई दिलचस्पी नहीं थी। सिर्फ़ गृहमंत्री शाह ही इसका रास्ता निकाल सकते थे, लेकिन वे तब बीमार थे।

तीन महीने बाद, सितम्बर 2020 में जब संसद में तीनों कृषि विधेयकों पर चर्चा शुरू हुई, तो शिरोमणि अकाली दल के नेता सुखबीर बादल ने लोकसभा में अचानक घोषणा की कि उनकी पत्नी हरसिमरत कौर, कृषि विधेयकों के विरोध में मोदी सरकार छोड़ रही थीं। कुछ ही देर में हरसमिरत ने अपना इस्तीफ़ा प्रधानमंत्री कार्यालय को सौंप दिया और ट्वीट किया: 'किसानों की बेटी और बहन के रूप में उनके साथ खड़े होने पर गर्व है।' शायद कम लोग जानते होंगे कि हरसमिरत ने एक दिन पहले ही अपने इस्तीफ़े की पेशकश कर दी थी। रक्षा मंत्री राजनाथ सिंह, भाजपा अध्यक्ष जे.पी. नड्डा और कृषि मंत्री नरेन्द्र सिंह तोमर के साथ बैठक में कौर ने अपना इरादा जता दिया था कि यदि कृषि विधेयकों को संसद में पास कराया गया, तो उनका सरकार में बने रहना मुश्किल होगा। उन्होंने चेतावनी के अंदाज़ में कहा, 'आग लगेगी! मैं इस

पर समझौता नहीं कर सकती।' तीनों नेता किसानों के गुस्से को कम दिखाने की कोशिश कर रहे थे, शायद वे ज़मीनी हक़ीकत से अनजान बन रहे थे। राजनाथ सिंह ने कहा, 'कुछ दिनों में सब ठीक हो जाएगा।'

हरसिमरत के इस्तीफ़े के एक हफ्ते बाद अकाली दल ने एक कदम और आगे बढ़ते हुए खुद को एनडीए से बाहर कर लिया, यानी सरकार से समर्थन वापस ले लिया। अकाली दल भाजपा के सबसे पुराने सहयोगी में से था, जो 1967 से भारतीय जनसंघ के ज़माने से उनके साथ थे। अकाली दल के सबसे बड़े नेता प्रकाश सिंह बादल की अगुवाई में 1997 के पंजाब विधानसभा चुनाव दोनों दलों ने मिलकर लड़े थे और पंजाब और दिल्ली में सरकार बनाई थी। प्रकाश सिंह बादल के भाजपा के नेता अटल बिहारी वाजपेयी के साथ बेहद अच्छे रिश्ते थे। एक अकाली नेता ने याद करते हुए बताया कि 'आपातकाल में जेल में साथ रहने के दौरान बना यह रिश्ता मजबूत था और जब भी बादल साहब, दिल्ली में होते वे अटल जी और आडवाणी जी से मिलते थे।'

साल 2014 में मोदी के प्रधानमंत्री बनने के बाद से अकाली-भाजपा रिश्तों में दूरियां बनने लगीं। यूं तो नब्बे के दशक में जब मोदी पंजाब में भाजपा के प्रभारी पार्टी सचिव थे, तब वे बादल साहब का बहुत सम्मान करते थे। लेकिन महत्वाकांक्षी नई पीढ़ी की मंज़िलें और रास्ते शायद अलग थे। कई आरोपों का सामना कर रहा बादल परिवार, मोदी के 'भ्रष्टाचार और परिवारवाद' के ख़िलाफ़ अभियान में एनडीए के निशाने पर था। सरकार में दूसरे सबसे ताकतवर नेता और गृहमंत्री अमित शाह भी इस रिश्ते को आगे बढ़ाने में ज़्यादा उत्साहित नहीं दिखते थे। शाह जब भाजपा अध्यक्ष थे, तो अपनी पंजाब यात्रा के दौरान उन्होंने भाजपा के नेताओं से कहा कि हमें इस गठबंधन पर फिर से विचार करना चाहिए। शाह ने ज़ोर देकर कहा, 'अगर हम हमेशा जूनियर पार्टनर बने रहेंगे तो आगे कैसे बढ़ेंगे? पंजाब में बादल परिवार के ख़िलाफ़ सत्ता विरोधी हवा है और उसका ख़ामियाज़ा हमें उठाना पड़ रहा है।'

दोनों दलों के बीच यह रिश्ता अब तक इसलिए चल रहा था क्योंकि मोदी सरकार के प्रमुख नेता अरुण जेटली, दिल्ली में अकालियों के दोस्त थे। मिलनसार जेटली का अकालियों से बरसों पुराना रिश्ता था। 2014 के चुनावों में प्रकाश सिंह बादल ने ही ज़ोर दिया था कि जेटली, अपना पहला लोकसभा चुनाव अमृतसर से लड़ें। उन्होंने जेटली को जिताने का भरोसा दिलाया। लेकिन जेटली, पटियाला के शाही परिवार और कांग्रेस के कद्दावर नेता कैप्टन अमरिंदर सिंह से चुनाव हार गए। इस हार के बावजूद जेटली ने बादल परिवार के प्रति अपना आभार व्यक्त किया और 2019 के अगले चुनावों तक यह गठबंधन बनाए रखा। अगस्त 2019 में जेटली के निधन के बाद अकाली दल को समझ आ गया कि अब यह रिश्ता कुछ दिनों का ही था। अकाली दल के सांसद रहे नरेश गुजराल ने कहा, 'सच तो यह है कि भाजपा अध्यक्ष बनने के बाद से ही अमित शाह इस गठबंधन के पक्ष में नहीं थे और वे इसे तोड़ने के लिए कोई बहाना तलाश रहे थे।'

2022 की शुरुआत में पंजाब विधानसभा चुनावों के वक्त अकाली दल को समझ आ गया था कि अब फ़ैसले का वक्त आ गया था और उन्हें पहल करनी चाहिए। कृषि क़ानूनों को लेकर लोगों में बढ़ते गुस्से के बाद अकाली दल के पास बहुत कम विकल्प थे। सुखबीर बादल ने तब भाजपा से अलग होने का ऐलान करते हुए कहा, 'किसानों से जुड़े ये बिल विनाशकारी हैं और पंजाब ने पिछले पचास साल में जो कुछ बनाया है, उसे ख़त्म कर देंगे। केन्द्र सरकार पंजाबियों और सिख समुदाय को लेकर असंवेदनशील है।'

2017 के चुनाव में कांग्रेस ने अकाली दल को सत्ता से बाहर कर दिया था और अब पंजाब में आम आदमी पार्टी की ताकत बढ़ने से अकाली दल तीसरे नंबर पर पहुंचने वाला था, ऐसे में किसानों की भावनाओं के सहारे वो अपनी ज़मीन बचाने की कोशिश कर रहे थे। मगर मतदाताओं में भरोसे की बहाली में बहुत देर हो गई थी, अकाली सरकार के वक्त की ज़्यादतियां अब भी उनके जेहन से उतरी नहीं थी। केन्द्र को अंदाज़ा नहीं था कि पंजाब के गांवों में कृषि बिल को लेकर पहले से ही नाराज़गी है और यह गुस्सा जल्दी ही दिल्ली की सीमाओं तक पहुंच जाएगा।

प्रधानमंत्री की छवि ऐसे नेता की बनाई गई, जिसे कोई चुनौती नहीं दे सकता, लेकिन यह पहला झटका हो सकता था, और वह कोई राजनीतिक विरोधी नहीं, बल्कि मौसम की मार झेलकर भी अन्याय के ख़िलाफ़ खड़ा रहने वाला किसान है। किसानों की ताकत 'दबंग नेता' मोदी को घुटनों पर ला सकती है।

═

14 सितम्बर 2020 को, छह महीने के बाद संसद की बैटक हुई। कोविड की वजह से इस बार दो सत्रों के बीच ज़्यादा वक्त हो गया था। कोविड का ख़तरा अभी टला नहीं था, इसलिए सांसदों को ज़्यादा सतर्कता बरतने के लिए कहा गया। संसद चलाने के तरीके और समय में बदलाव किया गया। लोकसभा सुबह और राज्यसभा शाम को चलेगी। दोनों सदनों में कोविड संक्रमण को फैलने से रोकने के लिए कांच के डिवाइडर बना दिए गए थे, मास्क ज़रूरी हो गया था। संसद में कोविड से जुड़ी परेशानियों और चिंताओं के हावी रहने की संभावना थी। कांग्रेस के वरिष्ठ सांसद दिग्विजय सिंह ने कहा, 'हम कई महीनों से अपने साथी सांसदों से नहीं मिले थे, कई लोगों को इस दौरान निजी नुकसान भी उठाना पड़ा था। हमने सोचा कि इस सत्र में कोविड को लेकर सरकार के कामकाज और हालात की समीक्षा हो सकेगी।'

सांसदों की चिंता सिर्फ़ कोविड महामारी को लेकर ही नहीं थी। प्रधानमंत्री मोदी ने चीन के राष्ट्रपति शी जिनपिंग के साथ कुछ 'खास' संबंध होने का दावा किया थाः इससे पहले 2014 में अहमदाबाद में साबरमती रिवरफ्रंट पर झूले पर एक साथ बैठे दोनों नेताओं की तस्वीरें वायरल

हुई थीं। मगर जून 2020 में दोनों देशों के बीच सीमा पर साठ साल में सबसे खराब झड़पें हुई। वास्तविक नियंत्रण रेखा के पश्चिमी इलाके में लद्दाख की गलवान घाटी में दोनों तरफ के सैनिकों के बीच लड़ाई हुई। फौजी एक दूसरे पर लोहे की छड़ों और डंडों से हमला कर रहे थे। इस झड़प में बीस भारतीय जवान शहीद हुए और चार चीनी सैनिक मारे गए। चीनी सेना की इस घुसपैठ की कोशिश से मोदी सरकार हैरान थी। लेकिन इसके बाद बुलाई गई सर्वदलीय बैठक में सरकार इंकार की मुद्रा में थी। प्रधानमंत्री ने ज़ोर देकर कहा, 'न तो वे (चीन) हमारी सीमा में घुसे हैं और न ही किसी चौकी पर कोई कब्ज़ा किया गया है।'

जब कांग्रेस सांसद मनीष तिवारी ने लद्दाख में चीनी घुसपैठ पर संसद में चर्चा की मांग की तो सरकार, राष्ट्रीय सुरक्षा का हवाला देते हुए इस पर बहस के लिए तैयार नहीं हुई। इससे नाराज़ कांग्रेस सांसद तिवारी ने मुझसे कहा, 'मैंने चीनी घुसपैठ को लेकर पैंसठ सवाल रखे थे, लेकिन सरकार ने एक का जवाब भी नहीं दिया। ऐसा लगता है कि सरकार अपनी फजीहत से बचने के लिए चीन के मुद्दे पर बात ही नहीं करना चाहती।' इससे प्रधानमंत्री की मजबूत नेता की छवि पर असर पड़ता। भाजपा के प्रवक्ताओं को चीनी घुसपैठ के विषय पर टीवी बहस में शामिल नहीं होने के सख्त निर्देश दिए गए थे। पार्टी चीनी सामान के बहिष्कार की बात कर रही थी और चीन के सोशल मीडिया एप 'टिक टॉक' पर पाबंदी लगाने का ऐलान ऐसे किया गया, मानो अब चीनी सेना का ख़तरा टल जाएगा। इस सब हंगामे का मकसद था कि सीमा के हालात पर लोगों का ध्यान ना जाए। 2023-24 तक, चीन के साथ भारत का व्यापार घाटा 85 अरब अमेरिकी डॉलर हो गया था, जिससे दोनों मुल्कों के रिश्तों की ताकत समझ आ सकती थी। दोनों मुल्कों की सेना के अफसरों के बीच कई बैठकों के बावजूद लद्दाख में गतिरोध पूरी तरह ख़त्म नहीं हुआ था।

किसी भी सच्चाई पर इंकार की मुद्रा और ध्यान भटकाने की कोशिश मोदी सरकार की रणनीति का हिस्सा होती है। शायद इसीलिए बाहरी खतरे से ध्यान भटकाने के लिए सरकार दूसरे बड़े मुद्दे को लेकर आ गई। 2020 में संसद के मानसून सत्र के पहले दिन ही कृषि मंत्री नरेन्द्र सिंह तोमर ने खेती-किसानी से जुड़े तीन विवादास्पद अध्यादेशों को क़ानून में बदलने के लिए तीन बिल लोकसभा में पेश कर दिए। कैबिनेट ने जून में इन अध्यादेशों को मंज़ूरी दी थी। लोकसभा में तो सरकार के पास बहुमत था, इसलिए बिलों को ध्वनि मत से पारित करा लिया गया। लेकिन जब राज्यसभा में इन बिलों को पेश किया गया तो दो बिलों पर विपक्ष ने आपत्ति जताते हुए इन्हें संसदीय समिति के पास भेजने की मांग की। राज्यसभा में उस वक्त उप-सभापति हरिवंश नारायण सिंह सदन चला रहे थे। हरिवंश भाजपा के सहयोगी दल जनता दल यूनाइटेड के सांसद थे। उन्होंने विपक्ष की मांग को ख़ारिज़ करते हुए बिलों को ध्वनि मत से पारित करने का प्रस्ताव रखा। इसका विरोध करते हुए तृणमूल कांग्रेस के सांसद डेरेक ओ

ब्रायन ने कहा, 'आप इतने महत्वपूर्ण विधेयक को ध्वनि-मत से कैसे पारित कर सकते हैं, इस पर मत-विभाजन कराइए।' जब उप-सभापति ने उनकी इस मांग को नहीं माना तो कई विपक्षी सांसद 'वैल' तक पहुंच गए और 'रूल बुक' को फाड़ने और उप-सभापति के माइक को छीनने की कोशिश की गई। लेकिन डेरेक ओ ब्रायन ने इस बात से इंकार किया कि उन्होंने रूल बुक को फाड़ा था। 'क्या कोई इसका वीडियो दिखा सकता है कि मैंने रूल बुक फाड़ी है? यदि ऐसा होगा तो मैं संसद से इस्तीफ़ा दे दूंगा। आप जानते हैं कि सरकार राज्यसभा टीवी के प्रसारण को बंद कर देती है ताकि जनता यह नहीं जान सके कि वे बिल पास कराने के लिए कैसे लोकतंत्र की हत्या कर रहे हैं।' ब्रायन गुस्से में बोल रहे थे, 'यदि एक भी सदस्य मत विभाजन की मांग करता है, तो सभापति उसे इस अधिकार से कैसे रोक सकते हैं और ऐसे ज़बरदस्ती ध्वनि मत से बिल को कैसे पास कराया जा सकता है?'

मैं राज्यसभा के उप-सभापति हरिवंश को उन दिनों से जानता हूं, जब वे रांची के एक प्रमुख हिंदी अखबार *प्रभात खबर* के प्रतिष्ठित संपादक थे। मृदुभाषी हरिवंश जनता दल यूनाइटेड नेतृत्व, खासतौर से बिहार के मुख्यमंत्री नीतीश कुमार के करीबी माने जाते हैं। राज्यसभा सांसद के रूप में उन्होंने प्रधानमंत्री मोदी से अपनी निकटता बढ़ा ली थी। जब मैंने हरिवंश जी से कृषि बिल विवाद के बारे में पूछा, तो वे कुछ बोलना नहीं चाहते थे। उन्होंने कहा, 'मेरी अंतरआत्मा साफ है। सबने सांसदों के व्यवहार को देखा है और मैंने नियमों के हिसाब से काम किया है। मैं इससे ज़्यादा क्या कह सकता हूं।' इस घटना पर तब के राष्ट्रपति रामनाथ कोविंद को लिखे पत्र में हरिवंश ने कहा, 'उच्च सदन के सदस्य लोकतंत्र के नाम पर हिंसक गतिविधियों में शामिल थे। उन्होंने अध्यक्ष को भी धमकाने की कोशिश की। हर नियम, सिस्टम की धज्जियां उड़ाई गईं।'

इस अराजकता के एक दिन बाद, राज्यसभा के सभापति वेंकैया नायडू ने आठ सांसदों को उनके नियम विरुद्ध व्यवहार के लिए निलंबित कर दिया। सभापति ने कहा, 'कृषि विधेयक पारित होने के दौरान जो कुछ हुआ, वह दुर्भाग्यपूर्ण है, उसे स्वीकार नहीं किया जा सकता और वह निंदनीय है। यह राज्यसभा के लिए बेहद बुरा दिन था।' निलंबित सांसदों में तृणमूल कांग्रेस के सदन में नेता डेरेक ओ ब्रायन का नाम भी शामिल था। ब्रायन का कहना था कि 'हमें निलंबित करने के बजाय सभापति वेंकैया नायडू को देश को यह बताना चाहिए कि इतने महत्वपूर्ण बिलों को पारित कराते समय वे खुद आसन पर क्यों नहीं थे? सच्चाई यह है कि एक किसान के बेटे के रूप में उप-राष्ट्रपति शायद इस काले दिन से खुद को जोड़ना नहीं चाहते थे और इसलिए वे दूर रहे!' विपक्षी सांसदों का मानना था कि उपसभापति हरिवंश को ऐन वक्त पर ध्वनि मत से बिल पास कराने के लिए सदन में आना पड़ा, क्योंकि सभापति इस विवाद से खुद को दूर रखना चाहते थे।

नाराज होने वालों में अकेले डेरेक ओ ब्रायन ही नहीं थे। राज्यसभा में अकाली दल के सांसद नरेश गुजराल भी कम नाराज नहीं थे, कृषि क़ानून उनकी पार्टी की प्राथमिकता थे, इसलिए उन्होंने अपनी बात रखने के लिए ज़्यादा समय मांगा। पहले उन्हें बारह मिनट का समय दिया गया था, बाद में उसे घटाकर ढाई मिनट कर दिया गया। गुजराल ने कहा, 'सत्ता पक्ष भी मेरी बात सुनना चाहता था, लेकिन शायद वेंकैया जी तैयार नहीं थे। ऐसा लगता है कि वे उस दिन किसी और के निर्देश पर काम कर रहे थे।'

इस बीच, प्रधानमंत्री मोदी संसद में हंगामे से बेपरवाह दिख रहे थे। लोगों का मानना है कि पिछले कई सालों में गुजरात के मुख्यमंत्री और फिर प्रधानमंत्री के तौर पर, मोदी अक्सर संसदीय परपंराओं की अनदेखी करते हैं। वे यूं तो संसद को लोकतंत्र का मंदिर बताते हैं, लेकिन असल में वे समझते हैं कि संसद को प्रधानमंत्री को ही 'बॉस' मानना चाहिए। मोदी, हमेशा बहुमत के जनादेश को अपने लिए वो 'लाइसेंस' मानते हैं जिसमें लोकतंत्र से ऊपर 'राजा' को माना जाए। मोदी कार्यकाल में विवादास्पद मुद्दों पर बहस अक्सर नहीं होती। बजट कई बार बिना चर्चा के पारित कर दिए जाते हैं। विरोध करने वाले विपक्षी सांसदों को निलंबित करने में हिचकिचाहट नहीं होती और बहुत कम विधेयकों को अब संसदीय समिति के पास भेजा जाता है (मोदी के दूसरे कार्यकाल में केवल 16 फ़ीसदी और पहले कार्यकाल में 25 फ़ीसदी विधेयकों को विस्तार से चर्चा के लिए संसदीय स्थायी समितियों के पास भेजा गया, जबकि इससे पहले मनमोहन सिंह के दूसरे कार्यकाल में 71 फ़ीसदी बिलों को संसदीय समितियों के पास भेजा गया)। प्रधानमंत्री कार्यालय में रहे एक अधिकारी के मुताबिक 'प्रधानमंत्री का मानना है कि अनियंत्रित संसद और विधानसभाएं सरकार को कड़े फ़ैसले करने से रोकती हैं।' मोदी की शैली में, संसद, सरकार के निर्णयों को आगे बढ़ाने के लिए एक 'रबर स्टैम्प' भर होती है। कड़े और बड़े निर्णयों को मोदी की पहचान माना जा सकता है, जिसे वो फ़ैसले लेने वाली सरकार मानते हैं। लोकतंत्र में आमतौर पर यह अराजक रवैया माना जाता है।

इस बार भी प्रधानमंत्री विपक्ष की बात मानने को तैयार नहीं दिख रहे थे। संसद में हंगामे और विरोध से बेपरवाह प्रधानमंत्री ने कृषि क़ानूनों को पारित होने को खेती-किसानी के लिए ऐतिहासिक क्षण बताया। प्रधानमंत्री ने अपने ट्वीट में कहा, 'दशकों से किसान बिचौलियों और दूसरी बाधाओं से परेशान था। इन बिलों के पास होने से उसे इस सबसे छुटकारा मिलेगा। बिल किसानों की आमदनी दोगुनी करने और उन्हें समृद्ध बनाने में मदद करेंगे।'

मोदी की राजनीति का फोकस 'गरीब' और 'किसान' ही हैं। उनके चुनावी भाषण गरीब और किसान को लेकर उनकी प्रतिबद्धता जताए बिना पूरे नहीं होते। लोकसभा चुनावों से ठीक पहले, फरवरी 2019 में उन्होंने 'प्रधानमंत्री किसान सम्मान निधि' योजना की शुरुआत की, इस योजना में किसानों को तीन किश्तों में छह हज़ार रुपये सालाना मिलेंगे। साल 2019 के चुनाव नतीजों को देखें, तो साफ है कि इस योजना का लाभ भाजपा को मिला।

मोदी ने केवल यह आर्थिक मदद ही नहीं की, बल्कि फरवरी 2016 में प्रधानमंत्री ने अगले छह साल में किसानों की आय दोगुनी करने का संकल्प भी किया। आज़ादी के 75 साल पूरे होने पर यह उपहार साल 2022-23 में मिलना था। यह वादा आकर्षक तो था, लेकिन हक़ीकत से थोड़ा दूर था। मोदी सरकार ने किसानों की आय दोगुनी करने के लिए एक समिति (डीएफआईसी) का गठन किया। इस समिति के मुताबिक साल 2015-16 में एक किसान परिवार की सालाना आमदनी 96,703 रुपये यानी करीब आठ हज़ार रुपये महीने थी। 2022-23 तक इसे दोगुनी करने का मतलब था, 2015-16 की कीमतों पर सालाना 1,72,694 रुपये या 2022 की कीमतों के हिसाब से करीब ढाई लाख रुपये है। इसके लिए किसानों की आय में सालाना 10.4 फ़ीसदी की बढ़ोतरी की ज़रूरत होगी। जबकि उस वक्त बढ़ोतरी की रफ्तार करीब 4 फ़ीसदी थी यानी लक्ष्य से काफी दूर। दिसम्बर 2022 में तत्कालीन कृषि मंत्री नरेन्द्र सिंह तोमर ने संसद में एक लिखित जवाब में यह माना कि किसानों की आय 10,218 रुपये महीने है, जो दोगुनी से दूर है।

किसानों की आमदनी के आंकड़े भले ही सरकार के पक्ष में नहीं हों, लेकिन मोदी की राजनीति में माहौल बनाना महत्वपूर्ण है। इसका मक़सद सुर्खियां बटोरने के साथ उसे दास्तान की तरह पेश करना होता है। इसीलिए कृषि क़ानूनों को इस तरह परोसा गया, मानो वो किसानों की जिंदगी बेहतर और समृद्ध कर देंगे। सरकारी प्रचार नें पुरानी फ़िल्म, *दो बीघा ज़मीन* के गरीब, मेहनतकश, बदहाल किसान की मटमैली तस्वीर की जगह अब नयी तकनीक और नीतियों की वजह से खुशहाल, खिलखिलाते चेहरे वाले किसान के रंगीन वीडियो ने ली थी। नीति आयोग के एक अधिकारी का कहना था कि 'यह मानना गलत होगा कि कृषि क़ानूनों पर कोई सलाह-मशविरा नहीं किया गया या पूरी तैयारी नहीं की गई थी। इस पर नीतियां बनाने वालों और बड़े अर्थशास्त्रियों के साथ मशविरा किया गया था।' दरअसल नीति आयोग की पहल पर कृषि क़ानूनों को अमली जामा पहनाने की कोशिश हुई थी। मोदी ने साल 2014 में सत्ता संभालने के बाद बरसों से चल रहे योजना आयोग को बदलकर नीति आयोग बनाया था। यह सच है कि कृषि क़ानूनों पर अर्थशास्त्रियों से सलाह-मशविरा किया गया, लेकिन जिन लोगों पर इसका असर होने वाला था, उनसे यानी किसान संगठनों को इस पर भरोसे में नहीं लिया गया। वरिष्ठ अधिकारी का कहना था कि 'हमें लगा कि आम किसान के बीच प्रधानमंत्री की विश्वसनीयता इतनी है कि वो उन पर भरोसा करेंगे।'

यह सोच कितनी सही थी, यह बाद में किसान विरोध से ज़ाहिर हो गया। संसद में सरकार ने संख्या की ताकत पर बिल भले ही पास करा लिये, लेकिन बिना सलाह के किसानों को इन क़ानूनों के लिए राजी कर लेना मुमकिन नहीं था।

पंजाब के गांवों में खेती-किसानी की उतनी ही अहमियत है जितनी गुजरात के शहरों में व्यापार-धंधे की। खेती पंजाब के किसान की पहचान है। एक किसान नेता ने मुझे कहा कि उनके लिए 'ज़मीन' और 'ज़मीर' की लड़ाई बराबर है। साठ के दशक में देश में हरित क्रांति की शुरुआत पंजाब से ही हुई थी। अस्सी के दशक तक पंजाब में खेती से उत्पादन में बढोतरी की दर देश के औसत से दोगुनी थी। पंजाब में एक लाख जोत पर जहां 17,459 ट्रैक्टर थे, वहीं पूरे देश में केवल 714 ट्रैक्टर होते थे। पंजाब की सामाजिक और आर्थिक खुशहाली की वजह मेहनतकश और उद्यमी जाट सिख किसान थे।

अस्सी के दशक के बाद पंजाब खेती के लिहाज से उस तरह का खुशहाल राज्य नहीं रहा। छोटे होते खेतों और बढ़ते कर्ज से वहां किसानों की आत्महत्या की ख़बरें भी आने लगी थीं। साल 2022 की एक रिसर्च रिपोर्ट के मुताबिक पंजाब के सिर्फ़ 6 ज़िलों में 2000 से 2018 के बीच 16,594 किसानों ने आत्महत्या की थी। एक ज़माने में खुशहाल किसान, जहां पंजाब की पहचान होता था, अब उसकी जगह नशीली दवाओं और अपराध के शिकंजे में फंसने वाले नौजवानों पर बनी फ़िल्मों ने ले ली थी। फ़िल्म *उड़ता पंजाब* ऐसे ही ढहते राज्य की कहानी थी।

इसके साथ ही पंजाब की स्थानीय राजनीति में भी काफी उथल-पुथल होने लगी थी। साल 2007 से 2017 तक सरकार में रहने वाले सबसे प्रमुख अकाली दल पर भ्रष्टाचार और परिवारवाद के आरोपों से जनता में नाराज़गी दिख रही थी। कांग्रेस को इस सत्ता विरोधी भावना का फायदा मिला लेकिन अंदरूनी कलह की वजह से मुख्यमंत्री कैप्टन अमरिंदर सिंह पर पार्टी की परवाह नहीं करने और जनता से जुड़ाव नहीं होने के आरोप भी लगे। इस सबसे परेशान नौजवान नयी बनी आम आदमी पार्टी की तरफ उम्मीदों से देखने लगा। उसे वो पार्टी सत्ता-विरोधी लड़ाई लड़ती दिखी। चंडीगढ़ के एक शिक्षाविद् डॉ. प्रमोद कुमार ने कहा, 'कृषि क़ानून पंजाब में ऐसे खराब वक्त में आए, जब वो परेशानी के दौर से ही नहीं गुज़र रहा था, बल्कि वो इसके ज्लावामुखी पर बैठा था।'

केन्द्र सरकार ने भले ही इन क़ानूनों को 'सुधार' और खेती की 'बेहतरी' के तौर पर पेश किया हो, लेकिन पंजाब के गांवों में किसानों को लगा कि यह उनके खेती के पारपंरिक तरीकों को नुक़सान पहुंचा सकते थे। डॉ. कुमार का तर्क था, 'इन सुधारों से खेती का फायदा भले ही हो जाए, लेकिन किसान ख़त्म हो जाएंगे।' पंजाब के किसानों को लगा कि केन्द्र ज़बरदस्ती उनके तौर-तरीकों में दख़ल दे रहा था। पंजाब के गांवों में खेती और किसान के बीच एक अहम किरदार 'आढ़तिया' या कमीशन एजेंट होते हैं, जो किसान और खरीदारों के बीच व्यापार के लिए बिचौलिये का काम करते हैं। मोदी सरकार का कहना था कि ये क़ानून किसानों को आढ़तियों के चंगुल से मुक्ति दिलाएंगे। लेकिन किसानों के लिए आढ़तियें सिर्फ़ दलाल नहीं थे। जिला स्तर पर मंडियों में बड़ी तादाद में लाइसेंसधारी आढ़तिये होते हैं जो फसल की खरीद

और बिक्री का काम तो देखते ही हैं। कई बार उनकी परेशानी के वक्त वे कर्ज दिलाने और ज़रूरी काम कराने में भी मदद करते हैं। पंजाब में ज़्यादातर आढ़तिये जाट सिख हैं जो किसानों के साथ जुड़े हुए हैं। किसान क़ानूनों का विरोध कर रहे संगरूर के एक प्रदर्शनकारी गुरमीत सिंह का कहना था कि 'दिल्ली में अपने बंगलों में बैठकर क़ानून बनाने वाले आढ़तियों को भले ही बिचौलिए समझते हों, लेकिन वो किसान के हर अच्छे बुरे वक्त में साथ देते हैं। उनके बिना ज़िंदगी मुश्किल है, क्या कोई कॉरपोरेट हमें गांव में शादी या बीमारी के लिए जरूरत पर आढ़तियों की तरह पैसा उधार देगा?'

केन्द्र ने जब पहली बार कृषि अध्यादेशों का ऐलान किया तो, कांग्रेस ने मोदी सरकार पर किसानों के हितों को मुकेश अंबानी और गौतम अडानी जैसे बड़े अरबपतियों को बेचने का आरोप लगाया। दोनों उद्योगपति अक्सर विपक्ष के निशाने पर रहते हैं। कांग्रेस नेता राहुल गांधी ने ट्वीट कर कहा, 'इन अडानी-अंबानी कृषि क़ानूनों को तुरंत रद्द किया जाए, हमें इससे कम कुछ भी मंज़ूर नहीं है।' किसी अनहोनी की आशंका से, अंबानी के रिलायंस समूह ने तुरंत एक बयान जारी करके स्पष्ट किया कि उसने कभी कोई कॉन्ट्रैक्ट खेती नहीं की थी और न ही उनका इरादा इस क्षेत्र में कभी आने का था। लेकिन अडानी समूह के लिए चिंता की वजह बड़ी थी, क्योंकि वो पहले से ही पंजाब और हरियाणा में अनाज भंडारण का काम कर रहा था। इसी दौरान किसानों के समूहों और संगठनों के बीच एक व्हाट्सएप अभियान से अफवाह फैलाई गई कि अडानी समूह पंजाब में कृषि बाज़ार को 'अपने नियंत्रण' में लेने की योजना बना रहा था। क्रांतिकारी किसान यूनियन के नेता डॉ. दर्शन पाल का कहना था, 'हमारे दिलो-दिमाग को लगता है कि अडानी और प्रधानमंत्री मोदी के बीच एक रिश्ता है। ये सभी सुधार केवल बड़े कारपोरेट्स घरानों को फायदा पहुंचाने के लिए हैं।' अब झूठ हो या सच, जंग की भूमिका बन गई थी।

राज्यसभा में कृषि क़ानूनों को पारित हुए अभी चार दिन बीते थे कि 24 सितम्बर 2020 को, पंजाब के किसानों ने तीन दिन का 'रेल रोको' आंदोलन शुरू कर दिया। इसे कमज़ोर और छोटा बताने के लिए सरकार ने कहा कि यह प्रदर्शन पंजाब के कुछ इलाकों तक ही 'सीमित' था। लेकिन मुख्यमंत्री कैप्टन अमरिंदर सिंह को ऐसा नहीं लग रहा था। उन्होंने पहले खेती-किसानी में निजी निवेश का समर्थन किया था, लेकिन जब इस मसले पर अकाली दल ने भाजपा के साथ गठबंधन तोड़ दिया, तो कैप्टन को भी रुख बदलना पड़ा। उन्होंने चेतावनी देते हुए कहा, 'पंजाब एक सीमावर्ती राज्य है। मोदी सरकार लोगों की भावनाओं के साथ नहीं खेले। अगर कृषि क़ानूनों को वापस नहीं लिया गया, तो यह मुद्दा भड़क जाएगा।'

कैप्टन को हालात समझ आ रहे थे। रेले रोको आंदोलन के कुछ समय बाद पंजाब और हरियाणा के किसान संगठनों ने देशभर में सड़क नाकाबंदी का आह्वान किया। कृषि क़ानूनों के विरोध में 'दिल्ली चलो' के नारे के साथ उन्होंने राष्ट्रीय राजधानी की तरफ कूच कर दिया।

कोविड-19 प्रोटोकॉल का हवाला देते हुए दिल्ली पुलिस ने प्रदर्शनकारियों को शहर में घुसने की इज़ाजत नहीं दी। किसानों को रोकने के लिए पुलिस को पानी की बोछारों और लाठी बरसाने का काम भी करना पड़ा। कैप्टन सिंह ने कहा, 'मैंने टेलीविजन पर यह सब देखा था और मुझे समझ आ गया था कि यह बड़ी मुसीबत बनने वाली थी। सिख बहुत स्वाभिमानी और देशभक्त लोग हैं, लेकिन आप उनके साथ ज़बरदस्ती करेंगे तो वे चुप नहीं बैठेंगे।' कैप्टन सिंह ने गृहमंत्री से बात करके जल्दी रास्ता निकालने का अनुरोध किया। गृह मंत्रालय के आदेश पर, दिल्ली पुलिस पीछे हट गई। लेकिन किसानों ने लंबे समय तक आंदोलन चलाने के लिए दिल्ली की सीमाओं पर डेरा डाल दिया। गृह मंत्रालय के एक आला अफसर का कहना था, 'हमें लगा, सर्दियां आ गई हैं और अब किसान बाहर डेरा डालने के बजाय वापस चले जाएंगे।'

गृह मंत्रालय का शायद यह एक और गलत आंकलन था। जब मैं दिसम्बर में प्रदर्शन का जायजा लेने के लिए सिंघु बॉर्डर पहुंचा तो समझ आया कि किसानों ने लंबे आंदोलन की तैयारी कर रखी थी। टेंटों के बाहर सिख लंगर चल रहे थे, जिनमें दिन-रात भोजन की व्यवस्था थी। राशन की बोरियों के ढेर लगे थे। स्वादिष्ट खीर बनाने के लिए बड़े-बड़े हांडे ताजा दूध से भरे जा रहे थे। ताज़ा सब्जियां थी। इंतज़ाम देख रहे एक स्वयंसेवक ने कहा, 'हमारे पास एक साल तक के लिए खाने-पीने के सामान का इंतज़ाम है। कोई भी किसान भूखा नहीं रहेगा। जब तक सरकार कृषि क़ानूनों को वापस नहीं लेगी, तब तक हम यहीं रहेंगे।' सिंघु बॉर्डर पर माहौल उत्सव जैसा था, भोजन, गीत-संगीत के साथ फिटनेस सेंटर भी और राजनीतिक गर्मी भी महसूस की जा सकती थी। हर शाम को किसान नेता मंच से भाषण देते। साफ था कि किसान मोदी सरकार के फ़ैसले पर पीछे हटने वाले नहीं थे।

अब कृषि क़ानून सिर्फ़ पंजाब के किसानों का मुद्दा नहीं रह गया था। धीरे-धीरे बात पड़ोसी इलाकों तक भी पहुंचने लगी थी। पश्चिमी उत्तरप्रदेश और हरियाणा में भी जाट मौटे तौर पर खेती-किसानी करते हैं। इस इलाके की राजनीति यहां की ताकतवर 'खाप पंचायतों' के इर्द-गिर्द घूमती रही है। अस्सी के दशक में महेन्द्र सिंह टिकैत एक मजबूत किसान नेता के तौर पर उभरे। टिकैत ने भारतीय किसान यूनियन बनाकर किसानों के बिजली बिल माफ़ कराने की मांग को लेकर मुज़फ्फरनगर में एक बड़ा आंदोलन चलाया। 1988 में दिल्ली के बोट क्लब पर हुई रैली की, अब तक भी चर्चा होती है, इस रैली में पांच लाख किसान जुटे थे। फिर धीरे-धीरे किसानों पर उनका नियंत्रण कमज़ोर होता गया और 2011 में उनके निधन के बाद यूनियन ख़त्म सी हो गई।

कुछ समय बाद उनके बेटे राकेश टिकैत सामने आए। अस्सी के दशक में दिल्ली पुलिस में कॉस्टेबल रहे राकेश टिकैत ने अपने पिता के आंदोलन में शामिल होने के लिए अपनी पुलिस वर्दी को उतार दिया। सीनियर टिकैत को चुनावी राजनीति पसंद नहीं थी, जबकि बेटे राकेश राजनीति के मैदान में उतरना चाहते थे। तीखे नैन-नक्श के साथ दाढ़ी रखे, कभी किसान की

पगड़ी तो कभी टोपी पहनने वाले युवा राकेश ने पश्चिमी उत्तरप्रदेश से दो बार चुनाव लड़ा, लेकिन दोनों बार हार देखनी पड़ी। पंजाब के किसानों के आंदोलन में उन्हें एक बार फिर अपने पैर जमाने का मौका दिखाई दिया। पंजाब के किसानों के दिल्ली कूच के ऐलान के कुछ दिनों बाद राकेश टिकैत ने अपने किसान संगठन को भी इस आंदोलन से जोड़ने का फ़ैसला किया। किसान यूनियन के नेता डॉ. दर्शन पाल ने बताया कि 'हमने उनसे शामिल होने के लिए नहीं कहा था, लेकिन वे अपनी मर्जी से आंदोलन में शामिल हुए।'

दिसम्बर 2020 में, दिल्ली के गाज़ीपुर बार्डर पर जब मैंने पहली बार टिकैत का साक्षात्कार लिया, तब वे वहां उस प्रदर्शन स्थल पर अपने समर्थकों के साथ मौजूद थे और उन पर मीडिया की नज़र थी। सफेद धोती-कुर्ता, हरे रंग की आंदोलन वाली टोपी, गले में हरा-सफेद गमछा, बेतरतीब सफेद होती दाढ़ी में टिकैत ठेठ देहाती लुक में थे। उन्होंने जोरदार नारों के बीच सरकार को चेतावनी दी, 'जाट और सिख भाई-भाई हैं। हम सब किसान-पुत्र हैं। मोदी सरकार को ये काला क़ानून वापस लेना होगा!' जब मैंने उनसे कृषि क़ानून से जुड़ी दिक्कतों के बारे में पूछा, तो मेरे सवाल को दरकिनार करते हुए उन्होंने कहाः 'ये सब बाद में... मुझे आज बहुत से लोगों से मिलना है।' फिर उन्होंने अपना मोबाइल फ़ोन दिखाते हुए बताया कि 'अभी मेरी शरद पवार से बात हुई है।' कांस्टेबल से शुरू हुआ सफ़र, आंदोलनकारी किसान नेता से अब पूरी तरह से राजनेता बनते टिकैत, खुद को बड़ी 'लीग' में शामिल होते महसूस कर रहे थे।

संयुक्त किसान मोर्चा अब सरकार के लिए बड़ी चुनौती के तौर पर सामने था, इसमें किसान, राजनेता, कार्यकर्ता और प्रदर्शनकारी, हर कोई शामिल था। 2020 दिसम्बर की कड़ाके की ठंड में दिल्ली की सीमा पर डटे किसान प्रदर्शनकारियों का जोश कम नहीं हो रहा था। कोविड-19 की वजह से छवि को लेकर परेशान मोदी सरकार को नए साल की शुरुआत के साथ अहसास हुआ कि ठंड में टैंट में बैठे गुस्साए किसानों से भी उसकी छवि खराब होने लगी थी। लेकिन सवाल था कि क्या खुद की राजनीतिक ताकत पर गर्व करने वाली सरकार सड़क पर प्रदर्शन कर रहे लोगों के सामने झुक सकती थी?

किसान आंदोलन ने केन्द्रीय कृषि मंत्री नरेन्द्र सिंह तोमर को अचानक सुर्खियों में ला दिया। साठ पार के तोमर, लंबे समय तक भाजपा संगठन से जुड़े और मध्यप्रदेश से तीन बार सांसद रहे थे। मध्यप्रदेश में कमलनाथ सरकार गिराए जाने पर उन्हें मुख्यमंत्री बनाए जाने की उम्मीद थी। प्रभावशाली ओबीसी समुदाय से आने वाले तोमर को प्रधानमंत्री पसंद करते थे और उन्हें 'किसान-पुत्र' के तौर पर पेश किया गया था, लेकिन पार्टी ने नेतृत्व में बदलाव के बजाय फिर से शिवराज सिंह चौहान को ही मुख्यमंत्री बनाए रखना तय किया। आमतौर पर

चुपचाप काम करने वाले तोमर अब प्रदर्शनकारी किसानों तक मोदी सरकार की पहुंच का 'चेहरा' बन गए थे।

दिसम्बर 2020 में तोमर ने 'देश के किसानों के नाम' एक भावनात्मक चिट्ठी लिखीः

'कृषि मंत्री के तौर पर मैं यह अपनी ज़िम्मेदारी मानता हूं कि कृषि क़ानूनों के नाम पर दिल्ली की सीमा पर बैठे किसानों और सरकार के बीच जो साज़िश रची जा रही है, उसे स्पष्ट किया जाए। मैं खुद किसान परिवार से हूं और बचपन से ही उन तकलीफों को महसूस किया है। मैं यह भी समझता हूं कि फसल उगाने या बेचने के लिए क्या-क्या करना पड़ता है। मंडियों और न्यूनतम समर्थन मूल्य के नाम पर झूठ परोसा जा रहा है जबकि हक़ीकत यह है कि इससे कुछ भी बदलने वाला नहीं है।'

इस चिट्ठी से पहले कृषि मंत्री तोमर और केन्द्रीय वाणिज्य मंत्री पीयूष गोयल आंदोलन पर बैठे किसान नेताओं के साथ कई बैठक कर चुके थे, लेकिन कोई बात आगे नहीं बढ़ी थी। इन बैठकों का ज़िक्र करते हुए राकेश टिकैत ने कहा, 'ये मंत्री हमें हमारी जगह दिखाना चाहते थे। हमसे ऐसे बात की जैसे हम उनके काबिल नहीं हैं।' लेकिन कृषि मंत्री का अलग पक्ष है। तोमर का कहना था, 'हम किसी भी बात पर विचार के लिए तैयार थे। हमने कहा कि सरकार उनकी चिंताओं को ध्यान में रखते हुए संशोधन करेगी। लेकिन वे कोई समझौता नहीं चाहते थे, और सिर्फ़ एमएसपी की क़ानूनी गांरटी पर ज़ोर दे रहे थे, जो संभव नहीं था।' दोनों के बीच अविश्वास इतना बढ़ गया कि बैठकों के दौरान भी किसान, सरकारी भोजन के बजाय अपने लंगर से खाना खा रहे थे।

मौटे तौर पर विवाद सिर्फ़ एमएसपी की 'क़ानूनी गारंटी' को लेकर था। जिसका मतलब केन्द्र एक न्यूनतम समर्थन मूल्य की सिफ़ारिश करता है जिस पर गेंहू और धान समेत तेईस फसलें किसानों से खरीदी जा सकती है। किसानों की मांग थी कि डॉ. एम.एस. स्वामीनाथन की अध्यक्षता वाले राष्ट्रीय किसान आयोग ने जो 'लागत-प्लस मूल्य निर्धारण' का फॉर्मूला बनाया था, उसके हिसाब से खरीदी मूल्य की क़ानूनी गारंटी मिले, चाहे मौजूदा बाज़ार की स्थितियां कैसी भी हों। कृषि मंत्रालय को सलाह देने वाले और खेती में सुधार की ज़रूरत पर जोर देने वाले अर्थशास्त्री अशोक गुलाटी का मानना है कि 'यह मांग न केवल अव्यावहारिक है, बल्कि एमएसपी की क़ानूनी गांरटी बाज़ार के बुनियादी मांग-आपूर्ति सिद्धान्त के ख़िलाफ़ है। इससे मुआवज़े को लेकर मुकदमेबाज़ी बढ़ेगी और किसान फिर नई-नई फसलों को उगाने पर कम ध्यान देंगे।' कांग्रेस नेता राहुल गांधी ने भी उनसे मुलाकात की थी। प्रोफेसर गुलाटी ने कहा, 'मैंने राहुल को बताया कि मौजूदा कृषि क़ानून कमोबेश कांग्रेस के घोषणापत्र में शामिल प्रस्तावों

जैसे ही हैं, इसलिए क्यूं ना उनका समर्थन करके कांग्रेस इसका श्रेय ले। लेकिन राजनीति एक अलग तरह का खेल है।' दिलचस्प यह भी है कि 2011 में नरेन्द्र मोदी ने गुजरात के मुख्यमंत्री रहते हुए एमएसपी की क़ानूनी गारंटी की सिफ़ारिश की थी।

कृषि मंत्री तोमर और वाणिज्य मंत्री गोयल जब इस मसले को सुलझाने की कोशिश कर रहे थे, तब वरिष्ठ मंत्री राजनाथ सिंह को बातचीत से बाहर रखा गया, जो संभवतः इसे आगे तक ले जा सकते थे। वाजपेयी सरकार में कृषि मंत्री रहे राजनाथ सिंह के किसान संगठनों और खासतौर से उत्तरप्रदेश में अच्छे संबंध थे। तोमर ने राजनाथ सिंह से बीच का रास्ता निकालने की गुज़ारिश की। लेकिन जब बातचीत का वक्त आया, तो राजनाथ सिंह इसमें सीधे तौर पर शामिल नहीं थे। भाजपा के एक नेता ने माना कि 'राजनाथ जी अपने सहमति वाले स्वभाव और वरिष्ठ मंत्री होने के नाते किसानों के मुद्दे को बेहतर तरीके से संभाल सकते थे।'

किसान नेता टिकैत का आरोप था कि बातचीत आगे नहीं बढ़ने पर सरकार ने किसानों को बांटने की कोशिश की। उन्होंने कहा, 'कई बार मुझे फ़ोन आए कि "आप दिल्ली चलिए, हम आपकी बात सीधे बड़े नेता से कराते हैं। कितने दिन संघर्ष करोगे, एक बार मिल लो, आपके लिए सब फिट हो जाएगा"।' टिकैत ने कहा, यह आंदोलन को तोड़ने की साज़िश थी, जिसमें शामिल होने से उन्होंने मना कर दिया। टिकैत बोले, 'मैंने उन्हें साफ कहा कि वन-टू-वन मीटिंग नहीं होगी, या तो आप सभी किसान नेताओं से मुलाकात करें या फिर किसी से भी न मिलें।' चर्चा यह भी थी कि टिकैत पश्चिमी उत्तरप्रदेश के कुछ भाजपा नेताओं से संपर्क में थे, जो उन्हें विरोध प्रदर्शन से बाहर आने के लिए मनाने की कोशिश कर रहे थे। खासतौर से जब 12 जनवरी 2021 को सुप्रीम कोर्ट ने कृषि क़ानूनों को लागू करने पर रोक लगा दी और किसानों की शिकायतों पर गौर करने के लिए एक 'विशेषज्ञ समिति' बनाने के आदेश दिए।

अदालत के आदेश से किसान संगठनों के हौंसले और बढ़ गए। किसान यूनियनों ने अदालत के आदेश से पहले ही 26 जनवरी 2021 को एक 'ट्रैक्टर रैली' निकालने की घोषणा की थी। रैली के आयोजकों में से एक प्रभज्योत ने बताया कि, 'अदालती फ़ैसले के बाद हम किसानों की एक विजय परेड निकालना चाहते थे। गणतंत्र दिवस पर परेड करने वाले फौजी भी तो किसान के बेटे ही हैं। हमारा नारा था: जय जवान,जय किसान।' थोड़ी बातचीत के बाद दिल्ली पुलिस ने प्रदर्शन स्थल से दिल्ली तक एक निश्चित रास्ते पर रैली निकालने की मंज़ूरी दे दी। यह रैली किसान आंदोलन के लिए एक अहम मोड़ होगी। बातचीत के नाकाम होने और किसानों को बांटने की कोशिश के असफल होने के बाद सरकार ने एक आख़िरी चाल चलीः मुख्य धारा मीडिया और सोशल मीडिया के रास्ते प्रदर्शनकारी किसानों को राष्ट्र विरोधी 'खालिस्तानी' के रंग में रंगना शुरू किया।

दिसम्बर 2020 में, केन्द्रीय क़ानून मंत्री रविशंकर प्रसाद ने आरोप लगाया कि किसान विरोध प्रदर्शन पर 'टुकड़े टुकड़े गैंग' ने कब्ज़ा कर लिया था। भारतीय जनता पार्टी ने 'टुकड़े-टुकड़े गैंग' शब्द का इस्तेमाल सबसे पहले 2016 में जवाहर लाल नेहरु विश्वविद्यालय के छात्रों के प्रदर्शन को लेकर किया था। ये छात्र 2001 में भारतीय संसद पर हमले के दोषी अफ़ज़ल गुरु की फांसी के ख़िलाफ़ अपना गुस्सा ज़ाहिर कर रहे थे। तबसे भाजपा इस शब्द का इस्तेमाल राजनीतिक विरोधियों को 'राष्ट्रद्रोही' या 'देश को तोड़ने वाली ताकत' के रूप में प्रस्तुत करने के लिए करती है। एक और केन्द्रीय मंत्री राव साहेब दानवे थोड़ा और आगे बढ़ गए, उन्होंने आरोप लगाया कि किसान विरोध के पीछे चीन और पाकिस्तान का हाथ था। अज्ञात ख़ुफ़िया सूत्रों के हिसाब से 'अल्ट्रा लेफ्ट नक्सल' के हाथ की ओर इशारा करते हुए कृषि मंत्री नरेन्द्र सिंह तोमर और केन्द्रीय मंत्री पीयूष गोयल ने मीडिया से कहा कि आप पता लगाइए कि इन प्रदर्शनों के पीछे कौन था। आंदोलन की अगुवाई पंजाब के जाट सिख किसान कर रहे थे, तो शक की सुई को 'खालिस्तानी समर्थकों' के साथ जोड़ने में देर नहीं लगी।

खालिस्तान, पंजाब में एक संवेदनशील मुद्दा है, जो अस्सी के दशक में प्रदेश में अलगाववादी हिंसा की याद दिलाता है। बहुत से लोगों ने किसान आंदोलन में 'खालिस्तानी हाथ' के आरोप को मोदी सरकार की आंदोलन को बदनाम करने की कोशिश माना। किसान इससे और भड़क गए, उन्होंने इस प्रचार अभियान से डरने या पीछे हटने से इंकार कर दिया। 'आप मीडिया वाले जो लोग हमें खालिस्तानी कह रहे हैं, वो यहां से चले जाएं। हम किसान हैं, आतंकवादी नहीं है।' उनका गुस्सा बढ़ता जा रहा था। और जब गुस्से की चिंगारी सुलग रही हो तो उसे आग में बदलने के लिए एक ही कारण काफी होता है। दिल्ली में, गणतंत्र दिवस की 'ट्रैक्टर परेड' ने वह मौका दे दिया।

'ट्रैक्टर परेड' से एक दिन पहले 25 जनवरी को, पंजाबी अभिनेता दीप सिद्धू ने बड़े ही नाटकीय ढंग से ऐलान किया कि किसान अगले दिन लाल किले की तरफ मार्च करेंगे। संयुक्त किसान मोर्चा से जुड़े किसी दूसरे संगठन ने इस ऐलान का समर्थन नहीं किया था। किसान विरोधी प्रदर्शन में शामिल होने को लेकर सिद्धू पर पहले से ही कई सवालिया निशान लगे थे। चरमपंथियों से रिश्ते रखने के आरोपी, सिद्धू को एक वायरल हुए वीडियो में सफेद पगड़ी और काले कपड़ों में पुलिस अफसरों से सड़क पर बैरियर हटाने के लिए बहस करते देखा गया था। मैं सिद्धू से 2019 के चुनाव में पहली बार गुरुदासपुर में मिला था। उस समय वे, भाजपा के टिकट पर चुनाव लड़ रहे फ़िल्म अभिनेता सनी देओल की टीम में शामिल थे। प्रचार अभियान के दौरान सनी देओल को पकड़ पाना आसान काम नहीं था, क्योंकि वे अक्सर निर्धारित वक्त से देर से पहुंचते थे। लेकिन सिद्धू ने हमें स्टार उम्मीदवार का साक्षात्कार दिलाने में मदद की। इसके बाद सिद्धू ने कई बार मुझे फ़ोन पर कहा कि उन्हें युवाओं का बहुत समर्थन मिल रहा था।

'मेरे साथ समर्थकों की पूरी फौज है और मैं पंजाब में अगला चुनाव आसानी से जीत जाऊंगा,' वे अपनी शेखी बघार रहे थे।

दीप सिद्धू की अगुवाई वाली इस टीम को गणतंत्र दिवस पर 'किसान परेड' के दौरान भड़की हिंसा के लिए जिम्मेदार माना गया। सिद्धू समर्थक माने जाने वाले कुछ लोगों ने परेड के लिए तय रूट को छोड़ दिया, पुलिस के साथ भिड़ने की कोशिश की और जबरन लाल किले में घुसकर एक खाली 'ध्वज-स्तम्भ' पर धार्मिक सिख झंडा फहरा दिया। संयुक्त किसान मोर्चा के एक नेता ने अपनी सफाई में ज़ोर देकर कहा, 'हमने अपने लोगों को स्पष्ट निर्देश के साथ, तयमार्ग पर चलने, हर ट्रैक्टर पर तिरंगा फहराने और अनुशासन बनाए रखने के लिए कहा था। हिंसा फैलाने वाले लोग हमारे नहीं थे, वो एक बेकाबू भीड़ थी, जिसका अपना कोई एजेंडा था।'

बैरिकेड्स तोड़ने और फिर आंसू गैस के गोले चलने से शांतिपूर्ण किसान आंदोलन पर हिंसक होने का दाग़ लग गया। सांप्रदायिक और अलगाववादी सोच के लोगों ने आंदोलन को 'हाईजैक' करने की धमकी दी। मोदी सरकार हरकत में आ गई थी। उस रात केन्द्रीय क़ानून मंत्री रविशंकर प्रसाद एक बार फिर टीवी न्यूज चैनलों पर दावा कर रहे थे, 'अब हमारी बात सच साबित हो गई, इस भयावह घटना के पीछे टुकड़े-टुकड़े गैंग का हाथ है।'

हिंसा भड़कने के कुछ ही देर में प्रशासन एक्शन में आ गया। ज़िला मजिस्ट्रेट ने गाजीपुर के धरना स्थल को खाली कराने के आदेश दिए, वहां की बिजली काट दी गई, टैंट हटा दिए गए और बैरिकेड्स से रास्ता बंद कर दिया गया। 28 जनवरी को दोपहर तक अर्द्धसैनिक बलों ने मंच को घेर लिया। किसान नेता राकेश टिकैत ने मंच से कहा कि वह गिरफ़्तारी देने के लिए तैयार थे। तब तक कुछ भाजपा समर्थक भी घटनास्थल पर पहुंचकर किसानों को हटाने की मांग और नारेबाज़ी करने लगे। यही वो समय था जब टिकैत अचानक भावुक हो गए। टिकैत ने अपने भावुक भाषण में भारतीय जनता पार्टी पर पश्चिमी उत्तरप्रदेश के जाटों को धोखा देने का आरोप लगाया, जिन्होंने हाल के चुनावों में भाजपा का साथ दिया था। 'इतना बड़ा धोखा, इतनी बड़ी गद्दारी,' टिकैत का गला भरभराया हुआ था, आंखें नम हो गई थीं। टीवी चैनलों पर इन भावुक तस्वीरों को देखकर प्रदर्शनकारी फिर से जोश में आ गए। टिकैत की गीली आंखों से लड़ाई जारी रखने की भावुक अपील वायरल हो गई। अगर गणतंत्र दिवस की हिंसा किसान प्रदर्शन के लिए बड़ा झटका थी, तो टिकैत के इस भाषण ने पूरी तस्वीर बदल दी। रातों-रात एक 'नया किसान नेता' मिल गया था।

दिल्ली के दूसरी तरफ सिंघु बॉर्डर पर जमा किसानों में भी गर्मी दिखाई दे रही थी। गणतंत्र दिवस की घटना के अगले दिन, करीब सौ लोगों की भीड़ धरना-स्थल पर अचानक पहुंच गई और नारेबाजी करने लगी। प्रदर्शनकारियों की तरफ पत्थर भी फेंके जा रहे थे। पता नहीं

था कि ये कौन लोग थे, लेकिन आंदोलनकारी किसानों की मानें तो ये बीजेपी के समर्थन वाले 'बाहरी' लोग थे। किसान नेता हरमीत सिंह ने दावा किया कि 'ये लोग हमें प्रदर्शन स्थल से हटाना चाहते थे और पुलिस बस देखती रही।' यह बात तब स्पष्ट हो गई कि पुलिस किसानों को बाहर निकालना चाहती थी, जब कुछ ही देर में वहां बैरिकेड्स लगा दिए गए, कांटेदार तारों और कंक्रीट सीमेंट के ब्लॉक्स लगाने के साथ सड़क पर नुकीली कीलें ठोक दी गईं। धरना स्थल को जंग के मैदान की तरह तब्दील किया जा रहा था। प्रदर्शनकारियों को अलग-थलग करने के इंतज़ाम किए गए थे। हरियाणा के दो दर्जन से ज़्यादा ज़िलों में इंटरनेट सेवाएं बंद कर गईं। लेकिन हुआ उल्टा, सरकार की सख्ती ने किसानों को और मजबूती से डटे रहने के लिए तैयार कर दिया। एक नौजवान किसान ने कहा, 'हमारे पास एक साल तक के भोजन और जरूरत का इंतज़ाम था। मैंने अपने पिता से वादा किया था कि मैं जंग जीते बिना वापस नहीं लौटूंगा।'

हकीकत में यह एक ऐसा युद्ध था, जिसे सरकार, जनता की नज़र में नहीं जीत पा रही थी। अब तक मोदी सरकार की कामयाबी उसकी हर चीज़ों पर नियंत्रण की ताकत को लेकर थी। लेकिन अब मुख्य सड़कों पर लोहे की नुकीली कीलें और बैरिकेड्स की भयावह तस्वीरें, किसानों को डराने के लिए प्रशासनिक ताकत बता रही थी कि केन्द्र आम लोगों के साथ कैसा बर्ताव कर रहा था। एक तरफ उत्तर-भारत की कड़ाके की ठंड में ठिठुरते बहादुर किसान थे तो दूसरी तरफ 'लुटियन दिल्ली' के गर्म बंगलों में मोदी और उनके बड़े लोग आराम कर रहे थे। यूं देखें तो दोनों के बीच कोई मुकाबला नहीं था। लेकिन इस बार मोदी के विरोधियों का संदेश और सहानुभूति आगे बढ़ रहे थे। एक 'तानाशाह' प्रधानमंत्री उत्तर भारत की 'किसान बैल्ट' में हर किसी की ज़ुबान पर चढ़ने लगा था।

प्रधानमंत्री मोदी ने संसद में बिना किसी संवेदना के, नाराज़गी के अंदाज़ में जवाब दिया। 8 फरवरी 2021 को संसद में राष्ट्रपति के अभिभाषण पर धन्यवाद प्रस्ताव का जवाब देते हुए प्रधानमंत्री ने प्रदर्शनकारियों पर हमला बोला, और उनके लिए एक नया शब्द 'आंदोलन-जीवी' गढ़ दिया। भाषण में किसानों की चिंता कहीं नहीं थी। प्रधानमंत्री ने कहा, 'ये परजीवी हर आंदोलन में मौज उड़ाते हैं। जब वे सामने नहीं दिखते, तब पर्दे की पीछे से काम करते हैं, दरअसल वो आंदोलन के बिना जी ही नहीं सकते।' एक और नया शब्द था, विदेशी विनाशकारी विचारधारा (**FDI**)। प्रदर्शनकारियों पर विदेशी ताकतों के साथ के आरोप थे। मोदी ने चेतावनी के स्वर में कहा, 'हमें ऐसी विचारधारा से बचने की ज़रूरत है।' लगा, मानो यह किसी प्रधानमंत्री कद के राजनेता का नहीं, बल्कि एक 'गर्म मिज़ाजी दंगाई राजनेता' का भाषण हो। मोदी किसान आंदोलन के सामने लड़खड़ाते से दिखे। उन्होंने काफी हद तक ज़मीन खो दी थी। अन्नदाता किसानों को प्रधानमंत्री आंदोलन-जीवी कह रहे थे। बातचीत की उम्मीद खत्म हो गई थी। किसान

अपने आंदोलन के साथ डटे हुए थे, प्रधानमंत्री उनसे बातचीत करने को तैयार नहीं थे—ऐसे में यह गतिरोध कब तक चलेगा, कहा नहीं जा सकता!

═

भारत-नेपाल सीमा पर रोहेलखंड में बसा लखीमपुर खीरी उत्तरप्रदेश का सबसे बड़ा ज़िला ही नहीं है, उसे 'चीनी की कटोरा' भी कहा जाता है। मोटे तौर पर इस इलाके की अर्थव्यवस्था गन्ने की खेती और उससे बनी चीनी और दूसरे उत्पादों पर निर्भर है। तराई इलाके की नदियों की वजह से यह ज़मीन काफी उपजाऊ है और इसलिए आज़ादी के वक्त, विभाजन के बाद पचास के दशक में पंजाब के उद्यमी किसान यहां आकर बसने लगे। लखीमपुर खीरी के सिख किसानों में ज़्यादातर के पास गन्ने के खेत हैं और वे पंजाब के किसानों जैसे हैं। दिल्ली की सीमा पर चल रहे किसान आंदोलन से उनका जुड़ाव है। आंदोलन की गूंज यहां सुनाई देती है। प्राइवेट चीनी मिलों के किसानों को बकाया भुगतान नहीं करने से यहां भी बेचैनी बढ़ गई थी। स्थानीय किसान अपनी परेशानी बताने का मौका ढूंढ रहे थे। उत्तरप्रदेश के उपमुख्यमंत्री केशव प्रसाद मौर्य के तीन अक्टूबर 2021 को उस इलाके में दौरे से किसानों को वह मौका मिल गया। बहुत से लोग अपने ट्रैक्टरों पर काले झंडे लगाकर हैलीपेड तक पहुंच गए। मौर्य के मेजबान केन्द्रीय गृह राज्य मंत्री और भाजपा सांसद अजय मिश्रा 'टेनी' थे। टेनी ने अपने गांव तिकुनिया में सालाना 'कुश्ती प्रतियोगिता' का आयोजन किया था, इसमें मौर्य को पुरस्कार वितरण करना था। लेकिन इस बार दंगल समारोह ने भीषण रूप ले लिया।

बताया जाता है कि उस दिन दोपहर में जब किसान अपने विरोध प्रदर्शन के बाद लौट रहे थे, तो आरोप है कि केन्द्रीय मंत्री अजय मिश्रा के बेटे आशीष मिश्रा की अगुवाई में एसयूवी गाड़ियों का एक काफ़िला पीछे से आया। उनमें से एक गाड़ी ने भीड़ में घुसकर किसानों को टक्कर मारी। जब किसानों ने रास्ता रोकने की कोशिश की तो दो और गाड़ियों ने तेज़ी से आगे बढ़कर किसानों को कुचल दिया, जिससे उनकी मौत हो गई। कुचले गए चारों सिख किसान थे। इसके बाद किसानों और काफ़िले के लोगों के बीच हुई झड़प में चार और लोग मारे गए, इनमें तीन स्थानीय भाजपा कार्यकर्ता और एक पत्रकार शामिल था। इस वीभत्स हिंसा का वीडियो सामने आने के बाद न्यूज चैनलों पर 'निर्मम हत्या' की खबरें तेज़ हो गईं। इनमें वो चैनल भी शामिल थे, जिन्हें कुछ लोग 'सत्ता के साथ' दिखने वाले चैनल मानते थे। कथित तौर पर केन्द्र सरकार के एक मंत्री के बेटे के वीआईपी काफिले ने निहत्थे, निर्दोष आंदोलनकारी किसानों की हत्या कर दीः मोदी सरकार के लिए इससे बुरी ख़बर नहीं हो सकती थी। बात तब और बिगड़ गई, जब एक पुराने वीडियो में केन्द्रीय मंत्री अजय मिश्रा किसानों को धमकाते हुए दिखाई दिएः 'सुधर जाओ, वरना सुधार देंगे'। मिश्रा बोले, 'अगर मैंने उन्हें अपनी असली ताकत दिखा दी

तो उन्हें गांव नहीं, ज़िला भी छोड़कर जाना पड़ेगा।' गुंडागर्दी करते मंत्री की इस खुली धमकी की वजह से मोदी सरकार को और शर्मिंदा होना पड़ा।

भाजपा के एक बड़े नेता ने माना कि 'हमें अहसास हो गया था कि लखीमपुर में जो कुछ हुआ, उसकी माफ़ी नहीं हो सकती; मुश्किल यह थी कि हमें नहीं पता था कि शुरू में हमें क्या कहना था।' नुक़सान की भरपाई के लिए भाजपा प्रवक्ताओं को संदेश था कि कोई भी टीवी बहस पर मंत्री या उनके बेटे का बचाव नहीं करेगा। प्रधानमंत्री और दूसरे बड़े मंत्रियों ने चुप्पी साध ली थी। जब मैंने मिश्रा से बात करने की कोशिश की, तो उनके सहयोगी ने रूखेपन से जवाब दिया, 'आप जैसे टीवी पत्रकार से हम सवाल क्यों लें?' इस मुद्दे पर केवल पड़ोसी पीलीभीत संसदीय क्षेत्र के भाजपा नेता और सांसद वरुण गांधी ने प्रतिक्रिया दी। वरुण ने ट्वीट किया, 'वीडियो बिल्कुल स्पष्ट है। हत्या के जरिए प्रदर्शनकारियों को चुप नहीं कराया जा सकता। निर्दोष किसानों के ख़ून की जवाबदेही तय होनी चाहिए।' भारतीय जनता पार्टी ने वरुण के बयान पर कोई टिप्पणी नहीं की। इसके बजाय, कुछ दिनों बाद वरुण और उनकी मां मेनका गांधी का नाम पार्टी की राष्ट्रीय कार्यकारिणी की नई सूची में शामिल नहीं था। फिर 2024 में वरुण गांधी को लोकसभा का टिकट नहीं दिया गया।

दिलचस्प बात यह है कि जब केन्द्र सरकार अजय मिश्रा और उनके बेटे पर कार्रवाई को लेकर टालमटोल कर रही थी, तब उत्तरप्रदेश के मुख्यमंत्री योगी आदित्यनाथ ने भरोसा दिलाया कि 'किसी को बख्शा नहीं जाएगा।' घटना के एक हफ्ते के भीतर ही मंत्री के फरार बेटे आशीष को पुलिस ने गिरफ़्तार कर लिया। मामले की जांच विशेष जांच टीम (एसआईटी) को सौंप दी गई। एसआईटी की रिपोर्ट में किसानों की मौत का कारण केवल लापरवाही से गाड़ी चलाना नहीं बल्कि पूर्व नियोजित साज़िश बताया गया था। इस मामले में पुलिस ने हत्या, आपराधिक साज़िश और दंगा करने के आरोप दर्ज किए। यानी मंत्री के बेटे को लंबे समय तक जेल में रहना पड़ेगा।

लेकिन मिश्रा के मंत्री पद से इस्तीफ़े की मांग के बावजूद मोदी सरकार ने कोई फ़ैसला नहीं किया। मिश्रा पर पहले ही एक हत्या का मामला चल रहा था। इसमें शिकायतकर्ता का आरोप था कि मिश्रा ने साल 2000 में पंचायत चुनाव के दौरान तिकुनिया में दिनदहाड़े मुख्य सड़क पर उनके बेटे को सिर में गोली मार दी थी। यह मामला सालों-साल चलता रहा, लेकिन जातिगत राजनीति के कारण मिश्रा के राजनीतिक रसूख में कमी नहीं आई और जुलाई 2021 में हुए कैबिनेट फेरबदल के बावजूद उनकी मंत्री की कुर्सी बरकरार रही। भाजपा ब्राह्मणों को नाराज़ नहीं करना चाहती थी। दो बार के सांसद मिश्रा ने ब्राह्मणों का समर्थन जुटाने और ताकत दिखाने के लिए रोहेलखंड इलाके में 'आशीर्वाद यात्रा' निकाली।

दरअसल मिश्रा की ताकत सिर्फ़ ब्राह्मण राजनीति ही नहीं थी, उन पर गृहमंत्री अमित शाह का आशीर्वाद भी था, जो उत्तरप्रदेश की राजनीति में गहरा दखल रखते थे। इस बात का

अंदाज़ा इससे लगाया जा सकता है कि लखीमपुर की घटना के कुछ दिनों बाद लखनऊ में गृहमंत्री अमित शाह के साथ मिश्रा पुलिस अफसरों के उस कार्यक्रम में मंच साझा कर रहे थे, जिसमें क़ानून व्यवस्था पर चर्चा होनी थी। शाह ने अपने किसी सहयोगी मंत्री को मिश्रा के बारे में बोला, 'ज़मीन से जुडा नेता है, डायनमिक लीडर है, चुनाव जीतना जानता है।' कुछ पत्रकारों ने जब मिश्रा को हटाने की विपक्ष की मांग पर शाह से सवाल किया, तो गृहमंत्री ने हमलावर अंदाज़ में जवाब दिया, 'किसी के बेटे ने कोई अपराध किया है, तो उसके पिता को इस्तीफ़ा क्यों देना चाहिए, मुझे बताइए कि क्या मिश्रा भी उस घटना में शामिल है?' राजनीतिक ताकत ने मिश्रा के अपराध को नज़रअंदाज़ कर दिया था। चुनावी हिसाब-किताब को समझने वाली यह मोदी-नेतृत्व वाली नई भारतीय जनता पार्टी है। इसके बाद पार्टी ने 2024 के लोकसभा चुनावों में मिश्रा को सिर्फ टिकट ही नहीं दिया, बल्कि उनके चुनाव प्रचार के दौरान अमित शाह ने लोगों को भरोसा दिलाया कि वे मिश्रा को फिर से सांसद चुने जाने पर 'बड़ा आदमी' बनाएंगे, लेकिन जनता ने उन्हें 34,000 वोटों से हरा दिया।

गृहमंत्री ने जिस तरह से लखीमपुर खीरी हिंसा से निपटने की कोशिश की, उससे गुजरात और अब केन्द्र में मोदी-शाह के काम करने का अंदाज़ा लगाया जा सकता है। एक विवादास्पद मंत्री को कैबिनेट फेरबदल में चुपचाप हटाया जा सकता होगा, लेकिन विपक्ष की मांग पर तो हर्गिज़ नहीं। एक बार गुजरात में सभी दलों की बैठक के दौरान एक कांग्रेसी नेता ने मुख्यमंत्री मोदी से पूछा कि भ्रष्टाचार के आरोपी एक मंत्री को क्यों नहीं हटाया गया? मोदी ने उनकी बात को ख़ारिज़ करते हुए कहा, 'सरकार हमें चलानी है, आपको और विपक्ष को नहीं।' मोदी शासन के लिए दूसरों में भय पैदा करने की कोशिश करते हैं। जब आप यह दिखाते हैं कि आप कुछ भी कर सकते हैं तो विरोधी हैरान होते हैं।

लखीमपुर खीरी कांड के कुछ दिनों बाद प्रधानमंत्री की मुलाक़ात एक खास मेहमान, जम्मू कश्मीर के राज्यपाल रहे और अब मेघालय के राज्यपाल सत्यपाल मलिक से हुई। सत्तर के दशक में लोकदल के युवा नेता के तौर पर उभरे मलिक की पहचान किसान-पुत्र के रूप में रही है। मलिक ने प्रधानमंत्री से अपील की, 'इतने सारे किसान मर गए हैं, आपको कृषि क़ानूनों को वापस लेना चाहिए, ताकि इस विरोध पर रोक लग सके, वरना इसका असर चुनावों पर पड़ सकता है।' प्रधानमंत्री ने उन्हें घूरते हुए जवाब दिया, 'सत्यपाल जी, आपको इतनी चिंता करने की ज़रूरत नहीं है। किसान जल्दी ही अपना प्रदर्शन छोड़कर, अपने घर लौट जाएंगे।' चाय आ गई थी, लेकिन प्रधानमंत्री जब बीच में ही उठ गए, तो राज्यपाल मलिक को भी तुरंत बाहर निकलना पड़ा। मलिक का कहना था, 'उन्होंने मेरी तरफ ऐसे देखा, मानो मैंने किसानों की मौत का मुद्दा उठाकर कोई पाप कर दिया हो। उस दिन प्रधानमंत्री आवास से निकलते वक्त मैंने मन बना लिया कि अब फिर प्रधानमंत्री से मुलाक़ात नहीं करूंगा। इससे पहले मैं

समझता था कि प्रधानमंत्री का दिल किसानों के लिए धड़कता है, लेकिन उस दिन समझ आया कि उन्हें सिर्फ अपनी कुर्सी और छवि की चिंता थी। वो दुनिया में कहीं भी, किसी की भी मौत पर टिप्पणी और ट्वीट कर सकते हैं, लेकिन हमारे उन किसानों के लिए उनके पास सहानुभूति के दो शब्द नहीं हैं, जो मर गए।' राजनीतिक लड़ाई में कभी पीछे नहीं हटने वाले मलिक ने किसानों के मुद्दे पर मोदी सरकार के ख़िलाफ़ बड़ा हमला किया था। केन्द्र सरकार के ख़िलाफ़ किसी राज्यपाल का यह व्यवहार सामान्य नहीं था। 'मैं पहले एक किसान हूं, फिर कोई सार्वजनिक पद पर बैठा शख्स। अगर प्रधानमंत्री चाहते हैं कि मैं इस्तीफ़ा दूं, तो मैं इसमें देर नहीं करूंगा, मुझे कुर्सी से कोई प्यार नहीं है।' मलिक ने मुझे उस वक्त दिए एक साक्षात्कार में साफगोई से कहा।

बाग़ी हो गए मलिक को सरकार ने इस्तीफ़ा देने के लिए नहीं कहा, लेकिन उन्होंने अक्टूबर 2022 में अपना कार्यकाल ख़त्म होने तक नाराजगी कम नहीं की। अप्रैल 2023 में वरिष्ठ पत्रकार करण थापर को दिए एक साक्षात्कार के बाद वे फिर से सुर्खियों में थे। साक्षात्कार में मलिक ने प्रधानमंत्री मोदी पर जम्मू-कश्मीर के राज्यपाल के रूप में उन्हें चुप कराने का आरोप लगाया। मलिक ने 2019 के चुनावों से पहले पुलवामा में हुए आंतकी हमले के लिए कथित सुरक्षा लापरवाही के बारे में विस्तार से बात की। क्या वो अब यह बात बोलकर मोदी से हिसाब बराबर करने की कोशिश कर रहे थे? मलिक ने ज़ोर देकर कहा, 'बदला नहीं, बदलाव होना चाहिए।' प्रधानमंत्री ने अपनी आदत के मुताबिक मलिक के अप्रमाणित आरोपों का कोई जवाब नहीं दिया। मोदी की राजनीति में किसी आलोचना का जवाब कमज़ोरी समझा जाता है और वे उन्हें चुनौती देने वाले किसी व्यक्ति को जवाब देने से बचते हैं।

═

कृषि क़ानूनों के ख़िलाफ़ चल रहे आंदोलन को अब एक साल पूरा होने को था और इसके ख़त्म होने के आसार फिलहाल नहीं दिख रहे थे। प्रदर्शनकारियों पर प्रधानमंत्री के रवैये और लखीमपुर खीरी कांड पर चुप्पी ने इसे और गंभीर बना दिया था। किसानों पर बेरहमी की तस्वीरों के वायरल होने से प्रदर्शनकारी किसानों का गुस्सा तो बढ़ा ही था, लेकिन आम लोगों में भी उनके पक्ष में माहौल बनने लगा। भारतीय जनता पार्टी के अक्टूबर 2021 में कराए गए 'मासिक ट्रैकर पोल' में बताया गया कि किसानों की बेचैनी का असर चुनाव नतीजों पर पड़ सकता है, खासतौर से उत्तरप्रदेश में तो इसका असर रहेगा ही। सर्वेक्षण में पूछे गए एक सवाल के जवाब में ज़्यादातर किसानों का मानना था कि सरकार को कृषि क़ानूनों को वापस ले लेना चाहिए। इसके बाद नवम्बर की शुरुआत में पार्टी के वरिष्ठ नेता और केन्द्रीय सड़क परिवहन मंत्री नितिन गडकरी ने प्रधानमंत्री से मुलाकात में कृषि क़ानूनों पर असंतोष की बात की और इन क़ानूनों

की रणनीतिक वापसी का सुझाव दिया। इससे पहले साल 2015 में सरकार ने विपक्षी दलों और किसान संगठनों के विरोध के बाद विवादास्पद भूमि अधिग्रहण क़ानून को वापस ले लिया था। इस बार मोदी झुकने को तैयार नहीं दिख रहे थे। बताया जाता है कि उन्होंने गडकरी से कहा, वे दबाव की राजनीति के आगे नहीं झुकेंगे। 'अगर हम दबाव में आते तो आपको लगता है कि हम यहां तक पहुंचते,' मोदी ने अपने वरिष्ठ सहयोगी से कहा।

गडकरी के साथ मोदी की बैठक के कुछ दिनों बाद राष्ट्रीय स्वयंसेवक संघ के प्रमुख डॉ. मोहन भागवत ने प्रधानमंत्री को फ़ोन किया। मोदी और भागवत के रिश्ते आपसी समझ के हैं और दोनों अपनी सीमाएं जानते हैं, लेकिन दोनों की हिन्दू राष्ट्र को लेकर प्रतिबद्धता एक जैसी ही है। संघ प्रमुख सरकार के रोज़मर्रा के कामकाज और नीतियों में दख़ल नहीं देते, तो प्रधानमंत्री संघ के सांस्कृतिक कार्यक्रमों से दूरी रखते हैं। वाजपेयी सरकार के वक्त संघ नेतृत्व कई बार सरकार की आलोचना करता था, लेकिन अब ऐसा नहीं होता। अब ज़्यादातर समय सरकार की ही चलती है, डॉ. भागवत 'लक्ष्मण रेखा' को नहीं लांघते। यहां तक कि कोविड संकट के दौरान प्रवासी मजदूरों की परेशानी पर संघ के कई बड़े पदाधिकारियों ने नाखुशी जाहिर की थी, लेकिन संघ प्रमुख ने उस बात को ज़्यादा तूल नहीं दिया। इस बार भारतीय किसान संघ की तरफ से सरसंघचालक पर किसानों के गतिरोध का हल निकालने के लिए दबाव बन रहा था। किसान संघ का ज़ोर था कि उपज की बिक्री और खरीद पर न्यूनतम समर्थन मूल्य की 'क़ानूनी गारंटी' होनी चाहिए। दूसरे किसान संगठनों की भी यही सबसे प्रमुख मांग थी।

जब संघ प्रमुख ने प्रधानमंत्री से कृषि क़ानूनों पर फिर से विचार करने के लिए जोर दिया तो शुरुआत में तो उन्होंने खारिज करते हुए कहा, 'यह सिर्फ़ कुछ आंदोलनजीवी हैं, जो इसका विरोध कर रहे हैं, लेकिन ज़्यादातर लोग इसके पक्ष में हैं।' आरएसएस प्रमुख की बातचीत के कुछ दिनों बाद प्रधानमंत्री कार्यालय को भी यह ख़तरे की घंटी सुनाई देने लगी थी। पार्टी के स्थानीय नेताओं के आधार पर मिली रिपोर्ट से 'फीडबैक' देने वालों ने भी 'पोल ट्रैकर' की रिपोर्ट को सही माना: उत्तरप्रदेश में ज़्यादातर किसान कृषि क़ानूनों को वापस लेना चाहते थे। भारतीय जनता पार्टी के एक वरिष्ठ नेता ने बताया, 'हमें इस बात पर आश्चर्य नहीं था कि पंजाब के किसान इसके ख़िलाफ़ थे, लेकिन यूपी से भी यही रिपोर्ट मिलना चिंता की बात थी।'

प्रधानमंत्री मोदी की छवि एक 'दंबग राजनेता' की है जो अक्सर संघर्ष में जीत हासिल करता है और दबाव के आगे नहीं झुकता। मोदी के लिए उत्तरप्रदेश सिर्फ़ युद्ध का मैदान भर नहीं है। वह अब उनकी कर्मभूमि भी है, जिसके साथ उन्होंने एक निजी और राजनीतिक गहरा रिश्ता बना लिया था। मौजूदा हालात का सामना करते हुए भी वे अपनी प्रतिष्ठा को दांव पर नहीं लगा सकते थे, साथ ही वे विपक्ष को भी एक मौका नहीं देना चाहते थे। आखिरकार, प्रधानमंत्री मोदी ने कृषि मंत्री नरेन्द्र सिंह तोमर, रक्षा मंत्री राजनाथ सिंह और गृहमंत्री अमित शाह के साथ एक

बैठक कर कृषि क़ानूनों को वापस लेने के अपने फ़ैसले के बारे में बताया। लेकिन ज़ोर अब भी इस बात पर था कि इस फ़ैसले को इस तरह से पेश किया जाए कि प्रधानमंत्री की 'नैतिक जीत' दिखाई दे। एक सहयोगी ने इसके कुछ दिनों बाद 19 नवम्बर 2021 को पड़ने वाली गुरुनानक जयंती के मौके पर ऐलान करने का सुझाव दिया। उनका मानना था कि 'ज्यादातर प्रदर्शनकारी सिख हैं, तो उस हिसाब से इसका फायदा हो सकता है।' राजनीति में हर चीज़ को नापतौल से देखने वाले मोदी ने इसे तुरंत मान लिया। मौके का फायदा उठाने में कुछ ही दूसरे राजनेता उनसे बेहतर हो सकते हैं। मोदी के लिए राजनीति एक ऐसी कला है जिसमें पटकथा और दूसरी चीज़ों को ध्यान में रखकर वे बेहतर प्रदर्शन करते हैं। उन्हें राजनीतिक ज़रूरत के वक्त लचीला होने में देर नहीं लगती।

'मैंने जो कुछ भी किया, किसानों के लिए किया। मैं जो कर रहा हूं, वह देश के लिए कर रहा हूं।' भावुक दिखते प्रधानमंत्री ने घोषणा की कि वे उन कृषि क़ानूनों को वापस ले रहे थे, जिनकी वजह से एक साल से आंदोलन चल रहा था। मई 2014 में सत्ता संभालने के बाद मोदी के लिए अब तक की यह सबसे बड़ी और शर्मनाक हार जैसी थी, बिना किसी हो-हल्ला के सुबह नौ बजे इसकी घोषणा की गई, जब लोग गुरुनानक जयंती मनाने की तैयारी में लगे थे। अक्सर टीवी के 'प्राइम टाइम' का इस्तेमाल प्रधानमंत्री किसी बड़े फ़ैसले को नाटकीय तौर पर रखने के लिए करते हैं। इस बार उन्हें हार में विनम्र दिखना था, यहां तक कि माफ़ी भी मांगनी पड़ी, जो आमतौर पर नहीं होता। 'मैं देश की जनता से माफ़ी मांगता हूं, कि तमाम कोशिशों के बावजूद हम किसानों को राजी नहीं कर पाए।'

लेकिन इस माफ़ी के वक्त भी लखीमपुरी खीरी की घटना या फिर विरोध प्रदर्शन के दौरान मारे गए किसानों पर कोई अफसोस नहीं जताया गया था। (संयुक्त किसान मोर्चा ने बाद में दावा किया कि आंदोलन के दौरान 702 किसानों की मौत हुई थी।) इसके बावजूद, मोदी ने ज़ोर देकर कहा, उनकी सरकार ने किसानों की मदद के लिए 'हरसंभव काम' किया था। प्रधानमंत्री मोदी ने दावा किया, 'अपने जीवन के पांच दशकों से अधिक समय में मैंने किसानों के संघर्ष को करीब से देखा है और यही वजह है कि मेरी सरकार ने हमेशा किसानों के मुद्दों को प्राथमिकता दी।' मोदी की यही पहचान है। किसान आंदोलन के दौरान आंसू गैस और लाठी चलवाने के बावजूद मोदी ने गरीब किसान को फिर से अपने साथ खड़े करने की कोशिश की।

कृषि क़ानूनों की वापसी ने मोदी की अजेय छवि में दरार डाल दी थी। उनकी हमलावर राजनीतिक शैली, उनके राजनीतिक विरोधियों को तो घेरने में कामयाब थी, लेकिन परेशान और बेचैन किसानों और उनके 'जय जवान, जय किसान' के नारों से वे निपट नहीं पा रहे थे। खासतौर से चुनावों से पहले यह मुमकिन नहीं लग रहा था, जिन्हें वे हर हाल मे जीतना चाहते थे। इस फ़ैसले से उन्हें फौरी राहत भले ही मिली हो, लेकिन उनकी किसान समर्थक

छवि फिर वैसी नहीं रही। सत्ता में सात साल तक सबसे ताकतवर प्रधानमंत्री रहे मोदी अब कमज़ोर नज़र आ रहे थे। बेशक, प्रधानमंत्री मोदी अब भी 'दिल्ली सल्तनत' के सबसे बड़े चेहरे थे, लेकिन विधानसभा चुनावों में बीजेपी को अपनी लोकसभा की कामयाबी को दोहरा पाना मुश्किल लग रहा था। दो अहम लडाइयों ने मोदी-शाह टीम के 'अजेय' होने के दावे को दरक दिया था।

5

पवार साहेब और ममता दीदी: खेला होबे

टेलीविजन न्यूज़ चैनल्स में काम करने वाले टीवी पत्रकार की हालत किसी अस्पताल के इमरजेंसी वार्ड में तैनात डॉक्टर जैसी होती है: हर वक्त कॉल पर। डॉक्टरों की तरह पत्रकारों को भी लगता है कि कभी-कभी फ़ोन को 'स्विच ऑफ' कर दिया जाए। 23 नवम्बर 2019 की सुबह मेरा मन अपने कुत्ते के साथ लंबी सैर पर जाने, अच्छा भरपेट नाश्ता करने और फिर दोपहर में थोड़ी झपकी लेने का था। शायद यही वजह रही होगी कि जब सवेरे साढ़े सात बजे मोबाइल की घंटी बजने लगी, तो मन हुआ कि फ़ोन को बंद कर दूं। फ़ोन स्क्रीन पर इंडिया टुडे 'असाइनमेंट डेस्क' का नंबर चमक रहा था। फ़ोन उठाया तो दूसरी तरफ से तेज़ आवाज़ थी: 'ब्रेकिंग न्यूज़। सर, हमें आपका तुरंत "लाइव फोनो" चाहिए,' मेरे सहयोगी की आवाज़ में सांस की तेजी महसूस हो रही थी। 'मुंबई में राजभवन में शपथग्रहण समारोह शुरू होने वाला है। देवेन्द्र फडनवीस और अजित पवार वहां पहुंचे हुए हैं,' उनकी आखिरी बात ने मुझे झटका सा दिया। एक मिनट रुकिए, शपथ ग्रहण? कौन? फडनवीस और अजित पवार इतने सवेरे शपथ ले रहे हैं? लगा, क्या मैं कोई नया राजनीतिक सपना देख रहा था?

पिछली रात देर तक मैं महाराष्ट्र में चल रही राजनीतिक उठापटक पर ही 'न्यूज़ शो' कर रहा था। 'एनसीपी-शिवसेना-कांग्रेस, महाविकास अघाड़ी गठबंधन मज़बूत हुआ; उद्धव ठाकरे महाराष्ट्र के नए मुख्यमंत्री हो सकते हैं,' यह देर रात तक की ख़बर थी। ऑफिस से लौटते वक्त, मैंने शिवसेना नेता को शुभकामना संदेश भी भेजा था। ठाकरे के 'धन्यवाद इमोजी' के साथ संदेश में 'जय महाराष्ट्र' लिखा था। अब सिर्फ़ आठ घंटे बाद, मैं एक बार फिर 'लाइव ऑन एयर' था, दर्शकों को यह बताने के लिए कि बीजेपी के देवेन्द्र फडनवीस नए मुख्यमंत्री के रूप

में शपथ ले रहे थे और एनसीपी के अजित पवार उनके साथ उप-मुख्यमंत्री होंगे। मुझे याद आया कि ब्रिटिश प्रधानमंत्री हेरॉल्ट विल्सन का यह बयान बहुत प्रसिद्ध हुआ कि 'राजनीति में एक सप्ताह बहुत लंबा समय होता है', लेकिन महाराष्ट्र में शायद 'कुछ घंटे' भी राजनीतिक बदलाव के लिए काफी थे।

राष्ट्रवादी कांग्रेस पार्टी (एनसीपी) के प्रमुख शरद पवार भी उस रात काफी देर से सोए थे। वे देर रात तक कांग्रेस और शिवसेना के नेताओं के साथ बैठक में गठबंधन के रास्ते में आने वाली गाठों को सुलझाने की कोशिश में लगे थे। मुंबई के नेहरू सेंटर में हुई बैठक में पवार और उस समय कांग्रेस के महाराष्ट्र में प्रभारी नेता मल्लिकार्जुन खड़गे के साथ विधानसभा अध्यक्ष पद को लेकर काफी गरमागरमी हो गई थीः कांग्रेस स्पीकर पद अपने पास रखना चाहती थी, जबकि एनसीपी झुकने के लिए तैयार नहीं थी। नाराज़ पवार अचानक बैठक से उठकर चले गए और उनके पीछे-पीछे उनके भतीजे और एनसीपी के नेता अजित पवार भी दौड़े। घर पहुंचने के बाद पवार मामले को सुलझाने के लिए देर तक फ़ोन पर बात करते रहे। अकेले अजित पवार से उनकी बात नहीं हो पाई थी, क्योंकि उनका फोन 'स्विच ऑफ' दिखा रहा था। पवार को बताया गया कि 'अजित दादा किसी ज़रूरी काम से अपने वकीलों से मिलने गए हैं।' पवार सारे फ़ोन निपटाने के बाद देर रात सोने चले गए, उन्हें उम्मीद थी कि शुरुआती रुकावटों के बावजूद गठबंधन पटरी पर था। सुबह करीब सात बजे पार्टी के एक विधायक ने उन्हें जगाया और बताया कि अजित पवार, भाजपा नेता देवेन्द्र फडनवीस के साथ राजभवन में थे और 'शपथग्रहण शुरू होने वाला है साहेब'। करीब अस्सी साल के शरद पवार 'साहेब' आसानी से परेशान नहीं होते। पांच दशकों के राजनीतिक सफ़र में उन्होंने बहुत से उतार-चढ़ाव देखे थे। 38 साल की उम्र में वे महाराष्ट्र के सबसे युवा मुख्यमंत्री बन गए थे, हालांकि वो एक से ज्यादा मौकों पर प्रधानमंत्री की कुर्सी तक पहुंचते-पहुंचते चूक गए। कैंसर से लंबी लड़ाई के बावजूद, पवार साहेब का दृढ़ निश्चय ही उनकी सबसे बड़ी खूबी और ताकत है। पवार ने अपनी बेटी सुप्रिया सुले को फ़ोन किया। सांसद सुप्रिया, उनके साथ ही दक्षिण मुंबई में उसी हरियाली भरे 'सिल्वर ओक एस्टेट कॉम्प्लेक्स' में रहती हैं। सुप्रिया पहले ही उठ गई थीं और उनके पति ने इस ख़बर के बारे में बताया, जो सवेरे की खबरों के लिए चैनलों को देख रहे थे। 'आप यकीन मानिए, मुझे नहीं पता था कि क्या हो रहा था,' सुप्रिया सुले ने कहा। 'अजित दादा का देवेन्द्र फडनवीस के साथ शपथ लेना, ईमानदारी से कहूं तो इस पर भरोसा ही नहीं हो रहा था।'

पवार परिवार एक ऐसा घनिष्ठ परिवार है जो राजनीतिक और व्यवसायिक संबंधों के बावजूद भावनात्मक तौर पर जुड़ा हुआ है। अजित पवार, जिन्हें परिवार के लोग और दोस्त, प्यार से 'अजित दादा' कहते हैं, शरद पवार के बड़े भाई अनंतराव के बेटे हैं। अपने भाई के निधन के बाद, शरद पवार ने अजित को अपने संरक्षण में रखा और उन्हें पुणे के पास अपने पारिवारिक

गढ़ बारामती को संभालने का काम सौंपा। सिर्फ़ 23 साल की उम्र में शरद पवार ने उन्हें स्थानीय 'चीनी सहकारी कारखाना बोर्ड' में पहुंचा दिया, जो मराठा-बहुल पश्चिमी महाराष्ट्र में अजित के राजनीतिक करियर की शुरुआत थी। उनके एक पारिवारिक मित्र ने दावा किया, 'साहेब के लिए अजित उनके बेटे की तरह है, जिसका वो हमेशा ख्याल रखते रहे।' शरद पवार के खुद के कोई बेटा नहीं है, उनकी इकलौती बेटी सुप्रिया हैं। लेकिन चाचा-भतीजे के स्वभाव में बहुत फ़र्क है। जहां पवार साहेब हिसाब-किताब और धैर्य के साथ राजनीति करने वाले नेता हैं, वहीं अजित पवार एक उतावले और जल्दी नाराज़ आने वाले नेता हैं। परिवार से जुड़े एक सदस्य ने बताया, 'साहेब का दोस्तों और संपर्कों का बड़ा दायरा है और वे किसी से भी संबंध बना सकते हैं। जबकि दादा इतने मिलनसार नहीं है, जब उन्हें अपनी बात मनवाने में दिक्कत होती है तो वे जल्दी ही गरम हो जाते हैं।' एक सरकारी अफसर ने बताया कि कैसे एक बार अजित पवार ने गालियां देते हुए गुस्से में एक फाइल को फेंक दिया था। उनका कहना था कि 'अजित, एक अच्छे प्रशासक हैं, जल्दी फ़ैसले करते हैं, लेकिन आसानी से आपा भी खो सकते हैं।' उनके ख़िलाफ़ भ्रष्टाचार के आरोप भी लगते रहे हैं। 2012 में, अजित पवार को महाराष्ट्र सरकार से इस्तीफ़ा देना पड़ा था, जब उन पर जल संसाधन मंत्री रहते हुए एक सिंचाई घोटाले में शामिल होने का आरोप लगा था।

शरद पवार की नज़र हमेशा राष्ट्रीय राजनीति यानी दिल्ली दरबार पर रही, इसलिए वे महाराष्ट्र से दिल्ली पहुंच गए, जबकि अजित का मन प्रदेश की राजनीति में लगता था। 2004 में अजित पवार कांग्रेस-एनसीपी गठबंधन की सरकार में पहली बार महाराष्ट्र के उप-मुख्यमंत्री बने थे। एनसीपी के एक नेता ने बताया, 'दादा, बहुत कुशल राजनेता हैं। जब साहेब दिल्ली में रहते थे तो दादा ही मुंबई और पुणे में पार्टी के सभी अहम कामकाज देखते थे। लोगों से लेकर पैसे तक सबकुछ वे ही संभालते थे। साहेब उन पर बहुत निर्भर थे।'

शायद यही वजह रही कि जब उस सुबह अजित पवार की बगावत की ख़बर आई तो ज़्यादा चर्चा इस बात की थी कि सहमति ना भी हो, लेकिन चाचा की जानकारी के बिना अजित दादा इतना बड़ा कदम नहीं उठा सकते। 'मैं अजित के भारतीय जनता पार्टी से हाथ मिलाने के लिए क्यों तैयार होता, जबकि मैंने ही तो कांग्रेस और शिवसेना के साथ मिलकर सरकार बनाने का समझौता किया था। उस सुबह अजित ने फडनवीस के साथ जो शपथ ली, उस पर मेरी मंज़ूरी नहीं थी,' जब हमने शरद पवार से इस अचानक शपथ के बारे में पूछा। फिर भी उनके जैसे चतुर राजनेता की राजनीतिक चाल को भांपना आसान काम नहीं है। कम बोलने वाले शरद पवार 'रहस्यमयी' राजनेता माने जाते हैं। महाराष्ट्र के राजनीतिक हलकों में अक्सर यह मज़ाक चलता है कि जब वे 'ना' कहते हैं तो इसका मतलब 'हां' समझिए और जब वे 'हां' कहें तो मतलब 'शायद' है। अगर इतनी भोर में सरकार का शपथ लेना आपको नाटकीय नहीं लगता, तो महाराष्ट्र

में सत्ता का खेल वाकई कैसे चल रहा था और इसकी कहानी कम चौंकाने वाली नहीं हैं। यह इक्कीसवीं सदी की भारतीय राजनीति में पर्दे के पीछे बदलते रिश्तों की बदसूरत तस्वीर है।

═

अक्टूबर 2019 में, महाराष्ट्र विधानसभा चुनावों में भारतीय जनता पार्टी और शिवसेना ने मिलकर चुनाव लड़ा और इस गठबंधन को स्पष्ट बहुनत मिला था, लेकिन भाजपा अपने दम पर स्पष्ट बहुमत से चूक गई। 288 सीटों वाली विधानसभा में उसने केवल 105 सीटें जीती, जो बहुमत के आंकड़े 145 से काफी कम थी। लेकिन उम्मीदों से उलट एनसीपी ने 54 सीटें हासिल कर ली थीं, यह उस पार्टी के लिए खासा मजबूत प्रदर्शन था, जिसे चुनाव विशेषज्ञों ने ख़ारिज़ कर दिया था। इसी दौरान सतारा में मूसलाधार बारिश के बीच एक जनसभा को संबोधित करते अस्सी साल के शरद पवार की एक तस्वीर वायरल हुई थी, जो उनकी कभी ना रुकने वाली योद्धा छवि को जता रही थी। वैसे देखा जाए तो, भाजपा-शिवसेना को मिलकर तुरंत सरकार बना लेनी चाहिए थी, क्योंकि उनके पास स्पष्ट बहुमत था। शिवसेना के 56 विधायकों के साथ उस गठबंधन के पास कुल 161 विधायक थे। लेकिन भारत में मसला जब नेतृत्व का हो, तो फिर सामान्य स्थिति काम नहीं आती। शिवसेना का दावा है कि दोनों दलों के बीच चुनावों से पहले मुख्यमंत्री की कुर्सी समेत सत्ता में 50-50 की हिस्सेदारी की बात तय हुई थी लेकिन भाजपा का कहना है कि ऐसी किसी 'व्यवस्था' पर कोई सहमति नहीं हुई थी। बताया जाता है कि यह डील फरवरी 2019 में मुंबई में उद्धव ठाकरे के आवास पर अमित शाह और ठाकरे के बीच हुई बातचीत में तय हुई थी। जब मैंने अमित शाह से इसके बारे पूछा, तो उन्होंने आक्रामक तरीके से जवाब दिया, 'उद्धव जी झूठ बोल रहे हैं। आप मुझे कोई ऐसा बयान या कोई कागज़ बताइए, जिसमें मैंने कहा हो कि मुख्यमंत्री शिवसेना का होगा। हमारा रुख स्पष्ट थाः जिसे ज़्यादा सीटें मिलेंगी, मुख्यमंत्री उसी पार्टी का होगा। इस पर कोई समझौता नहीं हो सकता था।' भाजपा को शिवसेना से ज़्यादा सीटें मिलने के बाद तत्कालीन मुख्यमंत्री देवेन्द्र फडनवीस को दावेदार के तौर पर देखा जा रहा था। चुनावों से ठीक पहले जब मैंने एक सार्वजनिक कार्यक्रम में शांत-स्वभाव वाले फडनवीस से मुख्यमंत्री पद पर खींचतान के बारे में सवाल किया था, तो उन्होंने यह कहते हुए ख़ारिज़ कर दिया कि 'यह कोई मुद्दा ही नहीं है। मुझे विश्वास है कि मैं एक बार फिर से मुख्यमंत्री पद की शपथ लूंगा, इसको लेकर शिवसेना और हमारे बीच कोई विवाद नहीं है।' उसी कार्यक्रम में दर्शकों में बैठे शिवसेना के युवा नेता आदित्य ठाकरे ने मुस्कुराते हुए जवाब दिया, 'मुझे लगता है कि यह काम पत्रकारों को हम पर छोड़ देना चाहिए।'

फिर अचानक ऐसा क्या हो गया कि एक ही 'भगवा विचारधारा' वाले सहयोगी एक महीने से भी कम समय में कड़वाहट के साथ अलग हो गए। भाजपा का कहना था कि शिवसेना

ने एनसीपी-कांग्रेस गठबंधन के साथ सरकार बनाने के लिए गोपनीय बातचीत शुरू करके धोखा दिया। फडनवीस ने कहा, 'उद्धव जी मुख्यमंत्री बनना चाहते थे। वे हमसे तो कहते रहे कि अलग होने की कोई बात ही नहीं है, लेकिन वे दूसरा रास्ता तलाश रहे थे।' लेकिन उद्धव ठाकरे के करीबी माने जाने वाले शिवसेना सांसद संजय राउत के पास अपनी एक कहानी थीः 'क्या आप जानते हैं कि उद्धव जी और मैंने सरकार बनाने पर फ़ैसला करने के लिए भाजपा के सभी आला नेताओं को दर्ज़नों बार फ़ोन किया होगा, लेकिन उन्होंने अपने फ़ोन बंद कर दिए थे? हम तो उप-मुख्यमंत्री पद के लिए भी तैयार थे, लेकिन बीजेपी हमसे बात नहीं करना चाहती थी।'

उग्र स्वभाव के संजय राउत महाराष्ट्र के इस सियासी घमासान में एक अहम किरदार माने जाते हैं। पत्रकार रहे राउत अस्सी के दशक में पहली बार शिवसेना प्रमुख बाला साहेब ठाकरे से मिले थे। राउत किसी मराठी पत्रिका के लिए उनका साक्षात्कार करने गए थे। बालासाहेब ठाकरे उनसे प्रभावित हुए और उन्होंने इस युवा पत्रकार को शिवसेना के मुखपत्र *सामना* के संपादन की ज़िम्मेदारी सौंप दी। हिन्दुत्व की राजनीति पर दमदार समर्थन और तीखी लेखन शैली ने राउत को ठाकरे परिवार की आवाज़ बना दिया। शिवसेना ने साल 2000 में उन्हें राज्यसभा भेजा, जहां राउत ने जल्दी ही राजनीति को बेहतर तरीके से समझने और चलाने के तौर पर पहचान बना ली। शरद पवार समेत बहुत से बड़े नेताओं के साथ राउत की दोस्ती हो गई थी। राउत ने याद करते हुए कहा, 'मैं संसद के सेन्ट्रल हॉल में पवार साहेब के साथ बैठा करता था। कई बार उनसे घर मिलने भी जाता था। हमारे बीचे भले ही वैचारिक मतभेद रहे हों, लेकिन पवार साहेब मुझे हमेशा समय देते थे।' बताया गया कि 2019 के महाराष्ट्र विधानसभा चुनावों से पहले ऐसी ही एक बैठक में पवार साहेब ने बीजेपी के ख़िलाफ़ एक महागठबंधन बनाने की संभावना की चर्चा की थी। पवार ने राउत को बताया कि 'भाजपा, शिवसेना को ख़त्म कर देगी, जैसे वह अपने दूसरे क्षेत्रीय सहयोगियों को एक-एक करके ख़त्म कर रही है। अगर हम चाहते हैं कि महाराष्ट्र की राजनीति दिल्ली से न चले, तो फिर विकल्पों पर विचार करने की ज़रूरत है।' यह सुझाव उद्धव ठाकरे को भी पसंद आया। गठबंधन पर अमित शाह के दबंग रवैये से परेशान ठाकरे काफी समय से खुद को सहज महसूस नहीं कर रहे थे। उद्धव ने दावा किया, 'मेरे प्रधानमंत्री मोदी से तो अच्छे संबंध हैं, लेकिन शाह के साथ वो बात नहीं है, वे हमेशा हमें हल्के में लेते थे।' कहा जाता है कि बातचीत के दौरान एक बार तीखी नोकझोंक में अमित शाह ने उद्धव ठाकरे से कहा, 'शिवसेना को भाजपा की ज़रूरत है न कि भाजपा को शिवसेना की। यह बाल ठाकरे का ज़माना नहीं है।' शाह की इस टिप्पणी को उद्धव ने दिल पर ले लिया। संजय राउत ने भी एक बार एक पत्रकार से कहा, शिवसेना और भाजपा के रिश्तों में परेशानी की वजह मोदी नहीं, अमित शाह थे।

महाराष्ट्र विधानसभा चुनावों के नतीजे के दिन जब अंतिम आंकड़े टीवी स्क्रीन पर चमके, तो शिवसेना प्रमुख को अहसास हुआ कि अब उनके पास भी कुछ विकल्प हो सकते थे। भले ही शिवसेना को सिर्फ़ 56 सीटें मिली हो, लेकिन 105 सीटों के साथ भाजपा, बिना शिवसेना के समर्थन के सरकार नहीं बना सकती। दूसरी तरफ एनसीपी को भी अगर शरद पवार के भाजपा के ख़िलाफ़ महागठबंधन के आइडिया को आगे बढ़ाना था तो उसे भी शिवसेना की ज़रूरत पड़ेगी। नतीज़ों के कुछ दिनों बाद संजय राउत के कहने पर ठाकरे ने फोन उठाया और शरद पवार से बात की। ठाकरे परिवार और पवार बरसों से महाराष्ट्र की राजनीति पर हावी रहे हैं। राजनीतिक मतभेदों के बावजूद शरद पवार और बाल ठाकरे के निजी रिश्ते अच्छे रहे थे। अब पवार ने उद्धव के सामने एक आकर्षक प्रस्ताव रखा: 'अगर बीजेपी आपके साथ सम्मान से बर्ताव नहीं करती, और आप वाकई में उनका साथ छोड़ना चाहते हैं तो हम गठबंधन क्यों नहीं बनाते?' उस वक्त तो उद्धव ने कोई वादा नहीं किया, लेकिन राउत के साथ बातचीत को आगे बढ़ाने का रास्ता खोल दिया।

उद्धव ठाकरे और शरद पवार की फ़ोन पर पहली बातचीत अब आगे बढ़ती दिख रही थी। राउत ने शिवसेना प्रमुख को शरद पवार से मिलने और गठबंधन को लेकर चर्चा के लिए राजी कर लिया। इस फ़ैसले में शिवसेना नेता को तैयार करने में उनकी पत्नी रश्मि की भी अहम भूमिका रही, जो मौजूदा राजनीतिक घटनाक्रम में दिलचस्पी ले रही थीं। ठाकरे परिवार के एक विश्वस्त ने बताया, 'उद्धव अगर सबसे ज़्यादा किसी पर भरोसा करते हैं तो वह उनकी पत्नी है। रश्मि ताई ने उन्हें भाजपा का साथ छोड़कर एनसीपी-कांग्रेस गठबंधन के साथ जुड़ने के लिए मना लिया।' मुंबई के एक पांच सितारा होटल में गठबंधन में शामिल सभी प्रमुख लोगों की एक बैठक हुई। उद्धव ने पवार की सत्ता में साझेदारी की पेशकश को मानने का संकेत दिया। लेकिन उनकी अहम शर्त थी, 'मैं सार्वजनिक गारंटी चाहता हूं कि मुख्यमंत्री की कुर्सी पूरे पांच साल के लिए शिवसेना के पास रहेगी।' एक मुस्कुराहट के साथ एनसीपी नेता शरद पवार ने 'हां' में जवाब दिया, लेकिन कांग्रेस ने नेतृत्व से इस महागठबंधन पर मंजूरी के लिए समय मांगा। शरद पवार कांग्रेस के साथ बातचीत शुरू करते, इससे पहले ही उद्धव ठाकरे थोड़ा आगे बढ़ गए, जिसकी उम्मीद नहीं थी। उन्होंने राउत से तुरंत सोनिया गांधी से फ़ोन पर बात कराने के लिए कहा। राउत के पास सोनिया गांधी का मोबाइल नंबर नहीं था, तो उन्होंने 10 जनपथ पर उनसे बात करने की कोशिश की। उद्धव ठाकरे की इससे पहले कभी सोनिया गांधी से ना तो कोई मुलाकात हुई थी और ना ही कभी बात हुई थी। विचारधारा को लेकर कांग्रेस और शिवसेना दोनों बरसों तक एक-दूसरे के विरोधी रहे हैं। अब अचानक शिवसेना नेता संभावित गठबंधन को लेकर सीधे सोनिया गांधी से बात करना चाहते थे। शायद सोनिया को भी इस फ़ोन की उम्मीद नहीं थी, इसलिए उन्होंने विनम्रता

से टालते हुए कहा कि वे इस मसले पर पहले पवार और अपनी पार्टी के नेताओं के साथ सलाह करके बात करेंगी।

सत्ता संघर्षों का लंबा अनुभव रखने वाले पवार का गांधी परिवार से रिश्ता उतार-चढ़ाव भरा रहा है। 1977 में आपातकाल के बाद चुनावों में इंदिरा गांधी की हार के तुरंत बाद पवार कांग्रेस से अलग हो गए। उन्होंने इंदिरा गांधी ही नहीं, अपने राजनीतिक गुरु वाई.बी. चव्हाण का साथ छोड़कर विरोधी जनता पार्टी के साथ गठबंधन कर लिया। 1980 में जब इंदिरा गांधी की सत्ता में वापसी हुई तो उन्होंने महाराष्ट्र में पवार सरकार को बर्खास्त कर दिया। फिर 1987 में जब राजीव गांधी प्रधानमंत्री थे, तब पवार कांग्रेस में लौटे, लेकिन गांधी परिवार के साथ बात ठीक से बन नहीं पा रही थी। गांधी परिवार की एक महत्वपूर्ण सदस्य सोनिया गांधी ने जब 1998 में कांग्रेस की बागडोर संभाली, तो पवार साहेब को लगा कि लोकसभा में पार्टी के नेता के तौर पर उनकी अनदेखी हो रही है। 1999 में उन्होंने सोनिया गांधी के ख़िलाफ़ खुली बगावत कर दी। पवार ने इस बात पर ज़ोर दिया कि कांग्रेस पार्टी प्रधानमंत्री पद के उम्मीदवार के तौर पर 'विदेशी मूल' की सोनिया गांधी का नाम आगे नहीं बढ़ा सकती। इस मुद्दे पर उन्हें पार्टी से निकाल दिया गया और उन्होंने 'राष्ट्रवादी कांग्रेस पार्टी' (एनसीपी) बना ली, लेकिन इसके तुरंत बाद महाराष्ट्र में हुए विधानसभा चुनावों के बाद कांग्रेस के साथ सरकार बनाने में पवार जरा भी नहीं झिझके। हर पल राजनीतिक पेंतरेबाज़ी दिखाने वाले शरद पवार को लेकर सोनिया गांधी ने अपने एक सहयोगी से कहा, 'कोई ऐसे शख्स पर कैसे भरोसा कर सकता है, जो लगातार यू-टर्न लेता रहता है?' कांग्रेस अध्यक्ष की मंडली में शामिल रहने के लिए सबसे ज़रूरी है—वफादारी। सोनिया गांधी की दुनिया उनके वफादारों और दूसरे लोगों के बीच साफतौर पर बंटी हुई है। एनसीपी नेता ने जोर देकर कहा कि वे दिल से कांग्रेसी थे। एकबारगी भावुक होते हुए पवार बोले, 'मैं साठ के दशक की शुरुआत में कांग्रेस में शामिल हुआ था, तब जवाहर लाल नेहरु प्रधानमंत्री थे। कांग्रेस मेरा पहला घर है।'

साल 2019 में लोकसभा चुनावों में करारी हार की जिम्मेदारी लेते हुए जब राहुल गांधी ने कांग्रेस अध्यक्ष पद से इस्तीफ़ा दिया, तो सोनिया गांधी ने अंतरिम अध्यक्ष का पद संभाला। इस वक्त पवार ने उनके सामने महाराष्ट्र में शिवसेना के साथ महागठबंधन बनाने का विचार रखा, तो उन्होंने तुरंत कोई प्रतिक्रिया नहीं दी। सोनिया जल्दबाज़ी में फ़ैसले नहीं लेने के लिए जानी जाती हैं, वह सावधानी से कदम बढ़ाती हैं। उन्होंने अपने 10 जनपथ के आवास पर अहमद पटेल और ए.के. एंटोनी समेत अपने विश्वस्त सहयोगियों की एक बैठक में इस मसले पर चर्चा की। बैठक में अहमद पटेल का मानना था कि महाराष्ट्र जैसे बड़े और अहम राज्य में भारतीय जनता पार्टी को सत्ता से बाहर रखने के लिए किसी के साथ भी सरकार बनाने के लिए तैयार रहना चाहिए। लेकिन ए.के. एंटोनी समेत कुछ और लोगों को लगता था कि शिवसेना जैसी

'साम्प्रदायिक पार्टी' के साथ गठबंधन अपनी राजनीतिक 'मौत को गले लगाना' जैसे होगा। सोनिया गांधी भी एंटोनी से सहमत दिख रही थीं। उन्होंने कहा कि 'मुझे कुछ और लोगों से बात करने दीजिए।' इनमें सबसे अहम थे उनके बेटे राहुल गांधी, जो भले ही अब पार्टी के अध्यक्ष नहीं थे, लेकिन फ़ैसले लेने वालों में वे सबसे अहम थे। राहुल का फ़ैसला और भी साफ था: 'शिवसेना जैसी हिंदुत्ववादी पार्टी के साथ गठबंधन का सवाल ही नहीं होता।'

कांग्रेस का साथ नहीं मिलने से पवार के लिए मुश्किल हो गई। लेकिन जैसे ही यह रणनीति नाकाम होती दिख रही थी, तभी इस कहानी में एक नाटकीय मोड़ आ गया। किसी ने 'बीजेपी-एनसीपी' के गठबंधन का प्रस्ताव रखा। पवार के भतीजे अजित पवार और एनसीपी के राज्यसभा सांसद प्रफुल्ल पटेल बीजेपी के साथ गठबंधन के लिए तुरंत तैयार हो गए। दोनों नेताओं का मानना था कि यह महाराष्ट्र की राजनीति में बड़ा बदलाव होगा, 'गेमचेंजर साबित हो सकता है और इसमें सबका फायदा है।' महाराष्ट्र की मराठा ग्रामीण राजनीति में प्रफुल्ल पटेल थोड़े अलग दिखते हैं। लंबे कद और चटकीले कपड़े पहने मुंबई में गुजराती उद्योगपति से नेता बने पटेल परिवार का तंबाकू का अच्छा खासा व्यापार है और विदर्भ के इलाके में बीड़ी बनाने के लिए तेंदू पत्ता के खेत हैं। उनके पिता मनोहर लाल पटेल कांग्रेस के विधायक और शरद पवार के मित्र थे। 1987 में जब पवार कांग्रेस में फिर से लौटे, तो उन्होंने युवा प्रफुल्ल पटेल को राजनीति में अपने साथ ले लिया और 1991 के चुनावों में उन्हें लोकसभा भेज दिया। प्राइवेट स्कूल में पढ़े-लिखे शालीन प्रफुल्ल भाई दिल्ली में अपने गुरु पवार साहेब की 'आंख-कान' बनकर काम करने लगे। एनसीपी के एक नेता ने कहा कि 'साहेब को वे लोग पसंद हैं जो किसी भी जोखिम को लेने के साथ तेज़तर्रार राजनीति कर सकते हैं। नब्बे के दशक की शुरुआत में जब वे दिल्ली आए, तो प्रफुल्ल भाई उनके लिए एकदम सही व्यक्ति थे।' पवार के इस दिल्ली के आदमी का राजधानी के राजनीतिक सर्किल में अच्छा संपर्क था। 2004 से 2014 के दौरान यूपीए सरकार में नागरिक उड्डयन मंत्री और गुजरात के प्रभारी एनसीपी नेता के रूप में प्रफुल्ल पटेल ने उस समय नरेन्द्र मोदी और अमित शाह से अच्छे संबध बना लिए थे। मोदी उस वक्त गुजरात में मुख्यमंत्री थे और शाह सरकार में नंबर दो की हैसियत रखते थे। पटेल कहते हैं, 'मैं हमेशा राजनीति से पार दोस्ती बनाए रखने में भरोसा करता हूं और इसलिए मोदी और शाह के साथ भी ऐसा ही रिश्ता था।' शाह अहमदाबाद ज़िला कोऑपरेटिव बैंक के निदेशक और अध्यक्ष भी रहे थे, तो दोनों के व्यवसायिक रिश्तों में भी समानता थी। हालांकि शाह और पटेल यूं तो दोनों गुजराती थे, लेकिन शख्सियत दोनों की एकदम उलट थी। एक तरफ चौबीसों घंटे राजनीति में सक्रिय रहने वाल अमित शाह थे, जिनके पास सामाजिक समारोहों के लिए समय नहीं होता था तो दूसरी ओर अंग्रेज़ीदां प्रफुल्ल पटेल को 'हाई-सोसायटी' और 'इलीट पार्टियों' में रहना अच्छा लगता था। लेकिन विरोधी दल और स्वभाव के बावजूद दोनों में रिश्ता बना रहा।

दिलचस्प बात यह है कि यह पहला मौका नहीं था जब बीजेपी-एनसीपी गठबंधन की बात सामने आई हो। इससे पहले 2014 में एनसीपी ने महाराष्ट्र में फडनवीस के नेतृत्व वाली बीजेपी सरकार का समर्थन किया था, लेकिन औपचारिक तौर पर गठबंधन आगे नहीं बढ़ पाया। 2017 में हुई दूसरी कोशिश भी नाकाम रही। इन दोनों मौकों पर अहम भूमिका में अहमदाबाद के एक व्यवसायी थे, जिनके पवार और प्रधानमंत्री दोनों से अच्छे संबध थे। प्रधानमंत्री मोदी को पवार के साथ गठबंधन करने का विचार पसंद आया। मोदी ने कहा, 'इस सरकार को शरदराव जैसे अनुभवी व्यक्ति की ज़रूरत है, गठबंधन सही कदम होगा।' संयोग से प्रधानमंत्री कार्यालय में मोदी के सबसे भरोसेमंद अफसरों में से एक पी.के. मिश्रा ने यूपीए सरकार के वक्त कृषि मंत्री शरद पवार के साथ कृषि सचिव के तौर पर काम किया था। अनौपचारिक प्रस्तावों में पवार की बेटी सुप्रिया सुले को केन्द्र सरकार में मंत्री बनाना और शरद पवार को कृषि पर एक राष्ट्रीय स्तर के निकाय में कैबिनेट रैंक के साथ प्रमुख बनाने की बात थी।

प्रधानमंत्री मोदी ने गृहमंत्री शाह और महाराष्ट्र में मुख्यमंत्री और भाजपा के नेता देवेन्द्र फडनवीस को बातचीत आगे बढ़ाने के निर्देश दिए, जबकि पवार की तरफ से प्रफुल्ल पटेल और अजित पवार को यह ज़िम्मेदारी सौंपी गई। फडनवीस का एनसीपी के साथ सरकार बनाने के लिए आगे बढ़ना यह बताता है कि सत्ता की राजनीति को पलटने में देर नहीं लगती। इससे पहले 2019 में महाराष्ट्र के चुनाव अभियान में फडनवीस के निशाने पर पवार परिवार ही था। उन्होंने सिंचाई घोटाले में उनकी कथित भूमिका पर अजित पवार के ख़िलाफ़ मुकदमा चलाने और दूसरे मामलों की फिर से जांच कराने का वादा किया था। इस दौरान जब भाजपा ने कई स्थानीय एनसीपी नेताओं को अपने साथ आने के लिए राजी कर लिया, तब फडनवीस ने दावा किया, 'उम्रदराज़ पवार के लिए अब वक्त ख़त्म हो गया है।' बात यहीं तक नहीं रुकी, इस जंग का आखिरी हथियार भी चला दिया गया। चुनावों से ऐन पहले पवार के ख़िलाफ प्रवर्तन निदेशालय (ईडी) ने जांच शुरू कर दी। पवार ने इस पर ईडी दफ्तर तक मार्च की धमकी देते हुए कहा, 'भाजपा मुझे राजनीतिक रूप में ख़त्म करना चाहती है, लेकिन मैं किसी भी जांच का सामना करने के लिए तैयार हूं।' लेकिन मुख्यमंत्री की शपथ लेने के लिए बेचैन फडनवीस, एक पखवाड़े बाद भी शिवसेना की पहल नहीं होने पर, नए राजनीतिक खेल के लिए तैयार हो गए। फडनवीस को लगता था कि मुख्यमंत्री होना, उनका 'अधिकार' था। मीडिया की नज़रों से दूर बीजेपी-एनसीपी गठबंधन को आगे बढ़ाने के लिए मुंबई और दिल्ली में कई बैठकें हुई। दिल्ली में एक प्रमुख कंपनी के गेस्ट हाउस में बैठकें हो रही थीं।

उस वक्त महाराष्ट्र विधानसभा को 'सस्पेंडेड' रखा गया था, तब इस राजनीतिक गहमागहमी के बीच राज्यपाल भगत सिंह कोश्यारी भी हरकत में आ गए। कोश्यारी उत्तराखंड में भाजपा के मुख्यमंत्री बने और आरएसएस के प्रमुख लोगों में से रहे हैं। चुनाव नतीजों के बाद उन्होंने

12 नवम्बर को महाराष्ट्र में राष्ट्रपति शासन लगा दिया था। राज्यपाल कोश्यारी का दावा था कि अभी तक कोई भी पार्टी या गठबंधन बहुमत साबित नहीं कर पाया है। राज्यपाल पर आरोप लगा कि वे केन्द्र की उस 'स्क्रिप्ट' के हिसाब से काम कर रहे थे, जिससे महाराष्ट्र में भाजपा की सरकार बन सके। मोदी के कार्यकाल में राज्यपालों पर खुले तौर पर पक्षपात करने के आरोप लगते रहे हैं। मुंबई में समुद्र तट पर बने राजभवन में रहने वाले कोश्यारी को भी इन आरोपों से अलग नहीं किया जा सकता। शिवसेना के संजय राउत ने आरोप लगाया कि 'राष्ट्रपति शासन के ऐलान के पीछे उनका इकलौता मकसद था कि भारतीय जनता पार्टी को किसी भी तरह संख्या बल जुटाने के लिए पर्याप्त समय मिल जाए।' लेकिन बीजेपी का आरोप था कि असल में एनसीपी राष्ट्रपति शासन लगाए जाने के लिए दबाव बना रही थी। बीजेपी के एक नेता ने दावा किया, 'एनसीपी नेताओं ने कहा कि वे बीजेपी के साथ गठबंधन के लिए कुछ समय चाहते हैं ताकि पवार साहेब इस मसले पर पूरे महाराष्ट्र का दौरा कर अपने कार्यकर्ताओं को नयी दोस्ती के लिए तैयार कर सकें।'

महाराष्ट्र में राष्ट्रपति शासन की घोषणा से सभी राजनीतिक दलों पर गतिरोध को जल्दी ख़त्म करने का दबाव बनने लगा। सबसे पहले कांग्रेस आगे बढ़ती दिखी। महाराष्ट्र कांग्रेस के विधायकों के एक प्रतिनिधिमंडल ने दिल्ली में सोनिया गांधी से मुलाकात की और चेताया कि अगर सरकार में शामिल होने के प्रस्ताव को ख़ारिज किया गया तो पार्टी टूट सकती थी। प्रदेश के पूर्व मुख्यमंत्री अशोक चव्हाण ने चेतावनी के स्वर में कहा, 'भारतीय जनता पार्टी ने पहले ही संकेत भेजने शुरू कर दिए हैं, पैसे और मंत्री पद का लालच दिया जा रहा है, हमें इस पर जल्दी फ़ैसला करने की ज़रूरत है।' श्रीमती गांधी ने अपनी कोर टीम से सलाह मशविरा किया। पार्टी के बड़े सलाहकार अहमद पटेल का सुझाव था कि संभावित सहयोगियों के साथ एक न्यूनतम साझा कार्यक्रम बनाना चाहिए। पटेल का मानना था कि 'उद्धव ठाकरे की शिवसेना, अब बाल ठाकरे की शिवसेना नहीं है। वो अधिक उदार होंगे।' फिर सोनिया गांधी और उद्धव ठाकरे के बीच फ़ोन पर बात कराई गई। उसके बाद राहुल गांधी और आदित्य ठाकरे के बीच बात हुई और दोनों दलों के बीच सहमति बन गई। 2019 के लोकसभा चुनावों में करारी हार के बाद, कांग्रेस को महाराष्ट्र में सरकार में हिस्सेदार होने की सख्त ज़रूरत थी।

इसके बाद जब शरद पवार की सोनिया गांधी से उनके आवास, 10 जनपथ पर मुलाकात हुई तो वे शिवसेना और कांग्रेस के बीच सहमति से अचरज में थे और उत्साहित भी थे। सोनिया गांधी ने पवार को कहा, 'हमारी पार्टी शिवसेना के साथ गठबंधन के लिए तैयार है और अहमद भाई आपके साथ आगे की बातचीत करेंगे।' दूसरी तरफ उनकी टीम अजित पवार और प्रफुल्ल पटेल के नेतृत्व में भाजपा की अगुवाई वाली सरकार की संभावनाओं पर बातचीत कर रही थी। जब सोनिया गांधी ने शिवसेना के साथ सरकार बनाने की हामी भर ली, तो शरद पवार जानते

थे कि अब आगे क्या करना था। पवार समझते थे कि वे भाजपा सरकार में कोई फ़ैसला नहीं ले पाएंगे, जबकि 'एनसीपी-शिवसेना-कांग्रेस' गठबंधन में वे 'किंगमेकर' होंगे और उनकी हर बात का वज़न होगा। पवार की राजनीति को करीब से समझने वाले एक शख्स ने कहा, 'जब आप ताश खेल रहे हों और अचानक आपके पास सभी इक्के आ जाएं तो फिर आप पहले से अनिश्चित बाज़ी पर दांव क्यों लगाएंगे?' इस सत्ता के खेल में हर कोई अपने लिए बड़े इनाम की कोशिश में लगा था। और इस तरह महाविकास अघाड़ी गठबंधन बन गया, जिसमें कांग्रेस, शिवसेना और एनसीपी शामिल थे।

कहानी में अभी क्लाइमेक्स आना बाकी था। गठबंधन के बाद अभी मुख्यमंत्री पद के लिए फ़ैसला होना था। इस पर चर्चा के लिए मुंबई के एक पांच सितारा होटल में पवार और उद्धव ठाकरे की एक और बैठक हुई। बैठक में पवार ने ठाकरे को कहा, 'आप इस गठबंधन का नेतृत्व करेंगे। आपको मुख्यमंत्री पद संभालना होगा। सब लोग किसी और नाम पर तैयार नहीं होगें।' उद्धव ठाकरे को इस बात को हजम करने में शायद कुछ वक्त लगा। क्योंकि उनके पिता और आदर्श रहे बाल ठाकरे ने 1995 में जब पहली बार भाजपा-शिवसेना गठबंधन की सरकार बनी थी, तो मुख्यमंत्री पद लेने से इंकार कर दिया था। 'मुख्यमंत्री कोई भी बने, लेकिन रिमोट कंट्रोल मेरे पास रहेगा,' सेना प्रमुख का यह बयान बरसों तक महाराष्ट्र की राजनीति में गूंजता रहा है। बाल ठाकरे, साफगोई और सख्त बोलने वाले जुझारू जननायक थे, जिनके साथ लोगों की भावनाएं जुड़ी हुई थीं, लेकिन फोटोग्राफी को ही अपना जुनून बनाने वाले शर्मीले उद्धव के चेहरे पर हमेशा मुस्कुराहट रहती है, वे लड़ाई-झगड़े से दूर रहते हैं। अब पवार का ऐसा प्रस्ताव उनके सामने था, जिसे उनके पिता एकदम खारिज़ कर देते। 'उस वक्त पवार साहेब से हाथ मिलाते हुए मेरे हाथ कांप रहे थे, मुख्यमंत्री बनने के बारे में ना मैंने कभी चाहा था और ना कभी इस बारे में सोचा था,' उद्धव ने अपने एक दोस्त को बताया। लेकिन महाराष्ट्र के बीजेपी नेताओं का इस बारे में कुछ और कहना है, 'उद्धव ठाकरे हमेशा से ही मुख्यमंत्री बनना चाहते थे, उनकी इस बात पर भरोसा मत कीजिए कि उन्हें सत्ता की चाहत नहीं थी,' उनका दावा था।

काफी दिनों बाद जब मैंने पवार से भाजपा के साथ बातचीत के बारे में पूछा, तो उन्होंने माना कि यह सिर्फ़ 'प्लान बी' था, अगर बाकी सब नाकाम रहा। उन्होंने कहा, 'प्लान ए' हमेशा से शिवसेना और कांग्रेस के साथ महागठबंधन बनाने का ही था। 'वहां कोई सरकार नहीं थी और महाराष्ट्र में राष्ट्रपति शासन की आशंका बढ़ रही थी। इसलिए मैंने अजित और प्रफुल्ल को भाजपा से बात करने के लिए हामी भर दी, ताकि उन संभावनाओं को भी तलाशा जा सके। लेकिन मैं गठबंधन के लिए कभी तैयार नहीं हुआ था।' इसे आप भले ही अनैतिक कहें, लेकिन सत्ता को हर हाल में हासिल करने की महारथ रखने वाले राजनेता की तुरुप की बाज़ी का यह 'डबल गेम' था।

राष्ट्रपति शासन लगने के आठ दिन बाद 20 नवम्बर को शरद पवार ने प्रधानमंत्री से मुलाकात का समय मांगा। संसद का शीतकालीन सत्र अभी शुरू ही हुआ था और चर्चा थी कि पवार कृषि और सहकारी क्षेत्र से जुड़े मसलों पर प्रधानमंत्री से बात करना चाहते थे। दिखावे के लिए महाराष्ट्र में परेशान किसानों की मदद के लिए प्रधानमंत्री को एक ज्ञापन सौंपा गया। दरअसल मुलाक़ात का असली मकसद तो प्रधानमंत्री मोदी को यह बताना था कि महाराष्ट्र में बीजेपी-एनसीपी के बीच गठबंधन संभव नहीं होगा। भाजपा के एक नेता ने इस मुलाकात के बाद कहा कि 'प्रधानमंत्री इस जवाब से निराश हो गए, लेकिन उन्होंने इसे ज़ाहिर नहीं किया।' लेकिन गृहमंत्री अमित शाह बहुत गुस्से में थे। शाह ने अपनी टीम से कहा, 'मैंने आपको पहले ही चेताया था कि पवार पर भरोसा नहीं किया जा सकता, उन्होंने कांग्रेस का समर्थन शिवसेना को दिलाने के लिए हमारा इस्तेमाल किया।' फडनवीस भी मुख्यमंत्री की कुर्सी छिनते देख नाराज़ थे। फडनवीस ने बताया, 'हमने उनसे हाथ मिलाया और एनसीपी के साथ सभी मुद्दों पर सहमति बन गई थी, यहां तक कि इस पर भी बात तय हो गई थी कि किस ज़िले का पालक मंत्री कौन होगा। पवार के अचानक धोखा देने से पहले तक, सबकुछ आसानी से और ठीक चल रहा था।'

जब अमित शाह ने फडनवीस के एनसीपी को तोड़कर अजित पवार के साथ गठबंधन के प्लान को मंज़ूरी दी, तो उसमें बदले की बू महसूस की जा सकती थी। फडनवीस का तर्क था कि 'अजित पवार कांग्रेस के साथ नहीं जाना चाहते।' 'ठीक है, लेकिन जल्दी करो', पवार को सत्ता के खेल में सबक सिखाने के लिए शाह ने फडनवीस को हरी झंडी दे दी। शाह के भरोसेमंद और संकटमोचक, भाजपा के महाराष्ट्र के प्रभारी भूपेन्द्र यादव को मुंबई जाकर अजित पवार के साथ बातचीत का जिम्मा सौंपा गया। 'ज़्यादातर विधायक मेरे साथ आएंगे,' अजित पवार भरोसा दिला रहे थे। महत्वाकांक्षी अजित पवार को उम्मीद थी कि भाजपा के साथ जाने से उनके ख़िलाफ़ चल रहे मामले ख़त्म हो जाएंगे या 'ठंडे बस्ते' में डाल दिए जाएंगे। जब 22 नवम्बर को शाह को बताया गया कि अजित पवार एक समझौते के लिए तैयार हो गए थे तो गृहमंत्री ने जल्दी आगे बढ़ने के लिए कहा। इस घटनाक्रम की जानकारी प्रधानमंत्री को दी गई और विश्वास जताया गया कि भाजपा के पास सरकार बनाने का दावा करने के लिए पर्याप्त विधायक थे। 'आज रात ही करिए, सुबह का इंतज़ार नहीं करना है। अगर शरद पवार को इसके बारे में पता चला, तो वे इसे रुकवा सकते हैं,' शाह ने फडनवीस को स्पष्ट निर्देश दिए। रात को साढ़े बारह बजे राज्यपाल कोश्यारी ने केन्द्र को एक चिट्ठी भेजकर महाराष्ट्र में राष्ट्रपति शासन ख़त्म करने की सिफ़ारिश की। बिना किसी देरी के केन्द्र ने इसे विचार के लिए राष्ट्रपति के पास भेज दिया और रात डेढ़ बजे राष्ट्रपति रामनाथ कोविंद ने इस पर अपनी मंज़ूरी दे दी। संविधान के किसी जानकार ने यह जानने की जहमत भी नहीं उठाई कि फडनवीस के दावे में कितना दम था और

अजित पवार के पास वाकई कितने विधायकों का समर्थन था। इसे राजनीतिक चालबाज़ी से क़ानून और संवैधानिक नैतिकता के नाम पर रातोंरात हुआ 'तख्तापलट' कहा जा सकता है।

लेकिन शाह, फडनवीस और अजित पवार ने मुंबई की राजनीतिक शतरंज के शातिर खिलाड़ी शरद पवार की काबिलियत का ठीक से अंदाज़ा नहीं लगाया था। अपने भतीजे की बगावत के बाद शरद पवार ने एनसीपी के सभी पाला बदलने वाले विधायकों से संपर्क किया। एक एनसीपी विधायक ने बताया, 'साहेब ने उन्हें याद दिलाया कि कैसे उन्होंने उनके पिता की तब मदद की थी, जब उनका व्यापार-धंधा चौपट हो गया था।' एनसीपी नेता और पवार के वफादार माने जाने वाले जितेन्द्र अव्हाड़ ने ज़ोर देकर कहा, 'साहेब के ज़्यादातर विधायकों के साथ निजी संबंध हैं और वे उनके परिवार की तरह हैं।' जैसे-जैसे पाला बदलने वाले विधायक फिर से साहेब के पास घर वापसी कर रहे थे, अजित पवार अकेले होते जा रहे थे। जब सुप्रीम कोर्ट ने दख़ल देते हुए राज्यपाल के आधी रात के फ़ैसले पर सवाल उठाया और विधानसभा में बहुमत साबित करने के आदेश दिए, तो अजित पवार और फडनवीस को समझ आ गया कि उनका 'खेल खत्म' हो गया था। शपथ ग्रहण के तीन बाद ही 26 नवम्बर को फडनवीस ने इस्तीफ़ा दे दिया। हारे हुए अजित पवार फिर से एनसीपी में लौट आए। 28 नवम्बर 2019 को मुंबई के प्रसिद्ध शिवाजी पार्क में शिवसेना के उद्धव ठाकरे ने महाराष्ट्र के मुख्यमंत्री पद की शपथ ली। उद्धव ने दावा किया कि उन्होंने महाराष्ट्र में भगवा झंडा फहराने की अपने पिता की इच्छा को पूरा कर दिया था। लेकिन जिस बात पर ध्यान नहीं दिया गया कि उद्धव ने यह मंज़िल उन लोगों के साथ मिलकर हासिल की, जिनका विरोध उनके पिता ज़िंदगीभर करते रहे थे।

सत्ता परिवर्तन को टेलीविजन पर देखते अमित शाह गुस्से में थे। 2014 में राजनीति के राष्ट्रीय मंच पर उभरने के बाद से मीडिया में अक्सर उनकी 'चाणक्य नीति' की तारीफ़ होती थी। महाराष्ट्र में इस राजनीतिक नाकामी ने उन्हें इसका बदला लेने के लिए बेचैन कर दिया था। साफ था कि अगले कुछ साल राज्य में बदले की राजनीति चलेगी और 2024 के राजनीतिक समीकरणों पर भी इसका असर पड़ेगा। महाराष्ट्र अब राजनीतिक कड़वाहट और परस्पर विरोधी महत्वाकांक्षाओं से उपजी अराजकता के दौर में पहुंच गया था। हर दिन होती राजनीतिक सौदेबाजी और बदलते राजनीतिक समीकरणों का असर देश भर की राजनीति पर दिखाई देने लगा था। बार-बार त्रिशंकु विधानसभाओं से वैचारिक राजनीतिक दलों के बजाय केवल सत्ता के हितों से पनपे नेताओं को वर्चस्व होने लगा है। लगता है कि महाराष्ट्र के जोड़-तोड़ में माहिर राजनेताओं से तालमेल बिठाना अब तो मैकियावेली के बस की बात भी नहीं होती। पिछले पचास साल में फडनवीस महाराष्ट्र के अकेले मुख्यमंत्री हैं, जिन्होंने 2014 में सत्ता संभालने के बाद पहली बार पांच साल का कार्यकाल पूरा किया है। भारत की आर्थिक राजधानी मुंबई पर नियंत्रण करने के लिए बड़े दांव और ख़तरे मोल लेने पड़ते हैं।

शरद पवार जहां अभी अपनी कामयाबी का जश्न मना रहे थे, वहीं गृहमंत्री शाह का ध्यान अब दूसरे राज्य के राजनीतिक अभियान पर चला गया था। एक ऐसा राज्य, जिस पर गृहमंत्री शाह समेत ज्यादातर बीजेपी नेताओं की अरसे से नज़र थी। सत्ता का खेल अब पश्चिमी भारत से पूर्वी तट पर पंहुच गया था। बंगाल की खाड़ी में सतह पर पानी में भले ही कोई हलचल नहीं दिख रही हो, लेकिन उसकी गहराई में कई रहस्य छिपे हुए थे।

भारतीय जनता पार्टी के लिए पश्चिम बंगाल का कुछ खास भावनात्मक और राजनीतिक महत्व है। इसकी राजनीतिक ताकत इसलिए भी है क्योंकि उत्तरप्रदेश और महाराष्ट्र के बाद यहां से सबसे ज़्यादा 42 सांसद लोकसभा पहुंचते हैं, लेकिन भाजपा के लिए इसकी अहमियत इसलिए भी है क्योंकि यह जनसंघ के संस्थापक डॉ. श्यामाप्रसाद मुखर्जी का गृह राज्य भी है। 1943 और 1946 के दौरान हिंदू महासभा के अध्यक्ष रहे डॉ. मुखर्जी संयुक्त बंगाल को एक 'स्वतंत्र प्रांत' में बदलने के विरोधी रहे थे। इसके बजाय 1947 में उन्होंने भारत में बंगाली हिंदुओं के लिए एक अलग राज्य बनाने के लिए बंगाल के बंटवारे पर ज़ोर दिया था। इस आंदोलन में हज़ारों लोग मारे गए थे। पश्चिम बंगाल में पार्टी की ताकत बढ़ाने को मुखर्जी की विरासत को फिर से जिंदा करने के अहम मिशन के रूप में देखा गया। यही वजह रही कि जब शाह भारतीय जनता पार्टी के राष्ट्रीय अध्यक्ष बने तो 'मिशन बंगाल' उनकी प्राथमिकताओं में सबसे ऊपर था। अगले पांच साल में शाह ने अपने गृह राज्य गुजरात के बाद सबसे ज़्यादा दौरे पश्चिम बंगाल में किए। बंगाल के एक भाजपा नेता ने कहा, 'बंगाल जीतने की बात करते वक्त अमित भाई की आंखों में एक अलग ही चमक होती है।'

साल 2019 के लोकसभा चुनावों ने भाजपा को आश्वस्त किया कि बंगाल पर विजय हासिल करना इतना मुश्किल काम भी नहीं था: भाजपा ने प्रदेश की 42 लोकसभा सीटों में से 18 सीटों पर जीत हासिल की और उसे 40 फ़ीसदी वोट मिला था। इससे पहले यहां भाजपा वोट और सीटों के लिहाज़ से कभी दहाई का आंकड़ा भी पार नहीं कर पाई थी। इस नतीजे को महत्वपूर्ण जीत के तौर पर पेश किया गया। उत्साहित शाह ने चुनावों में कामयाबी पर बधाई देने आए बंगाल के बीजेपी नेताओं को कहा, 'आज हमने देश पर जीत हासिल की है, कल बंगाल हमारा होगा।'

तृणमूल कांग्रेस की नेता और पश्चिम बंगाल की मुख्यमंत्री ममता बनर्जी के लिए 2019 के चुनावों के नतीजे चेतावनी भरे थे। 2011 में जबसे उन्होंने पहली बार वामपंथियों के लाल किले में सेंध लगाई थी, तबसे ममता बनर्जी बंगाल की निर्विवाद सुप्रीमो मानी जाने लगी थीं। उन्होंने मज़ाक में कहा, 'मैं बंगाल की सिर्फ़ दीदी नहीं, बल्कि दादा भी हूं, हर कोई मेरे

साथ हैं।' आमतौर पर सफेद साड़ी में रहने वाली ताकतवर ममता बनर्जी देश के उन गिने-चुने जननेताओं में से एक हैं जिनकी राजनीतिक सूझबूझ और दूरदर्शिता को हर कोई मानता है। उन्होंने 2011 से 2019 के आठ वर्षों में विधानसभा से लेकर पंचायत तक हर चुनाव में कामयाबी हासिल की। उन पर ताकत के इस्तेमाल, सरकारी मशीनरी के दुरुपयोग और विरोधियों को डराने-धमकाने के लिए अपनी पार्टी के कार्यकर्ताओं को खुली छूट देने के आरोप लगते रहे हैं। एक ज़माने तक ताकतवर रहे वामपंथी दलों ने ममता दी से हार मान ली, उनके कार्यकर्ताओं को या तो लोभ-लालच दिया गया या फिर तृणमूल कांग्रेस में शामिल होने के लिए धमकी दी गई। लेकिन बीजेपी से मुकाबला अलग तरह का था। बीजेपी में दीदी को चुनौती देने की राजनीतिक भूख थी और उसे पूरा करने के लिए ज़रूरी संसाधन भी। 2017 में बीजेपी ने ममता दी को पहला झटका दिया, जब उनके दाहिने हाथ माने जाने वाले मुकुल रॉय को पार्टी ने अपने पाले में कर लिया। संगठन के एक मजबूत नेता, मुकुल रॉय ने टीएमसी को बनाने में अहम भूमिका निभाई थी। उनके जाने से बनर्जी की सुरक्षित दीवार में एक दरार सी आ गईः सरकार चलाने और प्रबंधन में व्यस्त होने की वजह से वे धीरे-धीरे अपने दूसरे स्तर के नेताओं से दूर होती जा रही थीं। भाजपा के 'जयश्री राम' के नारे की गूंज प्रदेश के कुछ हिस्सों में सुनाई देने लगी थी। बंगाल में मुस्लिमों की बड़ी आबादी का फायदा उठाते हुए भाजपा ने उन इलाकों में अपनी ज़मीन बनाना शुरू किया, जहां ममता बनर्जी पर मुस्लिमों का साथ देने का आरोप लगाकर हिन्दू-मुस्लिम भावनाओं को भड़काना मुमकिन था। जब 2019 में एक चुनाव सर्वेक्षण में भारतीय जनता पार्टी को बढ़त मिलने की संभावना दिखाई गई तो गुस्से में ममता दी ने आरोप लगाया कि सर्वेक्षण करने वाली एजेंसी और इसे दिखाने वाले टीवी चैनल को भाजपा ने खरीद लिया है। उन्होंने गुस्से में कहा, 'उनको भाजपा ने खरीद लिया है, वे सब मोदी-शाह के एजेंट हैं।' हालांकि चुनाव नतीजों ने सर्वेक्षणों की चेतावनी को सही साबित किया। बंगाल में अब 'कमल' खिलने लगा था। 2019 के नतीजों के बाद उन्होंने काफी समय तक पार्टी सहयोगियों समेत किसी से बात नहीं की। ममता बनर्जी ने खुद को कालीघाट वाले अपने दफ्तर-कम-घर में समेट लिया। कोलकता में भाजपा के सत्ता के एक गंभीर दावेदार के रूप में उभरने को पचाना उनके लिए मुश्किल हो रहा था। अपने इस असुरक्षा भाव की वजह से वे हर किसी पर अविश्वास करने लगी थीं। तृणमूल कांग्रेस के एक पूर्व सांसद ने बताया, 'उस वक्त ममता दी ने गुस्से में एक व्हाट्सएप संदेश मुझे भेजा, जिसमें मुझ पर भाजपा के साथ मिलीभगत का आरोप लगाया था। मैंने दीदी को समझाने की कोशिश की, हमने अब भी भाजपा से ज्यादा लोकसभा सीटें जीती हैं, इसलिए निराश होने की ज़रूरत नहीं है। लेकिन वे मेरी बात सुनने को तैयार नहीं थीं, उन्होंने मुझ पर अमित शाह के साथ गुप्त सौदा करने के आरोप लगाया और मेरा फ़ोन नंबर भी ब्लॉक कर दिया।'

ऐसे वक्त में जब उन्हें लगता था कि वे हर तरफ से दुश्मनों से घिरी हुई थीं, ममता बनर्जी को किसी ऐसे व्यक्ति की ज़रूरत थी जिस पर वे पूरी तरह से भरोसा कर सकें। उनमें एक चेहरा उनके भतीजे अभिषेक बनर्जी का था, जो उनसे बेहिचक मिल सकते थे। चश्मा लगाए, शर्मीले और विनम्र अभिषेक ममता के बड़े भाई के बेटे हैं। ममता बनर्जी जहां कालीघाट की गंदी गलियों में वामपंथी कार्यकर्ताओं से लड़ते, लंबे संघर्ष के बाद सत्ता के शिखर पर पहुंची थीं, वहां अभिषेक को राजनीति में जगह आसानी से मिल गई थी। एमबीए करने के बाद अभिषेक ने अपनी बुआ ममता बनर्जी की 2011 में विधानसभा में जीत से ठीक पहले एक कंपनी 'लीप्स एंड बाउंड्स' शुरू की थी, जिससे उन्हें सत्ता तक पहुंचने में मदद मिली। साल के आखिर में अभिषेक ने राजनीति में 'लो-प्रोफाइल एंट्री' की। उन्होंने युवाओं के लिए तृणमूल के एक नए संगठन 'युवा' की शुरुआत की। फिर 2014 के चुनावों में पार्टी ने उन्हें डायमंड हार्बर लोकसभा सीट से टिकट दिया। ममता की लहर में वे सत्ताइस साल की उम्र में सबसे कम उम्र के सांसदों में से एक बन गए। 2019 आते-आते वे सिर्फ एक सांसद भर नहीं रह गए थे, अब वे तृणमूल कांग्रेस के संगठन के सबसे अहम नेता, अपनी बुआ के 'आंख-कान' और 'संकटमोचक' भी हो गए थे। ममता उन पर इस कदर भरोसा करने लगीं कि पार्टी के कई पुराने नेता अपने को पीछे छूटता महसूस करने लगे। इससे विपक्ष को मुख्यमंत्री पर हमला करने का बड़ा मौका मिल गया। भाजपा नेता दिलीप घोष ने कहा, 'यह अब पिशी-भाइपो (बुआ-भतीजा) की सरकार है।' अमित शाह ने और तीखा हमला किया, यह 'तोलाबाजी-तुष्टिकरण-भतीजाकरण' की सरकार है। अफवाहें थीं कि कोलकता में हरीश मुखर्जी रोड पर उनके शानदार अपार्टमेंट में अभिषेक से मिलने के लिए स्थानीय बड़े व्यापारियों को बुलाया जा रहा था। दिलीप घोष ने आरोप लगाया, 'अभिषेक ने सिंगापुर, बैंकॉक और दुबई समेत कई जगहों पर अपार संपत्ति बनाई है।' अभिषेक ने इन सभी आरोपों का खंडन किया। कुछ दिनों बाद मुझसे एक साक्षात्कार में अभिषेक ने कहा, 'भाजपा का काम केवल आरोप लगाना है, उन्हें अपने इन बेतुके आरोपों को साबित करना चाहिए।'

अपने भतीजे पर भ्रष्टाचार के आरोपों से शुरुआत में ममता बनर्जी परेशान हो गई थीं। अभिषेक के शौक मंहगे हैं, लेकिन मुख्यमंत्री की सार्वजनिक छवि सादगी वाली है, जिसके लिए वे सचेत रहती हैं। वे हमेशा कहती रहीं कि 'मैं एक सीधी-सरल व्यक्ति हूं।' मुख्यमंत्री बनने के बाद भी वे सरकारी बंगले यानी मुख्यमंत्री आवास के बजाय अपने पुराने कालीघाट के घर में ही रहती हैं। बनर्जी परिवार एक मज़बूत परिवार है और हमेशा एक दूसरे के साथ खड़ा रहता है। जब अभिषेक को निशाना बनाया गया तो ममता दी ने पार्टी के अंदर और बाहर उनका बचाव किया। फिर जब तेजी से उभरती भाजपा से बुआ को चुनौती मिल रही थी तो वक्त था भतीजे का उनके साथ खड़े रहकर बचाव करने का।

2021 ‘मिशन बंगाल’ में भाजपा से मुकाबले के लिए अभिषेक ने जाने-माने रणनीतिकार प्रशांत कुमार को टीएमसी में शामिल करने का सुझाव दिया। ममता दी को 2015 में, बिहार में नीतीश कुमार सरकार के शपथ-ग्रहण समारोह में उनके राज्यसभा सांसद डेरेक ओ ब्रायन ने प्रशांत से मिलवाया था। जनता के साथ रिश्तों पर ज़्यादा भरोसा रखने वाली, पुराने ज़माने की राजनेता बनर्जी, बड़ी-बड़ी बातें और एक मजबूत रिकॉर्ड रखने वाले प्रशांत किशोर से ज़्यादा प्रभावित नहीं हुई थीं। उन्होंने तब अपने एक सहयोगी को कहा था, ‘ये सब अपने काम के लिए बड़ा पैसा मांगते हैं। हम भाजपा की तरह अमीर पार्टी नहीं हैं।’ हालांकि युवा और तकनीक को ज़्यादा इस्तेमाल करने वाले अभिषेक, प्रशांत किशोर के उन चुनाव अभियानों से प्रभावित थे, जो उन्होंने 2014 में मोदी नेतृत्व वाली भाजपा के लिए और फिर 2015 में बिहार में नीतीश-लालू यादव के प्रचार के लिए किए थे। अभिषेक ने तब डेरेक को कहा था कि ‘वह एक ऐसे व्यक्ति हैं जिनकी हमें किसी दिन बंगाल में जरूरत पड़ सकती है।‘

उस समय किशोर एक के बाद दूसरी चुनावी कामयाबी को अपने सेहरे में बांध रहे थे। 2014 के चुनावों में मोदी टीम के एक महत्वपूर्ण सदस्य के रूप में अपनी प्रतिष्ठा बनाने के बाद किशोर ने देश में कई पार्टियों के विजयी प्रचार अभियानों के लिए काम किया था। प्रशांत किशोर के करियर में एक महत्वपूर्ण मोड़ तब आया, जब 2018 में नीतीश कुमार ने अपनी पार्टी जनता दल यूनाइटेड में शामिल करने के कुछ हफ्तों बाद ही उन्हें संगठन का राष्ट्रीय उपाध्यक्ष बना दिया। किशोर ने 2015 में नीतीश के चुनाव अभियान पर काम किया और नीतीश कुमार के साथ व्यक्तिगत समीकरण बना लिए थे। पटना के एक वरिष्ठ पत्रकार ने कहा, ‘प्रशांत एक पारंपरिक राजनेता नहीं थे, इसलिए नीतीश को उन्हें आगे बढ़ाने में कोई ख़तरा महसूस नहीं हुआ।’

अगला साल आते-आते तस्वीर उतनी अच्छी नहीं रही थी। किशोर को समझ आने लगा था कि एक राजनेता की जिंदगी किसी पेशेवर रणनीतिकार से बहुत अलग थी। पार्टी में कई लोगों को, वे बहुत महत्वाकांक्षी के तौर पर चुभने लगे थे, जो खुद को एक उम्रदराज मुख्यमंत्री के संभावित उत्तराधिकारी के तौर पर पेश कर रहे थे। पार्टी की एक बैठक में जनता दल यूनाइटेड के एक वरिष्ठ नेता ने प्रशांत किशोर के मुख्यमंत्री की ज़रूरत से ज्यादा निकटता पर सवाल उठाया। ‘हममें से कई लोग तो नीतीश जी से हफ्तों-हफ्तों नहीं मिल पाते, लेकिन यह आदमी जिसने कभी कोई चुनाव नहीं जीता, उसका मुख्यमंत्री आवास में इस कदर आना-जाना है, मानो वो ही असली मुख्यमंत्री हो। वो कौन होता है जो हमें बताए कि हमें क्या करना है?’ 2019 के चुनावों से पहले बिहार की राजनीतिक खींचतान में फंसे प्रशांत ने अब अपना ध्यान आंध्रप्रदेश की तरफ लगाया। यहां उनकी कंपनी **I-PAC** जगन मोहन रेड्डी के सफल चुनाव अभियान पर काम कर रही थी। चुनाव ख़त्म होने के बाद, किशोर की कंपनी दूसरे बड़े ग्राहक की तलाश में थी। यहीं पर उत्साही अभिषेक बनर्जी की एंट्री होती है। दोनों की जोड़ी तुरंत ही जम गई।

किशोर ने कहा, 'मैं अभिषेक की तृणमूल कांग्रेस को पेशेवर बनाने की इच्छा से प्रभावित था।' भाजपा की बढ़ती राजनीतिक गर्मी को महसूस करते हुए, ममता ने रणनीतिकार को जोड़ने के अपने भतीजे के सुझाव को मान लिया। यह करोड़ों रुपये का मंहगा अनुबंध था, लेकिन अभिषेक अपनी बुआ को समझाने में सफल रहे कि पार्टी को 2021 के विधानसभा चुनावों से पहले उन जैसे विशेषज्ञ की ज़रूरत थी।

ममता बनर्जी ने कांग्रेस से अलग होकर 1998 में तृणमूल कांग्रेस बनाई थी। क्षेत्रीय राष्ट्रवाद के मुद्दे पर जोर देती पार्टी, मोटे तौर पर जुझारू और ज़मीनी नेता ममता बनर्जी और प्रदेश की वामपंथी सरकार के ख़िलाफ़ उग्र विरोध के इर्द-गिर्द घूमती रही थी। ममता बनर्जी बहुत हिम्मती हैं, साहस से भरपूर हैं। उन्होंने कहा, 'क्या आप जानते हैं कि पुलिस ने कितनी बार मुझ पर लाठियां चलाई हैं। ये दिग्गज कांग्रेसी नेता दिल्ली के बंगलों में एसी कमरों में बैठे रहते हैं और मैं सड़कों पर लड़ाई लड़ रही हूं।' वामपंथी सरकार के ख़िलाफ़ सड़क पर उतरने और लड़ने वाली छवि का सीधा फायदा ममता को मिला। उनका 'पोरिबर्तन' (परिवर्तन) का नारा राज्य में विरोधी आवाज़ों के लिए एक ताकत का नाम बन गया। 2011 के चुनावों में दमदार तरीके से जीत हासिल करने और फिर पांच साल बाद इसे बनाए रखने के लिए ममता दी को अपने स्थानीय 'दादाओं' और ज़िले की राजनीति पर पकड़ रखने वाले बाहुबलियों पर लगाम कसना मुश्किल हो रहा था। पार्टी के इस सिंडिकेट पर हर सौदे पर 'कट-मनी' मांगने और जबरन वसूली के आरोप लग रहे थे। कोलकता की वरिष्ठ पत्रकार शिखा मुखर्जी ने कहा, 'बंगाल की ज़मीन पर हकीकत में कोई पोरिबर्तन नहीं था, केवल गिरोह चलाने वाले नेताओं की पार्टी बदल गई थी और गुंडागर्दी बढ़ रही थी, वही लोग फैसले करते थे।'

प्रशांत किशोर ने खुलासा किया, 'बंगाल में हमारी पहली बड़ी चुनौती पार्टी के शीर्ष नेतृत्व को मतदाताओं से जोड़कर छवि सुधारना था। अभी वे अपनी शिकायतें वहां तक नहीं पहुंचा सकते थे।' किशोर ने इसके लिए 2020 में कोलकता को ही अपना ठिकाना बना लिया, वे या तो अभिषेक के घर से या फिर शहर के एक पांच सितारा होटल के सुइट से कामकाज देख रहे थे। उनकी **I-PAC** की टीम में सौ से ज़्यादा लोग शामिल थे, जिनमें कई तो हाल में स्नातक किए बीस साल के युवा थे। उन्होंने 'सॉल्ट लेक सिटी' में अपना दफ्तर बनाया। टीम के इन युवाओं को सबसे पहला काम आम मतदाताओं तक पहुंचकर यह जानना था कि तृणमूल के स्थानीय नेताओं की छवि कैसी थी। इसे फिर 'दीदी के बोलो' (**TELL DIDI**) अभियान में बदल दिया गया, जिसमें आम आदमी अपनी शिकायतें ऑनलाइन पोर्टल या एक खास 'व्हाट्सएप नंबर' पर कर सकता था, जिसे सीधे मुख्यमंत्री सचिवालय देख रहा था। तृणमूल कांग्रेस के मीडिया प्रभारी सांसद डेरेक का कहना था, 'प्रशांत की टीम ने एक प्रभावी फीडबैक सिस्टम बनाया, जिससे हमें पार्टी को फिर से पटरी पर लाने में बड़ी मदद मिली।' पार्टी की

इमेज को सुधारने का काम यहां रुका नहीं, बल्कि यहां से शुरुआत हुई। अभिषेक बनर्जी की निगरानी में पार्टी के नेताओं और विधायकों को कुछ दिन अपने निर्वाचन क्षेत्रों में गुज़ारने और मतदाताओं से जुड़ने के लिए उनके घरों में रुकने के लिए कहा गया। प्रशांत किशोर ने याद करते हुए बताया, 'कई विधायकों को यह अच्छा नहीं लगा कि हम "बाहरी" लोग बता रहे हैं कि उन्हें क्या करना चाहिए। उन्होंने इसकी शिकायत ममता बनर्जी से भी की, लेकिन अच्छी बात यह रही कि उन्होंने हमें अपने हिसाब से काम करने की पूरी छूट दी।' पश्चिम बंगाल सरकार ने अपनी कल्याणकारी सामाजिक योजनाओं का लाभ सीधे आम आदमी तक पहुँचाने के लिए एक महत्वाकांक्षी कार्यक्रम 'दुआरे सरकार' (सरकार आपके द्वार) शुरू किया था। इसके लिए ज़िलों में शिविर लगाए गए, जहां सरकारी अधिकारी सरकार की योजनाओं के बारे में बताते थे। एक सरकारी अफसर ने बताया, 'ममता बनर्जी सरकार की कई कल्याणकारी योजनाओं में पैसा नकद मिलता था, खासतौर से महिलाओं की कई योजनाओं में। दुआरे सरकार कार्यक्रम से यह फायदा हुआ कि हम 'कट-मनी' लेने वालों, यानी बिचौलियों को रोक सके। यह एक गेम चेंजर साबित हुआ।'

मार्च में होने वाले विधानसभा चुनावों से पहले जनवरी 2021 में मैंने मुख्यमंत्री ममता बनर्जी का साक्षात्कार किया। 2019 में लोकसभा के झटके के बाद यह उनका पहला साक्षात्कार था। ममता ने आत्मविश्वास के साथ कहा, 'मैं भाजपा को खुली चुनौती दे रही हूं। वे चाहे जिसे ले आएं, मोदी जी, अमित शाह जी, नड्डा जी, कोई भी हमें बंगाल में नहीं हरा सकता, क्योंकि जनता हमारे साथ है।' ऐसा लग रहा था कि 2019 की हार के बाद उनकी तैयारी ने उन्हें नया आत्मविश्वास दिया था। साक्षात्कार के बाद ममता बनर्जी ने मुझे अपने फ़ोन पर एक चुनाव प्रचार वीडियो दिखायाः इसे आकर्षक धुन पर मुख्यमंत्री और उनकी रैलियों की रंगीन तस्वीरों को जोड़कर बनाया गया था। 'यह हमारा चुनावी थीम गीत है, क्या आपको पसंद आया,' उन्होंने पूछा। मेरी बंगाली बहुत अच्छी नहीं है, लेकिन गीत का थीम 'खेला होबे' (खेल शुरू हो गया है), जबरदस्त लग रहा था। टीएमसी के युवा कार्यकर्ता देबांग्शु भट्टाचार्य ने इसे बनाया था और सोशल मीडिया पर डाला था। 'मैंने टीएमसी की एक रैली से पहले इसे लिखा, दीदी को बहुत पसंद आया था, उन्होंने कहा मैं इसे चुनाव का थीम सोंग बनाउंगी,' भट्टाचार्य ने कहा। जब मैं निकलने लगा, तो ममता बनर्जी ने अंगूठा दिखाते हुए 'थम्स अप' किया। 'खेला होबे, राजदीप जी खेला होबे,' उन्होंने कहा। कुछ हफ्तों बाद प्रधानमंत्री मोदी ने जवाबी हमला किया: 'खेला शेष, दीदी (खेल खत्म हो गया)!' सबसे ज़बरदस्त और राजनीतिक तौर पर आक्रामक राज्य बंगाल, चुनावी लड़ाई की उल्टी गिनती के लिए तैयार था।

गृहमंत्री अमित शाह के लिए यह ख़बर कि प्रशांत किशोर ममता बनर्जी का चुनाव अभियान संभाल रहे थे, किसी 'लाल निशान' से कम नहीं थी। भाजपा की 2014 के चुनावों में जीत के बाद शाह और प्रशांत अलग हो गए थे। वैसे भी प्रधानमंत्री के कोर ग्रुप में केवल एक ही 'चाणक्य' रह सकता था। शाह जानते थे कि उनके सामने एक बड़ी चुनौती थी, लेकिन वे नया इतिहास लिखने की तैयारी कर रहे थे। उनके पास एक बड़ी चुनौती मुख्यमंत्री ममता बनर्जी के मुकाबले लोगों में लोकप्रिय होने वाले एक बड़े स्थानीय चेहरे की तलाश करना था। संभावित दावेदारों की सूची में सबसे ऊपर भारतीय क्रिकेट टीम के कप्तान रहे सौरव गांगुली का नाम था। बंगाल के लोकनायक जैसे गांगुली को लोग प्यार से 'दादा' बुलाते हैं। दूसरे क्रिकेट खिलाड़ियों से उलट, गांगुली राजनीति पर गहरी पकड़ रखते हैं। बंगाल के गौरव के तौर पर वे खासे लोकप्रिय हैं। वामपंथी दल और तृणमूल कांग्रेस ने उन्हें राज्यसभा भेजने का प्रस्ताव रखा था, जिसे उन्होंने नामंज़ूर कर दिया था। गांगुली का कहना था, 'मैं क्रिकेट में अपने योगदान को लेकर खुश हूं और बहुत से दूसरे काम कर रहा हूं, जिससे संसद के लिए बंधना मुश्किल हो जाएगा।' कोलकता के बेहाला इलाके में एक बहुमंजिला बंगले में रहने वाले सौरव समृद्ध बंगाली परिवार से हैं और उनका प्रिटिंग का व्यवसाय है। देश के सबसे सम्मानित कप्तानों में से एक गांगुली, क्रिकेट से संन्यास लेने के बाद बहुत से दूसरे कामों के साथ जुड़े हुए हैं। कोलकता के होर्डिंग्स पर कई उत्पादों के विज्ञापनों में उनका चेहरा अब भी नज़र आता है। वो एक सफल बंगाली टीवी क्विज़ शो की मेज़बानी कर रहे थे। एक स्थानीय फुटबाल टीम के अलावा कई कंपनियों में भी उनका पैसा लगा हुआ है। एक बंगाली पत्रकार ने मुझसे कहा, 'गांगुली को दो चीज़ें बेहतर आती हैं: कवर ड्राइव और व्यवसायिक अवसरों को पहचानना।'

साल 2015 में तृणमूल कांग्रेस नेतृत्व के समर्थन से गांगुली बंगाल क्रिकेट एसोसिएशन के अध्यक्ष बने। बंगाली अस्मिता को पहचान बनाने वाली ममता बनर्जी खेलों और फ़िल्मी सितारों को अपने साथ जोड़ने में लगी थीं। गांगुली के मन को बदलना आसान काम नहीं था, लेकिन अमित शाह के पास एक अचूक हथियार था। एक क्रिकेटर के तौर पर गांगुली का क्रिकेट बोर्ड के साथ अक्सर विवाद चलता रहा था। अब, अमित शाह भारतीय क्रिकेट कंट्रोल बोर्ड (बीसीसीआई) का अध्यक्ष का पद उन्हें इनाम के तौर पर देने वाले थे। शाह को उम्मीद थी कि इससे गांगुली को भाजपा के करीब लाना आसान हो जाएगा। 'क्या यह सच है कि आप बीसीसीआई के अध्यक्ष पद के लिए कोशिश कर रहे हैं और शायद एक दिन बंगाल के मुख्यमंत्री भी बन जाएं?' 2017 में कोलकता में एक पुस्तक विमोचन समारोह में मैंने गागुंली से पूछा था। 'आप पत्रकारों की यही परेशानी है, बेमतलब की अटकलें लगाते रहते हैं। मैं जहां हूं, वहां खुश हूं,' गांगुली के जवाब में चिड़चिड़ाहट महसूस हो रही थी। 'मुझे-राजनीति-में-कोई-

दिलचस्पी-नहीं', वाला उनका रुख एक दिखावा भर था; गांगुली महत्वाकांक्षी थे और अहम बात यह कि वे बीसीसीआई के सत्ता के केन्द्र बनने के ख़िलाफ़ नहीं दिखे।

बीसीसीआई के चुनावों में 'साज़िशें' और 'गुप्त सौदे' होना कोई नई बात नहीं है। अक्टूबर 2019 के चुनावों के दौरान, गांगुली को इंडियन प्रीमियर लीग (आईपीएल) की गवर्निंग काउंसिल के उपाध्यक्ष या अध्यक्ष बनाने की पेशकश की गई थी, उन्होंने उसे अस्वीकार कर दिया। उस वक्त क्रिकेट के हलकों में बड़ी चर्चा थी कि बीसीसीआई के पूर्व अध्यक्ष एन. श्रीनिवासन समेत एक प्रभावशाली वर्ग कर्नाटक के पूर्व टैस्ट खिलाड़ी बृजेश पटेल को अध्यक्ष बनाना चाह रहा था। बधाई संदेश आने लगे थे और पटेल को अध्यक्ष घोषित करने वाली प्रेस-विज्ञप्ति का मसौदा तैयार किया जा रहा था, उस वक्त पूरी योजना में एक नाटकीय बदलाव हुआ। मुंबई में बोर्ड की बैठक के बाद, गांगुली, ट्राइडेंट होटल के अपने सुइट में थे, तभी उनके फ़ोन की घंटी बजी। फोन पर दूसरी तरफ बीसीसीआई के अध्यक्ष रहे और अब केन्द्रीय वित्त राज्य मंत्री अनुराग ठाकुर थे। ठाकुर ने कहा, 'दादा, मुझे आपको यह बताते हुए खुशी हो रही है कि अमित शाह जी को लगता है कि बीसीसीआई का नेतृत्व करने लिए आप सही व्यक्ति होंगे।' गांगुली को शुरू में तो यह यकीन नहीं हुआ कि फोन किसी ने मज़ाक के लिए किया था या सच में असली प्रस्ताव था। जैसे ही उन्होंने इस प्रस्ताव पर हामी भरी, बृजेश पटेल को अध्यक्ष घोषित करने वाली विज्ञप्ति को तुरंत वापस लिया गया और उन्हें बीसीसीआई के बजाय आईपीएल गवर्निंग कांउसिल का प्रमुख बना दिया गया। मैच फिक्सिंग विवाद के बाद भारतीय क्रिकेट की प्रतिष्ठा बहाल करने वाले कप्तान गांगुली अब क्रिकेट प्रशासन की कमान सभालेंगे। सबसे अमीर और ताकतवर बीसीसीआई के अध्यक्ष बनने वाले वे पहले टैस्ट क्रिकेटर हैं। बोर्ड के सचिव और उनके सहायक के तौर पर शाह के छोटे बेटे जय शाह थे। क्रिकेट बोर्ड पर भाजपा का पूरा कब्ज़ा हो चुका था। तो आखिरी समय में बदलाव क्यों? एक शब्द का जवाबः राजनीति! अमित शाह ने 2021 के बंगाल चुनाव की बाज़ी चल दी थी। फ़ोन लाइनें व्यस्त हो गई थीं। गृहमंत्री ने अपने पद के प्रभाव का इस्तेमाल करते हुए श्रीनिवासन जैसे बोर्ड के प्रमुख सदस्यों को अनिच्छा से अपना मन बदलने को मजबूर कर दिया था। शाह की रणनीति साफ थीः गांगुली को पहले बीसीसीआई का अध्यक्ष बनाओ, फिर उन्हें विधानसभा चुनावों में भाजपा के संभावित मुख्यमंत्री उम्मीदवार के तौर पर पेश करो। इस सब खेल के संपर्क सूत्र अनुराग ठाकुर को शाह ने बताया कि 'बस गांगुली को यह याद दिलाए रखा जाए कि उन्हें यह पद हमने दिया था।'

औपचारिक तौर पर शाह समेत हर शख्स ने इस बात से इंकार किया कि गांगुली को बोर्ड का अध्यक्ष बनाने के लिए कोई 'डील' हुई थी। बोर्ड के निष्पक्ष और 'स्वतंत्र' चुनावों में कोई दवाब नहीं था। पूर्व क्रिकेट कप्तान गांगुली ने जोर देकर कहा, 'मेरी बात पर भरोसा कीजिए, कभी कोई लेन-देन जैसी बात नहीं हुई। किसी ने मुझसे कभी नहीं कहा कि बोर्ड अध्यक्ष बनने

के बदले मुझे भाजपा को समर्थन देना होगा।' कोई भी सौदा चाहे 'साफ' हो या 'अनकहा', लेकिन भाजपा के नेताओं को यकीन था कि गांगुली 2021 के बंगाल विधानसभा चुनावों में पार्टी के लिए प्रचार तो करेंगे। बंगाल भाजपा के एक नेता का कहना था, 'हर बात का ढोल पीटने की ज़रूरत नहीं होती, लेकिन यह उम्मीद तो थी कि ज़रूरत के वक्त गांगुली हमारे साथ रहेंगे।' दिसम्बर 2020 में, बंगाल के चुनाव ज़्यादा दूर नहीं थे, तब भाजपा नेतृत्व ने आगे बढ़ने का फ़ैसला किया। अनुराग ठाकुर ने गांगुली को फ़ोन कर भाजपा में शामिल होने के लिए कहा। गांगुली खुद को फंसा हुआ महसूस कर रहे थे। हालांकि प्रस्ताव तो आकर्षक था, लेकिन उन्हें इस बात का एहसास था कि औपचारिक रूप से किसी पार्टी में शामिल होने से बंगाली 'आइकन' के तौर पर उनकी प्रतिष्ठा इस बंटी हुई राजनीति में उलझ जाएगी। अपने पत्रकार मित्रों से बातचीत में उनका मानना था कि भाजपा के लिए बंगाल की लड़ाई आसान नहीं होगी। प्रदेश में ममता बनर्जी आगे लग रही थीं और उनसे गांगुली के संबंध भी अच्छे थे। गांगुली ने ठाकुर से कहा, 'मुझे नहीं लगता कि मैं इसके लिए तैयार हूं।' अमित शाह ने जनवरी 2021 में चुनाव तैयारियों की देखरेख के बहाने कोलकता का दौरा किया, लेकिन उनका असल एजेंडा एक और कोशिश करके गांगुली को भाजपा के साथ लाना था। जब शाह कोलकता पहुंचे, तब ख़बर मिली कि गांगुली को सीने में दर्द की शिकायत के बाद अचानक अस्पताल में भर्ती कराया गया था। उनकी एंजियोप्लास्टी करके एक स्टेंट डाला गया। दिल में ब्लॉकेज की वजह से उन्हें आराम करने की सलाह दी गई। ऐसे में चुनाव पर चर्चा के बजाय, शाह ने गांगुली की तबियत जानने के लिए फ़ोन किया। मैंने पूछा, क्या गृहमंत्री से मिलने से बचने के लिए आपको अस्पताल जाना पड़ा? उन्होंने कहा: 'आप फिर से बेवजह अटकलें लगा रहे हैं। मैं दिल की बीमारी का बहाना कैसे बना सकता हूं।'

गांगुली के बार-बार सफाई देने और इंकार करने के बावजूद उनके किसी भी वक्त भाजपा के मंच पर दिखाई देने की अफवाहें चलती रहीं। 7 मार्च, 2021 को कोलकता के ब्रिगेड मैदान में एक रैली के साथ भाजपा को अपने बंगाल अभियान की शुरुआत करनी थी। प्रधानमंत्री इस रैली को संबोधित करने वाले थे। रैली के दिन सवेरे भाजपा के एक नेता ने हमसे कहा, 'अगर गांगुली वहां पहुंचते हैं तो अचरज में ना आएं'। समाचार चैनलों पर ना केवल अटकलों का दौर चल रहा था, बल्कि गांगुली के आवास के बाहर कैमरे लगे हुए थे। गांगुली मेरा फ़ोन नहीं उठा रहे थे और न ही मेरे संदेशों का जवाब दे रहे थे। दोपहर दो बजे, आखिरकार उन्होंने जवाब दिया, 'मुझे कितनी बार कहना होगा, मैं राजनीति में शामिल नहीं हो रहा।' सौरव गांगुली के बजाय, 80 के दशक के सुपरस्टार मिथुन चक्रवर्ती को रैली मैदान में मंच पर भीड़ से मिलवाया गया। 'मिशन गांगुली' की नाकामी के बाद शाह ने दूसरे विकल्प के साथ जाना तय किया। मिथुन चक्रवर्ती ने कुछ दिनों पहले ही आरएसएस प्रमुख मोहन भागवत से मुलाक़ात की और

भाजपा को समर्थन देने का वादा किया था। सत्तर के दशक में चक्रवर्ती नक्सली आंदोलन से जुड़े थे। उस समय बहुत से बंगाली युवा इस सशस्त्र वामपंथी संघर्ष से प्रभावित हो रहे थे। चक्रवर्ती 2014 में तृणमूल कांग्रेस से राज्यसभा के सांसद तो बने, लेकिन संसद में उनकी मौज़ूदगी ना के बराबर रही, उन्होंने कभी कोई सवाल भी सदन में नहीं पूछा और 2016 में इस्तीफ़ा दे दिया। अब वे फिर से राजनीतिक सुर्खियों में थे। इस बार उन्होंने संघ के साथ अपने 'आध्यात्मिक संबंध' होने का दावा किया।

अक्टूबर 2022 में बीसीसीआई के नए अध्यक्ष के चुनाव में सौरव गांगुली के फिर से इस कुर्सी पर बैठने की उम्मीदें ख़त्म हो गईं। 2019 में, शाह को अपने राजनीतिक एजेंडे के लिए एक स्टार क्रिकेट की ज़रूरत थी। दुर्भाग्य से गांगुली उस वक्त काम नहीं आए। अब उन्हें 'कुर्बान' करने में कोई हर्ज नहीं था। बीसीसीआई चुनावों से पहले दिल्ली में अमित शाह के आवास पर बैठक चल रही थी। इस बैठक में बोर्ड के पूर्व अध्यक्ष श्रीनिवासन ने गांगुली को समर्थन नहीं देने की घोषणा कर दी। श्रीनिवास ने कहा कि 'बोर्ड के इतिहास में कोई भी दो बार अध्यक्ष नहीं रहा है। इसके साथ ही गांगुली अध्यक्ष रहते हुए भी आईपीएल टीमों और उत्पादों का विज्ञापन कर रहे थे और सलाह भी दे रहे थे। यह दोनों के हितों में टकराव है।' किसी ने उनकी बात पर आपत्ति ज़ाहिर नहीं की। इसके बजाय यह फ़ैसला किया गया कि गांगुली की ज़गह अब पूर्व खिलाड़ी और विश्व कप विजेता टीम में रहे रोज़र बिन्नी, बोर्ड के अध्यक्ष बनेंगे। एक रियायत के तौर पर गांगुली को आईपीएल के अध्यक्ष की पेशकश की गई, जिसे उन्होंने अस्वीकार कर दिया। गांगुली ने दिल्ली कैपिटल्स फ्रेंचाइज़ी के साथ क्रिकेट निदेशक बनना पसंद किया। गांगुली बाहर हो गए थे, लेकिन तीस साल के जय शाह को बोर्ड के ताकतवर सचिव बनाए रखने का निर्णय किया गया। आखिरकार वे गृहमंत्री के बेटे थे और प्रशासक के तौर पर उनके पास सभी अधिकार और संरक्षण था। राजनीति की तरह, क्रिकेट बोर्ड में भी कोई 'स्थायी दोस्त या दुश्मन' नहीं होता।

═

'दीदी ओ दीदी।'

2021 के बंगाल चुनाव के आखिरी दौर में प्रधानमंत्री मोदी ने ममता बनर्जी पर तीन शब्दों का तंज कसा था, लेकिन उसने प्रधानमंत्री को ही परेशान किया। राजनीतिक पर्यवेक्षक इसे महिला विरोधी बयान के तौर पर देख रहे थे। उन्होंने इसे एक अनुभवी महिला राजनेता के ख़िलाफ़ तंज और गाली के तौर पर माना, जो प्रधानमंत्री के लिए ठीक नहीं मानी जा सकती। लेकिन यह भाजपा की उस सोची-समझी रणनीति का हिस्सा थी, जिसमें ममता बनर्जी परेशान हो जाएं और गुस्से में कोई जवाब दे ताकि इसे मुख्यमंत्री और प्रधानमंत्री के बीच मुकाबले

में बदला जा सके। भाजपा के एक रणनीतिकार ने माना, 'सौरव गांगुली के चुनावी लड़ाई में शामिल होने से इंकार करने के बाद हमारे पास बहुत कम विकल्प बचे थे, अब इसे प्रधानमंत्री बनाम मुख्यमंत्री लड़ाई बनाने के अलावा कोई चारा नहीं था।' ममता बनर्जी को उकसाने पर जल्दी गुस्सा हो जाने के लिए जाना जाता है। 2019 के चुनाव अभियान में भाजपा ने अपने कार्यकर्ताओं को ममता बनर्जी की रैलियों और रोड़ शो में 'जयश्री राम' के नारे लगाकर बाधा पहुंचाने के लिए कहा था। इसी दौरान एक वीडियो वायरल हो गया था जिसमें ममता बनर्जी अपनी कार से उतरकर 'जय श्री राम' के नारे लगाने वालों से भिड़ गई थीं। इससे भाजपा को ममता बनर्जी को हिंदू विरोधी के रूप में पेश करने का मौका मिल गया। इस बार उनकी टीम सतर्क और सचेत थी। प्रशांत किशोर ने मुझे बाद में बताया, 'बंगाल में हमारी सबसे बड़ी चुनौती यह तय करना था कि हम कोई बड़ी गलती न करें। ममता दीदी पर लगातार हमलों के बीच उन्हें शांत रखना ज़रूरी था।' तृणमूल के रणनीतिकारों ने चतुराई दिखाई, प्रधानमंत्री के बयान को उनकी महिला नेता को परेशान करने और बंगालियों के उपहास से जोड़ दिया। क्षेत्रीय अस्मिता पर जोर दिया गयाः 'बांग्ला निजेर मेये कई चाय' (बंगाल अपनी बेटी चाहता है), यह जवाबी नारा था। मोदी और शाह को 'बाहरी' के तौर पर ब्रांड किया गया। टीएमसी को बंगाली गौरव को बनाए रखने, बंगाली संस्कृति को आगे बढ़ाने वाली और दिल्ली की अंहकारी पार्टी के ख़िलाफ़ क्षेत्रीय अस्मिता के लिए लड़ने वाली पार्टी के तौर पर पेश किया गया, एक ऐसी पार्टी जो प्रदेश के हितों की रक्षा करेगी। बंगाल बनाम दिल्ली एक ऐसा मुद्दा है जिसका पिछले कई सालों में राजनीतिक फायदे के लिए इस्तेमाल किया गया। वामपंथियों ने अपनी सरकार के दौरान इसको बार-बार भुनाया। बंगाल में भाजपा के चुनाव प्रभारी कैलाश विजयवर्गीय का कहना था, 'ऐसा नहीं है कि प्रधानमंत्री को ममता बनर्जी से कोई खास शिकायत हैं, लेकिन चुनाव प्रचार की गर्मी में प्रतिद्वन्दी के ख़िलाफ़ जोश में कुछ ऐसी बातें हो जाती हैं।'

मोदी-शाह की जोड़ी आसानी से हार मानने वालों में से नहीं है। कोविड महामारी की चेतावनियों के बावजूद इस आठ चरणों वाले चुनाव में प्रधानमंत्री मोदी ने बंगाल में बिना रुके और आक्रामक प्रचार जारी रखा, जब तक कि चुनाव आयोग के प्रोटोकॉल ने आखिरी चरण में उन्हें पीछे हटने के लिए मजबूर नहीं कर दिया। यह हर हाल में चुनाव जीतने की इच्छा तो थी हीः इसके अलावा 'पुराने घाव' भी मोदी बनाम दीदी टकराव को बढ़ा रहे थे। 2002 में जब ममता बनर्जी वाजपेयी के नेतृत्व वाली एनडीए सरकार में शामिल थीं, तो वे गुजरात में हुई सांप्रदायिक हिंसा के बाद मोदी को मुख्यमंत्री पद से बर्खास्त करने की मांग में शामिल हो गई थीं। भाजपा के एक नेता ने कहा, 'प्रधानमंत्री आसानी से भूलते या माफ़ नहीं करते हैं। वे आसानी से दीदी से हारने वाले नहीं हैं।' देश के गृहमंत्री होने के बावजूद, अब बंगाल में ज्यादा समय बिता रहे अमित शाह ने भी लड़ाई नहीं छोड़ी थी। दिसम्बर 2020 में, शाह, बनर्जी के एक विश्वस्त सहयोगी

सुवेन्दु अधिकारी को अपने पाले में लाने में कामयाब हो गए थे। सुवेन्दु अधिकारी पूर्वी मिदनापुर से तृणमूल कांग्रेस के कद्दावर नेता थे और उन्होंने साल 2007 में नंदीग्राम 'भूमि अधिग्रहण' आंदोलन में अहम भूमिका निभाई थी। इस आंदोलन ने ममता बनर्जी को सत्ता में पहुंचा दिया था। टीएमसी की युवा शाखा के प्रमुख के रूप में सुवेन्दु का अभिषेक बनर्जी से विवाद तब शुरू हुआ जब अभिषेक ने पार्टी के भीतर ही अपना एक अलग समानांतर युवा संगठन खड़ा कर दिया। मुख्यमंत्री के भतीजे को संरक्षण देने का मतलब था कि अधिकारी खुद को पार्टी की अगली पीढ़ी के सत्ता संघर्ष में मुश्किल में देख रहे थे। मुख्यमंत्री की एक दिल्ली यात्रा के गवाह रहे एक वरिष्ठ पत्रकार ने बताया, 'संसद के सेन्ट्रल हॉल में जब ममता बनर्जी अभिषेक बनर्जी समेत अपने सांसदों का अभिवादन कर रही थीं, तो उन्होंने अपने साथ खड़े सुवेन्दु अधिकारी से, सभी के लिए चाय का इंतज़ाम करने को कहा। उन्होंने फिर जोर देकर कहा, देख लीजिएगा कि चाय अच्छी हो, जबकि उस वक्त वे दूसरे सांसदों के साथ खुश होकर बात कर रही थीं।' एक सांसद ने हंसते हुए बताया, 'जब दीदी कोई संदेश देना चाहती हैं तो वे आंख से आंख नहीं मिलाती, बल्कि आपसे चाय के इंतज़ाम के लिए कहती हैं।' हालांकि गंभीर चेहरे वाले सुवेन्दु में गांगुली जैसी स्टार अपील तो नहीं थी, लेकिन भाजपा ने उसे बड़ी जीत के तौर पर लिया था। शाह ने ममता खेमे को कड़ा संदेश देने के लिए सुवेन्दु को नंदीग्राम से चुनाव लड़ने को कहा, जो अधिकारी परिवार का गढ़ माना जाता था। अधिकारी ने 2016 के विधानसभा चुनावों में यहां से 80 हज़ार वोटों से बड़ी जीत हासिल की थी। टीएमसी के रणनीतिकार प्रशांत ने कहा, 'जब हमें पता लगा कि भाजपा सुवेन्दु को अपना उम्मीदवार बना रही है तो हमें लगा कि ममता को यह चुनौती स्वीकार करना चाहिए और वहां से चुनाव लड़ना चाहिए।' प्रशांत किशोर ने कहा कि एक असली नेता को हमेशा निडर दिखना चाहिए। हालांकि ममता बनर्जी नंदीग्राम से चुनाव हार गईं, लेकिन उन्होंने बड़ी जंग जीत ली थी।

तीस फ़ीसदी से ज़्यादा मुस्लिम आबादी वाले राज्य में अमित शाह धार्मिक ध्रुवीकरण पर ज़्यादा भरोसा कर रहे थे। 2019 के लोकसभा चुनावों में भाजपा की बढ़त की एक बड़ी वजह मुख्यमंत्री के ख़िलाफ़ 'मुस्लिम तुष्टिकरण' करने का अभियान रहा। इस अभियान का असर खासतौर से दलित और आदिवासी इलाकों में पड़ा, जहां भाजपा के वोट शेयर में इज़ाफा हुआ। मुख्यमंत्री की इस्लाम समर्थक 'जिहादी दीदी' की छवि बनाने के लिए भाजपा ने अपने कार्यकर्ताओं से ममता बनर्जी की नमाज अता करने वाली तस्वीरों को व्हाट्सएप ग्रुप और दूसरे तरीकों से साझा करने को लिए कहा। उस समय तो ममता बनर्जी ने मुस्लिम समर्थक टैग पर गुस्से में प्रतिक्रिया दी, लेकिन अब नंदीग्राम में उन्होंने 'हिंदू चंडीपाठ' के श्लोंकों के सही पाठ के साथ अपने अभियान की शुरुआत की। मुख्यमंत्री ने पलटवार करते हुए कहा, 'मैं भी एक हिंदू महिला हूं। मेरे साथ हिंदू कार्ड खेलने की कोशिश मत करिए। क्या तुम जानते हो कि एक

अच्छा हिंदू कैसे बना जाता है?' भाजपा के भड़काऊ बयानों और अभियान से मुस्लिम वोट ममता बनर्जी के साथ मजबूती से खड़ा हो गया था। अब वो अपनी सरकार की योजनाओं का लाभ पाने वाली महिलाओं और हिंदू मतदाताओं को अपने पाले में लाने में लगी थीं। प्रशांत किशोर ने कहा, 'जब आपको अल्पसंख्यक वोटों का बड़ा हिस्सा मिलने का भरोसा हो जाता है तो आपको केवल यह रणनीति बनानी होती है कि बहुसंख्यक समदाय आपसे अलग-थलग ना हो, और उसका एक बड़ा हिस्सा अब भी आपको वोट दे।' अल्पसंख्यकों का बड़ा वोट, गरीब दलितों और आदिवासियों में बढ़े हिस्से के साथ महिलाओं का समर्थन मिलने से ममता दीदी भाजपा के 'विजय रथ' को पीछे धकेलने में लगी थीं।

10 मार्च 2021 को, नंदीग्राम में जब वो चुनाव प्रचार में लगी थीं, अचानक एक ख़बर आई, 'ममता बनर्जी घायल हो गई हैं, उन्हें अस्पताल ले जाया गया।' जब वो मौजूदा भीड़ का हाथ हिलाकर अभिवादन कर रही थीं, तो कार का दरवाज़ा उनके पैर पर टकराने से उन्हें चोट लग गई थी। 'यह उनकी हत्या की साज़िश है, कुछ अनजान लोगों ने उन्हें कार में धकेल दिया,' उनके साथ मौजूद तृणमूल सांसद सुखेंदु शेखर रे चिल्ला रहे थे। वीडियो फुटेज से लगा कि यह एक दुर्घटना थी, भीड़भाड़ वाली गली में कार का दरवाज़ा एक खंभे से टकराने से ऐसा हुआ। कुछ घंटों बाद अस्पताल में भर्ती ममता दी की तस्वीरें इंटरनेट पर छाई हुई थीं, जिनमें उनके पैर पर प्लास्टर चढ़ा हुआ था और वे तकलीफ में दिख रही थीं। एक्स-रे रिपोर्ट में उनके बाएं टखने में फ्रैक्चर दिखाया गया था। तीन दिन बाद, मुख्यमंत्री व्हीलचेयर पर अस्पताल से बाहर आईं। उन्होंने कहा, 'मैं अपने टूटे पैर के साथ व्हीलचेयर पर ही पूरे बंगाल में प्रचार करूंगी।' इसका असर बढ़ाने के लिए उन्होंने कहा, 'खेला होबे'। महीनों बाद जब मैंने पूछा कि क्या व्हीलचेयर का मकसद मतदाताओं की सहानुभूति हासिल करना था, तो वे नाराज़ हो गईं। उन्होंने जवाब दिया, 'अब भी मेरा बायां टखना देख लो, उसमें सूजन आई हुई है।' उन्होंने ज़ोर दिया, वे व्हीलचेयर से सभाओं में भाषण देने के बजाय पैदल चलना और लोगों से मिलना पसंद करती हैं। 'क्या आप जानते हैं कि मैं हर दिन 30 हज़ार कदम चलती हूं और अपनी स्मार्ट वॉच पर इसका हिसाब रखती हूं।' उनका कहना था कि 'जब तक दूसरा विकल्प हो, मेरा जैसा व्यक्ति क्यों व्हीलचेयर पर रहेगा।' अब इसे चाहे संयोग कहें या जानबूझकर लेकिन एक दृढ निश्चयी मुख्यमंत्री, व्हीलचेयर पर अपनी खास सफेद साड़ी और रबर की चप्पल पहने अकेली महिला की फोटो 2021 के बंगाल चुनाव अभियान की ऐसी तस्वीर बन गई, जिसने नतीजों को वोट से पहले ही तय कर दिया था।

ऐसा लग रहा था कि चुनावी हवा टीएमसी नेता के पक्ष में बहने लगी थी, लेकिन अमित शाह आश्वस्त थे कि भाजपा मशीनरी आखिर में जीत ही जाएगी। अप्रैल की शुरुआत में, एक प्रेस-कान्फ्रेंस के तुरंत बाद कोलकता के एक होटल में मैं गृहमंत्री से मिला, जहां शाह ने दावा

किया कि भाजपा 294 सदस्यों वाली विधानसभा में 200 से ज़्यादा सीटें जीतेगी। मैंने पूछा, 'आपको इतना भरोसा कैसे है जबकि महिलाओं और अल्पसंख्यकों का वोट अब भी ममता के साथ है?' गृहमंत्री ने मुझे खारिज़ करते हुए अपने अंदाज़ में जवाब दिया, 'आप स्टूडियो में चुनाव भविष्यवाणी करने वालों के साथ ज़्यादा वक्त बिताते हैं। ज़मीन पर आइए, असल में बदलाव हो रहा है।' मैंने गृहमंत्री से कहा, चुनावों के बाद इस पर बात करेंगे।

जब 5 मई को पश्चिम बंगाल में नतीजे आए तो एक पार्टी को दो सौ से ज़्यादा सीटें मिली थी, लेकिन वह पार्टी बीजेपी नहीं थी। तृणमूल कांग्रेस ने सत्ता की हैट्रिक लगाते हुए 215 सीटों के साथ ज़बरदस्त जीत हासिल कर ली थी। भाजपा ने अब तक के अपने सबसे बेहतर प्रदर्शन के साथ 77 सीटें जीती थीं, लेकिन वो अमित शाह के आत्मविश्वास से भरे दावे से बहुत दूर थी। दीदी ने अपनी उम्मीद से भी ज़्यादा सीटों के साथ, 'करो या मरो' का खेला जीत लिया था। 2015 में बिहार के बाद मोदी-शाह जोड़ी के लिए किसी बड़े राज्य के चुनावों में यह बड़ा झटका था। तृणमूल कांग्रेस की चुनावी रणनीति में अहम भूमिका निभाने वाले उत्साहित प्रशांत किशोर ने कहा, 'मीडिया ने जो अजेय होने की छवि बनाई थी, वो ख़त्म हो गई है। अब आप तय कीजिए कि असली चाणक्य कौन है?'

पहले महाराष्ट्र में 'साहेब' ने मात दी, तो अब पश्चिम बंगाल में 'दीदी' ने पटखनी दे दी। यह साफ हो गया था कि राज्यों के विधानसभा चुनाव राष्ट्रीय स्तर के आम चुनावों से बिल्कुल अलग खेल है। शरद पवार और ममता बनर्जी जैसे क्षत्रपों ने बता दिया कि वे क्षेत्रीय भावनाओं, अस्मिता और अपने दमदार नेटवर्क से भाजपा जैसी ताकतवर मशीनरी को भी हरा सकते हैं। अपने अस्तित्व पर ख़तरा दिखने पर क्षेत्रीय दल स्थानीय पहचान, गरिमा और संस्कृति के मज़बूत आधार के साथ करो या मरो की लड़ाई में पूरी ताकत लगा सकते हैं। बहुदलीय व्यवस्था की जड़ें भारत में गहरी हैं और लोकप्रिय स्थानीय नेताओं का मज़ाक उड़ाना या अपमान को मतदाता पसंद नहीं करता। 2024 के चुनावों में भी मतदाताओं का यही रुख रहेगा तो किसी एक पार्टी का एकछत्र राज होना नामुमकिन हो जाएगा। महाराष्ट्र और बंगाल में हार का मतलब था कि मोदी-शाह की जोड़ी को भारतीय जनता पार्टी की चुनावी मशीनरी को फिर से पटरी पर लाने की सख्त ज़रूरत है। कांटों के ताज वाला यह खेल अब वहां और मुश्किल होने वाला था, जिससे सिंहासन मिलता हैः उत्तरप्रदेश।

6

योगी है उपयोगी

भारत में शायद ही कोई प्रधानमंत्री नरेन्द्र मोदी की तरह मीडिया में अपनी 'नकारात्मक' छवि को लेकर इतना चिंतित रहा होगा। मोदी टीवी की ख़बरों पर बारीक नज़र रखते हैं और सोशल मीडिया पर भी उनका बड़ा ध्यान रहता है। एक आलोचक ने एक बार मोदी सरकार को 'ट्विटर की, ट्विटर द्वारा और ट्विटर के लिए', कहा था। मई 2021 में कोविड की दूसरी लहर के दौरान एक बड़े हिन्दी न्यूज़ चैनल पर अपने संसदीय क्षेत्र वाराणसी में गंगा से तीन शव निकाले जाने की लाइव तस्वीरें देखकर प्रधानमंत्री मोदी चौंक से गए थे। ख़बर थी: 'बिहार से लेकर उत्तरप्रदेश तक, गंगा में लाशें ही लाशें'। टीवी पर रिपोर्टर जिन लोगों से बात कर रहा था, वे राज्य और केन्द्र सरकार दोनों को ज़िम्मेदार ठहरा रहे थे। एक युवक ने अपने बुजुर्ग पिता के शव को नदी में फेंकते हुए कहा, 'यहां कोई व्यवस्था नहीं हैं, ना योगी जी की ना मोदी जी की, हम लाश बहाने के लिए मजबूर हैं।'

टीवी चैनल पर कोविड आपदा की भयावह तस्वीरें देखकर प्रधानमंत्री गुस्से में दिखाई दिए। 'आप लोगों ने कहा था कि हालात काबू में हैं, वाराणसी में यह क्या हो रहा है?' उनसे जुड़े एक आला अधिकारी ने बताया, 'जब मोदी जी गुस्से में होते हैं तो वे कम बोलते हैं। उनके लहज़े से समझ आता है कि प्रधानमंत्री जी गुस्से में हैं।' प्रधानमंत्री की हमेशा चौकस रहने वाली मीडिया टीम और सरकार के सूचना प्रसारण मंत्रालय के अफसर पहले से ही न्यूज़ चैनलों के संपादकों से बात कर रहे थे और उन्हें शवों की तस्वीरें दिखाने से बचने के निर्देश दे रहे थे। 'यह संवेदनशील मुद्दा है जो प्रसारण नियमों के भी ख़िलाफ़ है। आप इस तरह से शवों को नहीं दिखा सकते, क्या आप चाहते हैं कि आपका लाइसेंस निलंबित कर दिया जाए,' एक चैनल के संपादक को मंत्रालय के अफसर ने सीधी चेतावनी दी।

उधर, लखनऊ में मुख्यमंत्री योगी भी अपने आवास पर नदी में बहते शवों की भयावह तस्वीरें देख रहे थे। प्रधानमंत्री की तरह मुख्यमंत्री योगी आदित्यनाथ भी मीडिया में अपनी छवि को लेकर चौकस रहते हैं। 2017 में अचानक सत्ता में आने के बाद से ही योगी ने अपनी सरकार को लेकर बहुत कम 'नकारात्मक' ख़बरों को मीडिया में आने दिया है। मीडिया पर छवि को मैनेज करने के लिए सख्त नियम बनाए गए हैं। खबरों में सरकारी नज़रिए पर सवाल उठाने का मतलब सरकार से नाराज़गी मोल लेना होता है। ज़िला प्रशासन के अफसरों को ऐसी ख़बरों पर नज़र रखने और उनकी जांच करने के साथ, सरकार की छवि खराब करने पर उन्हें तलब करने के निर्देश हैं। सरकार की आलोचना करने वाली ख़बरों को लेकर सरकार ने कई पत्रकारों के ख़िलाफ़ पुलिस में रपट भी दर्ज कराई।

2019 में मिर्जापुर के एक पत्रकार पर सरकार को बदनाम करने की साज़िश का आरोप लगाया गया, क्योंकि उसने एक सरकारी स्कूल में बच्चों को मिलने वाले भोजन में रोटी और नमक परोसने का वीडियो बनाया था। इस पर तुरंत मामला दर्ज़ किया गया। 2020 में कानपुर में एक अखबार के रिपोर्टर ने रेत माफिया और ज़मीन हड़पने वालों का पर्दाफाश किया था, वह जब मोटरसाइकिल पर अपने दोस्त के साथ घर लौट रहा था, तब उसकी गोली मारकर हत्या कर दी गई। उसी साल, एक डिजिटल न्यूज़ एजेंसी 'स्क्रॉल' की कार्यकारी संपादक सुप्रिया शर्मा के ख़िलाफ उस रिपोर्ट को लेकर एफआईआर दर्ज की गई, जिस रिपोर्ट में बताया गया था कि वाराणसी में प्रधानमंत्री के गोद लिए गांव में लोग कोविड के लॉकडाउन में भूख से परेशान थे। पत्रकारों पर हमले को लेकर बनी एक कमेटी की रिपोर्ट में कहा गया कि 2017 से फरवरी 2022 के बीच योगी सरकार में पत्रकारों के ख़िलाफ़ 138 मामले दर्ज किए गए, 48 पत्रकारों पर हमले हुए और 66 पर मामले दर्ज किए गए या उन्हें गिरफ्तार किया गया। इनमें से ज़्यादातर 78 फ़ीसदी मामले कोविड महामारी के दौरान 2020 और 2021 के बीच दर्ज किए गए।

उस वक्त योगी सरकार के एक बड़े आईएएस अफसर, नवनीत सहगल (1988 बैच) इस सब पर नज़र रखते थे। उत्तरप्रदेश प्रशासन के किसी भी कामयाब अफसर की तरह उन्हें भी राज बदलने के बावजूद एक सरकार से दूसरी सरकार में अपनी मजबूत जगह बनाने की महारथ हासिल थी। एक ज़माने में सहगल बहुजन समाज पार्टी की नेता और मुख्यमंत्री मायावती के सबसे विश्वस्त अफसर माने जाते थे, फिर जब अखिलेश यादव की सरकार आई, तब भी वे महत्वपूर्ण पद पर रहे थे और अब योगी सरकार में उनकी ज़िम्मेदारी सूचना विभाग को देखने की रही। जब गंगा में बहती लाशों की तस्वीरें चल रही थीं तो मुख्यमंत्री ने स्पष्ट निर्देश दिया, 'ये क्या हो रहा है, इसे बंद करवाइए!'

सहगल के लिए यह बड़ी चुनौती थी। मुख्यमंत्री चाहते थे कि कोविड में यूपी की दुखद घटनाओं की ख़बरें पूरी दुनिया तक ना पहुंचें। सहगल ने लखनऊ और दिल्ली में अखबारों

और न्यूज़ चैनलों के संपादकों और मालिकों से सीधे निर्देश के साथ संपर्क किया: 'लाशों को दिखाना बंद करिए। आप बेवजह इसे सनसनीखेज़ बना रहे हैं। अगर आप इसी तरह करते रहे तो हमें कार्रवाई करनी पड़ेगी।' वे इन सब आरोपों को ख़ारिज़ करते हैं। अब सहगल दिल्ली में प्रसार भारती का जिम्मा संभालते हैं। उन्होंने बेबाकी से कहा, 'मैं तो बस यह बता रहा था कि यूपी के कुछ इलाकों में शवों के जल समाधि की परपंरा है, इसे कोविड से क्यों जोड़ा जा रहा है।'

उस वक्त सबके दिमाग में चुनाव चल रहे थे। 2022 की शुरुआत में उत्तरप्रदेश में विधानसभा चुनाव होने वाले थे और राजनीतिक नजरिए से कोविड की भयावह दूसरी लहर इससे ज़्यादा गलत समय पर नहीं हो सकती थी। भाजपा अपने इस मज़बूत गढ़ उत्तरप्रदेश को वायरस की तबाही के बावजूद खोना नहीं चाहती थी। 1985 में नारायण दत्त तिवारी के बाद से प्रदेश में कोई दोबारा मुख्यमंत्री नहीं चुना गया था, और इससे भी बढ़कर आज़ादी के बाद से प्रदेश में किसी मुख्यमंत्री ने पांच साल का कार्यकाल पूरा नहीं किया था। जब मुख्यमंत्री योगी और भाजपा इस इतिहास को बनाए रखने की कोशिश में लगे थे, तब प्रधानमंत्री का फोकस इस बात पर था कि कोविड की वजह से 'सुशासन गुरु' की उनकी छवि को कोई नुकसान नहीं पहुंचे। मोदी की कर्मभूमि वाराणसी अब तैरती हुई लाशों केन्द्र बना हुआ था, और मीडिया कवरेज में अब वो 'मिठास और खुशामद' नहीं थी। फिर भी मीडिया को भले ही कुछ फोन से नियंत्रण में किया जा सकता हो, लेकिन ज़मीनी हालात पर काबू के लिए ज़्यादा ध्यान देने की ज़रूरत थी।

संकट की इस घड़ी में प्रधानमंत्री मोदी ने अपने भरोसेमंद सहयोगी रहे अरविंद शर्मा को याद किया, जो हाल में ही सरकारी अफसर से राजनेता बने थे। 1988 बैच के गुजरात कॉडर के अधिकारी शर्मा ने मोदी के साथ गुजरात में और दिल्ली में काम किया था। मेहनती, विनम्र और काम को अंजाम तक पहुंचाने के साथ किसी बात पर सवाल ना करने वाले अफसर को प्रधानमंत्री अपने साथ रखते हैं और शर्मा हमेशा उनकी कोर टीम का हिस्सा रहे। जनवरी 2021 में, अरविंद शर्मा ने सिविल सेवाओं से रिटायरमेंट लिया और तीन दिन बाद ही भारतीय जनता पार्टी में शामिल हो गए। 'सरकारी ड्रैस' छोड़कर अब उनके सिर पर 'भगवा टोपी' आ गई थी। एक हफ्ते में ही उन्हें उत्तरप्रदेश विधान परिषद में मनोनीत कर दिया गया और साथ ही पार्टी के प्रदेश उपाध्यक्ष भी बन गए, इससे उनके योगी सरकार में शामिल होने की अटकलें भी शुरू हो गईं क्या वे उत्तरप्रदेश में प्रधानमंत्री की आंख-कान बनने आए हैं? या फिर योगी सरकार पर अंकुश लगाएंगे? इस सवाल का जवाब देने से बच रहे थे शर्मा जी। शर्मा ने जवाब दिया, 'मैं यहां प्रधानमंत्री की इच्छा के मुताबिक लोगों का काम करने आया हूं, कृपया अटकलबाज़ी न करें।' उत्तरप्रदेश में कोविड से मौत का सरकारी आंकड़ा मई के आखिर में बीस हज़ार तक पहुंच गया था, जब जून में कोविड के मामले तेज़ी से बढ़ने लगे

तो प्रधानमंत्री ने शर्मा को तलब किया और उनकी भूमिका स्पष्ट की: 'वाराणसी में भयावह होते हालात को काबू किया जाए।'

शर्मा को वाराणसी और आसपास के ज़िलों में कोविड के प्रबंधन का प्रभारी बनाने के लिए मुख्यमंत्री से सलाह नहीं ली गई, उन्हें केवल जानकारी दी गई। सरकार के एक आला अफसर ने सफाई देते हुए कहा, 'ऐसा नहीं है कि केन्द्र सरकार और राज्य सरकार एक दूसरे से उलट दिशा में या ख़िलाफ़ काम कर रहे हैं। हम यह सुनिश्चित करना चाहते थे कि चिंताजनक हालात पर काबू के लिए किसी अच्छे व्यक्ति को ज़िम्मेदारी दी जाए। प्रधानमंत्री फ़ैसला लेने का नियंत्रण छोड़ना पसंद नहीं करते। जब वे कुछ तय कर लेते हैं तो उसे तुरंत और हर हाल में पूरा करना चाहते हैं। वैसे भी योगी लखनऊ से सब काम देख रहे थे, हम वाराणसी को नज़रअंदाज़ नहीं कर सकते, वह प्रधानमंत्री का संसदीय क्षेत्र है।'

वाराणसी पहुंचते ही शर्मा ने तुरंत काम शुरू कर दिया। वाराणसी उस वक्त वेंटिलेटर्स और ऑक्सीजन सिलेंडर की भारी कमी का सामना कर रहा था। प्रधानमंत्री के आदेश का तुरंत असर दिखाई दिया। जब औरंगाबाद की एक एजेंसी को ऑक्सीजन प्लांट की तत्काल ज़रूरत बताई गई और देशभर से भी बैकअप आर्डर का हवाला दिया गया। उन्हें स्पष्ट निर्देश दिया गया कि यह कोई 'साधारण आर्डर' नहीं, बल्कि प्रधानमंत्री के संसदीय क्षेत्र के लिए है। अगले ही दिन, ऑक्सीजन प्लांट मशीन वाराणसी के रास्ते पर थी, जिससे शहर के बड़े सरकारी अस्पताल को काफी राहत मिली। गुजरात से चार सौ सिलेंडर के अलावा देश के अलग-अलग हिस्सों से भी वेंटिलेटर और ऑक्सीजन सिलेंडर वाराणसी के लिए मंगवाए गए। चौबीसों घंटे चलने वाले 'कोविड रिस्पॉंस सेंटर' से शर्मा और उनकी टीम ने हालात पर काफी हद तक काबू पा लिया।

मुख्यमंत्री योगी को वाराणसी में प्रधानमंत्री का दखल कोविड के प्रबंधन में सरकार के ख़िलाफ़ 'अविश्वास प्रस्ताव' जैसा महसूस हो रहा था। उत्तरप्रदेश जैसे बड़े राज्य में कोविड ने सरकार के चिकित्सा इंतज़ामों और स्वास्थ्य सिस्टम की पोल खोल दी थी। मार्च-अप्रैल 2021 में प्रदेश में हुए पंचायत चुनावों में ज़ोरदार मुकाबला हुआ था, लेकिन इससे कोविड के मामले भी तेजी से बढ़े। चुनाव ड्यूटी पर लगे शिक्षकों पर कोविड का हमला हुआ। इसके साथ ही पड़ोसी राज्य उत्तराखंड में अप्रैल में कुंभ मेले ने कोविड को तेज़ी से फैला दिया। फिर भी सरकार इस पर ज़ोर देती रही कि चिंता की कोई बात नहीं है। मुख्यमंत्री भी कोविड के शिकार हो गए और अगले दिन 15 अप्रैल को उन्होंने ट्वीट किया: 'चिंता करने की ज़रूरत नहीं है, उत्तरप्रदेश सरकार आपके साथ है।' लेकिन ज़मीनी हकीकत ऐसी नहीं थी, तस्वीर बेहद खराब थी। प्रदेश के ज़्यादातर अस्पतालों में मरीज़ों के लिए जगह नहीं बची थी, बिस्तरों और ऑक्सीजन की कमी से कोविड का इलाज करना मुश्किल हो रहा था। गांवों में हालात तो और ज़्यादा खराब

थे। कई ज़िलों में तो कोविड के टेस्ट के भी इंतज़ाम नहीं थे। बहुत सी मौतों में कारण कोविड नहीं बताया गया। फिर भी ऐसे हालात में मुख्यमंत्री 'सब ठीक है' का संदेश जारी कर रहे थे, मानो वे किसी दूसरी दुनिया में रह रहे हों। हकीकत से मुंह मोड़ना, सच्चाई को नकार कर बड़े पैमाने पर हालात अच्छे होने का प्रचार करना, सरकार के लिए सामान्य था।

लेकिन गंगा में तैरती लाशों की तस्वीरें सरकार के लिए 'अंतिम चेतावनी' जैसी थीं। क्या मोदी सरकार कोविड के दौरान उत्तरप्रदेश में मुख्यमंत्री बदलने के बारे में सोच रही थी? मैंने उत्तरप्रदेश की नुमाइंदगी करने वाले एक केन्द्रीय मंत्री से सीधा सवाल पूछा। 'मैं समझता हूं कि मोदी जी शुरू में यूपी सरकार के कामकाज से खुश नहीं थे, लेकिन मुझे नहीं लगता कि मुख्यमंत्री बदलने के बारे में कोई योजना थी। ऐसा नहीं था कि यह परेशानी केवल उत्तप्रदेश में ही हो। आप अगर एक मुख्यमंत्री बदलते हैं तो फिर दूसरों को भी जिम्मेदार मानना होगा।' केन्द्रीय मंत्री के इस लचर से जवाब के बावजूद सबसे बड़ी राजनीतिक ताकत वाला उत्तरप्रदेश देश के किसी दूसरे राज्य जैसा नहीं था। यहां से आने वाली 80 लोकसभा सीटें भाजपा की ताकत के लिए महत्वपूर्ण हैं। और ना ही योगी आदित्यनाथ सिर्फ़ एक और मुख्यमंत्री भर हैं। अपनी सरकार के कुछ सालों में भगवा पहने, कानों में कुंडल डाले और मुंडे सिर वाले इस छोटे कद के उग्र धर्मगुरु ने भाजपा कार्यकर्ताओं के बीच खुद को 'हिंदुत्व' का चेहरा बना लिया है। देशभर में चुनाव प्रचार में प्रधानमंत्री के अलावा सबसे ज़्यादा भीड़ लाने वाला चेहरा भगवाधारी योगी आदित्यनाथ का ही है। भाजपा के एक चुनाव रणनीतिकार ने बताया कि 'जब भी हम देशभर में कोई अभियान बनाते हैं तो उम्मीदवार योगी की कम से कम एक रैली ज़रूर चाहते हैं।'

'मोदी के बाद, कौन?' यह सवाल अक्सर हवा में रहता है। अटकलें थी कि गृहमंत्री अमित शाह अपने से करीब दस साल छोटे योगी आदित्यनाथ को प्रधानमंत्री पद के लिए अपनी चुनौती के तौर पर देखते हैं। क्या गुजरात की जोड़ी नंबर-1, साल 2022 में उत्तरप्रदेश के अहम विधानसभा चुनावों से पहले योगी को मात देने की कोशिश कर रही थी। इस सवाल का जवाब भले ही ना मिला हो, लेकिन यह 2024 के आम चुनावों में भी भाजपा को परेशान करता रहेगा।

टीकाकरण अभियान में देरी हो गई थी, लेकिन कोविड से मौतों पर जब काफी हद तक काबू पा लिया गया, तो 21 नवम्बर 2021 को मुख्यमंत्री योगी आदित्यनाथ ने अपने आधिकारिक ट्विटर हैंडल से एक तस्वीर जारी की, जिसमें प्रधानमंत्री मोदी और योगी साथ-साथ चल रहे हैं और मोदी का हाथ योगी के कंधे पर है। 'हम निकल पड़े हैं प्रण करके / अपना तन-मन अर्पण करके / ज़िद है एक सूर्य उगाना है / अंबर से ऊंचा जाना है / एक भारत नया बनाना है।' लेकिन तस्वीर के आगे यह कैप्शन बेमायना सा हो गया था। 'मिशन उत्तरप्रदेश' के लिए प्रधानमंत्री और मुख्यमंत्री एक ही मंच पर थेः एक, भाजपा के आगे बढ़ने का 'राष्ट्रीय चेहरा' तो दूसरा उत्तरप्रदेश का 'शुभंकर'। भाजपा की प्रचार मशीनरी बार-बार इसे 'डबल इंजन' की सरकार

कहती है। यानी इस बहाने वह गैर-भाजपा सरकारों को 'सिंगल इंजन' और भाजपा सरकारों को 'डबल इंजन' की ताकत वाली सरकार बताती है।

कुछ हफ्तों बाद, दिसम्बर 2021 में उत्तरप्रदेश के शाहजहांपुर में 594 किलोमीटर लंबे गंगा एक्सप्रेस-वे की आधारशिला रखने के बाद प्रधानमंत्री ने रैली में एक नया मुहावरा गढ़ा: 'उत्तरप्रदेश प्लस योगी, बहुत है उपयोगी'। ऐसा लग रहा था मानो कोविड संकट और उससे हुई मौतें अब बीते ज़माने की बात हो गई थीं। अब मुख्यमंत्री की नई तस्वीर गढ़ी जाने लगी थीः माफिया राज को ख़त्म करने वाला, और विकास की रफ्तार बढ़ाने वाला हिंदुत्ववादी चेहरा। उत्तरप्रदेश के 2022 के विधानसभा चुनावों के लिए खाका तैयार हो गया था।

═

मार्च 2017 में, पहली बार मुख्यमंत्री बनने के एक हफ्ते बाद ही योगी आदित्यनाथ ने प्रदेश के आला पुलिस अफसरों की बैठक बुलाई थी। ज्यादातर पुलिस अफसर नए मुख्यमंत्री से पहली बार मिल रहे थे, इसलिए थोड़ा घबराए हुए थे क्योंकि बैठक का कोई एजेंडा भी नहीं बताया गया था। सख्त चेहरे के साथ मुख्यमंत्री ने कमरे में चारों तरफ नज़र घुमाई और दृढ़ता के साथ कहा, 'मुझे अगले हफ्ते तक उत्तरप्रदेश के सभी गैंग और उनके गैंग लीडर्स की पूरी लिस्ट चाहिए।' कमरे में कुछ देर सन्नाटा सा था। मुख्यमंत्री ने अपनी मुट्ठी मेज पर थपथपाते हुए कहा, 'सभी गैंगस्टरों को साफ संदेश मिलना चाहिए कि योगी सरकार में किसी को बख्शा नहीं जाएगा। ज़ीरो टालरेंस!'

बैठक में मौजूद रहे एक अधिकारी ने बताया कि मुख्यमंत्री के सख्त लहज़े ने कुछ अफसरों को चिंता में डाल दिया था। 'जब एक सहयोगी ने इससे पुलिस ज़्यादतियों की आशंका ज़ाहिर की तो उसे तुरंत ही आदेश के ख़िलाफ ना जाने की हिदायत दी गई। हम उसी दिन समझ गए थे कि एक ऐसे मुख्यमंत्री के साथ काम करना है जो लीक पर चलने वाले लोगों में से नहीं है। योगी आदित्यनाथ अपनी बात साफ़गोई से रखने में परहेज़ नहीं करते।' जून 2017 में, टीवी के एक कार्यक्रम *आप की अदालत* में, मुख्यमंत्री ने एक ऐसी चेतावनी दी जो संवैधानिक पदों पर बैठने वाले लोग नहीं देते: 'अगर अपराध करेंगे तो ठोक दिए जाएंगे।' मुख्यमंत्री के इस 'ठोक देंगे' वाले रवैये को पुलिस को 'हत्या का लाइसेंस' देने के तौर पर देखा गया। मुख्यमंत्री के एक साल पूरा होने पर जारी पोस्टर में दावा किया गया, एक साल में 1,038 मुठभेड़ हुईं, जिनमें 32 लोग मारे गए और 238 घायल हुए। अंग्रेजी अखबार *इंडियन एक्सप्रेस* में छपी एक रिपोर्ट के मुताबिक उत्तरप्रदेश में साल 2017 से 2023 के बीच पुलिस मुठभेड़ (एनकाउंटर) में 186 हत्याएं हुईं (कानूनी प्रक्रिया के बाहर सुरक्षा एजेसियों द्वारा हत्या, लोकतंत्र में घृणित होनी चाहिए)। इसका मतलब हर पखवाड़े यूपी पुलिस ने एक से ज़्यादा कथित अपराधी को

एनकाउंटर कर मार दिया। इन पुलिस मुठभेड़ों में 5,046 घायल हुए, यानी हर पन्द्रह दिनों में 30 से ज्यादा कथित अपराधी पुलिस की गोली से घायल हुए। इनमें से ज़्यादातर मुठभेड़ मौतों को ना तो अदालतों में चुनौती दी गई और ना ही कोई सवाल उठाए गए। बिना किसी आपत्ति के औपचारिक नियमित मजिस्ट्रेट जांच पूरी कर ली गई। वरिष्ठ वकील संजय हेगड़े का आरोप है कि योगी सरकार में मुठभेड़ सामान्य प्रक्रिया हो गई है और पूरी आपराधिक न्याय प्रणाली को कमतर कर दिया गया है।

लेकिन आंकड़ों से तस्वीर पूरी साफ़ नहीं होती। पश्चिमी उत्तरप्रदेश में मेरठ, मुज़फ़्फ़रनगर, सहारनपुर और बागपत जैसे मुस्लिम बहुल ज़िलों में बड़ी संख्या में मुठभेड़ हुईं। इनमें मारे गए ज़्यादा गैंगस्टर्स मुस्लिम थे। उत्तरप्रदेश के गैंग अक्सर जातियों और समुदायों पर संगठित होते हैं। इनके बीच ख़ूनी मुकाबले राजनेताओं से उनकी करीबी और सामाजिक बंटवारे की कहानियां भी बताते हैं। उत्तरप्रदेश के गिरोह अक्सर जाति और समुदाय के आधार पर संगठित होते हैं। इसका अच्छा उदाहरण आदित्यनाथ के अपने निर्वाचन क्षेत्र गोरखपुर में है, जहां गैंगस्टर से राजनेता बने ब्राह्मण हरि शंकर तिवारी और ठाकुर वीरेंद्र प्रताप शाही के गिरोहों के बीच झगडों में दर्जनों लोग मारे गए। यूपी पुलिस के एक अधिकारी ने बताया, 'उत्तरप्रदेश में आपको गैंगवार को अक्सर जाति और समुदायों के नजरिए से देखना पड़ता है, क्योंकि उनके गैंगलीडर खुद को अपनी जाति या समुदाय के रक्षक के तौर पर पेश करते हैं।' पूर्वी उत्तरप्रदेश के दो बड़े गैंगस्टर-राजनेता, अतीक अहमद और मुख्तार अंसारी को 'मुस्लिम डॉन' कहा जाता था, लेकिन दोनों को मुस्लिम समाज के अलावा दूसरे समुदायों का भी समर्थन हासिल था। अप्रैल 2023 में, प्रयागराज के एक सरकारी अस्पताल के बाहर तीन हमलावरों ने अतीक अहमद की उस वक्त गोली मारकर हत्या कर दी, जब पुलिस उसे मेडिकल जांच के लिए ले जा रही थी। हत्या को लाइव टेलीविजन पर देखा गया था। इस सबसे बेफ़िक्र मुख्यमंत्री योगी ने इसे माफ़िया राज का अंत बताया।

योगी आदित्यनाथ का जन्म उत्तराखंड के एक सुदूर गांव में 1971 में हुआ था। उनके बचपन का नाम अजय मोहन बिष्ट था। राम जन्मभूमि आंदोलन के दौरान 1993 में उनके जीवन में बड़ा बदलाव तब आया जब वे गोरखनाथ मंदिर दर्शन के लिए गए थे और वहां उनकी मुलाकात महंत अवैद्यनाथ से हुई। महंत अवैद्यनाथ राम मंदिर आंदोलन के सबसे मुखर समर्थकों में से एक थे और उनकी आंदोलन में सक्रिय भूमिका रही थी। महंत अवैद्यनाथ ने 'युवा रामभक्त' को भरोसा दिलाया कि वह एक 'जन्मजात योगी' है और दीक्षा के बाद 1998 में उन्हें अपना उत्तराधिकारी घोषित किया। उसी साल भाजपा ने उनके गुरु अवैद्यनाथ की जगह योगी आदित्यनाथ को गोरखपुर से पार्टी का लोकसभा उम्मीदवार भी बनाया। वरिष्ठ पत्रकार और योगी आदित्यनाथ पर जीवनी लिखने वाले शरत प्रधान ने बताया कि गोरखधाम पीठ एक समतावादी व्यवस्था

का दावा करता है, जिसमें उसके दरबार में स्थानीय मुस्लिमों समेत सभी लोग आते हैं। प्रधान का मानना हैं कि 'एक धर्मगुरु के तौर पर योगी आदित्यनाथ भले ही सभी समुदायों के बीच सामाजिक और आध्यात्मिक काम करने का दावा करते हों, लेकिन एक राजनेता के तौर पर वे बेबाक कट्टरपंथी हिंदू हैं, जिनका धर्म उनके दिल के करीब है।'

अपने राजनीतिक जीवन की शुरुआत में योगी ने 'गो-रक्षा मंच' बनाया, जो जल्द ही 'हिंदू युवा वाहिनी' में बदल गया। आरोप है कि युवा वाहिनी ने हिंदू हितों के नाम पर मुस्लिमों के ख़िलाफ़ सांप्रदायिकता को बढ़ावा दिया। आरोप है कि 1999 में युवा वाहिनी के कार्यकर्ता एक काफिले में महाराजगंज के एक मुस्लिम बहुल गांव में घुस गए, जहां उन पर हिंदुओं को भड़काने और एक कब्र खोदने का आरोप भी लगा। जब योगी के इस काफिले को भाजपा सरकार का विरोध कर रहे समाजवादी पार्टी के कार्यकर्ताओं की एक टोली ने रोकने की कोशिश की तो कथित तौर पर उनको पीटा गया, गोली चलाई गई, जिसमें एक की मौत हो गई। योगी पर हत्या के आरोप को 2019 में इलाहाबाद उच्च न्यायालय की सांसदों और विधायकों की विशेष अदालत ने खारिज़ कर दिया। प्रधान का कहना है कि 'उस वक्त एक उग्र हिंदू भड़काऊ भाषण देने वाला नेता पैदा हुआ।'

अगले दशक में युवा वाहिनी का नाम गोरखपुर और उसके आसपास के इलाकों में सांप्रदायिक दंगों में शामिल होने के लिए लिया जाता रहा। हिंसा भड़काने में आदित्यनाथ की भूमिका अक्सर सवालों के घेरे में रही। 2005 में आदित्यनाथ को एक भड़काऊ भाषण देते सुना गयाः 'अगर एक हिंदू का ख़ून बहेगा, तो कम से कम दस लोगों की हत्या करवाएंगे।' उन्होंने ऐलान किया कि वे गोरखपुर ज़िले में ताजिया के जुलुस की इज़ाजत नहीं देंगे। आरोप है कि उन्होंने अपने समर्थकों को उनकी होली जलाने के लिए उकसाया। आदित्यनाथ की निजी सेना का मार्च चल रहा था। वह अक्सर 'लव जिहाद' के नाम पर हिंदू-मुस्लिम शादियों में घुस जाती। योगी 'लव जिहाद' शब्द का इस्तेमाल अपने भाषणों में अंतरधार्मिक विवाहों को निशाना बनाने के लिए करते थे। उनके समर्थक किसी मांस रखने या बेचने वाले पर गोहत्या का आरोप लगाकर धमकाते थे।

मुख्यमंत्री बनने के बाद आदित्यनाथ युवा वाहिनी के अपने उग्र अतीत को छोड़कर सबके लिए बराबर कानून-व्यवस्था में सख्त दिखना चाहते थे। उत्तरप्रदेश के एक पुलिस अधिकारी का कहना था, 'हमें निर्देश दिए गए थे कि क़ानून को अपने हाथ में लेने वाला कोई भी हो, यानी हिन्दू-मुसलमान, उसे गिरफ़्तार कीजिए।' यानी मुख्यमंत्री ना तो किसी का पक्ष लेने के लिए कह रहे थे और ना ही किसी के साथ भेदभाव करने की बात थी। इसके बावजूद यह धारणा ज़ोर पकड़ रही थी कि माफियाओं पर सख्ती, दरअसल मुसलमानों के ख़िलाफ़ जंग थी। मेरठ के एक सामाजिक कार्यकर्ता राशिद अहमद (बदला हुआ नाम) का कहना था, 'देखिए, आप

बरसों तक मुसलमानों के ख़िलाफ़ जहर उगलते रहे और हमला करते रहे, तो फिर अचानक एक दिन सबके लिए बराबर की क़ानून का शासन चलने वाले की छवि नहीं बना सकते। चाहे आप पंसद करें या नहीं, लेकिन मुसलमान उनसे सताए हुए महसूस करते हैं।' अहमद, योगी सरकार के पहले फ़ैसलों में से एक का ज़िक्र करते हुए कहते हैः 'अवैध बूचड़खानों को बंद करने के आदेश क्या यह भेदभाव वाली राजनीति नहीं है?' अहमद ने आरोप लगाया कि योगी, अपनी ठाकुर जाति के किसी भी गैरक़ानूनी कारोबार पर कार्रवाई नहीं करेंगे, लेकिन मुसलमान के कथित अवैध कारोबार पर पुलिस एक्शन में देर नहीं लगेगी। बरसों से मांस के कारोबार में लगे लोगों पर कार्रवाई कर उन्हें बेरोज़गार कर दिया गया।

मुख्यमंत्री ऐसी आलोचनाओं की परवाह नहीं करते। 2018 में पश्चिमी उत्तरप्रदेश के मुस्लिम इलाकों में काम करने वाले एक सामाजिक संगठन ने स्थानीय मुसलमानों पर पुलिस की कथित ज़्यादतियों को लेकर एक बड़ी रिपोर्ट बनाई थी और एक आला अधिकारी की मार्फ़त मुख्यमंत्री से मिलने का समय मांगा। काफी कोशिशों के बाद अधिकारी उनकी बात मुख्यमंत्री कार्यालय तक पहुंचाने के लिए तैयार हुए। लेकिन उस पर हफ्तों तक कोई जवाब नहीं मिला। जब उस आला अधिकारी ने इस मसले पर मुख्यमंत्री के करीबी एक बड़े अधिकारी से बात की, तो उन्हें सलाह दी गई कि इस मुद्दे को आगे न बढ़ाएं।

साल 2022 के विधानसभा चुनावों से पहले इस 'राजनीतिक हिन्दू' को बांटने वाली राजनीति को आगे बढ़ाया गया, जिसमें मुसलमानों को या तो 'शैतान' के तौर पर पेश किया गया, या फिर उनकी परवाह नहीं थी। एक मीडिया कॉन्क्लेव में जब उनसे सवाल किया गया कि विपक्ष का आरोप है कि मुख्यमंत्री भाजपा के ब्राह्मण नेतृत्व को नाराज़ करने की क़ीमत पर भी ठाकुर राज को बढ़ावा दे रहे हैं? तो उन्होंने जवाब देने में देर नहीं लगाईः 'यह लड़ाई उससे बहुत आगे जा चुकी है। यह लड़ाई अब अस्सी बनाम बीस की हो चुकी है।' ज़ाहिर है इशारा, उत्तरप्रदेश में मुसलमानों की 19-20 फ़ीसदी आबादी को लेकर था। संविधान की शपथ लेने वाले मुख्यमंत्री स्पष्ट कर रहे थे कि असली लड़ाई ब्राह्मणों और ठाकुरों के बीच नहीं थी। क्या वे हिंदुओं और अल्पसंख्यक मुसलमानों के बीच धार्मिक लड़ाई की बात कर रहे थे?

इस विवादित टिप्पणी पर विपक्षी नेताओं ने 'सांप्रदायिक वोट बैंक' राजनीति का आरोप लगाया, लेकिन इसके चौबीस घंटे में मुख्यमंत्री फिर से उसी ज़मीन पर थे। 'अस्सी बनाम बीस' के बयान पर सफाई मांगे जाने पर आदित्यनाथ पीछे हटने को तैयार नहीं थे। उन्होंने कहा, 'अस्सी बनाम बीस एक हकीकत है। 20 प्रतिशत वे लोग हैं जो राम जन्मभूमि, काशी विश्वनाथ धाम और मथुरा-वृन्दावन के विकास का विरोध करते हैं... जो माफिया और आंतकवादियों से सहानुभूति रखते हैं।' इसे सांप्रदायिकता को हवा देने और हिंदू वोट बैंक को एकजुट करने की बदनुमा कोशिश कहा जा सकता है। एक महीने बाद, उत्तरप्रदेश के दूसरे चरण की वोटिंग

से पहले, आदित्यनाथ ने सफाई दी, उनका बयान किसी जाति या धर्म को लेकर नहीं था। 'मैंने कहा अस्सी प्रतिशत लोग भाजपा के साथ हैं और बीस प्रतिशत लोग हमारा विरोध करते हैं और इस बार भी वो ऐसा करेंगे। इस बीस प्रतिशत में वे लोग शामिल हैं जो वैक्सीन, महिला सुरक्षा, गरीबों के लिए कल्याणकारी योजनाओं, राजमार्ग और मेडिकल कालेज जैसी योजनाओं का विरोध करते हैं।' इसे आप राजनीतिक चालाकी कह सकते हैं। पहले आप अपने कट्टर समर्थकों के साथ खड़े होने का माहौल बनाते हैं और फिर किसी आलोचना की परवाह किए बिना कहते हैं कि आपकी बात का ग़लत मतलब निकाला गया।

'चाल-चरित्र और चेहरे' की राजनीति करने वाले भाजपा की पिछली पीढ़ी के नेताओं से उलट आदित्यनाथ संवैधानिक मापदंडों से बेपरवाह दिखते हैं और न ही उन्हें इस बात का डर लगता है कि चुनाव आयोग उन पर कोई कार्रवाई कर सकता है। उनकी राजनीति बाबरी मस्जिद गिराए जाने के बाद के दौर की है। इसमें मुसलमानों पर हमला करना सामान्य होता जा रहा है। इसमें भगवा पहने हिंदू साधु का देश में सबसे बड़ी आबादी वाले राज्य का नेतृत्व करना किसी धर्मनिरपेक्ष गणराज्य को कमज़ोर करने के तौर पर नहीं देखा जाता। साधु-संत समाज अस्सी और नब्बे के दशक में रामजन्मभूमि आंदोलन में शामिल था और 'हिंदू ताकत' के तौर पर 'त्रिशूल' का इस्तेमाल दिखाने के लिए किया जाता था। आदित्यनाथ ने मुख्यमंत्री बनने के बाद अपनी सरकार की शैली बताने के लिए एक नया हथियार ढूंढ लिया थाः 'बुलडोजर'।

मुख्यमंत्री ने बुलडोजर शब्द का सार्वजनिक तौर पर इस्तेमाल पहली बार सितम्बर, 2017 में किया था। जब उन्होंने चेतावनी दी थी कि वे अपराधियों की संपत्ति पर बुलडोजर चलाएंगे। वैसे 2020 की शुरुआत में उन्होंने बुलडोजर का इस्तेमाल अपराधियों पर नहीं, सीएए विरोधी प्रदर्शनकारियों में दहशत फैलाने के लिए किया था, जिनमें ज़्यादातर मुसलमान थे। प्रदर्शनकारियों ने कई जगहों पर पुलिस के साथ झड़प की, जिससे दंगे और आगजनी की घटनाएं हुईं। इसके बाद योगी सरकार ने विरोध प्रदर्शन के दौरान बर्बरता के आरोपियों की तस्वीरों के 'नाम और पते' के साथ लखनऊ में बैनर लगवा दिए, जो 'बदनाम और शर्मिंदा' करने के लिए काफी थे। उन्हें नुक़सान की भरपाई का नोटिस जारी कर चेतावनी दी गई कि जुर्माना नहीं भरने पर उनकी संपत्ति ज़ब्त कर ली जाएगी। और आखिरी कदम के तौर पर घरों को बुलडोजर से गिराने की धमकी दी गई। लखनऊ की नेता-सामाजिक कार्यकर्ता सदफ जाफ़र, जिन्होंने बाद में 2022 में कांग्रेस के टिकट पर चुनाव लड़ा, ने गुस्से में कहा, 'यह पागलपन था। हमारे साथ अपराधियों जैसा सलूक किया जा रहा था, ये मुकदमा अदालत में नहीं योगी राज में चल रहा था, जहां सिर्फ़ एक का हुक्म चलता था।'

सुप्रीम कोर्ट ने इसमें दख़ल देते हुए राज्य सरकार को सीएए विरोधी प्रदर्शनकारियों से वसूले गए पैसे वापस करने का आदेश दिया तो उत्तरप्रदेश सरकार ने एक कदम आगे बढ़कर एक

क़ानून बना दिया, जो मुआवज़े के तौर पर संपत्ति जब्त करने का अधिकार देता है। 'बुलडोज़र न्याय' के इस सिस्टम पर योगी सरकार का बचाव था कि वो सिर्फ़ कानून व्यवस्था को लागू कर रही है। तत्कालीन सहायक पुलिस महानिदेशक (क़ानून और व्यवस्था) और 'बुलडोज़र अभियान' के प्रभारी प्रशांत कुमार ने दावा किया, 'मुख्यमंत्री के सख्त निर्देश हैं कि बुलडोजर का इस्तेमाल सिर्फ़ अपराधियों और माफिया के ख़िलाफ़ किया जाए।' 2020 में जिस अपराधी विकास दुबे की गैंग ने गोलीबारी में आठ पुलिसकर्मियों को मार दिया था, उसकी संपत्ति को बुलडोजर से गिरा दिया गया।

वैसे कट्टर अपराधियों और प्रदर्शनकारियों के बीच फ़र्क करने वाली रेखा धुंधली थी। जून 2022 में पैगंबर पर भाजपा के एक नेता की भड़काऊ टिप्पणी के बाद प्रदेश भर में पथराव की घटनाएं और विरोध प्रदर्शन हुए। इनके कथित मास्टरमाइंड की संपत्तियों को तेज़ी से गिरा दिया गया था। मुख्यमंत्री के मीडिया सलाहकार मृत्युंजय कुमार ने एक बुलडोजर की तस्वीर को ट्वीट करते हुए एक पूर्वाग्रह भरा पोस्ट कियाः 'याद रखें, हर शुक्रवार के बाद शनिवार आता है।' हरियाणा भाजपा के आईटी-सैल के प्रभारी अरुण यादव का ट्वीट थाः 'शुक्रवार पथराव दिवस है तो शनिवार को बुलडोजर दिवस घोषित किया जाना चाहिए!' बुलडोजर हमले को लेकर अब विपक्ष ने योगी आदित्यनाथ को 'बुलडोजर बाबा' का नाम दे दिया था। एक बार फिर सुप्रीम कोर्ट ने दखल देते हुए चेतावनी दी, 'विध्वंस क़ानून के मुताबिक हो, प्रतिशोध के लिए नहीं हो सकते।'

2022 के चुनावों के दौरान उत्तरप्रदेश के शहरों और गांवों की गलियों-मोहल्लों में जाने से समझ आने लगा था कि बुलडोजर अभियान ने मतदाताओं पर असर किया था। जिस राज्य में अखिलेश यादव के नेतृत्व वाली पिछली समाजवादी सरकार पर अपराधियों के प्रति नरम रवैया रखने और मुसलमानों के तुष्टिकरण के आरोप लगते थे, वहां आदित्यनाथ ने खुद की एक मज़बूत क़ानून-व्यवस्था वाले ताकतवर नेता के तौर पर जगह बना ली थी। मुस्लिमों पर सांप्रदायिक हमला करते यानी 'तालिबानी' मानसिकता को किसी भी हाल में बर्दाश्त नहीं करने वाला हिन्दू नायक के तौर पर आदित्यनाथ लोकप्रिय थे। नतीजतन, बड़ी निर्माण परियोजनाओं में काम आने वाली बुलडोजर, अब कमज़ोर लोगों पर बहुसंख्यवादी हमले और ताकतवर शासन का राजनीतिक प्रतीक बन गई थी।

चुनावों के दौरान जब मैंने मुज़फ्फरनगर के एक गांव में मिले एक जाट परिवार से पूछा कि आप किसे वोट देंगे, तो उन्होंने उत्साह से जवाब दिया, 'हम बुलडोजर को वोट देंगे!' जबकि 2020 में मोदी सरकार के कृषि क़ानूनों के ख़िलाफ़ किसानों के प्रदर्शन में उस परिवार ने हिस्सा लिया था। इन चुनावों में भाजपा का चुनाव चिन्ह कमल और बुलडोजर एक तरह से इस्तेमाल होने लगे थे। आदित्यनाथ की कुछ रैलियों में बुलडोजर की तस्वीरें भी थीं। मैंने परिवार के एक

पुरुष से पूछा कि जब वो कुछ महीने पहले कृषि कानूनों के ख़िलाफ़ थे, तो अब भाजपा को वोट क्यों देंगे? 'वो अलग बात हैं। यहां योगीजी ने क़ानून ठीक किया है। अब हमारी बेटी शाम को भी बिना डरे बाहर जा सकती है और पूरे गांव में शांति रहती है,' उसने बिना रुके जवाब दिया। दिल्ली में प्रदर्शन के वक्त नाराज़ जाट किसान अपने गांव में पहले राजनीतिक नजरिए से हिंदू था, फिर किसान। इस मजबूत हिन्दू पहचान की राजनीति को चुनौती देना, कमज़ोर और बंटे हुए विपक्ष के लिए आसान नहीं होने वाला था।

═

समाजवादी पार्टी के नेता अखिलेश यादव को आरामतलब ज़िंदगी पसंद है। उन्हें परिवार के साथ छुट्टियां बिताना अच्छा लगता है और उनकी पसंदीदा जगह लंदन हैं, जहां वे हर गर्मियों में काफी वक्त गुजारते हैं। उन्हें खेल पसंद हैं, खासतौर से क्रिकेट और टेनिस। जब अखिलेश उत्तरप्रदेश के मुख्यमंत्री थे, तब उन्होंने सरकारी आवास में एक फुटबॉल का मैदान और जिम बनवाया था। उनकी यह आराम-पसंद जीवनशैली उनके पिता और समाजवादी पार्टी के संस्थापक मुलायम सिंह यादव की देहाती परवरिश से बिल्कुल अलग है। मुलायम सिंह किसान परिवार में पैदा हुए थे। पश्चिमी उत्तरप्रदेश में अपने गांव सैफई से कॉलेज के लिए उन्हें रोजाना बीस किलोमीटर जाना पड़ता था। पहलवानी का शौक रखने वाले मुलायम सिंह को कॉलेज के रास्ते में झील को पार करना होता था, जो मानसून में भर जाती थी। इसका मतलब अपनी साइकिल को कंधों पर उठाना और उसे एक बरगद के पेड़ पर बांध देना होता था। बाद में साइकिल ही समाजवादी पार्टी का प्रतीक बन गई। लोग उन्हें 'नेताजी' कहकर सम्मान देते थे। मुलायम सिंह के राजनीतिक जीवन को लंबे समय तक देखने वाले वरिष्ठ पत्रकार राहुल श्रीवास्तव, नेताजी की सादगी की एक कहानी बताते हैं। मुलायम सिंह को उसी कॉलेज में नौकरी मिल गई थी, जहां उन्होंने पढ़ाई की थी। एक दिन वे कॉलेज के मालिक लालाजी के घर पर थे, तभी उनके टेलीफोन की घंटी बजी। लालाजी ने उन्हें फ़ोन उठाने को कहा, लेकिन मुलायम ने कभी फ़ोन देखा या बात नहीं की थी। फ़ोन उठाते वक्त वे डरे हुए थे। दूसरी तरफ से फोन पर हैलो-हैलो की आवाज़ आ रही थी। मुलायम को लगा कि वो हिलो-हिलो कह रहा है। गुस्साए मुलायम ने कहा, 'तुम हिलो, हम क्यों हिलें?' और फोन पटक दिया।

इसके विपरीत अखिलेश का जन्म वीआईपी सुविधाओं के बीच हुआ था। मुलायम सिंह अट्ठाईस साल की उम्र में विधायक बन गए थे। पार्टी में पदाधिकारी रहे एक नेता ने बताया कि 'अखिलेश को सबकुछ बहुत आसानी से मिल गया। मुलायम ने मुश्किल राजनीतिक लड़ाईयां लड़ी, लेकिन अखिलेश को तो एक तरह से सत्ता थाली में परोस दी गई।' अखिलेश 39 साल की उम्र में 2012 में यूपी के सबसे युवा मुख्यमंत्री बन गए थे। पार्टी के कार्यकर्ता अखिलेश

को प्यार से 'भैया' कहकर बुलाते हैं। पांच साल बाद जब चुनावों में वे सत्ता से बाहर हो गए तो उन्हें अपनी हार का कराण समझ नहीं आ रहा था। उन्होंने दावा किया, 'हमने इतना काम किया, फिर भी जनता ने नकार दिया। चुनाव में हमारा काम नहीं, मोदी जी का जादू चला है!'

आमतौर पर सहज दिखने वाले अखिलेश यादव को राजनीति की गहरी समझ अपने पिता से विरासत में मिली है। 2022 के चुनावों के वक्त जब योगी सरकार कोविड के संकट काल से गुजर रही थी तो अखिलेश को इस बार चुनावी पहिया अपने पक्ष में घूमता लग रहा था। अखिलेश के एक उद्योगपति मित्र ने 2021 की गर्मियों में कोविड की दूसरी लहर के दौरान खुश दिखते अखिलेश से मुलाकात को याद करते हुए बताया, 'अखिलेश ने मुझसे कहा, "कोविड ने योगी राज को भी ख़त्म कर दिया है"।' अखिलेश ने शायद एक सर्वेक्षण करवाया था, जिसमें सरकार के ख़िलाफ़ नाराज़गी बढ़ती दिख रही थी। जब अगस्त 2021 में *इंडिया टुडे* 'मूड ऑफ द नेशन' के सर्वेक्षण में भी मतदाताओं की नाराज़गी दिखाई गई तो उन्हें यकीन हो गया कि हवा बदल रही थी। उन्होंने कहा कि 'उत्तरप्रदेश को चलाना योगीजी के बस की बात नहीं है।' अखिलेश का कहना था कि उस वक्त कई भाजपा विधायक उनके संपर्क में थो, जो पाला बदलना चाहते थे। उन्होंने इस बदलाव को अपने पक्ष में करने के लिए ओबीसी से जुड़ी कई छोटी पार्टियों के साथ गठबंधन भी किया था।

हालांकि, चुनावी नतीजों से उत्साहित अखिलेश ने किसी भी राजनेता के तौर पर एक बड़ी ग़लती कीः उन्होंने 2022 के चुनाव परिणामों को हल्के में लिया। जब कोविड पर खराब इंतज़ामों को लेकर उन्हें योगी सरकार के ख़िलाफ़ लोगों को जागरूक करने के लिए सड़क पर उतरना चाहिए था, तब उन्होंने घर में रहना तय किया। फिर जब मुख्यमंत्री ने अपने अफसरों और सरकारी मशीनरी को हरकत में ला दिया और भाजपा के कार्यकर्ता पूरे प्रदेश में काम में जुट गए, तब समाजवादी पार्टी दिशाहीन और चुप सी थी, मानो पार्टी को अपने नेता की पहल और निर्देश का इंतज़ार था। प्रदेश में कोविड के कहर के वक्त, अखिलेश कई हफ्तों तक लंदन के एक आलीशान होटल में ठहरे हुए थे। अखिलेश ने ज़ोर देते हुए कहा, 'यह कहना गलत है कि मैं कोविड के वक्त ग़ायब रहा, मैं अपनी बेटी को छोड़ने लंदन गया था, उसका वहां कॉलेज में दाखिला हुआ था। यह माहौल आप मीडिया वालों ने इसलिए बनाया क्योंकि भाजपा यही चाहती थी।'

अखिलेश अपनी नाकामियों के लिए मीडिया को दोष नहीं दे सकते। 2021 की शुरुआत में, जब वैक्सीन लगना शुरू हुआ, तो उन्होंने लखनऊ में एक प्रेस कॉन्फ्रेंस में यह कहकर हलचल मचा दी कि वे बीजेपी की वैक्सीन नहीं लगवाएंगे। 'मैं आपको खुद के बारे में बता रहा हूं कि मैं अभी वैक्सीन नहीं लगवाऊंगा। क्या मैं बीजेपी की वैक्सीन पर भरोसा करूंगा?' उनकी आवाज़ में गुस्सा था। लेकिन कुछ ही महीनों बाद जब सरकार ने कोविड की दूसरी लहर के

बाद वैक्सीन अभियान को तेज़ कर दिया, तो अखिलेश ने यू-टर्न ले लिया। 'लोगों के गुस्से को देखते हुए, केन्द्र सरकार ने अब वैक्सीन का राजनीतिकरण छोड़ दिया है। मैं बीजेपी की वैक्सीन के ख़िलाफ़ था, लेकिन भारत सरकार की वैक्सीन का स्वागत करता हूं। मैं भी अब वैक्सीन लगवाऊंगा और लोगों से अपील करता हूं कि जो लोग अभी तक वैक्सीन की कमी की वजह से नहीं लगवा पाए हैं, वे अब वैक्सीन लगवा लें,' उन्होंने ट्वीट किया। जब मैंने उनसे अपने इस बदलाव पर सवाल किया, तो उन्होंने बेबाकी से कहा, 'राजनीति में परिस्थितियां बदलती रहती हैं।' वास्तव में अखिलेश ने अपने वैक्सीन विरोधी रुख से भाजपा को मजाक उड़ाने का मौका दे दिया था, यह उनकी बड़ी ग़लती थी। सोशल मीडिया के इस ज़माने में उनकी इस चूक ने सरकार को अपनी कमियों से ध्यान हटाने और विपक्ष को बचाव की मुद्रा में लाने का मौका दे दिया।

अखिलेश यादव जब अपने अंदाज़ में थे, तब उत्तरप्रदेश की दूसरी बड़ी खिलाड़ी मायावती राजनीतिक नक्शे से गायब लग रही थीं। समाजवादी पार्टी और बहुजन समाज पार्टी ने 2019 के लोकसभा चुनावों से पहले साथ आने का फ़ैसला किया, जिससे दोनों पार्टियों में बरसों से चल रही कड़वाहट ख़त्म हो गई थी। अखिलेश ने जब मायावती को सम्मान के साथ 'बुआ' (पिता की बहन) कहा, तो इसे एक गेम-चेंजर के तौर पर देखा गया। लेकिन मोदी लहर में 'बुआ' और 'भतीजा' दोनों ही बह गए। हार के कुछ दिनों बाद, मायावती ने गठबंधन ख़त्म होने का एकतरफा ऐलान करते हुए कहा कि बहुजन समाज पार्टी भविष्य में अपने दम पर चुनाव लड़ेगी। गठबंधन टूटने का आधिकारिक कारण समाजवादी पार्टी का व्यवहार बताया, जो अब उन्हें मंज़ूर नहीं था।

बहुजन समाज पार्टी की सुप्रीमो मायावती का समाजवादी पार्टी से रिश्ता टूटने की वास्तविक वजह यह बताई जाती है कि उन्हें केन्द्र की भाजपा सरकार के निशाने पर आने का डर था। 2019 के लोकसभा चुनावों में बसपा और समाजवादी पार्टी ने साथ चुनाव लड़ा था। बसपा के दस सांसद चुने गए थे, उनमें से एक और लोकसभा में बसपा संसदीय दल के नेता दानिश अली का कहना था, 'मायावती जी दो चीजों से डरती हैं—जेल जाने की आशंका और उनकी सिक्योरिटी ख़त्म होना।' दानिश अली के मुताबिक, मायावती को लगता था कि अगर उन्होंने भाजपा को राजनीतिक तौर पर चुनौती दी तो वे उनके ख़िलाफ़ ईडी की जांच शुरू करवा देंगे। बसपा नेता, उनके भाई समेत परिवार के कई सदस्यों पर भ्रष्टाचार के मामले चल रहे थे। जब प्रवर्तन निदेशालय ने उनके भाई को पूछताछ के लिए बुलाया तो मायावती घबरा गईं कि अब अगला नंबर उनका होगा। अली का कहना था कि 'समाजवादी पार्टी से नाता तोड़कर और चुप्पी साधकर मायावती ने खुद को किसी बड़ी कार्रवाई से बचा लिया।' उन्होंने बसपा-भाजपा के बीच 'मौन समझौते' का आरोप भी लगाया। दानिश अली एक किस्से का ज़िक्र करते हैं, दिसम्बर 2019 में लोकसभा में विवादास्पद सीएए पर बहस के दौरान, अली ने गृहमंत्री शाह के भाषण में टोकते हुए ज़ोर देकर कहा कि शाह अपने बयान से सांप्रदायिक कटुता फैला रहे

थे। शोरशराबे के बीच, तब एक सहयोगी ने अली को एक पर्ची दी, बहनजी उनसे ज़रूरी बात करना चाहती थीं। अली ने संसद में पार्टी कार्यालय पहुंचकर बहनजी को फ़ोन किया। 'यह कैसा व्यवहार है, आप गृहमंत्री के भाषण में कैसे टोकाटाकी कर सकते हो?' वे चिल्लाते हुए बोली थीं। जब अली ने समझाने की कोशिश की तो मायावती ने कहा बताया, 'मैं आपकी कोई बात नहीं सुनना चाहती। आप कभी भी गृहमंत्री से बहस नहीं करेंगे, जानते नहीं, ये कितने ख़तरनाक लोग हैं?' दिसम्बर 2023 में दानिश अली को पार्टी लाइन के ख़िलाफ़ जाने पर पार्टी से निलंबित कर दिया गया। दानिश अली ने आरोप लगाया, 'किसी भी विवादास्पद मुद्दे पर, चाहे वो आर्टिकल 370 हो, ट्रिपल तलाक हो या सीएए हो, मायावती चाहती थीं कि हम विरोध न करें। जब मैंने कहा कि हमें भाजपा की (बी-टीन) के तौर पर देखा जा रहा है तो उन्होंने चिल्लाते हुए मुझे कमरे से बाहर निकल जाने को कहा '

आश्चर्य की बात नहीं है कि 2022 में उत्तरप्रदेश विधानसभा चुनावों में मायावती ज़्यादातर नज़र ही नहीं आईं। वे दिल्ली और लखनऊ में अपने आलीशान आवास से बाहर नहीं निकलीं और शायद ही कभी अपने विधायकों से बातचीत की। पार्टी के मामलों पर उनकी पकड़ अब भी मजबूत थी, लेकिन संगठन से जुड़े छोटे-मोटे मुद्दों को संभालने के लिए अब वे अपने भतीजे आकाश आनंद को तैयार कर रही थीं। पार्टी के संस्थापक कांशीराम ने दलितों को सामाजिक और राजनीतिक ताकत देने के लिए जिस बहुजन समाज पार्टी को बनाया था, अब वो एक दलित की बेटी की 'जागीर' बन गई थी। मायावती का साक्षात्कार करना तो दूर की बात, अब उनसे मिलना भी मुश्किल हो गया था। उनके सबसे विश्वस्त और बातचीत करा सकने वाले वकील और राजनेता सतीश मिश्रा उनके सभी मामले संभाल रहे थे। जब मैंने 2022 के चुनावों में उनसे मायावती से मिलाने के लिए कहा, तो उनका छोटा सा जवाब था, 'मुझे देखने दीजिए, आजकल वे बहुत व्यस्त हैं।'

साल 2022 में मायावती के चुनाव अभियान का कोई शोर नहीं था, जिससे लगता था कि वे व्यस्त नहीं, उदासीन ज़्यादा थीं। पूरे प्रदेश में जोर-शोर से अभियान के बजाय उन्होंने कुछ बड़े शहरों में रैलियां करना तय किया। किसी ज़माने में बसपा के गढ़ रहे आगरा शहर में मैं एक ऐसी ही रैली में पहुंचा। आगरा अब तेज़ी से बीजेपी के गढ़ में बदलता दिख रहा था। भीड़ तो थी, लेकिन उनके कोर वोटर जाटवों में अब वैसा उत्साह नहीं दिख रहा था। मुझे रैली में एक वरिष्ठ पत्रकार ने इस बदलाव को समझाया था, 'उत्तरप्रदेश में दलितों ने सत्ता का स्वाद चखा है, एक समय था जब उन्हें लगता था कि मायावती के रास्ते ही सत्ता तक पहुंचा जा सकता है, अब वो चेहरा मोदी है।' दिलचस्प यह है कि आगरा में मायावती के निशाने पर बीजेपी के बजाय कांग्रेस ज़्यादा रही। मायावती ने कहा, 'कांग्रेस ने दलितों का उत्थान करने वाले डॉ. बाबासाहेब अम्बेडकर को कभी सम्मान नहीं दिया, इसीलिए कांग्रेस ने अपने शासन में उन्हें

भारतरत्न नहीं दिया।' बीजेपी भी ऐसा ही आरोप लगाती है। एक ज़माने तक कद्दावर नेता रही मायावती को बीजेपी की 'बी' टीम होने का आरोप परेशान करेगा। राजनीतिक तौर पर उनके कमज़ोर होने से 2024 के आम चुनावों में नए जातिगत गठबंधन बनने लगे।

═

कांग्रेस पार्टी के लिए उत्तरप्रदेश अब एक 'ब्लैक-एंड-व्हाइट' ज़माने की फ़िल्मों की तरह है, जिसे अक्सर अतीत के चश्मे से देखा जाता है। आज़ादी के बाद चार दशकों तक देश की राजनीति में पार्टी का मज़बूत आधार रहने वाले उत्तरप्रदेश के ज्यादातर हिस्से अब बीजेपी का गढ़ बन गए हैं। प्रदेश में कांग्रेस को फिर से खड़ा करने की कोशिशों को बड़ी कामयाबी नहीं मिली। 2012 के विधानसभा चुनावों में राहुल गांधी के नेतृत्व में कांग्रेस ने समाजवादी पार्टी और बहुजन समाज पार्टी दोनों को अपने निशाने पर रखा था, लेकिन करारी हार का सामना करना पड़ा। पांच साल बाद, 2017 के विधानसभा चुनावों में कांग्रेस ने समाजवादी पार्टी के अखिलेश यादव से हाथ मिलाया। बीच चुनावों में हुई इस दोस्ती को रणनीतिकार प्रशांत किशोर ने 'यूपी के लड़के' के रूप में ब्रांड किया था, लेकिन यह अभियान लोगों के बीच चल नहीं पाया और भारतीय जनता पार्टी बड़े बहुमत के साथ सत्ता में आ गई। फिर 2019 के आम चुनावों से दो महीने पहले कांग्रेस ने प्रियंका गांधी वाड्रा को उत्तरप्रदेश (पूर्व) का प्रभारी महासचिव बनाकर गुगली खेलने की कोशिश की, उनके साथ युवा नेता ज्योतिरादित्य सिंधिया को उत्तरप्रदेश (पश्चिम) का प्रभार सौंपा गया। अचानक हुई इन नियुक्तियों ने शायद पार्टी की उलझन और बढ़ा दी। प्रदेश कांग्रेस के एक वरिष्ठ नेता ने याद करते हुए कहा, 'यह जल्दी में किया गया बेवजह का फैसला था, जिस पर भरोसा करना भी मुश्किल रहा। न तो प्रियंका गांधी ने और न ही सिंधिया ने प्रदेश में ज़मीनी कार्यकर्ताओं से जुड़ने की कोई कोशिश की। अगर आपको उन्हें जिम्मेदारी देनी थी तो ज़मीन बनाने के लिए कुछ समय तो देना चाहिए था।'

खासतौर से ऐन चुनाव के वक्त प्रियंका को जिम्मेदारी देना हैरान करने वाला था। बरसों से कांग्रेस, 'फोटोजेनिक' और करिश्माई गांधी परिवार की बेटी प्रियंका को भाजपा के मुकाबले के लिए अपने 'ब्रह्मास्त्र' के तौर पर देखती थी। पार्टी को लगता था कि प्रियंका में दादी इंदिरा गांधी की याद दिलाने का आकर्षण है। 2017 के चुनावों से पहले प्रशांत किशोर ने प्रियंका गांधी को पार्टी के मुख्यमंत्री पद के चेहरे के तौर पर उतारने पर भी ज़ोर दिया था, लेकिन पार्टी नेतृत्व ने इसे खारिज़ कर दिया। प्रियंका अभी तक सिर्फ़ गांधी परिवार के गढ़ माने जाने वाले अमेठी-रायबरेली इलाके में ही प्रचार का काम देखती थीं, अब अचानक उनसे बढ़ती हुई भाजपा और मजबूत समाजवादी पार्टी-बहुजन समाजवादी पार्टी गठबंधन का मुकाबला करने की उम्मीद की जा रही थी। कांग्रेस पर नज़र रखने वाले एक जानकार ने कहा, 'प्रियंका को तैरना सीखने का

मौका दिए बिना गहरे पानी में फेंकना पागलपन जैसा था।' 2019 का चुनाव वैसे ही मुश्किल था, कांग्रेस ने सिर्फ एक सीट सोनिया गांधी का गढ़ रायबरेली जीती। मोदी की लहर वाले इस चुनाव अमेठी में राहुल गांधी को हार का सामना करना पड़ा।

2022 के विधानसभा चुनाव आते-आते प्रियंका ने उत्तरप्रदेश की उथल-पुथल वाले राजनीतिक हालात में अपने दम पर आगे बढ़ना सीख लिया था। नाराज़ सिंधिया ने अब बीजेपी का दामन पकड़ लिया था; राहुल गांधी कांग्रेस के राष्ट्रीय अध्यक्ष पद से इस्तीफ़ा दे चुके थे और केरल के वायनाड से सांसद बन गए थे। यानी कांग्रेस को यूपी में फिर से खड़ा करने की पूरी जिम्मेदारी अब प्रियंका के कंधों पर आ गई थी। 2019 में लोकसभा चुनावों में करारी हार के बाद उन्होंने प्रदेश में कमज़ोर पार्टी को जंग के लिए तैयार संगठन में बदलने की कोशिश की थी। सबसे पहले अहम फ़ैसलों में उन्होंने प्रदेश संगठन की जिम्मेदारी अभिनेता से राजनेता बने राज बब्बर से लेकर ओबीसी समुदाय के नेता और दो बार विधायक रहे अजय कुमार लल्लू को सौंप दी। यह राज्य में बदलते जातिगत राजनीतिक समीकरणों को साधने के लिए देर से की गई कोशिश थी। फिर उन्होंने संगठन में ब्लाक स्तर तक बदलाव करने, नए चेहरे लाने का निर्णय किया। जब पहली बार उन्होंने काम संभाला तो वे प्रदेश कांग्रेस की पुरानी कार्यसमिति के 500 से ज़्यादा सदस्यों को देखकर हैरान रह गईं। ये नेता पिछले तीस साल से एक ही पद पर जमे हुए थे और अगली पीढ़ी को जगह देने को तैयार नहीं थे। इनमें से कई पुराने नेताओं ने तो अपने ड्राइवरों और सुरक्षा गार्डों को भी ज़िला समिति का सदस्य बनवा दिया था। प्रियंका गांधी ने अपने एक सहयोगी को कहा, 'ऐसा लगता है कि पार्टी में कार्यकर्ता कम और नेता ज़्यादा हैं।' इस बदलाव से अब एक छोटी 75 सदस्यों वाली नई कार्यसमिति थी, जिसमें जिम्मेदारियों को बांटने और जातिगत संतुलन को साधने की कोशिश की गई थी।

लेकिन संगठन में बदलाव ने पार्टी की दरारों को सामने ला दिया। जून 2021 में, राहुल गांधी के वफादार माने जाने वाले शाहजहांपुर के जितिन प्रसाद पार्टी छोड़कर भाजपा में शामिल हो गए। जब उनके सहयोगी ने एक सीधा सवाल पूछा कि क्या आपने मंत्री पद पाने के लिए पार्टी छोड़ी? तो नाराज़ जितिन प्रसाद ने जवाब दिया, 'क्या मैं उस पार्टी में बना रहूं जहां बिना किसी सलाह मशविरा के फ़ैसले लिए जाते हैं।' कहा जाता है कि प्रसाद उनके गृह जिले शाहजहांपुर में उनकी जानकारी के बिना संगठन में हुई कुछ नियुक्तियों को लेकर नाराज़ थे। छह महीने बाद राहुल टीम के ही एक और नेता आर.पी.एन. सिंह पार्टी छोड़कर भाजपा में चले गए। नाराज़ सिंह ने कहा, 'अब वह पार्टी नहीं रही, जिसमें मैं तीस साल तक हिस्सा रहा हूं।' बताया गया कि सिंह ने राहुल गांधी से अपनी शिकायतें साझा करने की कोशिश की थी, लेकिन राहुल ने उन्हें कहा कि वे उत्तरप्रदेश के मामले में उनकी मां सोनिया गांधी और बहन प्रियंका से बात करें। सिंह अब भाजपा के राज्यसभा सांसद हैं।

सिंह और प्रसाद दोनों ही कोई ज़मीनी या जननेता नहीं हैं, बल्कि दोनों ही उत्तरप्रदेश के प्रभावशाली परिवारों में पैदा हुए उत्तराधिकारी भर हैं, जो लंबे समय से कांग्रेस में थे। राहुल गांधी के दख़ल के बाद 2009 में दोनों को मनमोहन सिंह सरकार में मंत्री बनाया गया था, लेकिन दोनों को अब कांग्रेस के टिकट पर जीतने का भरोसा नहीं था। निजी महत्वाकांक्षा पार्टी बदलने या छोड़ने का एक कारण हो सकती है, लेकिन यह भी भावना थी कि कांग्रेस अब दूसरी सोच-समझ के साथ काम कर रही थी। दोनों में से किसी ने प्रियंका पर कोई आरोप नहीं लगाया, लेकिन साफ था कि वे अपने राजनीतिक 'जूनियर' के फ़ैसले को मानने को तैयार नहीं थे। पार्टी के अंदरूनी सूत्रों की बात मानें तो गठन में अंदरूनी झगड़े इस कदर थे कि आर.पी.एन. सिंह पदाधिकारियों की उन बैठकों में लगातार गायब रहे जो प्रियंका गांधी ने बुलाई थीं। बताया जाता है कि मामला इस हद तक पहुंच गया कि उस समय झारखंड में पार्टी के प्रभारी महासचिव सिंह ने प्रियंका गांधी को फ़ोन पर देर तक खरी-खोटी सुनाई। बाद में उन्होंने अपने गुस्से के लिए माफ़ी भी मांगी और कहा कि उनकी मां ने भी उन्हें इस बर्ताव के लिए बहुत डांट पिलाई थी।

प्रियंका की आलोचना करने वाले लोग, उनके निजी सहायक संदीप सिह के बढ़ते दबदबे को लेकर भी नाराज़ थे। पूर्वी उत्तरप्रदेश के संदीप सिंह जेएनयू के छात्र नेता रहे थे और एक ज़माने तक अति-वामपंथी छात्र संगठन से जुड़े रहे थे, जिसने तत्कालीन प्रधानमंत्री मनमोहन सिंह को काले झंडे दिखाए थे। बाद में सिंह, 2019 में राहुल गांधी की चुनावी टीम का अहम हिस्सा बन गए। उन्होंने राहुल गांधी के कई भाषण भी लिखे। कहा जाता है कि 2019 के चुनावी अभियान का विवादित नारा 'चौकीदार चोर है', सिंह ने ही गढ़ा था। अब प्रियंका के करीबी सहयोगी और राजनीति पर चौकस निगाह रखने वाले संदीप कांग्रेस नेता के 'चौकीदार' जैसे थे। जब 2024 के चुनाव अभियान में मुझे प्रियंका का साक्षात्कार करना था, तो संदीप ने साक्षात्कार से पहले बातचीत के लिए लखनऊ-रायबरेली हाइवे पर एक ढाबे पर आधी रात को मिलने को कहा। एक पूर्व कांग्रेसी ने कहा कि 'प्रियंका के बारे में अच्छी बात यह है कि उनके भाई राहुल से उलट, आप उनसे मुलाकात कर सकते हैं, बात कर सकते हैं, लेकिन परेशानी की बात यह है कि वह आपसे उम्मीद करती हैं कि आप अपने इलाके के मुद्दों पर संदीप और उनकी टीम से ही बात करें। पार्टी के लिए बरसों मेहनत और काम करने वाले हम जैसे लोगों को निर्देश देने वाला वो नौसिखिया कौन होता है?' कांग्रेसी नेता की नाराज़गी दिख रही थी।

प्रियंका गांधी पार्टी की अंदरूनी चुनौतियों के बावजूद राजनीतिक लड़ाई लड़ते दिख रही थीं, जबकि ज़्यादातर विपक्षी नेता अभी सड़क पर उतरते नहीं लग रहे थे। सितम्बर 2020 में, प्रियंका गांधी हाथरस ज़िले के बूलगढ़ी गांव में कांग्रेस के प्रदर्शन में पहुंच गईं, जहां 14 सितम्बर को चार सवर्णों ने एक युवा दलित महिला के साथ कथित तौर पर सामूहिक बलात्कार किया था। पीड़िता ने दो सप्ताह बाद दम तोड़ दिया था। और एक भयावह कदम उठाते हुए पुलिस ने

29 सितम्बर की सुबह उसके परिवार की जानकारी या सहमति के बिना जल्दबाज़ी में अंतिम संस्कार कर दिया। पीडिता की मौत और जल्दी में अंतिम संस्कार की खबरें मीडिया में आक्रामक तरीके से चल रही थीं। उत्तरप्रदेश प्रशासन की भूमिका पर भी सवाल उठाए गए।

ऐसे वक्त में प्रियंका गांधी उत्तरप्रदेश के राजनीतिक मैदान में उतर गई थीं। उन्होंने एक टीवी पत्रकार से बातचीत में कहा, 'हाथरस में जो कुछ हुआ वो इस बात का सबूत है कि योगी सरकार क़ानून व्यवस्था को लेकर भले ही बड़ी-बड़ी बातें करे, लेकिन वह दलित बेटी की रक्षा करने में विफल रही है।' इस मुद्दे पर मायावती के ज़ोरदार तरीके से ना बोलने और अखिलेश यादव के तब लंदन में होने से प्रियंका गांधी अचानक विरोध का बड़ा चेहरा बन गईं। उनके एक पारिवारिक मित्र का कहना है, 'भले ही वे इसे ना मानें, लेकिन प्रियंका, राहुल गांधी की बहन या फिर राजीव-सोनिया की बेटी या इंदिरा गांधी जैसी दिखने वाली पोती से ज़्यादा राजनीतिक कद की इच्छा रखती हैं। उन्हें राजनीति की चमक अच्छी लगती है और एक्शन में दिखना चाहती हैं।' इस मौके का फायदा उठाते हुए, प्रियंका ने भाई राहुल के साथ बूलगढ़ी तक कांग्रेस मार्च निकालने का फ़ैसला किया। जब उत्तरप्रदेश पुलिस ने धारा 144 का उल्लंघन करने के मामले में रोका, तो गांधी परिवार ने दो दिन बाद फिर लौटने का फ़ैसला किया। इस बार भारी पुलिस बल की तैनाती के बावजूद इस काफिले ने लौटने से इंकार कर दिया। जैसे ही कांग्रेस कार्यकर्ताओं और पुलिस के बीच झड़प शुरू हुई, प्रियंका अपनी गाड़ी से उतरकर कार्यकर्ताओं को बचाने की कोशिश करने लगीं। एक पुलिस वाले ने कांग्रेस महासचिव को कुर्ते से पकड़कर, धक्का देकर दूर कर दिया। कैमरे में कैद हुई यह तस्वीर टीवी चैनलों पर बार-बार दिखाई जा रही थी। इस दबाव में यूपी पुलिस को माफ़ी मांगने और जांच के आदेश देने के लिए मजबूर होना पड़ा। आखिरकार उन्हें पीड़ित परिवार से मिलने की इजाजत मिल गई। यह प्रियंका गांधी के लिए बेलची वाला पल भले ही नहीं रहा हो, लेकिन इससे प्रियंका को 'वंशवादी' राजनीति के टैग से निकलकर राजनीतिक 'प्रोफाइल' बनाने का मौका मिल गया था। 1977 में करारी हार के बाद इंदिरा गांधी के लिए यह ऐतिहासिक क्षण था, जब 13 अगस्त 1977 को इंदिरा गांधी बिहार शरीफ के बेलची गांव में हाथी पर चढ़कर उन पीडित परिवारों से मिलने पहुंची थीं, जहां 27 मई 1977 को आठ दलितों सहित 13 लोगों को जिंदा जला दिया गया था। भारी बारिश के बीच जब इंदिरा गांधी की जीप फंस गईं, तब उन्हें हाथी पर बेठाकर गांव तक ले जाया गया था। इस घटना ने इंदिरा गांधी को अपनी बड़ी हार के झटके से बाहर निकाल दिया था।

एक साल बाद, अक्टूबर 2021 में प्रियंका गांधी फिर से सड़क पर थीं। इस बार वे पूर्वी उत्तरप्रदेश के एक 'फ्लैशपांइट' पर पहुँचीं। लखीमपुरी खीरी में केन्द्रीय मंत्री अजय मिश्रा टेनी के बेटे की अगुवाई में एक काफिले पर प्रदर्शनकारी किसानों को कुचलने की कोशिश का आरोप था। इस घटना और बाद में हुई झड़पों में आठ लोग मारे गए थे। इलाके में बड़ी संख्या में

पुलिस तैनात थी और धारा 144 लागू होने के बावज़ूद प्रियंका ने कांग्रेस सांसद दीपेन्द्र हुड्डा के साथ अपने सुरक्षा घेरे को चकमा देकर रात को इलाके में घुसने की कोशिश की। उत्तरप्रदेश पुलिस की पचास सदस्यीय टीम ने उनका पीछा कर तड़के चार बजे ज़िले की सीमा पर पकड़ लिया। पुलिस ने उन्हें जीप में धकेलने की कोशिश की और उनके सहायक संदीप को भी पीटा। जब प्रियंका ने गिरफ्तारी वारंट के बिना पुलिस हिरासत में जाने से इंकार किया तो पुलिस ने जल्दबाजी में व्हाट्सएप पर आदेश जारी किया। सीतापुर जिले के एक पुलिस गेस्ट हाउस में प्रियंका को तीन दिन तक रखा गया।

प्रियंका गांधी की 'गिरफ़्तारी' की ख़बर अब प्राइम टाइम न्यूज़ थी। गेस्टहाउस से भी उन्होंने कुछ टीवी चैनलों पर ऑनलाइन जुड़कर पुलिस पर उनके साथ बदसलूकी का आरोप लगाया। इससे आगे, उनके एक सहयोगी ने एक वीडियो जारी किया, जिसमें प्रियंका गांधी उस कमरे का फर्श साफ कर रही थीं, जहां उन्हें ठहराया गया था। प्रियंका ने कहा, 'मैं जहां भी रहती हूं और अगर वहां गंदगी है तो मैं उसे साफ करती हूं। मेरी यह आदत विपश्यना ध्यान से आई है, इसमें नाटक या दिखावे की कोई बात ही नहीं है। मैं खुद सफाई कर रही थी और एक सहयोगी ने वीडियो बनाकर मुझे बताए बिना इसे जारी कर दिया।' जाने या अनजाने, जो भी हो, लेकिन यह वीडियो टीवी के लिए था। भाजपा ने इसे फोटो की राजनीति कहा, लेकिन यह स्पष्ट था कि कांग्रेस नेता लोगों का ध्यान अपनी ओर खींच रही थीं।

2022 में उत्तरप्रदेश की लड़ाई में प्रियंका कांग्रेस का चेहरा बन गईं। हाथरस से लखीमपुर खीरी होते हुए उन्नाव तक, प्रियंका को योगी सरकार से मुकाबले के लिए सड़क पर उतरी नेता के तौर पर पेश किया जा रहा था। उन्नाव में उन्होंने एक बलात्कार पीड़िता की बात की, जिसे कथित तौर पर बलात्कार के बाद आरोपियों ने आग लगा दी और उसकी मौत हो गई। कांग्रेस का अच्छे वीडियो के साथ एक आकर्षक नारा आयाः 'लड़की हूं, लड़ सकती हूं।' उनकी टीम को भरोसा था, 'हमारे वीडियो वायरल हो रहे हैं, इस बार हम उत्तरप्रदेश में अपनी जगह बनाएंगे।'

लेकिन जब समर्थक जोर-शोर से प्रचार में जुटे थे, तब प्रियंका को हकीकत समझ आ रही थी कि यह हारने वाली लड़ाई थी। पर्दे के पीछे प्रियंका ने बसपा नेता मायावती से संपर्क किया और चुनावी गठबंधन की संभावनाएं तलाशी। उन्होंने पूर्व मुख्यमंत्री मायावती को लखनऊ या दिल्ली कहीं भी मिलने के लिए कम से कम चार बार फ़ोन किया, लेकिन हर बार किसी ना किसी बहाने से बातचीत को टाल दिया गया। प्रियंका ने अपने सहयोगियों से कहा, 'मुझे लगता है कि बहनजी की अपनी मजबूरियां होंगी।'

═

मार्च 2022 के पहले सप्ताह में उत्तरप्रदेश में सात चरणों का चुनाव अभियान ख़त्म होने वाला था, केन्द्रीय मंत्री अमित शाह वाराणसी में होटल ताज गंगा के लॉन में पत्रकारों और चुनाव विश्लेषकों के साथ चर्चा कर रहे थे। शाह खुद को बड़ा सटीक चुनाव विश्लेषक मानते हैं। 2014 के आम चुनावों से पहले जब वे राज्य के चुनाव प्रभारी बनाए गए थे, उस समय भाजपा को यूपी में 80 में से 70 से ज़्यादा सीटों की सबसे बड़ी जीत हासिल हुई थी, तब से उत्तरप्रदेश खासतौर से उनका गढ़ रहा है। शाह ने कहा कि 'हम निश्चित तौर पर जीत रहे हैं, लेकिन मैं कोई नंबर नहीं बताना चाहता।' वैसे यह अमित शाह को लेकर सामान्य नहीं था, क्योंकि शाह अक्सर सीटों की बड़ी संख्या बताकर अपनी ही पार्टी को बेहतर प्रदर्शन के लिए चुनौती देते हैं। क्या वह सतर्क थे? मीडिया के सवालों पर उनका जवाब था, 'देखो, नंबर देना आपका काम है; मेरा लक्ष्य पार्टी को चुनाव जिताना है।'

गृहमंत्री की ऐसी प्रतिक्रिया से भाजपा खेमे की चिंता समझी जा सकती है। पार्टी के अंदरूनी सर्वेक्षणों और रिपोर्ट के हिसाब से भाजपा विरोधी वोटों का एक बड़ा हिस्सा अखिलेश यादव के पास जा रहा था। मोटे तौर पर अब दो तरफा मुकाबला हो गया था, जिसमें मुसलमान, यादव और गैर-यादव ओबीसी का एक हिस्सा समाजवादी पार्टी के साथ होने लगा था। साथ ही समाजवादी पार्टी ने जाट प्रभुत्व वाली राष्ट्रीय लोकदल से भी गठबंधन किया है, इसका असर पश्चिमी उत्तरप्रदेश में है। योगी सरकार को खेतों में खड़ी फसलों को खा जाने वाले आवारा पशुओं से परेशान किसानों की नाराज़गी की सामना करना पड़ रहा था। इसकी बड़ी वजह पशुओं के वध पर रोक लगने को माना जा रहा था। वाराणसी और पूर्वी उत्तरप्रदेश के ज़्यादातर हिस्सों में अंतिम चरण में वोट डाले जाने थे और शाह अंतिम समय में पार्टी की बढ़त के लिए प्रधानमंत्री मोदी की लोकप्रियता पर भरोसा कर रहे थे। प्रधानमंत्री ने अपने संसदीय क्षेत्र में आखिरी मेगा रोड शो किया, जिसमें हमेशा की तरह खुली छत वाली गाड़ी में शहर भर में पहुंचे। सड़कों पर जमा लोग उन पर फूलों की बारिश कर रहे थे और इशारा पाते ही भीड़ जयश्री राम का नारा लगा रही थी। कैमरे को पसंद करने वाले प्रधानमंत्री ने भगवा टोपी और गले में गमछा पहन रखा था। 'उत्तरप्रदेश में साफतौर पर "मोदी असर" दिखाई देता है। प्रधानमंत्री जिस भी इलाके में जाते हैं, हमने वहां पार्टी के उम्मीदवार के लिए 2-3 प्रतिशत की बढ़त देखी है,' पार्टी के एक सर्वेक्षण करने वाले ने बताया। मोदी के शहर में दौरे के एक दिन बाद डेली मूड ट्रैकर ने भाजपा के लिए वोटों में बड़े उछाल की संभावना जाहिर की। शाह मतदान की संभावना से संतुष्ट लग रहे थे, लेकिन अपनी टीम को चेतावनी दी कि इस बात का ध्यान रखें कि 'मतदान के दिन कोई भी बूथ छूट न जाए, हर वोट मायने रखता है!'

उत्तरप्रदेश में मतदान टीम पर निगरानी के लिए गृहमंत्री ने मुख्य रूप से एक व्यक्ति पर भरोसा किया: सुनील बंसल। 2014 के चुनावों में शाह की टीम में चुने जाने से पहले सुनील बंसल आरएसएस के चुपचाप काम करने वाले प्रचारकों में से थे, जो पहले विद्यार्थी परिषद से

जुड़े रहे। वे राजस्थान से आते हैं। वे पर्दे के पीछे, सावधानी से और लंबे समय तक अपने प्लान पर काम करने वाले लोगों में से थे। उत्तरप्रदेश में चुनावी कामयाबी ने उन्हें शाह का 'वफादार' बनाया और पार्टी में एक मजबूत जगह तक पहुंचा दिया। प्रदेश में नौकरशाह तो मुख्यमंत्री को रिपोर्ट करते थे, लेकिन संगठन का बूथ स्तर का नेटवर्क बंसल की निगरानी में काम कर रहा था। सत्ता में वे एक ताकतवर शख्स हो गए थे। भाजपा के एक नेता का मानना था, 'प्रदेश में हर वरिष्ठ मंत्री की नियुक्ति बंसल की मंज़ूरी के बाद ही की जाती है। योगी भले ही मुख्यमंत्री हों, लेकिन संगठन में सत्ता के असली केन्द्र सुनील जी हैं।'

जब योगी सरकार का शपथग्रहण समारोह होना था, तो ज्यादातर मंत्री पहले लखनऊ में भाजपा के मुख्यालय में सुनील बंसल के दफ्तर में उनका 'आशीर्वाद' लेने पहुंचे, इनमें कैबिनेट के इकलौते मुस्लिम चेहरे दानिश अंसारी भी शामिल थे। दानिश अंसारी उस वक्त शायद बाज़ार में टहल रहे थे, जब उन्हें अचानक बंसल का फ़ोन आया और उन्हें तुरंत कार्यालय पहुंचने को कहा। उनको मंत्री बनाने की ख़बर सुनकर वे हैरान रह गए। उन्होंने हंसते हुए बताया, 'मुझे तो फिर इस मौके के लिए तुरंत नए कपड़े भी खरीदने पड़े।' अगस्त 2022 में जब ताकतवर सुनील बंसल को उत्तरप्रदेश से हटाकर पार्टी का राष्ट्रीय महासचिव बनाया गया, दरअसल तब ही 'योगी खेमे' और 'शाह-बंसल गुट' के बीच विभाजन के बीज बो दिए गए थे। लोग मानते थे कि 2024 के चुनाव में सत्ता के दो अलग-अलग केन्द्र एक दूसरे के ख़िलाफ़ काम करेंगे तो पार्टी के चुनावी प्रदर्शन पर असर पड़ेगा।

2022 के विधानसभा चुनावों में भाजपा को उम्मीदों से ज़्यादा सीटें मिली थीं। उत्तरप्रदेश में 403 सीटों की विधानसभा में भाजपा ने स्पष्ट बहुमत से ज़्यादा 255 सीटें जीती थीं। योगी आदित्यनाथ के फिर से मुख्यमंत्री बनने से प्रदेश का 37 साल का रिकॉर्ड टूट गया, जिसमें 1985 से कोई लगातार दूसरी बार मुख्यमंत्री नहीं बना था। भाजपा का वोट शेयर भी पिछली बार के 39.6 फ़ीसदी से बढ़कर 41.2 फ़ीसदी हो गया था, हालांकि उसकी सीटें इस बार 312 से कम हो गई थीं। गृहमंत्री शाह की आशंका सही साबित हुई, विपक्ष का वोट मौटे तौर पर समाजवादी पार्टी को मिला, इससे उसके वोट में 10.2 फ़ीसदी की बढ़ोतरी हुई थी। समाजवादी पार्टी ने इस बार 111 सीटों पर कब्ज़ा कर लिया, जबकि पिछली बार उसे सिर्फ 47 सीटें मिली थीं। एक समय की सबसे ताकतवर पार्टी माने जाने वाली बहुजन समाज पार्टी के खाते में सिर्फ़ एक सीट आई थी, जबकि 2007 में उन्होंने और बसपा ने स्पष्ट बहुमत हासिल किया था। कांग्रेस 2.33 फ़ीसदी के साथ केवल दो सीटें जीत पाई, उसने 399 सीटों पर चुनाव लड़ा था। उसके 387 उम्मीदवारों की ज़मानत ज़ब्त हो गई थी, इससे बुरी हार शायद ही कभी हुई हो।

उत्तरप्रदेश में बीजेपी की इस शानदार जीत को कैसे समझा जा सकता है। जब सत्ता विरोधी लहर हो, कोविड से होने वाली मौतों की बड़ी संख्या और 2020 में प्रवासियों का बड़ी तादाद

में पलायन, जब हज़ारों-हज़ार लोग पैदल ही अपने गांवों और घरों तक लौट आए थे। इसके साथ जातिगत राजनीति के मुश्किल समीकरणों के बाद भी ये नतीजे क्या कहानी कहते हैं? एक भाजपा नेता ने इस जीत को समझाते हुए कहा, 'प्रधानमंत्री मोदी और योगी जी के नेतृत्व के साथ बंसल और उनकी टीम के चुनाव प्रबंधन में कोई भी हमारा मुकाबला नहीं कर सकता।' हिंदुत्व विचार वाले कोर वोटर के साथ 15 करोड़ से ज्यादा मुफ्त राशन पाने वाले लोग और दूसरे लाभार्थियों ने इस जीत को पुख्ता किया। योगी की बुलडोज़र वाली छवि भले ही संवैधानिक रूप से सवालों के घेरे में हो, लेकिन राजनीति में उसका खासा असर दिखाई दिया। यूपी योगी **(UPYOGI)** हिन्दुत्व की ताकत की पहचान बन गया था। बीजेपी की राजनीति में मुख्यमंत्री योगी को अब हाशिए पर रखना मुश्किल था, अब वे लोकप्रिय नेता बन गए थे। उनकी सख्त क़ानून-व्यवस्था को लेकर बनी छवि मतदाताओं को अपनी ओर खींचने में अहम रही। उनकी ध्रुवीकरण वाली बयानबाजी मुस्लिम-विरोधी पूर्वाग्रहों को जोड़ रही थी।

इस हिसाब से कोई भी विपक्षी दल या उसका नेता भाजपा संगठन की ताकत और जन संपर्क के बराबर नहीं था। समाजावादी पार्टी के अखिलेश यादव ने खुद को विपक्ष का प्रमुख चेहरा तो बना लिया, लेकिन वे मुस्लिम-यादव वोट से आगे नहीं बढ़ पाए थे। मायावती का प्रभाव धुंधला होने लगा था, लगता था कि वे इस लड़ाई में थी ही नहीं और उन्होंने अपनी राजनीतिक साख खो दी थी। कांग्रेस की प्रियंका गांधी वाड्रा अपनी 'टीवी इमेज' को ज़मीनी स्तर पर नहीं उतार पाईं।

2022 के उत्तरप्रदेश के चुनाव नतीजों के एक दिन बाद, उत्साह से भरे अमित शाह ने गुजरात समेत उस साल होने वाले चुनावों पर चर्चा के लिए भाजपा पदाधिकारियों की एक बैठक बुलाई। 'इस बार मिशन 150 है। हमें गुजरात में सबसे ज़्यादा सीटें जीतने का रिकॉर्ड बनाना है।' लेकिन कांग्रेस दफ्तर पर हताशा और उदासी का माहौल था। उत्तरप्रदेश में ही पार्टी का सफाया नहीं हुआ था, बल्कि उसने पंजाब में भी अपनी सरकार गंवा दी थी। उसे टक्कर देकर आम आदमी पार्टी ने जीत हासिल की थी। छोटे राज्य गोवा में कांग्रेस को सत्ता-विरोधी लहर के दम पर भाजपा को हराने की उम्मीद थी, लेकिन उसने सत्ता में वापसी कर ली। कांग्रेस के एक पदाधिकारी का मानना था, वास्तव में ऐसा लगा कि 'हम बिना कप्तान के डूबते जहाज थे।' पार्टी को जिस कप्तान से भविष्य में नेतृत्व की उम्मीद थी, वह अभी 2019 में हार के झटके से ही उबर नहीं पाया था। उत्तरप्रदेश में प्रियंका के संघर्ष और सोनिया गांधी के आधे-अधूरे रिटायरमेंट के साथ राहुल गांधी फिर से फोकस में थे।

क्या अतीत की ग़लतियों से सबक लेने के बजाय कांग्रेस फिर से अपने 'शाश्वत उत्तराधिकारी' से चमत्कार की उम्मीद कर रही थी। यह एक खेल बदलने वाली असंभव सी राजनीतिक वापसी की पटकथा लिखने का समय था।

7

राहुल गांधी की 'मोहब्बत की दुकान'

देश की सबसे पुरानी पार्टी कांग्रेस की तरह 'कांग्रेस कार्यसमिति'(CWC) की अपनी पुरानी छवि धूमिल होने लगी है। 1998 में सोनिया गांधी के कांग्रेस अध्यक्ष बनने के बाद से दो दशक से ज़्यादा का वक्त हो गया, लेकिन पार्टी की सर्वोच्च कार्यसमिति के लिए चुनाव नहीं हुए। इसके बजाय, समिति गांधी परिवार के वफादारों से भरी पड़ी थी, जिन्हें 'मनोनीत' करके शामिल किया गया। बैठकें अब कभी-कभार ही होती थी। एक ज़माने में कार्यसमिति की बैठकों में महत्वपूर्ण मसलों पर जोरदार बहस हुआ करती थी, लेकिन अब हर बात पर पार्टी आलाकमान को अधिकृत करने के लिए सिर्फ़ एक लाइन के प्रस्ताव आते थे। शायद इसीलिए जब आम चुनावों में कांग्रेस की शर्मनाक हार के बाद राहुल गांधी ने 25 मई 2019 को कार्यसमिति की आपात बैठक बुलाई तो ज्यादातर नेता हैरान थे। कार्यसमिति के एक वरिष्ठ नेता ने कहा, 'सोनिया जी सब्र रखने की बात करतीं और जब तक कि कोई बड़ा संकट नहीं हो, वे यथास्थिति बनाए रखने के पक्ष में रहती थीं। लेकिन राहुल गांधी इससे बिल्कुल उलट हैं, वे कुछ नाटकीय करके चीजों को हिला देना चाहते हैं।'

राहुल गांधी ने दिसम्बर 2017 में कांग्रेस अध्यक्ष पद संभाला था, ज़ाहिर है वे बिना किसी चुनाव के अध्यक्ष बने थे। कांग्रेस में नेहरु-गांधी परिवार की पांचवी पीढ़ी के 'राज्याभिषेक' का इंतज़ार कई साल से चल रहा था, लेकिन राहुल गांधी ने अपनी मां सोनिया के सामने पद नहीं लेने की इच्छा जताई थी। अब आम चुनावों से अठारह महीने पहले, सैंतालिस साल के राहुल ने आखिरकार पार्टी की कमान संभाल ली। पार्टी ने युवा चेहरे का उत्साह से स्वागत इस उम्मीद से किया कि वे नरेन्द्र मोदी के नेतृत्व के सामने काफी समय से निष्क्रिय सी पड़ी पार्टी

को ऊर्जा देंगे और आगे बढ़ाने में मदद करेंगे। एक कांग्रेस सांसद ने कहा, 'मुझे याद है कि राहुल की अध्यक्षता में हुई पहली बैठक में, हमें उम्मीद जगी थी कि वे पार्टी को राजीव गांधी के दिनों में ले जाएंगे, जब एक पीढ़ी के बदलाव को लेकर बहुत जोश और उत्साह था।' जब कांग्रेस ने 2018 की गर्मियों में कर्नाटक में गठबंधन सरकार बनाई और फिर उसी साल दिसम्बर में हिन्दी पट्टी के राजस्थान, मध्यप्रदेश और छत्तीसगढ़ में जीत हासिल की, तो बेहतर भविष्य की उम्मीदें जागने लगी थीं। अब उन लोगों ने भी चुप्पी साध ली, जो राहुल गांधी के वोट हासिल करने की क्षमताओं पर सवाल कर रहे थे। इन चुनावों में जीत के बाद अब 'राहुल बनाम मोदी' के मुकाबले को मुश्किल नहीं माना जा रहा था। कार्यसमिति के एक सदस्य ने हंसते हुए कहा, 'दरअसल जनवरी, 2019 आते-आते तो कांग्रेस में कुछ नेता केन्द्र में सरकार बनने पर मंत्रालयों के बंटवारे को लेकर भी चर्चा करने लगे थे।' लेकिन मई 2019 के आम चुनावों ने कांग्रेस के सपनों का बुलबुला फोड़ दिया। सत्ता में रहने की आदी पार्टी के लिए कम से कम, अगले पांच साल फिर से विपक्ष में बैठना मुश्किलों भरा महसूस हो रहा था। 2014 की 44 सीटों से अब सिर्फ़ 8 सीटें ज्यादा केवल 52 सीटों पर जीत, पार्टी के लिए एक बड़ा झटका थी। साल 2014 के चुनावों में हार का ठीकरा तो मनमोहन सिंह की अगुवाई में कमज़ोर होते गठबंधन पर फोड़ दिया गया था, लेकिन क्या गांधी परिवार इस बार के नतीजों की ज़िम्मेदारी से बच सकता था?

चुनाव नतीजों के बाद 25 मई को कार्यसमिति की बैठक, हार पर पोस्टमार्टम के लिए बुलाई गई थी, जिसमें आत्मनिरीक्षण की शायद औपचारिकता पूरी करनी थी। लेकिन राहुल गांधी कुछ और सोच रहे थे। दिल्ली में 24 अकबर रोड पर पार्टी के मुख्यालय में होने वाली इस बैठक में राहुल गांधी ने एकबारगी कांग्रेस के दिग्गज उदास चेहरों की तरफ निगाह डाली, फिर एक तीखी टिप्पणी के साथ चुप्पी तोड़ीः 'मैं फेल हुआ, आप फेल हुए, हम सब फेल हुए।' बात यहां नहीं रुकी, अब राहुल ज़्यादा मुखर होकर आगे बढ़ेः 'इस कमरे में आपमें से कितने लोगों ने राफेल विमान सौदे में भ्रष्टाचार के ख़िलाफ़ अभियान में मेरा साथ दिया? आपमें से कितने लोगों ने मोदी सरकार के भ्रष्टाचार की बात की? भाजपा के ख़िलाफ़ लड़ाई में मुझे अकेला क्यों छोड़ दिया गया?' कांग्रेस के कुछ सदस्यों ने जब दख़ल देने की कोशिश की तो राहुल ने उसे खारिज़ करते हुए अपनी बात जारी रखीः 'इस कमरे में कुछ लोग हैं जिन्होंने पार्टी के बजाय अपने बच्चों के प्रचार और समर्थन पर ज़्यादा ध्यान दिया।' उनका इशारा राजस्थान के तत्कालीन मुख्यमंत्री अशोक गहलोत पर था, जिन्होंने जोधपुर सीट पर अपने बेटे वैभव के चुनाव प्रचार में कई दिन बिताए थे। राजस्थान में भाजपा और उसके सहयोगियों ने सभी 25 सीटों पर जीत हासिल कर ली थी। उस वक्त बैठक में मध्यप्रदेश के मुख्यमंत्री कमलनाथ भले ही मौजूद नहीं थे, लेकिन राहुल गांधी उनके बेटे नकुल नाथ को छिंदवाड़ा से उम्मीदवार बनाने की जिद का आरोप लगाने से नहीं चूके। राहुल ने कहा, 'कमलनाथ ने खुद कहा था कि मुख्यमंत्री होने के

नाते उन्हें अपने बेटे को चुनाव लड़ाने का अधिकार था।' (वैसे कांग्रेस ने मध्यप्रदेश में अकेले नकुल नाथ की छिंदवाड़ा सीट जीती थी, बाकी सभी 28 सीटों पर भाजपा ने कब्ज़ा किया था।) राहुल का हमला जारी था, बैठक में सन्नाटा पसर गया। कांग्रेस में गुटबाजी पर उंगली उठाना कोई नई बात नहीं है, लेकिन कार्यसमिति की बैठक में व्यक्तिगत हमले करना असामान्य है। कार्यसमिति की बैठक में मौजूद रहे एक नेता ने कहा, 'हमें उम्मीद थी कि बैठक में राहुल हमारा मनोबल बढ़ाएंगे, लेकिन इससे उलट उनकी टिप्पणियों से माहौल निराशा में बदल गया।' राहुल खुद उत्तरप्रदेश में गांधी परिवार का गढ़ माने जाने वाली अमेठी सीट से चुनाव हार गए थे। वे केवल दूसरी सुरक्षित सीट वायनाड से जीत पाए थे। 'अगर आप खुद अपनी सीट नहीं जीत सकते, तो दूसरे लोगों को कैसे दोष दे सकते हैं। क्यों नहीं मानते कि यह मोदी लहर का चुनाव था।' एक कांग्रेसी ने तर्क दिया, जो अब पार्टी छोड़ चुके हैं।

बैठक में राहुल गांधी ही अकेले नहीं थे, जो गुस्से में नज़र आ रहे थे। तीन घंटे की इस बैठक में गर्मी बढ़ने लगी थी। प्रियंका गांधी भी अपने भाई के समर्थन में उतर आईं। चुनावों से कुछ महीनों पहले संगठन की जिम्मेदारी संभालने वाली महासचिव भी काफी गुस्से में थीं। प्रियंका ने दावा किया कि उनके भाई ने पूरा चुनाव अपने दम पर लड़ा था। कांग्रेस कार्यसमिति के एक सदस्य के मुताबिक प्रियंका ने नाराज़गी ज़ाहिर करते हुए कहा, 'संगठन की कमज़ोरियों पर हमें उपदेश देने वाले बहुत से लोगों ने ही इसे बर्बाद किया है।'

बैठक में लोग अभी अपनी आलोचना से निकलने की कोशिश कर रहे थे कि तभी राहुल गांधी ने एक बड़ा धमाका कर दिया। राहुल ने कहा, 'पार्टी के नेता के तौर पर मैं इस हार की नैतिक जिम्मेदारी लेता हूं। मैं पार्टी अध्यक्ष पद से इस्तीफ़ा देना चाहता हूं। आपसे आग्रह है कि इस्तीफ़ा स्वीकार कर मेरी जगह किसी और को जिम्मेदारी सौंपें।' उन्होंने ज़ोर देकर कहा, 'वह व्यक्ति हमारे परिवार से न हो, ताकि कोई यह न कह सके कि कांग्रेस पर एक परिवार का नियंत्रण है।' राहुल के इस्तीफ़ा देने का ऐलान भी उतना ही अप्रत्याशित था, जितना इससे पहले की गई तीखी आलोचना। ऐसा लगा कि वहां बैठे लोग अचानक जागे। उन्होंने विरोध जताते हुए ज़ोर दिया, 'आपके इस्तीफ़े का सवाल ही नहीं उठता। आपको ही पार्टी को मजबूत करना है और इसे आगे ले जाना है।' इस वंदना में वो लोग भी शामिल हो गए, जिनकी आलोचना राहुल गांधी ने बैठक में की थी।

राहुल अपना मन बदलने को तैयार नहीं थे। शोरगुल के बीच, वे अचानक कमरे से निकलकर बाहर चले गए। बैठक में मौजूद लोग हैरान थे और भविष्य को लेकर थोड़ा परेशान थे कि आगे क्या होने वाला था। वैसे बैठक में राहुल गांधी के लहजे को लेकर हैरान नहीं होना चाहिए। अक्सर अपने विश्वस्त सहयोगियों के साथ बंद कमरों में होने वाली बैठकों में राहुल इन पुराने दिग्गजों (ओल्ड गार्ड) के ख़िलाफ़ बोलते रहे थे। उनकी मां सोनिया गांधी के इर्द-गिर्द घेरा

बनाने वाले ये ज़्यादातर लोग उनके पिता राजीव गांधी के प्रधानमंत्री काल में राजनीति में आए थे। राहुल गांधी ने बचपन में बड़ी हिंसा और विश्वासघात को देखा था, उनका बचपन त्रासदी और ख़ून-खराबे से भरा रहा। राहुल ने अपने पिता की आलोचना होते और मां के लिए ताने मारते लोगों को देखा था। इस वजह से वे उन लोगों से आहत और नाराज़ थे जिनके बारे में राहुल को लगता था कि उन्होंने उनके माता-पिता के भलेपन का हमेशा फायदा उठाया। 'इनमें से कितने लोग उस वक्त मेरे पिता के बचाव के लिए सामने आए, जब विश्वनाथ प्रताप सिंह ने बोफोर्स मामले में उन पर हमला किया था। कितने लोग मेरी मां के साथ खड़े थे, जब विदेशी मूल के नाम पर उन्हें निशाना बनाया जा रहा था?' राहुल ने एक बार अपने दोस्त से शिकायत की थी। यह अंदर का गुस्सा और तकलीफ कभी-कभी राजनेताओं के खिलाफ़ नाराज़गी के तौर पर भी सामने आ जाती थी।

कांग्रेस कार्यसमिति की बैठक में चल रहे सियासी हंगामे को देखने वालों में अहमद पटेल भी शामिल थे, जो पुराने नेताओं की जमात में से थे और उनके साथ राहुल सहज नहीं थे। अहमद भाई के तौर पर लोकप्रिय पटेल सोनिया गांधी के अध्यक्ष रहते वक्त कांग्रेस के सबसे ताकतवर नेता माने जाते थे। कांग्रेस अध्यक्ष के राजनीतिक सचिव होने के साथ वे सोनिया गांधी के ना केवल 'आंख-कान' थे, बल्कि 'संकटमोचक' भी और हर अहम बात में शामिल किए जाने वाले नेता थे। लेकिन 2017 में राहुल गांधी के अध्यक्ष बनने के बाद से उन्हें धीरे-धीरे हाशिए पर डाल दिया गया। अस्सी के दशक में राजीव गांधी ने उन्हें मौका दिया था और वे अब भी गांधी परिवार के भरोसेमंद माने जाते थे। उन्होंने एक बार मुझे बताया, 'राहुल की टीम में से किसी ने मुझे कहा कि मैं एक दलाल हूं, लेकिन उन्हें शायद इस बात का अहसास नहीं है कि मैं गांधी परिवार की ओर से काम करता हूं और हमेशा उनके हितों को ध्यान में रखता हूं।'

अब राहुल गांधी के अध्यक्ष पद छोड़ने पर अड़ जाने को लेकर अहमद पटेल चिंतित लग रहे थे। राहुल की नयी टीम और संगठन में फेरबदल के लिए पार्टी के पुराने दिग्गजों को पद छोड़ना पड़ सकता है। इस मसले पर दख़ल के लिए पटेल ने सोनिया गांधी से बात की। 'इस्तीफ़ा देने से क्या फायदा होगा? अगर राहुल अपना इस्तीफ़ा वापस नहीं लेते हैं तो पार्टी में टूट का ख़तरा हो सकता है। यही तो भाजपा चाहती है, यही उसकी रणनीति है।' श्रीमती गांधी ने अपने विश्वस्त सहयोगी की बात तो सुनी, लेकिन अपनी लाचारी जताते हुए कहा, 'मैंने पहले ही उन्हें समझाने की कोशिश की, लेकिन आप जानते हैं कि राहुल जब एक बार मन बना लेते हैं तो उन्हें बदलना मुश्किल होता है।' कार्यसमिति की हंगामेदार बैठक के बाद करीब एक महीने तक राहुल गांधी जनता की नज़रों से ग़ायब रहे। उन्होंने इस दौरान अपना ज़्यादातर वक्त अपने 12, तुगलक लेन के आवास में गुज़ारा और पार्टी अध्यक्ष की हैसियत से किसी भी पदाधिकारी से मुलाक़ात नहीं की।

अध्यक्ष पद छोड़ने के ऐलान के करीब 6 हफ्ते बाद, 6 जुलाई 2019 को राहुल गांधी ने एक भावनात्मक चिट्ठी में अपने इस्तीफ़े की औपचारिक घोषणा के साथ सभी अटकलों को खत्म कर दिया। इस चिट्ठी राहुल ने लिखाः 'कांग्रेस पार्टी के अध्यक्ष के रूप में 2019 के चुनावों में हार के लिए मैं जिम्मेदार हूं। पार्टी के भविष्य और उसे आगे बढ़ाने के लिए जवाबदेही अहम है। इसी वजह से मैंने कांग्रेस अध्यक्ष पद से इस्तीफ़ा दिया है।' राहुल ने चिट्ठी में आरोप लगाया कि भाजपा-आरएसएस ने देश की हर संवैधानिक संस्था को कमज़ोर किया है, इसके ख़िलाफ़ वैचारिक लड़ाई के लिए तैयार रहना चाहिए। 'भारत में आदत है कि शक्तिशाली लोग सत्ता से चिपके रहते हैं, और कोई सत्ता नहीं छोड़ता। लेकिन सत्ता की इच्छा छोड़े बिना और एक गंभीर वैचारिक लड़ाई के बिना हम अपने विरोधियों को नहीं हरा सकते।' चिट्ठी को ख़त्म करते हुए उन्होंने लिखा, 'मैं कांग्रेसी पैदा हुआ हूं, कांग्रेस मेरे ख़ून में है और मैं जिंदगी भर कांग्रेस में रहूंगा।'

यह पत्र राहुल गांधी की राजनीतिक सोच समझ और विश्वास का आइना जैसा था। वे सत्ता की गलाकाट राजनीति के बीच फंसे हुए तो थे, लेकिन उस कीचड़ से बाहर निकलने की इच्छा भी रखते थे। साल 2013 में जयपुर में कांग्रेस के महत्वपूर्ण अधिवेशन में जब गांधी परिवार के वफादार उन्हें प्रधानमंत्री पद का चेहरा बनाने की तैयारी कर रहे थे, और संगठन का उपाध्यक्ष बनाया गया था, उस दिन उन्होंने अपने भाषण में 'सत्ता को जहर' बताया था। राहुल ने कहा—'पावर इज पॉइज़न'। मुश्किल यह है कि जब राहुल गांधी अपने पत्र में कांग्रेस कार्यकर्ताओं से संघ परिवार से वैचारिक लड़ाई लड़ने का आह्वान कर रहे थे, उसी समय वे इस्तीफ़ा दे रहे थे, जबकि पार्टी को उस वक़्त उनकी बेहद जरूरत थी कि वे आगे बढ़कर लड़ाई की अगुवाई करें। वे सत्ता की राजनीति में थे, फिर भी इससे बाहर थे। पार्टी के 'शुभंकर' भी, लेकिन स्वयंभू 'राजनीतिक तपस्वी' भी। एक ऐसा विरोधाभास जिसने कांग्रेस को दिशाहीन और भ्रमित कर दिया था।

राहुल गांधी ने ऊंचे नैतिक मापदंडों को बनाए रखने के लिए इस्तीफ़ा दे दिया था, वहीं नए कांग्रेस अध्यक्ष का चेहरा ढूंढने का काम सोनिया गांधी ने अहमद भाई को सौंप दिया गया था। अहमद पटेल के लिए यह ज़िम्मेदारी कांग्रेस की उथल-पुथल को ठीक करने के साथ-साथ पार्टी में अपनी प्रासंगिकता बहाल करने का मौका भी था। राहुल गांधी ने यह साफ कर दिया था कि वे उनका उत्तराधिकारी चुनने की प्रक्रिया में शामिल नहीं होंगे। पटेल ने कुछ वरिष्ठ नेताओं के साथ मिलकर यह खोज शुरू की, लेकिन कोई ऐसा नाम सामने नहीं आया, जो सबको स्वीकार्य हो सके। पटेल की अपनी पसंद महाराष्ट्र से जुड़े, संगठन के मृदुभाषी नेता मुकुल वासनिक थे। वासनिक इसके लिए तैयार नहीं थे, उन्होंने साफ किया, 'मुझे इसमें नहीं पड़ना है।'

कार्यसमिति में इस्तीफ़े के ड्रामे के 77 दिन बाद 10 अगस्त 2019 को जब पार्टी की कार्यसमिति फिर से मिली, तब तक भी राहुल की जगह किसी नाम पर सहमति नहीं बन पाई थी। वासनिक चुपचाप बाहर हो गए थे। राहुल के कई समर्थक अब भी उनसे इस्तीफ़ा वापस

लेने की अपील कर रहे थे, लेकिन राहुल पीछे हटने को तैयार नहीं थे। बैठक में थोड़ी देर बाद अहमद पटेल ने सोनिया गांधी को आगाह किया कि गांधी परिवार के अलावा किसी और को अध्यक्ष बनाने से काम नहीं चलेगा। पटेल ने ज़ोर देकर कहा, 'आपको पद संभालना होगा, मैडम।' हो सकता है इस बारे में उन्होंने एक दिन पहले सोनिया गांधी से बात की हो। बताया जाता है कि जब सोनिया ने इस बारे में राहुल से सलाह ली, तब वे इसके सख्त ख़िलाफ़ थे, लेकिन प्रियंका को शायद कोई आपत्ति नहीं थी। 'मैं संभाल लूंगी, लेकिन केवल एक साल के लिए, जब तक कि आप कोई और नाम नहीं ढूंढ़ लेते,' सोनिया इस शर्त पर तैयार हो गई थीं। अनुभवी कांग्रेसी नेता ने उनके सुझाव पर तुरंत हामी भर दी। देर रात इस बात की घोषणा की गई कि सबसे लंबे समय तक पार्टी की अध्यक्ष रहीं सोनिया गांधी फिर से अंतरिम अध्यक्ष के तौर पर वापसी करेंगी। ऐसा लग रहा था कि कांग्रेस अपने पहले परिवार के साथ 'गर्भनाल' से जुड़ गई है। भाजपा को एक बार फिर कांग्रेस पर परिवारवाद का नारा ज़ोर से लगाने का मौका मिलेगा और कांग्रेस के पास शायद ही कोई जवाब हो।

═

यथास्थिति बनाए रखने वाली कांग्रेस जैसी पार्टी में बगावत को नापसंद किया जाता है। कांग्रेस में गुटबाज़ी भले ही तीखी हो, लेकिन जब बात हाईकमान की आती है, तो फिर ज्यादातर लोग रास्ते पर आ जाते हैं। यह कारण रहा होगा कि 23 अगस्त 2020 को पार्टी में बगावत के एक छोटे धमाके ने ही सबको चौंका दिया। तेईस कांग्रेसियों ने एक गुट बनाकर सोनिया गांधी को पत्र लिखा और संगठन के चुनाव और पार्टी में बड़े बदलाव की बात की। कांग्रेस के जानने वालों के हिसाब से पत्र के सार्वजनिक होने से कांग्रेसजनों में अविश्वास की भावना फैल गई। अविश्वास की एक वजह यह भी थी कि जब इस 'लैटर बम' को जारी किया गया, तब सोनिया गांधी अस्पताल में थीं। चिट्ठी पर दस्तख़त करने वालों में कई पूर्व केन्द्रीय मंत्री और मुख्यमंत्री शामिल थे। इस ग्रुप को 'जी-23' (G-23) नाम दिया गया, जिन्हें आप बागी ना भी कहें, लेकिन वो पार्टी में बदलाव चाहने वालों का समूह तो था ही। '2019 के आम चुनावों के नतीजों के चौदह महीनों बाद भी, कांग्रेस ने अपनी हार और लगातार कमज़ोर होती पार्टी के कारणों का कोई ईमानदार आत्ममंथन नहीं किया था। नेतृत्व पर अनिश्चितता से कार्यकर्ताओं का मनोबल गिरा। पार्टी और कमज़ोर हुई। कई राज्यों में नेताओं और पदाधिकारियों के छोड़कर जाने से भी उसका जनाधार कम हुआ है। पार्टी के सामने चुनौतियों की गंभीरता को देखते हुए एक नेतृत्व का सिस्टम खड़ा करना ज़रूरी हो गया था।' चिट्ठी पर दस्तखत करने वाले भले ही यह ना मानें, लेकिन 1999 में दिग्गज नेता शरद पवार के सोनिया के 'विदेशी मूल' के मुद्दे पर पार्टी छोड़ देने के बाद, सोनिया के नेतृत्व के लिए यह पहली गंभीर चुनौती थी।

जी-23 के प्रमुख सदस्य, वकील और राजनेता कपिल सिब्बल ज़ोर देकर कहते हैं, 'हम सुधार चाहते थे, हम बागी नहीं हैं। हम कांग्रेस में सोनिया गांधी के योगदान का सम्मान करते हैं और उसे सम्मान देते हैं, लेकिन हमें संगठन के कामकाज की शैली में तुरंत बदलाव की ज़रूरत महसूस हुई।' वैसे भी सिब्बल इस ग्रुप में अलग ही दिखते हैं। देश के बड़े वकीलों में से एक सिब्बल, संवैधानिक मूल्यों की प्रतिबद्धता रखते हैं और सरकारी भेदभाव या अत्याचार के पीड़ित लोगों के लिए मुकदमे लड़ते हैं। सिब्बल के इस कदम के पीछे कोई निजी महत्वाकांक्षा नहीं दिखती, बल्कि तेजी से गिरती पार्टी को फिर से सशक्त बनाने की इच्छा थी। वैसे जी-23 में शामिल दूसरे लोग राजनेता थे, जो सत्ता के लंबे समय से वनवास को ख़त्म करने के लिए संघर्ष कर रहे थे।

बागियों की इस जमात में सबसे हाई-प्रोफाइल अनुभवी नेता ग़ुलाम नबी आज़ाद थे, जो राज्यसभा में कांग्रेस के नेता भी थे। आज़ाद ने सत्तर के दशक में इंदिरा गांधी के नेतृत्व में अपनी राजनीतिक पारी शुरू की थी। पुराने ज़माने के आकर्षक, लंबे कद और मुस्कुराते चेहरे वाले कश्मीरी नेता परिवार के वफादार माने जाते थे। वे उन लोगों को हैरान कर रहे थे, जिनका राजनीतिक सफ़र गांधी परिवार के करीबी होने की वजह से चलता रहा है। तो सवाल था कि फिर इस वफ़ादार नेता ने बगावत का झंडा क्यों उठाया? 'मुझे सोनिया जी से कोई दिक्कत नहीं थी, मेरी परेशानी राहुल गांधी और उनके कामकाज के तरीके से थी। हर बार जब मैं मैडम से मिलता, तो वे मुझसे राहुल से बात करने के लिए कहतीं। और जब मैं राहुल से संपर्क करने की कोशिश करता, तो उनके सहयोगी उनकी मां यानी सोनिया जी से बात करने के लिए कहते। एक पार्टी सत्ता के दो केन्द्र के साथ कैसे चल सकती है? खासतौर से उन लोगों के लिए ये ज़्यादा मुश्किल है जिन्होंने उनकी दादी और पिता के साथ काम किया था,' आज़ाद की शिकायत थी। राहुल की अपने ही नेताओं से मुलाकात में मुश्किल, लंबे समय से कांग्रेस के गलियारे में फुसफुसाती रही है और नेता उससे निराश होते हैं। इनमें से कई ऐसे नेता और वरिष्ठ सांसद भी हैं जिनके पास राहुल गांधी का मोबाइल नंबर भी नहीं था। उन्हें राहुल से मुलाकात के लिए, उनकी टीम के कम अनुभवी और नए लोगों से संपर्क करना होता था और वह भी आसान नहीं था। जी-23 के एक नाराज़ सदस्य का कहना था, 'राहुल के साथ समस्या यह है कि वो कहते तो हैं कि सत्ता में उन्हें कोई दिलचस्पी नहीं है, लेकिन फिर भी वे कांग्रेस के सबसे ताकतवर नेता हैं।' हालांकि पार्टी के रोजमर्रा के कामकाज से राहुल दूर रहते हैं, लेकिन कांग्रेस के अहम फ़ैसलों और महत्वपूर्ण नियुक्तियों में उनके पास 'वीटो पावर' थी। आज़ाद के समर्थकों ने दावा किया, आज़ाद को सत्ता में बैठी द्रविड़ मुनेत्र कड़गम (डीएमके) पार्टी के समर्थन से तमिलनाडु से राज्यसभा भेजने का भरोसा दिलाया गया था। आज़ाद के डीएमके से लंबे समय से संबंध रहे थे। 'राहुल ने आज़ाद साहब का नाम उस लिस्ट से इसलिए हटा दिया, क्योंकि उन्हें लगता

था कि आज़ाद और प्रधानमंत्री मोदी के बीच खास दोस्ती थी। जब आपको अपने ही नेताओं पर शक हो तो आप राजनीति कैसे कर सकते हैं?' आज़ाद के समर्थक ने कहा। जम्मू कश्मीर के मुख्यमंत्री रहे आज़ाद ने जब अगस्त 2022 में पार्टी छोड़ दी, तब मैंने उनसे पूछा कि क्या राज्यसभा सीट नहीं मिलने के कारण आपने पार्टी छोड़ दी? 'बकवास,' उन्होंने गुस्से में जवाब दिया। आज़ाद ने कहा, 'क्या आपको लगता है कि पचास साल तक पार्टी में रहने के बाद मैं पार्टी इसलिए छोड़ दूंगा क्योंकि मुझे राज्यसभा नहीं भेजा गया? मैंने पार्टी इसलिए छोड़ी क्योंकि राहुल गांधी की कांग्रेस में आत्मसम्मान रखने वाले किसी व्यक्ति के लिए कोई जगह नहीं है।'

यह मसला सिर्फ़ आज़ाद का नहीं था। जी-23 के ज्यादातर नेता राहुल के राजनीति करने के तरीके से परेशान थेः निर्णय लेने में अनिश्चितता और काम में लापरवाही या उदासीनता। उदाहरण के लिए हरियाणा से दो बार कांग्रेस के मुख्यमंत्री रहे भूपिंदर सिंह हुड्डा इस बात से नाराज़ थे कि उन्हें 2019 के विधानसभा चुनावों से पहले पूरी ज़िम्मेदारी या प्रभार नहीं दिया गया। हुड्डा ने ज़ोर देकर कहा, 'अगर मुझे पूरी छूट मिलती तो हम हरियाणा निश्चित तौर पर जीत जाते।' सत्तर साल के हुड्डा, अहमद पटेल के करीबी सहयोगी माने जाते थे, यानी सत्ता के बदलते समीकरणों में वे दूसरी तरफ खड़े थे। जी-23 में एक और बड़ा नाम था, महाराष्ट्र के पूर्व मुख्यमंत्री और प्रतिष्ठित नेता पृथ्वीराज चव्हाण, जो 2014 के विधानसभा चुनावों में पार्टी की हार के बाद हाशिये पर चले गए थे। बताया गया कि चव्हाण अपनी शिकायतों के लिए महीनों से राहुल से मुलाकात का वक्त मांग रहे थे, लेकिन कामयाबी नहीं मिली। चव्हाण ने एक सहयोगी से शिकायती लहजे में कहा, 'जब कोई संवाद ही नहीं है, तो आप कैसे काम कर सकते हैं?'

मुखर और युवा माने जाने वाले दो सांसद तेज़तर्रार 'टेलीजेनिक' शशि थरूर और बेहतर वक्ता मनीष तिवारी भी लोकसभा में नेतृत्व के लिए नज़रअंदाज़ किए जाने से नाराज़ थे। उनके बजाय पश्चिम बंगाल से पांच बार सांसद रहे अधीर रंजन चौधरी को लोकसभा में कांग्रेस का नेता बनाया गया। पश्चिम बंगाल में सीपीआई (एम) और ममता बनर्जी सरकार दोनों पर हमलावर रहने वाले चौधरी की छवि सख्त नेता की है, लेकिन संसद में बेहतर तरीके से बात रखने के कौशल की ज़रूरत होती है। जी-23 के एक सदस्य ने हंसते हुए तंज में कहा, 'कांग्रेस पार्टी में, हमारे पास सही काम के लिए गलत आदमी को चुनने की आदत है।' कहा जाता है कि लोकसभा में नेता के नाम पर फ़ैसला कांग्रेस संसदीय दल की अध्यक्ष सोनिया गांधी ने सहयोगियों की सलाह के बिना किया था। जब नाराज़ थरूर ने इस पर कांग्रेस नेतृत्व से सवाल किया कि उन्हें इस पद के लिए क्यों नहीं चुना गया, तो उनकी चिंताओं को दरकिनार कर दिया गया। 'अधीर रंजन पांच बार के सांसद हैं और आपसे वरिष्ठ हैं,' उन्हें बताया गया। कुछ लोगों का मानना है कि अधीर को यह ज़िम्मेदारी इसलिए दी गई क्योंकि उनकी अपने संसदीय क्षेत्र बेहरामपुर से बाहर कोई

'मास अपील' नहीं है, जबकि संसद में विपक्ष की अगुवाई करने वाले थरूर और तिवारी राष्ट्रीय स्तर पर चर्चा का विषय बन सकते हैं। एक वरिष्ठ नेता ने कहा, 'कांग्रेस में प्रतिभाशाली लोग अपने साथ के लोगों को बेहद असुरक्षित बनाते हैं।'

इस मसले में दिलचस्प यह है कि कांग्रेस में सुधार की इच्छा रखने वाले ग्रुप में यह शुरुआती विचार पहली बार शशि थरूर के सुंदर आवास पर डिनर के दौरान आया था। थरूर ने ज़ोर देकर कहा, 'यह पार्टी या गांधी परिवार के ख़िलाफ़ कोई साज़िश नहीं थी, बल्कि संगठन की चिंता करने वाले नेताओं के बीच एक ईमानदार चर्चा थी। मैं एक सुधारवादी हूं, कोई क्रांतिकारी नहीं।' कांग्रेस सरकार में वित्त मंत्री रहे पी. चिदंबरम भी इस बैठक में शामिल हुए थे, लेकिन बाद में उन्होंने दस्तख़त करने वाले लोगों से खुद को अलग कर लिया। चिदम्बरम का कहना था कि 'मैं मानता हूं कि गांधी परिवार की सहमति के बिना कुछ नहीं किया जा सकता। और यह ठीक नहीं था कि सोनिया गांधी के अस्पताल रहने के दौरान कोई पत्र भेजा जाए और उसे सार्वजनिक किया जाए।'

जी-23 की यह बगावत जल्दी ही शांत हो गई। इस ग्रुप को कांग्रेस में बदलाव की मांग के लिए कार्यकर्ताओं और नेताओं का राजनीतिक समर्थन नहीं मिला। दिसम्बर, 2020 की सर्दियों में सोनिया गांधी के 10, जनपथ आवास पर पुदीने की चटनी के साथ सैंडविच और कुकीज के साथ अनौपचारिक चाय पर मुलाक़ात में बर्फ पिघलने में देर नहीं लगी। सोनिया गांधी ने अपने खास अंदाज़ में इस बगावती संकट को कम करने की कोशिश की। उन्होंने कहा कि वे किसी भी असंतुष्टि को लेकर कोई दुर्भावना नहीं रखती हैं। जी-23 के प्रमुख सदस्यों को कहा, 'मेरे दरवाज़े आपके लिए हमेशा खुले हैं और मैं आपको भरोसा दिलाती हूं कि आपकी चिंताओं का रास्ता निकाला जाएगा।' सोनिया और प्रियंका जहां 'शांतिदूत' की तरह थे, वहीं राहुल 'विद्रोही' दिख रहे थे। उन्होंने एक असंतुष्ट नेता से कहा, 'पार्टी नेतृत्व पर हमला करके, आप भाजपा के हाथों में खेल रहे हैं।' गांधी परिवार में ही बागियों को लेकर दो अलग नजरिए थे। कांग्रेस अध्यक्ष के तौर पर सोनिया गांधी की दो दशकों की कार्यशैली मौटे तौर पर सबके साथ सहमति बनाकर चलने की रही। वह उन लोगों को भी साथ लेकर चलने की राजनीति करती थीं, जिनसे वे नज़रें मिलाना भी पसंद नहीं करतीं। उदाहरण के तौर पर, साल 2012 में राष्ट्रपति पद के लिए प्रणब मुखर्जी पार्टी के उम्मीदवार थे, भले ही सोनिया गांधी, अपने पति से वफादारी नहीं निभाने वाले इस नेता पर पूरी तरह भरोसा नहीं कर सकती थीं। राजनीतिक परिपक्वता दिखाते हुए सोनिया गांधी ने उन शरद पवार के साथ भी शांति का हाथ बढ़ाया, जिन्होंने विदेशी मूल के सवाल पर उनके रास्ते में कांटे बिछाए थे। कांग्रेस कार्यसमिति के एक सदस्य ने कहा, 'सोनिया जी अपनी ताकत और सीमाएं दोनों समझती हैं, और जानती हैं कि कब किसके सामने गाजर फेंकनी हैं और कब डंडा चलाने की ज़रूरत है? इस मामले में वो पक्की राजनेता हैं।'

इससे उलट, राहुल गांधी वैचारिक रूप से उनके साथ नहीं दिखने वाले लोगों को लेकर अडिग थे और उतावले भी। राहुल बीजेपी-आरएसएस के हिंदू-राष्ट्र के एजेंडा को अपना दुश्मन नंबर-1 मानते हैं। राहुल समझते हैं कि उनके पूर्वजों ने संवैधानिक मूल्यों की रक्षा और हिंदू चरमपंथ के ख़िलाफ़ जमकर संघर्ष किया था। हिन्दुत्व से लड़ना उनका सबसे बड़ा वैचारिक मिशन है और जो कोई इससे थोड़ा भी अलग होता है, वह संदेह के दायरे में आता है। एक पूर्व कांग्रेसी ने कहा, 'राहुल गांधी एक राजनीतिक पार्टी में विचारक बनना चाहते हैं जिसकी एकमात्र विचारधारा सत्ता है।' उन्होंने कांग्रेस इसलिए छोड़ दी क्योंकि राहुल की टीम के लोगों ने उन पर भाजपा के साथ सांठगांठ करने का आरोप लगाया था। 'मैं अपने पुराने मित्र, भाजपा के सांसद के घर पर डिनर पर गया था। फिर एक व्हाट्सएप संदेश पर मुझे "दलबदलू" कहा गया। यह सिर्फ़ पागलपन था।' वैसे ये नेता बाद में भाजपा में शामिल हो गए। राहुल के समर्थकों ने इस आरोप को गलत बताया कि उनके नेता की वजह से पार्टी के भीतर टकराव हो रहा था। 'राहुल जी लोकतंत्र में भरोसा करते हैं और पार्टी में एक पीढ़ीगत और संगठन स्तर पर बदलाव लाना चाहते हैं।' राहुल के साथ लंबे समय से रहने वाले सहयोगी का कहना था, 'जब वे कहते हैं कि वह अपने लिए सत्ता नहीं चाहते, बल्कि समाज में बदलाव लाना चाहते हैं, तो वाकई उनका मतलब यही होता है।'

राहुल गांधी की ईमानदारी पर भले ही कम लोग संदेह करते हैं, लेकिन ज़्यादातर लोग उनकी राजनीतिक समझ पर सवाल उठाते हैं। एक तरफ सोनिया गांधी ने सौम्य, मिलनसार और अनुभवी राजनेता अहमद पटेल को अपने राजनीतिक सचिव के तौर पर चुना था, जिनके सभी राजनीतिक दलों में संबंध थे, वहीं राहुल गांधी ने राजनीतिक सहयोगी के तौर पर पार्टी के महासचिव (संगठन) के.सी. वेणुगोपाल पर भरोसा किया था। 'जब यूपीए सत्ता में थी और विपक्ष के किसी नेता या किसी उद्योगपति को मदद की ज़रूरत होती, तो अहमद भाई बेझिझक फोन उठाकर उनका काम करवा देते,' कांग्रेस के भूतपूर्व एमपी ने कहा। इसके विपरीत गंभीर-चेहरे वाले वेणुगोपाल दिल्ली की एलिट राजनीति के लिए एक 'आउटसाइडर' ही थे; उनके पास न तो पटेल की तरह विस्तृत नेटवर्क था, और न ही वे अच्छे हिन्दी वक्ता थे। कांग्रेस की राजनीतिक हालत पतली होने की बड़ी वजह उसका देश की हिन्दी पट्टी में तेजी से गिरना था। उत्तर भारत की राजनीति से अनजान केरल के एक नेता को संगठन में केन्द्रीय भूमिका में रखने पर भी बहुत से लोग अचरज करते थे। उत्तरप्रदेश के एक दलित नेता बृजलाल खबरी को अक्टूबर 2022 में कुछ समय के लिए प्रदेश कांग्रेस अध्यक्ष बनाया गया था। खबरी बताते हैं कि उन्हें वेणुगोपाल के साथ तालमेल में बहुत मुश्किल होती थी। देहाती खबरी केवल हिन्दी जानते थे।

'मैं वेणुगोपाल जी से केवल तीन-चार बार मिला, लेकिन कोई भी बात करने में बड़ी परेशानी होती थी, क्योंकि उन्हें हिन्दी नहीं आती थी और मुझे अंग्रेज़ी। जब भी मैं कोई राजनीतिक मसला उठाता तो वे बस सिर हिलाकर कहते, ठीक है, ठीक है।' एक साल से भी कम समय में जब खबरी को उनके पद से हटा दिया गया तो उन्हें अपने निष्कासन की जानकारी एक पत्रकार मित्र से मिली, जिसने उन्हें एक व्हाट्सएप संदेश भेजा था। खबरी बोले, 'किसी ने मुझे यह बताने या फ़ोन करने की भी ज़हमत नहीं उठाई कि मुझे क्यों हटाया जा रहा था।' जाहिर है कि देश की सबसे ज़्यादा आबादी वाला और राजनीतिक तौर पर सबसे प्रभावशाली प्रदेश कांग्रेस नेतृत्व की प्राथमिकता नहीं था। उत्तरप्रदेश से देश में सबसे ज़्यादा 80 लोकसभा सीटें हैं और उसने अब तक सबसे ज़्यादा प्रधानमंत्री बनाए हैं। प्रदेश कांग्रेस के एक नेता को तकलीफ थीः 'हमें उत्तर भारत से किसी समझदार, चतुर हिंदी भाषी नेता की ज़रूरत थी, लेकिन हमें एक ऐसा गैर-हिंदी भाषी नेता मिला, जो प्रदेश के ज़िलों के नाम तक नहीं जानता, उसे पार्टी को फिर से खड़ा करने की ज़िम्मेदारी सौंपी गई।' कहा जाता है कि वेणुगोपाल ने ही 2019 में राहुल को अमेठी के साथ केरल के वायनाड से भी चुनाव लड़ने के लिए तैयार किया था, लेकिन इसे राजनीतिक जानकारों ने देश के सबसे अहम राजनीतिक मैदान से पीछे हटने के संकेत के तौर पर देखा।

उत्तर भारत की जटिल और मुश्किल राजनीति से निपटने में कांग्रेस नेतृत्व के फ़ैसले लेने की क्षमता पर उत्तरप्रदेश के अलावा भी कई जगहों पर सवाल उठते रहे हैं।

2018 में जब कांग्रेस ने राजस्थान में विधानसभा चुनाव में जीत हासिल की, तो पार्टी हाईकमान ने दो बार मुख्यमंत्री रह चुके अनुभवी अशोक गहलोत को फिर से कमान सौंपी। जबकि वहां तेजतर्रार युवा नेता सचिन पायलट ने चुनाव में अहम भूमिका निभाई थी। आसानी से समझ नहीं आने वाले, कुर्ता-पायजामा पहने गहलोत अपने शांत स्वभाव से सबको सहज रखते हैं। गहलोत सत्तर के दशक में इंदिरा-संजय युग में छात्र राजनीति से आए। वह टीवी से पहले का ज़माना था, जब लोग कपड़ों को लेकर ज़्यादा परवाह नहीं करते थे। इसके विपरीत आकर्षक सचिन पायलट तो इक्कीसवीं सदी की राजनीति के विज्ञापन जैसे लगते हैं। राहुल गांधी की तरह वंशवादी, युवा, सुंदर, लंबा कद, स्मार्ट लुक, टेलीजेनिक और तकनीक के जानकार हैं। बहुत मिलनसार, उन्होंने मुख्यमंत्री बनने की इच्छा को कभी छिपाने की कोशिश नहीं की, लेकिन गहलोत की तरह दिल्ली के सत्ता के गलियारों में उनके पास ज़्यादा सहयोगी नहीं थे। बताया जाता है कि राजस्थान में सरकार बनाते वक्त राहुल गांधी ने समझौते के तौर पर सचिन पायलट को जल्दी ही मुख्यमंत्री बनाने का वादा किया था।

जुलाई 2020 आते-आते यह साफ हो गया था कि गहलोत जल्दी नहीं जाने वाले थे। पायलट सरकार में उप-मुख्यमंत्री तो थे, लेकिन सभी अहम फाइलें और नियुक्तियां मुख्यमंत्री कार्यालय के ही नियंत्रण में रहती थीं। पायलट के एक सहयोगी का आरोप था कि 'हमारे नेता तो अपनी

इच्छा से एक कांस्टेबल तक का तबादला नहीं कर सकते थे।' प्रदेश की राजनीति में पानी तब सिर से गुजरने लगा, जब गहलोत सरकार को गिराने के आरोप में विधायकों की खरीद-फरोख्त पर बातचीत को 'मोबाइल इंटरसेप्ट' किया गया, इसके बाद राजद्रोह के अपराध में एफआईआर दर्ज कराई गई और इनमें सचिन पायलट का नाम शामिल था। पायलट को जारी एक नोटिस में उन्हें पुलिस के सामने पेश होकर बयान दर्ज कराने के लिए कहा गया। पायलट ने कहा, 'हां, मेरे लिए यह बगावत का ट्रिगर पांइट था। जरा सोचिए, मैं उप-मुख्यमंत्री और प्रदेश कांग्रेस का अध्यक्ष हूं और पुलिस मेरे दरवाज़े पर आती है और मुझ पर राजद्रोह का आरोप लगाती है।'

नाराज़ पायलट को लगा कि मुख्यमंत्री ने उन्हें पार्टी से बाहर निकालने के लिए यह साज़िश रची थी, इसलिए उन्होंने बगावत कर दी और कम से कम एक दर्जन अपने वफादार विधायकों के साथ जयपुर छोड़ दिया और कसम खाई कि गहलोत को हटाए जाने से पहले जयपुर नहीं लौटेंगे। कुछ विधायकों को जब भाजपा शासित राज्य हरियाणा के मानेसर में होटल में ठहराया गया, तो यह संदेह बढ़ गया कि बगावत के बहाने भारतीय जनता पार्टी एक और कांग्रेस शासित सरकार को गिराने की कोशिश कर रही थी। गहलोत ने ज़ोर देकर कहा, 'हमारे पास बागी विधायकों और दिल्ली में भाजपा नेताओं के बीच फोन पर हुई बातचीत के रिकॉर्ड हैं, जिसमें पैसे के लेने-देन पर बात हो रही है।' राजनीतिक संकट बढ़ता देख, विधायकों की खरीद-फरोख्त से बचने के लिए गहलोत ने अपने वफादार विधायकों को जैसलमेर के एक रिजॉर्ट में भेज दिया। आरोप था कि भाजपा के नेता और केन्द्रीय मंत्री गजेन्द्र सिंह शेखावत इस योजना को अंजाम तक पहुंचाने में अहम भूमिका निभा रहे थे। शेखावत ने 2019 में जोधपुर में अशोक गहलोत के बेटे वैभव को हराया था और दिल्ली में केन्द्रीय मंत्री बने थे। लेकिन पायलट का कहना था कि उन्होंने कभी किसी भाजपा नेता से संपर्क नहीं किया। 'मेरे पास होटल के सभी बिल, क़ानूनी फीस और दूसरे भुगतानों के बिल भी हैं। मेरे विधायकों और मैंने हर चीज़ का भुगतान अपनी ज़ेब से किया है।'

इसे पार्टी में अंदरूनी बगावत कहें या संभावित 'ऑपरेशन लोटस' (विपक्षी दलों की सरकारों को गिराने के भाजपा के प्रयासों का चर्चित कोडनेम), इन घटनाओं ने कांग्रेस नेतृत्व को चिंता में डाल दिया था। इससे पहले, मार्च 2020 में, मध्यप्रदेश में कांग्रेस की कमलनाथ सरकार गिर गई थी, पार्टी अपनी एक और सरकार गिरने का ज़ोख़िम नहीं उठा सकती थी। पायलट के विद्रोह के एक महीने बाद अगस्त में, अहमद पटेल और प्रियंका गांधी के बीच-बचाव से दोनों नाराज़ गुटों के बीच थोड़ी शांति हुई। पटेल, मुख्यमंत्री गहलोत के करीब माने जाते थे और प्रियंका को उनकी मां सोनिया गांधी की आवाज़ के तौर पर देखा जाता था। राहुल गांधी ने इस मसले में पड़ने से साफ इंकार कर दिया। बताया गया कि पहले हुए समझौते में माना गया था कि गहलोत मुख्यमंत्री बने रहेंगे, लेकिन पायलट के विश्वस्त लोगों को मंत्री बनाया जाएगा। सचिन पायलट को भरोसा दिलाया गया था कि उन्हें 2023 में होने वाले विधानसभा चुनावों से

पहले मुख्यमंत्री बनाया जाएगा। बेचैन पायलट ने सितम्बर 2022 तक इंतज़ार किया। सोनिया गांधी ने गहलोत को दिल्ली में उनकी जगह पार्टी का राष्ट्रीय अध्यक्ष बनने के लिए कहा और पायलट को जयपुर में मुख्यमंत्री की कुर्सी संभालने के लिए तैयार रहने का संदेश दिया गया। गहलोत ने इस पर शुरू में तो सहमति जताई, लेकिन जब उन्हें पायलट को मुख्यमंत्री बनाए जाने की जानकारी मिली तो उन्होंने वो कदम उठाया, जिसके बारे में शायद ही किसी ने सोचा हो: गहलोत ने आलाकमान के फैसले के ख़िलाफ़ जाने का तय कर लिया।

कांग्रेस ने संकट खत्म करने के लिए मल्लिकार्जुन खड़गे और अजय माकन की दो सदस्यों वाली टीम को जयपुर भेजने का फ़ैसला किया। उनको जयपुर में विधायक दल की बैठक बुलाकर एक लाइन का प्रस्ताव पारित कराना था, जिसमें पार्टी हाईकमान को नया मुख्यमंत्री चुनने के लिए अधिकृत किया जाए। लेकिन जब दोनों पर्यवेक्षक मुख्यमंत्री के आवास पर विधायकों के इकट्ठा होने का इंतज़ार कर रहे थे, तब गहलोत के वफादार और सरकार में मंत्री शांति धारीवाल ने विधायकों की एक और बैठक बुलाई, जिसमें नई शर्तें रखी गईः वे पायलट खेमे से किसी को मुख्यमंत्री स्वीकार नहीं करेंगे और मुख्यमंत्री को लेकर फ़ैसला अध्यक्ष के चुनाव होने तक टाल दिया जाए। 'मैंने ऐसा पहले कभी नहीं देखा, विधायक शर्तें रखकर आलाकमान को ब्लैकमेल करने की कोशिश कर रहे थे,' परेशान खड़गे ने स्वीकार किया। फिर एक महीने बाद खड़गे ही पार्टी अध्यक्ष बन गए। गहलोत की चुनौती का सामना करने, उन्हें पद छोड़ने और पार्टी का राष्ट्रीय अध्यक्ष पद लेने पर मजबूर करने के बजाय कांग्रेस आलाकमान पीछे हट गया। गहलोत मुख्यमंत्री बने रहे।

बीमारी से जूझ रही और सत्तर पार कर चुकी सोनिया गांधी को, अहमद पटेल की गैर-मौजूदगी में पुराने नेताओं से भी अपना आदेश मनवाने में मुश्किल हो रही थी। उनके विश्वस्त रहे अहमद पटेल का नवम्बर 2020 में निधन हो गया था। मौजूदा संगठन प्रभारी के.सी. वेणुगोपाल के पास न तो वैसा अनुभव था और ना ही वो राजनीतिक ताकत, जिससे वे किसी वरिष्ठ नेता को उनके हिसाब से चलने के लिए दबाव डाल पाते। अक्सर कम बोलने वाले राहुल गांधी ने अब कांग्रेस की रोजमर्रा की राजनीति से खुद को दूर कर लिया था। एक समय की सबसे मजबूत कांग्रेस इस समय नेतृत्व के संकट से जूझ रही थी। एक वरिष्ठ कांग्रेस नेता ने माना, 'गहलोत के विरोध से साफ था कि कांग्रेस नेतृत्व कितना असहाय हो गया है। इसका संदेश यह भी था कि गांधी परिवार को भी चुनौती दी जा सकती है।' बताया जाता है कि अशोक गहलोत ने बाद में अपने असहयोग के लिए सोनिया गांधी से माफ़ी मांगी और यह सुनिश्चित कर लिया कि उनके ख़िलाफ़ कोई अनुशासनात्मक कार्रवाई नहीं की जाएगी। गहलोत ने एक बार फिर पायलट को पटखनी दे दी थी। दिसम्बर 2023 में हुए राजस्थान विधानसभा के चुनावों से करीब एक हफ्ते पहले राहुल गांधी की रैली में गहलोत और पायलट को मंच पर एक साथ देखा गया था, लेकिन

तब तक बहुत देर गई थी और यह नाकाफी था। बिखरी हुई कांग्रेस ने राजस्थान में सत्ता खो दी। गहलोत के 'समर्थक' वफादार मंत्रियों में ज़्यादातर चुनाव हार गए।

राजस्थान में जहां कांग्रेस पार्टी के अंदरूनी झगड़े को निपटाने में नाकाम रही, तो पंजाब में तो खुद को ख़त्म करने का काम कर लिया। 2017 में कांग्रेस ने कैप्टन अमरिंदर सिंह की अगुवाई में पंजाब विधानसभा का चुनाव जीता था। पटियाला के पूर्व राजा, कैप्टन अमरिंदर अपनी शानदार पगड़ी, बेदाग कुर्ते और स्टाइलिश दाढ़ी-मूंछों के साथ राजशाही जिंदगी जीने वाले प्रभावशाली नेता हैं। चंडीगढ़ के पास उनके शानदार फॉर्महाउस, व्हिस्की, कला और सैन्य इतिहासों पर किताबों से उनकी बेहतरीन पसंद का अहसास होता है। खुद अमरिंदर सिंह ने कई किताबें लिखी हैं। अपनी शाही जीवनशैली की वजह से कैप्टन सिंह पंजाब की गुटबाजी वाली राजनीति में अकेले दिखाई देते हैं। उनके विधायकों ने उन पर नौकरशाही के भरोसे रहने और उनसे मिलना नामुमकिन होने के आरोप लगाए थे। कैप्टन सिंह कहते हैं कि 'मैं आम राजनीतिक चाटुकारों का रोजाना दरबार नहीं लगाता, इसका मतलब यह नहीं होता कि मैं किसी की पहुंच से बाहर हूं या नहीं मिलता हूं।'

कैप्टन को भरोसा था कि वे विधायकों के असंतोष से निपट लेंगे, लेकिन उनकी ही पार्टी का एक नेता सार्वजनिक रूप से बगावती सुर दिखा रहा था। क्रिकेटर से टीवी पर कॉमेडियन शो-मैन, और फिर राजनेता बने नवजोत सिंह सिद्धू को ऐसी मिसाइल माना जाता है, जिस पर किसी का कोई नियंत्रण नहीं है। 2017 के चुनावों से पहले उन्होंने अकाली-भाजपा गठबंधन वाली सरकार में अकाली नेतृत्व के ख़िलाफ़ मोर्चा खोल दिया था, फिर वे भाजपा छोड़कर कांग्रेस में शामिल हो गए। उन्होंने कांग्रेस में जाने से पहले आम आदमी पार्टी के साथ जाने की कोशिश भी की। आप, अकाली सरकार और बादल परिवार के ख़िलाफ़ भ्रष्टाचार विरोधी अभियान चला रही थी। लेकिन सिद्धू ने जब खुद को मुख्यमंत्री के चेहरे के तौर पर पेश करने पर जोर दिया तो बातचीत टूट गई। सिद्धू को कांग्रेस में लाने का काम रणनीतिकार प्रशांत किशोर ने किया। किशोर उस समय कैप्टन सिंह के अभियान को संभाल रहे थे। किशोर ने कांग्रेस आलाकमान को इस बात का भरोसा दिलाया कि सिद्धू से चुनावी लड़ाई में बड़ा असर पड़ेगा। हर हाल में चुनाव जीतने की कोशिश में लगे कैप्टन सिंह सिद्धू को उप-मुख्यमंत्री बनाने पर भी तैयार हो गए थे, लेकिन बाद में वे पलट गए। प्रशांत क़िशोर मानते हैं कि '2017 में आप के ख़िलाफ़ लड़ाई मेरे लिए अब तक का सबसे मुश्किल चुनाव था। हम सिद्धू को इसलिए लाए, क्योंकि उनकी स्टार अपील थी और वे भीड़ जुटाने वाला चेहरा थे।'

बेशक सिद्धू एक स्टार थे। टीवी पर उनकी छवि एक तेज-तर्रार व्यंग्यकार कॉमेडियन शो-मैन की थी, जिसने उन्हें खेल और मनोरंजन दोनों क्षेत्र में खास पहचान दी। लेकिन कैप्टन सिंह को कभी इस बात इत्मीनान नहीं हुआ कि सिद्धू सेलिब्रिटी से राजनेता बन सकते हैं। कैप्टन

सिंह का मानना था कि 'जब आप सरकार में मंत्री होते हैं तो आपको अनुशासित रहना होता है, आप टीवी स्टुडियो के शो-मैन की तरह नही रह सकते।' उनका पहला टकराव इस बात पर हुआ कि सिद्धू टीवी शो में जाना चाहते थे। मुख्यमंत्री इसे हितों के टकराव के तौर पर देख रहे थे, जबकि सिद्धू अपनी जिद पर अड़े थे। सिद्धू का कहना था, 'मैं सवेरे 9 बजे से शाम 6 बजे तक अपना सरकारी काम करता हूं, इसके बाद क्या करूं, इससे किसी का कोई लेना-देना नहीं होना चाहिए।' इस मसले पर पंजाब महाधिवक्ता से क़ानूनी मंज़ूरी मिलने के बाद उन्हें टीवी शो में जाने की इज़ाजत मिल गई। लेकिन 2018 में बात तब बढ़ गई, जब सिद्धू मुख्यमंत्री के आदेशों की अवहेलना करते हुए इस्लामाबाद में पाकिस्तान के प्रधानमंत्री इमरान ख़ान के शपथ-ग्रहण समारोह में पहुंच गए। सिद्धू ने अपने बचाव में कहा, 'इमरान मेरे क्रिकेट के दिनों से पुराने दोस्त हैं, अगर उन्होंने बुलाया है तो मैं क्यों नहीं जाता?' इस समारोह में जब सिद्धू की पाकिस्तान के तत्कालीन सेना प्रमुख जनरल बाजवा से गले मिलने की तस्वीरें वायरल हुईं तो यह यात्रा मुख्यमंत्री सिंह के लिए शर्मिंदगी का मसला बन गई। भले ही एक पाकिस्तानी महिला पत्रकार के साथ उनके कथित संबंधों को लेकर अफवाहें चलती रही हों, लेकिन सेना में रहे, उग्र राष्ट्रवादी कैप्टन सिंह ने पाकिस्तान पर कड़ा रुख अपनाया था। एक बार पंजाब विधानसभा में पंजाबी भावनाओं को उकसाते हुए कैप्टन सिंह ने पाकिस्तान के सीमापार आतंकवाद को समर्थन देने पर चेताया था: 'मैं जनरल बाजवा को साफतौर पर कहना चाहता हूं, यदि आप पंजाबी हैं, तो हम भी पंजाबी हैं, और अगर आपने हमारी सीमा में घुसने की ज़ुर्रत की, तो हम ठीक करना जानते हैं।'

जैसे-जैसे दोनों सरदारों के बीच की 'जंग' सार्वजनिक हमलों में बदलती जा रही थी, तब सिद्धू ने अपना मंत्रालय बदलने से नाराज़ होकर कैबिनेट से इस्तीफ़ा दे दिया। उन्होंने अपना इस्तीफ़ा मुख्यमंत्री को भेजने के बजाय इसे राहुल गांधी को संबोधित करते हुए ट्विटर पर जारी कर दिया, मुख्यमंत्री को इसकी सूचना बाद में दी। मुख्यमंत्री सिंह ने इसे प्रोटोकॉल का उल्लघंन माना। 'क्या इस अस्थिर आदमी को समझ आता है कि कैबिनेट सिस्टम कैसे चलता है?' मुख्यमंत्री नाराज दिख रहे थे, लेकिन सिद्धू को मानो इसकी परवाह नहीं थी। राहुल को सीधे पत्र लिखकर सिद्धू ने जता दिया था कि उनका सीधा संपर्क गांधी परिवार से है और वे सिर्फ़ उनके प्रति जवाबदेह हैं, मुख्यमंत्री के लिए नहीं। दिल्ली में प्रियंका गांधी वाड्रा, सिद्धू की विश्वसनीय व्यक्ति थीं। पार्टी ने उन्हें मसला हल करने और शांति बनाने के लिए कहा बताया, क्योंकि सिद्धू अकेले उन पर भरोसा करते थे। सिद्धू बहुत से मौकों पर चंडीगढ़ से बिना बताए दिल्ली चले आए और प्रियंका गांधी के सामने अपनी नाराज़गी ज़ाहिर की। कांग्रेस के एक पदाधिकारी का कहना था, 'सिद्धू के मूड को बदलना या संभालना आसान काम नहीं हैं, लेकिन प्रियंका धैर्य के साथ बात करती थीं, इससे हमें कुछ समय के लिए राहत मिली।'

2021 में गर्मियां आते-आते मसला इतना बढ़ गया था, जहां से वापसी संभव नहीं थी। 2022 में पंजाब के विधानसभा चुनावों से पहले सिद्धू की नाराज़गी सड़क तक पहुंच गई। अपनी जन सभाओं में सिद्धू नशीले पदार्थों की तस्करी, भ्रष्टाचार और बेअदबी के आरोपों पर पिछली अकाली सरकार के ख़िलाफ़ कार्रवाई नहीं करने को लेकर मुख्यमंत्री की तीखी आलोचना कर रहे थे। और जब सोशल मीडिया पर प्रियंका और राहुल गांधी के साथ मुस्कुराते सिद्धू की तस्वीरें सामने आईं, तो पंजाब में बदलाव की अटकलें तेज़ हो गईं। नाराज़ कैप्टन ने सोनिया गांधी से स्थिति स्पष्ट करने के लिए दखल देने की मांग की। सिंह ने बताया, 'मैंने उनसे कहा कि अगर वे मेरा इस्तीफ़ा चाहती हैं, तो मैं तुरंत इस्तीफ़ा दे दूंगा, लेकिन एक नौसिखिया राजनेता के हमले का अपमान बर्दश्त नहीं कर सकता। लेकिन उसे अनुशासन खत्म करने का नोटिस देने के बजाय उनके बच्चे उसके साथ दिखाई दे रहे थे।' कैप्टन सिंह राजीव गांधी को दून स्कूल के वक्त से जानते थे, साथ ही उनके पारिवारिक मित्र भी थे। गांधी परिवार जब छुट्टियां मनाने के लिए हिमाचल प्रदेश जाता, तो कैप्टन ने कई बार उनके लिए हेलिकॉप्टर का इंतज़ाम भी किया था। एक बार किसी कांग्रेसी नेता ने कैप्टन को सलाह दी कि उन्हें भी दूसरे कांग्रेसी नेताओं की तरह राहुल गांधी को 'राहुल जी' कहकर संबोधित करना चाहिए, तो उन्होंने बेपरवाही से हंसते हुए कहा, 'मेरे बजाय राहुल को मुझे "अंकलजी" बुलाना चाहिए!'

प्रदेश में बढ़ते संकट को संभालने की कोशिश में सोनिया गांधी ने कैप्टन सिंह को भरोसा दिलाया कि वे अब भी हाईकमान की पसंद थे। उन्होंने दोनों पक्षों से बात कर मसले को सुलझाने के लिए तीन सदस्यों की एक कमेटी भी बना दी। यह सोनिया गांधी का अंदाज़ था, किसी चीज़ पर फैसला टाल कर विवाद को शांत करने की कोशिश करना। लेकिन पटियाला राजघराने से जुड़े सिंह को अंदाज़ा ही नहीं था कि उनसे राज छीना जाने वाला था। कांग्रेस के एक गुट का आरोप था कि अमरिंदर सिंह गृहमंत्री अमित शाह से संपर्क में थे और उन्होंने कोई डील कर ली थी। इसके साथ ही पार्टी के एक सर्वेक्षण में कहा गया कि मुख्यमंत्री आम लोगों और विधायकों के बीच काफी अलोकप्रिय थे। बताया गया कि राहुल गांधी ने पंजाब के प्रभारी महासचिव हरीश रावत से कहा, 'सर्वेक्षण के हिसाब से, मुझे नहीं लगता कि हम कैप्टन सिंह के नेतृत्व में पंजाब जीत सकते हैं।' एक तरफ मां सोनिया, मामले को शांत करने और समझौते की कोशिश कर रही थीं तो दूसरी तरफ बेटे राहुल चीजों को बदलने में लगे थे। ऐसा पहली बार नहीं हुआ, लेकिन इस बार भी कांग्रेस में भ्रम से संकट बना हुआ था।

जुलाई 2021 में, जब सिद्धू को पंजाब कांग्रेस का अध्यक्ष बनाया गया, तो इसकी जानकारी कैप्टन को नहीं दी गई। नाराज़ सिंह ने मुझसे कहा, 'क्या आप जानते है कि मुझे पहली बार तब पता चला जब आपने टीवी पर हरीश रावत का इंटरव्यू लिया था, जिसमें वे कह रहे थे एक समझौता फॉर्मूला बनाया गया है। इसके तहत सिद्धू पार्टी प्रमुख रहेंगे और कैप्टन मुख्यमंत्री

बने रहेंगे। क्या पार्टी ऐसे चलती है?' सिंह अब भी गुस्से में लग रहे थे। फिर सितम्बर 2021 में अचानक बुलाई गई कांग्रेस विधायक दल की बैठक के बारे में भी उन्हें नहीं बताया गया। बैठक में कहा गया कि ज़्यादातर विधायक कैप्टन के ख़िलाफ़ थे, इसलिए कांग्रेस आलाकमान ने मुख्यमंत्री बदलने का फ़ैसला किया। 'मैं उस वक्त घर पर नाश्ता कर रहा था, जब मेरे मीडिया सलाहकार ने बताया कि न्यूज़ चैनल्स पर ब्रेकिंग न्यूज़ चल रही थी, जिसके मुताबिक मुझे मुख्यमंत्री पद छोड़ने के लिए कहा जाएगा। क्या इससे ज़्यादा अपमानजनक कुछ हो सकता है? मैंने इतने साल इस पार्टी को दिए हैं।' बैठक का इंतज़ार करने के बजाय सिंह ने तुरंत सोनिया गांधी को बताया कि वे इस्तीफ़ा दे रहे थे। इससे पहले कैप्टन ने उस व्यक्ति पर हमला बोला, जिसे वे अपनी विदाई के लिए ज़िम्मेदार मानते थे। उन्होंने कहा, 'सिद्धू के समर्थन का कोई सवाल ही नहीं होता, जो साफतौर पर पाकिस्तान से मिला हुआ है और पंजाब और देश के लिए खतरा है।'

हैरानी की बात यह है कि कांग्रेस के पास लंबे समय तक मुख्यमंत्री रहे कैप्टन की जगह लेने के लिए कोई दूसरा मजबूत नाम नहीं था। सिद्धू को ज़्यादातर विधायक अपना नेता मानने वाले नहीं थे। किसी एक नाम पर आम सहमति बनाना मुश्किल हो रहा था। आखिर में आलाकमान ने एक ऐसे नाम के साथ गतिरोध तोड़ने की कोशिश की, जिसके बारे में शायद ही किसी को उम्मीद होः चरणजीत सिंह चन्नी। चन्नी तीन बार के विधायक तो थे, लेकिन प्रोफाइल में वे 'जूनियर' माने जाते थे। 'वे पंजाब के पहले दलित मुख्यमंत्री हैं और उनकी नियुक्ति गेम-चेंजर साबित होगी,' प्रभारी महासचिव हरीश रावत ने उत्साह से कहा। चन्नी के नाम का समर्थन राहुल गांधी ने किया था, जो नेतृत्व के स्तर पर दलितों की ज़्यादा नुमाइंदगी पर ज़ोर दे रहे थे। जब सिद्धू को चन्नी के नाम का पता चला तो वे भड़क गए और पार्टी छोड़ने की धमकी दी। उस समय शिमला में छुट्टियां मना रही प्रियंका गांधी ने फिर से सरदार सिद्धू को शांत करने की कोशिश की, लेकिन उन्होंने बिना किसी को बताए अध्यक्ष पद छोड़ने की घोषणा ट्विटर पर कर दी। लेकिन अब प्रियंका गांधी ने उनकी बगावत पर ध्यान नहीं दिया।

विधानसभा चुनावों से पांच महीने पहले नेतृत्व में बदलाव कांग्रेस के लिए बडा संकट होने वाला था। कांग्रेस का पंजाब का 'सोप ओपरा' कई महीनों से सबके सामने था और मतदाता अब कांग्रेस के दलित कार्ड के नाम से प्रभावित होने वाला नहीं था। इसके बाद हुए 2022 के पंजाब विधानसभा चुनावों में एक दशक पुरानी पार्टी आप ने बदलाव की बयार में कांग्रेस का सफाया कर दिया। आप ने 117 में से 92 सीटों के साथ भारी जीत हासिल की थी। नए मुख्यमंत्री चरणजीत सिंह चन्नी ने दो सीटों से चुनाव लड़ा और दोनों हार गए। और फिर अपने छोटे से कार्यकाल में भ्रष्टाचार के आरोपों के बाद रहस्यमय तरीके से देश छोड़कर चले गए। सिद्धू भी अमृतसर से चुनाव हार गए और फिर 1998 के एक रोडरेज मामले उन्हें एक साल के लिए जेल

जाना पड़ा। कांग्रेस छोड़ने के बाद कैप्टन अमरिंदर सिंह ने पहले अपनी पार्टी बनाई, लेकिन पटियाला में अपने गढ़ में हार के बाद भाजपा में शामिल हो गए।

असल सवाल तो यह है कि 'राजवंश' की पाचवीं पीढ़ी के 'आदर्शवादी राजनेता' के बारे में क्या, जो अब भी कांग्रेस के असली नेता थे? पार्टी एक के बाद एक चुनावी हार का सामना कर रही थी। पार्टी के कार्यकर्ता एक ऐसे सवाल से जूझ रहे थे, जिसका सामना करने से पार्टी बरसों से बचती रही थी: क्या राहुल गांधी वाकई एक गंभीर राजनेता थे, जिनमें एक कमज़ोर कांग्रेस को फिर से खड़ा करने की इच्छा और महत्वाकांक्षा थी? क्या उनके पास कोई सही राजनीतिक दिशा थी या फिर वे सिर्फ़ एक बोझ थे, जो सिर्फ़ अपने सरनेम की वजह से नेता बने हुए थे? पार्टी को लगातार दो बड़े आम चुनावों में करारी हार का सामना करना पड़ा, एक के बाद एक कई राज्यों में भी पार्टी की हार हुई। फिर पार्टी के मुखिया के पद से इस्तीफ़ा दिया, हताश कार्यकर्ताओं का मनोबल बढ़ाने में नाकाम रहे। कई गलत फ़ैसले किए, फिर भी कांग्रेस के सिस्टम में किसी ने उन पर सवाल नहीं उठाए। राहुल गांधी एक टूटी हुई नाव पर सवार अकेले नाविक की तरह थे, जो भंवर वाले पानी में डूबने वाली थी। सार्वजनिक जीवन में दो दशक के बावजूद राहुल गांधी सचमुच एक चौराहे पर थे। हो सकता है कि वे मोदी से मोहित लोगों के दिलों को नहीं जीत पाए हों, लेकिन क्या वे अपने लोगों की सद्भावना और सम्मान हासिल कर सकते थे? क्या उन्हें एक ऐसी यात्रा की ज़रूरत है जिसमें वे खुद को खोज कर आलोचकों के मुंह बंद कर सकें?

राजनीति में 'शारीरिक फिटनेस' को लेकर अगर नंबर दिए जाएं तो राहुल गांधी मुकाबले में आसानी से सबसे ऊपर हो सकते हैं। वे बेहद फिट हैं, खिलाड़ी और एथलेटिक हैं। वह जापानी मार्शल आर्ट एकिडो में ब्लैक बेल्ट हैं, साथ ही उन्होंने क्लोज-कॉमबेट मार्शल आर्ट जुजित्सु में भी प्रशिक्षण लिया है और एक बेहतर तलवारबाज और साइक्लिंग में भी विशेषज्ञता है। राहुल ने पेशेवर स्कूबा-डाइविंग का कोर्स भी कर रखा है। उनके एक दोस्त ने बताया, 'रोजाना जब राहुल जिम में होते हैं तो लगता है कि वे दूसरी दुनिया में हैं, बहुत फोकस होकर अपने को मजबूत रखते हैं।'

अब राहुल गांधी की इस फिटनेस के इम्तिहान का वक्त था। मई 2022 में, राजस्थान के उदयपुर में कांग्रेस के चिंतन शिविर में राहुल गांधी की देशव्यापी 'भारत जोड़ो' पदयात्रा शुरू करने का ऐलान किया गया। वैसे कांग्रेस में 2020 से ही एक जन-संपर्क यात्रा शुरू करने पर विचार चल रहा था, लेकिन कोविड-19 की वजह से उसे टाला जाता रहा। फिर उत्तरप्रदेश विधानसभा चुनावों में पार्टी की करारी हार यकीनन उसके लिए आखिरी चेतावनी जैसी थी।

हताश कांग्रेस किसी संजीवनी की तलाश में थी। यात्रा से पहले मैंने कांग्रेस का एक 'कॉन्सेप्ट नोट' देखा, जिसमें कहा गया था: 'भारत जोड़ो यात्रा 2024 के चुनावों से पहले का एक कार्यक्रम भर नहीं है। यह एक पवित्र मिशन है, एक राष्ट्रीय तीर्थयात्रा है, जिसके माध्यम से भारत खुद को फिर से खोजता है, इसमें समान विचारधारा वाले भारतीय साथी यात्री होंगे। कांग्रेस के लिए, यह लोगों और खुद के मूल सिद्धांतों से जुड़ने की यात्रा है।'

इस यात्रा के मूल विचारों में कहा गया:

- देश के मूड को नकारात्मकता, घृणा और हार की सोच से बाहर सकारात्मकता, एकता और उम्मीद की तरफ ले जाना है।
- भाजपा और संघ की विभाजनकारी राजनीति को चुनौती देने के लिए राष्ट्रीय संकल्प को मजबूत करना।
- भारत के विचार को बचाने के लिए संघर्ष कर रहे लोगों, संगठनों और दूसरी ताकतों के साथ जुड़ना।
- राष्ट्रवादी विरासत और कांग्रेस की संस्कृति को फिर से जिंदा करने और ताकत देने की कोशिश।
- सांस्कृतिक और वैचारिक विस्तार के लिए नए प्रतीकों को शामिल करना।
- कांग्रेस पार्टी और नेतृत्व की सार्वजनिक छवि में बड़े बदलाव की ज़रूरत।

कहा गया कि यात्रा के इस एजेंडा नोट को योगेन्द्र यादव ने तैयार किया था। यादव कहते हैं, 'मैंने राहुल के लिए एक कॉन्सेप्ट नोट तैयार किया होगा, लेकिन पदयात्रा का विचार पूरी तरह से उनका था। राहुल का ज़ोर पदयात्रा को लेकर था, जबकि पहले राजनीतिक गतिविधियों के चरणबद्ध अभियान का सुझाव था।' ज़ुबान में मिठास भरे, बुद्धिजीवी राजनीतिक विश्लेषक योगेन्द्र यादव अब भारत जोड़ो यात्रा टीम के मुख्य लोगों में से थे। आप के संस्थापक सदस्यों में से रहे यादव ने बाद में अपना राजनीतिक संगठन 'स्वराज अभियान' शुरू किया। स्वराज अभियान 2020 के किसान आंदोलन के अलावा कई सामाजिक अभियानों में जुड़ा रहा। दिलचस्प बात यह है कि मई 2019 के लोकसभा चुनावों के बाद यादव ने एक टीवी शो के दौरान मुझसे कहा, 'कांग्रेस पार्टी को ख़त्म हो जाना चाहिए।' और अब तीन साल बाद उस कोर टीम का हिस्सा बन गए, जो कांग्रेस को फिर से ज़िंदा करने और नेतृत्व को मजबूत करने में लगी थी। यादव ने कहा, 'मेरी प्रतिबद्धता किसी पार्टी के प्रति नहीं, बल्कि सिद्धान्तों के प्रति है। राहुल गांधी संविधान को लेकर जो लड़ाई लड़ रहे हैं, मेरा विश्वास उन सिद्धांतों पर है।'

यादव ने उस यात्रा को भले ही एक बौद्धिक चेहरा दिया हो, लेकिन कांग्रेस के दूसरे अनुभवी लोग भी इसे संभाल रहे थे। मध्यप्रदेश के दो बार मुख्यमंत्री रहे दिग्विजय सिंह और एसपीजी यानी विशेष सुरक्षा ग्रुप के बड़े अफसर के.बी. बायजू को यात्रा की योजना की जिम्मेदारी मिली थी। राहुल के मित्र बायजू को गांधी परिवार का विश्वस्त माना जाता है। लंबे समय से आरएसएस के मुखर आलोचक रहे दृढ़ निश्चयी दिग्विजय सिंह उन चुनिंदा पुराने कांग्रेसियों में से एक हैं जिनके राहुल के साथ बेहतर संबंध है। अनुभवी राजनेता सिंह के कई वामपंथी संगठनों से भी अच्छे रिश्ते रहे हैं जिनकी मदद इस यात्रा में ली जा सकती थी। सिंह कहते हैं कि 'हम यात्रा में उन सभी लोगों को शामिल करना चाहते हैं जिनकी आवाज़ को भाजपा ने बंद करने की कोशिश की।' आरएसएस से लगातार लड़ने और मुकाबले करने की वजह से ही सिंह, राहुल के पसंदीदा लोगों में से रहे। उन्हें यह मानने में कोई हिचक नहीं कि वे कट्टर धर्मनिरपेक्ष व्यक्ति हैं। राहुल ने एक सहयोगी से कहा, 'हमारे कई बड़े नेता मोदी से डरते हैं, लेकिन दिग्विजय जी नहीं।'

यात्रा के दौरान ख़बरें और सुर्खियां बनाने की जिम्मेदारी जयराम रमेश को सौंपी गई थी। मोदी सरकार की तीखी आलोचना करने की वजह से ही रमेश, राहुल के पसंदीदा लोगों में शुमार थे। आईआईटी से निकले अंग्रेज़ी दा बुद्धिजीवी रमेश नीतियां बनाने से लेकर यूपीए सरकार में मंत्री भी रहे और अब कांग्रेस के मीडिया विभाग में असरदार भूमिका निभाई। राहुल गांधी के राजनीतिक सफ़र के शुरुआती दिनों में 'नेहरुवादी' रमेश ने अहम भूमिका निभाई। साल 2004 में जब राहुल गांधी पहली बार अपनी पारिवारिक सीट अमेठी से चुनाव लड़ने गए तो रमेश उनके साथ थे और उनके प्रचार की जिम्मेदारी उनके पास थी। एक पुराने कांग्रेसी नेता का कहना था, 'राहुल गांधी की अडानी को लेकर नफ़रत में उनकी भूमिका अहम है, जयराम ने राहुल को यकीन दिलाया कि अडानी समूह प्रधानमंत्री मोदी के करीबी हैं।'

राहुल के करीबी और तेज़तर्रार जयराम पुराने कांग्रेसियों को ज़्यादा भाव नहीं देते, और इससे पार्टी में अंदरूनी झगड़े भी बढ़े। एक बार जब कांग्रेस के एक मुख्यमंत्री अडानी समूह के साथ कोई करार करने वाले थे, तब जयराम ने उसके ख़िलाफ़ झंडा उठा लिया, इस पर राहुल गांधी ने दख़ल दिया और वह सौदा रद्द हो गया। कांग्रेस के 'वॉररूम' की निगरानी करने वाले विचारक रमेश ने राहुल गांधी के वामपंथी नजरिए से जुड़े युवा प्रोफेशनल्स जुटाए। महत्वपूर्ण मुद्दों पर पार्टी लाइन तय करने के लिए जयराम एक बेहतर 'ड्राफ्ट्समैन' हैं, लेकिन कई लोगों को उनका तरीका ज़्यादा दखलंदाजी वाला लगता था और इस वजह से कई पुराने कांग्रेसी नेता नाराज़ रहते थे। उदाहरण के तौर पर पुराने कांग्रेसी रहे गुलाम नबी आज़ाद उनके पार्टी छोड़ने की वजह जयराम को मानते हैं। 'जयराम ही राहुल के सामने मेरे ख़िलाफ़ कहानियां गढ़ते रहे। वे भले ही अच्छी अंग्रेजी बोल और लिख सकते हैं, लेकिन क्या वे इससे अच्छे नेता बन गए? वे सिर्फ़ ड्राईंगरूम नेता हैं,' नाराज़ आज़ाद बता रहे थे।

कांग्रेस के मीडिया प्रभारी के तौर पर उनकी चुनौती एक ऐसे मीडिया को संभालने की थी, जिसका मोटे तौर पर कांग्रेस विरोधी रवैया रहता है। 'आपके सारे सवाल विपक्ष से ही क्यों होते हैं? राहुल गांधी अपनी यात्रा में हर राज्य में प्रेस-कॉन्फ्रेंस कर रहे हैं। क्या प्रधानमंत्री मोदी ने अपने पूरे कार्यकाल में एक भी प्रेस-कॉन्फ्रेंस की है?' जयराम का यह तंज उन पत्रकारों के लिए था, जो राहुल से ना मिल पाने की शिकायत कर रहे थे। भारत जोड़ो यात्रा के दौरान राहुल गांधी ने कई ज़्यादा चलने वाले युवा यूट्यूबर्स को तो साक्षात्कार दिए, लेकिन मुख्यधारा के मीडिया से बातचीत नहीं कर रहे थे। एक सहयोगी ने कहा, 'उन्हें लगता है कि आपने अपनी आत्मा भाजपा को बेच दी है।' जब मैंने जयराम रमेश से राहुल गांधी से एक साक्षात्कार के लिए पूछा, तो उन्होंने हाथ खड़े कर दिए। 'मैं यात्रा के दौरान आपके लिए कुछ भी इंतज़ाम कर सकता हूं, लेकिन मेरे लिए यह काम मुश्किल है, इसके लिए आपको राहुल से सीधे बातचीत करनी होगी,' रमेश ने हंसते हुए बात को टाल दिया।

राहुल गांधी के 'इनर सर्किल' तक पहुंचना भले ही अब भी मुश्किल हो, लेकिन कन्याकुमारी से कश्मीर तक की चार हज़ार किलोमीटर लंबी पदयात्रा का मतलब था कि राहुल अब पार्टी के कार्यकर्ताओं के लिए अपनी दीवार को तोड़ रहे थे। इस यात्रा में साथ चल रहे सैंकड़ों कांग्रेस समर्थकों को भारत यात्री नाम दिया गया। इन भारत यात्रियों के साथ एक बैठक में राहुल गांधी ने यात्रा को 'प्रायश्चित' और 'तपस्या' बताया। राहुल ने ज़ोर देकर कहा, 'हमने लोगों से संपर्क खो दिया, इसलिए हमें प्रायश्चित करने की ज़रूरत है। हम यात्रा में वोट नहीं मांग रहे हैं, लेकिन यह जनता से फिर से जुड़ने की तपस्या है।' बंद कमरे में एक बातचीत के दौरान जब कुछ सामाजिक कार्यकर्ताओं ने उनका स्वागत करते हुए 'पूरा समर्थन' देने का वादा किया, 'क्योंकि हमें आप पर पूरा भरोसा है' तो जवाब में हंसते हुए विनम्रता के साथ राहुल ने कहा, 'प्लीज, राजनेताओं पर विश्वास न करें।' उत्साह से भरे राहुल अपनी इस यात्रा से लोगों से जुड़ना और सीधा सपंर्क करना चाहते थे।

यात्रा का कार्यक्रम बहुत कठिन था। 7 सितम्बर 2022 से 30 जनवरी 2023 के बीच डेढ़ सौ से ज़्यादा दिनों तक हर सुबह सभी को चार बजे के अलार्म के साथ उठना होता था, कई बार इससे भी पहले। खासतौर से उत्तर भारत की कड़ाके की सर्दियों में, अक्सर घने अंधेरे में, हर दिन सवेरे 6 बजे शुरू होने वाली यात्रा में रोजाना करीब 25 किलोमीटर पैदल चलना होता था। एक भारत यात्री ने राहुल से अनुरोध किया, क्या कड़ाके की सर्दी में यात्रा का समय बदला जा सकता है? 'जब किसान खेत में पानी डालने के लिए सुबह चार बजे उठ सकता है, तो हम क्यों नहीं उठ सकते!' राहुल का जवाब था। राजनीतिक चुनौतियों का सामना करने से बचने की आलोचना झेलने वाले राहुल गांधी अब युवा कप्तान की तरह अपनी सेना की अगुवाई कर रहे थे। जो आलोचक यह मान रहे थे कि राहुल यात्रा को बीच में छोड़कर कभी भी छुट्टियां

मनाने विदेश चले जाएंगे, वे ग़लत साबित हो रहे थे। सफेद टी-शर्ट, जींस और स्नीकर्स वाली अपनी पसंदीदा ड्रैस में राहुल हर दिन यात्रा के शुरुआती बिंदू पर सबसे पहले पहुंचते थे। यात्रा में वे लुटियन्स बंगलों की शानदार व्यवस्था से दूर रात को एक वातानुकूलित कंटेनर में रुकते थे, जिसमें एक बिस्तर, एक सोफा और एक अटैच्ड बाथरूम था। दूसरे यात्री साधारण मोबाइल वैन में रुकते, जिसमें एक साथ चार से छह लोग होते और एक बाथरूम होता था। राहुल ने यात्रा के दौरान दाढ़ी नहीं बनाने का फ़ैसला किया, जो थोड़े दिनों में घनी, सफेद और अव्यवस्थित सी दिखने लगी थी। दिल्ली के लुटियंस इलाके के नखरेबाज़, शरारती बच्चे की जगह अब 'परशुराम-चे ग्वेरा' शैली का 'सत्ता विरोधी योगी' चेहरा सामने था। उत्तर भारत की कड़ाके की सर्दी में भी राहुल गांधी का जोर केवल सफेद टी-शर्ट पहनने पर था। उनका कहना था कि जब वे कुछ गरीब युवा लड़कियों से मिले जो कड़ाके की ठंड में फटे कपड़ों में कांप रही थीं। 'उस दिन मैंने कमस खाई कि मैं भी केवल टी-शर्ट पहनूंगा।' जब एक नौजवान राहुल से मिलने के लिए उनके सुरक्षा घेरे से जद्दोजहद कर रहा था, तब राहुल ने आकर उसे गले लगा लिया। मिलने वाले नौजवान की आंखों में नमी थी, उसने भरे गले से फ़ुसफ़ुसाते हुए कहा, 'नफ़रत के बाज़ार में आपने मोहब्बत की दुकान खोली है।' इसके साथ ही राहुल को उस यात्रा का लोकप्रिय स्लोगन मिल गया – 'मोहब्बत की दुकान'।

'मोहब्बत की दुकान' का नारा करुणा-प्रेम के राजनीतिक्र संदेश का प्रतीक था, जो भाजपा समर्थकों के 'मोदी है तो मुमकिन है' (जब तक प्रधानमंत्री मोदी है, तब तक कुछ भी संभव है) के विजयमंत्र का विकल्प बनाने की कोशिश थी। इस नारे के माध्यम से राहुल गांधी को मोहब्बत और स्नेह की बात करने वाले सौम्य राजनेता के तौर पर पेश करने की कोशिश की गई, वहीं प्रधानमंत्री मोदी को '56 इंच के सीने' के साथ 'राष्ट्रवादी दंबग' व्यक्तित्व के तौर पर पेश किया गया। विनम्रता बनाम अंहकार। समावेश बनाम बहिष्कार। कोमलता बनाम डींग हांकने वाला। और मोहब्बत बनाम नफ़रत। मोदी भक्तों के ख़िलाफ़ लड़ाई का खाका तैयार हो गया था। छोटी उम्मीदों के साथ शुरू हुई यात्रा धीरे-धीरे रफ्तार पकड़ने लगी थी। राहुल गांधी के बुज़ुर्गों को गले लगाने, सम्मान करने, बच्चों को गोदी उठाने और चूमने और किसानों से बात करते वीडियो बड़े पैमाने पर साझा किए जा रहे थे। ड्रोन से शूट किए गए, भीड़ के समुंदर बनते शॉट्स और बैकग्राउंड म्यूज़िक के साथ तैयार वीडियो यूट्यूब और सोशल मीडिया पर वायरल होने लगे थे। इस काम के लिए मुंबई की कंपनी 'तीन बंदर' को जिम्मा सौंपा गया था। कंपनी के सह-संस्थापक प्रशांत चारी कहते हैं कि 'वे राहुल गांधी के फोकस और अनुशासन से प्रभावित हुए। हम तेलंगाना से महाराष्ट्र के नांदेड में प्रवेश कर रहे थे, काफी देर हो गई थी। राहुल सुबह से चल रहे थे, लेकिन अब भी उनमें इतनी ऊर्जा थी वे राज्य की सीमा पार करके एक रैली कर सकते थे। वे कभी थकते नहीं दिखे,' चारी ने याद करते हुए बताया।

राहुल की ऊर्जा से मानो यात्रा को रफ्तार और प्रोत्साहन मिल रहा था। चाहे फिर वह कोच्चि में नाव दौड़ में हिस्सा लेना हो या मैसूर की बारिश में भीगते हुए भाषण देना, राहुल आम लोगों से जुड़ने के अपने लक्ष्य को लेकर गंभीर दिख रहे थे। चारी करते हैं कि 'हमने राहुल के साथ लोगों के मिलने और यात्रा के जितने वीडियो बनाए, वे सहज और स्वाभाविक लग रहे थे। यहां तक कि लद्दाख में बाइक रैली भी, जो राहुल को अचानक आया हुआ आइडिया था, उनकी कोशिश थी कि हिन्दुस्तान के हर हिस्से में लोगों से मिला जाए। यह सब इसलिए भी कामयाब हुआ क्योंकि उनके व्यक्तित्व में एक प्रामाणिकता और विश्वसनीयता लगती थी, जो लोगों ने पहले कभी नहीं देखी।' कभी तेज़ी से चलते, दौड़ते, तैरते, नाव चलाते, बाइक सवार, बच्चों को गोद में उठाए, बुज़ुर्गों को गले लगाते, हमेशा लोगों से घिरे हुए, लोगों की नज़र में यह 'नए राहुल' थे। अब तक खुद की बंद दुनिया में रहा कांग्रेस का यह 'शुभांकर' दुनिया के सामने खुद को खोल रहा था।

तो क्या माना जाए कि ये फोट-ऑप्स और साउंड बाइट्स, बयान एक सोची-समझी छवि बनाने की रणनीति का हिस्सा थे? 2020 में राहुल गांधी ने अपनी 'कम्युनिकेशन टीम' में बदलाव किया था। कर्नाटक युवा कांग्रेस में सोशल मीडिया टीम संभाल रहे चालीस साल के वाई.बी. श्रीवत्स को इस काम के लिए लाया गया। राहुल का संदेश साफ थाः 'इस अभियान को इस तरह से तैयार किया जाए कि दुनिया को पता चले कि वास्तव में मैं कौन हूं। यह दिखना चाहिए, महसूस होना चाहिए, ना कि बताया जाए।' श्रीवत्स ने इसके लिए अलग से एक छोटी टीम बनाई। राहुल गांधी को लगता था कि मुख्य धारा मीडिया मोदी सरकार के दौरान तटस्थ नहीं हो सकता, इसलिए श्रीवत्स ने डिजिटल और सोशल मीडिया पर वैकल्पिक रास्ते और मंच पहचानने का काम किया। इसके साथ ही इंस्टाग्राम और ट्विटर पर इसे तेजी से आगे बढ़ाने के लिए युवा कांग्रेस समर्थकों को शामिल किया गया। श्रीवत्स का कहना है कि 'आप उन वीडियो में जिस आदमी को देखते हैं वही असल राहुल गांधी हैं, जो आम लोगों की चिंताओं को समझना, जानना चाहते हैं और उसको लेकर प्रतिबद्ध हैं।' उदाहरण के तौर पर, जब राहुल गांधी बाइक मैकेनिकों से मिले तो उन्होंने उनके साथ बाइक ठीक करना सीखा और तीन घंटे इसमें लगाए। मकान बनाने वाले मजदूरों के साथ ईट-पत्थर से घर बनाने के कौशल को सीखने के लिए वे उनके साथ चार घंटे रहे। योगेन्द्र यादव ज़ोर देकर कहते हैं कि 'राहुल गांधी कोई भी काम केवल कैमरा पर दिखने या दिखाने के लिए नहीं कर रहे थे। मैं आपको भरोसा दिलाना चाहता हूं कि इनमें से कोई भी वीडियो पहले से डिजाइन किया हुआ नहीं है। राहुल कोई राजनीतिक रणनीतिकार नहीं बल्कि एक आध्यात्मिक शख्सियत हैं, जिन्हें गरीबों से सच्ची सहानुभूति है और प्रगतिशील विचार रखते हैं।'

गांधीवादी सिद्धान्तों से प्रेरित दिखने वाले राहुल के आध्यात्मिक झुकाव, कांग्रेस के सामने खड़ी असल मुश्किलों को नहीं छिपा सके। एक के बाद एक चुनाव हारती हताश पार्टी को क्या

उस आदर्शवादी नेतृत्व से कोई फायदा मिलेगा, जो सत्ता की राजनीति की दलदली दुनिया में फंसना नहीं चाहता।

हकीकत यह है कि वायनाड से सांसद राहुल के अब राजनीतिक गृह राज्य केरल से शुरू हुई यह यात्रा उन्नीस दिनों तक केरल से होकर गुजरी, लेकिन देश के सबसे अहम राजनीतिक लड़ाई के मैदान उत्तरप्रदेश के अलावा नवम्बर 2022 में विधानसभा चुनावों वाले गुजरात और हिमाचल प्रदेश को नहीं छुआ। यह बात सबको समझ आ रही थी। दिग्विजय सिंह ने कहा, 'हमने यात्रा की योजना चुनावों के हिसाब से नहीं बनाई थी बल्कि कन्याकुमारी से कश्मीर पहुंचने के रास्ते को ध्यान में रखा गया था।' गुजरात प्रदेश कांग्रेस के एक नेता ने उस दौरान पार्टी पदाधिकारियों के बीच चल रहे व्हाट्सएप संदेशों का ज़िक्र किया। इनमें महत्वपूर्ण सवाल था कि क्या राहुल गांधी को गुजरात में प्रचार करना चाहिए? गुजरात कांग्रेस के एक नेता ने बताया, 'पार्टी के एक नेता ने मुझसे कहा कि अगर राहुल गांधी यहां प्रचार करते और हम बुरी तरह हार जाते तो फिर दोष उनके सिर मढ़ा जाता, इसलिए यह खतरा क्यों मोल लिया जाए?' हार के डर वाली ऐसी मानसिकता के साथ आप कैसे चुनाव जीत सकते हैं। आखिरकार राहुल गुजरात में सिर्फ़ एक दिन प्रचार के लिए गए, जो शायद इस बात का संकेत था कि कांग्रेस नेतृत्व ने प्रधानमंत्री मोदी के गृह राज्य गुजरात में लड़ाई नहीं लड़ने का मन बना लिया था।

सवाल यह है कि फिर 2022 की इस कठिन यात्रा से राहुल गांधी और कांग्रेस को क्या हासिल हुआ? यह सच है कि शारीरिक सहनशक्ति के रूप में राहुल की छवि को ताकत मिली। इससे पहले राहुल गांधी को बार-बार 'पप्पू' (मूर्ख) कहकर मजाक उड़ाने और राजनीतिक पर्यटक, संसद सत्र के दौरान ब्रेक लेने पर भाजपा उनका लगातार मज़ाक उड़ाती रही थी। इस यात्रा ने इन सब पर रोक लगाने का काम किया और संदेश दिया कि अब वे कहीं जाने वाले नहीं थे और राजनीतिक लड़ाई के लिए तैयार थे। खास बात यह भी है कि इस यात्रा से उन्हें उस वक्त पार्टी का सम्मान मिला, जब लगातार चुनावी हार से नेहरू-गांधी परिवार की आभा फीकी होने लगी थी। पार्टी के जुझारू मीडिया प्रभारी पवन खेड़ा सवाल करते हैं, 'आप एक भी विपक्षी नेता का नाम बताइए, जिसने राहुल गांधी के मुद्दों को लगातार उठाया हो—चाहे वह कोविड हो, चीन हो, नौकरियां, किसान या भाई-भतीजावाद का मुद्दा हो। यह केवल राहुल हैं जो मोदी सरकार से सीधे भिड़ंत करते हैं और हर बार सही साबित हुए हैं।' इस यात्रा ने कार्यकर्ताओं में उस वक्त आत्मविश्वास जगाया, जब उनका मनोबल गिर रहा था। पार्टी में नई पीढ़ी की टीम का हिस्सा माने जाने वाले युवक कांग्रेस के मुखिया बी.वी. श्रीनिवास कहते हैं, 'हर बार जब राहुल गांधी कहते हैं, "डरो मत", तो हमें गर्व होता है और हमारा आत्मविश्वास बढ़ता है। अगर हमारा नेता ऐसा कर सकता है तो हम भी कर सकते हैं।' राहुल अपनी विरासत को फिर से हासिल कर रहे थे।

लेकिन क्या इस यात्रा ने देश का मूड बदल दिया था? या कांग्रेस की राजनीतिक किस्मत बदल सकती थी? भारतीय जनता पार्टी ने गुजरात विधानसभा में रिकॉर्ड जीत, अब तक की सबसे ज़्यादा सीटें हासिल कीं, और अपने सहयोगी दलों के साथ तीन पूर्वोत्तर राज्यों में भी सरकार बना ली, जहां फरवरी 2023 में यात्रा ख़त्म होने के कुछ हफ्तों बाद चुनाव हुए थे। हालांकि कांग्रेस हिमाचल प्रदेश में सरकार बनाने में कामयाब रही और मई 2023 में उसने कर्नाटक में भी बीजेपी से सत्ता छीन ली। मगर इससे यह दावे के साथ नहीं कहा जा सकता कि यात्रा से प्रधानमंत्री का प्रभाव कम हुआ हो या दोनों राष्ट्रीय दलों के बीच राजनीतिक खाई कम हुई हो। योगेन्द्र यादव इसका अलग तरह से विश्लेषण करते हैं, 'मुझे नहीं लगता कि आप इस यात्रा को केवल टीवी स्टुडियो की बहस में नफा-नुकसान के हिसाब से देखें। यात्रा ने उन लाखों लोगों में उम्मीदें जगाईं जो बांटने की राजनीति और सत्ता से अलग-थलग और निराश महसूस कर रहे थे। मोहब्बत जैसे शब्दों का इस्तेमाल और सामाजिक खाई को पाटने की कोशिश आज देश में हिम्मत का काम है। राहुल गांधी ने वो हिम्मत दिखाई है।'

साहसी, दृढ इच्छाशक्ति, ईमानदार और जनता से जुड़े राहुल गांधी के नये रूप से कम से कम कांग्रेस समर्थकों के दिलों-दिमाग में आत्मविश्वास बढ़ा है। फिर भी इस सवाल का जवाब आना अभी बाकी है कि भाजपा की अजेय चुनावी मशीन के खिलाफ़ राजनीतिक वापसी की क्या योजना बनाई जा रही थी?

═

2020 की गर्मियों में, जब देश 'कोविड लॉकडाउन' से जूझ रहा था, तब सोनिया गांधी कांग्रेस पार्टी की हालत और संगठन पर गांधी परिवार की पकड़ को लेकर निराश लग रही थीं। 2019 के लोकसभा चुनावों में पार्टी की करारी हार के बाद राहुल गांधी ने अध्यक्ष पद से इस्तीफ़ा दे दिया था, ऐसे वक्त में पार्टी को सोनिया गांधी से ही उम्मीद थी कि वे कांग्रेस को फिर से खड़ा करने का कोई 'टॉनिक' ढूंढ लेंगी। लंबे समय तक कांग्रेस की अध्यक्ष रहने के दौरान सोनिया ने यथास्थिति बनाए रखी, कोई बड़े बदलाव की कोशिश नहीं की। लेकिन जब मुश्किल समय हो तो उससे निकलने के लिए मुश्किल उपाय खोजने पड़ते हैं। इस मुश्किल वक्त में सोनिया ने चुनावी रणनीतिकार प्रशांत किशोर का रुख किया। हालांकि किशोर उस समय तृणमूल कांग्रेस के लिए 2021 के बंगाल विधानसभा चुनाव अभियान को देख रहे थे, लेकिन उन्होंने प्रियंका गांधी के माध्यम से सोनिया से भी करीबी पहचान बना ली थी। किशोर ने इससे पहले कांग्रेस के लिए 2017 के उत्तरप्रदेश चुनाव के दौरान काम किया था। तब उन्होंने अपनी रणनीति में प्रियंका गांधी को मुख्यमंत्री पद का उम्मीदवार बनाने पर जोर दिया था। सोनिया गांधी ने उस समय इस सुझाव को खारिज़ कर दिया था, लेकिन अब वे किशोर के सुझावों पर विचार के

लिए तैयार लग रही थीं। प्रशांत किशोर ने तीन दिनों में ज़ूम पर सोनिया गांधी के साथ करीब 12 घंटे की बैठकें कीं। इनमें कांग्रेस को फिर से खड़ा करने की एक दीर्घकालीन योजना रखी। इसमें करीब 'सौ स्लाइड्स' से उन्होंने नेतृत्व के मुद्दे पर विस्तार से चर्चा की थी। 'मैं उनके फोकस से बहुत प्रभावित हुआ। ऐसा लगा कि वो वाकई बदलाव चाहती हैं,' किशोर ने दावा किया। लेकिन बात आगे नहीं बढ़ पाई, क्योंकि तब तक सोनिया गांधी की तबियत और फिर जी-23 की बगावत ने प्राथमिकता ले ली थी। खुद किशोर भी पश्चिम बंगाल के सबसे मुश्किल चुनाव की तैयारी और उसकी रणनीति बनाने में व्यस्त हो गए थे।

करीब एक साल बाद, मई 2021 में, सोनिया गांधी की किशोर से फिर से बातचीत हुई। ममता बनर्जी की चुनाव में भारी जीत से किशोर की लोकप्रियता और बढ़ गई थी। कांग्रेस अध्यक्ष ने संकेत दिया कि किशोर अपनी चुनावी रणनीति के साथ आएं, लेकिन उन्हें एक बार पहले अपने बेटे से सलाह करनी थी। किशोर ने चीजों को जल्द आगे बढ़ाने की ज़रूरत पर ज़ोर दिया। 'मुझे समयबद्ध निर्णय चाहिएं।' करीब एक महीने बाद किशोर ने अपने रणनीतिक ब्लूप्रिंट के साथ राहुल से मुलाकात की। 'राहुल मौटे तौर पर मेरे सुझावों से सहमत थे लेकिन सोनिया की तरह उत्साहित नहीं थे,' किशोर ने बताया। संगठन को लेकर किशोर के सुझावों में एक महत्वपूर्ण सुझाव था कि पार्टी का अध्यक्ष नेहरु-गांधी परिवार से बाहर का बनाया जाए। राहुल गांधी कांग्रेस संसदीय दल के नेता की ज़िम्मेदारी संभालें और प्रियंका गांधी को संगठन में अहम भूमिका दी जाए। किशोर का कहना था, इसके अलावा उन्होंने पार्टी को फिर से पुनर्गठित करने और दूसरे संगठनों और कार्यक्रमों को लेकर भी पूरी एक रिपोर्ट रखी थी।

सोनिया गांधी ने इस पर तुरंत फ़ैसला करने के बजाय, प्रशांत किशोर को पार्टी में शामिल करने पर सहमति बनाने के लिए ए.के एंटोनी और अंबिका सोनी समेत कई वरिष्ठ नेताओं की एक कमेटी बना दी। किशोर की शुरुआती सफलता प्रधानमंत्री मोदी के साथ रही थी, और अब भी बहुत से कांग्रेसी उन्हें 'मोदी मैन' यानी मोदी का ही विश्वस्त मानते थे। कमेटी ने विचार के बाद सुझाया कि किशोर को पहले खुद को आने वाले उत्तरप्रदेश, पंजाब, उत्तराखंड और गोवा के विधानसभा चुनावों में साबित करना चाहिए। किशोर बताते हैं कि 'मैंने उन्हें स्पष्ट तौर पर कहा कि मैं कोई जादूगर या 'डे-ट्रेडर' नहीं हूं, जो तुरंत नतीजे दे सके। मैं दस साल की दीर्घकालिक योजना पर विचार कर रहा था, जिसे 2022 के आखिर में होने वाले गुजरात विधानसभा चुनावों से शुरू किया जा सकता था।' कांग्रेस ने इस विचार को ख़ारिज़ कर दिया और किशोर का ड्राफ्ट आगे बढ़ाने के बजाय ठंडे बस्ते में डाल दिया गया।

इससे नाराज़ प्रशांत किशोर ने अब आगे बढ़कर ममता बनर्जी के लिए गोवा में विस्तार करने की योजना बनाई। कांग्रेस में किशोर की एंट्री को लेकर बनी कमेटी के एक सदस्य ने कहा, 'हम ऐसे आदमी पर कैसे भरोसा कर सकते हैं जो पहले हमसे बात कर रहे हैं और अगले ही

दिन गोवा में हमें हराने के लिए तृणमूल के साथ योजना बना रहे हैं?' किशोर ने इस आरोप से इंकार किया कि उन्होंने कांग्रेस को नाराज़ करने के लिए ममता बनर्जी को गोवा चुनाव लड़ने के लिए तैयार किया। उन्होंने कहा कि 'हमारा मकसद भाजपा को हराना था। अगर कांग्रेस इसके लिए तैयार नहीं थी, तो बंगाल में भारी जीत के बाद ममता के लिए यह अच्छा मौका था।' लेकिन पश्चिमी तट के छोटे खूबसूरत राज्य की राजनीति, पूर्वी समुद्र तट से बिल्कुल अलग थी, नतीजतन गोवा में तृणमूल कांग्रेस का खाता भी नहीं खुल पाया।

इन नतीजों से बेचैन हुए किशोर ने कांग्रेस नेतृत्व को एक और दौर की बैठकें करने के लिए फ़ोन किए। कांग्रेस को मार्च 2022 में हुए सभी विधानसभा चुनावों में करारी हार का सामना करना पड़ा था। संगठन को फिर से जान देने के लिए वक्त तेज़ी से निकल रहा था। इस बार सोनिया गांधी ने फुर्ती दिखाई। गांधी के आवास 10 जनपथ पर कार्यसमिति के वरिष्ठ सदस्यों और कांग्रेस के मुख्यमंत्रियों की एक उच्च स्तरीय बैठक बुलाई गई। किशोर को इस बैठक में अपने '350 स्लाइडस का प्रजेंटेशन' देने को कहा गया। इस बैठक को गोपनीय रखने की ज़रूरत नहीं समझी गई। बैठक के आयोजन यानी श्रीमती गांधी के आवास के बाहर तीन दिनों तक टीवी कैमरों की नज़र में, किशोर ने कांग्रेस के पुनर्गठन की अपनी योजना को पार्टी के आला नेताओं के साथ साझा किया। 'ज़्यादातर सदस्य मेरे सुझावों से सहमत थे, यहां तक कि वरिष्ठ नेता पी. चिदंबरम को इस योजना पर अमल करने का जिम्मा सौंप दिया गया। लेकिन जब असल फ़ैसले की बात आई तो वे एक ऐसा ताकतवर वर्किंग ग्रुप नहीं बनाना चाहते थे जिसके पास पार्टी को पूरी तरह से पुनर्गठित करने का अधिकार हो।' किशोर बताते हैं, 'उन्होंने मुझे महासचिव (चुनाव) पद देने का प्रस्ताव रखा था, लेकिन मैं सिर्फ़ कागज़ों पर बड़ा पद नहीं लेना चाहता था।' कांग्रेस के एक वरिष्ठ नेता का आरोप था कि 'किशोर बहुत महत्वाकांक्षी हैं। वे सोनिया गांधी के बाद पार्टी में दूसरे नंबर पर सबसे महत्वपूर्ण व्यक्ति बनना चाहते हैं। कोई भी अचानक आकर इस तरह पार्टी पर कब्ज़ा नहीं कर सकता।' और बात फेल हो गई। किशोर और कांग्रेस अलग-अलग रास्ते पर थे।

'मिशन पीके' के नाकाम होने से कांग्रेस के हालात समझे जा सकते हैं। अगर देश की सबसे पुरानी पार्टी किशोर जैसे बाहरी व्यक्ति के साथ जुड़ने के लिए उत्साहित दिखती है यानी पार्टी में गंभीर आंतरिक संकट है। सोनिया गांधी ज़ोखिम लेने से बचती हैं और पार्टी में वरिष्ठता में मोटे तौर पर कोई फेरबदल के लिए तैयार नहीं होतीं, लेकिन इस मसले पर उनका नेतृत्व करना आश्चर्य से कम नहीं लगता। शायद उन्हें इस बात का अहसास हुआ होगा कि कांग्रेस को एक बड़े बदलाव की ज़रूरत थी। इसके बावजूद वे अपने बेटे राहुल को किशोर के पार्टी में आने पर सहमति के लिए तैयार नहीं कर सकीं। सच तो यह है कि जब किशोर कांग्रेस के पुनर्गठन पर 10 जनपथ में अपनी योजना बता रहे थे, उस बीच राहुल गांधी विदेश

यात्रा पर चले गए। किशोर कहते हैं कि 'मुझे नहीं पता कि वह मुझसे असुरक्षा थी या उनका अति आत्मविश्वास, शायद राहुल गांधी को लगता होगा कि कांग्रेस के बेहतर भविष्य के लिए उनके पास मुझसे ज़्यादा अच्छी योजना है, इसके लिए उन्हें शुभकामनाएं।' राहुल की टीम के एक सदस्य कहते हैं कि राहुल गांधी किशोर के कांग्रेस से जुड़ने को लेकर बहुत आश्वस्त नहीं थे। 'हमें लगता है कि वे उस तरह के भाड़े के सिपाही हैं जो किसी से भी अच्छा सौदा होने पर उनके साथ जा सकता है। यह भी मत भूलिए कि उन्होंने मोदी को प्रधानमंत्री के नाम पर प्रचारित कर नाम कमाया है।' साफ है कि राहुल और प्रशांत किशोर के बीच अविश्वास की गहरी खाई को पाटना मुश्किल था।

किशोर के बाहर हो जाने से साफ था कि कांग्रेस को अपना घर खुद ही ठीक करना होगा। पार्टी के नए अध्यक्ष की खोज भी लंबे समय से पूरी नहीं हो पाई थी। अगस्त 2019 में सोनिया गांधी ने इस शर्त के साथ 'अंतरिम अध्यक्ष' पद संभाला था कि अब संगठन के चुनावों के बाद नया अध्यक्ष मिल जाएगा, हालांकि संगठन चुनाव भी लंबे समय से नहीं हुए थे। दरअसल कांग्रेस नेतृत्व के मसले पर टालमटोल ही करती रही थी और बहुत से कार्यकर्ताओं को तो अब भी उम्मीद थी कि राहुल गांधी लौट आएंगे। जब राहुल गांधी ने स्पष्ट कर दिया कि वे कोई आधिकारिक पद नहीं लेंगे और इसके बजाय उन्होंने अपनी यात्रा शुरू करना पसंद किया, तब सोनिया गांधी ने फिर से अपने पुराने वफादारों की तरफ रुख किया। सोनिया गांधी की पहली पसंद 'सत्ता सिस्टम' का लंबा अनुभव रखने वाले राजस्थान के मुख्यमंत्री अशोक गहलोत थे, लेकिन जब उन्होंने मुख्यमंत्री की कुर्सी छोड़ने से इंकार कर दिया तो कांग्रेस नेतृत्व मुश्किल में पड़ गया।

अब शशि थरूर ने इस मैदान में उतरने का फ़ैसला किया। सांसद, लेखक, राजनयिक रहे और बेहतर वक्ता की कई भूमिकाओं वाले थरूर, पुरानी कांग्रेस में एक मूर्ति-भंजक या रूढ़ियों को तोड़ने वाले नेता हैं, जबकि कांग्रेस अपने नेताओं का विनम्र होना और सुर्खियों से दूर रहना पसंद करती है। स्टाइलिश ड्रैस में आकर्षक, बालों को खास तरीके से झटकने के अंदाज़ और बुद्धिमान, साफगोई से बात रखने वाले कांग्रेस सांसद थरूर ने 2009 में पहली बार सासंद बनने के साथ ही अपनी विशिष्ट पहचान बना ली थी। बड़ी तादाद में उनके प्रशंसकों में पुरुष और महिलाएं दोनों हैं, इसके साथ ही युवा, शहरी और अंग्रेज़ी दां लोगों में तो वे 'रॉकस्टार' जैसे हैं। एक बार नई दिल्ली के एक साहित्य समारोह में जब वे अपनी नयी किताब पर चर्चा कर रहे थे तो दर्शकों में मौजूद एक युवती ने पूछा, 'क्या आप शादी के प्रस्ताव के लिए तैयार हैं?' शशि थरूर की बड़ी अपील है। 2017 में थरूर 'ऑल इंडिया प्रोफेशनल्स कांग्रेस' के संस्थापक अध्यक्ष बने थे, जो कांग्रेस को समर्थन करने वाले कामकाजी प्रोफेशनल्स थे, लेकिन कांग्रेस के किसी अहम फ़ैसले में अपनी भूमिका बनाने में नाकाम रहे। थरूर के एक समर्थक का कहना है

कि 'वे ज़्यादातर मुद्दों पर अपनी समझ से चलने वाले उन लोगों में से हैं जो राजनीति के रास्ते से यहां तक नहीं पहुंचे थे।' पार्टी में उनके आलोचक उन पर सबको साथ लेकर चलने वाला 'टीम प्लेयर' नहीं मानते थे।

थरूर के लिए, कांग्रेस अध्यक्ष का चुनाव लड़ना पार्टी में केवल अपना प्रोफाइल बढ़ाने का मौका ही नहीं था, बल्कि कांग्रेस के मौजूदा नेतृत्व को चुनाव में फिक्स मैच के बजाय खुले मुकाबले की ज़रूरत पर ज़ोर देना भी था। थरूर का दावा था, 'मुझे लगता है कि मेरे चुनाव लड़ने से कांग्रेस के लोकतांत्रिक चरित्र को ना केवल मजबूती मिलेगी, बल्कि लोगों में यह भरोसा बढ़ेगा कि पार्टी में आंतरिक लोकतंत्र ज़िंदा है।' राहुल गांधी ने भी स्वतंत्र और निष्पक्ष चुनाव पर ज़ोर दिया था, लेकिन पार्टी में सब लोग ऐसा सोचने वाले नहीं थे। थरूर केरल के तिरुवनंतपुरम से तीन बार सांसद चुने गए थे। उनके ही गृह राज्य के पार्टी के एक प्रतिनिधि ने बताया, 'हमें 10 जनपथ के नजदीकी रहे कांग्रेस के एक वरिष्ठ नेता का फ़ोन आया था। जिसमें डॉ. थरूर के अध्यक्षीय चुनाव अभियान में शामिल नहीं होने के लिए एक तरह से चेतावनी दी गई थी।' जब थरूर दिल्ली में कांग्रेस मुख्यालय पहुंचे तो केवल तीन प्रतिनिधि उनसे मिलने आए। दिल्ली कांग्रेस के एक प्रतिनिधि ने खुलासा किया कि 'हमारे वरिष्ठ नेताओं ने चेतावनी के स्वर में कहा था कि अगर हम थरूर की बैठक में देखे गए तो हमारा करियर ख़त्म हो जाएगा।' साफ है कि कांग्रेस में ऐसे बहुत से लोग थे जिन्हें आतंरिक लोकतंत्र सुहाता नहीं था। थरूर को समझ आ रहा था कि वे एक 'हारी हुई लड़ाई' लड़ रहे थे, लेकिन उन्होंने देशभर में समर्थन जुटाने की पूरी कोशिश की।

अशोक गहलोत ने खुद को चुनावी दौड़ से बाहर कर लिया था। थरूर चुनावी मैदान से हटने को तैयार नहीं थे, तब दिग्विजय सिंह को अपने नामांकन पत्र तैयार रखने के लिए कहा गया। इस बीच कांग्रेस के महासचिव के.सी. वेणुगोपाल ने पार्टी के राज्यसभा में नेता, अस्सी साल के मल्लिकर्जुन खड़गे को जिम्मेदारी संभालने के लिए राजी किया। कर्नाटक के वरिष्ठ नेता और दलित चेहरा माने जाने वाले खड़गे कदम दर कदम कांग्रेस में आगे बढ़े थे। गांधी परिवार के कट्टर वफादार खड़गे ने अपने बच्चों के नाम भी गांधी परिवार से ही लिए थे, इंदिरा गांधी से प्रियदर्शिनी और प्रियंका गांधी से प्रियांक उनके बच्चों के नाम थे। यानी खड़गे कांग्रेस के ज़रूरी सभी मानकों पर खरे उतर रहे थे। वे गांधी परिवार के वर्चस्व को कभी चुनौती देने वाले नहीं थे यानी बदलाव भी हो जाएगा, और नेतृत्व की निरंतरता भी बनी रहेगी। उम्रदराज़ खड़गे शुरू में खुद को आश्वस्त नहीं कर पा रहे थे। 'आप मुझे इस उम्र में कांटों का ताज पहनने के लिए कह रहे हैं,' उन्होंने देर रात हो रही बैठक में वेणुगोपाल को कहा था। नामांकन की प्रकिया ख़त्म होने से एक दिन पहले खड़गे मैदान में उतरने को तैयार हो गए। उनके पर्चा दाखिल करने के वक्त कार्यसमिति के बहुत से सदस्य मौजूद थे। जाहिर था कि वे ही इस लड़ाई के 'विजेता'

थे। 'खड़गे अनौपचारिक तौर पर हमारे औपचारिक उम्मीदवार थे,' कांग्रेस कार्यसमिति के एक सदस्य ने चुटकी ली।

नतीजे उम्मीद के मुताबिक ही थे। खड़गे विजयी घोषित किए गए। खड़गे के पक्ष में 7,897 वोट मिले, जबकि थरूर को 1,072 वोट मिले थे। ये नतीजे कई लोगों की उम्मीद के मुताबिक नहीं रहे और भले ही इसे बेमेल मुकाबला कहें, लेकिन यह मोटे तौर पर एकतरफा नहीं था। साल 2000 में जब सोनिया गांधी अध्यक्ष बनी थीं, तब चुनाव में उनके ख़िलाफ़ खड़े हुए जितेन्द्र प्रसाद को सिर्फ़ 94 वोट मिले थे। यानी थरूर का प्रदर्शन सम्मानजनक कहा जा सकता है। कांग्रेस में चुनाव प्रक्रिया के प्रमुख मधुसुदन मिस्त्री ने ज़ोर देकर कहा, 'आप मीडिया के लोग जो मर्जी हो वो कहें, लेकिन हमारे चुनाव स्वतंत्र और निष्पक्ष थे। भाजपा में तो आरएसएस तय करता है कि पार्टी का नेतृत्व कौन संभालेगा।' दिलचस्प यह था कि जहां खड़गे के अभियान को पार्टी के आलाकमान और बड़े नेताओं का समर्थन हासिल था, वहीं राहुल गांधी ने किसी का पक्ष लेने से इंकार कर दिया। उन्होंने चुनाव के दौरान दिल्ली में रहने से बचने के लिए अपनी यात्रा को एक महीने पहले ही शुरू करने का निर्णय किया। कांग्रेस महासचिव वेणुगोपाल दावा करते हैं कि 'जब किसी ने राहुल जी से पूछा कि वे अध्यक्ष के तौर पर किसे पसंद करते हैं, तो उनका स्पष्ट जवाब था, "मेरा इस चुनाव से कोई लेना-देना नहीं है, मैं अपनी यात्रा पर फोकस कर रहा हूं"।' वेणुगोपाल अब पार्टी में मजबूत 'पावर सेंटर' बन गए थे। पुरानी व्यवस्था और नई व्यवस्था के बीच सेतू और हर बड़े फ़ैसले में शामिल थे।

नए अध्यक्ष खड़गे ने जब अपनी राजनीतिक ताक़त बढ़ाने के इरादे से अपने भरोसेमंद सहयोगियों के साथ नयी टीम बनाना शुरू किया, तो उस टीम में भी राहुल का दबदबा दिख रहा था। दिसम्बर 2022 में हुए चुनावों में गुजरात में तो कांग्रेस पूरी तरह साफ हो गई थी, लेकिन हिमाचल प्रदेश में उसने जीत हासिल कर ली थी। ऐसे नें पार्टी के नेताओं को दुविधा यह थी कि इस जश्न को कैसे पेश किया जाए। पार्टी के एक नेता ने बताया, 'हमने हिमाचल जीत पर खड़गे जी की फोटो के साथ उन्हें बधाई देने का पोस्टर जारी करने का मन बनाया, क्योंकि अध्यक्ष के तौर पर यह उनकी पहली जीत थी, लेकिन हमें कहा गया कि राहुल और प्रियंका को बधाई देना न भूलें। इस असमंजस को ख़त्म करने के लिए हमने तीनों के चेहरों के साथ बधाई देने के पोस्टर लगा दिए थे।' हकीकत तो यही है कि जब खड़गे पार्टी के अध्यक्ष थे, तब भी प्रमुख फ़ैसलों पर 'अंतिम मुहर' गांधी परिवार की ही होती थी। कांग्रेस के एक पुराने नेता ने इसे स्पष्ट कर दिया, 'खड़गे सुझाव देते हैं, राहुल मंज़ूरी देते हैं और वेणुगोपाल उस पर अमल करते हैं। यह सत्ता की चाबी को लेकर ज़िम्मेदारियों का बंटवारा था।'

अनिश्चितता और उथल-पुथल का वह दौर, जिसनें नेतृत्व की चूक और राजनीतिक ताकत के अस्तित्व को लेकर सवाल उठाए जाते थे, अब वो खत्म हो चुका था। देश की सबसे पुरानी

पार्टी फिर से पैर जमाते दिखी। कांग्रेस के पास अब एक अनुभवी अध्यक्ष था, लेकिन पार्टी का ताबीज़ तो राहुल गांधी ही थे। चाहे फिर लंदन में कैम्ब्रिज यूनिवर्सिटी में व्याख्यान के लिए जाना हो या एक दिन किसानों से मिलने, अगले दिन ट्रक ड्राइवरों से मिलते हुए या फिर ऊटी में चॉकलेट बनाने वालों से बातचीत के भावुक वीडियो साझा करना हो, राहुल गांधी एक अलग नेता के तौर पर अपनी छवि बनाने में लगे थे। अब वे पर्दे के पीछे रणनीति बनाने वाले नहीं, पार्टी के विचारक, सीधे जनता से जुड़ाव रखने वाले और राजनीतिक तूफान का सामना करने वाले नेता बन रहे थे। ऐसा लग रहा था कि कांग्रेस का शुभंकर सत्ता की राजनीति की परंपराओं और नियमों से बेपरवाह, अपनी शर्तों पर सार्वजनिक जीवन जी रहा हो। एक तरफ अपने समर्थकों के लिए प्यारी शख्सियत, दूसरी तरफ विरोधियों के लिए वंशवादी राजनेता, राहुल गांधी के नए अवतार पर जनता की राय भी एक सी नहीं थी। लंबे समय तक भाजपा की हमलावर राजनीति और उपेक्षा किए जाने के बावजूद डटे रहने से राहुल गांधी में ताकतवर तरीके से लड़ाई लड़ने की हिम्मत आ गई थी। उनके साथ राजनीतिक मैदान में दुर्व्यवहार किया गया, लेकिन उन्होंने उसका जवाब नहीं दिया, बल्कि पीड़ितों और उपेक्षितों का साथ देना पसंद किया। भले ही वे सार्वजनिक मंचों पर मोदी विरोधी छवि के साथ कट्टर आलोचक थे, लेकिन निजी ज़िंदगी में सतर्क रहते थे। मगर राहुल की ज़िंदगी में एक पहलू नहीं बदलाः जब वे निजी छुट्टियों पर गए तो उनकी पार्टी भी उतनी ही बेखबर थी, जितना कि मीडिया।

अगस्त 2023 में जब राहुल निजी यात्रा पर गोवा गए, तो प्रदेश कांग्रेस और स्थानीय मीडिया काफी उत्साहित थे। कांग्रेस के नेता ने मीडिया को बताया, 'वे इस यात्रा में व्यापारियों और कार्यकर्ताओं के अलावा कई लोगों से मुलाक़ात करेंगे।' कल्पना कीजिए कि इस बात से कितनी हैरानी होगी, जब गोवा के एक प्रमुख केबल चैनल 'प्रूडेंट' के संपादक प्रमोद आचार्य को एक तस्वीर मिली, जिसमें राहुल उत्तरी गोवा के मापुसा में जैक रसेल टेरियर के पिल्लों को प्यार करते-दुलारते दिख रहे थे। वहां कोई व्यापारी या कार्यकर्ता नहीं था। आचार्य ने हंसते हुए बताया, 'हमें शुरू में इन तस्वीरों के असली होने पर यकीन नहीं था, लेकिन बाद में मिले एक वीडियो में राहुल गांधी स्टेनली ब्रैगांका के घर पर पिल्लों के साथ खेल रहे थे, ब्रैगांका की पत्नी शरवानी एक डॉग-कैनेल चलाती है। हमें लगा था कि वे गोवा में कांग्रेस को फिर से खड़ा करने की योजना के साथ आए हैं, लेकिन उनके मन में शायद कुछ और ही था।' कुछ हफ्तों बाद, राहुल ने अपने यूट्यूब चैनल पर एक वीडियो शेयर किया, जिसमें वे अपनी मां सोनिया को एक प्यारा सा 'पपी- नूरी' उपहार में दे रहे थे। वीडियो पर राहुल ने लिखा, 'मैं चाहता हूं कि आप हमारे परिवार के नए और प्यारे सदस्य से मिलें। बिना शर्त बेपनाह प्यार और वफादारी, यह खूबसूरत जानवर हमें बहुत कुछ सिखा सकता है।' हर चीज़ को सिर्फ़ राजनीति के नज़रिए से देखने वाले लोग भले ही इस वीडियो पर हंस रहे हों, लेकिन इंस्टाग्राम पर युवाओं के बीच

ये तस्वीरें काफी वायरल हुईं। साफ है कि उनकी 'मोहब्बत की दुकान' का प्रचार-प्रसार हो रहा था और उन्हें नए प्रशंसक भी मिल रहे थे।

इस सबसे इतर सबसे बड़ा सवाल अब भी वही था कि उस कमजोर कांग्रेस पार्टी का भविष्य क्या है जो अब भी सत्ता में वापसी के लिए कड़ा संघर्ष कर रही थी? राहुल गांधी भले ही अपनी धुन में एक प्यारे पपी के साथ चल रहे हों, लेकिन कांग्रेस ही नहीं पूरा विपक्ष, मोदी के 'क्रूर ख़ूनी कुत्ते' से परेशान थाः क़ानूनी तौर पर मज़बूत 'प्रवर्तन निदेशालय' (ED), ऐसी सबसे ताकतवर सरकारी एजेंसी, तो राजनीति के खेल के नियमों को बदलने के लिए तैयार थी।

8

'हमारे साथ ईडी है': वॉशिंग मशीन राजनीति

मई 2023 की गर्मियों की शाम थी। नासिक में होटल में अच्छे ठंडे एयरकंडीशन कमरे के बावजूद एनसीपी नेता छगन भुजबल पसीने से तरबतर थे। भुजबल ने गिलास से अपनी पसंदीदा व्हिस्की का एक घूंट गले में उतारा, लेकिन वे परेशान और चिंतित दिख रहे थे। सफेद दाढ़ी, थकी हुई आंखों के साथ चेहरे पर कमज़ोरी झलक रही थी। हमेशा रहने वाली मुस्कुराहट और उत्साह गायब था, जो उनके जीवट की पहचान थी। कुछ दिन पहले मनी लॉन्ड्रिंग मामले में उन्हें प्रवर्तन निदेशालय का एक नोटिस मिला था। 2016 में दर्ज मामला अभी चल रहा था। मुंबई के एक 'डेवलपर' को सौ करोड़ रुपये से ज़्यादा के ठेके में गड़बडी का आरोप उनके बेटे और भतीजे समेत उन पर था, जिसमें भुजबल ढाई साल जेल में रहने के बाद जमानत पर छूटे थे। जेल का उनके स्वास्थ्य पर बड़ा असर पड़ा था। वे लगातार गोलियां खा रहे थे। 'जेल के दिनों को याद करके, मुझे आजकल रातों को नींद भी नहीं आती। मैं 75 साल का हो गया हूं, लेकिन अब भी ईडी मुझे निशाना बना रही है,' भुजबल ने अपनी तकलीफ ज़ाहिर की।

'आप इतने वरिष्ठ नेता हैं, मुझे भरोसा है कि शरद पवार आपकी मदद करेंगे,' मैंने कहा। 'जब आप मुसीबत में होते हैं, तो कोई साथ नहीं होता। जब मैं जेल में था, तो कौन मेरी मदद के लिए आया? मतलबी है सारी दुनिया,' भुजबल ने अपना दुख जताते हुए अपने सहयोगी से एक और ड्रिंक्स बनाने को कहा। भुजबल ने याद दिलाया कि कैसे एनसीपी के ही एक और वरिष्ठ नेता और महाराष्ट्र के गृहमंत्री रहे अनिल देशमुख मनी लॉन्ड्रिंग के आरोप मे तेरह महीने जेल में रहने के बाद रिहा हुए थे। रिहाई के बाद देशमुख ने आरोप लगाया था कि जेल के दौरान

उन्हें क़ानून से बचने के लिए भाजपा में शामिल होने का प्रस्ताव दिया गया था। 'अब वो मुझे देशमुख जी की तरह फंसाना चाहते हैं,' भुजबल ने आरोप लगाया।

1999 में शरद पवार ने जब कांग्रेस से अलग होकर एनसीपी बनाई थी, तब महाराष्ट्र के उप-मुख्यमंत्री रहे भुजबल, पवार के साथ चले गए थे। उन्होंने शिवसेना में बालासाहेब ठाकरे के प्रमुख सहयोगियों के रूप में अपना राजनीतिक करियर शुरू किया था। बेहद गरीबी में पले-बढ़े भुजबल मुंबई के भायकुला बाज़ार के पास एक छोटे से कमरे के मकान में रहते थे। उनका परिवार सड़क किनारे फूल और सब्जियां बेचता था। महाराष्ट्र के दूसरे राजनेताओं की तरह अब शिक्षा, खेती-किसानी और 'रियल एस्टेट' तक उनका बिजनेस फैला हुआ है। 'मैंने सब कुछ खुद मेहनत से कमाया है और मुश्किलें पार करके आगे बढ़ा हूं। एजेंसियां मेरे पीछे इसलिए पड़ी हैं क्योंकि मैं पिछड़े ओबीसी समाज से आता हूं। क्या आपको लगता है कि वे किसी सवर्ण राजनेता के साथ ऐसा बर्ताव करेंगे?' ओबीसी कार्ड भुजबल की राजनीतिक ताकत थी। मराठा प्रभुत्व वाली राजनीति में ताकत दिखाने के लिए वे अक्सर अपने ओबीसी कार्ड का इस्तेमाल करते थे।

भुजबल की कहानी भले ही सम्मोहक लगती हो, लेकिन उनका जेल जाना वैसी बहादुरी नहीं है। उनके ख़िलाफ़ भ्रष्टाचार के आरोपों के पुख्ता दस्तावेज़ बताए गए हैं। मैं उनके प्रति सहानुभूति दिखाने की पूरी कोशिश कर रहा था और उनकी तकलीफ को सब्र से सुन रहा था। 'अब केवल एक ही रास्ता है कि मोदीजी और भाजपा के साथ हाथ मिला लिया जाए। यहां तक पवार साहेब भी जानते हैं, केवल वे अपना मन नही बना पा रहे हैं,' जब वे अपनी कहानी सुना रहे थे, तब तक टेबल पर चिकन टिक्का और सीक कबाब की बड़ी प्लेंटे सजा दी गई थीं। अब तक व्हिस्की की बोतल करीब-करीब खाली हो चुकी थी। भुजबल एक अच्छे मेजबान हैं। लेकिन भाजपा के साथ जाने से आपको केस में क्या मदद मिलेगी, मैंने पूछा। 'तुम इतना मासूम क्यों बन रहे हो? सबको पता है कि क्या चल रहा है,' उन्होंने तुरंत जवाब दिया।

इस मुलाक़ात के कुछ हफ्ते बीते होंगे। जुलाई 2023 में एक रविवार को न्यूज़ डेस्क से फ़ोन था, 'सर, आपका तुरंत लाइव फोनो चाहिए। एनसीपी में टूट हो गई है। अजित पवार कुछ और एनसीपी नेताओं के साथ शपथ ले रहे हैं। पवार और उनके साथी एकनाथ शिंदे की अगुवाई में भाजपा-शिवसेना गठबंधन सरकार में शामिल हो रहे हैं।' जब मैंने कैबिनेट मंत्रियों की सूची पर निगाह डाली तो उसमें एक नाम था: छगन भुजबल। भुजबल फिर से सरकार में थे। कुछ दिनों बाद, मैं मुंबई के आलीशान मालाबर इलाके में भुजबल के सरकारी बंगले में मिला। वे पिछले तीन दशकों से मंत्री पद का राजपाट भोग रहे थे और यहां सहज दिख रहे थे। यह उस घबराए हुए विपक्षी राजनेता से बिल्कुल उलट तस्वीर थी, जिनसे कुछ महीने पहले मैं नासिक के उस अंधेरे से होटल के कमरे में मिला था। 'अब तो आपको अच्छी नींद आ रही होगी?' मैंने चुटकी

ली। 'हां, हां, मैं मज़े में हूं, मैं आपको बता नहीं सकता कि कैसा लग रहा है, यह फिर से जन्म लेने जैसा है,' उनके चेहरे पर मुस्कुराहट लौट आई थी।

फिर पता चला कि भुजबल साहेब की मुस्कुराहट बेवजह नहीं थी। दिसम्बर 2023 में, प्रवर्तन निदेशालय ने बॉम्बे हाईकोर्ट से अपनी वह याचिका वापस ले ली, जिसमें भुजबल और उनके भतीजे समीर को ज़मानत देने और पासपोर्ट को 'रिन्यू' करने, और विदेश यात्रा की इज़ाजत देने वाले 2018 के आदेश को रद्द करने की मांग की गई थी। अब मामला ठंडे बस्ते में डाल दिया गया था। भुजबल अब निशाने पर नहीं थे।

राजनीतिक दोस्त बदलने से सुकून महसूस करने वाले भुजबल अकेले नेता नहीं थे। विभाजित एनसीपी के नेता अजित पवार पर भी भ्रष्टाचार के कई आरोप थे। बॉम्बे हाईकोर्ट की निगरानी में सीबीआई उनके ख़िलाफ़ जल संसाधन मंत्री रहते हुए 70 हज़ार करोड़ रुपये के कथित सिंचाई घोटाले की जांच कर रही थी। इसके साथ ही प्रवर्तन निदेशालय यानी ईडी महाराष्ट्र राज्य सहकारी बैंक के कर्ज देने में गड़बड़ी के मामलों की जांच कर रहा था। इसमें भले ही सीधे तौर पर अजित पवार का नाम नहीं था, लेकिन इस मसले में जांच के दायरे में आई कंपनियों में से एक की बड़ी शेयरहोल्डर उनकी पत्नी सुनेत्रा पवार थीं। एनसीपी के एक नेता ने कहा, 'जब अजित दादा को बताया गया कि ईडी उनकी पत्नी को तलब कर गिरफ्तार कर सकती है,' तो दादा अचानक घबरा गए।

परेशान अजित पवार संकट से निकलने के लिए अपने चाचा शरद पवार के पास पहुंचे। उनके साथ एनसीपी के दो और सांसद प्रफुल्ल पटेल और सुनील तटकरे भी थे। जुलाई 2022 में, ईडी ने प्रफुल्ल पटेल की एक व्यावसायिक बिल्डिंग की चार मंज़िलों को सीज़ कर दिया था। मनी लॉन्ड्रिंग का यह मामला अंडरवर्ल्ड डॉन दाऊद इब्राहिम के गिरोह के इकबाल मिर्ची से जुड़ा था। ईडी तटकरे के ख़िलाफ़ भी भ्रष्टाचार और ज़मीन कब्ज़ाने के आरोपों की जांच कर रही थी। तीनों नेताओं ने एनसीपी के संस्थापक-अध्यक्ष शरद पवार से गुहार लगाई कि भाजपा के साथ गठबंधन कर लेना चाहिए। शरद पवार ने दावा किया, 'उन्होंने मुझसे कहा था कि बेहतर भविष्य के लिए भाजपा के साथ जाना ठीक रहेगा, लेकिन हकीकत में वे ईडी जांच से बचना चाहते थे। मैंने उनसे साफ कहा कि वे भाजपा के साथ जाने के लिए आज़ाद हैं, लेकिन मैं नहीं जाऊंगा।'

शरद पवार ने जब उनके प्रस्ताव को नहीं माना तो अजित पवार और पटेल ने भाजपा के साथ अपनी पिछली बातचीत को फिर से शुरू किया। सौदा साफ और आसान था। समर्थन देने के एवज़ में एनसीपी के करीब आधा दर्ज़न वरिष्ठ नेताओं के ख़िलाफ़ चल रहे ईडी के मामलों को वापस ले लिया जाएगा या फिर ठंडे बस्ते में डाल दिया जाएगा। प्रफुल्ल पटेल ऐसे किसी सौदे के आरोप को ख़ारिज़ करते हैं। 'यह मसला किसी एक को बचाने का नहीं, पार्टी के

अस्तित्व को बचाने का था। हमारे पास विभाजित विपक्ष और केन्द्र में मज़बूत नरेन्द्र मोदी के बीच विकल्प था। हमने राजनीतिक स्थिरता को चुना,' पटेल का तर्क था।

अजित पवार गुट की भाजपा के साथ इस नयी दोस्ती के कुछ दिन पहले ही प्रधानमंत्री मोदी ने एनसीपी नेताओं के ख़िलाफ़ घोटालों का ज़िक्र किया था। इसमें वह सिंचाई घोटाला भी था, जिसमें सिंचाई योजनाओं के नाम पर बहुत पैसा ख़र्च किया गया, लेकिन सिंचाई में कोई बढ़ोतरी नहीं हुई। इसको लेकर भ्रष्टाचार के बहुत आरोप लगाए गए थे। भोपाल में भाजपा बूथ-कार्यकर्ताओं की एक बैठक में प्रधानमंत्री ने एनसीपी के ख़िलाफ़ भ्रष्टाचार के मामलों में 'ज़ीरो टॉलरेंस' की चेतावनी दी थी यानी भ्रष्टाचार किसी भी हाल में बर्दाश्त नहीं किया जाएगा। प्रधानमंत्री ने कहा, 'हमारे पास उनके लिए एक घोटाला-मीटर होना चाहिए।' महाराष्ट्र के उप-मुख्यमंत्री और भाजपा नेता देवेन्द्र फड़नवीस ने कथित सिंचाई घोटाले में अजित पवार को जेल भिजवाने का वादा किया था, अब पवार उनके साथ ही उप-मुख्यमंत्री बनने वाले थे। 'हम महाराष्ट्र के विकास में भागीदार बन रहे हैं,' पार्टी के रुख में बेशर्मी भरा बदलाव दिख रहा था।

राजनीति की विडंबना यह है कि मुंबई भाजपा के नेता और पूर्व सांसद किरीट सोमैया ने ही हसन मुश्रिफ समेत एनसीपी के कई नेताओं के ख़िलाफ़ कार्रवाई के लिए जांच एजेंसियों पर दबाव डालने में अहम भूमिका निभाई थी। सोमैया ने ही मुश्रिफ की कथित धोखाधड़ी और मनी लॉन्ड्रिंग मामले के दस्तावेज़ों का खुलासा किया था। बाद में जब मुश्रिफ भाजपा गठबंधन सरकार में मंत्री बन गए तो सोमैया शर्मिंदगी तो महसूस कर रहे थे, लेकिन निराश नहीं थे। उन्होंने कहा, 'राजनीति में कभी-कभी पार्टी के लिए अपने व्यक्तिगत लक्ष्यों को छोड़ना पड़ता है। यह सच है कि मेरी लड़ाई अंज़ाम तक नहीं पहुंची, लेकिन महाराष्ट्र में हमने कम से कम सरकार तो बना ली।' फरवरी 2024 में, मुंबई पुलिस की आर्थिक अपराध शाखा ने सहकारी बैंक मामले में अजित पवार को लेकर एक 'क्लोज़र रिपोर्ट' फाइल कर दी, इसमें कहा गया कि 'तथ्यों की ग़लती की वजह से' आपराधिक मामला दर्ज किया गया था। सिंचाई घोटाले की जांच भी बंद हो गई थी। प्रवर्तन निदेशालय ने प्रफुल्ल पटेल, हसन मुश्रिफ और सुनील तटकरे के ख़िलाफ़ मामलों को आगे बढ़ाने की कोशिश नहीं की। एनडीए के साथ आने के कुछ दिनों बाद ही सीबीआई ने भी 'एयर इंडिया विलय' के मामले में पटेल को लेकर 'क्लोज़र रिपोर्ट' दाखिल कर दी। भुजबल की तरह, पार्टी में शामिल होने वाले सभी एनसीपी नेता अब चैन की नींद सो सकते थे।

═

दरअसल क़ानूनी पकड़ से राजनीतिक छूट का खाका एक साल पहले जून 2022 में ही तैयार हो गया था, जब महाराष्ट्र में उद्धव ठाकरे की सरकार का तख्ता पलट कर दिया गया था। ठाकरे

महाविकास अघाड़ी सरकार का नेतृत्व कर रहे थे। ठाकरे के ही सबसे करीबी सहयोगी और विश्वस्त माने जाने वाले एकनाथ शिंदे ने ठाकरे के ख़िलाफ़ बगावत कर सरकार गिरा दी। ललाट पर लाल तिलक, करीने से बनी दाढ़ी, छोटे कद के शिंदे की राजनीतिक ऊर्जा और मुख्यमंत्री की कुर्सी पर नज़र उस वक्त से थी, जब उद्धव ठाकरे दिसम्बर 2021 में एक सर्जरी के बाद से अस्पताल में स्वास्थ्य लाभ ले रहे थे। 'पार्टी और सरकार के लिए सारी मेहनत मैं कर रहा हूं, लेकिन इसका पूरा श्रेय उद्धव जी और अब उनके बेटे आदित्य को मिल रहा है। मैं बच्चे जैसे आदित्य के अधीन क्यों काम करूंगा?' एकनाथ शिंदे ने पार्टी के एक सहयोगी से शिकायत की। बताया गया कि मामला तब अचानक बढ़ गया जब ठाणे के इस कद्दावर नेता को मुख्यमंत्री ठाकरे के सरकारी आवास 'वर्षा' पर एक घंटे से ज़्यादा देर तक इंतज़ार कराया गया और फिर कहा गया कि उद्धव जी की तबियत ठीक नहीं थी, लेकिन वे ठाकरे की पत्नी रश्मि या आदित्य से मिल सकते थे। शिंदे का कहना था कि 'उस दिन मैंने तय किया कि अब बहुत हो गया, मैं अपने आत्म-सम्मान के साथ समझौता नहीं करूंगा।'

राज्यसभा सांसद और शिवसेना (यूबीटी) के प्रवक्ता संजय राउत ने इन आरोपों को ख़ारिज़ करते हुए कहा, 'क्या बकवास है! उद्धव जी ने शिंदेजी को अपना मंत्रालय चलाने और ठाणे में पार्टी को देखने की पूरी छूट दे रखी थी और उन पर पूरा भरोसा किया। इसमें किसी का कोई दख़ल नहीं था।' राउत की बात मानें तो शिंदे की बग़ावत तब शुरू हुई, जब एक प्रमुख बिल्डर समेत उनके दो सहयोगियों के ख़िलाफ़ ईडी ने एक गोपनीय जांच शुरू की। राउत ने कहा, 'शिंदे को डर था कि यह जांच जल्दी ही उन तक पहुंच जाएगी और उन्हें जेल भेज दिया जाएगा।' उद्धव खेमे की बात पर अगर भरोसा किया जाए, तो पार्टी छोड़ने से करीब एक महीने पहले रुआंसे से शिंदे ने शिवसेना प्रमुख से भारतीय जनता पार्टी के साथ गठबंधन की गुहार लगाई थी, नहीं तो उन्हें गिरफ़्तार कर लिया जाएगा। रोते हुए से शिंदे ने कहा, 'मैं अब दादा बन गया हूं और मैं जेल नहीं जाना चाहता।'

केन्द्रीय गृहमंत्री अमित शाह ने महत्वाकांक्षी शिंदे की बेचैनी को भांप लिया था। शाह को उद्धव ठाकरे-शरद पवार जोड़ी से 2019 में मात का अपना हिसाब पूरा करना था। जब उन्होंने भाजपा के बजाय महाविकास अघाड़ी की सरकार बना ली थी। शाह ने बताया कि नवम्बर 2019 में, ठाकरे के नेतृत्व वाली 'महाविकास अघाड़ी' सरकार के शपथग्रहण के कुछ देर बाद ही एकनाथ शिंदे को फ़ोन किया था। शाह ने खुलासा किया, 'मैंने उनसे कहा कि जब भी उन्हें ठाकरे परिवार में घुटन महसूस होने लगे, तो मुझे फ़ोन करें।' शाह के अलावा इस मामले की जानकारी सिर्फ देवेन्द्र फड़नवीस को थी, शिवसेना से धोखा खाए फड़नवीस अब भी गुस्से में थे। दिल्ली में जब शाह, फड़नवीस और शिंदे की मुलाक़ात हुई तो गृहमंत्री शाह ने गर्मजोशी के साथ शिंदे को भरोसा दिलाया कि अगर वे पार्टी तोड़कर सरकार बना सकते हैं तो उन्हें पूरा

समर्थन मिलेगा। 'यह आसान काम नहीं है, लेकिन मैं कोशिश करूंगा,' शिंदे ने वादा तो किया, लेकिन वे शिवसेना पर ठाकरे परिवार की पकड़ से वाकिफ़ थे।

साठ के दशक में मुंबई में भूमिपुत्र और मूल निवासियों की पार्टी के तौर पर शिवसेना बनी। शिवसेना के पास शाखा प्रमुखों और समर्पित कार्यकर्ताओं का एक नेटवर्क है। शिवसेना 'महाराष्ट्रीय फर्स्ट' की क्षेत्रीय और उग्र हिन्दुत्व की पहचान मानी जाती है। इसके कार्यकर्ता शिवसेना संस्थापक बालासाहेब ठाकरे के प्रति आस्थावान हैं। जब तक करिश्माई बालासाहेब ठाकरे जीवित थे, वे निर्विवाद 'सुप्रीम' थे। लोगों में उनका डर भी था और उनकी तारीफ़ भी की जाती थी। 2012 में उनके निधन के बाद, शिवसेना का नेतृत्व उनके बेटे उद्धव ठाकरे को मिल गया। एक 'वाइल्ड लाइफ' फोटोग्राफर से राजनेता बने उद्धव की पहचान बालासाहेब की बड़ी ताकतवर छवि से उलट, नरम आवाज़ और विनम्र शैली वाली थी। 2019 तक उद्धव के बेटे आदित्य भी राजनीति में उतर गए। अंग्रेजी स्कूल में पढ़े-लिखे, दुबले-पतले, जींस पहने, अच्छे वक्ता आदित्य, उस नई पीढ़ी के राजनेता हैं जो सड़क पर उतरकर प्रदर्शन करने के बजाय जलवायु परिवर्तन जैसे विषयों पर सम्मेलन में बोलने में ज़्यादा सहज महसूस करते हैं। कई शिवसैनिक कार्यकर्ता, अपनी 'ठोकशाही' (शिवसेना का ट्रेडमार्कः ताकत से शासन) की लड़ाकू राजनीति के साथ, आदित्य के शहरी तरीके से काम करने से खुद को जोड़ नहीं पा रहे थे। एक वरिष्ठ नेता ने कहा, 'बालासाहेब की वजह से हमारा पार्टी से भावनात्मक जुड़ाव तो है, लेकिन आप यह उम्मीद नहीं कर सकते कि यह वफादारी उनके पोते के साथ भी बनी रहे।'

अपनी लंबी आस्तीन वाली सफेद शर्ट और सफेद पतलून में शिंदे मुंबई के पास के बड़े ज़िले ठाणे में एक प्रभावशाली नेता हैं। किसी ज़माने में वे यहां की भीड़-भाड़ वाली सड़कों पर ऑटो रिक्शा चलाते थे, लेकिन अब एक प्राइवेट हेलिपैड वाले विशाल फॉर्म हाउस के साथ उनके पास कारों का बड़ा काफिला है, जो बताता है कि कैसे मराठी मानुष के नाम से शुरू हुई शिवसेना अब बड़े फायदे वाले 'राजनीतिक बिजनेस' में बदल गई है। सवाल यह था कि क्या ठाणे के वफादार क्षत्रप, चाहे कितने ही साधन संपन्न हो जाएं, एक बड़ी पारिवारिक विरासत को संभाल सकते हैं? और उससे भी बड़ा सवाल कि क्या सरकार में बैठी पार्टी को तोड़ सकते हैं? आमतौर पर कम बोलने वाले शिंदे के पास अपने नेता को हटाने के मिशन के लिए दो हथियार थे, पहला केन्द्रीय गृहमंत्री शाह का पूरा समर्थन और दूसरा, ईडी का मंडराता डर।

एनसीपी की तरह, शिवसेना के कई नेताओं पर भी ईडी की ख़तरा बना हुआ था। उनमें से एक नेता थे प्रताप सरनाइक। ठाणे के ही एक और महत्वाकांक्षी ऑटो चालक रहे सरनाइक तीन बार के विधायक थे। राजनीतिक संपर्कों का फायदा उठाकर सरनाइक ने मुंबई और ठाणे में रियल एस्टेट और हॉस्पिटेलिटी का बिजनेस खड़ा किया था। ठाकरे के मुखर समर्थक रहे सरनाइक के घर पर ठाकरे परिवार के साथ उनकी ढेरों तस्वीरें लगी हुई थीं। वे कहते हैं कि 'मैं

जो कुछ हूं, उनके आशीर्वाद और समर्थन से हूं।' लेकिन उद्धव ठाकरे के मुख्यमंत्री रहते हुए भी सरनाइक परेशानी में थे। 2021-22 में ईडी ने सरनाइक और उनके व्यावसायिक सहयोगियों पर छापे मारे और शिवसेना के इस विधायक की एक फर्म के 100 से ज्यादा प्लॉट्स को अपने कब्ज़े में ले लिया था। सरनाइक के करीबी ठाणे के ही एक बिल्डर को भी ईडी ने 'नेशनल स्पॉट एक्सचेंज लिमिटेड' मनी लॉन्ड्रिंग मामले में गिरफ़्तार किया था। अपने इर्द-गिर्द बुने जाल में फंसते सरनाइक ने जून 2021 में, उद्धव ठाकरे को एक ओपन लैटर लिखाः 'मेरी राय में यह ज़रूरी है कि हम माननीय प्रधानमंत्री नरेन्द्र मोदी के साथ समझौता कर लें। हमारे बहुत से समर्थकों को लगता है कि ऐसा करने से प्रताप सरनाइक, अनिल परब और रवीन्द्र वायकर और उनके परिवारों का उत्पीड़न बंद हो जाएगा। मैं पिछले सात महीनों से राज्य सरकार या किसी दूसरे नेता के समर्थन के बिना क़ानूनी लड़ाई लड़ रहा हूं।' (शिवसेना विधायक परब और वाईकर भी ईडी के निशाने पर थे। वाईकर मार्च 2024 में, शिवसेना (यूबीटी) छोड़कर शिंदे शिवसेना में शामिल हो गए थे, उन पर ईडी ने शिकंजा कस दिया था। वाईकर ने 2024 में मुंबई उत्तर-पश्चिम सीट से चुनाव लड़ा और सिर्फ़ 48 वोटों से जीत हासिल की। इसके बाद मुंबई पुलिस ने नगर निगम की ज़मीन पर एक होटल के अवैध निर्माण के लिए उनके ख़िलाफ़ चल रहे मामले को बंद कर दिया।)

सरनाईक की चिट्ठी ने लोगों को थोड़ा हैरान कर दिया। मुख्यमंत्री ठाकरे के करीबी एक शिवसेना विधायक का आरोप था कि प्रवर्तन निदेशालय उनके पीछे पड़ा था और उन्हें खुद को बचाने के लिए भाजपा के साथ जाने की वकालत कर रहा था। सरनाईक का कहना था, 'मैं उद्धव जी से कहता रहा कि हमें भाजपा के साथ जाना चाहिए। बड़े नेताओं के तो दिल्ली में संबंध हैं, उन्हें तो बचाया जा सकता है, लेकिन हमारे जैसे कार्यकर्ताओं और विधायकों को अंजाम भुगतना पड़ता है।' ठाकरे ने ईडी की जांच को रोकने में अपनी लाचारी जाहिर की। शिवसेना प्रमुख का जवाब था, 'वे तो मेरे और मेरे परिवार के पीछे भी पड़े हैं, हम सभी को लड़ाई लड़नी पड़ेगी।'

हताश सरनाईक ने अपने लिए दूसरे रास्तों को खोजना शुरू किया और जब शिंदे ने उन्हे पाला बदलने का मौका दिया तो उन्होंने उसे पकड़ने में देरी नहीं की। इससे पहले सरनाईक और शिंदे दोनों नेता ठाणे में एक दूसरे के ख़िलाफ़ मैदान में रहे थे, लेकिन जेल जाने के अंदेशे और परेशानी से बचने के लिए यह सब बेमायने था। गृहमंत्री शाह के साथ बैठक में फ़ैसला हो गया। उद्धव समर्थकों ने दावा किया कि सरनाईक गृहमंत्री के सामने रोने लगे, उन्हें इस बात की आशंका थी कि अगर वे पाला बदलने लिए तैयार नहीं हुए तो उन्हें जेल भेज दिया जाएगा। सरनाइक ने सफाई दी, 'हां, मैंने दलबदल करने वाले विधायकों के साथ जाने से पहले गृहमंत्री शाह से मुलाक़ात की थी, लेकिन मेरे ख़िलाफ़ बनाई जा रही कहानियों पर भरोसा मत करिए।

अमित भाई से मैंने केवल इस भरोसे के लिए अपील की थी कि प्रवर्तन एजेंसियां मुझे परेशान न करें। उन्होंने जब यह वादा कर दिया, तो फिर पीछे मुड़ने का सवाल नहीं था।' सरनाईक ने बताया कि उनके ख़िलाफ़ अब मामले अदालतों में चल रहे थे।

सरनाईक की तरह ही उद्धव के एक और विश्वस्त यशवंत जाधव भी परेशान थे। मई 2022 में, ईडी ने उन्हें हवाला के पैसे से मुंबई में संपत्ति खरीदने के मामले में तलब किया था। इससे पहले आयकर विभाग ने जाधव पर कार्रवाई करके कथित तौर पर उनके और सहयोगियों की 41 संपत्तियों को जब्त किया था। जाधव 'बृहन्मुंबई नगर निगम' की स्थायी समिति के अध्यक्ष रहे थे। उस दौरान उन्होंने कई बड़े ठेकों को देने में अहम भूमिका निभाई थी। आयकर विभाग को जाधव के घर मिली एक डायरी में करोड़ों रुपये का हिसाब लिखा हुआ मिला। इनमें एक में 50 लाख रुपये की घड़ी और दो करोड़ रुपये के गिफ्ट का भी ज़िक्र था, दोनों को बांद्रा में ठाकरे निवास मातोश्री में भेंट किया बताया था। पूछताछ में जाधव ने कहा कि वे अपनी मां को मातोश्री कहते हैं!

जाधव की पत्नी यामिनी सेन्ट्रल मुंबई के भायकुला से शिवसेना की विधायक थीं। पति-पत्नी दोनों को जब ईडी और आयकर विभाग से बार-बार तलब किया जाने लगा तो दोनों में घबराहट शुरू हो गई। ऐसे वक्त मे शिंदे का फ़ोन आना तो उन्हें वरदान जैसा लगा, उन्होंने शिंदे के साथ जाने में देर नहीं लगाई। 'हमने उद्धव जी को हिंदूत्व के रास्ते पर लौटने और भाजपा के साथ गठबंधन के लिए मनाने की कोशिश की, लेकिन वे तैयार नहीं हुए,' जाधव ने जोर देकर कहा, 'हम पहले हिंदूत्ववादी हैं।' अपनी इस दलबदल को भावनाओं से जोड़ने के लिए यामिनी ने एक वीडियो जारी कर दावा किया, वह कई महीनों से कैंसर का सामना कर रही थीं, लेकिन शिवसेना प्रमुख को तो उनसे मिलने की फुर्सत भी नहो थी। 'मैं अकेली पड़ गई थी,' उन्हें रोते हुए कहा। लेकिन ये आंसू और बयान भी सच्चाई को छिपा नहीं सके। जाधव अपने भविष्य पर ईडी और आयकर की तलवार लटकी रहने से बचना चाहते थे।

ऐसा ही मामला पांच बार शिवसेना की सांसद रही भावना गवली का भी था। अगस्त 2021 में, प्रवर्तन निदेशालय ने सांसद से जुड़ी कई संपत्तियों पर छापे मारे। पुलिस ने उन पर सरकारी अनुदान के दुरुपयोग और 14 करोड़ के गबन का आरोप लगाते हुए एफआईआर दर्ज़ की। उनके ख़िलाफ़ ये मामले भाजपा के पूर्व सांसद किरीट सोमैया ने चलाए थे। सोमैया का दावा था कि उनके पास इसके पुख़्ता सबूत थे। दूसरे नेताओं की तरह भावना गवली भी बचने के रास्ते तलाश रही थीं। इस दौरान जब मुख्यमंत्री बनने की इच्छा रखने वाले शिंदे के बेटे सांसद श्रीकांत शिंदे ने संपर्क किया तो वे बेहिचक शिंदे के पक्ष में खड़ी हो गईं। आरोप लगाया कि उन्होंने ईडी से परेशान नहीं किए जाने का आग्रह किया था, हालांकि सार्वजनिक तौर पर गवली ने कहा कि उन्होंने पाला इसलिए बदला क्योंकि वे प्रधानमंत्री मोदी की समर्थक थीं।

इस बात पर आश्चर्य नहीं होना चाहिए कि जब शिंदे ने जून 2022 में, शिवसेना से अलग होने का बड़ा फ़ैसला किया तो संख्याबल उनके पास था। शिवसेना के 56 विधायकों में से 40 और 19 सांसदों में से 12 सांसद उनके साथ आ गए थे। इन विधायकों को पहले सूरत के एक रिज़ॉर्ट में ले जाया गया, फिर वहां से वे गुवाहाटी के एक आलीशान होटल में पहुंचे और दस दिन बाद गोवा होते हुए उन्हें मुंबई पहुंचाया गया। जब विधायक भाजपा शासित एक राज्य से दूसरे राज्य में जा रहे थे, तो विधायकों को राज्य की 'सुरक्षा' दी गई थी। स्थानीय पुलिस अधिकारी उनके साथ रहते थे। बगावत की अगुवाई भले ही शिंदे कर रहे थे, लेकिन इसकी निगरानी दिल्ली से गृहमंत्री अमित शाह कर रहे थे। शिंदे समर्थक एक विधायक ने माना, 'अमित शाह जी ने हमारी बहुत मदद की।' गुवाहाटी के होटल में विधायकों का सत्कार असम के भाजपा मुख्यमंत्री हिमंत बिस्वा सरमा ने किया। दलबदल करने वालों में से एक विधायक ने कहा कि 'हमें भरोसा दिलाया गया कि हम सुरक्षित हाथों में थे।'

2022 की गर्मियों में विरोधी दलों के नेतृत्व वाली महाराष्ट्र सरकार को अस्थिर करना और फिर उसका गिरना ईडी की ताकत का 'बेहतर उदाहरण' माना जा सकता है। मोदी सरकार पर ईडी के दुरुपयोग और दो राजनीतिक गुटों में वर्चस्व की लड़ाई में जांच एजेंसियों के इस्तेमाल के आरोप लगे। शिवसेना के एक वरिष्ठ मंत्री दीपक केसरकर ने कहा, 'आप बार-बार यह ईडी-ईडी क्यों करते रहते हैं? हममें से कई लोगों पर ईडी के कोई मामले नहीं थे। हम इसलिए अलग हुए क्योंकि हम फिर से हिन्दूत्व वाले गठबंधन को खड़ा करना चाहते थे।' अमित शाह ने कहा कि 'जिन लोगों पर आरोप हैं, उनकी जांच चल रही है, किसी को भी नहीं छोड़ा जा रहा।' हकीकत यह है कि पाला बदलने वालों के ख़िलाफ़ मामलों की जांच या तो धीमी कर दी गई या उन्हें ठंडे बस्ते में डाल दिया गया। शिंदे के साथ आए लोगों में से किसी को अपराध में दोषी नहीं ठहराया गया और न ही जेल भेजा गया।

इससे उलट, ठाकरे परिवार के बचाव में उतरे अकेले कमांडर और उद्धव के वफादार संजय राउत को शिंदे सरकार बनने के कुछ समय बाद अगस्त 2022 में, ईडी ने गिरफ्तार कर लिया। राउत पर झुग्गी-झोपड़ी पुनर्विकास मामले में मनी लॉन्ड्रिंग का आरोप लगाया गया और उन्हें तीन महीने की जेल हो गई। राउत को जब जमानत दी गई, तो बॉम्बे हाईकोर्ट ने अपने सख्त आदेश में उनकी गिरफ़्तारी को शुरू से ही अवैध बताया। 'उन्हें बिना किसी कारण गिरफ़्तार किया गया था। यह साफ है... अदालत के दख़ल से उन्हें ईडी हिरासत में एक हवादार कमरा मिल सका। इस सबसे साफ है कि उनकी गिरफ़्तारी जबरदस्ती घसीटने और उनके अधिकारों को खत्म करने की कोशिश के अलावा कुछ नहीं है,' अदालत ने अपने आदेश में कहा था।

शिवसेना के राज्यसभा सांसद राउत ने आरोप लगाया कि उनकी गिरफ्तारी से पहले दिल्ली में भाजपा के कम से कम तीन नेताओं ने उनसे संपर्क साधा था, और उन्हें बचाने का प्रस्ताव

रखा था, बशर्ते वह ठाकरे परिवार का साथ छोड़ दें और महाविकास अघाड़ी सरकार को गिराने में मदद करें। उन्होंने ईडी पर भाजपा के 'आपराधिक सिंडीकेट' का हिस्सा होने का आरोप लगाया। फरवरी 2022 में, राज्यसभा के सभापति और उपराष्ट्रपति वेंकैया नायडु को एक चिट्ठी लिखकर राउत ने सांसदों को डराने-धमकाने और परेशान करने के लिए सत्ता के दुरुपयोग से सुरक्षा देने की मांग की थी। राउत ने अपनी गिरफ्तारी से कुछ दिन पहले एक प्रेस कॉन्फ्रेंस में चेतावनी दी थी कि उनके पास ऐसे वीडियो सबूत थे जिनमें ईडी के अफसर स्थानीय व्यापारियों को ब्लैकमेल करके पैसा वसूली कर रहे थे। ये वीडियो कभी जारी नहीं किए गए, लेकिन राउत ईडी से लड़ने को तैयार दिख रहे थे। राउत आरोप लगाते हैं, 'क्या आप जानते हैं कि जिस दिन ईडी ने मेरे घर पर छापा मारा और मुझे गिरफ़्तार किया, वे मुझसे कह रहे थे, "सर, ऊपर वालों से बात क्यों नहीं करते, वे इसे निपटा देंगे।"'

राउत के इस आरोप को ईडी के अफसर ख़ारिज़ करते हैं। उनका दावा है कि वे राजनीति के हिसाब से नहीं, सबूतों के आधार पर कार्रवाई करते हैं। लेकिन सत्ता के गलियारों में राजनेताओं के ख़िलाफ़ कार्रवाई के वक्त दो शब्दों की गूंज सुनाई देती हैः 'वॉशिंग मशीन'। 'सरकार में जाओ, सब पाप धुल जाते हैं। ईडी वॉशिंग पाउडर सर्फ के प्रसिद्ध विज्ञापन में ललिता जी की तरह है,' राउत ने हंसते हुए कहा। यह वाकई एक अच्छी वॉशिंग मशीन है, अगर आप विपक्ष में हैं तो गंदे और दाग़दार होकर जाओ और दूसरी तरफ से भाजपा के सदस्य के तौर पर बिल्कुल साफ निकलो।

कुछ लोग इस 'ईडी सुरक्षा' को स्वीकार भी करते हैं। 2019 के महाराष्ट्र विधानसभा चुनावों से पहले भाजपा में शामिल हुए कांग्रेस में मंत्री रहे हर्षवर्धन पाटिल ने एक सार्वजनिक सभा में कहा, 'मैं भाजपा में क्यों शामिल हुआ? अब सब ठीक हैं, मुझे चैन की नींद आती है, अब कोई पूछताछ के लिए नहीं आता।' बाद में शर्मिंदा पाटिल ने सफाई दी कि उनकी बातों का गलत अर्थ निकाला गया।

महाराष्ट्र में एमवीए सरकार के पूर्व मंत्री और शरद पवार खेमे में बने रहने वाले नेताओं में से एक जितेन्द्र आव्हाड ने एक दिलचस्प किस्सा साझा किया। एमवीए सरकार के तख्तापलट की साज़िशों के वक्त आव्हाड ने इस दलबदल में शामिल शिवसेना के एक नेता से मुलाकात की और उन्हें कहा कि आखिरी फ़ैसला लेने से पहले ठाकरे परिवार के साथ रहे उनके रिश्तों पर भी विचार कर लें। आव्हाड ने उन्हें चेतावनी दी, 'आज आप जो कुछ हैं, वे ठाकरे परिवार की बदौलत हैं, अगर आप उन्हें धोखा देंगे तो शिवसैनिक और जनता आपको माफ़ नहीं करेगी।' शिवसेना नेता ने आतमविश्वास के साथ कहाः 'चुनावों को तय करने दें कि कौन किसके साथ है। अभी मैं सिर्फ़ एक चीज़ जानता हूं: हमारे साथ ईडी है।'

आउच!

प्रवर्तन निदेशालय का मुख्यालय लुटिंयस दिल्ली के हरे-भरे डॉ. अब्दुल कलाम रोड पर है, जिसे पहले औरंगज़ेब रोड कहा जाता था। इससे पहले ख़ान मार्केट के पिछवाड़े में लोकनायक भवन के छोटे, गंदे से कमरों में चलने वाला यह दफ़्तर अब तीन मंज़िला इमारत के परिसर में कई विंग में फैला हुआ है। पते में बदलाव भी कई बार संस्थान की बढ़ती ताकत की ओर इशारा करता है। ईडी को 1956 में आर्थिक मामलों के विभाग में 'विदेशी मुद्रा विनिमयन अधिनियम', 1947 के उल्लंघन के मामलों की जांच के लिए एक छोटी इकाई के तौर पर शुरू किया गया था। एक साल बाद 1957 में यह प्रवर्तन निदेशालय तो हो गया, लेकिन प्रमुख वित्तीय अपराधों की जांच में कोई अहम भूमिका नहीं निभाई। यह समाजवादी विचारधारा का दौर था और ईडी विदेशी मुद्रा में छोटे लेन-देन पर कार्रवाई कर रहा था। सत्तर के दशक में इंदिरा गांधी के वक्त, आयकर विभाग के नाम से लोगों को डर लगता था। उस वक्त टैक्स की ऊंची दरों की वजह से राजनेताओं और व्यापारियों से बड़ी तादाद में कालेधन की जब्ती या छापे की कार्रवाई सुर्खियों में आ जाती थी। ईडी के पास 'विदेशी मुद्रा विनियमन अधिनियम' (फेरा) और 'विदेशी मुद्रा सरंक्षण और तस्करी गतिविधियां रोकथाम अधिनियम', 1974 (सीओएफईपीओएसए) जैसे क़ानूनों से ताकत मिलती थी, लेकिन निशाने पर राजनेता नहीं, बल्कि सोने के तस्कर और आयात-निर्यात कंपनियां होती थीं।

ईडी ने अपना राजनीतिक प्रोफाइल पहली बार 80 के दशक में प्रधानमंत्री राजीव गांधी के कार्यकाल में बनाया, जब प्रधानमंत्री ने भ्रष्टाचार खत्म करने के जनादेश के साथ विश्वनाथ प्रताप सिंह को अपना वित्त मंत्री बनाया। वी.पी. सिंह अपने भरोसेमंद अफसर भूरे लाल को प्रवर्तन निदेशक के तौर पर लाए। 1970 बैच के आईएएस अफसर भूरे लाल अपनी प्रभावशाली मूंछों वाले व्यक्तित्व के साथ जल्दी ही ऐसे नाम बन गए, जिनसे लोग थर्राते थे। उन्होंने अंबानी से लेकर थापर तक कई प्रमुख उद्योगपतियों और व्यवसायियों पर छापे मारने, जांच शुरू करने के लिए अपनी सरकारी ताकत का भरपूर इस्तेमाल किया। हर कार्रवाई के साथ पूरा प्रचार तंत्र होता था। वी.पी. सिंह ईडी का इस्तेमाल अपनी छवि 'मिस्टर क्लीन' के रूप में बनाने में कर रहे थे। इस रास्ते ने बड़े करीने से सिंह को बोफोर्स घोटाले में राजीव गांधी को चुनौती देने और कमज़ोर करने और फिर 1989 में उन्हें प्रधानमंत्री की कुर्सी तक पहुंचाने में मदद की। और इस तरह ईडी के पहले कदम राजनीति में घुसपैठ कर गए।

नब्बे के दशक में आर्थिक उदारीकरण के आगे बढ़ने के साथ इस बात पर चर्चा होने लगी कि व्यापार के ख़िलाफ़ कड़े क़ानूनों की समीक्षा की जानी चाहिए और विदेशी मुद्रा को दुर्लभ संसाधन के बजाय पॉजिटिव तरीके से परिसंपत्ति माना जाना चाहिए। 1999 में (FERA) की जगह कम कड़े क़ानून 'विदेशी मुद्रा प्रबंधन अधिनियम' (FEMA) को लाया गया। FEMA क़ानूनों के उल्लघंन में सीधे जेल नहीं हो सकती थी, इसे दीवानी अपराध को तौर पर देखा

गया। लेकिन FEMA लागू होने वाला अकेला नया क़ानून नहीं था। दुनिया भर में नशीली दवा की तस्करी और मनी लॉन्ड्रिंग से इसके रिश्तों पर शोर के बाद इस पर नकेल कसने के लिए PMLA, 2002 लाया गया। इसमें ज़मानत के लिए कड़ी शर्तें लगाई गई थीं और आरोपी को खुद को निर्दोष साबित करना होता था। PMLA की धारा 45 के मुताबिक मनी लॉन्ड्रिंग मामले में किसी आरोपी को तभी ज़मानत मिल सकती है जब दो शर्तें पूरी होती होः पहला, यह आश्वस्त किया जा सके कि आरोपी ने अपराध नही किया है, और दूसरा ज़मानत के दौरान उसके अपराध करने की संभावना नहीं हो। वाजपेयी की एनडीए सरकार ने इस बिल को पास कराया और फिर 2005 में यूपीए सरकार ने इसे अधिसूचित किया। ऐसे मौके कम होते हैं जब दो विरोधी बड़े दल किसी एक मसले पर सहमत दिखाई दें। 'यह कोई हमारा मूल आइडिया नहीं था, बल्कि "अंतरराष्ट्रीय वित्तीय कार्रवाई फोर्स" के सदस्य के रूप में यह हमारी जिम्मेदारी थी,' वकील-राजनेता और यूपीए सरकार में वित्त मंत्री रहे पी. चिदंबरम ने ज़ोर देकर कहा। लेकिन क्या उन्हें इस कड़े क़ानून के बेज़ा इस्तमाल की आशंका नहीं रही थी? 'मुझे कैसे पता होता कि अगली सरकार क़ानून को ही अपना हथियार बना लेगी?' चिदंबरम का जवाब था।

कोई भी अधिनियम एक सरकार से दूसरी सरकार में बदलाव के लिए बढ़ सकता है। 2015 से 2019 के बीच इसमें कई संशोधनों के लिए इसे 'मनी बिल' के तौर पर लाया गया, ताकि राज्यसभा में इसकी मंज़ूरी की ज़रूरत ना पड़े। मनी लॉन्ड्रिंग के दायरे को बढ़ाते हुए 2019 में एक बदलाव किया गया। इसमें PMLA की धारा 3 के तहत अपराध की आय में कोई भी संपत्ति शामिल है जो सीधे या परोक्ष तौर पर इससे जुड़े किसी भी अपराध के रास्ते से हासिल की गई है। इसका मतलब यह हुआ कि यह अधिनियम किसी एक आतंकवादी और कोई साधारण कार डीलर के बीच कोई फ़र्क नहीं करता, और किसी भी शख्स को चाहे अनजाने में ही, मनी लॉन्ड्रिंग के संदेह में गिरफ़्तार किया जा सकता है या उसकी संपत्ति को ज़ब्त या फ्रीज़ किया जा सकता है। PMLA के विशेषज्ञ वकील अभिमन्यु भंडारी कहते हैं, 'यह बेहद कठोर क़ानून है। गुरुग्राम में एक प्रापर्टी डीलर के ख़िलाफ़ धोखाधड़ी के मामले में एफआईआर दर्ज की जा सकती है, लेकिन आपने उससे कोई फ्लैट खरीदा है, तो ईडी उस अपराध की आय से जोड़कर आपको भी इसमें शामिल कर सकता है। इससे आप जिस किसी को चाहें फंसा सकते हैं।'

जुलाई 2022 में, PMLA के कुछ कड़े प्रावधानों को ख़त्म करने के बजाय सुप्रीम कोर्ट में जस्टिस ए.एम. खानविलकर की अध्यक्षता वाली तीन जजों की बैंच ने इस अधिनियम की संवैधानिकता को बरकरार रखा, यानी ईडी के जांच के अधिकारों और कड़े ज़मानत प्रावधानों की पुष्टि की। सुप्रीम कोर्ट ने ईडी अधिकारियों को पुलिस से अलग मानते हुए PMLA की धारा 50 को भी बनाए रखा, जो ईडी अधिकारियों को किसी भी व्यक्ति से शपथ लेकर बयान दर्ज करने का अधिकार देता है, जो अदालत में माने जाएंगे, जबकि पुलिस के पास यह अधिकार

नहीं है। यह फ़ैसला जस्टिस खानविलकर ने अपने सेवानिवृत होने से दो दिन पहले सुनाया था। जस्टिस खानविलकर उस बैंच का भी हिस्सा थे, जिसने 2002 के गुजरात दंगों में मारे गए पूर्व सांसद एहसान जाफरी की विधवा ज़किया जाफरी की याचिका ख़ारिज़ की थी। ज़किया जाफरी ने अपनी याचिका में गुजरात दंगों के मामलों में नरेन्द्र मोदी समेत चौसठ लोगों को क्लीन चिट मिलने को चुनौती दी थी। अदालत के फ़ैसले के आधार पर, गुजरात पुलिस ने अगले ही दिन सामाजिक कार्यकर्ता तीस्ता सीतलवाड़ और आईपीएस अफसर रहे आर.बी. श्रीकुमार को झूठे सबूत तैयार करने के आरोप में गिरफ्तार कर लिया। फरवरी 2024 में जस्टिस खानविलकर को भारत का लोकपाल बनाया गया, जो सेवानिवृति के बाद महत्वपूर्ण पद कहा जा सकता है। अपील दायर होने के बाद उनका पीएमएलए पर फ़ैसला सुप्रीम कोर्ट की संविधान पीठ के सामने समीक्षा के लिए है। समीक्षा प्रक्रिया में देरी से, अगस्त 2024 में सुप्रीम कोर्ट ने ज़ोर देकर यह कहा कि पीएमएलए मामलों में भी ज़मानत नियम है और जेल अपवाद है।

सुप्रीम कोर्ट के वरिष्ठ वकील और कार्यपालिका-न्यायपालिका गठजोड़ के मुखर आलोचक रहे दुष्यंत दवे ने कहा, 'पीएमएलए पर फ़ैसला सर्वोच्च न्यायालय पर एक काले धब्बे जैसा है। ईडी को अपने राजनीतिक आकाओं की सेवा के लिए एक हथियार बनाया गया है।' जस्टिस खानविलकर के फ़ैसले के बाद आई, दवे की चेतावनी दूरदर्शी साबित होगी। ईडी अब देश की सबसे ताकतवर और डर पैदा करने वाली एजेंसी बन गई है। इतनी बड़ी एजेंसी, लगभग हर बड़े संदिग्ध वित्तीय अपराध की जांच की निगरानी करती है। ऐसा 'नया भगवान', जो सबकुछ नियंत्रित करता है। सरकार को बस एक विनम्र लेकिन अपनी शक्तियों का बेरोकटोक इस्तेमाल करने वाले अफसर की ज़रूरत है, जो जैसा कि विपक्ष आरोप लगाता है, सरकार के राजनीतिक विरोधियों पर मुकदमा चलाने के लिए अपनी ताकत का इस्तेमाल करे। देश के बड़े नौकरशाही सिस्टम में ऐसा अफसर ढूंढना कोई मुश्किल काम नहीं है जो अपने मालिक की आवाज़ बन सके। मोदी सरकार को जल्दी ही ऐसा आदर्श चेहरा मिल जाएगा।

═

नब्बे के दशक में टी.एन. शेषन के आने से पहले बहुत कम लोग जानते थे कि देश के मुख्य चुनाव आयुक्त कौन हैं। शेषन ने चुनाव आयोग की ताकत और तस्वीर को शोहरत दिलाई। कम लोग ही जानते थे कि ईडी के प्रमुख कौन थे, जब तक कि गंजे, भारी मूंछों वाले, तेज़ निगाह वाले संजय मिश्रा ने नवम्बर 2018 में यह ज़िम्मेदारी नहीं संभाली थी। शेषन को ख़बरों में बने रहने में मज़ा आता था लेकिन ताकतवर मिश्रा ने सुर्खियों से दूर रहकर इस केन्द्रीय एजेंसी की छवि ही बदल दी। भारतीय राजस्व सेवा में 1984 बैच के अधिकारी, लखनऊ में जन्मे और बायोकेमेस्ट्री में डिग्री रखने वाले मिश्रा ने आयकर विभाग में सहायक निदेशक के तौर पर

अपना काम शुरू किया था। उनके सहयोगी उन्हें चुपचाप मगर अपने काम को बेहतर तरीके और सतर्कता से करने वाले अधिकारी के तौर पर याद करते हैं। 'वे नियमों के सख्त पाबंद हैं, जिन्हें कोई आसानी से धमका नहीं सकता, उनकी पसंद-नापसंद को बदलना आसान नहीं।'

इंडियन एक्सप्रेस में छपे उनके प्रोफाइल में एक घटना का ज़िक्र है कि कैसे उस वक्त आगरा-जयपुर डिवीजन के प्रभारी रहे ईडी के सहायक निदेशक मिश्रा ने 20 लाख रुपये के हवाला लेन-देन की सूचना पर छापा मारा था। कार्रवाई के दौरान जानकारी मिली कि संदिग्ध पाकिस्तान के सिंध से एक व्यवसायी था, जो धार्मिक उत्पीड़न की वजह से भागकर भारत आ गया था। मिश्रा ने मामला दर्ज कराते वक्त इस बात का ध्यान रखा कि संदिग्ध पर कठोर कार्रवाई न हो। ईडी पर नज़र रखने वाले एक पत्रकार का कहना है कि मिश्रा की छवि ईमानदार अधिकारी की होने का मतलब यह था कि राजधानी में अच्छे नेटवर्क वाले फिक्सर्स के लिए उन तक पहुंचना आसान नहीं था। पत्रकार के मुताबिक 'एक बिचौलिए ने एक बार दिवाली के उपहार के तौर पर उन्हें एक मंहगी घड़ी भेजी थी। मिश्रा ने उसे सख्त चेतावनी के साथ लौटा दिया कि आइंदा उन्हें रिश्वत देने की कोशिश न करें।'

मिश्रा प्रचार से दूर, मगर अपने काम पर हर वक्त निगाह के साथ तेज राजनीतिक समझ वाले ऐसे कुशल और शांत अधिकारी थे, जिन्हें खरीदना मुश्किल था, मोदी सरकार को इस महत्वपूर्ण एजेंसी को संभालने के लिए ऐसे ही अधिकारी की तलाश थी। दिलचस्प यह है कि मिश्रा ने 1994 से नौ साल तक अहमदाबाद में आयकर विभाग में जांच विभाग में ऐसा काम किया कि कांग्रेस और भाजपा नेताओं की नज़रों में आ गए। शुरुआती दौर में कांग्रेस के अहमद पटेल उनके राजनीतिक तौर पर संवेदनशील मामलों पर काम करने के तरीके से बहुत प्रभावित हुए। उन्हें पहला बड़ा मौका कांग्रेस सरकार में ही मिला, जब वित्त मंत्री प्रणब मुखर्जी के वक्त उन्हें वित्त मंत्रालय में संयुक्त सचिव बनाया गया।

2013 आते-आते जब दिल्ली में सत्ता के गलियारों में बदलाव की हवा महसूस होने लगी थी, तब मिश्रा ने तेजी से उभरती 'टीम-मोदी' के साथ संबंध बना लिए। कहा गया कि गुजरात के एक व्यावसायिक घराने ने इसमें अहम भूमिका निभाई। उनके एक सहयोगी ने कहा कि 'संजय लो-प्रोफाइल भले ही हैं लेकिन वे तेजतर्रार और महत्वाकांक्षी हैं और ऊपर बढ़ने के लिए राजनीतिक सीढ़ी के इस्तेमाल को समझते हैं।' जब 2018 में पहली बार उन्हें ईडी का निदेशक बनाया गया, तो कई लोगों ने उन्हें शक की निगाह से देखा क्योंकि उन्हें अब तक 'अहमद भाई के आदमी' के तौर पर देखा जाता था, लेकिन कुछ ही महीनों में संदेह के बादल छंट गए। विपक्षी नेताओं से जुड़े मामले अब तेज़ी से आगे बढ़ने लगे थे। जून 2020 में, ईडी की टीम ने अहमद पटेल के घर पर दस्तक दी। ईडी टीम देश से भाग चुके संदेसरा बंधुओं की एक बॉयोटेक कंपनी से जुड़े मनी लॉन्ड्रिंग मामले में पटेल का बयान दर्ज करने पहुंची थी। 'यह

महत्वपूर्ण फ़ैसला था, क्योंकि मिश्रा जानते थे कि टीम मोदी-शाह सबसे ज़्यादा अहमद पटेल को नापसंद करती थी। उन्हें यकीन था कि पटेल की वजह से ही सोनिया गांधी के निर्देश पर उन्हें गुजरात में परेशान किया गया।' ईडी पर नज़र रखने वाले शख़्स ने कहा कि 'ईडी के पटेल के दरवाजे तक पहुंचने के साथ ही मिश्रा ने वफादारी का आखिरी इम्तिहान पास कर लिया था।' साफ है कि मिश्रा समझते थे कि 'ब्रेड के किस तरफ मक्खन' लगाना है। उन्होंने अपने बॉस के हितों के लिए निष्ठा और निर्दयता से आगे बढ़ने का काम किया।

दो साल के कार्यकाल की नियुक्ति के बावजूद, उनका कार्यकाल तीन बार बढ़ाया गया और वे करीब पांच साल तक कुर्सी पर बने रहे। सुप्रीम कोर्ट ने उनके पहले एक्सटेंशन के बाद पद छोड़ने का आदेश दिया, तो मोदी सरकार नवम्बर 2021 में एक अध्यादेश लेकर आ गई, जिसमें ईडी निदेशक का कार्यकाल पांच साल तक बढ़ाने का अधिकार मिल गया, बाद में इसे संसद से पारित करा लिया गया। सुप्रीम कोर्ट ने जुलाई 2023 में, मिश्रा के कार्यकाल को बार-बार बढ़ाने के आदेश को अवैध ठहराया, लेकिन उन्हें सितम्बर तक काम करने की इज़ाजत दी क्योंकि सरकार ने अदालत में बताया कि मनी लॉन्ड्रिंग के मामलों पर निगाह रखने वाली अंतरराष्ट्रीय संस्था 'फाइनेंशियल एक्शन टॉस्क फोर्स' के मसले में मिश्रा की जानकारियों की ज़रूरत है। मिश्रा के रिटायर होने के बाद भी मोदी सरकार ने उनकी जगह किसी दूसरे को पूर्णकालिक निदेशक नहीं बनाया। वकील और एक्टिविस्ट प्रशांत भूषण कहते हैं, 'मिश्रा का कार्यकाल बार-बार बढ़ाने का मतलब साफ है कि मोदी सरकार ईडी निदेशक को विपक्षी नेताओं के ख़िलाफ़ कार्रवाई करने के लिए पुरस्कृत और प्रोत्साहित कर रही थी। लगता था कि अदालतें भी अपने आदेशों के इस दुरुपयोग को रोकने में बेबस सी लग रही हैं।'

मैंने मिश्रा से उनका पक्ष जानने के लिए कई संदेश भेजे, मगर वे मुलाकात के लिए तैयार नहीं हुए। उनके अधीन काम करने वाले एक अफसर ने कहा कि मिश्रा के कार्यकाल को एजेंसी के इतिहास में 'स्वर्णिम काल' के तौर पर देखा जाना चाहिए। एक अधिकारी ने दावा किया, 'हमारे लिए उनके निर्देश स्पष्ट थे: किसी को नहीं छोड़ना है। पीएमएलए क़ानून सख्त है, आपको दिखाना है कि आप इसके लिए गंभीर हैं।'

हालांकि पिछले एक दशक में ईडी के कामकाज का तरीका उसकी 'राजनीतिक' भूमिका पर सवाल खड़े करता है। सितम्बर 2022 में, *इंडियन एक्सप्रेस* की एक जांच रिपोर्ट से पता चलता है कि 2014 में मोदी सरकार आने के बाद से ईडी की जांच के दायरे में आए 121 राजनेताओं में से 95 फ़ीसदी 115 विपक्षी नेता थे। इन पर ईडी ने मामले दर्ज किए, छापे मारे, पूछताछ की या उन्हें गिरफ़्तार किया। जबकि यूपीए सरकार के 2004 से 2014 के दस साल में ईडी ने सिर्फ़ 26 नेताओं की जांच की, इनमें विपक्ष के 14 यानी 54 फ़ीसदी नेता शामिल थे। ईडी का अपनी सफाई में कहना है कि सभी मामले पूरी जांच के बाद ही दर्ज किए जाते हैं। ईडी के एक आला

अधिकारी का कहना है, 'मनी लॉन्ड्रिंग के ज़्यादातर मामलों में सुनवाई के बाद दोष साबित हुए हैं। अदालत ने हमारे सभी आरोप-पत्रों का संज्ञान लिया है। अगर यह राजनीतिक विद्वेष के मामले होते तो अदालत आरोपियों को बार-बार ज़मानत देने से इंकार करने के बजाय मामलों को खारिज़ कर देती।'

साल 2023 में जारी आंकड़ों में ईडी ने दावा किया कि उसने 2005 से आर्थिक अपराधों के लिए 5,906 मामले दर्ज किए, इनमें से जिन 25 मामलों की सुनवाई पूरी हुई उनमें से 24 में सज़ा मिली है। लेकिन सज़ा के ये आंकड़ें साफ तस्वीर पेश नहीं करते। पिछले सत्रह साल में एजेंसी केवल 0.42 फ़ीसद मामलों को ही निपटा पाई; बाकी ज़्यादातर मामले लंबी मुक़दमेबाज़ी और देरी में फंस गए, जिसमें लंबी 'प्रक्रिया ही सजा' बन गई। ईडी का तर्क है कि कुल दर्ज मामलो में से केवल 176 या सिर्फ़ तीन फ़ीसद में ही राजनेता शामिल हैं। ईडी के एक अधिकारी का कहना है, 'राजनेताओं के ख़िलाफ़ मामलों को मीडिया ज़ोर-शोर से दिखाता है, लेकिन उन दूसरे सैकड़ों लोगों की चर्चा नहीं होती, जिन पर हम कार्रवाई कर रहे हैं।' सरकार ने संसद में एक सवाल के जवाब में बताया कि 2014 से 2022 के आठ साल में ईडी के छापों में 27 गुना की बढ़ोतरी हुई है। इस दौरान 3,010 तलाशी की गई, जबकि यूपीए सरकार के 2004 से 2014 के बीच दस साल में सिर्फ 112 छापे पड़े थे। 'आपराधिक आमदनी' की कुर्की से यूपीए सरकार में जहां 5,436 करोड़ रुपये मिले, वो रकम मोदी सरकार में 1,00,000 करोड़ रुपये तक पहुंच गई। ईडी का दावा है कि 'हम पीएमएलए मामलों में ज़्यादा सक्रिय हो गए हैं, इसलिए हमें निशाना बनाया जा रहा है।'

हालांकि ईडी का यह तर्क राजनीतिक क्षेत्र में बेमानी लगता है। मामले दर मामले पर नज़र डाली जाए तो साफ हो जाता है कि इसके निशाने पर मौटे तौर पर विपक्षी राजनेता और उनकी सरकारें होती हैं, जिन्हें पीएमएलए के तहत शिकंजे में लिया जाता है, जबकि बीजेपी शासित सरकारों, बीजेपी नेताओं या दल बदलकर बीजेपी के साथ आनेवाले नेताओं के ख़िलाफ कार्रवाई अक्सर नहीं होती या दिखावा भर होती है। ऐसा लगता है कि ईडी एक सुनियोजित तरीके से काम करता है और सरकार के हथियार से ज़्यादा कुछ नहीं है जो विपक्ष पर फंदा डालने के लिए तैयार रहती है। कांग्रेस नेता और वरिष्ठ वकील अभिषेक मनु सिंघवी कहते हैं कि 'अगर राजनीति किसी खेल की टीम की तरह 'ग्यारह बनाम ग्यारह' का खेल होता तो हम इसे खेल सकते थे, लेकिन जब एक पक्ष के पास "बारहवां खिलाडी" (ईडी) होता है, जिसके पास आपके खिलाड़ी को कभी भी अयोग्य साबित करने की ताकत होती है या फिर अंपायर ही पक्षपात करता हो तो क्या हो सकता है?'

उदाहरण के तौर पर कर्नाटक कांग्रेस के कद्दावर नेता और उप-मुख्यमंत्री डी.के. शिवकुमार का ही मामला लें। 'डीके' नाम से लोकप्रिय नेता ने पिछले कुछ साल में एक 'साधन संपन्न'

राजनेता के रूप में अपनी प्रतिष्ठा बनाई थी, वे कांग्रेस के उन कुछ नेताओं में से हैं जिनकी पहुंच धनबल वाले बड़े लोगों तक है। साल 2017 में आयकर विभाग ने उनके बेंगलुरु और दिल्ली के घरों पर छापे मारे और 8.59 करोड़ बरामद करना बताया गया। खास बात यह है कि ये छापे उस वक्त मारे गए जब डीके ने गुजरात में एक अहम राज्यसभा चुनाव से पहले चवालीस विधायकों को बेंगलुरु के पास एक रिजॉर्ट तक पहुंचाने में महत्वपूर्ण भूमिका निभाई थी। यह मुकाबला गृहमंत्री अमित शाह और कांग्रेस नेता अहमद पटेल के बीच था। अहमद पटेल ने कड़े मुकाबले में जैसे ही मामूली अंतर से यह जीत हासिल की, डीके निशाने पर आ गए। आयकर छापों को आधार बनाकर उनके ख़िलाफ़ ईडी ने मनी लॉन्ड्रिंग का मामल दर्ज किया। डीके ने आरोप लगाया, 'कर्नाटक के भाजपा नेता ने उस समय चेताया था कि मुझे राजनीतिक तौर पर खत्म कर दिया जाएगा।'

एक साल बाद डीके फिर से एजेंसियों के निशाने पर आ गए। 2018 के विधानसभा चुनावों में कर्नाटक में त्रिशंकु विधानसभा बनी यानी किसी के पास सरकार बनाने के लिए स्पष्ट बहुमत नहीं था। बीजेपी सबसे बड़ी पार्टी बनकर तो उभरी थी, लेकिन उसे बहुमत के लिए नौ विधायकों की ज़रूरत थी। भारतीय जनता पार्टी के बी.एस. येदियुरप्पा सरकार बनाने का दावा पेश करने के लिए तैयार थे, लेकिन उन्हें कांग्रेस या जनता दल (सेक्युलर) के विधायकों के एक ग्रुप का समर्थन चाहिए था। डीके का आरोप है, 'भाजपा के एक वरिष्ठ नेता ने मुझसे संपर्क साधा और कहा कि अगर मैं अपने समर्थक विधायकों के साथ भाजपा के पक्ष में आ जाता हूं, तो मुझे उप-मुख्यमंत्री की कुर्सी और महत्वपूर्ण विभाग मिल जाएंगे और मेरे ख़िलाफ़ चल रहे मामले भी बंद हो जाएंगे। अगर मैंने साथ नहीं दिया तो मुझे जेल भेज दिया जाएगा।' कांग्रेस नेता ने यह प्रस्ताव स्वीकार नहीं किया। येदियुरप्पा की सरकार केवल तीन दिन चली और फिर जनता दल (सेक्युलर) और कांग्रेस ने मिलकर सरकार बना ली। लेकिन 2019 में जब भाजपा ने लोकसभा चुनावों में बड़ी जीत हासिल की, तो हालात बदल गए। इस बार डीके भी कांग्रेस को टूटने से नहीं रोक पाए। कर्नाटक में भाजपा की नई सरकार आने के कुछ हफ्तों बाद ही सितम्बर 2019 में, ईडी ने डीके को गिरफ़्तार कर लिया। एक महीने बाद उन्हें ज़मानत तो मिल गई, लेकिन उन्हें और उनके परिवार के दूसरे सदस्यों को लगभग हर हफ्ते एजेंसियों के समन मिलते रहे। डीके कहते हैं, 'एक दिन सीबीआई, अगले दिन आयकर विभाग तो फिर ईडी... यहां तक कि मेरी बेटी को भी नहीं बख्शा गया।'

डीके एक हवाईअड्डे के लाउंज में एक वरिष्ठ केन्द्रीय मंत्री से अचानक हुई मुलाक़ात का ज़िक्र करते हैं, जहां उन्हें 2018 में भाजपा से हाथ मिलाने से इंकार करने की याद दिलाई गई। डीके दावा करते हैं, 'मुझे साफतौर पर बताया गया कि मुझे भाजपा नेतृत्व की अवहेलना करने

और कांग्रेस से नाता नहीं तोड़ने की कीमत चुकानी पड़ रही है।' मार्च 2023 में, सुप्रीम कोर्ट ने डीके के ख़िलाफ़ मनी लॉन्ड्रिंग के मामले को ख़ारिज़ करते हुए कहा कि ईडी बरामद मनी के स्रोत को मनी लॉन्ड्रिंग के तौर पर साबित नहीं कर पाया।

अब डीके के मामले की तुलना अगर असम के मुख्यमंत्री हिमंत बिस्वा सरमा से करें। सरमा भी कांग्रेस के एक 'साधन संपन्न' नेता रहे, जो गांधी परिवार से मतभेद के बाद 2016 के विधानसभा चुनावों से ठीक पहले भाजपा में शामिल हो गए थे। महत्वाकांक्षी सरमा को कांग्रेस आलाकमान से उम्मीद थी कि लंबे समय से राज्य के मुख्यमंत्री रहे तरुण गोगोई का उत्तराधिकारी उन्हें बनाया जाएगा, लेकिन नेतृत्व से कोई आश्वासन नहीं मिल रहा था। सरमा भी डीके की तरह 'अच्छे नेटवर्क' वाले नेता हैं और उनके बहुत से व्यापारिक हित जुड़े रहे हैं। जब वे गोगोई सरकार में मंत्री थे, तब सरमा को भाजपा ने 'चिटफंड मामले' और 'गुवाहाटी के जल आपूर्ति परियोजना घोटाले' में शामिल होने का आरोप लगाया था। इस मामले में अमेरिकी बहुराष्ट्रीय कंपनी लुइस बर्जर इंटरनेशनल द्वारा राजनेताओं को कथित रूप से रिश्वत दी गई थी। सीबीआई ने 2014 में चिटफंड मामले में सरमा से पूछताछ की थी और छापे मारे थे, लेकिन उनके भाजपा में शामिल होने के बाद जांच रुक गई। लुइस बर्जर मामले में भी किसी केन्द्रीय एजेंसी ने उनसे पूछताछ नहीं की। सरमा के पाला बदलने के बाद न तो सीबीआई और न ही ईडी ने कथित घोटाले की जांच को आगे बढ़ाने में दिलचस्पी दिखाई। सरमा कहते हैं, 'इस मामले में मेरा नाम कभी भी किसी फाइल रिकॉर्ड में आरोपी के तौर पर नहीं था, यह सिर्फ़ मेरी छवि खराब करने की कोशिश है।' उनके दोस्तों से अब दुश्मन बने कांग्रेसी नेताओं के लिए यह वॉशिंग मशीन राजनीति का बेहतरीन उदाहरण है। 'भाजपा 2015 में एक बुकलैट जारी करती हैं, जिसमें सरमा का नाम घोटाले में मुख्य आरोपी के तौर पर होता है और जब वह पार्टी में शामिल हो जाते हैं तो किसी को यह मामला याद नहीं रहता। अगर यह वॉशिंग मशीन नहीं है तो क्या है?' असम से कांग्रेस के सांसद गौरव गोगोई सवाल करते हैं।

प्रवर्तन एजेंसियों का दावा भले ही यह हो कि इन मामलों में जांच बंद नहीं हुई है, लेकिन लगता है कि प्रदेश और राष्ट्रीय राजनीति को प्रभावित करने के लिए ईडी की शक्तियों का दुरुपयोग किया जा रहा है। हकीकत यह है कि विपक्षी नेताओं को निशाना बनाने वाले मामलों में ईडी ज़्यादा सक्रिय रहा, जबकि सत्ता में बैठे किसी राजनेता के उस खेमे में गए लोगों के ख़िलाफ़ मामलों में उसने चुप्पी सी साध ली। इससे विपक्षी पार्टियों की सरकारों को अस्थिर करने के मोदी सरकार के नापाक इरादे दिखाई देते हैं। यहां तक कि ईडी के नोटिस, छापे की कार्रवाई और गिरफ्तारी का समय यह सब भी राजनीतिक कैलेंडर से मेल खाता है।

ईडी केसबुक के कुछ उदाहरणः

- मार्च 2024 में, लोकसभा चुनावों के ऐलान के कुछ दिनों में, दिल्ली के मुख्यमंत्री अरविन्द केजरीवाल को शराब नीति जांच में ईडी ने गिरफ़्तार कर लिया। प्रवर्तन निदेशालय अगस्त 2022 से इस कथित रिश्वत मामले की जांच कर रहा था और फरवरी 2023 में दिल्ली के उप-मुख्यमंत्री मनीष सिसोदिया समेत आप के कई नेताओं को पहले ही गिरफ़्तार कर चुका था। केजरीवाल ने इन चुनावों के लिए दिल्ली की सभी सात सीटों पर कांग्रेस के साथ चुनावी गठबंधन किया था। केजरीवाल ने आरोप लगाया, 'एक बड़े अधिकारी ने मेरी टीम से साफतौर पर कहा था कि अगर मैं कांग्रेस के साथ गठबंधन तोड़ता हूं तो मुझे गिरफ्तार नहीं किया जाएगा।' ईडी ने इसके जवाब में कहा कि केजरीवाल को पूछताछ के लिए नौ समन जारी किए गए थे, लेकिन मुख्यमंत्री किसी पर भी पेश नहीं हुए। इस मामले में कोई नकद बरामदगी नहीं हुई और न ही पैसे को लेकर कोई सुराग मिला लेकिन ईडी ने ज़ोर देकर कहा कि केजरीवाल से पूछताछ से उनकी भूमिका का पता चलेगा।
- मार्च 2024 में, शराब मामले में ही तेलंगाना के पूर्व मुख्यमंत्री और भारत राष्ट्र समिति (बीआरएस) के प्रमुख के. चन्द्रशेखर राव की बेटी के. कविता को भी गिरफ़्तार किया गया। 2023 में तेलंगाना के विधानसभा चुनावों से पहले, बीआरएस-बीजेपी के चुनावों के बाद गठबंधन की चर्चाएं जोरों पर थी, उस दौरान ईडी ने कई बार पूछताछ के बावजूद के. कविता को गिरफ़्तार नहीं किया। बीआरएस की विधानसभा चुनावों में हार के बाद ईडी फिर से सक्रिय हो गई। के. कविता ने अपनी गिरफ़्तारी को अवैध बताया और सभी आरोपों से इंकार किया। ईडी का दावा है कि उन्होंने केजरीवाल और उप-मुख्यमंत्री मनीष सिसोदिया को 100 करोड़ रुपये की रिश्वत देने की बात 'कबूल' की है।
- जुलाई 2020 में, राजस्थान में जब मुख्यमंत्री अशोक गहलोत की सरकार को उनके उप-मुख्यमंत्री सचिन पायलट की बगावत का सामना करना पड़ा, तब ईडी ने 2007-09 में उर्वरक मामले में कथित गड़बड़ी की जांच के सिलसिले में गहलोत के भाई अग्रसेन के यहां छापा मारा। कांग्रेस का आरोप था कि इस 'छापा राज' को केन्द्र ने गहलोत सरकार को गिराने की कोशिश के लिए किया था। अक्टूबर 2023 में, राजस्थान विधानसभा चुनावों से कुछ हफ्ते पहले, मुख्यमंत्री के बेटे वैभव गहलोत को विदेशी मुद्रा के लेनदेन के आरोप में ईडी ने तलब किया।
- फरवरी 2021 में, पश्चिम बंगाल विधानसभा चुनाव के कुछ हफ्ते पहले सीबीआई और फिर ईडी ने कोयला चोरी मामले के आरोप में तृणमूल कांग्रेस के नेता और सांसद

अभिषेक बनर्जी की पत्नी रुजिरा बनर्जी को समन भेजा। बनर्जी से इस बारे में कई बार पूछताछ के बावजूद यह मामला अभी तक चल रहा है।

- अगस्त 2023 में, विधानसभा चुनावों से ऐन पहले छत्तीसगढ़ के मुख्यमंत्री भूपेश बघेल के करीबी सहयोगियों पर ईडी के छापे मारे गए। इनमें बघेल के फाइनेंसर भी शामिल थे, यानी ऐसे महत्वपूर्ण समय में इसे कांग्रेस के फंड को कमज़ोर करने की कोशिश कहा जा सकता है। मतदान से कुछ दिन पहले ईडी ने एक बयान जारी किया कि वह दुबई में 'ऑनलाइन सट्टेबाज़ी साइट' की जांच के सिलसिले में बघेल को 508 करोड़ रुपये रिश्वत के आरोप की जांच कर रही है। ईडी ने दावा किया कि साइट का इस्तेमाल बेनामी बैंक खातों से पैसा निकालने के लिए किया जा रहा था। मुख्यमंत्री बघेल ने अपने बचाव में जोर देकर कहा कि उनकी सरकार ने इस मामले में पहले ही 72 एफआईआर दर्ज की हैं और केन्द्र से आरोपियों के ख़िलाफ़ कार्रवाई करने को कहा है, लेकिन उनके इस बचाव के आने तक देर हो गई थी। भारतीय जनता पार्टी की मीडिया टीम ने पहले ही व्हाट्सएप ग्रुप और स्थानीय न्यूज़ चैनलों पर बघेल के दुबई कनेक्शन की खबरें दे दी थीं। बघेल के एक सहयोगी का कहना था कि 'छत्तीसगढ़ में वरिष्ठ भाजपा नेताओं की तस्वीरें इस महादेव ऐप प्रमोटरों के साथ हैं, जिनमें एक राज्यपाल भी शामिल हैं, फिर भी चुनावों के दौरान हमें कटघरे में खड़ा किया गया।'
- फरवरी 2024 में, आम चुनावों से ठीक पहले, ईडी ने झारंखड मुक्ति मोर्चा के नेता और मुख्यमंत्री हेमंत सोरेन को कथित ज़मीन घोटाले में गिरफ़्तार किया। कांग्रेस के साथ प्रदेश में सरकार चला रहे सोरेन का आरोप था कि उन्होंने इससे पहले पाला बदलने के कई प्रस्तावों को ठुकरा दिया था। भाजपा ने 2023 में उनकी सरकार को गिराने की नाकाम कोशिश की थी। सोरेन को ज़मानत देते हुए झारखंड हाईकोर्ट ने कहा, यह मानने के कारण हैं कि सोरेन पीएमएलए मामले के दोषी नहीं थे, जिनका उन पर आरोप लगाया गया था।

इससे ठीक उलट, जो विपक्षी नेता भारतीय जनता पार्टी में शामिल हो गए, या उनके साथ गठबंधन कर लिया, तो उन्हें क़ानून से सुरक्षा मिली हुई है। अप्रैल 2024 में, *इंडियन एक्सप्रेस* में छपी रिपोर्ट में बताया गया कि कैसे भ्रष्टाचार के मामलों की जांच का सामना कर रहे 25 विपक्षी नेताओं में से 23 को राहत मिल गई, ये नेता भाजपा में शामिल हो गए थे। उनके ख़िलाफ़ मामलों की जांच या तो धीमी कर दी गई या फिर उन्हें ठंडे बस्ते में डाल दिया गया।

- सितम्बर 2021 में, ईडी ने पश्चिम बंगाल में नारद स्टिंग मामले में नकद लेनदेन में उनकी कथित भूमिका को लेकर तृणमूल कांग्रेस के कई नेताओं के ख़िलाफ़ मनी लॉन्ड्रिंग के मामले दायर किए गए। इनमें एक अहम नाम सुवेन्दु अधिकारी का गायब था, जो दिसम्बर 2020 में, टीएमसी से अलग हो गए और विधानसभा चुनावों में भाजपा का प्रमुख चेहरा बन गए। इससे पहले उनका नाम सीबीआई चार्जशीट में था और उनकी फाइल को लोकसभा अध्यक्ष के पास मंजूरी के लिए छोड़ दिया गया।
- 2018 में, आंध्रप्रदेश में तेलुगुदेशम पार्टी (टीडीपी) के नेता और राज्यसभा सांसद सी.एम. रमेश की संपत्तियों पर आयकर छापे मारे गए थे, उस वक्त टीडीपी भाजपा से अलग हो गई थी। रमेश से जुड़ी एक फर्म पर 100 करोड़ रुपये की हेराफेरी का आरोप था। जून 2019 में, रमेश टीडीपी छोड़कर भाजपा में शामिल हो गए। फिर मामले में आगे कोई कार्रवाई नहीं होने पर रमेश ने 2024 का चुनाव भाजपा के टिकट पर लड़ा और जीत हासिल की।
- मार्च 2024 में, सीबीआई ने महाराष्ट्र में एनसीपी के वरिष्ठ नेता प्रफुल्ल पटेल के ख़िलाफ़ भ्रष्टाचार के मामले की जांच बंद कर दी। पटेल पर यूपीए सरकार के दौरान केन्द्रीय विमानन मंत्री रहते हुए एयरक्राफ्ट लीज में अनियमितता का आरोप था। जुलाई 2023 में अजित पवार वाले एनसीपी गुट के भाजपा के साथ जाने में प्रफुल्ल पटेल की अहम भूमिका रही थी।
- नवम्बर 2020 में, पंजाब के पूर्व मुख्यमंत्री कैप्टन अमरिंदर सिंह के बेटे रणिंदर सिंह से ईडी ने मनी लॉन्ड्रिंग के आरोप में पूछताछ की थी। एक साल बाद अमरिंदर सिंह ने कांग्रेस छोड़ दी और फिर भाजपा में शामिल हो गए। उसके बाद से उनके बेटे के ख़िलाफ़ मामला आगे नहीं बढ़ा।

वरिष्ठ वकील और राजनेता कपिल सिब्बल कहते हैं कि 'केन्द्रीय एजेंसियों खासतौर से ईडी के कामकाज को समझने के लिए आपको बस हर मामले के घटनाक्रम को देखना होगा। यह सत्तारूढ़ दल की ऐसी अराजक शक्ति है जो किसी नियम या सीमा को नहीं जानती, यह विरोधियों के ख़िलाफ काम करती है और अपने लोगों पर इसकी नज़र नहीं जाती। सवाल है कि ऐसा कैसा होता है कि भाजपा सांसदों और विधायकों को छुआ तक नहीं जाता, जबकि विपक्षी नेताओं को परेशान किया जाता है?'

दिलचस्प यह है कि 2019 के बाद से ईडी ने अपनी असली ताकत दिखाना शुरू किया। यह बदलाव नॉर्थ ब्लॉक में सत्ता परिवर्तन के साथ हुआ, जब राजनीतिक रूप से कमज़ोर निर्मला सीतारमण को अरुण जेटली की जगह वित्त मंत्रालय मिला और अमित शाह ने राजनाथ सिंह

की जगह गृह मंत्रालय संभाला। जेटली-सिंह के दौरान ईडी अपेक्षाकृत थोड़ा शांत तरीके से काम कर रही थी, लेकिन अमित शाह के आने के बाद इसे रोकना मुमकिन नहीं था। वैसे तो आधिकारिक तौर पर प्रवर्तन निदेशालय (ईडी) वित्त मंत्रालय में राजस्व विभाग के अधीन काम करता है, लेकिन अब कथित तौर पर वह सीधे गृहमंत्री से आदेश ले रहा था।

इसे इस मामले से समझिए, अगस्त 2019 में, मोदी सरकार के दोबारा शपथ लेने कुछ महीनों बाद वरिष्ठ कांग्रेस नेता पी. चिदंबरम की गिरफ़्तारी होती है। यूपीए सरकार में वित्त और गृहमंत्री रहे चिदंबरम पर 2014 से कार्रवाई की तलवार लटक रही थी, लेकिन राजनीतिक विरोधी होने के बावजूद वरिष्ठ वकील रहे वित्त मंत्री अरुण जेटली और चिदंबरम एक ही क़ानूनी बिरादरी के हिस्सा थे और एक-दूसरे से मिलते-जुलते रहते थे; जेटली की बेटी की शादी के समारोह में चिदंबरम एक प्रमुख मेहमान रहे थे। सीबीआई ने पहले 2017 में चिदंबरम के आवास पर छापा मारा, लेकिन गिरफ़्तारी नहीं की थी। गृहमंत्री शाह को लगता था कि जुलाई 2010 में, एक फर्जी मुठभेड़ मामले में सीबीआई ने जब उन्हें गिरफ्तार किया था तो इसमें गृहमंत्री रहे चिदंबरम का हाथ था। उस वक्त उन्हें तीन महीने से ज़्यादा जेल में रहना पड़ा था। गुजरात भाजपा के एक नेता ने कहा, 'मोदी जी और अमित भाई दोनों की याददाश्त अच्छी है, वे आसानी से भूलते या माफ़ नहीं करते हैं।' चिदंबरम को सीबीआई ने 21 अगस्त 2019 को गिरफ़्तार किया था। इसके पांच दिन बाद गंभीर रूप से बीमार चल रहे जेटली का निधन हो गया था। 55 दिन जेल में रहने के बाद ईडी ने फिर से उन्हें पूछताछ के लिए हिरासत में ले लिया और चिदंबरम को 105 दिन जेल में बिताने पड़े, जो 2010 में अमित शाह की कैद से 12 दिन ज़्यादा थे। शाह को इस 'जीत' के लिए नौ साल तक इंतज़ार करना पड़ा।

पूर्व वित्त मंत्री चिदंबरम के ख़िलाफ़ मामला 2007 का है, जब सीबीआई और ईडी आईएनएक्स मीडिया को 'विदेशी निवेश संवर्धन बोर्ड' (एफआईपीबी) की मंज़ूरी में कथित अनियमितताओं की जांच कर रहे थे। इस कंपनी का मालिकाना हक पीटर मुखर्जी और इंद्राणी मुखर्जी के पास था। 2015 में पीटर मुखर्जी, इंद्राणी की बेटी शीना बोरा की हत्या में मुख्य आरोपी हो गए। जुलाई 2019 में, मुकदमे का सामना कर रही इंद्राणी अचानक आईएनएक्स मामले में सरकारी गवाह बन गईं और दावा किया कि उन्होंने एफआईपीबी मंज़ूरी को ठीक करने के लिए चिदंबरम के बेटे कार्ति चिदंबरम को रिश्वत दी थी। चिदंबरम इस मामले पर बात नहीं करना चाहते, लेकिन उनके सहयोगी ने कहा, 'कल्पना कीजिए कि एक पूर्व गृहमंत्री को हत्या के आरोपी के संदिग्ध दावों के आधार पर गिरफ्तार किया जाए, जबकि एफआईपीबी फ़ाइल की मंज़ूरी पर वित्त मंत्रालय के आला अफसरों के दस्तख़त थे।' ईडी के एक अधिकारी का कहना है कि 'पिता-पुत्र की जोड़ी के ख़िलाफ़ मामला सबूतों पर आधारित है और उसकी जांच चल रही है।' आधिकारिक मंत्रः 'कुछ भी बंद नहीं हुआ है।' दिलचस्प यह भी है कि

चिदंबरम पर आरोप लगाने वाली इंद्राणी मुखर्जी को 2022 में ज़मानत मिल गई और हाल में नेटफ्लिक्स पर उनसे जुड़ी एक डॉक्यूमेंट्री भी बनी।

राजनीतिक कारणों से ईडी जांच का एक बहुचर्चित मामला गांधी परिवार से जुड़ा है। जून 2022 में, सोनिया गांधी और राहुल गांधी को *नेशनल हेराल्ड* मामले में मनी लॉन्ड्रिंग के आरोपों पर एजेंसी के सामने पेश होने के लिए नोटिस भेजे गए। इस मामले की शुरुआत 2013 में तब हुई, जब भाजपा नेता डॉ. सुब्रह्मनियम स्वामी ने एक ट्रायल कोर्ट में शिकायत दर्ज कराई, जिसमें गांधी परिवार पर *नेशनल हेराल्ड* अखबार और संपत्ति के अधिग्रहण में धोखाधड़ी और पैसे के दुरुपयोग के आरोप लगाए गए थे। स्वामी का आरोप था कि गांधी परिवार ने अखबार के पूर्ववर्ती प्रकाशकों, एसोसिएटेड जर्नल्स लिमिटेड को 'यंग इंडिया' नाम के एक 'नॉट फॉर प्रोफिट' संगठन के माध्यम से खरीदा था, जिसमें उनकी सबसे बड़ी हिस्सेदारी थी। हर दिन बदलते स्वभाव के स्वामी का गांधी परिवार से उतार-चढ़ाव भरा रिश्ता रहा है। हालांकि उन्होंने राजीव गांधी के करीबी होने का दावा किया था, लेकिन वे पिछले कई साल से सोनिया गांधी पर हमले करते रहे हैं। 1999 में स्वामी ने सोनिया गांधी और अखिल भारतीय द्रविड़ मुनेत्र कड़गम (एआईएडीएमके) की नेता और पांच बार तमिलनाडु की मुख्यमंत्री रही जे. जयललिता के लिए एक 'चाय-पार्टी' का आयोजन किया था। इस मुलाकात का नतीजा वाजपेयी सरकार का गिरना रहा, मगर यह मेल-मिलाप ज़्यादा दिन नहीं चला और स्वामी फिर से गांधी परिवार के ख़िलाफ़ जंग पर निकल पड़े।

एक 'खतरनाक दुश्मन' के तौर पर पहचान रखने वाले डॉ. स्वामी *नेशनल हेराल्ड* मामले में कार्रवाई की मांग करते रहे। मनी लॉन्ड्रिंग के आरोपों की जांच कर रही ईडी ने 2015 की शुरुआत में मामले को बंद कर दिया, लेकिन कुछ महीनों बाद इसे फिर से खोल दिया। दिसम्बर 2015 में, सोनिया और राहुल गांधी को ज़मानत मिल गई, लेकिन पीएमएलए मामला लंबे समय तक चलता रहा। गांधी परिवार के वकील रहे सिंघवी कहते हैं, 'यह सिर्फ़ पागलपन है। किसी भी संपत्ति का हस्तांतरण नहीं हुआ, किसी एक ने भी धोखे की शिकायत नहीं की और फिर भी ईडी मामले को बंद करने को तैयार नहीं है।' ईडी अधिकारियों ने दावा किया कि अभी जांच जारी है और जब तक जांच पूरी नहीं हो जाती, तब तक मामले को बंद नहीं किया जा सकता।

मामला तब बढ़ गया, जब मां-बेटे सोनिया-राहुल दोनों को जून 2022 में, ईडी मुख्यालय में पूछताछ के लिए बुलाया गया। अब तक, मोदी सरकार और कांग्रेस के बीच बढ़ती दुश्मनी के बावजूद गांधी परिवार को नहीं छुआ गया था। कांग्रेस नेता शक्ति सिंह गोहिल का कहना था, 'उन्हें बुलाना प्रधानमंत्री की प्रतिशोध की कार्रवाई थी, क्योंकि मोदी को 2002 के दंगों के मामले में जांचकर्ताओं ने बुलाया था।' गोहिल का इशारा 2002 के गुजरात दंगों की साज़िश के आरोपों की जांच कर रही विशेष जांच टीम (एसआईटी) की मोदी से दिनभर की पूछताछ

की ओर था। मोदी ने जहां पूछताछ में आठ घंटे बिताए थे, तो राहुल गांधी से चार दिनों तक पूछताछ में 36 घंटे से ज्यादा लगे। गांधी परिवार की लीगल टीम के एक सदस्य का कहना था, 'तथ्य यह है कि ईडी के पास केवल दो पन्नों की प्रश्नावली थी और उन्हीं सवालों को बार-बार चार दिनों तक पूछा गया। यानी यह केवल उन्हें परेशान करने और डराने के लिए था।' कहा जाता है कि ईडी अक्सर पूछताछ को लंबा खींचता है और पूछताछों के बीच भी अंतराल ज़्यादा रखा जाता है ताकि आरोपी को तनाव में रखा जा सके। ईडी पर नज़र रखने वाले एक पत्रकार के मुताबिक, एक मामले में अपनी ताकत का अहसास कराने के लिए ईडी अधिकारियों ने एक आरोपी को पूछताछ कक्ष में करीब 6 घंटे तक बैंच पर खड़ा रखा था, हालांकि ईडी ने इस आरोप को ख़ारिज़ किया।

करीब एक महीने बाद, सोनिया गांधी से तीन दिनों तक पूछताछ की गई, लेकिन इस बार ईडी की टीम ने सहूलियत के साथ काम किया। श्रीमती गांधी की तबियत खराब थी और उनका अस्पताल आना-जाना लगा रहता था। ईडी मुख्यालय में सोनिया गांधी के साथ जाने वाले प्रियंका गांधी के एक सहयोगी ने कहा, 'हमने ईडी अधिकारियों को चेतावनी दी थी कि अगर सोनिया जी को कुछ हुआ तो वे इसके जवाबदेह होंगे।' गांधी परिवार लंबे समय तक चली इस पूछताछ के दौरान शांत दिख रहा था, लेकिन कमजोर कांग्रेस को इससे ऊर्जा मिल गई। कांग्रेस पार्टी के कार्यकर्ता और नेता सड़कों पर उतर आए, विरोध प्रदर्शन किए गए और गिरफ़्तारियां दी गईं। इस दौरान मीडिया, गांधी परिवार के भविष्य पर अटकलें लगाने लगा था। अभिषेक सिंघवी कहते हैं, 'एक बात साफ कर दें: यह मामला गिरफ़्तारी या दोष साबित करने का नही था, क्योंकि इसमें ऐसा कुछ था ही नहीं। इसका मकसद सिर्फ़ राजनीतिक माहौल को गर्म रखना है, सुर्खियों में रहना है।' इस मामले में गिरफ़्तारी क्यों नहीं की गई, के सवाल पर ईडी अधिकारियों ने चुप्पी साध ली: 'इंतज़ार कीजिए, और देखिए; अभी क़ानूनी प्रक्रिया चल रही है।'

एक सबसे ताकतवर जांच एजेंसी के ऐसे जवाब उसके अपारदर्शी तरीके से काम करने को बताता है, जो किसी के प्रति जवाबदेह नहीं लगती। मसला चाहे गांधी परिवार का हो या फिर किसी और विपक्षी नेता का, ईडी की कार्रवाई के दायरे में, उसे दोषी ठहराया गया हो या रिहा किया गया हो, कोई खास फर्क नहीं पड़ता। दरअसल क्रिमिनल लॉ में, खासतौर से पीएमएलए के तहत इसके कड़े जमानत प्रावधानों और अपराधों के बड़े दायरे में, 'प्रक्रिया ही सज़ा' है। मार्च 2023 में, चौदह विपक्षी दलों ने सुप्रीम कोर्ट के दरवाज़े पर दस्तक दी। कहा गया कि जिन नेताओं ने मोदी सरकार के ख़िलाफ़ आवाज़ उठाने की हिम्मत की, केन्द्र सरकार उन विपक्षी नेताओं को गिरफ़्तार करने और उनके ख़िलाफ़ आपराधिक कार्रवाई शुरू करने के लिए ईडी का मनमाने ढंग से इस्तेमाल कर रही है। याचिका में कहा गया कि नेताओं की गिरफ्तारी से पहले और बाद के लिए दिशा-निर्देश जारी किए जाएं। याचिका को ख़ारिज़ करते हुए मुख्य

न्यायाधीश जस्टिस डी.वाई. चन्द्रचूड़ ने कहा कि 'राजनेता भी नागरिक हैं और सबके लिए एक ही क़ानून है। ऐसे देश में जहां लाखों लोग सालों से विचाराधीन हैं, उसमें राजनेताओं को विशेष अधिकार या छूट नहीं दी जा सकती।' मुख्य न्यायाधीश का रुख बेबाक था। हालांकि, आदेश का मतलब उस सिस्टम में कोई ढील नहीं है जहां सत्ता में बैठे लोगों को संरक्षित रखा जाए और विपक्षी नेताओं को दबाव का सामना करना पड़ रहा है। सिंघवी कहते हैं, 'ईडी की भेदभावपूर्ण कार्रवाईयों से साफ है कि अब लोकतंत्र की सबके लिए बराबर की अवधारणा के लिए जगह नहीं बची है। उम्मीद है कि अदालतें भी इसे एक दिन महसूस करेंगी।'

सबके लिए 'बराबर सुविधा' यानी (लेवल प्लेइंग फील्ड) चुनावी लोकतंत्र की मूल अवधारणा मानी जाती हैं। क़ानून के सामने सब बराबर के संवैधानिक सिद्धांत को मोदी सरकार के दस साल में थोड़ा-थोड़ा करके ख़त्म किया गया है। ईडी की चुन-चुनकर की जाने वाली कार्रवाई का मतलब साफ है कि विपक्षी दलों की कोई सरकार राहत की सांस नहीं ले पा रही है क्योंकि वे लगातार गिरफ़्तारी के खतरे को महसूस कर रहे हैं। फरवरी 2024 में, समाचार वेबसाइट 'द न्यूज़ मिनट' और 'न्यूज़लॉन्ड्री' की जांच से पता चलाः

साल 2018-19 और 2022-23 के बीच भारतीय जनता पार्टी को करीब 335 करोड़ रुपये का चंदा देने वाली कम से कम तीस कंपनियों को इस दौरान केन्द्रीय एजेंसियों की जांच का सामना करना पड़ा था।

- इनमें से कम से कम 23 कंपनियों ने 2014 से लेकर जब उन पर छापेमारी की गई, उस बीच भाजपा को कोई चंदा नहीं दिया था।
- इनमें से चार कंपनियों ने केन्द्रीय एजेंसियों की जांच के दौरान चार महीनों में कुल 9.05 करोड़ का चंदा दिया।
- इनमें से जो छह कंपनियां पहले से ही चंदा दे रही थीं, छापों के बाद और ज़्यादा चंदा दिया।
- छह ऐसी कंपनियां भी थीं, जिन्होंने पहले तो भाजपा को चंदा दिया, लेकिन पिछले एक साल में चंदा नहीं देने के बाद केन्द्रीय एजेंसी की जांच का सामना कर रही थीं।
- इनमें से केवल तीन कंपनियों ने इस दौरान कांग्रेस को चंदा दिया।

मार्च 2024 में, सुप्रीम कोर्ट ने भारतीय स्टेट बैंक को 'इलेक्टोरल बॉन्ड' के माध्यम से राजनीतिक दलों को मिले पैसे की जानकारी देने का आदेश किया। इन बॉन्ड्स की पचास फ़ीसदी से ज़्यादा रकम भाजपा को मिली थी। इससे साफ है कि चुनावी राजनीति में कोई बराबरी का खेल नहीं होता, कोई लेवल प्लेइंग फील्ड नहीं है। एक बार फिर ईडी कार्रवाई से जुड़े संभावित

लेन-देन का तरीका स्पष्ट हो जाता है। 2019 और 2024 के बीच चुनावी बॉन्ड खरीदने वाली शीर्ष तीस कंपनियों में से कम से कम चौदह कंपनियों पर केन्द्रीय या राज्य की जांच एजेंसियां कार्रवाई कर रही थीं।

- तमिलनाडु की लॉटरी कंपनी 'फ्यूचर गेमिंग एंड होटल्स प्राइवेट लिमिटेड' की ईडी जांच कर रही थी, इस कंपनी ने 1,368 करोड़ रुपये के इलेक्टॉरल बॉन्ड खरीदे थे। ईडी ने मनी लॉन्ड्रिंग के मामले में इस कंपनी की 409 करोड़ रुपये की संपत्ति ज़ब्त की थी। फ्यूचर गेमिंग के बॉन्ड के पैसे का एक बड़ा हिस्सा चेन्नई में डीएमके सरकार और बंगाल में तृणमूल कांग्रेस को दिया गया था। यह इस बात का सबूत है कि समझौता करने वाले व्यवसायी सत्ता के साथ रहते हैं चाहे वो राज्य सरकार हो या फिर केन्द्र।
- ग्यारह इन्फ्रास्ट्रक्चर कंपनियों ने ईडी या सीबीआई की जांच कार्रवाई के तुरंत बाद 506 करोड़ रुपये के बॉन्ड खरीदे।
- तेलंगाना में 'मेघा इंजीनियरिंग एंड इन्फ्रास्ट्रक्चर लिमिटेड' ने 584 करोड़ रुपये के इलेक्टॉरल बॉन्ड खरीदे, यह भाजपा को चंदा देने वाली सबसे बड़ी कंपनी थी। 2019 में, ईडी और आयकर विभाग ने इस कंपनी की जांच की थी और अब यह देशभर में इन्फ्रास्ट्रक्चर की कई बड़ी योजनाओं पर काम कर रही है।
- हैदराबाद के व्यवसायी सरथ रेड्डी की कंपनी अरबिंदो फार्मा ने भाजपा को बॉन्ड से 25 करोड रुपये का चंदा दिया। दिलचस्प बात यह है कि मई 2023 में ईडी ने, दिल्ली शराब मामले में उनकी ज़मानत का विरोध नहीं किया था और कुछ महीनों बाद, जब रेड्डी सरकारी गवाह बन गए, तो उनकी गवाही का इस्तेमाल दिल्ली के मुख्यमंत्री अरविंद केजरीवाल को गिरफ़्तार करने के लिए किया गया।

एक मीडिया कार्यक्रम में इस मुद्दे को लेकर सवाल पर वित्त मंत्री निर्मला सीतारमण ने कहा, 'मुझे लगता है कि आप यह कयासबाजी कर रहे हैं कि ईडी के छापे या कार्रवाई या उन्हें बचाने के बदले कंपनियां यह चंदा देती हैं। आप शायद जानते हैं कि उन्होंने चंदा दिया, इसके बावजूद ईडी की कार्रवाई उन पर चल रही है।' पूर्व वित्त मंत्री पी. चिदंबरम ने जवाब में कहा, 'यह कुछ और नहीं बल्कि बॉन्ड के जरिए रिश्वतखोरी को वैध बनाना है।' कांग्रेस नेता जयराम रमेश ने आरोप लगाया, 'यह भाजपा की "हफ्ता वसूली" रणनीति है। ईडी, सीबीआई या आयकर विभाग के जरिए "छापा मारो" और फिर कंपनी के बचाव के लिए "हफ्ता (चंदा) मांगो"।' पार्टी ने एक लाइन में हमला किया, 'चंदा दो, धंधा लो।' भाजपा के रविशंकर ने पलटवार किया, कांग्रेस 'भ्रष्टाचार की गंगोत्री' है।

वॉशिंग मशीन। एक्सटोर्शन डिपार्टमेंट (ईडी)। इलेक्शन डिपार्टमेंट। जांच एजेंसियों की चुनिंदा कार्रवाई या बचाव राजनीतिक सिस्टम की गंदगी को बता रही थी। आरोप-प्रत्यारोप का दौर तेज़ था, लेकिन इस शोर-शराबे से सच्चाई छिप नहीं रही थी। ईडी एक ऐसे राजनीतिक मुकाबले के बीच था, जहां खेल के सभी इक्के सत्ताधारी दल के पास थे। मोदी सरकार के ईडी को हथियार की तरह इस्तेमाल से राजनीतिक खेल के नियम पूरी तरह से बदल गए थे। भारतीय राजनीति में समान अवसर की संवैधानिक प्रतिबद्धता को मानो दफ़ना दिया गया था। सत्तारूढ़ पार्टी के पास अब एक अतिरिक्त खिलाड़ी था, जिसके पास अपनी पसंद के हिसाब से समय और स्थान पर किसी भी प्रतिद्वन्दी को परेशान करने, नुकसान पहुंचाने या ध्वस्त करने की बेशुमार ताकत थी। कांग्रेस ने भी सत्ता में रहते हुए एजेंसियों का दुरुपयोग किया था, खासतौर से इंदिरा गांधी के नेतृत्व में आपातकाल के दौरान। लेकिन बीते वक्त की गलतियां आज बेशर्मी से इरादतन कार्रवाई को सही नहीं ठहरा सकतीं।

सुप्रीम कोर्ट के वरिष्ठ वकील संजय हेगड़े कहते हैं, 'अत्याचार का मतलब अपने दुश्मनों के ख़िलाफ़ चुनिंदा रूप से कठोर क़ानूनों का इस्तेमाल करने की क्षमता है।' ऐसे माहौल में विपक्ष के पास क्या मौका था, जो खुद एकजुट और भरोसेमंद नहीं था?

9

'ये अडानी की सरकार है': 'INDIA' बनने की कहानी

अरबपति गौतम अडानी एक मृदुभाषी, शर्मीले और कम बोलने वाले व्यक्ति हैं। 2012 में जब उन्होंने अपना पचासवां जन्मदिन मनाया, तो उनके करीबी दोस्त और परिवार के लोग इसे बड़ी धूमधाम के साथ मनाना चाहते थे। लेकिन तब अहमदाबाद के इस व्यवसायी ने विनम्रता से इंकार कर दिया। अडानी ने अपने खास अंदाज़ में कहा, 'मेरा श्रेष्ठ आना अभी बाकी है, अभी जश्न मनाने की ज़रूरत नहीं है।' अब तक मीडिया से दूर रहने वाले गौतम भाई यानी अडानी के लिए दिसम्बर 2022 में, अपनी इस छवि से बाहर निकलने के अलावा कोई रास्ता नहीं था। *फोर्ब्स* पत्रिका ने भारत के सबसे अमीर शख्स के रूप में उभरने और 'रियल टाइम' अरबपतियों की सूची में दुनिया के दूसरे सबसे अमीर बनने की सुर्खियों में गौतम अडानी को शुमार किया था। उनके बंदरगाहों से लेकर बिजली तक के समूह की पूंजी केवल तीन साल में नौ गुना बढ़ गई थी। *फोर्ब्स* के आंकड़ों के मुताबिक 2022 के आखिर में उनकी व्यक्तिगत कुल संपत्ति 125.8 अरब डॉलर हो गई थी। 2008 के बाद पहली बार सबसे ज़्यादा अमीरों की सूची में बदलाव हुआ: गौतम भाई ने रिलायंस इंडस्ट्रीज के मुकेश अंबानी को पीछे छोड़ दिया था।

इंडिया टुडे पत्रिका के 'न्यूज़मेकर ऑफ द ईयर' के सम्मान से लेकर इंडिया टीवी के लोकप्रिय शो 'आप की अदालत में' आने तक, अडानी इस सीजन के सबसे चमकते सितारे थे। हर मीडिया कंपनी अडानी की जिंदगी की कहानी को समझना और जानना चाहती थी। दसवीं कक्षा में ही पढ़ाई छोड़ देने वाला दुनिया का सबसे अमीर भारतीय बनना किसी परी कथा के सच होने जैसा था। अडानी के एक सहयोगी ने बताया, 'हमें दुनिया भर से हज़ारों बधाई संदेश

मिल रहे थे। गौतम भाई उत्साहित थे, लेकिन इसे दिखाना नहीं चाहते थे। उन्होंने कई संपादकों और राजनेताओं से निजी तौर पर बात कर, सहयोग के लिए शुक्रिया अदा किया।'

चार हफ्ते तक यह जोश रहा। फिर 24 जनवरी 2023 को, अमेरिका की एक फर्म हिंडनबर्ग रिसर्च ने एक धमाकेदार रिपोर्ट छापी, जिसमें अडानी पर ऑफशोर शेल कंपनियों के रास्ते 'स्टॉक में हेरफेर' और 'धोखाधड़ी' में शामिल होने का आरोप लगाया गया था। इससे अडानी के शेयरों में तेजी से गिरावट आई और उनकी निजी संपत्ति सिर्फ़ एक महीने में 80 अरब डॉलर कम हो गई। एक राजनेता, खासतौर से खुश थे, उन्हें लगा कि इस विवाद पर उन्हें एक बड़ा हमला करने का हथियार मिल गया था, जिसके खुलासे का वे सालों से इंतज़ार कर रहे थे। 'मुझे याद है कि अडानी की कहानी सामने आने के एक हफ्ते बाद मैं राहुल गांधी से मिला था और उनकी पहली प्रतिक्रिया थी, "क्या मैं सही नहीं था?"' कांग्रेस के एक पदाधिकारी ने बताया।

2014 के लोकसभा चुनावों से पहले जब उन्हें कांग्रेस नेतृत्व का मौका मिला था, तब से राहुल गांधी, अडानी समूह और नरेन्द्र मोदी के साथ उनके कथित संबंधों पर निशाना साध रहे थे। राहुल ने अपने एक सहयोगी को कहा, 'यदि आप मोदी को निशाना बनाना चाहते हैं तो उसका रास्ता उनके अमीर दोस्तों से होकर जाएगा। अडानी और मोदी दोनों एक-दूसरे के लिए इनाम जैसे हैं, यानी दोनों से एक-दूसरे को फायदा होता है। यह मोदी शैली का कुलीनतंत्र पूंजीवाद है यानी राजनीतिक ताकत से पूंजी बढ़ाना।' अडानी की संपत्ति और उनके राजनीतिक रिश्तों पर राहुल जुनूनी हद तक चले गए थे। इस पर वे कोई दूसरी बात सुनने को तैयार नहीं लगते थे। एक पूर्व कांग्रेसी ने गांधी परिवार के एक पारिवारिक मित्र को सलाह दी कि पार्टी को अडानी पर हमला 'थोड़ा नरम' रखना चाहिए, क्योंकि वह एक अच्छे नेटवर्क वाले ऐसे उद्यगपति हैं, जो कांग्रेस की भी मदद करते थे। वह नेता याद करते हुए कहते हैं कि 'अगली बात मुझे पता चली कि मुझे उनके दायरे से बाहर कर दिया गया है, मुझ पर अडानी पर नरम रुख अपनाने का आरोप लगाया गया।'

राहुल गांधी को अडानी इतने नापसंद क्यों हैं? केन्द्र में जब यूपीए सरकार थी, तब पहली पीढ़ी के उद्यमी अडानी ने कई तरह के संपर्कों से राहुल गांधी से मुलाक़ात की कोशिश की थी। इसकी शुरुआत रॉबर्ट वाड्रा से हुई, जिसे अडानी ने गुजरात में अपने मूंदड़ा बंदरगाह पर आमंत्रित किया था। अडानी ने इसे एक 'रुटीन' दौरा बताया। कारोबारी दिग्गज का कहना था कि 'मैंने बहुत से लोगों को यह देखने के लिए बुलाया था कि हमने क्या काम किया है, रॉबर्ट वाड्रा उनमें से सिर्फ़ एक थे।' इसके बाद, दिल्ली में राहुल से मुलाकात के लिए कई कोशिशें की गईं, पहले अहमद पटेल, फिर कमलनाथ के जरिए, जिन्हें अडानी का नजदीकी माना जाता रहा है। वाणिज्य मंत्री के तौर पर कमलनाथ बड़े कारोबारियों के प्रबल समर्थक माने जाते रहे। लेकिन कोई भी राहुल गांधी से अडानी की मुलाकात कराने में कामयाब नहीं हो पाया। अडानी

से निजी रिश्ते रखने वाले एक और राजनेता शरद पवार से भी रास्ता निकालने के लिए सलाह ली गई। लेकिन सतर्क पवार ने इससे दूर रहना ही बेहतर समझा।

दरअसल अडानी-गांधी विवाद 2014 के चुनावों से पहले का है, जब पार्टी के एक सहयोगी ने राहुल गांधी को बताया था कि मोदी और अडानी की निकटता, कैसे एक दूसरे को फायदा पहुंचा रही थी। हालांकि अडानी को अपना शुरुआती कारोबार नब्बे के दशक में गुजरात में मिला था, जब वहां चिमनभाई पटेल के नेतृत्व में कांग्रेस सरकार थी, लेकिन उनके कारोबार में तेजी से बढ़ोतरी 2002 के बाद मोदी के बढ़ते राजनीतिक रसूख से मेल खाती है। इसी दौरान अडानी ने कन्फेडरेशन ऑफ़ इंडियन इंडस्ट्री (सीआईआई) के विरोध में गुजरात के रिसर्जेंट ग्रुप (आरजीजी) की स्थापना की थी। सीआइआई ने 2002 में गुजरात दंगे ठीक से न सँभालने के लिए मोदी की आलोचना की थी। अडानी के चेयरपर्सन रहते हुए, आरजीजी मोदी के गुजरात विकास मॉडल की प्रमुख कहानी बन गई। राहुल गांधी को प्रस्तुत की गई रिपोर्ट में गुजरात में अडानी की बड़ी इन्फ्रास्ट्रक्चर परियोजनाओं के बारे में बताया गया था और ऐसी बहुत सी परियोजनाओं का ज़िक्र था, जिनमें मोदी सरकार ने कथित तौर पर बहुत कम दाम पर ज़मीनें दीं। राहुल गांधी को वो तस्वीरें भी दिखाई गईं, जिसमें गोवा में अडानी के बेटे की शादी समेत कई दूसरे मौकों पर मोदी और अडानी एकसाथ दिखाई दे रहे थे। 2013 में जब नरेन्द्र मोदी को भारतीय जनता पार्टी ने अपना प्रधानमंत्री पद का उम्मीदवार बनाया, तो चुनाव प्रचार के दौरान मोदी ने अडानी के निजी विमानों में से एक का इस्तेमाल किया, राहुल ने इसे भाई-भतीजावाद का सबूत माना। 2024 में, स्क्रोल में प्रकाशित एक रिपोर्ट में इशारा किया गया कि प्रधानमंत्री मोदी जिस भी देश में जाते या जिस भी देश के प्रमुख से मिलते, कुछ समय बाद उसी देश के साथ अडानी के विदेशी प्रोजेक्ट की घोषणा हो जाती। हालांकि अडानी ग्रुप का दावा है कि उसने ये सारे प्रोजेक्ट्स ईमानदारी से हासिल किये हैं लेकिन कांग्रेस के नेता का कुछ और ही सोचना है। गांधी परिवार के एक मित्र ने कहा, 'राहुल को दृढ़ता से लगता है कि भारत भाई-भतीजावादी ऐसे पूंजीपतियों के कब्ज़े में रहा है जिनकी संपत्ति राजनीतिक रिश्तों की वजह से सार्वजनिक संसाधनों पर कब्ज़ा करने से हासिल हुई है।' राहुल गांधी ने सबसे पहले अपने ऐसे अभियान की शुरुआत 2008 में ओड़िशा में की थी, जब वे उन आदिवासियों के आंदोलन का समर्थन करने पहुंचे, जो पर्यावरण के नजरिए से संवेदनशील नियामगिरी पहाड़ियों में 'वेदांता बॉक्साइट खनन परियोजना' का विरोध कर रहे थे। उस समय केन्द्र में कांग्रेस की अगुवाई वाली यूपीए सरकार थी और पर्यावरण मंत्रालय ने वेदांता की बोली को ख़ारिज़ कर दिया था।

वहीं, अडानी को लगता था कि राहुल गांधी के आसपास ऐसे 'वामपंथी' सलाहकार थे जिन्होंने राहुल के दिमाग में उनके ख़िलाफ़ 'जहर' भर दिया था, और मोदी के ख़िलाफ़ अपनी

लड़ाई में राहुल को मोहरे की तरह इस्तेमाल कर रहे थे। जब मैंने उनसे मोदी से संबंधों के बारे में पूछा तो उन्होंने पलटकर जवाब दिया, 'ऐसा कैसे हो सकता है, मैंने देश के 24 राज्यों में इन्फ्रास्ट्रक्चर की कई परियोजनाएं शुरू की हैं, जिनमें सभी को मैंने उचित तरीके से नीलामी में हासिल किया है। इनमें से कई राज्यों में कांग्रेस की सरकारें हैं। मुझ पर सिर्फ़ भाजपा के साथ काम करने का आरोप कैसे लगाया जा सकता है?' अडानी की नाराज़गी खासतौर पर कांग्रेस सांसद जयराम रमेश को लेकर थी, जो राहुल गांधी की तरह ही अडानी समूह के बिज़नेस मॉडल के मुखर आलोचक थे। केन्द्रीय पर्यावरण मंत्री के तौर पर जयराम रमेश ने कई प्रमुख व्यापारिक घरानों के साथ उन परियोजनाओं को मंज़ूरी देने पर बहस की थी, जिनमें वन अधिकार नियमों का उल्लंघन होने की बात कही गई थी। छत्तीसगढ़ जैसे राज्यों में बड़े पैमाने पर खनन में रुचि रखने वाले अडानी अक्सर पर्यावरण मंत्री के निशाने पर रहते थे। बाद में कांग्रेस के मुख्य प्रवक्ता और पार्टी विचारक के तौर पर जयराम के हमले ज्यादा आक्रामक हो गए थे। अडानी ने अपने एक व्यावसायिक सहयोगी से कहा, 'राहुल तो हर वक्त हमारी आलोचना करते हैं, लेकिन असल में जयराम हमारे ख़िलाफ़ एजेंडा तैयार करते हैं।'

जयराम रमेश और राहुल गांधी दोनों ही कांग्रेस में 'गांधीवादी धारा' (बेयरफुट डेवलपमेंट) से आते हैं। हालांकि वे उद्योगों के ख़िलाफ़ नहीं हैं, लेकिन यह विचारधारा सार्वजनिक रूप से 'कॉरपोरेट' उद्योगों के बजाय 'वामपंथी' अर्थशास्त्रियों के पक्ष में खड़ा होना पसंद करती है। राहुल अपने इस विचार पर खड़े रहते हैं, भले ही इसे 'शैंपेन साम्राज्यवाद' या अभिजात्य वर्ग की वामपंथी सनक के तौर पर मज़ाक उड़ाया जाता रहा हो। हिंडनबर्ग रिपोर्ट ने वह मौका दे दिया, जिसका वे मोदी सरकार को शर्मिंदा करने के लिए इंतज़ार कर रहे थे। इस रिपोर्ट के लिए इससे बेहतर समय नहीं हो सकता था, जब 2023 में संसद के बजट सत्र के कुछ दिन ही बचे थे और देशभर में 'भारत जोड़ो' यात्रा समाप्त होने वाली थी। संसद में राष्ट्रपति के अभिभाषण पर धन्यवाद प्रस्ताव की बहस चल रही थी। अपनी काली-सफेद अस्त-व्यस्त दाढ़ी के साथ 'कार्ल मॉर्क्स' और अभी-अभी पदयात्रा से लौटे योद्धा की छवि के बीच राहुल गांधी ने अपने चालीस मिनट के भाषण में ज़्यादातर समय मोदी-अडानी समीकरण पर ही बात की। राहुल ने कहा, 'लोग मोदी-अडानी संबंधों के बारे में जानना चाहते हैं। अडानी के लिए नियमों की अनदेखी की गई। तमिलनाडु, केरल से लेकर हिमाचल तक हम सिर्फ़ एक ही नाम सुनते हैं: "अडानी"। लोग मुझसे पूछते थे कि अडानी किसी भी व्यवसाय में आते हैं लेकिन कभी असफल नहीं होते। हार्वर्ड जैसे बिजनेस स्कूलों में अडानी पर एक केस स्टडी होनी चाहिए कि व्यवसाय और राजनीति के बीच रिश्ते कैसे काम आते हैं... नरेन्द्र मोदी को तो इसमें स्वर्ण पदक मिलना चाहिए। असली जादू तो 2014 में शुरू हुआ, जब नरेन्द्र मोदी दिल्ली आए। 2014 में अडानी दुनिया के अमीरों की सूची में 609वें स्थान पर थे, आज वे सबसे ऊपर पहुंच गए हैं।' महीनों

से मोदी सरकार पर हमला करते रहे राहुल ने कहा, 'यह अडानी की सरकार है।' अब वे इस नारे को संसद तक ले आए थे।

संसद में राहुल गांधी ने अडानी और मोदी की निजी विमान में पांच सितारा सुविधाओं में आराम करते हुए तस्वीरें दिखाईं। उन्होंने हवाई अड्डों समेत कई बड़ी परियोजनाओं का ज़िक्र किया, जिनमें पक्षपात का आरोप लगाया गया था। कांग्रेस नेता ने खासतौर से मुंबई अंतरराष्ट्रीय हवाई अड्डे पर बात की और आरोप लगाया कि देश के सबसे व्यस्त हवाई अड्डे को हैदराबाद के 'जीवीके' समूह से ले लिया गया। राहुल का आरोप था कि ईडी और सीबीआई जैसी केन्द्रीय एजेंसियों का इस्तेमाल करके इसका 'अपहरण' कर अडानी को दे दिया गया। इस पर महीनों अटकलें चलती रहीं कि इन्फ्रास्ट्रक्चर में काम करने वाले एक प्रमुख कॉरपोरेट ने देश की आर्थिक राजधानी के फायदे वाले हवाई अड्डे को क्यों बेच दिया? जीवीके ने इसको लेकर खंडन जारी किया, लेकिन राहुल गांधी के आरोप अख़बारों के पहले पन्ने पर सुर्खियां बन गए थे। 'अडानी का नाम संसद में आने के बाद लड़ाई खुलकर सामने आ गई थी,' कांग्रेस के एक सांसद ने कहा। 'इससे पार्टी के कार्यकर्ताओं को समझ आ गया कि हमारे नेता मोदी से लड़ाई में पीछे हटने वाले नहीं हैं।'

सत्ता पक्ष नाराज हो गया। जबरदस्त जवाबी हमला किया गया। केन्द्रीय मंत्री किरेन रिजिजू ने राहुल गांधी को प्रधानमंत्री के ख़िलाफ़ सबूत पेश करने की चुनौती दी। लोकसभा अध्यक्ष ओम बिरला ने सदन में तस्वीरें लहराए जाने की निंदा की। विपक्ष पहले से ही लोकसभा अध्यक्ष पर पक्षपात करने का आरोप लगा रहा था। अध्यक्ष ने राहुल गांधी के भाषण से अडानी के सभी संदर्भों को हटाने के निर्देश दिए। न्यूज़ चैनलों को लोकसभा अध्यक्ष के कार्यालय से चेतावनी दी गई कि वे अपने प्राइम टाइम कार्यक्रमों में हटाए गए शब्दों का इस्तेमाल न करें। संसद में हुई तीखी नोक-झोंक के गवाह रहे एक वरिष्ठ पत्रकार ने कहा, 'उस शाम संसद में काफी गर्मागर्म बहस हुई। लग रहा था कि सरकार इस बात से नाखुश थी कि लोकसभा अध्यक्ष ने राहुल गांधी को संसद में मोदी-अडानी पर बोलने से पहले ही क्यों नहीं रोक दिया?'

अगले दिन प्रधानमंत्री मोदी ने पलटवार किया। विवादस्पद 'A' शब्द उनके बयान में नहीं था और न ही कांग्रेस नेता के विशिष्ट आरोपों का कोई जवाब दिया। अपने चिर-परिचित लोक लुभावन और तंज के साथ एक गुस्से भरे भाषण में प्रधानमंत्री ने देश के लोगों के साथ अपने जुड़ाव का ज़िक्र किया। उन्होंने कहा, 'मोदी देश के पच्चीस करोड़ परिवारों का एक सदस्य है। 140 करोड़ लोगों का भरोसा मेरी सबसे बड़ी सुरक्षा है, जिसे आपका झूठ नहीं तोड़ सकता। मुफ़्त राशन पाने वाले 80 करोड़ लोग शायद ही इन झूठे आरोप लगाने वालों पर विश्वास करें।' अडानी के तेजी से आगे बढ़ने पर राहुल गांधी ने हार्वर्ड विश्वविद्यालय की स्टडी कराने का जो तंज किया था, उस पर प्रधानमंत्री ने कहा, 'यहां कई लोगों को हार्वर्ड की स्टडी का बड़ा क्रेज

है। एक अध्ययन कांग्रेस के पतन पर हो सकता है। मेरा मानना है कि हर बड़ा विश्वविद्यालय कांग्रेस के पतन और उसके लिए ज़िम्मेदार लोगों पर भी स्टडी करेगा।'

आमतौर पर, मोदी-गांधी के बीच राजनीतिक भाषणबाज़ी निराशाजनक रूप से एकतरफा होती है। 'जात्रा-शैली' में नाटकीय और भड़काऊ भाषण देने बनाम एक अकुशल नेता, जिसकी सार्वजनिक वक्ता के तौर पर ताकत नहीं रही। फिर भी यह ऐसा दौर था, जब राहुल गांधी ने कई बार तीखे हमले किए। हालांकि मोदी-अडानी रिश्ते के आरोप नए नहीं थे। राजनीति में मोदी के चमकने के साथ अडानी की संपत्ति के तेजी से आगे बढ़ने पर राजनीतिक चर्चाएं होती रही हैं। लेकिन इस बार तीसरे पक्ष के तौर पर हिंडनबर्ग की रिपोर्ट ने उन हमलों के लिए गोला-बारूद दे दिया था, जो लड़ाई अब तक प्रधानमंत्री के ख़िलाफ़ राहुल गांधी का व्यक्तिगत अभियान माना जाता था। यहां तक कि मोदी-अडानी रिश्ते पर चर्चा से हिचकने वाले मीडिया घरानों को भी अब इस पर बहस के लिए मजबूर होना पड़ा था। कांग्रेस की सोशल मीडिया प्रमुख सुप्रिया सुनेत्र ने कहा, 'मुझे लगता है कि राहुल गांधी का निशाना मोदी पर ठीक वहां लगा है, जहां उन्हें चोट महसूस होती है। प्रधानमंत्री को बेवजह का हंगामा करने के बजाय हमारे आरोपों का जवाब देना चाहिए।' हालांकि उस वक्त भाजपा अडानी मुद्दे पर बहस के लिए अपने प्रवक्ताओं को भेजने के लिए तैयार नहीं थी, इसके बजाय पार्टी की मीडिया मशीनरी ने कथित तौर पर कुछ चैनलों को फोन करके दूसरे विषयों पर चर्चा करने के लिए कहा। संसद में भाजपा सांसद बार-बार सदन में हंगामा कर रहे थे और राहुल गांधी के लंदन में एक भाषण में देश में लोकतंत्र पर भारत विरोधी टिप्पणी पर माफी मांगने पर ज़ोर दे रहे थे। ऐसा लग रहा था कि मोदी सरकार के पास अडानी संबंधों पर छिपाने के लिए काफी कुछ था, लेकिन मुद्दे से ध्यान भटकाने की कोशिशें काम करती नहीं दिख रही थीं। इस बार कांग्रेस जनता में इस मुद्दे पर अपनी बात रख पाने की लड़ाई जीतती दिख रही थी।

सरकार को हिंडनबर्ग रिपोर्ट से ध्यान हटाने के लिए एक बड़े मुद्दे की तलाश थी। मार्च के तीसरे सप्ताह में अडानी विवाद के बाद यह बड़ा मुद्दा मिल ही गया। 23 मार्च 2023 को गुजरात के भाजपा विधायक पूर्णेश मोदी की याचिका पर सूरत की एक अदालत ने आपराधिक मानहानि के मामले में राहुल गांधी को दोषी ठहराया। राहुल गांधी को दो साल की कैद और 15 हज़ार रुपये जुर्माना भरना था। यह मामला 2019 में कर्नाटक की चुनावी रैली में राहुल गांधी के उस भाषण को लेकर था, जिसमें राहुल ने कहा, 'मेरा एक सवाल है, इन सभी चोरों के नाम में मोदी-मोदी क्यों हैं? नीरव मोदी, ललित मोदी, नरेन्द्र मोदी। अगर हम थोड़ा और आगे बढ़ेंगे तो ऐसे कई और मोदी सामने आएंगे।' यह राजनीतिक गर्मी भरे चुनावी अभियान में एक तंज था। पहली नज़र में, इस आपराधिक मानहानि के लिए दो साल की सज़ा ज़रूरत से ज़्यादा लगती है। शायद पिछले सौ साल में भी इस क़ानून के तहत यह सज़ा किसी को नहीं दी गई।

मामले के तथ्यों ने इस पर सवालों के घेरे खड़े किए थे। अप्रैल 2019 में, मुक़दमा दायर होने के बाद, राहुल गांधी जून 2021 में, सूरत के मुख्य न्यायिक मजिस्ट्रेट ए.एन. दवे की अदालत में व्यक्तिगत रूप से पेश हुए थे और अपना बयान दर्ज कराया था। फिर अचानक, पूर्णेश मोदी ने गुजरात हाईकोर्ट में मुकदमे पर रोक लगाने की मांग की, इस याचिका को मार्च 2022 में, मंज़ूर कर लिया गया। हैरानी इस बात पर थी कि मुक़दमे पर रोक लगाने की मांग आरोपी ने नहीं बल्कि शिकायतकर्ता ने की थी। लेकिन फरवरी 2023 में राहुल गांधी के लोकसभा में चर्चित भाषण के कुछ दिनों बाद पूर्णेश मोदी ने मामले से रोक हटाने के लिए फिर से अदालत का रुख किया। तब तक ए.एन. दवे की जगह हरीश वर्मा आ गए थे, उनकी अदालत ने कुछ हफ्तों में ही राहुल गांधी को दोषी करार दिया। वर्मा को जल्दी ही ज़िला न्यायाधीश बना दिया गया। राहुल के वकील डॉ. अभिषेक मनु सिंघवी कहते हैं, 'मामले का घटनाक्रम ही सारी कहानी कह देता है। राहुल गांधी के कट्टर आलोचक भी मानेंगे कि जो कुछ हुआ वो अन्यायपूर्ण था।'

दोष साबित होने के अदालती आदेश के चौबीस घंटे में, लोकसभा सचिवालय ने राहुल गांधी को सदस्यता से अयोग्य घोषित करने की अधिसूचना जारी कर दी। जनप्रतिनिधित्व अधिनियम, 1951 की धारा 8(3) के मुताबिक, 'किसी अपराध में दोषी और कम से कम दो साल के कारावास की सज़ा होने पर दोष साबित होने की तारीख से सदस्यता से अयोग्य घोषित कर दिया जाएगा और उसकी रिहाई से छह साल तक अयोग्य माना जाएगा।' शायद तेजी से कार्रवाई करने के दबाव में लोकसभा अध्यक्ष कार्यालय ने अडानी से जुड़ी टिप्पणी को हटाने के दो महीने से भी कम वक्त में कांग्रेस नेता को अयोग्य घोषित करने के लिए रूलबुक का इस्तेमाल किया। राजस्थान के कोटा से सांसद बने ओम बिरला को कमोबेश गुमनामी से निकालकर हाई-प्रोफाइल पद पर बिठाया गया था। एक विपक्षी सांसद ने हंसते हुए तंज किया, 'वे ऐसे व्यक्ति हैं जो प्रधानमंत्री की नज़र पड़ने पर भी खड़े हो जाते हैं।'

अतीत में बहुत से मौके गंवाने की आलोचना झेलने वाले राहुल गांधी इस बार जुझारू रूप से सामने आए। उन्होंने पलटवार किया, मोदी-अडानी मुद्दे पर सच बोलने के लिए उन्हें प्रताड़ित किया जा रहा था। विपक्ष भी उनके साथ खड़ा दिखाई दिया और मोदी सरकार पर राजनीतिक प्रतिशोध का आरोप लगाया। 22 अप्रैल को राहुल ने लुटिंयस दिल्ली में अपना आधिकारिक बंगला खाली कर दिया। हाउस स्टॉफ को विदाई देते और ट्रकों में सामान लादते हुए देखने की उनकी तस्वीरें वायरल हो गईं। कहा जाता है कि अप्रैल में भाजपा के 'आंतरिक ट्रैकर पोल' में बताया गया कि पार्टी समर्थकों में भी ज़्यादातर की राय थी कि राहुल की बेदखली अनुचित थी और इससे राजनीतिक प्रतिशोध की बू आती है। भाजपा प्रवक्ता ने माना, 'हमने इस मुद्दे पर माहौल को ठीक से नहीं समझा। राहुल को सहानुभूति इसलिए मिली क्योंकि उन्हें सांसद के तौर पर अयोग्य ठहराया गया था।'

भारतीय जनता पार्टी की रणनीति गलत साबित हुई। अडानी मुद्दे से ध्यान हटाने की बेचैनी में पार्टी ने राहुल गांधी को पीड़ित बनने का मौका दे दिया। इससे भी खराब पार्टी के लिए यह रहा कि इस सबने राहुल को मोदी के मुख्य प्रतिद्वन्दी के तौर पर खड़ा कर दिया, एक ऐसा मजबूत नेता जो असहज सवाल उठाने से नहीं डरता, भले उसे इसका नुक़सान उठाना पड़े। अगस्त 2023 में, सुप्रीम कोर्ट ने निचली अदालत के आदेश पर रोक लगा दी, लेकिन संसद से निकाले जाने के इन महीनों में उन्हें मोदी विरोधी ताकतों के लिए मुख्य चेहरा बना दिया। अब अहम सवाल यह था कि क्या राहुल गांधी और उनकी पार्टी 2024 के आम चुनावों में इस सहानुभूति को वोटों में बदल पाएंगे?

═

देश में चुनावी नज़रिए से कर्नाटक जैसे राज्य कम ही हैं, जिन्हें समझना थोड़ा मुश्किल हो सकता है। करीब चार दशकों से यहां के मतदाताओं ने विधानसभा और लोकसभा चुनावों में अलग-अलग विकल्प चुने हैं। जंगलों के बीच बहती नदियां, धुंध भरी पहाड़ियों में बहते झरनों से सजा कर्नाटक जादुई सा महसूस होता है। राहुल गांधी की सांसदी जाने के बाद कांग्रेस के लिए यह बड़ा इम्तिहान था। एक साल बाद आम चुनाव होने थे और कांग्रेस के महासचिव रणदीप सुरजेवाला के मुताबिक कर्नाटक में 2023 के विधानसभा चुनाव पार्टी के लिए 'करो या मरो' की लड़ाई थे। वैसे कांग्रेस ने दिसंबर 2022 में हिमाचल प्रदेश में जीत हासिल की थी, लेकिन इससे पहले 2018 की सर्दियों के बाद से किसी भी प्रमुख राज्य में सीधी चुनावी लड़ाई में भाजपा को नहीं हराया था। सुरजेवाला कहते हैं, 'मुझे याद है कि मैंने अपने प्रदेश के नेताओं से कहा कि वे केवल बेंगलुरु में सरकार बनाने के लिए नहीं लड़ रहे हैं, बल्कि उनके पास देश में कांग्रेस को फिर से ज़िंदा करने का काम था।'

वैसे, कर्नाटक उन कुछ राज्यों में से एक हैं, जहां कांग्रेस के पास भारतीय जनता पार्टी से लड़ने लायक ताकत है। अनुभवी कुरबा योद्धा सिद्दारमैया और तेजतर्रार डी.के. शिवकुमार जैसे दो मजबूत क्षत्रप हैं। चतुर और अनुभवी सिद्दारमैया का लोगों से जमीनी जुड़ाव है, जबकि शिवकुमार संगठन के लिए बेहद 'साधन संपन्न' नेता हैं। हालांकि दोनों नेताओं के बीच तीखे मतभेद थे, लेकिन वे चुनावी लड़ाई में इसे अलग रखने को तैयार दिख रहे थे। चुनाव से करीब एक साल पहले राहुल गांधी ने दोनों नेताओं को साथ बिठाकर समझौता करा दिया था। सुरजेवाला कहते हैं, 'मुझे लगता है कि जब ये दोनों दिग्गज एक साथ आ गए, तभी हमने आधी लड़ाई जीत ली थी।'

कांग्रेस के पास एक और चुनावी ताकत थी, जिसकी चर्चा कम थीः पार्टी के नए चुनावी रणनीतिकार सुनील कनोगुलु। बेंगलुरु के कनोगुलु 2022 में कांग्रेस की चुनावी रणनीति समिति

के मुखिया के तौर पर शामिल हुए, इससे कुछ पहले ही पार्टी की रणनीतिकार प्रशांत किशोर के साथ बातचीत टूट गई थी। कनोगुलु पहली बार प्रशांत किशोर की शुरुआती टीम का हिस्सा बने थे, जिसने नरेन्द्र मोदी के 2014 के लोकसभा चुनाव अभियान पर काम किया था। 'हाई-प्रोफाइल' किशोर से उलट, मोटा चश्मा पहने कनोगुलु सुर्खियों से दूर रहना पंसद करते हैं। 'लो-प्रोफाइल' कनोगुलु 'बैकरुम ऑपरेटर' के तौर पर चुपचाप काम करते हैं, वे किसी कैमरे के सामने बोलने को तैयार नही होते। मोदी को छोड़कर किशोर तो आगे बढ़ गए थे, लेकिन कनोगुलु भाजपा के साथ ही बने रहे। 2017 के उत्तरप्रदेश विधानसभा चुनावों में उन्होंने अमित शाह के साथ मिलकर काम किया, पार्टी ने यहां बड़ी जीत हासिल की थी। इसके बाद उनके रास्ते में कई और मोड़ आए, जब कांग्रेस के साथ जुड़ने से पहले उन्होंने तमिलनाडु में दोनों द्रविड़ पार्टियों के साथ अलग-अलग वक्त पर काम किया। कांग्रेस को वे वैचारिक तौर पर अपनी पार्टी मानते हैं। कर्नाटक उनकी लिए अपनी काबिलियत दिखाने का मौका था, जो भाजपा के किसी को कोई रियायत नहीं देने और सबकुछ भूल जाने वाले नज़रिए से थोड़ा अलग था।

तेज़ी से सोचने वाले कनोगुलु ने कांग्रेस की सुस्त चुनावी योजना में भाजपा की कामयाबी की खासियतों और तजुर्बे को शामिल करने का काम किया। ज़मीनी सर्वेक्षणों के आधार पर टिकट बंटवारे में कई तरह के बदलाव किए गए और आकर्षक मीडिया अभियान तैयार किया गया। ऐसा ही एक लोकप्रिय अभियान था, 'पे-सीएम' पोस्टर वॉर, जो भाजपा के तत्कालीन मुख्यमंत्री बसवराज बोम्मई के खिलाफ़ भ्रष्टाचार के आरोपों पर तंज भरा अभियान था। अचानक रातोंरात इस अभियान के पोस्टर मुख्यमंत्री आवास और भाजपा के दफ्तर समेत पूरे बेंगलुरु शहर में लगाए गए। इन पोस्टरों में 'क्यूआर कोड' स्कैन कर, रिश्वतखोरी के ख़िलाफ़ शिकायत दर्ज करने के लिए कहा गया था। 'पे-सीएम' के नारे की गूंज तब और बढ़ गई, जब कर्नाटक ठेकेदारों की संस्था ने आरोप लगाया कि उन्हें सरकारी ठेके हासिल करने के लिए 40 प्रतिशत कमीशन देना पड़ता है। शिवकुमार ने माना कि 'सुनील का आइडिया था कि भाजपा से लड़ाई में हमें पहल करनी चाहिए। भाजपा इस पर प्रतिक्रिया देती तब तक यह लोगों की ज़ुबान पर चढ़ गया था। इससे हमें बढ़त मिल गई।'

कर्नाटक में भारतीय जनता पार्टी के ख़िलाफ़ कांग्रेस का सबसे धारधार हथियार भ्रष्टाचार का मुद्दा रहा। इसके साथ ही पार्टी ने मतदाताओं को पांच 'गारंटी' भी दी। इस 'गारंटी' शब्द का इस्तेमाल कांग्रेस ने पहली बार 2021 में असम में और फिर 2022 में हिमाचल प्रदेश के चुनावों में किया था। इसका मकसद था लोगों को इस बात का भरोसा दिलाना कि देश की सबसे पुरानी पार्टी अपने वादों पर काम करेगी। इस बार वादों की सूची भी लंबी हो गई थी। मुफ़्त बिजली, महिलाओं को दो हज़ार रुपये महीने नकद की सहायता, गरीबों को दस किलो मुफ़्त चावल, महिलाओं के लिए मुफ़्त बस यात्रा और बेरोज़गार युवाओं को नकद सहायता

देने की बात कही गई। कांग्रेस की पांच गारंटियों को इस आश्वासन से और मज़बूती मिली कि गैस सिलेंडर पांच सौ रुपये में दिया जाएगा। सुरजेवाला कहते हैं कि 'इस बात का श्रेय तो हमें दें कि प्रधानमंत्री हमारे आइडिया की नकल कर "मोदी की गारंटी" लेकर आये, लेकिन इससे बहुत पहले "कांग्रेस की गारंटी" थी।'

कांग्रेस जब अपनी रणनीति पर काम कर रही थी, उस वक्त भाजपा एक बार फिर लड़खड़ा रही थी, लेकिन इसमें कुछ अप्रत्याशित नहीं था। कर्नाटक भाजपा का गढ़ जैसा कभी नहीं रहा। पार्टी ने यहां अपने दम पर कभी बहुमत हासिल नहीं किया। भाजपा का मोटे तौर पर वोट बैंक राजनीतिक रूप से ताकतवर लिंगायत समुदाय है, लेकिन इसका नुक़सान यह होता है कि दूसरे समुदायों में फिर उसकी अपील असर नहीं डालती, या उन्हें रोकती है। प्रदेश में भाजपा के सबसे बड़े नेता बी.एस. येदियुरप्पा लिंगायतों के सबसे बड़े चेहरे माने जाते थे। चतुर और बुद्धिमान राजनेता येदियुरप्पा दो दशकों से भी ज्यादा समय तक पार्टी के सबसे बड़े नेता रहे थे। लेकिन एक क्षत्रप के पास प्रदेश संगठन पर पूरा नियंत्रण 'मोदी-शाह मॉडल' की राजनीति के विपरीत हैं, जहां किसी दूसरी ताकत को संदेह की नज़रों से देखा जाता है। जुलाई 2021 में, जब येदियुरप्पा परिवार के बढ़ते 'कमीशन-राज' की शिकायतें पीएमओ को मिलीं, तो भाजपा नेतृत्व ने आखिरकार कार्रवाई करने का फ़ैसला किया। नई पीढ़ी को मौका देने के नाम पर अठहतर साल के येदियुरप्पा को कुर्सी छोड़ने के लिए कहा गया, लेकिन वे हार मानने को तैयार नहीं थे। हालात संभालने के लिए येदियुरप्पा ने एक संत की मदद भी ली, लेकिन केन्द्र अपने फ़ैसले पर अड़ा रहा। अगर येदियुरप्पा कुर्सी नहीं छोड़ते तो उनके समर्थकों में यह डर हमेशा बना रहता कि उनके ख़िलाफ़ मामलों को फिर से खोला जा सकता है। नई भाजपा में सिर्फ़ विपक्ष ही नहीं है, जिसे ईडी की कार्रवाई का ख़तरा है, बल्कि इससे पार्टी के सहयोगियों को भी डराया जा सकता है। रुआंसे येदियुरप्पा ने बेमन से कुर्सी, कमज़ोर राजनेता माने जाने वाले बसवराज बोम्मई को सौंप दी। यह इस बात का संकेत थी कि कर्नाटक में पार्टी येदियुरप्पा के वफादारों और केन्द्र के बीच तीखे संघर्ष में फंस गई थी।

कर्नाटक भाजपा में कुर्सी के खेल में एक प्रमुख व्यक्ति बी.एल. संतोष थे, जो पार्टी के ताकतवर राष्ट्रीय महासचिव (संगठन) थे। संतोष के पास भाजपा और आरएसएस के बीच समन्वय की ज़िम्मेदारी थी। संघ प्रचारक संतोष का करियर भी मोदी की तरह आगे बढ़ा था। गोल चेहरे पर पतली मूंछें रखे, विचारकों की तरह निगाहों वाले संतोष हमेशा बेदाग सफेद शर्ट और धोती पहनते हैं और हमेशा लाल तिलक उनके ललाट पर रहता है। कर्नाटक में पार्टी संगठन के साथ काम करने के बाद वे अपने गृह राज्य की राजनीति में ज़्यादा दखल चाहते थे, ठीक वैसे ही जैसे एक ज़माने में मोदी ने गुजरात में रखा था। भाजपा पर नज़र रखने वाले बेंगलुरु के एक प्रेक्षक ने कहा कि 'संतोष बहुत महत्वाकांक्षी हैं। मोदी जी की तरह ही वे भी केवल शांत

प्रचारक नहीं बने रहना चाहते हैं, बल्कि एक दिन कर्नाटक का मुख्यमंत्री बनने का सपना देखते हैं।' टीम मोदी शाह का ध्यान राष्ट्रीय घटनाक्रम पर ज़्यादा था इसलिए कर्नाटक अभियान की ज़िम्मेदारी संतोष पर छोड़ दी गई थी।

संतोष सिर्फ़ उम्मीदवारों को चुनने का काम हीं नहीं देख रहे थे, उनकी बड़ी जिम्मेदारी हिंदुत्व के एजेंडा को प्रदेश में फिर से जिंदा करने की भी थी। 2023 के कर्नाटक चुनावों में भाजपा ने धार्मिक मुद्दे उठाने की तैयारी कर ली थी। संघ से जुड़े मतदाताओं को ध्रुवीकृत करने और बोम्मई सरकार के ख़िलाफ़ भ्रष्टाचार के मुद्दे से ध्यान हटाने के लिए सांप्रदायिक तापमान बढ़ाने की कोशिश भी की गई। इसे मोदी-शाह अभियान का ही हिस्सा माना गया। आलोचक अक्सर भाजपा नेतृत्व पर चुनावों में धार्मिक घृणा और सांप्रदायिक विद्वेष बढ़ाने का आरोप लगाते रहे हैं। मुस्लिम लड़कियों को स्कूलों में हिजाब पहनने से रोकने से लेकर हलाल मांस के बहिष्कार की बात और मुस्लिम दुकानदारों को पारपंरिक मंदिर उत्सवों में शामिल होने से रोकने तक, हिंदू-मुस्लिम विभाजन को भड़काने की हरसंभव कोशिश के आरोप भी लगे। उग्रवादी हिंदुत्व और चरमपंथी सोच के लोगों के मंच संभालते ही, बोम्मई चुपचाप किनारे हो गए थे। 'ये आप लोग हैं जो हिजाब-हलाल को मुद्दा बनाते रहते हैं। मैं सिर्फ सरकार चलाने पर ध्यान दे रहा हूं,' पत्रकारों को बोम्मई का जवाब था। हालांकि ऑफ द रिकॉर्ड उन्होंने अपने सहयोगियों के सामने माना कि हिंदुत्व का मुद्दा 'धर्मनिरपेक्ष' कर्नाटक में काम नहीं करेगा।

कर्नाटक चुनावों के अंतिम चरण में, भाजपा अभियान में बढ़ती घबराहट हताशा में बदलने लगी थी। प्रदेश कांग्रेस ने अपने घोषणापत्र में बजरंग दल पर प्रतिबंध लगाने का वादा किया, दक्षिणपंथी हिंदुत्व संगठनों की तुलना उसने 'इस्लामिक पॉपुलर फ्रंट' से की और आरोप लगाया कि दोनों ही तरह के संगठन दुश्मनी और नफ़रत को बढ़ावा दे रहे थे। भाजपा ने बजरंग दल के मुद्दे को लपक लिया, बताया गया कि इस मसले पर कांग्रेस के केन्द्रीय नेतृत्व से सहमति नहीं ली गई थी। कर्नाटक में एक दौरे पर, प्रधानमंत्री मोदी ने अपने भाषणों की शुरुआत 'जय बजरंग बली' के उद्घोष के साथ की। जहां तक चुनाव प्रचार की बात है मोदी ने बार-बार यह जताया है कि चुनाव जीतने के लिए उन्हें धार्मिक विभाजन की किसी भी हद तक जाने में कोई गुरेज़ नहीं है।

प्रधानमंत्री की रैलियों में भारी भीड़ देख कांग्रेस शुरू में परेशान थी। क्या बजरंग बली का नारा चुनावी हवा को बदल सकता है और सस्ते गैस सिलेंडर जैसी गारंटियों से भी ध्यान भटका सकता है? क्या भगवान हनुमान चुनावी हथियार तो साबित नहीं होंगे? कांग्रेस की रणनीति टीम के एक सदस्य के मुताबिक प्रधानमंत्री की रैली के बाद जब हमने एक स्पॉट पोल किया, तब थोड़ा भरोसा हुआ। बजरंग बली केवल भाजपा समर्थकों के लिए मुद्दा थे।

2023 के कर्नाटक चुनावों के नतीजों से भी इस बात की पुष्टि हो गईः कांग्रेस ने 135 सीटों के साथ स्पष्ट बहुमत हासिल किया, भाजपा काफी दूर 66 सीटों पर रह गई। एलपीजी गैस

सिलेंडर की गारंटी ने हिंदुत्व के कट्टर नफ़रती नारे को मात दे दी। प्रधानमंत्री का 'डबल इंजन' सरकार का नारा भी काम नहीं आया, जिसका मतलब था कि भाजपा का वोट केन्द्र की ताकत बनेगा। 'अगर आप कर्नाटक में विकास चाहते हैं तो "डबल इंजन" के लिए वोट करें। अगर कांग्रेस सरकार बनाती है तो सिद्दारमैया सरकार केन्द्र की सभी योजनाओं को रोक देगी,' भाजपा अध्यक्ष जे.पी. नड्डा ने अपने चुनावी भाषण में इस बात पर जोर दिया यानी इशारा था कि भाजपा को वोट यानी केन्द्र की मदद जारी रहेगी। लेकिन नतीजों ने भाजपा के डबल इंजन को पटरी से उतार दिया था। हिन्दुत्व की बजाय गारंटी को हां, कर्नाटक के मतदाता ने दिल्ली के बजाय बेंगलुरु को चुना। राष्ट्रीय के बजाय स्थानीय। हिमाचल के बाद कांग्रेस ने अपने दम पर लगातार दूसरी बार भाजपा को सीधी लड़ाई में मात दी थी। सवाल था, क्या यह कांग्रेस के लिए जीत के तूफान में बदल सकता है? क्या कांग्रेस ने 2024 की लड़ाई में खुद को चैलेंजर नंबर 1 बना लिया था? या क्या दूसरे विपक्षी नेता अपने लिए कुछ और नतीजों के इंतज़ार में थे? सबसे अहम यह है कि यदि ज़रूरत पड़ी तो क्या सभी विपक्षी नेता एकजुट होकर भाजपा के ख़िलाफ़ मैदान में उतर पाएंगे, जिनकी परस्पर विरोधी महत्वाकांक्षाएं और बदलती विचारधाराएं हैं?

गर्मियों में पटना गर्म कड़ाही की तरह तप रहा था। जून 2023 के तीसरे हफ्ते में, राजनीतिक गप्पबाजी और चर्चाओं वाले इस शहर में राजनीतिक तापमान बढ़ने लगा था। लंबे समय से बिहार के मुख्यमंत्री रहे नीतीश कुमार एक बड़े राजनीतिक स्पैक्ट्रम की तैयारी में नेताओं की मेज़बानी में लगे थे। पटना हवाईअड्डे से शहर तक सड़कों पर देश के अलग-अलग हिस्सें से आए नेताओं के कट-आउट सजे हुए थे। इनमें 26 छोटी-बड़ी पार्टियों के नेता शामिल थे। मेहमानों की सूची देश के विपक्षी नेताओं की सूची लग रही थी। एक टेबल पर ममता बनर्जी का दरबार था, तो अगली टेबल पर उनके धुर-विरोधी रहे वामपंथी नेता सीताराम येचुरी और डी. राजा बातचीत में मशगूल थे। हाल की कर्नाटक जीत के वजह से बहुत से लोगों की नज़रें राहुल गांधी पर थीं, जबकि आम आदमी पार्टी के नेता अरविंद केजरीवाल दूसरे कोने में कागज़ पर कुछ उधेड़बुन में थे। हिंदुत्व का झंडा उठाते रहे शिवसेना के उद्धव ठाकरे की घबराहट उनकी चहलकदमी में दिख रही थी, जबकि कश्मीर की तूफ़ानी नेता महबूबा मुफ़्ती के चेहरे पर मुस्कुराहट थी। अखिलेश यादव लंच में लगे थे और तेजस्वी यादव अपनी फैंसी घड़ी दिखा रहे थे। सभा में मौजूद बुज़ुर्ग नेता शरद पवार, मल्लिकार्जुन खड़गे, लालू प्रसाद और फ़ारुक़ अब्दुल्ला थोड़े शांत दिख रहे थे, शायद इसलिए क्योंकि उन्होंने अपने राजनीतिक सफ़र में बहुत उतार-चढ़ाव देखे थे। अलग-अलग रंगों और विचारों वाले इन विपक्षी नेताओं के इस जमघट की इकलौती वजह थी: प्रधानमंत्री नरेन्द्र मोदी को हराने के लिए हाथ मिलाने की संभावना।

जब पत्रकारों ने बैठक के इरादे और संभावना पर सवाल किए तो नीतीश कुमार ने याद दिलाया, 'क्या 1977 में इंदिरा गांधी को हराने के लिए वामपंथी और दक्षिणपंथी एकसाथ नहीं आए थे?'

लेकिन 2023 की गर्मियां 1977 की दोपहर जैसी सुर्ख नहीं थी, जब जनता पार्टी की बिखरी हुई सेना ने ताकतवर इंदिरा गांधी को हरा दिया था। इन सबको एकजुट करने के लिए, यहां कोई जयप्रकाश नारायण या 'जेपी' जैसा दिग्गज नेता नहीं था, जिसका नैतिक कद और जीवन सार्वजनिक सेवा में गुजरा हो। विपक्ष के पास प्रादेशिक स्तर के प्रभावशाली नेता तो थे, लेकिन अखिल भारतीय अपील रखने वाले नरेन्द्र मोदी के मुकाबले लायक कोई नहीं लगता था और पार्टियों के पास भी भाजपा जैसा संगठन, संसाधन या मशीनरी नहीं थी, जो उससे बराबरी की लड़ाई लड़ सके।

उदाहरण के लिए, पश्चिम बंगाल की मुख्यमंत्री ममता बनर्जी एक दशक से ज़्यादा से कोलकाता में सरकार चला रही थीं, लेकिन राष्ट्रीय स्तर पर वे अपने पैर जमाने में अब तक नाकाम रही थीं। 2021 में तीसरी बार विधानसभा चुनाव जीतने के बाद रणनीतिकार प्रशांत किशोर और उनके भतीजे अभिषेक बनर्जी ने गोवा में तृणमूल कांग्रेस को आगे बढ़ाने के लिए उन्हें राजी कर लिया। प्रशांत किशोर का मानना था कि 'छोटे से राज्य गोवा में ईसाई और मुस्लिमों की बड़ी अल्पसंख्यक आबादी है, इससे वहां पैर जमाने में मदद मिल सकती है।' बंगाल में जीत की हैट्रिक से उत्साहित ममता बनर्जी ने उनकी बात मान ली। प्रचार अभियान में गोवा के ग्रामीण इलाको में ममता बनर्जी के पोस्टर लग गए थे, जबकि स्थानीय नेताओं को टीएमसी में लाने के लिए किशोर ने राजधानी पणजी के पास डोना पाउला में एक पांच सितारा लग्जरी होटल में डेरा डाल लिया था। किशोर की नज़र पूर्व उप-मुख्यमंत्री और गोवा फॉरवर्ड के प्रमुख, दक्षिण गोवा के महत्वाकांक्षी नेता पचास वर्षीय विजय सरदेसाई पर थी, लेकिन डील नहीं हो पाई। सरदेसाई ने कहा कि 'किशोर ने मुझे मुख्यमंत्री का चेहरा बनाने और पूरी आर्थिक मदद करने की पेशकश की थी, लेकिन वे चाहते थे कि हम अपनी पार्टी का विलय तृणमूल कांग्रेस में कर दें। जिसके लिए हम तैयार नही थे। गोवा, कोलकाता के हिसाब से क्यों चलना चाहिए?' यहां तक कि त्यौहारों के दौरान जब ममता बनर्जी गोवा आईं तो बंगाली और कोंकणी शैली की साड़ियां भी इस समस्या को नहीं सुलझा पाईं।

गोवा के नेता का तर्क दरअसल वो कैच-22 स्थिति है जिसका सामना राष्ट्रीय स्तर पर बढ़ने की कोशिश करने वाले क्षेत्रीय दलों को करना पड़ता है। ममता बनर्जी की टीएमसी की पहचान बंगाली लोक संस्कृति है, गोवा में भले ही मछली और फुटबॉल को लेकर जुनून हो, लेकिन उसकी राजनीति, पंचायतों और गांवों के छोटे-छोटे समुदायों के साथ गहरे रिश्तों से बुनी है—बाहरी लोगों का इसे तोड़ पाना मुश्किल है। सरदेसाई का कहना है, 'किशोर ने सोचा होगा कि वे पैसे की ताकत से चुनाव खरीद सकते हैं, लेकिन गोवा में स्थानीय संबंध किसी भी

चीज़ से ज़्यादा मायने रखते हैं।' इस मसले पर टीमसी-किशोर खेमे की अपनी अलग कहानी है, उनका दावा है कि 'गोवा फॉरवर्ड के नेता ने कांग्रेस के साथ बेहतर डील के लिए टीएमसी से बातचीत का इस्तेमाल किया।' टीएमसी नेता ने कहा कि 'वे हमारे साथ आने को लेकर गंभीर नहीं थे। उन्होंने राहुल गांधी को डील टेबल पर लाने के लिए ममता दी के नाम का इस्तेमाल किया।' जब विधानसभा चुनावों के नतीजे आए, तो टीएमसी को एक भी सीट नहीं मिल पाई थी। चालीस सीटों वाली विधानसभा में भाजपा ने आसान जीत हासिल कर ली, भाजपा-विरोधी वोट बंटने से उनका काम और आसान हो गया। सरदेसाई जोर देकर कहते हैं कि 'टीएमसी गोवा में भाजपा की "बी" टीम थी, जो सेक्यूलर वोटों को बांटने के लिए आई थी।'

एक और महत्वाकांक्षी नेता अरविंद केजरीवाल पर भी 'बी टीम' होने का आरोप था, और आए दिन उन्हें इस आलोचना का सामना करना पड़ा। जहां ममता बनर्जी अपनी बंगाली छवि से बाहर नहीं निकल पाईं, वहीं चतुर केजरीवाल ने आम आदमी पार्टी बनने के दस साल में राष्ट्रीय स्तर पर प्रमुखता बना ली थी। आम आदमी पार्टी में पढ़े-लिखे युवा और बदलाव चाहने वाले लोग हैं, जो वंशवाद, धर्म, जाति या क्षेत्र की पहचान पर ज़ोर नहीं देते। केजरीवाल ने लगातार तीन चुनाव जीते, उनमें से दो दिल्ली में भारी बढ़त के साथ और फिर मार्च 2022 में, दिल्ली से जुड़े महत्वपूर्ण सीमावर्ती राज्य पंजाब में भी सरकार बना ली। पंजाब की जीत से केजरीवाल को भरोसा हो गया कि वे भविष्य में भाजपा और प्रधानमंत्री मोदी को सबसे मजबूत चुनौती दे सकते हैं। आप के पूर्व नेता आशुतोष कहते हैं कि 'जब राजनीतिक क्षमता की बात आती है तो अरविंद ने हमेशा खुद को मोदी के बराबर माना है। एक "डेविड" जिसे खुद पर भरोसा है कि वह "गोलियथ" को हरा सकता है। यही वजह रही कि 2014 के चुनाव में उन्होंने वाराणसी में मोदी से मुकाबला किया, भले ही हम जानते थे कि यह जीत नामुमकिन थी।'

केजरीवाल की नज़रें अब मोदी के गृहराज्य गुजरात पर थीं, जहां नवम्बर 2022 में, विधानसभा चुनाव होने वाले थे। मुख्यमंत्री आवास पर एक बैठक में उनके पार्टी के सहयोगी तब हैरान रह गए, जब आप की गुजरात में रणनीति से लेकर बूथ स्तर तक के काम पर बड़ा प्रजेंटेशन रखा गया। एक सहयोगी ने कहा, 'हमने लंबे समय से अरविंद को इतना उत्साहित नहीं देखा, जितना उस दिन वे गुजरात को लेकर बात कर रहे थे।' बैठक में एक सहयोगी ने सवाल किया, गुजरात में आप की मौजूदगी पर हम उस आलोचना का जवाब कसे देंगे कि भाजपा-विरोधी वोटो को बांटकर हम कांग्रेस को नुकसान पहुंचा रहे हैं? 'पिछले पच्चीस सालों से गुजरात में कांग्रेस, भाजपा से नहीं लड़ पाई है, अब हमें इसका मौका मिलना चाहिए,' केजरीवाल ने बेबाक जवाब दिया।

बहुत से लोग शायद यह नहीं जानते होंगे कि गुजरात में सार्वजनिक रूप से बीजेपी के मुकाबले में खुद को चैलेंजर नंबर 1 बनाते, केजरीवाल पर्दे के पीछे से कांग्रेस के साथ सीटों के

बंटवारे पर काम कर रहे थे। उन्होंने इस मसले पर राहुल गांधी के साथ बात बढ़ाने की कोशिश की, लेकिन राहुल ने नकार दिया। बताया जाता है कि राहुल ने अपने सहयोगियों से कहा, 'मैं कांग्रेस अध्यक्ष नहीं हूं और मैं गठबंधन पर फ़ैसला नहीं करता, तो फिर मुझे केजरीवाल से क्यों मिलना चाहिए?' राहुल का रास्ता बंद होने पर केजरीवाल ने सोनिया गांधी से संपर्क किया। दोनों की फोन पर बातचीत हुई, लेकिन उन्होंने कोई भरोसा देने बजाय वरिष्ठ नेताओं के साथ बात करके जवाब देने की बात की, लेकिन कोई जवाब नहीं आया। अपने स्वभाव के मुताबिक चौकस सोनिया, चुनाव से पहले कोई वादा करने को तैयार नहीं थीं। इस बातचीत के विफल होने का बड़ा फायदा भाजपा को मिला। 182 सदस्यों वाली विधानसभा में रिकॉर्ड 156 सीटों के साथ अपने गढ़ में उसकी जीत और आसान हो गई। आम आदमी पार्टी को भी 5 सीटें और 13 फ़ीसदी वोट मिले, यानी उसने भी अपने लिए थोड़ी जगह बना ली। प्रदेश के आदिवासी इलाके में केजरीवाल ने कई सीटों पर कांग्रेस को पीछे छोड़ दिया। 'हम ऐसे व्यक्ति पर कैसे विश्वास कर सकते हैं, जो पूरे देश में हमारे ही वोट बैंक को नुक़सान पहुंचा रहा है,' कांग्रेस के एक नेता ने तर्क दिया। राजनीति में ज़्यादा जगह पाने के लिए केजरीवाल को हमेशा 'गैर-भरोसेमंद' होने की छवि का नुक़सान उठाना पड़ा है।

'भरोसेमंद' शब्द का खामियाज़ा विपक्षी खेमे के एक और शख्स को उठाना पड़ रहा था, जो प्रधानमंत्री पद के लिए खुद को दावेदार मानते हैं। राजनीतिक मौसम में तमाम बदलावों के बावजूद सबसे लंबी पारी खेल चुके शरद पवार पटना के लंच में सबसे वरिष्ठ नेता थे, जिनका राजनीतिक करियर साठ के दशक में शुरू हुआ था। जब वे महाराष्ट्र में सबसे कम 38 साल की उम्र में युवा मुख्यमंत्री बने, तो पवार की पहचान ऐसे नेता के रूप में बनी, जो जब भी संभव हो, पाला बदल सकता है। अब 83 साल का उम्र में पवार शायद किसी भी राजनीतिक महत्वाकांक्षा को आगे बढ़ाने के लिए कम इच्छुक नज़र आ रहे थे। जुलाई 2022 में, वे राष्ट्रपति पद के लिए विपक्ष के साझा उम्मीदवार बनने के लिए तैयार हो गए थे, लेकिन ऐन वक्त पर पीछे हट गए। एक विपक्षी नेता ने याद करते हुए कहा, 'शुरू में उन्होंने हामी भर दी थी, लेकिन जब हम उनका नाम प्रस्तावित करने वाले थे, तो अचानक उन्होंने मना कर दिया।' फिलहाल किंग नहीं, किंगमेकर की भूमिका उन्होंने अपने लिए चुनी थी। उन्होंने अपने एक करीबी मित्र को कहा, 'मैं इतने कम सांसदों के साथ प्रधानमंत्री कैसे बन सकता हूं? मेरी केवल इतनी कोशिश है कि इस समय विपक्ष एकजुट रहे।' लेकिन जो बात अनकही थी कि वे अपनी बेटी और सांसद, मुखर सुप्रिया सुले के लिए गठबंधन में सुरक्षित भविष्य सुनिश्चित करना चाहते थे।

पवार भले ही अब चुनौती देने की इच्छा नहीं रखते हों, लेकिन पटना की बैठक के मेजबान के मन में ज़रूर इच्छा थी। नीतीश कुमार उन राजनेताओं में से हैं, जिन्होंने सत्तर के दशक में आपातकाल के वक्त अपने करियर की शुरुआत की थी। उस समय ज़्यादातर लोग समाजवादी

नेता जयप्रकाश नारायण के 'संपूर्ण क्रांति' अभियान से प्रेरित होकर राजनीति में आए थे। उस समय के 'आदर्शवादी' छात्र नेता, अब हर हाल में राजनीतिक अस्तित्व की लड़ाई के लिए तैयार नीतीश कुमार ने बिहार में नवीं बार मुख्यमंत्री की शपथ ली थी। राजनीतिक पाला बदलने में माहिर होने की वजह से लोग अब उन्हें 'पलटू कुमार' कहते हैं। तमाम राजनीतिक बदलावों के बीच भी नीतीश कुमार ने एक महत्वाकांक्षा मजबूती से बना रखी हैः एक दिन प्रधानमंत्री बनना। यही वजह है कि तेज़ी से बढ़ते मोदी ने उनकी पीढ़ी के दूसरे राजनेताओं की तरह उन्हें भी भौचक्का कर दिया। वैसे भी मोदी, अपेक्षाकृत राजनीतिक तौर पर कम वज़न वाले राज्य गुजरात से आते हैं, न कि बिहार या उत्तरप्रदेश जैसे हिंदीभाषी राज्यों से (जिनके पास लोकसभा की करीब एक चौथाई हिस्सेदारी है)। नीतीश कुमार वाजपेयी सरकार में केन्द्रीय मंत्री भी रह चुके और मुख्यमंत्री भी, जबकि मोदी कभी केन्द्र सरकार में नहीं रहे। उन्होंने एक बार प्रधानमंत्री को ख़ारिज़ करते हुए कहा था, 'ये मोदी जी आप मीडिया वालों की देन हैं।'

नीतीश कुमार, मोदी को पसंद नहीं करते और उन्होंने इसे कभी छिपाया भी नहीं। 2013 में जब भारतीय जनता पार्टी ने मोदी को प्रधानमंत्री पद का उम्मीदवार बनाया तो नीतीश कुमार 'सेक्यूलर' छवि की मशाल उठाकर एनडीए से बाहर निकलने वाले पहले नेता थे। तब लंदन में बैठे भाजपा नेता अरुण जेटली ने नीतीश कुमार को फ़ोन करके कहा था कि 'वे जल्दबाज़ी में कोई फ़ैसला नहीं करें।' जेटली और नीतीश कुमार के बीच अच्छे संबंध थे। 'अरुणजी, मैं आपका सम्मान करता हूं, लेकिन मैं इनके (मोदी) साथ काम नहीं कर सकता। वे साम्प्रदायिक हैं, डेमोक्रेटिक नहीं हैं, तानाशाह हैं,' कुमार ने सीधा जवाब दिया था।

भारतीय जनता पार्टी से रिश्ता टूटने के बाद नीतीश कुमार अपने पुराने राजनीतिक प्रतिद्वन्दी लालू यादव के पास चले गए। उनके गठबंधन ने 2015 के विधानसभा चुनावों में जीत हासिल की, लेकिन रिश्तों में तनाव बना हुआ था। 'मंडल आंदोलन' से निकले दोनों नेता हर समय बिहार में अपनी जगह मजबूत करने और शीर्ष पर रहने की कोशिश में कभी स्थायी साझेदार नहीं हो सकते थे। 2017 में नीतीश कुमार ने कहा, यादव परिवार के भ्रष्टाचार से उन्हें 'घुटन' होने लगी थी, और वे मोदी की ताकत को मानते हुए, फिर से एनडीए में लौट आए। इसके बावजूद भविष्य में मोदी-विरोधी राजनीति का नेतृत्व करने की उम्मीद से उन्होंने कांग्रेस और राहुल गांधी से दरवाज़े बंद नहीं किए। फिर 2018 में नीतीश कुमार, प्रशांत किशोर (तब जेडीयू में रहे) के साथ करीब एक सप्ताह दिल्ली में रहे और 2019 के आम चुनावों के लिए कांग्रेस के साथ गठबंधन की कोशिश की। लेकिन जब सतर्क राहुल उनसे नहीं मिले, तो परेशान नीतीश खुद को अलग-थलग महसूस करने लगे। बिहार कांग्रेस के एक नेता ने कहा, 'मुझे लगता है कि नीतीश की एनडीए में वापसी के बाद राहुल उन पर पूरी तरह भरोसा नहीं कर पाए। वैसे भी राहुल नीतीश के बजाय लालू यादव के साथ ज़्यादा सहज रहे हैं।'

राजनीति में कुछ भी स्थायी नहीं होता, खासकर बिहार जैसी अस्थिर राजनीति में। जुलाई 2022 में, एक बार फिर नीतीश कुमार ने वफादारी बदल ली। शिवसेना के टूटने और कुछ हफ्ते पहले महाराष्ट्र में सरकार गिरने से नीतीश कुमार को लगने लगा था कि भाजपा उनके ख़िलाफ़ एकनाथ शिंदे जैसी तख्तापलट की योजना बना रही थी: 2020 के बिहार विधानसभा चुनावों में उनकी पार्टी जनता दल यूनाइटेड को सिर्फ़ 43 सीटें मिली थीं, जो भाजपा के साथ गठबंधन के बाद से अब तक का पार्टी सबसे कम नंबर था। चर्चा चलती रही कि भाजपा ने नीतीश कुमार को निशाना बनाने के लिए युवा नेता चिराग पासवान का इस्तेमाल किया था, जिससे नीतीश कुमार नाराज़ थे। जेडी(यू) के एक पूर्व नेता ने कहा, 'उम्र बढ़ने के साथ नीतीश किसी पर भरोसा नहीं करते और उन्हें हर समय अपने ख़िलाफ़ साज़िश होती नज़र आती है।'

मोदी-विरोधी ग्रुप में लौटकर, नीतीश कुमार को राष्ट्रीय राजनीति में विपक्षी गठबंधन के संयोजक के तौर पर अहम भूमिका निभाने का अवसर महसूस हुआ। कर्नाटक में कांग्रेस की जीत के कुछ दिनों में ही, वे मैदान में उतर गए, विपक्षी नेताओं से मुलाकात की और उन्हें एक धर्मनिरपेक्ष लोकतांत्रिक गठबंधन में शामिल होने का न्यौता दिया। दिल्ली के एक नेता ने याद करते हुए बताया कि मुलाकात के दौरान नीतीश कुमार भावुक हो गए थे। 'इस तानाशाह को हटाने का, हमारे पास यह आखिरी मौका है,' बिहार के नेता का यह भावुक भाषण था। पटना में मंच पर देशभर से आए विपक्षी नेताओं से घिरे बैठे नीतीश कुमार अपने लक्ष्य के एक कदम और करीब पहुंच गए थेः मोदी से मुकाबले के लिए विपक्ष का राष्ट्रीय चेहरा।

पटना की यह बैठक 2024 के आम चुनावों में प्रधानमंत्री मोदी को संभावित चुनौती देने के लिए किसी बड़ी घोषणा का आखिरी कदम नहीं था। बल्कि यह तो बस शुरुआत थी कि आम चुनावों में बचे एक साल से पहले एक लक्ष्य वाले सभी लोग कुछ आगे बढ़ने का काम करेंगे। लालू प्रसाद ने उत्साह से कहा, 'हर क्रांति पटना से शुरू होती है।' किडनी ट्रांसप्लांट के बाद थोड़ा कमज़ोर दिखते बिहार के पूर्व मुख्यमंत्री एक बेहतर चुनावी मुकाबले की संभावना देख रहे थे। विपक्षी गठबंधन तैयार हो चुका था। साथियों का जमावड़ा हो गया था।

एक महीने बाद गठबंधन के साथी फिर मिले। इस बार बेंगलुरु में ताज वेस्टएंड के ज़्यादा शानदार माहौल में। कर्नाटक में सफल राजनीतिक जीत का मतलब था कि कांग्रेस अब बेहतर मेजबानी को तैयार थी। वीवीआईपी लोगों की इस बैठक के लिए आलीशान पांच सितारा होटल की घेराबंदी कर दी गई थी, लेकिन मेन्यू में सीटों का बंटवारा और संयोजक चुनने का ज़िक्र नहीं था। केवल दो प्रमुख घोषणाएं की गईः एक महीने में फिर से मुंबई में बैठक होगी, दूसरा दिलचस्प था गठबंधन का नाम। कांग्रेस अध्यक्ष मल्लिकार्जुन खड़गे ने नाम का ऐलान कियाः 'इंडिया नेशनल डेवलपमेंट इनक्लूसिव एलायंस,' और इसका छोटा आकर्षक नाम बनाः 'INDIA'।

कहा गया कि INDIA नाम ममता बनर्जी का आइडिया था, जिसका कांग्रेस ने समर्थन किया। वैसे हर कोई इससे सहमत नहीं था, खासतौर से नीतीश कुमार। औपचारिक रूप से संयोजक नहीं बनाए जाने से नाराज़ नीतीश कुमार का गुस्सा इसलिए बढ़ गया कि उनके सुझाए नाम 'आईएमएफ' या 'इंडिया मेन फ्रंट' को बहुत कम लोगों ने पसंद किया (इसमें वाशिंगटन के इंटरनेशनल मॉनिटरी फंड की गूंज सुनाई देती थी)। उन्होंने एकतरफा फैसले का विरोध किया, लेकिन वामपंथी नेता सीताराम येचुरी ने उन्हें बैठक छोड़कर न जाने के लिए मना लिया। नीतीश ने चिढ़ते हुए कहा, 'इस गठबंधन पर कांग्रेस का कब्ज़ा हो रहा है।'

शुरुआती छोटी-मोटी परेशानियों ने बड़ी तस्वीर पर असर नहीं डाला। यह विपक्ष के लिए एक महत्वपूर्ण क्षण था। सात राज्यों के मुख्यमंत्रियों वाली पार्टियों समेत, लोकसभा के 142 सदस्यों की ताकत वाले 26 दलों का बड़ा गठबंधन बन गया था। ना केवल नाम लोकप्रिय हो गया, बल्कि अगले दिन इसे एक अच्छी टैगलाइन भी मिल गईः 'जुड़ेगा भारत, जीतेगा इंडिया'। तृणमूल कांग्रेस के डेरेक ओ ब्रायन ने उत्साह से कहा, '2024 में यह INDIA बनाम मोदी होगा।' यह बेवजह का आशावाद था या फिर मूड बदलने का इशारा? भारत को जवाब का इंतज़ार था।

10

कौन बनेगा चैलेंजर: राज्य के राजा

कामयाबी के मंत्र के सवाल पर अमित शाह ने भाजपा के अपने एक जूनियर सहयोगी से कहा था, 'ज़िंदगी हो या राजनीति, कभी भी किसी चीज़ को हल्के में न लें।' 2023 के बीते आधे साल में राजनीतिक हालात को देखते हुए गृहमंत्री को चिंताएं समझ आ रही थीं। वह सिर्फ़ कर्नाटक विधानसभा चुनावों में हार से ही परेशान नहीं थे। दिल्ली में ओलंपिक पदक विजेताओं समेत कई महिला पहलवान भाजपा के सांसद और भारतीय कुश्ती महासंघ (WFI) के प्रमुख बृजभूषण शरण सिंह के ख़िलाफ़ आंदोलन पर थे। सड़क पर उतरे इन नाराज़ पहलवानों ने सिंह पर यौन उत्पीड़न का आरोप लगाया था, आंदोलन काबू से बाहर होने लगा था। देश के कुछ बड़े खिलाड़ियों के सड़क पर विरोध प्रदर्शन के वायरल वीडियों और तस्वीरों से आम लोगों की राय में डर पैदा होने लगा था और इसने मोदी सरकार को बहुत शर्मिंदा किया। ज़्यादातर चैंपियन पहलवान हरियाणा से थे, जहां भाजपा की सरकार थी और राजनीति और खेल के बीच रिश्तों को सामने आने में ज़्यादा वक्त नहीं लगा। हालात को काबू में लाने का काम खेल मंत्री अनुराग ठाकुर को सौंपा गया था, उन्होंने दावा किया, 'हरियाणा में कांग्रेस और हुड्डा पहलवानों के विरोध प्रदर्शन का समर्थन कर रहे हैं और यह राजनीति से प्रेरित है।'

असली कहानी ज़्यादा धुंधली है। इस तूफ़ान का केन्द्र आपराधिक रिकॉर्ड वाले बाहुबली बृजभूषण शरण सिंह, उत्तरप्रदेश से छह बार सांसद रहे थे। मैं उनसे पहली बार नब्बे के दशक में तब मिला था, जब उन पर दिल्ली में अपने आधिकारिक आवास में मुंबई अडंरवर्ल्ड के लोगों को पनाह देने के आरोप में आतंकवादी और विघटनकारी गतिविधियां (रोकथाम) अधिनियम (टाडा) लगाया गया था। उनकी सफाई थी, 'पूरा मामला मनगढ़ंत है। मेरे संसदीय क्षेत्र से बहुत

से लोग मेरे घर रहने आते हैं, हरेक पर मैं कैसे नज़र रख सकता हूं?' बृजभूषण को बाद में आतंकवाद के मामले में छोड़ दिया गया, लेकिन अपहरण से लेकर हत्या तक कई आरोपों में उन पर जांच चल रही थी। खास बात यह कि उन्हें भाजपा में गृहमंत्री शाह के 'प्रभावशाली गुट' के तौर पर देखा जाता था, उत्तरप्रदेश के इस ठाकुर नेता का इस्तेमाल योगी आदित्यनाथ के बढ़ते असर पर रोक लगाने के लिए किया जा सकता था। यौन उत्पीड़न के आरोप लगने पर उन्होंने मदद के लिए शाह का रुख किया और ज़ोर देकर कहा, 'मैंने कुछ ग़लत नहीं किया है।' गृहमंत्री ने बृजभूषण को फिलहाल शांत रहने और बचने की सलाह दी। जब मैंने सांसद से उनके दिल्ली आवास पर बात करने की कोशिश की, तो एक सुरक्षा गार्ड ने चेताया, 'अगर आप यहां फिर से दिखे, तो आपका कैमरा तोड़ देंगे!'

साफ-सुथरे दिखते चश्मा पहने कांग्रेस के युवा सांसद दीपेन्द्र हुड्डा के लिए पहलवानों का विरोध, उनके समाज के साथ खड़े दिखने और रक्षक होने का दावा करने का एक मौका था। विरोध करने वाली सभी महिला पहलवान जाट समाज से थीं, उनमें से कुछ तो हरियाणा में हुड्डा परिवार के गढ़ रोहतक से ही थीं। राष्ट्रीय कुश्ती महासंघ को जागीर की तरह चलाने वाले बृजभूषण ने दीपेन्द्र को बाहर कर दिया। महत्वाकांक्षी और मेहनती दीपेन्द्र हुड्डा 2020 तक हरियाणा कुश्ती महासंघ के अध्यक्ष रहे थे। हुड्डा ने कहा कि 'यह मसला राजनीति का नहीं है, हमारी महिला पहलवान हमारे समाज और प्रदेश का गौरव हैं।' जनवरी 2020 में, जब पहलवानों ने अपना विरोध प्रदर्शन शुरू किया, तब उनका ज़ोर राजनेताओं को आंदोलन से दूर रखने पर था। लेकिन अप्रैल में जब खेल मंत्रालय के आश्वासन के बावजूद बृजभूषण के ख़िलाफ़ कोई कार्रवाई नहीं की गई, तो आंदोलन ने राजनीतिक मोड़ ले लिया। कहा जाता है कि हुड्डा और खेलों से जुड़े एक प्रमुख औद्योगिक घराने के समर्थन से पहलवानों ने अपना विरोध और तेज़ कर दिया। एक नाटकीय कदम उठाते हुए पहलवानों ने अपने ओलिंपिक और विश्व चैंपियनशिप के पदक गंगा में विसर्जित करने की धमकी दी। कॉमनवेल्थ गेम्स में अनेकों गोल्ड मेडल जीत चुकी विनेश फोगट ने कहा, 'ममता बनर्जी और अरविंद केजरीवाल ने हमें फोन करके ऐसा कदम न उठाने की विनती की। प्रियंका गांधी हमसे मिलीं। उन सबने हमारे सहयोग का वादा किया, लेकिन बीजेपी में से किसी ने हमसे मिलने की कोई कोशिश नहीं की।'

ओलिंपिक में कांस्य पदक जीतने वाली साक्षी मलिक ने कहा, 'हमारी बात पर ध्यान देने और सांसद पर कार्रवाई करने के बजाय सरकार चरित्र-हनन पर उतर आई है।' हरियाणा सरकार के अधिकारियों को पहलवानों के घर पर भेजा गया ताकि परिवारों पर विरोध वापस लेने का दबाव बनाया जा सके। कई ओलंपियन राज्य सरकार की नौकरी में थे, उन्हें चेतावनी दी गई कि अगर उन्होंने आंदोलन ख़त्म नहीं किया, तो उनकी नौकरी जा सकती है। अल-जज़ीरा की वेबसाइट पर एक स्टोरी में बताया गया कि शिकायत करने वाले एक युवा को कथित तौर पर

धमकी दी गई, 'आपको डोप के मामले में फंसा देंगे।' इसके तुरंत बाद राष्ट्रीय डोपिंग रोधी एजेंसी (NADA) के अफसर आवासीय कुश्ती अकादमी पहुंचे, जहां शिकायत करने वाली पहलवान प्रशिक्षण ले रही थी और उसे 'डोप टैस्ट' के लिए मजबूर किया गया। कुछ दिनों बाद मिले नोटिस में दावा किया गया था कि उसके सैम्पल में प्रतिबंधित पदार्थ के संकेत मिले थे। हरियाणा के कुश्ती कोच के एक प्रतिनिधिमंडल ने कथित डोपिंग आरोपों के मुद्दे पर खेल मंत्री अनुराग ठाकुर से मुलाक़ात की, लेकिन नोटिस वापस नहीं लिया गया। वह निलंबित रही। सात महीने बाद नाडा ने उसे 'क्लीन चिट' दे दी, लेकिन तब तक बहुत देर हो चुकी थी। उसकी तीन साल की 'स्पॉंसरशिप डील' को रद्द कर दिया गया था और उसका करियर ख़त्म होने की कगार पर पहुंच गया। 'साम-दाम-दंड, उन्होंने सबकुछ करने की कोशिश की,' ओलिंपिक पदक विजेता बजरंग पूनिया ने आरोप लगाया। खेल मंत्रालय पूनिया को विरोध प्रदर्शनों का 'सरगना' मानता था। यूं तो पूनिया ने मोदी समर्थक होने का दावा किया था, लेकिन जब उन्होंने पीएमओ से दख़ल की मांग की तो उन्हें कोई जवाब नहीं मिला।

राजधानी के केन्द्र में जंतर-मंतर पर अस्थायी टेंट लगाकर प्रदर्शन कर रहे पहलवानों ने कोई समाधान नहीं दिखने पर, उद्घाटन के दिन संसद भवन की ओर मार्च का फ़ैसला किया। दिल्ली पुलिस ने दबिश देकर पहलवानों को हिरासत में ले लिया। विरोध को ख़त्म करने के आदेश सीधे गृह मंत्रालय से आए थे। महिला पहलवानों को सड़क पर घसीटने की तस्वीरें और पुलिस की गाड़ियों के वीडियो वायरल हो गए थे। कुछ दिनों पहले जिन ओलम्पिक विजेताओं को प्रधानमंत्री ने देश के लिए पदक जीतने पर अपने आवास पर सम्मानित किया था, उनके साथ अब सड़क के गुंडों जैसा बर्ताव किया जा रहा था। इस विरोध ने पहलवानों को मोदी सरकार विरोधी भावना का प्रतीक बना दिया। कांग्रेस ने बजरंग पूनिया को 2023 के राजस्थान विधानसभा चुनावों में टिकट दिया और साक्षी मलिक को 2024 के लोकसभा चुनावों में मथुरा से लड़ने का प्रस्ताव रखा, लेकिन दोनों ने प्रस्ताव को ठुकरा दिया। विनेश ने राजनीति में कदम रखने का फैसला किया और 2024 में हरियाणा विधानसभा चुनावों में जुलाना से कांग्रेस की सीट पर चुनाव लड़ा। पेरिस ओलम्पिक में स्वर्ण पदक के लिए उन्हें विवादास्पद तरीके से अयोग्य घोषित कर दिया गया था और उन्हें लगा कि उनके पास खोने के लिए कुछ नहीं है। उन्होंने कहा, 'अगर जरूरत के समय प्रधानमंत्री हमारे साथ खड़े होते तो मैं कभी राजनीति में नहीं आती।'

पहलवानों की मांगों पर उनकी चुप्पी ने प्रधानमंत्री मोदी के 'बेटी बचाओ, बेटी पढ़ाओ' के नारों को कमज़ोर कर दिया था। जनता की सहानुभूति पूरी तरह पहलवानों के साथ थी। भाजपा के एक नेता ने माना, 'कांग्रेस ने पहलवानों का समर्थन किया हो, लेकिन लोगों की नज़र में हम लड़ाई हार गए थे, ओलंपियन बनाम नेता कोई मुक़ाबला नहीं है।' किसान आंदोलन के बाद अब पहलवानों के विरोध को एक निरंकुश, गलत सलाह मानने वाली सरकार ने गलत

तरीके से संभालने की कोशिश की, जो असहमति के सामने अनिश्चित और कमज़ोर लग रही थी। सरकार के इस झूठ का असर चुनावों में होना था। 2024 के आम चुनावों में हरियाणा और राजस्थान के जाट-प्रभुत्व इलाके में कांग्रेस का दबदबा रहा।

दुर्भाग्य से गृहमंत्री के लिए अभी कुछ और बुरी ख़बरें बाकी थीं। जब वह कर्नाटक में चुनाव प्रचार कर रहे थे, तब मणिपुर में मैतेई-कुकी समुदायों के बीच नस्लीय हिंसा भड़क गई, जिसमें कई लोग मारे गए और हज़ारों लोग बेघर हो गए थे। हरियाणा की तरह मणिपुर में भाजपा की सरकार थी। एक ज़माने में कांग्रेस में रहे प्रदेश के मुख्यमंत्री एन. बीरेन सिंह भी शाह की बढ़ती ताकत का हिस्सा माने जाते थे। इस मसले पर जब भाजपा के कई विधायकों ने मुख्यमंत्री बदलने की बात की, तो शाह ने उसे खारिज़ कर दिया। गृहमंत्री ने विधायकों से कहा, 'मुख्यमंत्री बदलने से कुछ नहीं होगा। यह बहुत संवेदनशील मुद्दा है।' 63 साल के बीरेन सिंह, कठोर राजनेता और दिलचस्प शख्सियत हैं, वह नेशनल लेवल पर 'स्टार फुटबॉलर' रहे हैं। उनके इम्फाल के आवास पर एक अहम तस्वीर है, जिसमें वह 1981 की सीमा सुरक्षा बल की टीम के साथ डूरंड कप पकड़े हुए हैं। डूरंड कप भारत की सबसे पुरानी सालाना घरेलू फुटबॉल प्रतियोगिता है। उन्होंने मुस्कुराते हुए कहा, 'फुटबॉल मेरा पहला प्यार है, राजनीति इसके बाद आई।' बरसों तक कांग्रेस में रहे बीरेन सिंह 2017 के विधानसभा चुनावों से पहले भाजपा में आ गए थे। सिंह के साथ ही उनके दामाद आर.के. इमो सिंह भी भाजपा में शामिल हो गए थे, वह भी प्रसिद्ध कांग्रेस परिवार से रहे हैं और मणिपुर क्रिकेट संघ के अध्यक्ष हैं। उन्हें बीसीसीआई में जय शाह गुट का हिस्सा माना जाता है। इम्फाल के वरिष्ठ पत्रकार प्रदीप फंजौबेम कहते हैं, 'मणिपुर में हर राजनेता का दिल्ली से कोई न कोई संबंध है, सब गोरखधंधा है, इसे समझना आसान काम नहीं।'

मई 2023 में गृहमंत्री हालात का जायजा लेने के लिए तीन दिन के दौरे पर मणिपुर गए थे, लेकिन प्रधानमंत्री ने खुद को इससे दूर रखा, यहां तक कि राज्य में फैली हिंसा पर उन्होंने कोई ट्वीट तक नहीं किया। जुलाई में, जब मणिपुर के कांगपोकपी ज़िले में दो महिलाओं को एक बड़ी भीड़ के नग्न परेड कराने का भयावह वीडियो वायरल हुआ, तब प्रधानमंत्री ने अपनी चुप्पी तोड़ी। प्रधानमंत्री पूर्वोत्तर का विशेष ध्यान रखने को लेकर गर्व करते हैं, किसी दूसरे प्रधानमंत्री ने इस क्षेत्र का कभी इतनी बार दौरा नहीं किया है। लेकिन जब मणिपुर में इसके इम्तिहान की बारी आई तो मोदी सरकार लड़खड़ाती और इसे खारिज़ करती हुई दिखी। मार्टिन लूथर किंग जूनियर ने कहा था, 'किसी व्यक्ति की पहचान इससे नहीं होती कि वह आराम और बेहतर वक्त में कहां खड़ा है, बल्कि उसकी शख्सियत की पहचान इससे होती है कि वह चुनौती और संकट के समय कहां रहा।' देश में किसानों का विरोध हो, पहलवानों का आंदोलन या फिर मणिपुर जैसी घटनाएं, जब चुनौती और विवाद का सामना करना पड़ता है, तो मोदी का एक स्याह पहलू सामने आता है: पलायनवादी, गैर ज़िम्मेदार और असंवेदनशील। मोदी से उलट, राहुल

गांधी एक बार फिर एक्शन में दिखे, राहुल मणिपुर के राहत शिविरों तक पहुंचे और विभिन्न समुदायों के विस्थापितों से मुलाक़ात की। भाजपा के राष्ट्रीय प्रवक्ता नलिन मेहता ने सफाई में कहा, 'हम फोटो-ऑप राजनीति में विश्वास नहीं करते हैं।' लेकिन कभी-कभी किसी तस्वीर की गूंज दूर तक और देर तक सुनाई देती है। आंसू भरी मणिपुरी महिलाओं को गले लगाते राहुल की तस्वीर अपने आप में पूरी कहानी बयां कर रही थी। खामोश मोदी बनाम सहानुभूतिपूर्ण राहुल गांधी—मणिपुर ने दो बड़े नेताओं के संकट के समय में विपरीत नजरिए को रेखांकित किया। धारणा और छवि बदलने लगी थी।

मणिपुर के गंभीर हालात में मुझे पहली बार अनुभव हुआ कि वहां सरकार जैसी कोई चीज़ नहीं है। जून 2023 के आखिर में, एक मानवाधिकार कार्यकर्ता और मित्र ने फोन पर आग्रह किया, 'क्या आप वुंगाजिन वाल्टे की कहानी को रिपोर्ट कर सकते हैं?' मुझे नहीं पता था कि वाल्टे कौन थे? लेकिन जब उसने डरावनी कहानी सुनाई तो मैं अपने भीतर के सन्नाटे के साथ बाहर आ गया। दक्षिण दिल्ली की एक भीड़-भाड़ वाली कॉलोनी में मुश्किल से उस ग्राउंड फ्लोर के छोटे से फ्लैट में पहुंचा, जहां मणिपुर से तीन बार के भाजपा के विधायक वाल्टे रह रहे थे। मौत के चंगुल से निकले वाल्टे, बीरेन सिंह के विश्वस्त रहे हैं। वाल्टे कुकी समुदाय से हैं। मुख्यमंत्री बीरेन सिंह के सरकारी आवास से थोड़ी दूर पर हथियारों से लैस मैतेई समुदाय की भीड़ ने उन्हें निशाना बनाया था। वाल्टे की हालत देखने की हिम्मत मुझमें नहीं थी, पूरा शरीर घायल, मुड़ा हुआ, अपंग, तकलीफ को समझना मुश्किल नहीं था, उनकी आवाज़ पर असर पड़ा था, बताया गया कि उन्हें बिजली के झटके दिए गए थे। उन्हें इम्फाल से निकालकर हवाई जहाज से दिल्ली के एक अस्पताल में पहुंचाया गया। एक रिश्तेदार के घर पर रह रहे वाल्टे परिवार के लोग चिंता और तकलीफ से बेहाल थे। मैनू वाल्टे ने रोते हुए कहा, 'मेरे पति को लगभग मार ही दिया गया, लेकिन अभी तक किसी को गिरफ़्तार नहीं किया गया और ना ही कोई हमें देखने आता है।' आंसू रोकना मुश्किल था। अगर एक भाजपा विधायक के परिवार की यह हालत थी, तो सोच सकते हैं कि राहत शिविरों में मणिपुर के आम लोगों की हालत क्या होगी। मणिपुर भारत के कोने में बसा एक छोटा सा राज्य है, लेकिन 2024 की लड़ाई से पहले यह मरहम लगाने में राजनीतिक नेतृत्व की विफलता का प्रतीक बन गया था। 2024 के आम चुनावों में, मणिपुर में भाजपा का सफाया हो गया, राज्य की दोनों सीटें पार्टी हार गई।

═

भारतीय जनता पार्टी का चुनावी वॉर-रूम अपने आंतारेक पोल सर्वेक्षणों को गंभीरता से लेता है। यह फीडबैक कई निजी सर्वेक्षण एजेंसियों और ज़मीन पर काम कर रहे संघ-भाजपा के बड़े नेटवर्क से मिलता है। जून 2023 में, पार्टी के मासिक ओपिनियन-ट्रैकर पोल से पता चला कि

वह मध्यप्रदेश, छत्तीसगढ़, राजस्थान के साथ तेलंगाना में पीछे चल रही थी, जहां नवंबर में विधानसभा चुनाव होने थे। दक्षिण के राज्य कर्नाटक में, जहां हर पांच साल में सरकार बदलती है, एक कमज़ोर स्थानीय संगठन से रणनीति गड़बड़ाने की बात तो समझ आती है, लेकिन हिंदीभाषी राज्यों में वह कांग्रेस से कैसे हार सकती थी। एक साल बाद, 2024 के आम चुनावों से पहले यह बड़े ख़तरे की घंटी थी।

प्रधानमंत्री आवास पर जून की शुरुआत में बुलाई गई आला नेताओं की एक बैठक में पोल के निष्कर्षों पर गहन चर्चा हुई। उसी समय 'इंडिया गठबंधन' भी शक्ल ले रहा था। बंद कमरे में मोदी, शाह, भाजपा के राष्ट्रीय अध्यक्ष जगत प्रकाश नड्डा और संगठन महासचिव बी.एल. संतोष थे। बीजेपी के इन 'बिग फोर' के पास पूरी पार्टी का नियंत्रण था और हरेक के पास एक विशेष ज़िम्मेदारी। मोदी भाजपा चुनावी मशीन के सारथी, सर्वोच्च नेता और अंतिम फ़ैसला करने वाले थे, शाह रणनीतिकार और ज़मीन से जुड़े रहने वाले मुख्य आयोजक, तो नड्डा ऐसे भरोसेमंद अनुयायी, जो हर आदेश को पूरा करने के लिए तैयार रहते थे। कर्नाटक में हार से थोड़ा परेशान संतोष भाजपा और आरएसएस के बीच तालमेल को देख रहे थे। जब अमित शाह ने मध्यप्रदेश और छत्तीसगढ़ के परेशान करने वाले आंकड़ों का ज़िक्र किया, तो प्रधानमंत्री बेअसर दिखाई पड़े। उन्होंने ज़ोर देकर कहा, 'बस हमें मेहनत और करनी पड़ेगी।' भाजपा के एक पदाधिकारी का कहना था, 'मोदी जी और अमित भाई का संदेश हमेशा यह रहता है कि हर चुनाव एक नई लड़ाई जैसा है। अगर आप एक चुनाव हार जाते हैं तो हार मानकर बैठिए मत, बस यह सुनिश्चित करना है कि अगली लड़ाई बेहतर तरीके से लड़ी जाए।'

संघ परिवार का गढ़ माना जाने वाला बड़ा राज्य मध्यप्रदेश पार्टी के लिए चिंता का सबब था। भाजपा केवल जनमत सर्वेक्षण में ही नहीं पिछड़ रही थी, बल्कि मुख्यमंत्री शिवराज सिंह चौहान की लोकप्रियता की रेटिंग भी गिर रही थी। कुछ महीने पहले भी, चौहान पर सर्वेक्षण रिपोर्ट ठीक नहीं थी, जिसके बाद यह अटकलें लगाई जा रही थीं कि 2018-19 के छोटे से अंतराल को छोड़कर 18 साल सत्ता में रहने के बाद, पार्टी आलाकमान लंबे समय से मुख्यमंत्री रहे शिवराज को बदल सकता है। भाजपा के उच्च सूत्रों ने इस बात की पुष्टि की कि नेतृत्व में बदलाव को लेकर फरवरी 2023 में ही फ़ैसला किया गया था, लेकिन शिवराज के समर्थन में संघ के आला नेताओं के दख़ल के बाद, अंतिम समय में रोक दिया गया। अब नए सर्वेक्षणों के बाद चौहान के भविष्य को लेकर फिर से चर्चा शुरू हो गई, कहा गया कि 'मामाजी' को लेकर लोगों में गुस्सा तो कम था, लेकिन थकावट नज़र आ रही थी। शिवराज जी मध्यप्रदेश में 'मामाजी' के नाम से लोकप्रिय नेता हैं। लेकिन विकल्प नहीं दिख रहे थे। अमित शाह के ज़मीनी हालात पर रिपोर्ट रखने तक मुख्यमंत्री बदलने के फ़ैसले को टाल दिया गया। जून 2023 में, प्रधानमंत्री महत्वपूर्ण अमेरिका यात्रा पर जा रहे थे। शाह को चुनाव की पूरी ज़िम्मेदारी सौंप

दी गई। प्रधानमंत्री ने अमेरिका के लिए जहाज में चढ़ने से पहले कहा, 'अमित भाई के निर्देशों के मुताबिक योजना बनाइए,' 'बिग फोर' के अन्य सदस्यों ने सिर्फ़ सिर हिलाकर हामी भर दी।

चुनावी जंग को लेकर गृहमंत्री का एक अलग जज़्बा है। अस्सी के दशक की शुरुआत में अहमदाबाद में जब उन्होंने कॉलेज में पहला चुनाव लड़ा था, तबसे जीत ही उनके लिए सबकुछ है। किसी भी हाल में मुकाबले को जीतना और उसके लिए किसी भी हद तक जाने की मानसिकता, उन्हें दूसरों से अलग करती है। प्रधानमंत्री के भरोसे से उत्साहित शाह ने अपना काम शुरू कर दिया। सबसे पहले उन्होंने सभी चुनावी राज्यों में मतदाताओं के मूड का एक बड़ा सर्वेक्षण करवाया। इसमें स्थानीय और बूथ कार्यकर्ताओं के आंकलन को भी शामिल किया गया था। शाह के भरोसेमंद भूपेन्द्र यादव को मध्यप्रदेश का प्रभारी बनाया गया। राजस्थान के वरिष्ठ नेता ओम माथुर को छत्तीसगढ़ की जिम्मेदारी दी गई। केन्द्रीय मंत्री प्रहलाद जोशी को राजस्थान संभालने के लिए कहा गया। देशभर से पार्टी के प्रमुख नेताओं को चुनाव से तीन महीने पहले ही अलग-अलग ज़िलों में तैनाती के निर्देश दिए गए। जैसे, गोवा के वरिष्ठ मंत्री विश्वजीत राणे को इंदौर ज़िले की सभी छह सीटों की ज़िम्मेदारी मिली। राणे को प्रदेश प्रभारी को रिपोर्ट करने के साथ बूथ स्तर पर बैठकों का आयोजन करना था और साथ ही साप्ताहिक रिपोर्ट देनी थी, इसके अलावा गृहमंत्री की अध्यक्षता में लगातार होने वाली वीडियो कॉन्फ्रेंस में शामिल होना होगा। कांग्रेस में रहे राणे कहते हैं, 'अमित भाई के साथ रात-दिन जैसी कोई सोच नहीं है। वह आपसे आधी रात को भी कुछ करने के लिए कह सकते हैं और बस यह देखना है कि वह पूरा हो जाए। मैंने इतने गहन तरीके से काम कभी नहीं देखा।'

चुनाव से दो महीने पहले उम्मीदवारों के चयन से लेकर, कड़े मुकाबले वाली सीटों पर ज़्यादा ध्यान देने तक, शाह एक उत्साही माहौल बनाने में लगे थे, ताकि लगे कि भाजपा कर्नाटक के झटके से उबर गई है और फिर से मजबूती के साथ चुनाव मैदान में है। कार्यकर्ता का मनोबल बढ़ाने की रणनीति के तहत शाह ने केन्द्रीय मंत्रियों को विधानसभा चुनाव लड़ाने की सिफ़ारिश की। ऐसे ही एक मंत्री ने बताया, 'शाह ने आधी रात को फोन कर उन्हें अपना फ़ैसला बताया। मैंने जब उनसे पूछा कि उनके विधानसभा चुनाव लड़ने को लोग डिमोशन की तरह तो नहीं देखेंगे, क्योंकि मैं एक सांसद और मंत्री था। उनका जवाब सीधा था, "राजनीति में कोई डिमोशन-प्रमोशन नहीं होता; आप पहले बीजेपी के कार्यकर्ता हैं और फिर नेता, अब जाकर चुनाव जीतो।"' एक समय में केन्द्र में मंत्री रहे और अब विधायक ने कहा, 'यह चुनाव प्रबंधन के अमित शाह स्कूल में मेरे लिए एक और सबक था।'

चुनावी राज्यों के आंतरिक सर्वेक्षण से एक और दिलचस्प बात सामने आई। प्रदेश स्तर के नेताओं की लोकप्रियता तो ऊपर-नीचे थी, लेकिन प्रधानमंत्री की रेटिंग बहुत मजबूत थी। निष्कर्ष यह था कि 2023 के विधानसभा चुनाव सिर्फ़ प्रधानमंत्री के नाम पर लड़े जाने होंगे।

‘कोई डबल-इंजन नहीं, इस बार हर राज्य में सिर्फ़ एक ही इंजन चलेगा, मोदी जी का इंजन,’ शाह का अपनी टीम को साफ संदेश था। कर्नाटक में असरदार रही कांग्रेस की गारंटी के मुकाबले के लिए भाजपा ने केन्द्र सरकार की विभिन्न योजनाओं को लेकर एक जवाबी नारा दिया: ‘मोदी की गारंटी’। शाह का तर्क था, ‘लोग मोदी जी पर भरोसा करते हैं, उनकी गारंटी हमेशा विपक्ष की किसी भी पेशकश से ज़्यादा वज़नदार साबित होगी।’ सरल, फोकस्ड और असरदार। विधानसभा चुनावों और 2024 के आम चुनावों दोनों के लिए ‘मोदी की गारंटी’ भाजपा का मुख्य चुनावी नारा बन गई। लेकिन दोनों के नतीज़े अलग रहे।

मध्यप्रदेश में विधानसभा चुनावों से ठीक पहले रतलाम में एक रैली में प्रधानमंत्री ने घोषणा की कि उनकी सरकार ‘प्रधानमंत्री गरीब कल्याण अनाज योजना’ के तहत मिलने वाले ‘मुफ़्त राशन’ को अगले पांच साल के लिए बढ़ाएगी। यह योजना कोविड के दौरान शुरू की गई थी और इसका लक्ष्य 80 करोड़ गरीब लोगों को फायदा पहुंचाना था। प्रधानमंत्री ने कहा ‘अगले पांच साल तक मेरे देश के 80 करोड़ लोगों के घरों में चूल्हे जलते रहेंगे, यह मोदी की गारंटी है।’ चुनावों में पार्टियों के घोषणापत्र वादों से भरे होते हैं, जिनमें सभी पूरे नहीं होते। मोदी ने दावा किया कि ‘यह सिर्फ़ चुनावी वादा या भाजपा के एजेंडा का मुद्दा नहीं है, यह प्रधानमंत्री की प्रतिबद्धता है, मोदी की गारंटी है।’ सभी तानाशाहों की तरह, मोदी अपने बारे में थर्ड पर्सन के तौर पर बात करते हैं और पार्टी को दरकिनार करते हुए सीधे मतदाता से जुड़ते हैं।

मोदी-केन्द्रित अभियान का मतलब था कि कोई भी स्थानीय नेता प्रचार सामग्री में सामने नहीं होगा। यहां तक कि चार बार के मुख्यमंत्री रह चुके नेता को भी पार्टी के एकमात्र चेहरे के तौर पर नहीं पेश किया जाएगा। बदलते समय का संकेत साफ था, राज्य में करीब एक साथ पांच जगहों से जन-आशीर्वाद यात्राएं शुरू की गईं लेकिन पिछले चुनावों से उलट, इसका नेतृत्व शिवराज सिंह चौहान के बजाय प्रदेश के अलग-अलग नेताओं ने किया। जब चौहान सरकार ने सब्सिडी वाली भोजन योजना का नाम बदलकर ‘मामा की थाली’ रखने का सुझाव दिया, तो इस प्रस्ताव को ख़ारिज़ कर दिया गया। हालांकि केन्द्र ने नरमी दिखाते हुए मुख्यमंत्री की महिलाओं के लिए उनकी ‘लाडली बहन योजना’ को आगे बढ़ाने की इजाज़त दे दी। मार्च 2023 में शुरू की गई इस योजना में कमज़ोर वर्ग की महिलाओं को हर महीने एक हज़ार रुपये नकद देने का वादा किया गया था। जून 2023 तक, 21 से 60 साल तक की करीब एक करोड़ तीस लाख महिलाओं ने इसमें अपना नामांकन कराया था। लाडली बहन की लाभार्थी महिलाएं मध्यप्रदेश में भाजपा के लिए निर्णायक वोट साबित हुईं।

राजनीतिक संकट में फंसे चौहान विनम्रता दिखाते हुए चुपचाप ‘पार्टी लाइन’ पर रहे और मध्यप्रदेश में सामूहिक नेतृत्व के साथ जाने के लिए तैयार हो गए। लेकिन पड़ोसी राज्य राजस्थान में भाजपा की इकलौती उत्तर भारतीय महिला क्षत्रप, स्टाइलिश, मुखर और तेवर दिखाती

वसुंधरा राजे, बिना संघर्ष के हार मानने को तैयार नहीं थीं। दो बार मुख्यमंत्री रहीं वसुंधरा प्रदेश में भाजपा की सबसे लोकप्रिय नेता थीं। वह सिर्फ़ एक और नेता के तौर पर दिखने को राजी नहीं थीं, उन्होंने चुनाव अभियान में उतरने से पहले भविष्य में उनकी भूमिका स्पष्ट करने पर ज़ोर दिया, लेकिन शाह अडिग थे। वसुंधरा से वैसे भी कभी उनके रिश्ते मधुर नहीं रहे थे। शाह ने पार्टी में उनके 'टीम-प्लेयर' नहीं होने की आलोचना की थी। जब निराश वसुंधरा पार्टी नेतृत्व के साथ मसलों को सुलझाने के लिए एक हफ्ते तक दिल्ली में डेरा डाले रहीं, तो उन्हें न तो गृहमंत्री और न ही प्रधानमंत्री से मुलाकात का समय मिला। प्रदेश भाजपा के एक नेता ने कहा, 'मुझे लगता है कि वसुंधरा जी को संदेश संतोष जी के माध्यम से दिया गया। उन्हें टीम में रहना होगा और नेतृत्व पर फ़ैसला चुनावों के बाद होगा।' आखिर में वसुंधरा भाजपा के परिवर्तन यात्रा अभियान में शामिल तो हुईं, लेकिन उनका चिर-परिचित जोश नहीं दिख रहा था।

शाह के लिए सबसे मुश्किल काम शायद छत्तीसगढ़ था, जहां 2018 के पिछले चुनावों में कांग्रेस भारी बहुमत के साथ सत्ता में आई थी। भाजपा के एक पदाधिकारी ने कहा, 'यह मानना चाहिए कि पार्टी में हममें से ज़्यादातर लोगों ने छत्तीसगढ़ को लेकर तो हार मान ली थी। तीन महीने पहले हुए पार्टी के आंतरिक सर्वेक्षण भी कांग्रेस की आसान जीत बता रहे थे।' लेकिन शाह, बिना लड़ाई लड़े हार मानने को तैयार नहीं थे। उनका तर्क था, 'छोटा राज्य है, वोटों में तीन-चार प्रतिशत का बदलाव भी माहौल को बदल देगा।' राज्य की राजनीति आदिवासी ज़िलों और मैदानी इलाकों में बंटी थी। 2018 के चुनावों में कांग्रेस ने आदिवासी इलाकों में रिकॉर्ड जीत हासिल की थी, बस्तर में 12 में से 11 सीटें और सरगुजा में सभी 14 सीटें कांग्रेस ने जीती थीं। विष्णुदेव साय ने याद करते हुए कहा, 'छत्तीसगढ़ की हमारी पहली चुनावी रणनीति बैठक में ओम माथुर जी ने आदिवासी सीटों पर फोकस रखने को कहा, आदिवासी वोटों को जीतने के लिए जो कुछ करना पड़े, किया जाना चाहिए।' साय, बाद में प्रदेश के पहले आदिवासी मुख्यमंत्री बने।

आदिवासी ज़िलों में प्रचार अभियान में जाना-पहचाना तरीका इस्तेमाल किया गया: धार्मिक डर का फायदा उठाना और सांप्रदायिक उन्माद बढ़ाना। भाजपा ने आदिवासियों में बढ़ते धर्मांतरण पर एक दुष्प्रचार अभियान चलाया। राष्ट्रीय स्वयंसेवक संघ, आदिवासियों के लिए चलाए जा रहे अपने वनवासी कल्याण आश्रम के माध्यम से आदिवासियों के ईसाई धर्म में शामिल होने का मुद्दा पहले से ही चला रहा था। चुनावों के दौरान, संघ की पूरी मशीनरी ने धर्मांतरण पर ज़ोर-शोर से प्रचार किया, बूथ स्तर पर व्हाट्सएप ग्रुप पर चर्च की गतिविधियों के बारे में नफ़रत फैलाने की कोशिश की गई। एक ऐसे ही वीडियो में कहा गया, 'वे आपकी ज़मीन और आपके भगवान छीन लेंगे,' जिसका मकसद साफ था: आदिवासियों को धर्म के आधार पर बांटना। भाजपा ने मतदाताओं को याद दिलाया कि मोदी सरकार ने ही द्रौपदी मुर्मु को राष्ट्रपति

बनाया था। प्रधानमंत्री ने आदिवासी कल्याण की बड़ी योजनाओं का ऐलान किया, ताकि मोदी सरकार की आदिवासियों को लेकर प्रतिबद्धता बताई जा सके। अभियान के आखिरी चरण में, अमित शाह ने स्थानीय इकाई को निर्देश दिया कि वे गोंडवाणा गणतंत्र पार्टी और हमार राज पार्टी जैसे छोटे दलों के उम्मीदवारों को आगे बढ़ाएं, उन्हें मदद करें, ताकि भाजपा विरोधी वोटों को बांटा जा सके। इस रणनीति को मोदी-शाह जोड़ी ने राजनीति के अपने शुरुआती सालों में गुजरात के नगरपालिका और पंचायत चुनावों में आजमाया था। भाजपा विरोधी इलाकों में अपने विरोधियों को आगे करके दूसरे प्रतिद्वन्दियों के वोटों को विभाजित किया जाए। 'भाजपा को मेन पोल बनाओ, बाकी के वोट कटाओ,' यह उनकी जांची-परखी रणनीति थी। 'लाडली बहना योजना' की तरह, राज्य में शादीशुदा महिलाओं के लिए 'महतारी वंदन योजना' की भाजपा की घोषणा, छत्तीसगढ़ में बड़े पैमाने में लोगों तक पहुंचने में अहम रही और मतदान के दिन यह महत्वपूर्ण साबित हुई। इस योजना में लाभार्थी महिलाओं को हर महीने एक हज़ार रुपये की मदद और उनका आर्थिक सशक्तिकरण की बात की गई थी। इसके लिए प्रदेश भर में महिलाओं से फॉर्म भरवाने के लिए शिविर लगाए गए। राज्य के धान किसानों तक पहुंचने के लिए, भाजपा ने न्यूनतम समर्थन मूल्य से ऊपर एक विशेष बोनस देने का वादा किया। दिल्ली में भले ही केन्द्र सरकार किसानों की एमएसपी बढ़ाने की मांग को मानने के लिए तैयार नहीं थी, लेकिन छत्तीसगढ़ में चुनाव जीतना ज़रूरी था। भाजपा के एक पोलस्टर ने कहा, 'यदि आप यह समझना चाहते हैं कि भाजपा-आरएसएस चुनाव मशीनरी कैसे काम करती है तो उनके छत्तीसगढ़ चुनाव अभियान का एक केस स्टडी करें। आदिवासी बनाम गैर-आदिवासी, हिंदू बनाम ईसाई, छोटे दलों और निर्दलियों की मदद, महिलाओं और किसानों को नकद सहायता का वादा, मुझे नहीं लगता कि ऐसा कुछ भी रहा होगा जो भाजपा ने सत्ता में वापसी के लिए नहीं किया होगा।' सरकार चलाते वक्त पार्टी की कमियां भले ही नज़र आती हों, लेकिन चुनाव अभियान के दौरान मोदी की भाजपा का हर सिस्टम चालू रहता है।

इसके विपरीत, कांग्रेस कर्नाटक में हाल में मिली जीत को भी भुनाने में नाकाम रही। कर्नाटक में पार्टी की जीत में भूमिका निभाने के बाद, उत्साही सुनील कनोगुलु और उनकी टीम मध्यप्रदेश में कांग्रेस के अभियान के लिए भोपाल पहुंचे। लेकिन वहां 77 साल के पार्टी के दिग्गज नेता और मुख्यमंत्री पद के दावेदार और अभियान के संचालक कमलनाथ के अड़ियल रुख का सामना करना पड़ा। नाथ ने कनोगुलु से कहा, 'आपको उन्हें रिपोर्ट करना होगा,' उन्होंने 29 साल की निकिता खन्ना की तरफ इशारा किया। वह कमलनाथ के एक मित्र की अमेरिका से लौटी बेटी थी। निकिता ने संयुक्त राष्ट्र की एक संस्था के साथ काम किया था, लेकिन चुनाव का कोई अनुभव नहीं था। निकिता का कहना है, 'दूसरे लोगों के साथ मैं भी चुनाव वॉर रूम में शामिल थी, हम एक टीम थे।' जब कनोगुलु ने कमलनाथ की बात मानने से इंकार कर दिया,

तो वे भड़क गए। नाथ ने कांग्रेस अभियान सिर्फ़ अपने हिसाब से चलाने पर ज़ोर दिया। वह अपने वफादारों के अलावा, किसी बाहरी व्यक्ति से सलाह या निर्देश लेने को तैयार नहीं थे।

दूसरे चुनाव रणनीतिकारों की तरह, कनोगुलु ने डेटा और ज़मीनी सर्वेक्षणों पर भरोसा किया। डेटा से पता चला कि चौहान और भाजपा आगे बढ़ रहे थे, खासतौर से लाडली बहन योजना के सफल तरीके से चलने से, तो उन्होंने अभियान का फोकस बदलने का सुझाव दियाः सलाह थी, 'महिला मतदाता' महत्वपूर्ण हैं। 'मुझे आप जैसे बैकरूम काम करने वाले लोगों से सलाह की ज़रूरत नहीं हैं। क्या आप जानते हैं कि मैंने कितने चुनाव लड़े और जीते हैं? मैं तबसे चुनाव जीत रहा हूं, जब आप पैदा भी नहीं हुए थे,' नौ बार सांसद रहे नाथ का गुस्सा दिखाई दे रहा था। जब मैंने नाथ से कनोगुलु से नोक-झोंक के बारे में पूछा, तो उन्होंने टालते हुए कहा, 'मैं सिर्फ़ यह जानना चाहता था कि उनकी टीम के पास क्या रणनीति है, लेकिन उनके पास बताने के लिए कुछ ठोस नहीं था।'

दोनों के बीच शांति की आखिरी कोशिश के तौर पर कांग्रेस नेतृत्व ने कर्नाटक चुनावों में कामयाबी का हिस्सा रहे रणदीप सुरजेवाला को प्रभारी महासचिव के रूप में भोपाल जाने के लिए कहा। हालांकि, तब तक बहुत देर हो चुकी थी। एक सुबह, कमलनाथ के लोग, वहां पहुंचे, जहां कनोगुलु और उनके पचास लोगों की टीम काम कर रही थी और उन्हें चौबीस घंटे के भीतर जगह खाली करने को कहा। उन्होंने धमकी दी कि 'अगर आप नहीं जाएंगे तो हम आपके कंप्यूटर बाहर फेंक देंगे।' अभियान पर एक महीने तक काम करने के बाद, इससे घबराए कनोगुलु जल्दबाजी में भोपाल से चले गए। बाद में उन्होंने एक दोस्त से कहा, 'अगर कांग्रेस बीजेपी से हारती है, तो यह कमलनाथ जैसे नेताओं की वजह से है जो वक्त के साथ नहीं बदलते और सोचते हैं कि वह सबकुछ जानते हैं।'

मध्यप्रदेश में कांग्रेस अभियान का पूरा फोकस कनलनाथ पर था। किसी दूसरे नेता के लिए इसमें कोई जगह नहीं थी। सत्तर के दशक में संजय गांधी के 'जोशीले सैनिकों' में से एक, हमेशा मुस्कुराते चेहरे के साथ आकर्षक कमलनाथ अपने बड़े व्यावसायिक संबंधों के लिए जाने जाते हैं। 1984 के सिख-विरोधी दंगों के आरोपों में घिरे होने के बावज़ूद उन्होंने 1998 से अपने संसदीय क्षेत्र छिंदवाड़ा से लगातार जीत हासिल कर, ताकतवर राजनेता के रूप में अपनी साख साबित की है। इसमें कोई शक नहीं, एक 'संसाधन संपन्न' चुनाव प्रबंधक के रूप में कमलनाथ के पास फिर से चुनाव जीतने के लिए आवश्यक अनुभव था। लेकिन इस कड़े मुकाबले में कांग्रेस के लिए ज़रूरी टीम नेता नहीं थे। जब इंडिया गठबंधन ने अपने अभियान की शुरुआत के लिए भोपाल में एक संयुक्त रैली का प्रस्ताव रखा, तो कथित तौर पर उन्होंने यह कहकर 'वीटो' कर दिया कि इससे अभियान भटक जाएगा। उन्होंने समाजवादी पार्टी के साथ प्रस्तावित सीट समझौते पर बढ़ने से इंकार कर दिया। इसके बजाय, कमलनाथ ने प्रतिस्पर्धी

हिंदुत्व की राजनीति को अपनी तरह से चलाने का तय किया, कभी भी खुद को हनुमान भक्त बताने का मौका नहीं छोड़ा, यहां तक कि अपनी हिंदू पहचान जताने के लिए साधु-संतों के साथ भी कार्यक्रम किए। 'इसको ऐसे समझिए, हिंदू धर्म पर भाजपा का कोई एकाधिकार नहीं है। क्या आपको पता है कि छिंदवाड़ा में सबसे बड़ा हनुमान मंदिर मैंने बनवाया है? क्या आपको पता है कि राजीव गांधी ने अयोध्या में बाबरी मस्जिद का ताला खुलवाया था?' उनका तर्क था। लेकिन हिंदीभाषी इलाकों में कांग्रेस का 'सॉफ्ट हिंदुत्व' का कार्ड कभी नहीं चला, कमलनाथ की यह रणनीति पूरी तरह फेल हो गई। भोपाल के सत्ता के गलियारों में अफवाह चलने लगी कि नाथ ने ईडी की गिरफ्त से बचने के लिए भाजपा के साथ कोई गुप्त समझौता किया होगा। उनके एक रिश्तेदार की कथित धोखाधड़ी और मनी लॉन्ड्रिंग मामले में चल रही ईडी-सीबीआई जांच ने इन अटकलों को और हवा दी। नाथ ने इसे खारिज करते हुए कहा, 'क्या बकवास है! क्या आपको सच में लगता है कि मैं उन लोगों को हराना नहीं चाहता, जिन्होंने गलत तरीकों से मेरी सरकार गिराई थी?'

गहराई से देखें, तो मध्यप्रदेश में कांग्रेस की हार के लिए सिर्फ़ कमलनाथ को दोषी ठहराना उचित नहीं होगा। अगर पार्टी भाजपा सरकार के ख़िलाफ़ बढ़ती नाराज़गी का फायदा नहीं उठा पाई, तो इसकी बड़ी वजह दो दशकों से सत्ता से बाहर रहने के बाद राज्य और दूसरी जगहों पर संगठन लगातार कमज़ोर होता चला गया था। 2018 के चुनाव के बाद जब भाजपा से बढ़त हासिल कर कांग्रेस ने पन्द्रह महीनों के लिए प्रदेश में सरकार बनाई, तो उसे सिर्फ़ अपवाद माना जाना चाहिए। सच्चाई यह है कि मध्यप्रदेश में संगठन पर कमलनाथ और दिग्विजय समर्थकों का कब्ज़ा था और ये दोनों नेता शायद ही उस बदलाव की नुमाइंदगी करते थे, जो मतदाता चाहता था। भाजपा ने जहां सामूहिक नेतृत्व के साथ मोदी कार्ड का आक्रामक तरीके से इस्तेमाल किया और अपनी ताकत के साथ लचीलापन भी रखा, वहीं कांग्रेस ना तो अपनी पुरानी सोच को बदल पाई और ना ही गुटबाजी वाले प्रदेश संगठन को संभालने के लिए उसके पास कोई भरोसेमंद नेतृत्व था। इसके विपरीत, गुजरात की तरह मध्यप्रदेश में भी भाजपा को संघ परिवार के मजबूत नेटवर्क का फायदा मिला। इसमें आश्चर्य नहीं होना चाहिए कि कांग्रेस का 2023 के विधानसभा चुनावों में सफाया हो गया और फिर 2024 के आम चुनावों में भी मध्यप्रदेश में वही नतीजा रहा।

मध्यप्रदेश में यदि कांग्रेस ने मौका चूका तो पड़ोसी छत्तीसगढ़ एक आत्मघाती गोल साबित हुआ। अगस्त 2023 में, विधानसभा चुनावों से तीन महीने पहले तक, हर सर्वेक्षण में भूपेश बघेल की कांग्रेस सरकार के लिए स्पष्ट जीत की बात की गई थी। इससे पिछले 2018 के चुनावों में उसने भाजपा का सफाया करके सरकार बनाई थी। बघेल के करीबी सहयोगी विनोद वर्मा कहते हैं कि 'आप एक दर्जन आंतरिक सर्वेक्षणों को देख लें, चाहे वह भाजपा के हों या फिर कांग्रेस

के, हरेक ने हमारी जीत तय बताई थी। मुझे लगता है कि जब हर कोई आपकी जीत बता रहा हो, तो आप अति-आत्मविश्वास के शिकार हो जाते हैं।'

2013 में जीरम घाटी में हुए नक्सली हमले में छत्तीसगढ़ कांग्रेस का लगभग पूरा नेतृत्व ख़त्म हो गया था। 2018 में प्रदेश की बागडोर संभालते हुए, भूपेश बघेल एक लोकप्रिय और ज़मीनी नेता साबित हुए। जीरम घाटी के भयावह हत्याकांड के बाद कांग्रेस की यह मजबूत वापसी थी। इस बार भी कांग्रेस को यकीन था कि बघेल एक बार फिर कांग्रेस की वापसी करेंगे, लेकिन उम्मीदों से अलग, स्थानीय स्तर पर असंतोष पनप रहा था। बघेल का आक्रामक रवैया, कांग्रेस की उस संस्कृति के मुताबिक नहीं थी, जो मजबूत क्षत्रपों को आगे बढ़ाने के लिए नहीं जानी जाती। मुख्यमंत्री ने नौकरशाही की मदद से पकड़ मजबूत की, जिससे जिला-स्तर पर कांग्रेस के ज़्यादातर कार्यकर्ता अलग-थलग पड़ गए, जिन्हें उम्मीद थी कि सत्ता में उनकी भी हिस्सेदारी होगी। रायपुर के एक पत्रकार ने टिपण्णी की, 'उनके कामकाज का तरीका तानाशाही था; यहां तक कि उनके कई मंत्री भी उनके गुस्से का सामना करने से डरते थे।' जब आदिवासी समूहों ने बस्तर के इलाके में 'सर्व आदिवासी समाज' के बैनर पर खुद को संगठित किया, तब मुख्यमंत्री पर ग्राम पंचायतों को ज़्यादा स्वायतता देने सहित दूसरी मांगों को अनदेखा करने का आरोप लगाया गया। 2018 के चुनावों में कांग्रेस ने जहां आदिवासी इलाके में 26 में से 25 सीटें जीतकर भाजपा का सफाया कर दिया था, वहां 2023 में उसे सिर्फ़ चार सीटें मिल पाईं।

कांग्रेस में भूपेश बघेल के मुख्य प्रतिद्वन्दी शाही घराने से रहे राजनेता त्रिभुवनेश्वर शरण सिंह देव थे। तीखे नाक-नक्श और करीने से कंघी किए गए बालों के साथ, दिल्ली विश्वविद्यालय में पढ़ाई किए देव, भले ही अब नाम के महाराजा हों, लेकिन उनका तौर-तरीका अभिजात वर्ग सा है। उनके परिवार ने कभी आदिवासी बहुल सरगुजा ज़िले पर राज किया था। 2018 में मुख्यमंत्री पद की लड़ाई में देव ने बघेल को मुख्यमंत्री की कुर्सी दे दी, कहा गया कि राहुल गांधी ने एक समझौता कराया था कि दोनों नेता ढाई-ढाई साल के लिए मुख्यमंत्री रहेंगे। लेकिन 2021 में जब सत्ता सौंपने का वक्त आया, तो बघेल ने ज़्यादातर विधायकों के समर्थन का दावा करते हुए कुर्सी छोड़ने से इंकार कर दिया। शुरू में तो कांग्रेस नेतृत्व, बदलाव के लिए इच्छुक दिखाई दिया और कहा गया कि बघेल ने इस्तीफ़ा भी दे दिया था, लेकिन आखिरी वक्त पर उन्होंने अपना मन बदल लिया। देव ने दिल्ली में कांग्रेस के आला नेताओं से मुलाक़ात की और भरोसा दिलाया गया कि उन्हें जल्दी ही मुख्यमंत्री बना दिया जाएगा। देव के एक समर्थक ने शिकायती लहजे में कहा, 'हमारे नेता को शपथ-ग्रहण की तारीख तय करने के लिए भी कहा गया था, लेकिन अचानक आलाकमान ने पूरी तरह से यू-टर्न ले लिया।' जबकि आधिकारिक कारण यह बताया गया कि बघेल की प्रमुख ओबीसी नेता के रूप में बड़ी साख है। कांग्रेस के लिए बघेल को बड़ा फंड दिलाने वाला नेता माना जाता है और पार्टी नेतृत्व उन्हें पसंद करता है। खासतौर से बघेल

ने, यूपी और हिमाचल प्रदेश में उनके अभियानों में पूरा साथ देकर प्रियंका गांधी वाड्रा के साथ मजबूत समझ बना ली थी। कांग्रेस के एक नेता ने कहा कि 'यह बताने में भले ही अच्छा नहीं लगे, लेकिन बघेल जी हमारे भरोसेमंद एटीएम की तरह थे, उन्होंने हर चुनाव में पूरी मदद की।'

हमेशा विनम्र रहने वाले मृदुभाषी देव हार गए और फिर उनकी तसल्ली के लिए एक रास्ता निकाला गया: जून 2023 में, उन्हें उप-मुख्यमंत्री बना दिया गया। लेकिन तब तक पार्टी में बंटवारे की लाइन खिंच चुकी थी और हरेक गुट दूसरे को कमज़ोर करने में लगा था। अंदरूनी कलह को रोकने के लिए, पार्टी के केन्द्रीय नेतृत्व के निर्देश पर पहले से तय अभियान के नारे 'भूपेश है, तो भरोसा है' को बदल दिया गया और नया नारा था, 'कांग्रेस है, तो भरोसा है'। पोस्टरों और प्रचार सामग्री पर अब सिर्फ़ मुख्यमंत्री का अकेला चेहरा नहीं था, उसमें प्रदेश के दूसरे नेताओं की तस्वीरें भी शामिल कर दी गईं। बघेल के एक वफादार नेता ने बताया, 'हमारे अपने सर्वेक्षणों में कहा गया था कि चुनाव अभियान से बघेल का चेहरा हटाने से कम से कम बीस सीटों का नुक़सान होगा। तब भी दिल्ली के नेताओं ने छत्तीसगढ़ में सामूहिक नेतृत्व के साथ चुनाव लड़ने की समझदारी दिखाई।' विधानसभा चुनावों के करीब आने के साथ, बघेल खुद भ्रष्टाचार के आरोपों और ईडी की जांच के जाल में फंस गए, जिससे कांग्रेस इस महत्वपूर्ण समय में 'बैकफुट' पर आ गई। पार्टी को छत्तीसगढ़ में बुरी तरह हार का सामना करना पड़ा, यहां तक कि देव के गढ़ माने जाने वाले सरगुजा में भी पार्टी हार गई, जहां उसने पांच साल पहले बड़ी जीत दर्ज की थी। भाजपा ने इस बार 90 में से 54 सीटें जीतकर स्पष्ट से ज्यादा बहुमत हासिल किया।

छत्तीसगढ में कांग्रेस के हाथ से अगर जीती हुई बाज़ी फिसल गई थी, तो राजस्थान में उसने अपनी बड़ी हार को किसी हद तक रोक लिया था। ज़्यादातर चुनावी पंडितों ने उसकी संभावनाओं को नकार दिया था। 2023 की शुरुआत में, कांग्रेस को आंतरिक सर्वेक्षणों में भाजपा से काफी पीछे दिखाया गया था। वैसे भी पिछले तीन दशकों से राजस्थान में हर पांच साल में सरकारें बदलती रही हैं। मुख्यमंत्री अशोक गहलोत और उनके प्रतिद्वन्दी युवा सचिन पायलट के बीच सार्वजनिक विवादों से भी मुश्किलें बढ़ी थीं। अपनी पोजीशन बचाने के लिए गहलोत ने तेज़-तर्रार चुनाव विशेषज्ञ नरेश अरोड़ा से संपर्क साधा, जो 2016 से कांग्रेस के साथ काम कर रहे थे। अरोड़ा, 'मिशन कर्नाटक' में डी.के. शिवकुमार की टीम के हिस्सा थे। 'जब मैं जनवरी 2023 में पहली बार गहलोत जी से मिला, तो मैंने उनसे सीधा सवाल किया था: क्या हम जीतने के लिए चुनाव लड़ रहे हैं या सिर्फ़ शर्मनाक हार से बचने के लिए?' चिकनी-चुपड़ी बातें करने वाले अरोड़ा ने कहा। 'जब गहलोत ने यह साफ कर दिया कि वे जीत की रणनीति चाहते थे, तो मैं इसमें कूद पड़ा।' उनकी कंपनी डिज़ायन बॉक्स के दो हज़ार लोगों की टीम पूरे राज्य में डेटा इकट्ठा कर रणनीति बनाने में जुट गई।

2023 में नौ महीनों के लिए, गहलोत की छवि बदल गई थी। एक विनम्र लो-प्रोफाइल राजनेता को मोदी जैसे बड़े कद के मुख्यमंत्री की इमेज में बदल दिया गया। मोदी ने यदि 'आयुष्मान भारत स्वास्थ्य बीमा योजना' को राष्ट्रीय स्तर पर अपनी पहचान बनाया था तो गहलोत की 'चिरंजीवी स्वास्थ्य बीमा योजना' के फायदे बढ़ाकर उसे चुनावी मुद्दा बनाने की कोशिश की गई। अरोड़ा कहते हैं, 'राज्य स्तर पर भी हर कल्याण योजना मोदी के साथ जुड़ी थी, हमें इस छवि को बदलने की ज़रूरत थी।' फिर लोगों तक पहुंचने की योजना तैयार की गई। इसमें राजस्थान भर में महंगाई राहत शिविर स्थापित करना शामिल था, जिससे लाभार्थियों को विभिन्न सरकारी योजनाओं के तहत राहत मिल सके, जिसमें मुद्रास्फीति विरोधी उपाय के रूप में 500 रुपये में एलपीजी सिलेंडर तक पहुंच शामिल है। बुद्धिमान, वरिष्ठ और उदार गहलोत को गरीब समर्थक, परोपकारी मुख्यमंत्री के तौर पर पेश करने का असर दिखने लगा, जिसमें भरोसा था कि वह स्थिर सरकार देंगे। चुनावों से पहले हर सर्वेक्षण ने गहलोत को अपने प्रतिद्वन्दियों की तुलना में ज़्यादा लोकप्रिय दिखाया। कर्नाटक में सफल रही गारंटी और कल्याणकारी योजनाओं के वादे यहां भी काम करते दिख रहे थे। गहलोत फैक्टर के जवाब में भाजपा को 'मोदी की गारंटी' के साथ मैदान में उतरना पड़ा।

फिर भी, जैसा कि कांग्रेस में अक्सर होता है, एक व्यक्ति पर फोकस अभियान पर पार्टी के एक वर्ग ने नापसंदगी ज़ाहिर की। 'यह अरोड़ा, केवल मुख्यमंत्री को दिखाने पर भारी पैसा खर्च करना चाहता है। उसे किसी और की परवाह नहीं हैं, यहां तक कि पार्टी संगठन की भी नहीं,' प्रदेश कांग्रेस अध्यक्ष गोविंद सिंह डोटासरा की शिकायत थी। डोटासरा और अरोड़ा के बीच पहले से ही झगड़ा चल रहा था। अरोड़ा कहते हैं कि 'मैंने उन्हें समझाने की कोशिश की कि आप एक जहाज के दो कप्तान नहीं रख सकते। अगर गहलोत जीतते हैं तो कांग्रेस जीतेगी, लेकिन कांग्रेस ने गहलोत को निराश किया।'

गहलोत प्रदेश में पार्टी के सबसे बड़े नेता हैं और गुटबाज़ी से निपटने में भी माहिर हैं। मुख्यमंत्री का कद बढ़ने के साथ उनके कई विधायकों पर भ्रष्टाचार और उपेक्षा के आरोप लगने लगे। लेकिन दाग़ी विधायकों पर कार्रवाई करने के बजाय मुख्यमंत्री कार्यालय उन्हें बचाते और शह देते हुए दिखा। जब एक आंतरिक सर्वेक्षण में 113 में से 39 विधायकों के टिकट काटने की सिफारिश की गई तो गहलोत कार्रवाई करने को तैयार नहीं थे। न ही कांग्रेस नेतृत्व इस पर कोई फैसला ले रहा था। गहलोत ने उनका बचाव किया, 'यह कहना तो बहुत आसान है कि "एक मौजूदा विधायक का टिकट काट दिया जाए", लेकिन याद रखिए कि इन विधायकों ने मेरा तब साथ दिया था, जब भाजपा हर तरह का प्रलोभन देकर उन्हें तोड़ने की कोशिश कर रही थी।' आखिर में केवल आठ विधायकों के नाम सूची से काटे गए। यह ग़लती महंगी साबित हुई। कई मौजूदा विधायक चुनाव हार गए। पार्टी आलाकमान नाराज़ पायलट की शिकायतों को भी दूर

नहीं कर पाया, गुर्जरों में उनका काफी असर है। पायलट ने पार्टी के एक सहयोगी से शिकायत की: 'चुनाव के आखिरी दिनों में मुझे पूरे राज्य में प्रचार के लिए कहा गया और सिर्फ़ एक हेलिकॉप्टर दिया गया। इससे पहले, मुझे किसी भी फ़ैसले के वक्त बाहर रखा गया।' हालांकि गहलोत खेमे का कहना था कि पायलट कोई दिलचस्पी नहीं ले रहे थे, क्योंकि वह चाहते थे कि मुख्यमंत्री हार जाएं। तथ्य यह है कि चुनाव अभियान के आखिरी पखवाड़े में, जब अरोड़ा ने 'गारंटी यात्रा' की योजना बनाई तो स्टार प्रचारकों की लिस्ट के नेता भी उपलब्ध नहीं थे। अरोड़ा ने कहा, 'यह मत समझिए कि भाजपा ने राजस्थान में कांग्रेस को हराया, वह कांग्रेस से ही हारी, खासतौर से जो लोग दिल्ली में बैठते हैं और ज़मीनी हालात के बारे में कुछ नहीं जानते, उन्होंने खुद को ही हरा दिया।' लेकिन 2024 के आम चुनावों में चुस्त और फोकस्ड कांग्रेस संगठन ने राजस्थान में 25 में से 11 लोकसभा सीटें जीत लीं, जबकि ज़्यादातर चुनाव पंडितों ने कांग्रेस के पूरी तरह साफ होने की भविष्यवाणी की थी। सवाल यह है कि क्या कांग्रेस की अंदरूनी कलह ने 2023 में उसकी जीत की संभावनाओं को ख़त्म कर दिया?

राजस्थान में कांग्रेस भले ही हालात नहीं बदल सकी, लेकिन तेलंगाना में वे कामयाब हो गए। यहां भी, 2023 में शुरुआती सर्वेक्षणों में पार्टी की संभावनाओं को नकारा गया था। 2014 में कांग्रेस ने ही तेलंगाना बनाया था, लेकिन यह नया राज्य अब के. चन्द्रशेखर राव या 'केसीआर' का गढ़ बन गया था। दुबले-पतले, तेज़-तर्रार राजनेता केसीआर तेलंगाना आंदोलन के नेता रहे और पिछले दस साल से यहां पूरी तरह अपने नियंत्रण में सरकार चला रहे थे। अक्टूबर 2022 में, जब केसीआर ने अपनी 'तेलंगाना राष्ट्रीय समिति' पार्टी का नाम बदलकर 'भारत राष्ट्र समिति' रखा, तो उनका दावा था कि भाजपा के लिए असल चुनौती हम होंगे।

महत्वाकांक्षी और उत्साही केसीआर के पास पैसे की कोई कमी नहीं थी। उनके एक सहयोगी ने बताया कि तेलगांना के मुख्यमंत्री, 2024 के 'इंडिया' गठबंधन के अभियान के लिए पैसा देने को तैयार थे, बशर्ते उन्हें गठबंधन का संयोजक बनाया जाए। बीआरएस में रहे एक नेता कहते हैं कि 'केसीआर खुद को मोदी समेत दूसरे नेताओं के मुकाबले एक बेहतर प्रशासक मानते हैं।' खुद को असली किसान नेता के रूप में पेश करते हुए वे अपने राष्ट्रीय मिशन को पड़ोसी राज्य से शुरू करना चाहते थे, इसके लिए उन्होंने 'मिशन महाराष्ट्र' योजना भी बना ली थी। 2023 में नांदेड़ जैसे महाराष्ट्र के कई शहरों में बीआरएस के पोस्टर लगे हुए थे और पार्टी के खास गुलाबी पोस्टर छा गए थे। केसीआर ने मतदाताओं तक पहुंचने के लिए नारा दिया: 'अबकी बार, किसान सरकार'।

लेकिन जब हैदराबाद के बाहरी इलाके के एक फार्महाउस में केसीआर महाराष्ट्र और उससे आगे की योजना पर विचार कर रहे थे, तब शायद वे अपनी घरेलू ज़मीन के खिसकने से बेखबर थे। तेलंगाना के इलाके में किसी ज़माने में प्रमुख पार्टी रही कांग्रेस एक बार फिर से पैर पसार रही

थी। मध्यप्रदेश में कांग्रेस नेताओं से निकाले जाने के बाद चुनावी रणनीतिकार सुनील कनोगुलु ने अपना ठिकाना हैदराबाद को बना लिया था, जहां सत्ता हासिल करने की चाह में बैठे युवा नेता ने उनका गर्मजोशी से स्वागत किया। 2023 तक, रेवंत रेड्डी को तेलंगाना के बाहर शायद ही कोई जानता था। जोश से भरे करिश्माई रेवंत ने तेलुगुदेशम में शामिल होने से पहले अपना सफर अखिल भारतीय विद्यार्थी परिषद (एबीवीपी) से शुरू किया था, फिर 2018 में वे कांग्रेस में शामिल हो गए। 2015 में उनकी बेटी के सगाई सम रोह से ठीक पहले केसीआर सरकार ने उन्हें 'कैश-फॉर-वोट' के आरोप में गिरफ़्तार किया था। हालांकि उन्हें सगाई समारोह में शामिल होने के लिए कुछ घंटों की ज़मानत मिल गई थी, लेकिन तभी उन्होंने बदला लेने की कसम खा ली थी। रेड्डी कहते हैं, 'उस दिन से मेरे पास केवल एक ही मिशन थाः केसीआर को हराना और मेरे परिवार के साथ जो हुआ, उसके लिए सबक सिखाना।'

कनोगुलु और उनकी टीम से मिली बारीक जानकारियों और बैकरूम सपोर्ट से रेड्डी ने केसीआर से लड़ाई शुरू कर दी। रेड्डी ने मुख्यमंत्री पर तेलंगाना में परिवार राज को बढ़ावा देने का आरोप लगाया। 2023 में एक जनसभा में उन्होंने केसीआर को चुनौती दी, 'आपके पास (119 सदस्यों वाली विधानसभा में) 104 विधायक हैं और अगर आप असली मर्द हैं और जीत पर पूरा भरोसा है तो अपने सभी मौजूदा विधायकों को टिकट दे दें।' आमतौर पर चतुराई से काम लेने वाले, अति-आत्मविश्वासी केसीआर इस बार जाल में फंस गए। कुछ हफ्तों बाद उन्होंने ऐलान किया कि वे अपने सभी मौजूदा विधायकों को फिर से टिकट दे रहे थे (बाद में केवल दो को टिकट नहीं दिया)। 'जिस दिन उन्होंने यह घोषणा की, हमें पता था कि हमारे पास मौजूदा विधायकों के ख़िलाफ़ सत्ता विरोधी लहर को भुनाने का मौका मिल गया था। केसीआर ने सबसे बड़ा सेल्फ-गोल किया,' रेड्डी ने मुस्कुराते हुए कहा। उनका आंकलन सही साबित हुआ। कांग्रेस गठबंधन ने 119 सदस्यों वाली विधानसभा में 64 सीटें जीत लीं, जबकि बीआरएस को केवल 39 सीटें ही मिल पाईं। 2014 में तेलंगाना को अलग राज्य बनाने वाली कांग्रेस को पहली बार सरकार बनाने का मौका मिला था।

चार प्रमुख राज्यों के विधानसभा चुनावों के नतीजे रविवार, 3 दिसम्बर 2023 को आए। इन चुनावों को 2024 के फाइनल से पहले 'सेमीफाइन्ल' के तौर पर देखा जा रहा था। बेहतर प्रदर्शन को लेकर आश्वस्त कांग्रेस के एक पदाधिकारी ने दोपहर में मीडिया और पार्टी समर्थकों में लड्डू बांटने का ऑर्डर दिया था। 'अगर हम दो राज्य भी जीतते हैं तो यह हमारे लिए अच्छी ख़बर होगी, तीन जीते तो यह बोनस होगा और अगर चारों जीत जाते हैं तो मोदी के अंत की शुरुआत होगी,' कांग्रेसी नेता ने कहा। दूसरी तरफ आमतौर पर वोटों की गिनती के दिन उत्साह से भरे रहने वाले भाजपा दफ्तर में थोड़ी शांति थी। भाजपा प्रवक्ता सैयद ज़फर इस्लाम ने कहा, 'चलिए, कुछ घंटे इंतज़ार करते हैं, फिर पता चल जाएगा कि किसे जश्न मनाना चाहिए।'

दोपहर तक चुनावी हवा का रुख साफ हो गया। राजस्थान के कड़े मुकाबले में भाजपा आगे चल रही थी, इससे भी ज़्यादा अप्रत्याशित रूप से छत्तीसगढ़ में भी कमल खिलने लगा था। केवल दक्षिण में तेलगांना से ही कांग्रेस के लिए अच्छी ख़बर थी। भाजपा के पक्ष में 3-1 के नतीजे निर्णायक जीत थे, जहां पांच साल पहले तीनों हिंदीभाषी राज्यों में वह चुनाव हार गई थी। कांग्रेस मुख्यालय में लड्डू का ऑर्डर फिर पूरा नहीं हो पाया। इसके बजाय भारतीय जनता पार्टी के दफ्तर में लड्डू और जलेबियों के साथ जश्न शुरू हो गया। पार्टी को यकीन हो गया कि सर्दियों में 2023 के चुनावों ने 2024 की गर्मियों के तूफान की तैयारी कर दी है। लंबे समय से बुरे वक्त का सामना कर रही कांग्रेस का जो साल उम्मीदों के साथ शुरू हुआ था, वह निराशा के दलदल में खत्म हो रहा था।

═

पटना के 1, अणे मार्ग, बिहार में मुख्यमंत्री का विशाल और भारी सुरक्षा वाला बंगला, करीब दो दशकों से नीतीश कुमार का आधिकारिक निवास रहा है। सड़क के उस पार, 7, सर्कुलर रोड पर एक और बंगला है, जो 2013 में उन्हें कुछ समय के लिए तब मिला था, जब वे मुख्यमंत्री नहीं रहे थे। मुख्यमंत्री जहां कभी 'जनता दरबार' लगाते थे, अब वहां पहुंचना मुश्किल था। केवल कुछ करीबी सहयोगी ही यहां आसानी से आ सकते थे। 3 दिसम्बर को जब चुनाव नतीजे आए, तो जनता दल यूनाइटेड के तीन प्रमुख नेता उनसे बंद कमरे में बातचीत के लिए आए। मंत्री संजय झा, अशोक चौधरी और विजय चौधरी नीतीश कुमार की ऐसी तिकड़ी थे, जो मुख्यमंत्री के आंख और कान बन गए थे। जेडीयू के एक पूर्व सहयोगी ने कहा, 'मुख्यमंत्री उनकी सलाह के बिना कुछ नहीं करते; उनका नीतीश जी पर पूरा नियंत्रण हैं और वो उन तीनों पर निर्भर हैं।'

पटना के सत्ता गलियारों में कई महीनों से नीतीश कुमार के स्वास्थ्य की चर्चा भी ज़ोरों पर रही। एक वरिष्ठ आईएएस अधिकारी ने नीतीश से बातचीत का ज़िक्र करते हुए कहा, 'वह आजकल चीजें भूल जाते है और बड़बड़ाते रहते हैं।' मुंबई में विपक्षी 'इंडिया' गठबंधन की बैठक में नीतीश ने तमिलनाडु के मुख्यमंत्री एम.के. स्टालिन के नेतृत्व में डीएमके प्रतिनिधिमंडल से मुलाक़ात की थी। स्टालिन के कमरे से बाहर जाने के कुछ देर बार नीतीश कुमार ने अपनी पार्टी के लोगों की तरफ मुड़कर पूछा, 'ये कौन थे? मैं इनका नाम भूल गया!' हालांकि किसी ने नहीं बताया कि क्या गड़बड़ थी, लेकिन नीतीश की भूलने की बीमारी वास्तविक चिंता का कारण बन रही थी। चीज़ों को ठीक से नहीं समझ पाना और भूलने की बीमारी कई बुज़ुर्गों को परेशान करती है और रोज़मर्रा का ज़िंदगी पर इसका असर पड़ता है।

चिंता की मौजूदा वजह 'इंडिया' गठबंधन में नीतीश कुमार की अपनी स्थिति थी। मुख्यमंत्री ने अलग-अलग विचारों और ताकतों वाले लोगों को एक साथ लाने में अहम भूमिका निभाई

थी। लेकिन छह महीने पहले पटना में शुरू हुई यह कहानी आगे नहीं बढ़ पा रही थी। नीतीश कुमार को संयोजक बनाने की बात पर भी मुहर नहीं लगी थी। यह घोषणा सितंबर में मुंबई में हुई गठबंधन की बैठक में की जानी थी, लेकिन आम सहमति नहीं बन पाने से, आखिरी वक्त पर इसे सार्वजनिक करने से रोक दिया गया। यह साफ नहीं है कि घोषणा को किसने रोका था, लेकिन फिर भी एक छोटे गुट पर उंगलिया उठ रही थीं, जो नीतीश की महत्वाकांक्षा से परेशान थे। 'इंडिया' गठबंधन के एक सदस्य ने तकलीफ ज़ाहिर करते हुए कहा, 'अगर उस दिन नीतीश कुमार को संयोजक बना दिया जाता, तो वे हमें कभी नहीं छोड़ते और 2024 का चुनाव हमारा होता।'

गठबंधन में परेशानी की एक वजह कांग्रेस का 2023 के विधानसभा चुनावों पर ज़्यादा ध्यान था। एक वरिष्ठ सहयोगी ने कहा, 'जब भी हमने आम चुनावों के लिए सीट बंटवारें और गठबंधन के न्यूनतम साझा कार्यक्रम पर तत्काल बातचीत की जरूरत बताने की कोशिश की, तो कांग्रेस नेतृत्व ने कहा कि अभी वह विधानसभा चुनावों में व्यस्त है। यह बहुत निराशाजनक था।' साफ था कि कांग्रेस विधानसभा चुनावों में अपने अच्छे प्रदर्शन की उम्मीद कर रही थी ताकि सीट-बंटवारे में नेतृत्व करने के उनके दावे मजबूत होते। लेकिन महत्वपूर्ण हिंदीभाषी राज्यों में करारी हार ने उनकी इस उम्मीद को ख़त्म कर दिया। कांग्रेस के एक नेता ने कहा, 'हमें अब पता था कि इंडिया गठबंधन में हर पार्टी की मांगों को मानने का भारी दबाव होगा।'

कांग्रेस को शायद इस बात का अंदेशा नहीं था कि दिसंबर 2023 के नतीजों से पहले ही नीतीश की टीम एनडीए में वापसी के लिए भाजपा से बातचीत शुरू कर चुकी थी। नीतीश के करीबी सहयोगी संजय झा इस बातचीत को देख रहे थे। दिवंगत अरुण जेटली के करीबी और भारतीय जनता युवा मोर्चा के नेता रहे झा ने 2013 में पाला बदल लिया था और नीतीश के साथ उस वक्त आ गए थे, जब शुरू में जनता दल युनाइटेड और भाजपा में टूट हुई थी। बताया जाता है कि उनके इस पाला बदलने में जेटली की सहमति रही थी। बिहार के एक वरिष्ठ पत्रकार ने दावा किया, 'झा हमेशा भाजपा और जद(यू) के बीच मध्यस्थ रहे हैं; उनके दोस्त दोनों तरफ हैं।' 2023 के चुनाव नतीजों से कुछ हफ्ते पहले नवम्बर में, झा ने अशोक चौधरी और विजय चौधरी के साथ, भाजपा अध्यक्ष जगत प्रकाश नड्डा समेत कई भाजपा नेताओं से मुलाक़ात की। इस तिकड़ी ने नीतीश को कमोबेश आश्वस्त कर दिया था कि इंडिया गठबंधन एक हारने वाला प्रस्ताव था। 'जब तक कांग्रेस और ममता बनर्जी जैसे नेता हैं, वह आपको कभी संयोजक नहीं बनाएंगे,' उन्होंने नीतीश कुमार के सामने बात रखी।

नीतीश कुमार जब हालात का जायजा ले रहे थे, तब चुनावों की हार के बाद कांग्रेस परेशान थी, अब उसके पास विकल्प और वक्त कम बचा था। दिसबंर में नतीजों के एक दिन बाद, जब कांग्रेस अध्यक्ष मल्लिकार्जुन खड़गे के दफ़्तर से इंडिया गठबंधन के सहयोगियों को एक ज़रूरी

बैठक के लिए फ़ोन किया गया, तो उनमें से कई ने जवाब नहीं दिया, जबकि कुछ ने वक्त की कमी का हवाला देते हुए आने में मुश्किल जताई। मध्यप्रदेश में कांग्रेस के उन्हें एक भी सीट नहीं देने से दुखी, सौम्य और अच्छे स्वभाव वाले अखिलेश यादव ने भी कहा कि वह व्यस्त थे। ममता ने भी अपनी असमर्थता जाहिर की। बैठक के लिए ना कहने वालों की लाइन लंबी थी। 'हम अब सभी की सुविधा के मुताबिक एक बैठक करेंगे,' कांग्रेस ने प्रतिक्रिया दी।

दिल्ली में जब दिसम्बर में अशोका होटल में बैठक हुई तो लगा कि कांग्रेस ने जल्दबाजी में यह आयोजन किया था। एक सहयोगी ने शिकायत की, कि 'उन्होंने लंच या चाय की व्यवस्था भी ठीक से नहीं की।' खासतौर से जुलाई में बेंगलुरु के ताज वेस्ट एंड होटल के शानदार आयोजन के मुकाबले में यह कहीं नहीं था। कांग्रेस के एक प्रवक्ता ने कहा, 'हमने उस वक्त कर्नाटक में सरकार बनाई थी, तो जश्न का माहौल था, लेकिन अब विधानसभा चुनावों में हार के बाद स्वाभाविक रूप से माहौल में उदासी थी।' सत्ता की राजनीति में, समारोहों के मेन्यू, किसी पार्टी की खुशहाली और हालात भी बताते हैं। लेकिन छोटा मेन्यू इंडिया गठबंधन की बड़ी चिंता नहीं थी। बैठक में ममता बनर्जी ने अचानक एक 'बाउंसर' फेंका। उन्होंने सुझाव दिया कि गठबंधन नेतृत्व के लिए तुरंत एक 'चेहरा' चुन ले और उन्होंने प्रधानमंत्री पद के उम्मीदवार के तौर पर मल्लिकार्जुन खड़गे का नाम प्रस्तावित किया। उनके सुझाव का आम आदमी पार्टी के नेता अरविंद केजरीवाल ने तुरंत समर्थन किया। वैसे एक दिन पहले ही मीडिया से चाय पर मुलाकात के वक्त बनर्जी ने इंडिया गठबंधन के लिए प्रधानमंत्री पद के उम्मीदवार के लिए किसी का नाम पेश किए जाने की संभावना से इंकार किया था। लेकिन चौबीस घंटे से भी कम समय में उन्होंने अपना विचार बदल दिया। खड़गे के एक सहयोगी ने माना, 'ममता दी ने जो किया, हम उससे अचंभित थे। हमें नहीं पता था कि अब क्या कहना है।'

कांग्रेस अध्यक्ष और ज़्यादातर दूसरे नेता चुप रहे, वहीं नीतीश कुमार का गुस्सा फूट पड़ा। वे नाराज़ थे। विपक्षी नेताओं को साथ लाने की कोशिशों के बाद एक महत्वपूर्ण क्षण में उन्होंने खुद को हाशिये पर जाते देखा। 'यहां हमारे लिए अब कोई जगह नहीं है; आपका कहना सही था,' उन्होंने बड़बड़ाते हुए अपने सहयोगी से कहा।

किसी के पास इस बात का कोई स्पष्ट जवाब नहीं था कि ममता बनर्जी ने अचानक खड़गे का नाम क्यों सामने रखा, लेकिन यह दिख रहा था कि ममता अपने प्रतिद्वन्दी नीतीश को नेतृत्व की भूमिका देने को तैयार नहीं थीं। शायद अस्सी साल के खड़गे उन्हें एक सुरक्षित दांव लगे। तृणमूल कांग्रेस के एक सांसद ने जोर देकर कहा, 'ममता दी को लगा कि खड़गे जैसे अनुभवी दलित नेता को प्रधानमंत्री पद का दावेदार बनाना एक स्मार्ट रणनीति होगी, जो भाजपा को परेशान कर सकती है और इसका असर होगा। याद रखिए, देश में अभी तक कोई दलित प्रधानमंत्री नहीं रहा।'

इसे चालाकी भरी राजनीति कहें या चतुर रणनीति, लगा मानो ममता बनर्जी ने इंडिया गठबंधन के 'कबूतरों के बीच बिल्ली' को छोड़ दिया था। खासतौर से नीतीश के लिए अब यहां कुछ नहीं बचा था। भाजपा के साथ जाने के अलावा उनके पास कोई रास्ता नहीं था। उसी रात, झा की तिकड़ी ने भाजपा के बिहार के प्रभारी महासचिव विनोद तावड़े को फ़ोन करके एनडीए में लौटने की इच्छा ज़ाहिर की। जेडीयू के नेता राजीव रंजन सिंह, जिन्हें ललन सिंह के नाम से जाना जाता है, इस कदम के पक्ष में नहीं थे, उन्हें जल्दी ही पार्टी के राष्ट्रीय अध्यक्ष पद से हटा दिया गया। 'वह पार्टी को तोड़ने के लिए लालू यादव से बातचीत कर रहे थे,' ललन सिंह के ख़िलाफ़ तिकड़ी ने इस कानाफूसी को शुरू किया। असुरक्षित और मानसिक रूप से कमज़ोर होते नीतीश ने इस कहानी को मान लिया।

इस बीच भाजपा और जनता दल यूनाइटेड की बातचीत तावड़े से नड्डा और फिर अमित शाह तक बढ़ गई। शाह को नीतीश कुमार की राजनीतिक उलटफेर पसंद नहीं थी। उन्होंने कहा कि 'अगर वह गठबंधन करना चाहते हैं तो इस बार मुख्यमंत्री पद हमें देना चाहिए,' लेकिन कुछ दिनों पहले तक प्रधानमंत्री पद की दौड़ में शामिल, नीतीश कुमार इसके लिए तैयार नहीं थे। व्यवहारिक शाह जानते थे कि लोकसभा चुनावों से पहले उन्हें इंडिया गठबंधन को करारा झटका देने की ज़रूरत थी, इसलिए पीछे हट गए। शाह के लिए यह निर्णायक इसलिए था क्योंकि नीतीश के इंडिया गठबंधन से निकलने से उनमें निराशा आएगी। नीतीश ही तो गठबंधन के 'मुख्य वास्तुकार' थे। जनवरी 2024 की शुरुआत में दोनों नेताओं, नीतीश कुमार और प्रधानमंत्री मोदी के बीच बातचीत फाइनल हो गई। बताया गया कि प्रधानमंत्री ने मुलाकात में कुछ ज़्यादा नहीं कहा, लेकिन नीतीश, प्रधानमंत्री की तारीफ करते रहे। उन्होंने मिठास के लिए एक तोहफा मांगाः बिहार के पूर्व मुख्यमंत्री और मंडल आंदोलन के प्रतीक कर्पूरी ठाकुर के लिए भारत रत्न। 'कल्पना कीजिए, प्रधानमंत्री को चुनौती देने वाला नेता, उनसे भारत रत्न के लिए आग्रह कर रहा है, नीतीश जी के अब यह हाल हो गए हैं,' एक पूर्व सहयोगी ने कहा।

विडंबना यह है कि मोदी-नीतीश के बीच फ़ोन पर बातचीत के कुछ दिनों बाद इंडिया गठबंधन की एक बैठक वीडियो कॉन्फ्रेंसिग के जरिए हुई। बैठक से ममता बनर्जी ने दूरी बनाए रखी, कांग्रेस ने नीतीश को संयोजक पद देने की पेशकश की। 'नहीं, नहीं, यह किसी और को करने दो, मैं तभी कोई पद लूंगा, जब सबको मेरा नाम स्वीकार्य हो,' बिहार के मुख्यमंत्री ने कहा। उन्होंने मन बना लिया था, वे केवल समय बिता रहे थे। राष्ट्रपति भवन की तरफ से 23 जनवरी को कर्पूरी ठाकुर को भारत रत्न देने की घोषणा की गई। इसके पांच दिन बाद, नीतीश कुमार ने रिकॉर्ड नौंवी बार बिहार के मुख्यमंत्री की शपथ ली। दस साल में पांचवीं बार उन्होंने पाला बदला था।

बातचीत में शामिल भाजपा के एक नेता ने कहा, 'जिस दिन नीतीश जी ने विपक्षी गठबंधन छोड़ा, हमें यकीन था कि 2024 में हमारे लिए यह खेल, और मैच तय हो गया था।' यह बेमायने नहीं था। भारतीय राजनीति में, वैसे तो कुछ भी तय नहीं होता, लेकिन विधानसभा चुनावों के निराशाजनक नतीजों के बाद नीतीश कुमार का जाना, विपक्ष के लिए एक बड़ा झटका माना जा रहा था। अब इस परेशान करने वाले बड़े सवाल का जवाब मिल गया था: कौन बनेगा चैलेंजर? सच कहें तो मोदी को चुनौती देने वाला कोई नहीं था।

या फिर ऐसा लग रहा था!

11

मोदी की गारंटी बनाम संविधान ख़तरे में है: विमर्श का युद्ध

मोदी-शाह के युग में भारतीय जनता पार्टी की चुनावी मशीन 'बिना ऑफ बटन' की हाई-स्पीड ट्रेडमिल की तरह है। अथक। अटल। असीमित। 2023 दिसम्बर के विधानसभा चुनाव के नतीज़ों के बाद की सुबह, भाजपा के लोकसभा सांसदों के व्हाट्सग्रुप पर एक छोटा सा संदेश था: 'प्रधानमंत्री जी का सम्मान करने और इस बड़ी जीत का जश्न मनाने के लिए कृपया सुबह 11 बजे तक संसद भवन आएं।' पिछली सरकारों ने आमतौर पर विधानसभा चुनावों की जीत का जश्न संसद के बाहर पार्टी कार्यक्रमों के रूप में मनाया था, ताकि संसदीय कामकाज में कोई बाधा नहीं पहुंचे। लेकिन मोदी सरकार के लिए हर चुनावी जीत, संसद के अंदर और बाहर दोनों जगह खुशी मनाने और खुद को बधाई देने का मौका था। इसकी पूरी तैयारी थी। प्रधानमंत्री जब एक 'सम्राट' की तरह लोकसभा में आते हैं, तो पार्टी के सदस्य एक साथ खड़े होते हैं, मेजें थपथपाते हैं और मुख्य कलाकार के लिए मंच तैयार करते 'बैक-ग्राउंड' गायकों की तरह मोदी-मोदी के नारे लगाते हैं।

वह दिन भी अलग नहीं था। संसदीय कार्य मंत्री प्रह्लाद जोशी की अगुवाई में सांसदों ने 'तीसरी बार मोदी सरकार', 'बार-बार मोदी सरकार', 'मोदी! मोदी! हैट-ट्रिक! हैटट्रिक', के नारे लगाने शुरू कर दिए। अपनी पहली पंक्ति की सीट पर प्रधानमंत्री ऐसे बैठे दिखाई दिए, मानो उन्होंने नारे सुने ही नहीं, जबकि संसद के कैमरों का फोकस पूरी तरह उन पर ही था। लोकसभा अध्यक्ष ओम बिरला बिना कुछ कहे अपनी सदाबहार सौम्यता के साथ मुस्कुराए, तो नारों की

आवाज़ और ऊंची हो गई। इरादा साफ था। भाजपा का घिरे हुए विपक्ष और मतदाताओं को संदेश था: तीन प्रमुख राज्यों में जीत से उत्साहित मोदी के नेतृत्व में भाजपा 2024 के लोकसभा चुनावों में जीत की मुश्किल हैट-ट्रिक लगाने को तैयार थी।

कांग्रेस के सांसद गौरव गोगोई ने टिप्पणी की, 'भाजपा ने पवित्र संसद परिसर को भी लोकतंत्र के मंदिर से राजा के दरबार में बदल दिया है, यह बेतुका है।' लेकिन भाजपा नेतृत्व इस आलोचना से बेपरवाह दिखाई दिया। भाजपा के एक सांसद ने बताया कि प्रधानमंत्री की टीम की 'मोदी-मोदी' के नारों पर कड़ी नज़र थी। पीछे बैठने वाले एक सांसद ने कहा, 'ऐसा लगता है कि मानो आप बिग-बॉस स्टुडियो में हैं और कोई हर समय आप पर नज़र रख रहा है।'

'बिग बॉस' शायद सबसे सटीक उपमा है। निर्विवाद सुप्रीमो मोदी, और उनके विश्वस्त चुनाव प्रभारी शाह जोड़ी नंबर-1 हैं, जिन्हें कोई चुनौती नहीं दे सकता, और उन्हें रोक पाना नामुमकिन है। वे दिग्गज पेशेवर राजनीति के पहलवानों की ऐसी 'टैग-टीम' है, जो अस्सी के दशक में गुजरात के नगरपालिका चुनावों से एक साथ मुकाबला कर रहे हैं। वे रुकने या पीछे हटने के मूड में नहीं दिखते। मुख्यमंत्रियों के नाम तय करने से लेकर सभी बड़े फ़ैसले, यह जोड़ी सीमित सलाह और पूरी गोपनीयता के साथ करती है। जैसे 2022 में गुजरात में मुख्यमंत्री का नाम तय किया गया। कृषि मंत्री नरेन्द्र तोमर के साथ पार्टी पर्यवेक्षकों को नए चुनकर आए भाजपा विधायकों से मिलने के लिए दिल्ली से गुजरात के गांधीनगर भेजा गया था। विधायक दल की बैठक शुरू होने तक तोमर को नेतृत्व की पसंद के बारे में कोई जानकारी नहीं थी। प्रधानमंत्री कार्यालय का संदेश था, हम आपको उचित समय पर सूचित करेंगे। दिल्ली के फ़ैसले के इंतज़ार में बेसब्र तोमर करीब 45 मिनट तक विधायकों को संबोधित करते रहे। अब तो उनके पास शायद कहने के लिए भी कुछ नहीं बचा था, तभी अचानक उनके हाथ में नाम की एक पर्ची थमा दी गई। उन्होंने नाम का ऐलान किया—भूपेन्द्र पटेल, तो कमरे में सन्नाटा सा छा गया। पहली बार विधायक बने पटेल आखिरी पंक्ति में बैठे थे। दिल्ली में आलाकमान ने कमोबेश एक अनजान विधायक को चुना था। अस्सी के दशक में इंदिरा गांधी पर मुख्यमंत्रियों को चुनने में प्रदेश संगठन को दरकिनार करने का आरोप लगता था। मोदी-शाह टीम ने इंदिरा शैली की हाईकमान संस्कृति को ज़्यादा अधिकार के साथ अपनाया था।

2023 की सर्दियों में तीन हिंदीभाषी राज्यों के मुख्यमंत्री भी उसी गोपनीय तरीके से चुने गए थे। छत्तीसगढ़ में तीन बार मुख्यमंत्री रहे डॉ. रमन सिंह की जगह कम उम्र के विष्णु देव साय का नाम तय किया गया, जो राज्य के पहले आदिवासी मुख्यमंत्री थे। हालांकि सिंह को हटाने की चर्चा चल रही थी, वे पहले भी राज्यपाल बनने की दौड़ में लगे हुए थे। लेकिन चौंकाने वाली बात रही मध्यप्रदेश में, जहां लंबे समय से मुख्यमंत्री रहे शिवराज सिंह चौहान को नज़रअंदाज़

किया गया। भाजपा ने यहां कड़े मुकाबले में दो-तिहाई सीटों के साथ बड़ी जीत हासिल की थी और 'मैन-ऑफ-द-मैच', चौहान को ही फिर से कुर्सी मिलने की उम्मीद थी। आखिरकार, इस जीत में उनके दिमाग की उपज रही 'लाडली बहन योजना' का मतदाताओं पर बहुत असर रहा था, योजना में महिलाओं को हर महीने नकद राशि दी जा रही थी। नतीजों के बाद, चौहान उत्साहित समर्थकों से मालाएं पहनते, महिला मतदाताओं के साथ तस्वीरें खिंचवाने, अफसरों के साथ समीक्षा बैठकें करने और शपथ-ग्रहण के लिए शुभ मुहुर्त तय करने में लगे थे, जब उन्हें बताया गया कि पार्टी ने किसी और का नाम तय कर दिया था। उज्जैन के बाहुबली मोहन यादव की मध्यप्रदेश से बाहर कोई पहचान नहीं थी, और उन्हें चौहान के बराबर की शख्सियत नहीं माना जा सकता था। एक समर्थक ने बताया, 'शिवराज जी ने आरएसएस और दिल्ली में अपने संपर्कों के साथ जमकर पैरवी की, लेकिन आलाकमान टीम ने उनकी किस्मत का पहले ही फ़ैसला कर दिया था।' यादव का नाम चुनावी रणनीति के तहत किया गया। भाजपा उत्तरप्रदेश और बिहार के प्रभावशाली यादव समुदाय तक पहुंचना चाहती थी। उनके शपथ समारोह के दिन यादव वोटों को आकर्षित करने के लिए बिहार के यादव-बहुल इलाकों में 'एलईडी स्क्रीन्स' लगाई गई थीं। मिलनसार और अडिग पार्टी कार्यकर्ता रहे चौहान को आखिर लाइन में आना पड़ा, उन्होंने लोकसभा चुनाव बड़े अंतर के साथ जीता और फिर कृषि मंत्री बनाए गए। लेकिन पड़ोसी राज्य राजस्थान में वसुंधरा राजे को यह समझाना ज़्यादा मुश्किल काम था कि अब उनका समय पूरा हो गया था। भाजपा ने जैसे ही आधी से ज़्यादा सीटें जीतीं, वसुंधरा राजे ने अपने वफ़ादार विधायकों को इकट्ठा करना शुरू कर दिया, ताकि आलाकमान पर दबाव बनाया जा सके, लेकिन कोई फायदा नहीं हुआ। रक्षा मंत्री राजनाथ सिंह, उन नेताओं में से थे जिनके राजे के साथ अच्छे संबंध माने जाते हैं, उन्हें केन्द्रीय पर्यवेक्षक बनाकर भेजा गया। 'तो आप किसे मुख्यमंत्री बना रहे हैं?' राजनाथ सिंह के जयपुर पहुंचने पर कथित तौर पर उत्तेजित वसुंधरा ने उनसे पूछा। राजनाथ ने कहा, चुनाव विधायकों पर छोड़ा गया है, लेकिन हकीकत में फ़ैसला दिल्ली में पहले ही हो चुका था। संगठन में रहे, पहली बार विधायक बने भजन लाल शर्मा नए मुख्यमंत्री होंगे। विधायक दल की बैठक में, नाराज़ राजे को अंतिम समय पर एक पर्ची थमा दी गई और उन्हें नाम का प्रस्ताव रखने के लिए कहा गया। उनके एक वफादार विधायक ने कहा, 'वसुंधरा अपनी अनदेखी से नाराज़ थीं, लेकिन बोलने की हिम्मत नहीं जुटा पाईं।' फिर अपने को समेटकर राजे ने बेटे दुष्यंत सिंह के झालावाड़-बारां निर्वाचन क्षेत्र को छोड़कर लोकसभा चुनावों में कहीं और प्रचार नहीं करने का फ़ैसला किया। यहां तक कि कुछ कांग्रेस उम्मीदवारों को उनका 'मौन' समर्थन मिला। राजे की खामोश बगावत पार्टी को मंहगी पड़ी। 2019 में राजस्थान में सभी 25 सीटों पर जीत हासिल करने वाली भाजपा को सिर्फ़ 14 सीटों पर संतोष करना पड़ा।

हिंदीभाषी राज्यों में एक आदिवासी, एक ओबीसी और एक ब्राह्मण मुख्यमंत्री, यह मोदी-शाह की जाति आधारित सोशल इंजीनियरिंग का हिस्सा था, जिसका मकसद मिशन 2024 से पहले नेतृत्व में पीढ़ीगत बदलाव लाना था। उनकी यह योजना आम चुनावों से करीब दो साल पहले 2022 की गर्मियों में शुरू हो गई थी। भाजपा ने तब महत्वपूर्ण उत्तरप्रदेश विधानसभा चुनाव जीते थे और चुनावी रफ्तार पकड़ी थी, लेकिन इस बात की चिंता शुरू हो गई थी कि केन्द्र में दस साल से सरकार के ख़िलाफ सत्ता विरोधी भावना से नुक़सान हो सकता है। चुनौती यह थी कि संगठन में आरामपरस्ती आने से पहले कैसे फिर से सक्रिय किया जाए। मई 2022 में, पार्टी पदाधिकारियों की एक बैठक में शाह ने कहा, 'अगर हमें 2024 में बड़ी जीत हासिल करनी है तो संगठन को फिर से दुरुस्त करना होगा।'

उस समय तक 'चार सौ पार' का लक्ष्य तय नहीं किया गया था, लेकिन गृहमंत्री यह सुनिश्चित करना चाहते थे कि भाजपा 2019 के 303 सीटों के आंकड़े को पार कर जाए। पार्टी पदाधिकारियों के सामने उन्होंने उन 224 सीटों का ज़िक्र किया, जिन्हें पार्टी ने 2019 में 50 फ़ीसद से ज़्यादा वोटों के साथ जीता था। शाह ने कहा कि 'अब हमें उन 100 सीटों पर ध्यान देना है, जो पिछली बार हार गए थे।' 2019 में भाजपा ने ज़्यादातर सीटें उत्तर और पश्चिम भारत में जीती थीं, यहां उसे 80 फ़ीसद से ज़्यादा सीटें मिली और आधा दर्जन राज्यों में विपक्ष को खाली हाथ रहना पड़ा। इन इलाकों में और बढ़ने की गुंज़ाइश कम थी। लेकिन पूर्व और दक्षिण के इलाकों में अभी आगे बढ़ने की संभावनाएं थीं।

भाजपा ने लोगों तक पहुंचने के लिए एक महत्वाकांक्षी 'आउटरीच' कार्यक्रम 'लोकसभा प्रवास योजना' शुरू की। इसका मकसद उन संसदीय क्षेत्रों में पार्टी को मज़बूत करना था, जहां 2019 में वह दूसरे या तीसरे स्थान पर रहे या फिर जीत का फासला कम रहा। उन्होंने ऐसी 144 मुश्किल सीटों की पहचान की (बाद में यह संख्या बढ़कर 160 हो गई) और उन पर फोकस करने के लिए कहा गया। इन सीटों के तीन-चार सीटों को मिलाकर ग्रुप बना दिए गए और हर समूह की ज़िम्मेदारी एक सांसद या वरिष्ठ मंत्री को सौंपी गई। प्रभारी नेता को इन निर्वाचन क्षेत्रों में हर महीने दौरा करना था, बूथ स्तर पर पार्टी कार्यकर्ताओं से बातचीत और सरकारी योजनाओं की ज़मीन पर डिलीवरी का आंकलन करना था और इसकी विस्तार से रिपोर्ट केन्द्रीय नेतृत्व को देनी थीं। नई भाजपा में सरकार और पार्टी के कामकाज के बीच रेखाएं तेज़ी से धुंधली होने लगी थीं। प्रवास योजना में शामिल मंत्रियों को 144-पॉइंट का कार्यक्रम फॉर्म दिया गया। इस योजना में कई वरिष्ठ मंत्रियों को भी शामिल किया गया था। विदेश मंत्री एस.जयशंकर को तिरुवनंतपुरम की ज़िम्मेदारी दी गई, तो वित्त मंत्री निर्मला सीतारमण को तेलंगाना की निगरानी के लिए कहा गया। इस कार्यक्रम पर एक मंत्री ने टिप्पणी की, 'हमसे सप्ताह के कामकाजी दिनों में मंत्री की जिम्मेदारी संभालने और सप्ताह के आखिर में पार्टी का काम करने की उम्मीद की जाती थी यानी कोई छुट्टी नहीं, कोई ऑफ नहीं!'

शाह के मिशन 2024 का एक और अहम पहलू यह था, जिसे पार्टी के लोग 'एम एंड ए' (**'M&A' approach: Mergers and Acquisitions**) दृष्टिकोण कहते थेः यानी 'विलय और कब्ज़ा'। शाह ने तीन बड़े राज्यों की पहचान की थी, जहां सीटों में दोहरे अंकों के नुकसान की आशंका से इंकार नहीं किया जा सकताः महाराष्ट्र, बिहार और कर्नाटक। महाराष्ट्र में 2019 में भाजपा नेतृत्व वाले एनडीए ने 48 में से 42 सीटें जीती थीं, लेकिन इस बार ज़्यादा चुनौती थी। शिवसेना को तोड़कर और 2022 में सरकार बनाने के बावज़ूद, भाजपा को इस बात की चिंता थी कि इस बार उसके ख़िलाफ़ एक मजबूत विपक्षी गठबंधन था। अपने खेमे को और मज़बूत करने के लिए पार्टी ने जुलाई 2023 में, एनसीपी में टूट कराने की कोशिश की, (जैसा कि पिछले अध्याय में विस्तार से बताया गया है, ईडी को डर और सुरक्षा के हथियार के तौर पर इस्तेमाल किया गया।) इसका मतलब था अजित पवार के साथ गठबंधन। कुछ समय पहले भाजपा ने उन्हें सबसे भ्रष्ट बताया था। विभाजन और दलबदल से 'भाजपा-शिवसेना-एनसीपी' का मजबूत गठबंधन बनाया गया।

बिहार में, भाजपा ने लोक जनशक्ति पार्टी के युवा नेता चिराग पासवान को जोड़ने का फ़ैसला किया। चिराग ने खासतौर से दलित युवाओं के बीच अच्छी पकड़ बनाई थी। 2020 के बिहार विधानसभा चुनावों से पहले चिराग पासवान को मुख्यमंत्री नीतीश कुमार का कद छोटा करने के लिए अकेले चुनाव में जाने के लिए प्रोत्साहित किया गया। बिहार भाजपा के एक नेता ने स्वीकार किया, 'अमित शाह जी ने चिराग को जेडी(यू) उम्मीदवारों के ख़िलाफ़ कड़ी टक्कर देने के लिए कहा, लेकिन इसमें भाजपा को निशाना नहीं बनाने के निर्देश भी थे।' इसका मक़सद भाजपा को सबसे बड़ी पार्टी बनाना और नीतीश कुमार की चुनाव बाद सौदेबाज़ी की ताकत को कम करना था। इसमें ज़ोखिम ज़्यादा था, लेकिन मोदी-शाह टीम इस जुए को खेलने के लिए तैयार थी। गुजरात के वक्त से ही उनकी शैली, पार्टी के भीतर और बाहर अपने प्रतिद्वन्दियों को लगातार किनारे पर रखने की रही है। चुनाव ख़त्म होने के एक साल बाद, चिराग ने खुद को सचमुच सड़क पर पाया। एक ज़माने में बॉलीवुड में अपना करियर बनाने की नाकाम कोशिश करने वाले आकर्षक दिखते राजनेता को अब जिंदगी का असल ड्रामा समझ आया। सरकारी अफसर, उनके 12, जनपथ के सरकारी आवास पर पहुंचें, जहां उनके दिवंगत पिता रामविलास पासवान बरसों से रह रहे थे, उन्हें तुरंत घर खाली करने को कहा गया। खुद को मोदी का 'हनुमान' बताने वाले हताश चिराग ने, शाह के दफ्तर समेत भाजपा के कई वरिष्ठ नेताओं से संपर्क करने की कोशिश की, लेकिन कोई मदद नहीं मिली। कई नेताओं ने तो उनका फ़ोन भी नहीं उठाया। रातों-रात ट्रकों में भरकर घर का सामान बाहर भेजना पड़ा। मोदी सरकार ने चिराग के चाचा पशुपति कुमार पारस को केन्द्र में मंत्री बना दिया। भतीजे को पूछने वाला कोई नहीं था। चिराग पासवान ने बाद में स्वीकार किया, 'यह अपमानजनक था, लेकिन जिंदगी में यह सब आपको मजबूत बनाता है।' मोदी-शाह टीम का

पासवान के साथ यह बर्ताव उनकी सुविधा के मुताबिक 'इस्तेमाल करो और फेंक दो' (यूज़ एंड थ्रो) की राजनीति का उदाहरण है।

जुलाई 2023 तक, जब नीतीश कुमार विपक्ष के पाले में चले गए, तो मोदी-शाह टीम को फिर से पासवान की ज़रूरत थी। पासवान परिवार से मधुर संबंध रखने वाले पार्टी के राष्ट्रीय अध्यक्ष जगत प्रकाश नड्डा को, उन्हें मनाने का काम सौंपा गया। अपने राजनीतिक अकेलेपन को ख़त्म करने के लिए बेचैन, पासवान ने फिर से राष्ट्रीय मुख्यधारा में लौटने के मौके का फायदा उठाया। वापसी के बाद एनडीए की एक बैठक में मोदी ने पासवान का हाथ पकड़कर गले लगाया। बिहार के नेता ने कहा, 'वह मेरे लिए पिता जैसे है।' इस्तेमाल करो। फेंको। फिर इस्तेमाल करो। बदलती निष्ठाओं के बीच, एनडीए मजबूत हुआ। जब जनवरी 2024 में नीतीश कुमार फिर लौटे, तो चक्र पूरा हो गया था। भाजपा को करीब से देखने वाले एक पर्यवेक्षक ने कहा, 'मोदी-शाह नेतृत्व का यह लचीलापन ही है कि उनके लिए कोई स्थायी दुश्मन नहीं है।'

कर्नाटक में भी वैचारिक लचीलापन काम आया। 2023 के विधानसभा चुनावों में भाजपा ने कर्नाटक के पूर्व मुख्यमंत्री और जेडी(एस) के नेता एच.डी. कुमारास्वामी को बार-बार निशाना बनाया और उन पर भ्रष्टाचार और वंशवाद की राजनीति का आरोप लगाया, लेकिन कर्नाटक में कांग्रेस की जीत ने भाजपा की योजनाओं पर पानी फेर दिया था। अब 2024 के लोकसभा चुनावों में भाजपा राज्य में एक और झटका बर्दाश्त करने को तैयार नहीं थी। 2019 के पिछले चुनावों में उसने यहां 28 लोकसभा सीटों में से 25 जीती थीं। गोल-मटोल से और सहज कुमारास्वामी एक बेहतर 'सौदागर' थे। वह अलग-अलग वक्त पर भाजपा और कांग्रेस दोनों के साथ गठबंधन कर मुख्यमंत्री रहे थे। बेंगलुरु के बाहरी इलाके में अपने खेतनुमा फॉर्महाउस में कुमारास्वामी परेशान नज़र आ रहे थे। कांग्रेस की निगाह उनके जेडी(एस) विधायकों पर थी और वह अपने को राजनीति में बेमायने होते देख रहे थे। बाद में उन्होंने बताया, 'हां, मैंने अमित शाह जी से बातचीत की और वे भी बातचीत के लिए इच्छुक थे।' गृहमंत्री ने जेडी(एस) का भाजपा में विलय का प्रस्ताव रखा। कुमारास्वामी तो तैयार थे, लेकिन उनके पिता एच.डी. देवेगौड़ा ने गठबंधन की बात की। जनवरी 2024 में, इस साझेदारी की घोषणा की गई, हालांकि इस पर बातचीत कई महीनों पहले शुरू हो गई थी। जब प्रधानमंत्री मोदी दिल्ली में 'परिवारवाद' को निशाना बना रहे थे, तब बेंगलुरु में एक राजनीतिक परिवार को भाजपा के साथ जोड़ते वक्त कोई हिचक नहीं थी। कर्नाटक में भाजपा के प्रमुख बी.वाई. विजयेन्द्र ने सफाई देते हुए कहा, 'राजनीति में आपको भविष्य के बारे में सोचना चाहिए, अतीत से बंधे रहने की ज़रूरत नहीं है।' विजयेन्द्र खुद भी कर्नाटक के पूर्व मुख्यमंत्री बी.एस. येदियुरप्पा के बेटे के तौर पर ही तो राजनीतिक वंशवाद का फायदा उठा रहे थे। मोदी के लिए चुनावी जीत ही सबसे महत्वपूर्ण है। चुनावी जीत ही उनकी राजनीति का सार है। सरकार, नारे, आदर्श, नीतियां, ध्रुवीकरण और

हिंसा, यह सब किसी भी कीमत पर चुनाव जीतने के लिए ज़रूरी है, सत्ता के लिए एकतरफा, कड़े मुकाबले के लिए उन्मादी सनक, भारतीय राजनीति में इससे पहले शायद ही देखी गई हो। 2024 के चुनाव में भाजपा-जेडी(एस) गठबंधन विजयी रहा, दक्षिणी कर्नाटक में गठबंधन ने वो सीटें भी हासिल कर लीं, जो भाजपा शायद हार जाती।

हालांकि गठबंधन की सभी कोशिशें कामयाब नहीं हो पाईं। पंजाब में, शाह ने शुरुआती ना-नुकुर के बाद भाजपा के पुराने सहयोगी अकाली दल के साथ फिर से बातचीत पर सहमति जता दी। इससे पहले अकाली दल पंजाब में बड़े भाई की भूमिका में था और उसने 13 में से 10 सीटों पर चुनाव लड़ा जबकि बाकी 3 पर भाजपा ने अपने उम्मीदवार उतारे थे, इस बार शाह 50-50 पर अड़े थे। पंजाब भाजपा अध्यक्ष सुनील जाखड़ को बाकी चीज़ों को देखने के लिए कहा गया। भाजपा ने आखिरी पेशकश अकाली दल के लिए 7 और भाजपा के लिए 6 सीटों की रखी: 'ले लो या छोड़ दो'। अकाली इस पर सहमत नहीं हुए, उनका मानना था कि सीट बंटवारा आत्म-सम्मान से जुड़ा था। शाह अड़े रहे। बातचीत टूट गई। बरसों बाद दोनों दलों ने अलग-अलग लोकसभा चुनाव लड़ा। भाजपा को एक भी सीट पर जीत नहीं मिली, जबकि अकाली केवल एक सीट जीत पाए।

गृहमंत्री शाह गठबंधन के मामलों की निगरानी कर रहे थे, जबकि एक उच्चस्तरीय 'ज्वाइनिंग कमेटी' बनाई गई, जो दूसरी पार्टियों से आने वाले लोगों को चुनकर उन्हें पार्टी में शामिल करने का फ़ैसला करेगी। इस कमेटी में केन्द्रीय मंत्री भूपेन्द्र यादव, असम के मुख्यमंत्री हिमंता बिस्वा सरमा, राष्ट्रीय महासचिव विनोद तावड़े और महासचिव (संगठन) बी.एल. संतोष शामिल थे। प्रदेश की इकाईयां सिफ़ारिश भेज सकती थीं, जिनकी कमेटी जांच करेगी। मुख्य पैमाना वोट जुटाने का कौशल था। कमेटी के एक सदस्य ने कहा, 'कोई एक वोट भी हासिल कर लेता है, तो वह उपयोगी है।' एक अन्य ने तंज में कहा, 'हम अब भारतीय जनता पार्टी नहीं रह गए हैं, बल्कि "भरती" जनता पार्टी हो गए हैं।' कांग्रेस से आने वाले लोगों पर ज़्यादा ध्यान दिया गया। अब तक कम से कम कांग्रेस के दस पूर्व मुख्यमंत्री भाजपा में शामिल हो चुके थे।

वैसे, ज़रूरी नहीं था कि हर हाई-प्रोफाइल की एंट्री हो ही गई। जैसे, मध्यप्रदेश के पूर्व मुख्यमंत्री और नौ बार सांसद रहे कमलनाथ विधानसभा चुनावों में हार के बाद मार्च 2024 की शुरुआत में, भाजपा में शामिल होने की तैयारी कर रहे थे। गांधी परिवार के करीबी माने जाने वाले कमलनाथ को पार्टी में शामिल करने से यह माहौल बनाना आसान होता कि कांग्रेस पार्टी डूबता जहाज है। बताया जाता है कि कमलनाथ ने एक साझा कारोबारी मित्र की मदद से प्रधानमंत्री से संपर्क किया था। दिल्ली में एक भव्य कार्यक्रम में कमलनाथ और उनके बेटे और छिंदवाड़ा से सांसद नकुल नाथ को शामिल करने की योजना बनाई गई थी। जब कमलनाथ अपने निजी विमान से दिल्ली पहुंचे, तब उनके शामिल होने को लेकर तारीख और समय पर

काम चल रहा था, लेकिन आखिरी समय में यह राय मिली कि कमलनाथ को शामिल करने को लेकर पार्टी कार्यकर्ता में नाराज़गी है और खासतौर से सिख समुदाय 1984 से सिख-विरोधी दंगों में उनकी कथित भूमिका को लेकर नाराज़ है। भाजपा के एक वरिष्ठ नेता ने बताया, 'उन्हें शामिल करने के लिए बहुत दबाव के बावजूद हमने जोख़िम नहीं लिया।' पार्टी ने आधिकारिक तौर पर इस बात का खंडन किया कि मध्यप्रेश कांग्रेस नेता के साथ पार्टी कोई डील करने वाली थी। अनुभवी कांग्रेसी नेता ने भी दलबदल की किसी भी योजना की बात को ख़ारिज़ कर दिया और ज़ोर देकर कहा कि वे पार्टी के वफादार हैं। नाथ भले ही कांग्रेस में रह गए हों, लेकिन पूरे प्रदेश में सैकड़ों कांग्रेसी कार्यकर्ताओं ने पाला बदल लिया, जिससे पार्टी और कमज़ोर हो गई। नाथ खुद 2024 के चुनाव अभियान में अपने गढ़ छिंदवाड़ा के बाहर शायद ही दिखे हों। मध्यप्रदेश में भाजपा ने सभी 29 सीटों पर कब्ज़ा कर लिया।

टीम मोदी-शाह की विलय और कब्ज़ा करने की रणनीति का मिला-जुला असर रहा। जहां कर्नाटक जैसी जगहों पर यह कारगर रही, उसने पार्टी को महत्वपूर्ण सीटें दिलाईं, लेकिन महाराष्ट्र जैसे प्रदेशों में यह नहीं चल पाई और इससे पार्टी के कार्यकर्ताओं में अंसतोष बढ़ा। भाजपा में यूं तो कोई सार्वजनिक तौर पर नहीं बोलेगा, लेकिन विचारधारा वाली पार्टी अब सिर्फ़ चुनावी गणित के हिसाब में बदल गई थी, उससे अलग-अलग स्तर पर आरएसएस और भाजपा के नेताओं में बेचैनी साफ दिख रही थी। भाजपा के एक नेता ने कहा, 'जरा सोचिए, पार्टी को अपना जीवन समर्पित करने वाले कार्यकर्ता को अब कांग्रेस नेताओं का प्रचार करने के लिए कहा जा रहा है, जिन्हें पाला बदलते ही भाजपा का टिकट मिल गया, क्या इससे कार्यकर्ता का मनोबल नहीं गिरता?' 2024 के चुनाव में भाजपा के 441 उम्मीदवारों में से 25 फ़ीसद कुल 116 उम्मीदवार दूसरी पार्टियों से आए नेता थे, जिनमें ज़्यादातर कांग्रेस से थे। पार्टी के एक पदाधिकारी ने दुखी होते हुए कहा, 'कांग्रेस मुक्त भारत' के बजाय हम 'कांग्रेस युक्त भाजपा' बन रहे हैं। लेकिन मोदी-शाह टीम को इस आलोचना से कोई फर्क नहीं पड़ रहा था, क्योंकि उनके पास हमेशा एक तुरुप का इक्का था: प्रधानमंत्री मोदी की लोकप्रियता।

═

नरेन्द्र मोदी में राजनीतिक प्रचार को लेकर जुनून है, जिसमें ऊर्जा और आत्मविश्वास है। गुजरात के दिनों के मोदी के एक पुराने सहयोगी ने बताया कि एक युवा प्रचारक के तौर पर भी उन्हें किसी भी चीज़ में हारना पसंद नहीं था। उन्होंने याद करते हुए बताया कि 'एक बार मैंने उनसे शर्त लगाई थी कि अहमदाबाद में एक सार्वजनिक सभा के मैदान तक पहुंचने में कौन तेज़ चल सकता है। जब मैं उनसे थोड़ा आगे पहुंच गया, तो वे नाराज़ हो गए और एक-दो दिन तो उन्होंने मुझसे बात तक नहीं की।' किसी भी कीमत पर जीतने के रवैये से समझा जा सकता है

कि क्यों मोदी कभी चुनावी मोड से बाहर नहीं निकलते और अपने लोगों को ज्यादा से ज़्यादा वोट हासिल करने के लिए प्रेरित करते हैं।

मंत्रियों और सांसदों की प्रवास योजना अभी ख़त्म हुई थी कि नवम्बर 2023 में, मोदी सरकार ने एक और आउटरीच कार्यक्रम शुरू कर दिया। प्रधानमंत्री ने हरी झंडी दिखाकर 'विकसित भारत संकल्प यात्रा' शुरू की, जिसका मकसद सरकार की कई योजनाओं जैसे उज्जवला योजना, आवास योजना और आयुष्मान भारत को लेकर जागरुकता बढ़ाना था और इस बात की निगरानी भी करनी थी कि सरकार की योजनाएं ज़रूरतमंद लोगों तक पहुंच रही हैं और उनमें कोई गड़बड़-झाला नहीं है। ज़िलों में शिविर लगाए गए, जहां लोग सरकारी अफसरों के सामने ना केवल अपनी परेशानी रख सकते थे, बल्कि वहीं उनका निपटारा भी किया जाना था। भाजपा के पास सरकारी योजनाओं के लाखों लाभार्थियों की सूची थी, जिन्हें पार्टी अपने वोट बैंक के तौर पर देख रही थी। योजना की बारीकी से निगरानी करने वाले भाजपा के एक नेता ने बताया, 'व्हाट्सएप ग्रुप बनाने से लेकर कॉल सेंटर स्थापित करने तक, हम देशभर में लाखों लाभार्थियों के संपर्क में थे।' देशभर में 150 कॉल सेंटर बनाए गए। हर कॉल सेंटर तीन लोकसभा सीटों पर निगरानी रखने के लिए था, इसके लिए हर सेंटर पर 75 युवा लोगों की टीम थी, जिन्हें 7000-10,000 रुपये महीने पर रखा गया था। भाजपा के सभी संदेशों को आगे बढ़ाने के लिए वे फ़ोन पर काम कर रहे थे। भाजपा के लिए काम करने वाली कंपनियों में से एक राजनीतिक परामर्श फर्म, 'जार्विस टेक्नोलॉजी एंड स्ट्रैटेजी कंसल्टिंग', देशभर के लाभार्थियों से जुड़ने वाले कॉल सेंटर की परियोजना को देख रही थी। इस काम में बहुत पैसे और लोग लगे थे, जो पिछले दस साल में टीम मोदी-शाह की बड़े पैमाने पर चुनाव प्रबंधन शैली की खासियत थी। इस चुनाव जीतने की इतनी बड़ी मशीनरी में काफी ऊर्जा और प्लानिंग रही है, जिसने किसी सरकार, रोजाना के प्रशासन और नीति बनाने वाली किसी भी चुनाव तैयारी को पीछे छोड़ दिया है।

और फिर भी, 2024 में कुछ कमी रह गई थी। 2019 में, भाजपा की कमयाबी के लिए लाभार्थियों तक पहुंच को अहम माना गया। पार्टी के मुताबिक सरकारी योजनाओं के 20 करोड़ से ज़्यादा लाभार्थियों से उसको मतदाताओं को बढ़ाने में मदद मिली। पांच साल बाद, लाभार्थियों की यह मशीन लड़खड़ाने लगी थी। उदाहरण के लिए, कॉल सेंटर लाभार्थियों को विकास यात्रा के रास्ते पर सेल्फी क्लिक करने और इसे अपने फेसबुक या इंस्टाग्राम पेज पर अपलोड करने के लिए प्रोत्साहित कर रहे थे। लेकिन इस बार लाभार्थियों की भागीदारी कम दिख रही थी। भाजपा के राजनीतिक अभियानों से जुड़े रणनीतिकार रजत सेठी कहते हैं, 'मुझे लगता है कि पिछले दशक में भाजपा के लिए तकनीक के बढ़ते इस्तेमाल और इंवेट आधारित राजनीति की आउटसोर्सिंग का काम पूरा हो चुका था। तकनीक से सिस्टम बेहतर तो होता है, लेकिन इससे लोगों से संपर्क ख़त्म हो गया।' कार्यकर्ताओं का आरोप था कि अब विधायक

और सांसद नज़र नहीं आते, जबकि सरकारी योजनाओं का फायदा उठाने के लिए मंझले स्तर पर पार्टी नेताओं के कमीशन लेने की शिकायतें बढ़ गई थीं। हालांकि पारपंरिक कारीगरों और शिल्पकारों को मदद करने के लिए प्रधानमंत्री विश्वकर्मा योजना और स्वयं सहायता समूहों के माध्यम से 'लखपति दीदी' जैसी नई योजनाओं की घोषणाएं भी की गईं, लेकिन ज़मीनी स्तर पर हर जगह नहीं थी। उदाहरण के लिए, वेबसाइट पर पंजीकरण करना आवेदकों के लिए मुश्किल भरा था। भाजपा के एक वरिष्ठ अधिकारी ने माना, 'चाहे वह हमारा कार्यकर्ता हो या श्रमिक हो, हर कोई चाहता है कि सिर्फ़ मोबाइल एप पर ही नहीं, उससे बातचीत करके उसे समझा जाए। शायद हम बहुत जल्दी, बहुत बड़ा बनने की कोशिश की कीमत चुका रहे हैं।' कल्याणकारी योजनाओं के लाभार्थी अब भी पार्टी की ताकत थे, लेकिन उनके वोटों को अब हल्के में नहीं लिया जा सकता।

ज़ोर-शोर से शुरू की गई विकसित भारत संकल्प यात्रा भी विवादों से अछूती नहीं रही। इसे सरकारी और पार्टी दोनों के कार्यक्रम के तौर पर बताया गया। मंच पर नौकरशाह, भाजपा नेताओं के साथ कंधे से कंधा मिलाते नज़र आ रहे थे तो मंच से इतर संयुक्त सचिव और उप सचिव स्तर के अधिकारियों को सरकार की उपलब्धियों को दिखाने के लिए 'ज़िला रथ प्रभारी' बनाया गया था। विपक्ष ने आरोप लगाया कि राजनीतिक यात्रा को बढ़ावा देने के लिए सरकारी पैसे का दुरुपयोग किया जा रहा है, जिसका मकसद सत्ताधारी पार्टी को फायदा पहुंचाना है। जनवरी 2024 में, यात्रा के पचास दिन पूरे होने पर, सरकार के प्रेस सूचना ब्यूरो ने एक बयान जारी कर दावा किया कि इस यात्रा में दस करोड़ लोग शामिल हुए। इसके बाद पार्टी नेताओं और मंत्रियों ने प्रधानमंत्री को बधाई संदेश जारी किए। इसके अलावा, रक्षा मंत्रालय को रेलवे स्टेशनों और हवाई अड्डे जैसे प्रमुख स्थानों पर 822 'सेल्फी पांइट' बनाने की जिम्मेदारी दी गई, वहां लोग प्रधानमंत्री के कट-आउट के साथ तस्वीरें ले सकते थे। रक्षा मंत्रालय के एक अन्य आदेश में सालाना छुट्टी पर जाने वाले सैनिकों को सरकारी योजनाओं के प्रचार-प्रसार के लिए समय निकालने को कहा गया था। नौकरशाही और यहां तक कि सेना का राजनीतिकरण चिंता की बात थी। कांग्रेस के मीडिया प्रमुख पवन खेड़ा ने पूछा, 'क्या यह सरकारी मशीनरी के दुरुपयोग और सेवा नियमों को तोड़ने की शर्मनाक कोशिश नहीं है?' भाजपा के राष्ट्रीय अध्यक्ष जे.पी. नड्डा ने एक ट्वीट में जवाब दिया, 'मैं हैरान हूं कि सरकारी अफसरों के ज़मीनी स्तर पर लोगों तक पहुंचने से कांग्रेस को परेशानी हो रही है। अगर यह सरकार का सबसे अहम काम नहीं है, तो क्या है?' तथ्य यह है कि जब प्रधानमंत्री इंदिरा गांधी ने 1971 के चुनावों में चुनाव प्रचार के लिए अपने सहायक यशपाल कपूर (जो उस वक्त सरकार में थे) की सेवाएं ली थीं, तो इसे 'चुनावी कदाचार' करार दिया गया। 12 जून 1975 के अपने ऐतिहासिक फ़ैसले में इलाहाबाद उच्च न्यायालय ने उन्हें प्रधानमंत्री पद से बर्खास्त कर दिया था। मोदी के चुनावी मकसद से

सरकारी मशीनरी का इस कदर बड़े पैमाने पर इस्तेमाल के सामने इंदिरा गांधी की कार्रवाई कोई यातायात उल्लंघन जैसा मामला लगता है।

भारतीय जनता पार्टी के 2024 के चुनाव अभियान की परेशानियों को यह राजनीतिक घमासान शायद ही छिपा सके: 2047 तक विकसित भ रत, जब देश आज़ादी की 100वीं सालगिरह मनाएगा। इससे पहले अमृत काल और मोदी की गारंटी, जिंदगी बदलने वाला उनका व्यक्तिगत वादा: 'मोदी की गारंटी'। इससे पहले 2022 तक मोदी ने नए भारत के सपने पर ज़ोर दिया था। अब वे ज़्यादा महत्वाकांक्षी हो गए थे और अपने समर्थकों को 2047 तक का तय लक्ष्य देकर और बड़े सपने देखने की बात कर रहे थे। मोदी सरकार से जुड़े एक अन्य शोध और वकालत समूह ब्लूक्राफ्ट डिजिटल फाउंडेशन ने 'विकसित भारत राजदूत' कार्यक्रम शुरू किया, जिसका उद्देश्य कॉलेज के छात्रों और युवा पेशेवरों को प्रधानमंत्री के दृष्टिकोण को फैलाने के लिए आकर्षित करना था। चुनावों से पहले सामुदायिक जुड़ाव को बढ़ावा देने के लिए देशभर में सार्वजनिक बैठकों से लेकर मैराथन दौड़ तक लगभग पचास ऐसे प्रोग्राम शुरू किये गए। आध्यात्मिक नेता श्री श्री रविशंकर, बैडमिंटन चैंपियन साइना नेहवाल और फिल्म अभिनेता राजकुमार राव और विक्रांत मैसी जैसी हस्तियों को दर्शकों से बातचीत करने के लिए बुलाया गया। 'हम चाहते थे कि युवा भारत को पता चले कि "विकसित भारत" का क्या मतलब है। हमारा प्रयास सिर्फ वोट मांगने से कहीं आगे था; हम युवाओं से वास्तव में विकसित भारत की कल्पना करने के लिए कह रहे थे,' ब्लूक्राफ्ट के निदेशक मुंबई स्थित भाजपा के वकील-राजनेता हितेश जैन ने कहा। 'सपनों के सौदागर' को अपने लोगों का भरोसा हासिल हो, लेकिन सपनों के बुनने की भी अपनी सीमा होती है। कोविड की महामारी के साथ देश ने अभी पांच मुश्किल सालों का सामना किया है। विकसित भारत के मुद्दे के सामने बेरोज़गारी और मंहगाई जैसी कड़वी सचाई मुश्किल पैदा कर रही थीं। भाजपा के एक चुनावी रणनीतिकार ने माना, 'हम 2027 में भारत की तस्वीर की बात कर रहे थे, लेकिन ज़्यादातर मतदाता की चिंता यह थी कि अगले छह से बारह महीनों में उनकी ज़िंदगी कैसे बदलेगी? शायद यही वजह रही होगी कि 2024 की कहानी बदल गई।'

फरवरी 2024 में, पार्टी के चुनिंदा सांसदों के सामने प्रधानमंत्री ने अपने विकसित भारत के विज़न को रखा। राम मंदिर का प्राण-प्रतिष्ठा समारोह अभी- अभी हुआ था और इसे हिंदू सभ्यता के महान क्षण के रूप में मनाया जा रहा था। इस जोश के बीच उम्मीद थी कि मोदी राम मंदिर निर्माण को अपना तुरुप का पत्ता बनाएंगे। लेकिन प्रधानमंत्री ने अलग नजरिया रखा, उन्होंने सांसदों को सलाह दी कि वे अपने चुनाव अभियान में लाखों भारतीयों को गरीबी से बाहर निकालने में सरकारी उपलब्धियों और भारत को दुनिया की पांचवीं सबसे बड़ी अर्थव्यवस्था बनाने पर ज़ोर दें। 'जो पिछले साठ साल में नहीं हुआ, हमने दस साल में करके दिखाया। वोटर

को विकसित भारत चाहिए।' चुनावों से ऐन पहले, राम मंदिर और हिंदुत्व की राजनीति पीछे छूट रही थी और इसकी जगह सर्वोच्च नेता के तौर पर मोदी की राष्ट्रवादी-लोकलुभावन रणनीति ले रही थी। विकसित भारत की शक्ति और गौरव, सिर्फ़ मोदी ही बहाल कर सकते थे।

एक और रोचक कहानी है। राम मंदिर के प्राण प्रतिष्ठा समारोह से कई हफ्तों पहले संघ परिवार ने मंदिर मुद्दे को आम लोगों तक ले जाने की तैयारी कर ली थी। विश्व हिन्दू परिषद् ने लोगों से अपने आसपास के मंदिर में जाने और 'श्रीराम ज्योति' जलाने का अभियान चलाया था। श्रीरामजन्मभूमि ट्रस्ट ने पांच लाख गांवों में घर-घर बांटने के लिए 'अक्षत' विश्व हिन्दू परिषद के कार्यकर्ताओं को दिए। जनवरी से अप्रैल के बीच पचास लाख लोगों को अयोध्या लाने के लिए एक सामूहिक तीर्थ यात्रा की योजना बनाई गई। अयोध्या में प्राण प्रतिष्ठा और अनुष्ठानों के मुख्य यजमान तो प्रधानमंत्री थे ही, इससे पहले उन्होंने देश के दूसरे महत्वपूर्ण मंदिरों के दर्शन किए। इसके बावजूद अब प्रधानमंत्री मोदी, अपने सांसदों से मंदिर निर्माण को मुद्दा बनाने के बजाय, गरीबों के लिए सरकार की कल्याणकारी योजनाओं और इन्फ्रास्ट्रक्चर पर हुए काम पर ज़ोर देने की बात कर रहे थे: चाहे वह ग़रीबों के लिए मुफ़्त राशन हो, देशभर में राजमार्गों का निर्माण हो या उनकी महत्वाकांक्षी योजना—हर घर नल, जिसमें गांवों में हर घर तक नल का पानी पहुंचाने का वादा किया गया था। 'देश में केवल चार जातियां हैं, गरीब, युवा, किसान और महिलाएं, वे हमारी प्राथमिकता हैं,' उन्होंने लाभार्थियों के एक कार्यक्रम में वीडियो कॉन्फ्रेंस में कहा। मोदी ने इसके लिए एक संक्षिप्त नाम गढ़ा: ज्ञान (**GYAN**), जिसमें गरीब, युवा, अन्नदाता (किसान) और नारी (महिलाएं) शामिल थे। मंदिर के उत्साह और जोश के बाद यह फिर से कल्याणकारी राजनीति की तरफ वापसी थी, जिसका मक़सद, मतदाताओं का दायरा बढ़ाना और खासतौर से गरीबों तक पहुंचना था। भाजपा के एक चुनावी रणनीतिकार ने कहा, राम अहम है, लेकिन रसोई में राशन के बिना नहीं। 'मुझे लगता है प्रधानमंत्री ने मंदिर राजनीति की सीमाओं को समझ लिया है: वह अपने कोर वोटर को तो साथ रख सकता है, लेकिन उससे वोटों में बड़ा इज़ाफ़ा नहीं होगा।' तीस साल पहले नब्बे के दशक में हिंदूत्व के सांस्कृतिक-वैचारिक एजेंडा का जोश अब ठंडा पड़ने लगा था। आप एक ही तीर को दो बार नहीं चला सकते। हिंदूत्व को ज़मीनी सच्चाई के साथ संतुलित करने की ज़रूरत थी कि कैसे ज़रूरी लाभ देकर मतदाताओं को लुभाया जाए।

इस बात पर आश्चर्य नहीं होना चाहिए कि जब 2024 के चुनावों के लिए भाजपा ने अपना संकल्प पत्र (घोषणा-पत्र) जारी किया, तो उसका फोकस मोदी की गारंटी था। पार्टी अब पूरी तरह से एक ही नेतृत्व के रास्ते पर चलने लगी थी। साठ-सत्तर पन्नों के घोषणा पत्र में केवल प्रधानमंत्री की तस्वीरों के साथ सरकार की गारंटियों का ज़िक्र था। कस्बों, शहरों के प्रमुख स्थानों पर सड़कों पर लगे होर्डिंग्स में प्रधानमंत्री की आदमकद तस्वीरों के साथ 'मोदी की

गारंटी' का नारा छाया हुआ था। भाजपा की प्रचार टीम के एक सदस्य ने बताया, 'हमने 2019 के मुकाबले इस बार दोगुना मोदी पोस्टर छापे, जिनकी तादाद लाखों में थी।' इसका मक़सद था कि हर जगह मोदी ही दिखाई दे ताकि चुनाव अभियान शुरू होने से पहले ही विपक्ष नज़र ही नहीं आए और उसका मनोबल गिर जाए। मोदी का चेहरा हर जगह था: होर्डिंग से लेकर अख़बारों, एयरपोर्ट के कियोस्क से लेकर रेलवे स्टेशन तक। लेकिन इलाके और आबादी के हिसाब से गारंटी बदल गई थी। जैसे मेट्रो शहर बेंगलुर में विश्व-स्तरीय इन्फ्रास्ट्रक्चर की गारंटी थी; तो जम्मू में अनुच्छेद 370 को हटाने का मुद्दा बनाया गया; और बिहार में पानी और पक्के घर की गारंटी की बात की गई। मोदी, भाजपा के पाइड पाइपर, प्रधानमंत्री, प्रधान सेवक, फील गुड गुरु और सपनों के सौदागर, सबकुछ एक विशाल व्यक्तित्व में समाहित था। पार्टी के 2019 के सफल अभियान में जहां राष्ट्रवाद मुख्य संदेश था, तो 2024 में विकसित भारत के वादे के साथ कल्याणकारी योजनाएं थीं। भाजपा के एक नेता ने कहा, 'हमारे सर्वेक्षणों के मुताबिक प्रधानमंत्री की लोकप्रियता अपने प्रतिद्वन्दियों से बहुत आगे थी, तो हम उन्हें अपना शुभंकर क्यों नहीं बनाते?' मोदी की गारंटी और विकसित भारत के प्रचार अभियान को बढ़ाने के लिए एक वॉर-रूम बनाया गया, जिसे पूर्व आईएएस अधिकारी और आईआईटी से पढ़े केन्द्रीय मंत्री अश्विनी वैष्णव देख रहे थे, जिन्हें भाजपा के एक नेता ने मोदी का नया चहेता (ब्ल्यू आईड बॉय) बताया। कारोबार और प्रशासन के लंबे अनुभव के साथ खिचड़ी बालों वाले, तेज़ तर्रार वैष्णव एक बैकरूम बॉय हैं, जो पैसे और तकनीकी मीडिया प्रबंधन में माहिर हैं, जो किसी भी अभियान के लिए सबसे ज़रूरी माने जाते हैं।

प्रधानमंत्री ने पार्टी के कई और बड़े नेताओं को पहली बार चुनावी मैदान में उतरने के लिए कहा। केन्द्रीय मंत्री पीयूष गोयल को सुरक्षित मानी जाने वाली सीट मुंबई उत्तर दी गई, भूपेन्द्र यादव को राजस्थान के अलवर से और धर्मेन्द्र प्रधान को उड़ीसा के संबलपुर से चुनाव लड़ने का कहा गया। भाजपा के एक रणनीतिकार का कहना था कि 'इसका उद्देश्य ज़्यादा से ज़्यादा मंत्रियों को अपनी चुनावी ताकत दिखाने और साथ ही उन राज्यों में चुनावी हलचल पैदा करना था।' दस साल से ज़्यादा समय से कर्नाटक से निर्दलीय राज्यसभा सांसद रहने के बाद 2018 में भाजपा में शामिल हुए कारोबारी-राजनेता राजीव चन्द्रशेखर को प्रधानमंत्री ने 2021 के कैबिनेट फेरबदल में अपनी सरकार में शामिल किया था, इससे उनकी बढ़ती राजनीतिक ताकत का अहसास होता था। तकनीकी जानकार राजीव चन्द्रशेखर अपने गृह नगर और भाजपा की मज़बूत लोकसभा सीट बेंगलुरु से टिकट चाहते थे। लेकिन पार्टी की स्थानीय इकाई को शायद यह पसंद नहीं था। उन्होंने अंग्रेज़ीदां चन्द्रशेखर को 'बाहरी' के तौर पर देखा। इसके बजाय चन्द्रशेखर को केरल में तिरुवनंतपुरम सीट पर कांग्रेस के शशि थरूर के ख़िलाफ़ कड़े मुकाबले में उतारा गया। भजापा यह दिखाना चाहती थी कि केरल उसके लिए महत्वपूर्ण था, यहां से उसने पहले कभी

कोई लोकसभा सीट नहीं जीती थी। चन्द्रशेखर भले ही कभी केरल में नहीं रहे, लेकिन उनका परिवार वहां से था। चन्द्रशेखर के सहयोगी ने ज़ोर देकर कहा, 'पहली बार के उम्मीदवार ने तीन बार के हाई-प्रोफाइल सांसद से दमदार मुकाबला किया, हमारे पास खोने के लिए कुछ नहीं था।' जुझारू और सख्त बोलने वाले चन्द्रशेखर ने थरूर से हर कदम पर मुकाबला करते हुए मज़बूत लड़ाई लड़ी। यह अंग्रेज़ी बोलने वाले अभिजात वर्ग, नेहरूवादी पोस्टर ब्वॉय बनाम नए भारत के कारोबारी और धनबल के ख़िलाफ़ एक जंग थी। कांटे की टक्कर में थरूर सिर्फ़ 16 हज़ार वोटों से जीत पाए। 'यह बहुत मुश्किल लड़ाई थी, उन्होंने मेरे ख़िलाफ़ हरसंभव कोशिश की,' चन्द्रशेखर मोदी सरकार के चुनाव हारने वाले 17 मंत्रियों में से एक थे, और एक दर्जन मंत्रियों को टिकट नहीं दिया गया था यानी मंत्रिपरिषद् के 72 में से 29 या तो हार गए या उन्हें बदल दिया गया, हवा के बदलते रुख को समझने के लिए यह काफी था।

सभी मंत्रियों को इस बात पर यकीन था कि मोदी की शख़्सियत स्थानीय मुद्दों पर हावी रहेगी और विपक्ष डर जाएगा। 'चार सौ पार' का नारा, इस एक नेता, एक राष्ट्र रणनीति का हिस्सा था। फरवरी की शुरुआत में प्रधानमंत्री मध्यप्रदेश के आदिवासी बहुल इलाके झाबुआ में थे। अपने चुनाव अभियान की शुरुआत करते हुए यहां मोदी ने मतदाताओं से पिछले चुनाव के मुकाबले इस बार हर सीट पर 370 वोट ज़्यादा डालने की अपील की ताकि भाजपा 370 सीटें जीत सके और अपने सहयोगियों के साथ चार सौ पार कर सके। चुनाव को खुद के दम पर आगे बढ़ाते हुए मोदी ने तीन महीने के लंबे मुश्किल चुनाव अभियान में देशभर में पूरी ऊर्जा के साथ 206 रैलियां और रोड शो किए, लगता है चुनाव लड़ना और जीतना ही उनका धर्म है। आश्चर्यभरे अंदाज़ में एक मंत्री ने कहा, 'एक प्रचार करने वाले के तौर पर, उनकी अलग पहचान है। मैंने उन्हें विमान में थके हुए देखा है, लेकिन जैसे ही उतरते हैं और भीड़ को देखते हैं, वे पूरी तरह तरोताज़ा हो जाते हैं।'

क्या भारतीय जनता पार्टी की ताकतवर चुनाव मशीनरी के साथ प्रचार में कुशल नेता के ख़िलाफ़, एक लुटा-पिटा सा विपक्ष, अजेय मोदी के एक बड़ी जीत की ओर बढ़ते कदम को रोक सकता था?

═

कांग्रेस सांसद अजय माकन को हरफनमौला कहा जा सकता है, इस पुरानी बड़ी पार्टी में उन्होंने बहुत सी ज़िम्मेदारियां निभाई हैं। दिल्ली से तीन बार सांसद और विधायक रहे माकन, दिल्ली विधानसभा के सबसे युवा स्पीकर, पार्टी की मीडिया टीम के प्रमुख और मनमोहन सिंह सरकार में मंत्री रहे थे। लेकिन 2024 के चुनावों में साठ साल के माकन को अपने राजनीतिक जीवन की सबसे बड़ी चुनौती का सामना करना पड़ा। पार्टी के कोषाध्यक्ष के तौर पर उनसे यह उम्मीद थी

कि आम चुनाव लड़ने के लिए कांग्रेस के पास पर्याप्त पैसा हो। यह किसी भी तरह से आसान काम नहीं था। 2014 में सत्ता से बाहर होने के बाद से कांग्रेस को औद्योगिक घरानों से मिलने वाला चंदा कम होने लगा था। किसी ज़माने में कांग्रेस का साथ देने वाले कारोबारी समूह पार्टी को मदद करने और मोदी सरकार की नाराज़गी झेलने के डर से हिचक रहे थे। देश के दो सबसे बड़े कॉरपोरेट दिग्गजों गौतम अडानी और मुकेश अंबानी ने कांग्रेस को बिल्कुल चंदा नहीं दिया था। राहुल गांधी की भाई-भतीजावाद (क्रोनी कैपिटलिस्ट) की तीखी आलोचना से पार्टी को चंदा मिलना और मुश्किल हो गया था। अपने फंड को बढ़ाने और पार्टी को चर्चा में लाने के लिए बेताब कांग्रेस ने दिसंबर 2023 में, अपनी तरह का पहला 'क्राउड-फंडिग' अभियान शुरू किया। माकन और उनकी टीम ने 'देश के लिए दान' **(Donate for Desh)** अभियान चलाया, जिसमें पार्टी के 138 साल पूरे होने के बहाने लोगों से 138 रुपये के गुणक में योगदान देने के लिए कहा। कांग्रेस समर्थकों के बीच लोकप्रियता भुनाने के लिए 670 रुपये या ज़्यादा देने वालों को राहुल गांधी के दस्तखत वाली सफेद टी-शर्ट उपहार में देने का भी वादा किया गया। एक ज़माने तक बड़े कारोबारी घरानों से मोटा चंदा पाने वाली पार्टी के लिए छोटे से चंदे के बदले टी-शर्ट देना इस बात का संकेत था कि पार्टी मुश्किल दौर से गुज़र रही थी। पचास दिनों के इस अभियान में पार्टी ने 25 करोड़ रुपये जुटाए। माकन कहते हैं, 'यह पैसा काफी नहीं था, लेकिन यह क्राउड फंडिग के नाम पर कार्यकर्ताओं को प्रेरित करने और पार्टी से जोड़ने की कोशिश थी।'

पार्टी की वित्तीय चिंताएं बढ़ने वाली थीं। फरवरी 2024 में, आम चुनावों की उलटी गिनती शुरू हो गई थी। कांग्रेस बीट कवर करने वाले पत्रकारों को माकन ने एक संदेश भेजा: 'बड़ी ब्रेकिंग न्यूज, एक घंटे में प्रेस कॉन्फ्रेंस। कृपया लाइव कवरेज करें।' प्रेस कॉन्फ्रेंस में उन्होंने नाटकीय अंदाज़ में घोषणा की, आयकर विभाग ने कांग्रेस के 11 बैंक खातों को फ्रीज़ कर दिया। इससे पहले विभाग ने 2018-19 के टैक्स रिटर्न को देर से दाखिल करने पर ज़ुर्माना लगाया था। माकन ने एक दिन पहले ज्यादातर समय चार्टेड अकाउंटेट से फोन पर बिताया था, जो बैंक अधिकारियों से मामले को सुलझाने की कोशिश कर रहे थे। अकाउंटेंट ने बताया, 'वे कह रहे हैं कि जब तक हमें कोर्ट के आदेश नहीं मिल जाते, आप पैसे को हाथ नहीं लगा सकते।' माकन ने जवाब दिया, 'आप बैंक परिसर से बाहर मत निकलिए, हम इसे सुलझाने की कोशिश कर रहे हैं।' एक महीने बाद भी जब मसला सुलझता नहीं दिखा, तो कांग्रेस नेतृत्व ने इस मुद्दे को और बड़ा कर दिया। आमतौर पर नहीं दिखने वाली सोनिया गांधी, कांग्रेस अध्यक्ष मल्लिकार्जुन खड़गे और राहुल गांधी के साथ पार्टी मुख्यालय में नज़र आईं, और भाजपा पर मुख्य विपक्षी दल को कमज़ोर करने का आरोप लगाया। 'आयकर विभाग ने हमारे खातों से 135 करोड़ रुपये ज़बरन निकाल लिए हैं, इसके बाद भी खातों को काम में नहीं लेने दिया जा रहा। इसके

अलावा 31 साल बाद वित्तीय वर्ष 1993-94 समेत के 3,500 करोड़ रुपये की वसूली के नए नोटिस भेजे हैं, यह पूरी तरह से टैक्स-टेरेरिज़्म है,' माकन ने गुस्से में कहा।

कांग्रेस और आयकर विभाग के बीच का यह विवाद और इसकी टाइमिंग से समझा जा सकता है कि 2024 की लड़ाई किसी भी तरह से बराबरी के मैदान (लेवल प्लेइंग फील्ड) में नहीं थी। कांग्रेस के ज़्यादातर उम्मीदवारों को पार्टी से चुनाव के लिए 2 से 3 करोड़ रुपये का चंदा मिला था, जबकि भाजपा के पास अपने उम्मीदवारों के लिए डबल-डिजिट में करोड़ों का बजट था (कोई भी चुनावी खर्च की सही रकम तो नहीं बताता, लेकिन भाजपा के एक सांसद ने कहा कि उसे पार्टी से दस करोड़ रुपये मिले हैं।) नए चुनकर आए एक कांग्रेसी सांसद ने कहा कि मैं अपने क्षेत्र में बड़ी रैली नहीं करना चाहता था, क्योंकि उसमें बहुत खर्चा होता। 'हताशा में, मैंने अपने एक मित्र स्थानीय ठेकेदार से आधा पैसा चुकाने को कहा। लेकिन जब वह आखिरी समय पर पीछे हट गया, तो फिर मैंने केवल डोर-टू-डोर अभियान के साथ ही चलने का फ़ैसला किया और उसने बेहतर काम किया,' उन्होंने राहत की सांस लेते हुए कहा।

आम चुनावों से पहले कांग्रेस की परेशानियों में पैसे का संकट ताज़ा था। दिसम्बर 2023 में, तीन हिंदीभाषी राज्यों में हार से पार्टी के मनोबल को बड़ा झटका लगा था। फिर बिहार के मुख्यमंत्री नीतीश कुमार के इंडिया गठबंधन से अलग होकर, 2024 में भाजपा से हाथ मिलाने से संकट और बढ़ गया। इसके बाद नाराज ममता बनर्जी ने ऐलान किया कि वह कांग्रेस के साथ साझा चुनाव नहीं लड़ेंगी। उन्होंने देश में कांग्रेस को 40 सीटें मिलने पर भी संदेह जाहिर किया। बताया गया कि दिसंबर में इंडिया गठबंधन की एक बैठक में टीएमसी और कांग्रेस नेताओं के बीच सीट-बंटवारें पर चर्चा हो रही थी, उस वक्त राहुल गांधी, ममता बनर्जी के सामने अपनी सीट पर बेपरवाही से बैठे थे। एक पर्यवेक्षक के अनुसार, तीन बार मुख्यमंत्री रह चुकीं और देश की इकलौती महिला मुख्यमंत्री के प्रति यह अनादर का भाव था। बनर्जी ने कहा, 'मैं आपको दो सीटें दे सकती हूं, बाकी पर हम लड़ेंगे।' राहुल को अच्छा नहीं लगा। उन्होंने चेतावनी दी, 'मत भूलिए, हम बंगाल में आपको नुक़सान पहुंचा सकते हैं।' कांग्रेस नेता की इस बात से मुख्यमंत्री को झटका लगा और उन्होंने नाराज़गी ज़ाहिर करते हुए पलटवार किया, 'आप नुकसान पहुंचाइए, हम संभाल लेंगे।' बनर्जी का गुस्सा कांग्रेस के लोकसभा में नेता और पश्चिम बंगाल के अध्यक्ष अधीर रंजन को लेकर भी था, जो आए दिन उन पर हमलावर रहते थे। बताया जाता है कि ममता दी ने खड़गे को फ़ोन करके कहा, 'अगर आप गठबंधन चाहते हैं तो पहले अधीर रंजन को हटाएं।' पार्टी अध्यक्ष ने मामला सुलझाने का वादा किया, लेकिन दोनों पक्षों के बीच सीट-बंटवारे को लेकर गतिरोध बना रहा। इस रिश्ते में आखिरी कील तब लगी, जब चुनावों से पहले राहुल गांधी ने अपनी भारत जोड़ो न्याय यात्रा के रूट में पश्चिम बंगाल को शामिल किया। बनर्जी ने एक सहयोगी से शिकायत की, 'उन्हें इस तरह बंगाल आने की क्या

ज़रूरत है, यहां हम मुख्य पार्टी हैं। उन्हें कोई फ़ैसला लेने से पहले हमसे सलाह तो लेनी चाहिए थी।' कांग्रेस में कुछ लोग मानते थे कि बनर्जी ने भाजपा के साथ पिछले दरवाज़े से 'सौदा' कर लिया, ताकि इंडिया गठबंधन को नुक़सान पहुंचाया जा सके और फिर इससे बाहर निकलने का रास्ता तलाश रही थीं। तृणमूल के एक नेता ने पूछा, 'जब दोनों पक्षों में भरोसे की इतनी कमी है तो आप किसी साझेदारी की उम्मीद कैसे कर सकते हैं?' आखिर में टीएमसी अकेले चुनाव लड़ेगी जबकि कांग्रेस वामदलों के साथ जाएगी और इस निर्णय से इंडिया गठबंधन को चार से पांच सीटों का नुक़सान हो सकता है।

तमाम तरह के भ्रमों के बीच कांग्रेस आगे के रास्तों को लेकर अनिश्चित दिखी। उसे तय करना था कि पहले इंडिया गठबंधन को मज़बूत करे या फिर अपनी ताकत बढ़ाए। जनवरी में राम मंदिर के प्राण-प्रतिष्ठा समारोह से दूर रहने के पार्टी के फ़ैसले से वैचारिक स्तर पर विभाजन दिखाई देने लगा। बंद कमरे में हुई एक बैठक में, कई कांग्रेस नेता प्राण-प्रतिष्ठा समारोह में इसलिए शामिल होने के पक्ष में थे, क्योंकि बहिष्कार से उसे हिंदू विरोधी माना जाएगा। सभी दलों में दोस्त रखने वाले पत्रकार से राजनेता बने राज्यसभा सांसद राजीव शुक्ला भी समारोह में शामिल होने के पक्ष में थे। शुक्ला ने कहा, 'हमारी लड़ाई भाजपा से है, राम से नहीं।'

धार्मिक पहचान की राजनीति पर कांग्रेस दुविधा में रहती है। 2023 में चुनावी रोडमैप को अंतिम रूप देने के लिए रायपुर में पार्टी के अधिवेशन में, पार्टी के पोस्टरों और विज्ञापनों में बड़े स्वतंत्रता सेनानियों की तस्वीरें शामिल थीं, लेकिन इसमें मौलाना आज़ाद की तस्वीर नहीं थी। छत्तीसगढ़ के स्थानीय नेताओं ने आज़ाद को मुस्लिम नेता के तौर पर देखते हुए कोई जोखिम उठाना ठीक नहीं समझा। कांग्रेस के एक नेता ने बताया कि, 'हमें आखिरी वक्त पर दख़ल देना पड़ा ताकि यह सुनिश्चित किया जा सके कि मंच पर आज़ाद की तस्वीर प्रमुखता से हो।' पार्टी का एक हिस्सा भाजपा के अति हिंदूत्ववाद से प्रभावित था और उसे समझ नहीं आ रहा था कि इसे कैसे चुनौती दी जाए। लेकिन खड़गे और राहुल गांधी में इसको लेकर कोई संदेह नहीं था। अलग-अलग नज़रिए के बावज़ूद, राहुल गांधी राहुल गांधी के समर्थन से पार्टी अध्यक्ष इस बात पर अड़े रहे कि चुनाव से पहले, राम मंदिर समारोह मोटे तौर पर संघ परिवार के लिए एक राजनीतिक मंच है। अपने शुरुआती सालों में अम्बेडकर की शिक्षा से प्रभावित रहे खड़गे ने कहा, 'प्रधानमंत्री मोदी धर्म और राजनीति को मिलाना चाहते हैं, तो हमें उनके एजेंडा में पड़ने की क्या ज़रूरत है और क्यों समर्थन करना चाहिए?' यह निर्णय करना आसान नहीं था, लेकिन साफ था कि कांग्रेस आखिर एक फ़ैसला लेने और खुद को हिंदूत्व की राजनीति से दूर रखने के लिए तैयार थी।

खासतौर पर राहुल गांधी के लिए, इस फ़ैसले को सच्चाई के साथ खड़े होने के तौर पर देखा गया। 2017 के गुजरात चुनावों में, राहुल ने मंदिर-मंदिर अभियान शुरू किया और पार्टी

ने उनकी जनेऊधारी ब्राह्मण, यानी हिंदू छवि पर ज़ोर दिया था। उस समय हिंदू वोटों के लिए भाजपा से मुकाबले की एक हताश कोशिश लग रहा था, इसका कुछ फायदा भी हुआ। लेकिन अब पार्टी नेतृत्व हिंदू धर्म और हिंदूत्व के बीच फ़र्क दिखाना चाहता था, भले ही इसके मायने राम मंदिर समारोह का बहिष्कार करना और जोखिम लेना हो। हिंदू धर्म का आध्यात्मिक तौर पर पार्टी गहराई से सम्मान करती थी, लेकिन हिंदूत्व केवल राजनीतिक फायदे के लिए भाजपा का हथियार था। कार्यसमिति के सदस्य और पार्टी अध्यक्ष कार्यालय के एक अहम चेहरे गुरदीप सप्पल कहते हैं, 'राम मंदिर उद्घाटन समारोह से दूर रहने का फ़ैसला हमारे लिए एक निर्णायक क्षण था। अब हमारे पास धर्म निरपेक्षता बनाम सॉफ्ट हिंदूत्व की बहस को लेकर स्पष्टता थी जो पहले नहीं दिखती थी।'

हालांकि पार्टी प्रमुख की बात से सब लोग सहमत नहीं थे। पार्टी छोड़ने वालों में सबसे पहले गांधी परिवार के करीबी माने जाने वाले मिलिंद देवड़ा थे, जिन्हें हाल ही में पार्टी का संयुक्त कोषाध्यक्ष बनाया गया था। पिछली दो बार से महाराष्ट्र से राज्यसभा उम्मीदवारी में उनका नाम नहीं होने से वे बेचैन थे। मुकेश अंबानी जैसे कॉरपोरेट के साथ सहज रहने वाले, अमेरिका से पढ़ाई करके आए मिलिंद, राहुल गांधी की बड़े कारोबारियों के ख़िलाफ बयानों से मुश्किल में लगते थे। उन्होंने राम मंदिर फ़ैसले का इस्तेमाल सत्ता में बैठी शिवसेना (शिंदे) में शामिल होने के लिए बहाने के रूप में किया। पार्टी ने उन्हें राज्यसभा सीट देने का वादा किया था। देवड़ा ने कहा, 'यह मसला किसी पद को लेकर नहीं था, मुझे लगा कि कांग्रेस ने लोगों से अपना संपर्क खो दिया है। चाहे वह राम मंदिर का मसला हो या फिर आर्थिक नीति, कांग्रेस इतिहास के गलत पन्ने की तरफ थी।' देवड़ा के इस्तीफ़े का समय अहम था। उस दिन राहुल गांधी इम्फाल से अपनी भारत जोड़ो न्याय यात्रा शुरू करने वाले थे। जनवरी की ठंड और कुहासे भरी दिल्ली की सुबह में निजी चार्टर विमान से सभी बड़े कांग्रेसी नेता इम्फाल के लिए उड़ान भर रहे थे। इस सूची में मिलिंद देवड़ा का नाम भी था। विमान के इंतज़ार में वीआईपी लाउंज में बैठे कांग्रेसी नेताओं ने जब ताज़ा खबरों के लिए टीवी चालू किया। वो हैरान थे कि खबरों में यात्रा सुर्खियों में नहीं थी, बल्कि देवड़ा का इस्तीफ़ा बड़ी ख़बर था! कुछ सप्ताह बाद, महाराष्ट्र से ही एक और बड़े नेता, पूर्व मुख्यमंत्री अशोक चव्हाण भी दलबदल करने वालों में शामिल थे। चव्हाण ने कहा, 'मैं पार्टी की दिशा से खुश नहीं था। मैंने पार्टी नेतृत्व को अपना नजरिया समझाने की कोशिश की, लेकिन कोई सुनने को तैयार नहीं था। भाजपा ने गर्माहट के साथ मेरा स्वागत किया, तो मैंने सोचा क्यों न इसे आजमाया जाए।' दिलचस्प यह है कि इस्तीफ़ा देने से कुछ दिनों पहले चव्हाण महाराष्ट्र में सीट बंटवारे की बातचीत में शामिल थे। महाराष्ट्र कांग्रेस के एक नेता कहते हैं, 'उन्होंने इस बात की भनक ही नहीं लगने दी कि वे पार्टी छोड़ने वाले थे, यह सब बहुत अचानक से हुआ।' एक बेहतर संगठन चलाने वाले और अच्छे नेटवर्क वाले

चव्हाण को भाजपा ने इनाम के तौर पर राज्यसभा भेज दिया। वैसे भाजपा ने 2010 में आदर्श सहकारी आवास सोसायटी घोटाले में कथित भूमिका को लेकर चव्हाण को निशाना बनाया था, और उन्हें मुख्यमंत्री पद छोड़ना पड़ा था। लेकिन अब इस फाइल को ठंडे बस्ते में डाल दिया गया, क्योंकि पार्टी को चव्हाण के गृह जिले नांदेड़ में अपनी पकड़ मजूत करनी थी। 'वॉशिंग मशीन' फिर से काम कर रही थी।

हाई-प्रोफाइल नेताओं के पार्टी छोड़ने से कांग्रेस में निराशा और हताशा बढ़ गई। प्रदेश इकाइयों से मिले फीडबैक का इशारा था कि पार्टी को 2019 में हासिल 52 सीटों को पार करने में संघर्ष करना पड़ सकता है। फरवरी में कार्यसमिति की एक बैठक में एक वरिष्ठ सांसद ने चिंता ज़ाहिर की, 'कांग्रेस सिर्फ़ 25 या 27 सीटों पर सिमट सकती है।' यहां तक कि कर्नाटक और तेलंगाना में जीत में अहम भूमिका निभाने वाले रणनीतिकार सुनील कनोगुलु भी अपने आंकलन को लेकर सतर्क थे। उनकी टीम संसदीय क्षेत्रों के सर्वेक्षण और चुनाव प्रबंधन में लगी थी, लेकिन उन्होंने राष्ट्रीय स्तर पर कोई रणनीति बनाने से इंकार कर दिया, उनका कहना था कि अब इसके लिए बहुत कम समय बचा था। खड़गे ने जब पार्टी के वरिष्ठ नेताओं को चुनाव लड़ने के लिए कहा, तो उनमें से कई ने विनम्रता से इंकार कर दिया। एक पूर्व मख्यमंत्री ने तो कांग्रेस अध्यक्ष से साफ कहा, 'इस एकतरफा माहौल में चुनाव लड़ना वक्त और पैसे दोनों की बर्बादी है।'

लेकिन कांग्रेस के एक नेता अडिग रहे। निराशा के माहौल के बीच, राहुल गांधी ने जनवरी 2024 में, अपनी मणिपुर से मुंबई तक की भारत जोड़ो न्याय यात्रा के साथ आगे बढ़ने का फ़ैसला किया। आम चुनावों के इतने करीब यात्रा शुरू करना भी एक विवादास्पद फ़ैसला था। कांग्रेस के कुछ नेता चाहते थे कि राहुल गांधी इस वक्त चुनावी रणनीति और टिकट बांटने जैसे पेचीदा मसले पर ध्यान दें। उनका तर्क था, 'महत्वपूर्ण फ़ैसलों के वक्त राहुल जी दूर कैसे रह सकते हैं?' लेकिन गांधी अड़े हुए थे। पिछली भारत जोड़ो यात्रा की कामयाबी से वे अपने विचारों को लेकर ज़्यादा आश्वस्त थे और उसी रास्ते चलने पर अड़े हुए थे। उनका कहना था कि 'यात्रा, जनता से जुड़ने का एकमात्र तरीका है और जनसंपर्क से ही पार्टी को फिर से खड़ा किया जा सकता है।' यह नये राहुल गांधी थे, जो अपने दम पर खड़े थे, लोगों से जुड़ने की कोशिश कर रहे थे। शायद हिंसा के शिकार के रूप में अपने बचपन की चोट और गुस्से को, कमज़ोर और असहाय लोगों को न्याय दिलाने के बड़े मकसद में बदल रहे थे। जब पार्टी ने उम्मीदवारों के नाम तय करने के लिए स्क्रीनिंग कमेटी की बैठकें शुरू की, तब राहुल सड़क पर थे और अंतिम निर्णय लेने की ज़िम्मेदारी उन्होंने पार्टी अध्यक्ष खड़गे पर छोड़ दी थी। एक वरिष्ठ नेता ने बताया, 'पूर्व छात्रनेता कन्हैया कुमार को दिल्ली में टिकट पर ज़ोर देने के अलावा राहुल उम्मीदवारों को चुनने के काम से दूर रहे। एक मौके पर, हमें उन्हें वीडियो कॉन्फ्रेंसिंग के जरिए जुड़ने के लिए मजबूर करना पड़ा।'

कन्याकुमारी से कश्मीर तक की पिछली भारत जोड़ो यात्रा एक महत्वाकांक्षी पदयात्रा थी, लेकिन इस बार समय की कमी की वजह से उसमें बदलाव करना पड़ा। अब पहचान बन गई सफेद टी-शर्ट में राहुल इस बार कुछ जगहों पर पैदल पहुंचे, तो कुछ जगहों पर ज़्यादा दूरी के लिए बस का इस्तेमाल किया। यात्रा की शुरुआत इम्फाल से करना महत्वपूर्ण था। मणिपुर मई 2023 से, जातीय हिंसा में जल रहा था। प्रधानमंत्री मोदी ने एक बार भी राज्य का दौरा नहीं किया था, लेकिन राहुल गांधी ने राहत शिविरों में जाना तय किया। अपने घरों से निकाले गए हज़ारों लोग, दुख और मुश्किल से इन शिविरों में रह रहे थे। विस्थापित लोगों के प्रति सहानुभूति दिखाने के लिए राहुल ने इस न्याय यात्रा की शुरुआत मणिपुर से की ताकि राज्य की तकलीफ पर राष्ट्रीय स्तर पर जागरुकता लाई जा सके।

'न्याय' को चुनावी मुद्दा बनाना एक जोख़िम भरा विकल्प था। कांग्रेस में भी कुछ लोगों को इस बात पर संदेह था कि यह आम मतदाता को सीधे समझ आएगा। 2019 के लोकसभा चुनावों में कांग्रेस ने इसे मुख्य नारे के तौर पर इस्तेमाल किया, लेकिन कोई फायदा नहीं दिखाई दिया। पार्टी ने इस विचार को सबसे गरीब आदमी को बुनियादी आमदनी सहायता योजना के तौर पर घोषणापत्र में शामिल किया और इसे शक्ल देने के लिए नोबेल पुरस्कार विजेता और अर्थशास्त्री अभिजीत बनर्जी को शामिल किया, लेकिन पुलवामा-बालाकोट के बाद कट्टर राष्ट्रवाद की गूंज में मतदाताओं को न्याय की आवाज़ दर्ज ही नहीं हुई। इस बार कांग्रेस ने फिर से न्याय की बात उठाई, लेकिन एक महत्वपूर्ण बदलाव किया। न्याय को पार्टी ने विशेष गारंटी के साथ जोड़ दिया, जिसमें 1) महिलाओं को सालाना एक लाख रुपये देने का वादा; 2) युवाओं को सालाना एक लाख रुपये के वजीफे के साथ रोज़गार की गारंटी; 3) मनरेगा के तहत श्रमिकों के लिए 400 रुपये रोजाना की गारंटी और 4) ओबीसी, दलितों और आदिवासियों को सामाजिक और आर्थिक न्याय दिलाने के लिए जाति-जनगणना करना शामिल था। आलोचकों को हैरानी थी कि कांग्रेस सरकार इन लोकलुभावन वादों को कैसे पूरा करेगी, लेकिन घोषणापत्र समिति के सदस्यों ने कहा कि उन्होंने इसका हिसाब-किताब कर लिया था। घोषणापत्र समिति के अध्यक्ष और पूर्व वित्त मंत्री पी. चिदंबरम ने दावा किया, 'कांग्रेस ने घोषणापत्र के हर वादे के लिए जरूरी बजट को ध्यान में रखकर तैयार किया है। वादों को पांच साल में लागू और पूरा करना था, इसलिए हमें लक्ष्य पूरा करने का भरोसा था।'

इन वादों में सबसे विवादास्पद मसला जाति-जनगणना था। कई लोगों ने इसे समाज को बांटने वाला और नुकसान देने वाला विचार माना। वैसे 2009 में, तब केन्द्रीय मंत्री रहे, कांग्रेस नेता वीरप्पा मोइली ने 2011 की जनगणना में जाति-जनगणना कराने पर ज़ोर दिया था। लेकिन कई कांग्रेसी नेताओं के विरोध के बाद इसका जातिगत डेटा जारी नहीं किया गया। अब राहुल गांधी ने ना केवल इसे फिर से जिंदा कर दिया था, बल्कि अपनी न्याय यात्रा का मुख्य मुद्दा भी

बना दिया। इस दिशा में एक महत्वपूर्ण बदलाव, 2022 में उदयपुर में हुए कांग्रेस के 'चिंतन शिविर' में हुआ। चिंतन शिविर में राहुल गांधी ने भावुकता के साथ कांग्रेस पार्टी को बदलने और अमीर-गरीब के बीच खाई को ख़त्म करने पर जोर दिया। एक साल से कम समय बाद, फरवरी 2023 में, रायपुर सम्मेलन में, कांग्रेस ने संगठन स्तर पर ऐतिहासिक बदलाव का फ़ैसला किया। पार्टी ने कार्यसमिति और पार्टी के सभी प्रमुख पदों पर दलितों, आदिवासियों, ओबीसी, अल्पसंख्यकों और महिलाओं को 50 फ़ीसदी आरक्षण देने के लिए पार्टी संविधान में बदलाव किया। खासतौर से ओबीसी एक बड़ी आबादी थी, जो मोदी युग में भाजपा की तरफ आकर्षित हुई थी। ओबीसी नेतृत्व वाली हिंदुत्व की राजनीति को चुनौती देने के लिए, कांग्रेस को गैर-सवर्णों को ज़्यादा प्रतिनिधित्व वाले एक नए जाति गठबंधन की ज़रूरत थी। दिलचस्प बात यह है कि इस विचार को वामपंथी शिक्षाविदों के एक समूह ने जन्म दिया था, जिसमें फ्रांसीसी राजनीतिक वैज्ञानिक और दक्षिण एशिया विशेषज्ञ क्रिस्टोफ़ जाफ़रलो भी शामिल थे। जब राहुल गांधी सितंबर 2023 में पेरिस गए थे, तो उन्होंने प्रो. जाफ़रलो के साथ लंबी बैठक की थी। जाफ़रलो ने कहा, 'मैं कुछ समय से लिख रहा हूं कि हिंदुत्व का मुकाबला करने का सबसे अच्छा तरीका जाति के इर्द-गिर्द एक काउंटर-नैरेटिव बनाना है, लेकिन मुझे नहीं लगता कि यह कहना सही होगा कि मैंने राहुल के विचारों को प्रेरित किया। वह पहले से ही उस रास्ते पर थे।' कांग्रेस नेताओं ने कहा कि राहुल का जाति जनगणना सूत्रीकरण उनका अपना एजेंडा था। गुरदीप सिंह ज़ोर देते हुए कहते हैं कि 'यह गलती न करें, यह बदलाव राहुल जी ने अपने विश्वास की वजह से किया है ना कि सुविधा के कारण।'

बरसों से, भारतीय जनता पार्टी ने राहुल गांधी को 'पप्पू' कहकर मज़ाक उड़ाया था, उसकी कोशिश राहुल को गैर-गंभीर राजनेता के रूप में खारिज करने की थी। भारत जोड़ो यात्रा ने यदि लोगों को राहुल गांधी के बारे में अपनी धारणा बदलने के लिए मजबूर किया था, तो न्याय यात्रा ने राहुल को एक नई पहचान दी। सामाजिक न्याय और आर्थिक समानता की ज़मीनी लड़ाई लड़ने वाले नेता के तौर पर गांधी, कांग्रेस जैसी पारंपरिक पार्टी के लिए अनजान रहे इलाके में घुस रहे थे। ओबीसी आरक्षण, खासतौर से, उत्तर भारत की मंडलवादी पार्टियों की पहचान रही है, नब्बे के दशक में जिनका उदय, कांग्रेस के पतन के साथ हुआ था। अब राहुल गांधी आरक्षण का समर्थन आर्थिक असमानता को दूर करने के लिए कर रहे थे, जितनी आबादी, उतना हक़। इस आक्रामक नारे को लेकर कई कांग्रेसियों को चिंता थी कि कहीं यह उल्टा न पड़ जाए। 'कांग्रेस जाति के मामले में हमेशा ही रूढ़िवादी पार्टी रही है, जाहिर है कुछ प्रतिरोध होगा। लेकिन राहुल गांधी की सोच शुरू से ही स्पष्ट थी: कांग्रेस को सोशल इंजीनियरिंग और बदलाव की ताकत बनना चाहिए,' समृद्ध भारत फाउंडेशन के निदेशक पुष्पराज देशपांडे कहते हैं। संवैधानिक मूल्यों को बढ़ावा देने के लिए, एक ट्रस्ट के रूप में फाउंडेशन कांग्रेस

और राहुल गांधी के साथ मिलकर काम कर रहा था। 2024 के चुनाव अभियान में कम से कम तीन टाउन-हॉल मीटिंग का आयोजन किया गया, जहां कांग्रेस नेता दलित, आदिवासी और ओबीसी समुदाय के प्रभावशाली लोगों से मिले। भाजपा के सोशल मीडिया इनफ्लूएंसर्स ने फाउंडेशन को बदनाम करने के लिए जोर-शोर से अभियान चलाया, जिसमें कहा गया कि इसको अरबपति कारोबारी जॉर्ज सोरोस जैसी भारत विरोधी ताकतों से मदद मिल रही थी। देशपांडे ज़ोर देकर कहते हैं, 'हमारी सारी फंडिग स्थानीय है और किसी विदेशी काराबोरी या संस्था से कोई लेना-देना नहीं है।'

एक राजनीतिक क्रांतिकारी की छवि ने राहुल की भाषण शैली को भी बदल दिया। वह अब सीधे और सहज तरीके से बात करते हैं। अनौपचारिक, बेबाक, कभी मोटर साइकिल पर तो कभी किसी ढाबे पर, वह लोगों से मिलने के लिए हमेशा तैयार रहते हैं। जिससे समझ आता है कि कोई राजनेता, औपचारिक भाषणों के बजाय लोगों से सीधा संवाद करने में ज़्यादा सहज है। उदाहरण के लिए, हिन्दी न्यूज़ पोर्टल 'लल्लनटॉप' पर एक वीडियो में दिखाया गया था कि एक दुकानदार पैसे नहीं होने से टमाटर नहीं खरीद पाने के कारण टूट गया था, इसे देखने के बाद राहुल ने अचानक सुबह पांच बजे, दिल्ली की आज़ादपुर मंडी में सब्जी बेचने वालों और सामान उठाने वालों से मिलने का फ़ैसला किया। जब राहुल मंडी पहुंचे, तो लोग उन्हें घेरकर इकट्ठा हो गए। बिहार के एक दलित लोडर ने कांग्रेस नेता का हाथ पकड़ते हुए कहा, 'हम खुश हैं कि आप आ गए, हमें कोई याद नहीं करता।' इससे विपरीत, मोदी, मंहगे कपड़े पहने 'राजा' की तरह और उनके सुरक्षा दल के साथ बेहतर कोरियोग्राफ किए गए कार्यक्रमों में पहुंचने और उनके एकतरफा दंबग दिखते वीडियो इससे ज़्यादा असरदार नहीं हो सकते थे।

न्याय यात्रा के दौरान, राहुल अचानक जीप पर चढ़कर, माइक उठाते, भीड़ में किसी को पुकारते, उसके पास जाते, उसके कंधों पर हाथ रखते और अक्सर, जातीय राजनीति पर बातचीत शुरू कर देते। अगर भारत जोड़ो यात्रा सद्भाव के 'मोहब्बत की दुकान' की थीम के इर्दगिर्द थी, तो न्याय यात्रा में जाति पर ज़ोर था, जिससे कभी टकराव जैसी स्थिति बन सकती थी। रायबरेली में एक मौके पर, राहुल ने एक अनावश्यक विवाद पैदा कर दिया, जब उन्होंने एक टीवी पत्रकार से उनके टीवी चैनल के मालिक की जाति बताने को कहा, 'क्या वे ओबीसी हैं? नहीं। क्या वे दलित हैं? नहीं,' उन्होंने पूछा। रिपोर्टर के जवाब देने से पहले ही दर्शकों में मौजूद कुछ कांग्रेस कर्यकर्ताओं ने उसके साथ मारपीट की। यह एक परेशान करने वाली घटना थी, जिसने विघटनकारी और कई बार विभाजनकारी राजनीतिक संदेशों के खतरे को उजागर किया था। सफाई में कांग्रेस के एक नेता ने कहा, 'रायबरेली में जो हुआ, वह दुर्भाग्यपूर्ण था, लेकिन यह मत भूलिए कि राहुल जी को इतने लंबे समय तक दुश्मन जैसे व्यवहार वाले मीडिया से क्या-क्या सहना पड़ा है।'

टीम राहुल और कांग्रेस के लिए न्याय यात्रा का असर ठीक-ठाक था, जबकि पहले इसके शुरू होने के समय को लेकर संदेह किया जा रहे थे। एक ख़ाका तैयार हो गया। अगर 2014 और 2019 में, भाजपा, राहुल गांधी की छवि एक 'नामदार' (वंशवादी) के रूप में बनाने में कामयाब हुई थी, जो कुलीन सत्ता का अंदरूनी था, जो 'बाहरी' चायवाले मोदी के ख़िलाफ़ खड़ा था, तो अब उन्हें एक अस्त-व्यस्त दिखते, यथास्थिति को चुनौती देते वंचितों के लिए लड़ रहे एक नाराज़ विद्रोही की छवि के साथ पेश किया गया। उदाहरण के लिए, राहुल गांधी ने न्याय यात्रा के दौरान सेना में भर्ती होने वाले जवानों की वकालत की। जून 2022 में, मोदी सरकार ने नई 'अग्निपथ' योजना शुरू की जिसमें चार साल की सेवा के लिए जवानों की भर्ती होनी थी। इन सैनिकों को 'अग्निवीर' का नाम दिया गया। इस योजना को शुरू करने का इससे ज़्यादा खराब समय नहीं हो सकता था। इससे ढाई साल पहले, कोविड महामारी की वजह से सेना में भर्ती टाली गई थी। अब अग्निपथ योजना ने अनिश्चितता के माहौल को और बढ़ा दिया। मेजर जनरल यश मोर कहते हैं, 'कई युवाओं के लिए यह बड़ा झटका था। कई ने अपना इम्तिहान पास कर लिया था और फौज में भर्ती का इंतज़ार कर रहे थे और अब अचानक उनकी उम्र सीमा पार हो गई, क्योंकि लंबित भर्ती प्रक्रिया को रद्द कर दिया गया, वे कहीं और नहीं जा सकते।' मोदी सरकार के कई और बड़े फ़ैसलों की तरह, इस फ़ैसले के बारे में सेना के नेतृत्व को अंधेरे में रखा गया। बिना किसी सलाह या तैयारी के चुपके से की गई इस घोषणा का विरोध तो होना ही था। उत्तर भारत के कई हिस्सों में युवाओं ने हिंसक विरोध प्रदर्शन किए, जिन्हें आशंका थी कि सेना के जवान के तौर पर स्थायी करियर की उनकी उम्मीदें ख़त्म हो गई थीं। हरियाणा और राजस्थान जैसे प्रदेशों में, जहां परपंरागत रूप से नौजवान बड़ी तादाद में फौज में शामिल होते हैं, यहां बेरोज़गारी की दर भी ज़्यादा है, अग्निवीर का एक बड़ा मुद्दा था। कांग्रेस के सांसद दीपेन्द्र हुड्डा का कहना था कि 'फौज में शामिल होने हमारे समाज की परपंरा जैसा है। हरियाणा में हर साल पांच हज़ार से ज़्यादा युवा फौज में शामिल होते हैं। आप अचानक उनकी जिंदगी को कैसे रोक सकते हैं!' हुड्डा की टीम ने इस मुद्दे को प्रमुखता देने के लिए पूरे हरियाणा में सेना परीक्षा कोचिंग केन्द्रों पर सबको साथ लेने की कोशिश की, जो इस बात का संकेत था कि अब कांग्रेस प्रतिक्रिया में ज़्यादा चुस्त हो गई थी।

राहुल गांधी ने अपनी यात्राओं के दौरान मिले प्रदर्शनकारियों से उनके मुद्दे को उठाने की बात की। टीम राहुल ने देशभर में उन युवाओं की सूची तैयार की, जिन्हें नई भर्ती प्रक्रिया की वजह से नौकरी नहीं मिल पाई थी और उनके साथ नियमित तौर पर जुड़े रहने के लिए व्हाट्सएप ग्रुप बनाए गए। कुछ युवा प्रदर्शनकारियों को राहुल के साथ बातचीत के लिए 10, जनपथ पर बुलाया गया। जब मुलाक़ात के दौरान एक युवा रोने लगा, तो राहुल ने उसे भरोसा दिलाया कि वह मोदी सरकार को इस योजना को ख़त्म करने के लिए मजबूर करेंगे। कांग्रेस नेता के लगातार

अभियान का असर रक्षा मंत्रालय पर पड़ा और उसने चुनावों के बाद अग्निवीर योजना की समीक्षा और ज़रूरी बदलावों की सिफ़ारिश की। अगर मोदी ने खुद को कट्टर राष्ट्रवादी के तौर पर पेश किया था, तो राहुल खुद की सत्ता-विरोधी लोगों के योद्धा के रूप में पहचान बना रहे थे। टीम के एक सदस्य ने कहा, 'मोदी जी ने केवल देशभक्ति की बात की, जबकि राहुल जी ने जो कहा, उस पर अमल किया।'

चुनाव अभियान शुरू होने से पहले ही राहुल के नेतृत्व में 'न्याय' राजनीतिक बातचीत का हिस्सा बन गया, जो भाजपा के मोदी की गारंटी और विकसित भारत के नारे का जवाब था। कांग्रेस के मीडिया प्रमुख पवन खेड़ा ने कहा, '2019 में मोदी और भाजपा ने एजेंडा तय किया था, इस बार हमारे पास मुद्दों को लेकर तस्वीर साफ है, जिसने हमें माहौल की लड़ाई में सक्षम बनाया।' एक महत्वपूर्ण बदलाव कांग्रेस के फ़ैसले लेने को लेकर भी रहा, 2019 के मुकाबले अब पार्टी ज्यादा केन्द्रित और तालमेल के साथ काम कर रही थी। पार्टी में कम्युनिकेशन के प्रमुख जयराम रमेश अपने तीखे ट्वीट्स और बेहतर बयान वाले प्रमुख चेहरे थे, तो वहीं प्रचार का काम अजय माकन, गुरदीप सप्पल, पवन खेड़ा और सोशल मीडिया प्रमुख सुप्रिया श्रीनेत की टीम देख रही थी। मज़बूती से अपनी बात रखने वाली सुप्रिया श्रीनेत कहती हैं, 'इस बार हम बेखौफ़ थे, इसलिए जब हमला हुआ तो हमने पलटवार में संकोच नहीं किया।' टीवी पर बहस के दौरान हमलावर रहने वाली श्रीनेत का यह नयी कांग्रेस का नज़रिया था।

2019 में, कांग्रेस का सोशल मीडिया अभियान 'चौकीदार चोर है' के नारे के इर्दगिर्द घूमता रहा, यह मोदी पर अपमानजनक हमला था, जिसका उलटा असर हुआ। विपक्ष के एक हिस्से ने मोदी की वैवाहिक स्थिति का मुद्दा उठाया, इस निजी मामले को मतदाताओं ने पसंद नहीं किया। 2022 में, जब सुप्रिया श्रीनेत ने सोशल मीडिया विभाग संभाला, तो उनका निर्देश स्पष्ट थाः ज़ोरदार रहें, लेकिन अभियान को राजनीतिक रखें, व्यक्तिगत ना बनाएं। सबसे पहले उन्होंने युवा एनिमेटर्स को काम पर रखा। इंस्टाग्राम रील्स और मीम्स में प्रधानमंत्री के कैरिकेचर बनाने का आइडिया जोख़िम भरा था, लेकिन इसने कांग्रेस के अभियान को नयापन दिया। मोदी को एक फूले हुए गुब्बारे के तरह दिखाने वाले एनिमेशन वीडियो, जिसे राहुल गांधी अक्सर, प्रधानमंत्री के 'झूठ का गुब्बारा' कहते थे। इस वीडियो में एक बच्चा गुब्बारे में पिन चुभाता है। ये वीडियो वायरल हो गया और इसे लाखों बार देखा गया। श्रीनेत कहती हैं, 'हमें एक बात समझ आई कि मोदी को एक चीज़ पसंद नहीं है, उनका अंहकार टूटना, इसलिए हमने वही करने का फ़ैसला किया।'

इसका मकसद निजी हमलों से बचना था, क्योंकि उससे प्रधानमंत्री को 'विक्टिम कार्ड' खेलने का मौका मिलता था, लेकिन राजनीतिक रूप से निशाना साधने में कोई कसर नहीं छोड़ी जाए। जब मोदी ने परिवारवाद की बात की, तो कांग्रेस ने उन लोगों की सूची पोस्ट कर

दी, जो वंशवादी अब भाजपा के साथ थे। भ्रष्टाचार के मामले में भी अब कांग्रेस बचाव की मुद्रा में नहीं थी। अजित पवार जैसे सहयोगियों पर भाजपा के पुराने ट्वीट् और बयानों को वॉशिंग मशीन की छवि के साथ प्रसारित किया गया। जब भाजपा ने एक विज्ञापन अभियान में कहा कि 'इंडिया गठबंधन सरकार का मतलब, हर साल एक नया प्रधानमंत्री', होगा तो कांग्रेस ने तुरंत जवाब दियाः 'चलो, मान लिया, सरकार तो हमारी ही बनेगी।' महंगाई और बेरोज़गारी पर आम लोगों की वीडियो बाइट्स को उनकी टीम ने सोशल मीडिया पर फैलाने का काम किया। श्रीनेत ने कहा, 'मुझे लगता है कि नयापन लिए हमारे वीडियो युवाओं का ध्यान खींच रहे थे, जबकि भाजपा अतीत में फंसी हुई थी और अब भी राहुल गांधी पर पप्पू और शहज़ादा कहकर हमला कर रही थी।' श्रीनेत ने कहा, राहुल और भारत दोनों आगे बढ़ गए थे, लेकिन भाजपा नहीं। डेटा उनकी इस बात की पुष्टि करता है। कांग्रेस के प्रचार अभियान में इंस्टाग्राम वीडियो पर औसत लाइक 1,22,000 थे जबकि भाजपा के इससे बहुत कम सिर्फ 26,945 थे। यू-ट्यूब पर भी, 2024 के मार्च से मई के बीच भाजपा के 15 करोड़ के मुकाबले, कांग्रेस को 61 करोड़ 30 लाख़ व्यूज़ मिले। यह उस पार्टी के लिए नाटकीय बदलाव था, जो अब तक सोशल मीडिया के खेल में भाजपा से काफी पीछे थी।

कहा जाता है कि पुरानी आदतें आसानी से नहीं बदलती। सबकुछ योजना के हिसाब से नहीं चला। शुरू में आउटडोर विज्ञापनों पर ध्यान नहीं दिया गया, पार्टी ने चुनाव के पहले तीन चरणों में आउटडोर प्रचार पर पैसा ही खर्च नहीं किया। 'सिस्टम में कई लोगों का मानना था कि हमारी लड़ाई बेमायने थी, इसलिए वे पैसा खर्च करने में हिचक रहे थे। यदि देखें तो इसकी वजह से हमें पन्द्रह से बीस सीटों का नुकसान हुआ होगा,' कांग्रेस के एक पदाधिकारी ने माना। हालांकि, आखिरी चरण तक, अंदरूनी झगड़ों वाली पार्टी, लड़ाई के लिए तैयार थी। अजय माकन ने कहा, '2019 में हमारे सिस्टम में कई खामियां थीं और बहुत से खर्चों का कोई हिसाब नहीं था। इस बार हमने सुनिश्चित किया कोई लीकेज ना हो और पूरे अभियान की ऑडिटिंग हो।'

इतना ही अहम, लेकिन आमतौर पर नज़रअंदाज़ किए जाने वाले पार्टी वॉर-रूम की भूमिका रही, जिसे कर्नाटक काडर के आईएएस अधिकारी रहे शशिकांत सेंथिल देख रहे थे। सेंथिल ने अनुच्छेद 370 को रद्द करने और सीएए के पास होने के विरोध में सरकारी नौकरी छोड़ दी थी और 2021 में कांग्रेस में शामिल हो गए थे। सेंथिल का कहना था, 'विविधता वाले लोकतंत्र के मूलभूत ढांचे को ख़त्म करने की कोशिश हो रही है।' एक मज़बूत, ऊर्जा से भरे संगठन के व्यक्ति, आशावादी और कट्टर भाजपा विरोधी सेंथिल ने बड़े पैमाने पर लोगों तक पहुंचने में अहम भूमिका निभाई। सत्ता का कोई दिखावा नहीं करने और कम बोलने वाले सेंथिल दिल्ली की सड़कों पर घिसी हुई चप्पलों के साथ घूम रहे थे। अड़तीस राज्य स्तरीय वॉर रूम में 700 से ज़्यादा लोगों की टीम ज़मीनी स्तर पर अभियान को देख रही थी। इसका मुख्यालय लुटियंस

दिल्ली में तेलगांना कांग्रेस के मंत्री उत्तम कुमार रेड्डी के बंगले में बनाया गया था। इसके पास एक बड़ा काम 12 भाषाओं में आठ करोड़ कार्ड लोगों तक पहुंचाने थे, जिनमें न्याय के वादे किए गए थे। ए4 फॉर्मेट में छपे ये कार्ड उम्मीदवारों तक पहुंचाए गए और हर चरण में कम से कम दस दिन पहले मतदाताओं के घर तक पहुंच गए। कांग्रेस के पास भाजपा की बराबरी लायक बूथ-स्तर का प्रबंधन तो नहीं था, लेकिन एक बार आखिरी दरवाज़े तक पहुंचने की कोशिश कर रही थी। तमिलनाडु से अब सांसद सेंथिल कहते हैं, 'अगर भाजपा मशीनरी के पास तकनीक की ताकत थी, तो हमने लोगों पर ज़ोर दिया और कार्यकर्ताओं से लगातार संपर्क रख उन्हें भागीदारी का अहसास दिलाया। हम वॉर-रूम नहीं, संपर्क केन्द्र की तरह काम कर रहे थे।'

पैंतालीस साल के सेंथिल राहुल गांधी के इर्दगिर्द रहने वाले कांग्रेस नेताओं की उस पीढ़ी की नुमाइंदगी करते हैं जिनमें कोई भी खास अहमियत रखने वाला वंशवादी नहीं है। इनमें ज़्यादातर लोग राजनीतिक कार्यकर्ता हैं, जो जनहित अभियान से जुड़ना चाहते हैं। वैभव वालिया और वरुण संतोष जैसे वॉर-रूम सदस्य, अपने कुर्ता-जींस-झोला लुक में, उस पीढ़ीगत बदलाव का हिस्सा हैं, जो उन शानदार ड्रैस में पारिवारिक विरासत वाले बाबा लोग राजनेताओं से उलट हैं, जिनके साथ राहुल गांधी कभी घूमते थे। पार्टी के कई वरिष्ठ नेता उनसे चौकस रहते थे, उनकी चिंता थी कि ये लोग महत्वपूर्ण मुद्दों पर पार्टी को कट्टर वामपंथी रुख अपनाने के लिए प्रेरित कर रहे थे। 2024 के चुनावों से पहले पार्टी छोड़ने वाले एक कांग्रेसी नेता कहते हैं, 'नई कांग्रेस पर एनजीओ मानसिकता वाले लोगों ने कब्ज़ा कर लिया है जो अपनी संकीर्ण विचारधारा से परे नहीं देख सकते।' ऐसी आलोचना को हंसी में उड़ाते हुए सेंथिल कहते हैं, 'मुझे लगता है कि असल में भाजपा एक कमांड एंड कंट्रोल पार्टी है, जबकि कांग्रेस वाकई लोगों से जुड़ा संगठन है और मैं उसका एक छोटा हिस्सा हूं।'

एक मिशन को लेकर फिर से खड़े हुए एक नेता के नेतृत्व में फिर से जागती कांग्रेस बनाम एक करिश्माई दिग्गज राजनेता के नेतृत्व में आजमाई हुई भाजपा चुनाव मशीनः 2024 की लड़ाई के लिए मंच तैयार था।

═

भारत शायद इकलौता देश है, जहां समय के साथ चुनावी प्रक्रिया को छोटा करने के बजाय बढ़ाया गया है। 16 मार्च 2024 को चुनाव आयोग ने चवालीस दिनों तक सात चरणों में होने वाले मतदान की घोषणा की। यह देश में 1951-52 में चार महीने तक चले, पहले चुनावों के बाद दूसरी सबसे लंबी अवधि थी। इसमें 543 सीटों के लिए साढ़े दस लाख मतदान केन्द्र बनाए गए, जहां 97 करोड़ पंजीकृत मतदाता आठ हज़ार से ज़्यादा उम्मीदवारों की चुनावी किस्मत का फ़ैसला करेंगे। भारत में चुनाव एक बड़ा काम है, लेकिन क्या इसके लिए इतने लंबे कार्यक्रम

की ज़रूरत थी, खासतौर से गर्मियों में, जब भयंकर गर्मी का असर मतदान पर पड़ता है। हैरानी की बात है कि महाराष्ट्र जैसे राज्य में, जहां कभी राजनीतिक हिंसा नहीं होती, वहां भी पांच चरणों में चुनाव होने थे। विपक्ष को लगता था कि चुनाव कार्यक्रम भाजपा को फायदा पहुंचाने के लिए बनाया गया था, ताकि प्रधानमंत्री पूरे देश में चुनाव अभियान कर सकें और विपक्ष के पास इतना खर्च करने के लिए नहीं है। शिवसेना के संजय राउत ने पूछा, 'आप चाहते हैं कि जून तक खत्म होने वाले चुनाव के लिए हम मार्च में प्रचार शुरू करें। प्रधानमंत्री तो अपने सरकारी विमान में हर जगह दौरा करेंगे, लेकिन हमें तो सीमित संसाधनों में काम चलाना होगा, क्या इन्हें स्वतंत्र और निष्पक्ष कहा जा सकता है?'

'समान अवसर' नहीं होने के तर्क पर जवाब के बजाय चुनाव आयोग ने खुद को नौकरशाही की दीवार के पीछे छिपाना ठीक समझा। चुनावी कार्यक्रम की घोषणा की प्रेस कॉन्फ्रेंस के बाद चुनाव आयोग ने मीडिया से पूरी तरह दूरी बनाए रखी। चुनावों के ऐलान से कुछ दिन पहले ही, केन्द्र ने तीन में से दो चुनाव आयुक्तों की नियुक्ति की। इससे पहले केन्द्र ने चुनाव आयुक्तों की नियुक्ति के क़ानून में बदलाव किया था और चयन समिति में सुप्रीम कोर्ट के मुख्य न्यायाधीश को हटाकर एक कैबिनेट मंत्री को रखा गया था। विपक्ष ने चुनाव आयोग को बार-बार पत्र लिखकर वीवीपैट की सौ फ़ीसद गिनती की मांग करने के लिए समय मांगा था, लेकिन चुनाव आयोग से उन्हें समय नहीं मिला। कांग्रेस नेता जयराम रमेश ने कहा, 'हम इलेक्ट्रॉनिक वोटिंग मशीनों के ख़िलाफ़ नहीं हैं, लेकिन हम स्वतंत्र और निष्पक्ष चुनाव के लिए वीवीपैट की पूरी गिनती चाहते हैं। चुनाव आयोग हमसे मिलने के लिए तैयार क्यों नहीं है?' विपक्ष के एक नेता ने चुनाव आयोग को 'चाय-बिस्किट' संस्था कहा। उनका कहना था कि 'जब भी हम उनसे मिलते हैं, वे विनम्रता से हमें चाय-बिस्किट देते हैं, लेकिन हमारी चिंताओं को दूर करने के लिए कुछ नहीं करते।'

हालांकि लंबे चुनाव कार्यक्रम से विपक्ष को बेहतर तरीके से काम करने का समय मिलेगा। विपक्षी खेमे में बेचैनी तब और बढ़ गई, जब चुनावों की घोषणा के ठीक पांच दिन बाद ईडी ने दिल्ली शराब नीति मामले में मनी-लॉन्ड्रिंग के आरोप में दिल्ली के मुख्यमंत्री अरविंद केजरीवाल को गिरफ़्तार कर लिया। संसदीय लोकतंत्र में इससे पहले शायद ही कभी ऐसा हुआ हो। ईडी के निशाने पर केजरीवाल कई महीनों से थे, उन्हें पूछताछ के लिए कई समन भेजे गए ताकि वे एजेंसी के सामने पेश हो जाएं, इसलिए जब उनकी गिरफ़्तारी हुई तो बड़ी हैरानी वाली बात नहीं थी। वैसे खुद केजरीवाल भी इसकी तैयारी कर रहे थे, उन्होंने जोर देकर कहा कि 18 महीने पहले शुरू हुई जांच में उन्हें फंसाने के लिए कोई 'मनी ट्रेल' नहीं था। 'वे बस मुझे 2024 के चुनावों में प्रचार करने से रोकना चाहते हैं।' उन्होंने आरोप लगाया, 'भाजपा ने मेरी टीम के लोगों से कहा कि अगर मैं इंडिया गठबंधन से अलग हो जाऊंगा तो बच जाऊंगा, वरना जेल भेज दिया जाएगा।'

चुनावों के ऐलान के एक हफ्ते में विपक्ष के एक हाई-प्रोफाइल नेता गिरफ़्तार करना एक सोचा-समझा ज़ोखिम था, जिसे मोदी सरकार लेने को तैयार थी। चुनाव अभियान से कुछ दिन पहले एक मौजूदा मुख्यमंत्री की गिरफ़्तारी में शर्मनाक राजनीतिक चाल की बू आ रही थी और एक बार फिर सत्ता के दम पर विपक्ष को कुचलने की प्रतिशोध की कार्रवाई को बताता है। कहा जाता है कि इसकी वजह आम आदमी पार्टी के नेता को लेकर प्रधानमंत्री मोदी की व्यक्तिगत नाराज़गी थी। केजरीवाल उसी दिन से निशाने पर थे, जब 2014 में उन्होंने मोदी के ख़िलाफ़ वाराणसी से चुनाव लड़ा। दिल्ली भाजपा के एक नेता ने माना कि 'मोदी जी दूसरे विपक्षी नेताओं से तो बात कर सकते हैं, लेकिन केजरीवाल के नाम से ही उनका पारा चढ़ जाता है।' एक टीवी न्यूज़ चैनल के संपादक ने याद करते हुए कहा, 'जब उनके चैनल पर प्राइम टाइम में केजरीवाल का साक्षात्कार चलाया गया, तो एक सरकारी अधिकारी ने उन्हें फ़ोन कर चेतावनी दी थी कि आप हर समय ऐसी पार्टी का प्रचार करते दिखते हैं जिसका एक भी सांसद नहीं है, सावधान रहें।'

इंडिया गठबंधन के नेताओं के लिए केजरीवाल की गिरफ़्तारी एक अच्छा संकेत नहीं था। ज़ाहिर है कि चुनावी बिगुल बजने का मतलब यह नहीं था कि अब जांच एजेंसिया दबाव कम करेंगी। जनवरी में, इंडिया गठबंधन के एक और सहयोगी झारखंड के मुख्यमंत्री हेमंत सोरेन को कथित भूमि घोटाले में ईडी ने गिरफ़्तार किया था। विवादों में घिरे इन सहयोगियों के पास अब एकजुट होने के अलावा कोई विकल्प नहीं था। जब आम आदमी पार्टी ने दिल्ली में 'लोकतंत्र बचाओ' रैली का फ़ैसला किया, तो इंडिया गठबंधन के ज़्यादातर सहयोगी शक्ति प्रदर्शन के लिए वहां पहुंचे। तब तक इस बात पर अनिश्चितता बनी हुई थी कि क्या अतीत की दुश्मनी को भूलकर कांग्रेस दिल्ली में आप के साथ गठबंधन करेगी। आप के एक नेता ने टिप्पणी की, 'मुझे लगता है कि कांग्रेस को इस हकीकत से वास्ता कराने के लिए गिरफ़्तारी की ज़रूरत थी कि इस बार हमें साथ तैरना या डूबना था।'

एक और बड़ा मुद्दा, जनवरी 2024 में चंडीगढ़ मेयर चुनाव का था, जहां भाजपा के अल्पसंख्यक प्रकोष्ठ के सदस्य और पीठासीन अधिकारी अनिल मसीह ने आठ वोटों को अमान्य घोषित कर दिया, जिससे भाजपा ने कांग्रेस-आप के साझा उम्मीदवार को हरा दिया था। पर्दे के पीछे की कहानी समझने की ज़रूरत है। आप-कांग्रेस गठबंधन के पास पार्षदों का बहुमत था, लेकिन भाजपा बिना लड़े हार मानने को तैयार नहीं थी। राष्ट्रीय महासचिव विनोद तावड़े को चुनावों की निगरानी के लिए चंडीगढ़ भेजा गया था। तावड़े आप के दो पार्षदों को पाला बदलने के मनाने में कामयाब रहे, लेकिन भाजपा को अब भी कुछ और लोगों की ज़रूरत थी। कथित तौर पर उत्साही मसीह ने भाजपा नेता से कहा, 'चिंता मत करिए, मैं जो ज़रूरी होगा, करूंगा।' पहले सिर्फ़ दो वोटों को ही अवैध घोषित करने की योजना थी, लेकिन अति-उत्साही मसीह ने आठ वोटों को अवैध घोषित कर दिया। लेकिन वोटों को अवैध घोषित करने का

तरीका कैमरे में कैद हो गया। सुप्रीम कोर्ट के दखल से फ़ैसला बदलना पड़ा। आप सांसद संजय सिंह ने टिप्पणी की, 'कल्पना कीजिए, अगर चंडीगढ़ के मेयर चुनाव में धांधली हो सकती है तो आम चुनावों में क्या होगा?'

चंडीगढ़ जैसे ही हालात सूरत लोकभा सीट पर दोहरए गए। कांग्रेस उम्मीदवार का नामांकन पीठासीन अधिकारी ने ख़ारिज़ कर दिया, क्योंकि उनके तीन प्रस्तावकों ने एक जैसे हलफ़नामे पेश करके दावा किया कि उन्होंने दस्तवेज़ों पर दस्तख़त नहीं किए थे और उनके दस्तख़त जाली थे। जब गुजरात कांग्रेस ने प्रस्तावकों से जिरह करनी चाही तो बताया गया के वे लोग 'गायब' थे और यहां तक कि उनका उम्मीदवार भी 'गायब' था। जब तक वे सामने आते, तब तक बहुत देर हो चुकी थी। दूसरे बचे हुए उम्मीदवारों ने भी अपने नाम वापस ले लिए थे और भाजपा उम्मीदवार निर्विरोध चुने हुए घोषित कर दिए गए, लोकसभा चुनावों में ऐसा आमतौर पर नहीं होता। गुजरात कांग्रेस के नेता शक्तिसिंह गोहिल ने शिकायती स्वर में कहा, 'हस्ताक्षर जाली का दावा करने वाले गायब लोग पुलिस सुरक्षा में घूम रहे थे, लेकिन हमें उनसे मिलने नहीं दिया गया।' भाजपा शासित गुजरात में राज्य मशीनरी को कोई चुनौती नहीं दे सकता थाः आश्चर्य नहीं होना चाहिए कि भाजपा प्रदेश की 26 में से 25 सीटें जीत गई।

इस वजह से मार्च के आखिर में दिल्ली के रामलीला मैदान में हुई 'लोकतंत्र बचाओ' रैली, विपक्ष के लिए साझा आधार तलाशने का मंच बन गई। बैटक में हर नेता ने मोदी के नेतृत्व वाली भाजपा की तानाशाही के ख़िलाफ़ आवाज़ उठाई। लोकतंत्र बनाम तानाशाही का नारा इंडिया गठबंधन के लिए एक ऐसा खाका बन गया, जो 1977 का दौर को फिर से लाने की कोशिश थी। लेकिन मोदी पर इंदिरा गांधी की तरह आपातकाल का दाग़ नहीं था, उनके लोक लुभावन भाषणों को अब भी समर्थन था। दिग्गज कम्युनिस्ट नेता डी. राजा ने जोर देकर कहा, 'अब चीज़ें बदल जाएंगी, यह चुनाव जनता बनाम मोदी होगा।' तृणमूल कांग्रेस के डेरेक ओ ब्रायन ने कहा, 'रुको और देखो, मोदी की गारंटी का मतलब है ज़ीरो वारंटी।'

मतदान के करीब दस दिन पहले, अप्रैल के पहले हफ्ते में, राजस्थान के नागौर से भाजपा की उम्मीदवार ज्योति मिर्धा (पहले कांग्रेस में थीं) ने मतदाताओं से अपील की कि भाजपा के 'चार सौ पार' के लक्ष्य को हासिल करने में मदद करें। मिर्धा ने कहा, 'देश हित में कई कठोर फ़ैसले लेने की ज़रूरत है और इसके लिए संविधान में कई बदलाव करने होंगे।' वैसे, ऐसा कहने वाली वे पहली नेता नहीं थीं। मार्च की शुरुआत में, कर्नाटक से भाजपा सांसद अनंत कुमार हेगड़े ने भी कुछ इस तरह की ही बात की थी। मुखर वक्ता हेगड़े, विवादों में घिरे रहते हैं और उनकी तीखी टिप्पणियों की वजह से पार्टी ने उनका टिकट काट दिया था। लेकिन मिर्धा की टिप्पणी वायरल हो गई। फैज़ाबाद-अयोध्या के भाजपा सांसद लल्लू सिंह भी इस कोरस में शामिल हो गए थे। एक वायरल वीडियो में सिंह कह रहे थे, '272 सांसदों के साथ सरकार तो

बनाई जा सकती है, लेकिन संविधान में बदलाव के लिए हमें दो-तिहाई बहुमत चाहिए।' कांग्रेस ने उनके इस बयान को लपक लिया। पार्टी ने ट्वीट किया, 'इन बयानों से साफ है कि भाजपा और प्रधानमंत्री मोदी, संविधान और लोकतंत्र से नफ़रत करते हैं। बाबा साहेब के संविधान को ख़त्म करके भाजपा लोगों के अधिकार छीनना चाहती है।'

इसके चौबीस घंटे बाद राजस्थान के चित्तौड़गढ़ में एक रैली में कांग्रेस के राष्ट्रीय अध्यक्ष मल्लिकार्जुन खड़गे ने संविधान का मुद्दा उठाया। खड़गे ने चेतावनी के स्वर में कहा, 'संविधान ख़तरे में है और इस सरकार में आरक्षण भी सुरक्षित नहीं है। इसलिए वे चार सौ पार चाहते हैं।' रैली में उनके साथ मौजूद राजस्थान प्रदेश कांग्रेस के अध्यक्ष गोविन्द सिंह डोटासरा ने कहा, खड़गे का यह भाषण चुनाव अभियान का एक महत्वपूर्ण मोड़ था। उन्होंने कहा, 'अब हर कोई मोदी कीं गारंटी के बजाय संविधान की बात कर रहा था।' खड़गे सिर्फ़ कांग्रेस अध्यक्ष ही नहीं, दलित भी थे। 'आरक्षण ख़तरे में' का मुद्दा अब राजनीतिक शोर में दबा नहीं। भाजपा गुस्से में थी। भाजपा प्रवक्ताओं ने कांग्रेस पर जानबूझकर झूठ फैलाने का आरोप लगाया। छत्तीसगढ की एक रैली में गृहमंत्री अमित शाह ने जोर देकर कहा, 'मैं स्पष्ट करना चाहता हूं कि जब तक भाजपा राजनीति में है, हम आरक्षण को कुछ नहीं होने देंगे। हम कांग्रेस को भी इसे ख़त्म नहीं करने देंगे।'

गृहमंत्री सही थे। कोई भी पार्टी ऐसे राजनीतिक माहौल में आरक्षण को ख़त्म करने का जोख़िम नहीं उठा सकती थी। विपक्ष एक काल्पनिक डर को हवा दे रहा था। लेकिन चुनावी शोर में, ऐसे भावनात्मक मुद्दे अपने आप रफ़्तार पकड़ लेते हैं। 'संविधान ख़तरे में' है, नारे के साथ भी ऐसा ही हुआ। जैसा कि पहले अध्याय में ज़िक्र किया गया है कि 'चार सौ पार' के नारे को प्रधानमंत्री मोदी ने जनवरी 2024 में हरी झंडी दी थी, क्योंकि वे पुराने रिकॉर्ड को तोड़ना चाहते थे। लेकिन टीम मोदी-शाह इसे स्पष्ट करने में नाकाम रही कि भाजपा के 400 सीटों के बहुमत का मतदाता और देश के लिए क्या मतलब होगा? भाजपा के एक नेता ने माना, 'हमने चार सौ पार तो कहा, लेकिन इस मैजिक नंबर के साथ कोई वादा नहीं किया। शायद हमें कहना चाहिए था, "अबकी बार चार सौ पार तो पीओके पर वार" या ऐसा ही कुछ और!' सत्ता में दस साल के बाद भाजपा चुनाव के लिए कोई आकर्षक विमर्श (नैरेटिव) ढूंढने में लगी थी। धीरे-धीरे राजनीतिक नेतृत्व और मतदाता के बीच होता अलगाव दिखने लगा था।

'चार सौ पार' के इस नारे ने विपक्ष को वो राजनीतिक हथियार दे दिया, जिसकी उसे तलाश थी। अचानक मिला यह मुद्दा, चुनाव के अंतिम चरण तक पहुंचते-पहुंचते चरम पर पहुंच गया। राहुल गाधी अपनी रैलियों में संविधान की प्रति दिखा रहे थे। बीस सेंटीमीटर लंबा और आठ सेंटीमीटर चौड़ा संविधान का यह लेदर पॉकेट संस्करण, एक ताकतवर चुनावी हथियार बन गया। जाति जनगणना और आरक्षण बढ़ाने के लिए आक्रामक रूप से दबाव बनाने के बाद, 'संविधान ख़तरे में है' के नारे अगला मज़बूत कदम थे। कांग्रेस के एक पदाधिकारी ने बताया, 'जयराम

रमेश ने राहुल गांधी को संविधान का एक पॉकेट प्रति भेंट की थी। उनका आइडिया था कि रैलियों में इसे दिखाना, सामाजिक न्याय के मुद्दे पर लोगों को जोड़ने का एक अच्छा तरीका है।'

कांग्रेस और विपक्ष ने खासतौर से हिंदी पट्टी में संविधान बहस से राजनीतिक फायदा उठाया, लेकिन इसे आगे बढ़ाने वाले असल लोग एनजीओ कार्यकर्ता, यूट्यूब पत्रकार और दलित समूहों से जुड़े प्रभावशाली लोग थे। मुख्यधारा मीडिया के शोर से दूर, व्यापक रूप से देखे जाने वाले वैकल्पिक मंचों, डिजिटल और सोशल मीडिया पर मानो 'मौन क्रांति' चल रही थी। अम्बेडकर की तस्वीरों वाली टी-शर्ट पहने पैंतीस साल के सुमित चौहान ने, यूट्यूब पर दलित समुदाय से आने वाले जाति-विरोधी पत्रकार के तौर पर पहचान बनाई है। दमदार वीडियो की वजह से उनके यूट्यूब पर दस लाख से ज़्यादा फॉलोअर्स हैं, साथ ही उनके हिंदी भाषी पोर्टल द न्यूज़ वीक प्लेटफॉर्म पर इससे दोगुने फॉलोअ्र्स हैं। मुख्यधारा मीडिया के चैनलों में सात साल काम करने के बाद उन्होंने 2019 में हाशिये पर रहने वाले समाज, खासतौर से दलितों से जुड़े कंटेट क्रिएटर के रूप में अपनी पहचान बनाई है। मुख्यधारा मीडिया को वह मनु-स्ट्रीम मीडिया कहते हैं। चौहान का कहना है कि 'हम दलितों के ख़िलाफ़ अत्याचारों को लेकर बरसों से चिंता जताते रहे हैं। हमारे लिए भाजपा, हिंदू राष्ट्र और जाति-वर्चस्व की नुमाइंदगी करती है।' जब चुनावों में यह विवाद शुरू हुआ, इससे पहले से ही कई दलित-नेतृत्व वाले यूट्यूब चैनलों पर भाजपा सरकार के संविधान बदलने के ख़तरे पर चर्चा हो रही थी। चौहान का मानना है कि 'हिंदुत्व विरोधी भावना पहले से ही ज़मीन पर थी, विपक्षी दलों ने इसका फायदा उठाया।'

चुनावों में संविधान ख़तरे में है, अभियान का कितना असर हुआ, इसका सटीक अनुमान लगाना तो मुश्किल है, लेकिन नतीजों से पता चलता है कि मतदान के पहले चरण में विपक्ष को स्पष्ट बढ़त मिली। राजस्थान से यह विवाद शुरू हुआ था, वहां कांग्रेस को पहले चरण वाली 12 सीटों में से आठ सीटों पर जीत हासिल हुई। उत्तरप्रदेश के पहले चरण में भी नतीजे वैसे ही आश्चर्यजनक थे। दलित और मुस्लिम बहुल इलाके वाले पश्चिमी उत्तरप्रदेश में समाजवादी पार्टी-कांग्रेस गठबंधन ने 8 में से 6 सीटों पर कब्ज़ा कर लिया। कुल मिलाकर पहले चरण में इंडिया गठबंधन ने 102 में से 64 सीटें जीतीं, जबकि भाजपा को केवल 35 सीटें मिलीं। चुनावी मैदान में ऐसा होने की उम्मीद नहीं दिख रही थी। ज़्यादातर सर्वेक्षण करने वालों और विश्लेषकों ने विपक्ष को ख़ारिज़ कर दिया था, उसने कई महत्वपूर्ण राज्य में भी बढ़त हासिल की। भगवा पार्टी को अब जवाबी शैली और रणनीति में तुरंत बदलाव की ज़रूरत थी। मोदी की गारंटी काम नहीं कर रही थी। अब बुनियादी मुद्दों पर लौटने का समय आ गया था।

गुजरात और महाराष्ट्र की सीमा से लगा राजस्थान का आदिवासी बहुल ज़िला बांसवाड़ा, पुराने बांस के जंगलों और पारपंरिक हस्तशिल्प के लिए जाना जाता है। राष्ट्रीय स्तर पर पहली बार वह सुर्खियों में साठ के दशक में उस वक्त आया, जब बांसवाड़ा के शाही परिवार के स्टाइलिश बल्लेबाज़ हनुमंत सिंह ने अपने पहले टैस्ट में ही शतक मारा था। लेकिन 21 अप्रैल 2024 को यह छोटा शहर फिर से ख़बरों के पहले पन्ने पर आ गया। प्रधानमंत्री मोदी ने जिले में एक चुनावी रैली में कहा, अगर कांग्रेस फिर से सत्ता में आई तो वह आपकी संपत्ति जब्त कर मुसलमानों में बांट देगी। मोदी ने मुसलमानों को 'घुसपैठिया' और 'ज़्यादा बच्चे पैदा करने वाले' कहा। 'जब कांग्रेस सत्ता में थी, तो उसने कहा था कि सरकार की संपत्तियों पर पहला हक़ मुसलमानों का था। इसका मतलब हुआ कि वे आपकी संपत्ति उन लोगों को देंगे, जिनके ज़्यादा बच्चे हैं। जो घुसपैठिए हैं। क्या आप चाहते हैं कि आपका पैसा घुसपैठियों को दे दिया जाए? कांग्रेस के घोषणापत्र में यही कहा गया हैः हमारी माताओं, बेटियों के पास जितना सोना है, उसका नाप-जोख करके इकट्ठा किया जाएगा और बांटा जाएगा। वे आपके पैसे को उन लोगों में बांट देंगे। ये अर्बन नक्सल आपकी माताओं और बहनों के मंगलसूत्र को भी नहीं छोड़ेंगे। वे इसके लिए कहीं तक जा सकते हैं...'

भारत के प्रधानमंत्री ने अभी एक भयावह जहरीला और घृणा फैलाने वाला भाषण दिया, जिसमें सांप्रदायिकता फैलाने वाली उत्तेजना और शर्मनाक झूठ शामिल था। विकसित भारत के सपने को तो भूल जाइए, देश के स्वयंभू 'प्रधान सेवक' बेबाकी से मुस्लिम विरोधी बयानबाजी पर लौट आए। पहली बार 2002 में गुजरात हिंसा के बाद राष्ट्रीय स्तर पर उन्हें आलोचना झेलनी पड़ी थी। यह उग्र और कट्टरपंथी भाषण था, जिसमें देश के बीस करोड़ मुसलमानों को घुसपैठिया और हिंदुओं की संपत्ति लूटने वाला खलनायक बनाया गया और कथित तौर पर ज़्यादा बच्चे पैदा करने के लिए उनका मज़ाक उड़ाया गया था। समाज में डर बढ़ाने की बेशर्म कोशिश हो रही थी।

प्रधानमंत्री ने अपनी कल्याणकारी योजनाओं, गारंटियों और विकसित भारत के महत्वाकांक्षी नज़रिए वाले अभियान से अचानक रुख बदलकर मतदाताओं को भड़काने का फ़ैसला क्यों किया? मोदी अचानक नफ़रत क्यों फैलाने लगे थे? इसका जवाब भाषण की टाइमिंग में छिपा है। मतदान का पहला चरण पूरा हुए अभी दो दिन हुए थे, इस चरण में कम मतदान हुआ था। भाजपा के अंदरूनी ट्रैकर सर्वेक्षणों में इस पर चिंता ज़ाहिर की गई थी। इसमें मुसलमानों ने बड़ी तादाद में वोट किया, लेकिन भाजपा का कोर मतदाता गायब रहा, शयाद उसको भरोसा था कि पार्टी चार सौ पार ज़रूर जीतेगी। उत्तर भारत में भीषण गर्मी भी शायद इसकी एक वजह रही हो, लेकिन मतदाताओं में उत्साह कम था। इसके अलावा कांग्रेस का अभियान और घोषणापत्र नकद गारंटियों और संविधान ख़तरे में है, पर केन्द्रित था, जो लोगों को लुभा रहा था। आक्रामक

राहुल गांधी, महंगाई, रोज़गार, संपत्ति का एक्सरे और नकद गारंटी का 'खटाखट' मिलने का वादा करके गरीब समर्थक एजेंडे पर ज़ोर दे रहे थे। खासतौर से 'खटाखट' शब्द चल गया था। जब भी राहुल गांधी आम बोलचाल में 'खटाखट-खटाखट' बोलते, तो जनता में जवाबी उत्साह दिखता। राहुल के कम्युनिकेशन प्रमुख श्रीवत्स याद करते हैं, 'इंस्टाग्राम और दूसरे सोशल मीडिया चैनलों पर हमारे लोगों की प्रतिक्रिया से पता चला कि "खटाखट" लोकप्रियता हासिल कर रहा था और इसके ज़िक्र वाला हर वीडियो वायरल हो रहा था।' इससे उत्साहित कांग्रेस ने खटाखट अभियान को तेज़ कर दिया और इसे हरसंभव प्लेटफॉर्म पर आगे बढ़ाया। श्रीवत्स कहते हैं, 'खटाखट अभियान अपने आप ही बढ़ गया, किसी ने इसकी योजना नहीं बनाई थी।'

भारतीय जनता पार्टी को इस लोकलुभावन आर्थिक राजनीति के जवाबी तोड़ की ज़रूरत थी। कांग्रेस के वादों को सिर्फ़ रेवड़ी कहकर ख़ारिज़ करना अब काम नहीं आ रहा था। भाजपा के एक रणनीतिकार ने बताया, 'मतदान के पहले चरण के बाद ज़मीनी सर्वेक्षणों से साफ था कि यह बात यहां खत्म नहीं हो रही थी, डन डील नहीं थी, जिसकी हम उम्मीद कर रहे थे। भाजपा विरोधी वोट एकजुट हो रहे थे, जबकि हमारे मतदाता बूथ तक नहीं पहुंचे।' इसका मतलब आजमाए हुए नुस्खे पर लौटने की ज़रूरत थी। भाजपा और संघ परिवार के लिए इसके मायने मुसलमानों पर हमलावर होना है। बरसों से भगवा बिरादरी के लिए मुसलमानों को दुश्मन के तौर पर पेश करना, विचारधारा का हिस्सा माना जाता है। भाजपा के आगे बढ़ने का रास्ता, उसकी मुख्य प्रतिद्वन्दी पार्टी कांग्रेस को मुस्लिम तुष्टिकरण से जोड़ने से निकलता है। कांग्रेस पर तुष्टिकरण का 'टैग' अस्सी के दशक में शाहबानो मामले के बाद से चिपका हुआ है। उस वक्त राजीव गांधी सरकार ने एक तलाकशुदा मुस्लिम महिला के भरण-पोषण के अधिकार पर सुप्रीम कोर्ट के फ़ैसले को पलट दिया था। मोदी तुष्टिकरण के आरोप को फिर से हवा दे रहे थे, लेकिन इस बार अशिष्टता, अभद्रता और खुलेआम झूठ भी चल रहा था। मुसलमानों को सरकारी संसाधनों पर पहला हक़ का ज़िक्र, डॉ. मनमोहन सिंह के उस भाषण को लेकर था, जो उन्होंने 2006 में राष्ट्रीय विकास परिषद में दिया था। लेकिन उसमें संदर्भों को बाहर रखा गया। डॉ. सिंह ने, ना केवल मुस्लिम अल्पसंख्यकों का ज़िक्र किया था, बल्कि उसके साथ एससी, एसटी, ओबीसी, दूसरे अल्पसंख्यकों और महिलाओं को भी सरकार की प्राथमिकता में रखने की बात की थी। इसी तरह कांग्रेस के घोषणापत्र में सोना और संपत्ति का सर्वेक्षण और उसे मुसलमानों में बांटने के वादे की बात बेतुकी थी। यह काल्पनिक, अजीब पागलपन सा था। कांग्रेस के 46 पन्नों के न्याय पत्र में संपत्ति और आमदनी में बढ़ती असमानता की बात की गई थी, जिसे नीतियों में ज़रूरी बदलाव करके दूर करने का वादा था, लेकिन निजी संपत्ति को ज़ब्त करने का ज़िक्र नहीं था। हिंदू महिलाओं के मंगलसूत्र को ज़ब्त करने की बात तो दूर, मुसलमानों को अलग से फायदा पहुंचाने की बात भी नहीं थी। यहां तक कि मुसलमानों के ज़्यादा बच्चे पैदा करने

के आरोप को भी सरकार के राष्ट्रीय परिवार स्वास्थ्य सर्वेक्षण ने ख़ारिज़ कर दिया था, जिसमें सभी समुदायों में प्रजनन दर में गिरावट दिखाई गई थी। तो प्रधानमंत्री जान-बूझकर झूठ क्यों फैला रहे थे। 'देखिए, चुनाव प्रचार में कई बात आवेश में कही जाती हैं। जब कांग्रेस संविधान बदले जाने और भाजपा सरकार आरक्षण ख़त्म कर देगी, का विमर्श चला रही थी, तो क्या यह सरासर झूठ नहीं था, जिसे स्पष्ट करने की ज़रूरत थी,' भाजपा के एक वरिष्ठ नेता ने तर्क दिया।

लेकिन बांसवाड़ा में कोई सामान्य क्षणिक आवेश का भाषण नहीं कहा जा सकता। पहले चरण के निराशाजनक मतदान के बाद भाजपा के कार्यकर्ताओं में जोश भरने के लिए जानबूझकर उठाया गया कदम था। इसे आंशिक रूप से रणनीति कहें, आंशिक रूप से दंगा भड़काने की प्रवृत्ति और थोड़ी हताशा से भरा यह भाषण, विपक्ष, खासतौर से कांग्रेस के विमर्श से फिर से जीतने के लिए था। बांसवाड़ा में दिया गया भाषण आचार संहिता का खुला उल्लंघन कहा जा सकता है, लेकिन चुनाव आयोग ने मोदी को फटकार लगाने से इंकार कर दिया। शुरू में इस पर कोई टिप्पणी नहीं करने के बाद चुनाव आयोग ने भाषण देने वाले की निंदा, फटकार या सज़ा देने के बजाय, भाजपा के राष्ट्रीय अध्यक्ष जे.पी. नड्डा को नोटिस भेजा। सुरक्षित खेलने की कोशिश करते हुए आयोग ने राहुल गांधी के भाषणों पर कांग्रेस अध्यक्ष खड़गे को भी नोटिस भेजा। बांसवाड़ा का बयान, सांप्रदायिक रूप से जहरीले भाषण का गंभीर उदाहरण था, जिस पर चुनाव आयोग को तुरंत कार्रवाई करनी चाहिए थी। इसके बजाय, चार हफ्ते बाद, आयोग ने एक कमज़ोर बयान जारी किया, जिसमें सभी पक्षों से जाति और धर्म के आधार पर भाषण देने पर संयम बरतने को कहा गया। यह चुनावों की सर्वोच्च संस्था के लिए एक और सीढ़ी नीचे गिरने जैसा था, जो अपने राजनीतिक सुप्रीमो से निपटने के लिए तैयार नहीं थी।

बांसवाड़ा का भाषण अकेली घटना नहीं थी। बांसवाड़ा के बाद के हफ्ते पर न्यूज़ पोर्टल 'स्क्रॉल' ने मोदी के भाषणों की विस्तार से समीक्षा की थी। लगभग हर भाषण में प्रधानमंत्री ने न केवल कांग्रेस पर मुस्लिम हितों का ध्यान रखने का आरोप दोहराया, बल्कि ऐसे दावे भी किए, जो झूठ या अधूरे सच थे। मध्यप्रदेश के सागर में एक भाषण में मोदी ने आरोप लगाया कि कर्नाटक में कांग्रेस सरकार ने अवैध तरीके से धर्म के आधार पर आरक्षण लागू किया था। तथ्य यह है कि 1962 में कर्नाटक में कांग्रेस सरकार ने एक सरकारी पैनल की सिफ़ारिश के आधार पर कुछ मुस्लिम जातियों को ओबीसी सूची में शामिल किया था, लेकिन 1994 में एच.डी. देवेगौड़ा की जेडी(एस) सरकार ने सभी मुस्लिम समुदायों को ओबीसी सूची में शामिल कर दिया और उनके लिए अलग से 4 फ़ीसद उप-कोटा बनाया। जेडी(एस) अब भाजपा को साथ चुनाव लड़ रही थी। इसके बाद सरगुजा में मोदी ने कहा कि 'अगर कांग्रेस सत्ता में आई तो वह विरासत टैक्स लगाने की योजना बना रही है। जो संपत्ति आपने जमा की है, वह आपके बच्चों को नहीं मिलेगी। कांग्रेस इसे आपसे छीन लेगी।' गुजरात के बनासकांठा में तो मोदी

कुछ और आगे बढ़ गए। उन्होंने चेतावनी दी, 'खबरदार, कांग्रेस आपकी भैंस छीन लेगी। अगर आपके पास दो भैंस हैं, तो कांग्रेस एक छीन लेगी।' यह टिप्पणी ओवरसीज कांग्रेस के अध्यक्ष सैम पित्रोदा के समाचार एजेंसी एएनआई को दिए साक्षात्कार के कुछ घंटों बाद आई। पित्रोदा ने कहा था कि 'विरासत कर' एक आकर्षक आइडिया था। नाराज़ पित्रोदा ने दावा किया कि उनके बयान को तोड़-मरोड़कर पेश किया गया। उन्होंने कहा, 'यह पूरी तरह से मीडिया की साज़िश है जो मोदी सरकार के एजेंट की तरह काम कर रहा है। मैं विरासत कर पर अमेरिका को लेकर चर्चा कर रहा था और न्यूज एजेंसी ने ऐसे बताया कि जैसे मैं भारत के संदर्भ में बात कर रहा था।' मुश्किल में पड़ी कांग्रेस ने तुरंत ही पित्रोदा के बयान से खुद को अलग कर लिया।

शुरू में कांग्रेस ने मोदी के बयानों पर कोई प्रतिक्रिया नहीं देने का फ़ैसला किया था। कांग्रेस मीडिया सेल के एक सदस्य ने मुझे बताया, 'हम समझ गए थे कि अगर हम भाजपा की हिन्दू-मुस्लिम राजनीति का जवाब देते हैं, तो हम अपने समाज के कल्याणकारी मुद्दे से दूर हो जाएंगे, हम सिर्फ़ उनके विमर्श पर नहीं चलना चाहते थे।' दिलचस्प बात यह है कि जब कांग्रेस ने बांसवाड़ा हमले पर पलटवार किया, तो प्रियंका गांधी ने इसका नेतृत्व किया। लंबे कद, आकर्षक और मुखर प्रियंका के लिए भीड़ उमड़ती है, लेकिन अतीत में पार्टी नेतृत्व उन्हें चुनावी मैदान में उतारने का इच्छुक नहीं लग रहा था, शायद एक डर कि कहीं उनकी चमक, उनके भाई की आभा को कम कर सकती है। लेकिन इस बार, नेतृत्व तैयार था। बेंगलुरु की एक रैली में प्रियंका ने मोदी के मंगलसूत्र के बयान पर पलटवार किया। उन्होंने अपने पिता राजीव गांधी की हत्या का ज़िक्र करते हुए कहा, 'मेरी मां का मंगलसूत्र इस देश पर कुर्बान है। जब युद्ध हुआ था, तब इंदिरा गांधी ने अपना सोना कुर्बान कर दिया था।' यह भावनात्मक प्रतिक्रिया जनता के दिलों को छूने वाली थी। मंगलसूत्र का विरोध कांग्रेस के अभियान में प्रियंका की भूमिका को भी तय करेगा। अगर राहुल गांधी सामाजिक न्याय की लड़ाई लड़ने वाले थे, और खड़गे को ज़मीनी स्तर के दिग्गज राजनेता के तौर पर पेश किया गया तो प्रियंका करिश्माई नेता थीं, जो संवेदनशील मुद्दों को अपने 'पर्सनल टच' के साथ उठा सकती थीं। कांग्रेस के एक उत्साही नेता ने कहा, 'अब हमारे पास भाजपा के डबल इंजन से मुकाबले के लिए अपना त्रिशूल है।'

संविधान, खटाखट और मंगलसूत्र जैसे धारदार राजनीतिक शब्दों का हथियार के तौर पर इस्तेमाल कर कांग्रेस ने चुनावी विमर्श पर कब्ज़ा कर लिया था। हर बार, भाजपा बैकफुट पर जाती हुई दिखी। हालांकि मोदी ने ज़ोर देकर कहा कि उनकी सरकार संविधान बदलने नहीं जा रही, लेकिन ज़मीन पर उस अभियान का तोड़ मुश्किल था। उन्होंने राहुल गांधी के खटाखट वाली बात को मज़ाक उड़ाया, लेकिन वो लोगों के दिमाग में बस गया था। मंगलसूत्र के मुद्दे को अपनी मां के साथ जोड़कर प्रियंका ने उस बहस को सुलझा दिया था। 2019 में पुलवामा आतंकी हमले मे मोदी और भाजपा को चुनावी विमर्श बनाने में निर्णायक बढ़त दिलाई थी।

'घर में घुसकर मारा', जैसे मोदी के वन-लाइनर की देशभर में गूंज ने उनकी छवि को एक उग्र राष्ट्रवादी के तौर पर मज़बूत किया था। 2024 में राहुल गांधी के भाषण, खासतौर से यूट्यूब और सोशल मीडिया पर लोगों को ज़्यादा आकर्षित कर रहे थे। विमर्श की लड़ाई और नेतृत्व का मुकाबला अब एकतरफा नहीं थे।

मोदी जैसे कुशल प्रचारक भी परेशान होने लगे थे, इसका संकेत मई के पहले सप्ताह में हैदराबाद रैली में मिला, जब प्रधानमंत्री ने कांग्रेस पर हमला करने के लिए अडानी-अंबानी जोड़ी का हवाला दिया, 'पांच साल तक इन लोगों (कांग्रेस) ने अडानी-अंबानी को गाली दी, लेकिन चुनाव के ऐलान के बाद से यह सब बंद हो गया। कितना माल उठाया है? काले धन के कितने बोरे भरकर रुपये आए हैं? कांग्रेस को कितने टेंपो भरकर पैसे पहुंचे हैं? आपको देश को जवाब देना होगा,' उन्होंने रैली में जोर से कहा। यह समझ से परे, अचानक आया आरोप था। दस साल तक, मोदी ने राहुल गांधी के लगातार उकसाए जाने के बावजूद कभी विवादास्पद **(A–A)** शब्द नहीं बोले थे। उनके लिए यह जुबान कठोर और समझ से परे थी। राहुल गांधी ने तुरंत जवाब दियाः 'आप यह भी जानते हैं कि वे टेंपों में पैसे देते हैं। क्या यह आपका निजी अनुभव है? देश जानता है कि भाजपा के भ्रष्टाचार के टैंपों का कौन ड्राईवर है और कौन हेल्पर?' मैंने भाजपा के जितने नेताओं और रणनीतिकारों से बात की, किसी को समझ नहीं आया था कि मोदी ने अडानी-अंबानी को चुनावी जुबानी जंग में क्यों घसीटा। भाजपा के एक रणनीतिकार ने माना कि 'हम कांग्रेस की पिच पर खेलने और खुद को बेवजह विवाद में डालने के बारे में क्यों सोचेंगे। मुझे लगता है कि "संविधान ख़तरे में है" का नारा प्रधानमंत्री को गहरे तक चुभ गया था और वे किसी तरह इसकी सुर्खियों को बदलने की कोशिश कर रहे थे।'

विपक्ष के संविधान के नारे से मुकाबले में मुश्किल में पड़ने के बावजूद, भाजपा का कहना है कि बांसवाड़ा में उनकी रणनीति ने मतदाताओं को उत्साहित किया। मोदी के भड़काऊ भाषण के बाद के चुनाव के तीन चरणों में, हिंदी पट्टी के प्रदेशों में मतदान प्रतिशत बढ़ा और पार्टी ने 60 फ़ीसद से ज़्यादा सीटें जीतीं, अपने पारपंरिक गढ़ मध्यप्रदेश और गुजरात जैसे राज्यों में जीत हासिल की, और उत्तरप्रदेश और राजस्थान में पहले चरण में हुए नुकसान को पूरा करने का काम किया। इस चुनावी मैराथन के पड़ाव पर भाजपा को भरोसा था कि टीम मोदी-शाह लगातार तीसरी बार जीत हासिल करेगी। क्या बदल सकता था? निर्णायक आखिरी पड़ाव पर कहानी में नाटकीय उलटफेर होने वाला था।

12

'हवा बदल रही है': राज्यों ने बदला राज

लखनऊ में राजनीतिक गपबाज़ी, उसके मशहूर 'इत्र' बाज़ारों की नशीली खुशबू से ज़्यादा फैली महसूस होती है। गली-मोहल्लों में 'बन-मस्का' और 'टुंडे कबाब' से लेकर सरकारी पैंतरेबाज़ी और विधानभवन में फेरबदल तक, यह शहर खाने-पीने के शौकीनों के लिए जितना मज़ेदार है, उतना ही राजनीति का स्वाद रखने वालों के लिए भी है। मई 2024 की, शुरुआत में गर्मी बढ़ने के साथ, चुनावी गर्मी भी बढ़ने लगी थी। क्या योगी आदित्यानाथ को प्रचार से बाहर रखा गया या मुख्यमंत्री जी ने खुद को ही इससे दूर कर लिया था? भाजपा के केन्द्रीय नेतृत्व, खासतौर से गृहमंत्री अमित शाह के साथ योगी की कथित लड़ाई पर उत्तर प्रदेश के सत्ता के गलियारों में कानाफूसी हो रही थी कि क्या चुनाव के बाद पार्टी को बड़ी जीत मिलने पर लखनऊ में सत्ता में बदलाव की संभावना थी।

कोई नहीं बता सकता कि 'योगी बाहर होने वाले हैं', अफवाह, किसने, कैसे या क्यों फैलाई। लखनऊ में सरकार में बैठे लोगों ने दावा किया, यह चर्चा 2023 की सर्दियों में हुए चुनावों के बाद शुरू हुई, जब मध्यप्रदेश में शिवराज सिंह को हटाया गया और राजस्थान में वसुंधरा राजे हाशिए पर चली गईं। भाजपा ने आम आदमी पार्टी के नेता अरविंद केजरीवाल पर अंगुली उठाई, जब उन्होंने चुनाव अभियान में शामिल होने के लिए सुप्रीम कोर्ट से मिली ज़मानत के एक दिन बाद दावा किया था कि केन्द्र 2024 के लोकसभा चुनावों के बाद भगवाधारी मुख्यमंत्री को बाहर का रास्ता दिखाने की तैयारी कर रहा था। 'अगर भाजपा की सरकार बनती है, तो वे सबसे पहले योगी आदित्यनाथ को हटाएंगे और फिर अमित शाह को देश का प्रधानमंत्री बनाएंगे। प्रधानमंत्री मोदी, अमित शाह के लिए वोट मांग रहे हैं। क्या अमित शाह मोदी की गारंटी पूरी

करेंगे?' दिल्ली के मुख्यमंत्री ने सवाल किया। यह राजनीतिक चतुराई भरी, लेकिन शरारती टिप्पणी थी, जिसका मकसद भाजपा के कार्यकर्ताओं में गफलत पैदा करना था और ये गपशप के बाज़ार को गर्म करने के लिए काफी थी। अगले दिन, यूपी के दूसरे प्रमुख राजनीतिक खिलाड़ी और समाजवादी पार्टी के नेता अखिलेश यादव ने इस पर चुटकी लेते हुए पूछा, 'बताइए, भाजपा के होर्डिंग्स में योगी की तस्वीर क्यों नहीं दिखती? उत्तर प्रदेश का डबल इंजन अचानक सिंगल इंजन कैसे बन गया? क्या बीजेपी योगी के साथ भी वैसा ही करेगी, जैसा उन्होंने मध्य प्रदेश में शिवराज चौहान के साथ किया?' सवाल में मुस्कान भरी हुई थी।

गपशप तब मज़ेदार लगती है, जब लगे कि इसमें कुछ सच्चाई है। शाह-योगी कहानी इस पैमाने पर फिट बैठती है। भविष्य में नरेन्द्र मोदी का उत्तराधिकारी कौन होगा? अगली पीढ़ी की इस पर लड़ाई, राजनीतिक कयासों का विषय थी। शाह, मोदी के असली नंबर 2, भाजपा के संकटमोचक, प्रबंधक और चुनावों के लिए मुख्य रणनीतिकार थे, जबकि योगी आदित्यनाथ, सीटों के नंबर के हिसाब से देश के निर्णायक राज्य में बेहद लोकप्रिय नेता थे। अब एक बड़े चुनाव के बीच, अंदरूनी खींचतान फिर से ज़ोर पकड़ रही थी। कई स्रोतों से बातचीत के बाद मुझे पता चला कि योगी भाजपा के लोकसभा उम्मीदवारों की पसंद से नाखुश थे। उन्होंने केन्द्रीय नेतृत्व को कई नाम सुझाए थे, लेकिन वो पार्टी आलाकमान को मंज़ूर नहीं थे, उनमें से ही एक नाम जनरल वी.के. सिंह का भी था। पूर्व सेना प्रमुख और केन्द्रीय मंत्री रहे सिंह ने 2019 में गाज़ियाबाद सीट से चुनाव 5 लाख 60 हज़ार वोटों से जीता था। 2024 के उम्मीदवारों की सूची में सिंह का नाम गायब होने से योगी भड़क गए। योगी ने पार्टी की अंदरूनी बैठक में चेतावनी दी, 'आप उनके जैसे कद के किसी व्यक्ति को कैसे हटा सकते हैं? इससे ग़लत संदेश जाएगा।' उनकी चेतावनी पर ध्यान नहीं दिया गया। कथित तौर पर केन्द्रीय नेतृत्व जनरल सिंह के पक्ष में नहीं था।

मुख्यमंत्री के उम्मीदवारों की अनदेखी से निराश योगी खेमे ने इसके लिए गृहमंत्री के इर्दगिर्द रहने वाले लोगों को ज़िम्मेदार ठहराया, खासतौर से सुनील बंसल को। बंसल भाजपा के ताकतवर महासचिव हैं और आदित्यनाथ के समर्थक उन्हें 'छोटा चाणक्य' कहते हैं। एक राष्ट्रीय समाचार नेटवर्क के निदेशक भी उनके निशाने पर थे, जिसकी शाह तक आसान पहुंच थी और उनके आलोचकों ने उन पर 'सौदा' करने का आरोप लगाया। योगी के एक समर्थक ने कहा, 'दिल्ली में एसी कमरों में बैठे ये लोग, उत्तर प्रदेश में ज़मीनी स्तर पर क्या हमसे ज़्यादा जानते हैं?'

इसमें कोई शक नहीं कि अमित शाह की उत्तर प्रदेश में खास रुचि थी। देश में राजनीतिक रूप से सबसे अहम राज्य के प्रभारी महासचिव के तौर पर उन्होंने 2014 में भाजपा को शानदार जीत दिलाकर राष्ट्रीय स्तर पर पहचान बनाई थी। प्रदेश की भाजपा इकाई में शाह के जो

वफ़ादार थे, उनमें से एक सबसे महत्वपूर्ण सुनील बंसल थे। बंसल केन्द्रीय नेतृत्व के करीब होने से ताकतवर थे, लेकिन अगस्त 2022 में, उन्हें भाजपा के संगठन सचिव पद से हटा दिया गया, इसके बजाय उन्हें पश्चिम बंगाल, ओड़िशा और तेलंगाना की ज़िम्मेदारी दी गई। उनके जाने से, योगी ही प्रदेश में शक्ति के इकलौते केन्द्र हो गए। वे 2022 में पार्टी की शानदार जीत का चेहरा थे। एक विधायक ने अफसोस ज़ाहिर करते हुए कहा, 'योगी भाजपा के किसी नेता से सलाह लिए बिना खुद फ़ैसला करते हैं; किसी मंत्री, सांसद या विधायक की सरकार में कोई भूमिका नहीं है। केवल चुनिंदा नौकरशाह ही सबकुछ हैं। कम से कम जब बंसल जी थे, तो हम उनसे शिकायत कर सकते थे, अब तो कोई नहीं है।'

आरोप है कि मुख्यमंत्री पार्टी के ब्राह्मण और ओबीसी नेताओं की क़ीमत पर, अपने ठाकुर समुदाय के लोगों को बढ़ावा दे रहे थे। योगी सरकार में उप-मुख्यमंत्री और पार्टी के ओबीसी चेहरा केशव प्रसाद मौर्य इस असंतुष्ट गुट की अगुवाई कर रहे थे। मौर्य को यकीन था कि 2022 के विधानसभा चुनावों में, योगी के वफ़ादारों ने ही उन्हें हराने की साज़िश रची थी। मुख्यमंत्री और उनके डिप्टी भले ही लखनऊ के वीवीआईपी इलाके में सिर्फ़ 75 मीटर की दूरी पर रहते हों, लेकिन करीब पांच साल में वे एक दूसरे के आवास पर नहीं गए थे। योगी केवल एक बार 2021 में मौर्य के नवविवाहित बेटे और बहू को आशीर्वाद देने गए थे। वे शादी और रिसेप्शन समारोह में नहीं गए, जिसमें संघ परिवार के कई बड़े लोग शामिल हुए थे। प्रदेश के एक वरिष्ठ नेता ने माना, 'संघ के कुछ वरिष्ठ नेताओ ने योगी को अपने उप-मुख्यमंत्री के साथ कम से कम सार्वजनिक तौर पर सौहार्द्रपूर्ण संबंध रखने को कहा, लेकिन सच्चाई यह है कि संबंध पूरी तरह टूट गए थे।'

योगी के नेतृत्व वाले उत्तर प्रदेश में भाजपा की हालत, गुजरात में मोदी के दौरान पार्टी की दुर्दशा से अलग नहीं थी। उस समय मोदी पर आरोप था कि उनके लिए चुनौती बनने वाले लोगों को हाशिए पर डाल दिया गया। उग्र हिंदुत्व रुख की वजह से पार्टी कार्यकर्ताओं का समर्थन हासिल करने वाले भगवाधारी स्वयंभू 'साधु' योगी आदित्यनाथ, पर भी अब उनके साथी 'वन-मैन शो' चलाने का आरोप लगा रहे थे। निर्णय लेने की प्रक्रिया दिल्ली और लखनऊ में केन्द्रित होने के साथ भाजपा के भीतर दरारें बढ़ती गईं। ज़िला स्तर के भाजपा नेताओं और कार्यकर्ताओं की शिकायत थी कि शीर्ष पर सत्ता संघर्ष चलने से ज़मीन पर उनकी शिकायतें सुनने वाला कोई नहीं था। तीन दशकों से ज़्यादा समय से उत्तर प्रदेश की राजनीति पर नज़र रखने वाले पत्रकार राहुल श्रीवास्तव कहते हैं, '2024 में उत्तर प्रदेश में हज़ारों राजनीतिक विद्रोह चल रहे थे।'

पूर्वी उत्तर प्रदेश के एक सुंदर लेकिन थोड़े ऊबड़-खाबड़ शहर जौनपुर में भी सत्ता का खेल खेला जा रहा था। भाजपा के केन्द्रीय नेतृत्व ने मुंबई में लंबे समय तक कांग्रेस में रहे कृपाशंकर सिंह को टिकट दिया था, सिंह 2021 में भाजपा में शामिल हुए थे। सिंह उन 100 से ज़्यादा

उम्मीदवारों में से थे, जिन्होंने पिछले दशक में कांग्रेस छोड़ी थी और टिकट मिला था। इससे पार्टी के भीतर बेचैनी बढ़ रही थी और संघ के लिए चिंता का विषय था, जिसमें सबसे ऊपर वफादारी होती है। मूल रूप से जौनपुर के रहने वाले सिंह 70 के दशक में मुंबई चले गए थे और वहां कांग्रेस का उत्तर भारतीय चेहरा बने। विडंबना यह है कि 'आय से अधिक संपत्ति' के मामले में भाजपा ने उनके ख़िलाफ़ आरोप लगाए थे, जिससे उन्हें बरी कर दिया गया था। अब वे भगवा सेना का हिस्सा बन गए थे और मुंबई में पाली हिल के आलीशान अपार्टमेंट से जौनपुर की धूल भरी पगडंडियों पर चले आए थे। ज़्यादातर लोगों को उनको टिकट मिलने पर आश्चर्य था और पार्टी हलकों में अटकलें थी कि सिंह ने टिकट पाने के लिए, मुंबई के 'बड़े पैसे वाले कनेक्शन' का इस्तेमाल किया था, उन्होंने इस आरोप का ज़ोरदार खंडन किया। सिंह ने चुनाव प्रचार के दौरान मुझसे कहा, 'मैं अब मोदी जी का सिपाही हूं और यह मेरी धरती है।'

टिकट मिलने से सिंह बहुत खुश थे, लेकिन यह आसान सीट नहीं थी। 2019 में इस सीट पर बहुजन समाज पार्टी ने जीत हासिल की थी, इस बार उसने जेल में बंद गैंगस्टर-राजनेता धनंजय सिंह की पत्नी श्रीकला रेड्डी सिंह को अपना उम्मीदवार बनाया था। कुछ दिनों बाद जौनपुर के निर्विवाद बाहुबली धनजंय सिंह को ज़मानत पर जेल से रिहा किया गया, बताया जाता है कि केन्द्रीय गृहमंत्री ने उनसे सख्ती से कहा: 'आपको अपनी पत्नी का नाम वापस लेना होगा।' काफी कोशिशों के बाद, वह अनिच्छा से मैदान से हट गईं और धनंजय सिंह ने भाजपा को अपना समर्थन देने की घोषणा की। धनंजय सिंह का पूर्वांचल में कम से कम तीन सीटों पर असर है, इसलिए वो महत्वपूर्ण माने जाते हैं।

मुख्यमंत्री योगी इस घटनाक्रम से खुश नहीं थे। माफिया के ख़िलाफ़ अभियान को अपनी पहचान बनाने के बाद, योगी को लगा कि उनके गृह क्षेत्र पूर्वांचल में एक ठाकुर और हिस्ट्रीशीटर को दिल्ली में भाजपा नेतृत्व मनाने में लगा था। योगी आदित्यनाथ ने जौनपुर में एक रैली में हिस्सा तो लिया, लेकिन वे कथित तौर पर धनंजय के हाथ मज़बूत करने को तैयार नहीं थे। उन्होंने उसके साथ मंच साझा करने से भी इंकार कर दिया। उत्तर प्रदेश में ठाकुरों के बीच प्रतिद्वन्दिता कई बार परेशानी पैदा कर सकती है। इस सबके बीच फंसे कृपाशंकर सिंह पहले से ही बाहरी होने के टैग का सामना कर रहे थे। 2024 के चुनाव में जौनपुर सीट वह समाजवादी पार्टी के बाबू सिंह कुशवाहा से 99,335 वोटों से हार गए। भाजपा की अंदरूनी कलह के बीच, ओबीसी वोट और बसपा के दलित वोट का एक बड़ा हिस्सा कुशवाहा के साथ चला गया।

उत्तर प्रदेश में सत्ता की राजनीति का एक और उदाहरण, बड़ी पहचान रखने वाले भाजपा बाहुबली से जुड़ा था। छह बार सांसद रह चुके बृजभूषण शरण सिंह पर कई पदक विजेता महिला पहलवानों ने यौन उत्पीड़न समेत कई गंभीर आरोप लगाए थे और वे बड़े विवाद में फंस गए थे। बृजभूषण ने अनिच्छा से कुश्ती महासंघ के मुखिया के पद से इस्तीफ़ा दे दिया, लेकिन वे

सेन्ट्रल उत्तर प्रदेश में अपनी कैसरगंज़ सीट छोड़ने को तैयार नहीं थे। भाजपा का केन्द्रीय नेतृत्व दुविधा में था: बृजभूषण की बात मानने से पार्टी पर कथित तौर पर यौन उत्पीड़न के आरोपी का पक्ष लेने का आरोप लगता, लेकिन साथ छोड़ने से उनके प्रभाव वाली दो या तीन सीटों पर चुनाव में असर पड़ सकता था। उलझन में फंसे भाजपा नेतृत्व ने समझौते का रास्ता निकाला। भाजपा अध्यक्ष जे.पी. नड्डा ने प्रस्ताव दिया, 'हम आपके बेटे करण को टिकट देंगे।' हालांकि अंतिम फ़ैसला शाह ने किया, लेकिन टिकट की सूचना देने की औपचारिकता मिलनसार भाजपा अध्यक्ष पर छोड़ दी गई थी। अपने ख़िलाफ़ उत्पीड़न के आरोपों को झूठा बताने वाले बृजभूषण, नड्डा के प्रस्ताव पर राजी नहीं थे। 'अगर आप टिकट नहीं देंगे, तो मैं निर्दलीय चुनाव लड़ूंगा और जीतूंगा। आपको जो करना है, करो, मैं आपकी बात नहीं मानूंगा।' निराश नड्डा ने गृहमंत्री को फ़ोन कर दख़ल देने को कहा। शाह के एक फ़ोन से आखिरी वक्त पर काम बन गया। शाह के करीबी माने जाने वाले बृजभूषण ने बाद में मुझसे कहा, 'नेताजी के कहने पर मैं तैयार हो गया, आख़िर कौन अपने बेटे को आगे बढ़ता नहीं देखना चाहता।'

लेकिन कहानी यहां ख़त्म नहीं होती। अपने बेटे के प्रचार के वक्त बृजभूषण ने योगी आदित्यनाथ की 'बुलडोज़र' नीति के ख़िलाफ़ आवाज़ उठाई। कैसरगंज़ के इस बाहुबली की योगी से लंबे समय से प्रतिद्वन्दिता चल रही थी। वह योगी को अपना जूनियर मानते थे। अस्सी के दशक के आखिर में बृजभूषण राम मंदिर आंदोलन से राजनीति में आए थे। 'मैं जानता हूं कि घर बनाना कितना मुश्किल होता है, इसलिए मैं आपका दुख दर्द समझता हूं और इसी वजह से मैं बुलडोज़र के ख़िलाफ़ हूं,' उन्होंने गोंडा की एक चुनावी सभा में कहा। उनके शानदार फ़ॉर्महाउस पर जब मैंने उनका साक्षात्कार किया, तो बृजभूषण ने दावा किया, वे भाजपा के उन कुछ नेताओं में से थे, जिनके समर्थकों में स्थानीय मुसलमान भी शामिल थे। उन्होंने कहा, 'लोग मेरे साथ हैं, भले ही कुछ ताकतवर लोग मुझे ख़त्म करने की साज़िश कर रहे हों।' मैंने उनसे पूछा कि क्या वह आदित्यनाथ का ज़िक्र कर रहे थे। उनका जवाब था, 'अब कुछ बातें कैमरे पर नहीं कही जातीं।' पार्टी नेतृत्व ने जब उन्हें हाशिए पर डाल दिया, तो नाखुश बृजभूषण सिर्फ़ अपने बेटे की जीत सुनिश्चित करने तक ही सीमित रहे। जहां करण भूषण सिंह ने कैसरगंज़ सीट 1 लाख 48 हज़ार वोटों से जीती, वहीं सेन्ट्रल उत्तर प्रदेश में भाजपा को अप्रत्याशित हार का सामना करना पड़ा।

उत्तर प्रदेश में सिर्फ़ नेतृत्व ही उलझन में नहीं था। पार्टी संगठन की ताकत भाजपा-संघ कार्यकर्ता भी खुद को अलग-थलग महसूस कर रहे थे। मेरठ में भाजपा ने मौजूदा सांसद की जगह अस्सी के दशक में मशहूर टीवी धारावाहिक *रामायण* में भगवान राम की भूमिका निभाने वाले अरुण गोविल को टिकट दिया, लेकिन वहां जश्न के बजाय माहौल उदासी भरा था। भाजपा के स्थानीय कार्यकर्ताओं के लिए, उदास चेहरे वाले गोविल 'बाहरी' थे, जिनका इलाके से बहुत

कम जुड़ाव था। मेरठ में भाजपा के एक पदाधिकारी ने कहा, 'भले ही वे स्टार हों, लेकिन क्या वे हमारे बीच में रहेंगे?' गोविल देश के लिए भले ही टीवी के राम थे, लेकिन मेरठ में भाजपा कार्यकर्ताओं के लिए, वे शीर्ष से थोपे गए सेलिब्रिटी भर थे। कहा गया कि वो हाथ मिलाते वक्त दस्ताने पहनते थे और लोगों के माला पहनाने से कतराते थे। जब एक टीवी चैनल ने उनके साक्षात्कार के लिए कहा, तो उनके सहयोगी ने इसके लिए फीस की बात की। ऑन-स्क्रीन राम को ऑफ-स्क्रीन राजनीति की ज़रूरतों के साथ तालमेल बिठाना बाकी था। गोविल आखिरकार 10,000 से ज़्यादा वोटों से जीत गए।

चुनावी दौड़ में एक बाहरी को पैराशूट उम्मीदवार बनाने का एक और अच्छा उदाहरण था, जब भाजपा ने श्रावस्ती से अपने मौजूदा सांसद का टिकट काटकर साकेत मिश्रा को उम्मीदवार बनाया। साकेत, श्रीरामजन्मभूमि तीर्थ ट्रस्ट के अध्यक्ष और प्रधानमंत्री कार्यालय में ताकतवर नौकरशाह रहे नृपेन्द्र मिश्र के बेटे हैं। आईआईएम कोलकाता से स्नातक और ग्लोबल इनवेस्टमेंट बैंकर, साकेत ने 'राष्ट्र-निर्माण में हिस्सेदारी' के लिए घर लौटने से पहले काफी समय तक विदेशों में काम किया था। वह 2018 में भाजपा में शामिल हुए और पूर्वांचल विकास बोर्ड के सलाहकार के तौर पर काम किया। लेकिन श्रावस्ती में भाजपा के लोगों ने उन्हें वीवीआईपी संबंधों की वजह से टिकट मिलने के तौर पर देखा। प्रदेश भाजपा के एक पदाधिकारी ने कहा, 'हम कांग्रेस को "बाबा लोगों" की पार्टी कहते हैं, लेकिन अब हमारे पास भी अपने बड़े लोग हैं।' साकेत श्रावस्ती सीट करीब 77 हज़ार वोटों से हार गए।

भाजपा के कई उम्मीदवारों को लेकर बढ़ते असंतोष का मतलब था कि निराश कार्यकर्ता और बंटे हुए नेता एक साथ नहीं आ पा रहे थे। अति-आत्मविश्वास और मोदी फैक्टर पर निर्भरता से भाजपा की चुनावी रणनीति में आरामपरस्ती आ गई थी। इसके अलावा यह भरोसा था कि टिकटों को लेकर छोटी-मोटी खींचतान के बावजूद, कुशल रणनीतिकार शाह और उनके चुनावी कौशल से जीत उनकी ही होगी। यह उत्साह और आत्मविश्वास बुरी तरह से गलत साबित हुआ। लेकिन हमेशा हार पार्टी की खामियों की वजह से नहीं होती। कभी-कभी प्रतिद्वन्दी भी उन ख़ामियों का अप्रत्याशित तौर पर फायदा उठा लेता है। और 2024 में उत्तर प्रदेश में, 51 साल के अखिलेश यादव, अपने दमखम के साथ योग्यता को साबित करने के लिए तैयार थे।

═

अखिलेश यादव ने आत्मविश्वास भरी मुस्कुराहट के साथ कहा, 'हवा बदल रही है; अपना समय आ रहा है।' हम लखनऊ शहर में रोड शो कर रहे थे, इसके लिए हज़रतगंज की चमकदार सड़कों से गोमतीनगर की जगमगाती रोशनी की ओर बढ़ रहे थे। रास्ते भर समाजवादी पार्टी के कार्यकर्ता अपने अखिलेश भैया की झलक पाने के लिए उत्साहित थे। बीच-बीच में अखिलेश

यादव बस रोककर बाहर निकलकर भीड़ को अभिवादन के लिए हाथ हिलाते। उन्होंने मुस्कुराते हुए पूछा, 'क्या आपने ऐसा जोश पहले देखा है?' मैं उनके समर्थकों के उत्साह से हैरान तो था, लेकिन मुझे नहीं लगता था कि यह चुनावी जीत में तब्दील होगा। पिछले दस साल में अखिलेश को दो विधानसभा और दो लोकसभा चुनावों समेत चार बार भाजपा के हाथों हार का सामना करना पड़ा था। ऐसा लगता था कि समाजवादी पार्टी के नेता का जोश ज़मीनी हकीकत से मेल नहीं खाता। उन्होंने आश्वस्त होते हुए कहा, 'इस बार उनके सामने, हमारा पीडीए बहुत मज़बूत होगा, बस आप इंतज़ार करिए और देखें।'

अखिलेश ने 'पीडीए' शब्द अपने सोशल इंजीनियरिंग की योजना के लिए गढ़ा था, जिसका मक़सद पिछड़ा, दलित, अल्पसंख्यक और आधी आबादी (महिलाओं) को एक मंच पर लाना था। कागज़ पर यह गठबंधन शक्तिशाली लगता था, जिसे पार्टी को अपने पिता दिवंगत मुलायम सिंह यादव के राजनीतिक आधार (एम-वाई) मुस्लिम-यादव के संकीर्ण दायरे से दूर ले जाने के लिए तैयार किया गया था। लेकिन यह कोई नया प्रयोग नहीं था। 2022 के विधानसभा चुनावों में अखिलेश यादव ने गैर-यादव ओबीसी नेताओं तक पंहुच बनाकर अपना दायरा बढ़ाने की कोशिश की थी। लेकिन वे भाजपा के विजय रथ को रोकने में कामयाब नहीं हो पाए थे। दरअसल समाजवादी पार्टी को ज़्यादा समावेशी बनाने की कोशिश 2013 में ही शुरू हो गई थी, जब मुख्यमंत्री अखिलेश यादव ने कर्पूरी ठाकुर की जयंती मनाई थी। जननायक के तौर पर लोकप्रिय कर्पूरी ठाकुर 1970-71 में बिहार के मुख्यमंत्री बने थे और उन्हें पड़ोसी राज्य बिहार के ईबीसी समुदाय का नेता माना जाता है। जुलाई 2024 की, *कारवां* पत्रिका की कवर स्टोरी में बताया गया कि समाजवादी पार्टी ने 2024 के चुनावों से पहले अठारह महीनों में ईबीसी, ओबीसी और दलित हस्तियों को जोड़ने की पूरी कशिश की। अखिलेश के टिकट बंटवारे में भी इन सामाजिक समीकरणों को समेटने की समझदारी दिखती है। उन्होंने ज़ोर देकर कहा, 'मैंने इस बार केवल पांच यादव (सभी उनके परिवार के सदस्य) और चार मुस्लिमों को टिकट दिया है। मेरी सूची में 15 दलित और 27 गैर-यादव ओबीसी हैं।' ऐसे राज्य में जहां जातिगत समीकरण महत्वपूर्ण हैं, अखिलेश अपना हिसाब-किताब ठीक कर रहे थे। उदाहरण के लिए, उन्होंने कुर्मी समाज को 12 टिकट दिए, उससे इस बड़े समुदाय में उनकी पार्टी का आधार फिर से खड़ा हो गया।

समाजवादी पार्टी के नेता गठबंधन का खेल भी समझदारी से खेल रहे थे। 2019 के आम चुनावों में, अखिलेश ने मायावती के साथ गठबंधन किया था, लेकिन 'बुआ-भतीजा' का यह मेल असहज था, क्योंकि बसपा नेता अपने राजनीतिक प्रतिद्वन्दी को बराबर जगह देने को तैयार नहीं दिख रही थीं। इस बार, अखिलेश ने कांग्रेस और राहुल गांधी के साथ गठबंधन करना तय किया। 2017 में, इस जोड़ी को 'यूपी के लड़के' के रूप में ब्रांड किया गया था, लेकिन भाजपा की ताकत के सामने वे लड़खड़ा गए। अखिलेश ने आरोप लगाया कि कांग्रेस

नेतृत्व ने उनका फ़ोन नहीं उठाया और संदेशों का जवाब भी नहीं दिया, जबकि कांग्रेस ने दावा किया कि अखिलेश प्रदेश में उनकी पार्टी को ख़त्म करना चाहते थे। मौजूदा हालात ने उन्हें फिर से इंडिया गठबंधन की छतरी तले एक साथ ला दिया। कांग्रेस ज़मीनी स्तर पर लगातार कमज़ोर हो रही थी, लेकिन अखिलेश उन्हें 80 में से 17 सीटें देने को तैयार हो गए। राहुल गांधी की यात्राओं ने उन्हें खासतौर पर अल्पसंख्यकों के बीच लोकप्रिय बना दिया था और केवल गठबंधन ही एक महत्वपूर्ण वोट बैंक को मज़बूत कर सकता था। उत्तर प्रदेश के प्रभारी कांग्रेस महासचिव अविनाश पांडे कहते हैं, 'शुरुआती कड़ी सौदेबाजी के बाद, अखिलेश हमारे सबसे सरल सहयोगियों में से एक थे। प्रदेश में बड़ी पार्टी होने के बावज़ूद कोई दिखावा या अंहकार नहीं था।' बातचीत में कुछ मज़ेदार पल भी आए। जैसे, कांग्रेस की सूची में ग़लती से दिवंगत महावीर प्रसाद का नाम भी शामिल हो गया। पार्टी में शायद कोई यह भूल गया कि उनका निधन दस साल पहले हो चुका था! (कांग्रेस इस कहानी को ख़ारिज़ करते हुए कहती है, यह अफवाह किसी शरारती तत्व ने फैलाई है।)

फिर भी ज़मीनी स्तर पर बदलाव के लिए कोई बेचैनी न हो, तो कोई भी जातीय गणित या गठबंधन काम नहीं कर सकता। इतने बड़े राज्य में सात चरणों का मतदान पश्चिमी उत्तर प्रदेश से शुरू हुआ और यहीं से बदलती हवा के संकेत मिले। हवा में एक अनिश्चितता महसूस की जा सकती थी। 'संविधान ख़तरे में है' की कहानी, खासतौर से दलित इलाकों में, जंगल की आग की तरह फैल गई। *इंडिया* टुडे की संवाददाता प्रीति चौधरी, सहारनपुर के एक गांव में 62 साल की सोमवती और उनके पोते राजबीर से मुलाक़ात को याद करती हैं। दोनों ने कहा कि वे गठबंधन (समाजवादी पार्टी-कांग्रेस गठबंधन) को वोट देंगे। सोमवती ने हमेशा बहन जी (मायावती) और बीएसपी के हाथी को वोट दिया था, जबकि पहली बार वोटर बने, उनके पोते मोदी के भाषणों से प्रभावित थे। तो इस बार वे अपना वोट क्यों बदल रहे थे? सोमवती ने कहा, 'हमने नुक्कड़ सभा में सुना है कि अगर भाजपा आएगी तो वे आरक्षण को ख़त्म कर देंगे और यहां तक कि एससी/एसटी क़ानून को भी ख़त्म कर देंगे।' अनपढ़ बुज़ुर्ग महिला को संविधान के बारे में कोई जानकारी नहीं थी, लेकिन उन्हें इस बात की चिंता थी कि आरक्षण का फायदा मिलना बंद हो जाएगा। चौधरी कहती हैं, 'ज़्यादातर गांववालों के लिए शिक्षा और नौकरियों में आरक्षण ही सबसे अहम है; यही उनकी लाइफलाइन है।' मायावती को भाजपा की 'बी' टीम के रूप में बताने के साथ, समाजवादी पार्टी-कांग्रेस को पूरे प्रदेश में दलित वोट का बड़ा हिस्सा मिला। कांग्रेस के इमरान मसूद सहारनपुर में 60 हज़ार से ज़्यादा वोटों से जीते। ज़मीन पर 'दलित-मुस्लिम' रणनीतिक गठबंधन निर्णायक साबित हुआ।

दलित अगर आरक्षण को लेकर चिंतित थे, तो देश के नौजवान नौकरियों को लेकर नाराज़ और बेचैन थे। उन सभी ने 2022 में उत्तर प्रदेश के विधानसभा चुनावों में भाजपा को वोट दिया

था, लेकिन अब उनमें से कम से कम आधे कांग्रेस को वोट देने की सोच रहे थे। 'मैंने 2019 और 2022 में, दो बार भाजपा को वोट दिया, क्योंकि मुझे लगा कि वे नौकरियां सुनिश्चित करेंगे, लेकिन हमें बस पेपर लीक और फिर पेपर लीक मिले हैं। अगर कोई सरकार परीक्षा ठीक से नहीं करा सकती, तो फिर हमसे वोट कैसे मांग सकती है!' एक युवक ने गुस्से में कहा। सरकारी भर्ती परीक्षाओं के पेपर लीक होने की परेशानी देशभर में थी, लेकिन उत्तर प्रदेश में यह महामारी जैसा बन गया था। चुनावों से कुछ हफ्तों पहले, उत्तर प्रदेश कॉस्टेबल भर्ती परीक्षा का पेपर लीक हो गया था, जिसका असर 48 लाख से ज़्यादा परीक्षार्थियों पर पड़ा। एक पूरी पीढ़ी के लिए, पेपर लीक, भ्रष्टाचार और सरकारी अक्षमता का प्रतीक बन गया था। एक और युवक ने चुटकी लेते हुए कहा, 'राहुल गांधी और अखिलेश कम से कम जनता की बात तो कर रहे हैं, मोदी जी तो केवल मन की बात करते हैं।' 2014 से उत्तर प्रदेश के सफ़र में, कोई कभी-कभार अंसतोष की बात सुनाई देती थी, लेकिन प्रधानमंत्री की ऐसी तीखी आलोचना शायद ही कभी सुनी हो। अब मोहभंग हुए युवा मतदाता, मोदी का भी मज़ाक उड़ा रहे थे। 39 साल के आईआईटी स्नातक, और इंस्टाग्राम पर बड़ी तादाद में 'फॉलोअर' रखने वाले कांग्रेस के तनुज पूनिया ने बाराबांकी सीट दो लाख से ज़्यादा वोटों से जीती।

उत्तर प्रदेश चुनाव अभियान के दौरान एक अहम तस्वीर फूलपुर में राहुल-अखिलेश गठबंधन की साझा रैली की थी। दोनों नेता देर से पहुंचने वाले थे और जनता बेचैन हो रही थी, फिर भी वे नेताओं के इंतज़ार में रुके रहे। जब हेलिकॉप्टर उतरा, तो आसपास के इलाकों से आए युवाओं की भीड़ अनियंत्रित हो गई और बैरिकेड्स को तोड़कर मंच की तरफ बढ़ गई। सुरक्षा कारणों से सभा को बीच में ही रोकना पड़ा। ऐसी उन्मादी भीड़ उत्तर प्रदेश में लंबे समय से नहीं देखी गई थी, वह भी खासतौर से कांग्रेस के किसी कार्यक्रम में। जब हम सभा से बाहर निकलने की कोशिश कर रहे थे, तो पीले रंग की चमकीली शर्ट पहने, जिस पर 'रॉक ऑन' लिखा था, एक युवक, कैमरा देखकर, उत्साह से हमारी ओर मुड़ा। 'सर, आपने राहुल जी और अखिलेश जी को देखा? पूरा खटाखट मज़ा आ गया!' राहुल गांधी ने नकद गारंटी को जिस 'खटाखट' शब्द से जोड़ा था, अगर वो आम बोलचाल का हिस्सा बन गया था, तो साफतौर पर बदलाव की हवा चल रही थी। कभी मज़ाक का पात्र रहे 'यूपी के लड़के' वास्तव में आ गए थे। युवा, आकर्षक, जीवंत दिखते राहुल गांधी और अखिलेश यादव, भाजपा के उन नेताओं पर भारी पड़ रहे थे, जो अपने बड़ी-बड़ी गाड़ियों के काफिले में पुराने खोखले वादों के साथ भव्य समारोहों में शामिल होते थे।

उत्तर प्रदेश में मेरे लिए दूसरा खास पल मोदी के संसदीय क्षेत्र वाराणसी में था। हम अस्सी घाट पर चाय पी रहे थे, तभी कुछ स्थानीय लोग अचानक 'चाय पर चर्चा' के लिए हमारे साथ आ गए। इस बात पर राय बंटी हुई थी कि दस साल के मोदी राज ने वाराणसी कैसे बदल दिया

था। मोदी समर्थकों का कहना था कि प्रधानमंत्री ने वाराणसी को आस्था-पर्यटन के केन्द्र के रूप में विकसित किया, जिससे यहां पर्यटकों की तादाद बढ़ी थी। लेकिन आलोचकों का दमदार दावा था कि जो कुछ हुआ, उसने ऐतिहासिक शहर का गुजरातीकरण कर दिया था। उन्होंने दुख जताते हुए कहा, 'सभी नए होटल, रेस्तरां बाहरी लोग लगा रहे हैं; सभी ठेके गुजराती व्यापारियों को दिए जा रहे हैं।' गरमागरम बहस तब जाकर शांत हुई जब किसी ने मीठा पान पेश किया। 2014 से ही चाय की दुकान मेरे लिए एक ज़रूरी पड़ाव रही है, लेकिन यह पहली बार था कि जब मैंने हिंदुत्व के नाम पर कसम खाने वाले, रोजाना के ग्राहकों के बीच अंसतोष और नाराज़गी देखी। वाराणसी के पत्रकार उत्पल पाठक कहते हैं, 'आपको मोदी और भाजपा में फ़र्क करना होगा, लोग अब भी मोदी की तारीफ करते हैं, लेकिन उन्हें स्थानीय बीजेपी नेता पसंद नहीं हैं, उन्हें वे भ्रष्ट और नाकारा मानते हैं।'

4 जून को जब नतीजे आए, तो इस बदलाव पर मुहर लग गई। समाजवादी पार्टी ने 37 सीटें और कांग्रेस ने 6 सीटें जीती थी। बीजेपी को 33 सीटों के साथ दूसरे स्थान पर संतोष करना पड़ा, पार्टी का वोट शेयर आठ फ़ीसद कम हो गया था। भाजपा, राम मंदिर के शहर की सीट अयोध्या-फैज़ाबाद भी हार गई। वाराणसी में भाजपा के चुनाव प्रबंधकों ने रिकॉर्ड तोड़, अबकी बार दस लाख पार, जीत का दावा किया था, वहां जीत का अंतर घटकर सिर्फ़ डेढ़ लाख वोट रह गया था, जो एक मौजूदा प्रधानमंत्री के लिए बड़ी 'हार' जैसा था। बीजेपी के एक नेता ने कहा, 'मुझे लगा था कि हमारा वोट शेयर कुछ कम हो सकता है, लेकिन इतनी सीटें हारने का अंदाज़ा नहीं था।' अखिलेश उम्मीद के मुताबिक खुश थेः 'क्या मैंने आपको नहीं कहा था: हवा बदल रही है!'

चुनाव नतीज़ों के पोस्टमार्टम के बाद भाजपा ने उत्तर प्रदेश में हार के लिए बहुत से मुद्दे गिनाएः अति-आत्मविश्वास; सुस्त कॉडर; दलितों पर संविधान-आरक्षण विवाद का असर; मुस्लिम वोटों की एकजुटता; सरकारी नौकरियों का नहीं भरा जाना; कुर्मी जैसे गैर-यादव ओबीसी का खिसकना और मौजूदा सांसदों के ख़िलाफ़ सत्ता विरोधी लहर। यह एक लंबी सूची थी, लेकिन कोई भी असल मुद्दे का सामना नहीं करना चाहता थाः सभी अहम मुद्दों पर फ़ैसला करने वाली टीम मोदी-शाह ने मुख्यमंत्री योगी आदित्यनाथ को अलग-थलग कर दिया था। आरएसएस के एक वरिष्ठ नेता ने कहा कि जब 2022 में चौधरी भूपेन्द्र सिंह को उत्तर प्रदेश भाजपा का अध्यक्ष बनाया गया, तो स्थानीय नेताओं को पूछा तक नहीं गया। यह भाजपा का कांग्रेसीकरण हो रहा था, जैसे इंदिरा गांधी के दौर में कांग्रेस की सारी ताकत प्रधानमंत्री कार्यालय के इर्दगिर्द होती थी, जिससे प्रदेश के नेताओं का कद कम होता गया और पार्टी कार्यकर्ताओं से उनका नाता टूट गया। संघ हमेशा 'सामूहिक नेतृत्व' की बात करता है और 'व्यक्ति पूजा' से परहेज़ किया है, लेकिन अब उसे अपने ही कार्यकर्ताओं के बीच सिर्फ़ एक व्यक्ति की पूजा का सामना करना पड़ रहा था।

महत्वपूर्ण है कि चौथे चरण के मतदान के बाद *इंडियन एक्सप्रेस* को एक साक्षात्कार में भाजपा अध्यक्ष जे.पी. नड्डा ने कहा कि अब पार्टी आरएसएस से आगे बढ़ गई थी। 'शुरुआत में हम कम सक्षम और छोटे थे और हमें आरएसएस की ज़रूरत थी। आज हम बड़े हो गए हैं और हम खुद सक्षम हैं। भाजपा खुद चलती है,' नड्डा की टिप्पणी ने संघ के भीतर बेचैनी की भावना को बढ़ा दिया। आम धारणा यह थी कि पार्टी प्रमुख, मोदी-शाह की लाइन को दोहरा रहे थे। आरएसएस नेता ने कहा, 'देखिए, अगर उन्हें हमारी ज़रूरत नहीं है, तो ठीक है। हम अपना सामाजिक कार्य जारी रखेंगे।' उन्होंने कहा कि मध्यप्रदेश और गुजरात जैसे राज्यों में, आरएसएस का नेटवर्क मज़बूत था और अभियान में पूरी तरह शामिल था, वहां भाजपा ने चुनावों में जीत हासिल की। लेकिन उत्तर प्रदेश और हरियाणा जैसे राज्यों में, संगठन अलग-थलग महसूस हुआ, तो वहां कार्यकर्ताओं ने हिस्सा नहीं लिया। आरएसएस नेता ने साफतौर से कहा, 'सोचिए, अगर भाजपा गुजरात और मध्य प्रदेश में नहीं जीतती तो वह कहां होती।'

सच तो यह है कि खासतौर से उत्तर प्रदेश के नतीजे गृहमंत्री शाह के लिए एक चेतावनी थे और इसे राजनीति के चाणक्य की प्रतिष्ठा पर धब्बे की तरह देखा गया। उनके समर्थकों का कहना है कि शाह ने हरसंभव कोशिश की, यहां तक कि भाजपा के बेहतर नतीजों के लिए पश्चिमी उत्तर प्रदेश में जाट-बहुल राष्ट्रीय लोकदल के साथ आखिरी समय में गठबंधन भी कर लिया। भाजपा-आरएलडी का 'सौदा', शाह की राजनीति में 'साम-दाम' की नीति अपनाने को बताता है। जनवरी के तीसरे सप्ताह में, समाजवादी पार्टी और आरएलडी ने सीट-बंटवारे के समझौते की घोषणा की। टेक्सास में जन्मे, और लंदन स्कूल ऑफ इकॉनामिक्स से स्नातक पैंतालिस साल के जयंत चौधरी की आरएलडी उस वक्त तक इंडिया गठबंधन का हिस्सा थी। लेकिन सीट बंटवारे को लेकर बातचीत लंबी खिंचने से, जयंत चौधरी का धैर्य जवाब दे रहा था। गृहमंत्री शाह को जब यह पता चला, तो उन्होंने अपने एक खास व्यक्ति को आरएलडी के साथ बातचीत शुरू करने को कहा। चौधरी को कुछ समय से भाजपा नेताओं से संकेत मिल रहे थे, लेकिन इस बार खुद गृहमंत्री बातचीत के लिए फ़ोन पर थे। बातचीत में दो लोकसभा सीटों का प्रस्ताव रखा गया। आरएलडी नेता ने कुछ और सीटें देने पर जोर दिया, लेकिन शाह से बातचीत में कुछ हासिल करना थोड़ा मुश्किल होता है। जब कहा गया कि, 'इसे ले लीजिए या फिर छोड़ दीजिए' तो चौधरी ने रिश्ते की मिठास के लिए एक मांग की: अपने दादा और जाट किसान नेता दिवंगत चौधरी चरण सिंह को भारत रत्न सम्मान। गृहमंत्री ने इस पर हामी भर दी और बात पक्की हो गई। भारत रत्न के लालच ने भाजपा को इंडिया गठबंधन का एक और सहयोगी दिला दिया था। चौधरी ने अपने एक सहयोगी को कहा, 'चुनाव में कौन जीतने वाले के साथ नहीं रहना चाहता। भाजपा विजेता दिख रही है, तो फिर मुझे उनके साथ क्यों नहीं रहना चाहिए?' इंडिया गठबंधन में, आरएलडी नेता को पांच और साल विपक्ष में बिताने की

संभावना दिख रही थी, जबकि भाजपा के साथ वे केन्द्रीय मंत्री बन सकते थे। सत्ता का लालच बाकी सब पर भारी पड़ा।

दुर्भाग्य से भाजपा के लिए, चौधरी का अपना जाट वोट बैंक, इस बदलाव से पूरी तरह आश्वस्त नहीं था। पांच साल पहले ही, 2019 में उनके पिता अजित सिंह, मुजफ्फरनगर में एक प्रतिष्ठा की लड़ाई में भाजपा के दिग्गज जाट नेता संजीव बालियान से 6000 वोटों के मामूली फासले से चुनाव हार गए थे। वहां देर रात तक वोटों की गिनती चलती रही थी। अब चौधरी से ना केवल उस व्यक्ति के लिए प्रचार की उम्मीद थी जिसने उनके पिता को हराया, बल्कि उस पार्टी के लिए भी जिसने 2014 में अजित सिंह को उनके आधिकारिक बंगले से बाहर निकाल दिया था। जाट सम्मान दांव पर था। पत्रकार प्रीति चौधरी याद करती हैं, 'मैं बालियान और जयंत के साथ उनकी प्रचार बस में चुनाव कवर कर रही थी, लेकिन पूरे सफर में दोनों ने एक-दूसरे से कोई बात नहीं की।' बालियान इस बार मुजफ्फरनगर सीट हार गए, जबकि आरएलडी ने अपनी दोनों सीटें जीत लीं। पार्टी का जाट वोट, भाजपा उम्मीदवारों की तरफ नहीं आया। बालियान के ख़िलाफ़ सत्ता विरोधी लहर भी चल रही थी। 2020-21 के किसानों के विरोध की वजह से पश्चिमी उत्तर प्रदेश के जाट, भाजपा से सहज नहीं थे। राजनीति में अंकगणित के साथ केमेस्ट्री यानी रिश्तों में सहजता भी मायने रखती है।

उत्तर प्रदेश में हुई करारी हार भी 2024 में भाजपा की कम हुई सीटों की एक बड़ी वजह थी। अभियान की शुरुआत में, टीम मोदी-शाह के लिए काम करने वाली एक कंसल्टेंसी फर्म के सर्वेक्षण में कम से कम 70 सीटें मिलने की बात की गई थी। अब उससे आधी सीटें मिलने से, वो बुलबुला फूट गया था। इस अजेय मशीन को गंभीर चुनौती मिली थी और उनकी सीमाओं का पता चल गया था। लेकिन उत्तर प्रदेश ही शाह के लिए एक सिरदर्द नहीं था। भाजपा के इस बड़े रणनीतिकार को एक और हक़ीकत का सामना करना पड़ा।

═

पश्चिमी महाराष्ट्र में बारामती पवार परिवार का गढ़ है, जो राज्य की राजनीति में सबसे स्थायी परिवार माना जाता है। पुणे से करीब 100 किलोमीटर दूर बारामती शहर में शॉपिंग मॉल, मल्टीप्लेक्स थियेटर के साथ-साथ बॉयो-टेक्नॉलोजी संस्थान भी है। पवार मज़बूत राजनीतिक उद्यमी हैं। कॉलेज़ों से लेकर अस्पतालों तक, दूध की डेरियों से लेकर अंगूर के बागीचों तक, शहर में हर चीज़ पर उनकी छाप दिखती है। इस छोटे से मुफस्सिल कस्बे को हर चीज़ दिलाने की पवार की कोशिशों का इनाम भी मतदाताओं ने उन्हें दिया है। 1967 में परिवार के मुखिया, शरद पवार के यहां से पहली बार चुनाव लड़ने से अब तक बारामती में पवार का दबदबा बना हुआ है। पवार की बेटी सुप्रिया सुले बारामती से तीन बार सांसद रही हैं और उनके भतीजे

अजित पवार 1991 से यहां से विधायक हैं। एक स्थानीय पत्रकार ने कहा, 'बारामती में पवार की सहमति के बिना कुछ नहीं चलता, वे यहां नए ज़माने के शासक हैं।'

लेकिन 2024 में पवार को एक ऐसी अंदरूनी जंग का सामना करना पड़ा, जिसकी कल्पना शायद किसी ने नहीं की होगी। 2023 में, अपने चाचा से अलग होने के अजित पवार के फ़ैसले ने दादा (अजित) को साहेब (शरद) के ख़िलाफ़ खड़ा कर दिया। पवार की पार्टी राष्ट्रवादी कांग्रेस पार्टी (एनसीपी) दो फाड़ हो गई, दोनों गुट पार्टी के नाम और चिन्ह को लेकर एक-दूसरे से जूझ रहे थे। जैसा पहले ज़िक्र किया गया, गृहमंत्री शाह ने अजित पवार को भाजपा के साथ आने के वक्त एक कड़ी शर्त रखी, अजित को अपनी पत्नी सुनेत्रा को अपनी चचेरी बहन सुप्रिया के ख़िलाफ़ चुनाव में उतारना होगा। पुरानी दुश्मनी से अब भी दुखी शाह किसी भी कीमत पर शरद पवार को उनके घर में ही हराना चाहते थे। महाराष्ट्र सरकार में भाजपा के उप-मुख्यमंत्री देवेन्द्र फड़नवीस की भी यही इच्छा थी। बताया गया कि जब एक प्रमुख उद्योगपति ने पवार परिवार की अंदरूनी लड़ाई को टालने के लिए दख़ल की कोशिश की, तब शाह का संदेश साफ था, 'इस बार बारामती पर कोई समझौता नहीं होगा।'

सुप्रिया ताई (बहन) बनाम सुनेत्रा वाहिनी (भाभी) 2024 में महाराष्ट्र की राजनीति में सबसे ज़्यादा दांव पर लगी पारिवारिक लड़ाई थी। एक पारिवारिक मित्र ने टिप्पणी की, 'वे लोग एक खुशहाल परिवार की तरह सभी त्योहारों पर मिलते हैं, चाहे वो गणेश चतुर्थी हो, दिवाली हो, लेकिन चुनाव में एक-दूसरे को हराने के लिए जी-जान से लड़ रहे हैं, यह पागलपन है।' पश्चिमी महाराष्ट्र में पचास साल से प्रतिष्ठित राजनीतिक विरासत जोख़िम में थी।

मुंह के कैंसर से पीड़ित रहे 83 साल के शरद पवार ने अपनी बेटी सुप्रिया की चुनावी लड़ाई को अपने लिए प्रतिष्ठा का सवाल बना लिया था, उनकी जीत ही उनके घावों के लिए मरहम का काम करेगी। चौसठ साल के अजित पवार के लिए एनसीपी से अलग होना, अपने चाचा की छाया से बाहर निकलने और महाराष्ट्र में नेतृत्व के दावे का एक मौका था। दंबग अजित का नेटवर्क बहुत बड़ा है और वे चुनावों के प्रबंधन को समझते हैं। जब वे सुबह 6 बजे अपने विशाल बंगले में साक्षात्कार के लिए राजी हो गए, तब उनके समर्थकों की कतार उनसे मिलने के लिए लगी हुई थी। मैंने उनसे पूछा कि शाह ने जो मुझे बताया पहले उसकी पुष्टि करें। क्या गृहमंत्री ने वरिष्ठ पवार से बदला लेने की इच्छा से उन्हें चचेरी बहन के ख़िलाफ़ अपनी पत्नी को उम्मीदवार बनाने के लिए मजबूर किया था? अजीत ने कहा, 'मुझे कोई भी मजबूर नहीं कर सकता, मैं वही कर रहा हूं, जो हमारी पार्टी के लिए सबसे अच्छा है, परिवार बाद में आता है।' लेकिन राजनीति में नई, रिटायर्ड, विनम्र सुनेत्रा वोट मांगने वाली राजनेता की अपनी नई भूमिका में असहज दिख रही थीं। कम बोलने वाली सुनेत्रा, मीडिया फोकस से परेशान थीं। 'कृपया, मुझसे ज़्यादा सवाल न पूछें,' उन्होंने आग्रह किया।

इसके विपरीत, ज़िंदादिल और मिलनसार सुप्रिया सुले को कैमरे से कोई परेशानी नहीं होती। मुंबई के एक अंग्रेज़ी माध्यम स्कूल में पढ़ी सुप्रिया संसद में विभिन्न मुद्दों पर असरदार तरीके से बोलती हैं। लेकिन ज़्यादातर समय मुंबई और दिल्ली में रहने की वजह से, वह बारामती में चुनाव प्रचार के लिए अजित पवार के संपर्कों पर निर्भर थीं। अजित ने कथित तौर पर अपने समर्थकों को सुप्रिया की बैठकों से दूर रहने के लिए कहा था। एक स्थानीय एनसीपी नेता ने कहा, 'दादा, एक ज़मीनी नेता हैं, लेकिन दंबग हैं और बारामती में बहुत से लोग उनसे डरते हैं।'

जहां अजित पवार लोगों के इस डर का फायदा उठा रहे थे, वहीं शरद पवार उनसे सहानुभूति की उम्मीद कर रहे थे, क्योंकि जिस पार्टी को उन्होंने बनाया, उसे उनके महत्वाकांक्षी भतीजे ने तोड़ दिया और सार्वजनिक रूप से उनसे राजनीति से संन्यास लेने को कहा। सीनियर पवार को न केवल राजनीतिक परिवार के मुखिया के तौर पर देखा जाता है, बल्कि बारामती के बाज़ारों में उनकी प्रतिष्ठा ऐसे नेता की है, जिसने एक गुमनाम कस्बे को राष्ट्रीय नक्शे पर ला दिया था। अपने चचेरे भाई के विश्वासघात के बावज़ूद, सुप्रिया सुले ने अपने प्रतिद्वन्दी के ख़िलाफ कुछ भी बोलने से इंकार किया। सुप्रिया ने ज़ोर देकर कहा, 'मैं नकारात्मक अभियान नहीं चलाऊंगी और सार्वजनिक रूप से कोई गंदी बात नहीं कहने वाली। लोगों को मेरे सांसद के काम के आधार पर मुझे वोट देने दें।' उन्होंने माना कि परिवार के सदस्य के सामने चुनाव लड़ना आसान नहीं था। इसके अलावा उनके सामने एक और बड़ी परेशानी थी, एनसीपी का जाना-पहचाना चुनाव चिन्ह 'घड़ी' अब अजित पवार गुट के पास था। हर भाषण में उन्हें मतदाताओं को याद दिलाना पड़ता था कि वह इस बार नए चुनाव चिन्ह 'तुतारी' (संगीत वाद्ययंत्र) पर चुनाव लड़ रही थीं।

एनसीपी के मतदाता जहां, चुनाव चिन्ह को लेकर भ्रम में थे, वहीं भाजपा मतदाता, बदलते राजनीतिक समीकरणों से हैरान थे। आखिरकार, प्रधानमंत्री मोदी समेत भाजपा के नेताओं ने पहले अजित पवार पर बड़े पैमाने पर भ्रष्टाचार के आरोप लगाए थे। 2014 की एक चुनावी रैली में, देवेन्द्र फड़नवीस ने अजित पवार को जेल भेजने की बात की थी। जब इस दुविधा को भाजपा के एक स्थानीय नेता ने पार्टी आलाकमान के सामने रखा तो शाह ने उन्हें चुप करा दिया। शाह ने चेतावनी दी, 'अगर आप अजित पवार के लिए काम नहीं करेंगे, तो आपको विधानसभा का टिकट नहीं मिलेगा।' घबराए राजनेता ने अनिच्छा से उनकी बात मान ली।

पूरे पश्चिमी महाराष्ट्र में ऐसी ही कहानी चल रही थी। भाजपा कार्यकर्ताओं से उन्हीं एनसीपी नेताओं के लिए प्रचार करने को कहा जा रहा था, जिनका वे बरसों से विरोध करते रहे थे। सतारा के एक भाजपा नेता ने गुस्से में कहा, 'दिल्ली में एक तरफ प्रधानमंत्री भ्रष्टाचार और वंशवाद की राजनीति के ख़िलाफ़ लड़ने की बात करते हैं और दूसरी तरफ यहां हमें अजित पवार के साथ खड़े होने को कहा जा रहा है, जिन्हें हमारे नेता अक्सर भ्रष्टाचार और वंशवाद की राजनीति के लिए निशाना बनाते रहे हैं।'

पवार परिवार का सत्ता का खेल सुर्खियों में बना रहा, लेकिन महाराष्ट्र के इस इलाके के मतदाता आजीविका के गंभीर संकट का सामना कर रहे थे। लंबे समय से कम बारिश से पानी की भयंकर कमी हो गई और गांववालों की परेशानियां बढ़ गई थीं। गांव के लोग पानी के लिए लंबी लाइनों में खड़े थे, उन्हें प्राइवेट टैंकर से एक ड्रम पानी के लिए हर हफ्ते दो सौ रुपये देने पड़ते थे। हम कुछ गांववालों से मिले, लेकिन उनकी दिलचस्पी चुनावों में नहीं थी, उनकी चिंताएं और भी थीं। एक अधेड़ उम्र की महिला ने गुस्से में कहा, 'मुझे इससे कोई फ़र्क नहीं पड़ता कि कौन पवार जीतेगा, मुझे तो पानी चाहिए।' लेकिन ऐसे लोगों की तादाद ज़्यादा नहीं थी। ज्यादातर लोगों ने कहा, वे सुप्रिया को वोट देंगे। एक बुज़ुर्ग किसान ने कहा, 'यह हमारी अस्मिता का सवाल है, हमें ऐसे गद्दार नहीं चाहिएं, जो अपने ही परिवार को धोखा देते हैं।'

'गद्दार' ऐसा ताकतवर शब्द, जो महाराष्ट्र की राजनीति में अराजकता और कटुता का प्रतीक बन गया था, यह उस घटिया सौदेबाजी की याद दिलाता है जिसने सत्तारूढ़ गठबंधन को परेशान किया। टीम मोदी-शाह के निर्देशों पर राज्य के दो क्षेत्रीय दलों को दोफाड़ कर दिया गया था, और इस काम को देवेन्द्र फड़नवीस ने अंज़ाम दिया। 'बांटो और राज करो' की उनकी योजना को सोची-समझी राजनीतिक रणनीति के रूप में छिपाने की कोशिश की गई हो, लेकिन मतदाता को यह खेल समझ आ गया था। राज्य की राजनीति में गुस्सा और सत्ता विरोधी हवा बह रही थी। मतगणना के दिन, सुप्रिया और उनकी भाभी के बीच में शुरुआत में कुछ मुकाबला सा लग रहा था, लेकिन धीरे-धीरे सुप्रिया आगे निकल गईं और फिर डेढ़ लाख वोटों से चुनाव जीत गईं। बारामती में पवार के बीच लड़ाई, फिलहाल के लिए तय हो गई थी। महाराष्ट्र में भाजपा के नेतृत्व वाले गठबंधन को 48 में से केवल 17 सीटें मिलीं, जबकि 2019 में उसने 41 सीटें जीती थीं। भाजपा सिर्फ़ 9 सीटें जीत पाई। विदर्भ में दलित मतदाताओं के कांग्रेस के साथ जाने और मराठवाड़ा में मराठा आरक्षण से जातिगत फूट होने तक, महाराष्ट्र की राजनीति गहरे मंथन के दौर से गुजर रही थी।

उत्तर प्रदेश की तरह यहां भी, सत्ता की अंदरूनी लड़ाई भाजपा का नुकसान कर रही थी। बेहतर प्रदर्शन करने वाले केन्द्रीय मंत्री नितिन गड़करी को लगता था कि मुंबई और दिल्ली में बैठी ताकतें नागपुर के उनके गढ़ में हराने के लिए लगी हुई थीं। राजधानी के सत्ता के गलियारों में गडकरी को साफ बोलने वाला इकलौता मंत्री माना जाता है, जो मोदी-शाह की टीम की लाइन पर आंख मूंदकर नहीं चलते। उनके गढ़ में ही बहुत से मतदाताओं के नाम मतदाता सूची से गायब पाए गए थे। वे प्रचार के दौरान उत्साहित नहीं दिखते थे, लेकिन उन्होंने 1 लाख तीस हज़ार वोटों से जीत हासिल की। गंभीर डायबिटीज के रोगी गडकरी अपनी एक रैली में, भीषण गर्मी की वजह से बेहोश हो गए थे। उन्होंने एक भाजपा नेता से कहा, 'मैं पार्टी का वफ़ादार सिपाही हूं, लेकिन मुझसे एक सीमा से ज़्यादा पूरे महाराष्ट्र के प्रचार में शामिल होने की उम्मीद न करें।'

महाराष्ट्र में हार, मोदी-शाह टीम और भाजपा की प्रदेश इकाई के लिए एक बड़ा झटका थी, जिसकी संभावना नहीं लग रही थी। पराजित फड़नवीस ने अपने इस्तीफ़े की पेशकश की, जिसे ठुकरा दिया गया। पार्टी में उनके आलोचकों ने उन पर दूसरे नेताओं को दरकिनार करने और किसी से सलाह किए बिना फ़ैसले करने का आरोप लगाया। सदमे में आए शाह चुप रहे। पवार को मात देने की योजना बुरी तरफ नाकाम रही।

देश के दो सबसे बड़े चुनावी राज्यों में हवा नाटकीय रूप से बदल गई थी।

═

अयोध्या में राम मंदिर का उद्घाटन हुए अभी एक पखवाड़ा बीता था कि फरवरी 2024 के पहले सप्ताह में, भाजपा के चुनावी रणनीतिकारों के लिए सुखद ख़बर थी। पार्टी के साप्ताहिक ट्रैकर सर्वेक्षण में पश्चिम बंगाल में भाजपा आगे बढ़ रही थी, मंदिर मुद्दे को लेकर काफी चर्चा थी और प्रधानमंत्री मोदी की लोकप्रियता भी चरम पर बताई गई। सर्वेक्षण में पश्चिम बंगाल में कम से कम 25 सीटें मिलने की भविष्यवाणी की गई। भारतीय जनता पार्टी के पास सिर्फ़ एक ही सर्वेक्षण टीम नहीं है। राजनीतिक सलाह देने वाली फर्म, 'नेशन विद नमो' (जिसे पहले एसोसिएशन ऑफ बिलियन माइंड्स कहा जाता था), पूरी तरह से टीम मोदी-शाह की 'इन-हाउस ग्राउंड-फीडबैक' एजेंसी के रूप में काम करती है। इसके अलावा दूसरी कंपनियों में एक 'एक्सिस माई इंडिया' है, जो बड़े जनमत सर्वेक्षण करती है। 'वराहे एनालिटिक्स', खासतौर से दक्षिणी राज्यों में डेटा पर काम करता है। सभी सर्वेक्षणों का इशारा एक ही था। बंगाल में भाजपा सत्तारूढ़ तृणमूल कांग्रेस के काफी आगे थी। पार्टी नेतृत्व का मानना था, बंगाल जैसे बड़े राज्य में हम दूसरी जगह के नुकसान को पूरा कर सकते हैं। 2019 में, भाजपा ने बंगाल में 42 में से 18 सीटें जीती थीं। लंबे समय से राज्य में संघर्ष कर रही पार्टी के लिए यह बड़ा बदलाव था। अब वो और बड़ा लक्ष्य बना रही थी।

दिलचस्प यह है कि टीएमसी के आंतरिक सर्वेक्षण भी भाजपा के बढ़ते ग्राफ को दिखा रहे थे। इससे पहले तक उन्हें लगता था कि वह भाजपा को पीछे छोड़ देगी, इसलिए मुख्यमंत्री ममता बनर्जी शुरुआत में कांग्रेस-वामपंथी गठबंधन से निपटने की तैयारी में लगी थीं। उनकी रणनीति ममता विरोधी वोटों को प्रतिद्वन्दियों के बीच बांटने की थी। हालांकि राम मंदिर के उत्साह से भाजपा के आगे बढ़ने से समीकरण बदलने लगे थे। लोकसभा चुनावों के ऐलान से कुछ दिन पहले, केन्द्र सरकार ने नागरिकता संशोधन क़ानून (सीएए) के नियमों को तैयार करने का फ़ैसला किया। इससे पहले जनवरी 2020 में अधिनियम की अधिसूचना जारी की गई थी, तब से 1521 दिनों में उसे नौ बार एक्सटेंशन दिया गया। शाह ने घोषणा की, 'हमने एक और वादा, प्रतिबद्धता को पूरा कर दिया है।' इसका फ़ैसला बांग्लादेश से पलायन करके आए बंगाल के बड़े हिंदु मतुआ समुदाय को लुभाने के लिए किया गया था।

लेकिन पार्टी ने खुद को सिर्फ़ हिन्दू कार्ड खेलने तक ही सीमित नहीं रखा। फरवरी के मध्य में, सुंदरबन के एक नदी के किनारे के द्वीप संदेशखाली के एक गांव की महिलाओं ने तृणमूल कांग्रेस के स्थानीय कद्दावर नेता शेख शाहजहां और उनके लोगों पर ज़मीन हड़पने और यौन शोषण के आरोप लगाए। संदेशखाली करीब एक महीने तक राष्ट्रीय मीडिया की सुर्खियां बना रहा। महिला मतदाता, मुख्यमंत्री ममता बनर्जी का सुरक्षित वोट बैंक था, लेकिन संदेशखाली में लगे आरोपों से इसको नुकसान पहुंचा। अगर महिला मतदाता उनसे दूर हो गईं तो बनर्जी मुश्किल में पड़ सकती थीं। जब मैंने संदेशखाली की घटनाओं पर उनसे प्रतिक्रिया मांगी, तो उन्होंने गुस्से में जवाब दिया, 'आप दिल्ली में बैठे लोग, भाजपा के दुष्प्रचार में आ गए हैं; यह सब बंगाल को बदनाम करने की साज़िश है।'

2021 के पश्चिम बंगाल विधानसभा चुनावों की तरह, बनर्जी इस बार भी अपने ही चिर-परिचित पिच पर खेलते हुए मोदी सरकार को बंगाल विरोधी के तौर पर पेश कर रही थीं। तृणमूल कांग्रेस के अभियान पर काम कर रहे (I-PAC) के सदस्य प्रतीक जैन ने कहा, 'हमारे ट्रैकर पोल के हिसाब से जो लोग दीदी को सीएम देखना चाहते थे, वही मोदी को पीएम देखना चाहते थे, यही हमारे लिए बड़ी दुविधा थी।' अपने महिला वोट को जोड़े रखने के लिए ममता बनर्जी ने पहले कदम के तौर पर 'लाखिर भंडार' योजना में महिलाओं के लिए मासिक सहायता को दोगुना करके एक हज़ार रुपये कर दिया। उन्होंने बंगाल की महिलाओं से कहा, 'मोदी सरकार हमें फंड देने से रोकती है, लेकिन मैं हमेशा आपके साथ खड़ी रहूंगी।'

तीन बार मुख्यमंत्री, चार बार केन्द्रीय मंत्री और सात बार सांसद रह चुकी अनुभवी राजनेता ममता अपने काम को व्यवस्थित तरीके से कर रही थीं और चतुराई से योजना बना रही थीं, लेकिन भाजपा ने खुद ही अपने नुकसान का बटन दबा दिया। पार्टी की प्रदेश इकाई में हमेशा ही गुटबाज़ी चलती रही है। एक तरफ आरएसएस से जुड़े पुराने लोग और दूसरी तरफ टीएमसी के दलबदलुओं के बीच झगड़ा चलता रहता है। मुश्किल तब और बढ़ गई, जब भाजपा ने अपनी पहली सूची में भोजपुरी गायक-अभिनेता पवन सिंह का नाम शामिल किया। सिंह को टीएमसी के अभिनेता-राजनेता और भाजपा सांसद रहे शत्रुघ्न सिन्हा के ख़िलाफ़ आसनसोल से चुनाव लड़ना था। आरोप है कि तब पार्टी में ही उनके प्रतिद्वन्दी ने पवन सिंह के बंगाली महिलाओं को अशोभनीय तरीके से दिखाने वाले उनके भद्दे और अश्लील म्यूज़िक वीडियो लीक करवा दिए। इसके ख़िलाफ़ महिला संगठनों, टीएमसी सांसदों और भाजपा के भी स्थानीय नेताओं के मुखर विरोध के बाद पार्टी को उनका नाम घोषित करने के चौबीस घंटे के भीतर नाम वापस लेने पर मजबूर होना पड़ा। यह बंगाल में भाजपा के लिए एक शुरुआती झटका था।

भाजपा जैसी सुव्यवस्थित पार्टी में आमतौर पर पवन सिंह जैसे प्रकरण के बारे में सोचा भी नहीं जा सकता, लेकिन इस घटना ने पार्टी में दरारों को सामने ला दिया। गायक-अभिनेता पवन सिंह कहीं से भी चुनाव लड़ने के इच्छुक थे। बिहारी बाबू सिन्हा के ख़िलाफ़ उन्हें उतारने का

विचार दिल्ली में जल्दबाज़ी में, पृष्ठभूमि की जांच किए बिना और प्रदेश इकाई से औपचारिक सहमति लिए बिना रखा गया था। गृहमंत्री शाह ने बंगाल में टिकट बंटवारे का काम अपने भरोसेमंद सहयोगी और पार्टी महासचिव सुनील बंसल पर छोड़ दिया था। बंसल, बंगाल में भाजपा के विपक्ष के नेता सुवेंदु अधिकारी की सलाह पर काम कर रहे थे। अधिकारी, 2020 में तृणमूल से भाजपा में शामिल हुए थे और भाजपा में अपना प्रभुत्व बनाना चाहते थे। उन पर पार्टी के पुराने नेताओं को दरकिनार करने के आरोप लगाए गए। पार्टी के प्रदेश अध्यक्ष और मिदनापुर से सांसद दिलीप घोष को उनकी इच्छा के ख़िलाफ़ दुर्गापुर चुनाव लड़ने के लिए भेज दिया गया। एक सर्वेक्षण के मुताबिक उनका आधार कमज़ोर हो रहा था। भाजपा दोनों ही सीटें हार गई। भाजपा के प्रदेश के एक नेता की शिकायत थी, 'अधिकारी और पार्टी आलाकमान के इर्दगिर्द की ताकतवर मंडली ने बंगाल में जो कुछ हो रहा था, उससे हमें अलग कर दिया था।' पहले 'आलाकमान' शब्द का इस्तेमाल, कांग्रेस पर गांधी परिवार की पकड़ बताने के लिए किया जाता था, अब मोदी-शाह युग में यह भाजपा में भी आ गया है।

भाजपा जब अंदरूनी संघर्षों से जूझ रही थी, तब टीएमसी जिम्मेदारी के स्पष्ट विभाजन के साथ अपने अभियान को आगे बढ़ा रही थीः ममता बनर्जी स्टार प्रचारक थीं, तो भतीजे अभिषेक बनर्जी संगठन की पूरी ज़िम्मेदारी संभाल रहे थे। कुछ स्टार चेहरों को अपने साथ लाने के लिए पार्टी ने एक गुगली फेंकी, जब उसने 2011 के विश्व कप विजेता टीम में रहे यूसुफ पठान को बहरामपुर से कांग्रेस के पांच बार के सांसद अधीर रंजन चौधरी के ख़िलाफ़ मैदान में उतार दिया। बनर्जी, चौधरी को हराने के लिए दृढ़ थीं, जो लगातार उन पर हमला करते हुए उनका अपमान कर रहे थे। 'हमने सोचा कि मुस्लिम समुदाय से एक सेलिब्रिटी चेहरे को लाना जीत के लिए अच्छा रहेगा,' पोल रणनीतिकार जैन ने कहा; मुस्लिम तृणमूल के एक और टिकाऊ वोट बैंक का हिस्सा हैं। गुजरात में वडोदरा के पठान ने इंडियन प्रीमियर लीग में कोलकाता नाइटराइडर्स (केकेआर) के लिए खेला था, बाकी क्रिकेट के दूसरे प्रारूपों से उन्होंने काफी पहले ही संन्यास ले लिया था। यूसुफ कहते हैं, 'मैं दिग्गजों के एक क्रिकेट कार्यक्रम के लिए श्रीलंका जा रहा था, तब अचानक मुझसे किसी ने संपर्क करके कहा, वह ममता दी और अभिषेक के कार्यालय से बोल रहा है और मेरे चुनाव लड़ने की संभावना पर बात करना चाहता है। मेरी पहली प्रतिक्रिया तो मजबूती से "ना" कहने की थी।' लेकिन जब फ़ोन करने वाले ने ज़ोर दिया तो यूसुफ ने अपने भाई और क्रिकेट स्टार रहे इरफान से सलाह मांगी। यूसुफ ने केकेआर के दो कार्यक्रमों में पश्चिम बंगाल की मुख्यमंत्री से दो बार मुलाक़ात की थी। इरफान ने एक बॉलीवुड स्टार के साथ मिलकर यूसुफ को चुनाव लड़ने को राजी किया, जो पहले तैयार नहीं थे। चुनाव में 'सेलिब्रिटी' रणनीति काम आई। पहली बार चुनावी मैदान पर उतरे यूसुफ ने दिग्गज चौधरी को 80 हज़ार वोटों से हरा दिया। क्रिकेट के मैदान पर स्टार अब राजनीतिक पिच पर एक मुस्लिम चेहरा बन गया था और उसने सफलतापूर्वक मुस्लिम वोट को अपने पीछे एकजुट कर लिया।

लेकिन 2024 में, पश्चिम बंगाल में लड़ाई के भीतर असली लड़ाई कृष्णानगर में लड़ी गई। यहां, जालंगी नदी के दक्षिणी तट पर, ममता बनर्जी ने अपने चुनाव अभियान की शुरुआत की और प्रधानमंत्री एक ही सीट पर दो अलग-अलग मौकों पर प्रचार के लिए पहुंचे, जो कि आमतौर पर नहीं होता। यहां टीएमसी की सुर्खियां बटोरने वाली मुखर महुआ मोइत्रा का भविष्य दांव पर था। महुआ मोइत्रा उन कुछ सांसदों में से हैं, जिन्होंने अपनी पहली संसदीय पारी में बहुत से उतार-चढाव देखे हैं। मोइत्रा ने पहली बार 2019 में लोकसभा चुनाव जीता था। उनका संसद में भावुक पहला भाषण इंटरनेट पर वायरल हो गया था, जिसमें उन्होंने मोदी सरकार पर हमला बोलते हुए बढ़ते फासीवाद के शुरुआती संकेतों की चेतावनी थी। एक स्टार का जन्म हुआ। 'बचपन से ही मुझे बातें करना का शौक रहा है, इसलिए भाषण मेरे लिए स्वाभाविक है, लेकिन मैं उस भाषण पर मिली प्रतिक्रिया से हैरान थी क्योंकि जब सत्ता के सामने सच बोलना भी साहसिक काम माना जाता है, तब आपको अहसास होता है कि डर कितना गहरा है,' उन्होंने कहा।

देश के वामपंथी, उदारवादी अभिजात वर्ग के लिए, हिन्दुत्व की राजनीति का बढ़ता प्रभुत्व तनाव का विषय था, ऐसे में मोइत्रा का उदय ताज़ा हवा के झोंके सा था। कुछ लोग उन्हें 'ख़ान मार्केट गैंग' भी कहते हैं। दक्षिणपंथी विचारकों की राजनीतिक दुनिया में एक उनचास साल की, अच्छा बोलने वाली महिला ने ज़ोरदार जवाब दिया था। एक बेहतर अमेरीकी कालेज में पढ़ी, पूर्व निवेश बैंकर और अंग्रेज़ीदां तेज़ सांसद, मोइत्रा, अपनी बेहतरीन साड़ियों, ब्रांडेड सामान के साथ तीक्ष्ण बुद्धि वाली शहरी संस्कारों वाली महिला हैं, जो किसी राजनीतिक परिवार से नहीं थीं। मोइत्रा रूढ़िवादी हिंदू राजनीति पर सवाल खड़े कर सकती थीं। मोइत्रा ने कहा, 'मैं ठेठ कोलकाता के बॉक्सवाला परिवार में एक चाय बागान में पली-बढ़ी हूं। मैंने हमेशा सुना कि भारतीय राजनीति गंदी है, और उसके लिए राजनीतिक परिवार और करोड़ों रुपये चाहिएं। मैंने इस धारणा को गलत साबित करने के लिए राजनीति में आने का फ़ैसला किया।'

ठीक चार साल बाद, दिसम्बर 2023 में, 17वीं लोकसभा के कार्यकाल पूरा होने से कुछ महीनों पहले मोइत्रा खबरों में थीं, लेकिन इस बार सभी गलत कारणों से। उन्हें संसद से निष्काषित कर दिया गया। संसदीय आचार समिति ने उन पर रिश्वत लेने, संसद का लॉग-इन और पासवर्ड का विवरण, दुबई के एक कारोबारी के साथ साझा करने का आरोप लगाया। प्रसिद्धि और बदनामी के बीच रेखा बहुत महीन हो सकती है। एक उभरते राजनीतिक सितारे के संसदीय करियर पर अचानक अंधेरा छा गया था। 'यह पूरी तरह से अजीब है। आचार समिति का गठन लोकसभा अध्यक्ष ओम बिड़ला ने "कंगारू कोर्ट" की तरह किया था, जिसका एजेंडा मुझे किसी भी कीमत पर बाहर निकालना था। मुझे उन लोगों से जिरह भी नहीं करने दी गई, जिन्होंने मुझ पर यह घिनौने आरोप लगाए,' मोइत्रा नाराजगी से कहती हैं। मोइत्रा संसद के अंदर और बाहर, मोदी सरकार पर लगातार निशाना साधने के लिए जानी जाती थीं, खासतौर

पर उन्होंने बड़े कारोबारी गौतम अडानी के विदेशी फंडिग के स्रोत और प्रधानमंत्री के साथ उनके कथित संबंधों को निशाना बनाया था। उन्होंने भाजपा सांसद निशिकांत दुबे पर अपनी डॉक्टरेट की डिग्री में जालसाजी करने का आरोप लगाया था। मोइत्रा जब भी संसद में बोलतीं, सत्ता पक्ष की तरफ से दुबे उन्हें टोकने की कोशिश करते। सांसद और लोकसभा अध्यक्ष के बीच भी रिश्तों में कोई मिठास नहीं थी। विपक्ष को बोलने के समान अवसर नहीं देने पर दोनों के बीच अक्सर टकराव होता था। उनके आलोचकों का कहना था कि मोइत्रा शुरुआती प्रशंसा में बह गई थीं और 'ध्यान आकर्षित करने वाली दिवा' की तरह व्यवहार करती थीं। उन्होंने कहा, 'अगर आप जिस पर यकीन करते हैं, उस पर कायम रहते हैं तो परवाह न करें, लोगों को जो कहना है, कहने दें।'

महुआ मोइत्रा का निष्कासन चौंकाने वाला था। अक्टूबर 2023 में, दिल्ली के एक युवा वकील जय देहाद्राय, ने मुझे और कुछ और पत्रकारों को फ़ोन करके कहा कि उनके पास एक टीएमसी सांसद के ख़िलाफ विस्फोटक सामग्री थी। मोइत्रा ने जय को अपना 'पूर्व प्रेमी' कहा था। मैंने तृणमूल कांग्रेस देखने वाले अपने एक सहयोगी को उनसे संपर्क करने के लिए कहा। लेकिन देहाद्राय के खुलासा करने से पहले ही भाजपा सांसद निशिकांत दुबे ने एक प्रेस-कॉन्फ्रेंस कर दावा किया कि मोइत्रा संसद में सवाल पूछने के लिए पैसे लेने की दोषी थीं। देहाद्राय और दुबे के आरोप मिलते-जुलते थे, जो अपने पालतु कुत्ते, रॉटवीलर हेनरी को लेकर मोइत्रा के साथ झगड़ा कर रहे थे। लगता था कि देहाद्राय और दुबे, मोइत्रा के ख़िलाफ़ एक साथ काम कर रहे थे। दोनों मुख्य शिकायतकर्ता बन गए। इस कथित रिश्वत मामले के केन्द्र में रहे दुबई के कारोबारी दर्शन हीरानंदानी ने भी मोइत्रा के पासवर्ड तक अपनी पहुंच होने की बात हलफनामा देकर स्वीकार की थी, लेकिन अजीब बात यह थी कि उन्हें आचार समिति के सामने नहीं बुलाया गया। पर्दे के पीछे के इस नाटक में दर्शन के पिता और मुंबई में प्रमुख रियल एस्टेट के कारोबारी निरंजन हीरानंदानी, ईडी के जांच के दायरे में आ गए। मोइत्रा का कहना था, 'दर्शन एक मित्र हैं, जिन्हें मोदी सरकार के दबाव में हलफनामे पर दस्तख़त करने के लिए मजबूर किया गया। इसमें कोई नकद लेनदेन शामिल नहीं था, यह सब अडानी की ओर से रची गई कहानी थी।' दुबे का कहना है कि 'कैश के बदले सवाल पूछताछ मामले में सार्वजनिक हित में काम कर रहे थे।' दुबे ने ज़ोर देकर कहा, एक सांसद को अपने अनुचित आचरण की क़ीमत तो चुकानी होगी।

मोइत्रा का कहना है कि इसका सबसे खराब या लोएस्ट पांइट, जनवरी 2024 में आया, जब वह हिस्टेरेक्टॉमी के बाद, अस्पताल में भर्ती थीं और उन्हें एस्टेट विभाग से बेदखली का नोटिस दिया गया। उन्होंने दिल्ली उच्च न्यायालय में अपील की, लेकिन कोई फायदा नहीं हुआ। क्या किसी सांसद के साथ ऐसा बर्ताव किया जाएगा, जब तक कि उसका एजेंडा केवल उन्हें अपमानित करना ना हो।

उनके सबसे बुरे वक्त में मोइत्रा को, बंगाल की मुख्यमंत्री कट्टर सहयोगी की तरह मिलीं। ममता बनर्जी खुद को वंचितों के साथ रखने में गौरव महसूस करती हैं और बंगाल के लोगों की चुनी गई सांसद के उत्पीड़न से नाराज़ थीं। कृष्णानगर से चुनाव अभियान की शुरुआत करते हुए बनर्जी ने कहा, 'भाजपा ने आपके सांसद को ग़लत तरीके से निकालकर उन्हें निशाना बनाया है। अब आपको, उनकी संसद सदस्यता और अपना गौरव बहाल करना होगा।' घायल बंगाली गौरव और अत्याचारी दिल्ली के बीच की लड़ाई का फ़ैसला अब जनता की अदालत में होना था। प्रधानमंत्री मोदी भी कृष्णानगर की जंग के मैदान में उतर आए। उन्होंने ज़िले में न केवल दो-दो सभाएं की, बल्कि भाजपा की उम्मीदवार राजमाता अमृता रॉय के साथ एक वीडियो कॉन्फ्रेंस भी की। अमृता रॉय, खुद को यहां के शाही परिवार से जोड़ती हैं। विधायक और सांसद के तौर पर मोइत्रा इस इलाके में दस साल से भी ज़्यादा समय से सक्रिय हैं, वहीं रॉय एक राजनीतिक नौसिखिया थीं, उनको मोदी की अपील और बीजेपी मशीनरी पर भरोसा था। भाजपा के एक पदाधिकारी ने कहा, 'बंगाल में टिकट बंटवारे में हमने कई गलतियां कीं, यह भी एक और गलती थी।' बनर्जी के मजबूती से उनके साथ खड़ी होने से, जोश से भरी मोइत्रा ने 56,000 से ज़्यादा वोटों से जीत हासिल की। तृणमूल सांसद ने कहा, 'मेरी नेता सभी शेरनियों को मात देने वाली शेरनी है... जो ज़रूरत पड़ने पर एक दर्ज़न मोदी से मुकाबला कर सकती हैं।'

भारतीय राजनीति में 'जेंडर पावर' एक दोधारी तलवार जैसी है। पितृ सत्तात्मक रूढ़िवादिता इस असमान लड़ाई में गहरे तक जड़ें जमा चुकी है। अगर कोई महिला नेता अपनी बात पर अड़ी रहती है, तो उस पर ज्यादा हमले होते हैं। देश की इकलौती महिला मुख्यमंत्री के रूप में, बनर्जी अक्सर इस सोच की पीड़ित रही हैं, उन्हें तीखे 'सेक्सिस्ट' लहज़े में निशाना बनाया गया है, जो शायद किसी पुरूष मुख्यमंत्री के साथ कोई नहीं करेगा। मोइत्रा को भी मीडिया और राजनीतिक ट्रायल का सामना करना पड़ा। मामले के तथ्यों के साथ-साथ, उनके चरित्र पर सवाल उठाए गए। मोइत्रा को कोई पछतावा नहीं है। उन्होंने कहा, 'मुझे बिल्कुल पछतावा नहीं है। मैं इनमें से कुछ भी किसी और तरीके से नहीं करती और मुझे उम्मीद है कि मैं दूसरे लोगों को भी कभी हार नहीं मानने की भावना से जीने के लिए प्रेरित करूंगी'।

मोइत्रा 2024 में जीतने वाली 12 टीएमसी महिला सासंदों में से एक थीं। प्रतिशत के हिसाब से किसी भी पार्टी से ज़्यादा, तृणमूल कांग्रेस ने बंगाल में कुल 28 सीटें जीती थी। बीजेपी, अपने सर्वेक्षण से बहुत कम, केवल 12 सीटें ही जीत पाई। टीएमसी के राज्यसभा में नेता डेरेक ओ ब्रायन ने मुस्कुराते हुए कहा, 'भाजपा को शायद अपनी सर्वेक्षण टीम को बदलने की ज़रूरत है, वे बंगाल में लगातार गलतियां कर रहे हैं।' 2021 की तरह, एक बार फिर खुद के लिए बड़ी जीत का अनुमान लगाने के बाद, भाजपा बंगाल में हार गई। एक बार फिर, भगवा सेना को, पोलस्टर्स

ने बुरी तरह धोखा दिया, जो राजनीतिक रूप से जागरूक बंगाल के मतदाता के मन को नहीं पढ़ पाए। उत्तर प्रदेश और महाराष्ट्र के बाद, बंगाल भाजपा के लिए एक और बड़ा झटका था। लेकिन बात यहीं खत्म नहीं हुई। 2019 में भाजपा ने जिन राज्यों में बड़ी जीत हासिल की थी, इस बार, वहां भी जीत मुश्किल लग रही थी।

═

'मुझे डर है कि हम 25-0 से हारने जा रहे हैं,' फरवरी 2024 में, दिल्ली में कांग्रेस पार्टी के पदाधिकारियों की एक बैठक में राजस्थान के एक वरिष्ठ कांग्रेसी नेता ने तकलीफ ज़ाहिर की। बैठक में कई कांग्रेसी नेताओं ने खुद चुनाव लड़ने से भी इंकार कर दिया था। पूरी तरह से आत्मसमर्पण करने वाला निराशावादी नजरिया आश्चर्यजनक नहीं था। भाजपा ने 2014 और 2019 दोनों चुनावों में राजस्थान की सभी 25 सीटें जीती थीं और 2023 के विधानसभा चुनावों में सत्ता में वापसी की। राम मंदिर को भावनात्मक मुद्दे के तौर पर देखने और प्रधानमंत्री मोदी की बढ़ती रेटिंग के साथ भाजपा अजेय लग रही थी। लेकिन इस निराशा के बीच, एक कांग्रेसी नेता इतनी आसानी से हार मानने को तैयार नहीं था। राजस्थान में प्रदेश कांग्रेस अध्यक्ष, 59 साल के गोविंद सिंह डोटासरा एक जुझारू नेता हैं, जिन्होंने अपना राजनीतिक सफ़र सीकर ज़िले से ग्राम प्रधान के रूप में शुरू किया था। सार्वजनिक समारोहों में अक्सर पारंपरिक गुलाबी पगड़ी पहने डोटासरा, तीन बार के विधायक और जाट नेता थे, जिन्हें प्रदेश के बाहर कम लोग जानते थे, जब तक कि उन्हें 2020 में अचानक प्रदेश में पार्टी का प्रमुख नहीं बना दिया गया। राज्य में अशोक गहलोत और सचिन पायलट गुटों में बंटी कांग्रेस को किसी ऐसे ही व्यक्ति की ज़रूरत थी। सीधे-सादे और देहाती डोटासरा के पास न तो पायलट के जैसा ज्ञान था और न ही गहलोत जैसा अनुभव, लेकिन राजनीति में ज़रूरी एक खास गुण उनमें थाः दृढ़ व्यवहार। वह कहते हैं, 'जब मैंने अपने ही एक नेता से यह सुना कि राजस्थान में हमारा सफाया हो जाएगा, तो मैं भड़क गया। जो भी हो, लड़ना तो है, यह मूंछ का सवाल है।'

मार्च की शुरुआत में डोटासरा और कांग्रेस को एक बड़ा मौका मिल गया। शेखावाटी इलाके में जाट समुदाय में अच्छी पकड़ रखने वाले चूरू से दो बार के भाजपा सांसद राहुल कस्वां ने संकेत दिया कि वह भाजपा छोड़कर कांग्रेस में शामिल होने को तैयार थे, बशर्ते उन्हें लोकसभा टिकट की गारंटी दी जाए। युवा, महत्वाकांक्षी नेता कस्वां को वसुंधरा राजे के खेमे का माना जाता था। वह उन खबरों से परेशान थे, जिसमें पार्टी विरोधी गतिविधियों के आरोप में उनका टिकट काटा जा सकता था। कस्वां का पार्टी के वरिष्ठ नेता राजेन्द्र सिंह राठौड़ से सत्ता संघर्ष चल रहा था। राठौड़ ने उन पर विधानसभा चुनावों में उन्हें हराने की साज़िश करने का आरोप लगाया था। उनके साथी जाट नेता के पाला बदलने की इच्छा ने

प्रदेश कांग्रेस अध्यक्ष को उत्साहित कर दिया, जिनका कस्वां परिवार से व्यक्ति संबंध भी था। भाजपा सांसद, उप राष्ट्रपति जगदीप धनखड़ के भी रिश्तेदार थे और उन्होंने भाजपा के शीर्ष नेतृत्व के साथ उनकी तरफ से मध्यस्थता करने के लिए उनसे संपर्क किया था। प्रदेश की लड़ाई में उलझने से बचने के लिए धनखड़ ने कस्वां परिवार से कहा, 'मुझे इससे दूर ही रखें।' दिल्ली में टीम मोदी-शाह के फ़ैसले के बाद जिस दिन कस्वां को टिकट नहीं देने की ख़बर आई—डोटासरा को आधी रात को दस्तक मिली। कस्वां के पिता ने अपने बेटे को कांग्रेस से टिकट देने की बात की। डोटासरा ने कहा, 'ऐसे वक़्त में जब हर कोई कांग्रेस छोड़कर भाजपा में शामिल हो रहा था, यह हमारा मनोबल बढ़ाने वाला टॉनिक था।' अड़तालीस घंटे के अंदर कांग्रेस अध्यक्ष मल्लिकार्जुन खड़गे की मौजूदगी में दिल्ली में जल्दबाजी में एक ज्वाइनिंग समारोह आयोजित किया गया।

इसका संदेश सिर्फ़ यह नहीं था कि लोकसभा चुनाव से कुछ दिन पहले एक भाजपा सांसद, कांग्रेस में शामिल हो गए। राजस्थान के प्रभावशाली जाट समुदाय के लिए संकेत था कि अब कांग्रेस इकलौती ऐसी पार्टी थी, जिसके पास प्रदेश में प्रभावी जाट नेतृत्व था। भाजपा ने जब अपना मुख्यमंत्री ब्राह्मण भजनलाल शर्मा को चुना तो जाति की दरारें और चौड़ी हो गईं। प्रदेश भाजपा के एक नेता ने माना, 'हमें कम से कम एक जाट को उप-मुख्यमंत्री तो बनाना चाहिए था, हमारे पास कांग्रेस के अभियान के मुकाबले किसी बड़े पद पर कोई जाट चेहरा नहीं था।' जाति को लेकर संवेदनशील राज्य में कांग्रेस को अपनी जीत का टिकट मिल गया था।

राजस्थान के शेखावाटी इलाके में जाटों ने कांग्रेस को भरपूर वोट दिया। दलित समुदाय, 'संविधान ख़तरे में हैं', के मुद्दे पर पार्टी के पीछे खड़ा हो गया था तो पूर्वी राजस्थान में गुर्जर-मीणा इलाकों में भी कांग्रेस को बढ़त मिल रही थी। यानी जिस पार्टी का सफाया होने की आशंका थी, माहौल उस कांग्रेस के पक्ष में बदल रहा था। हताशा में, भाजपा के एक वरिष्ठ नेता ने इस उम्मीद से वसुंधरा राजे को फ़ोन किया कि वे लड़खड़ाते चुनाव अभियान को सहारा देंगी। मुख्यमंत्री नहीं बनाने से नाराज़ राजे ने, नेतृत्व के लिए बगावती अंदाज़ में जवाब दिया, 'मैं अब केवल एक विधायक हूं और इसलिए केवल अपने बेटे के लोकसभा क्षेत्र में प्रचार करूंगी।'

मई के पहले सप्ताह में, जब राजस्थान में मतदान पूरा हो गया, तो उत्साहित डोटासरा ने मुझे फ़ोन किया, 'हमें राजस्थान में कम से कम दस सीटें मिलेंगी, अगर इससे एक भी कम मिली, तो मैं राजनीति छोड़ दूंगा।' मैंने पूछा कि क्या मैं उनके दावे को रिकॉर्ड कर लूं, यदि गलत साबित हुए तो मैं मतगणना के दिन इसका इस्तेमाल कर सकता था। 'ज़रूर करिए, लेकिन अगर मेरे आंकड़े सही निकले तो फिर मेरा ज़िक्र करना ना भूलें!' 4 जून को जब कांग्रेस ने राजस्थान में 11 सीटें जीतीं, जो 2019 से एक बड़ा बदलाव था। उस दिन सबसे पहले फ़ोन करने वालों में डोटासरा थे, उन्होंने हंसते हुए कहा, 'उम्मीद है कि अगली बार आप राजस्थान में मुझे अपना

पोलस्टर बनाएंगे।' राजस्थान में भाजपा को अपने अति-आत्मविश्वास और अंदरूनी कलह की कीमत चुकानी पड़ी।

केवल राजस्थान ही नहीं था, जहां चुनावों में 'जाट फैक्टर' ने अहम भूमिका निभाई। पड़ोसी राज्य हरियाणा में भी, जहां जाटों की आबादी 27 फ़ीसद है और राजनीति में उनका बड़ा असर है, वहां भी हालात धीरे-धीरे बदलने लगे। जैसा कि पिछले अध्यायों में बताया गया है कि हरियाणा में जाट कई मुद्दों पर मोदी सरकार के ख़िलाफ़ लामबंद हो रहे थे। किसान आंदोलन से लेकर महिला पहलवानों के विरोध और अग्निपथ योजना के ख़िलाफ़ प्रदर्शनों से साफ था कि जाटों में गुस्सा बढ़ रहा था। 2014 में भाजपा ने गैर-जाट जातियों को मजबूती से अपने साथ लाकर हरियाणा में सरकार बनाई थी और 2019 के लोकसभा चुनावों में भी सभी 10 सीटें जीत ली थीं। 2016 में जब जाट आरक्षण आंदोलन में हिंसा भड़क उठी और ज़मीनी स्तर पर जाट बनाम गैर जाट में खाई बढ़ गई, तो भाजपा ने इसका राजनीतिक फायदा उठाया। लेकिन दस साल में सत्ता-विरोधी भावना भी दिख रही थी। बढ़ती बेरोज़गारी भी एक बड़ी चुनौती थी। 'सेंटर फॉर मॉनिटरिंग इंडियन इकॉनमी' के आंकड़ों के मुताबिक, 2022 में हरियाणा में बेरोज़गारी दर 37.4 फ़ीसद थी, जो देश में सबसे ज़्यादा थी। हरियाणा में भाजपा सरकार का नारा था, 'बिना पर्ची, बिना खर्ची, नौकरी पक्की', अब भ्रष्टाचार के आरोपों के बीच यही नारा पार्टी को मुश्किल में डाल रहा था। सरकारी लाभ के लिए ऑनलाइन पोर्टल के काम नहीं करने से शिकायतों की सूची बढ़ती जा रही थी। हिंदी समाचार वेबसाइट 'लल्लनटॉप' के पत्रकार अभिनव पांडे कहते हैं, 'मैंने जितने प्रदेशों की यात्रा की, उनमें हरियाणा में युवाओं में गुस्सा सबसे ज़्यादा था। कई युवा हताशा में नशे की तरफ बढ़ रहे थे, जो यहां पहले कभी नहीं सुनाई दिया।'

पिछले दशक में हरियाणा में भाजपा के मुख्यमंत्री रहे सत्तर साल के मनोहर लाल खट्टर को राजनीति में वज़नदार नेता नहीं माना जाता है। गंभीर और शांत स्वभाव वाले खट्टर अस्सी के दशक में मोदी के साथ संघ प्रचारक थे और दोनों कुछ समय के लिए एक ही कमरे में रहे थे। भाजपा के एक नेता ने कहा, 'वह व्यक्तिगत तौर पर ईमानदार और प्रधानमंत्री के वफादार हैं।' लेकिन 2023 की शुरुआत में, पार्टी के सर्वेक्षणों में कहा गया कि मुख्यमंत्री की लोकप्रियता तेज़ी से कम हो रही थी। खट्टर को बदलने का फ़ैसला लेने के बाद भी करीब एक साल तक इसे रोके रखा गया क्योंकि मोदी अपने पुराने साथी को अलग नहीं करना चाहते थे और पार्टी में कोई आवाज़ उठाने को तैयार नहीं था। जब मार्च 2024 में, खट्टर की जगह ओबीसी चेहरे नायब सिंह सैनी को मुख्यमंत्री बनाया गया, तब आम चुनावों में कुछ हफ्ते ही बचे थे। भाजपा के एक केन्द्रीय अधिकारी ने माना, 'हरियाणा में बदलाव में हमने बहुत देरी कर दी।'

इसके विपरीत कांग्रेस तैयारी में जुट गई थी। प्रदेश में गुटबाज़ी के लिए जानी जाने वाली पार्टी एकजुट मोर्चा बना रही थी। वह अपने इंडिया गठबंधन के सहयोगी आप को एक सीट

देने के लिए भी तैयार हो गई। चुनाव का नेतृत्व हुड्डा, पिता-पुत्र की जोडी कर रहे थे। केन्द्रीय नेतृत्व ने दोनों को पूरा नियंत्रण सौंप दिया था। दो बार मुख्यनंत्री रहे भूपिंदर सिंह हुड्डा, कांग्रेस के बगावती गुट, जी-23 का हिस्सा रहे थे, लेकिन प्रदेश में पार्टी का चेहरा बनाए जाने और बेटे दीपेन्द्र को राज्यसभा भेजने की संभावना से, वे शांत हो गए थे। अनुभवी राजनेता हुड्डा को दिल्ली जिमखाना में कभी-कभार टेनिस खेलने और इंडिया इटरनेशनल सेंटर में कॉफी पीना पसंद है। वे राहुल गांधी की नई कांग्रेस में पार्टी के बचे हुए पुराने दिग्गजों में से एक हैं। होशियार हुड्डा जानते थे कि 2024 के लोकसभा चुनावों में बेहतर प्रदर्शन ही उनके फिर से मुख्यमंत्री बनने की संभावनाओं को मजबूत करेगा। दीपेन्द्र हुड्डा हर चुनावी सभा में कह रहे थे, 'चंडीगढ़ का रास्ता दिल्ली से होकर जाता है।'

हरियाणा के नतीजों में कांग्रेस और भाजपा में कड़ी टक्कर दिखाई दी। दोनों ने 5-5 सीटें जीती थीं और क्षेत्रीय दलों का सफाया हो गया था। दीपेन्द्र ने राज्य में सबसे ज़्यादा 3 लाख 20 हज़ार वोटों के अंतर से रोहतक सीट जीत ली थी। राजस्थान की तरह यहां भी जाट-दलित गठबंधन ने कांग्रेस को ताकत दी थी। दोनों राज्यों में कांग्रेस ने साबित कर दिया कि वह उत्तर भारत में भाजपा से सीधी लड़ाई में जीत सकती है। इससे पहले 2014 और 2019 में आमने-सामने की टक्कर एकतरफा रही थी। भाजपा के रणनीतिकारों को अपने उत्तरी गढ़ों में इस तरह ज़मीन खोने की आशंका नहीं थी। दोनों राज्यों में टिकटों के बंटवारे में ग़लती और दंबग हाईकमान संस्कृति ने एक बार फिर पार्टी को नुकसान पहुंचाया था। बैकफुट पर आई भाजपा को अब आगे बढ़ने के लिए नए इलाके खोजने की ज़रूरत थी, जिसमें अब तक अभेद्य रहा दक्षिण भी शामिल था।

यहां एक सवाल हैः प्रधानमंत्री मोदी ने 2024 की शुरुआत में राम मंदिर के उद्घाटन की तैयारियों और फिर आम चुनावों से पहले किस राज्य का दौरा सबसे ज़्यादा किया?

उत्तरः तमिलनाडु।

रामायण से जुड़ते तारों वाले मंदिरों में पूजा-अर्चना करने से लेकर स्थानीय सांस्कृतिक प्रतीकों पर ज़ोर देने और शानदार रोड शो करने तक, मोदी ने इस दक्षिणी राज्य के सात बार दौरे किए। यह आउटरीच, भाजपा के 'मिशन साउथ' का हिस्सा था, जिसका मक़सद पार्टी का समर्थन आधार बढ़ाना और मोदी की राष्ट्रीय स्वीकार्यता को विस्तार देना था। मोदी के पहले कार्यकाल के दौरान, उनके एजेंडे पर दक्षिण राज्य प्रमुखता से नहीं था, उनका पूरा ध्यान हिंदी भाषी इलाकों में बढ़त को मज़बूत करना था। लेकिन 2019 में मिली बड़ी जीत के बाद सोच की दिशा बदल गई। विंध्य के उत्तर में सुरक्षित महसूस करने के बाद मोदी ने अखिल भारतीय स्तर पर मान्यता के लिए कदम बढ़ाए।

फोकस तमिलनाडु और केरल पर था। केरल में, भाजपा ईसाई समुदाय को लुभाने के साथ-साथ लेफ्ट बनाम कांग्रेस के एकाधिकार को तोड़ने की उम्मीद कर रही थी। 2023 के क्रिसमस पर, प्रधानमंत्री मोदी ने अपने आवास पर, पादरी, शिक्षाविदों और प्रभावशाली लोगों समेत ईसाई समुदाय के करीब 75 लोगों से मुलाक़ात की, ताकि 'सबका साथ' का संदेश भेजा जा सके। पूर्व एथलीट अंजू बॉबी जॉर्ज और अभिनेता डिनो मोरिया जैसे 'सेलिब्रिटी' भी यहां रौनक बढ़ा रहे थे। कार्यक्रम के आयोजकों में, कांग्रेस के पूर्व मुख्यमंत्री ए.के.एंटनी के बेटे अनिल एंटनी भी शामिल थे। स्टैनफोर्ड से पढ़े उनतीस साल के अनिल, अप्रैल 2023 में भाजपा में उस वक्त शामिल हुए थे, जब पार्टी केरल के कुछ ईसाई चेहरों को आगे करने की सोच रही थी। हाई-टी पर दो घंटे की लंबी क्रिसमस मीटिंग का मकसद फायदे से ज़्यादा दिखना था। कार्यक्रम में शामिल एक ने कहा, 'पीएम बहुत विनम्र थे, लेकिन यह त्यौहार का मौका था और कोई ऐसा विवादास्पद मुद्दा नहीं उठाना चाहता था जो किसी को असहज करे। हम सभी ने अपनी तरफ से बेहतर पेश आने की कोशिश की।' निजी बातचीत में मोदी भले ही आकर्षक लगते हैं लेकिन अल्पसंख्यकों के डर को ख़त्म करने के लिए, इस क्रिसमस केक को साझा करने से ज़्यादा की ज़रूरत होती है।

मोदी के आकर्षण का सीमित असर दिखाई दिया। अभिनेता-राजनेता सुरेश गोपी, केरल से पार्टी के पहले सांसद चुने गए और प्रदेश में पार्टी का वोट शेयर करीब बीस फ़ीसद तक बढ़ गया, लेकिन केरल के अल्पसंख्यकों का एक बड़ा हिस्सा अब भी भगवा ताकत पर भरोसा नहीं कर पा रहा था। कोच्चि के वरिष्ठ पत्रकार पी.पी. जेम्स कहते हैं, 'त्रिशूर में गोपी की जीत की बड़ी वजह उनकी स्टार अपील और स्थानीय स्तर पर सरकार से नाराज़गी रही।' कुछ इलाकों को छोड़कर, ज़्यादातर ईसाई कांग्रेस के साथ रहे। मणिपुर में चर्चों को जलाने की तस्वीरें, छत्तीसगढ़ और मध्यप्रदेश में मिशनरी स्कूलों को निशाना बनाने और ईसाई एनजीओ के विदेशी फंड में कटौती की शिकायतों का मतलब था कि भाजपा केरल में ज़मीनी स्तर पर विश्वास की कमी को पूरी तरह से दूर नहीं कर सकती। पथनमिट्टा सीट पर तीसरे स्थान पर रहे, लेकिन 26 प्रतिशत वोट शेयर हासिल करने वाले एंटनी ने कहा, 'हम रातोंरात चीज़ों को बदलने की उम्मीद नहीं कर सकते, खासतौर से केरल जैसे राज्य में, जहां कांग्रेस और वामपंथी कॉडर की जड़ें गहराई तक हैं, लेकिन हम अपने सामाजिक आधार को बढ़ाने की हरसंभव कोशिश कर रहे हैं।'

तमिलनाडु उन राज्यों में से एक है, जहां मोदी की लोकप्रियता कांग्रेस नेता राहुल गांधी से लगातार कम रही है। भाजपा के लिए यह केरल जितनी बड़ी चुनौती थी। चेन्नई के पत्रकार जी.सी.शेखर के मुताबिक, 'जब मोदी पिछली बार तमिलनाडु आए थे और उनको काले झंडों और "वापस जाओ" के नारों का सामना करना पड़ा था, तो निश्चित रूप से उन्हें ठेस लगी होगी, वह उस छवि को हर हाल में बदलना चाहते थे।'

2024 के आम चुनावों से एक साल पहले ही इस बात के संकेत मिल गए थे, जब मई 2023 में नए संसद भवन के उद्घाटन पर उस मौके को यादगार बनाने के लिए तमिल संस्कृति के प्रतीक को चुना। मोदी के दूसरे कार्यक्रमों की तरह, उद्घाटन भी अच्छी तरह कोरियोग्राफ किया कार्यक्रम था, जिसकी योजना हफ्तों पहले बनाई गई थी। विभिन्न मठों के अधीनम पुजारियों को एक विशेष चार्टेड विमान से एक साथ लाया गया और वे समारोह के मुख्य अतिथि थे। प्रधानमंत्री को भगवा वस्त्रधारी पुजारियों के आशीर्वाद देने और 'सेंगोल' भेंट किए जाने की तस्वीरें और वीडियो मीडिया में छाए रहे। सेंगोल, तमिल साम्राज्यों से जुड़ा, सोने और चांदी से मढ़ा हुआ एक पवित्र राजदंड है। तमिलनाडु की इस ऐतिहासिक कलाकृति को नए संसद भवन में लोकसभा अध्यक्ष की कुर्सी के साथ रखा गया था—इसका प्रतीकात्मक महत्व था। 'सेंगोल' की कहानी को सरकार ने अपने तरीके से पेश किया। सरकार ने दावा किया कि यह राजदंड मूल रूप से 14 अगस्त 1947 को अंग्रेजों के सत्ता हस्तांतरण के वक्त जवाहर लाल नेहरू को प्रतीक के तौर पर सौंपा गया था, लेकिन इसे बाद में इलाहाबाद के नेहरु संग्रहालय में रख दिया गया। इतिहासकारों और विपक्षी डीएमके-कांग्रेस के बीच इस बात पर विवाद था कि 'सेंगोल' क्या नेहरू को सिर्फ एक उपहार था या वास्तव में आधी रात को मिली आज़ादी के महत्वपूर्ण क्षण की नुमांइदगी करता था? इसमें कोई संदेह नहीं कि अपने स्वभाव के मुताबिक, मोदी इस मौके का उपयोग अपने राजनीतिक फायदे के लिए कर रहे थे। जहां तक मोदी का सवाल है, 'सेंगोल' तमिलनाडु में केवल प्रधानमंत्री की चमक बढ़ाने का साधन था, तमिलनाडु के मतदाताओं के सिर पर लहराती बड़ी छड़ी, जिसका संदेश था कि 'मुझे वोट दो, क्योंकि मैंने आपके सांस्कृतिक प्रतीक को संसद में पहुंचा दिया है।' भाजपा के एक पदाधिकारी का कहना था, 'सेंगोल पर डीएमके और कांग्रेस की आपत्तियों ने हमारी मदद ही की; इससे हमें तमिलनाडु में बात करने का एक और मुद्दा मिल गया।'

तमिलनाडु में अपना असर बढ़ाना, बरसों से भाजपा का एक अधूरा सपना रहा है। सामाजिक न्याय और आंदोलनों की विरासत वाले, जुझारू और मजबूत द्रविड़ क्षेत्रीय दलों वाले राज्य में भाजपा को गंगा किनारे वाले ब्राह्मणवादी, हिंदी भाषी और हिन्दूत्व की पार्टी के तौर पर जाना जाता है और उसे बाहरी के रूप में बताया गया था। दिलचस्प बात यह है कि पूरे राज्य में भाजपा कहीं नहीं थी, लेकिन संघ ने 'हिंदू मुन्नी' जैसे सहयोगी संगठनों की मदद से कई जगहों खासतौर से कन्याकुमारी में अपनी जगह बना ली थी। दिसंबर 2022 में, मोदी सरकार ने वाराणसी में एक महीने तक चलने वाले 'काशी संगमम' की शुरुआत की, जिसे उत्तर और दक्षिण भारत के बीच ऐतिहासिक और सभ्यतागत संबंधों को बढ़ावा देने के लिए तैयार किया गया था। तमिलनाडु से हज़ारों की तादाद में लोगों को तीर्थयात्रा के लिए वाराणसी और अयोध्या ले जाया गया, जिसमें आरएसएस ने पर्दे के पीछे अहम भूमिका निभाई। संघ के एक नेता ने कहा, 'हम हमेशा

से धार्मिक और सांस्कृतिक आयोजनों में तमिलनाडु के समाज के साथ गहराई से जुड़े रहे हैं।' संघ परिवार के पास तमिलनाडु में ज़मीन पर तो कार्यकर्ता थे, लेकिन कोई असरदार नेतृत्व नहीं था। 2019 के चुनावों से पहले, भाजपा ने कुछ लोगों के रास्ते सुपरस्टार रजनीकांत को नेतृत्व सौंपने की कोशिश की। तमिलनाडु में भाजपा के एक नेता ने बताया, 'हम कई मौकों पर करीब पहुंच गए, लेकिन वे आखिरी समय में पीछे हट गए।' अब 2024 में भाजपा को भरोसा था कि उन्हें चालीस साल के आक्रामक, युवा पुलिस अधिकारी से राजनेता बने कुप्पुस्वामी अन्नामलाई में भविष्य का नेता मिल गया था। अन्नामलाई का राजनीति में तेज़ी से बढ़ता कद किसी भी पारंपरिक ढांचे में फिट नहीं बैठता। इंजीनियर और कर्नाटक में आईपीएस कैडर में आने से पहले, उन्होंने लखनऊ आईआईएम से पढ़ाई की। एक सीधे-सादे लेकिन सख्त अधिकारी की छवि वाले अन्नामलाई ने आखिर सरकारी नौकरी छोड़ने का फ़ैसला कर लिया, क्योंकि उन्हें नियमों और प्रोटोकाल के जाल में बेबसी महसूस हो रही थी। दक्षिण बेंगलुरु में पुलिस उपायुक्त रहते उन्होंने 2019 में इस्तीफ़ा दे दिया। अन्नामलाई कहते हैं कि 'मैं समाज के लिए कुछ सार्थक करना चाहता था, इसलिए शुरुआत में मैंने नौ महीने छुट्टी ली और कोयंबटूर में एक एनजीओ–वी द लीडर्स बनाया, जिसका मकसद कौशल, गांवों में बदलाव और जैविक खेती जैसे मुद्दों पर युवाओं के साथ काम करना था।'

यह साफ नहीं है कि आरएसएस-भाजपा ने अन्नामलाई को ढूंढा या उन्होंने संघ परिवार की तरफ पहल की। लेकिन यह स्पष्ट है कि संघ तमिलनाडु में जिस नए नेतृत्व की तलाश में था, महत्वाकांक्षी अन्नामलाई उसके लिए पूरी तरह उपयुक्त थे। उन्होंने कहा, 'मैं राष्ट्र निर्माण के लिए मोदी जी की प्रतिबद्धता से प्रभावित था। मेरे लिए हिंदुत्व से बढ़कर, राष्ट्र पहले है।' जब 2021 में उन्हें तमिलनाडु भाजपा का अध्यक्ष बनाया गया, मोदी ने उन्हें स्थानीय राजनीति में उथल-पुथल मचाने का निर्देश दिया ताकि पार्टी को द्रविड़ राजनीति के राष्ट्रीय विकल्प के रूप में स्थापित किया जा सके।

यह सफ़र आसान नहीं था। 2021 में, अन्नामलाई ने तमिलनाडु विधानसभा का चुनाव लड़ा और डीएमके उम्मीदवार से करारी हार का सामना करना पड़ा। 2023 में, आम चुनावों की तैयारी के लिए, अन्नामलाई ने राज्यव्यापी पदयात्रा शुरू की। इस यात्रा में उन्होंने भ्रष्टाचार और सत्ताधारी डीएमके और विपक्षी एआईएडीएमके दोनों की परिवारवादी राजनीति पर जमकर हमला किया। इस यात्रा से वे तमिलनाडु की द्रविड़ राजनीति में तुरंत सुर्खियों में आ गए। जब डीएमके नेता उदयनिधि स्टालिन ने सनातन धर्म पर हमला किया और उसकी तुलना मलेरिया, एचआईवी से करते हुए उसे मिटाने की बात की, तो अन्नामलाई ने इसके ख़िलाफ़ विरोध प्रदर्शन का नेतृत्व किया। सोशल मीडिया के इस ज़माने में उनके तीखे बयानों से वे 'डिजिटल सनसनी' बन गए और उनका हर वीडियो वायरल हो रहा था। एक ऐसा व्यक्ति जिसने कभी चुनाव नहीं

जीता हो और उसकी पार्टी तमिलनाडु में हार गई हो, अन्नामलाई इंटरनेट पर हंगामा किए हुए थे। 'मुझे लगता है कि ऐसा इसलिए हुआ क्योंकि मैं गैर-परपंरावादी राजनेता हूं और बिना लाग-लपेट के सच कहता हूं,' अन्नामलाई कहते हैं। 'मैं पीछे नहीं हटता, क्योंकि मैं दूसरे लोगों की तरह हमेशा राजनीतिक फायदे को ध्यान में रखने पर भरोसा नहीं करता।' नये ऊर्जावान, मीडिया की पसंद वाले ठीक उस तरह के नेता हैं, जैसा मोदी के नेतृत्व वाली भाजपा को चाहिए। प्रदेश भाजपा के एक पदाधिकारी ने कहा, 'वह हमारे "सिंघम" थे, एक ऐसा नौजवान जिसने लोगों का ध्यान खींचा, जिसकी हमें ज़रूरत थी।'

लेकिन सुर्खियां बटोरना वोट हासिल करने से बिल्कुल अलग है। 2021 में अपनी हार के बावजूद, 2024 में अन्नामलाई फिर से चुनाव मैदान में थे और इस बार कोयबंटूर से चुनाव लड़ रहे थे। भाजपा इस सीट पर जीत की संभावना देख रही थी। पार्टी की पहले एआईएडीएमके के साथ गठबंधन करने की योजना थी। ऐसी पार्टी जो अब भी 2016 में अपनी दिग्गज नेता जे. जयललिता के निधन से उबरने के लिए संघर्ष कर रही थी। दोनों पार्टियों के बीच पर्दे के पीछे बातचीत शुरू हो गई थी लेकिन आत्मविश्वास से भरे अन्नामलाई ने मोदी को जीत का भरोसा दिलाया। उन्होंने कहा, 'जब तक हम अपने दम पर नहीं लड़ेगें, तो आगे कैसे बढ़ेंगे?' प्रदेश इकाई गठबंधन चाहती थी, लेकिन मोदी अपने युवा नेता पर भरोसा कर रहे थे, इसलिए उन्होंने एक सीमा के बाद उस पर ज़ोर नहीं दिया। मार्च-अप्रैल में भाजपा के पोल सर्वेक्षणों में पार्टी और प्रधानमंत्री की रेटिंग में उछाल बताया गया था। इससे नेतृत्व को लगा कि ऐतिहासिक सफलता मिल सकती थी। अभियान को बढ़ाने के लिए और संसाधन और ताकत लगाई गई। शहर में 1998 में हुए सीरियल ब्लास्ट के पीड़ितों को प्रधानमंत्री ने श्रद्धांजलि दी। इस्लामिक गुट 'अल-उम्मा' पर इन विस्फोटों को कराने का आरोप था, जिसमें 58 लोग मारे गए थे। बाद में उत्साहित मोदी ने, 2024 के चुनाव अभियान के दौरान अपना पहला साक्षात्कार तमिल चैनल थांती टीवी को दिया। पारपंरिक तमिल पोशाक वेष्टि पहने मोदी ने शुरुआत तमिल में बोलकर की, फिर हिंदी में दिए इस साक्षात्कार में वह तमिल लोगों के प्रति अपने प्रेम को ज़ाहिर करते रहे। भाजपा के एक रणनीतिकार ने दावा किया, 'उस साक्षात्कार और कोयंबटूर में मोदी के रोड शो के बाद, हमारे सर्वेक्षणों में बताया गया कि हनें प्रदेश में 4-5 सीटें और 20 फ़ीसद से ज़्यादा वोट शेयर मिल सकता है।'

पश्चिम बंगाल की तरह, तमिलनाडु में भी सर्वेक्षण गलत साबित हुए। राज्य के बाकी हिस्सों की तरह कोयंबटूर में भी जीतना आसान नहीं था। इस औद्योगिक शहर में और आसपास के इलाकों में डीएमके और एआईएडीएमके दोनों का मजबूत संगठन है। यहां कम्युनिस्टों का भी खासा असर हैः 2019 में सीपीआई(एम) ने यह सीट जीती थी। शहर में एक छोटा उद्योग चलाने वाले एम. रघु कहते हैं, 'मोदी 1998 के भूत को फिर से जिंदा करना चाहते थे, लेकिन यहां के

लोग अब आगे बढ़ चुके हैं। कोविड के बाद से कोयंबटूर को अपने उद्योग-धंधों को फिर से खड़ा करना है, न कि हिंदू-मुस्लिम राजनीति करनी है।' एक सवाल के जवाब में अन्नामलाई ने अतीत के सांप्रदायिक दागों की याद दिलाने के आरोप को ख़ारिज़ किया। उन्होंने कहा, 'हम आतंक के ख़िलाफ़ ज़ीरो टॉलरेंस की बात करते हैं, निश्चित रूप से इस पर किसी को कोई परेशानी नहीं हो सकती।'

डीएमके को अन्नामलाई की द्रविड़ राजनीति पर बार-बार और तीखा हमला करने से परेशानी थी। 'वह अंहकार की भाषा बोलते हैं, जिसे कोई भी स्वाभिमानी तमिल स्वीकार नहीं करेगा। वह पेरियार से लेकर अन्नादुरई और करुणानिधि तक हमारे आदर्शों का अपमान कर रहे हैं; उनके साथ कौन बातचीत करेगा?' कोयंबटूर में पार्टी के प्रभारी और डीएमके के मंत्री टी.आर.बी. राजा का तर्क था। प्रतिष्ठा की लड़ाई वाले इस मुकाबले में डीएमके और इंडिया गठबंधन के सदस्यों ने जीत सुनिश्चित करने के लिए हरसंभव कोशिश की। यह कोशिश काम आई। डीएमके ने कोयंबटूर सीट जीत ली, इसके उम्मीदवार गणपति राजकुमार ने अन्नामलाई को 1 लाख 18 हज़ार वोटों से हराया। हालांकि अन्नामलाई को साढ़े चार लाख वोट मिले, लेकिन वे जीत के लिए काफी नहीं थे। लंबे समय के इंतज़ार के बाद भी तमिलनाडु में भाजपा को जीत नहीं मिली। खराब तबियत के बावजूद मुख्यमंत्री एम.के. स्टालिन के नेतृत्व में डीएमके गठबंधन ने सभी 39 सीटें जीत लीं, जिससे साबित हुआ कि पार्टी का मजबूत कैडर अब भी एकजुट था और सहयोगियों के बीच भी वोट-ट्रांसफर करीब-करीब ठीक हो गया। हालांकि अन्नामलाई पूरी तरह निराश नहीं थे। उन्होंने कहा, 'यह पहली बार है जब हमारा वोट शेयर दोहरे अंकों में पहुंच गया; इससे भविष्य के लिए हमें मंच मिल गया है। एक बात और तय हो गई कि अब हम "बाहरी" लोगों या "केवल उत्तर भारत" की पार्टी नहीं हैं।'

भविष्य का तो नहीं कहा जा सकता, लेकिन कम से कम 2024 में, मोदी का तमिलनाडु अभियान हक़ीकत से ज़्यादा प्रचार पर आधारित था। अपनी खास राजनीतिक संस्कृति वाला दक्षिणी राज्य, भाजपा की हिंदुत्व विचारधारा का विरोधी बना रहा। ताकतवर द्रविड़ वोट बैंक, उत्तर से आने वाले आगंतुकों के ख़िलाफ़ मज़बूती से खड़ा रहा। आश्चर्य तो इस बात पर है कि चैन्नई के बजाय कम चर्चा में रहे उस क्षेत्र में भाजपा के पक्ष में हवा बह रही थी।

═

चौबीस घंटे चलने वाले समाचारों की दुनिया कभी रुकती नहीं, जिसका मतलब है कि एक टेलीविजन पत्रकार कभी 'स्विच ऑफ' नहीं कर सकता। मार्च 2024 की शुरुआत में, मैं अपनी सुबह की सैर पर था और दिल्ली में मुश्किल से मिलने वाली बंसत की ठंडक वाली हवा का आंनद ले रहा था, तभी मेरा मोबाइल फ़ोन बज़ने लगा। दफ्तर से, फोन पर मुझसे लाइव

प्रतिक्रिया देने के लिए कहा जा रहा था। 'बड़ी ब्रेकिंग न्यूज़ है: ओड़िशा में बीजू जनता दल के साथ भाजपा का गठबंधन हो गया है!' चैनल के असाइनमेंट डेस्क से फ़ोन था। टी-शर्ट और ट्रैक पैंट पहने, मैं अनिच्छा से 'ऑन एयर' आने के लिए सहमत हो गया। इसके लिए सवेरे की एक्सरसाइज़ भी छोड़ने का मन बनाया। एक या दो घंटे के बाद, समाचार अब भी फ्लैश हो रहा था, मेरे पास भाजपा के महासचिव सुनील बंसल का फ़ोन आया, जो ओड़िशा में पार्टी के चुनाव प्रभारी भी थे। बसंल ने कहा, 'यह ख़बर गलत है; हमने कोई गठबंधन नहीं किया है।' एक चतुर बैकरूम नेता और अमित शाह के वफ़ादार माने जाने वाले, बंसल पार्टी को आगे बढ़ाने के लिए उत्तर प्रदेश से पूर्वी तट पर पहुंच गए थे। उनकी ख़बर आमतौर पर सटीक होती है। सिर्फ़ अड़तालीस घंटे बाद, भाजपा और बीजू जनता दल, दोनों ने औपचारिक तौर पर घोषणा की कि वे 2024 के चुनाव अलग-अलग लड़ेंगे। यह फ़ैसला आम चुनाव की तस्वीर को बदलने का काम कर सकता था।

तो करीब-करीब तय हो चुका, गठबंधन अचानक क्यों छोड़ दिया गया? दिल्ली और भुवनेश्वर में कई स्रोतों से बात करने के बाद, साफ था कि इस गठबंधन पर प्रधानमंत्री मोदी और ओड़िसा के मुख्यमंत्री नवीन पटनायक के बीच काम चल रहा था। दोनों के बीच लंबे समय से चल रहे रिश्ते को एक वरिष्ठ नौकरशाह ने 'निजी मित्रता' कहाः पटनायक देश में लंबे समय तक मुख्यमंत्री रहने वालों में से एक थे और मोदी भी पहले गुजरात और फिर केन्द्र में दो दशकों से सरकार में थे। एक नौकरशाह ने कहा, 'मोदी के पटनायक से अच्छे संबंध थे, क्योंकि वे उन्हें अपने लिए ख़तरा नहीं मानते थे। मोदी उन मुख्यमंत्रियों से नहीं निपट सकते, जिनसे उन्हें ख़तरा महसूस होता है।' यही वजह है कि जब पटनायक ने 2023 के आखिर में पहली बार चुनावी गठबंधन की संभावना जताई, तो मोदी ने कोई आपत्ति नहीं की। साल 2000 से ओड़िशा के मुख्यमंत्री, 77 साल के पटनायक का स्वास्थ्य खराब चल रहा था और वे एक कठिन लड़ाई से बचना चाहते थे। मोदी भी विपक्षी इंडिया गठबंधन के मुकाबले के लिए टीम को मजबूत करना चाहते थे। यह दोनों के लिए फायदे का सौदा लग रहा था। 5 मार्च को, मोदी ने नवीन के पिता और ओड़िशा की राजनीति की शानदार शख्सियत बीजू पटनायक की 108वीं जयंती के कार्यक्रम में हिस्सा लिया। ओड़िशा के जाजपुर में हुए इस कार्यक्रम में मोदी ने नवीन पटनायक के साथ मंच साझा किया था। दोनों नेताओं ने कार्यक्रम में एक-दूसरे की जमकर तारीफ की। प्रधानमंत्री ने नवीन पटनायक को ओड़िशा का लोकप्रिय मुख्यमंत्री बताया। समारोह से लौटते वक्त उन्होंने पटनायक से फुसफुसाकर कहा, 'चिंता मत करो, जल्दी कर देंगे।' इस गठबंधन को मोदी ने हरी झंडी दे दी थी और भाजपा सुप्रीमो की मुहर लग गई थी।

लेकिन भाजपा की प्रदेश इकाई या आरएसएस से इसे मंज़ूरी नहीं मिली थी। संघ का ओड़िशा में, खासतौर से आदिवासी इलाकों में काफी प्रभाव है। प्रदेश अध्यक्ष मनमोहन सामल

गठबंधन के पूरी तरह ख़िलाफ़ थे। उन्होंने केन्द्रीय नेतृत्व को लिखे एक पत्र में कहा, 'यह हमारे कार्यकर्ताओं का मनोबल गिराएगा, जिन्होंने पिछले दस सालों में ओड़िशा में हमें एक जुझारू ताकत बनाने के लिए कड़ी मेहनत की है।' इसमें निर्णायक मोड़ तब आया, जब मार्च के दूसरे हफ्ते में भाजपा के आंतरिक ट्रैकर सर्वेक्षण में पार्टी को न केवल लोकसभा बल्कि विधानसभा चुनावों में बढ़त दिखाई गई थी (ओड़िशा में लोकसभा और विधानसभा के चुनाव एकसाथ होने थे)। भाजपा के सर्वेक्षण करने वाले उत्तर प्रदेश, बंगाल और तमिलनाडु का अनुमान लगाने में भले ही गलत रहे, लेकिन यहां बिल्कुल सही थे। जब गृहमंत्री शाह को सर्वेक्षण के बारे में जानकारी मिली तो उन्होंने प्रधानमंत्री से मुलाकात कर सुझाव दिया कि वे गठबंधन को लेकर फिर से विचार करें। खबरों के मुताबिक, प्रधानमंत्री ने कहा, 'मैंने नवीन बाबू को हां कह दी है।' शाह ने ज़रूरत पड़ने पर चुनाव के बाद समझौता करने का प्रस्ताव रखा। कुछ आग्रह के बाद मोदी, अपने संभावित चुनाव-पूर्व सहयोगी को छोड़ने पर सहमत हो गए। मोदी का निर्णय इस बात का सबूत था कि क्यों उनके कई प्रशंसक उनके लचीलेपन को मानते हैं तो आलोचक इसे चालाकी कहते हैं। मुश्किल समय में मोदी जीत को ही हर चीज़ से ऊपर रखते हैं। जहां उनके प्रशंसक इसे हकीकत की राजनीति के तौर पर सराहते हैं, वहीं उनके आलोचक इसे अनैतिक राजनीति कहते हैं, जिसमें कोई स्थायी मित्र नहीं होता, सिर्फ स्थायी हित होते हैं।

इस रुख में अचानक बदलाव को करीब से देख रहे थे, वी. कार्तिकेयन पांडियन, जिन्हें ज़्यादातर लोग ओड़िशा का असली मुख्यमंत्री मानते थे। 2000 बैच के आईएएस अधिकारी पांडियन तेरह साल से मुख्यमंत्री कार्यालय में थे और वे पटनायक की छाया की तरह हमेशा उनके साथ रहते थे। पांडियन, भाजपा के साथ गठबंधन के प्रबल समर्थक थे और इसे दोनों दलों के लिए फायदे का सौदा मानते हुए इसे पक्का करने के लिए दिल्ली और भुवनेश्वर के बीच भागदौड़ कर रहे थे। ओड़िशा कैडर के एक पूर्व अधिकारी ने कहा, 'नवीन बाबू उन पर पूरा भरोसा करते हैं। यह कोई आम नेता-अफसर समीकरण नहीं बल्कि पिता-पुत्र जैसा गहरा रिश्ता है।' नवंबर 2023 में पांडियन के इस खास रिश्ते को औपचारिक रूप दिया गयाः पांडियन भुवनेश्वर में पटनायक के घर नवीन आवास पर उनके पैर छूकर औपचारिक रूप से बीजू जनता दल में शामिल हो गए। उम्रदराज होते मुख्यमंत्री की सक्रियता कम होने से, अब पांडियन को उत्तराधिकारी माना जाने लगा, इससे चुनाव के दौरान पार्टी को परेशानी हो सकती थी। पांडियन कहते हैं कि 'बीजू जनता दल में शामिल होना नवीन बाबू के प्रति मेरे प्यार और स्नेह की वजह से एक भावनात्मक निर्णय था। मैं उनका बोझ कम करना चाहता था और मुझे भरोसा था कि ओड़िया लोगों का भरोसा हमारे साथ है।'

पांडियन का विश्वास ग़लत साबित हुआ। बीस साल की अपनी सरकार में पटनायक और पांडियन के साथ उनके अफसरों की टीम ने देश के सबसे ग़रीब राज्यों में से एक में विकास

के लिए कई शानदार काम किए थे। समुद्री तूफान के प्रबंधन से लेकर स्वास्थ्य सेवाओं तक, महिला स्वयं सहायता समूहों से लेकर विश्व स्तरीय खेल इन्फ्रास्ट्रक्चर तक, ओड़िशा तेज़ी से आगे बढ़ रहा था। भुवनेश्वर आज एक बदला हुआ शहर है, इसकी चौड़ी सड़कें, साफ-सुंदर पार्क, आधुनिक दिखती दुकानें इस बात को बताती हैं कि पटनायक सरकार ने बेहतर काम किया। लेकिन एक बेहतर विकास, हमेशा वोटों की गारंटी में तब्दील नहीं होता, खासतौर से दो दशक तक सत्ता में रहने के बाद। सत्ता विरोधी लहर या फिर ऊब, धीर-धीरे बढ़ रही थी। इससे भी ज़्यादा पांडियन की असरदार मौज़ूदगी प्रदेश की राजनीति पर भारी पड़ रही थी, और जल्दी ही पांडियन की तमिल पहचान और भविष्य में उनकी भूमिका चुनावों में सबसे बड़ा मुद्दा बन गई। भले ही उनका दावा हो कि वे 'जन्म से हिंदुस्तानी और सांस से ओड़िया हैं।' ओड़िशा के कस्बों और गांवों में अब एक नारा गूंजने लगा था, जो लोगों की बेचैनी को दिखा रहा था: 'अमे जदी बोट देबा नवीन कू, वोट जीबा पांडियन कू' (अगर हम नवीन को वोट देंगे, तो वो पांडियन को जाएगा)। ओड़िया सामाचार वेबसाइट ओमकाम न्यूज़ के संपादक जजाति करण कहते हैं, 'मुझे लगता है कि पांडियन ने एक अहम गलती की कि वे पार्टी की रैलियों में मंच पर सामने आ गए। अगर वे पीछे से काम करते रहते तो शायद कोई फ़र्क नहीं पड़ता।' राजनेता के तौर पर पांडियन की अलोकप्रियता बीजेडी के लिए कमज़ोरी बन गई।

भाजपा इस बात को समझ गई और उसने तुरंत इस पर काम किया। जैसे कि संभावना थी कि पार्टी ने लगातार पांडियन पर निशाना साधा, साथ ही पार्टी नेतृत्व ने पटनायक को भी नहीं बख्शा। जैसे-जैसे प्रचार अभियान आगे बढ़ा, मोदी-पटनायक की दोस्ती अतीत की बात हो गई। एक रैली में मोदी ने मुख्यमंत्री को ओड़िशा के सभी ज़िलों के नाम बताने की चुनौती दी, जिसका मतलब था कि वे अपने गृह राज्य के बारे में नहीं जानते हैं। एक और रैली में प्रधानमंत्री ने पटनायक की तबियत पर निशाना साधते हुए कहा, उनका हाथ हर समय क्यों कांपता रहता है, क्या इसके पीछे कोई साज़िश थी? पटनायक के कांपते हाथों को पांडियन के सहारा देने का वीडियो भाजपा हैंडल ने सोशल मीडिया पर साझा किया। मुख्यमंत्री ने खंडन जारी करते हुए कहा: 'प्रधानमंत्री कहते हैं कि वे मेरे अच्छे दोस्त हैं, तो उन्हें बस फोन उठाकर मेरी तबियत के बारे में बताना था।' प्रचार अभियान में टीम मोदी-शाह का कोई दोस्त नहीं होता। बेरहम, बेशर्म, असभ्य और नीचे किसी भी सीमा तक गिरने को तैयार, उनका ध्यान बस वोटों पर होता हैं। निजी रिश्तों के लिए उनकी सत्ता की किताब में कोई जगह नहीं है।

पटनायक और बीजू जनता दल के लिए, अपनी खोई ज़मीन फिर से हासिल करने में बहुत देर हो चुकी थी। भाजपा ने 'ओड़िशा के लिए ओड़िया' की कहानी पर ज़ोर दिया। नतीजे चौंकाने वाले थे। भाजपा ने न केवल लोकसभा में 21 में से 20 सीटें जीत लीं, बल्कि विधानसभा में 147 में से 78 सीटों पर कब्ज़ा कर शानदार जीत दर्ज की। यहां तक कि भाजपा नेतृत्व भी इन

नतीजों से हैरान था। चुनाव नतीजों से आहत पांडियन ने राजनीति छोड़ने की घोषणा कर दी। उन्होंने कहा, 'मुझे अफसोस इस बात का है कि हम भाजपा के झूठे प्रचार का मुकाबला नहीं कर पाए।' ऐसे समय में जब भगवा सेना अपने गढ़ों में ताकत खो रही थी, तब ओड़िशा भाजपा की मदद के लिए आगे आया। राज्य की 20 सीटों ने एक गुजराती को तीसरी बार प्रधानमंत्री बनने में मदद की। आश्चर्य की बात नहीं है कि जब चुनावी जीत के बाद एनडीए संसदीय दल की बैठक में मोदी पहुंचे, तो सेन्ट्रल हॉल में 'जय श्रीराम' की जगह 'जय जगन्नाथ' के नारे गूंज उठे। प्रधानमंत्री ने अपना भाषण भी 'जय जगन्नाथ' से शुरू किया। ओड़िशा में सबसे पूजनीय माने जाने वाले भगवान ने मोदी को वहां पहुंचाने में मदद की, जहां दूसरे देवताओं ने विफल कर दिया था।

═

सत्ता से बाहर होने वालों के लिए राजनीति क्रूर हो सकती है। अगस्त 2023 में, आंध्रप्रदेश के पूर्व मुख्यमंत्री चन्द्रबाबू नायडू ने दिल्ली में वरिष्ठ पत्रकारों को एक लंच पर मुलाकात के लिए आमंत्रित किया। बहुत कम पत्रकार आए, जबकि बड़े पैमाने पर शानदार और स्वादिष्ट आंध्रा भोजन की तैयारी की गई थी। नायडू उस समय सत्ता से बाहर थे और ख़बरों में नहीं थे। अपनी ट्रेडमार्क क्रीम रंग की लंबी आस्तीन वाली शर्ट पहने नायडू थोड़ा निराश दिखाई दिए। वह गृहमंत्री अमित शाह से मिलने और 2024 के चुनावों में तेलुगुदेशम पार्टी और भाजपा के बीच साझेदारी की संभावनाओं पर चर्चा के लिए दिल्ली आए थे। शाह ने उन्हें दो दिन इंतज़ार कराया और जब मुलाक़ात हुई तो उन्होंने गठबंधन को लेकर किसी तरह की कोई पक्की बात नहीं की। उन्होंने कहा, 'तेलंगाना चुनाव खत्म होने दें, फिर हम बात कर सकते हैं।' तेलंगाना में चुनाव अभी तीन महीने बाद नवंबर में होने थे।

दिल्ली से लौटने के कुछ हफ्तों बाद आंध्र के नेता खबरों में थे। नायडू को 9 सितम्बर की सुबह तीन बजे आंध्र पुलिस ने उस वक्त गिरफ़्तार कर लिया, जब वे चुनाव से पहले के अभियान पर निकले थे और नांदयाल में डेरा डाले बस में सो रहे थे। उन पर उस कथित घोटाले में शामिल होने का आरोप लगाया गया, जो 2014 में उनके मुख्यमंत्री रहने के दौरान हुआ था। नायडू की गिरफ़्तारी के समय और तरीके से तमिलनाडु के पूर्व मुख्यमंत्री एम. करुणानिधि की उन तस्वीरों की यादें ताज़ा हो गईं, जब 2001 में रात दो बजे स्थानीय पुलिस ने उन्हें बिस्तर से घसीटते हुए बाहर निकालकर गिरफ़्तार किया गया था। उस समय एआईएडीएमके नेता और मुख्यमंत्री जे. जयललिता पर बदले की भावना से काम करने का आरोप लगा था। 2023 में YSR कांग्रेस पार्टी (YSRCP) के नेता और आंध्रप्रदेश के तत्कालीन मुख्यमंत्री जगन मोहन रेड्डी पर भी बदले की राजनीति के आरोप लगे। करुणानिधि की राजनीतिक क़िस्मत बदलने

में तो कुछ साल लग गए, लेकिन चौहतर साल के नायडू ने इसका फायदा उठाया और 2024 के लोकसभा और विधानसभा चुनावों में वापसी कर ली। आंध्र प्रदेश के वरिष्ठ पत्रकार कृष्ण राव कहते हैं, 'इस तरह से किसी वरिष्ठ नेता को गिरफ्तार करना जगन की सबसे बड़ी गलती थी। जनता की सहानुभूति पूरी तरह नायडू के साथ हो गई।'

ट्रैकर पोल के नतीजे भी इस बात की पुष्टि करते हैं। सितंबर के मध्य तक, रेड्डी की टीम के साप्ताहिक पोल में टीडीपी से काफी आगे थे। सिर्फ़ चार हफ्ते बाद, नायडू आगे निकल गए और यह बढ़त आने वाले महीनों में बढ़ती गई। अपने प्रतिद्वन्दी को रातोंरात गिरफ्तार करने का फ़ैसला रेड्डी के काम करने की निरंकुश शैली को बता रहा था। वह सनकी और जिद्दी हो सकते हैं, कई बार अपने शुभचिंतकों की सलाह भी सुनने से इंकार कर देते हैं। अब टीडीपी के साथ, लेकिन पहले YSRCP के साथ रहे एक नेता ने कहा, 'हमने उनसे संपर्क करने की कोशिश की, लेकिन उन्होंने हमारी बात नहीं सुनी।' रेड्डी को यकीन था कि नायडू ने कांग्रेस के साथ मिलकर उन्हें 2012 में सोलह महीने जेल में रखने की साज़िश की थी। यह उसका बदला था। थके और हताश नायडू को 53 दिनों तक जेल में रहना पड़ा, इस दौरान उनकी सेहत भी खराब हो गई। जेल में पहले हफ्ते ही उनकी मुलाक़ात लोकप्रिय अभिनेता और जन सेना प्रमुख पवन कल्याण से हुई। इस मुलाकात के तुरंत बाद पवन कल्याण ने आंध्र प्रदेश चुनावों के लिए टीडीपी के साथ गठबंधन की घोषणा कर दी। अभिनेता-राजनेता कल्याण कहते हैं, 'मैं नायडू जी की दुर्दशा से नाराज़ और दुखी था। मैंने तभी गठबंधन का फ़ैसला कर लिया। बस, बहुत हो गया।'

नायडू का ज़ोरदार स्वागत हुआ। आंध्र प्रदेश में माहौल पूरी तरह बदला हुआ और एकतरफा लग रहा था। दिसंबर की शुरुआत में जब नायडू दिल्ली आए, तो उनकी चाल में दमखम दिखाई दे रहा था। भाजपा नेतृत्व ने उनके साथ गठबंधन की बात मान तो ली, लेकिन उसका ऐलान अभी नहीं किया गया। 17वीं लोकसभा अभी चल रही थी और भाजपा को राज्यसभा में एक महत्वपूर्ण विधेयक को पारित कराने के लिए वाईएसआरसीपी के समर्थन की ज़रूरत थी। टीम मोदी-शाह ने अपनी लेन-देन, सांठ-गांठ और 'इस्तेमाल करो और फेंको' की राजनीति और गठबंधन बनाने का काम जारी रखा। (जब जगन मोहन रेड्डी, जुलाई 2024 में अपने पार्टी कार्यकर्ताओं पर हमलों के विरोध में दिल्ली आए, तो प्रधान्मंत्री और गृहमंत्री से उन्हें मिलने का समय नहीं मिला। लोकसभा में केवल चार सांसदों के साथ अब जगन की भाजपा के लिए कोई अहमियत नहीं रह गई थी।)

आम चुनावों के ऐलान से कुछ दिनों पहले मार्च 2024 में, इस समझौते की घोषणा की एक और बड़ी वजह थी। प्रधानमंत्री मोदी और चन्द्रबाबू नायडू के बीच संबंध उतार-चढ़ाव वाले रहे थे। 2002 में गुजरात हिंसा के बाद, वाजपेयी की एनडीए सरकार में सहयोगी रहे नायडू ने, मोदी के इस्तीफ़े की मांग की थी। फिर मोदी के नेतृत्व वाली भाजपा सरकार के साथ साझेदारी के बाद,

उन्होंने 2018 में प्रधानमंत्री पर विभाजित आंध्र के लिए विशेष दर्जा देने के वादे पर धोखा देने का आरोप लगाया और सरकार से अलग हो गए। नायडू ने उस वक्त मोदी को आतंकवादी तक कहा था। जब मैंने उनसे 2024 के चुनाव अभियान के दौरान उनकी आतंकवादी टिप्पणी के बारे में पूछा, तो उनके सहयोगियों ने इस सवाल को हटाने का आग्रह किया। हालांकि भाजपा को अपने चार सौ पार के लक्ष्य के लिए ज़्यादा से ज़्यादा सहयोगियों की ज़रूरत थी तो नायडू उसके लिए उपयोगी सहयोगी हो सकते थे, लेकिन मोदी टीडीपी नेता के पिछले अपमानों को नहीं भूले थे। भाजपा के 'बिग-बॉस' की याददाश्त लंबी है और उनके आलोचक उन पर बदले की भावना रखने का आरोप लगाते हैं। नायडू को कुछ वक्त इंतज़ार कराना, इस बात को याद रखने के लिए काफी था कि 'असली बॉस' कौन था?

फिर भी, 2024 में अभियान के दौरान, मोदी अपने दुश्मन से दोस्त बने नेता को लेकर रणनीतिक तौर पर गर्मजोशी दिखा रहे थे। नए गठबंधन की पहली प्रजागलम (लोगों की आवाज़), संयुक्त रैली में मोदी और नायडू ने एक-दूसरे की तारीफ की। जब नायडू ने संभावित बातचीत पर कुछ सुझावों के साथ एक कागज़ की एक चिट आगे बढ़ाई, तो मोदी ने सहमति में तुरंत सिर हिलाया और मजबूती से हाथ मिलाया। डील तय हो गई थी और अब वोट देने का समय था। रेड्डी सरकार के ख़िलाफ़ सत्ता-विरोधी लहर का फायदा मिला। गठबंधन ने लोकसभा और विधानसभा दोनों चुनावों में जीत हासिल की। लोकसभा की 25 में से 21 सीटें जीत ली थीं। ओड़िशा की सफलता के साथ, आंध्र प्रदेश की जीत एनडीए को बहुमत दिलाने के लिए काफी थी। भाजपा खुद भले ही 272 के बहुमत के आंकड़े से दूर सिर्फ़ 240 पर रह गई थी, लेकिन गठबंधन ने बहुमत को पार कर लिया था।

नतीजों के बाद, अपने कार्यकर्ताओं को संबोधित करते हुए, मोदी ने 2024 को तीसरी बार एनडीए सरकार के लिए जनादेश कहा, न कि भाजपा सरकार के लिए। कार्यक्रम में किसी ने भी अपने उत्साही भाषणों में 'चार सौ पार' का ज़िक्र नहीं किया। कुछ दिनों बाद जब एनडीए की संसदीय दल की बैठक में मोदी को प्रधानमंत्री चुना गया, तो वे नायडू और बिहार के मुख्यमंत्री नीतीश कुमार के साथ मंच साझा कर रहे थे। एन फैक्टर—नीतीश और नायडू अब मोदी 3.0 की किस्मत का फ़ैसला करेंगे। एक समय पर दबदबे वाले सुप्रीमो, जिनके अजेय और स्थायित्व के आभामंडल ने बाकी सभी को बौना कर दिया था, का कद छोटा कर दिया और अब वे उन लोगों पर निर्भर थे, जिन्हें कभी उनके साथ रहना मंज़ूर नहीं था।

दिलचस्प बात यह है कि मुझे राष्ट्रपति भवन के प्रांगण में होने वाले मोदी के शपथ-ग्रहण समारोह का निमंत्रण मिला था। आमतौर पर मैं ऐसे आधिकारिरक आयोजनों से दूर ही रहता हूं—वे बेहद उबाऊ होते हैं, लेकिन इस बार मैंने इसे सत्ता की बदलती धुरी के अवसर के रूप में देखा। मुझे आश्चर्य हुआ कि मैं नायडू समेत नई दिल्ली के नए राजनीतिक अभिजात वर्ग

के साथ आगे की पंक्तियों में से एक में बैठा था। भारत ने मोदी के ख़िलाफ विपक्ष को बढ़ाया और एक गठबंधन सरकार के लिए वोट दिया। एक ऐसी सरकार जो देश की विविधता की झलक देगी। मतदाताओं ने कई नये सांसदों को चुना था, उनमें से कई दिग्गज थे और लोकतंत्र में विविधता की उम्मीद के नए प्रतीक थे। यह उम्मीद और साहस की उन कहानियों में से हैं, जिनकी ओर अब हम मुड़ते हैं।

13

'डेमोक्रेसी ज़िंदा है': उम्मीद की कहानियाँ

'ऐ बाबू, ये पब्लिक है पब्लिक
ये जो पब्लिक है ये सब जानती है...
अजी अंदर क्या है,
अजी बाहर क्या है...
ये सब कुछ पहचानती है'
(रोटी, 1974)

मई 2024 की एक गर्म शाम को, अमेठी में कांग्रेस का कार्यालय, उत्तर प्रदेश में भव्य पुरानी इमारत, पार्टी की खस्ता हालत को बताती है। जीर्ण-शीर्ण होती इमारत, दीवारों से पेंट उखड़ रहा है, टूटा-फूटा सा धूल भरा फर्नीचर बिखरा हुआ है और पास में ही एक खुली नाली बह रही है। जब मैं वहां पहुंचा तो देखा कि मुट्ठी भर कांग्रेसी कार्यकर्ता इधर-उधर घूम रहे थे और चाय के प्यालों के साथ बहस कर रहे थे। बढ़ती गर्मी के साथ उनकी आवाज़ें भी बढ़ रही थीं। बिजली वहां नियमित नहीं आती, इसलिए एक इलेक्ट्रिशियन, जेनरेटर को ठीक करने में लगा था। एक छोटे से कमरे में, दीवारों पर गांधी परिवार की सीपिया रंग की तस्वीरें लगी थीं, एक शख्स अपने आसपास के शोर से अजीब तरह से बेफ़िक्र बैठा था। ठिगने कद के 62 साल के किशोरी लाल शर्मा, कार्टूनिस्ट आर.के. लक्ष्मण के अमर हो गए 'आम आदमी' से मिलते-जुलते हैं। किशोरी लाल को उनके राजनीतिक जीवन का सबसे बड़ा आश्चर्य हुए चौबीस घंटे भी नहीं बीते थेः उन्हें कांग्रेस ने अमेठी से लोकसभा का उम्मीदवार बनाया था।

'जब खड़गे जी ने पहली बार मुझे फ़ोन करके बताया कि मुझे अमेठी से पार्टी का उम्मीदवार बनाया गया है, तो लगा कि कोई मज़ाक कर रहा था। फिर, जब श्रीमती गांधी, प्रियंका जी और राहुल जी ने मुझे बधाई देने के लिए फ़ोन किया, तो मुझे अहसास हुआ कि अभी क्या हुआ था। मैं उन सभी का कर्ज़दार हूं; वे मेरे नेता हैं और हमेशा रहेंगे,' उन्होंने अपनी घनी, लटकती सी 'वालरस' मूंछों के बीच झांकती एक सौम्य मुस्कराहट के साथ कहा। मूलतः लुधियाना के निवासी किशोरी लाल पिछले चालीस साल से अमेठी में रह रहे थे, जो सेन्ट्रल उत्तर प्रदेश में गांधी परिवार का गढ़ माना जाता है। राजीव गांधी से लेकर सोनिया गांधी और फिर उनके बच्चों तक, वह हमेशा गांधी परिवार के वफादार रहे हैं और इस छोटे से जर्जर शहर में बस गए। एक स्थानीय कांग्रेस कार्यकर्ता ने कहा, 'चाहे कोई शादी समारोह हो या फिर किसी का निधन, किशोरी लाल वहां ज़रूर होंगे। वे ज़्यादातर लोगों को उनके पहले नाम से जानते हैं।'

बेहतर बैकरूम ऑपरेटर को अब सामने मुख्य भूमिका में लाया जा रहा था। उन्होंने अचानक मीडिया का फोकस मिलने से असहज होने की बात मानी। उन्होंने कहा, 'मैंने कभी इस तरह का साक्षात्कार नहीं दिया है, मुझे सच में नहीं पता कि मुझे क्या कहना है।' लेकिन उनके बाहर से विनम्र व्यक्तित्व के पीछे एक तेज़ राजनीतिक दिमाग़ छिपा हुआ था। साक्षात्कार शुरू होने से पहले, किशोरी लाल ने जल्दी से अपनी बेदाग़ सफेद गांधी टोपी पहन ली और सुनिश्चित किया कि पीछे गांधी परिवार की तस्वीर फ्रेम में आ रही हो। उन्होंने दोहराया कि 'मैं जहां हूं, सिर्फ़ उनके कारण हूं।' किशोरी लाल के इस विनम्र रवैये की वजह से बीजेपी ने उनकी खिल्ली उड़ाई। हाई-प्रोफाइल अमेठी सीट से उनकी उम्मीदवारी पर सवाल उठाते हुए, पड़ोसी रायबरेली सीट से बीजेपी के उम्मीदवार ने किशोरी लाल को 'चपरासी' और प्रियंका गांधी वाड्रा का 'क्लर्क' कहा।

अमेठी में किशोरी लाल के सामने केन्द्रीय मंत्री और टीवी स्टार से राजनेता बनी स्मृति ईरानी थीं, जो कई मायनों में उनसे बिलकुल उलट लगती थीं। सिर्फ़ पांच साल पहले, 2019 में स्मृति ईरानी ने राहुल गांधी को 55,000 वोटों से हराकर देश के चुनावी इतिहास की सबसे बड़ी जीत हासिल की थी। इस जीत से उन्हें राष्ट्रीय स्तर पर पहचान मिली। बहुत मेहनती, महत्वाकांक्षी ईरानी में मौजूदा राजनीति में कामयाब होने के सभी ज़रूरी गुण हैं: ऊर्जावान हैं, दूरदर्शी हैं, धाराप्रवाह हैं और आधा दर्ज़न से अधिक भाषाएं बोलती हैं। अमेठी में घर खरीदने के बाद, वह हर महीने कम से कम एक बार अपने संसदीय क्षेत्र का दौरा करती थीं और इसके विकास में हर मुमकिन कोशिश का दावा करती थीं। इसके विपरीत, राहुल गांधी 2019 में अपनी हार के बाद से अमेठी से ज़्यादातर समय ग़ायब रहे, भाजपा ने उन पर 'भागने' का आरोप लगाया। स्टार मंत्री ने घोषणा की, 'मैं किसी विशेषाधिकार वाले राजवंश की सदस्य नहीं हूं, जो अमेठी को एक पर्यटक स्थल समझता हो, लोगों के लिए मेरा काम खुद बोलता है।' गांधी परिवार पर तीखे हमले ईरानी की लोकप्रियता की पहचान थे। इससे भाजपा के कार्यकर्ताओं के बीच उनका

खासा आकर्षण बना। एक उत्साही प्रचारक के तौर पर ईरानी एसयूवी गाड़ियों के काफिले में अमेठी की कच्ची धूल भरी सड़कों पर घूम रही थीं, उनके समर्थक 'भारत माता की जय' और 'मोदी ज़िंदाबाद' के नारे लगा रहे थे। मंत्री जी को भरोसा था कि भाजपा की मजबूत चुनावी मशीनरी उन्हें जीत दिलाएगी। स्थानीय समुदायों से गहराई से जुड़े, ग्राम प्रधानों का नेटवर्क, अब पार्टी के साथ था। प्रचार के आखिरी दिन, गृहमंत्री अमित शाह ने अमेठी में भारी शोरगुल वाला रोड़ शो किया। उस वक्त यह लड़ाई एक सामान्य कार्यकर्ता और एक बड़े चमकते सितारे नेता के बीच थी। ऊपरी तौर पर भाजपा के लिए यह कोई मुकाबला जैसा नहीं था।

ईरानी की दमदार मौजूदगी ने अमेठी को गांधी परिवार के लिए प्रतिष्ठा की लड़ाई बना दिया। नामांकन के आख़िरी दिन तक, ज़्यादातर लोगों को उम्मीद थी कि राहुल गांधी केरल में ज़्यादा सुरक्षित माने जाने वाली वायनाड सीट के अलावा अमेठी से भी चुनाव लड़ेंगे। 2019 में इसे लड़ाई की अगली कड़ी के तौर पर पेश किया गया, जो इस बार उनके लिए हिसाब बराबर करने का एक मौका था। कांग्रेस अध्यक्ष खड़गे ने कहा, उन्होंने राहुल गांधी से अमेठी से चुनाव लड़ने का आग्रह किया था। खड़गे ने कहा, 'मैं बहुत उत्सुक हूं कि राहुल जी अमेठी से और प्रियंका जी रायबरेली से लड़ें। इससे हमारे कार्यकर्ताओं में जोश बढ़ेगा।' लेकिन गांधी परिवार शायद कुछ और सोच रहा था। आखिरी समय में राहुल को, गांधी परिवार की एक और सुरक्षित सीट रायबरेली से उम्मीदवार बनाया गया, जबकि प्रियंका चुनावी मैदान से बाहर रहीं। प्रदेश कांग्रेस के नेता प्रमोद तिवारी ने कहा, 'हमें स्मृति ईरानी को इतनी अहमियत क्यों देनी चाहिए? गांधी परिवार राष्ट्रीय स्तर के नेता हैं, जिन्हें अमेठी तक सीमित रखने की ज़रूरत नहीं है।'

प्रियंका की भूमिका रहस्यमय बनी रहीः चुनावों में वे स्टार प्रचारक तो थीं, लेकिन खुद चुनावी लड़ाई में नहीं उतरीं। 2019 में अपने भाई की हार ने उन्हें झकझोर दिया था। उन्होंने इसे निजी नुक़सान की तरह लिया। अमेठी की हार के बाद अपने उदासी भरे सफ़र को प्रियंका याद करती हैं, उनके साथ किशोरी लाल थे। वह परेशान थे, आंखें नम थीं। उन्होंने कमस खाई, 'अगली बार ऐसा नहीं होने देंगे। स्मृति ईरानी को हराएंगे। राहुल भैया को भारी बहुमत से जिताएंगे।' 'नहीं, अगली बार स्मृति ईरानी को आप हराएंगें!' प्रियंका ने कहा। किशोरी लाल हैरान थे, जब प्रियंका ने समझायाः 'अमेठी से अगला चुनाव आप लड़ेंगे, और मेरा वादा है कि आप स्मृति को हराएंगे।' यह बड़ा खुलासा थाः अमेठी से किशोरी लाल को लड़ाने का फ़ैसला 2019 में ही शायद कर लिया गया था।

राहुल की बहन का मिशन बदला लेने का था। किशोरी लाल टिकट पर चेहरा थे, लेकिन भीड़ प्रियंका को देख रही थी। वह इस इलाके को अच्छे से जानती थीं, उन्होंने यहां पहली बार 1999 में अपनी मां के चुनाव के लिए काम किया था। उनके सहायक संदीप भी इसी इलाके से थे। उन्होंने गांव-गांव जाकर बातचीत करने का कार्यक्रम बनाया। अमेठी और रायबरेली में

रोज़ाना करीब एक दर्जन बैठकें होनी थीं। एक बार सभा के दौरान जब बिजली चली गई, तो वे माइक एक तरफ रखकर जीप की छत पर चढ़ गईं और वहां से ज़ोरदार ऊंची आवाज़ में भाषण दिया। प्रियंका एक शानदार प्रचारक हैं और उन्होंने अमेठी के मतदाताओं के साथ आसानी से तालमेल बिठाया। जब एक भावुक भाषण में उन्होंने अपने पिता के साथ अमेठी में अपने बचपन की यादों का ताज़ा किया, तो वह वीडियो वायरल हो गया।

इसके विपरीत, अति-आत्मविश्वासी ईरानी को एक बड़ी बाधा का सामना करना पड़ा। आम धारणा बन गई थी कि ईरानी बहुत अंहकारी थीं और उनके पसंदीदा लोगों के अलावा किसी का उनसे मिलना मुश्किल होता था। चुनाव के समय अहंकार की बात बड़ी परेशानी बन सकता है। स्थानीय पत्रकारों का कहना था कि वे ईरानी से संपर्क करने से डरते थे। एक ने कहा, 'अगर हम उनसे कोई ऐसा सवाल पूछते, जो उनको पसंद नहीं है, तो वह बहुत रूखा बर्ताव करती हैं।' स्थानीय भाजपा नेतृत्व का एक गुट भी उन्हें लेकर उदासीन था, क्योंकि ईरानी उनमें से कुछ के प्रति तिरस्कारपूण रवैया रखती थीं। अमेठी के शाही परिवार से रहे, पूर्व सांसद संजय सिंह, 2022 के विधानसभा चुनावों में हार से दुखी होकर चुनाव प्रचार से दूर रहे। भाजपा के एक ज़िला पदाधिकारी ने शिकायती लहज़े में कहा, 'वह बड़ी नेता हैं, लेकिन उन्हें हमारा भी सम्मान रखना चाहिए।' अमेठी में मसालों के बड़े कारोबारी राजेश मसाला, जैसे चुनिंदा लोगों को ईरानी का पसंदीदा माना जाता था।

अमेठी के मुख्य बाज़ार में मंहगाई हमेशा बहस का मुद्दा रहती है। 2019 के अपने चुनाव अभियान में स्मृति ईरानी ने 13 रुपये किलो चीनी दिलाने का वादा किया था। अब, कांग्रेस के कार्यकर्ता हर मोहल्ले में रियायती दर पर चीनी बेचकर मतदाताओं को टूटे हुए वादे की याद दिला रहे थे। कई लोगों को इस बात पर निराशा थी कि राहुल भैया मैदान में नहीं थे। आखिरकार, कांग्रेस के प्रथम परिवार के साथ अमेठी का अटूट रिश्ता रहा है। एक बुज़ुर्ग दुकानदार ने कहा, 'अगर गांधी परिवार न होता, तो अमेठी के बारे में कौन जानता?' कांग्रेस के मतदाताओं को इस बात का अफ़सोस ज़रूर था कि उन्होंने 2019 में राहुल भैया की हार रोकने के लिए जरूरी कदम नहीं उठाए। वैसे इस हार का कारण मोदी लहर को माना गया। 'इस बार कोई लहर नहीं है, इस बार जनता चुनाव लड़ रही है,' नौकरी नहीं मिलने पर, गन्ने का रस बेचकर काम चलाने वाले स्नातक राजू ने ज़ोर देकर कहा। राजू ने अनुरोध किया, 'अगर किशोरी लाल जीतते हैं, तो आपको स्टुडियो से मेरा इंटरव्यू करना होगा।'

मतगणना के दिन, जैसे-जैसे नतीजे आने लगे, मेरी नज़र अमेठी पर थी। शुरुआती रुझानों में ही किशोरी लाल को बढ़त मिल रही थी। मुझे आश्चर्य हुआ, क्या वह वाकई जीत सकते थे? दोपहर होते-होते यह साफ हो गया कि इस बड़े मुकाबले में किशोरी लाल, ईरानी से आगे चल रहे थे और आखिर में उन्होंने 1 लाख 67 हज़ार वोटों के अंतर से बड़ी जीत हासिल कर

ली। जब उनकी जीत पर मुहर लग गई, तो मैंने उन्हें लाइव इंटरव्यू के लिए हमारे साथ जुड़ने के लिए फ़ोन किया। 'बधाई हो, अब आप एक दिग्गज हैं,' मैंने कहा। इस बार उन्होंने बिना किसी हिचक के सहमति जताई और कहा, 'जब मैं दिल्ली आऊं, तो आपको मेरे और परिवार के साथ डिनर करना है। हम साथ में बटर चिकन और नान खाएंगे!' मैं राजू के साथ स्टुडियो से इंटरव्यू का वादा तो पूरा नहीं कर पाया, लेकिन मैं उसे शोर भरे जश्न में गन्ने के रस के कुछ ज़्यादा गिलास बेचता हुआ महसूस कर रहा था।

कहावत है कि घमंडी का सिर नीचा होता है। अमेठी ने राजनीति में अहंकार और करिश्में की हदें उजागर कर दीं। ईरानी का दबंग अंदाज़, किशोरी लाल के विनम्र स्वभाव से बिल्कुल उलट था। 2019 में जो मतदाता 'मोदी लहर' में बह गए थे, वही अब बदलाव की बात कर रहे थे। उनके बीच का फ़र्क साफ था: मृदुभाषी, कैमरे से शर्मीले और ज़मीन से जुड़े बेटे किशोरी लाल बनाम तेज़तर्रार, भाषणों में माहिर, सेलिब्रिटी सी चमक-दमक और दिल्ली से ऊंची उड़ान भरने वाली स्मृति ईरानी। भले ही किशोरी लाल में ईरानी की तरह स्टार राजनेता के आकर्षक गुणों में से कोई नहीं था, लेकिन उनके पास एक अनमोल और अक्सर कम करके आंका जाने वाला जीत का गुण था: विनम्रता। जब वह जीत के बाद गांधी परिवार से मिलने गए, तो उन्हें केवल एक सलाह दी गई, 'जैसे हो, वैसे ही रहो। घमंड नहीं करना है कि आप एमपी हो गए हो।' टेलीविजन चैनलों की बहस पर उनके प्रतिद्वन्दी भले ही 'फैमिली क्लर्क' कहकर उनका मज़ाक उड़ाते रहे हों, लेकिन मतदाताओं के लिए किशोरी लाल एक मिलनसार पड़ोसी जैसे थे। और चुनाव के वक्त, मतदाताओं की सोच, स्टूडियो में होने वाली फ़िज़ूल की बातों से ज़्यादा मायने रखती है।

═

बेंगलुरु से 45 किलोमीटर दूर, रामनगर में ऊबड़-खाबड़ ग्रेनाइट की पहाड़ियां, हिन्दी सिनेमा की ज़ुबान पर चढ़ी कहानियों का हिस्सा हैं। यह इलाका सत्तर के दशक की ब्लॉकबस्टर फ़िल्म *शोले* में दिखाया गया था, इसका चट्टानी इलाका कुख्यात गब्बर सिंह की यादें ताज़ा करता है, जो फिल्म में खलनायक डकैत था और हिंदुस्तानियों की एक पूरी पीढ़ी का घरेलू नाम बन गया। 2024 में, इस बड़े ग्रामीण बेंगलुरु संसदीय क्षेत्र में चुनावी लड़ाई किसी फ़िल्मी पटकथा से कम नहीं थी: बड़े राजनीतिक दिग्गजों और राजनीति में पहली बार आने वाले एक प्रसिद्ध डॉक्टर के बीच का मुकाबला।

मौजूदा सांसद डी.के. सुरेश 2019 में मोदी लहर के दौरान कर्नाटक से जीतने वाले इकलौते कांग्रेस सांसद थे। सुरेश, कर्नाटक के सबसे ताकतवर राजनीतिक भाइयों की जोड़ी का हिस्सा हैं। उनके भाई डी.के. शिवकुमार कर्नाटक के उप-मुख्यमंत्री और संभवतः देश के सबसे ज़्यादा

संसाधनों वाले राजनेता हैं। डीके के नाम से मशहूर प्रभावशाली शिवकुमार ने 2023 के चुनावों में 1,413 करोड़ रुपये की संपत्ति घोषित की थी और वे देश के सबसे अमीर विधायक बन गए। शिवकुमार का कारोबार रियल एस्टेट से लेकर शिक्षा और खनन तक फैला हुआ है। उन्होंने अपने खास अंदाज़ में कहा, 'जन्म से मैं किसान हूं, पेशे से कारोबारी और पसंद से शिक्षाविद् हूं और राजनीति मेरा जुनून है।'

डीके से थोड़ा कम लोकप्रिय, चौड़े कंधों वाले सुरेश वन लाइनर बातों में नहीं फसंते, लेकिन कम विवादास्पद नहीं रहे हैं। फरवरी 2024 में, उन्होंने उत्तर-दक्षिण विभाजन विवाद को हवा दी। सुरेश ने आरोप लगाया कि 'केन्द्र दक्षिण के हिस्से के पैसे को हिंदीपट्टी में भेज रहा हैः हिंदी पट्टी ने देश के बाकी हिस्सों के लिए जो स्थिति थोपी है, उसके बाद अलग देश की मांग करने के अलावा कोई रास्ता नहीं है।' ऐसी विभाजनकारी टिप्पणियां, ग्रामीण बेंगलुरु में सुरेश के प्रतिद्वन्दी उम्मीदवार डॉ. सी.एन. मंजूनाथ कभी नहीं करेंगे। प्रसिद्ध हृदय रोग विशेषज्ञ डॉ. मंजूनाथ ने बेंगलुर ग्रामीण संसदीय क्षेत्र में देश का सबसे अच्छा हृदय रोग केन्द्र बनाया था, जिसका स्लोगन, 'पहले उपचार, बाद में भुगतान' है। राजनीति से उनका रिश्ता शादी की वजह से है: वे पूर्व प्रधानमंत्री जेडी(एस) के सुप्रीमो एच.डी. देवेगौड़ा के दामाद हैं। जेडी(एस) के साथ भाजपा के गठबंधन ने उनके लिए चुनाव के दरवाज़े खोल दिए। जेडी(एस) के समर्थन से भाजपा के टिकट से चुनाव लड़ने पर उन्होंने कहा, 'मैं पहले और आखिर में एक डॉक्टर हूं; राजनीति में आना जनता की सेवा करने का एक और तरीका है।' जहां उग्र स्वभाव वाले, अनुभवी राजनेता सुरेश अपने समर्थकों को निर्देश दे रहे थे, वहीं जैकेट और टाई में मृदुभाषी डॉ. मंजूनाथ चुनाव प्रचार के शोरगुल से दूर दिख रहे थे।

चुनाव प्रचार के दौरान शिवकुमार ग़लत कारणों से सुर्खियों में आए। एक वायरल वीडियो में, वे एक अपार्टमेंट के लोगों को चेतावनी देते दिख रहे थे कि यदि वे उनके भाई को वोट नहीं देंगे तो कावेरी से नियमित पानी और अपने घर के ऑक्यूपेंसी सर्टिफिकेट की उम्मीद न करें। ग्रामीण बेंगलुरु पीने के पानी के गंभीर संकट का सामना कर रहा था और उनकी इस चेतावनी को ब्लैकमेल की राजनीति के तौर पर देखा गया। फिर शिवकुमार ने सफाई दी, 'मैं तो केवल मज़ाक कर रहा था, मैं भरोसा दिलाता हूं कि लोगों को चुनाव से पहले पानी मिलेगा।' फिर भी उनके गलत अंदाज़ ने मतदाताओं को असहज कर दिया था।

देशभर में बढ़ती लेन-देन वाली राजनीति कर्नाटक में भी थी। 2023 के विधानसभा चुनावों में गरीबों के लिए कांग्रेस की गारंटी ने उसे बड़ी जीत दिलाई थी। दोनों उम्मीदवार ढेरों वादे कर रहे थे और कथित तौर पर चुनाव प्रचार में भी बहुत पैसा खर्च कर रहे थे। एक वरिष्ठ पत्रकार ने बताया, 'मुझे ऐसे बहुत से मामले पता हैं, जहां मतदाताओं को उनके वोट के लिए 2,000 से 5,000 रुपये तक की पेशकश की गई। कर्नाटक में आप तब तक

चुनाव नहीं जीत सकते, जब तक कि आपके पास खर्च करने के लिए कम से कम पचास करोड़ रुपये न हो।'

धनबल यानी पैसे की ताकत का जातिगत समीकरणों से गहरा नाता है। सुरेश और डॉ. मंजूनाथ, दोनों ही खासतौर से दक्षिणी कर्नाटक में ज़मीन की ताकत रखने वाले प्रभावशाली वोक्कालिग्गा समुदाय से थे। बरसों तक देवेगौड़ा वोक्कालिग्गा समुदाय के सबसे बड़े नेता रहे, जब तक कि डीके भाइयों ने उनके वर्चस्व को चुनौती नहीं दी और बेंगलुरु ग्रामीण को अपना गढ़ नहीं बना लिया। जातिगत गणित वाली राजनीति में, चिकित्सा के क्षेत्र में बेहतर ट्रैक रिकॉर्ड रखने वाले डॉ. मंजूनाथ ने जातियों के पार जाकर मतदाताओं को आकर्षित किया। लेकिन सुरेश को भरोसा था। उन्होंने ज़ोर देकर कहा, 'उन्होंने चिकित्सा के क्षेत्र में अच्छा काम किया होगा, लेकिन मैं इस इलाके के हर कोने को जानता हूं और मैं कम से कम 3 लाख वोटों से जीतूंगा।'

तीन बार से सांसद और राजनीति के दिग्गज को आश्चर्य का सामना करना पड़ाः वह 2 लाख 60 हज़ार वोटों से हार गए। डॉ. मंजूनाथ की जीत में, भाजपा का चुनाव चिन्ह, उनके ससुर का जातिगत आधार, प्रभावशाली वोक्कालिग्गा और लिंगायत का गठजोड़ और खुद डॉक्टर मंजूनाथ की प्रतिष्ठा सब चीजें शामिल रहें। मिलनसार डॉक्टर मतदाताओं को बदलाव के लिए मनाने में कामयाब हो गए।

कर्नाटक के मतदाताओं के एक साल के भीतर लोकसभा और विधानसभा चुनावों (विधानसभा में कांग्रेस जीती थी) में अलग-अलग विकल्प चुने जाने से, एक बार फिर साबित हुआ कि हर चुनावी लड़ाई अलग होती है। इन नतीजों में दंबग भाइयों के लिए एक गंभीर संदेश थाः सत्ता का भरोसा नहीं और मतदाताओं को कभी हल्के में नहीं लिया जा सकता। शानो-शौकत और अंदाज़ से सुर्खियां तो मिल सकती हैं, लेकिन असली मुद्दों का एक जटिल हिसाब-किताब, मतदाता, मतदान केन्द्र में अकेले वोट डालते वक्त विकल्प तय करता है।

═

'वह एक युवा सामाजिक कार्यकर्ता हैं और बहुत अच्छा बोलता है। आपको उसे अपने टीवी शो पर ज़रूर बुलाना चाहिए!' एक दोस्त ने उत्साह से कहा। साल 2015 में स्टुडियो में बहस का मुद्दा दलित राजनीति का भविष्य था। वह चन्द्रशेखर आज़ाद के साथ मेरी पहली मुलाक़ात थी। स्टुडियो में कदम रखते हुए, हट्टे-कट्टे आज़ाद, अपनी शानदार मूंछों और गर्दन पर लंबे नीले दुपट्टे के साथ एक प्रभावशाली व्यक्ति लग रहे थे। उन्होंने युवाओं का एक संगठन 'भीम आर्मी' बनाई और हिंदू सवर्णों के वर्चस्व को चुनौती देने के लिए अपने नाम में 'रावण' उपनाम जोड़ा। 'अगली बार जब आप मुझे टीवी पर बहस के लिए बुलाएं, तो किसी और को साथ न रखें, मैं आमने-सामने बातचीत करना चाहूंगा,' उन्होंने कहा।

मैं साफगोई से बोलने वाले आजाद के आत्मविश्वास से भरे व्यवहार से प्रभावित हुआ। दिलचस्प बात यह है कि जब मैंने *टाइम्स ऑफ इंडिया* के लिए कांशीराम का पहली बार इंटरव्यू किया था, तब उन्होंने भी ऐसी ही शर्त रखी थी। 'मेरा इंटरव्यू पहले पेज पर छपना चाहिए, अख़बार के पीछे के किसी कोने में नहीं!' उन्होंने चेतावनी दी थी। पश्चिमी उत्तर प्रदेश के सहारनपुर ज़िले में पले-बढ़े आज़ाद का कहना था कि वे अम्बेडकर और कांशीराम से प्रेरणा लेते हैं। उन्होंने दावा किया, 'मैं उनके जैसा सच्चा नेता बनना चाहता हूं, किसी पार्टी का ग़ुलाम नहीं।'

2017 में मैंने फिर आज़ाद का इंटरव्यू लिया। इस बार वे कहीं छिपे हुए थे, क्योंकि सहारनपुर में जातिगत हिंसा भड़कने के बाद पुलिस ने उनके ख़िलाफ़ वारंट जारी किया था। आज़ाद ने कहा, 'मैं आपको बताना चाहता हूं कि मुझे जेल जाने का डर नहीं है, इससे लोगों के बीच मेरी लोकप्रियता अब और बढ़ेगी।' निडर, साहसी और विशेष व्यक्तित्व। वह अपना प्रभाव बनाना चाहते थे। उन्हें राष्ट्रीय सुरक्षा क़ानून के तहत एक साल जेल में रहना पड़ा, लेकिन जातीय उत्पीड़न के ख़िलाफ़ संघर्ष जारी रखा। 2020 में वह सीएए के ख़िलाफ़ आंदोलन को लेकर जेल गए। उन्होंने कहा, 'पुलिस ने मुझे लाठियों से मारा, मेरे चार दांत तोड़ दिए, लेकिन मैं उनके दबाव में नहीं आया।' 2021 में उन्हें *टाइम* पत्रिका ने भविष्य को आकार देने वाले 100 उभरते नेताओं की सालाना सूची में शामिल किया था। 'क्या मैंने आपको नहीं कहा था कि एक दिन मैं अपना नाम बनाऊंगा!' उन्होंने दावा किया।

ज़ाहिर है कि नाम बनाने की जल्दी में, आज़ाद ने 2022 के उत्तर प्रदेश के विधानसभा चुनावों में गोरखपुर से मुख्यमंत्री योगी आदित्यनाथ के ख़िलाफ़ मैदान में उतरने का फ़ैसला किया, उनकी यहां ज़मानत ज़ब्त हो गई। लेकिन उन्होंने बेबाकी से इसे राजनीतिक हिंदुत्व के उदय के ख़िलाफ एक प्रतीकात्मक लड़ाई कहा। वह समय के लिहाज से महत्वपूर्ण था। उत्तर प्रदेश की तीन बार मुख्यमंत्री और बहुजन समाज पार्टी की नेता मायावती और उनकी पार्टी भाजपा के साथ सौदेबाज़ी के आरोप में तेजी से ढलान पर थीं। खासतौर से, युवा दलित नए नेतृत्व की तलाश में था और आज़ाद इस खालीपन को भरने के लिए उत्सुक थे। साल 2023 तक, उनकी आज़ाद समाज पार्टी एक दर्ज़न से ज़्यादा राज्यों में फैल चुकी थी और उनकी सभाओं में भीड़ उमड़ रही थी। लेकिन क्या यह भीड़ वोटों में तब्दील होगी? उन्होंने कहा, 'मैं 2024 के चुनावों के लिए इंडिया गठबंधन के साथ गठबंधन की पेशकश कर रहा हूं, लेकिन वे मुझे लटकाए हुए हैं।' बताया गया कि उन्होंने समाजवादी पार्टी के नेता अखिलेश यादव को यह प्रस्ताव दिया था, उन्होंने चाय पर बुलाने के लिए भी कहा था, वह मुलाक़ात कभी नहीं हुई। 'मुझे लगता है कि वे सभी मुझसे डरते हैं। शेन वार्न ने एक बार कहा था कि उन्हें सचिन तेंदुलकर को गेंदबाज़ी करने की सोचकर ही डरावने सपने आने लगते हैं। मुझे लगता है कि मैं उनके लिए सचिन जैसा ही हूं,' उन्होंने हंसते हुए कहा। आज़ाद तेंदुलकर के बड़े प्रशंसक हैं।

इंडिया गठबंधन के नेताओं का अलग नजरिया था। उत्तर प्रदेश सरकार ने जब आज़ाद को विशेष सुरक्षा प्रदान की, तो यह बात तेज़ी से फैल गई कि वह भाजपा की बी टीम थे। समाजवादी पार्टी के एक नेता ने कहा, 'भाजपा दलित वोटों को बांटने के लिए उनका इस्तेमाल करना चाहती है, हम उन पर कैसे भरोसा कर सकते हैं?' जून 2023 में, आज़ाद पर गोली चलाई गई थी और उनके काफ़िले पर हथियारबंद लोगों ने हमला किया था, आज़ाद इस आरोप से घबराए नहीं। 'ये वही लोग हैं जिन्होंने कभी कांशीराम को सीआईए एजेंट कहा था। उन्हें ऐसे किसी भी व्यक्ति से ख़तरा लगता है जो उनकी ताकत को चुनौती देता है। मैं एक नेता हूं, कोई सीढ़ी नहीं, जिसका कोई इस्तेमाल कर सके,' उन्होंने जवाब दिया।

इंडिया गठबंधन के उन्हें साथ लेने का इंतज़ार करने के बजाय, आज़ाद ने 2024 के आम चुनावों में, उत्तर प्रदेश के बिजनौर ज़िले की नगीना सीट से अपने दम पर लड़ने का फ़ैसला किया। बिजनौर का राजनीतिक इतिहास दिलचस्प है, 1989 में बसपा नेता मायावती ने पहली बार यहां से चुनाव में जीत हासिल की थी। क्या आज़ाद प्रदेश की पहली दलित मुख्यमंत्री और कांशीराम की मूल राजनीतिक उत्तराधिकारी जैसी सफलता हासिल कर सकते थे? उन्होंने ज़ोर देकर कहा, 'मैं खुद को केवल दलित नेता के रूप में नहीं देखता। मैं दलितों, मुसलमानों और पिछड़ी जातियों समेत सभी वंचितों की नुमाइंदगी कर रहा हूं, यह हाशिए पर पड़े लोगों का गठबंधन है।' नगीना की सड़क पर, साफ था कि आज़ाद का मतलब काम से था। उनकी मोहल्ला बैठकों पर नीला रंग छाया हुआ रहता, हर लैंप पोस्ट पर उनके चिन्ह केतली का प्रतीक दिखाई दे रहा था। उनकी लोकप्रियता का अंदाज़ा इस बात से लगाया जा सकता था कि युवा उनके साथ सेल्फी के लिए कतार में खड़े थे और उस फोटो को अपने मोबाइल का वॉलपेपर बनाते थे। आज़ाद को सोशल मीडिया पर 44 लाख से ज़्यादा लोग फॉलो करते हैं, जिनमें अकेले इंस्टाग्राम पर उनकी तादाद 22 लाख है।

2019 के चुनाव में नगीना सीट, बसपा ने समाजवादी पार्टी के साथ लड़कर जीती थी, उनके उम्मीदवार को 5 लाख 50 हज़ार से ज़्यादा वोट मिले थे, लेकिन इस बार बसपा केवल 13,272 वोटों के साथ चौथे स्थान पर पहुंच गई। आज़ाद को 5 लाख 12 हज़ार वोट मिले और उनकी जीत का अंतर 1 लाख 51 हज़ार वोटों का था। आज़ाद ने चुटकी लेते हुए कहा, 'वर्ण व्यवस्था को उखाड़ फेंकने की कांशीराम की चुनावी रणनीति में पहला चुनाव हारने के लिए, दूसरा चुनाव दूसरों को हराने के लिए और तीसरा जीतने के लिए लड़ा जाता है। मुझे लगता है कि मैंने बस दूसरा चरण छोड़ दिया।' सत्ता का विरोध करने वाला सितारा वास्तव में आ गया था।

एक ऐसे राजनीतिक माहौल में जहां निराश और कमजोर दिखता मतदाता आजमाए और परखे हुए विकल्पों से अलग कुछ तलाश रहा था, वहां 38 साल के एक नौजवान ने बताया कि आंदोलन की राजनीति को कभी कमतर नहीं आंकना चाहिए। ज़मीन पर एक नई ऊर्जा

महसूस की जा सकती है: किसी व्यक्तित्व की ताकत को सोशल मीडिया के रास्ते बेहतर और असरदार तरीके से रखा जा सकता है और तमाम बाधाओं से लड़ता एक अकेला चुनौती देने वाला, युवाओं के बीच ज़बरदस्त समर्थन हासिल कर सकता है।

═

वोटों की गिनती के दिन वायरल हुए बहुत से वीडियो में एक सबसे अलग लग रहा था। हल्के रंग की साड़ी पहने एक युवती अपनी महिला साथियों के साथ नाच रही थी जबकि पुरूष सड़क किनारे से यह देख रहे थे, थोड़ा अचंभे में थे। पूर्वी राजस्थान में भरतपुर से सांसद संजना जाटव कहती हैं, 'हमारे समाज में खुशी के मौके पर इस तरह से नाचना परपंरा है!' जाटव के पास जश्न मनाने की हर वजह थी। एक गरीब दलित परिवार से आई दो बच्चों की मां, छब्बीस साल की संजना ने राजस्थान में सबसे कम उम्र की सांसद बनकर इतिहास रच दिया था। सबसे कम उम्र के सांसद का रिकॉर्ड पहले अपने नाम रखने वाले कांग्रेस नेता सचिन पायलट कहते हैं, 'वह कुछ और ही है, वह असली योद्धा है।' जाटव के लिए प्रचार करते वक्त पायलट यह देखकर हैरान रह गए कि वह कितनी सहजता से लोगों से घुलमिल जाती है। 'वह अच्छी तरह जानती थी कि किससे क्या कहना है, और कौन सी बातचीत इंस्टाग्राम रील बन सकती है,' वह हंसते हैं।

यह लड़ाई, आसान नहीं होने वाली थी। भरतपुर, राजस्थान के मुख्यमंत्री भजन लाल शर्मा भी इसी इलाके से आते हैं। इस आरक्षित सीट पर जातियों के बीच संघर्ष तीखा रहता है। जाटव 2023 के विधानसभा चुनाव में केवल 407 वोटों से हार गई थीं। उनकी मामूली हार के एक महीने बाद ही उन के पिता का दिल का दौरा पड़ने से निधन हो गया। वह परेशान थीं, लेकिन अडिग थीं। जब 2024 में कांग्रेस नेतृत्व ने उन्हें लोकसभा चुनाव लड़ने को कहा, तो उन्होंने इसे चुनौती के तौर पर लिया और अपने सीमित संसाधनों के साथ वे समर्थन हासिल करने के लिए गांव-गांव तक गई। उनकी इस शिद्दत को देखकर, पूर्व राजघरानों से ताल्लुक रखने वाले जितेन्द्र सिंह और विश्वेंद्र सिंह जैसे नेता भी उनके अभियान में जुड़ गए। उन्होंने हर जनसभा में कहा, 'मैं आपकी बेटी हूं, उम्मीदवार नहीं।' यह गर्मजोशी भावनात्मक जुड़ाव पैदा कर रही थी और चुनावी शोरगुल के बीच अलग दिख रही थी।

लेकिन बातचीत के कौशल से ज़्यादा, यह संजना जाटव का दृढ़ संकल्प था, जिसने उन्हें अलग खड़ा कर दिया। अठारह साल की उम्र में, पड़ोस के गांव में शादी, दो साल बाद, पंचायतों में महिला आरक्षण के महत्वपूर्ण सुधार का फायदा लेते हुए वह ज़िला परिषद की सदस्य बन गई। पति की हौसला अफजाई और सहयोग से उन्होंने पहले स्नातक और फिर एलएलबी किया, और मातृत्व को आगे बढ़ने में आड़े नहीं आने दिया। उनके पति, कप्तान सिंह राजस्थान पुलिस

में कॉस्टेबल हैं। आरोप है कि उनके सरकारी नौकरी में होने की वजह से पत्नी को चुनावी दौड़ से बाहर रखने का दबाव बनाया गया, लेकिन वह चट्टान की तरह उनके साथ खड़े रहे और हरदम हौंसला बढ़ाया। जाटव कहती हैं कि 'मैं यहां इसलिए हूं क्योंकि कप्तान सिंह ने हमेशा मेरा साथ दिया और मुझे लक्ष्य ऊंचे रखने के लिए प्रोत्साहित करते रहे।' जब उनकी पत्नी पचास हज़ार वोटों से जीतकर सांसद बनी तो कप्तान सिंह ने फेसबुक पर पोस्ट किया: 'आज मेरी धर्मपत्नी संजना जाटव ने मेरी शान बढ़ाई!' एक गरीब दलित परिवार की महिला, एक रूढ़िवादी पुरूष प्रधान इलाके से चुनाव लड़ रही, संजना जाटव की कामयाबी बताती हैं कि कैसे हमारे कमज़ोर तबके के रोल मॉडल धीरे-धीरे देश के राजनीतिक नक्शे की नयी तस्वीर बना रहे हैं। चमकदाक शोर-शराबे वाले रोड शो से दूर, ऐसे अनजान नायक भी हैं, जो आत्मा को झकझोर देने वाली कहानियां रच रहे हैं। अक्सर अपने अभियान और मकसद को समाज तक पहुंचाने के लिए सोशल मीडिया की पहुंच और ताकत का इस्तेमाल करते हैं। जाटव के इंस्टाग्राम पर 63 हज़ार से ज़्यादा फॉलोअर्स हैं। जब मैंने पूछा कि आपको किससे आगे बढ़ने की प्रेरणा मिलती है, तो उनका जवाब था, 'लड़की हूं लड़ सकती हूं।' कांग्रेस महासचिव प्रियंका गांधी ने यह नारा सबसे पहले 2022 में उत्तर प्रदेश के विधानसभा चुनावों में दिया था। कांग्रेस नेता प्रियंका उन लोगों में से हैं, जिन्होंने जाटव को टिकट देने के लिए दबाव डाला। सचिन पायलट सही कहते है: भरतपुर के भुसावर गांव की यह युवा महिला स्वाभाविक नेता है जो मुकाबले की राजनीति में गहरी रूचि रखती है।

═

बत्तीस साल के राजकुमार रोत जानते हैं कि धूम कैसे मचाई जाती है। 18वीं लोकसभा में सांसद के तौर पर शपथ लेने वाले दिन, फोटोजैनिक रोत, दक्षिणी राजस्थान की भील जनजाति की खास रंगीन पोशाक पहने हुए ऊंट पर सवार होकर संसद भवन पहुंचे। रोत कहते हैं, 'मैं सभी को यह याद दिलाना चाहता था कि इस देश के आदिवासियों की अलग संस्कृति है, खास जीवन शैली है, जो हमसे कोई नहीं छीन सकता।' रोत राजस्थान-गुजरात-मध्यप्रदेश की सीमा पर बसे आदिवासी बहुल बांसवाड़ा-डूंगरपुर सीट से चुनाव जीते थे। उन्होंने नई बनी भारत आदिवासी पार्टी (बीएपी) के टिकट पर चुनाव लड़ा था।

रोत कहते हैं, 'लड़ने का कीड़ा मुझमें हमेशा से था।' रोत ने अपना राजनीतिक सफ़र छात्र नेता के तौर पर शुरू किया और 2016 में 'भील प्रदेश विद्यार्थी मोर्चा' बनाया। राजस्थान के आदिवासी इलाकों में भील समुदाय की तादाद अच्छी है, लेकिन राज्य की राजनीति में उनका असर कभी नहीं रहा। डूंगरपुर के एक छोटे से गांव में पले-बढ़े रोत को बचपन में ही गहरी सामाजिक असमानताओं की तकलीफ का अहसास होने लगा था। वे कहते हैं, 'स्कूल में मेरे

कुछ दोस्त थे, जिनके घर पर मुझे नहीं बुलाया जाता था, क्योंकि वे ऊंची जाति के राजपूत थे और उन्हें आदिवासियों के साथ खाना खाते नहीं देखा, खान-पान नहीं होता था।'

इन शुरुआती अनुभवों ने रोत को राजनीतिक रास्ते तलाशने की ओर बढ़ाया और अपने आदिवासी समुदाय की गरिमा की बहाली और उनके अधिकारों की लड़ाई के लिए तैयार किया। 2018 में, वह भारतीय ट्राइबल पार्टी (बीटीपी) में शामिल हो गए, और 26 साल के रोत, चोरासी सीट से चुनाव लड़कर, राजस्थान के सबसे कम उम्र के विधायक बने। बीटीपी गुजरात की पार्टी थी, जिसे भीलों के लिए अलग से 'भीलिस्तान' बनाने की मांग को लेकर स्थानीय कद्दावर नेता छोटू वसावा ने बनाया था। जब वसावा पार्टी का, पड़ोसी राज्य राजस्थान में विस्तार करने की सोच रहे थे, तो उन्होंने रोत और उनके युवा आदिवासी कार्यकर्ताओं को अपने साथ जोड़ लिया, लेकिन महत्वाकांक्षी रोत जल्द ही वसावा से अलग हो गए। उन्होंने कहा कि वे परिवार के नेतृत्व वाली पार्टी के आदेशों पर नहीं चलना चाहते। बीटीपी का मतलब सिर्फ़ वसावा और उनका परिवार था। 'भारतीय आदिवासी पार्टी (बीएपी), हमने 2023 में बनाई, यह आदिवासियों की विचारधारधारा और उनकी मांगों पर काम कर रही है,' उन्होंने घोषणा की।

बीएपी ने 2023 में राजस्थान में दो और मध्यप्रदेश में एक विधानसभा सीट जीतकर आगे बढ़ने का रास्ता बना लिया। लेकिन असली परीक्षा 2024 में लोकसभा चुनाव में होनी थी। तब रोत के ख़िलाफ़ एक ताकतवर भाजपा उम्मीदवार महेन्द्रजीत सिंह मालवीय खड़े थे। अशोक गहलोत सरकार में मंत्री रहे महेन्द्र सिंह, चुनावों से पहले कांग्रेस छोड़कर, भाजपा में शामिल हो गए थे। अनुभवी आदिवासी नेता, कांग्रेस के 'धनकुबेरों' मे से एक माने जाते थे और कहा गया कि अपने हितों को बचाने के लिए वे भाजपा में शामिल हो गए। चुनावों में, जब महेन्द्र सिंह एसयूवी के बड़े काफिले में चुनाव प्रचार कर रहे होते थे, तब रोत और उनके कार्यकर्ता युवा शक्ति के प्रतीक, अपनी मोटरसाइकिलों पर गांवों में जाते। टी-शर्ट और जींस पहने, सिर पर गमछा लपेटे, बांसवाड़ा में अपनी हीरो स्प्लेंडर पर प्रचार करते रोत एक गिरोह के नेता लगते थे। राजस्थान के एक पत्रकार अविनाश कल्ला ने कहा, 'हम उन्हें बांसवाड़ा के बाइकर्स कहते हैं।' मालवीय के पास जहां धनबल था, वहीं रोत आदिवासियों के मुद्दों के लड़ने वाले के तौर पर लोकप्रिय हो गए थे। 'क्या आप जानते हैं कि जब हम रैलियां करते थे, तो गांव के लोग अपने पैसे से टेंट लगाते थे? चुनाव जीतने के लिए करोड़ों रुपयों की नहीं, लोगों की ताकत की ज़रूरत होती है।'

दिलचस्प बात यह है कि यहां, कांग्रेस ने पहले स्थानीय नेता अरविंद डामोर को उम्मीदवार बनाया था, लेकिन आखिरी समय में उन्होंने इंडिया गठबंधन के हिस्से के रूप में बीएपी और रोत को समर्थन देने का फ़ैसला किया। यह निर्णय कांग्रेस के प्रदेश अध्यक्ष गोविन्द सिंह डोटासरा का था। डोटासरा कहते हैं कि '2024 का चुनाव हमारे जीतने की ताकत को लेकर था और

रोत अपनी युवा अपील से जीतने वाले उम्मीदवार लग रहे थे।' हालांकि कांग्रेस उम्मीदवार के नाम वापस नहीं लेने से मुकाबला त्रिकोणिय हो गया। लेकिन रोत अपने आदिवासियों की ज़मीन और विकास पहले अभियान की थीम पर ही रहे। उन्होंने 2 लाख 47 हज़ार वोटों के अंतर से यह बड़ी जीत हासिल की। बांसवाड़ा में ही प्रधानमंत्री ने मुसलमानों को 'घुसपैठिए' और 'मंगलसूत्र' छीनने वाला चर्चित भाषण दिया था। देशभर में उनके हिंदुत्व के मुद्दे को जोरदार तरीके से उठाने से ज़मीन पर छोटे-छोटे विद्रोह की चिंगारी भड़क उठी थी। 'अभी तो यह शुरुआत है। हम जल्दी ही देश के हर आदिवासी कोने में फैल जाएंगे। बीएपी पूरे देश में आदिवासियों की आवाज़ बनेगी,' रोत ने कहा।

यह आवाज़ धीरे-धीरे थोड़ी तीखी होती जा रही थी। अपनी एक विवादास्पद टिप्पणी में, युवा सांसद ने कहा, 'आदिवासी हिंदू नहीं हैं, बल्कि वे इस ज़मीन के मूल निवासी हैं।' जब राजस्थान में भाजपा के एक मंत्री ने इस पर आपत्ति जताई और रोत से धार्मिक पहचान के लिए डीएनए टेस्ट कराने को कहा, तो नाराज़ रोत ने पलटकर जवाब दिया: 'मैं ही नहीं, बल्कि हर आदिवासी आपको अपने ख़ून का सैंपल भेजेगा। हम आपके धर्म और वर्ण व्यवस्था का हिस्सा नहीं हैं। हमारे अपने रीति-रिवाज हैं।' अब बढ़ता आक्रोश इस बात का संकेत था कि देश में आदिवासी राजनीति धीरे-धीरे कैसे बदल रही है। भाजपा ने देश को पहला आदिवासी राष्ट्रपति दिया है और किसी ज़माने में कांग्रेस आदिवासी इलाकों में सबसे बड़ी राष्ट्रीय पार्टी होती थी, लेकिन अब आदिवासियों के पास नई पीढ़ी में ज़्यादा मुखर नेतृत्व है जो पारपंरिक विकल्पों से परे देख रहा है। रोत कहते हैं, 'हमें हिंदुत्व नहीं चाहिए, हमें रियायतें नहीं चाहिएं, हमें अपनी ज़मीन और अधिकार चाहिए।'

आदिवासियों के बीच भी तीखे मतभेद हैं और ऐसे में आदिवासियों के लिए कोई असरदार राष्ट्रीय पार्टी बनाने के लिए संघर्ष करना पड़ सकता है, लेकिन आदिवासियों के समूहों से ही निकलने वाले युवा नेता अब सत्ता के बड़े खेल में किसी का मोहरा बनने को तैयार नहीं हैं। रोत अपनी जोशीली वकालत के साथ आदिवासी अधिकारों के लिए नई व्यवस्था के ताबीज़ हैं। लेकिन उनका दूसरा नरम पक्ष भी है। जब कुछ साल पहले उनकी शादी हुई तो उन्होंने प्रसिद्ध डूंगरपुर महल में प्री-वेडिंग शूट कराने का फ़ैसला किया। 'राजनीति में, मैं हमेशा अपने आदिवासी भाई-बहनों के साथ खड़ा रहूंगा, लेकिन निजी स्तर पर मेरे कुछ रॉयल दोस्त भी हैं!' उन्होंने कहा। एक आदिवासी, जो राजसी विशेषाधिकारों के लिए खड़ा है, लेकिन फिर भी महल में शादी की तस्वीरों को लेकर गर्व महसूस करता है। रोत शायद सत्ता की राजनीति के नियमों को फिर से परिभाषित कर रहे हैं।

बीस बसंत देख चुकी एक युवती, लंदन के प्रतिष्ठित स्कूल ऑफ ओरिएंटल स्टडीज (एसओएएस) में राजनीति विज्ञान में पीएचडी करने का सपना देखती है, लेकिन कुछ साल बाद खुद को पश्चिमी उत्तर प्रदेश के कैराना के बड़े फैले हुए गन्ने के खेतों में घूमती और लोकसभा के लिए चुनावी लड़ाई में शामिल पाती है। तीस साल की इकरा हसन की कहानी कुछ अलग सी है: एक ही वक्त में प्रेरणा देने वाली और विचलित करने वाली भी। एसओएस से मास्टर्स डिग्री करने के बाद, इकरा आगे पढ़ाई की योजना बना रही थी, लेकिन कोविड महामारी की वजह से, उसे 2021 की गर्मियों में घर लौटना पड़ा। लेकिन उसकी चिंताएं यहां ख़त्म नहीं हुईं। कुछ ही महीनों बाद, 2022 के उत्तर प्रदेश विधानसभा चुनावों से पहले, उनके भाई नाहिद हुसैन को 'उत्तर प्रदेश गैंगस्टर्स और असामाजिक गतिविधियां (रोकथाम) अधिनियम, 1986' के तहत गिरफ़्तार कर लिया गया। नाहिद कैराना से तीन बार समाजवादी पार्टी के विधायक रहे थे। 'ऐसा लगा कि एक ही दिन में मेरी दुनिया उजड़ गई थी। मेरे पिता का निधन बहुत पहले हो गया था, मां बीमार थी और मेरा भाई सिर्फ़ इसलिए जेल में था क्योंकि उसने योगी सरकार को चुनौती दी थी। हमारे बैंक खाते फ्रीज़ कर दिए गए, हमारी संपत्तियों पर मुक़दमा चल रहा था। पढ़ाई-लिखाई की बात तो भूल जाइए, मुझे सिर्फ़ परिवार को एकजुट रखने पर काम करना था,' हसन कहती हैं।

उनकी पहली चुनौती अपने भाई के 2022 के विधानसभा चुनाव का अभियान संभालना था। हालांकि वह एक ऐसे जाने-माने राजनीतिक परिवार से आती हैं--जहां उनके दादा, पिता और मां, सभी सांसद रह चुके हैं, लेकिन अभी तक राजनीति विज्ञान की किताबों में डूबी, इस शर्मीली युवती के लिए चुनाव अभियान को संभालना एक अलग खेल था। 'मुझे समझ आया कि ज़मीनी हकीकत और किताबी दुनिया में कितना फ़र्क होता है। अचानक, मैं एक बहुत ही पितृ-सत्तात्मक व्यवस्था में जाति और समुदायों की राजनीति का सामना कर रही थी। बहुत से वरिष्ठ नेताओं के लिए मैं अभी बच्ची ही थी।' इकरा की मेहनत रंग लाई और उनके भाई नाहिद जेल में रहते हुए भी चुनाव जीत गए। इसके तुरंत बाद 2024 में जब उन्हें कैराना लोकसभा सीट से चुनाव लड़ने का मौका दिया गया, तो वे तैयार हो गईं। वह कहती हैं कि 'मुझे लगता है कि मेरे पास कोई दूसरा विकल्प नहीं था। हम उत्तर प्रदेश में दिन-रात योगी सरकार से लड़ रहे थे, इसलिए मुझे लगा कि अब इस लड़ाई को मतदाताओं तक ले जाना ही ठीक है।'

कैराना, लोकसभा सीट भाजपा का गढ़ थी। 2019 में भाजपा के प्रदीप चौधरी ने इकरा की मां बेगम तबस्सुम हसन को 92 हज़ार वोटों से हराया था। सांसद चौधरी फिर से भाजपा के टिकट पर मैदान में थे, इसलिए इकरा के लिए अपनी मां की हार का बदला लेना, इस चुनाव को लड़ने की एक और वजह थी। कैराना, एक बड़ी जाट और मुस्लिम आबादी वाला शहर है,

जहां ज्यादातर लोग खेती-किसानी करते हैं। यह 2013 में मुजफ्फरनगर सांप्रदायिक दंगों का केन्द्र रहा था, जिसने दो समुदायों को आमने-सामने खड़ा कर दिया। ग्यारह साल बाद, हसन को इस बंटवारे को पाटने के लिए कड़ी मेहनत करनी पड़ी। वह जानती थीं कि चुनाव जीतने के लिए उन्हें हर समुदाय का दिल जीतना होगा। कैराना में करीब 40 फ़ीसद मुस्लिम आबादी है, जबकि जाट, गुर्जर, सैनी, राजपूत और दलित का भी बड़ा हिस्सा यहां रहता है। 'मैंने पहले दिन से ही अपने अभियान को बिरादरी के बजाय मुद्दों पर केंद्रित किया, जिसका धर्म से कोई लेना-देना नहीं था। कैराना में सबसे बड़ी समस्या चीनी मिलों से किसानों को गन्ने की फसल का उचित और समय पर पैसा दिलाना है। योगी सरकार ने किसानों की आमदनी दोगुना करने का वादा किया था, लेकिन उन्होंने बेरोज़गारी को दोगुना कर दिया,' इकरा ने कहा।

पारंपरिक सलवार-कमीज़ पहने, उन्होंने पुराने ढंग से प्रचार किया। कोई बड़े तमाशे वाले रोड शो या शोरगुल वाली रैलियों के बजाय, उन्होंने घर-घर जाकर प्रचार किया, जिससे मतदाता शांत स्वभाव और ईमानदार 'इकरा बहन' से तुरंत आकर्षित हो गए। इकरा कहती हैं, 'मुझे नहीं लगता कि मेरे क्षेत्र में कोई एक भी घर ऐसा बचा होगा, जिसके दरवाजे पर मैंने दस्तक न दी हो। मैं चाहती थी कि लोग समझें कि मैं उनमे से एक हूं और हर समय उनके लिए मौजूद रहूंगी।' इससे लोगों को उनके प्रतिद्वन्दी भाजपा नेता के बीच का फ़र्क समझ आ गया। भाजपा सांसद पर आरोप था कि उनके पास लोगों से मिलने का वक्त ही नहीं था। हसन के व्यक्तिगत जुड़ाव और कड़ी मेनत का असर दिखाई दिया। उन्होंने कैराना सीट 69,000 वोटों के अंतर से जीती। इकरा को कुल 5 लाख 28 हज़ार वोट मिले थे। 'कैराना की बहन' अब सांसद थीं। उनकी जीत की वजह सिर्फ़ मुस्लिम वोट ही नहीं थे, बल्कि कई हिंदू जातियों का भरोसा भी उन्होंने हासिल किया था। उत्तर प्रदेश के ज़्यादातर हिस्सों की तरह यहां भी बीएसपी के वोटों में गिरावट आई थी, वो उनके लिए बोनस जैसा था। लेकिन अहम बात यह कि कैराना आखिरकार मुजफ्फनगर दंगों के भूत को भगा रहा था।

एक युवा मुस्लिम महिला, हालांकि राजनीतिक परिवार से थी, ने हिंदुत्व लॉबी की नुमाइंदगी करने वाले एक मजबूत भाजपा उम्मीदवार को हराया था, जिसे बरसों से सांप्रदायिक ध्रुवीकरण का फायदा मिल रहा था। शायद 2020-21 से लगातार चल रहे किसानों के आंदोलन ने भी मतदाताओं को अपनी धार्मिक पहचान से परे देखने और अपनी रोजी-रोटी के मुद्दों पर ध्यान देने के लिए राजी कर लिया था। ऐसा लगा कि एक बंटा हुआ समाज, एक निडर, ना रुकने वाली, पढ़ी-लिखी महिला की जीत से धीरे-धीरे बेहतर महसूस कर रहा था।

18वीं लोकसभा में सिर्फ़ चौबीस मुस्लिम सांसद हैं, जो अब तक की सबसे कम तादाद है और इकरा हसन, केवल तीन महिला मुस्लिम सासंदों में से एक हैं। 'मैं चाहती हूं कि कई और हिन्दू, मुस्लिम युवा महिलाएं राजनीति में आएं। अब भी राजनीति कुछ हद तक लड़कों का

क्लब है, जिसे बदलने की ज़रूरत है,' यह कहना है उस सांसद का, जिन्होंने कई रूढ़ियां तोड़ी हैं और दूसरी लड़कियों को अपने पदचिन्हों पर चलने के लिए प्रेरित किया होगा।

═

मोदी युग की चुनावी राजनीति में इससे मुश्किल कोई काम नहीं है कि गुजरात जैसे राज्य में कोई गैर-भाजपा उम्मीदवार लोकसभा चुनाव जीत जाए। 2014 में मोदी लहर पर सवार भाजपा ने गुजरात की सभी 26 सीटें जीती थीं, 2019 में और ज्यादा अंतर से सभी सीटें जीत लीं। गुजराती अस्मिता के प्रतीक और 'स्वयंभू' गुजरात के शेर मोदी और उनकी भाजपा की भारी चुनाव मशीनरी के सामने कोई विपक्षी उम्मीदवार के चुनाव जीतने की संभावना बहुत कम थी। जब तक कि उम्मीदवार गेनीबेन ठाकोर न हों, जो अब कांग्रेस की सांसद हैं और 2009 के बाद से गुजरात में लोकसभा चुनाव जीतने वाली इकलौती गैर-भाजपा उम्मीदवार हैं।

अहमदाबाद के वरिष्ठ पत्रकार महेश लांगा कहते हैं, 'गेनीबेन ठाकोर 2024 की लड़ाई की असली दिग्गज हैं। उनकी यह जीत सिर्फ़ अपने प्रतिद्वन्दी भाजपा उम्मीदवार पर ही नहीं है, बल्कि यह लड़ाई उन्होंने उस आर्थिक और राजनीतिक सिस्टम के लोगों के ख़िलाफ़ भी जीती है, जो सत्ता में बैठी पार्टी के अलावा कुछ सोचते ही नहीं। उनकी उपलब्धि अद्भुत है।' बनासकांठा से जीत, उनकी कोई एक बार की जीत नहीं है। करीब तीन दशक से ठाकोर लगातार चुनाव जीत रही हैं। 1995 में पंचायतों में महिला आरक्षण की शुरुआत के साथ उन्होंने उन्नीस साल की उम्र में, अपना पहला चुनाव लड़ा और शानदार जीत हासिल की। वह बताती हैं कि 'मैंने अपना पहला चुनाव तालुका पंचायत में जीता और तालुका पंचायत अध्यक्ष बनी। तब से, मैंने ज़िला चुनाव, विधानसभा चुनाव और अब लोकसभा चुनाव जीता है।'

यह खासतौर से इसलिए भी महत्वपूर्ण उपलब्धि है क्योंकि उनका तीस साल का राजनीतिक सफ़र, गुजरात में भाजपा के उदय के साथ चल रहा है। गुजरात में कांग्रेस अपने पहले की ताकत की धुंधली छाया रह गई है, जो नेतृत्व की कमी और संगठन की लगातार कम होती ताकत से जूझ रही है। 'गुजरात में कांग्रेस का नेता होना आसान काम नहीं है। भाजपा यहां जो चाहे कर सकती है। यदि आपके घर का कोई सदस्य सरकारी नौकरी में है, तो पाला नहीं बदलने पर उसकी नौकरी से छुट्टी करने की धमकी दी जाती है। यहां साम-दाम-दंड-भेद की राजनीति चलती है,' मुखर ठाकोर ने कहा।

उत्तर गुजरात का ग्रामीण ज़िला बनासकांठा, खासतौर से एक बड़ी चुनौती है। इलाके की राजनीतिक अर्थव्यवस्था के केन्द्र में देश की सबसे बड़ी सहकारी डेयरियों में से एक बनास डेयरी है, जिसका सालाना कारोबार 15,000 करोड़ रुपये से ज़्यादा है। यह गुजरात के विशाल जिला स्तरीय दूध संघ के नेटवर्क का हिस्सा है, जो प्रतिष्ठित अमूल ब्रांड के तहत अपने उत्पादों का

कारोबार करता है। लाखों किसान सहकारी समिति के सदस्य हैं, जो अपनी कमाई के लिए इस पर पूरी तरह निर्भर है। भाजपा का डेयरी नेटवर्क पर कड़ा नियंत्रण है। स्थानीय कद्दावर नेता और गुजरात विधानसभा के अध्यक्ष शंकर चौधरी बनास डेयरी के अध्यक्ष हैं। विपक्षी पार्टियों का आरोप था कि चुनाव के समय भाजपा, किसान मतदाताओं को प्रभावित करने के लिए डेयरी प्रबंधन पर अपनी ताकत का इस्तेमाल करती है। यहीं पर एक रैली प्रधानमंत्री ने वह विवादित भाषण दिया था, जिसमें उन्होंने मतदाताओं को चेतावनी थी कि 'अगर उनके पास दो भैंस हैं, तो कांग्रेस सत्ता में आने पर उनमें से एक भैंस छीन लेगी।'

तो ठाकोर ने अपने ख़िलाफ़ इन ताकतों पर कैसे काबू पाया। मध्यमवर्गीय परिवार में पैदा हुईं गनीबेन ठाकोर, प्रभावशाली ओबीसी क्षत्रिय ठाकोर समुदाय से हैं। उनके पिता पुराने ज़माने के गांधीवादी सामाजिक कार्यकर्ता थे, जिन्होंने उन्हें सार्वजनिक जीवन में उतरने को प्रेरित किया। वे कहती हैं कि 'मेरे पास निजी संपत्ति नहीं है, लेकिन लोगों की दुआएं मेरे साथ हैं। लोग जानते हैं कि अगर वे गेनीबेन का वोट देंगे, तो वह अच्छे और बुरे समय में उनकी सेवा के लिए मौजूद रहेंगी।' उन्होंने अपने विधायक फंड में से ज़्यादातर पैसा लड़कियों की शिक्षा पर खर्च किया, उससे स्कूल और छात्रावास बनवाए। 'मैं अपने चुनावों के लिए क्राउडफंडिग से पैसा जुटाती हूं। लोग मुझे 100 रुपये से लेकर 10,000 रुपये तक चंदा देते हैं। वे मुझे पैसे देते हैं, मैं उनकी सेवा में अपना जीवन लगाती हूं,' उनका अंदाज़ नाटकीय है।

एक तरह से, गेनीबेन की कामयाबी यह याद दिलाती है कि बिना किसी बड़े पैसे की पार्टी मशीनरी के भरोसे भी लोकसभा चुनाव लड़ना और जीतना संभव है। किसी अभियान के लिए क्राउडफंडिग के जरिए पैसा जुटाना, गांधीवादी नजरिया माना जाता है, जिसका मतलब है कि मतदाता राजनीतिक ट्रस्टीशिप के रूप में अपने पैसे से योग्य उम्मीदवार के समर्थन के लिए तैयार है। चंदा जुटाना लोगों की इस प्रतिबद्धता को बताता है कि वे राजनीति में निवेश और उसकी ज़िम्मेदारी के लिए तैयार हैं। आज़ादी के आंदोलन में गांधी जी लोगों से पैसा और गहने आदि भी लेते थे, ताकि लगे कि यह लोगों का आंदोलन है, लोगों का, लोगों के लिए, लोगों द्वारा एक असली जन आंदोलन है। क्या गेनीबेन दूसरों के लिए रोल मॉडल बन सकती हैं? 'मैं बस इतना जानती हूं कि मैं लोगों की सेवा करती रहूंगी, इससे मुझे खुशी मिलती है,' वह जवाब देती हैं। यह फिर से मूल मसलों पर लौटने का नजरिया है, जिसने उन्हें बाधाओं को पार करने और ऐतिहासक जीत की पटकथा लिखने लायक बनाया। महात्मा को इस पर अभिमान होगा।

═

नब्बे के दशक में, जब कश्मीर घाटी में उग्रवाद चरम पर था, देर रात मेरे होटल के कमरे पर दस्तक ने मुझे थोड़ा चिंता में डाल दिया। दरवाज़ा मज़बूती से बंद था, मैंने चाबी के छेद से

झांका, पठान सूट पहने एक गंजा, बिना दाढ़ी वाला आदमी, हाथ हिलाता हुआ दिखा। 'चिंता मत करो सर, मैं आतंकवादी नहीं हूं!' उसने हंसते हुए मुझे आश्वस्त किया। इंजीनियर राशिद उर्फ शेख अब्दुल राशिद से यह मेरी पहली मुलाक़ात थी। उनके उपनाम से याद आता है कि सार्वजनिक जीवन में आने से बहुत पहले, वह जम्मू-कश्मीर की एक निर्माण कंपनी में इंजीनियर के तौर पर काम करते थे। 'तब मैंने लोगों के लिए पुल बनाए, अब मैं लोगों के बीच पुल बना रहा हूं,' उन्होंने छोटी सी टिप्पणी की। हमारी दोस्ती हो गई। उत्तर कश्मीर के लंगेट शहर के राशिद साफ़गोई से बात करने वाले राजनेता हैं, जिन्होंने ख़ूनी घाटी की अशांत और जटिल दुनिया में मेरे लिए खिड़की खोली।

दो बार निर्दलीय विधायक चुने जाने के बाद, वह 2024 में तिहाड़ जेल से बारामुला का लोकसभा चुनाव लड़ रहे थे। जम्मू कश्मीर से अनुच्छेद 370 को निरस्त किए जाने के तुरंत बाद 2019 में राशिद को हिरासत में लिया गया था। राशिद पर 'गैरक़ानूनी गतिविधियां (रोकथाम) अधिनियम' (यूएपीए) के तहत आरोप लगाए गए थे और नेशनल जांच एजेंसी (एनआईए) के मुताबिक, उन पर आतंकवाद के लिए पैसा जुटाने और अलगाववादियों और पाकिस्तान से गड़बड़ी करने वालों के साथ काम करने का आरोप था। राशिद ने ज़ोर देकर कहा, आरोप झूठे थे और उन्होंने जो कुछ भी कहा या किया था उसका आतंकवाद से कोई संबंध नहीं था। उन्होंने आरोप लगाया कि 'मुझे मेरी राजनीति की वजह से परेशान किया जा रहा है, क्योंकि मैं दिल्ली और श्रीनगर में सत्ता में बैठे लोगों के सामने सच बोलता हूं।' कश्मीर पर लंबे समय से नज़र रखने वाले एक शख्स ने कहा, 'राशिद की राजनीति नरम अलगाववाद और बदलती निष्ठाओं के साथ देखी जा सकती है।' वह तेज़तर्रार नेता हैं, जिन्होंने हमेशा कश्मीरियों की स्वायतता और अधिकारों के लिए आवाज़ उठाई है। लेकिन उन्होंने हमेशा इस मुद्दे के लिए वोट की वकालत की, गोली की नहीं।

अब, वह घाटी के दो सबसे बड़े राजनीतिक चेहरों, पूर्व मुख्यमंत्री और नेशनल कॉन्फ्रेंस के नेता उमर अब्दुल्ला और पीपुल्स कॉन्फ्रेंस के नेता सज्जाद लोन के ख़िलाफ़ बारामुला से चुनाव लड़कर अपनी बात साबित करने के लिए वापस आ गए थे। कागज़ों पर यह लड़ाई बराबरी की नहीं लग रही थी। एक निर्दलीय उम्मीदवार, पार्टी सिस्टम की मदद से मैदान में उतरे दो बड़े प्रतिद्वन्दियों के ख़िलाफ़ जेल से चुनाव लड़ रहा था। फिर भी उनकी यह कमज़ोरी उनके लिए तुरुप का पत्ता साबित हुई। जेल में रहते हुए, राशिद ने मतदाताओं के साथ एक भावनात्मक कार्ड खेला। बहुत से कश्मीरियों के लिए, जेल की सलाखें, एक दमनकारी भारत सरकार की प्रतीक हैं। तीन दशकों से, हज़ारों कश्मीरियों को जेल में रखा गया है, उनमें से सभी, उन पर लगे आरोपों के मुताबिक दोषी नहीं हैं। 'जेल का बदला, वोट से लो,' राशिद के 22 साल के बेटे अबरार चुनाव प्रचार में नारे लगा रहे थे।

राशिद के बेटे अबरार सीमित साधनों से पहाड़ियों में चुनाव प्रचार कर रहे थे। एनजीओ नेटवर्क से पैसा जुटाते, अबरार कहते हैं कि उन्होंने सबसे ज़्यादा पैसा 27 हज़ार रुपये किराए की कार के पेट्रोल पर खर्च किए। उन्होंने रिटायर्ड सरकारी शिक्षक रहे अपने दादा की पेंशन से अभियान का कुछ खर्चा निकाला। राजनीतिक प्रतिद्वन्दियों का आरोप था कि सुरक्षा एजेंसियों ने घाटी की मुख्य धारा की पार्टियों को हराने के लिए राशिद के चुनाव में मदद की, उनके बेटे ने इसे सिरे से ख़ारिज़ कर दिया। अबरार कहते हैं, 'हमारे पास पोस्टर-बैनर के लिए भी पैसे नहीं थे, सबकुछ कार्यकर्ताओं के जरिए किया गया, यहां तक कि लाउडस्पीकर भी हमें जनता के चंदे से मिले थे और जब नहीं मिला, तो मैंने बिना माइक के ही भाषण दिया।'

आम लोगों से समर्थन कोई अचरज की बात नहीं थी। अपने राजनीतिक जीवन में, राशिद जनता के नेता माने जाते थे, ऐसा राजनेता जो पारपंरिक या स्टीरियोटाइप को चुनौती देता है। राशिद ने दावा किया कि उन्होंने विधायक निधि का पैसा अपने ज़िले के ग़रीब बच्चों को मुफ्त शिक्षा के इंतज़ाम पर खर्च किया था। सत्ता या सुरक्षा के तामझाम से दूर, राशिद कभी किसी मोटरसाइकिल पर पीछे बैठकर या स्थानीय लोगों के साथ गली के किनारे कहवा पीते हुए दिखते हैं। उन्होंने कहा, 'जब लोगों ने आपको चुना है तो फिर सुरक्षा की क्या ज़रूरत है? उनका समर्थन ही मेरी सबसे बड़ी सुरक्षा है।'

इसके विपरीत, उमर अब्दुल्ला और सज्जाद लोन, दोनों ही बड़े राजनीतिक परिवारों से थे और अपने सोशल स्टेटस से पहचाने जाते थे। बेहतर दिखने और अच्छे से बोलने वाले दोनों लोग घाटी के अभिजात वर्ग की नुमाइंदगी करते थे। दोनों को ही 2019 में, अनुच्छेद 370 के निरस्त होने के बाद राजनीतिक गतिविधियों को लेकर गिरफ़्तार किया गया और कई महीनों बाद रिहा किया गया। जबकि राशिद पांच साल से तिहाड़ जेल में है और अपने परिवार तक से बात नहीं कर पा रहे। वहीं उनके प्रतिद्वन्दियों को कम से कम आज़ादी मिल गई। अबरार कहते हैं, 'क्या आप जानते हैं कि मैं पिछले पांच साल में केवल एक बार अपने पिता से मिला हूं? वे फोन पर भी हमसे बात नहीं कर सकते।' राशिद को पीड़ित होने का 'विक्टिम कार्ड' उनके जेलरों ने अनजाने में ही दे दिया था। बहुत से मतदाताओं की नज़र में, निर्दलीय उम्मीदवार का समर्थन विरोध का प्रतीक था। यह सत्ता विरोधी वोट था, भारत सरकार के ख़िलाफ़ नाराज़गी का वोट।

जब बारामुला के नतीज़े आए, तो लगा चिनार के हर पेड़ पर से विरोध के वोट की गूंज सुनाई दे रही थी। राशिद ने जेल से एक लाख से ज़्यादा वोटों से जीत हासिल की। यह उन लोगों के लिए चौंकाने वाला नतीजा था, जो अब्दुल्ला और लोन के बीच मुकाबला होने की सोच रहे थे। तमाम मुश्किलों और सीमित संसधानों के बावजूद भी यूएपीए बंदी ने धुरंधर प्रतिद्वन्दियों को हरा दिया। विनम्र उमर अब्दुल्ला की प्रतिक्रिया उत्साहजनक थी, उन्होंने ट्वीट कर कहा:

'मुझे नहीं लगता कि इस जीत से उन्हें जेल से जल्दी रिहाई मिलेगी और न ही उत्तर कश्मीर के लोगों को वह नुमाइंदगी मिलेगी, जिसका उन्हें अधिकार है, लेकिन मतदाताओं ने अपनी बात कह दी है और लोकतंत्र में यही मायने रखता है। वाकई यही महत्वपूर्ण है।' राशिद को अदालत में अपनी बेगुनाही के लिए लंबी लड़ाई लड़नी पड़ सकती है, लेकिन अपने कश्मीरी लोगों की अदालत में वह बरी हो गए हैं।

═

मणिपुर सिर्फ़ दो लोकसभा सीटों के साथ यूं तो देश के चुनावी नक्शे पर एक बिंदू जैसा है, लेकिन 2024 में मणिपुर एक ऐसी सरकार का चेहरा बन गया, जिसे अपनी राजनीतिक ताकत के आगे कुछ नहीं दिखाई देता। मई 2023 में यहां मैतेई और कुकी लोगों के बीच जातीय हिंसा में 200 से ज़्यादा लोग मारे गए और हज़ारों लोग बेघर हो गए। जब हथियारबंद लोग सड़कों पर उतर आए, तब ताकतवर सरकार कहीं नज़र नहीं आ रही थी। सुरक्षाबल हालात को काबू में लाने के लिए संघर्ष कर रहे थे। इस हिंसक आग लगने के बाद प्रधानमंत्री नरेन्द्र मोदी ने एक बार भी राज्य का दौरा नहीं किया। गृहमंत्री अमित शाह ने मुख्यमंत्री एन. बीरेन सिंह को हटाने से साफ इंकार कर दिया। ऐसा लग रहा था मानो मणिपुर एक ऐसा नासूर बन गया था जिसे कोई ठीक नहीं करना चाहता। दूर बैठे देश के लोगों की चुप्पी भी तब टूटी, जब कथित तौर पर सामूहिक बलात्कार के बाद दो महिलाओं की नग्न परेड के वीडियो सामने आए।

शुरुआत में तो यह तय नहीं था कि मणिपुर में चुनाव होंगे या नहीं। कुकी-ज़ो समूहों ने चुनावों के बहिष्कार की बात की थी और सुरक्षा एडवायज़री में उम्मीदवारों को उग्रवादियों का निशाना बनाए जाने की चेतावनी दी गई थी। प्रतिशोध के डर से, कई संभावित राजनीतिक उम्मीदवारों ने चुनावी मैदान से दूर रहने का फ़ैसला किया। इस बारूदी सुरंग में कदम रखने वाले थे दिल्ली में जवाहरलाल नेहरू विश्वविद्यालय में सामाजिक मनोविज्ञान के प्रोफेसर अट्ठावन साल के बिमोल अकोईजम। प्रतिष्ठित शिक्षाविद् और फ़िल्म निर्माता, अकोईजम ने विभाजन पर बहुत शोध किया था, इसके साथ दूसरी कई अहम परियोजनाओं पर काम करने का लंबा अनुभव था। बुद्धिजीवी और सामाजिक कार्यकर्ता अकोईजम ने मणिपुर हिंसा को लेकर बहुत से लेख लिखे और टीवी पर अपनी बातों को दमदार तरह से रखा था। वे कहते हैं, 'मैं क़ानून-व्यवस्था बनाए रखने में सरकार की विफलता से नाराज़ और निराश था।' जब 2024 की जनवरी में, कांग्रेस की तरफ से इनर मणिपुर से चुनाव लड़ने का प्रस्ताव आया तो उन्होंने इस पर अपनी पत्नी ओलिविया के साथ लंबी चर्चा की। वे चुनाव लड़ने के लिए बहुत इच्छुक नहीं थे। उन्होंने कहा, 'मुझे लगा कि बाहर रहकर राजनीतिक हालात की आलोचना करने से बेहतर होगा कि सिस्टम में घुसकर अपने लोगों के लिए बदलाव की कोशिश की जाए।'

यह बदलाव आसान कतई नहीं था। उनको धमकी दी गई, उनकी एक चुनावी सभा में गोलियां चलाई गईं और नामांकन वापसी का दबाव डालने के लिए कुछ हथियारबंद लोग इम्फाल में उनके घर में घुस गए। अकोईजम कहते हैं, 'मुझे 48 घटे तक भूमिगत रहना पड़ा और फिर पर्चा वापसी की तारीख के बाद ही बाहर आया। इन धमकियों ने हार न मानने के मेरे संकल्प को और मज़बूत कर दिया।'

उनके ख़िलाफ़ सरकार में मंत्री और पूर्व आईपीएस अधिकारी रहे भाजपा के बसंत कुमार सिंह मैदान में थे, जिनके पास समर्थकों का एक बड़ा नेटवर्क था। इनर मणिपुर लोकसभा में आने वाली 32 विधानसभा सीटों में से 29 पर भाजपा विधायक हैं। प्रदेश का पूरा सिस्टम सीमित संसाधनों वाले अकोईजम के ख़िलाफ़ एकजुट हो गया था। उन्होंने कहा, 'मेरे पास एक चीज़ थी, आम लोगों की ताकत, यह उनका चुनाव था, मेरा नहीं। आपको यह जानकर अचरज होगा कि बहुत से युवा मणिपुरियों ने मेरे समर्थन में व्हाट्सएप ग्रुप बनाए। यहां तक कि देश और दुनियाभर से मणिपुरी लोग आए, कुछ तो ऑस्ट्रेलिया और सिंगापुर तक से भी, सिर्फ मुझे वोट देने के लिए आए।'

डोर-टू-डोर अभियान के दौरान, एक बुज़ुर्ग सब्जी बेचने वाले ने मेरे पास आकर 100 रुपये थमा दिए, ये उसका समर्थन करने का प्रतीक था। अकोईजम के अभियान में मतदाता ही आगे थे। एक साल तक लगातार डर और हिंसा के माहौल ने आम मतदाताओं और उनके परिवारों पर असर डाला था। वे बदलाव चाहते थे। लेकिन यह बदलाव सिर्फ बीरेन सिंह सरकार की नाकामियों और सत्ता विरोधी लहर का नहीं था, बल्कि दाग़दार हो गए मणिपुर की चुप्पी साधने वाली राजनीतिक संस्कृति के ख़िलाफ़ था। इम्फाल के वरिष्ठ पत्रकार प्रदीप फंजौबेम कहते हैं, 'मुझे लगता है कि अकोईजम सही वक्त पर सही जगह पर थे। वह एक नया चेहरा थे, ऐसे समय में बाहरी व्यक्ति, जब लोगों ने सामान्य राजनीतिक चेहरों को खारिज़ कर दिया था।'

दिलचस्प बात यह है कि गृहमंत्री अमित शाह ने इम्फाल में अपने प्रचार के दौरान, अकोईजाम के जेएनयू कनेक्शन की बात की, उन्हें देश-विरोधी और 'टुकड़े-टुकड़े गैंग' का सदस्य बताया, लेकिन सत्ता विरोधी माहौल में व्यक्तिगत अपमान करने का कोई नतीजा नहीं निकला। अकोईजम ने कहा, 'मुझे लगता है कि इन बेबुनियाद आरोपों से हमें कुछ हज़ार वोट ज़्यादा ही मिले।' अकोईजम एक लाख से ज़्यादा वोटों से जीते और कांग्रेस ने मणिपुर की दोनों सीटें भाजपा से छीन लीं।

अकोईजम समझते हैं कि सार्वजनिक जीवन में उनका असली इम्तिहान अब शुरू हुआ है। मणिपुर जातीय आधार पर बहुत ज़्यादा बंट गया है, जिसमें मैतेई और कुकी अब भी आमने-सामने हैं। वे सबको साथ लाना चाहते हैं। वे कहते हैं, 'मैं हर मणिपुरी का सांसद हूं। मैतेई, कुकी, नागा, पंगल, मारवाड़ी, ये सभी मेरे मतदाता हैं।' वे उनकी ज़िंदगी में बदलाव के अपने मिशन में

सफल हों या न हों, लेकिन उनकी चुनावी जीत ने बता दिया है कि मतदाता अपना विरोध, वोट के जरिए कैसे दर्ज कराते हैं। अकोईजम कहते हैं कि 'जब लोग बोलते हैं तो जादू हो सकता है।'

खूबसूरत, लेकिन सदमे में डूबे मणिपुर के लोगों ने अपनी आवाज़ बुलंद की है। क्या सत्ता में बैठे लोग, हाशिये पर रहने वालों की आवाज़ सुनेंगे?

═

मई 2024 के पहले रविवार को, अयोध्या मानो भगवा रंग में डूबी हुई थी। संघ परिवार के कार्यकर्ता पूरे उत्तर प्रदेश से शहर में उमड़े पड़े थे। सड़कों को साफ किया गया था। दुकानें सजी हुई थीं और रात में आसमान मंदिरों की लाइटों से जगमगा रहा था। प्रधानमंत्री मोदी चुनावी रोड शो कर रहे थे। जनवरी में राम मंदिर के प्राण-प्रतिष्ठा समारोह के बाद वह पहली बार अयोध्या आए थे। हज़ारों लोग कतार बनाकर राजनीतिक हिंदुत्व के 'स्वयंभू भगवान' के दर्शन के लिए खड़े थे। हर गली-मोहल्ले में प्रधानमंत्री के आदमकद कट-आउट लगे थे, जिन पर रामलला को घर वापस लाने के लिए धन्यवाद देने और उसके बदले में चार सौ पार की जीत का वादा करने वाले पोस्टर लगे हुए थे। जब मोदी ने चमचमाती पीली वैन पर चढ़कर, भीड़ की तरफ भाजपा का कमल चिन्ह दिखाया, तो समर्थक गुलाब की पंखुडियां बरसा रहे थे और 'जय श्री राम' और 'भारत माता' की जय के नारे लगा रहे थे. पुलिस को इन उन्मादी समर्थकों को रोकने में काफी मशक्कत का सामना करना पड़ा। मोदी के पीछे उत्तर प्रदेश के मुख्यमंत्री योगी आदित्यनाथ थे, जो जानबूझकर स्टार से एक कदम दूर थे।

इन दो दिग्गजों के बीच फैज़ाबाद-अयोध्या लोकसभा सीट से दो बार सांसद और पांच बार विधायक रहे लल्लू सिंह थे। सिंह ने भीड़ की ओर कभी-कभार हाथ हिलाया, ज़्यादातर वक्त मोदी का उत्साह ही दिख रहा था। न्यूज़ चैनलों पर रोड शो का सीधा प्रसारण हो रहा था। लोगों के उत्साह का ज़ोरदार तरीके से ज़िक्र, ऑन एयर कमेंट्री में किया जा रहा था।

मैं और मेरी टीम पूरे दिन अयोध्या में एक चुनावी कार्यक्रम को शूट कर रहे थे। हमने एक उत्तेजक सवाल: राम या रोज़गार पर बहस की और इस पर कई तरह की आवाज़ें थीं। देश के अलग-अलग हिस्सों से रामलला के दर्शन के लिए आए ज़्यादातर तीर्थयात्री काफी उत्साहित थे। वे राम मंदिर बनाने के लिए शुक्रिया अदा कर रहे थे। स्थानीय दुकानदार भी खुश थे, क्योंकि पर्यटकों और तीर्थयात्रियों की आवक बढ़ने से उनका कारोबार भी बढ़ा है। कुछ स्थानीय लोगों ने एलपीजी की बढ़ती कीमतों और भ्रष्टाचार की शिकायतें कीं। लेकिन भाजपा कार्यकर्ताओं ने इन आवाज़ों को खारिज कर दिया। फिर जैसे ही, हम कैमरा बंद करने वाले थे, तभी एक ऑटो-चालक फ्रेम में आया और अपनी बात कहने पर ज़ोर दिया। उसने ज़ोर से कहा, 'भाई साहब, न मथुरा, न काशी, अबकी बार अवधेश पासी!'

मेरी पहली प्रतिक्रिया था, अवधेश कौन? चुनावी मैदान में पैराशूट से उतरते, दिल्ली के कई पत्रकारों की तरह, मैं, फैज़ाबाद की जाति और समुदायों की जटिल राजनीति की हकीकत को नहीं समझ पाया था। हमारा ध्यान खासतौर से मीडिया से बने अयोध्या में मोदी-उन्माद और मतदताओं पर राम मंदिर के प्रभाव को समझने पर था। फिर भी, ऑटो-चालक के नारे ने हमें अयोध्या कांड के दूसरे पहलू को जानने के लिए मजबूर किया। वह व्यक्ति इस बात की शिकायत कर रहा था कि 'कैसे शहर में होटल बनाने के लिए, प्रभावशाली स्थानीय भाजपा नेताओं और बाहरी लोगों के बीच ज़मीनों के बड़े-बड़े सौदे हो रहे थे, कैसे नगर-निगम के अधिकारी, पर्यटकों के लिए सड़कों को चौड़ी करने के लिए पुराने घरों को गिरा रहे थे और कैसे मंदिर अधिकारियों से संबंध रखने वले लोग संपत्ति की बढ़ती कीमतों से फायदा उठा रहे थे।' उसने जोर देकर कहा, 'सब पैसे का खेल है।'

मोदी के आकर्षक रोड शो के बाद, अगली सुबह हम अयोध्या जिले की तहसील मिल्कीपुर में थे। अयोध्या के मंदिर की धूमधाम से उलट, मिल्कीपुर में कोई पर्यटक नहीं था। कोई कैमरा यहां की गंदी पगडंडियों को शूट करने नहीं आया, किसी वीवीआईपी ने यहां फोटो पोज़ नहीं दिया। लेकिन मीडिया के ध्यान नहीं देने के बावजूद फैज़ाबाद से समाजवादी पार्टी के उम्मीदवार अवधेश प्रसाद पासी यहां डोर-टू-डोर अभियान शुरू कर रहे थे।

सत्तर साल के वरिष्ठ राजनेता अवधेश प्रसाद फ़ैज़ाबाद लोकसभा सीट में शामिल पांच विधानसभा क्षेत्रों में से एक मिल्कीपुर से विधायक थे। समाजवादी पार्टी की खास लाल टोपी और मुड़ा हुआ कुर्ता-पजामा पहने प्रसाद हमें देखकर खुश नज़र आए। उन्होंने ठहाका लगाते हुए कहा, 'कोई तो नेशनल मीडिया हमसे भी बात करने आया है।' खिचड़ी बालों वाले प्रसाद, कोई नौसिखिया राजनेता नहीं थे, बल्कि नौ बार विधायक रह चुके थे। आपातकाल के दौरान उन्हें जेल जाना पड़ा और जेल में रहते हुए 1977 में उन्होंने अपना पहला विधानसभा चुनाव जीता, जो जनता पार्टी की जीत का उथल-पुथल भरा साल था। उस वक्त के युवा राजनीतिक कार्यकर्ता अवधेश प्रसाद, लोकदल नेता और पूर्व प्रधानमंत्री चौधरी चरण सिंह के चेले (अनुयायी) थे। अपने गुरु को लेकर इतनी श्रद्धा थी कि वे अपने पिता के अंतिम संस्कार में भी शामिल नहीं हुए, क्योंकि वे 1981 के उपचुनाव में अमेठी में थे, जहां राजीव गांधी ने अपने पहले चुनाव में लोकदल के शरद यादव को हराया था। प्रसाद तब शरद यादव के चुनाव अभियान के प्रबंधक थे और चरण सिंह का निर्देश था कि आखिरी वोट की गिनती तक मतगणना कक्ष से बाहर नहीं निकलना था। 1992 में जब मुलायम सिंह ने समाजवादी पार्टी बनाई तो वे मुलायम सिंह के साथ थे। यूपी के कई क्षेत्रीय दलों में से समाजवादी पार्टी एक थी, जो जनता पार्टी के देशभर में बंटने के बाद बनी थी। यादव-प्रभुत्व वाली पार्टी में पासी उपजाति के दलित चेहरे प्रसाद, नेताजी के साथ तब भी जुड़े रहे, जब ज्यादातर दलित मतदाताओं की पसंद बहुजन समाज पार्टी बन गई

थी। वे कहते हैं, 'हमारी राजनीति वफ़ादारी की है, अवसरवादिता की नहीं।' यही वजह रही कि जब अखिलेश यादव ने उन्हें चुनाव लड़ने को कहा, तो वह बिना किसी हिचक के फैज़ाबाद की चुनौती स्वीकार करने के लिए तैयार हो गए।

उनके चुनाव अभियान को देखकर मुझे लगा कि प्रसाद, राम मंदिर को लेकर उत्साह से परेशान नहीं थे। उनका तर्क था, 'भाजपा राम के नाम पर राजनीति करती है, वोट का व्यापार करती है। असली रामभक्त तो हम हैं, मेरे परिवार में कई लोगों के नाम राम से जुड़े हैं।' और फिर उनकी पंचलाइन आईः 'बीजेपी कहती है, हम राम को लाए हैं, सच्चाई यह है कि वे महंगाई और बेरोज़गारी लाए हैं।' विमर्श की लड़ाई में एक सीधा-सादा विश्वसनीय ईमानदार चेहरा प्रसाद, हिंदू धर्म के आध्यात्मिक-सांस्कृतिक घर माने जाने वाले अयोध्या में भाजपा के हिंदू राष्ट्रवाद के मुद्दे पर चर्चा कर रहे थे। प्रसाद ने कहा, 'कृपया मुझे दलित नेता के तौर पर न देखें, मैं पक्का समाजवादी हूं, शुरू से आखिर तक।'

पिछले तीन दशकों से उत्तर प्रदेश की राजनीति, धार्मिक और जातिगत पहचानों और मंडल-कमंडल की ताकतों के बीच बनती-बिगड़ती रही है। इस माहौल में अखिलेश यादव का उम्मीदवार का चुनाव एकदम सही लगता था। अवधेश प्रसाद दलित हैं। इस संसदीय क्षेत्र में **26** फ़ीसद दलित, **14** फ़ीसद मुस्लिम आबादी और काफी तादाद में यादव और कुर्मी ओबीसी आबादी है। दूसरी तरफ भाजपा के उम्मीदवार, लल्लू सिंह एक ठाकुर हैं, यहां सवर्णों की तादाद थोड़ी कम है। अयोध्या-फ़ैज़ाबाद, एक तरह से अखिलेश के अपने पीडीए (पिछड़ा, दलित, अल्पसंख्यक और आधी आबादी गठबंधन) के लिए एक आदर्श इलाका माना जा सकता है।

सत्तर साल के चतुर राजनेता अपनी संभावनाओं के लिए आश्वस्त दिख रहे थे, लेकिन अयोध्या में मोदी के रोड शो की मीडिया में छाई तस्वीरें उनके दिमाग में घूमती रहीं। तमाम तरह के जातिगत समीकरणों और स्थानीय सत्ता-विरोधी माहौल के कारण फ़ैज़ाबाद, भाजपा के लिए आसान नहीं था, लेकिन क्या राम मंदिर अपने पवित्र इलाके में पर्याप्त वोट दिलाएगा? हालांकि मेरा मन कह रहा था कि ऑटो-चालक का आकर्षक नारा राम मंदिर की चमचमाती लाइटों के पार तक गूंज सकता है। लेकिन मोदी समर्थकों का उत्साह देखकर, मैं दूसरी तरफ चला गया।

फ़ैज़ाबाद के जब नतीजे आए तो चौंकाने वाले थे। प्रसाद ने असली रामभक्त होने के अपने दावे को सच कर दिया था। उन्होंने पचास हज़ार से ज़्यादा वोटों से जीत हासिल की और न केवल अपने प्रतिद्वन्दी भाजपा के लल्लू सिंह को हराया, बल्कि पूरी हिन्दू मशीनरी को पराजित किया था। जातिगत समीकरणों और स्थानीय मुद्दों ने हिंदू एकजुटता के नारे को मात दे दी थी। मंडल ने कमंडल पर बढ़त हासिल कर ली थी। किसी ने मुझे चुनावी पत्रकारिता के पुराने नियम को याद दिलायाः 'एक, सड़क किनारे खड़े किसी की राय को कभी नज़रअंदाज़ न करें, जैसा कि

इस मामले में, एक ऑटो चालक, जो अंदरूनी समझ को आपसे साझा करता है; और दूसरा, कभी आत्मसंतुष्ट और दिखावे वाले पक्षपाती माहौल की गूंज में मत फसिए।'

इस चुनावी हवा में बहता एक अहम सवाल मेरे सामने है: भारतीय मीडिया ने **2024** के नतीज़ों को इतना ग़लत कैसे समझा? इस अध्याय में बताई गई, उम्मीदों की दस कहानियों के बाद, अब समय आ गया है कि हम इस गहरे अंधेरे से निकलने के रास्ते पर रोशनी डालें। अंतरात्मा को झकझोरने वाले अस्तित्व के संकट की दुविधा है। अब समय आ गया है कि न्यूज़रूम में मौजूद सबसे अहम सवाल का सामना किया जाए!

14

'गोदी मीडिया': मीडिया का कब्ज़ा

बीबीसीः जब आप पीछे मुड़कर देखते हैं (गुजरात नरसंहार पर), तो क्या आपको ऐसा लगता है कि आप कुछ अलग करते?

नरेन्द्र मोदीः हां, एक चीज़ में मैं बहुत कमज़ोर था, और वह था कि मीडिया को कैसे संभालना था।

—*भारतः मोदी से सवाल, बीबीसी, 2023 में प्रसारित*

'सर, मुझे लगता है कि दिल्ली पुलिस आपको गिरफ़्तार करने आ रही है, थोड़ा ध्यान रखें, सावधानी बरतें!' फ़ोन लाइन पर आवाज़ चिंतित लग रही थी। गृह मंत्रालय को कवर करने वाले मेरे एक सहयोगी ने मुझे यह बताने के लिए फ़ोन किया कि नॉर्थ ब्लॉक में अफ़वाह थी कि देशद्रोह के आरोप में मुझे गिरफ़्तार करने के लिए दिल्ली पुलिस को हरी झंडी मिल गई थी। मुझे एकबारगी को उस पर विश्वास नहीं हुआ। गिरफ़्तारी? देशद्रोह? जेल? मैं? यकीन नहीं हो रहा था, इससे मैं थोड़ा हैरान और सच कहूं तो डर गया था। एक दिन पहले ही, 28 जनवरी, 2021 को, दिल्ली पुलिस ने कांग्रेस सांसद शशि थरूर, वरिष्ठ पत्रकार मृणाल पांडे और ज़फर आगा, *कारवां* पत्रिका के संपादक विनोद जोस, पत्रिका के मालिक अनंत नाथ और मेरे ख़िलाफ़ एफआईआर दर्ज की थी। इस एफआईआर में हम पर दिल्ली में आंदोलनकारी किसानों की गणतंत्र दिवस पर निकाली गई ट्रैक्टर रैली के दौरान एक किसान की मौत के बारे में ट्वीट पर जानबूझकर गलत सूचना फैलाने का आरोप लगाया गया था।

यह सिर्फ़ दिल्ली पुलिस ही नहीं थी। कुछ घंटों में ही उत्तरप्रदेश में नोएडा पुलिस, मध्य प्रदेश के एक पुलिस स्टेशन और हरियाणा के गुरुग्राम में भी करीब-करीब ऐसी ही तीन एफआईआर दर्ज की गई। तीनों राज्यों में एक बात समान थी: तीनों में ही भाजपा सरकारें थीं। एक वकील मित्र ने सलाह दी, 'घर से निकलो और किसी गैर-भाजपा शासित राज्य के लिए फ्लाइट पकड़ लो। बस दिल्ली से बाहर निकलो।' इस बीच मेरे सहयोगी सुरेन्द्र नागर, मेरे लिए मुंबई का टिकट बुक करने में लग गए, वहां शिवसेना के नेतृत्व में महाविकास अघाड़ी की सरकार थी। मैं हैरान हो गया, गुस्से से जवाब दिया, 'क्या आप वाकई मुझे भागने और छिपने के लिए कह रहे हैं? साथ ही अगर वे मुझे गिरफ़्तार करते हैं तो उन्हें शशि थरूर को भी गिरफ़्तार करना होगा? क्या आपको लगता है कि सरकार दुनियाभर में पहचानी जाने वाली प्रमुख विपक्षी आवाज़ को सिर्फ़ इसलिए गिरफ़्तार करेगी, क्योंकि उन्होंने एक किसान की मौत के बारे में ट्वीट किया था? और क्या मृणाल जी जैसी वरिष्ठ और प्रतिष्ठित पत्रकार को छूने की हिम्मत करेंगे? मुझे लगता है कि वे हमें गिरफ़्तारी की धमकी देकर डराने की कोशिश कर रहे हैं, ऐसा कुछ नहीं होगा।'

संभावित गिरफ़्तारी पर मेरे उदासीन नज़रिए का मेरी पत्नी सागरिका और बेटी तारिणी पर कोई असर नहीं पड़ा। तारिणी ने अभी-अभी लॉ की डिग्री हासिल की थी और एक प्रमुख कॉरपोरेट लॉ फर्म के लिए घर से ही काम कर रही थी। कोविड सोशल डिस्टेंसिंग नियम अब भी लागू थे--हालात के प्रति मेरी लापरवाही से वह नाराज़ थी। 'आपको कैसे पता कि वे आपको गिरफ़्तार नहीं करेंगे? आप क़ानून या पुलिस के साथ कोई ख़तरा मोल नहीं ले सकते?' उसका तर्क था। पुलिस को मुझे गिरफ़्तार करने की चुनौती की मेरी बहादुरी ने उसके तेज़ क़ानूनी दिमाग़ को गरमा दिया था। सागरिका ने भी व्यावहारिक होते हुए कहा, 'कृपया दिखावा ना करें, बस वही करें, जो वकील कहता है। अपना बैग पैक करो और कुछ दिन ऐसी जगह चले जाओ, जहां पुलिस आपको ट्रैक न कर सके। आपको पता है कि मोदी सरकार की नज़र आप पर है। बस अब बहुत हो गया!' उन्होंने बढ़ती चिड़चिड़ाहट के साथ कहा।

बीच का रास्ता निकाला गया। मैं शहर छोड़कर नहीं जाऊंगा, बल्कि दिल्ली के सैनिक फार्महाउस में अपने एक दोस्त के पास जाऊंगा। सैनिक फार्म, संकरी गलियों के साथ विशाल बंगलों, हरियाली और घने जंगलों वाली बड़ी कॉलोनी है, जिसे मूल रूप से कुछ रिटायर्ड जनरलों और रियल एस्टेट में उनके दोस्तों ने खोजा था, जो राजनीतिक तौर पर अच्छे नेटवर्क वाले थे। पिछले कुछ सालों में इसमें लगातार अतिक्रमण होते रहे, वह बढ़ता रहा और निर्माण होते रहे, लेकिन इसका नियमित होना या वैधता सवालों के घेरे में है। किसी भी तरह की जांच और विवाद से बचने के लिए, सैनिक फार्म में बिजली, पानी और निजी सुरक्षा के अपने इंतज़ाम थे। मज़ाक में इसे 'रिपब्लिक ऑफ सैनिक फार्म' भी कहते हैं, जहां सरकार का शासन नहीं चलता, भले ही यहां रहने वाले बहुत से लोग सरकार में रसूखदार अफसर रहे हों।

फार्महाउसों की इस विशाल, अनियमित भूलभुलैया में, बाहर की चमकदार शहर की रोशनी से दूर रहना मुमकिन था।

सर्दियों की उस ठंडी शाम में, मैं सैनिक फार्महाउस के अंधेरे में, क़ानून और प्रतिशोध के राजनीतिक सिस्टम से भागते हुए एक भगोड़े जैसा महसूस कर रहा था, जो मुझे पकड़ने के लिए बाहर था। उस रात, जब मैं अपने दोस्त के यहां, गर्म कंबल में दुबका हुआ, ओल्ड मॉन्क और कोक पी रहा था, तो बाहर की मौन आवाज़ें मेरे मन के मकड़जाल को साफ करने में लगी थीं। मैंने ऐसा कौन सा अपराध किया था, जिसके लिए मुझे देशद्रोही बताया गया? इस 'नए' भारत में राष्ट्र-विरोधी करार दिए जाने के क्या मायने थे? जैसे ही मैं झपकी लेने लगा, मेरे थके हुए दिमाग़ में एक उथल-पुथल वाले सप्ताह की सारी बातें घूमने लगीं।

---

26 जनवरी, एक ऐसा दिन, जब भारत गणराज्य, अपनी सैन्य शक्ति और सांस्कृतिक विरासत का प्रदर्शन करता है। राजपथ पर होने वाला समारोह--जिसका नाम अब मोदी सरकार ने 'कर्तव्य पथ' रख दिया था--देशभक्ति की भावना जगाने के साथ, राज्य की ताकत और भव्यता को दिखाने के लिए होता है। औपनिवेशिक साम्राज्य को चुनौती देने वाले स्वतंत्रता सेनानियों ने इस संवैधानिक गणराज्य की नींव रखी थी, उसे राष्ट्रवादी भावनाओं को बढ़ाने के लिए सोवियत शैली की तरह सैनिक समारोह और राज्य की झांकियों की ज़रूरत है या नहीं, यह बहस का विषय हो सकता है। लेकिन हर कोई इस शानदार परेड को पसंद करता है, भले ही केवल 'वीवीआईपी' इसे करीब से देख सकते हों, और बाकी देश अपने घरों में टीवी पर विस्मय से देखता है। एक तरह से, यह परेड, नई दिल्ली के लुटिंयस अभिजात लोगों का देश पर प्रभुत्व बताती है। वही सामाजिक वर्ग, जिसे प्रधानमंत्री नरेन्द्र मोदी की सरकार तिरस्कार करने का दावा करती है।

आज, एक 'अभिजात वर्ग' की जगह दूसरे 'अभिजात वर्ग' ने ले ली है। एक ज़माने तक नेहरूवादी विशेषाधिकार वाली 'खास मंडली' ने हिन्दुत्व को आगे बढ़ाने का दावा करने वालों को रास्ता दे दिया है। लुटिंयस का अभिजात वर्ग, अब 'टीम मोदी' है।

2021 की गणतंत्र दिवस परेड बहुत अलग थी। जब जवान राजपथ पर मार्च कर रहे थे, तब मोदी सरकार के कृषि क़ानूनों के ख़िलाफ़ अपना विरोध जताने के लिए किसानों ने दिल्ली में ट्रैक्टर रैली निकालने का फ़ैसला किया। एक रिपोर्टर के तौर पर मुझे लगा कि किसान विरोध प्रदर्शन बड़ी घटना होगी और उसे टीवी स्टुडियो के बजाय फील्ड में जाकर कवर करना बेहतर होगा। इसलिए 25 जनवरी की ठंडी रात में, घने कोहरे में डूबे शहर से, हम हरियाणा के पास सिंघू बॉर्डर के लिए निकल पड़े। किसानों के इस ग्राउंड ज़ीरो तक पहुंचने के लिए हम सावधानी

से गाड़ी चला रहे थे। आधी रात के बाद हमें हाईवे के पास ही एक 'बी-एंड-बी' होटल में ठहरने का ठिकाना मिला और हम मुश्किल से कुछ घंटे सो पाए।

अगले दिन सवेरे 8 बजे हम, रंगीन पगड़ियां पहने, नारे लगाते किसानों की भीड़ के बीच थे। ज़्यादातर किसान अपने ट्रैक्टरों पर तैयार थे, तो कुछ मोटर साइकिलों और घोड़ों पर भी सवार थे। बगावती, लेकिन उत्सव जैसा माहौल था, लाउडस्पीकरों पर देशभक्ति गीत बज रहे थे। भगत सिंह के पोस्टर थे, आसमान में तिरंगा लहरा रहा था। जश्न के माहौल से उस बात का अंदाजा हम नहीं लगा पाए कि आगे क्या होने वाला था। करीब दोपहर में, पहली बार ख़बर मिली कि सेन्ट्रल दिल्ली में किसानों का प्रदर्शन हिंसक हो गया था।

एक सहकर्मी ने दिल्ली के बीचों-बीच आईटीओ मेट्रो स्टेशन पर किसानों के साथ पुलिस की झड़प और आंसू गैस के इस्तेमाल की तस्वीरें साझा कीं। प्रदर्शनकारियों ने पुलिस बैरिकेड्स तोड़ दिए थे, कुछ ने अपने ट्रैक्टरों से पुलिस पिकेट को टक्कर मारी थी और खाकी वर्दी वालों के साथ घमासान लड़ाई हो गई थी। इस बीच, हम भीड़ भरी सड़कों से अपना रास्ता बनाने के लिए संघर्ष कर रहे थे। मोबाइल नेटवर्क बंद कर दिया गया था और क़ानून-व्यवस्था की बहाली के लिए मुख्य सड़क से यातायात को दूसरी तरफ भेजा जा रहा था। हमने अपनी गाड़ियां छोड़ीं और पैदल ही तेजी से सेन्ट्रल दिल्ली की तरफ चलने लगे। जब हम हिंसा के केन्द्र आईटीओ भवन पहुंचे तो करीब दो बजे थे। तब तक पुलिस ने वहां हालात पर काबू पा लिया था, लेकिन जंग के मैदान जैसा लग रहा था। ज़्यादातर प्रदर्शनकारी तितर-बितर हो चुके थे। सड़कों पर टूटे बैरिकेड्स, पत्थर, आंसू गैस के गोलों से उस अफरातफरी का अंदाज़ा लगाया जा सकता था, जो कुछ घंटों पहले वहां हुई थी। मुख्य सड़क पर अब भी जमा भीड़, उस इलाके को खाली करने से इंकार कर रही थी।

पुलिस की घेराबंदी के बीच से हमने देखा कि युवा प्रदर्शनकारी एक शव को घेरे हुए थे, जो ज़मीन पर सफेद कपड़े में लिपटा हुआ था। उनमें से कुछ ने चिल्लाते हुए कहा, 'पुलिस ने हमारे दोस्त को गोली मार दी, उस वक्त वह ट्रैक्टर चला रहा था।' दूसरे ने ज़ोर देकर कहा, 'हम तब तक नहीं जाएंगे, जब तक हमें न्याय नहीं मिल जाता।' मैं ताजा हालात की रिपोर्टिंग कर रहा था और जब मैंने सवाल किया कि इस हिंसा के लिए कौन ज़िम्मेदार था, तो गुस्साए लोग और भड़कने लगे।

'तुम सब गोदी मीडिया हो, सिर्फ़ सरकार की बात रखते हो; यहां से चले जाओ,' एक और गुस्साए प्रदर्शनकारी ने हमारा कैमरा छीनने की कोशिश की। 'गोदी मीडिया' शब्द का इस्तेमाल उन पत्रकारों को निशाना बनाने के लिए किया जा रहा था, जिन पर मोदी सरकार की गोदी में बैठने (साथ देने) का आरोप था। यह पहली बार था, जब किसी ने मुझे 'गोदी' पत्रकार कहा था। मैं हैरान था और मैंने आरोप के ख़िलाफ़ खुद के बचाव की कोशिश की,

लेकिन समझ आया कि हालात हमारे ख़िलाफ़ थे और हम पर हमला करने वाली भीड़ से बचने के लिए दूर होना पड़ा।

इसके तुरंत बाद मैंने वह ट्वीट किया, जो पीड़ित के साथ वालों ने मुझसे कैमरे पर कहा था, 'एक व्यक्ति, 45 साल के नवनीत सिंह की मौत पुलिस की कथित गोलीबारी से हो गई। किसानों ने कहा, यह "बलिदान" व्यर्थ नहीं जाएगा।' थोड़ी देर बाद, पुलिस ने दावा किया कि प्रदर्शनकारी किसान की मौत तब हुई, जब उसका ट्रैक्टर बैरिकेड्स से टकराते वक्त पलट गया। मुझे लगा कि गुस्साई भीड़ ने शायद मुझे गुमराह किया था, तो मैंने उस ट्वीट को हटा दिया और उन विरोधाभासी रिपोर्ट की तरफ इशारा किया, जो ज़मीन पर चल रही थीं। ऐसे उत्तेजित माहौल में, लाइव न्यूज़ करते समय रिपोर्टिंग में ज़्यादा सावधानी और संवेदनशीलता की ज़रूरत होती है। हालांकि उस समय माहौल में बढ़ती गर्मी और तेजी से बदलते हालात के बीच हर आरोप की पुष्टि करना लगभग असंभव जैसा होता है। फील्ड पर रिपोर्टर जो देख, सुन रहे होते हैं, वही रिपोर्ट करना होता है और बदलती घटनाओं के साथ उसे अपडेट करते हैं। मैं भी यही करने की कोशिश कर रहा था, लेकिन ऐसे तनावपूर्ण माहौल में अलग-अलग बातों को ठीक से समझना मुश्किल था। यह सच है कि ऐसे माहौल में, मैंने एक अपुष्ट और संभवतः भ्रामक दावे को ट्वीट करके और चैनल पर ख़बर के तौर पर बताकर ग़लती की थी, लेकिन क्या मैं देशद्रोह का दोषी था? या क्या यह माहौल को भड़काने के लिए जानबूझकर, दुर्भावना से की गई कोशिश थी? क्या ऐसे उन्मादी माहौल में रिपोर्टिंग में ग़लती को देशद्रोही व्यवहार के सबूत के तौर पर देखा जा सकता है? निश्चित रूप से नहीं।

किसी भी स्तर पर मैंने प्रदर्शनकारियों को भड़काने की कोशिश नहीं की, बल्कि उस उग्र भीड़ ने हिंसा भड़काने में किसानों की भूमिका पर सवाल उठाने पर मुझे उस जगह से धकिया दिया था। भाजपा-शासित राज्यों में पुलिस ने देशद्रोह के आरोप में जो मुझ पर कई एफआईआर दर्ज कीं, उससे मैं परेशान था, मुझे निशाना बनाया गया। 9 फरवरी 2021 को, सुप्रीम कोर्ट ने हमारी गिरफ़्तारी पर रोक लगाने और कोई कार्रवाई से बचाने के लिए दख़ल दिया। सुनवाई के दौरान, मुख्य न्यायाधीश जस्टिस एस.ए. बोबड़े ने सॉलिसिटर जनरल तुषार मेहता से पूछा कि क्या सरकार का इरादा हमें गिरफ़्तार करने का था? सरकार की तरफ से मेहता ने इस पर कोई ठोस बात नहीं की, बल्कि मामले पर बहस के लिए और समय मांगा। सुनवाई ज़ूम लिंक पर होने से तनाव शायद कम था, लेकिन साफ था कि सरकार हमें सज़ा देना चाहती थी। उस शाम सरकार में मंत्री और मेरे मित्र ने फ़ोन किया। उन्होंने चेतावनी दी, 'राजदीप, तुम्हें ज़्यादा सावधान रहने की ज़रूरत है। यह मोदी राज है और तुम निशाने पर हो।'

मेरी बेटी का यह डर कि पुलिस किसी को भी राजद्रोह के आरोप में मनमाने तरीके से गिरफ़्तार कर सकती थी, किसी हद तक सही साबित हुआ। क़ानून के साथ मेरे संघर्ष के कुछ

दिनों बाद, 13 फरवरी को दिल्ली पुलिस ने बेंगलुरु में 'जलवायु परिवर्तन' पर काम करने वाली 22 साल की दिशा रवि को देशद्रोह के आरोप में गिरफ़्तार कर लिया, उन पर किसानों के विरोध का समर्थन करने वाले एक दस्तावेज़ को ऑनलाइन साझा करने का आरोप था। दिशा ने एक 'टूलकिट' को साझा करने का अपराध किया था, जिसमें प्रदर्शनकारियों के सोशल मीडिया अभियान की योजना और कार्यक्रमों की जानकारी दी गई थी।

इस मामले में किसी युवा कार्यकर्ता पर राजद्रोह और साज़िश के आरोप के बाद गिरफ़्तारी होनी चाहिए, यह पहली नज़र में ही बेतुका लगता था। ऐसे बहुत से दस्तावेज़ इंटरनेट पर चल रहे थे। इसके अलावा, दिशा की साझा की गई जानकारी और लाल किले पर उस हिंसा के बीच कोई सीधा संबंध नहीं दिखता था, जिसे किसान प्रदर्शनकारियों में से कुछ चरमपंथियों ने भड़काया था। पंजाब के गांवों से आए प्रदर्शनकारी किसान, शायद ही दुनियाभर के युवा जलवायु एक्टिविस्ट के सोशल मीडिया 'टूलकिट' का पालन करें। दिशा को जमानत मिलने से पहले आठ दिन पुलिस हिरासत में गुजारने पड़े। मैं उनसे कई महीनों बाद किसी मीडिया कार्यक्रम मिला, जहां वे विशेष अतिथि थीं: एक दुबली-पतली, मृदुभाषी युवती, जो अचानक उन पर इतने फोकस से हैरान दिख रही थीं। उन्होंने बताया कि कैसे गिरफ़्तारी ने उन्हें आहत किया और अंदर तक हिला दिया। दिशा ने कहा, 'मैंने बस एक दस्तावेज़ में कुछ लाइनें संपादित कर उसे साथी कार्यकर्ताओं में साझा किया था।'

अपनी गिरफ़्तारी के तरीके और पुलिस के डराने-धमकाने की बात करते वक्त दिशा की आंखें भर आई थीं। उन्होंने कहा, 'यह एक बुरे सपने जैसा था और मुझे उम्मीद है कि किसी और को इससे ना गुजरना पड़े।' दुख की बात है कि दिशा अकेली नहीं हैं। वेबसाइट 'आर्टिकल 14' ने एक डेटाबेस तैयार किया था, उसके मुताबिक 2010 से 2021 के बीच आईपीसी की धारा 124(ए) के तहत 13,000 लोगों के ख़िलाफ़ 800 से ज़्यादा राजद्रोह के मामले दर्ज किए गए। इन 11 साल में, सोशल मीडिया पर राष्ट्र-विरोधी या पाकिस्तान समर्थक संदेशों वाले पोस्ट करने के आरोप में राजद्रोह के 106 मामले दर्ज हुए, एक को छोड़कर, बाकी सभी मामले 2014 के बाद दर्ज किए गए थे। इस दौरान राजनेताओं और सरकार की आलोचना करने के लिए 405 लोगों के ख़िलाफ़ मामले दर्ज किए गए थे। इनमें से 96 फ़ीसद मामले–149 लोगों पर प्रधानमंत्री मोदी के ख़िलाफ़ आलोचनात्मक या अपमानजनक टिप्पणी करने का आरोप है और 144 पर उत्तरप्रदेश के मुख्यमंत्री योगी आदित्यनाथ के ख़िलाफ़ ऐसी ही टिप्पणी करने के मामले थे। यूपीए-2 के दौरान राजद्रोह के ज़यादातर मामले तमिलनाडु में न्यूक्लियर प्लांट का विरोध करने वालों और माओवादियों के ख़िलाफ़ दर्ज किए गए थे। मोदी सरकार में 2014 से 2020 के बीच, आंदोलनकारियों, पत्रकारों, सामाजिक कार्यकर्ताओं और बुद्धिजीवियों के ख़िलाफ़ 519 मामले दर्ज किए गए। डेटा बताता है कि देशद्रोह के आरोपियों को ट्रायल कोर्ट से

ज़मानत नहीं मिलने तक औसतन पचास दिन जेल में रहना पड़ता है और हाई कोर्ट से ज़मानत मिलने तक 200 दिन जेल में बिताते हैं। देशद्रोह के मामले में सज़ा की दर 0.1 फ़ीसद रही है।

आखिर में, मई 2022 में, सुप्रीम कोर्ट ने राजद्रोह क़ानून को स्थगित कर दिया और इससे जुड़े सभी मामलों पर रोक लगा दी, साथ ही केन्द्र और राज्य सरकारों को कोई भी नया मामला दर्ज नहीं करने का निर्देश दिया। क़ानून के दुरुपयोग की निंदा करते हुए 11 मई 2022 को, मुख्य न्यायाधीश जस्टिस एन.वी. रमन्ना ने कहा, 'गांधी और बाल गंगाधर तिलक को चुप कराने के लिए राजद्रोह क़ानून का इस्तेमाल किया गया था। क्या आज़ादी के 75 साल बाद भी सरकार अंग्रेज़ों के इस क़ानून को बनाए रखना चाहती है? पुलिस, सरकार का विरोध करने वाले लोगों को फंसाने के लिए, राजद्रोह क़ानून का दुरुपयोग करती है। देशद्रोह के आरोप लगाने के लिए कोई जवाबदेही नहीं है। यह ऐसा है कि जैसे किसी बढ़ई को लकड़ी काटने के लिए आरी दी जाए और वह पूरे जंगल को काट देता है।' अदालती दख़ल ने राजद्रोह के आरोपियों को कुछ राहत दे दी, खासतौर से उन लोगों को जो बिना किसी मुकदमे के महीनों से जेल में थे, लेकिन यह राहत लंबे समय के लिए नहीं थी। 2023 में, मोदी सरकार ने एक नया, 'स्वदेशी' भारतीय न्याय संहिता (बीएनएस) पारित कर दिया। बीएनएस, अधिनियम की धारा 150 फिर से औपनिवेशिक क़ानून को ज़िंदा करती है, यहां राजद्रोह को ज्यादा व्यापक शब्द से बदल दिया गया हैः 'विध्वंसक गतिविधियां'। मेरे ख़िलाफ़ राजद्रोह के आरोप अभी तक हटाए नहीं गए हैं, लेकिन मैं खुद को खुशकिस्मत मानता हूं। हमारे राजद्रोह के मामले में, हमें कपिल सिब्बल और कई वरिष्ठ वकीलों की एक बेहतरीन टीम मिली, जिन्होंने गिरफ़्तारी पर तुरंत रोक का काम किया। एक मान्यता प्राप्त पत्रकार के रूप में मुझे कुछ विशेषाधिकार हासिल हैं, लेकिन उन बहुत से अनाम भारतीयों का क्या, जिनके पास मेरे जैसे लाभ नहीं है? जब मैं उन लोगों की लंबी सूची देखता हूं, जिन पर राजद्रोह के आरोप लगाए गए हैं, उनमें से कई गरीब आदिवासी समुदायों से हैं, तो मुझे लगता है कि जैसे 'राष्ट्र-विरोधी' आरोप लगना, 'सम्मान' की बात है। एक लोकतंत्र में चुनावी बहुमत का सम्मान किया जाना चाहिए, क्योंकि यहां वोट ही निर्णायक होता है। लेकिन कोई चुनावी जीत, चाहे कितनी भी मुश्किल से लड़ी गई हो और सही हो, एक गंभीर हक़ीकत को नहीं छिपा सकती। इस नए भारत में असहमति को अक्सर अपराध के तौर पर देखा जाता है और सरकार से मुश्किल पैदा करने वाले सवाल पूछना, आपको जेल में डाल सकता है। खासकर तब, जब आप ऐसे पत्रकार हैं, जिसे सत्ता में बैठे लोग पसंद नहीं करते या स्वीकृति नहीं देते। किसानों ने भले ही मुझे 'गोदी मीडिया' कहकर धकिया दिया हो, लेकिन सरकार और उनके 'चीयरलीडर्स' के लिए मैं 'राष्ट्र-विरोधी' था और आज भी हूं।

═

अगस्त 2019 में, डॉ. प्रणॉय रॉय और उनकी पत्नी, राधिका रॉय के साथ परिवार के करीब एक दर्जन लोग राधिका का 70वां जन्मदिन मनाने के लिए केन्या जा रहे थे। डॉ. राय नई दिल्ली टेलीविजन (एनडीटीवी) के सह-संस्थापक रहे हैं, जिस ब्रांड ने देश में निजी समाचार चैनल की क्रांति की शुरुआत की थी। स्वाभाविक तौर पर माहौल खुशनुमा था। जब एयरपोर्ट पर परिवार के सदस्य इमिग्रेशन से गुजर रहे थे, तब डॉ. रॉय और राधिका रॉय को काउंटर पर रोक दिया गया। इमिग्रेशन अधिकारी ने माफ़ी के अंदाज़ में कहा, 'हमारे पास आपको विदेश यात्रा की अनुमति नहीं देने के आदेश हैं, सर।' अक्सर अंतरराष्ट्रीय सफ़र पर रहने वाले रॉय दंपत्ति हैरान रह गए। जब उनसे इस रोक का कारण पूछा गया तो अधिकारी कोई स्पष्टीकरण नहीं दे सके। ना ही वे रॉय दंपत्ति की विदेश यात्रा पर रोक से जुड़ा कोई लिखित आदेश बता पाए। अधिकारी ने कहा, 'यदि आप चाहें तो आपके परिवार के बाकी लोग यात्रा पर जा सकते हैं।' कोई भी आत्मसम्मान वाला व्यक्ति इस प्रस्ताव को स्वीकार नहीं करता। पूरा परिवार निराशा के साथ घर लौट गया।

कुछ साल बाद, वाराणसी की एक फ्लाइट में, मैं, एक आदमी के बगल में बैठा था, जो मुझे देखकर मुस्कुराता रहा। मुझे लगा कि उसने शायद मुझे पहचान लिया था। हम बातें करने लगे। उन्होंने बताया कि वे एक सरकारी अधिकारी थे और कस्टम और इमिग्रेशन डिपार्टमेंट में काम करते थे। उनके साथ उनकी छोटी बेटी और पत्नी भी थीं। 'हम छुट्टी मनाने और काशी विश्वनाथ मंदिर में दर्शन करने जा रहे हैं,' उन्होंने कहा। मैंने उन्हें शुकामनाएं दीं और नेटफ्लिक्स वीडियो देखने लगा, तभी उन्होंने मुझे टोककर पूछा, 'आप एनडीटीवी के द *बिग फाइट* में भी थे ना?' मैंने हामी में सिर हिलाया, तो उनका स्वर धीमा हो गया। 'मैं एक बात बताना चाहता हूं कि मैं उस टीम में शामिल था, जिसने प्रणॉय रॉय को मुंबई में विदेश यात्रा पर जाने से रोका था। यह मेरे करियर का सबसे बुरा दिन था। मुझे पता था कि मैं ग़लत कर रहा था, लेकिन मेरे पास कोई और रास्ता नहीं था,' उन्होंने आह भरी। और फिर आखिरी बात, 'अगर आप मिस्टर रॉय से मिलें, तो कृपया मेरी तरफ से सॉरी कहें!'

जून 2017 में, सीबीआई ने एनडीटीवी के प्रमोटरों के ख़िलाफ़ आईसीआईसीआई बैंक को लोन न चुकाने के कारण नुक़सान पहुंचाने का मामला दर्ज किया था। रॉय दंपत्ति ने दिल्ली हाइकोर्ट में इस मामले पर बहस की और बताया कि कर्ज़ का ब्याज सहित भुगतान समय से पहले कर दिया गया था। उसी महीने, सीबीआई ने उनके घर पर छापा मारा। एक महीने बाद, सीबीआई की जांच, ईडी की जांच का आधार बन गई। अगले कई साल तक इस मामले में कोई प्रगति नहीं हुई। इस मसले पर रॉय दंपत्ति ने सरकार में जिन मंत्रियों से बात की, उनमें से ज़्यादातर ने माना कि मामले में कोई दम नहीं था और उन्हें चिंता करने की ज़रूरत नहीं थी। फिर अचानक उन्हें एक अंतरराष्ट्रीय उड़ान पर चढ़ने से रोक दिया गया। प्रेस क्लब में आयोजित एक

एकजुटता बैठक में प्रमुख न्यायविद फली नरीमन ने कहा, 'यह बेहद निंदनीय है।' कोविड के बाद 2021 में, ईडी की कार्रवाई शुरू हो गई। अगले बारह महीनों में प्रणय रॉय को एक दर्ज़न से ज्यादा बार पूछताछ के लिए ईडी के मुख्यालय पर पेश होना पड़ा। राधिका रॉय को भी कम से कम चार मौकों पर बुलाया गया, हालांकि अधिकारियों ने ज़्यादा विनम्रता दिखाई। लंबी पूछताछ के बावजूद, सीबीआई या ईडी ने कोई चार्जशीट दाखिल नहीं की। इस बीच आयकर विभाग की तरफ से ढेरों नोटिस आ गए, जिनको टालने के लिए महंगे मुकदमे की ज़रूरत थी। 'रॉय और एनडीटीवी के साथ जो हुआ, वह इस बात का उदाहरण है कि सरकारें मीडिया को कैसे परेशान कर सकती हैं, जहां प्रक्रिया ही सज़ा है,' रॉय के पारिवारिक मित्र और जाने-माने संपादक एन. राम का मानना था।

रॉय के अपराध का उनके वित्तीय मामलों से कोई लेना-देना नहीं था, बल्कि पूरी तरह से उनकी पत्रकारिता के ब्रांड से जुड़ा मसला था, माना जाता था कि वहां वाम-उदारवादी नज़रिए को ज़्यादा जगह दी जाती थी। मोदी सरकार ने नेटवर्क को कट्टर भाजपा विरोधी या खासतौर से मोदी विरोधी के रूप में देखा। यह आरोप एनडीटीवी (तब स्टार न्यूज़) पर 2002 में गुजरात हिंसा के कवरेज से जुड़ा था। तब मैं गुजरात में कई हफ्तों और महीनों तक रहा, और हमारे रिपोर्टर्स की टीम के साथ सांप्रदायिक दंगों को कवर किया, जिसमें लाखों दर्शकों के ड्राईंगरूम तक हर जानकारी को सामने लाने की कोशिश की थी। 24X7 प्राइवेट न्यूज़ चैनलों के युग में देश में सामूहिक हिंसा का यह पहला ऐसा मामला था। गोधरा में एक ट्रेन में आग से, 59 कारसेवकों को जलाकर मार दिया गया था। इसके बाद गुजरात में हुए सांप्रदायिक दंगों में 1,000 से ज़्यादा लोग मारे गए थे, जिनमें ज़्यादातर मुसलमान थे। मौत की भयावह तस्वीरें, सामूहिक बलात्कार और हत्या की घटनाओं ने पूरे देश को झकझोर दिया था। इसको लेकर सज़ा और जवाबदेही की मांग उठने लगी थी। गुजरात के तत्कालीन मुख्यमंत्री, नरेन्द्र मोदी सबके निशाने पर थे और विपक्षी कांग्रेस उनके इस्तीफ़े की मांग कर रही थी। यहां तक कि प्रधानमंत्री अटल बिहारी वाजपेयी ने भी तब मुख्यमंत्री मोदी को 'राजधर्म' का पालन करने की आवश्यकता की याद दिलाई थी। सत्तर के दशक में गुजरात में लंबे समय तक रहे पुलिस महानिरीक्षक मेरे दिवंगत दादा पी.एम. पंत से मुझे यह सीख मिली थी कि 'प्रशासन की मिलीभगत या अक्षमता के बिना कोई सामूहिक दंगा नहीं होता।' इस बात पर आश्चर्य नहीं होना चाहिए कि मोदी को यकीन था कि मीडिया, खासतौर से एनडीटीवी, दंगों के कवरेज में उनके प्रति उदार नहीं था। केन्द्र में सत्ता संभालने के बाद, उनके पास बदला लेने की ताकत थी। प्रतिशोध की राजनीति, मोदी की रणनीति का एक अहम हिस्सा है। आरोप है कि वह अपनी राजनीतिक लड़ाई के लिए राज्य की शक्ति का बेशर्मी से इस्तेमाल करते हैं। गांधीनगर और दिल्ली में उनके मंत्रिमंडल के सहयोगी, उनके ग़लत पक्ष में जाने से डरते हैं।

शुरुआत में सत्ता के गलियारों में एनडीटीवी को घुसने नहीं देने की कोशिश की गई। ज़्यादातर मंत्री एनडीटीवी पर दिखने से बचते रहे। जून 2017 में, जब न्यूज़ एंकर निधि राज़दान ने, भाजपा प्रवक्ता संबित पात्रा को बहस में गरमागरमी के बाद शो छोड़ने के लिए कहा, तो भाजपा मीडिया सेल ने पार्टी के सभी लोगों को एनडीटीवी प्लेटफॉर्म का बहिष्कार करने का फरमान जारी कर दिया। जब एक भाजपा प्रवक्ता नलिन कोहली, स्वतंत्रता दिवस के अवसर पर एनडीटीवी के कार्यक्रम पर दिखाई दिए, तो पार्टी मुख्यालय से उन्हें चैनल से तुरंत हटने के लिए संदेश और फ़ोन आने लगे। बात यहीं ख़त्म नहीं हुई। नेटवर्क को कोई भी सरकारी विज्ञापन या मदद नहीं दी गई। निजी कंपनियों से भी एनडीटीवी पर किसी कार्यक्रम को प्रायोजित नहीं करने का आग्रह किया गया। विज्ञापन, खासकर सरकारी विज्ञापन, किसी चैनल के राजस्व मॉडल में सबसे अहम होते हैं, जिससे एनडीटीवी के लिए इसे चलाए रखना और भी चुनौतीपूर्ण हो गया।

2018 में प्रधानमंत्री मोदी ने नई दिल्ली में संसद भवन एनेक्सी में तमिलनाडु के कुछ वरिष्ठ पत्रकारों को बुलाया था। मोदी ने पूछा कि क्या उनको किसी परेशानी या दिक्कत का सामना करना पड़ रहा था? वहां मौजूद वरिष्ठ संपादक एन. राम ने उनसे मीडिया से मुलाक़ात ख़त्म होने के बाद बात करने को कहा। मोदी वरिष्ठ पत्रकार राम का बहुत सम्मान करते थे। जब वे दोनों वहां से उस तरफ बढ़े, जहां पत्रकार हाई-टी के लिए जमा थे, राम ने पूछा कि सरकार एनडीटीवी को बर्बाद करने पर क्यों तुली थी? उन्होंने कहा कि उनकी कार्रवाई ने मीडिया नेटवर्क को 'ढहने की कगार' पर पहुंचा दिया था। इस पर कथित तौर पर मोदी ने कहा, 'वे पहले ही ढह चुके हैं!'

एनडीटीवी का किला वास्तव में ध्वस्त होने में चार साल लग गए। रॉय दंपत्ति उस वक्त देश के बाहर बताए गए थे, जब उन्हें अपने मोबाइल पर 'ब्रेकिंग न्यूज़' मिली। देश के सबसे अमीर कारोबारी अरबपति गौतम अडानी के अडानी समूह के एनडीटीवी के अधिग्रहण की बोली लगाने की ख़बर थी। एक अप्रत्याशित कदम में अडानी समूह ने घोषणा की, वह एक छोटी कंपनी विश्वप्रधान कॉमर्शियल प्राइवेट लिमिटेड (वीसीपीएल) के माध्यम से एनडीटीवी में एक बड़ी हिस्सेदारी खरीद रहे थे। देश के एक दूसरे अरबपति व्यवसायी मुकेश अंबानी के नियंत्रण वाली कंपनी वीसीपीएल ने एनडटीवी के प्रमोटर्स को 2009 में 350 करोड़ रुपये का कर्ज़ दिया था, इसमें कहा गया था कि एक 'कनवर्टेबल वारंट' से इस कर्ज़ को 'इक्विटी' में बदला जा सकता था। करीब दस साल तक अंबानी ने एनडीटीवी को लेकर कोई दखल नहीं दिया। कारोबार पर नज़र रखने वाले कई लोग, दो कथित कॉरपोरेट प्रतिद्वन्दियों के बीच इस सौदे से हैरान थे, लेकिन राजधानी में राजनीतिक सत्ता के अभिजात वर्ग को इस पर कोई हैरानी नहीं थी। सरकार के एक वरिष्ठ मंत्री ने मुझसे कहा, 'जब मुकेश भाई अपनी हिस्सेदारी गौतम भाई को सौंपते हैं, तो आप मानकर चलिए कि कुछ दूसरी ताकतें भी इस खेल में शामिल हैं और मामला बहुत ऊपर से शुरू हुआ है।'

समझौते से पहले की बातचीत को जानने वाले एक प्रमुख कारोबारी कार्यकारी ने दावा किया, 'गौतम भाई शुरू में मीडिया व्यवसाय में आने के इच्छुक नहीं थे, लेकिन सरकार के सबसे पसंदीदा कारोबारी होने से, वह मुख्यधारा के उस टीवी मीडिया नेटवर्क को संभालने के लिए बेहतर विकल्प थे, जिसे सरकार-विरोधी रुख वाला चैनल माना जाता था।' चार महीने बाद, दिसंबर 2022 में, अधिग्रहण पूरा हो गया। अडानी एनडीटीवी के सबसे बड़े शेयरधारक हो गए थे, उन्होंने संस्थापकों के ज़्यादातर शेयर भी हासिल कर लिए थे। इस अधिग्रहण के साथ, अब देश के दो सबसे बड़े मीडिया नेटवर्क का नेतृत्व मोदी सरकार के करीबी कारोबारी दिग्गजों के पास था। (2014 में मुकेश अंबानी ने 'नेटवर्क 18' का अधिग्रहण किया था, जिसमें सीएनएन-आईबीएन जैसे चैनल शामिल थे और मैंने प्रधान संपादक के तौर पर इन्हें स्थापित करने में मदद की थी।)

एक वरिष्ठ वकील कहते हैं, 'मेरा भरोसा कीजिए, रॉय कंपनी पर अपनी पकड़ बनाए रखने के लिए लड़ना चाहते थे, लेकिन उन्हें सलाह दी गई कि इसे छोड़ देना ही बेहतर होगा। आप एक व्यक्ति से तो लड़ सकते हैं, लेकिन पूरे सिस्टम से नहीं लड़ सकते।' संस्थापक और प्रमोटर प्रणॉय और राधिका रॉय भारी मन से उस कंपनी को अलविदा कह रहे थे, जिसे उन्होंने 1988 में दक्षिण दिल्ली की एक छोटी सी कॉलोनी के बेसमेंट में शुरू किया था और तीन दशकों से ज़्यादा समय तक, उच्चतम पेशेवर मानकों के साथ, उसे देश का सबसे भरोसेमंद और मान्यता प्राप्त मीडिया ब्रांड बनाये रखा। साल 1991 के बाद की उदारीकरण की नीतियों से प्राइवेट ब्राडकास्टर्स को दूरदर्शन के एकाधिकार को तोड़ने का रास्ता मिला। दूसरे मीडिया दिग्गज अरुण पुरी, सुभाष चन्द्रा और राघव बहल समेत प्रणॉय रॉय ने देश में टीवी मीडिया की तस्वीर ही बदल दी। राधिका रॉय ने बाद में एक दोस्त से कहा, 'यह क्रूर और विनाशकारी था।' वह अकेली नहीं थीं। एनडीटीवी के साथ काम कर चुके कई पेशेवरों ने इस अधिग्रहण को एक युग के अंत के तौर पर देखा। मैं 1994 में एनडीटीवी में, मुंबई में *टाइम्स ऑफ इंडिया* में प्रिंट पत्रकारिता की स्थिर दुनिया (जिसे बोरीबंदर की ओल्ड लेडी कहा जाता था) को छोड़कर टीवी न्यूज़ की रोमांचक, लेकिन अनिश्चित दुनिया में आया था। मैं इस अविश्वसनीय यात्रा का हिस्सा बनने वाले खुशकिस्मत लोगों में से था, जिसमें 24X7 टीवी समाचार ने एक नया आसमां बनाया था। नई चुनौतियों का सामना करने से पहले मैंने एनडीटीवी में बेहद संतोषजनक 11 साल बिताए। जब अधिग्रहण के बाद नेटवर्क से लोगों के बाहर निकलने का सिलसिला शुरू हुआ तो मैं उदासी के साथ पुरानी यादों में खो गया था।

इसमें कोई संदेह नहीं था कि गौतम अडानी के पास पैसे की ताकत थी, लेकिन एक राजनीतिक रूप से जुड़े कारोबारी नेता, क्या किसी समाचार ब्रांड को विश्वसनीयता दे सकते थे? एनडीटीवी के शत्रुतापूर्ण अधिग्रहण से मीडिया उद्योग में एक तरह का डर फैल गया। अब

कोई भी खुद को सुरक्षित महसूस नहीं कर रहा था। पत्रकार ऐसी ख़बरें करने से डरने लगे, जिससे मोदी सरकार नाराज़ हो। ज़्यादातर न्यूज़ चैनल, खुले तौर पर सरकारी मुखपत्र जैसे हो गए, पक्षपाती दिख रहे थे। दूसरी कोविड लहर की भयावहता के दौरान, ज़्यादातर समाचार नेटवर्क, महामारी से निपटने के मोदी सरकार के तरीकों पर सवाल उठाने या प्रधानमंत्री की तेजी से गिरती लोकप्रियता वाले सर्वेक्षणों को दिखाने से हिचक रहे थे। जब मणिपुर में आग लगी हुई थी, तो मीडिया ने उस हिंसा को तब दिखाया, जब दो महिलाओं की नग्न परेड का वीडियो सामने आया। प्रवर्तन एजेंसियां जब विपक्षी नेताओं को चुनिंदा तौर से निशाना बना रही थीं, तो सत्ता के बेजा इस्तेमाल के लिए 2011 जैसा, 'इंडिया अंगेस्ट करप्शन' मीडिया का कोई अभियान नहीं चला। विपक्षी सरकारों को गिराने के लिए पैसे के इस्तेमाल के आरोपों पर कभी कार्रवाई नहीं की गई। जब चुनावी बॉन्ड की जानकारी से कारोबारियों और राजनीतिक दलों के बीच संभावित सौदेबाज़ी सामने आई, तब कहीं इस पर सुर्खियों का शोर नहीं था।

मीडिया ब्रांड, जो मज़बूत लड़ाई लड़ सकते थे, वे कुछ हद तक अपनी विश्वसनीयता और लंबे समय से चलने की ताकत से सुरक्षित थे। कई छोटे मीडिया संस्थानों और स्वतंत्र पत्रकारों के ख़िलाफ़ बदले की ज्यादा कार्रवाई हुई। अक्टूबर 2023 में, ऑनलाइन पोर्टल 'न्यूज़क्लिक' से जुड़े करीब 80 पत्रकारों और कर्मचारियों के घरों पर दिल्ली पुलिस की स्पेशल सेल ने छापा मारा, इनमें कई तो अभी ट्रेनी या प्रोबेशन पर थे। इसके संस्थापक और प्रधान संपादक प्रबीर पुरकायस्थ को आतंकवाद विरोधी क़ानून, (UAPA) के तहत गिरफ़्तार किया गया और उनके दफ़्तरों को सील कर दिया गया। आयकर विभाग के दख़ल के बाद उनकी संपत्ति को भी फ्रीज़ कर दिया गया, चार करोड़ रुपये ज़ब्त किए गए और बैंक खातों में सिर्फ़ 40 पैसे छोड़े! न्यूज़क्लिक के ख़िलाफ़ मामला, *न्यूयॉर्क टाइम्स* के उस लेख के आधार पर बनाया गया, जिसमें आरोप था कि शंघाई में अमेरिकी करोड़पति नेविल रॉय सिंघम, चीन के समर्थन वाले अंतरराष्ट्रीय न्यूज़ नेटवर्क के हिस्से के रूप में न्यूज़क्लिक समेत कई कंपनियों को फंड कर रहे थे। इसकी आपराधिकता का कोई सबूत नहीं था, क्योंकि पोर्टल को मिलने वाले विदेशी फंड को भारतीय रिज़र्व बैंक से मंज़ूरी मिली हुई थी। इसकी संपादकीय सोच मोदी सरकार विरोधी और वामपंथी विचाराधारा समर्थक थी। 'न्यूज़क्लिक' को चीनी फंडिग से चलने वाला बताकर, उसके संपादक को जेल में डाल दिया गया और आंतकवादी विरोधी क़ानूनों के तहत आरोपों से उन लोगों के लिए डर का माहौल पैदा करने की कोशिश थी, जो सत्ता के ख़िलाफ़ असहमति की आवाज़ उठा सकते थे।

विडंबना यह थी कि यह दूसरा मौका था, जब सीपीआईएम के बरसों से सदस्य रहे, जेएनयू से पढ़े, इंजीनियर, सफेद दाढ़ी वाले पुरकायस्थ, को जेल में डाला गया था। 1975 में आपातकाल के दौरान भी उन्हें जेल में रखा गया था। तब आधी रात को उन्हें गिरफ़्तार किया

गया था और अभी सवेरे ही उन्हें पकड़ा गया। तब उन्होंने एक साल जेल में बिताया था और अब मुश्किल सात महीनों के बाद ज़मानत मिली। 'आपातकाल में जेल के दौरान मैंने एक बात सीखी, वह यह है कि जिंदगी में आपका नियंत्रण आज के दिन पर है, क्योंकि रिहाई के बारे में किसी को कुछ नहीं पता। तब वह एक घोषित आपातकाल था और अब अघोषित!' 75 साल के पुरकायस्थ ने कहा।

जिन लोगों पर छापेमारी की गई, उनमें मेरे एक पूर्व सहकर्मी और दोस्त अभिसार शर्मा भी थे, जो न्यूज़क्लिक के कर्मचारी तो नहीं थे, लेकिन उनके वीडियो न्यूज़क्लिक पर चलते थे। पिछले दशक में कई स्वतंत्र पत्रकारों की तरह, शर्मा ने खुद का यूट्यूब चैनल शुरू किया, जो 2020 में किसान आंदोलन के दौरान काफी लोकप्रिय रहा था। पुलिस सुबह साढ़े छह बजे उनके घर में घुसी, उनके मोबाइल फ़ोन, रिकॉर्डिंग का सामान और लैपटॉप छीन लिए। 'मुझे स्पेशल सेल के मुख्यालय ले गए और दो दिन तक पूछताछ की। पुलिस ने मुझे बताया कि वे मेरे आतंकी संबंधों की पड़ताल कर रहे थे क्योंकि मैंने किसान आंदोलन और शाहीन बाग विरोध को कवर किया था। उन्होंने ये भी कहा कि *न्यूयॉर्क टाइम्स* में छपी खबर के मुताबिक मैंने चीन से फंड भी लिया था। जब मैंने उनसे लेख दिखाने के लिए कहा, तो पता चला कि यह एक दक्षिणपंथी वेबसाइट *ऑपइंडिया* में लिखा गया था, मेरा नाम उसके शीर्षक में तो था, लेकिन लेख में नहीं था!' वे याद करते हुए हंसते हैं। शर्मा को प्रवर्तन दल ने छोड़ दिया, लेकिन उनके महंगे उपकरण अब भी पुलिस हिरासत में हैं। न्यूज़क्लिक पर छापे में, पुलिस ने चार सौ से ज़्यादा उपकरण ज़ब्त किए। वे कहते हैं, 'पुलिस वाले वाकई बहुत विनम्र और सौम्य थे। आप समझ सकते थे कि वे सिर्फ ऊपर के आदेश पर काम कर रहे थे, ताकि यह संदेश जा सके कि जो भी कोई सरकार विरोधी ख़बर करेगा, उसके साथ अपराधियों जैसा सुलूक किया जाएगा।'

वरिष्ठ पत्रकार परंजॉय गुहा ठाकुरता से भी दस घंटे से ज़्यादा पूछताछ और छापेमारी की गई। गुहा ठाकुरता ने बरसों तक अडानी समूह को लेकर कई खोजी स्टोरीज की हैं। उन्होंने कहा, 'मुझे लगता है कि इसमें कोई संबंध हो सकता है क्योंकि न्यूज़क्लिक ने अडानी समूह पर कई वीडियों और स्टोरीज प्रकाशित किए हैं जिनमें बताया गया था कि कारोबारी समूह को प्रधानमंत्री की कथित नजदीकी का कैसे फायदा हुआ।' शर्मा की तरह गुहा ठाकुरता भी न्यूज़क्लिक में काम नहीं करते थे। हालांकि, जांच पूरी होने के तुरंत बाद उनका मोबाइल और सिमकार्ड तुरंत वापस कर दिए गए, जबकि कई लोगों के नहीं लौटाए गए। 'मैं उन कुछ खास लोगों में से था शायद, जिनका फ़ोन वापस किया गया। मुझे लगता है कि पुलिस को लगा होगा कि मेरे मोबाइल में कुछ भी आपत्तिजनक नहीं था। वे मुझसे चाय, कॉफी और फलों के रस के लिए पूछते रहे। उन्होंने छोले-भटूरे भी ऑफर किए, लेकिन मुझे भूख नहीं थी।'

2021 में, वह उन कुछ पत्रकारों, कार्यकर्ताओं और विपक्षी नेताओं में शामिल थे, जिन्होंने दावा किया था कि उनके फ़ोन को सरकारी एजेंसियों ने इज़राइली स्पाईवेयर 'पेगासस' का इस्तेमाल कर हैक किया था। कथित तौर पर 'पेगासस' की निगरानी में आने वालों में से एक और मोदी-विरोधी मानी जाने वाली वेबसाइट 'द वायर' के पत्रकार भी शामिल थे। इसके संस्थापक-संपादक सिद्धार्थ वरदराजन याद करते हैं कि कैसे उनके फ़ोन की फोरेंसिक जांच से पता चला था कि वे और उनके सह-संपादक एम.के. वेणु 2019 और 2021 के बीच पेगासस की नज़र में थे। वरदराजन कहते हैं कि '2023 में, मुझे फिर से एपल से अलर्ट मिला और फिर फोरेंसिक जांच ने पेगासस के नए हमले की पुष्टि की। हां, मुझे लगता है कि मोदी सरकार ने मुझे निशाना बनाया है। इस पर गौर कीजिए कि भाजपा शासित राज्यों में पुलिस ने हमारे ख़िलाफ़ कितने मामले दर्ज किए हैं।'

किसी के दबाव में नहीं आने वाले गुहा ठाकुरता ने कुछ प्रतिष्ठित नागरिकों के साथ सुप्रीम कोर्ट का दरवाज़ा खटखटाया और कथित जासूसी को अंसवैधानिक करार देने के लिए दख़ल का आग्रह किया। अदालत ने केन्द्र को नागरिकों की निजता के उल्लंघन को रोकने के लिए न्यायिक निगरानी का सिस्टम बनाने को कहा। सुप्रीम कोर्ट ने आरोपों की जांच के लिए एक विशेषज्ञ समिति नियुक्त की, लेकिन उसकी रिपोर्ट कभी सार्वजनिक नहीं की गई। अगस्त 2022 में, सुप्रीम कोर्ट ने कहा, मोदी सरकार ने पेगासस स्पाईवेयर मामलों की जांच में सहयोग नहीं किया। केन्द्रीय सूचना प्रौद्योगिकी मंत्री अश्विनी वैष्णव ने संसद में, पेगासस कहानी को ख़ारिज़ कर दिया, यह पहली बार 'द वायर' में छपी थीं। उन्होंने कहा, 'यह भारतीय लोकतंत्र और दूसरी संस्थाओं को बदनाम करने की कोशिश है। कई सनसनीखेज और अतिरंजित आरोप लगाए गए हैं।'

दिलचस्प बात यह है कि 'द वायर' के संपादक ने बताया कि जांच के दौरान, वैष्णव के भी दो नंबर पेगासस डेटाबेस में मिले, उस समय तक वे मंत्री नहीं थे और भाजपा में शामिल नहीं हुए थे और कारोबारी थे। वरदराजन कहते हैं कि 'वैष्णव के लिए हमारी जांच को वैध मानने का मतलब होगा कि उनकी सरकार ने उन पर भी जासूसी की है!' पेगासस की जांच, दुनियाभर के एक दर्ज़न से ज़्यादा मीडिया संस्थानों में की गई और इसके सनसनीखेज तथ्यों ने निगरानी करने वाली ताकतों के दुरुपयोग पर दुनिया भर में नाराज़गी सामने आई। लेकिन मोदी सरकार ने किसी भी जांच से परहेज़ किया। निश्चित रूप से, इज़रायल से स्पाइवेयर खरीदने के लिए सरकारी पैसे के इस्तेमाल के आरोप गंभीर थे, और इसकी गहन और पारदर्शी जांच होनी चाहिए थी। 1972 में, अमेरिकी राष्ट्रपति रिचर्ड निक्सन पर अपने प्रतिद्वन्दी डेमोक्रेटिक पार्टी के कार्यालयों में सेंध लगाने के लिए महाभियोग लगाने जैसी बात हुई, जबकि भारत में सुप्रीम कोर्ट ने इसकी रिपोर्ट के कुछ हिस्से अदालत की वेबसाइट पर अपलोड करने के निर्देश

दिए थे, लेकिन पेगासस रिपोर्ट को एक सीलबंद लिफ़ाफे में रखा गया था। इस मसले पर हर कार्रवाई, बल्कि निष्क्रियता, इस बात का इशारा कर रही थी कि पेगासस मामले में सरकार के पास छिपाने के लिए बहुत कुछ है।

सरकार के इंकार के बावजूद, एक पैटर्न साफ दिखाई दे रहा था कि मीडिया में सरकार की आलोचना करने वालों पर कार्रवाई का खतरा मंडरा रहा था। जुलाई 2021 में, बड़े हिंदी समाचार समूह 'दैनिक भास्कर' पर आयकर अधिकारियों ने छापे मारे। यह छापेमारी, उन रिपोर्ट्स के कुछ हफ्तों बाद हुई, जिनमें कोविड की दूसरी लहर से निपटने में मोदी सरकार की लापरवाही का खुलासा किया गया था। इन ख़बरों में गंगा में तैरती लाशों और मौतों की कम संख्या की रिपोर्टिंग शामिल थी। फरवरी 2023 में, जब 2002 के गुजरात दंगें से निपटने की आलोचना करने वाली एक डाक्यूमेंट्री 'बीबीसी' पर प्रसारित हुई तो उसके कुछ दिनों बाद बीबीसी के दफ्तरों पर आयकर अधिकारियों ने तलाशी अभियान चलाया। सरकार के एक संदेश के बाद यूट्यूब और ट्विटर पर डॉक्यूमेंट्री को ऑनलाइन ब्लॉक कर दिया गया। 2021 में, मोदी सरकार ने 'राष्ट्रीय सुरक्षा' के कारण मलयालम समाचार चैनल मीडिया वन के प्रसारण लाइसेंस को आगे बढ़ाने से इंकार कर दिया। कहा गया कि चैनल प्रमोटरों के इस्लामिक संगठन 'जमात-ए-इस्लामी-हिंद' (जेईआईएच) के साथ संबंध हैं। दो साल बाद, सुप्रीम कोर्ट ने केन्द्र के आदेश को ख़ारिज़ कर दिया। अदालत के मुताबिक रिकॉर्ड पर ऐसा कोई सबूत नहीं मिला, जिससे यह साबित हो सके कि चैनल के शेयरधारक जेईआईएच के समर्थक थे और वह संगठन भी प्रतिबंधित नहीं था। कोर्ट ने चेतावनी दी, 'राष्ट्रीय सुरक्षा के दावे यूं ही हवा में नहीं किए जा सकते।' गृह मंत्रालय के इस मनमाने आदेश की वजह से दर्जनों पत्रकारों को अपनी नौकरी से हाथ धोना पड़ा था।

मसला सिर्फ़ मीडिया तक ही नहीं था। कई सामाजिक कार्यकर्ताओं, एनजीओ और नीति शोध संस्थानों, सभी को 'एजेंसी पावर' के प्रकोप को झेलना पड़ा, चाहे फिर वह ईडी हो या आयकर विभाग। इससे भी बदतर बात यह थी कि प्रेस आज़ादी पर हमला, अब सिर्फ़ केन्द्र तक सीमित नहीं रह गया था। विपक्षी दलों की राज्य सरकारों सहित पूरे देश में, आधिकारिक लाइन पर नहीं चलने वाले पत्रकारों पर ख़तरा था। गुहा ठाकुरता कहते हैं, 'हम एक ऐसे युग में जी रहे हैं जहां किसी भी सरकार और उसके सहयोगियों को बेनकाब करने वाली खोजी पत्रकारिता को एक अपराध माना जाता है।'

मई 2023 में, 'रिपोर्टर्स विदाउट बॉर्डर्स' के प्रेस फ्रीडम इंडेक्स में भारत 150वें स्थान से गिरकर 161वें स्थान पर पहुंच गया, यह दुनियाभर के 180 देशों की रैंकिंग करता है। रैंकिंग से इस बात का पता चलता है कि दुनिया के सबसे बड़े लोकतंत्र में स्वतंत्र और निष्पक्ष रूप से रिपोर्ट करने में काफी चुनौतियां हैं, लेकिन इससे यह नहीं पता चलता कि डर से भरे माहौल में एक पेशेवर पत्रकार होने की क्या क़ीमत चुकानी पड़ती है, जहां पहले के मुकाबले कम संतुलन

है। अंतरराष्ट्रीय स्तर पर निगरानी करने वाली संस्था 'कमेटी टू प्रोटेक्ट जर्नलिस्ट्स' की 2024 की रिपोर्ट में कहा गया है कि 2023 में सात भारतीय पत्रकार जेल में थे। इनमें से चार जम्मू-कश्मीर से थे। इस अशांत संघर्ष क्षेत्र में सार्वजनिक सुरक्षा अधिनियम में किसी को भी बिना मुकदमे के दो साल तक हिरासत में रखा जा सकता है।

अक्टूबर 2020 में, केरल के एक पत्रकार सिद्दीक कप्पन को 'पीएफआई' से कथित संबंधों के आरोप में यूएपीए के तहत गिरफ़्तार किया गया। कट्टरपंथी इस्लामिक संगठन 'पीएफआई' को बाद में भारत सरकार ने प्रतिबंधित कर दिया। कप्पन को उस वक्त हिरासत में लिया गया, जब वह देशभर में सुर्खियों में आए, उत्तरप्रदेश के हाथरस जिले में हत्या और सामूहिक बलात्कार की ख़बर को कवर करने जा रहे थे। जब कप्पन रिहा होने वाले थे, तभी ईडी ने उन पर मनी लॉन्ड्रिंग के आरोप लगा दिए। उन पर किसी अपराधिक गतिविधि में शामिल होने के बहुत कम सबूत थे, फिर भी उन्हें दो साल से ज्यादा समय तक जेल में रहना पड़ा। कप्पन के जेल में रहने के दौरान उनकी मां का निधन हो गया, लेकिन वह आखिरी क्षणों में भी उनके साथ नहीं रह सके। केरल के पत्रकारों का एक समूह, कप्पन की पत्नी रेहाना को कुछ संपादकों से मिलाने के लिए दिल्ली लेकर आया। जब मैंने इस मामले को सुना, तब मैं उस तीन बच्चों की मां के संघर्ष को समझ पाया, जो पुलिस सिस्टम के ख़िलाफ अकेले लड़ रही थी। आंसू भरी आंखों से रेहाना ने कहा, 'हमने बहुत कुछ सहा है। मैं बस इतना कह सकती हूं कि मेरे पति एक अभिमानी भारतीय हैं और वह आतंकवादी नहीं हैं।'

कमरे से बाहर निकलते वक्त मैं निराशा महसूस करते हुए सोच रहा था, क्या नए भारत में एक 'मुस्लिम पत्रकार' होना, राज्य की सत्ता के सामने ज़्यादा असहाय बनाता है। सत्ता को चुनौती देने की हिम्मत रखने वाले स्वतंत्र मीडिया के भविष्य पर अंधेरा छाया हुआ लगता है। मुख्यधारा के मीडिया के बड़े हिस्से में निराशाजनक रूप में एकतरफा कवरेज हो रहा था। क्या ऐसे में 2024 में चुनावों में खेल के लिए बराबरी का मैदान (लेवल प्लेइंग फील्ड) मिल पाएगा? मैं हैरान था।

═

तो, मोदी सरकार में तीसरा सबसे शक्तिशाली व्यक्ति कौन है? 2024 के चुनावी संग्राम से पहले भाजपा के एक सांसद ने मुझसे यह गुगली सवाल पूछा था। एक सुप्रीमो और उनके भरोसेमंद नंबर-2 के इर्दगिर्द घूमने वाली सत्ता की धुरी में क्या तीसरे व्यक्ति के लिए भी कोई जगह थी? ज़्यादातर केन्द्रीय मंत्रियों को हां में हां मिलाने वाले लोग के तरह पर देखा जाता था, उनके मंत्रालयों पर सुप्रीम पीएमओ के अफसरों की कड़ी निगरानी रहती थी। सोशल मीडिया अभी शुरुआती दौर में ही था। फेसबुक और ट्विटर जैसे प्लेटफॉर्म, भारतीय मीडिया में अभी-अभी

काम में आने लगे थे। चौवन साल के इलेक्ट्रॉनिक्स इंजीनियर हीरेन जोशी, प्रधानमंत्री के मीडिया प्रभारी हैं। जोशी ने 2008 में गांधीनगर में मुख्यमंत्री कार्यालय (सीएमओ) जाने से पहले कुछ समय तक भीलवाड़ा इंजीनियरिंग कॉलेज में पढ़ाया था। शुरुआत में जोशी का काम मोदी की डिजिटल पहुंच को बढ़ाना था। मोदी उन पहले राजनेताओं में से थे, जिन्होंने जोशी की मदद से डिजिटल पर अपनी बढ़त बना ली थी। 2014 में जब मोदी ने प्रधानमंत्री की शपथ ली, तो जोशी पूरी गुजरात टीम के साथ दिल्ली में पीएमओ में चले आए। प्रधानमंत्री के ट्वीट और फेसबुक पोस्ट लिखने के साथ, सोशल मीडिया प्रोफाइल की देखरेख करने वाले जोशी को, जल्दी ही तमाम मुश्किलों वाले 'हाइड्रा-हेडेड' मीडिया और मोदी के विजय रथ को चलाने वाले कम्युनिकेशन इंजन को देखने का अधिकार मिल गया। उदारहण के लिए, प्रधानमंत्री के मासिक कार्यक्रम *मन की बात* के प्रसारण के वक्त प्रदेश भाजपा नेताओं से यह उम्मीद की जाती है कि प्रसारण को सुनने के लिए देशभर में श्रोता इकट्ठा हों। फिर उन जगहों और कार्यक्रमों के वीडियो और तस्वीरें अपलोड कर उसी समय पीएमओ की मीडिया टीम को भेजी जाती हैं। भाजपा सांसद ने कहा, 'हीरेन, मोदी सरकार के दो सबसे अहम तत्वों, इसकी मीडिया मशीन और सुप्रीम नेता तक पहुंच को नियंत्रित करते हैं, इसीलिए मैं उन्हें सरकार का तीसरा सबसे शक्तिशाली व्यक्ति कहता हूं।'

मूंछों के साथ सख्त चेहरे वाले जोशी में कुछ ऐसे गुण थे, जिनकी वजह से वे प्रधानमंत्री मोदी के प्रिय थे। अपने बॉस के वफादार और काम को समर्पित जोशी, अपनी पहचान बनाने की जल्दी में नहीं थे, बल्कि वह बंद दरवाज़ों के पीछे 'सत्ता का खेल' खेलना पसंद करते थे। पिछले प्रधानमंत्रियों के पास भी मीडिया सलाहकार होते थे, लेकिन आमतौर पर वे वरिष्ठ पत्रकार, यह जिम्मेदारी संभालने से पहले ही जाने-पहचाने चेहरे होते थे। उनमें से कुछ ने इसे लंबे पत्रकारिता के करियर के बाद एक आरामदायक नौकरी के रूप में लिया, तो कुछ ने इसे सरकारी छवि बनाने और नीति-निर्धारण में योगदान देने के अवसर के तौर पर लिया। इन अनुभवी पत्रकारों का आमतौर पर काम, अपने निजी नेटवर्क का इस्तेमाल, साथी संपादकों और रिपोर्टरों के साथ मधुर संबंध बनाए रखना होता था। यह आपस में जुड़े हुए मीडिया 'इको सिस्टम' का भी हिस्सा था, जिसे कुछ फ़ोन कॉल या दिल्ली जिमखाना और इंडिया इंटरनेशनल सेंटर में अच्छे लंच के साथ देखा जा सकता था। दूसरी तरफ, एक डिजिटल तकनीक विशेषज्ञ, जो पत्रकार नहीं थे, जोशी, राजधानी के मीडिया सर्किल में बाहरी व्यक्ति थे। बिना किसी पिछले दायित्व या व्यक्तिगत संबंधों के, वह अपनी ताकत का इस्तेमाल बेबाकी से कर सकते थे। वे पत्रकारों और पत्रकारिता पर कोई एहसान करने के लिए यहां नहीं थे, बल्कि उनका काम था मोदी की छवि बेहतर करना और यह सुनिश्चित करना कि मोदी ब्रांड को बनाने और बनाए रखने में मीडिया बिरादरी की तरफ से कोई विरोध नहीं हो।

इस बारे में बहुत कहानियां हैं कि कैसे एक इंजीनियर से संचार-प्रमुख बने जोशी ने अपनी बेलगाम शक्ति से मुख्यधारा के विरासत मीडिया को अपने नियंत्रण में कर लिया। जोशी के पास पीएमओ में एक बड़ी टीम थी, जो उनकी वॉचलिस्ट के हिसाब से हर टेलीविज़न शो पर नज़र रखती थी। यहां तक कि पीएमओ का मीडिया सेल पत्रकारों के ट्वीट और फेसबुक पोस्ट की भी लगातार जांच करता था। मोदी सरकार को ट्वीट को लेकर खास जुनून है। बताया जाता है कि प्रधानमंत्री को हर शाम उनसे जुड़े सभी महत्वपूर्ण ट्वीट के बारे में जानकारी दी जाती है। प्रधानमंत्री की उपलब्धियों को आगे बढ़ाने के लिए, केन्द्रीय मंत्रियों, भाजपा नेताओं, मोदी समर्थकों, सेलिब्रिटी, प्रभावितों, सेरोगट हैंडल्स और पत्रकारों की भी पूरी लिस्ट बनाई गई है। इस समूह के एक जैसे ट्वीट को सार्वजनिक डोमेन में डालना आम है। पीएमओ बीट के एक रिपोर्टर ने बताया, 'अगर हम उन ट्वीट्स को आगे नहीं बढ़ाते तो फिर हमें ब्रेकिंग न्यूज़ नहीं मिलेगी।'

इससे उलट, मुख्यधारा के मीडिया के वे पत्रकार निशाने पर थे, जो सरकार के ख़िलाफ राय रखते थे या ट्वीट करते थे। 2017 के उत्तरप्रदेश विधानसभा चुनावों के दौरान समाजवादी पार्टी को कवर करते हुए, एक बिज़नेस अख़बार में काम करने वाली खोजी पत्रकार रोहिणी सिंह ने कुछ ट्वीट पोस्ट किए, जिनमें अखिलेश यादव को आगे बताया गया था और कहा गया कि मोदी की लोकप्रियता वोटों में शायद तब्दील नहीं होगी। उनके इन 'आक्रामक' ट्वीट्स का एक डोज़ियर, अखबार प्रबंधन को भेजा गया और कथित तौर पर उनसे ट्वीट्स को हटाने और उनके ख़िलाफ़ उचित कार्रवाई करने को कहा गया। पीएमओ को, पहले से ही इस अखबार की राजनीतिक रिपोर्टिंग से परेशानी थी, अखबार को संदेश दे दिया गया कि अखबार के बिजनेस वैश्विक सम्मेलन में न तो प्रधानमंत्री मोदी और न ही सरकार के कोई मंत्री शामिल होंगे। सरकार के अनौपचारिक बहिष्कार का मतलब था कि उनके सालाना बजट के लिए आयोजित प्रमुख कार्यक्रम में स्पॉन्सर भी नहीं मिलेंगे यानी राजस्व का बड़ा नुकसान। उत्तरप्रदेश में भाजपा की जीत के तुरंत बाद, रोहिणी सिंह को फटकार लगाई गई और प्रायश्चित के तौर पर उनसे मोदी सरकार के लिए स्टोरीज़ करने को कहा गया। ऐसा करने के बजाय रोहिणी ने नौकरी छोड़ने का फ़ैसला किया। सिंह का आरोप था, 'उन्होंने यह अफवाहें भी फैलाईं कि मैंने अखिलेश यादव से कैसे अहसान लिए थे। भाजपा के आईटी सेल के सदस्य की यह बेशर्म चरित्र हनन की कोशिश थी।'

सरकार के निशाने पर रहने वाली, सिंह अकेली पत्रकार नहीं थीं। एक प्रमुख अंग्रेज़ी चैनल के वरिष्ठ पत्रकार के साथ 2024 के आम चुनावों में एक गंभीर मामला हुआ। पिछले उदाहरणों का ज़िक्र करते हुए, पत्रकार ने अपने लाइव प्रसारण में मोदी के बांसवाड़ा में विवादास्पद भाषण पर चुनाव आयोग के नोटिस नहीं भेजने की नाकामी पर बात की थी। चैनल के बड़े संपादक ने उन्हें बताया कि पूरे चुनाव अभियान के दौरान उन्हें 'ऑफ एयर' किया जा रहा था। ज़ाहिर तौर

पर चैनल, अब भी मोदी के इंटरव्यू के लिए इंतज़ार कर रहा था और पीएमओ की नाराज़गी का ज़ोखिम नहीं उठाना चाहता था। नेटवर्क के एक वरिष्ठ संपादक ने कहा, 'पत्रकार को ऑफ एयर करने का निर्णय, सरकार के शीर्ष के आदेश के तहत लिया गया था।'

बताया जाता है कि कुछ समय बाद, जब भी कोई लेख, ट्वीट या न्यूज़ शो मोदी सरकार के हितों के ख़िलाफ़ होता था, तो जोशी, मीडिया मालिकों को सीधे फ़ोन करके कार्रवाई के लिए कहने लगे थे। 'हम यहां किससे मज़ाक कर रहे हैं?' कांग्रेस के मीडिया प्रमुख पवन खेड़ा कहते हैं। 'मीडिया में हर कोई जानता है कि संपादकों और गोदी मीडिया एंकरों को, जोशी और उनके सहयोगी फ़ोन कर बताते हैं कि कौन से विषय पर चर्चा होनी है और प्राइम टाइम बहस में क्या लाइन लेनी है। यहां तक कि वे चैनल के टॉप बैंड और हेडलाइन की भाषा भी तय करते हैं।' भाजपा मीडिया टीम को इस आलोचना की परवाह नहीं है। 'क्या आप हमें बता रहे हैं कि अहमद पटेल जैसे लोग, मीडिया मालिकों को इसके लिए फ़ोन नहीं करते थे कि सोनिया गांधी के बारे में कुछ भी नकारात्मक नहीं कहा जाए? कांग्रेस, हमें उपदेश देने वाली कौन होती है?' भाजपा के एक प्रमुख प्रवक्ता ने सवाल किया।

यह सच है कि मीडिया का 'प्रबंधन' करना 2014 में शुरू नहीं हुआ था, लेकिन यह अब ज़्यादा बेशर्म और डराने वाला हो गया था। मनमोहन सिंह सरकार में, खासकर यूपीए-2 के दौरान, न्यूज़ चैनलों पर प्राइम टाइम को छोड़ दिया था, जो भ्रष्टाचार और अन्य विफलताओं के आरोपों पर सरकार को परेशान कर रहे थे। लेकिन मोदी सरकार का इरादा वह ग़लती करने का नहीं था।

मोदी की मीडिया रणनीति 'साम-दाम-दंड-भेद' अपनाने की रही। संसद में दिए एक जवाब के मुताबिक, 2017 से 2022 के बीच मोदी सरकार ने टीवी विज्ञापनों पर करीब 526 करोड़ रुपये और अख़बारों पर करीब 1,829 करोड़ रुपये खर्च किए। किसी मीडिया कॉन्क्लेव या विशेष कार्यक्रम में मंत्रियों और भाजपा नेताओं को आमंत्रित करने के लिए भाजपा के मीडिया प्रभारी अनिल बलूनी से संपर्क करना होता था। उत्तराखंड से सासंद, पूर्व पत्रकार, मृदुभाषी बलूनी उन आयोजकों को प्राथमिकता देते, जो पार्टी और सरकार की छवि को बेहतर तरीके से रखते थे। कथित 'गोदी एंकर' जो सरकार की बात और लाइन पर चलते थे, उनकी पहुंच मोदी के 'इनर सर्किल' तक होती थी, जो सरकार के लिए असहज सवाल करते थे, उन्हें बाहर रखा जाता था। मैं भी बाद वाले पत्रकारों की श्रेणी में आता हूं। जब मैंने जोशी से इस किताब के इंटरव्यू के लिए कहा, तो उनका सपाट जवाब था, 'ईमानदारी से मैं कहना चाहता हूं कि इस किताब से हमारा कोई भला नहीं होगा। यह आपके ट्वीट्स की तरह, पीठ पर हमले की कोशिश होगी, इसलिए मैं इस पर अपनी मुहर नहीं लगाना चाहता। लेकिन मैं इसके लिए आपको शुभकामनाएं देता हूं।' हमारे व्हाट्सएप बातचीत में हमेशा विनम्र, लेकिन अपने लक्ष्यों के प्रति साफतौर से कठोर, जोशी ने अपने बॉस की आवाज़ मे बोलने की महारत हासिल कर ली थी।

विपक्ष में कुछ लोग यदि जोशी को पीएमओ में एक 'कठपुतली' की तरह देखते थे, तो भाजपा आईटी सेल के प्रमुख आक्रामक अमित मालवीय पर सरकार की आलोचना करने वाले को सोशल मीडिया पर व्यक्तिगत तौर पर निशाना बनाने वाला माना जाता था। मालवीय और मेरे बीच कई बार टीवी शो पर आमना-सामना हो गया था। उन्हें बदतमीजी करने की आदत सी थी, लेकिन बात यहीं तक नहीं रुकी। कई बार उन्होंने मुझे आपत्तिजनक व्हाट्सएप संदेश भेजे और मुझे 'रिटायर' होने या 'मुझे हटा देने की धमकी' भी दी। ना चाहते हुए भी, फिर मैंने उन्हें व्हाट्सएप पर ब्लॉक कर दिया। वह सत्तारूढ़ पार्टी की मीडिया मशीन के एक ऐसे ताकतवर सदस्य थे, जिनके पास समान विचारधारा वाले सोशल मीडिया पर ट्रोल करने वालों की एक बड़ी सेना थी। उनके ग़लत पक्ष की तरफ आना एक अप्रिय अनुभव था, जिसके लिए मैंने शायद खुद को तैयार नहीं किया था।

2021 में, पश्चिम बंगाल में चुनाव प्रचार के दौरान, गृहमंत्री शाह मुझे इंटरव्यू देने के लिए तैयार हो गए, और इसके लिए अपने काफिले के साथ चलने को कहा। शाह ने कहा, 'मेरे अगले प्रचार अभियान में हम हेलिकॉप्टर में इंटरव्यू कर सकते हैं।' मैं खुश था। गृहमंत्री एक बेशकीमती साक्षात्कारकर्ता थे। हम मंत्री के काफ़िले में साथ थे, जब मालवीय ने अचानक उतरने के लिए कहा। शायद उन्हें मेरे इंटरव्यू करने के बारे में भनक लग गई थी। मालवीय के इस व्यवहार से मैं हैरान था। मालवीय पश्चिम बंगाल में भाजपा के चुनाव सह-प्रभारी थे, लेकिन निश्चित तौर पर उनके पास, देश के सबसे शक्तिशाली गृहमंत्री पर वीटो करने की ताकत नहीं थी। लेकिन समझ आया कि उनके पास वह ताकत थी। शर्मीले दिखने वाले शाह ने, फिर किसी और समय, इंटरव्यू करने का वादा किया।

मीडिया मैनेजमेंट, सिर्फ़ पत्रकारों को अपने हिसाब से काम कराने तक सीमित नहीं है। प्रधानमंत्री का शोर मचाने के लिए मोदी मशीन ने एक पूरा इकोसिस्टम तैयार कर दिया है। सरकार के सोशल मीडिया अभियान किसी योजनाबद्ध तरीके से काम करते हैं, इसका उदाहरण 'मोदी का परिवार' नारे को लेकर हुई चर्चा से समझा जा सकता है। मार्च 2024 की शुरुआत में, चुनावों के ऐलान से कुछ दिन पहले, विपक्षी नेता लालू प्रसाद यादव ने प्रधानमंत्री पर अपना परिवार नहीं होने का तंज किया था, मोदी के वंशवाद की राजनीति पर हमले के जवाब में यादव ने यह कहा था। चौबीस घंटे के भीतर, भाजपा के सभी नेताओं और समर्थकों ने प्रधानमंत्री के साथ एकजुटता दिखाने और जवाबी कार्रवाई के तौर पर अपने सोशल मीडिया हैंडल पर 'मोदी का परिवार' जोड़ दिया था। बताया गया कि भाजपा आईटी सेल और मालवीय इस अभियान को आगे बढ़ा रहे थे, लेकिन इसका आइडिया जोशी और पीएमओ में उनकी टीम का था। एक मंत्री ने कहा, 'हमें सीधे पार्टी मीडिया सेल से निर्देश मिलते हैं, लेकिन हम जानते हैं कि यह वास्तव में कहां से आते हैं।' मोदी पंथ (कल्ट) एक ऐसी शोर करती प्रचार मशीन

है, जिसे देश ने पहले कभी नहीं देखा। मीडिया स्पेस पर कब्ज़ा करना और उस पर हावी होना, मोदी शासन का मुख्य उद्देश्य है। कई मायनों में, मोदी, मीडिया द्वारा, मीडिया के लिए और मीडिया व्यक्तित्व हैं। हर सरकारी विज्ञापन, प्रचार फ़िल्म, हर तस्वीर, प्रधानमंत्री का हर बयान, हमेशा ज़्यादा से ज्यादा कवरेज को सुनिश्चित करने के लिए बहुत सावधानी से तैयार किए जाते हैं। जोशी और उनके जैसे लोग ऐसे कुशल कोरियोग्राफर हैं, जो अपने प्रभाव का इस्तेमाल करके, यह सुनिश्चित करते हैं कि मोदी की छवि पर कभी नकारात्मक प्रचार का असर नहीं पड़े। 2002 में गुजरात हिंसा के तुरंत बाद, मीडिया ने मोदी को परेशान किया था और सरकार की भूमिका पर उनसे तीखे सवाल पूछे गए थे। 2002 के बाद, मोदी से पत्रकारिता की पूछताछ की परिणति सीएनएन-आईबीएन के उस इंटरव्यू के दौरान हुई, जब कड़े और सख्त सवाल पूछने वाले करण थापर उनसे बात कर रहे थे, और उसे बीच में ही रोक दिया गया। मोदी ने उस समय अपने एक सहयोगी से कहा, 'ऐसा फिर कभी नहीं होना चाहिए।' संदेश स्पष्ट थाः मोदी कभी-कभार साक्षात्कार दे सकते हैं, लेकिन अपनी शर्तों पर। इससे समझा जा सकता है कि मोदी ने सत्ता के एक दशक में एक भी प्रेस कॉन्फ्रेंस नहीं करने का फ़ैसला किया। न ही उन्होंने संसद में प्रश्नकाल के दौरान एक भी सवाल का जवाब दिया है। इसके बजाय, मोदी के अपनी बात रखने के पसंदीदा तरीकों में ट्वीट, भाषण और उनका रेडियो शो, *मन की बात* है। इस तरह के एकतरफा संवाद का मतलब है कि विमर्श को नियंत्रित किया जा सकता है और कोई परेशान करने वाला सवाल नहीं होगा।

लेकिन 2024 के चुनावों के दौरान, रणनीति में बदलाव आया। एक और बड़े बहुमत से जीत को लेकर आश्वस्त, मोदी ने दो महीने के प्रचार अभियान में कई साक्षात्कार दिए, करीब 82 साक्षात्कार। सरकार में रहने के दौरान ज़्यादातर समय मीडिया से दूर रहने के बाद, यह अप्रत्याशित लाभ हो सकता था। भाजपा के एक रणनीतिकार ने कहा, 'इसका मकसद विपक्ष पर जोरदार तरीके से हमलावर होना, उसके लिए कोई जगह नहीं छोड़ना था, ताकि यह संदेश जा सके कि देश में केवल एक ही नेता हैः नरेन्द्र मोदी।' मोदी की हर बातचीत में दृश्य सबसे महत्वपूर्ण थे। अभियान के दौरान, जोशी और उनकी टीम ने हर साक्षात्कार को सावधानी से तैयार किया था ताकि प्रधानमंत्री की आभा चमकती रहे और मतदाता-दर्शक को उनके प्रति आकर्षण बना रहे। सरकार के ख़िलाफ़ कभी-कभार आलोचनात्मक ख़बर करने या संपादकीय लिखने वाले *इंडियन एक्सप्रेस* और *द हिंदू* जैसे राष्ट्रीय समाचार पत्रों को औपचारिक अनुरोध के बावजूद मौका नहीं दिया गया। साक्षात्कार एक पूर्व निर्धारित स्क्रिप्ट के हिसाब से होते थेः जोशी ने टीवी चैनलों और साक्षात्कार करने वालों का चयन, चुनाव कैंलेडर के हिसाब से किया था, जैसे मार्च के आखिर में, पहला साक्षात्कार, तमिल चैनल थांती टीवी के साथ इसलिए किया गया, क्योंकि तमिलनाडु में मतदान पहले चरण में होना था।

अप्रैल में मतदान शुरू होने से पहले, सरकार के अनुकूल माने जाने वाली समाचार एजेंसी एएनआई को साक्षात्कार दिया गया। एएनआई को सभी समाचार चैनल सब्सक्राइब करते हैं, जिसका मतलब है सभी जगह कवरेज होगा। ऐसा शायद पहली बार हुआ कि ज़्यादातर साक्षात्कार पीएमओ द्वारा शूट और संपादित किए गए। पीएमओ के पास अब अपनी इन-हाउस टीवी प्रोडक्शन टीम थी, जिसमें कैमरामैन, वीडियो एडिटर, और साउंड रिकॉर्डिस्ट शामिल थे, किसी भारतीय प्रधानमंत्री के लिए यह पहली बार था। एक वरिष्ठ पत्रकार ने टिप्पणी की, 'यह एक ऐसे शो की तरह है, जिसे पीएमओ ने निर्देशित और तैयार किया है, जिसमें केवल एक चमकता सितारा है और एंकर केवल सहायक के रूप में है।' इन साक्षात्कारों की शैली और सामग्री का विश्लेषण भी चौंकाने वाला है। हर साक्षात्कार नरम और बहुत विनम्र लहजे में था। कोई ऊंची आवाज़ नहीं, कोई तर्क नहीं, जवाब पर सवाल यानी क्रॉस-क्वेश्चन नहीं था। पत्रकारिता की कहावत, 'सवाल पूछो और सवाल का जवाब दो,' को ख़त्म कर दिया गया। कठोर, प्रतिकूल साक्षात्कार का युग पूरी तरह से और वास्तव में दफ़न हो गया था।

आश्चर्य की बात नहीं है कि साक्षात्कारों में मोदी से पूछे गए सभी सवालों की जांच की गई और जहां ज़रूरी था, वहां जवाबों को संपादित किया गया। अस्सी से ज़्यादा साक्षात्कारों में, मणिपुर हिंसा पर एक भी सवाल नहीं पूछा गया, जहां दो सौ से ज़्यादा लोग मारे गए थे और ना ही लद्दाख में चीन के साथ अनसुलझे गतिरोध पर कोई सवाल था। मोदी के अडानी के साथ संबंध पर एक सवाल धीरे से पूछा गया, लेकिन बिना किसी फॉलो-अप या तथ्य-जांच के। इसके बजाय कम से कम आधा दर्ज़न इंटरव्यू करने वालों ने प्रधानमंत्री की ऊर्जा के रहस्य के बारे में जरूर पूछा, एक से अधिक ने कहा कि 'उन्होंने मोदी जी जैसा प्रधानमंत्री कभी नहीं देखा,' और एक ने उन्हें 'ऐसे नेता के तौर पर पेश किया, जिनके बिना देश विकसित भारत का सपना नहीं देख सकता।' यह कभी ख़त्म नहीं होता दिखने वाला 'स्तुति गान', केवल मुख्यधारा मीडिया के इस भरोसे को बता रहा था कि मोदी के नेतृत्व में भाजपा को फिर से शानदार जीत मिलेगी। एक साक्षात्कार तो पूरी तरह इस बात के लिए समर्पित लगा कि मोदी 3.0 कैसा लगेगा। एक प्रसन्न प्रधानमंत्री, अगले एक हज़ार साल के विजन की रूपरेखा बता रहे थे और एंकर का सिर, प्रशंसा में हिल रहा था।

इसके विपरीत, राहुल गांधी ने मुख्यधारा या डिजिटल मीडिया को एक भी साक्षात्कार देने से इंकार कर दिया। अपनी भारत जोड़ो यात्रा के दौरान, उन्होंने यूट्यूब के इन्फ्लुएंसर्स को चुना, जिनकी बात ज़्यादातर युवा सुनते हैं। उनके यूट्यूब इंटरव्यू, ज़्यादातर गैर-विवादास्पद, फीचर जैसे प्रारूप में तैयार किए गए थे: मसलन राहुल के पसंदीदा भोजन और उनकी शादी की योजना से जुड़े हल्के-फुल्के सवाल पूछे गए थे। कड़े राजनीतिक सवाल, इंटरव्यू के मेन्यू से बाहर थे।

लेकिन 2024 के चुनाव अभियान के दौरान, राहुल गांधी ने खुद को किसी भी साक्षात्कार से दूर रखा। इसके बजाय उन्होंने सीधे प्रेस कॉन्फ्रेंस की और साथ ही व्यक्तिगत वीडियो साझा करना पसंद किया। राहुल टीम के एक सदस्य ने याद करते हुए कहा, उन्हें एक-दो साक्षात्कार के लिए मनाने की कोशिश की गई, लेकिन कोई फायदा नहीं हुआ। 'मुझे क्यों मीडिया को समय देना चाहिए, जो पिछले दस साल से मुझ पर और कांग्रेस पार्टी पर हमला कर रहा है? हम उन्हें क्यों प्रतिष्ठा दें?' राहुल और मीडिया के बीच असहज और तनावपूर्ण संबंध, कांग्रेस नेता की मीडिया संस्थानों के प्रति हमेशा की शिकायत की भावना को बताता है। उनका मानना था कि मीडिया भाजपा के इशारे पर खेल रहा था।

राहुल गांधी का यह अडियल रुख, विपक्ष के एक वर्ग की प्रतिक्रिया को बताता है। सितंबर 2023 में, विपक्ष के इंडिया गठबंधन ने उन न्यूज़ एंकरों की सूची जारी की, जिनके शो का बहिष्कार किया जाना था। पहली बार इस तरह का कदम उठाया गया था और दिखने में यह अलोकंतात्रिक और असहिष्णु लग रहा था। भले ही विपक्ष कुछ एंकरों के ज़्यादा पक्षपाती रवैये से नाराज़ था, फिर भी उनके आधिकारिक बहिष्कार का ऐलान क्यों किया गया? 'यह बहिष्कार नहीं, बल्कि सविनय अवज्ञा आंदोलन जैसा था। आप क्या चाहते हैं कि हम उन लोगों के साथ जुड़े रहें, जिनका एजेंडा ही विपक्ष को बदनाम करना और जहरीले विमर्श बनाना है?' कांग्रेस के पवन खेड़ा ने पूछा।

विपक्ष की एक मीडिया समिति ने चैनलों पर चली ऐसी सुर्खियों की सूची तैयार की, जिन्हें भड़काऊ कहा जा सके। उनका दावा था कि यह साबित करता है कि कुछ समाचार चैनल विपक्ष विरोधी और विभाजनकारी एजेंडे को बढ़ा रहे थे। जैसे 2022 के उत्तरप्रदेश के चुनावों से पहले एक शो में कहा गया: 'हिंदुओं के ख़िलाफ़ महागठबंधन।' इस नफरती प्रचार के ख़तरे अब सामने आने लगे थे, जब जुलाई 2023 में, रेलवे सुरक्षाबल के एक जवान ने ट्रेन में चार यात्रियों की गोली मारकर हत्या कर दी। जिस ट्रेन में वह सुरक्षा ड्यूटी पर था, उसने मुस्लिम दिखने वाले लोगों की तलाश की, उनके नाम पूछकर पहचान की और फिर गोलियों से भून दिया। उसने इस काम को यह कहकर उचित ठहराया कि ये लोग पाकिस्तान से काम कर रहे थे और बाद में बताया गया कि उसकी बेबुनियाद जानकारी का स्रोत 'भारतीय मीडिया' था। यह दुखद क्षण था, जिसे लेकर मीडिया नेटवर्क के नाम पर नफ़रत फैलाने वाले चैनलों से खुद के भीतर झांकने की मांग होनी चाहिए थी। लेकिन अफसोस, न तो अपराधियों ने कोई आत्मंथन किया और न ही मीडिया उद्योग में दूसरे लोगों ने भी कोई आवाज़ उठाई। हालांकि टीवी मीडिया की निगरानी करने वाली संस्था 'न्यूज़ ब्रॉडकास्टिंग एंड डिजिटल स्टेंडर्ड्स अथॉरिटी' (एनबीडीएसए) कभी-कभी आपत्तिजनक सामग्री पर दंड देने की कार्रवाई करता है, लेकिन यह नाकाफ़ी साबित हुई है।

बताया गया कि जयराम रमेश जैसे कांग्रेस नेताओं ने कुछ खास एंकरों के बहिष्कार के फ़ैसले का विरोध किया था। जबकि मीडिया के एक वर्ग की भूमिका को माफ़ नहीं किया जा सकता। ऐसे बहिष्कारों की सीमित उपयोगिता हो सकती है, खासतौर से चुनावी गर्मी से भरे अभियान में। प्रधानमंत्री के बहुत से साक्षात्कारों से तुलना करने पर मुख्यधारा के मीडिया से जुड़ने को लेकर राहुल गांधी का रवैया अड़ियल था, लेकिन इससे कुछ लोगों को लगा कि इसका मतलब कांग्रेस इस विमर्श की लड़ाई को हारने वाली थी। आखिरकार, भाजपा जब आसानी से पलटकर दावा करती है कि मोदी जैसे कुशल कम्युनिकेटर खुद को मीडिया के लिए आगे ला रहे थे, जबकि उनके प्रतिद्वन्दी मीडिया के सवालों से भाग रहे थे। दुनिया में किसी भी सामान्य राजनीतिक माहौल में इसके मायने होंगे कि खेल, सेट और दूसरी सभी संभावनाओं में मीडिया के पक्ष में रहना बेहतर होता।

हालांकि, आश्चर्यजनक तौर पर यह पूरी तरह काम नहीं आया। इसके बजाय, प्रधानमंत्री के ज़्यादातर साक्षात्कारों की चाटुकारिता और प्रधानमंत्री मोदी के अहंकारी जवाबों ने ज़्यादातर मौकों पर उलटा असर किया। उदाहरण के लिए, ईश्वर के 'नॉन-बायलॉजिकल दूत' होने के दावे पर वे मीम्स और मजाक का कारण बन गए। मोदी के 'नॉन-बायलॉजिकल' होने के दावे का इस्तेमाल विपक्ष अब आत्मप्रशंसा वाले प्रधानमंत्री का मज़ाक उड़ाने के लिए करता है। जब मोदी ने 'कौन राहुल?' कहकर हंसी उड़ाई, तो तालियों के बजाय उस पर मज़ाक ज़्यादा हुआ। पांच साल पहले तक मोदी के हर साक्षात्कार की चर्चा होती थी, वहीं अब उनके प्रतिद्वन्दी की सड़क पर सहज बातचीत के सामने उनकी अच्छे से तैयार, अटपटी और तारीफ की बातचीत फीकी पड़ रही थी। प्रधानमंत्री के विभिन्न सोशल मीडिया प्लेटफॉर्म पर कुल फॉलोअर्स और सब्सक्राइबर्स भले ही बहुत ज़्यादा रहे हों, लेकिन राहुल गांधी के सोशल और डिजिटल मीडिया इंप्रेशन, शेयर, लाइक्स, इंस्टाग्राम और यूट्यूब पर पहली बार मोदी से आगे निकल गए। शायद दर्शकों की पसंद बदल गई थी या मुख्यधारा मीडिया, खासतौर से टीवी न्यूज़ चैनलों की विश्वसनीयता का संकट सामने आ गया था। दर्शकों की राजनीतिक प्राथमिकताओं के आधार पर मुख्यधारा मीडिया को गोदी या दरबारी के रूप में खारिज़ करने के साथ वैकल्पिक विमर्श और बातचीत की जगह बनने लगी थी। 2024 का चुनाव, लंबे समय से इंतज़ार करती डिजिटल क्रांति को रफ़्तार देने के लिए एकदम सही मंच था।

═

पटना से करीब 50 किलोमीटर दूर हाजीपुर कस्बे के चौक पर, मुझे खबरों की बदलती पसंद का रियलिटी चैक हुआ। मैं वहां पहली बार वोट देने वाले मतदाताओं से लाइव बातचीत कर रहा था, तभी उनमें से एक नौजवान ने 'तानाशाही' पर तीखी टिप्पणी शुरू कर दी। मैं उसके

जुनून और उत्साही तर्कों से प्रभावित हुआ। मैंने कहा, 'लगता है कि आप राजनीति विज्ञान पढ़ रहे हो?' 'अरे, मैं बायोलॉजी पढ़ता हूं, लेकिन मैं ध्रुव राठी के यूट्यूब वीडियो देखता हूं। मुझे यकीन है कि आपने भी सुने होंगे!' उसने जवाब में कहा।

हां, कई बार सुने थे। फरवरी 2024 में, मोदी को नापसंद करने वाले मुंबई के एक मित्र ने, मुझे ध्रुव राठी का एक यूट्यूब वीडियो व्हाट्सएप पर भेजा, जिसका शीर्षक भड़काऊ लगता था, 'क्या भारत तानाशाह बन रहा है?' 'तुम लोगों में टीवी पर ऐसा करने की हिम्मत कब होगी?' मेरे दोस्त ने गुस्से में कहा। सनसनीखेज़ सुर्खियां और आकर्षक तस्वीरें यूट्यूब पर वायरल होने के लिए डिजाइन किए गए हैं। लाइव और बेबाक डिजिटल प्लेटफॉर्म ने कई बार टैब्लॉयड टीवी को भी बेदम कर दिया।

29 मिनट के इस वीडियो को कुछ ही घंटों में बीस लाख से ज़्यादा बार देखा गया। इसे कई व्हाट्सएप ग्रुप पर तेजी से फॉरवर्ड किया गया। कुछ हफ़्ते बाद, राठी इसके आगे की कहानी यानी सीक्वल के साथ आए। अरविंद केजरीवाल की गिरफ़्तारी पर इस वीडियो को कुछ ही घंटों में पचास लाख बार देखा गया। चुनाव अभियान शुरू होने तक, इन दोनों वीडियोज को अकेले यूट्यूब पर पांच करोड़ से ज़्यादा बार देखा गया। रोहतक में जन्मे 29 साल के यूट्यूबर राठी, आपके बेहद करीब रहने वाले मोबाइल पर पहुंच चुके थे। यह देश का पहला यूट्यूब आम चुनाव था।

राठी ने बाद में मुझे कहा, 'ईमानदारी से कहूं, मुझे इस तरह की प्रतिक्रिया की उम्मीद नहीं थी। ऐसा लगा कि लोग खुश थे कि कोई तो वह बात खुलकर कह रहा था, जिसे वे अंदर से महसूस कर रहे थे। यह सच है कि लोकतंत्र ख़तरे में है।' मैंने देखा कि उसकी सफलता की वजह उसके संदेशों की सादगी और साफगोई में थी। खुलापन। स्पष्ट। हमलावर। कठोर। लेकिन सबसे अहम बात, हिंदी में। आमतौर पर टीवी चैनलों के सामने विश्वसनीयता का संकट हिंदी न्यूज़ चैनलों पर ज्यादा बढ़ गया, जहां ज़्यादातर एंकरों को भाजपा के कट्टर समर्थकों की तरह देखा गया। इससे भी बदतर, कुछ लोग सांप्रदायिक कट्टरपन को खुलेआम बढ़ावा दे रहे थे और धार्मिक कट्टरता के प्रचार करने वाले हो गए थे। हिंदी आम आदमी के बोलचाल की ज़ुबान है और मोदी सरकार का पूरा ध्यान खासतौर से हिंदी समाचारों के विमर्श पर था। ज़्यादातर हिंदी टीवी न्यूज़ एंकर, असहमति के किसी भी विचार को चिल्लाकर दबा देते थे, तब राठी को सत्ता-विरोधी आवाज़ के तौर पर देखा गया। बेशक वह भी एक पक्ष को चुन रहे थे, लेकिन उनकी शैली स्पष्ट और बेरोक थी। तटस्थता का कोई दिखावा नहीं था, ना कोई बड़ा उपदेश था। वह पत्रकार होने का दावा भी नहीं कर रहे थे, बस ज़मीनी पत्रकारों के डेटा को बढ़ा-चढ़ाकर बता रहे थे और उसे तर्कसंगत बना रहे थे। कोई उनकी राय से असहमत हो सकता था, लेकिन पैकेजिंग और प्रस्तुति ताज़गी भरी और ध्यान खींचने वाली थी। यह एक तरह से 'पीढ़ीगत बदलाव'

का संकेत था। देश के युवा और बेचैन लोगों को ख़बरों और राय पर किसी तरह का 'फिल्टर' पसंद नहीं था। वे चाहते थे कि पत्रकार वैसा रहे, जो दरअसल प्रेस का मायने होता है: 'सत्ता विरोधी और सवाल करने वाला।'

असली 'तानाशाही' वीडियो चंडीगढ़ मेयर चुनाव में खुलेआम गड़बड़ी से शुरू हुआ था, जब तक कि सुप्रीम कोर्ट के फ़ैसले ने उस धांधली को सही नहीं कर दिया। राठी ने कहा, 'मुझे लगता है कि जिन्होंने भी उस वीडियो को देखा, वह गुस्से में थे और अपना गुस्सा निकालना चाहते थे। यह सिर्फ़ अलग से कोई एक मामला नही था। मुख्यमंत्रियों की गिरफ़्तारी, चुनावी बॉन्ड को ज़ब्त करना और विधायकों की खरीद फरोख्त, इन सबसे नाराज़गी बढ़ रही थी। मुझे लगा कि मैं अगर अब भी नहीं बोलूंगा, तो यह इस प्लेटफॉर्म की बर्बादी होगी।' राठी ज़ोर देकर कहते हैं कि वह वामपंथी या दक्षिणपंथी, यहां तक कि मोदी-विरोधी भी नहीं हैं, लेकिन वह मोदी के मूल्यों के ख़िलाफ़ हैं। वे कहते हैं कि 'मैं फ्री-स्पीच, आज़ादी और सहिष्णुता के मूल्यों में भरोसा करता हूं, वे 2024 में दांव पर हैं।' उनके वायरल वीडियो, मुख्यधारा के मीडिया के विमर्श को सीधे चुनौती देते और उस खास मौके का जवाब देने के लिए बने थे।

दिलचस्प बात यह है कि 2024 में अपनी क़ामयाबी से पहले, मैकेनिकल इंजीनियर राठी ने खुद को यूट्यूब शिक्षक के रूप में देखा था, जो विज्ञान और तकनीक, समाज और संस्कृति के जटिल विषयों पर आसानी से बात करता था। 2014 में उनका पहला वीडियो एक मज़ेदार यात्रा ब्लॉग था। 2020 में अपनी एक छोटी टीम के साथ वह पूरी तरह से यूट्यूब पर जुड़ गए थे, अब उनकी टीम में 15 लोग हैं। जर्मनी से इंजीनियरिंग की डिग्री हासिल करने और यूरोप में कहीं रह रहे हैं, लेकिन अभी घर लौटने के बारे में तय नहीं किया है। वे कहते हैं कि 'वैसे, सिवाय कुछ ट्रोलिंग के, मुझे कोई धमकी नहीं मिली है, लेकिन फिर भी बेहतर है कि मैं अपना सही पता नहीं बताऊं।'

राठी आराम से यूरोप में रह रहे हैं, लेकिन देश में दूसरे 'डिजिटल विद्रोही' भी हैं। इस समय 70 करोड़ से ज़्यादा लोगों के पास मोबाइल है और पचास करोड़ से ज्यादा यूट्यूब पर सक्रिय आबादी वाले देश में, हज़ारों यूट्यूबर और इंस्टाग्राम पर रहने वाले अपने फॉलोअर्स और समुदायों के समूह बना रहे हैं। ऑनलाइन प्लेटफॉर्म बना रहे हैं, जो ख़बरों के तेजी से लोकतंत्रीकरण को बताता है, जहां पारपंरिक सूचना पर एकाधिकार को चुनौती दी जा सकती है और विमर्श बनाया जा सकता है। स्थापित पत्रकारों से लेकर कुछ युवा प्रभावशाली लोगों तक, दक्षिणपंथी विचारधारा का झंडा उठाने वालों से लेकर कट्टरपंथी वामपथियों, दलित-ओबीसी समुदाय के पत्रकारों तक, कंटेट क्रिएटर्स की बड़ी तादाद का साथ देते हुए, यूट्यूब और इंस्टाग्राम वैचारिक रूप से तटस्थ प्लेटफॉर्म हैं, जिन पर अभी किसी का नियंत्रण नहीं है।

ऐसे समय में जब सूचना और प्रसारण मंत्रालय का एक निर्देश देश के साढ़े तीन सौ से ज़्यादा न्यूज़ चैनलों को एक लाइन पर खड़ा कर सकता है, ये साइट्स अलग-अलग नज़रियों को सुनने के लिए एक बेशकीमती मंच देती हैं।

भाजपा और कांग्रेस ही नहीं, क्षेत्रीय दलों को भी डिजीटल प्लेटफॉर्म पर आई तेज़ी का अहसास है और वे जानते हैं कि इस पर क्या दांव पर लगा है। उन्होंने 2024 में अपने राजनीतिक विज्ञापनों के फंड का एक बड़ा हिस्सा यूट्यूब और इंस्टाग्राम पर लगाया। 'गूगल एडवरटाइंज़िग ट्रांसपेरेंसी सेन्टर' ने बताया कि फरवरी और मई के बीच के महत्वपूर्ण चुनावी महीनों में, कांग्रेस ने वीडियो सामग्री के लिए गूगल विज्ञापनों पर 24.5 करोड़ रुपये और भाजपा ने करीब 50.4 करोड़ रुपये खर्च किए, इसके अलावा कथित तौर पर यूट्यूब-इंस्टाग्राम स्पेस पर हावी होने के लिए दूसरे नामों से भी पैसा खर्च किया गया। फिर भी, टीवी की तरह, भाजपा सोशल मीडिया पर एकतरफा एजेंडा बनाने में कामयाब नहीं हो पाई। डिजिटल मार्केटिंग के एक एग्ज़ीक्यूटिव ने बताया, 'यूट्यूब कंटेंट की बढ़ोतरी इतनी स्वाभाविक है कि कोई एक इस क्रांति को नियंत्रित नही कर सकता।'

इस क्रांति के प्रमुख चेहरों में से एक हैं उनचास स ल के रवीश कुमार, जो एनडीटीवी के एंकर रहे और 2019 में पत्रकारिता के लिए उन्हें प्रतिष्ठित रेमन मैग्सेसे पुरस्कार मिला है। यदि राठी अचानक ही, दुर्घटनावश डिजिटल समाचारों की दुनिया में आ गए थे, तो रवीश कुमार मुख्यधारा के पत्रकार रहे, जिन्होंने यूट्यूब की दुनिया में इसलिए कदम रखा, क्योंकि उनके पास कोई विकल्प नहीं था। 2022 में अडानी के एनडीटीर्वि के अधिग्रहण ने रवीश को नेटवर्क में दो दशक से ज्यादा समय के बाद इस्तीफ़ा देने के लिए मजबूर किया। बरसों तक, वे एनडीटीवी के हिंदी चैनल, एनडीटीवी इंडिया के चेहरा रहे थे, उनकी खास शैली और परीक्षा पेपर लीक, सरकारी नौकरियों में भर्ती में देरी, शहरी इन्फ्रास्ट्रक्चर के ढहने जैसे लोगों से जुड़े मुद्दों पर उनका फोकस करना, उन्हें ब्रेकिंग न्यूज़ के शोर से अलग खड़ा करता है। 'देखिए, अडानी के अधिग्रहण का पत्रकारिता से कोई लेना-देना नहीं है, इसके बाद एनडीटीवी में रहने के कोई मायने नहीं हैं। यह ऐसा है कि जैसे आपको भाजपा मुख्यालय में प्रूफरीडर बना दिया गया हो,' रवीश ने जोर देकर कहा।

निजी परेशानियों के दौर में, जब पटना में उनकी मां गंभीर रूप से बीमार थीं, रवीश को अपने एनडीटीवी के वफादार दर्शकों में कट्टर समर्थक मिले। यूट्यूब की दुनिया में आने के दस दिनों के भीतर उनके 23 लाख से ज़्यादा सब्सक्राइबर हो गए। 2024 का चुनाव अभियान शुरू होने तक यह संख्या एक करोड़ को पार कर गई। वे कहते हैं, 'मुझे लगता है कि यह उन दर्शकों की बग़ावत थी, जिन्होंने अडानी के अधिग्रहण के असल मायने समझ लिए थे और उनकी आवाज़ बनने वाले एक एंकर के साथ एकजुटता दिखाते हुए टीवी से मेरे यूट्यूब चैनल पर बदलने का

फ़ैसला किया।' आखिरकार ये कुमार ही थे, जिन्होंने 2016 में 'गोदी मीडिया' शब्द गढ़ा था, उनके शब्दों में, 'एक मालिक के सामने मीडिया का पूर्ण आत्मसमर्पण।'

रवीश मानते हैं कि अंतरराष्ट्रीय स्तर पर प्रशंसा के बावजूद प्राइम टाइम टीवी से यूट्यूब पर आने का सफ़र आसान नहीं रहा। रोज़ाना सवेरे 6 बजे उठकर अपनी वीडियो स्क्रिप्ट लिखना, खबरों पर बारीकी से जानकारी जुटाना, एक छोटी सी टीम के साथ संपादन और वीडियो तैयार करना, एक बड़े मीडिया ब्रांड और न्यूज़रूम का हिस्सा होने से बहुत अलग बात है। किसी सिस्टम की मदद के बिना घर से काम करना मुश्किल होता है, लेकिन आज़ादी की कीमत चुकानी पड़ती है। मैं पूछता हूं, 'क्या उनकी पत्रकारिता अब सिर्फ़ मोदी विरोधी बयानबाज़ी तक सीमित हो गई है?' जैसा कि बहुत से आलोचक आरोप लगाते हैं। 'अगर सरकार से, किसी भी सरकार से सवाल पूछना, लोगों से जुड़े विषय उठाना, मुझे मोदी विरोधी बनाता है, तो फिर कहने के लिए क्या बचा है?' वे जवाब देते हैं।

एक तरह से, रवीश कुमार का टीवी न्यूज़ एंकर-रिपोर्टर से यूट्यूब पर ओपिनियन-मेकर में सफल बदलाव यह बताता है कि मुख्यधारा के मीडिया ने 2014 के बाद कैसे खुद को सरकार का 'चीयरलीडर' बना लिया, जहां से लौटना अब मुश्किल लगता है। वही मीडिया, जिसने 2011 में अण्णा हज़ारे के नेतृत्व वाले 'इंडिया अंगेस्ट करप्शन' आंदोलन का समर्थन करने के लिए एक सुर में आवाज़ उठाई थी और दिल्ली में एक युवती के साथ हुए क्रूर सामूहिक बलात्कार और हत्या के बाद सड़कों पर उतर आया था। अब वो एकतरफा और कई बार सांप्रदायिक रूप से द्वेषपूर्ण विमर्श बनाने में मशगूल है। यह मसला सामान्य वामपंथी बनाम दक्षिणपंथी वैचारिक लड़ाई का नहीं था, बल्कि सत्ता के सामने मीडिया का आत्मसमर्पण था। तब डिजिटल आने की वजह, खासतौर से हिंदी मीडिया में, वैकल्पिक नजरिये को सुनने की बेताब इच्छा का नतीजा था। अहम बात यह है कि 2019 से अलग, इसने 2024 के 'मीडिया युद्ध' में कम से कम एक बराबरी के खेल की संभावना को बढ़ा दिया।

यूट्यूब का तेज़ी से बढ़ना 2024 के चुनावों और उसके बाद बने रहना भी तय था, लेकिन यह नहीं कहा जा सकता था कि यह कब तक अनियंत्रित रह सकता है। मोदी सरकर के 'ब्रॉडकास्टिंग सर्विसेज़ रेग्ययूलेशन बिल 2023', के मसौदे में ऑनलाइन कंटेट, वीडियो अपलोड करने, पॉडकास्ट बनाने या करंट अफेयर्स के बारे में लिखने वाले को डिजिटल न्यूज़ ब्रॉडकास्टर मानने की बात की गई थी, ताकि उन्हें सरकारी ढांचे के नियमन में लाया जा सके। 'विनियमन' अक्सर नियंत्रण और सेंसरशिप की ओर पहला कदम होता है। इन शब्दों का इस्तेमाल वह राजनीतिक नेतृत्व करते हैं, जो स्वाभाविक तौर पर सत्तावादी और दमनकारी सोच के होते हैं। दिसंबर 2023 में, संसद में एक सवाल के जवाब में सूचना प्रसारण मंत्री अनुराग ठाकुर ने माना कि दिसंबर 2021 से भारत की संप्रभुता और अखंडता को ध्यान में रखते हुए 122 यूट्यूब न्यूज़ चैनलों को

ब्लॉक कर दिया गया था। अगस्त 2024 में, ड्राफ्ट बिल को इसकी मंशा और विषय-वस्तु की आलोचना के बाद वापस ले लिया गया था, लेकिन जो लोग सरकारी सेंसरशिप से बचने के लिए यूट्यूब का रास्ता अपना रहे थे, उन्हें लग रहा होगा, क्या उनकी बारी भी जल्दी ही आएगी?

हालांकि, बड़े सवाल किसी प्लेटफॉर्म से जुड़े भर नहीं थे, बल्कि सामान्य तौर पर मीडिया के इर्दगिर्द घूमते हैं। मीडिया उस रास्ते पर कब तक चल पाएगा, जहां दबंग सत्ता का कोई प्रतिरोध नहीं है? पत्रकार कब तक खुद को सेंसर करेंगे और समाचार संस्थान सत्ता को सच बताने से डरेंगे? क्या मीडिया मालिक और पत्रकार याद रखेंगे कि उनकी पहली जवाबदेही अपने पाठकों और दर्शकों के प्रति है? लोगों की सेवा करने वाली, सच्चाई बताने वाली असली पत्रकारिता, मोदी सरकार की नज़र में अच्छे बने रहने की कोशिश से ज़्यादा बड़ा काम है। हो सकता है कि एक असाधारण चुनावी फ़ैसले ने एक मज़बूत प्रतिरोध का रास्ता दिखाया हो। अगर 'गैर-बराबरी' के खेल मैदान और तमाम बाधाओं के बावजूद, विनम्र मतदाता शक्तिशाली राजनेताओं को जवाबदेह ठहरा सकता हो, तो क्या भारतीय मीडिया अब ऐसा नहीं कर सकता? सभी पक्षों के प्रति निष्पक्ष और सभी पक्षों के लिए संतुलित हो, और शायद थोड़ा साहसी भी।

'मैनेज्ड' मीडिया के अंधेरे के बीच, बदलाव के लिए उम्मीद भरी आवाज़ें उठ रही हैं।

फिर, सुबह होगी!

उपसंहार

मोदी बनाम राहुल: आगे क्या है?

अक्सर पूछे जाने वाला सवाल: क्या मोदी युग समाप्त होने वाला है?

नरेन्द्र मोदी के सत्ता में हर कीमत पर बने रहने की ज़रूरत को लेकर एक कहानी है, जो शायद मनगढ़ंत है। एक युवा के तौर पर, जब मोदी, अहमदाबाद में अपने चाचा की कैंटीन में कुछ समय के लिए काम करते थे, तो वडनगर शहर में अपने घर से राज्य परिवहन की बस से आते-जाते थे। जब वे अहमदाबाद में उतरते तो सीट को आरक्षित रखने के लिए उसी बस में अपना झोला या बैग छोड़ देते थे, क्योंकि वह बस उन्हें वापस वडनगर ले जाती थी। कहानी का सबक क्या है? एक बार मोदी कुर्सी पर बैठ गए, तो फिर कोई भी उनसे कुर्सी नहीं छीन सकता! यह कहानी मुझे गुजरात कांग्रेस के एक नेता ने सुनाई थी, इसलिए इसे 'चुटकी भर नमक' जितना लिया जा सकता है, लेकिन इसके भीतर का संदेश साफ है! सहज रूप से दंबग, आत्ममुग्ध और बॉस की तरह, नरेन्द्र मोदी, अपनी किस्मत पर पूरे नियंत्रण के बिना असहज महसूस करते हैं। उनमें व्लादिमीर पुतिन जैसी निरंकुश सत्ता की चाहत है और तुर्किए के रेसेप तैयप एर्दोआन जैसा विश्वास है कि वे ही 'चुने हुए' नेता हैं!

योगेन्द्र यादव अकेले राजनीतिक विश्लेषक थे, जिन्होंने एक अख़बार के कॉलम में, 2024 के चुनाव के आंकड़ों का एकदम सही आंकलन किया था। यादव ने इन नतीजों को मोदी के लिए व्यक्तिगत और राजनीतिक हार कहा। यादव ने लिखा:

> इस बारे में कोई भ्रम नहीं होना चाहिए। यह चुनाव सर्वोच्च नेता द्वारा गणतंत्र को ईंट-दर-ईंट ध्वस्त करने और भारत के संवैधानिक लोकतंत्र को कमज़ोर करने और जनता

> का समर्थन हासिल करने के लिए था। लेकिन जनता ने उन्हें वह ताकत देने से इंकार कर दिया। यदि मुकाबला थोड़ा और निष्पक्ष होता तो वे विपक्ष में बैठे होते। आखिरकार, वे उस कुर्सी को फिर से पाने में कामयाब रहे, जिसकी उन्हें बहुत आवश्यकता थी, लेकिन जनता ने उन्हें वह इकबाल देने से मना कर दिया, जिसकी उन्हें लालसा थी।

यादव का यह मानना सही है कि 'चार सौ पार' के सपने को उड़ाकर मतदाताओं ने मोदी को कमतर आंका हैं और उनके नैतिक और राजनीतिक ताकत को नुक़सान पहुंचाया है। लेकिन, आखिर में भारत में चुनावी लोकतंत्र का मतलब है कि कौन पहले नंबर पर रहा है। 2014 में शुरू हुआ भाजपा का 'जातीय-धार्मिक हिंदुत्व राष्ट्रवाद' का युग एक दशक बाद भी चल रहा है और देश के बड़े हिस्से में मध्यमवर्गीय हिंदू का वोट भाजपा के साथ बना हुआ है। मोदी के अजेय होने का आभामंडल कम हुआ है और 'आएगा तो मोदी ही' या 'केवल मोदी है' भावना भी धीरे-धीरे फीकी पड़ रही है, लेकिन मोदी इस लड़ाई में पूरी तरह हारे नहीं हैं। भाजपा के 240 सांसद अब भी कांग्रेस के 99 सांसदों से दोगुने हैं, और वह भी उस दौर में जब दुनिया भर में मौजूदा सांसद हार रहे हैं।

लंबे समय से सार्वजनिक जीवन में रहने वाले राजनेताओं को राजनीति में जीने की कला आती है। इस किताब में भी ऐसे कई किरदारों का ज़िक्र हैः गांधी परिवार, मल्लिकार्जुन खड़गे, शरद पवार, ममता बनर्जी, नीतीश कुमार, चन्द्रबाबू नायडू, सिद्धारमैया और निश्चित रूप से मोदी-शाह की जोड़ी को भी इसमें शामिल किया जा सकता है। इन अनुभवी राजनेताओं में हरेक में एक बात समान हैः सबसे प्रतिकूल हालात में भी टिके रहने की ज़बरदस्त ताकत। मैं न तो सट्टा लगाने वाले लोगों में से हूं और न ही भविष्यवाणी करने वालों में से, लेकिन मेरा मानना है कि मोदी 3.0 को अंततः एनडीए गठबंधन में कोई मुश्किल नहीं आएगी। एक ध्रुवीकरण करने वाले ताकतवर शख्स के अंहकार का इम्तिहान, विरोधी लेते रहेंगे, लेकिन सत्ता में बने रहने का दृढ़ संकल्प 2024 के फ़ैसले से हिला नहीं हैं, अभी तक तो नहीं।

क्या मोदी के नेतृत्व में गठबंधन पांच साल पूरे करेगा? यह एक ऐसा सवाल है, जिसका जवाब, चुनाव नतीजों के कुछ दिन बाद पूरी हुई, यह किताब ढूंढने की कोशिश नहीं करती। यह भारतीय राजनीति के एक नाटकीय दौर की रिपोर्टिंग और समझने की कोशिश है न कि 'क्रिस्टल बॉल गेज़िंग' की तरह, उस पर पूरी तरह से ध्यान केन्द्रित रखने का प्रयास। खासकर भारत जैसे देश में, जहां पिछले एक दशक में साफतौर पर दिखता है कि 'राजनीति में चौबीस घंटे भी कभी-कभी बहुत लंबा समय होता है'। लेकिन मोदी के तीन दशकों के राजनीतिक करियर को करीब से देखने के नाते, मैं उन्हें सिर्फ़ इसलिए ख़ारिज़ नहीं करूंगा, क्योंकि उन्हें एक और बड़ा जनादेश नहीं मिला। जैसा कि इस किताब में बताया गया है, टीम मोदी-शाह की निर्मम

राजनीति, सत्ता में बने रहने के लिए, कुछ भी करने को तैयार रहने से मेल खाती है। हालांकि ऐसा लगता है, सरकार के माय-वे-और-हाईवे वाले नजरिए पर अब गठबंधन की राजनीति की वास्तविकताओं का असर दिखने लगा है और विवादास्पद क़ानूनों को ठंडे बस्ते में डाला जा रहा है या फिर संसदीय जांच के लिए भेजा जा रहा है। उदाहरण के लिए सरकार में, मध्य-स्तर पर नौकरशाहों के लिए प्रस्तावित 'लेटरल-एंट्री' भर्ती योजना को सरकार में अंदरूनी और बाहरी विरोध के बाद अड़तालीस घंटों में वापस ले लिया गया। मोदी सरकार के पिछले कार्यकालों में इतनी तेजी से वापसी के बारे में कल्पना भी नहीं की जा सकती।

भाजपा गठबंधन के प्रमुख सहयोगी भी अपनी नई भूमिका में ढल रहे हैं और अपनी बढ़ी हुई ताकत से सौदेबाज़ी का पूरा फायदा उठा रहे हैं। नई सरकार के शपथग्रहण के बाद चन्द्रबाबू नायडू के साथ बैठक में कुछ नया देखने को मिला। उनके हाव-भाव में चुनावी कामयाबी के बाद का आत्मविश्वास दिख रहा था। नायडू को अहसास है कि वे फिर से वाजपेयी के ज़माने वाली स्थिति में आ गए हैं, जब सभी रास्ते हैदराबाद की तरफ जाते थे। आंध्र के नेता का पहला लक्ष्य अपने 'आंध्र पुनर्निर्माण परियोजना' के लिए केन्द्र से ज्यादा से ज़्यादा वित्तीय सहायता हासिल करना है। नायडू ने कहा, 'मुझे केन्द्र में मंत्री पद में कोई दिलचस्पी नहीं है। मैं चाहता हूं कि आंध्र कि हितों को प्राथमिकता दी जाए।' जब उनसे पूछा गया कि क्या इस सौदेबाजी से उनकी धर्मनिरपेक्ष छवि से समझौता किया जा रहा था? नायडू ने ज़ोर देकर कहा वे कभी 'सांप्रदायिक राजनीति' बर्दाश्त नहीं करेंगे। उन्होंने कहा कि 'हम हमेशा संविधान का पालन करेंगे।' एक अनुभवी क्षेत्रीय क्षत्रप नायडू, सत्ता के गलियारों में अपना प्रभाव दिखाना जानते हैं। जाहिर है, केन्द्र ने वरिष्ठ नौकरशाहों को सख्त निर्देश दिए हैं कि नायडू जब दिल्ली आएं, तो उन्हें तुरंत समय दिया जाए और किसी भी हालत में उनकी मुलाक़ातों को नहीं टाला जाए। बजट 2024 से साफ है कि नायडू अपना हिस्सा हासिल करना जानते हैं।

मोदी के पद पर बने रहने के लिए चुनौती, गठबंधन के सहयोगी या विपक्ष नहीं है, बल्कि 'भगवा संगठन' में उनके अपने साथी हैं। इस किताब में मैंने टीम मोदी-शाह की 'क्रूर और चालाकी' भरी राजनीति के कई किस्सों का ज़िक्र किया है। सिर्फ़ विपक्षी सरकारें नहीं हैं, जिन्हें लालच-प्रलोभन और केन्द्रीय एजेंसियों का दुरुपयोग कर गिराया गया है। भाजपा के मुख्यमंत्रियों को मनमाने ढंग से बदला गया, कई वरिष्ठ नेताओं को दरकिनार किया गया है और कुछ को अपमानित भी किया गया। मोदी के सत्तावादी व्यक्तित्व ने संघ परिवार जैसे संगठन को भी ऐसे अंधेरे किनारे पर कर दिया, जहां वह उजाले का इंतज़ार करते रहे। एक केन्द्रीय मंत्री ने मोदी के पहले दशक को एक ऐसा 'तूफ़ान' बताया, जिसमें बाकी सभी के लिए छिपने और आड़ लेने के अलावा कोई रास्ता नहीं था। 2024 के नतीज़ों के बाद, मंत्री जी मुस्कराते हैः 'अब हम एक शांत किनारे की झलक पा सकते हैं।'

भारतीय जनता पार्टी में कुछ ही लोग, मोदी के वर्चस्व को चुनौती दे सकते हैं, लेकिन आरएसएस ने चिंता जाहिर की कि फ़ैसले केवल एक ही व्यक्ति ले रहा है और यह 'वन-मैन शो' चिंता की बात है। 2024 के चुनाव नतीजों पर अपनी पहली सार्वजनिक प्रतिक्रिया में संघ प्रमुख मोहन भागवत ने कहा, 'एक सच्चा सेवक, कभी अंहकार नहीं दिखाता और सार्वजनिक जीवन में हमेशा मर्यादा बनाए रखता है।' यह उस चुनाव अभियान के बाद अहम टिप्पणी थी, जब मोदी ने खुद के 'नॉन-बायलोजिकल' होने की बात की थी। लेकिन बात यहीं पर नहीं रुकी। सितंबर 2024 के भाषण में डॉ. भागवत ने कहा, 'कोई भी अपने काम से देवता और पूज्य बन सकता है, लेकिन हम देवतुल्य हैं या नहीं, यह दूसरे लोग तय करेंगे। हमें यह घोषणा नहीं करनी चाहिए कि हम भगवान बन गए हैं।' भागवत के इस बयान से साफ हैं कि संघ के मुखिया के तौर पर, आरएसएस एक निर्विवाद राजनीतिक सुप्रीमो से खोई हुई ज़मीन वापस पाने की कोशिश कर रहा है।

मोदी-आरएसएस रिश्तों को लेकर हमेशा अटकलें चलती रहती हैं। मोदी ने अपनी शुरुआत संघ प्रचारक के तौर पर की थी। वह जानते हैं कि संघ, अपने 'हिंदू राष्ट्र' के एजेंडा को साकार करने के लिए वैचारिक एजेंडा को आगे बढ़ाना चाहता है। उनकी सरकार ने दस सालों में आरएसएस को भारतीय राजनीति पर अपनी छाप बनाने का पूरा मौका दिया है। जुलाई 2024 में, मोदी सरकार ने, सरकारी कर्मचारियों के संघ में शामिल होने के चालीस साल पुराने प्रतिबंध को हटा दिया, जो सांस्कृतिक संगठन के नाम पर काम करने वाले, संघ को मुख्यधारा में लाने की दिशा में एक महत्वपूर्ण कदम था। इससे पहले तक संघ के 'बहुंसख्यकवादी' नज़रिए को संदेह की नज़र से देखा जाता था। 2025, संघ का शताब्दी वर्ष है। बॉलीवुड के एक निर्माता ने बताया कि आरएसएस नेतृत्व ने कुछ साल पहले मुंबई के एक पांच सितारा होटल में फ़िल्म निर्माताओं और मनोरंजन से जुड़े चैनलों के अधिकारियों से मुलाकात की और उनसे राष्ट्रवादी नायकों और हिंदू प्रतीकों पर फ़िल्में और सीरियल बनाने को कहा। उनका मानना था कि कांग्रेस सरकारों के दौरान उन नायकों को कभी भी उनका हक़ नहीं मिला। आरएसएस के बड़े पदाधिकारी ने कहा, 'हम इतिहास को सही नज़रिए से फिर से लिखना चाहते हैं।' इन फ़िल्मों को सरकार से संरक्षण मिलने का भरोसा दिलाया गया। यह समझा जा सकता है कि हाल के दिनों में भगवा सिनेमा की भरमार क्यों है? इन फ़िल्मों में संघ के विश्व दृष्टिकोण से भारतीय इतिहास और संस्कृति के बारे में दिखाया गया है।

कुछ हलकों में आशंकाओं के बावजूद, आरएसएस को पता है कि फिलहाल मोदी ही उनके लिए 'सबसे बेहतर विकल्प' हैं। जैसा कि सीएसडीएस के 2024 के चुनावों के बाद हुए सर्वेक्षणों में बताया गया कि मोदी की लोकप्रियता अभी भी उनकी पार्टी से ज़्यादा है। भाजपा के हर चार मतदाताओं में से एक ने कहा कि उन्होंने सिर्फ़ मोदी की वजह से भाजपा

को वोट दिया, 2019 में तीन में से एक मतदाता ने यह बात मानी थी। मोदी की लोकप्रियता का शिखर अब भले ही उतना न रहा हो, लेकिन उनका शिखर गिरना भी उतना अचानक नहीं होगा, जितना उनके आलोचक चाहते हैं। इसकी एक वजह यह भी है कि भाजपा में अभी उन्हें सीधी चुनौती देने वाला कोई नहीं है। 2024 के नतीजों ने अमित शाह के चुनाव प्रबंधन के कौशल की सीमाओं को भी उजागर कर दिया है। कट्टर हिंदूत्व के शुभंकर माने जाने वाले योगी आदित्यनाथ को भी 2024 में उत्तर प्रदेश में पार्टी की हार के बाद फिर से अपना आधार बनाना होगा। दूसरे दावेदारों--नितिन गडकरी, राजनाथ सिंह, शिवराज सिंह चौहान--में से कोई भी मोदी की 'अखिल भारतीय अपील' की बराबरी नहीं करता। जब तक कि आरएसएस खुद को ऊपर रखते हुए, सीधे तौर पर मुखर होने का निर्णय नहीं करता, जिसकी अभी संभावना ही कही जा सकती है, मोदी अपनी कुर्सी पर बने रहेंगे। सितंबर 2025 में मोदी 75 साल के हो जाएंगे, लेकिन एक अनुभवी राजनेता के लिए उम्र सिर्फ़ एक संख्या भर है। अगस्त 2024 में, एक वैश्विक व्यापार शिखर सम्मेलन में मोदी ने 2029 में 'फिर से सभा को संबोधित' करने के लिए आने का वादा किया। ज़ाहिर है 'रिटायरमेंट' पर जल्दी ही विचार नहीं किया जा रहा।

═

अक्सर पूछे जाने वाला सवाल: क्या राहुल गांधी आखिरकार एक सशक्त राजनेता के रूप में उभरे हैं?

राहुल गांधी का लंबे समय से एक गैर-गंभीर राजनेता के रूप में मज़ाक उड़ाया जाता रहा, लेकिन अब राहुल का नया अवतार और चुनावी-विमर्श तय करने वाले नेता के तौर पर उनका उभरना, 2024 के आम चुनावों की सबसे बड़ी कहानियों में से एक मानी जा सकती है। आरएसएस-भाजपा के 'सांस्कृतिक, नैतिक और सभ्यतागत' विचार को चुनौती देने पर अड़े रहकर, उन्होंने अपनी राजनीति को एक वैचारिक दिशा दी है। एक ऐसा मौका तब आया, जब जुलाई 2024 में, 18वीं लोकसभा के पहले सत्र में नई संसद में मोदी और राहुल आमने-सामने थे, जिसने नजरिए में एक महत्वपूर्ण बदलाव का संकेत दिया। उम्रदराज, कटु आलोचना करने वाले भाजपा सुप्रीमो के ख़िलाफ़ एक युवा और उत्साही प्रतिद्वन्दी से असल मुकाबला था, जिसने मोदी को दख़ल देने और विपक्ष के नेता के आरोपों का जवाब देने के लिए मजबूर किया। राहुल सकारात्मक ऊर्जा के साथ खड़े दिख रहे थे। उस आमने-सामने के मुकाबले में ऐसा लगा कि जैसे सत्ताधारी दल और विपक्ष के बीच, ज़रूरी राजनीतिक संतुलन, अस्थायी रूप से बहाल हो गया हो, और आखिर, विपक्ष ने कई मुद्दों पर आवाज़ उठाना शुरू कर दिया था।

2014 और 2019 के चुनावों पर अपनी पिछली किताबों में, मैंने लिखा था: 'राहुल गांधी ने अवसर चूकने का कभी कोई मौका नहीं गंवाया।' पुस्तक के आयोजनों में, मैं इस टिप्पणी को खूब दोहराता हूं और दर्शक खूब हंसते हैं। लेकिन अब नहीं! एक उद्धरण (जिसे गलत तरीके से महात्मा गांधी का बताया जाता है) का दावा है: 'पहले वे आपको अनदेखा करते हैं, फिर आप पर हंसते हैं, फिर वे आपस में लड़ते हैं और फिर आप जीत जाते हैं।' राहुल गांधी को कभी नज़रअंदाज़ नहीं किया गया, क्योंकि वे देश के एक प्रतिष्ठित राजनीतिक परिवार से ताल्लुक रखते हैं। उनके प्रतिद्वन्दियों ने उनका मज़ाक उड़ाया, उन्हें उपनाम 'पप्पू' दिया गया। बीजेपी ने उनके ख़िलाफ़ अभियान चलाया, जिसमें मीडिया ने भी साथ दिया और राहुल ने भी खुद कई गलतियां की। याद कीजिए, 2013 में, उन्होंने मनमोहन सिंह सरकार के अध्यादेश को प्रतीकात्मक तौर पर फाड़ दिया था। पिछले कुछ सालों में, उन्होंने व्यक्तिगत और राजनीतिक मोर्चों पर कई लड़ाई लड़ी हैं। पांचवी पीढ़ी के एक 'राजवंश' के तौर पर, राहुल, कांग्रेस के 'इतने गौरवशाली नहीं रहे अतीत' के कुछ बोझ को ढो रहे है। शायद उनके शुरुआती दौर में राजनीतिक पाखंड के अनुभव से, पुराने जमाने के चाटुकार नेताओं के प्रति उनकी नापसंदगी बनी रही। आखिरकार, गांधी-नेहरू परिवार के इर्दगिर्द रहने वाले 'गुटों और मंडलियों' ने कांग्रेस और उसके नेतृत्व को कमज़ोर कर दिया। एक किशोर के रूप में, उन्होंने अपनी दादी और पिता की गोलियों और बमों से निर्मम हत्या के आघात को झेला है। निश्चित तौर पर उनकी हिंसक मौतों ने उन पर गहराई तक असर डाला है। शायद यह भी समझा जा सकता है कि गला-काट राजनीति को लेकर उनमें घृणा क्यों हैं? बरसों तक ऐसा लगा, जैसे अतीत का बोझ, उन पर बहुत भारी पड़ गया था। उन्होंने पार्टी को चेतावनी दी कि 'सत्ता जहर है', फिर भी वे सत्ता के मोह से पूरी तरह अलग होने को तैयार नहीं थे।

अब लगता है कि राहुल गांधी अपनी राजनीतिक पहचान को स्वीकार कर चुके हैं। एक पूर्व सहयोगी ने कांग्रेस नेता से पूछा, वह किन मूल्यों पर लोगों से मिलना और जुड़ना चाहते हैं? राहुल ने दृढ़ता से जवाब दिया: 'प्रेम, करूणा, सच और साहस।' वह आगे बढ़कर नेतृत्व करने के लिए तैयार हैं, लेकिन सत्ता के पारपंरिक रास्तों पर नहीं चलना चाहते। अडानी-अंबानी के नाम पर, 'क्रोनी कैपिटलिज्म' पर उनके तीखे हमलों ने पार्टी में कई लोगों को असहज कर दिया। 'कुलीनतंत्र' के इस युग में, बड़े कारोबारियों से मुकाबला करना जोख़िम भरी राजनीति है। कांग्रेस के एक वरिष्ठ नेता ने माना कि उन्हें नहीं समझ आ रहा था कि अपने अच्छे दोस्तों 'गौतम भाई' और 'मुकेश भाई' से कैसे निपटना था, क्योंकि उनके ख़िलाफ़ माहौल बनाया जा रहा था। उन्होंने बताया कि 'मैं वास्तव में अडानी के किसी समारोह में शामिल नहीं हुआ, क्योंकि मुझे नहीं पता था कि राहुल जी इस पर कैसी प्रतिक्रिया देंगे।' जैसा कि इस पुस्तक से पता चलता है, न तो अडानी और न ही अंबानी ने, 2024 में कांग्रेस के अभियान के लिए कोई

चंदा दिया। कांग्रेस ने अपने कॉरपोरेट साथियों से खुद को अलग कर लिया था। दरअसल, 'राहुल बनाम अडानी' की बड़ी राजनीतिक जंग में एक अप्रत्याशित सा 'छद्म युद्ध' बन गया।

अपने मजबूत संकल्प के साथ अडिग राहुल गांधी अपनी धुन पर चल पड़े। पांच साल पहले, यह काफी नहीं था। 2024 में, लोगों ने उन्हें एक नए नजरिए से देखा। उनकी 'भारत जोड़ो' यात्रा एक ऐतिहासिक यात्रा थी, जिसने कांग्रेस नेता को अपनी पुरानी छवि के जाल से बाहर निकालने में मदद की। इससे समझ आया कि राजनीतिक कायाकल्प का रास्ता, आम लोगों के साथ बिना किसी 'फिल्टर' के जुड़ने से ही निकल सकता है। यह 'मोहब्बत की दुकान' ही थी, जिसे उन्होंने 2024 के अभियान में ऐसे समय अपनाया, जब उनकी पार्टी के ज़्यादातर नेताओं को हार तय दिख रही थी और वे भाजपा के चुनावी रथ का मुकाबला करने के लिए तैयार नहीं थे। राहुल गांधी के 'खटाखट' नकद गारंटी के वादे की, भाजपा ने 'रेवड़ी या मुफ़्त' के लोकलुभावने वादे के रूप में आलोचना की, लेकिन 2024 के विमर्श युद्ध में, कांग्रेस नेता ने गति और दिशा निर्धारित कर दी। 'संविधान ख़तरे में', का उनका जोशीला नारा, संभवतः एक अहम मोड़ था, जिसने उन्हें और कांग्रेस पार्टी को 'जाति-आरक्षण' के लिए सत्ता-विरोधी, सामाजिक न्याय के लिए लड़ने वाला बना दिया। इससे प्रधानमंत्री को अपने 'विकसित भारत' के नारे से हटकर, भड़काऊ सांप्रदायिक नारे लगाने के लिए मजबूर किया और हताशा में उन्होंने फिर धार्मिक घृणा की लाइन को पकड़ लिया।

अब भी ऐसे लोग हैं जो सवाल करते हैं कि क्या राहुल गांधी, अपने किसी काम को लगातार जारी रख सकते हैं? क्या उनका दिल अब भी इस 'मुकाबले वाली राजनीति' में है? और क्या वे एक अलग विपक्षी गठबंधन का नेतृत्व करने लायक परिपक्व हो गए हैं? और क्या एक अधिक रूढ़िवादी, व्यापार-अनुकूल कांग्रेस पार्टी, सामाजिक न्याय और आर्थिक असमानता से जुड़े एक स्पष्ट वामपंथी झुकाव के साथ तालमेल बिठाएगी? क्या कांग्रेस नेता की नकद सहायता की योजना से सरकारी खज़ाने को नुकसान होगा? और बरसों से उदारीकरण बाज़ार से जुड़े सुधारों को ख़त्म कर देगा? क्या उनका जाति आरक्षण का मुद्दा समाज को और बांट देगा? और महत्वाकांक्षी मध्यम वर्ग में उनके विकास को रोकने का डर पैदा करेगा? क्या कांग्रेस अपने कमज़ोर संगठन के साथ, निचली जातियों, खासकर हिंदी-पट्टी में, लगातार समर्थन जुटा सकती है? फिर राहुल गांधी का सोशल इंजीनियरिंग का प्रयोग, मौजूदा हिंदुत्व पर फोकस राजनीतिक व्यवस्था में केवल एक अस्थायी रोक जैसा है। ये ऐसे सवाल हैं, जिनका जवाब केवल राहुल गांधी और उनकी पार्टी, भविष्य में उनके एक्शन से दे सकती है, लेकिन 'केबीसी' (कौन बनेगा चैलेंज़र) का अहम सवाल, फिलहाल काफी हद तक तय हो चुका है। राहुल गांधी विपक्ष के चेहरे हैं और संसद के अंदर और बाहर इंडिया गठबंधन के नेता हैं। कुछ हद तक राहुल ने अपनी विरासत को हासिल कर लिया है।

हालांकि, इस बात का कोई भी आंकलन, अभी जल्दी होगा कि क्या मोदी युग भविष्य में राहुल गांधी युग का मार्ग प्रशस्त करेगा? राहुल के 'दरबारी'--मोदी के 'ढोल बजाने' वालों की तरह ही चापलूस--उन्हें पहले से ही अगला प्रधानमंत्री बना चुके हैं, जबकि इस सबसे पुरानी पार्टी के सामने एक कड़वी सचाई यह है कि उनके नेतृत्व में पार्टी ने लगातार तीसरी बार लोकसभा चुनावों में हार का सामना किया है। मोदी की तरह राहुल भी, भारतीय राजनीति पर असर डालने वाले 'हम बनाम वे' के 'हाइपर-ध्रुवीकरण' से नहीं निकल पाए हैं। आरएसएस-भाजपा के हिंदुत्व की आलोचना को अलग-अलग विचारों वालों के तिरस्कार तक नहीं ले जाया जा सकता। ऐसे समय में जब भारतीय राजनीति का केन्द्र, व्यावहारिक विकल्पों की तलाश कर रहा है, राहुल को यह दिखाने की ज़रूरत है कि वे सबके बीच पुल बनाने का काम कर सकते हैं और गठबंधन के नेता हो सकते हैं, वे अंहकार और राजवंश के विशेषाधिकार में नहीं फंस सकते। 'भारत जोड़ो' की अवधारणा को विचार से ज़मीनी कार्रवाई में बदलने की ज़रूरत है। सामाजिक और आर्थिक न्याय और धार्मिक बहुलता के विचारों को आकर्षक नारों और अनिर्धारित एजेंडों से आगे बढ़ना होगा, और सार्थक बदलाव के लिए रचनात्मक कार्यक्रम बनाना चाहिए।

यह साफ है कि 2024 के जनादेश ने राहुल गांधी और कांग्रेस को उन राज्यों में अपनी ताकत बढ़ाने के लिए एक आधार दिया, जहां अगले बड़े चुनावी मुकाबले होने हैं। लोगों से जुड़ने वाले एक नए नेता राहुल गांधी का असर और वोटों को फिर से हासिल करने वाले संगठन के रूप में कांग्रेस कितना आगे बढ़ पाएगी, यह इस बात पर निर्भर करेगा कि वह 2024 में बने माहौल को किस हद तक भुनाने में कामयाब होती है। यदि ज़्यादा विधानसभा चुनावों में उसकी जीत होती है तो लोकसभा में उसके प्रदर्शन को अपवाद नहीं माना जाएगा। वरना बरसों से पार्टी को परेशान करने वाली संगठन की कमज़ोरियां, चुनावी किस्मत में थोड़े से बदलाव के लिए कांग्रेस को फिर से कमज़ोर कर देंगी।

इसके अलावा, बिना तालमेल वाले इंडिया गठबंधन में, क्षेत्रीय ताकतों के साथ समन्वय करने वाली कांग्रेस, एक प्रभावी और टिकाऊ विपक्ष बनाने में रोड़ा बन सकती है, भले ही वह सबसे बड़ी और मजबूत पार्टी हो। 'मोदी-विरोध' ही वह बड़ा कारण है, जो 2024 में इन अलग-अलग पार्टियों को एक साथ ला सकता है, लेकिन अभी कोई साझा उद्देश्य या पहचान नहीं बनी है। जब 2024 के अगस्त में, कोलकाता के एक सरकारी अस्पताल में एक युवा महिला डॉक्टर के साथ बलात्कार के बाद हत्या की गई, तो प्रदेश कांग्रेस, ममता बनर्जी सरकार के ख़िलाफ़ सड़कों पर उतर आई। हरियाणा विधानसभा चुनावों के लिए आप-कांग्रेस में संभावित गठबंधन नहीं बन पाया। जब अरविंद केजरीवाल ने दिल्ली के मुख्यमंत्री पद से इस्तीफ़ा दिया, तो कांग्रेस ने खुद को आप नेता से दूर कर लिया।

परस्पर विरोधी महत्वाकांक्षाएं और व्यक्तिगत प्रतिद्वन्दिता रातों-रात ख़त्म नहीं होतीं। यही वजह है कि विपक्ष को ज़्यादा सतर्क रहने की ज़रूरत है। और 2024 के नतीजों को मोदी राज के 'अंत की शुरुआत' समझने की भूल नहीं करनी चाहिए। चुने हुए 'तानाशाह' चुपचाप छाया में नहीं चले जाते!

═

अक्सर पूछे जाने वाला सवाल: क्या भारत में लोकतंत्र मोदी युग में भी टिक पाएगा?

यह ऐसा सवाल है जिसका उत्तर सेमिनारों के उस सर्किट में मिल सकता हैं, जहां विचारधारा और गहरी चिंता जाहिर करते उपदेश, कभी-कभी ज़मीनी हक़ीकत को ईमानदारी से समझने पर हावी हो जाते है। मैं कोई अकादमिक नहीं हूं, बल्कि एक पत्रकार हूं, जिसकी रूचि भारतीय राजनीति में होने वाले उतार-चढ़ावों में है। यह तीसरी पुस्तक (त्रयी) 2014 में शुरू हुए उस सफ़र का प्रतीक है, जिस चुनाव ने भारत को बदलने की कोशिश की और भारतीय राजनीति में एक उथल-पुथल भरे दशक की शुरुआत की। एक राजनीतिक पर्यवेक्षक के तौर पर, भारतीय लोकतंत्र में बहुत कुछ ऐसा है, जो परेशान करता है। धन-बल का बेतहाशा इस्तेमाल, संस्थानों पर हमलावर होना, प्रवर्तन एजेंसियों को हथियार बनाना, खोखली होती विचारधारा, जाति और धर्म के नाम पर बंटता समाज, संकीर्णता, भ्रष्टाचार, आम आदमी की सेवा के लिए आए लोगों की सरासर बेइमानी, नेताओं का बढ़ता निरंकुश व्यवहार, असहमति की आवाज़ों को कुचलने की कोशिश और मीडिया के एक बड़े हिस्से की सत्ता के सामने सच बोलने में नाकामी। हालांकि, इनमें से कई नासूर जैसी बीमारियां 2024 से पहले की हैं, लेकिन अब ये निर्दयता के साथ खतरनाक तरीके से बढ़ रही हैं।

ऐसे हालात में, भारतीय लोकतंत्र के भविष्य पर किसी भी चर्चा को 2024 के फ़ैसले से आगे देखने की ज़रूरत है। जब एक समझदार मतदाता ने भारत में लोकतंत्र को तानाशाही में बदलने से रोकने की कोशिश की है और विपक्ष को ज़रूरी ऑक्सीजन देकर, चुनावी निरंकुशता पर लगाम लगाई है, लेकिन एक चुनाव परिणाम, 75 साल पूरे करते भारतीय गणतंत्र के सामने आने वाली कई चुनौतियों का समाधान नहीं कर सकता है।

कहा जा सकता है कि मोदी का यह दशक, अच्छा, बुरा और बदसूरत रहा है। दुनिया भर में अनिश्चितता के माहौल के बीच एक 'स्थिर सरकार' आश्वस्त करने वाली है। कुछ लोग ही इस बात को नकारेंगे कि मोदी के बेहतर प्रचार वाले व्यक्तित्व ने भारत को अंतरराष्ट्रीय स्तर पर ज़्यादा स्पष्ट उपस्थिति और घरेलू स्तर पर ज़्यादा आर्थिक ताकत दी है। तानाशाह अपने आस-पास के माहौल पर अपनी छाप छोड़ना पसंद करते हैं। मोदी राज में बड़े पैमाने

पर बुनियादी ढांचे की परियोजनाओं, बैंकिंग क्षेत्र में सुधार, बेहतर जीएसटी, कल्याणकारी योजनाओं में बढ़ोतरी और डिजिटल क्षेत्र में तेज़ी दिखाई दी। ये सब कदम समय के साथ, बढ़ती अर्थव्यवस्था को फायदा पहुंचाएंगे। लेकिन चढ़ता शेयर बाज़ार, चमचमाते राजमार्ग और अरबों डॉलर के मूल्यांकन वाले यूनिकॉर्न उद्यम, कई अंधेरे धब्बों को नहीं छिपा सकते। देश की बड़ी युवा आबादी के लिए बेहतर नौकरियों की कमी एक बड़ी चुनौती है, लेकिन इस समस्या का कोई रामबाण इलाज नहीं है। भारत का 'रिफॉर्म एजेंडा' रुक-रुककर आगे बढ़ रहा है। सरकारी सिस्टम, इंस्पेक्टर राज और कमज़ोर न्यायिक प्रणाली अब भी आसानी से व्यापार के रास्ते में बाधाएं हैं। छोटे और सूक्ष्म उद्योग और असंगठित क्षेत्र में काम-धंधे, कोविड के बाद से संघर्ष कर रहे हैं। देश के कई हिस्सों में किसानों की आत्महत्या और ग्रामीण संकट भी एक बड़ी परेशानी का सबब है। भारत की करीब आधी आबादी खेती-किसानी पर निर्भर है, लेकिन यह राष्ट्रीय आमदनी का सिर्फ़ छठा हिस्सा भर है। खेती-किसानी के लिए बहुत ज़रूरी माने जाने वाले सुधार नाकाम हो गए, क्योंकि उससे जुड़े लोगों को पहले भरोसे में नहीं लिया गया। 2015 में, बड़े ताम-झाम के साथ शुरू किया गया मोदी सरकार का 'स्मार्ट सिटीज' मिशन महत्वाकांक्षा और हकीकत के बीच के फासले को बताता है। नगरपालिका स्तर पर भ्रष्टाचार में डूबा शहरी बुनियादी ढांचा, ध्वस्त होने की कगार पर है। नए भारत के सबसे तेज़ी से बढ़ने वाली अर्थव्यवस्था और दुनिया की पांचवें नंबर पर आने वाली अर्थव्यवस्था के उत्साह के बीच, अक्सर यह आसानी से भुला दिया जाता है कि हम 2024 में प्रति व्यक्ति सकल घरेलू उत्पाद में 125वें स्थान पर और वैश्विक भूख सूचकांक में 125 देशों में से 111वें स्थान पर हैं।

एक बढ़ती अर्थव्यवस्था को समान अवसरों के साथ सबका ध्यान रखने वाला, समतावादी समाज बनाना चाहिए, न कि एक अरबपति राज, जो सिर्फ बड़े लोगों के लिए चमकता है, जबकि एक बड़ी आबादी के लिए मजदूरी में कोई अहम बदलाव नहीं होता। इसका जवाब अविवेकी आर्थिक लोकलुभावनवाद नहीं है, बल्कि एक ऐसे समावेशी सुधार एजेंडे की ज़रूरत है, जो सबसे ज़्यादा शिक्षा और स्वास्थ्य के मानकों पर फोकस करे।

सत्ता के ज़्यादा केन्द्रीकरण वाला मोदी मॉडल, चिंता की बात है, फ़ैसले करने की एक ऐसी शैली, जिसे मनमानी, अपारदर्शी और मौलिक रूप से अलोकतांत्रिक कहा जाना चाहिए। इसने विपक्षी नेताओं की गिरफ़्तारी, इकलौते मुस्लिम बहुल राज्य को केन्द्र शासित प्रदेश में बदल दिया, अचानक आधी रात को लॉकडाउन, भाई-भतीजावाद के आरोप, संस्थाओं को कमज़ोर करना और डर और धमकी का माहौल बनाया। इससे भारतीय लोकतंत्र की आधारशिला, यानी संघीय भावना को झटका लगा है। हर चुनाव के दौरान, भाजपा की 'डबल इंजन' की अवधारणा स्वाभाविक रूप से त्रुटिपूर्ण और भेदभावपूर्ण है। 'डबल इंजन' के असली मायने क्या हैं? क्या इसका मतलब यह है कि विपक्ष शासित राज्यों के पास कोई 'इंजन' नहीं है? विपक्ष

शासित राज्यों को क्यों निशाना बनाना चाहिए? और क्यों उन्हें उनका हक नहीं मिलना चाहिए जबकि भाजपा शासित राज्यों का ज़्यादा ध्यान रखा जाना चाहिए? उत्तर-दक्षिण विभाजन की आशंका से इंकार नहीं किया जा सकता, खासतौर से अगली जगणना के बाद, सीटों के परिसीमन से आर्थिक रूप से आगे दक्षिणी राज्यों की राजनीतिक ताकत और हिस्सेदारी कम हो सकती है। 'एक राष्ट्र एक चुनाव' का आइडिया संघीय मजबूती को और कमज़ोर करेगा। उम्मीद है कि एक गठबंधन सरकार और मजबूत विपक्ष, सिस्टम को एकतरफा बनाने की कोशिशों को रोक पाएगा।

मोदी के वर्षों के 'बदसूरत' पहलू ही गणतंत्र पर सबसे बड़ा दाग़ है। मोदी और उनके समर्थकों की सत्ता पर पूरी तरह नियंत्रण की चाह में समय-समय पर फैलाई गई विभाजनकारी, पहचान तय करने वाली और नफ़रत ने देश को बुरी तरह जख्मी किया है। उनके खुले तौर पर विभाजनकारी, बांसवाड़ा में भड़काऊ भाषण, जिसकी निंदा नहीं की गई, ने राजनीतिक बयानबाजी को एक नए निचले स्तर पर पहुंचा दिया और गहरे और बुरे पूर्वाग्रहों को सामने ला दिया। नफ़रत फैलाने वाले भाषणों को आम समझना एक चुनौती है, जिसका सामना निर्णायक न्यायिक और सिविल सोसायटी के दख़ल से होना चाहिए। 'सबका साथ, सबका विकास, सबका विश्वास' एक निरर्थक नारा लगता है, जबकि हकीकत यह है कि सत्ता में बैठी पार्टी हिंदू 'बहुसंख्यकवाद' के नज़रिए को बढ़ावा देती है और संसद में उसका एक भी मुस्लिम सांसद नहीं है। संघ परिवार से जुड़े विभिन्न संगठनों का अल्पसंख्यकों पर लगातार हमला और मुसलमानों को निशाना बनाना, भारत के विविधता और बहुत से धर्मों वाले समाज के विचार पर हमला है। और 2024 के लिए, एक सांप्रदायिक चुनाव अभियान ने किसी को भी यह भरोसा दिलाने की कोशिश नहीं की कि आने वाले दिनों में सहिष्णुता और आपसी सम्मान के मूल उदारवादी मूल्यों को बचाकर रखा जाएगा। एक बेहतर भारत को हमारे संस्थापक पूर्वजों के नजरिए और उनके संवैधानिक मूल्यों पर केन्द्रित होना चाहिएः 'आज़ादी, समानता और हां, बंधुत्व।' 'संविधानवाद' और 'हिंदू बहुसंख्यकवाद' के बीच लड़ाई अभी ख़त्म नहीं हुई है। संविधान पर बहस को फिर से नए नजरिए के साथ देखने की ज़रूरत है ताकि यह सुनिश्चित किया जा सके कि यह सड़कों तक ना आ जाए और कलह और हिंसा में न बदल जाए।

मैं, निजी तौर पर, 2024 के फ़ैसले के उन पहलुओं से उत्साहित हूं, जिसने एक बार फिर साबित किया कि ऐसे तनावपूर्ण समय में भी अहिंसक संदेश देना संभव है और भारत की विविधता, अब भी हमारे 'बहुलवादी लोकाचार' को कमज़ोर करने की कोशिशों का विरोध करती है। लेकिन आत्मसंतुष्टि के लिए कोई जगह नहीं है। यदि संवैधानिक ज़िम्मेदारियों को छोड़ दिया जाता है तो आम आदमी को, एक बार फिर अपने नेताओं को ज़्यादा जवाबदेह बनने और अपना अंहकार छोड़ने के लिए मजबूर करने का संकल्प दिखाना होगा। जैसा कि इस किताब

में बार-बार ज़ोर दिया गया है, 2024 के बड़े दांव वाले मुकाबले में कोई 'बराबरी के खेल का मैदान' (लेवल प्लेइंग फील्ड) नहीं था। फिर भी करोड़ों भारतीयों ने चुपचाप, हमारे गणतंत्र के संस्थापकों से मिली ताकत का इस्तेमाल, लोकतांत्रिक भावना की जीत को सुनिश्चित करने के लिए किया: 'हमारे वोट की ताकत'। हमें अब उस विशिष्ट, अडिग भारतीय भावना और अपने दिलों में एक बेहतर भारत की शाश्वत उम्मीद के साथ आगे बढ़ना चाहिए!

आभार

पेशे से पत्रकार और एक अंशकालिक लेखक के रूप में, पिछले कुछ साल मेरे लिए मुश्किल भरे रहे हैं। मैं उन लोगों का वाकई आभारी हूं, जिन्होंने मुझे उस समय आखिरी पायदान तक पहुंचा दिया, जब मैं सोच रहा था कि क्या मेरे पास चुनावों पर तीसरी पुस्तक (त्रयी) को पूरा करने की क्षमता है। इसके लिए हार्पर कॉलिन्स की टीम को विशेष धन्यवाद, खासतौर से उदयन मित्रा और अनंत पद्मनाभन, जो हमेशा हौंसला बढ़ाते रहे हैं। मेरी संपादक शतरूपा घोषाल बेहद समझदार और मेहनती हैं: उनके निरंतर सवालों और सुझावों ने निसंदेह इस रचना को बेहतर बनाने में मदद की है। हेमाली और रजंना के नेतृत्व में 'ए सूटेबल एजेंसी' की टीम बहुत सहायक रही है। इंडिया टुडे ग्रुप की कली पुरी ने मुझे आज के मुख्यधारा मीडिया के 'इको-सिस्टम' की तुलना में ज़्यादा आज़ादी और काम करने का मौका दिया, उसके लिए मैं आभारी हूं। प्रवीण शेखर ने अपने शोध का काम बहुत गहराई से किया और सुरेन्द्र नागर ने हमेशा जागरुकता के साथ सहयोग दिया है। चुनाव डेटा पर 'विश्वकोश' माने जाने वाले श्रेयस सरदेसाई, विशेष धन्यवाद के पात्र हैं। मैं मीडिया क्षेत्र में अपने बहुत से पत्रकार साथियों को धन्यवाद देना चाहता हूं, जिनका अनुभव और नजरिया इसमें जुड़ा है, इनमें से कुछ को मैंने पुस्तक में उद्धृत किया है और कुछ ने 'गुमनाम' रहना पसंद किया। मैं उन राजनेताओं का भी शुक्रिया अदा करना चाहता हूं, जिन्होंने अपनी कहानियां, 'ऑन रिकॉर्ड' या 'ऑफ रिकॉर्ड' मेरे साथ साझा कीं। हम ऐसे युग में जी रहे हैं जहां बहुत कम सार्वजनिक हस्तियां खुलकर बोलने को तैयार है, इसलिए जिन्होंने ऐसा किया, वे बेहद अहम हैं।

आख़िर में, अपने परिवार के लिए विशेष आभार। सागरिका घोष न केवल तीस साल से ज़्यादा समय से मेरी पत्नी, सबसे अच्छी दोस्त और साथी रही हैं, बल्कि पुस्तक को लिखने में एक बेशकीमती मार्गदर्शक भी हैं। ऐसे वक्त में भी जब आसमान में अंधेरा छा रहा हो, मेरे बच्चे ईशान और तारिणी, मुझे उम्मीदों और खुशी के ढेर सारे कारण देते हैं।

पत्रकारिता के पैंतीस साल से ज़्यादा समय तक, मेरी चुनाव यात्राएं मुझे इस अविश्वसनीय देश के कोने-कोने तक ले गईं। इस सफ़र के दौरान जिन लोगों ने मेरे लिए अपने दिल और दरवाज़े खोले, यह क़िताब आपके लिए है!

परिशिष्ट

RESULTS

1: State/UT-wise result for major national parties and their allies in the 18th Lok Sabha election

		NDA (National Democratic Alliance)						INDIA (Indian National Developmental Inclusive Alliance)						Others	
		BJP		BJP Allies		NDA Separate		INC		INC Allies		INDIA Separate			
State/Union Territory name	Total Seats	Seats Won	Vote Share (%)	Seats Won	Vote Share (%)	Seats Won	Vote Share (%)	Seats Won	Vote Share (%)	Seats Won	Vote Share (%)	Seats Won	Vote Share (%)	Seats Won	Vote Share (%)
Andaman & Nicobar Islands	1	1	50.58	0	0.00	0	0.00	0	38.54	0	0.00	0	2.97	0	7.91
Andhra Pradesh	25	3	11.29	18	42.19	0	0.00	0	2.70	0	0.39	0	0.08	4	43.35
Arunachal Pradesh	2	2	48.53	0	0.00	0	0.00	0	30.40	0	0.00	0	0.00	0	21.07
Assam	14	9	37.43	2	8.91	0	0.07	3	37.44	0	2.07	0	1.80	0	12.28
Bihar	40	12	20.52	18	26.69	0	0.00	3	9.20	6	30.05	0	0.02	1	13.52
Chandigarh	1	0	47.67	0	0.00	0	0.00	1	48.22	0	0.00	0	0.00	0	4.11

		NDA (National Democratic Alliance)						INDIA (Indian National Developmental Inclusive Alliance)						Others	
		BJP		BJP Allies		NDA Separate		INC		INC Allies		INDIA Separate			
State/Union Territory name	Total Seats	Seats Won	Vote Share (%)	Seats Won	Vote Share (%)	Seats Won	Vote Share (%)	Seats Won	Vote Share (%)	Seats Won	Vote Share (%)	Seats Won	Vote Share (%)	Seats Won	Vote Share (%)
Chhattisgarh	11	10	52.65	0	0.00	0	0.00	1	41.05	0	0.00	0	0.24	0	6.06
Dadra & Nagar Haveli and Daman and Diu	2	1	52.81	0	0.00	0	0.00	0	25.08	0	0.00	0	0.00	1	22.11
Delhi	7	7	54.38	0	0.00	0	0.00	0	18.89	0	24.15	0	0.01	0	2.57
Goa	2	1	50.92	0	0.00	0	0.00	1	39.62	0	0.00	0	0.00	0	9.46
Gujarat	26	25	61.79	0	0.00	0	0.00	1	31.28	0	2.69	0	0.01	0	4.23
Haryana	10	5	46.10	0	0.00	0	0.00	5	43.68	0	3.93	0	0.22	0	6.07
Himachal Pradesh	4	4	56.43	0	0.00	0	0.00	0	41.68	0	0.00	0	0.00	0	1.89
Jammu & Kashmir	5	2	24.43	0	0.00	0	0.00	0	19.39	2	22.27	0	8.51	1	25.40
Jharkhand	14	8	44.55	1	2.62	0	0.00	2	19.25	3	19.79	0	0.53	0	13.26
Karnataka	28	17	46.09	2	5.60	0	0.00	9	45.39	0	0.00	0	0.01	0	2.91
Kerala	20	1	16.67	0	2.53	0	0.00	14	35.05	4	10.08	1	33.36	0	2.31

		NDA (National Democratic Alliance)						INDIA (Indian National Developmental Inclusive Alliance)						Others	
		BJP		BJP Allies		NDA Separate		INC		INC Allies		INDIA Separate			
State/Union Territory name	Total Seats	Seats Won	Vote Share (%)	Seats Won	Vote Share (%)	Seats Won	Vote Share (%)	Seats Won	Vote Share (%)	Seats Won	Vote Share (%)	Seats Won	Vote Share (%)	Seats Won	Vote Share (%)
Ladakh	1	0	23.58	0	0.00	0	0.00	0	27.59	0	0.00	0	0.00	1	48.83
Lakshadweep	1	0	0.00	0	0.41	0	0.00	1	52.29	0	0.00	0	46.91	0	0.39
Madhya Pradesh	29	29	59.28	0	0.00	0	0.00	0	32.44	0	0.13	0	0.14	0	8.01
Maharashtra	48	9	26.17	8	17.36	0	0.00	13	16.92	17	26.99	0	0.06	1	12.50
Manipur	2	0	16.58	0	18.80	0	8.51	2	47.63	0	0.00	0	0.00	0	8.48
Meghalaya	2	0	0.00	0	24.25	0	2.60	1	34.06	0	0.00	0	2.85	1	36.24
Mizoram	1	0	6.82	0	0.00	0	0.00	0	20.07	0	0.00	0	0.00	1	73.11
Nagaland	1	0	0.00	0	46.13	0	0.00	1	52.83	0	0.00	0	0.00	0	1.04
Odisha	21	20	45.41	0	0.00	0	0.03	1	12.53	0	0.54	0	0.15	0	41.34
Puducherry	1	0	35.83	0	0.00	0	0.00	1	52.73	0	0.00	0	0.00	0	11.44
Punjab	13	0	18.56	0	0.00	0	0.02	7	26.31	0	0.00	3	26.24	3	28.87
Rajasthan	25	14	49.22	0	0.00	0	0.00	8	37.93	2	3.79	1	2.48	0	6.58
Sikkim	1	0	4.95	0	0.00	1	42.71	0	0.58	0	0.00	0	0.00	0	51.76
Tamil Nadu	39	0	11.26	0	6.93	0	0.00	9	10.67	30	36.24	0	0.00	0	34.90

		NDA (National Democratic Alliance)						INDIA (Indian National Developmental Inclusive Alliance)						Others	
		BJP		BJP Allies		NDA Separate		INC		INC Allies		INDIA Separate			
State/Union Territory name	Total Seats	Seats Won	Vote Share (%)	Seats Won	Vote Share (%)	Seats Won	Vote Share (%)	Seats Won	Vote Share (%)	Seats Won	Vote Share (%)	Seats Won	Vote Share (%)	Seats Won	Vote Share (%)
Telangana	17	8	35.19	0	0.00	0	0.01	8	40.10	0	0.00	0	0.36	1	24.34
Tripura	2	2	70.76	0	0.00	0	0.00	0	11.51	0	12.40	0	0.00	0	5.33
Uttar Pradesh	80	33	41.36	3	2.33	0	0.00	6	9.46	37	34.07	0	0.11	1	12.67
Uttarakhand	5	5	56.87	0	0.00	0	0.00	0	32.70	0	0.00	0	0.00	0	10.43
West Bengal	42	12	38.74	0	0.00	0	0.00	1	4.67	0	6.28	29	45.84	0	4.47
Grand Total	**543**	**240**	**36.56**	**52**	**7.26**	**1**	**0.06**	**99**	**21.19**	**101**	**14.01**	**34**	**6.21**	**16**	**14.71**

Source: Results available on the Election Commission of India (ECI) webpage (https://results.eci.gov.in/PcResultGenJune2024/index.htm)

Note: Vote shares have been rounded to two decimal points. NDA Separate and INDIA Separate include parties/candidates that were part of NDA and INDIA respectively but contested separately against the main/official NDA and INDIA candidates. An exception however has been made for Rajasthan's Banswara parliamentary constituency where the official INDIA candidate from Bharat Adivasi Party has been included in the INDIA Separate category as there was an INC 'rebel' candidate also in the fray who contested on the INC's election symbol.

BJP Allies include: Andhra Pradesh - JSP: Jana Sena Party, TDP: Telugu Desam Party; Assam - AGP: Asom Gana Parishad, UPPL: United People's Party, Liberal; Bihar - HAM (S): Hindustani Awam Morcha (Secular), JD (U): Janata Dal (United), LJP (RV): Lok Janshakti Party (Ram Vilas), RLM: Rashtriya Lok Morcha; Jharkhand - AJSUP: All Jharkhand Students Union Party; Karnataka - JD (S): Janata Dal (Secular); Kerala - BDJS: Bharath Dharma Jana Sena; Lakshadweep - NCP: Nationalist Congress Party; Maharashtra – NCP, RSPS: Rashtriya Samaj Paksha, SHS: Shiv Sena; Manipur - NPF: Naga People's Front; Meghalaya - NPEP: National People's Party; Nagaland - NDPP: Nationalist Democratic

Progressive Party; Tamil Nadu - AMMK: Amma Makkal Munnetra Kazhagam, PMK: Pattali Makkal Katchi, TMC (M): Tamil Maanila Congress (Moopanar), Independent supported by NDA; Uttar Pradesh - ADAL: Apna Dal, RLD: Rashtriya Lok Dal, SBSP: Suheldev Bharatiya Samaj Party.

NDA Separate includes: Andhra Pradesh - RPI (Athawale): Republican Party of India (Athawale); Assam - RPI (Athawale); Maharashtra – NPEP; Manipur - RPI (Athawale); Meghalaya - UDP: United Democratic Party; Odisha – AJSUP; Punjab - RPI (Athawale); Sikkim - SKM: Sikkim Krantikari Morcha; Telangana - RPI (Athawale).

INC Allies include: Andhra Pradesh - CPI: Communist Party of India, CPI (M): Communist Party of India (Marxist); Assam - AJP: Assam Jatiya Parishad; Bihar – CPI, CPI (M), CPI(M-L) (L): Communist Party of India (Marxist-Leninist) (Liberation), RJD: Rashtriya Janata Dal, VIP: Vikassheel Insaan Party; Delhi - AAP: Aam Aadmi Party; Gujarat – AAP; Haryana – AAP; Jammu and Kashmir - JKNC: Jammu & Kashmir National Conference; Jharkhand - CPI(M-L) (L), JMM: Jharkhand Mukti Morcha; Kerala - IUML: Indian Union Muslim League, KEC: Kerala Congress, RSP: Revolutionary Socialist Party; Madhya Pradesh – AIFB: All India Forward Bloc; Maharashtra - NCP (SP): Nationalist Congress Party (Sharadchandra Pawar), SHS (UBT): Shiv Sena (Uddhav Balasaheb Thackeray); Rajasthan – CPI (M), RLP: Rashtriya Loktantrik Party; Tamil Nadu - CPI, CPI (M), DMK: Dravida Munnetra Kazhagam, IUML, MDMK: Marumalarchi Dravida Munnetra Kazhagam, VCK: Viduthalai Chiruthaigal Katchi; Tripura – CPI(M); Uttar Pradesh – AITC: All India Trinamool Congress, SP: Samajwadi Party; West Bengal – AIFB, CPI, CPI (M), RSP.

INDIA Separate includes: Andaman and Nicobar – CPI (M); Andhra Pradesh: AIFB, CPI (M) (L), RSP, SP, VCK; Assam – AAP, AITC, CPI, CPI (M); Bihar – AIFB; Chhattisgarh – CPI; Delhi – AIFB; Gujarat – SP; Haryana - NCP (SP); Jammu and Kashmir – AIFB, JKPDP: Jammu & Kashmir Peoples Democratic Party; Jharkhand – CPI, CPI (M), Karnataka – CPI (M), VCK; Kerala – CPI, CPI (M), KC (M): Kerala Congress (Mani), VCK; Lakshadweep – NCP (SP); Madhya Pradesh – CPI; Maharashtra – AIFB, CPI, CPI (M); Meghalaya – AITC; Odisha – AIFB, CPI, CPI (M), CPI (M-L) (L), SP; Punjab – AAP, CPI, CPI (M), RSP; Rajasthan – Bharat Adivasi Party (BAP); Telangana – AIFB, CPI (M), RSP, VCK; Uttar Pradesh – AIFB, CPI; West Bengal – AIFB, AITC, CPI (M-L) (L).

Others include remaining parties, Independents and the None of the Above (NOTA) option.

2: Region-wise seats won by BJP, INC, their allies and others

East India was the only region where INC could not make any seat gains

	Total Seats	BJP			BJP Allies			INC			INC Allies			Others		
		2014	2019	2024	2014	2019	2024	2014	2019	2024	2014	2019	2024	2014	2019	2024
North West India	46	29	32	23	4	2	0	4	8	13	0	0	2	9	4	8
Northern Hindi States	174	145	131	88	11	25	21	6	3	17	5	0	45	7	15	3
Eastern and Tribal States	88	25	46	50	0	1	1	5	6	5	2	1	3	56	34	29
North East India	25	8	14	13	1	1	2	8	4	7	0	0	0	8	6	3
West India	78	53	51	36	19	18	8	2	2	15	4	4	17	0	3	2
South India	132	22	29	30	18	2	20	19	29	42	3	34	34	70	38	6

Source: Election results by ECI

Note: Composition of BJP Allies and INC Allies is not the same across the three elections. For example, unlike 2024, SP was not an ally of INC in 2014 and 2019.

North West India: Punjab, Haryana, Delhi, Uttarakhand, Himachal Pradesh, Jammu and Kashmir, Ladakh and Chandigarh

Northern Hindi States: Uttar Pradesh, Bihar, Madhya Pradesh and Rajasthan

Eastern and Tribal States: West Bengal, Odisha, Jharkhand and Chhattisgarh

North East India: Assam, Arunachal Pradesh, Manipur, Meghalaya, Tripura, Nagaland, Mizoram and Sikkim

West India: Maharashtra, Gujarat, Goa, Dadra and Nagar Haveli and Daman and Diu.

South India: Tamil Nadu, Karnataka, Andhra Pradesh, Kerala, Telangana, Andaman and Nicobar Islands, Lakshadweep and Puducherry

3: Region-wise vote share of BJP, INC, their allies and others

BJP suffered a major vote share loss in northwest and north India, gained the most in south India

	BJP (%)			BJP Allies (%)			INC (%)			INC Allies (%)			Others (%)		
	2014	2019	2024	2014	2019	2024	2014	2019	2024	2014	2019	2024	2014	2019	2024
North West India	32.1	44.1	39.8	9.6	7.9	0.0	26.9	31.1	30.9	0.9	0.0	7.6	30.5	17.0	21.8
Northern Hindi States	43.6	47.2	41.5	2.4	7.0	6.7	15.9	16.5	18.4	4.8	4.8	21.9	33.2	24.5	11.5
Eastern and Tribal States	24.9	42.6	42.8	0.0	0.6	0.4	17.2	13.1	13.1	1.4	2.5	6.2	56.4	41.2	37.5
North East India	28.1	33.7	35.0	4.2	9.5	10.2	29.8	33.6	35.1	1.1	0.0	2.5	36.8	23.3	17.2
West India	38.5	39.8	38.4	14.9	14.9	11.3	23.4	22.0	22.0	10.7	11.5	18.5	12.5	11.7	9.8
South India	15.6	17.5	23.9	5.8	8.7	12.5	18.6	20.4	24.8	1.1	14.9	11.3	58.9	38.5	27.5

Source: Election results by ECI

Note: Vote shares have been rounded to one decimal point.

Composition of BJP and INC allies is not the same across the three elections.

4: BJP and Congress vote shares, 2024 vs 2019

BJP's overall vote share fell by 0.8 percentage points despite the party contesting five seats more than 2019

Congress's overall vote share increased by 1.7 percentage points despite it contesting 93 fewer seats than 2019

BJP's contested vote share fell by 1.3 percentage points, Congress's increased by a whopping 10 points

	2019 LS (%)	2024 LS (%)	Change (% points)
Overall BJP Vote Share	37.4	36.6	-0.8
Contested BJP Vote Share*	46.1	44.8	-1.3
Overall INC Vote Share	19.5	21.2	+1.7
Contested INC Vote Share*	24.8	34.6	+9.8

Source: Election results by ECI

Note: Vote shares have been rounded to one decimal point

*Vote share only in seats contested by the party

BJP contested on 441 seats in 2024 and 436 in 2019. INC contested on 328 seats in 2024 and 421 in 2019.

5: BJP vs Congress contests

Congress's winning rate in its direct contests with BJP increased by nearly four times; it won 29 per cent of such contests as opposed to 8 per cent in 2019

Overall vote share gap between BJP and Congress in BJP vs Congress contests reduced to 10 percentage points from 21 points in 2019

	2019 LS	2024 LS
BJP vs INC Contest Seats*	**190**	**215**
Seats won by INC	15	62
Seats won by BJP	175	153
Vote Share of INC	35.3%	40.9%
Vote Share of BJP	56.5%	51.0%

Source: Election results by ECI

*Seats where the top two parties ended up being BJP and INC

SOME SLICES FROM CSDS SURVEY DATA

6: Narendra Modi and Rahul Gandhi as Prime Ministerial choices

Modi's popularity declined from 2019 high, Rahul Gandhi's increased further and doubled since 2014; gap between the two leaders reduced from 24 percentage points in 2019 to 14 points.

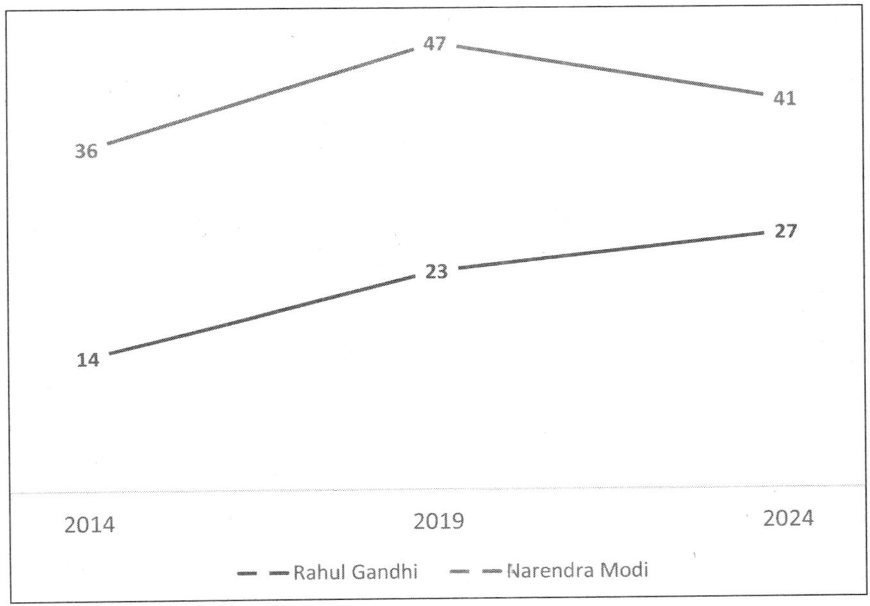

Source: CSDS-Lokniti NES Post Polls

Question asked by CSDS: Who do you want to see as the Prime Minister after this Lok Sabha election?

Figures are percentages.

Note: CSDS offered no names to the respondent while asking the question. The responses were spontaneous.

The rest of the respondents took other leaders' names or did not take any name.

7: Unemployment and Inflation as most important voting issues

50 per cent of the voters cited unemployment and inflation as the most important voting issues compared to just 16 per cent in 2019; those citing unemployment more than doubled in proportion compared to 2019 and those citing inflation increased by six times

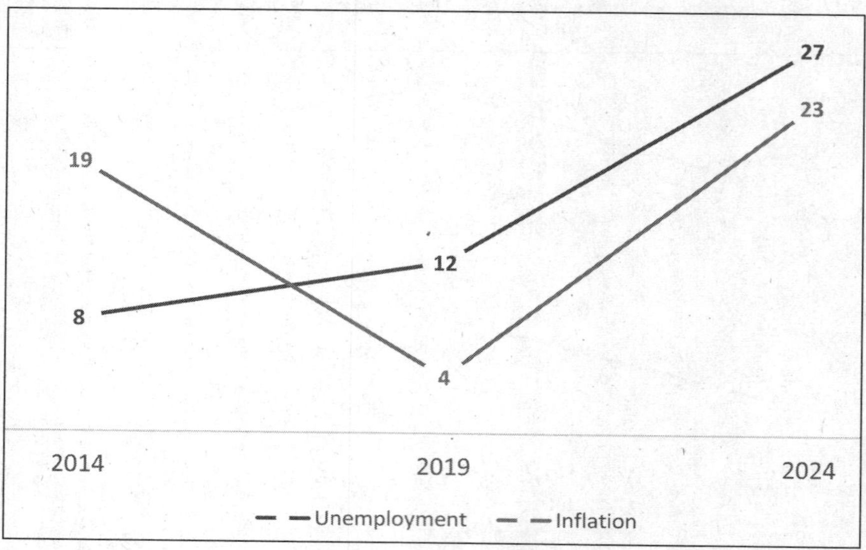

Source: CSDS-Lokniti NES Post/Pre-Polls

Questions asked: What was/will be the single most important issue for you while voting in this election?

Figures are percentages.

Note: CSDS offered no choices to the respondent while asking the question. The responses were spontaneous.

8: Modi effect on NDA voters

Modi's impact on BJP voters appears to have waned as only one in four of them voted for the party because of his being NDA's PM candidate; in 2019 one in every three BJP voters had cited Modi as a factor for voting for BJP. The Modi impact on BJP allies' voters, however, grew stronger.

	Would not have voted for NDA had Modi not been its PM candidate (%)		
	2014	2019	2024
BJP voters	27	32	25
BJP allies' voters	20	24	27

Source: CSDS-Lokniti NES Post Polls

Question asked by CSDS: If Narendra Modi was not the BJP's Prime Ministerial candidate, would you have still voted for the same party as you have done, or your decision would have changed?

9: Hindu Upper Caste Vote Choice, 2009-2024

Under Modi, Hindu upper castes have been the BJP–NDA's most loyal vote bank

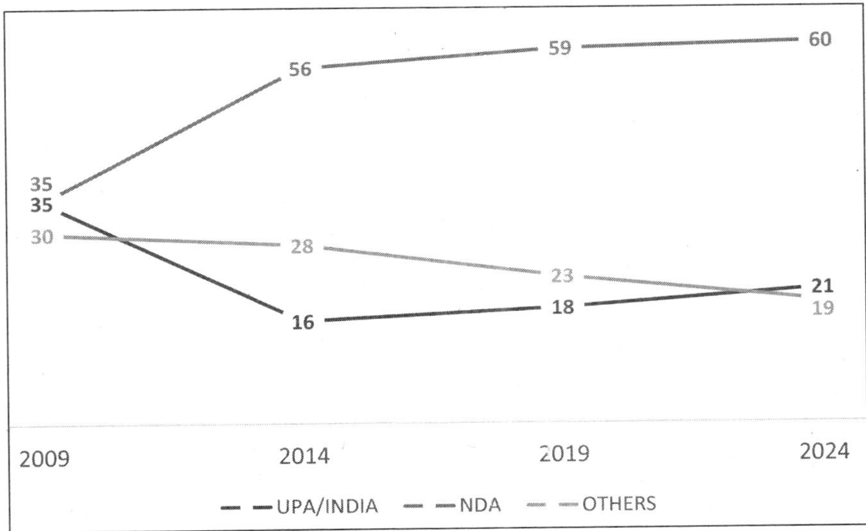

Source: CSDS-Lokniti NES Post Polls

Note: Figures are percentages

10: Hindu Upper OBC Vote Choice, 2009-2024

NDA lost some ground among Upper OBCs, Congress alliance gained tremendously among them registering its best performance since 2009

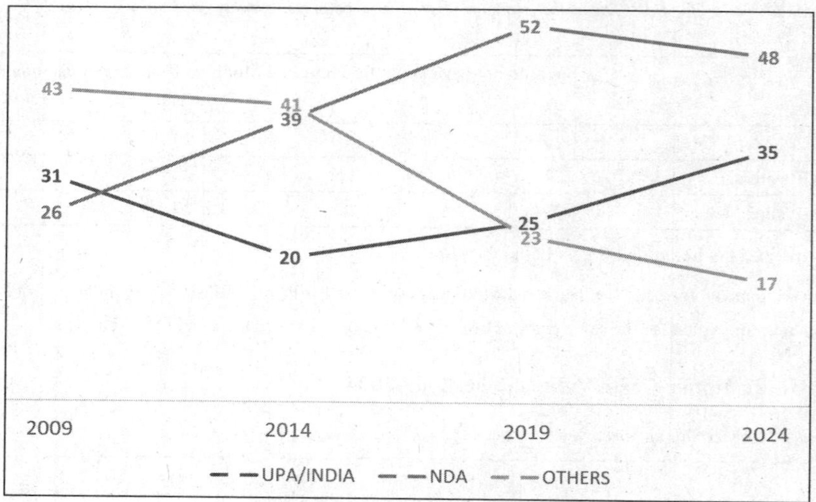

Source: CSDS-Lokniti NES Post Polls

Note: Figures are percentages; OBC stands for Other Backward Classes

11: Hindu Lower OBC Vote Choice, 2009-2024

NDA consolidated its performance among lower OBCs, Cong alliance also did much better than last time among them

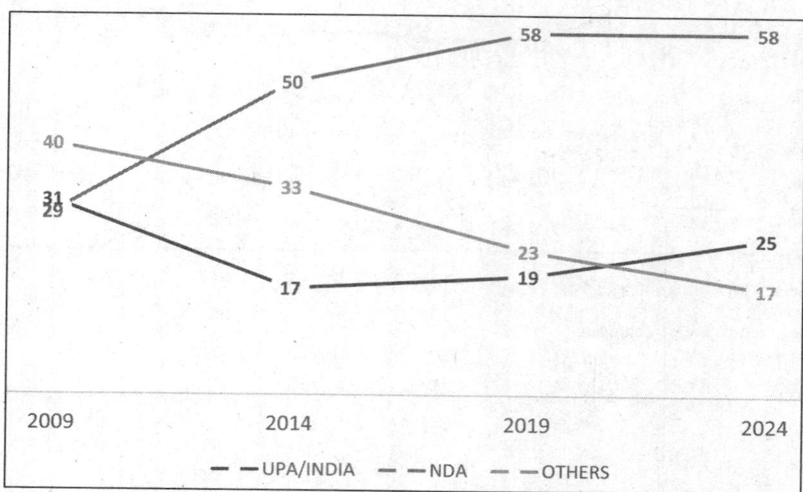

Source: CSDS-Lokniti NES Post Polls

Note: Figures are percentages

12: Hindu Dalit Vote Choice, 2009-2024

NDA's march among Dalits came to a halt; Congress and allies continued to regain lost ground, BSP's decline continued

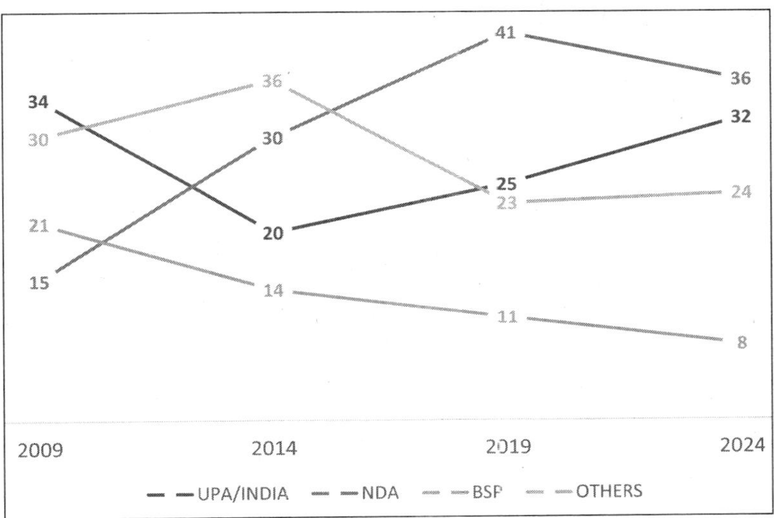

Source: CSDS-Lokniti NES Post Polls

Note: Figures are percentages

13: Hindu Adivasi Vote Choice, 2009-2024

Adivasi support for NDA consistently rising since 2014 and reached an all-time high nationally; Congress alliance performed poorly among them, on the whole.

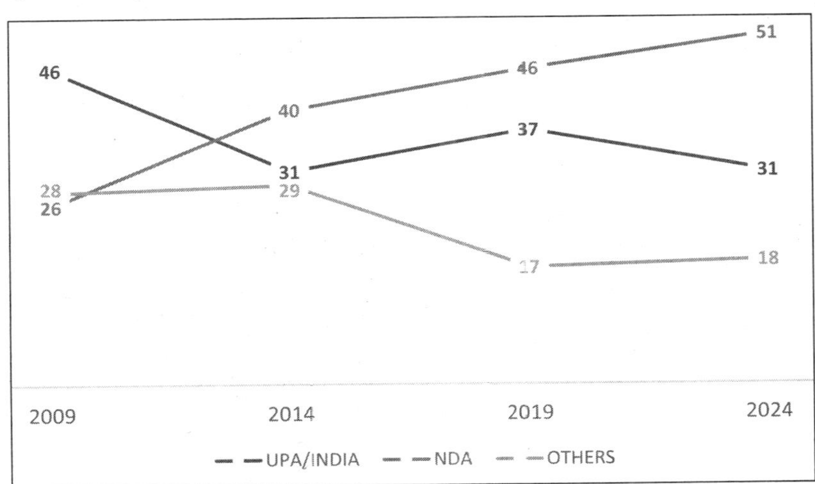

Source: CSDS-Lokniti NES Post Polls

Note: Figures are percentages

14: Muslim Vote Choice, 2009-2024

Muslims consolidated behind INDIA to defeat BJP, 20-point jump in Congress alliance's vote. Muslim support for non-aligned parties crashed

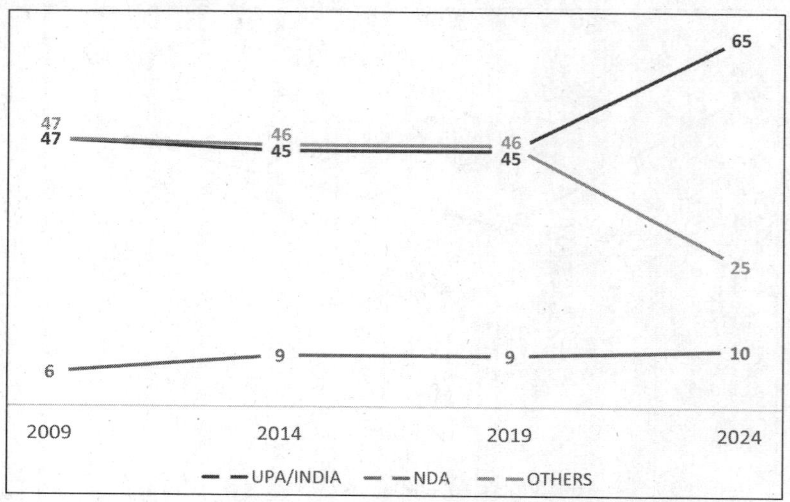

Source: CSDS-Lokniti NES Post Polls

Note: Figures are percentages

15: Vote for BJP and INC by Age Group, 2019 vs 2024

Even though young voters continued to be BJP's strongest supporters in 2024, support for party among them declined compared to 2019; support for Congress increased by around 2-3 points across all age groups

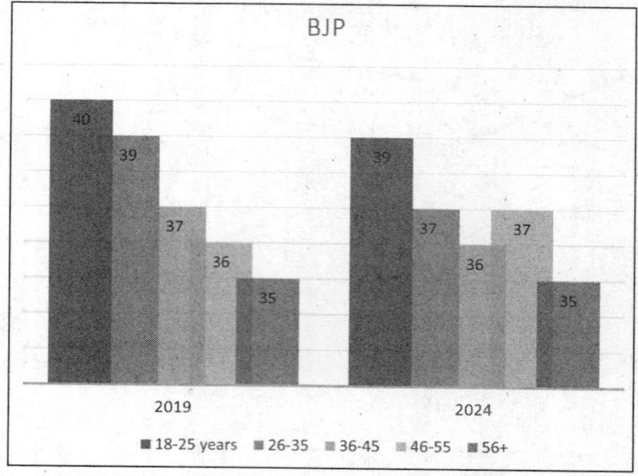

Source: CSDS-Lokniti NES Post Polls

Note: Figures are percentages

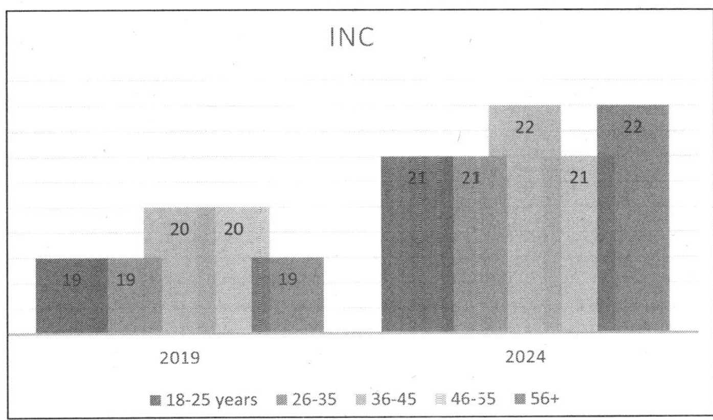

Source: CSDS-Lokniti NES Post Polls

Note: Figures are percentages

16: Vote for BJP among young voters in comparison to its overall vote share

Although the BJP's vote share declined among both 18-25-year-olds and 26-35-year-olds compared to 2019, the drop among the latter age group was greater than the decline among the former. Moreover, unlike 2014 and 2019, 26-35-year-olds were nearly as likely to vote for the BJP this time as the average BJP voter. 18-25-year-olds on the other hand continued to support the party significantly more than the average BJP voter, although among them too this tendency declined a bit.

	2014	**2019**	**2024**
Overall BJP Vote Share	**31.0**	**37.4**	**36.6**
BJP Vote Share among 18-25-year-olds	34	40	39
BJP Vote Share among 26-35-years-olds	33	39	37

Source: CSDS-Lokniti NES Post Polls

Note: Figures are percentages

17: Vote for BJP-NDA by Gender, 2009-2024

It's a myth that women are favoring the BJP more than men under Prime Minister Modi. At the all-India level, neither the BJP, nor the NDA have ever got a greater share of women's vote than men's vote according to CSDS post-poll data, although the gap has narrowed.

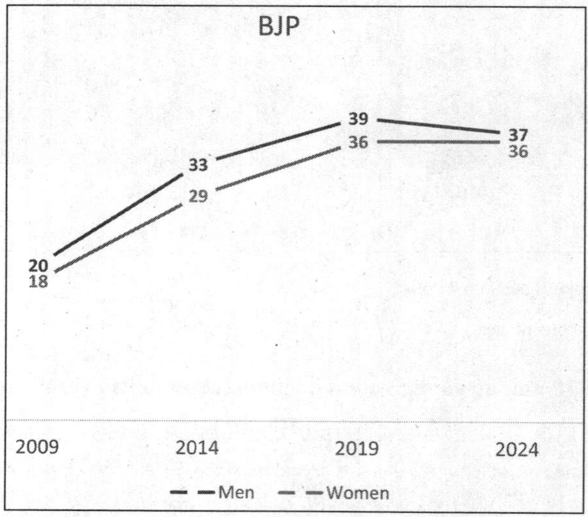

Source: CSDS-Lokniti NES Post Polls

Note: Figures are percentages

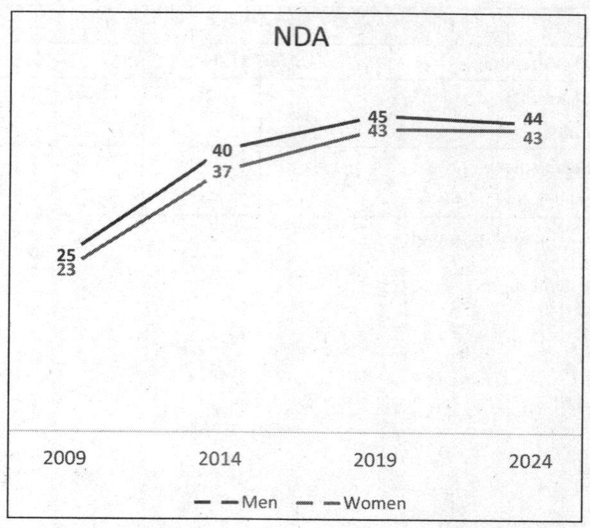

Source: CSDS-Lokniti NES Post Polls

Note: Figures are percentages

18: Vote for INC-UPA/INDIA by Gender, 2009-2024

INC has enjoyed a very slight advantage among women nationally in most Lok Sabha elections since 2009, however along with its allies there is no clear pattern

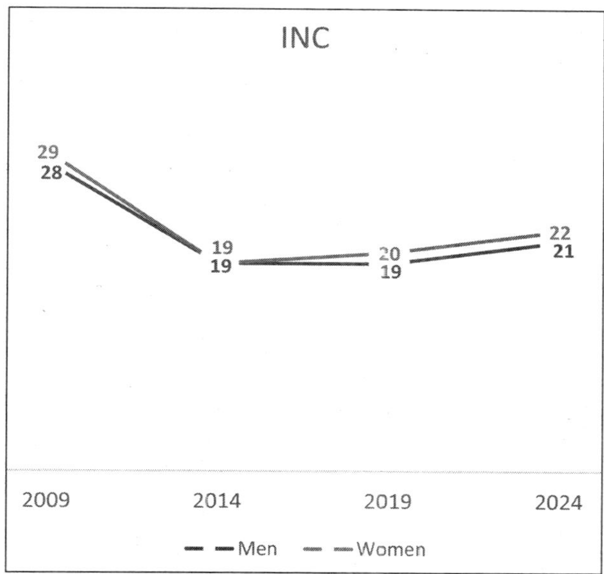

Source: CSDS-Lokniti NES Post Polls

Note: Figures are percentages

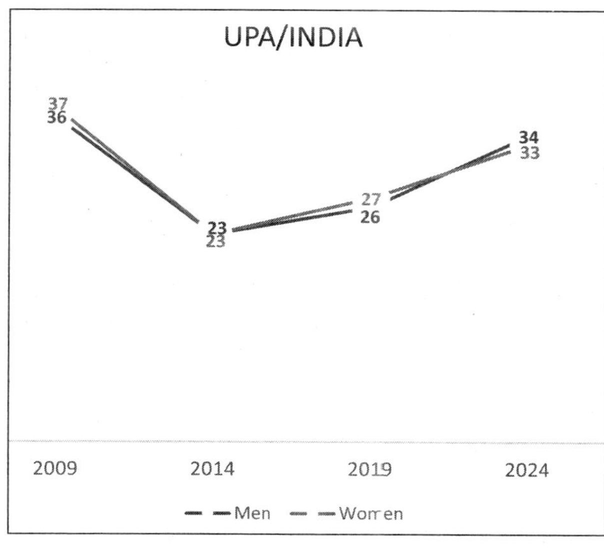

Source: CSDS-Lokniti NES Post Polls

Note: Figures are percentages

NOTE

Survey data shown is from National Election Studies (NES) 2019, 2014, 2009. All surveys were conducted by the Lokniti programme of the Centre for the Study of Developing Societies, Delhi. The data shown have been taken either from the CSDS-Lokniti website (www.lokniti.org) or from CSDS articles published in newspapers and academic journals over the years.

The sample size and coverage details of the surveys are as follows:

NES 2024: Sample size (N) – 19,663; Coverage – 23 States/UTs; 191 Parliamentary Constituencies

NES 2019: N - 24,236; Coverage - 26 States/UTs; 208 Parliamentary Constituencies

NES 2014: N - 22,295; Coverage - 26 States/UTs; 306 Parliamentary Constituencies

NES 2014 Pre-Poll: N - 20,957; Coverage - 21 States/UTs; 301 Parliamentary Constituencies

NES 2009: N - 36,169; Coverage - 29 States/UTs; 536 Parliamentary Constituencies

For detailed methodology and sampling method adopted for NES 2024, visit https://www.thehindu.com/opinion/op-ed/lokniti-programme-of-the-centre-for-the-study-of-developing-societies-csds-methodology/article68254913.ece; For detailed methodology of NES 2019, 2014 and 2009, visit www.lokniti.org

लेखक के बारे में

राजदीप सरदेसाई एक पुरस्कार विजेता वरिष्ठ पत्रकार, एंकर और टीवी समाचार प्रस्तुतकर्ता हैं। वर्तमान में इंडिया टुडे समूह के सलाहकार संपादक और प्रमुख समाचार एंकर सरदेसाई को प्रिंट और टेलीविज़न में तीन दशकों से ज़्यादा का पत्रकारिता का अनुभव है। वह IBN18 नेटवर्क के संस्थापक-संपादक थे और उससे पहले NDTV 24×7 और NDTV INDIA के प्रबंध संपादक रहे। उन्होंने पत्रकारिता में उत्कृष्टता के लिए पचास से अधिक पुरस्कार जीते हैं।

राजदीप की भारतीय चुनावों पर पिछली किताबें, *2019: हाउ मोदी वुन इंडिया* और *2014: द इलेक्शन दैट चेंज इंडिया*, राष्ट्रीय स्तर पर बेस्टसेलर रही हैं। वह *डेमोक्रेसीज़ इलेवनः द ग्रेट इंडियन क्रिकेट स्टोरी* के लेखक भी हैं।

अनुवादक के बारे में

विजय त्रिवेदी पत्रकारिता का करीब 40 साल का अनुभव और टेलीविज़न का जाना-पहचाना चेहरा। राजनीतिक रिपोर्टिंग, संसदीय कवरेज, शीर्ष राजनेताओं, कई प्रधानमंत्रियों और मुख्यमंत्रियों सहित, शीर्ष राजनेताओं, बॉलीवुड सितारों, खिलाड़ियों, नौकरशाहों और मशहूर हस्तियों के बेबाक साक्षात्कारों की अनूठी शैली के लिए जाने जाते हैं।

एनडीटीवी इंडिया और स्टार न्यूज़ में लंबे समय तक रहे। इसके बाद *न्यूज़ नेशन, न्यूज़ स्टेट, फर्स्ट इंडिया, न्यूज़ इंडिया 24×7* का नेतृत्व किया। डिजिटल एजेंसी एच.एस न्यूज़ और समाचार एजेंसी यूनीवार्ता की ज़िम्मेदारी संभाली। *ज़ी न्यूज़* की शुरुआती टीम में रहे। *नवभारत टाइम्स, इंडिया टुडे* और *राजस्थान पत्रिका* के साथ जुड़े रहे। पत्रकारिता के क्षेत्र में कई सम्मान हासिल किए। उनके टीवी शो काफी लोकप्रिय रहे हैं।

भारत रत्न अटल बिहारी वाजपेयी पर *हार नहीं मानूंगा, यदा यदा ही योगी, बीजेपीः कल, आज और कल* और राष्ट्रीय स्वयंसेवक संघ के सौ साल के सफ़र पर *संघम शरणम गच्छामि*, जैसी बेस्टसेलर पुस्तकों का लेखन किया है।

HarperCollins *Publishers* India

At HarperCollins India, we believe in telling the best stories and finding the widest readership for our books in every format possible. We started publishing in 1992; a great deal has changed since then, but what has remained constant is the passion with which our authors write their books, the love with which readers receive them, and the sheer joy and excitement that we as publishers feel in being a part of the publishing process.

Over the years, we've had the pleasure of publishing some of the finest writing from the subcontinent and around the world, including several award-winning titles and some of the biggest bestsellers in India's publishing history. But nothing has meant more to us than the fact that millions of people have read the books we published, and that somewhere, a book of ours might have made a difference.

As we look to the future, we go back to that one word—a word which has been a driving force for us all these years.

Read.